Make Instruction Needs-Based

- Identify where your students are struggling and customize your instruction to address their needs.
- Gauge how your entire class or individual students are doing by viewing the easy to use grade book.
- Ensure your students are getting the additional reinforcement and direction they need between class meetings.

Getting Started is as EASY as 1, 2, 3 . . . 4!

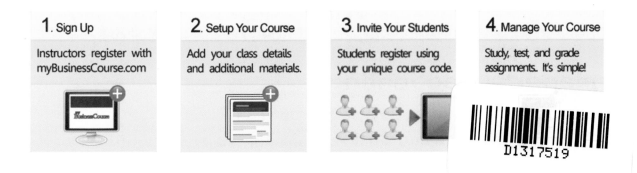

1. Sign Up
Instructors register with myBusinessCourse.com

2. Setup Your Course
Add your class details and additional materials.

3. Invite Your Students
Students register using your unique course code.

4. Manage Your Course
Study, test, and grade assignments. It's simple!

D1317519

Provide Instruction and Practice 24/7

- Assign homework from your Cambridge Business Publishers textbook and have myBusinessCourse grade it for you automatically.
- With our eLectures, your students can revisit accounting topics as often as they like or until they master the topic.
- Guided Examples show students how to solve select problems.
- Make homework due before class to ensure students enter your classroom prepared.
- Upgrade to include the eBook and you have all the tools needed for an online course.

Want to learn more about myBusinessCourse?

Contact your sales representative or visit **www.mybusinesscourse.com**.

STUDENTS: Find your access code on the myBusinessCourse insert on the following pages. If you have a used copy of this textbook, you can purchase access online at **www.mybusinesscourse.com**.

Cambridge Business Publishers Series in Accounting

Financial Accounting

- **Financial Accounting for Undergraduates, 2e** by Ferris, Wallace, and Christensen
- **Financial Accounting, 4e** by Dyckman, Magee, and Pfeiffer
- **Financial Accounting for MBAs, 5e** by Easton, Wild, Halsey, and McAnally
- **Financial Accounting for Executives & MBAs, 3e** by Simko, Ferris, and Wallace
- **Cases in Financial Reporting, 7e** by Engel, Hirst, and McAnally

Managerial Accounting

- **Managerial Accounting, 6e** by Hartgraves & Morse
- **Cases in Managerial and Cost Accounting, 1e** by Allen, Brownlee, Haskins, and Lynch

Combined Financial & Managerial Accounting

- **Financial & Managerial Accounting for MBAs, 3e** by Easton, Halsey, McAnally, Hartgraves, and Morse

Intermediate Accounting

- **Cases in Financial Reporting, 7e** by Engel, Hirst, and McAnally

Cost Accounting

- **Cases in Managerial and Cost Accounting, 1e** by Allen, Brownlee, Haskins, and Lynch

Financial Statement Analysis & Valuation

- **Financial Statement Analysis & Valuation, 3e** by Easton, McAnally, Sommers, and Zhang
- **Cases in Financial Reporting, 7e** by Engel, Hirst, and McAnally

Advanced Accounting

- **Advanced Accounting, 2e** by Hamlen, Huefner, and Largay
- **Advanced Accounting, 2e** by Halsey & Hopkins

my BusinessCourse

FREE WITH NEW COPIES OF THIS TEXTBOOK

Scratch here for access code

Scratch here for access code

Start using *my* BusinessCourse Today: www.mybusinesscourse.com

 my BusinessCourse is a web-based learning and assessment program intended to complement your textbook and faculty instruction.

Student Benefits

- eLectures
- Guided examples
- Immediate feedback with auto graded homework from the textbook
- Opportunities for additional practice and exam preparation
- Optional upgrade includes eBook

Instructor Benefits

- Easy-to-use course management system
- Homework automatically graded
- Provide students with additional help when you are not available
- Detailed diagnostic tools to assess class performance
- Resources for a complete online course

Interactive content that runs on any device.

Built for PCs, iPads, Laptops, Tablets, Smartphones

You can access *my* BusinessCourse 24/7 from any web-enabled device, including iPads, smartphones, laptops, and tablets.

If you purchased a used book and the protective coating that covers the access code has been removed, your code may be invalid.

Access to *my* BusinessCourse is free ONLY with the purchase of a new textbook.

2013-2014 UPDATE

Advanced Accounting

Second Edition

SUSAN S. HAMLEN
State University of New York—Buffalo

RONALD J. HUEFNER
State University of New York—Buffalo

JAMES A. LARGAY III
Lehigh University

Cambridge
BUSINESS PUBLISHERS

Cambridge Business Publishers

ADVANCED ACCOUNTING, Second Edition, by Susan S. Hamlen, Ronald J. Huefner, and James A. Largay III.

COPYRIGHT © 2013 by Cambridge Business Publishers, LLC. Published by Cambridge Business Publishers, LLC. Exclusive rights by Cambridge Business Publishers, LLC for manufacture and export.

ALL RIGHTS RESERVED. No part of this publication may be reproduced, distributed, or stored in a database or retrieval system in any form or by any means, without prior written consent of Cambridge Business Publishers, LLC, including, but not limited to, in any network or other electronic storage or transmission, or broadcast for distance learning.

STUDENT EDITION ISBN: 978-1-61853-097-4

Bookstores & Faculty: to order this book, call 800-619-6473 or email customerservice@cambridgepub.com.

Students: to order this book, please visit the book's Website and order directly online.

Printed in Canada.

10 9 8 7 6 5 4 3 2

Welcome to *Advanced Accounting*. We wrote this book with two major objectives in mind. First, we seek to reflect the changing topical emphases and content in the advanced accounting course; coverage is completely updated for new developments concerning applicable reporting issues and requirements, including the newest FASB and GASB pronouncements and proposals. We extensively discuss International Financial Reporting Standards where appropriate throughout the book. Second, we write from the perspective of enhancing teachability; many of the topics in this course are complex and require careful explanation. We highlight the major issues in each topic and provide the student with the background and logical structure needed to analyze these issues, rather than merely explaining current practice. This view equips students to analyze and assess future reporting developments.

This book is the product of extensive market research including focus groups, market surveys, class tests, manuscript reviews, and interviews with faculty from across the country. We are grateful to the students and faculty who provided us with useful feedback during the preparation of this book.

TARGET AUDIENCE

Advanced Accounting is intended for use, at either the undergraduate or graduate level, in the course commonly known as advanced accounting. It is also designed to be used in courses focusing on mergers and acquisitions that are often part of the MBA curriculum or that are offered as a nondegree, professional development program.

HOW THIS BOOK EFFECTIVELY TEACHES ADVANCED ACCOUNTING TOPICS

Conceptual focus

Conceptual explanations focus on the logic underlying reporting standards rather than merely explaining procedures. We develop each topic by explaining the underlying business activity, the reporting goals, and how standards and procedures achieve these goals. Each topic is clearly developed in terms students can understand. We use illustrations from actual practice to enhance understanding and familiarize students with the information presented in real financial statements. Accounting standards are increasingly **principles based**, requiring substantial **judgment** in their application. And standards change every year. Conceptual understanding prepares students to evaluate and effectively apply future standards throughout their professional careers.

Logical flow of topical coverage

The organization of chapters reflects the logical flow of topics:

- **Mergers and acquisitions** material is covered in Chapters 1-6.
- **Foreign currency translation, foreign currency transactions and hedging,** and **other financial derivatives** (futures, options, and swaps) are in Chapters 7-9.

- Reporting standards for **state and local government and NFP organizations** are in Chapters 10-13.
- **Partnerships, bankruptcy and reorganization**, and the **SEC** are covered in Chapters 14-16.

Relevant real company illustrations

Each chapter begins with a description of a familiar **focus company**, and how its activities and reporting practices relate to that chapter's topics. For example, in Chapter 2, **IBM**'s extensive acquisitions illustrate accounting for mergers and acquisitions. Noncontrolling interests are common in the resort industry, and in Chapter 5 **Las Vegas Sands Corporation** illustrates reporting for noncontrolling interests in subsidiaries. In Chapter 9, **Kellogg's** hedging practices illustrate hedge accounting for futures, options and swaps. In Chapter 13, **Beta Alpha Psi**'s financial statements illustrate NFP reporting standards. Throughout each chapter, examples from actual practice highlight major topics, using either the focus company or other companies in the same industry.

Following is a list of focus companies by chapter.

Chapter 1	Coca-Cola	**Chapter 9**	Kellogg's
Chapter 2	IBM	**Chapter 10**	Mecklenburg County, NC
Chapter 3	General Motors	**Chapter 11**	Alameda County, CA
Chapter 4	Time Warner	**Chapter 12**	St. Louis, MO
Chapter 5	Las Vegas Sands Corporation	**Chapter 13**	Beta Alpha Psi
Chapter 6	Nike	**Chapter 14**	Suburban Propane Partners
Chapter 7	Wal-Mart	**Chapter 15**	Borders Group Inc.
Chapter 8	McDonald's	**Chapter 16**	Securities and Exchange Commission

Emphasis on current issues and trends

Business applications, taken from current news and actual financial statements, illustrate reporting practice, current issues and controversies. **Reporting perspectives** comment on topics such as the strengths and weaknesses in reporting standards, motivations for changes in standards, ethical issues, implications for information quality, and proposals for new standards.

 Extensive discussion and illustration of **international financial reporting standards and proposals** appear in each of the business combinations, foreign currency translation and transactions, and futures, options and swaps chapters.

Clear and logical development of business combinations topics

Reporting issues related to business combinations cover a variety of topics. Consolidation procedures are difficult to comprehend and can be confusing to students. We emphasize the **measurement aspects** of combinations—reporting assets and liabilities acquired, determining acquisition cost, valuing noncontrolling interests, eliminating intercompany accounts.

To make consolidation procedures more comprehensible, eliminations subsequent to acquisition (covered in Chapters 4-6) presume that the parent uses the **complete (full) equity method**. Exclusive use of the complete (full) equity method allows students to focus on the goals of consolidation and the key issues in consolidation procedures. Once students develop a solid understanding of the consolidation process, changes in procedures required when the parent uses the **cost method** can be introduced. The appendix to Chapter 4 explains the elimination entries necessary to adjust the parent's accounts to the complete equity method before proceeding with consolidation. The appendix also compares complete equity method eliminations to cost method eliminations.

Additional pedagogy

To reinforce concepts presented in each chapter and ensure student comprehension, we include two or more **in-chapter review problems** that require students to recall and apply the accounting techniques and concepts described in the chapter. The solutions to the review problems are included after each chapter's assignments.

Learning Objectives identify the primary learning outcomes for each chapter. An end-of-chapter **Review of Key Concepts** summarizes the key topics of each chapter.

Extensive class-tested end-of-chapter material

Outstanding assignment material is an essential component of a successful textbook. End-of-chapter **questions, exercises and problems** cover all major topics and have a range of difficulty levels, allowing students ample opportunity to practice their understanding of the chapter. Some problems require students to use real company data in applying their knowledge. Assignment material is class-tested, with an emphasis on relevance and accuracy.

Certain **business combination problems continue from chapter to chapter**. For example, P3.2 covers consolidation at the date of acquisition, and P4.7 covers consolidation of the same two companies in subsequent years. P4.2 covers subsequent year consolidation of a wholly owned subsidiary, and P5.7 addresses subsequent year consolidation of the same subsidiary, when the subsidiary has outside ownership. In P2.5, an acquisition is reported as a merger, and in P3.11 the same acquisition is reported as a stock investment and consolidation. P3.4, P4.4, P5.2, P5.4 and P5.5 use the same acquisition data to illustrate consolidation of a bargain purchase at the date of acquisition, subsequent years, and with a noncontrolling interest. Each of these problems can also be assigned separately. In working through these problems, students gain a clearer understanding of accounting for business combinations.

FEATURES NEW TO THIS EDITION

- We use **FASB Codification** references for all relevant U.S. GAAP
- We adjusted the organization of chapters to better reflect the logical flow of topics:
  - ○ Foreign currency translation (Chapter 7) immediately follows the business combinations chapters, illustrating translation and consolidation procedures for international subsidiaries.
  - ○ Reporting for futures, options and swaps (Chapter 9) immediately follows Chapter 8's coverage of foreign currency transactions and hedging, where hedging, hedge accounting, and forward contracts are introduced.
- A major rewrite of Chapter 7, Consolidating Foreign Currency Financial Statements, focuses on the features of **remeasurement and translation** and logical implications of the choice of functional currency.
- A major rewrite of Chapter 9, Futures, Options and Interest Rate Swaps, **provides a smooth transition from the material on foreign currency derivatives and hedge accounting** covered in Chapter 8, Foreign Currency Transactions and Hedging.
- A new appendix to Chapter 4 discusses consolidation eliminations when the parent uses the **cost method**
- End of chapter **multiple choice questions** are provided for each learning objective.
- New topics in this edition include **hedge accounting by state and local governments**, current issues in **pension accounting by state and local governments**, and accounting for **acquisitions made by private NFP organizations**
- The state and local government chapters are completely updated for the **new classifications of fund balance**, effective in 2011, and the **new format for the basic financial statements**, effective in 2012.

STANDARDS UPDATES IN THIS EDITION

Chapter coverage includes all relevant FASB Accounting Standards Updates, including:

- Accounting Standards Update No. 2009-17—Consolidations (Topic 810), **qualitative identification of a controlling interest in a variable interest entity**
- Accounting Standards Update No. 2011-08—Intangibles—Goodwill and Other (Topic 350), **qualitative determination of whether the goodwill impairment test is required**
- Accounting Standards Update No. 2010-07—Not-for-Profit Entities (Topic 958), **combinations of NFP organizations**
- Accounting Standards Update No. 2010-23—Health Care Entities (Topic 954), **measurement of charity care**
- Accounting Standards Update No. 2011-07—Health Care Entities (Topic 954), **uncollectible amounts related to patient service revenue**
- Accounting Standards Update No. 2011-05—Comprehensive Income (Topic 220), **presentation of net income and comprehensive income**

New GASB standards significantly change the reporting model for state and local governments:

- *SGAS 53*—Accounting and Financial Reporting for Derivative Instruments, **hedge accounting**
- *SGAS 54*—Fund Balance Reporting and Governmental Fund Type Definitions, **classification of fund balance**
- *SGAS 63*—Financial Reporting of Deferred Outflows of Resources, Deferred Inflows of Resources, and Net Position, **state and local government financial statement format**

New IFRS relate to advanced accounting topics:

- *IFRS 9*—Financial Instruments, **measurement and classification of debt and equity investments, impairment, and hedge accounting**
- *IFRS 10*—Consolidated Financial Statements, **criteria for consolidation**
- *IFRS 11*—Joint Arrangements, **reporting for joint ventures**

The web site for this text provides updates for changes in standards occurring subsequent to the publication date.

SUPPLEMENT PACKAGE

For Instructors

 Instructor CD-ROM: This convenient supplement provides the text's ancillary materials on a portable CD-ROM. All the faculty supplements that accompany the textbook are available, including PowerPoint, Solutions Manual, Test Bank, Excel Templates, and Computerized Test Bank.

Solutions Manual: Created by the textbook authors, the *Solutions Manual* contains complete solutions to all the assignments in the textbook.

Test Bank: Written by the textbook authors, the test bank includes multiple-choice questions and problems.

 Excel Templates: Excel spreadsheets for select assignments are provided on the book's website. These spreadsheets will save time in data entry and allow students to dedicate additional time to learning the material. The Excel spreadsheets are identified by the Excel icon.

PowerPoint: The PowerPoint slides outline key elements of each chapter.

Computerized Test Bank: This computerized version of the test bank enables an instructor to add and edit questions; create up to 99 versions of each test; attach graphic files to questions; import and export ASCII files; and select questions based on type or learning objective. It provides password protection for saved tests and question databases and is able to run on a network.

Website: All instructor materials are accessible via the book's Website (password protected). **www.cambridgepub.com**

myBusinessCourse: A web-based learning and assessment program intended to complement your textbook and classroom instruction. This easy-to-use course management system grades homework automatically and provide students with additional help when you are not available. In addition, detailed diagnostic tools assess class and individual performance. myBusinessCourse is ideal for online courses or traditional face-to-face courses for which you want to offer students more resources to succeed. Assignments with the ✔ in the margin are available in myBusinessCourse.

For Students

 Excel Templates: Excel spreadsheets for select assignments are provided on the book's website. These spreadsheets will save time in data entry and allow students to dedicate additional time to learning the material. The Excel spreadsheets are identified by the Excel icon.

Website: Practice quizzes, Excel templates, and other useful links are available to students free of charge on the book's Website.

BusinessCourse: A web-based learning and assessment program intended to complement your textbook and faculty instruction. This easy-to-use program grades homework automatically and provides you with additional help when your instructor is not available. Assignments with the ✔ in the margin are available in myBusinessCourse. Access is free with new copies of this textbook (look for page containing the access code towards the front of the book). If you buy a used copy of the book, you can purchase access at **www.mybusinesscourse.com**.

ACKNOWLEDGEMENTS

Many individuals helped us develop this textbook. We gratefully acknowledge their assistance, and list their names and affiliations below. We also thank Gene Bryson for his help with accuracy checking the textbook and solutions manual.

Mark Anderson, *University of Texas—Dallas*
Mark Bauman, *University Northern Iowa*
John Bildersee, *New York University*
Gene Bryson, *University of Alabama—Hunstville*
Tina Carpenter, *University of Georgia*
Jean Crawford, *Alabama State University*
Hemang Desai, *Southern Methodist University*
John Dexter, *Northwood University*
Judi Doing, *University of Arizona*
Linda Flaming, *Monmouth University*
Ronald Guidry, *Illinois State University*
Judith Harris, *NOVA Southeastern University*
Kenneth Hiltebeitel, *Villanova University*
Teresa Iannaconi, *KPMG LLP*
Patricia Johnson, *Canisius College*
Gordon Klein, *University of California— Los Angeles*

Lisa Koonce, *University of Texas—Austin*
Stanley Kratchman, *Texas A&M University*
Robert Larson, *University of Dayton*
Hugo Nurnberg, *CUNY—Baruch*
Bruce Oliver, *Rochester Institute of Technology*
Tina Quinn, *Arkansas State University*
Kenneth Shaw, *University of Missouri*
Pamela Smith, *Northern Illinois University*
John Surdick, *Xavier University*
Diane Tanner, *University of North Florida*
David Wallin, *Ohio State University*
Jamie Wang, *University of Wisconsin—Parkside*
Jan Williams, *University of Baltimore*
Sung Wook Yoon, *California State University— Northridge*
Ling Zhou, *Tulane University*

We express our appreciation for the support of the School of Management, State University of New York at Buffalo, and the Department of Accounting, Lehigh University. In addition, we are extremely grateful to George Werthman, Jill Fischer, Jocelyn Mousel, Rich Kolasa, Debbie McQuade, Terry McQuade, and the entire team at Cambridge Business Publishers for their encouragement, enthusiasm, and guidance. Comments are invited and encouraged from all instructors, students, and readers.

Susan S. Hamlen (hamlen@buffalo.edu)
Ronald J. Huefner (rhuefner@buffalo.edu)
James A. Largay III (jal3@lehigh.edu)

Brief Contents

Content

Chapter 3

Consolidated Financial Statements: Date of Acquisition   76

Chapter 4

Consolidated Financial Statements Subsequent to Acquisition   112

Chapter 5

Consolidated Financial Statements: Outside Interests   162

Chapter 6
Consolidated Financial Statements: Intercompany Transactions 210

Chapter 7
Consolidating Foreign Currency Financial Statements 250

Chapter 8

Foreign Currency Transactions and Hedging 304

Chapter 9

Futures, Options and Interest Rate Swaps 350

Chapter 10

State and Local Governments: Introduction and General Fund Transactions 386

Chapter 11

State and Local Governments: Other Transactions   **438**

Chapter 12

State and Local Governments: External Financial Reporting   **484**

Chapter 15

Bankruptcy and Reorganization   622

Chapter 16

The SEC and Financial Reporting   660

1

Intercorporate Investments: An Overview

LEARNING OBJECTIVES

LO1 Describe the reporting for trading, available-for-sale, and held-to-maturity intercorporate investments. (p. 5)

LO2 Explain the reporting for equity method intercorporate investments. (p. 8)

LO3 Describe the reporting for controlling interests in other companies. (p. 14)

LO4 Discuss International Financial Reporting Standards (IFRS) for intercorporate investments. (p. 16)

THE COCA-COLA COMPANY
www.coca-cola.com

The Coca-Cola Company is the world's largest producer of nonalcoholic beverages. In addition to Coca-Cola, its brands include Sprite, Dasani, Minute Maid and Nestea. Coca-Cola produces beverage syrup in concentrated form, and sells it to franchised bottlers. The bottlers mix the syrup with water and other ingredients, and bottle or can the finished beverages for delivery to retailers, restaurants, and food distributors.

Coca-Cola's investments in its bottlers and other companies take a variety of forms. At the end of 2010, Coca-Cola owned several legally separate bottling companies, including Coca-Cola Bottlers Philippines, Inc., and BCI Coca-Cola Bottling Company of Los Angeles. These companies are **subsidiaries** of Coca-Cola Company. Coca-Cola has a **significant interest** in some of its bottlers through equity ownership. It is involved in several **joint ventures**, where Coca-Cola shares decision-making authority with another company, and has certain financial relationships with other companies, called **variable interests**, which must be disclosed in its financial statements. Coca-Cola also holds **marketable debt and equity investments** in other companies, categorized as trading, available-for-sale, or held-to-maturity. These accounts appear as current and noncurrent assets on Coca-Cola's balance sheet.

Coca-Cola's financial statements illustrate the variety of intercorporate investments. Each investment type involves a different set of reporting requirements. This chapter presents an overview of reporting for the major types of investments in other companies. Source: The Coca-Cola Company 2010 annual report.

CHAPTER ORGANIZATION

Introduction	Marketable debt and equity investments	Investments with significant influence	Controlling investments	International Financial Reporting Standards
• Motivations for intercorporate investments • Types of investments	• Trading investments • Available-for-sale investments • Held-to-maturity investments	• Equity method investments • Joint ventures	• Statutory mergers, statutory consolidations, and asset acquisitions • Stock acquisitions • Variable interest entities	• Marketable debt and equity investments • Investments with significant influence • Joint ventures • Controlling investments

INTRODUCTION

Companies invest in other companies for many reasons, using a variety of financing arrangements, operating relationships and legal structures. Intercorporate investments are pervasive business activities, affect financial performance in profound ways, and have detailed and complex reporting requirements. How firms value investments and report gains and losses depends on the purpose of the investment and whether the investor has significant influence or control over the investee.

Motivations for Intercorporate Investments

Intercorporate investments achieve a variety of business purposes.

- A company purchases debt or equity securities of another company as a temporary investment of excess cash or as part of a longer-term risk-adjusted portfolio, expecting to receive dividends and capital gains.
- A company makes strategic investments to develop relationships with suppliers or customers or to gain access to new product or geographic markets.
- A company obtains a controlling interest in another company to facilitate activity along its supply chain.

The balance sheet and footnotes to **The Coca-Cola Company**'s December 31, 2010 annual report illustrate some of the most common types of intercorporate investments.

The Coca-Cola Company, Balance Sheet, Investments Lines Only		
December 31 *(in millions)*	2010	2009
Trading securities	$ 209	$ 61
Available-for-sale securities	485	398
Held-to-maturity securities	111	199
Equity method investments	6,954	6,217
Other investments, principally bottling companies	631	538

Coca-Cola holds trading, available-for-sale, and held-to-maturity investments in the securities of other companies to generate investment income and capital gains. It reports most of these investments at fair value.

Coca-Cola uses the **equity method** to account for investments in which it has significant influence. Coca-Cola has a 30 percent ownership interest in Coca-Cola Amatil, one of the largest bottlers in the Asia-Pacific region, a 32 percent interest in the bottler Coca-Cola FEMSA, operating in Latin America, and a 23 percent interest in Coca-Cola Hellenic, operating in 28 European countries. Coca-Cola holds these investments for strategic reasons and exerts significant influence over the operations of these companies. Coca-Cola shares decision making authority in joint ventures with other companies. Multon is a Russian juice business run jointly with Coca-Cola Hellenic Bottling Company S.A. Beverage Partners Worldwide is a joint venture with Nestlé S.A., distributing Nestea products in non-U.S. markets. These investments are also reported using the equity method.

In recent years, beverage companies have changed strategy with respect to their bottlers, in some cases concluding that full ownership rather than significant influence results in more flexible, efficient and timely manufacture and delivery of products. For many years Coca-Cola held between 30 and 35 percent ownership in Coca-Cola Enterprises (CCE), a major bottler. In 2010 it acquired full ownership of CCE's North American production, sales, and distribution operations. Coca-Cola also has controlling ownership of many other companies.

Coca-Cola has financial relationships with other companies, involving profit or debt guarantees. In some cases these relationships give Coca-Cola the power to direct these companies' activities, even though it does not have any ownership interests. The individual assets and liabilities of all these companies are included with Coca-Cola's assets and liabilities on its balance sheet, through a process known as **consolidation**. There is no separate investment line for these companies.

Types of Investments

For reporting purposes, intercorporate investments are divided into the following categories:

- *Trading* debt or equity securities are held on a short-term basis to generate profits through realized gains. Investors typically buy and sell these securities frequently.

- *Held-to-maturity* investments are *debt* securities intended to be held to maturity. There are only limited circumstances where the investor may sell the security before maturity, such as financial distress on the part of the issuer, or if the investor reorganizes through acquisition or disposal of a unit and must rebalance its portfolio to maintain its current credit rating.

- *Available-for-sale* investments are debt or equity securities held for income or gains in value that are not classified as trading or held-to-maturity.

- *Equity method* investments are stock investments that provide the investor with a significant influence over the investee, typically by holding 20 to 50 percent of the investee's voting stock. This category includes *joint ventures*, where the investor shares joint control of an entity.

- Debt or equity securities can be held as *hedges* of the investor's financial risk. For example, a U.S. company with payables denominated in euros may neutralize the risk of a weakening U.S. dollar by investing in euro-denominated debt securities, which gain in value to offset the loss on the payables if the U.S. dollar weakens.

- A company can acquire the assets and liabilities of another company; the acquired company is usually absorbed into the acquiring company and loses its separate legal identity. These transactions are called *statutory mergers*, *statutory consolidations*, or *asset acquisitions*, depending on the acquisition structure.

- A company can gain a *controlling interest* in another legally separate company, either through ownership of all or the majority of its voting stock—termed a *stock acquisition*—or through a legal agreement that gives the investor the right to the majority of the investee's risks and rewards. These acquired companies are called *subsidiaries*. Entities controlled through a legal agreement rather than equity ownership are also known as *variable interest entities*.

FASB ASC Topic 825 allows companies to elect fair value reporting (the "fair value option") for eligible noncontrolling intercorporate investments. Investments for which the fair value option is chosen are reported at fair value and value changes appear in income. The discussion below assumes the investor does *not* elect the fair value option. Controlling equity investments are not eligible for the fair value option.

MARKETABLE DEBT AND EQUITY INVESTMENTS

LO1 Describe the reporting for trading, available-for-sale, and held-to-maturity investments in other companies.

Many businesses invest in the debt and equity securities of other companies to generate investment income and capital gains. Examples of debt securities include commercial paper, corporate bonds, and redeemable preferred stock. Equity investments typically take the form of shares of a company's common or preferred stock, but often involve put or call options on the shares, allowing the investor to sell or buy shares at a fixed price. Such investors have no significant influence over the investee, either because the investments are debt securities, or the equity investment is a small fraction of total ownership, generally less than 20 percent. *ASC Topic 320* describes reporting requirements for these securities.

The FASB is currently considering major changes in reporting requirements for investments covered by *ASC Topic 320*. As this edition goes to press, no Accounting Standards Update has been issued. The discussion below reflects GAAP in effect in 2013.

ASC Topic 320 divides investments with readily determinable market values into three categories or portfolios: trading, available-for-sale, and held-to-maturity investments. When market value is not determinable, investments are reported at cost. Because intermediate accounting courses detail the reporting for these investments, we provide only a brief discussion.

Trading Investments

Trading investments can be in the form of debt or equity securities. These investments appear on the balance sheet as current assets reported at fair value, with unrealized gains and losses reported on the income statement as market prices change. Investment income, in the form of interest or dividends, is reported in income as earned. An illustration is based on the information in Exhibit 1.1.

EXHIBIT 1.1   Securities Portfolio

Security	Date Acquired	Cost	Dec. 31, 2012 Fair Value	Date Sold	Selling Price
A.........	10/15/12	$100,000	$125,000	1/15/13	$120,000
B.........	10/15/12	500,000	485,000	1/15/13	496,000
C.........	10/15/12	200,000	N/A	12/5/12	214,000

When these securities are classified as trading securities, the journal entries related to these securities are as follows:

2012			
Oct. 15	Investment in trading securities.............................	800,000	
	Cash...		800,000
	To record investment in trading securities costing a total of $800,000 in cash.		
2012			
Dec. 5	Cash...	214,000	
	Investment in trading securities........................		200,000
	Gain on sale of trading securities		14,000
	To record sale of trading security C.		
2012			
Dec. 31	Investment in trading securities.............................	10,000	
	Unrealized gain on trading securities		10,000
	To record unrealized value change in securities A and B; unrealized gain of $25,000 on security A and unrealized loss of $15,000 on security B.		
2013			
Jan. 15	Cash...	616,000	
	Investment in trading securities........................		610,000
	Gain on sale of trading securities		6,000
	To record sale of trading securities A and B; cash received = $120,000 + $496,000, credit to Investment = $125,000 + $485,000.		

All unrealized and realized gains and losses on trading securities are reported on the income statement.

Available-for-Sale Investments

Investments in available-for-sale (AFS) securities may also be debt or equity securities that are reported at fair value as current or noncurrent assets on the balance sheet. As market prices change, unrealized gains and losses on AFS securities are reported in other comprehensive income (OCI), which is closed to accumulated other comprehensive income (AOCI) in the equity section of the balance sheet. When AFS securities are sold, the investor transfers the unrealized gain or loss from AOCI to the income statement. Interest or dividend income is reported in income as earned.

Assume that the securities in Exhibit 1.1 are classified as AFS securities. Journal entries are as follows:

2012			
Oct. 15	Investment in AFS securities	800,000	
	Cash		800,000
	To record investment in AFS securities A, B and C.		
2012			
Dec. 5	Cash	214,000	
	Investment in AFS securities		200,000
	Gain on sale of AFS securities (income)		14,000
	To record the sale of AFS security C. When AFS securities are *purchased and sold in the same reporting period, gains and losses* *can be reported directly in income without going through OCI.*		
2012			
Dec. 31	Investment in AFS securities	10,000	
	Unrealized gains on AFS securities (OCI)		10,000
	To record unrealized value changes for AFS securities A and B in *OCI; OCI is closed to AOCI on the balance sheet.*		
2013			
Jan. 15	Cash	616,000	
	Investment in AFS securities		610,000
	Gain on sale of AFS securities (income)		6,000
	To record sale of AFS securities A and B.		
Jan. 15	Unrealized gains on AFS securities (AOCI)	10,000	
	Gain on sale of AFS securities (income)		10,000
	To reclassify unrealized gains on sales of AFS securities from *AOCI to income.*		

The principal difference in reporting for trading and available-for-sale investments is the timing of gain and loss recognition on the income statement. For trading securities, gains and losses affect net income *as prices change*. For AFS securities, gains and losses affect net income *when they are sold*.

Impairment Testing for AFS Securities   Although available-for-sale debt and equity securities are already carried at fair value on the balance sheet, *ASC Section 320-10-35* requires impairment testing for these securities. Impairment losses differ from other declines in value because they are reported on the income statement, not in other comprehensive income. There are two steps to the impairment test.

1.   Determine whether the investment is impaired. Impairment occurs if the security's fair value is below its *cost*.

2.   Decide whether the impairment is "**other than temporary**." If the investor intends to sell the security soon after the balance sheet date, the impairment is clearly other than temporary. If not, the investor must assess whether, during the time it intends to hold the security, it will recover the security's cost.

Suppose the $15,000 decline in value of AFS security B at December 31, 2012, is determined to be other than temporary. The entry to adjust securities A and B to fair value is:

2012			
Dec. 31	Investment in AFS securities	10,000	
	Loss on security B (income)	15,000	
	Unrealized gain on security A (OCI)		25,000
	To record unrealized gain on security A and impairment loss on *security B.*		

For future impairment testing, security B's "cost" is $485,000. Any subsequent increases in fair value are not reported. Note that the amount of the impairment loss reported on the income statement is the decline in value below *cost*, not carrying value. If unrealized gains or losses have previously been recorded, and the security incurs an other-than-temporary impairment loss, any amounts recorded in AOCI are reclassified to income. Suppose an AFS investment, carried at $200,000, was originally acquired for $160,000. Its fair value is currently $90,000. The $70,000 loss (= $160,000 − $90,000) is determined to be other-than-temporary. The entry to record the impairment loss is:

Unrealized gain on AFS securities (OCI)	40,000	
Impairment loss on AFS securities (income)	70,000	
Investment in AFS securities		110,000
To record impairment loss on AFS securities.		

Held-to-Maturity Investments

Investments in held-to-maturity (HTM) securities can only be debt securities, since equity securities have no maturity date. They appear on the balance sheet as noncurrent assets until the year of maturity, and are reported at amortized cost. No gains or losses are reported unless the securities are not held to maturity as intended, and this only occurs under the limited circumstances discussed above. When debt securities are purchased above or below face value, the premium or discount is amortized over time as interest income is reported.

Assume investment of $965,349 in a $1,000,000 face value corporate bond on January 1, 2012, a price producing a 6 percent yield to maturity. The bond pays 5 percent interest annually on December 31, matures on December 31, 2015, and is classified as an HTM security. We use the effective interest method to amortize the discount. Journal entries to maturity are as follows:

2012			
Jan. 1	Investment in HTM securities.	965,349	
	Cash		965,349
	To record investment in HTM securities.		
2012			
Dec. 31	Cash.	50,000	
	Investment in HTM securities.	7,921	
	Interest income		57,921
	To record interest income for 2010; $50,000 = 5% × $1,000,000;		
	$57,921 = 6% × $965,349.		
2013			
Dec. 31	Cash.	50,000	
	Investment in HTM securities.	8,396	
	Interest income		58,396
	To record interest income for 2011; $58,396 = 6% × $973,270		
	(= $965,349 + $7,921).		
2014			
Dec. 31	Cash.	50,000	
	Investment in HTM securities.	8,900	
	Interest income		58,900
	To record interest income for 2012; $58,900 = 6% × $981,666		
	(= $973,270 + $8,396).		
2015			
Dec. 31	Cash.	50,000	
	Investment in HTM securities.	9,434	
	Interest income		59,434
	To record interest income for 2013; $59,434 = 6% × $990,566		
	(= $981,666 + $8,900).		
Dec. 31	Cash.	1,000,000	
	Investment in HTM securities		1,000,000
	To record receipt of the face value of the matured bond;		
	$1,000,000 = $990,566 + $9,434.		

Impairment Testing for HTM Investments Although companies normally report HTM securities at amortized cost, *ASC Section 320-10-35* requires that they be evaluated for impairment. If the fair value of the security declines below amortized cost, and the decline is judged to be "**other than temporary**," we write the security down to fair value and report the impairment loss on the income statement. Any subsequent increases in fair value are not reported. The Codification offers the following guidance in measuring other-than-temporary impairment:

> If the present value of cash flows expected to be collected is less than the amortized cost basis of the security, the entire amortized cost basis of the security will not be recovered (that is, a credit loss exists), and an other-than-temporary impairment shall be considered to have occurred. *(ASC para. 320-10-35-33C)*

In the illustration above, assume that a significant decrease in the bond issuer's profitability, and analysts' severe downgrade of company prospects, reduced the December 31, 2013, fair value of the corporate bond to $200,000 when the amortized cost of the bond is $981,666. If the decline in fair value is attributed to other-than-temporary impairment, the investor reports the impairment loss in income, as follows:

2013			
Dec. 31	Impairment loss on HTM securities	781,666	
	Investment in HTM securities		781,666
	To record other-than-temporary impairment of HTM securities;		
	$781,666 = $200,000 − $981,666.		

REVIEW 1   •   Trading, AFS, and HTM Investments

Assume **The Coca-Cola Company** makes the following intercorporate investments on January 2, 2013:

Security	Type	Cost
A	Trading	$ 300,000
B	AFS	1,000,000
C	HTM	486,384

Security C is a 3-year $500,000 face value corporate bond paying 4% interest annually on December 31 and yielding 5% to maturity. Coca-Cola sells Security A for $265,000 on June 15, 2013, and acquires Security D on October 15, 2013, for $250,000. Security D is classified as a trading security.

December 31, 2013, fair values are as follows:

Security	Type	Fair Value
B	AFS	$920,000
C	HTM	495,000
D	Trading	260,000

Cash dividends of $12,000 are received on the investments in Securities B and D on December 1, 2013. Interest of $20,000 is received on Security C on December 31, 2013.

Required: Prepare all entries related to the above investments for 2013.

Solutions are located after the chapter assignments.

INVESTMENTS WITH SIGNIFICANT INFLUENCE

LO2 Explain the reporting for equity method intercorporate investments.

Unless a company elects the *ASC Section 825-10-25* fair value option, *ASC Topic 323* requires that the **equity method** be used to account for large equity investments that allow the investor to exercise *significant influence* over the operating and financial decisions of the investee. **Significant influence** is assumed to be present if the investor owns between 20 and 50 percent of the investee's voting stock. Ownership of less than 20 percent of the investee's voting stock implies no significant influence, unless such influence can be demonstrated. The Codification offers guidelines that indicate the investor's ability to exert significant influence, including:

- representation on the investee's board of directors
- involvement in the development of investee operating and financial policies
- significant transactions between investor and investee

The 20 to 50 percent ownership test is a guideline; the *key issue* is whether the investor *in fact* exerts significant influence over the investee's operations. Significant influence may exist with less than 20 percent ownership of the investee's voting shares, or there may be circumstances where a large minority ownership does not indicate significant influence. *ASC para. 323-10-15-10* provides guidance on this point. For example, if the investor has given up significant shareholder rights, has tried but failed to gain representation on the investee's board, or if other owners not influenced by the investor control the investee's operations, the equity method is not appropriate even if the investor holds 20 to 50 percent of the voting stock.

Accounting Using the Equity Method

When the investor can influence the investee's operating and financial decisions and the amount and timing of dividends the investee pays, performance of the investment is not accurately measured by dividend payout. Instead, investment performance should parallel the investee's performance. The equity method achieves this goal with the following procedures:

- Increase (decrease) the investment account by the investor's share of the investee's income (loss).
- The investor reports its share of the investee's income (loss) in income.
- Reduce the investment account for dividends from the investee.

The investor's investment balance therefore changes in proportion to the changes in the investee's retained earnings.

Suppose that on January 2, 2013, The Coca-Cola Company acquires 300,000 voting shares of Rocky Mountain Bottlers for $40 per share, or a total investment of $12 million in cash. Because Rocky Mountain has one million voting shares, Coca-Cola's 30 percent ownership indicates significant influence and use of the equity method is appropriate. Rocky Mountain reports net income of $2 million for the year ended December 31, 2013. It declares a cash dividend of $0.50 per share on November 1, 2013, and pays the dividend on December 2, 2013. Coca-Cola records the following entries for 2013 relative to its equity method investment in Rocky Mountain:

2013			
Jan. 2	Investment in Rocky Mountain Bottlers...........................	12,000,000	
	Cash		12,000,000
	To record the investment.		
2013			
Nov. 1	Dividends receivable	150,000	
	Investment in Rocky Mountain Bottlers......................		150,000
	To record the declared dividend; $150,000 = $0.50 × 300,000.		
2013			
Dec. 2	Cash..	150,000	
	Dividends receivable		150,000
	To record receipt of the declared dividend.		
2013			
Dec. 31	Investment in Rocky Mountain Bottlers.........................	600,000	
	Equity in income of Rocky Mountain Bottlers.................		600,000
	To accrue the earnings of the investee; $600,000 = 30% × $2,000,000.		

The December 31, 2013, investment balance, reported on Coca-Cola's balance sheet in noncurrent assets, is $12,450,000 (= $12,000,000 − $150,000 + $600,000). Equity in income of Rocky Mountain Bottlers of $600,000 appears as a component of Coca-Cola's income for 2013.

Equity in Net Income Calculation

The discussion above computed equity in net income as the investor's share of the investee's reported net income, based on the assumption that the investee's reported net income accurately measures the performance of the investment. When investment cost differs from the investee's book value, or the investor and investee transact business with each other, the investor must make adjustments to the investee's reported income.

At the date of acquisition, investment cost usually exceeds the book value of the investee, calculated as its reported assets less liabilities. The investee reports its noncurrent assets such as plant and equipment at cost less accumulated depreciation, not current fair value. Internally developed intangible assets, such as favorable contractual agreements, customer base, technology and reputation do not appear as assets on the investee's balance sheet. Reported liabilities may also not reflect fair values—the investee may have unrecorded contingent liabilities such as lawsuits—but these differences are typically not as significant. For these reasons an investee's shares almost always sell at a price in excess of book value.

Companies usually take large noncontrolling interests in other entities for strategic reasons that facilitate business activities between the companies. Common transactions involve intercompany sales of raw materials or finished goods inventories. For example, Coca-Cola sells syrup to its 30-percent-owned bottler, Coca-Cola Amatil. When related entities sell merchandise to each other, the profit on these transactions is not considered to be earned until the merchandise is sold to an unrelated outside party.

Amortization of Investment Cost in Excess of Book Value Acquired   To accurately measure investment performance, we must consider any investment cost in excess of investee book value. The investee's reported income reflects appropriate write-offs of its reported assets, in the form of depreciation, amortization, and impairment losses. If investment cost reflects additional assets not recorded on the investee's books, equity in net income should in turn reflect write-offs of these additional assets. In the above discussion, we calculated Coca-Cola's share of Rocky Mountain Bottlers' income as a proportion of Rocky Mountain's reported net income. If Coca-Cola's investment cost at the date of investment differs from Rocky Mountain's underlying book value, we must make adjustments to accurately measure investment performance.

Suppose that on January 2, 2013, Rocky Mountain reports total assets of $80 million and total liabilities of $50 million, indicating a book value of $30 million. Coca-Cola therefore paid $3 million (= $12 million − 30% × $30 million) more for its 30 percent investment than its share of Rocky Mountain's underlying book value. Analysis of Rocky Mountain's assets and liabilities reveals undervaluation of its plant and equipment by $1 million and unreported technology valued at $5 million. We can explain the $3 million excess over acquired book value as follows:

Price paid		$12,000,000
Share of Rocky Mountain's net assets acquired:		
Book value (30% x $30,000,000)	$9,000,000	
Revaluation of plant and equipment (30% x $1,000,000)	300,000	
Unreported technology (30% x $5,000,000).	1,500,000	10,800,000
Additional investment cost (goodwill).		$ 1,200,000

Of the total $3 million excess cost, $1,800,000 (= $300,000 + $1,500,000) is explained by specific asset undervaluations. The remaining unexplained cost is attributed to goodwill, representing the additional cost not explained by underreported or unreported identifiable assets.

Rocky Mountain does not report depreciation, amortization and impairment losses on the additional assets embedded in Coca-Cola's investment cost, because these assets do not appear on Rocky Mountain's books. Coca-Cola therefore adjusts its equity in the net income of Rocky Mountain for depreciation and amortization of revaluations of limited life assets. Chapter 4 in this text covers these requirements in detail; we briefly summarize that discussion here.

The Codification requires that previously unreported intangible assets be identified as having limited lives or indefinite lives. Examples of previously unreported limited life intangibles include favorable lease agreements and customer lists. Examples of indefinite life intangibles include brand names, franchises, and in-process research and development. Limited life intangibles are amortized over their estimated lives, generally on a straight-line basis.

For investments reported using the equity method, equity in net income is adjusted for depreciation and amortization on revaluations of *tangible assets* and *limited life intangible assets*, but any adjustment for goodwill impairment is *prohibited*. Similarly, the investor should not adjust equity in net income for impairment losses on the investee's previously unreported intangibles.

Continuing Coca-Cola's investment in 30 percent of Rocky Mountain Bottlers' voting stock, assume that the revalued plant and equipment has a remaining life of 10 years as of January 2, 2013, straight-line, and the previously unreported technology is a limited life intangible asset with a five-year life. Coca-Cola's 2013 equity in the income of Rocky Mountain Bottlers is reduced by the implied depreciation on the plant and equipment revaluation of $30,000 (= $300,000/10) and amortization of previously unreported technology of $300,000 (= $1,500,000/5). In practice, however, the investor often attributes the excess cost entirely to goodwill. This shortcut avoids any income adjustments for revaluation write-offs.

Unconfirmed Inventory Profits An investor may sell inventory to its investee, termed **downstream** sales, or an investee may sell merchandise to the investor, termed **upstream** sales. Both companies record the sales as if they are selling to outside customers. If both companies sell the merchandise at a markup over cost, they will report a gross margin on these intercompany sales as part of their income. However, if the inventories are not yet sold to an unrelated outside party at year-end, this gross margin is not yet earned and must be removed when calculating equity in the net income of the investee.

Suppose that during 2013 Rocky Mountain Bottlers sells canned beverages to Coca-Cola (upstream) for $800,000, an average markup of 20 percent on cost. Coca-Cola still holds $210,000 of this inventory at year-end. During 2013 Coca-Cola sells finished products to Rocky Mountain (downstream) for $500,000, an average markup of 25 percent on cost. Rocky Mountain holds $100,000 of this inventory at year-end. The total unconfirmed profit on the ending inventories is as follows:

Unconfirmed gross profit on $210,000 upstream sales:
$210,000 − $210,000/1.20 = $35,000
Unconfirmed gross profit on $100,000 downstream sales:
$100,000 − $100,000/1.25 = $20,000

Coca-Cola's 2013 equity in the income of Rocky Mountain Bottlers is reduced by $10,500 (= 30% × $35,000) and $6,000 (= 30% × $20,000). In 2014, when the beginning inventories are sold to outside customers, the profit is confirmed and equity in net income is increased by $10,500 and $6,000.

To summarize, Coca-Cola's equity in the 2013 income of Rocky Mountain is calculated as follows:

Coca-Cola's share of Rocky Mountain's reported net income (30% x $2,000,000)	$600,000
Revaluation write-offs:	
Plant and equipment.	(30,000)
Previously unreported technology	(300,000)
Unconfirmed inventory profits:	
Upstream sales.	(10,500)
Downstream sales	(6,000)
Equity in net income of Rocky Mountain	$253,500

Coca-Cola's end-of-year entry to recognize its share of Rocky Mountain's income is:

2013			
Dec. 31	Investment in Rocky Mountain Bottlers	253,500	
	Equity in income of Rocky Mountain Bottlers		253,500
	To accrue Coca-Cola's share of the earnings of the investee.		

The investment balance at year-end is $12,103,500 (= $12,000,000 - $150,000 + $253,500).

The equity method required for *external* reporting of *significant influence investments* differs from the complete (full) equity method used *internally* by a *controlling* parent company to facilitate consolidation procedures. Chapters 4 through 6 provide further discussion of these differences.

Other Comprehensive Income and the Equity Method

Using the equity method, the investor reports its share of the investee's performance each year on its own books. A company's performance is measured by its income, which accumulates in retained earnings, but other elements of performance are reflected in accumulated other comprehensive income, an equity account on its balance sheet. To fully report the investee's performance, the investor adjusts its investment and other comprehensive income for its share of the investee's yearly OCI.

Assume that in 2013 Rocky Mountain reported $200,000 in unrealized gains on AFS securities. In addition to the entries above, Coca-Cola makes the following entry to reflect these gains:

2013			
Dec. 31	Investment in Rocky Mountain Bottlers	60,000	
	Unrealized gains on equity method investments (OCI)		60,000
	To report 30% share of Rocky Mountain's unrealized gains on AFS securities.		

Impairment Testing

ASC para. 323-10-35-32 requires impairment testing of equity method investments. If the fair value of the investment declines below its carrying value, and the decline is judged to be other than temporary, the investment is written down and the loss appears on the investor's income statement. Any subsequent increases in fair value are not reported.

- -

Reporting Perspective

Typically the cost of equity method investments exceeds the underlying book value of the investee, because the investee has assets valued by the market but not reported on its balance sheet. When using the equity method, the investor identifies the specific assets that are undervalued or not reported on the investee's books. The investor then reports equity in the net income of the investee as its share of the investee's reported net income, adjusted for write-offs of those undervalued or unreported assets with limited lives. Equity in net income is *not* adjusted for impairments of indefinite life intangibles, including goodwill.

Why are impairments in the investee's goodwill and other indefinite life intangibles not included when computing equity in net income? One logical explanation is that the impairment test for the investment as a whole should reflect any impairment losses in the investee's underlying assets. If the investment is subject to other-than-temporary impairment, expectations concerning the investee's future performance have significantly declined. A financially distressed investee's goodwill is therefore impaired. There are also practical arguments for not reporting impairments of the investee's indefinite life intangibles in equity in net income: (1) the investor may not have enough information to assess impairment losses on the investee's intangible assets; (2) the investor has a significant influence over the investee's operations, but may not have access to the detailed information on future cash flows necessary to properly test for impairment.

- -

BUSINESS APPLICATION   Impairment Testing

In 2010 **The Coca-Cola Company** recorded impairment losses of $26 million on its investments in debt and equity securities, as part of other income (loss). Note 1 to the 2010 financial statements describes Coca-Cola's impairment testing.

> Each reporting period we review all of our investments in equity and debt securities, except for those classified as trading, to determine whether a significant event or change in circumstances has occurred that may have an adverse effect on the fair value of each investment. When such events or changes occur, we evaluate the fair value compared to our cost basis in the investment. . . . The fair values of most of our investments in publicly traded companies are often readily available based on quoted market prices. For investments in nonpublicly traded companies, management's assessment of fair value is based on valuation methodologies including discounted cash flows, estimate of sales proceeds and appraisals, as appropriate.
>
> In the event the fair value of an investment declines below our cost basis, management determines if the decline in fair value is other than temporary. . . . Management's assessment as to the nature of a decline in fair value is based on, among other things, the length of time and the extent to which the market value has been less than our cost basis, the financial condition and near-term prospects of the issuer, and our intent and ability to retain the investment for a period of time sufficient to allow for any anticipated recovery in market value.

Coca-Cola uses a variety of methods to measure the fair value of its investments, and forecasts the future financial condition of the investee and the investment holding period to determine if declines in value are other than temporary. Source: The Coca-Cola Company 2010 annual report.

Joint Ventures

A **joint venture** is an entity formed by a small group of individuals or firms that contribute resources and jointly share in managing and controlling the venture. Joint ventures are traditionally established to carry out a single business transaction or activity, often over a limited period of time. Frequently, the owners of a joint venture are themselves large firms, either partnerships or corporations. A **corporate joint venture** exists when the venture is organized as a corporation. Participants form joint ventures for activities when it is mutually desirable to combine expertise, special technology, capital, or access to certain markets. Examples include research projects or development of new products, in which two areas of technology must be joined, and large-scale construction projects, in which the capital and facilities of two or more contractors are needed. Although joint ventures are frequently short-lived, they can last several years and their initial projects may lead to ongoing business activities.

We discussed Coca-Cola's joint ventures with Nestlé and Coca-Cola Hellenic earlier in this chapter. These joint ventures expand Coca-Cola's markets internationally. U.S. companies follow the guidelines of *ASC Topic 323*: investments of 20 to 50 percent interest in an investee are presumed to give the investor significant influence and require use of the equity method.

Reporting Perspective

If two companies form a joint venture with equal interests, U.S. GAAP allows both companies to report the venture using the equity method. As a result, the separate assets and liabilities of the joint venture do not appear on *any* balance sheet. Each investor reports its interest as a one-line equity investment in the asset section of its balance sheet. Similarly, the separate revenues and expenses of the joint venture do not appear on *any* income statement. Each investor reports its equity in the joint venture's net income on one line in its income statement.

Coca-Cola and Nestlé each have 50 percent ownership in Beverage Partners Worldwide (BPW). Suppose Coca-Cola instead had 60 percent ownership, and Nestlé 40 percent. Nestlé would continue to account for its investment using the equity method, assuming it retained significant influence over BPW. Coca-Cola, on the other hand, now owns a 60 percent controlling interest and would consolidate BPW on its financial statements. Consolidation involves combining the separate assets, liabilities, revenues and expenses of BPW with Coca-Cola's own accounts on its financial statements. The next section introduces reporting for controlling equity investments.

REVIEW 2   ●   Reporting for Equity Method Investments

On January 5, 2014, Fizzy Cola Corporation, headquartered in Minneapolis, MN, acquires 25 percent of the voting stock of Armadillo Bottlers, located in Austin, TX, to support expansion in southwestern U.S. markets. Fizzy Cola pays $15 million in cash for the stock. Armadillo's book value is $20 million at the acquisition date, and its assets and liabilities are fairly stated except for unreported customer-related intangible assets valued at $10 million, with average expected lives of five years. In 2014, Armadillo reports net income of $3 million.

Armadillo sells canned and bottled beverages to Fizzy Cola at a markup of 30 percent on cost. Fizzy Cola sells syrup to Armadillo at a markup of 20 percent on cost. At December 31, 2014, Fizzy Cola's inventory includes $325,000 in merchandise acquired from Armadillo. Armadillo's inventory includes $480,000 in merchandise purchased from Fizzy Cola. Armadillo pays total cash dividends of $500,000 on December 1, 2014. Fizzy Cola accounts for its investment in Armadillo using the equity method.

Required: Prepare Fizzy Cola's entries to record the above information for 2014.

Solutions are located after the chapter assignments.

CONTROLLING INVESTMENTS

LO3 Describe the reporting for controlling interests in other companies.

Investments in other companies may give the investor control over the operating and financial decisions of the investee. The investment structures may take different forms, as follows:

● **Statutory merger**, **statutory consolidation**, or **asset acquisition**, where the investor directly acquires the assets and liabilities of the investee. Statutory mergers occur when the investor acquires the investee and becomes the remaining legal entity. In a statutory consolidation, a new entity is formed to acquire both the investor and investee. In asset acquisitions, the investor acquires a subset of the investee's assets.

● **Stock acquisition**, where the investor acquires a controlling interest in the voting stock of the investee.

● **Variable interest entity**, where the investor may not hold the investee's stock, but legal agreements give it the power to direct the investee's activities, the obligation to absorb its losses and the right to receive its benefits. The investee's actual equity holders do not have the usual rights and responsibilities pertaining to equity ownership.

Investors should be able to evaluate a company's complete financial performance by looking at its financial statements. If the company controls the resources of another company, investors should see the results of decisions affecting these resources in the controlling company's financial statements. Therefore, regardless of the investment structure used to obtain control, reporting policies are generally the same—the assets, liabilities, revenues and expenses of the controlled investee are combined with those of the investor for presentation in its financial statements.

Statutory Mergers, Statutory Consolidations, and Asset Acquisitions

When the investor acquires the assets and liabilities of the investee, it records these assets and liabilities directly on its books at fair value. Consider again Coca-Cola's acquisition of Rocky Mountain Bottlers, but assume Coca-Cola acquires *all* of Rocky Mountain's assets and liabilities in a statutory merger. Information on this acquisition is in Exhibit 1.2 below.

EXHIBIT 1.2   Coca-Cola's Acquisition of Rocky Mountain Bottlers

Coca-Cola pays $40,000,000 in cash to acquire the assets and liabilities of Rocky Mountain Bottlers on January 2, 2013. Fair values of Rocky Mountain's reported assets and liabilities on that date are as follows:

Rocky Mountain Bottlers	Fair value
Current assets	$20,000,000
Plant and equipment	61,000,000
Current liabilities	15,000,000
Long-term liabilities	35,000,000

Coca-Cola identified and valued Rocky Mountain's previously unreported intangible assets as follows:

Technology	$ 5,000,000

The acquisition price is analyzed as follows:

Price paid		$40,000,000
Fair value of identifiable net assets acquired:		
Current assets	$20,000,000	
Plant and equipment	61,000,000	
Technology	5,000,000	
Current liabilities	(15,000,000)	
Long-term debt	(35,000,000)	36,000,000
Goodwill		$ 4,000,000

Coca-Cola makes the following January 2 entry on its books:

Current assets	20,000,000	
Plant and equipment	61,000,000	
Technology	5,000,000	
Goodwill	4,000,000	
Current liabilities		15,000,000
Long-term debt		35,000,000
Cash		40,000,000
To record the acquisition of Rocky Mountain Bottlers for $40,000,000 in cash.		

Coca-Cola records Rocky Mountain's assets and liabilities directly on its books. Rocky Mountain ceases to exist as a separate entity, and Coca-Cola reports Rocky Mountain's subsequent activities directly in its own financial records. Coca-Cola reports its acquisition of Rocky Mountain's assets and liabilities the same way it reports any other acquisition of property.

Stock Acquisitions

When an investor obtains control over another company by investing in its *voting stock*, the investee remains a separate legal entity. U.S. GAAP states that generally the investor has control over an investee when it owns the *majority* of its voting stock. Control may be obtained with a large minority ownership, but under U.S. GAAP this reporting option is almost never used.

When the investor has a controlling interest in the voting stock of an investee, the investor is known as the **parent**, the acquired company is the **subsidiary**, and the two companies remain as separate legal entities, recording transactions on their own books. At the end of each reporting period, the accountant **consolidates** the separate financial records of the parent and subsidiary for presentation in the annual report.

Suppose Coca-Cola acquires and holds all of the *voting stock* of Rocky Mountain Bottlers, paying the former stockholders of Rocky Mountain $40,000,000 cash. Coca-Cola makes the following entry on its own books:

Investment in Rocky Mountain Bottlers	40,000,000	
Cash		40,000,000
To record acquisition of all Rocky Mountain's stock for $40,000,000 cash.		

Rocky Mountain Bottlers continues to exist as a separate entity, and reports its financial activities on its own books. At the end of each reporting period, a *consolidation working paper* is used to combine the financial results of Coca-Cola and Rocky Mountain, as if Coca-Cola had reported Rocky Mountain's acquired assets and liabilities, and subsequent activities, directly on its books. Chapters 3 through 6 discuss this process.

Variable Interest Entities

Variable interest entities (VIEs) are similar to stock acquisitions, in that the investee is a separate legal entity controlled by another company. However, control occurs through legal relationships rather than stock ownership. Two reporting questions arise: (1) Is the entity a variable interest entity, and (2) must the investor consolidate the entity with its own financial statements? Chapter 3 provides detailed answers to these questions. The following discussion is a brief introduction.

According to *ASC para. 810-10-15-14*, if the entity must obtain guarantees from other parties in order to obtain financing, or if the equity holders do not have the usual rights and responsibilities pertaining to equity ownership, such as voting rights and the right to residual returns, the entity is a VIE. A common example is a leasing arrangement where a company creates a separate legal entity to purchase long-term assets, funded by loans guaranteed by the company. That entity leases the assets to the company, and uses the lease payments to pay interest and principal on the debt. The entity has a small outside equity ownership, but rights to dividends or returns in liquidation may be contractually guaranteed or limited, leaving the equity owners with rights similar to debtholders. The question is whether the entity can finance its activities without additional support, such as guaranteed loans or future funding commitments, from affiliated entities. If not, the entity is a VIE.

ASC para. 810-10-25-38A requires the entity that has the power to direct the VIE's activities, absorbs the majority of the VIE's expected losses and/or receives a majority of the VIE's residual gains, to consolidate the VIE. Consolidation procedures parallel those for stock investments.

INTERNATIONAL FINANCIAL REPORTING STANDARDS FOR INTERCORPORATE INVESTMENTS

LO4 Discuss International Financial Reporting Standards (IFRS) for intercorporate investments.

International financial reporting standards (IFRS) for intercorporate investments are found in the following pronouncements:

- *IAS 28*, Investments in Associates
- *IAS 39*, Financial Instruments: Recognition and Measurement
- *IFRS 3(R)*, Business Combinations
- *IFRS 9*, Financial Instruments
- *IFRS 10*, Consolidated Financial Statements
- *IFRS 11*, Joint Arrangements

In light of the 2008 credit crisis, both the FASB and the IASB recently proposed significant changes in reporting for investments in debt and equity securities that do not involve significant or controlling interests. The IASB's financial instruments project has three phases: classification and measurement, impairment, and hedge accounting. The classification and measurement phase was completed in 2009, with the issuance of *IFRS 9*. The guidance in the other two phases will be added to IFRS 9 as they are completed. Although *IFRS 9* will eventually replace *IAS 39*, in 2011 its effective date was moved from 2013 to 2015. The discussion below includes current *IAS 39* guidance as well as *IFRS 9* requirements.

The IASB also changed the requirements for joint ventures (*IFRS 11*) and for deciding when to consolidate an equity investment (*IFRS 10*). Both of these standards become effective in 2013, and the discussion below reflects their requirements.

Marketable Debt and Equity Investments

IFRS for marketable investments in debt and equity securities, found in *IAS 39*, generally parallel current U.S. GAAP. Investments are classified as trading, available-for-sale, and held-to-maturity. Trading and available-for-sale securities are reported at fair value, with unrealized gains and losses on trading securities reported in income, and unrealized gains and losses on available-for-sale securities reported in equity until the securities are sold. Held-to-maturity debt securities are carried at amortized cost.

IFRS for impairment losses focuses on specific objective evidence of the decline in fair value, citing observance of particular "*loss events*," such as a decline in credit rating or if the investee misses scheduled debt payments. U.S. GAAP requires loss recognition when the decline is "*other than temporary*," which may involve more judgment. Unlike U.S. GAAP, IFRS allows impairment losses on held-to-maturity debt investments to be *reversed*, thereby increasing income, if a subsequent event reduces the previously recognized impairment loss. Like U.S. GAAP, IFRS does not allow reversal of impairment losses on equity investments.

IFRS 9, effective in 2015, changes the measurement and classification of financial assets that do not give the investor significant influence or control over the investee. The default for all investments in marketable debt and equity financial instruments is to report these investments at fair value, with all value changes reported in income (FV-NI). Changes in the value of equity investments not held for trading may be reported in other comprehensive income (FV-OCI). The gains and losses reported in OCI are not reclassified to income when realized. Debt instruments held for principal and interest payments, with no intent to sell, may be reported at amortized cost.

New standards for impairment testing are under consideration, but the IASB's focus is on recognition of expected credit losses on debt instruments reported at amortized cost. The new model is expected to result in more accurate and timely recognition of impairment losses. Current *IAS 39* guidance looks to "loss events" to identify when impairment losses should be reported. The new model requires monitoring of estimated principal and interest cash flows over the life of the debt instrument, with a decline in present value reported as impairment loss.

Investments With Significant Influence

IFRS for investments providing the investor with a significant influence over the investee are found in *IAS 28*. The investee in this case is defined as an **associate**. While U.S. GAAP focuses on ownership in voting shares, IFRS takes a more principles-oriented view. Ownership of 20 percent or more of the voting shares presumes significant influence, but there are other circumstances that indicate significant influence, taking one of the following forms *(para 7)*:

- representation on the board of directors or equivalent governing body of the investee;
- participation in the policy-making process;
- material transactions between the investor and the investee;
- interchange of managerial personnel; or
- provision of essential technical information.

For example, suppose an investor that holds less than 20 percent of an investee's voting stock is the sole provider of technical support necessary to the investee's operations. While U.S. GAAP could conclude there is no significant influence, IFRS might disagree.

IFRS requires the equity method for significant influence investments, using procedures very similar to U.S. GAAP. *IAS 36* and *IAS 39* provide guidance for impairment recognition. *IAS 39* states that impairment testing is performed if one or more significant events occur that indicate the investment has become impaired. The quantitative impairment test, found in *IAS 36*, compares the investment's book value to its recoverable amount, which is the *higher of its market value or value-in-use*. **Value-in-use** is the present value of the investment's future expected cash flows while held by the investor. U.S. GAAP requires impairment recognition only when the decline in value is *other than temporary*. This difference in criteria is likely to result in differences in impairment loss recognition between IFRS and U.S. GAAP.

Joint Ventures

IFRS 11, effective in 2013, defines *joint arrangements* as investments in which contractual agreements require the investors to unanimously consent to decisions concerning the investee. For example, if decisions regarding the activities of an entity are made by majority vote, and two parties each have a 50 percent interest in the entity, it is a joint arrangement. Joint arrangements may be *joint operations* or *joint ventures*, with joint operations giving the investors rights to the entity's individual assets and obligations for its liabilities, and joint ventures giving the investors rights to the entity's net assets. Most joint arrangements are joint ventures, involving rights to the entity's returns and amounts received on disposal. Similar to U.S. GAAP, *IFRS 11* requires that joint ventures be reported using the equity method.

Prior to *IFRS 11*, investors could also use *proportionate consolidation* to report joint ventures. **Proportionate consolidation** includes the *investor's share* of the joint venture's assets, liabilities, revenues and expenses in the investor's financial statements. In contrast, the equity method replaces the joint venture's individual assets and liabilities with a single asset representing the net investment in the joint venture, and replaces the joint venture's individual revenues and expenses with a single revenue or expense, representing equity in the net income (loss) of the joint venture. Reported net income and total equity are the same, but proportionate consolidation allows the financial health of the joint venture to affect the investor's balance sheet. When proportionately consolidated, a highly leveraged joint venture increases the reported leverage of the investor by including the investor's share of the joint venture's debt in the liabilities reported on its consolidated balance sheet. If the same joint venture is accounted for using the equity method, there is no effect on the investor's reported leverage. In abolishing proportionate consolidation for joint ventures, the IASB concluded that an investor should not report assets and liabilities that are not controlled by the investor.

BUSINESS APPLICATION   **France Telecom Group's Equity Investments**

France Telecom's 2010 annual report lists the following interests in associates:

Entities jointly controlled	Main co-shareholder	% interest	Country
Everything Everywhere	Deutsche Telecom (50%)	50%	UK
Mobinil and subsidiaries	Orascom Telecom (35%)	36%	Egypt
Mauritius Telecom and subsidiaries	Gov. of Mauritius (33%)	40%	Mauritius
Getesa	Gov. of Equatorial Guinea (60%)	40%	Eq. Guinea
Entities under significant interest			
Medi Telecom	Groupe Caisse de Depot et De Gestion (30%)		Morocco
	Groupe FinanceCom (30%)	40%	
Sonaecom	Sonae SGPS (53%)	20%	Portugal
Orange Tunisie	Investec SA (51%)	49%	Tunisia
Cie Europeenne de Telephonie	Compagnie du Telephone (39%)	61%	France
Arkadin	Natural persons (64%)	20%	France
Orange Austria (ex-One)	Mid Europa Partners (65%)	35%	Austria

Note that although it owns 61% of Cie Europeenne de Telephonie, the investment is classified as a "significant interest."

Until 2010, France Telecom proportionately consolidated several jointly controlled companies. It now uses the equity method for these investments, giving the following reason:

> In light of the publication by the IASB of the standard Joint Arrangements expected in 2011 and given the IASB's intention to remove the proportionate consolidation method, the Group has decided to account for its interests in jointly controlled entities using the equity method from January 1, 2010. This change in accounting alternative results in the financial statements providing more relevant and comparative information since the main competitors of the Group apply this method.

France Telecom reports its joint ventures as a noncurrent asset on its balance sheet, rather than including joint venture assets and liabilities proportionately with those of France Telecom. At the end of 2010, Everything Everywhere reported total liabilities of €4,746 million. By using the equity method instead of proportionate consolidation, France Telecom avoids reporting their 50% share of these liabilities on its balance sheet. Source: France Telecom Group 2010 annual report.

Controlling Investments

IFRS 3(R), "Business Combinations," describes IFRS for assets and liabilities acquired in statutory mergers, consolidations, and asset acquisitions, and consolidation of controlling stock investments. These standards are similar to U.S. GAAP.

IFRS for determining *when* an entity should be consolidated are in *IFRS 10,* "Consolidated Financial Statements," effective in 2013. This standard applies to any entities with which the reporting entity has a relationship, whether it involves ownership of stock or some sort of contractual relationship. There is no separate standard for special purpose entities or other structured relationships. *IFRS 10* requires consolidation of an entity when it *controls* the entity. Control occurs when the investor has all of the following *(IFRS 10, para 7):*

- power over the investee—the investor has existing rights that give it the ability to direct the activities that significantly affect the investee's returns
- exposure, or rights, to variable returns from its involvement with the investee
- the ability to use its power over the investee to affect the amount of the investor's returns.

The IFRS consolidation standard requires qualitative analysis of the reporting entity's relationship with another entity. Although U.S. GAAP is also based on the concept of control, U.S. GAAP focuses on the "bright line" of majority equity ownership. There is also a separate set of conditions for consolidation of special purpose entities. As a result, IFRS and U.S. GAAP can disagree on whether a particular entity should be consolidated.

Reporting Perspective

The IASB's reasons for abolishing proportionate consolidation for joint ventures in *IFRS 11* center on the concept that the equity method better reflects the assets and liabilities under the reporting entity's *control*. This logic parallels consolidation requirements following business combinations. Consolidation includes another entity's assets and liabilities, revenues and expenses with those of the reporting entity. *IFRS 10*, as well as prior IFRS, requires consolidation if the reporting entity controls another entity. This concept applies whether control is achieved through ownership of another entity's stock or because of a contractual financial relationship.

REVIEW OF KEY CONCEPTS

Describe the reporting for trading, available-for-sale, and held-to-maturity intercorporate investments. LO 1
(p. 5) Investments in securities held for income and value increases are grouped into **trading, available-for-sale,** and **held-to-maturity** portfolios. Trading and available-for-sale investments in debt and equity securities appear on the balance sheet at fair value. Unrealized gains and losses on trading securities are reported in income. Unrealized gains and losses on AFS debt and equity securities are reported outside the income statement in other comprehensive income, and are reclassified to income when the securities are sold. Held-to-maturity debt securities are reported at amortized cost and are regularly tested for impairment. The FASB is currently deliberating significant changes in standards for financial instruments.

Explain the reporting for equity method intercorporate investments. (p. 8) The **equity method** is used to report LO 2
equity investments that enable the investor to significantly influence the investee's operating and financial decisions. Significant influence is generally present when the investor owns between 20 and 50 percent of the investee's voting stock. The investor's equity in the investee's income or loss appears on the investor's income statement, increasing or decreasing the investment balance, and dividends received reduce the balance. Equity in the investee's income is the investor's share of the investee's reported income, net of amortization of the excess of investment cost over the investee's book value and unconfirmed profits on intercompany transactions. Other-than-temporary impairment losses are reported in income. Some companies pool resources and create a business enterprise to complete a particular project or expand into new markets. This enterprise is a **joint venture** if control is shared by the participating companies. U.S. investors typically use the equity method to report joint ventures.

Describe the reporting for controlling interests in other companies. (p. 14) Controlling investments in other LO 3
companies take the form of **statutory mergers, statutory consolidations, asset acquisitions,** majority **stock investments,** and **variable interest entities.** The acquisition structures of statutory mergers, consolidations and

asset acquisitions differ, but they all involve investors acquiring the assets and liabilities of another company. The investor reports each acquired asset and liability at fair value. With controlling stock investments and variable interest entities "controlled" through legal financial agreements, the investor and investee remain legal entities with separate books, and the investor accounts for its investment as a noncurrent asset on its own books. **Consolidation procedures** bring the financial statements of the investor and investee together at the end of each reporting period for external reporting purposes.

LO 4 **Discuss International Financial Reporting Standards (IFRS) for intercorporate investments. (p. 16)** **International Financial Reporting Standards** (IFRS) for intercorporate investments currently parallel U.S. GAAP on many dimensions. Criteria for impairment loss recognition differ, and in some cases IFRS allows reversal of impairment losses. The decision to use the equity method of reporting focuses on whether the investor has significant influence, instead of assuming that influence exists when the investor holds 20 percent or more of the investee's stock. Similarly, the decision to consolidate the investee under IFRS depends on whether the investor controls the investee, not on whether the investor owns the majority of the investee's stock. *IFRS 9*, effective in 2015, significantly changes financial instrument classification, valuation, and impairment recognition.

MULTIPLE CHOICE QUESTIONS ·······························

Use the following information to answer questions 1 – 4:

On January 1, 2013, a company's balance sheet reports its investments in financial instruments as follows:

Assets	
Investment in trading securities	$160,000
Investment in AFS securities	100,000
Investment in HTM securities.	207,544
Equity	
Accumulated other comprehensive income:	
Unrealized gains on AFS securities	$ 4,000 credit

Additional information:

a. The HTM securities are $200,000 face value debt securities purchased on January 1, 2011 at a yield of 4%. The securities have a 4-year total life and pay interest annually on December 31, at a coupon rate of 6%.

b. The trading securities on hand on January 1 were sold in 2013 for $180,000.

c. More trading securities were purchased for $100,000. They are still on hand at December 31, 2013, and have a fair value of $125,000.

d. AFS securities, originally purchased for $26,000 and with a January 1, 2013 carrying value of $25,000, were sold for $29,000.

e. AFS securities on hand at December 31, 2013 have a fair value of $81,000.

LO 1 **1.** The gain on trading securities, reported on the 2013 income statement, is

    a. $20,000
    b. $25,000
    c. $45,000
    d. $60,000

LO 1 **2.** The gain on AFS securities, reported on the 2013 income statement, is

    a. $ 3,000
    b. $ 4,000
    c. $ 9,000
    d. $10,000

LO 1 **3.** Investment in HTM securities, reported on the December 31, 2013, balance sheet is

    a. $203,846
    b. $204,938
    c. $207,544
    d. $207,997

4. Accumulated other comprehensive income, reported in the December 31, 2013 balance sheet, is a credit balance of   LO 1

    a. $ 6,000
    b. $10,000
    c. $11,000
    d. $12,000

5. ABC Company uses the equity method to account for its 40% interest in the voting stock of XYZ Company. ABC paid $5,000,000 for the investment at the beginning of the current year, and XYZ's total book value at the time was $6,000,000. The discrepancy between acquisition cost and share of book value acquired was attributed to goodwill. XYZ reported income of $600,000 and paid dividends of $200,000 during the year. ABC will report its investment in XYZ on its end-of-year balance sheet at what amount?   LO 2

    a. $4,920,000
    b. $5,240,000
    c. $5,000,000
    d. $5,160,000

6. Under current standards, when is an impairment loss reported on a significant influence investment in the stock of another company, following U.S. GAAP and IFRS?   LO 2, 4

	U.S. GAAP	IFRS
a.	Book value > higher of market value or value-in-use	Other than temporary impairment
b.	Other than temporary impairment	Book value > higher of market value or value-in-use
c.	If a "loss event" occurs	Not reported
d.	Other than temporary impairment	If a "loss event" occurs

7. Fizzy Cola acquired 35% of the voting stock of National Bottlers on January 1, 2014 at a cost of $50,000,000, and reports its investment using the equity method. At the date of investment, National's assets and liabilities were reported at amounts approximating fair value. In 2014, National reported net income of $7,000,000 and declared and paid dividends of $2,000,000. National sells product to Fizzy at a markup of 25% on cost. Fizzy had $6,000,000 of product purchased from National in its ending inventory, measured at cost to Fizzy. What is Fizzy's Investment in National balance, reported on its December 31, 2014, balance sheet?   LO 2

    a. $50,000,000
    b. $51,330,000
    c. $52,030,000
    d. $51,750,000

8. Fizzy Cola acquires Juicee Ltd. for $25,000,000, and accounts for its investment as a statutory merger. Juicee's balance sheet at the date of acquisition is as follows: LO 3

Current assets	$ 100,000	Liabilities	$3,000,000
Property, net	4,000,000	Equity	1,100,000
Total	$4,100,000	Total	$4,100,000

The fair value of Juicee's current assets is $75,000 less than book value. The fair value of its property is $1,500,000 less than book value. The book value of its liabilities approximates fair value. How much goodwill does Fizzy report for this acquisition?

    a. $19,475,000
    b. $22,325,000
    c. $22,475,000
    d. $25,475,000

9. Under *IFRS 9*, effective in 2015 with early adoption allowed, companies that invest in equity securities can generally choose from which of the following options for reporting their investment?   LO 4

    a. FV-NI only
    b. FV-NI or FV-OCI
    c. Amortized cost or FV-NI
    d. Amortized cost or FV-OCI

LO 4   **10.** Following IFRS, when should a company use the equity method to report an intercorporate investment?

     a. The company significantly influences the decisions of the investee.
     b. The investee is the company's major supplier.
     c. The company owns 20 – 50% of the investee's voting stock.
     d. The company is holding the investment in its long-term portfolio.

Assignments with the ✓ in the margin are available in an online homework system.
See the Preface of the book for details.

EXERCISES ••

LO 1   **E1.1**   **Investment in Trading Securities**   The Coca-Cola Company's December 31, 2010 balance sheet reports investments in trading securities at $209 million, with net unrealized losses of $3 million.

COCA-COLA
[KO]

Required

     a. How much did Coca-Cola pay for the trading securities reported on its 2010 balance sheet?
     b. How are unrealized gains and losses on trading securities reported in Coca-Cola's financial statements?
     c. Assume the trading securities on hand at the end of 2010 were acquired during 2010. Prepare the summary journal entries made by Coca-Cola to record events related to these trading securities.
     d. Assume the securities are sold for $215 million in 2011. Prepare the journal entry to record the sale.

LO 1   **E1.2**   **Investment in Available-for-Sale Securities**   The Coca-Cola Company's December 31, 2010 balance sheet reports investments in available-for-sale securities at $485 million, with gross unrealized gains of $267 million and gross unrealized losses of $5 million. Coca-Cola's 2010 statement of shareholders' equity reports a net change in unrealized gains on available-for-sale securities as a $102 million credit to accumulated other comprehensive income. Coca-Cola also recorded other-than-temporary impairment losses of $26 million in 2010, on AFS securities with a carrying value of $131 million prior to the impairment charge. Coca-Cola did not sell any AFS securities in 2010.

COCA-COLA
[KO]

Required

     a. Assume the impaired AFS securities originally cost $150 million. Prepare the entry Coca-Cola made in 2010 to record the impairment loss on AFS securities.
     b. Given the entry you made in *a.*, prepare the adjusting entry made at the end of 2010 to record the unrealized gain or loss on AFS securities.
     c. Assume that in 2011 Coca-Cola sells AFS securities carried at $50 million on December 31, 2010, for $55 million. The original cost of these securities was $44 million. Prepare the journal entry to record the sale of the securities.

LO 1   **E1.3**   **Held-to-Maturity Investments**   On January 1, 2013, a company pays $5,222,591 for a 5-year corporate bond with a face value of $5 million. The bond pays interest at 5 percent on December 31 of each year, and the principal is due on December 31, 2017. The investment yields a 4 percent compound annual return to maturity. The company classifies the bond as a held-to-maturity investment.

Required

Prepare the journal entries to record the investment on January 1, 2013, receipt of the interest payments on December 31 of each year 2013 through 2017, and receipt of the bond principal on December 31, 2017, using the effective interest method.

✓ LO 1   **E1.4**   **Investment in Trading, AFS and HTM Securities**   Zyggy Corporation has the following investment activity during 2012, 2013, and 2014:

• Purchased trading investment of $200,000 in the stock of Allen Corporation on February 3, 2012. The investment was sold on June 18, 2012, for $210,000.
• Purchased trading investment of $400,000 in the stock of Becker Corporation on October 29, 2012. The investment had a December 31, 2012, fair value of $380,000 and was sold on March 1, 2013, for $405,000.
• Purchased AFS investment of $600,000 in the stock of Corey Corporation on November 1, 2012. Its fair value on December 31, 2012, and 2013 was $640,000 and $510,000, respectively. The investment was sold on February 15, 2014 for $560,000.
• Purchased AFS investment of $500,000 in the stock of Donata Corporation on April 4, 2014. Its fair value on December 31, 2014, was $535,000.

• Purchased HTM investment on January 2, 2013, of $194,449 in Eiffel Corporation's $200,000 face value, 3 percent bond, yielding 4 percent to maturity, interest paid annually on December 31.

Required

For each of the above investments, determine the accounts and balances reported on Zyggy's December 31, 2012, 2013, and 2014 balance sheets and its 2012, 2013, and 2014 income statements.

E1.5 **Equity Method Investment with Intercompany Sales and Profits** The Coca-Cola Company owns 32 percent of the voting stock of **Coca-Cola FEMSA**, acquired at book value. Assume that Coca-Cola FEMSA reports income of $5 million for 2013. Coca-Cola FEMSA regularly sells canned beverages to Coca-Cola at a markup of 35 percent on cost. During 2013 Coca-Cola FEMSA's sales to Coca-Cola totaled $25 million. Coca-Cola's January 1, 2013, inventories include $1,350,000 purchased from Coca-Cola FEMSA. Coca-Cola's December 31, 2013, inventories include $1,215,000 purchased from Coca-Cola FEMSA.

LO 2 ✅

COCA-COLA
[KO]

Required

Prepare the 2013 journal entry on Coca-Cola's books to recognize its income from Coca-Cola FEMSA under the equity method.

E1.6 **Equity Method Investment with Cost in Excess of Book Value** Revco Corporation purchases 40 percent of the voting stock of Ronco Pharmaceuticals on January 1, 2013, for $5 million in cash. Ronco's book value at the date of acquisition is $6 million. Investigation reveals that Ronco's reported patents (10-year life) are undervalued by $4 million and it has unreported technology (5-year life) valued at $1 million. Ronco pays dividends of $250,000 and reports net income of $900,000 for 2013. Any unallocated excess of Revco's cost over Ronco's book value is attributed to goodwill.

LO 2

Required

Prepare the journal entries on Revco's books to report the above information assuming Revco accounts for its investment in Ronco using the equity method.

E1.7 **Equity Method and Other Comprehensive Income** Mitchell Corporation pays $6 million to acquire a 25 percent interest in Turner Corporation's stock on January 1, 2014, and reports the investment using the equity method. Turner's net assets are fairly reported, except for $2 million of unreported intangibles (4-year life). During 2014, Turner reports net income of $900,000, which includes $25,000 in realized and unrealized gains on trading securities and $40,000 in realized gains on sales of AFS securities. Turner also reports $30,000 in unrealized losses on AFS securities and pays dividends of $240,000 in 2014.

LO 2

Required

Prepare Mitchell's journal entries to record the above events for 2014.

E1.8 **Equity Method Investment Cost Computation** Traynor Corporation reports its 40 percent investment in Victor Company on its December 31, 2014, balance sheet at $14,608,000. Traynor acquired its interest in Victor on January 2, 2012, and uses the equity method to account for the investment. Victor's assets and liabilities were fairly stated on January 2, 2012, except for unreported intangibles (5-year life) of $4 million. Victor reported net income of $1.2 million, $1.5 million, and $1.4 million, and paid dividends of $200,000, $250,000, and $230,000 in 2012, 2013, and 2014, respectively.

LO 2

Required

How much did Traynor Corporation pay for its investment in Victor Company on January 2, 2012?

E1.9 **Joint Venture** On January 2, 2014, Adena Corporation and Dillon Company form a joint venture to develop a new product. Each contributes $2.5 million and has a 50 percent interest in the venture. At December 31, 2014, the joint venture's balance sheet is as follows *(in millions)*:

LO 2

Cash	$ 1.8	Debt	$ 8.4
Equipment	12.2	Equity	5.6
Total	$14.0	Total	$14.0

The joint venture reported net income of $600,000 during 2014. Each investor uses the equity method to report its interest in the joint venture.

Required

Show how the joint venture is reported on each investor's financial statements for 2014. Where are the joint venture's individual assets and liabilities reported by the venturers?

LO 2 E1.10 Equity Method Investment with Indefinite Life Intangibles Several Years Later Saxton Corporation purchased 25 percent of Taylor Company's voting stock on January 1, 2010, for $3 million in cash. At the date of acquisition, Taylor reported its total assets at $60 million and its total liabilities at $56 million. Investigation revealed that Taylor's plant and equipment (15-year life) was undervalued by $1.8 million, it had an unreported customer database (2-year life) valued at $500,000, and unreported indefinite-life brand names valued at $1.5 million. Taylor pays $100,000 in dividends and reports net income of $250,000 in 2013. Impairment losses on the brand names for 2013 are $200,000.

Required

Prepare the necessary journal entries on Saxton's books to report the above information for 2013 assuming Saxton uses the equity method to report its investment.

LO 3 E1.11 Statutory Merger and Stock Investment (see related E1.10) Saxton Corporation purchases all of Taylor Company's assets and liabilities on January 1, 2010, for $12 million in cash. At the date of acquisition, Taylor's reported assets consist of current assets of $10 million and plant and equipment of $50 million. It reports current liabilities of $16 million and long-term debt of $40 million. Investigation reveals that Taylor's plant and equipment is undervalued by $1.8 million, it has an unreported customer database valued at $500,000, and unreported indefinite life brand names valued at $1.5 million.

Required

a. Prepare the necessary journal entry on Saxton's books to record its acquisition of Taylor on January 1, 2010.
b. Assume that Saxton purchases all of Taylor's voting stock on January 1, 2010, for $12 million in cash. Prepare the necessary journal entry on Saxton's books to record the acquisition.

LO 3 E1.12 Statutory Merger Organic Juices, Inc. acquires Healthy Snax Corporation for $50 million in cash, in a statutory merger. Healthy Snax' balance sheet at the date of acquisition is as follows *(in millions)*:

Current assets	$10	Current liabilities	$12
Plant and equipment	65	Long-term debt	36
Intangible assets	5	Capital stock	18
		Retained earnings	24
		Treasury stock	(10)
Total assets	$80	Total liabilities and equity	$80

A consulting firm values Healthy Snax' plant and equipment at $40 million and its intangibles at $25 million. There are no unreported identifiable intangibles, and all other assets and liabilities are fairly reported.

Required

Prepare the journal entry Organic Juices makes to record its acquisition of Healthy Snax.

PROBLEMS

P1.1 Investments in Marketable Securities A company has the following investment activity during   LO 1
2013 and 2014:

Security	Type	Date of Acquisition	Cost	Fair value at 12/31/13	Date of Sale	Selling Price	Fair value at 12/31/14
A.........	Trading	3/5/13	$350,000	N/A	6/3/13	$325,000	N/A
B.........	Trading	7/14/13	225,000	$252,000	1/15/14	235,000	N/A
C.........	Trading	9/1/14	400,000	N/A	N/A	N/A	$410,000
D.........	AFS	8/2/13	175,000	190,000	4/2/14	213,000	N/A
E.........	AFS	11/20/13	300,000	250,000	N/A	N/A	215,000
F.........	AFS	4/6/14	710,000	N/A	N/A	N/A	690,000

Required

a. Prepare the journal entries to record the above information for 2013 and 2014, including appropriate adjustments to other comprehensive income, assuming the company's reporting year ends December 31.
b. Show how this information is presented in the company's financial statements for 2013 and 2014.
c. If the company designated all the securities as trading securities, how would your answer to part *b* change? Comment on the income effect of classifying the AFS securities as trading securities.

P1.2 Held-to-Maturity Intercorporate Debt Investments On January 2, 2011, a company invests in   LO 1
the following corporate debt securities, classified as held-to-maturity per *ASC Topic 320*:

1. 5-year $1,000,000 face value corporate bond paying 6 percent interest annually on December 31. The bond is priced to yield 5 percent to maturity.
2. 4-year $500,000 face value corporate bond paying 4 percent interest annually on December 31. The bond is priced to yield 5 percent to maturity.

Required

a. Calculate the cost of each investment.
b. Calculate interest income for 2011 and 2012.
c. At what value are these investments reported on the company's December 31, 2013, balance sheet?
d. On December 31, 2014, the company determines that an impairment loss should be reported on the $1,000,000 bond. What factors indicate impairment loss? If the bond is estimated to have a value of $500,000 on December 31, 2014, what is the amount of the impairment loss, and where will it be reported on the 2014 financial statements?

P1.3 Held-to-Maturity Intercorporate Debt Investment, Impairment Losses Hansen Natural   LO 1
Corporation is a public U.S. company that produces and distributes "alternative" energy drinks. Its 2010 balance sheet includes $165 million in held-to-maturity bonds. Hansen reports its HTM securities as follows:

HANSEN
NATURAL
CORPORATION
[HANS]

> Held-to-maturity securities are recorded at amortized cost which approximates fair market value. The Company evaluates whether the decline in fair value of its investments is other-than-temporary at each quarter-end. This evaluation consists of a review by management, and includes market pricing information and maturity dates for the securities held, market and economic trends in the industry and information on the issuer's financial condition and, if applicable, information on the guarantors' financial condition. Factors considered in determining whether a loss is temporary include the length of time and extent to which the investment's fair value has been less than its cost basis, the financial condition and near-term prospects of the issuer and guarantors, including any specific events which may influence the operations of the issuer and our intent and ability to retain the investment for a reasonable period of time sufficient to allow for any anticipated recovery of fair value. (*Note 1 to Hansen Natural Corporation 2010 financial statements*)

Assume that the HTM bonds on Hansen's 2010 balance sheet have a 2-year remaining life, were acquired at par, and pay interest each December 31 at 4 percent. Hansen determines that due to an other-than-temporary decline in the issuer's liquidity, the fair value of the bonds is $131 million.

Required

a. Prepare Hansen's journal entry to record the impairment loss for 2010. Where is the loss reported in Hansen's financial statements?
b. What is Hansen's new yield on the bonds? Round to the nearest percent.
c. Assume Hansen receives its interest payment on December 31, 2011, as usual. Calculate reported interest revenue, and prepare Hansen's journal entry to record receipt of the interest. At what value does the investment appear on Hansen's December 31, 2011, balance sheet?
d. Assume that on December 31, 2011, the issuer's financial health has improved and the bonds' fair value is now $165 million. How does Hansen report this information?

LO 2   P1.4   Equity Method Investment Several Years after Acquisition   On January 2, 2011, Best Beverages acquired 45 percent of the stock of Better Bottlers for $30 million in cash. Best Beverages accounts for its investment using the equity method. At the time of acquisition, Better Bottlers' balance sheet was as follows *(in millions)*:

Better Bottlers Balance Sheet, January 2, 2011	
Assets	
Current assets	$ 20
Property and equipment, net	415
Patents and trademarks	150
Total assets	$585
Liabilities and equity	
Current liabilities	$ 42
Long-term debt	518
Total liabilities	560
Capital stock	12
Retained earnings	13
Total equity	25
Total liabilities and equity	$585

Valuation of Better Bottlers' assets and liabilities revealed that its reported patents and trademarks (10-year life) had a fair value of $160 million and it had unrecognized brand names (15-year life) worth $9 million. Better Bottlers' December 31, 2014, retained earnings balance is $25 million. For 2014, it reported net income of $2.5 million and paid $650,000 in dividends.

Required

a. Prepare the 2014 entries to report the above information on Best Beverages' books.
b. Calculate the Investment in Better Bottlers balance, reported on Best Beverages' December 31, 2014 balance sheet.

LO 2   P1.5   Equity Method Investment Several Years after Acquisition   Rance Corporation paid $10 million in cash to acquire 30 percent of the voting stock of Seaway Company on January 2, 2012. Rance uses the equity method to report its investment. Seaway's book value at date of acquisition was $25 million. Analysis of Seaway's assets and liabilities reveals that Seaway's property and equipment (10-year life) was overvalued by $4 million, and its reported intangibles (2-year life) were undervalued by $6 million.

During the years 2012 and 2013, Seaway reported total income of $14 million, paid dividends of $5 million, and reported net unrealized gains on AFS securities of $1 million. During 2014, Seaway reported income of $4 million, paid dividends of $1.5 million, and reported net unrealized losses on AFS securities of $800,000.

Rance sells merchandise to Seaway at a markup of 20 percent on cost. Seaway sells merchandise to Rance at a markup of 25 percent on cost. Below are the inventories on hand at each balance sheet date, related to these sales.

December 31	2012	2013	2014
Ending inventory held by Rance Corporation	$750,000	$925,000	$625,000
Ending inventory held by Seaway Company	480,000	420,000	696,000

Required

a.   Calculate Rance's equity in net income of Seaway for 2014.

b.   Prepare Rance's journal entries to report its investment in Seaway for 2014.

c.   Calculate the investment balance at December 31, 2014.

P1.6   **Equity Method Investment with Several Assets in Excess of Book Value**   Bristol Corporation   **LO 2**
acquired 40 percent of the voting stock of Manchester Corporation on January 2, 2013, for $3.2 million in
cash. Manchester's balance sheet and estimated fair values of its assets and liabilities on January 2, 2013,
are as follows:

MANCHESTER CORPORATION
Balance Sheet
January 2, 2013

(in thousands)	**Book Value**	**Fair Value**
Assets		
Cash and receivables.	$ 400	$ 400
Inventory (FIFO)	1,200	800
Investments	300	300
Land.	800	2,000
Property and equipment.	4,200	1,500
Less: Accumulated depreciation	(1,300)	
Total assets	$5,600	
Liabilities and Equity		
Current liabilities.	$ 900	$ 900
Long-term liabilities	3,000	3,000
Common stock, $2.00 par	500	
Additional paid-in capital	1,000	
Retained earnings	800	
Accumulated other comprehensive income.	(600)	
Total liabilities and equity.	$5,600	

In addition to its reported assets, Manchester has unreported franchise agreements (5-year life) valued at $1
million and brand names (indefinite life) valued at $2.2 million. Its property and equipment has a 20 year
average remaining life. Manchester reported income of $1.8 million for 2013.

Required

a.   How many shares of Manchester stock did Bristol acquire?

b.   Compute Bristol's equity in Manchester's net income for 2013.

P1.7   **Equity Method Investment, Intercompany Sales**   Harcker Corporation acquires 40 percent of   **LO 2**
Jackson Corporation's voting stock on January 3, 2014, for $40 million in cash. Jackson's net assets were
fairly reported at $100 million at the date of acquisition. During 2014, Harcker sells $65 million in merchandise to Jackson at a markup of 30 percent on cost. Jackson still holds all of this merchandise in its
ending inventory. Also during 2014, Jackson sells $54 million in merchandise to Harcker at a markup of
35 percent on cost. Harcker still holds all of this merchandise in its ending inventory. Jackson reports 2014
net income of $30 million.

Required

a.   Calculate Harcker's equity in Jackson's net income for 2014.

b.   Assume Harcker reports total 2014 sales revenue and cost of sales of $131 million and $110 million, respectively, while Jackson reports total 2014 sales revenue and cost of sales of $264 million and $229 million, respectively. Compute each company's gross margin on sales as reported following U.S. GAAP. Now
compute gross margin on sales again, excluding intercompany transactions. Comment on the results.

LO 2, 3   P1.8   Equity Investments, Various Reporting Methods   On January 2, 2013, Parker Corporation invests in the stock of Quarry Corporation. Quarry's book value is $4 million and its assets and liabilities are fairly reported. Quarry reports income of $3 million and pays dividends of $1 million in 2013. Parker's December 31, 2013, balance sheet and 2013 income statement, ignoring its investment in Quarry's stock, follow.

PARKER CORPORATION
Balance Sheet (in thousands)
December 31, 2013

Current assets	$ 40,000	Current liabilities.	$ 20,000
Property, net.	450,000	Long-term liabilities	200,000
Identifiable intangibles	5,000	Capital stock	90,000
		Retained earnings	185,000
Total assets	$495,000	Total liabilities and equity.	$495,000

PARKER CORPORATION
Income Statement (in thousands)
Year ended December 31, 2013

Sales revenue.	$900,000
Cost of sales.	(750,000)
Operating expenses	(140,000)
Net income.	$ 10,000

Quarry Corporation's financial statements for 2013 are as follows:

QUARRY CORPORATION
Balance Sheet (in thousands)
December 31, 2013

Current assets	$ 5,000	Current liabilities.	$ 3,000
Property, net.	85,000	Long-term liabilities	81,000
		Capital stock, $1 par	1,000
		Retained earnings	5,000
Total assets	$90,000	Total liabilities and equity.	$90,000

QUARRY CORPORATION
Income Statement (in thousands)
Year ended December 31, 2013

Sales revenue.	$60,000
Cost of sales.	(20,000)
Operating expenses	(37,000)
Net income.	$ 3,000

Required

Prepare Parker's December 31, 2013, balance sheet and 2013 income statement under each of the following circumstances:

a. Parker's investment consists of 100,000 shares costing $15/share, and Parker classifies it as an AFS investment. The shares have a market value of $12/share on December 31, 2013.

b. Parker's investment consists of 400,000 shares costing $15/share, and Parker accounts for it using the equity method.

c. Parker acquires all of Quarry's shares for $15 million, retires the shares and merges with Quarry. Goodwill is unimpaired in 2013.

P1.9 **Joint Venture** On January 3, 2012, Allen Corporation and Barkely Corporation invested $5 million   LO 2
each in cash to form Albar Enterprises, a joint venture that develops new products benefitting both corporations. Each corporation holds an equal ownership interest in Albar Enterprises. Albar Enterprises' balance sheet on December 31, 2012, follows (*in millions*):

Cash..........................	$ 0.5	Current payables	$ 26.5
Merchandise...................	12.0	Noncurrent debt...............	150.0
Equipment	120.0	Equity	6.0
Patents.......................	50.0		
Total	$182.5	Total	$182.5

The joint venture distributed $0.2 million in cash to each of its investors at the end of 2012.

December 31, 2012, balance sheets for each corporation are below. Each shows its investment in Albar Enterprises at original cost. The cash distribution has not yet been recorded.

Balance Sheet (in millions)	Allen Corp.	Barkely Corp.
Current assets	$ 1.0	$ 0.4
Plant and equipment, net.....................	150.0	65.0
Investment in Albarcol Enterprises...............	5.0	5.0
Intangibles	200.0	3.5
Total assets	$356.0	$73.9
Current liabilities.............................	$ 14.0	$ 0.2
Noncurrent liabilities.........................	265.0	55.0
Capital stock	10.0	1.0
Retained earnings	67.0	17.7
Total liabilities and equity......................	$356.0	$73.9

Both corporations use the equity method to report their investment in Albar Enterprises. Barkely estimates that the fair value of its investment in Albar declined to $0.5 million as of December 31, 2012, and that the decline is other-than-temporary. Allen does not report a decline in the value of its investment.

Required

a. Present the December 31, 2012, balance sheets of each corporation, after appropriate adjustments for their joint venture investment.
b. What is the amount of the impairment loss reported by Barkely on its 2012 income statement? Is it appropriate for Barkely to report an impairment loss on its investment in the joint venture, while Allen does not? Explain.

P1.10 **Balance Sheet after Business Acquisition** Wilson Corporation acquires Greatbatch Company for   LO 3 ✔
$50 million cash in a statutory merger. The balance sheets of both companies at the date of acquisition are as follows:

Balance Sheet (in millions)	Wilson	Greatbatch
Current assets	$ 60	$ 5
Property and equipment.............................	500	90
Intangibles	20	3
Total assets	$580	$98
Current liabilities....................................	$ 25	$ 2
Long-term debt	400	65
Capital stock	50	12
Retained earnings	120	15
Accumulated other comprehensive income.................	(15)	4
Total liabilities and equity...........................	$580	$98

Greatbatch's property and equipment is overvalued by $30 million, its reported intangibles are undervalued by $20 million, and it has unreported intangibles, in the form of customer databases and marketing agreements, valued at $7 million.

Required

Prepare Wilson's balance sheet immediately following the statutory merger.

LO 3 **P1.11 Business Acquisition** In 2007 **Clearly Canadian Beverage Corporation** acquired **My Organic Baby Inc.** (MOB), a leading Canadian producer of organic baby food. The total purchase price was $4,913,000, consisting of $369,000 in cash, and new no-par common stock with a market value of $4,544,000. The fair values of MOB's acquired assets and liabilities are as follows *(in thousands)*:

CLEARLY CANADIAN BEVERAGE [CCBEF]

MY ORGANIC BABY INC.

Net assets reported on MOB's books	
Cash and receivables	$ 466
Inventory	142
Plant and equipment	21
Other tangible assets	131
Accounts payable	686
Identifiable intangible assets not reported on MOB's books	
Distribution relationships	715
Trademarks, copyrights and brands	834
Other intangible assets	1,961

Required

Assuming Clearly Canadian records this acquisition as a statutory merger, prepare the journal entry it made in 2007 to record its acquisition of My Organic Baby, Inc.

✓LO 1 **P1.12 Trading and AFS Investments, Impairment** On its January 1, 2013, balance sheet, Ericsson Corporation reports the following balances related to its investments:

Trading investments	$ 56,000
AFS investments	160,000
Accumulated other comprehensive income (unrealized losses on AFS investments)	30,000 debit

During 2013, Ericsson sold for $43,000 trading securities carried at $40,000 on its beginning balance sheet. It sold the remaining trading securities held at the beginning of the year for $20,000. It purchased trading securities costing $60,000; their fair value at the end of 2013 was $52,000. Ericsson sold for $52,000 AFS securities carried at $50,000, with unrealized gains of $1,000 included in the beginning AOCI balance. It did not purchase any new AFS securities. At the end of 2013, AFS securities with a book value of $85,000 have a fair value of $88,000. It is determined that AFS securities with a book value of $25,000 and unrealized losses of $5,000 have a fair value of $10,000; this decline in value is determined to be other-than-temporary.

Required

Prepare journal entries to record the events of 2013, and determine the balances related to trading and AFS securities reported on Ericsson's income statement and balance sheet.

REVIEW SOLUTIONS ··

Review #1 Solution

2013			
Jan. 2	Investment in trading securities	300,000	
	Investment in AFS securities	1,000,000	
	Investment in HTM securities.	486,384	
	Cash		1,786,384
2013			
June 15	Cash.	265,000	
	Loss on sale of trading securities (income)	35,000	
	Investment in trading securities.		300,000
2013			
Oct. 15	Investment in trading securities	250,000	
	Cash		250,000
2013			
Dec. 1	Cash.	12,000	
	Dividend income		12,000
2013			
Dec. 31	Investment in trading securities	10,000	
	Unrealized loss on AFS securities (OCI).	80,000	
	Unrealized gain on trading securities (income)		10,000
	Investment in AFS securities.		80,000
Dec. 31	Cash.	20,000	
	Investment in HTM securities.	4,319	
	Interest income		24,319

$20,000 = 4% × $500,000; $24,319 = 5% × $486,384.

Review #2 Solution

2014			
Jan. 5	Investment in Armadillo Bottlers	15,000,000	
	Cash		15,000,000
	To record investment in Armadillo.		
2014			
Dec. 1	Cash.	125,000	
	Investment in Armadillo Bottlers		125,000
	To record dividends received; $125,000 = 25% × $500,000.		
2014			
Dec. 31	Investment in Armadillo Bottlers	211,250	
	Equity in income of Armadillo Bottlers		211,250
	To record equity in Armadillo's income for 2014.		

Equity in net income for 2014 is calculated as follows:

Fizzy Cola's share of Armadillo's reported net income (25% × $3 million).	$750,000
Amortization of previously unreported intangibles (25% × $10 million/5).	(500,000)
Unconfirmed profit on downstream sales (25% × ($480,000 − ($480,000/1.2)))	(20,000)
Unconfirmed profit on upstream sales (25% × ($325,000 − ($325,000/1.3)))	(18,750)
Equity in net income.	$211,250

2 Mergers and Acquisitions

'

LEARNING OBJECTIVES

LO1 Measure and account for the various assets and liabilities acquired in mergers and acquisitions. (p. 40)

LO2 Measure and report the various types of consideration paid. (p. 48)

LO3 Account for changes in the values of acquired assets and liabilities, and contingent consideration. (p. 51)

LO4 Account for bargain purchases. (p. 53)

LO5 Explain the reporting requirements and issues related to in-process research and development and preacquisition contingencies. (p. 55)

IBM CORPORATION

www.ibm.com

International Business Machines Corporation (IBM) is a world leader in systems, software, and technology services. Its business is organized in five segments: Global Technology Services, Global Business Services, Systems and Technology, Software, and Global Financing. Per its 2010 annual report, IBM uses acquisitions to increase revenues in its high margin services and software businesses.

Despite the volatility of the information technology (IT) industry over the past decade, IBM has consistently delivered superior performance, with a steady track record of sustained earnings per share growth. The company has shifted its business mix, exiting commoditized segments while increasing its presence in higher-value areas such as services, software and integrated solutions. As part of this shift, the company has acquired over 100 companies this past decade, complementing and scaling its portfolio of products and offerings.

IBM made 17 acquisitions costing $6,538 million in 2010: thirteen acquisitions by the Software segment, one each by the Global Technology Services and Global Business Services segments, and two by the Systems and Technology segment. The majority of these investments were cash acquisitions of privately held companies. The table below summarizes IBM's acquisition activity for the last few years. Clearly IBM uses acquisitions to achieve its strategic goals.

	2010	2009	2008	2007	2006	2005
Number of acquisitions	17	6	15	12	13	16
Aggregate purchase price *(in millions)* . . .	$6,538	$1,471	$6,796	$1,144	$4,817	$2,022

How does IBM report its acquisitions? Does it include all the assets and liabilities of these acquired companies on its balance sheet? If so, how are they valued? How are costs incurred in connection with acquisitions reported?

Most large companies use acquisitions to expand or refocus their business activities. This chapter explains that the reporting for acquisitions is controversial and has evolved significantly over the years. Because acquisitions often have a major impact on company financial performance, this subject deserves careful scrutiny.   *Source:* IBM Corporation annual reports, 2010 and 2007.

CHAPTER ORGANIZATION

Introduction	U.S. GAAP for statutory mergers and consolidations	IFRS for statutory mergers and consolidations
• Motivations for combinations	• Valuation of net assets acquired	• Requirements of *IFRS 3(R)*
• Types of combinations	• Valuation of consideration paid	
• Overview of reporting for combinations	• Post-acquisition changes in estimated values of net assets acquired or consideration paid	
• Evolution of reporting for business combinations	• Bargain purchases	
• Current status of reporting for business combinations	• Special issues: research and development and preacquisition contingencies	

INTRODUCTION

A **business combination**—also referred to as a *merger*, *acquisition*, or *takeover*—occurs when one company obtains control over another company. Chapter 1 introduced the general reporting requirements for controlling interests in other companies. This chapter provides a detailed analysis of these requirements for acquisition of the assets and liabilities of another company.

Motivations for Mergers and Acquisitions

To survive and prosper, business firms need reliable and cost-effective sources of supply, efficient and high quality production, distribution, and administrative capabilities, and sufficient customers. Firms also seek to grow larger and diversify into new products or markets. How are these goals to be accomplished? One strategy is to deal with other companies as suppliers, subcontractors, customers and to grow internally by adding new facilities and capabilities. Another is the acquisition of other established firms. Combining with another company enables a firm to instantly control a source of supply, acquire additional production or distribution facilities, achieve customer relationships, expand into new geographic markets, or diversify into new lines of business. The acquiring firm seeks a business combination when the firm's management believes that it can accomplish its objectives more efficiently and at lower cost than it could via internal growth or market transactions with other firms.

Growth is a major objective of most corporate enterprises and takes many forms. Growth in sales is needed to increase the firm's share of the market and to solidify the firm's position. Growth in earnings and earnings per share is essential for the firm's securities to become more attractive in the capital markets. Growth in diversification is pursued to reduce or spread business risk, insulate earnings from downturns in business, and decrease the cost of capital. Although firms can achieve growth in these areas internally as well as externally, they may prefer combination with existing firms to expansion from within, for some of the following reasons:

- A going concern has its own historical records, experienced personnel, and network of suppliers, customers, and creditors. Combination with such a firm eliminates the need to start from scratch. Although managerial and other changes may be necessary, the inescapable fact is that growth from within, whether for reasons of market share or diversification, usually requires duplication of many of the efforts already made by an existing firm. The cost of duplicating these efforts could exceed the cost of acquiring the firm outright.

- Combination with an existing firm often leads to lower levels of actual or potential competition. When two competing firms combine, competition is reduced. Similarly, if a new firm enters an industry by acquiring an existing firm, the number of competing firms remains unchanged. But entry into an industry by forming a new firm increases the number of competitors, thereby making it more difficult for the entering firm to succeed.

- The combination can lead to increased sales overall, if the combined firms have complementary products or services. For example, an organization providing tax services may acquire a large CPA firm specializing in business valuation or enterprise risk services. The combined organization offers a variety of financial services to clients. To the extent that the enterprise risk clients are persuaded to switch from outside tax services to those of the combined firm, sales increase.

Mergers and acquisitions (M&A) are pervasive, and are also a global phenomenon. The table below summarizes the largest acquisitions in recent years, measured in U.S. dollars.

EXHIBIT 2.1   Top M&A Deals Worldwide, 2000–2010

Year	Acquirer	Target	Price (USD billions)
2000	America Online	Time Warner	$165
2007	RFS Holdings	ABN-AMRO Holding	99
2000	Glaxo Wellcome Plc	SauersKline Beecham Plc	76
2004	Royal Dutch Petroleum Co.	Shell Transport & Trading Co.	75
2006	AT&T Inc.	BellSouth Corporation	73
2001	Comcast Corp.	AT&T Broadband & Internet Svcs	72
2009	Pfizer Inc.	Wyeth	67
2004	Sanofi-Synthelabo SA	Aventis SA	60
2002	Pfizer Inc.	Pharmacia Corp.	60
2008	InBev NV	Anheuser-Busch Cos. Inc.	60
2004	JP Morgan Chase	Bank One	59

Source: Thomson Reuters

Pfizer Inc.'s 2009 acquisition of **Wyeth** illustrates some of the common motivations for acquisitions. Despite being the largest pharmaceutical company worldwide, Pfizer faced a significant decline in revenues in 2011 due to loss of patent rights for the cholesterol drug Lipitor, comprising 25 percent of its sales. Analysts expected Pfizer to fall to fifth place in the industry, behind **Roche, Novartis, Sanofi,** and **GSK.** Pfizer's acquisition of Wyeth allowed it to retain top status in the industry. In addition to size, other acquisition benefits were mentioned in the financial press:

- The acquisition brings Pfizer into the vaccines, consumer healthcare, and veterinary drug markets. In particular, Wyeth's line includes the Prevnar vaccine for childhood infections and the rheumatoid arthritis drug Enbrel.
- Wyeth has several promising Alzheimer's drugs in development.
- The acquisition was expected to eliminate duplication and streamline operations, resulting in a 15 percent reduction in the combined workforce and a $4 billion reduction in costs.

Types of Combinations

Four types of business combinations can be identified from legal and organizational perspectives:

1. A **statutory merger** results when one company is absorbed into another company in exchange for cash, debt or stock. The acquiring company may purchase the assets and liabilities of the acquired company directly, or it may acquire and then retire the stock of the acquired company. In either case, the acquired company ceases to exist as a legal entity. Only the surviving firm remains as a legal entity.
2. A **statutory consolidation** takes place when a new corporation is organized to absorb the activities of two or more existing corporations. The shares of the existing companies are retired, and only the new corporation continues to exist as a legal entity.
3. An **asset acquisition** reflects the acquisition by one firm of assets (and possibly liabilities) of another firm, but not its shares. The selling firm may continue to survive as a legal entity, or it may liquidate entirely. The acquirer typically targets key assets for acquisition, or buys the acquiree's assets but does not assume its liabilities. Often the assets acquired are in the form of a division or product line.
4. A **stock acquisition** occurs when the acquiring firm obtains all or most of the voting shares of another firm. Each firm continues as a *separate legal entity*, and the investment in the acquired firm is treated as an intercorporate investment.

The first two types of combinations are *statutory* in the sense that the reorganization, issue and retirement of shares are governed by the laws of a state. Even though the absorbed firms cease to exist as legal entities, their operations may continue undisturbed as divisions of the combined firm. In an asset acquisition, no stock is acquired, and the acquirer may not buy the entire company. *All assets acquired and all liabilities assumed* in a business combination *are recorded directly on the books of the acquiring company* in the *statutory merger, statutory consolidation*, and *asset acquisition* cases.

In a business combination that is a *stock acquisition*, a *parent/subsidiary relationship* is created between the acquiring and acquired companies. The acquired company remains as a separate legal entity and is treated as an intercorporate investment by the acquiring firm. Consequently, the acquiring firm *does not record the assets and liabilities of the acquired firm on its books*. Rather, the acquiring firm records the shares of stock acquired in an **Investment in Subsidiary** account. This account gives a one-line summation of the acquiring company's interest in the underlying assets and liabilities of the acquired company. A stock acquisition does not affect the books of the acquired company; there is merely a change in ownership of its already-issued stock.

We shall see in subsequent chapters that the parent/subsidiary relationship resulting from a controlling stock investment normally requires the preparation of consolidated financial statements. In a consolidated balance sheet, the underlying asset and liability accounts of the subsidiary replace the Investment in Subsidiary account on the acquiring company's books.

Overview of Reporting for Combinations

From a reporting perspective, all acquisitions involve combining the assets and liabilities of the acquired company with those of the acquiring company. The assets and liabilities acquired are reported at their *fair value* at the date of acquisition. Consider the following example.

EXHIBIT 2.2   Combination Illustration

Suppose IBM pays $10,000,000 in cash to acquire DataFile Inc. on July 1, 2012. Fair values of DataFile's assets and liabilities are as follows:

Account	Fair value
Current assets	$ 5,000,000
Equipment	45,000,000
Patents and copyrights	10,000,000
Current liabilities	15,000,000
Long-term debt	35,000,000

If IBM absorbs the assets and liabilities of DataFile through a *statutory merger*, IBM makes the following entry on its books:

Current assets	5,000,000	
Equipment	45,000,000	
Patents and copyrights	10,000,000	
Current liabilities		15,000,000
Long-term debt		35,000,000
Cash		10,000,000

To record the acquisition of DataFile for $10,000,000 in cash.

IBM records DataFile's assets and liabilities directly on its books. DataFile ceases to exist as a separate entity, and IBM reports DataFile's subsequent activities directly in its own financial records. The *acquiring* company does not revalue its own assets and liabilities to fair value. Only the *acquired* assets and liabilities are reported at fair value at the date of acquisition. IBM reports acquisition of DataFile's assets and liabilities the same way it reports any other acquisition of property. When a company buys equipment, it reports the equipment at the price paid, which presumably is its fair value. The company probably owns other equipment, and reports it at historical cost less accumulated depreciation. The company does not revalue this equipment to current fair value when it purchases additional equipment.

Even if a new corporation absorbs both companies, as in a statutory consolidation, one of the companies is identified as the acquirer. The new corporation's balance sheet reports the acquirer's assets and liabilities at their book values shown in the acquirer's financial records. However, the new corporation's balance sheet reports the acquired company's assets and liabilities at fair value at the date of acquisition.

Now assume IBM acquires all of the *voting stock* of DataFile Inc., paying the former stockholders of DataFile $10,000,000 in cash. This is a *stock acquisition*, and IBM makes the following entry:

Investment in DataFile Inc.	10,000,000	
Cash		10,000,000

To record acquisition of all of DataFile's stock for $10,000,000 in cash.

In this case, DataFile continues to exist as a separate entity, and reports its financial activities on its own books. Because IBM will likely include the activities of DataFile in its financial statements, a *consolidation working paper* is used to combine the financial results of IBM and DataFile, just as if IBM had reported DataFile's acquired assets and liabilities, and subsequent activities, directly on its books.

Note, however, that whether the acquisition is initially reported as a statutory merger or statutory consolidation, or as a stock acquisition, the combined results are *exactly the same*. The only difference is that in a stock acquisition, a working paper combines the accounts of the two companies. In a statutory merger, consolidation, or asset acquisition, the acquirer reports the acquired assets and liabilities directly on its books, automatically combining the assets and liabilities of two companies.

Typically the price paid by the acquiring company exceeds the total fair value of the specific net assets acquired. A company's value includes its reputation and competitive strengths, which GAAP does not recognize as specific assets. The excess amount paid is attributed to goodwill, an intangible asset. For example, in Exhibit 2.2 above, suppose the fair value of the patents and copyrights is only $2,000,000. Then the acquisition cost is $8,000,000 greater than the fair values of the net assets acquired, as calculated below.

Acquisition cost		$10,000,000
Fair value of identifiable net assets acquired:		
Current assets	$ 5,000,000	
Equipment	45,000,000	
Patents and copyrights	2,000,000	
Current liabilities	(15,000,000)	
Long-term debt	(35,000,000)	2,000,000
Goodwill		$ 8,000,000

If this acquisition is a statutory merger, IBM makes the following entry to record the acquisition:

Current assets	5,000,000	
Equipment	45,000,000	
Patents and copyrights	2,000,000	
Goodwill	8,000,000	
Current liabilities		15,000,000
Long-term debt		35,000,000
Cash		10,000,000
To record the acquisition of DataFile Inc. for $10,000,000 in cash.		

Many reporting issues arise during the acquisition of a business. How are fair values of acquired assets and liabilities measured? Should we include assets and liabilities not currently reported on the acquired company's balance sheet, such as research and development (R&D) or other specific intangibles? What does the purchase price include? Should we include consulting fees or fees for registering any stock issued by the acquiring company? What happens when the purchase price is less than the sum of the fair values of the net assets acquired? If the acquirer does not purchase all of the acquired company's stock, how do the financial reports reflect this outside or "noncontrolling" interest?

Before addressing the current reporting requirements for acquisitions, it is useful to look at the evolution of reporting for business combinations over the years. Analysis of past practice is necessary when dealing with the results of acquisitions that took place under previous reporting requirements. It also highlights the reporting issues accountants have dealt with and continue to address today.

Evolution of Reporting for Business Combinations

Reporting for business combinations has changed dramatically in the twenty-first century. Major issues focus on identifying and valuing what was acquired, valuing and reporting the consideration paid, and valuation of and subsequent reporting of differences between the price paid and the net assets acquired. From 1970 through 2001, two accounting methods existed for recording business combinations, the **purchase method** and the **pooling-of-interests method**.

Purchase Method The *purchase method* views a business combination as an investment in either the assets or the equity shares of another business. Like any purchase transaction in accounting, the **cost**, or value given up, needs to be determined. Cost is easy to determine for cash acquisitions. When the acquirer issues debt or equity securities to buy a business, the fair market value of those securities generally measures cost.

Because many assets and liabilities are acquired in a business combination, the next step under the purchase method is to *allocate* the acquisition cost to the individual assets and liabilities. This allocation needs to be done immediately if the acquired company is to be absorbed into the acquiring company, as with a statutory merger. If the acquired company is to be maintained as a subsidiary, as in a stock acquisition, the entire acquisition cost is recorded as *Investment in Subsidiary* on the acquiring company's books. However, the allocation as of the acquisition date must be done eventually, as part of the process of preparing consolidated financial statements.

The cost of an acquisition usually exceeds the acquired company's book value—assets less liabilities reported on the acquired company's balance sheet. Remaining acquisition cost was typically assigned to the rather vague intangible asset known as **goodwill**, and it was not unusual to have acquisitions where goodwill absorbed a large majority of the purchase price. Accounting standards in effect from 1970 to 2001 required that goodwill be straight-line amortized over *not more than 40 years*. Many companies chose the maximum life of 40 years, a decision that minimized the effect of goodwill amortization expense on future earnings. Others chose to write goodwill off quickly, to avoid subsequent income effects entirely.

Acquisitions recorded under the purchase method reported combined net income in the acquisition year that included the acquirer's income for the entire year and the acquiree's income *after the acquisition date*.

Pooling-of-Interests Method   Whereas the purchase method views a business combination as an *acquisition* of one business by another, the *pooling-of-interests method* views it as a *union of two previously separate companies*, achieved through the exchange of equity shares. Treating this transaction as a "joining together" rather than a "purchase" avoids the question of acquisition *cost*. The pooling-of-interests method combines the balance sheets of the two companies, with appropriate adjustments in the equity section to account for the exchange of shares. Existing carrying amounts—"book values"—of assets and liabilities are simply added together. Since no cost figure is computed, no asset revaluations occur and no goodwill is recorded.

The pooling-of-interests method was used only when the combination involved an exchange of stock. By combining the book values of the two companies, the market value of the exchanged stock was ignored. Ownership and control of the combined company did not change, since the shareholders of the acquired company received shares in the acquiring company. Leaving the acquired company at book value was therefore justified by reasoning that no "acquisition" had occurred. Management often preferred pooling: the absence of goodwill and its amortization led to *higher future reported earnings* than under the purchase method. In addition, because the fair value of consideration paid was typically in excess of the reported book values of net assets acquired, *assets were lower* under the pooling-of-interests method. Consequently the return on assets ratio often used by investors to evaluate companies was higher under the pooling-of-interests method.

Acquisitions recorded under the pooling-of-interests method reported net income in the acquisition year that included the acquirer's and acquiree's income for the *entire* year, no matter when during the year the acquisition occurred. Even when the pooling took place at the end of the accounting year, the combined company's income statement included the profits of both companies for all twelve months. This practice further increased the value of the pooling-of-interests method in the eyes of management.

Reporting Differences   The following example illustrates the significant differences between the purchase and pooling-of-interests methods. Company A issues stock with a fair market value of $2,000,000 to acquire full ownership of Company B. Company B's assets and liabilities have book values and fair values as follows:

Company B Balance Sheet	Book Value	Fair Value
Assets.	$1,000,000	$1,500,000
Liabilities.	(700,000)	(700,000)
Net assets	$ 300,000	$ 800,000

Under the purchase method, the transaction is valued at $2,000,000, the fair value of the issued stock. The amount in excess of the fair value of net assets acquired, $1,200,000 (= $2,000,000 − $800,000), is goodwill. Under the pooling-of-interests method the transaction is valued at $300,000, the book value of the net assets acquired, and there is no revaluation of Company B's assets and liabilities. For a statutory merger, Company A records the acquisition as:

	Purchase Method		Pooling-of-interests Method	
Various assets	1,500,000		1,000,000	
Goodwill	1,200,000		—	
Various liabilities		700,000		700,000
Stockholders' equity		2,000,000		300,000

The purchase method revalues Company B's assets to fair value, an amount significantly greater than book value, and reports $1,700,000 more in assets than the pooling-of-interests method. Subsequent writeoff of these additional assets recognized under purchase accounting, whether in the form of depreciation, amortization, or impairment losses, has a dampening effect on the future income of the combined company.

Valuation Controversy The purchase and pooling-of-interests methods gave two very different accounting outcomes for a business combination. Not surprisingly, this led to ongoing controversy over the preferred method of accounting for business combinations. The controversy first flared up in the late 1960s when a large number of business combinations occurred, leading to widespread use—and abuse—of the pooling-of-interests method. Companies applied pooling retrospectively so that combined income could be reported for a given year, even though the combination did not actually occur until early the following year. When a combination involved both cash and equity shares, some companies used a hybrid part-purchase, part-pooling method to minimize goodwill. Even when companies used the purchase method, they sometimes chose not to amortize goodwill on the grounds that it had an indefinite life.

Accounting standard-setters—then the Accounting Principles Board—responded by issuing two standards in 1970. *APB Opinion No. 16* (*APBO 16*) established twelve criteria that had to be met to qualify for the pooling-of-interests method, and outlawed retrospective pooling and partial pooling methods. The companion *APB Opinion No. 17* required that goodwill be *amortized*, and that its estimated life could not exceed 40 years.

Though many felt that pooling of interests was an inherently defective accounting method, *APBO 16* stopped short of banning it. This approach seemed to solve the problem for a time. The number of poolings dropped steadily after 1970, to 10% or less of all business combinations by the mid-1980s.

By the mid-1990s, the issue erupted again, as "mega-mergers" of some of the country's biggest companies began to occur. The size of the companies involved and the high level of stock prices meant that these transactions often had values in the billions of dollars, far in excess of existing book values. Many of these large transactions were structured as poolings. Concern grew that huge amounts of transaction value were being suppressed by the pooling method, and there were renewed calls for its abolition.

At the same time, the purchase method had its own problems. Huge amounts were recorded as goodwill, as companies made little effort to identify and assign value to specific intangibles acquired. Goodwill life estimates were not made very seriously, and were often chosen to manage reported earnings. Companies sometimes allocated as much cost as possible to *in-process research and development*, which could be expensed immediately, rather than to goodwill. Others announced large-scale restructurings following the acquisition, again resulting in large immediate write-offs. Although write-offs from these approaches adversely affected current earnings, future earnings benefited as the written-off assets no longer had to be depreciated or amortized.

Given the increasing concern over accounting for business combinations and the continuing number of large transactions, the FASB proposed in 1999 to significantly change the accounting for business combinations by requiring the purchase method for all business combinations, *effectively eliminating the pooling-of-interests method*. To reduce the residual assigned to goodwill, the FASB proposed that companies *carefully analyze specific intangibles acquired*, assign cost to them, and amortize them over appropriate lives. Goodwill would be amortized over not more than 20 years.

The corporate community was not very happy with these proposals. They argued that the rules would discourage merger activity and harm the economy. Members of Congress supported their corporate constituents and hinted at legislation to prevent the new rules from being implemented.

In the face of considerable opposition to its original proposal, the FASB crafted a compromise. They retained elimination of the pooling method and identification of specific intangibles, but the proposal that goodwill be amortized over a period not exceeding 20 years was dropped, and replaced by a provision that *goodwill not be amortized at all*! In place of amortization, goodwill must be assessed regularly to determine whether its value has been *impaired*. The FASB adopted these modified provisions in 2001 when it issued *SFAS 141*, Business Combinations and *SFAS 142*, Goodwill and Other Intangible Assets. In 2008, the FASB issued *SFAS 141R*, making significant changes in the business combination standards.

Current Status of Reporting for Business Combinations

ASC Topic 805 contains current standards for reporting business combinations. Standards for valuing acquired intangible assets, including goodwill, are in *ASC Topic 350*. *ASC Topic 810* describes consolidation procedures for stock acquisitions. The major valuation requirements found in *ASC Topic 805* were significantly changed in 2008, and reflect convergence with IFRS.

Definition of Business Combination   The requirements of *ASC Topics 805* and *810* apply only to *business combinations*. A **business combination** occurs when *control is obtained* over one or more businesses. Control may be obtained by direct acquisition of the assets and liabilities of the acquired company—statutory merger, consolidation, or asset acquisition—or by obtaining a controlling interest in the voting shares of the acquired company—stock acquisition. To determine whether a business combination has occurred, we need a definition of **control**, and we need to identify the attributes that constitute a *business*.

This chapter focuses on statutory mergers, consolidations, and asset acquisitions: the acquired company or division ceases to exist and the acquiring company absorbs its financial records. It is therefore obvious that the acquiring company obtains control of the acquired company. When the acquisition is structured as a *stock acquisition*, the question of control becomes more relevant. Discussion of the concept of control and related reporting issues appears in Chapter 3. The ASC glossary provides this definition of a **business**:

> An integrated set of activities and assets that is capable of being conducted and managed for the purpose of providing a return in the form of dividends, lower costs, or other economic benefits directly to investors or other owners, members, or participants.

Certain transactions do *not* constitute a business combination. Formation of a **joint venture** by two or more existing companies is not a business combination. **Establishing a new business** as a separate subsidiary is not a business combination. In both of these cases, a new business is formed without an acquisition transaction. **Combining two or more companies already under common control**—such as two or more existing subsidiaries, or merging an existing subsidiary into the parent company—similarly does not constitute a business combination because there is no change in control. *ASC Topic 805* does not prescribe the accounting for these transactions. However, acquiring a division or product line of another company *is* a business combination, even though the division or product line is not a separate legal entity.

The remainder of this chapter discusses and illustrates the requirements of *ASC Topic 805*, focusing on the initial recording of acquisitions *reported as statutory mergers, consolidations, or asset acquisitions,* where the acquired assets and liabilities are recorded directly on the acquirer's books.

VALUATION OF ASSETS ACQUIRED AND LIABILITIES ASSUMED

LO1 Measure and account for the various assets and liabilities acquired in mergers and acquisitions.

The **acquisition method** is used to report all business combinations. This method calls for careful identification and valuation of the *fair value of the assets acquired and liabilities assumed* at the *acquisition date*.

Acquisition Date

FASB ASC para. 805-10-25-7 defines the **acquisition date** as the *date the acquiring company obtains control of the acquired company*, usually the date when the consideration is paid to the former owners of the acquired company. When control was attained at an earlier date, based on agreement with the former owners of the acquired company, the earlier date is used.

When the parties agree on an official acquisition date prior to completing all aspects of the transaction, the acquisition date typically is the beginning of an accounting period for the acquiring entity. This accounting convenience avoids including the acquired entity at some interim date during the reporting year. Subject to provisions needed to protect the interests of the equity holders of the two entities, effective control over the acquired entity must occur on or before this chosen date.

Identifying the Acquiring Company

As discussed earlier in the chapter, only the assets and liabilities of the *acquired company* are revalued to fair value at the acquisition date. It is therefore imperative that the acquiring and acquired companies be identified. When no equity interests are exchanged, determining the acquiring company is easy. The acquiring entity is the one distributing cash or other assets, and/or incurring liabilities. Business combinations that involve an equity exchange can be more difficult to resolve. The following characteristics typically describe the **acquiring company**:

- It is the entity that **issues the equity interests**.
- It is the **larger entity**, as measured by assets, revenues, or earnings.
- Its owners have the **larger voting interest** in the combined company.
- An individual or organized group of its prior owners constitute a **large minority ($\leq 50\%$) interest** in the combined entity, and there are no other significant concentrations of voting interests.
- It constitutes or selects a **majority of the governing body**—the Board of Directors—of the combined entity.
- Its senior management **dominates the senior management** of the combined entity.
- Its stockholders **did not receive a premium** over market value in the exchange, whereas stockholders of the acquired entity did receive a premium.

When these indicators do not all point in the same direction, the accountant must assess all the facts and circumstances to identify the acquiring company. Should a *new entity* be formed to serve as the combined entity—as in a statutory consolidation—one of the prior entities must still be designated as the acquiring company, following the guidelines above.

Combinations involving *more than two entities* make identification of the acquiring company even more difficult. In such cases, additional characteristics used to identify the acquiring company include:

- It is the entity which initiated the combination.
- It is the largest entity.

Once we identify the acquiring company and the acquisition date, we measure the assets acquired and liabilities assumed at fair value. If the acquisition cost is *greater than* the fair value of the identifiable net assets acquired, **goodwill** is reported. If the acquisition cost is *less than* the fair value of identifiable net assets acquired, the acquisition is a **bargain purchase** and a *gain* is reported.

BUSINESS APPLICATION   Reverse Acquisitions

Usually the company issuing the equity interests is the acquirer. But in a **reverse acquisition**, the equity issuer does not control the combined entity. Now the *former* shareholders receiving the issued stock *own the majority* of the shares in the combined company, or the management of the *other company* dominates the senior management of the combined company. Reverse acquisitions are particularly popular as a technique for taking a private company public without the cost and regulatory requirements involved with an initial public offering (IPO). Here a private company acquires a publicly traded company, but the public company controls the combined entity. The publicly traded company is usually a shell, with very few products or transactions, which then absorbs the private company's products, operations, and management.

Private Chinese companies have used reverse acquisitions to trade on U.S. markets without being subject to the SEC's usual rigorous regulatory and auditing standards. In 2010, the PCAOB issued an alert to investors, warning that financial information provided by these companies may not be reliable.

Measurement of Previously Reported Assets and Liabilities

The acquired company's balance sheet reports its assets and liabilities according to GAAP. Most of the reported values will likely *not* reflect fair value at the date of acquisition. Cash is obviously reported at fair value, and current liabilities probably reflect the amount needed to satisfy creditors. Most short-term investments are also reported at current fair values. However, even current assets such as receivables and inventories may not be reported at fair value. For example, LIFO inventories typically reflect very old historical costs, unless the entire inventory has been recently replaced. Long-term assets, such as buildings, equipment, and reported intangibles, are reported at historical cost less accumulated depreciation or amortization.

The fair value of acquired assets is based on the acquirer's planned use of those assets. Tangible operating property held by the acquired company changes in value if the acquirer intends to dispose of it or change its planned usage.

The meaning of *fair value*, and the methods of estimating it, vary from item to item. *FASB ASC Topic 820*, Fair Value Measurements and Disclosures, provides a detailed definition and framework for determining fair value for a variety of asset types. **Fair value** may be estimated by use of quoted market prices, appraisals, estimated selling prices, estimated replacement costs, and the present value of future cash flows discounted at an appropriate interest rate. Exhibit 2.3 presents common means of determining fair values of assets and liabilities.

EXHIBIT 2.3 Estimation of Fair Values	
Asset or Liability	**Fair Value Estimated by**
Accounts receivable	Discounted expected cash inflows
Marketable securities	Quoted market prices
Inventories: Raw materials	Current replacement cost
Inventories: Work in process	Estimated selling price, less costs to complete and sell, less reasonable profit
Inventories: Finished goods	Estimated selling price, less costs to sell, less reasonable profit
Property, plant and equipment to be used	Current replacement cost
Property, plant and equipment to be sold	Estimated selling price less costs to sell
Other assets	Appraised value
Most liabilities	Discounted expected cash outflows

Identification and Measurement of Previously Unreported Intangibles

Tangible assets acquired and most liabilities assumed should be fairly easy to identify. Virtually all of these appear on the books of the acquired company. Intangible assets, however, present special problems. The existence of significant *unrecorded* intangible assets may be both a major reason why the business combination occurred and a major factor in the total acquisition cost. Such intangibles include brand names, market share, customer base, good locations, technology, skilled workforce, and the like. Although most of these intangibles developed internally during the life of the acquired company, very few are recorded as assets on the acquired company's books under GAAP.

ASC Topic 805 specifies the requirements for reporting previously unrecognized acquired intangibles. Two criteria are employed to identify intangibles requiring separate recognition:

• The intangible asset arises from *contractual or other legal rights*, or

• The intangible is *separable*, that is, it can be separated or divided from the acquired entity and sold, rented, licensed, or otherwise transferred.

Meeting *either* criterion is sufficient to require separate recognition of an intangible. A firm must report an intangible asset arising from **contractual or other legal rights** *even if it is not separable*. *ASC para. 805-20-55-2* provides three examples:

• An operating lease with terms that are favorable to terms that could be obtained in the current market, even though the lease terms prohibit transfer of the lease to an outside party

- A license to operate a nuclear power plant, even though it cannot be sold or transferred to an outside party
- A patent licensed to others for a percentage of future revenues; even though the patent and the license cannot be separately sold, each is separately reported.

The **separability criterion** applies when the intangible could be separated from the acquired company and transferred through sale, licensing, leasing, or other means. Evidence of separability comes from similar observable market transactions; it does not matter whether the acquired company actually intends to sell the intangible asset or such market transactions occur regularly. However, when contractual terms prevent the company from selling the intangible asset, it does not meet the separability criterion.

Examples of Identifiable Intangible Assets The Codification offers many examples of reportable intangibles, grouped into broad categories as follows:

- **Contract-based intangible assets**, such as lease agreements, franchise agreements, licensing agreements, construction permits, employment contracts, broadcast rights, and mineral rights.
- **Marketing-related intangible assets**, such as brand names, trademarks, internet domain names, newspaper mastheads and non-competition agreements.
- **Customer-related intangible assets**, such as customer lists, order backlogs, and customer contracts.
- **Technology-based intangible assets**, such as patent rights, computer software, databases, and trade secrets.
- **Artistic-based intangible assets**, such as television programs, motion pictures, videos, recordings, books, photographs, and advertising jingles.

Most of these intangibles meet the criteria for separate reporting based on the *existence of contractual or legal rights*. This category of intangibles is wide-ranging, as many business features and activities involve contractual agreements. Far fewer examples of intangibles meeting the *separability* criterion exist; they include customer lists, noncontractual customer relationships, databases, and unpatented technology.

Unreported Intangibles Many intangibles do not meet the contractual or separability criteria and are not reported as assets acquired. Whether or not they meet the accounting definition of acquired intangible assets, the acquiring company views these intangibles as valuable, because they contribute to future cash flows. The consideration paid will reflect the value of these intangibles, and will likely exceed the fair value of the reported net assets acquired. The difference is reported as **goodwill**.

ASC paras. 805-20-55-6 and *7* provide examples of intangibles that are included in goodwill.

- An **assembled workforce**, the group of employees already in place and able to run the business, including management, sales, technical and other personnel
- **Potential contracts** being negotiated with prospective customers

Other examples include long-standing customer relationships, favorable locations, and business reputation.

Valuation of Intangibles Although the Codification does not provide specific guidance for valuing acquired intangible assets, the general measurement guidelines of *ASC Topic 820* apply. *ASC paras. 820-10-35-37* through *57* define the **fair value hierarchy**, in order of priority:

- **Level 1**: Quoted prices in an active market for identical assets
- **Level 2**: Quoted market prices for similar assets, adjusted for the attributes of the assets in question
- **Level 3**: Valuation based on unobservable estimated attributes

In all cases, the asset is valued in the context of its highest and best use. If the company obtains the most value from the asset by selling it, market values are used. If the asset's value is maximized through its use within the company, market values of products it produces or the estimated present value of expected future cash inflows may be used.

The Codification identifies three approaches to valuation:

- **Market:** Quoted market prices of identical or similar assets
- **Income:** Valuation models used to calculate the present value of future cash flows or earnings
- **Cost**: Estimation of replacement cost of the services provided by the asset

Acquired intangibles are less likely than tangible assets to be bought and sold in active markets. These assets tend to be specific in nature, deriving value from their use within the company. Quoted prices for similar assets may be appropriate, but in many cases companies employ valuation models using estimated future cash flows. For example, in its 2009 annual report, **Sun Microsystems, Inc.** (now merged with **Oracle Corporation**) describes its valuation of acquired in-process R&D (IPRD), an intangible asset:

> The value assigned to IPRD was determined by considering the importance of each project to the overall development plan, estimating costs to develop the purchased IPRD into commercially viable products, estimating the resulting net cash flows from the projects when completed and discounting the net cash flows to their present value. The revenue estimates used to value the purchased IPRD were based on estimates of the relevant market sizes and growth factors, expected trends in technology and the nature and expected timing of new product introductions.
>
> The rates utilized to discount the net cash flows to their present values were based on weighted-average cost of capital. The weighted-average cost of capital was adjusted to reflect the difficulties and uncertainties in completing each project and thereby achieving technological feasibility, the percentage of completion of each project, anticipated market acceptance and penetration, market growth rates and risks related to the impact of potential changes in future target markets. Based on these factors, discount rates that generally range from 12% to 22% were deemed appropriate for valuing the purchased IPRD.

Illustration of Reporting Assets Acquired and Liabilities Assumed

To illustrate the reporting for assets acquired and liabilities assumed, we use the statutory merger information in Exhibit 2.4.

EXHIBIT 2.4   Combination Illustration with Identifiable Intangibles

IBM pays $25,000,000 in cash to acquire DataFile Inc. on July 1, 2012. Fair values of DataFile's reported assets and liabilities follow:

Account	Fair value
Current assets	$ 2,000,000
Plant and equipment	60,000,000
Patents and copyrights	5,000,000
Current liabilities	10,000,000
Long-term debt	40,000,000

In addition, IBM identified and valued DataFile's previously unreported intangible assets as follows:

Brand names	$ 1,000,000
Favorable lease agreements	600,000
Assembled workforce	5,000,000
In-process contracts with potential customers	2,000,000
Contractual customer relationships	3,000,000

Other than the assembled workforce and in-process contracts, all of the previously unreported intangibles meet the contractual or separability criteria for reporting as identifiable intangibles. IBM records the acquisition as follows:

Current assets	2,000,000
Plant and equipment	60,000,000
Patents and copyrights	5,000,000
Brand names	1,000,000
Favorable lease agreements	600,000
Contractual customer relationships	3,000,000
Goodwill	3,400,000
Current liabilities	10,000,000
Long-term debt	40,000,000
Cash	25,000,000
To record the acquisition of DataFile for $25,000,000 in cash.	

Goodwill in this acquisition is the difference between the acquisition price and the fair value of the reportable net assets acquired, and is calculated as follows:

Acquisition cost		$25,000,000
Fair value of identifiable net assets acquired:		
Current assets	$ 2,000,000	
Plant and equipment	60,000,000	
Patents and copyrights	5,000,000	
Brand names	1,000,000	
Favorable lease agreements	600,000	
Contractual customer relationships	3,000,000	
Current liabilities	(10,000,000)	
Long-term debt	(40,000,000)	21,600,000
Goodwill		$ 3,400,000

Although unreportable intangible assets are one reason for the existence of goodwill, another explanation is that the acquiring company *paid too much* for the acquired company. Subsequent goodwill impairment testing should reveal this fact, as discussed in Chapter 4.

BUSINESS APPLICATION   Unreported Intangibles

The composition of goodwill is often discussed in financial statement footnotes. Below are some recent examples:

IBM (*2010 annual report, describing $4,754 million in goodwill recognized on 2010 acquisitions*):

> The primary items that generated the goodwill are the value of the synergies between the acquired companies and IBM and the acquired assembled workforce, neither of which qualify as an amortizable intangible asset.

Walt Disney (2010 annual report, describing $2.3 billion in goodwill recognized on its 2009 acquisition of Marvel):

> The goodwill reflects the value to Disney from leveraging Marvel intellectual property across our distribution channels, taking advantage of Disney's established global reach.

continued

continued from prior page

Walt Disney *(2007 annual report, describing $5.6 billion in goodwill recognized on its 2006 acquisition of Pixar):*

The goodwill that arose from the Acquisition reflected the value to Disney from:
- Acquiring a talented, assembled workforce, particularly the creative and technological talents of key senior management and film directors with a successful track record of producing high quality feature animation
- Securing all of the economic results of future films produced by Pixar
- Obtaining the benefits of leveraging future Pixar-created intellectual property across Disney's diversified revenue streams and portfolio of entertainment assets
- Improving the results of Disney feature animation films

Dell Inc. (2011 annual report, describing $2.3 billion in goodwill recognized on its fiscal 2010 acquisition of Perot Systems):

The goodwill of $2.3 billion represents the value from combining Perot Systems with Dell to provide customers with a broader range of IT services and solutions as well as optimizing how these solutions are delivered. The acquisition has enabled Dell to supply even more Perot Systems customers with Dell products and extended the reach of Perot Systems' capabilities to Dell customers around the world.

Sprint *(2006 annual report, describing $15.6 billion in goodwill recognized on its 2005 acquisition of Nextel):*

We paid a premium (i.e., goodwill) over the fair value of the net tangible and identified intangible assets of Nextel for a number of potential strategic and financial benefits that we believe will be realized as a result of the merger, including, but not limited to, the following:
- the combination of extensive network and spectrum assets, which we believe will enable us to offer consumers, businesses and government agencies a wide array of broadband wireless and integrated communications services;
- the combination of Nextel's strength in business and government wireless services with our position in consumer wireless and data services, including services supported by our global IP network, which we believe will enable us to serve a broader customer base;
- the size and scale of the combined company, which is comparable to that of our two largest competitors, which we believe will enable us to achieve more operating efficiencies than either company could achieve on its own; and,
- the ability to position us strategically in the fastest growing areas of the communications industry.

Reporting Perspective

Before *SFAS 141* became effective in 2002, accounting standards did not require companies to report acquired specific intangibles. Virtually all intangibles were combined under the generic title of Goodwill. For some acquisitions, 90 percent or more of net assets acquired were reported as goodwill. This did not provide very useful information about the composition and value of assets acquired and liabilities assumed. Current standards require that identifiable intangible assets be separately recognized.

continued

continued from prior page

Therefore, we expect acquisitions reported after 2002 to result in significantly increased recognition of specific intangible assets, and less recognition of goodwill. However, studies of actual acquisitions indicate no evidence that reported goodwill has declined. One such study, *"SFAS 141: The First 5 Years,"* available from **intangiblebusiness.com**, finds that goodwill reported by U.S. corporations in the Standard & Poor's 100 index over the period 2002–2006 accounted for an average of 65 percent of total purchase price, and that this proportion has not declined in the years since implementation of *SFAS 141*. The study identifies specific examples of goodwill overstatement. Walt Disney's $7.5 billion acquisition of Pixar in 2006 resulted in recognition of $5.6 billion in goodwill. Google's $1.2 billion acquisition of YouTube, also in 2006, reported $1.1 billion in goodwill. Both acquisitions appear to reflect a pervasive inability or reluctance to separately value specific acquired intangibles, such as brand names or customer lists.

IBM's acquisitions, shown below, tend to confirm this point. The specific identifiable intangible assets IBM reports include completed technology, client relationships, in-process R&D, and strategic alliances. Goodwill as a percent of total net assets acquired has actually *increased*, even though reporting requirements now emphasize identification of specific intangible assets acquired.

IBM Acquisitions, 1999 -2010 (in millions)	Pre-*SFAS 141*		Post-*SFAS 141*					
	1999	**2001**	**2003**	**2005**	**2007**	**2008**	**2009**	**2010**
Tangible net assets	$ 477	$ 96	$ 312	$ 426	$ (56)	$ (327)	$ 237	$ 204
Identifiable intangible assets	359	370	484	165	201	1,550	231	1,580
Goodwill	715	616	1,740	1,431	999	5,573	1,003	4,754
Total acquisition cost	$1,551	$1,082	$2,536	$2,022	$1,144	$6,796	$1,471	$6,538
Identifiable intangible assets as a percent of acquisition cost	16%	34%	19%	8%	18%	22%	16%	24%
Goodwill as a percent of acquisition cost.	46%	57%	69%	71%	87%	82%	68%	73%

REVIEW 1 • Reporting assets acquired and liabilities assumed

IBM acquires Lotus in an acquisition reported as a statutory merger, for $1.2 billion in cash. At the acquisition date, the reported assets and liabilities of Lotus have fair values as follows:

(in millions)	**Fair value**
Cash and receivables.	$ 400
Inventories	800
Property, plant and equipment.	3,500
Accounts payable.	300
Long-term debt	3,850

In addition, the following items are not currently reported on Lotus' balance sheet:

(in millions)	**Fair value**
Favorable lease agreements	$150
Skilled workforce	15
Favorable press reviews on products	5

Required: Prepare the entry IBM makes to record its acquisition of Lotus.

Solutions are located after the chapter assignments.

MEASUREMENT OF ACQUISITION COST

LO2 Measure
and report the
various types of
consideration
paid.

The Codification requires that the acquisition cost, or consideration transferred, in a business combination be measured at *fair value at the acquisition date*. **Acquisition cost** includes the following items:

- Assets, such as cash, transferred by the acquirer to the former owners of the acquiree
- Liabilities incurred by the acquirer and owed to the former owners of the acquiree
- Stock issued by the acquirer to the former owners of the acquiree

Prior practice allowed stock value to be measured at the *agreement date*. For example, in **Walt Disney Company**'s May 5, 2006, acquisition of **Pixar**, Disney exchanged 2.3 shares of its common stock for each share of Pixar common stock, a total of 279 million shares issued. The stock value was measured at the average price for the five day period starting two days before the acquisition announcement date of January 24, 2006. Although the acquisition was recorded on May 5, Disney concluded that the value of the stock at the announcement date more than three months previously was a more accurate measure of acquisition cost.

ASC Topic 805 requires that the *stock be valued on the date that the acquirer achieves control*. Using the acquisition date value adds uncertainty to the acquisition cost, as the market value of the stock issued is unknown until control changes hands. **Walt Disney**'s 2009 acquisition of **Marvel Entertainment, Inc.** is an example. Under terms of the agreement, announced at the end of August, 2009, Disney paid Marvel shareholders $30 per share in cash plus 0.745 Disney shares for each Marvel share owned. The total acquisition cost of $4 billion was based on Disney's August 28, 2009 closing price of $26.84 per share. The acquisition was completed on December 31, 2009, when Disney's stock price was $32.25 per share, adding over $300 million to the acquisition cost.

Contingent Consideration

Acquisition cost may also include **contingent consideration**, where the acquirer agrees to make additional payments to the former owners of the acquiree if certain events occur or conditions are met. For example, the acquirer may agree to pay more to the former owners of the acquired company if the acquired company achieves a specified performance target. Alternatively, if the former owners receive payment in the form of the acquirer's stock, they may ask that the market value of the stock be guaranteed at some minimum value for a specified time period. In each case, the acquiring company must make an additional payment to the former owners of the acquired company if the performance target is met, or if the market value of the acquirer's stock goes below the guaranteed minimum.

To report the terms of the acquisition in an accurate and timely manner, the Codification requires that contingent consideration be reported *at the date of acquisition*. Because the exact amount is unknown at that time, the acquirer must make a good-faith estimate of the *present value of the expected payment*, considering both its *probability* and its *timing*.

Earnings Contingency   A **contingency based on earnings** typically derives from the beliefs of the former shareholders of the acquired company that they are entitled to more consideration for their shares because their company will substantially bolster postcombination earnings. Although there may be no evidence on this point, to close the deal the acquiring company may agree that if earnings equal or exceed a given amount in a specified period of time, additional consideration will be paid to the former shareholders of the acquired company. Such payments add to the cost of the acquired company. The parties, in effect, agree that the total value of the acquired company is not known until the contingency period ends.

Earnings contingencies, commonly known as **earnouts**, may cover up to five postcombination years and specify a variety of performance goals, such as revenue, cash from operations, and earnings before deducting interest, taxes, depreciation, and amortization (EBITDA). For example, when **Oracle** acquired **Pillar Data** in 2011, the entire acquisition price was an earnout. Three years after the acquisition, Pillar investors will receive cash equal to three times the difference between Pillar's net revenues in 2014 and net losses from 2011 to 2014. If losses exceed revenues, the acquisition price is zero.

To illustrate the valuation and reporting for an earnout, assume that on January 1, 2013, Buyer agrees to pay Seller's former shareholders one dollar in cash for every dollar in cash from operations above $40,000,000 reported in the first year after the acquisition. In valuing an actual earnout, the acquirer may have many predictions of future cash from operations. For purposes of this illustration, assume Buyer expects only three possible outcomes for performance results in the first year ending December 31, 2013:

Cash from operations	Probability
$25,000,000	0.20
45,000,000	0.60
75,000,000	0.20

The expected payment is calculated as follows:

$$
\begin{aligned}
(\$45,000,000 - \$40,000,000) \times 60\% &= \$\ 3,000,000 \\
(\$75,000,000 - \$40,000,000) \times 20\% &= \underline{\ \ 7,000,000} \\
&\ \ \ \ \ \underline{\underline{\$10,000,000}}
\end{aligned}
$$

If the appropriate discount rate is 5 percent, the present value of the expected payment is:

$$\$10,000,000/(1 + 0.05) \quad = \quad \$9,523,810$$

The earnout of $9,523,810 increases the acquisition price, and is reported by the acquirer as a liability.

Security Price Contingency   **Security price contingencies** guarantee the former shareholders of the acquired company that the market value of securities (stock or debt) issued to them in exchange for their stock is at least a specified amount at a specified time. Security contingencies are not as common as earnouts, and often require that the acquiring company issue additional shares to the former shareholders of the acquired company, to bring the total value of shares issued to a minimum level.

For example, on January 1, 2013, Buyer issued 1,000,000 shares with a market price of $20 per share to the former shareholders of Seller. Buyer also agrees to issue additional shares to maintain the value of shares issued at $20,000,000 at the end of the first year following the acquisition. Buyer's management estimates the stock price at December 31, 2013, as follows:

Stock price per share	Probability
$16	0.10
18	0.25
25	0.65

The expected obligation from the stock price contingency is calculated as follows:

$$
\begin{aligned}
(\$20,000,000 - \$16,000,000) \times 10\% &= \$400,000 \\
(\$20,000,000 - \$18,000,000) \times 25\% &= \underline{\ \ 500,000} \\
&\ \ \ \underline{\underline{\$900,000}}
\end{aligned}
$$

If the appropriate discount rate is 5 percent, the present value of the expected payment is:

$$\$900,000/(1 + 0.05) \quad = \quad \$857,143$$

The security price contingency of $857,143 increases the acquisition price, and is reported by the acquirer as additional paid-in capital.

Acquisition-Related Costs

Costs related to acquisitions include more than just payments to the former owners of the acquired company. Acquirers generally employ outside consultants, lawyers, accountants, and advisory services, and incur costs to register newly issued securities. For example, in 2010 **Dell Inc.** incurred $116 million in acquisition-related costs related to its acquisition of **Perot Systems**: $93 million to settle prior compensation agreements for former Perot employees hired by Dell, and $23 million in other items such as bankers' fees and consulting fees.

These **out-of-pocket costs** to outside consultants, lawyers, accountants, and others are not included in acquisition cost. Although these costs are a necessary part of an acquisition, they do not increase the value of the acquired business. Therefore companies expense these acquisition-related costs as incurred. Similarly, costs of internally provided services, such as salaries for employees in the acquisitions department of the acquiring company, are expensed as incurred.

Registration costs for securities issued in an acquisition are treated the same as for any issue of securities—they reduce the net value of the equity accounts affected. For example, if an acquirer issues no-par stock with a fair value of $50,000,000, and registration costs are $2,000,000, the capital stock account is credited for $48,000,000. Stock registration fees do not affect the total acquisition cost—cash paid for the fees *adds* to the acquisition cost, but the fees are *netted out* of the total fair value of stock issued. In our example, consideration paid is $50,000,000, reported as $48,000,000 in capital stock and $2,000,000 in cash. If registration costs are instead $1,000,000, consideration paid is still $50,000,000, reported as $49,000,000 in capital stock and $1,000,000 in cash.

Companies often incur additional **acquisition-related restructuring costs**, including shutting down departments, reassigning or eliminating jobs, and changing suppliers or production practices in connection with business combinations. Unless represented by acquisition-date liabilities, these costs are expensed as incurred, and do not affect acquisition cost. In the past, firms have sought to capitalize these "acquisition-related" restructuring costs, effectively reporting them as goodwill and not as expenses, to improve their reported performance.

Illustration of Reporting Consideration Given in an Acquisition

Return to the July 1, 2012, business combination described in Exhibit 2.4. Instead of simply paying $25,000,000 in cash to the former owners of DataFile, IBM structures the deal as follows:

Cash paid to former owners of DataFile.	$ 3,000,000
Fair value of stock issued to former owners of DataFile: 1,000,000 shares, par value $0.50	20,000,000
Cash paid for registration fees on stock issued.	600,000
Cash paid for outside merger advisory services	1,200,000
Expected present value of earnout agreement	1,500,000
Expected present value of stock price contingency agreement	800,000

IBM pays total cash of $4,800,000, increasing acquisition cost for the $3,000,000 paid to the former owners of DataFile, netting the $600,000 in registration fees against additional paid-in capital, and expensing $1,200,000 in outside consulting fees. IBM reports both forms of contingent consideration as acquisition costs, at estimated fair value, even though it has not yet paid this consideration. Using the asset and liability data on page 44, IBM records the acquisition as follows:

Current assets	2,000,000	
Plant and equipment	60,000,000	
Patents and copyrights	5,000,000	
Brand names	1,000,000	
Favorable lease agreements	600,000	
Contractual customer relationships	3,000,000	
Goodwill	3,700,000	
Merger expenses	1,200,000	
Current liabilities		10,000,000
Long-term debt		40,000,000
Earnout liability		1,500,000
Common stock, $0.50 par.		500,000
Additional paid-in capital—stock issue.		18,900,000
Additional paid-in capital—stock contingency		800,000
Cash		4,800,000
To record the acquisition of DataFile Inc.		

We can separately calculate goodwill as follows:

Acquisition cost		
Cash to former owners of DataFile...................................	$ 3,000,000	
Cash paid for registration fees.......................................	600,000	
Fair value of stock issued, net	19,400,000	
Fair value of earnout...	1,500,000	
Fair value of stock contingency	800,000	
Total acquisition cost..		$25,300,000
Fair value of identifiable net assets acquired		
Current assets	$ 2,000,000	
Plant and equipment...	60,000,000	
Patents and copyrights...	5,000,000	
Brand names	1,000,000	
Favorable lease agreements..	600,000	
Contractual customer relationships	3,000,000	
Current liabilities..	(10,000,000)	
Long-term debt..	(40,000,000)	(21,600,000)
Goodwill..		$ 3,700,000

Reporting Perspective

Standards effective in 2009 changed the reporting of business combinations in fundamental ways:

- Out-of-pocket fees for outside consultants, lawyers, accountants, and others were previously included in acquisition cost, increasing goodwill. Treating these costs as expenses may direct additional attention to the size of these outlays, as they now impact income immediately.

- In-process R&D was previously expensed, and is now capitalized as an indefinite-lived asset, requiring impairment testing subsequent to acquisition.

- Contingent consideration was previously reported as incurred. More timely recognition at the acquisition date requires estimation of expected future cash outflows and selection of the appropriate discount rate.

Although the new requirements are designed to improve information on acquisitions, they require new valuation skills and considerable judgment, which can markedly affect reported assets, liabilities, and income.

SUBSEQUENT CHANGES IN ASSET, LIABILITY, OR CONTINGENT CONSIDERATION VALUES

LO3 Account for changes in the values of acquired assets and liabilities, and contingent consideration.

The above discussion indicates, perhaps surprisingly, that most of the numbers reported in an acquisition are estimates. Assets and liabilities acquired are reported at fair value as of the date of acquisition, based on the information known at the time. Reporting contingent consideration at the date of acquisition requires estimates of expected future performance or future stock prices. Subsequent reporting for changes in these estimates depends on whether new information obtained is a clarification of circumstances that existed at the *date of acquisition*, or reflects events and circumstances that occur *after the acquisition*. Value changes resulting from clarification of facts existing as of the *date of acquisition* are treated as *corrections to the initial acquisition entry*. Value changes caused by events occurring *after the acquisition* are reported *in income*.

Measurement Period

ASC Section 805-10-25 defines the **measurement period** as the period during which value changes can be reported as corrections to the initial acquisition entry. During this period, the acquirer may obtain additional facts pertaining to the acquisition-date fair values of assets acquired and liabilities assumed and the consideration paid, and use this information to adjust these values.

Although the Codification does not specify exactly when the measurement period is over, it does state that *the measurement period ends when no more information can be obtained concerning estimated values as of the acquisition date*. Information obtained soon after the acquisition occurs is more likely to relate to values as of the acquisition date, so *ASC para. 805-10-25-14* puts a limit on the measurement period at **one year from the acquisition date**. However, note carefully that the choice between reporting value changes as corrections of the acquisition entry or as gains or losses depends on whether the changes *affect value as of the acquisition date*, or value changes caused by *subsequent events*. Accountants *cannot* assume that all value changes within the first year are corrections of the original acquisition entry.

Reporting Subsequent Changes in Asset and Liability Values

Return again to the example in Exhibit 2.4 on page 44. Three months after the acquisition, new information reveals that equipment not belonging to DataFile was mistakenly included in the original valuation, and the actual fair value of the acquired equipment was $40,000,000 at the date of acquisition, not $60,000,000. In that case, IBM corrects the original acquisition entry:

Goodwill	20,000,000	
Plant and equipment		20,000,000
To correct the value of equipment acquired.		

For an acquisition reporting goodwill, increases in the value of acquired assets during the measurement period *reduce* reported goodwill. Increases in the value of liabilities assumed *increase* reported goodwill.

But if DataFile's equipment actually was worth $60,000,000 at date of acquisition and subsequently loses value because of a fire at the storage warehouse and is now worth $40,000,000, the following entry records the asset impairment:

Loss on equipment	20,000,000	
Plant and equipment		20,000,000
To report impairment of equipment.		

Changes in value caused by events subsequent to the acquisition are reported in income and do not adjust the original acquisition entry.

Reporting Subsequent Changes in Contingent Consideration Value

The values reported at date of acquisition for earnouts and stock price contingencies are estimates, based on the best judgment of management. These estimates will undoubtedly change based on events that occur after the date of acquisition. Additionally, the present values of the estimates will change with the passage of time.

As discussed above, it is important to distinguish changes in estimated value that result from *clarification of facts that existed at the date of acquisition* from changes that result from *events that occur subsequent to the acquisition*. Changes in the value of contingent consideration resulting from clarification of facts as of the acquisition date are reported as measurement period adjustments, while changes in value due to events occurring after the acquisition date are treated as follows:

- If the contingent consideration is reported as equity, as in a stock price contingency, no value changes are reported. Final settlement is reported in equity.
- If the contingent consideration is reported as a liability, as in an earnout agreement, changes in value are reported in income at each reporting date until the contingency is resolved.

The acquisition facts on page 50 show that IBM reports an earnout agreement at $1,500,000, and a stock price contingency at $800,000. Four months after the acquisition, new information is uncovered concerning expected performance as of the date of acquisition, and the expected earnout value increases by $400,000. IBM reports the change in earnout value as a correction to the original acquisition entry, as follows:

Goodwill	400,000	
Earnout liability		400,000
To record the change in value of the earnout during the measurement period.		

If instead the change in estimated earnout value is due to an improvement in business conditions after the acquisition, the entry is as follows:

Loss on earnout	400,000	
Earnout liability		400,000
To record the change in value of the earnout due to subsequent events.		

Companies do not report changes in the expected value of stock price contingencies. If, at settlement, the fair value of consideration paid differs from the original amount recorded, equity accounts are adjusted to reflect the value change.

REVIEW 2 • Reporting assets and liabilities acquired, consideration paid, and subsequent events

Refer to the information on IBM's acquisition of Lotus, in review problem #1 above. Instead of paying $1.2 billion in cash, IBM incurs the following costs to acquire Lotus *(in millions)*:

	Fair value
Cash paid to former owners of Lotus.	$ 600
Fair value of stock issued (15,000,000 shares, $1 par, $100 fair value per share)	1,500
Earnout agreement.	400
Cash paid for acquisition-related advisory services	200
Cash paid for registration fees for shares issued.	100

Required:
1. Prepare the entry IBM makes to record the acquisition.
2. Now assume that one month after the acquisition, new information reveals that the fair value of the property, plant and equipment acquired was $4 billion at the date of acquisition, not $3.5 billion. Six months after the acquisition, changes in the customer base since the acquisition reduce the expected present value of the earnout to $300 million. Prepare the entries necessary to report both value changes.

Solutions are located after the chapter assignments.

BARGAIN PURCHASES

LO4 Account for bargain purchases.

Because *ASC Topic 805* focuses on the fair values of assets and liabilities acquired, rather than allocating the cost of the acquisition to the acquired company's net assets as done under prior practice, there likely will be differences between the value of net assets acquired and the acquisition cost. We have already discussed and illustrated many cases where acquisition cost *exceeds* the fair value of identifiable net assets acquired, resulting in reporting the asset *goodwill*. However, in some cases the acquisition cost is *less than* the fair value of identifiable net assets acquired. These acquisitions are called **bargain purchases**.

An acquiring company may pay less than the fair value of identifiable net assets acquired if the acquisition is a "forced sale," where the seller is attempting to avoid bankruptcy or other serious financial losses and there is no time to shop around for a better price. One example occurred in 2009 when **Republic Airlines** acquired **Frontier Airlines**. Frontier was in bankruptcy, illiquidity in the credit market limited the competitive bidding process, and Frontier was expected to generate future losses. As a result, Republic paid a price that was determined to be lower than the fair value of Frontier's net assets.

In these cases, the acquisition price does not reflect the fair values of assets acquired and liabilities assumed. Because the Codification emphasizes accurate reporting of asset and liability values, rather than adjusting their values downward, a **gain** on the bargain purchase is reported. In its acquisition of Frontier, Republic recorded a bargain purchase gain of $203.7 million.

Before labeling an acquisition as a bargain purchase, however, the acquirer must carefully evaluate the assets acquired and liabilities assumed, and the consideration paid. An acquisition that looks like a bargain purchase may actually be the result of overvaluing acquired assets or undervaluing assumed liabilities. Identification and valuation of previously unreported assets and liabilities deserve particular scrutiny. The value of consideration paid may be understated as well.

Suppose that, after careful evaluation, the acquisition is still a bargain purchase. The assets acquired and liabilities assumed are reported at fair value, the consideration is reported at fair value, and a *gain on acquisition is reported in income*.

To illustrate, return to the acquisition facts in Exhibit 2.4 on page 44. If we now assume that IBM paid $20,000,000 in cash to the former owners of DataFile, we make this entry to record the bargain purchase:

Current assets	2,000,000	
Plant and equipment	60,000,000	
Patents and copyrights	5,000,000	
Brand names	1,000,000	
Favorable lease agreements	600,000	
Contractual customer relationships	3,000,000	
Current liabilities		10,000,000
Long-term debt		40,000,000
Cash		20,000,000
Gain on bargain purchase		1,600,000
To record the acquisition of DataFile Inc. for $20,000,000 in cash.		

We can calculate the gain separately as follows:

Acquisition cost		$20,000,000
Fair value of identifiable net assets acquired:		
Current assets	$ 2,000,000	
Plant and equipment.	60,000,000	
Patents and copyrights.	5,000,000	
Brand names	1,000,000	
Favorable lease agreements.	600,000	
Contractual customer relationships	3,000,000	
Current liabilities.	(10,000,000)	
Long-term debt.	(40,000,000)	21,600,000
Gain on bargain purchase		$ 1,600,000

Reporting Perspective

The requirement that a gain be reported on bargain purchases appears to open the door to earnings manipulation. Acquirers may intentionally over-report bargains to present a better financial picture to investors. However, the FASB made two arguments against this position. First, in business valuation, analysts generally ignore one-time or unusual gains. Second, in order to inflate a bargain gain, the fair values of identifiable net assets would have to be overstated. This would reduce future earnings as the inflated values are depreciated, amortized, or incur impairment losses. The FASB also addressed an apparent inconsistency in reporting—if gains on bargain purchases are reported, why aren't losses on overpayments also reported? Overpayment is instead reported as goodwill. The FASB believes overpayment is not likely to be intentional, and is difficult to quantify. Overpayment is instead addressed through recognition of subsequent impairment losses on goodwill and net assets acquired.

SPECIAL ISSUES: RESEARCH AND DEVELOPMENT AND PREACQUISITION CONTINGENCIES

Estimating the fair values of acquired assets and liabilities requires considerable judgment. This section highlights the particularly contentious reporting issues involved in reporting an acquired company's research and development, and contingent assets and liabilities.

LO5 Explain the reporting requirements and issues related to in-process research and development and preacquisition contingencies.

In-Process Research and Development

Especially in high-tech companies, ongoing research and development projects are of significant value to future performance. However, U.S. GAAP requires that costs of *internally* generated research and development be expensed as incurred. Prior to 2009, if such costs were part of a business combination, they were expensed at date of acquisition, unless the project had reached technological feasibility or the assets involved had alternative uses. This treatment mirrored the reporting for internally generated R&D.

The Codification now requires that in-process research and development acquired in a business combination be reported as an *asset*, at fair value, regardless of whether the R&D has an alternative future use. The requirement that in-process R&D be reported on the balance sheet is another example of the Codification's focus on accurate measurement of assets acquired and liabilities assumed. Although such projects may have a low probability of success, and estimated fair value is likely to be subject to more measurement error than other assets, the FASB believes that omitting these items from the balance sheet can mislead investors. In addition, capitalization of in-process research and development costs with no alternative future use is in agreement with international reporting standards. We discuss these standards at the end of the chapter.

BUSINESS APPLICATION   **In-Process R&D**

Before 2009, companies often allocated acquisition cost to an in-process R&D "asset," which was immediately expensed at the date of acquisition, reducing future write-offs of assets acquired. **Eastman Kodak Company** is a good example. In the notes to its financial statements, for each acquisition, Kodak separates out that portion of acquisition cost charged to "research and development assets that were written off at the date of acquisition." Kodak explains the process as follows:

> This amount was determined by identifying research and development projects that had not yet reached technological feasibility and for which no alternative future uses exist. The value of the projects identified to be in progress was determined by estimating the future cash flows from the projects once commercialized, less costs to complete development and discounting these cash flows back to their present value. The discount rate used for these research and development projects was 22%.

In prior practice, many companies tried to reduce goodwill by overstating in-process R&D, thereby converting periodic amortization charges into a one-time nonrecurring item.

Preacquisition Contingencies

An acquired company can have business situations that will result in a gain or loss if and when future events occur. A common example is an unsettled lawsuit. When the acquired company is the plaintiff in the lawsuit, a **contingent asset** may exist. When the acquired company is the defendant, a **contingent liability** can arise. Intermediate accounting courses examine these situations in the context of *ASC Topic 450*.

ASC paras. 805-20-25-18 through *20* distinguish between (1) known assets and liabilities with "determined" or "determinable" fair values and (2) other contingencies. We summarize the guidance as follows.

- The Codification uses a warranty liability to illustrate category (1) above. It requires that the fair value of acquired contingencies be recognized at date of acquisition when this value can be determined during the **measurement period**, not to exceed one year after acquisition. We interpret "determined" to mean a very narrow range of estimates (even warranty liabilities are not certain) or that published market prices exist.

● Recognition of category (2) contingencies, such as the unsettled lawsuit mentioned above, occurs when the following two criteria are satisfied during the measurement period:

    a. It is probable that a contingent asset or liability existed on the acquisition date, and

    b. The value of the asset or liability can be reasonably estimated.

These requirements generally bring the recognition and measurement issues in preacquisition contingencies under the umbrella of *ASC Topic 450*.

Companies must develop a systematic and logical method to identify and account for subsequent changes in the value of contingencies. A rational approach is to report these changes in the same way as changes in other estimated values related to the combination. Changes occurring within the measurement period are corrections in the original acquisition entry. Otherwise, the changes are reported in income. As emphasized throughout this chapter, the focus on complete reporting of assets acquired and liabilities assumed, even when this requires a significant amount of judgment, extends to the required treatment of preacquisition contingencies.

INTERNATIONAL FINANCIAL REPORTING STANDARDS FOR BUSINESS COMBINATIONS

IFRS for reporting statutory mergers, consolidations and asset acquisitions are found in the following pronouncements:

● *IFRS 3(R),* Business Combinations
● *IAS 38*, Intangible Assets

IFRS 3(R) covers the same reporting issues as *FASB ASC Topic 805*, and has similar requirements to U.S. GAAP for the issues studied in this chapter. The acquiring company reports the identifiable net assets of the acquired company at fair value at date of acquisition, including any previously unreported identifiable intangible assets. Goodwill arises if the acquired company's fair value exceeds the fair value of its identifiable net assets. Indicators of the acquiring company include size, contribution of management expertise, composition of the management team, and identity of the issuer of new stock. Acquisition-related costs are reported as expenses. Consideration in the form of earnouts or stock price contingencies is reported at expected present value. The definition of the measurement period, used to guide the reporting for subsequent changes in estimated reported values at the acquisition date, mirrors the definition in U.S. GAAP.

BUSINESS APPLICATION   Nokia's acquisitions

Nokia Group is a global leader in mobile communications. The company is headquartered in Finland, and its financial information is measured in euros and reported according to IFRS. Its stock is listed on the Helsinki, Frankfurt, and New York stock exchanges.

Similar to U.S. companies, goodwill continues to be a large percentage of acquisition cost for companies using IFRS. In 2010, Nokia acquired four companies for a total cost of €108 million, and recognized goodwill of €82 million. In 2009, Nokia acquired five companies for a total cost of €29 million, and recognized goodwill of €32 million, implying that the fair value of identifiable net assets was negative. Over the two year period, goodwill comprised over 83 percent of the total cost of Nokia's acquisitions.

continued

continued from prior page

In 2008, Nokia acquired NAVTEQ, a provider of digital map information, for €5,342 million. Nokia recorded the following NAVTEQ assets and liabilities (in millions):

Current assets	€ 427
Tangible noncurrent assets	273
Identifiable intangibles:	
Map database.	1,389
Customer relationships.	388
Developed technology	110
License and other.	64
Goodwill	3,673
Current liabilities.	(157)
Noncurrent liabilities.	(825)
Total net assets acquired.	€5,342

Although goodwill comprises the majority of NAVTEQ's acquisition cost, identifiable intangibles also are a significant part of net assets acquired. Even though the fair value of NAVTEQ's recorded net assets was negative, the company was worth €5,342 million to Nokia.

IAS 38 criteria for capitalization of identifiable intangibles follow the contractual or separability conditions, found in U.S. GAAP. Although internally-generated *research* is expensed under IFRS, in-process research acquired in a business combination is capitalized, regardless of whether it has an alternative future use. The FASB's decision to capitalize R&D with no alternative future use was influenced by the need to converge with international standards. IFRS for *internally* generated *development* costs allow capitalization of these costs under certain circumstances; U.S. standards require expensing of all internally generated development costs except for specific items such as certain software development costs. Therefore, companies reporting under IFRS have more experience with the issues related to capitalization of R&D.

Reporting Perspective

Similar to *SFAS 141*, a major goal of *IFRS 3*, effective in 2004, was to motivate companies to more accurately report the assets acquired and liabilities assumed and reduce the tendency to categorize most differences between acquisition price and the book value of net assets acquired as goodwill. Observation of international application of the new standards reveals the same problems as in the U.S. **intangiblebusiness.com** conducted a study of the financial statements of the FTSE 100—the largest companies listed on the London Stock Exchange—for 2005 and 2006. The findings are published in *"IFRS 3: The First Year,"* available from **intangiblebusiness.com**. On average, goodwill comprises 53 percent of the purchase price, with identifiable intangibles making up only 30 percent. In addition, many companies did not appropriately describe the intangibles they recognized. A few examples of "less inadequate" reporting, however, include **Cadbury Schweppes'** 2005 acquisition of organic chocolate maker **Green & Blacks** for £38 million, where 66 percent of the acquisition price was allocated to brands, and only 18 percent to goodwill. The poor implementation of *IFRS 3* requirements probably reflects companies' attempts to improve reported financial performance. Accounting for acquisition cost as goodwill rather than identifiable intangibles reduces the probability of write-offs, whether they are amortization or impairment charges.

REVIEW OF KEY CONCEPTS ••••••••••••••••••••••••••••••••••••••

LO 1   **Measure and account for the various assets and liabilities acquired in mergers and acquisitions. (p. 40)**
FASB ASC Topic 805 provides the reporting requirements for assets and liabilities acquired, and consideration
paid in a business combination. One company must be identified as the **acquirer**; it reports the acquired assets
and liabilities at **fair value at date of acquisition**. Complete reporting of assets acquired and liabilities assumed
involves revaluing the assets and liabilities reported on the acquired company's balance sheet, and identifying and
valuing previously unreported assets and liabilities. A major issue involves previously unreported **identifiable
intangibles**. These intangibles are reported if they meet **contractual** or **separability** criteria.

LO 2   **Measure and report the various types of consideration paid. (p. 48)** **Acquisition cost** is measured as the fair
value of assets transferred, liabilities incurred by the acquirer, and stock issued to the former owners of the acquired company. **Contingent consideration**, in the form of **earnouts** or **stock price contingencies**, is recorded at
estimated expected present value. **Acquisition-related costs** for consulting, legal, and other advisory services are
expensed as incurred.

LO 3   **Account for changes in the values of acquired assets and liabilities, and contingent consideration.
(p. 51)** **Subsequent changes** in the values of assets and liabilities acquired and consideration paid are reported as
adjustments to the original acquisition entry if the new information behind the changes pertains to their acquisition
date values and the changes occur within the **measurement period**. Value changes that arise from events subsequent to the acquisition date are reported in income.

LO 4   **Account for bargain purchases. (p. 53)** The acquisition cost is usually greater than the fair value of identifiable
net assets acquired, and is reported as **goodwill**. In some cases, especially in forced sales, the acquisition cost is less
than the fair value of net assets acquired. These situations are called **bargain purchases**. If, after careful review of
estimated values, an acquisition is identified as a bargain purchase, a **gain** is recognized in income.

LO 5   **Explain the reporting requirements and issues related to in-process research and development and preacquisition contingencies. (p. 55)** In identifying and measuring acquired assets and liabilities, **in-process research
and development projects** and **preacquisition contingencies** are particularly difficult to evaluate. In-process
research and development is reported as an acquired asset, even if the R&D has no alternative use. An acquired
contingent asset or liability is reported if, during the measurement period, its fair value is either determinable or it
is probable that it exists.

MULTIPLE CHOICE QUESTIONS ••••••••••••••••••••••••••••••••

Use the following information to answer questions 1 – 7 below. All amounts are in thousands.

PR Company pays $10,000 in cash and issues no-par stock with a fair value of $40,000 to acquire all of SX
Corporation's net assets. SX's balance sheet at the date of acquisition is as follows:

	SX Corporation	
	Book value	Fair value
Current assets	$ 2,000	$ 4,200
Property, plant & equipment, net	10,000	6,000
Identifiable intangible assets	4,000	14,000
Total assets	$16,000	
Current liabilities	$ 1,600	$ 2,000
Long-term debt	12,000	11,600
Capital stock	5,000	
Retained earnings	8,000	
Accumulated other comprehensive income	(1,000)	
Treasury stock	(9,600)	
Total liabilities & equity	$16,000	

PR's consultants find these items that are not reported on SX's balance sheet:

	Fair value
Potential contracts with new customers	$8,000
Advanced production technology	4,000
Future cost savings	2,000
Customer lists	1,000

Outside consultants are paid $200 in cash, and registration fees to issue PR's new stock are $400. All questions below relate to the entry or entries PR makes to record the acquisition on its books.

1. PR recognizes previously unrecorded intangibles of   LO 1

   a. $ 1,000
   b. $ 5,000
   c. $13,000
   d. $15,000

2. PR credits capital stock in the amount of   LO 2

   a. $40,000
   b. $50,000
   c. $39,600
   d. $39,200

3. PR records expenses of   LO 2

   a. $ 0
   b. $200
   c. $400
   d. $600

4. Three months after the acquisition, a fire damages SX's equipment, reducing its fair value from $6,000 to   LO 3
   $4,000. How does PR report this event?

   a.   Loss of $2,000, reported on the income statement
   b. $2,000 increase in goodwill
   c. $2,000 decrease in goodwill
   d.   Not reported

5. Three months after the acquisition, PR receives information revealing that the identifiable intangible assets   LO 3
   reported on SX's books at the date of acquisition were really worth $12,000 instead of $14,000. How does
   PR report this information?

   a.   Loss of $2,000, reported on the income statement
   b. $2,000 decrease in goodwill
   c. $2,000 increase in goodwill
   d.   Not reported

6. Now assume the acquisition cost to PR is $60,000 (not the right answer). Other facts are the same as origi-   LO 1
   nally reported. Goodwill reported on this acquisition is

   a. $35,600
   b. $35,800
   c. $44,400
   d. $49,400

7. Now assume PR paid $8,000 in cash for SX's net assets. There are no consultant fees, and no shares are is-   LO 4
   sued. Assume that SX's previously unrecorded intangible assets, capitalizable per GAAP, have a fair value
   of $500. PR records a bargain gain of

   a. $ 0
   b. $3,100
   c. $3,600
   d. $4,100

LO 1   **8.** Which one of the following is *most* likely to be reported as part of goodwill?

 a.   Brand names
 b.   Broadcast rights
 c.   Non-competition agreements
 d.   Favorable location

LO 5   **9.** What is the current standard for reporting acquired in-process R&D?

 a.   Not reported; becomes part of goodwill
 b.   Capitalized as an asset only if it is more likely than not that the outcome will be a viable project
 c.   Capitalized as an asset only if it has a future alternative use
 d.   Capitalized as an asset regardless of its probability of success or possible future use

LO 5   **10.** Which of the following items related to an acquired company is *most* likely to be recorded by the acquirer?

 a.   Warranty liability
 b.   Pending lawsuit, where the acquired company is the defendant
 c.   Pending lawsuit, where the acquired company is the plaintiff
 d.   Fines that might be assessed by environmental agencies

**Assignments with the ✅ in the margin are available in an online homework system.
See the Preface of the book for details.**

EXERCISES •

LO 1, 2   **E2.1   Recording a Merger and a Stock Acquisition**   The Poonamalie Company paid $4,000,000 in cash to the shareholders of the Slys Company for all of Slys' outstanding shares. Attorneys' fees related to the combination were $175,000, paid in cash. A comparison of the book and fair values of Slys' assets and liabilities appears below:

	Book Value	Fair Value
Cash and receivables.	$ 120,000	$ 120,000
Equity method investments	175,000	200,000
Inventory.	610,000	400,000
Plant assets.	1,600,000	1,000,000
Current liabilities.	(340,000)	(340,000)
Long-term debt	(1,090,000)	(1,100,000)
Net assets	$1,075,000	$ 280,000

Required

 a.   Prepare the journal entry made by Poonamalie to record the business combination as a statutory merger.
 b.   Prepare the journal entry made by Poonamalie to record the business combination as a stock acquisition.

LO 1   **E2.2   Post-Combination Balance Sheet: Three Types of Combinations**   Presented below are the balance sheets of Allen Corporation and Benson Corporation, *immediately prior* to a business combination. The fair values of Benson's net assets equal their book values, and there are no previously unreported identifiable intangible assets.

	Allen Corp.	Benson Corp.
Cash..	$ 400,000	$ 50,000
Other current assets............................	600,000	150,000
Property, plant and equipment...................	1,200,000	400,000
Total assets	$2,200,000	$600,000
Current liabilities..............................	$ 300,000	$100,000
Long-term liabilities	600,000	250,000
Common stock....................................	200,000	100,000
Additional paid-in capital	300,000	50,000
Retained earnings	800,000	100,000
Total liabilities and equity.....................	$2,200,000	$600,000

Required

a. Prepare the acquisition entry and the balance sheet of Allen Corporation after each of the following business combinations:
   (1) Allen acquires Benson for $300,000 cash in a transaction recorded as a statutory merger.
   (2) Allen acquires Benson for $300,000 cash in a transaction recorded as a stock acquisition.
   (3) Allen acquires the noncash net assets of Benson for $250,000 cash.
b. Why are Allen's total assets in part *a*(2), the stock acquisition, different from the total assets in part *a*(1) and part *a*(3)?
c. Prepare the balance sheet of Benson after the asset acquisition transaction in part *a*(3).

E2.3 Recording an Acquisition In fiscal 2010, **Dell Inc.** acquired **Perot Systems** for $3,878 million in cash. Perot's net assets acquired had the following fair values at the acquisition date:

LO 1, 2

DELL INC.
[DELL]

	Total (in millions)
Cash and cash equivalents	$ 266
Accounts receivable, net	410
Other assets..	58
Property, plant, and equipment	323
Identifiable intangible assets	1,174
Deferred tax liability, net.....................................	(424)
Other liabilities	(256)
Total identifiable net assets	1,551
Goodwill...	2,327
Total purchase price.....................................	$3,878

Identifiable intangible assets are:

	Estimated Cost (in millions)
Customer relationships	$1,081
Technology..	44
Non-compete agreements	39
Tradenames	10
Total amortizable intangible assets	$1,174

Dell incurred $93 million in cash compensation payments to former Perot Systems employees, related to previous compensation agreements with Perot. Dell spent another $23 million for bankers' fees, consulting fees, and integration costs.

Required

Prepare Dell's journal entry to record its acquisition of Perot Systems.

LO 4 **E2.4** **Bargain Purchase** Sontag Corporation's net assets have fair values as described below.

	Fair Value
Marketable securities.	$100,000
Land	800,000
Buildings.	500,000
Equipment.	300,000
Other net assets	200,000

The Pratt Company pays $3,000,000 for Sontag Corporation, and records the acquisition as a statutory merger. Pratt Company determines that identifiable intangibles valued at $1,300,000, not previously reported on Sontag's books, also are recognized as acquired assets.

Required

a. Prepare a schedule to calculate the gain on acquisition.
b. Prepare Pratt's journal entry to record the merger.

LO 1, 4 **E2.5** **Goodwill and Bargain Purchase** Panda Corporation paid $1,000,000 in cash for all of Sim Corporation's assets and liabilities in a statutory merger. The following table shows three possible cases for the merger:

	Fair Value		
Account	**Case 1**	**Case 2**	**Case 3**
Current assets	$300,000	$ 400,000	$ 50,000
Plant assets	600,000	800,000	1,430,000
Identifiable intangible assets	700,000	300,000	200,000
Liabilities.	(800,000)	(500,000)	(300,000)
Fair value of identifiable net assets	$800,000	$1,000,000	$1,380,000

Required

In each of the above cases, prepare the journal entry Panda makes to record the acquisition.

LO 3 **E2.6** **Changes in Acquisition Values** In 2013, Plummer Corporation acquired the net assets of Singer Company. The purchase price was $85 million. Plummer's annual reports for 2013 and 2014 provide the following information (in millions):

	2013	**Changes**	**2014**
Net assets acquired:			
Cash and receivables.	$ 10	$ —	$ 10
Inventories	70	(5)	65
Plant and equipment, net.	120	(30)	90
Identifiable intangible assets	35	6	41
Goodwill.	500	34	534
Current liabilities.	(50)	—	(50)
Long-term liabilities	(600)	(10)	(610)
Acquisition cost.	$ 85	$ (5)	$ 80

The change in acquisition cost is a reduction in the fair value of an earnings contingency.

Required

a. Did the changes in value between 2013 and 2014 occur within the measurement period? Explain.
b. Prepare the entry Plummer made in 2014 to adjust the 2013 acquisition values.

LO 2 **E2.7** **Acquisition Cost** Potluck Corp. acquired all of the net assets of Sauers Corp. on June 30, 2013, in an acquisition reported as a statutory merger. The fair values of Sauers Corp.'s identifiable net assets at the date of acquisition are as follows:

Tangible assets.	$25,000,000
Intangible assets.	90,000,000
Liabilities.	55,000,000

Potluck pays $100 million in cash and issues 1,500,000 shares of stock to the former owners of Sauers. Potluck's stock has a par value of $1/share. The market price of the shares at the date of acquisition, $40/share, is used to value the shares issued. Registration fees for the stock are $750,000, and legal and consulting fees connected with the acquisition are $900,000, both paid in cash.

Required

Record the acquisition on June 30, 2013.

E2.8 **Identification of Reportable Intangibles** DeLight Consulting is acquiring another consulting firm, Waterman Consulting for $2.4 million in cash. Although the fair values of Waterman's tangible net assets amount to $400,000, the parties have identified several intangible assets attributable to Waterman, as follows: **LO 1**

	Fair Value
Signed customer contracts for consulting projects, with expected gross billings of $10 million	$1,000,000
Skilled work force (Waterman does not use employment contracts).	200,000
Well-publicized internet domain name.	150,000
Expected future business value of having ex-Waterman personnel employed in key positions in potential client firms.	125,000
Office leases, at rents below current market, five years remaining.	100,000
Registered company name and trademark	60,000
Proprietary databases of industry data	50,000
Recent favorable press reports on a Waterman consulting project.	35,000

Required

a. Identify which of the above items meet the criteria for recognition as assets per *FASB ASC Topic 805*.
b. Calculate the goodwill to be reported in this acquisition.

E2.9 **Preacquisition Contingency** On January 3, 2012, Prance Corporation purchased all of the business operations of Step Corporation for $1,800,000 cash. The acquisition is recorded as a statutory merger. Step's identifiable assets and liabilities are listed below at their fair values: **LO 5** ✓

Current assets	$ 850,000
Noncurrent assets	1,600,000
Estimated liability: defective product lawsuits	280,000
Other liabilities	500,000

The $280,000 estimated liability represented Step's best estimate of likely losses due to lawsuits pending as of January 3, 2012. Later in 2012, as favorable information regarding the January 3, 2012, status of defective products became available, the estimated liability was reduced to $200,000. Then, in late 2013, after observing large judgments awarded by courts in similar lawsuits against competitors, management revised the estimated liability upward to $350,000.

Required

Prepare the entries made by Prance to record the above events.

E2.10 **Contingent Consideration** The Plank Company surrenders $5,000,000 cash plus 250,000 shares of its own $1 par value stock worth $10,000,000 for Stud Company, in a statutory merger. Management of Plank also makes the following guarantees to the former shareholders of Stud: **LO 2**

1. If total earnings from continuing operations of the combined entity exceed $2,000,000 over the next two years, additional shares of Plank will be issued to the former shareholders of Stud. Sufficient shares will be issued so that the market value of the additional shares equals the amount by which total earnings exceed $2,000,000. In no case, however, will additional shares having a market value

in excess of $500,000 be issued to satisfy this provision. Plank's management expects the following outcomes related to this earnings contingency:

Value of additional shares issued at the end of two years	Probability
$200,000	0.25
400,000	0.40
500,000	0.35

2. If the total market value of the original shares issued to Stud is less than $10,000,000 at the end of two years, Plank will issue sufficient additional shares to the former owners of Stud in order to restore the market value of all Plank shares issued in the acquisition to $10,000,000. Plank's management expects the following outcomes related to this contingency:

Value of originally issued shares at the end of two years	Probability
$ 6,000,000	0.10
9,000,000	0.20
12,000,000	0.70

Stud has the following assets and liabilities reported on its balance sheet at the date of acquisition:

	Book Value	Fair Value
Current assets	$ 2,000,000	$ 2,000,000
Property, plant and equipment.	15,000,000	12,000,000
Liabilities.	8,000,000	8,000,000

Stud has previously unreported intangible assets with a fair value of $3,000,000 that meet the criteria for recognition per *FASB ASC Topic 805*.

Required

a. Prepare the journal entry made by Plank at the acquisition date, following the requirements of *FASB ASC Topic 805*. A discount rate of 10 percent is appropriate when valuing the contingent consideration (round to the nearest thousand).
b. Assume the current fair value of contingency (1) increases by $100,000 during the first year following the acquisition. Prepare the journal entry made by Plank to record the value change, assuming:
    (1) The value change occurs within the measurement period.
    (2) The value change occurs after the end of the measurement period.

LO 1, 5 **E2.11 In-Process R&D, Other Previously Unreported Intangibles, Goodwill** Thorn Company acquires Underbrush Company for 2,000,000 shares of $0.50 par common stock with a market price of $15/share. Underbrush has the following assets and liabilities reported on its balance sheet at the date of acquisition:

	Book Value	Fair Value
Current assets	$ 400,000	$500,000
Plant assets	1,200,000	700,000
Liabilities.	500,000	450,000

Following are previously unreported assets identified as belonging to Underbrush:

	Fair Value
Contracts under negotiation with potential customers	$ 5,000,000
In-process research & development	2,500,000
Patent rights.	3,000,000
Skilled workforce	10,000,000

Required

Prepare the journal entry to record the acquisition on Thorn's books, as a statutory merger.

E2.12 Valuation of Earnings Contingency As part of the acquisition agreement, Parma Corporation agrees to pay the former shareholders of Stow Company $0.50 in cash for every dollar of EBITDA above $5,500,000 reported at the end of the first year following acquisition. Parma projects the following EBITDA outcomes for the year:

EBITDA	Probability
$3,500,000	0.05
4,500,000	0.30
5,500,000	0.20
6,500,000	0.25
7,500,000	0.20

Required

Using a 6 percent discount rate, what is the appropriate value to be reported as an earnings contingency liability on Parma's books at the date of acquisition?

PROGRAMS
PROBLEMS ••

P2.1 Acquisition Entries, Various Types of Combinations, Acquisition Costs Plastic Corporation is contemplating a business combination with Steel Corporation at December 31, 2011. Steel's condensed balance sheet on that date appears below *(in millions)*:

Assets	Book Value	Fair Value
Cash and receivables..	$ 35,000	$35,000
Inventory...	35,000	45,000
Equity method investments	18,000	20,000
Land...	8,000	11,000
Buildings and equipment.....................................	7,000	14,000
Patents..	5,000	10,000
Total assets	$108,000	

Liabilities and Stockholders' Equity		
Liabilities...	$ 22,000	$ 22,000
Common stock..	50,000	—
Retained earnings	36,000	—
Total liabilities and equity....................................	$108,000	

Required

Prepare the journal entry to record the business combination of Plastic and Steel for each of the following purchase prices and combination methods.

- a. Plastic merges with Steel by acquiring all of Steel's stock for $125,000 cash, in a statutory merger. Other direct cash acquisition costs are $25,000.
- b. Plastic merges with Steel by acquiring all of Steel's stock for $100,000 cash, in a statutory merger. Other direct cash acquisition costs are $10,000.
- c. Plastic acquires all of Steel's stock for $135,000 cash, in a stock acquisition. Other direct cash acquisition costs are $15,000.

LO 1 **P2.2** **Identification of Acquirer and Balance Sheet Valuation** Presented below are the book values and fair values of the assets and liabilities of Axtel, Inc. and Barcel, Inc. on October 4, 2013, immediately prior to a business combination.

	Axtel, Inc.		Barcel, Inc.	
	Book Value	**Fair Value**	**Book Value**	**Fair Value**
Current assets	$ 40,000	$100,000	$ 50,000	$ 25,000
Property, plant and equipment.	200,000	400,000	150,000	175,000
Total assets	$240,000		$200,000	
Current liabilities.	$ 70,000	$ 70,000	$ 30,000	$ 30,000
Common stock.	80,000		60,000	
Retained earnings	90,000		110,000	
Total liabilities and equity.	$240,000		$200,000	

Previously unreported identifiable intangibles, capitalized per GAAP, are:

Axtel, Inc. $75,000
Barcel, Inc.   80,000

Required

a. Prepare the balance sheet of the acquiring firm following each of the following business combinations:
   (1) Axtel borrows $250,000 on a long-term basis and buys full ownership of Barcel for $250,000 cash. The transaction is recorded as a statutory merger.
   (2) Barcel borrows $505,000 on a long-term basis, and buys full ownership of Axtel for $505,000 cash. The transaction is recorded as a statutory merger.
b. Comment on how the fair value data for Axtel and Barcel were used in each of the above transactions. Why are the two balance sheets different, even though each transaction results in the union of the same two companies?
c. Suppose that a new company, Coppel, Inc., is formed with a nominal investment of $1,000 by Axtel. Coppel's stock is then issued in exchange for the stock of Axtel and Barcel. Axtel stockholders receive 60 percent of the Coppel stock. Prepare the balance sheet of the acquiring firm.

LO 1, 2, 3 **P2.3** **Acquisition Adjustments and Merger Costs** The following disclosure appeared in the annual report of **GameStop Corp.** for its fiscal year ended February 2, 2008 ("fiscal 2007"). All amounts are in thousands of dollars.

**GAMESTOP
CORP.**
[GME]

**GAME BRANDS
INC.**

On January 13, 2007, the Company purchased **Game Brands Inc.** ("Game Brands"), a 72-store video game retailer operating under the name Rhino Video Games, for $11,344. The acquisition was accounted for using the purchase method of accounting and, accordingly, the results of operations for the period subsequent to the acquisition are included in the consolidated financial statements. The excess of the purchase price over the net assets acquired, in the amount of $8,083 was recorded as goodwill in fiscal 2006. In addition, merger-related costs and liabilities of $612 related to the Game Brands purchase were accrued for and included in accrued liabilities in the February 3, 2007 consolidated balance sheet. As of February 2, 2008, the cash payments made for the Game Brands merger costs were $206 and the remaining merger accrual balance of $406 was reversed as a purchase price adjustment to reduce goodwill. Additional purchase price adjustments to reduce goodwill for Game Brands were $1,061 during fiscal 2007.

The company's balance sheet showed goodwill of $1,403,907 at February 3, 2007 ("fiscal 2006").

Required

a. GameStop reported $8,083 in goodwill on its acquisition of Game Brands, Inc. Why does its fiscal 2006 balance sheet show a goodwill balance of $1,403,907?
b. Based on the above disclosure, and assuming no impairments, acquisitions or divestitures involving goodwill, what is the goodwill balance at February 2, 2008?

    c.   The disclosure refers to "purchase price adjustments to reduce goodwill." Identify the circumstances under which purchase price adjustments to reduce goodwill occur.

    d.   At the time of this acquisition, merger costs were included as acquisition costs, and treated in the same way as cash payments to the owners of the acquired company. If merger costs were treated as required by current U.S. GAAP, what would be the goodwill balance at February 2, 2008?

P2.4 **Type of Business Combination, Identification of Acquiring Company** **GameStop Corp.** is the world's largest retailer of new and used video game systems and software and personal computer entertainment software. It operates over 5,000 stores under the GameStop and EB Games trade names. The following excerpts appeared in its annual report for the year ended February 2, 2008 ("fiscal 2007"). All dollar amounts and number of shares are in thousands :

LO 1, 2

GAMESTOP
CORP.
[GME]

ELECTRONICS
BOUTIQUE
HOLDINGS CORP.
BABBAGE'S ETC.
FUNCO, INC.

> The Company is a Delaware corporation, formerly known as GSC Holdings Corp., formed for the purpose of consummating the business combination (the "merger" or "mergers") of GameStop Holdings Corp., formerly known as GameStop Corp. ("Historical GameStop"), and **Electronics Boutique Holdings Corp.** ("EB" or "Electronics Boutique"), which was completed on October 8, 2005. The merger of Historical GameStop and EB has been treated as a purchase business combination for accounting purposes, with Historical GameStop designated as the acquirer. Therefore, the historical financial statements of Historical GameStop became the historical financial statements of the Company.
>
> Historical GameStop's wholly-owned subsidiary **Babbage's Etc. LLC** ("Babbage's") began operations in November 1996. In October 1999, Babbage's was acquired by, and became a wholly-owned subsidiary of, **Barnes & Noble, Inc.** ("Barnes & Noble"). In June 2000, Barnes & Noble acquired **Funco, Inc.** ("Funco") and thereafter, Babbage's became a wholly-owned subsidiary of Funco. In December 2000, Funco changed its name to GameStop, Inc. Historical GameStop was incorporated under the laws of the State of Delaware in August 2001 as a holding company for GameStop, Inc. In February 2002, Historical GameStop completed a public offering of 41,528 shares of Class A common stock at $9.00 per share (the "Offering"). Upon the effective date of the Offering, Historical GameStop's Board of Directors approved the authorization of 5,000 shares of preferred stock and 300,000 shares of Class A common stock. At the same time, Historical GameStop's common stock outstanding was converted to 72,018 shares of common stock.
>
> Until October 2004, Barnes & Noble held 72,018 shares of Historical GameStop common stock. In October 2004, Historical GameStop's Board of Directors authorized a repurchase of 12,214 shares of common stock held by Barnes & Noble. Historical GameStop repurchased the shares at a price equal to $9.13 per share for aggregate consideration of $111,520. The repurchased shares were immediately retired. On November 12, 2004, Barnes & Noble distributed to its stockholders its remaining 59,804 shares of Historical GameStop's common stock in a tax-free dividend. All of the outstanding shares of Historical GameStop's common stock were exchanged for the Company's common stock. On October 8, 2005, Historical GameStop and EB completed their previously announced mergers pursuant to the Agreement and Plan of Merger, dated as of April 17, 2005 (the "Merger Agreement"). Upon the consummation of the mergers, Historical GameStop and EB became wholly-owned subsidiaries of the Company. Both management and the respective boards of directors of EB and Historical Gamestop believed that the merger of the companies would create significant synergies in operations when the companies were integrated and would enable the Company to increase profitability as a result of combined market share.
>
> Under the terms of the Merger Agreement, Historical GameStop's stockholders received one share of the Company's common stock for each share of Historical GameStop's common stock owned. Approximately 104,135 shares of the Company's common stock were issued in exchange for all outstanding common stock of Historical GameStop based on the one-for-one ratio. EB stockholders received $19.08 in cash and .39398 of a share of the Company's common stock for each EB share owned. In aggregate, 40,458 shares of the Company's Class A common stock were issued to EB stockholders at a value of approximately $437,144 (based on the closing price of $10.81 per share of Historical GameStop's Class A common stock on April 15, 2005, the last trading day before the date the merger was announced). In addition, approximately $993,254 in cash was paid in consideration for (i) all outstanding common stock of EB, and (ii) all outstanding stock options of EB. Including transaction costs of $13,558 incurred by Historical GameStop, the total consideration paid was approximately $1,443,956.

Required

a.   Trace the corporate history, beginning with the founding of Babbage's Etc. LLC in November 1996.
b.   What type of business combination was the merger of Historical GameStop and Electronics Boutique?
c.   Why was Historical GameStop designated as the acquiring company?
d.   How much was recorded as the acquisition price of Electronics Boutique?

LO 1, 2   P2.5   Identifiable Intangibles and Goodwill   Prince Corporation acquires Squire Service Corporation for one million shares of Prince stock, valued at $35 per share. Squire is merged into Prince, although it continues to do business under the Squire Service name. Professional fees connected with the acquisition are $1,200,000 and costs of registering and issuing the new shares are $600,000, both paid in cash. Squire performs vehicle maintenance services for owners of auto, truck and bus fleets. Squire's balance sheet at acquisition is as follows:

Cash........................	$ 300,000	Current liabilities..............	$ 3,100,000
Accounts receivable...........	2,700,000	Long-term liabilities	8,600,000
Parts inventory	5,200,000	Stockholders' equity	14,100,000
Equipment..................	17,600,000		
Total assets	$25,800,000	Total liabilities and equity.......	$25,800,000

In reviewing Squire's assets and liabilities, you determine the following:

1.   On a discounted present value basis, the accounts receivable have a fair value of $2,600,000, and the long-term liabilities have a fair value of $8,000,000.
2.   The current replacement cost of the parts inventory is $6,000,000.
3.   The current replacement cost of the equipment is $19,500,000.
4.   Squire occupies its service facilities under an operating lease with ten years remaining. The rent is below current market levels, giving the lease an estimated fair value of $1,250,000.
5.   Squire has long-term service contracts with several large fleet owners. These contracts have been profitable; the present value of expected profits over the remaining term of the contracts is estimated at $2,000,000.
6.   Squire has a skilled and experienced work force. You estimate that the cost to hire and train replacements would be $750,000.
7.   Squire's trade name is well-known among fleet owners and is estimated to have a fair value of $200,000.

Required

a.   Calculate the amount of goodwill that Prince records for the acquisition.
b.   Prepare Prince's journal entry or entries to record the merger with Squire.

LO 1   P2.6   Goodwill   Lisa Corporation made an offer to acquire the assets and assume the liabilities of Toga Corporation. Toga's balance sheet as of December 31, 2012, appears below. Toga has no unrecorded liabilities or contingent liabilities. The market values of Toga's current liabilities approximate their book values. Lisa Corporation offered Toga Corporation's Board of Directors $780,000,000 cash for 100 percent ownership interest.

TOGA CORPORATION Balance Sheet (*in thousands*) December 31, 2012	
Assets	
Accounts receivable......................................	$ 40,000
Inventories	90,000
Long-term marketable debt securities.......................	95,000
Property, plant and equipment.............................	275,000
Total assets	$500,000
Liabilities and Shareholders' Equity	
Current liabilities..	$ 70,000
Capital stock	230,000
Retained earnings	200,000
Total liabilities and shareholders' equity	$500,000

The fair values of Toga's assets as of December 31, 2012, are estimated to be as follows:

(in thousands)	Fair Value
Accounts receivable.	$ 40,000
Inventories	135,000
Long-term marketable debt securities.	115,000
Property, plant and equipment.	410,000
Total fair market value	$700,000

Required

a. Identify five business factors or conditions that generally give rise to goodwill.
b. Determine the amount of goodwill that would be recorded on the books of Lisa Corporation if the $780,000,000 cash offer is accepted by Toga Corporation.
c. Explain why the goodwill determined in part *b* was not included on Toga Corporation's balance sheet.

P2.7 **Bargain Purchase and Preacquisition Contingency** On January 2, 2014, Fisher Corporation ac- LO 1, 3, 4, 5
quired all of the voting common stock of Grant Corporation for its own stock worth $10,000,000, in a tax-free statutory merger. Grant's condensed balance sheet on January 2, 2014, appears below:

Assets	Book Value	Fair Value
Cash and receivables.	$ 6,400,000	$6,400,000
Inventory.	3,800,000	5,800,000
Depreciable plant assets	4,000,000	6,500,000
Other (nondepreciable) assets	3,000,000	3,000,000
Total assets	$17,200,000	

Liabilities and Stockholders' Equity	Book Value	Fair Value
Current liabilities.	$ 5,000,000	$5,000,000
Long-term debt	1,800,000	1,800,000
Capital stock	2,000,000	
Retained earnings	8,400,000	
Total liabilities and equity.	$17,200,000	

Note: On December 31, 2013, a lawsuit alleging defective products and claiming damages of $1,000,000 was filed against Grant. The estimated liability and related loss, believed to be $800,000, have not yet been accrued. Since the lawsuit had been anticipated, Fisher accepts responsibility for the liability.

Required

a. Prepare the journal entry made by Fisher to record the acquisition of Grant. There are no unrecorded identifiable intangibles.
b. During 2014, new facts are discovered that reset the value of the lawsuit at the date of acquisition to $300,000. Prepare the journal entry to record the change in the value of the lawsuit.
c. Assume that at the end of 2015, based on events occurring after the acquisition date, the lawsuit was settled out of court for $400,000 in cash. Prepare the journal entry to record this event.

P2.8 **Post-Combination Balance Sheet, Goodwill** Softdata, Inc. acquires all the net assets of Datalink LO 1, 2
Corporation, recording the combination as a statutory merger. The balance sheets of Softdata and Datalink *immediately prior* to the acquisition, along with fair value information for Datalink's reported assets and liabilities, are as follows:

(in millions)	Softdata Book Value	Datalink Book Value	Datalink Fair Value
Current assets	$ 100	$ 20	$ 18
Property, plant and equipment......................	2,000	800	600
Patents and trademarks...........................	500	100	250
Total assets	$2,600	$920	
Current liabilities.................................	$ 200	$ 15	$ 15
Long-term liabilities	1,500	970	900
Common stock, $1 par............................	10	2	
Additional paid-in capital	650	48	
Retained earnings	245	(100)	
Treasury stock	(5)	(15)	
Total liabilities and equity.........................	$2,600	$920	

Datalink also has the following previously unreported intangible assets that meet U.S. GAAP requirements for asset recognition:

(in millions)	Fair Value
Brand names	$10
Software..	50

Softdata issues 500,000 shares of stock with a fair value of $70 million, and pays cash of $12 million to the former owners of Datalink. Stock registration fees are $1 million and legal and consulting fees are $2 million, all paid in cash.

Required

Record the acquisition entry and prepare Softdata's balance sheet immediately after it acquires Datalink.

LO 1, 2, 3 **P2.9** **Merger Entry, Valuation Adjustments** On August 12, 2005, **Sprint** acquired all of **Nextel**, forming **Sprint Nextel**. Total consideration paid for the merger was as follows *(in millions)*:

SPRINT NEXTEL
[S]

Cash payment to Nextel shareholders...	$ 969
Stock issued to Nextel shareholders..	35,645
Conversion of Nextel stock-based awards to Sprint Nextel awards..................	1,124
Total...	$37,738

Direct acquisition costs for financial advisory, legal and other services were $78 million. The value of the 1,414 million shares issued was calculated as the average of the closing stock prices on the NYSE for the period two days before through two days after the December 15, 2004 announcement of the merger. The stock had a par value of $2/share. The value of the stock-based awards (employee stock options) was calculated following the requirements of *ASC Topic 718*. Estimated fair values of Nextel's identifiable net assets as of September 30, 2005, are listed below, as well as purchase price adjustments made in the fourth quarter of 2005.

(in millions)	Preliminary Purchase Price Allocation		
	As of 9/30/2005	Adjustments	As of 12/31/2005
Current assets	$ 5,501	$ 4	$ 5,505
Property, plant and equipment...............	8,454	(80)	8,374
Spectrum licenses and other indefinite life intangibles	14,640	—	14,640
Customer relationships and other definite life intangibles...................	10,448	—	10,448
Investments	2,680	(2)	2,678
Other assets...........................	111	—	111
Current liabilities........................	(2,902)	(18)	(2,920)
Long-term debt	(8,984)	—	(8,984)
Other long-term liabilities.................	(8,199)	105	(8,094)
Deferred compensation included in shareholders' equity	518	(33)	485
Totals	$22,267		$22,243

Required

In answering the following questions, assume the merger was accounted for under current U.S. GAAP.

a. Calculate the amount of goodwill reported on this acquisition, as of September 30, 2005.
b. What factors do you believe prompted Sprint to pay a premium over the fair values of Nextel's identifiable net assets (goodwill)?
c. Sprint used prior GAAP to value the shares issued to Nextel's former shareholders. What is current GAAP regarding valuation of stock issued for acquisitions? Discuss the relative merits of prior and current GAAP on this issue.
d. If Sprint recorded this acquisition as a statutory merger, what entry did it make, using September 30, 2005, fair values? Assume direct acquisition costs were paid in cash.
e. Prepare the entry Sprint made to record the fair value changes during the fourth quarter of 2005 as purchase price adjustments occurring during the measurement period.

P2.10 Earnings Contingency, In-Process R&D, Bargain Purchase On January 2, 2012, Fiser, Inc. acquired Vixen Pharmaceuticals for $1.25 billion cash, in a statutory merger. Vixen had two promising products for treating common infections under review by the U.S. Food and Drug Administration. The balance sheets of Fiser and Vixen, *immediately prior* to the acquisition, are below. Fair value information appears for Vixen's reported assets and liabilities.

LO 1, 2, 4, 5 ✓

(in thousands)	Fiser, Inc. Book Value	Vixen Pharmaceuticals	
		Book Value	Fair Value
Current assets	$ 5,000,000	$ 200,000	$ 200,000
Property, plant and equipment...........	60,000,000	10,000,000	5,000,000
Patents.............................	10,000,000	500,000	3,000,000
Total assets	$75,000,000	$10,700,000	$8,200,000
Liabilities..........................	$35,000,000	$ 7,850,000	$7,850,000
Capital stock	25,000,000	5,000,000	
Retained earnings	15,000,000	(2,150,000)	
Total liabilities and equity...............	$75,000,000	$10,700,000	

$1 billion of the purchase price was allocated to previously unreported in-process research and development attributed to Vixen's products under development. The purchase price was low due to Vixen's poor performance in previous years—Vixen reported a retained earnings deficit of $2.15 billion as of the date of acquisition. To close the deal, Fiser agreed to pay the former owners of Vixen $2 for every dollar of total revenue above $50 million reported on sales of Vixen's products over the next two years. This payment, if made at all, would occur at December 31, 2013. Fiser expects that there is only a 10 percent chance the payment will be made, as follows:

Total expected revenue on Vixen's products, 2012 - 2013	Probability
Below $50 million	0.90
$60 million	0.08
$80 million	0.02

Required

a. Calculate the present value of the earnout agreement, using a 5 percent discount rate.
b. This acquisition is a bargain purchase. Calculate the gain on acquisition reported by Fiser.
c. Prepare the entry Fiser made to record the acquisition.
d. Prepare Fiser's post-combination balance sheet.

LO 1, 2, 3, 4   **P2.11 Bargain Gain, Contingent Consideration, and Changes in Estimates**   On December 31, 2009, **Manitex International, Inc.** acquired the assets and certain liabilities of Terex Load King Trailers, manufacturer of custom trailers and hauling systems, from Genie Industries. The purchase consideration was as follows *(in thousands)*:

**MANITEX
INTERNATIONAL,
INC.**
[MNTX]

	Fair Value
Cash	$ 100
130,890 shares of Manitex International, Inc. stock	250
Interest-bearing promissory note	2,580
Contingent consideration	30
Total purchase consideration	$2,960

Manitex also incurred $54 in legal fees related to the Load King acquisition. Manitex common stock has no par value. The promissory note is the present value of amounts owed to Genie over the period 2009–2016. The contingent consideration is described as follows:

> The agreement has a contingent consideration provision which provides for a onetime payment of $750 if net revenues are equal to or greater than $30,000 in any of the next three years, i.e., 2010, 2011 or 2012. Given the disparity between the revenue threshold and the Company's projected financial results, it was determined that a Monte Carlo simulation analysis was appropriate to determine the fair value of contingent consideration. It was determined that the probability weighted average earnout payment is $30. Based thereon, we determined the fair value of the contingent consideration to be $30.

The purchase price allocation is as follows *(in thousands)*:

Purchase Price allocation:

Inventory.	$1,841
Machinery and equipment	1,716
Land and buildings.	2,610
Accounts receivable.	464
Prepaid expenses.	5
Trade names and trademarks	420
Unpatented technology	670
Accounts payable.	(144)
Accrued expenses	(150)
Deferred tax liability	(1,557)
Gain on bargain purchase	(2,915)
Net assets acquired	$2,960

Required

a. Prepare the entry made by Manitex to record its acquisition of Terex Load King.

b. Assume that within the measurement period, new information indicates that the date-of-acquisition fair values of some items have changed to *(in thousands)*:

Inventory.	$1,000
Machinery and equipment	800
Land and buildings.	1,200
Contingent consideration.	35

Prepare the entry to adjust the asset and contingent consideration values.

c. Now assume the fair value changes in *b*. occur outside the measurement period. Prepare the entry to adjust the asset and contingent consideration values.

d. If the contingent consideration was a stock price contingency instead of an earnout, how would your answer to *c*. change?

P2.12 Multiple Asset Acquisitions, Analysis of Combination Terms Wind Energy America Inc. (WNEA) is a small, publicly traded company entering the field of energy production from wind power. As of 2010, its stock trades in the over-the-counter market, and it is subject to SEC regulations regarding financial statement disclosure. The company existed under the name **Dotronix** since 1980. It was initially involved in the production of cathode ray tubes, digital signs, and non-prescription healthcare products. By early 2007, it discontinued or disposed of all its previous product lines, changed its name to Wind Energy America, Inc., and entered the wind power industry. By year-end June 30, 2007, it made a few small investments, and added more during the nine months ended March 31, 2008. The company's balance sheet showed the following at June 30, 2007, and March 31, 2008:

LO 1, 2, 4

WIND ENERGY
AMERICA INC.
[WNEA]

DOTRONIX

NORTHERN
ALTERNATIVE
ENERGY

BOREAL ENERGY

NAVITAS
ENERGY, INC.

	March 31, 2008	June 30, 2007
Total current assets	$ 46,782	$ 144,595
Investments in wind farms	4,900,000	1,750,000
Investments in wind projects	13,346,175	250,000
Investment in Grand Sierra Resort Corp	415,000	415,000
Investment in Navitas Energy, Inc	11,287,250	0
Goodwill	1,387,750	0
Total assets	$31,382,957	$ 2,559,595
Total liabilities.	$ 127,359	$ 172
Common stock, $.05 par (49,509,829 and 15,764,842 shares issued as of March 31, 2008 and June 30, 2007, respectively.	2,475,491	788,242
Additional paid-in capital	44,347,056	16,972,389
Accumulated deficit	(15,566,949)	(15,201,208)
Total liabilities and stockholders' equity	$31,382,957	$ 2,559,595

The company had an operating loss of $365,741 for the nine months ended March 31, 2008, and has yet to report any operating revenues from its wind power business. Its stock generally traded between $1.10 and $2.60 during the third quarter of 2007, between $1.30 and $2.00 during the fourth quarter of 2007, and between $0.92 and $1.70 during the first quarter of 2008.

The company had the following asset acquisitions during the nine months ended March 31, 2008:

- December 2007 acquisition of wind farms from **Northern Alternative Energy** in exchange for 4,000,000 shares of company stock
- February 2008 acquisitions of wind project assets from **Boreal Energy** in exchange for 18,500,000 shares of company stock
- March 2008 acquisition of a 15% interest in the stock of **Navitas Energy, Inc.** from Boreal Energy in exchange for 10,000,000 shares of company stock
- Additional wind project asset acquisitions for cash of $851,175

Besides the issuance of shares for asset acquisitions given above, the company also sold 1,159,987 common shares for $945,416 cash and issued 85,000 shares as compensation to executives; these shares were valued at $.90 each.

Required

a. Reconcile the information on shares issued as given above with the data on the company's balance sheets.

b. Determine the dollar amount assigned to the 32,500,000 shares issued in acquisition transactions by analysis of (1) the asset accounts, and (2) the equity accounts. The company's statement of cash flows gives the dollar value of shares issued for the acquisition of assets as $28,050,000.

c. What per-share valuation was attached to each of the three acquisitions described above? Assume the recorded goodwill pertains to the wind projects acquired from Boreal.

d. The company's Management Discussion and Analysis section of its 2008 annual report states that "the company did not seek or obtain any independent appraisal of the Boreal assets purchased in this transaction." How might the company have arrived at the recorded values?

e. Subsequent to March 31, 2008, the company entered into an exchange with **Gamesa Corp.**, the parent company of Navitas Energy. The company exchanged its 15% interest in Navitas for various assets described as follows:

> *160 acres of land in Lincoln County, Minnesota, where wind turbines will be operated; the Midwest Center for Wind Energy (MCWE), a hotel, office and maintenance facility located where existing WNEA wind projects operate and where an additional 300 megawatts will be built; two Gamesa G-52 wind turbines, ready to be commissioned, located at the MCWE site; two Gamesa G-80 wind turbines, ready to be commissioned, located in Osceola County, Iowa; substation and transmission facilities in Minnesota and Iowa; and the Viking Wind Energy Project, located in Martin County, Minnesota with transmission service with a nameplate capacity of up to 100 megawatts, expected to be operational by 2010.*

What accounting issues will the company face in recording this transaction?

REVIEW SOLUTIONS ··

Review 1 Solution *(in millions)*

Cash and receivables.	400	
Inventories	800	
Property, plant and equipment.	3,500	
Favorable lease agreements	150	
Goodwill	500	
Accounts payable		300
Long-term debt		3,850
Cash		1,200
To record acquisition of Lotus.		

···

Review 2 Solution *(in millions)*

1)	Cash and receivables.	400	
	Inventories	800	
	Property, plant and equipment.	3,500	
	Favorable lease agreements	150	
	Goodwill	1,800	
	Merger expenses	200	
	Accounts payable		300
	Long-term debt		3,850
	Earnout liability		400
	Cash		900
	Common stock, $1 par		15
	Additional paid-in capital.		1,385
	To record acquisition of Lotus.		
2)	Property, plant and equipment.	500	
	Goodwill.		500
	To record change in value of property, plant and equipment during measurement period.		
	Earnout liability.	100	
	Gain on earnout.		100
	To record subsequent change in value of earnout.		

3

Consolidated Financial Statements: Date of Acquisition

LEARNING OBJECTIVES

LO1 Explain the purpose of consolidated financial statements and how the concept of control determines when to consolidate. (p. 78)

LO2 Describe the motivations for off-balance-sheet financing. (p. 79)

LO3 Apply the concept of control to equity investments. (p. 81)

LO4 Apply the concept of control to non-equity investments (variable interest entities). (p. 81)

LO5 Prepare consolidated balance sheets using a consolidation working paper. (p. 85)

LO6 Explain IFRS for consolidations. (p. 95)

GENERAL MOTORS COMPANY
www.gm.com

General Motors Company (GM) is a worldwide producer and marketer of cars, trucks, and automotive parts. It also provides automotive financing services through its finance subsidiary, GM Financial. In 2010, GM made vehicles sold in North America under the following brands: Buick, Cadillac, Chevrolet and GMC, and had the largest U.S. market share in passenger cars and trucks, with Ford and Toyota in second and third place, respectively. GM also operates in Europe, Latin America, Africa, the Mid-East, and Asia Pacific, with additional brands not as familiar to U.S. customers, including Opel, Vauxhall, and Holden.

In 2009, General Motors Corporation—now called "old GM" in its annual report—filed for Chapter 11 bankruptcy. With financial support from the U.S. government, General Motors Company was formed to acquire the assets and certain liabilities of General Motors Corporation. GM's stock was again publicly traded after a 2010 offering of preferred and common stock, and is currently listed on the New York Stock Exchange. As of the end of 2010, the U.S. government owns 27 percent of GM's stock.

GM presents its financial results in the form of consolidated financial statements that include the financial records of entities legally separate from GM. GM's 2010 annual report describes its consolidation policy as follows:

The consolidated financial statements include our accounts and those of our subsidiaries that we control due to ownership of a majority voting interest. We continually evaluate our involvement with variable interest entities (VIEs) to determine whether we have variable interests and are the primary beneficiary of the VIE. When [these] criteria [are] met, we are required to consolidate the VIE.

GM owns 31 percent of GM Egypt and 49 percent of Shanghai General Motors Co., Ltd. (SGM). It includes GM Egypt's accounts in its consolidated financial statements. GM uses the equity method to account for its investment in SGM.

How did GM decide which entities to include in its 2010 consolidated financial statements? The basis of presentation in an annual report can have major effects on the overall financial performance of a company, as reflected in its consolidated financial statements. Consolidation policy has been the subject of serious debate among accounting regulators over the years, and is continually evolving. This chapter discusses the issues involved and explains current practice.

Once management identifies which entities to be included, how are the financial records of these entities incorporated into the consolidated financial statements? Accountants must accurately combine the financial records of the various entities. This chapter introduces you to the procedures involved. *Source:* General Motors Company annual report, 2010.

CHAPTER ORGANIZATION

Criteria for consolidation	Consolidation procedures	IFRS for consolidation
• Concept of control • Motivations for off-balance-sheet financing • Application to equity investments • Application to non-equity investments (variable interest entities)	• Preliminary issues: differences in currency, GAAP, year-end • Objectives of consolidation • Consolidation working paper • Consolidation illustration: goodwill and identifiable intangibles • Consolidation illustration: bargain purchase	• *IFRS 10* requirements • Convergence with U.S. GAAP

INTRODUCTION

This chapter concentrates on business combinations structured as **stock acquisitions**, where the acquirer obtains a controlling interest in another company by *purchasing and retaining its outstanding voting shares*. The acquirer is known as the **parent**, the acquired company is the **subsidiary**, and the two companies remain as separate legal entities, recording transactions on their own books. When appropriate, the accountant **consolidates** the separate financial records of the parent and subsidiary for presentation in the annual report.

Most business combinations are stock acquisitions. Stock ownership allows the acquirer to obtain control while holding less than 100 percent of the company, thereby reducing the investment needed. Because the two companies remain as separate legal entities, the subsidiary's creditors generally can only look to the assets of the subsidiary for satisfaction of debts. The parent and its subsidiaries also can retain separate names, which may be useful for marketing purposes. For example, Adam Opel AG is a German subsidiary of General Motors, but its cars bear the Opel name.

In other situations, one company can control another separate legal entity *without* equity ownership. Such entities are commonly known as **special purpose entities, structured entities,** or **variable interest entities**. Whether these entities should be consolidated in the financial statements of the "controlling" company has been and continues to be a contentious issue, and contributed to some of the accounting scandals of the early twenty-first century. This chapter also covers reporting requirements for these relationships.

Experience has shown that the subject of reporting for controlled investments in separate legal entities should be approached one step at a time. The parent and the subsidiary each have their own separate set of books. It is the accountant's job to consolidate these ever-changing financial records at each point in time when financial statements are to be published. Because this can be a complex process, this chapter covers consolidation *immediately following an acquisition*. This decision is made for pedagogical reasons only; in the business world, consolidation occurs at the *end of the reporting period*, not at the time of a merger or acquisition.

Consolidation at date of business combination allows us to focus on problems of consolidating the balance sheet only; because no time has elapsed since the acquisition, we can ignore for now the income statement and the statement of cash flows. We can also disregard for the moment the possibility of transactions between the parent and subsidiary. And for simplicity we limit our discussion in this chapter to 100-percent, or **wholly-owned**, subsidiaries.

Subsequent chapters focus on other topics related to consolidation. Chapter 4 discusses consolidation at any point in time *subsequent to acquisition*, which requires preparation of a consolidated income statement and a consolidated statement of cash flows in addition to the consolidated balance sheet. Chapter 5 examines controlled stock investments where the acquirer holds l*ess than 100 percent* of the voting stock of the acquired company. Chapter 6 covers additional consolidation procedures that are necessary when the combined companies do business with each other, in the form of *intercompany transactions*.

Before we discuss consolidation procedures, we must identify the circumstances under which consolidation takes place. In other words, *when* is it appropriate to combine the results of two or more separate legal entities for presentation in financial statements?

CRITERIA FOR CONSOLIDATION

LO1 Explain the purpose of consolidated financial statements and how the concept of control determines when to consolidate.

As discussed in Chapter 2, the requirements of *FASB ASC Topics 805* and *810* apply only to **business combinations**. A business combination occurs when *control is obtained* over one or more businesses. The definition of a *business* was discussed in Chapter 2. Here we discuss the concept of *control*, and the related reporting issues.

Underlying the concept of consolidation is the idea that aggregated information is more relevant to investors when one company has control over another company. *ASC Topic 810* addresses this issue as follows:

> The purpose of consolidated financial statements is to present, primarily for the benefit of the owners and creditors of the parent, the results of operations and the financial position of a parent and all its subsidiaries as if the consolidated group were a single economic entity. There is a presumption that consolidated financial statements are more meaningful than separate financial statements, and that they are usually necessary for a fair presentation when one of the entities in the consolidated group directly or indirectly has a controlling financial interest in the other entities. *(ASC para. 810-10-10-1)*

Investors should be able to evaluate the complete financial performance of a company by looking at its financial statements. If the company controls the resources of another company, investors should see the results of decisions affecting these resources in the controlling company's financial statements.

The Concept of Control

The definition of control found in *FASB ASC Topic 810* relies on the following previous authoritative guidance:

- *Accounting Research Bulletin No. 51 (ARB 51)*, Consolidated Financial Statements, as amended
- *Statement of Financial Reporting Standards No. 94 (SFAS 94)*, Consolidation of All Majority-Owned Subsidiaries, as amended
- *FASB Interpretation No. 46 (FIN 46)*, Consolidation of Variable Interest Entities, as amended

ASC Topic 810 elaborates on what is meant by "controlling financial interest."

> The usual condition for a controlling financial interest is ownership of a majority voting interest, and, therefore, as a general rule ownership by one entity, directly or indirectly, of more than fifty percent of the outstanding voting shares of another entity is a condition pointing toward consolidation. (*ASC para. 810-10-15-8*)

Issued in 1958, *ARB 51* originally permitted exceptions to the above requirement, including situations where control was **temporary**, or where **control was not present** even with majority ownership of the voting shares: for example, if the subsidiary was under bankruptcy protection. However, *ARB 51* also allowed exceptions for foreign subsidiaries, for subsidiaries with large noncontrolling interests, and for subsidiaries in "nonhomogeneous" areas of business, such as a finance subsidiary owned by a manufacturing company.

For decades after *ARB 51* was issued, companies took advantage of the exceptions to avoid including the financial results of certain controlled businesses, such as finance subsidiaries, in their annual reports. Over time, financial statement users and accounting regulators concluded that companies were withholding information from investors by taking advantage of the exceptions allowed by *ARB 51*. There was a marked tendency to exclude subsidiaries when including the results of these controlled companies diminished reported performance. *SFAS 94*, issued in 1987, eliminated most of the exceptions. The rationale for eliminating the "nonhomogeneity" exception was stated in *SFAS 94* as follows:

> Present practice has been criticized not only because apparently similar enterprises use different consolidation policies but also because excluding some subsidiaries from consolidation results in the omission of significant amounts of assets, liabilities, revenues, and expenses from the consolidated statements of many enterprises. Omissions of large amounts of liabilities, especially those of finance and similar subsidiaries, have led to the criticism that not consolidating those subsidiaries is an important factor in what is often called "off-balance-sheet financing." (*para 7*)

Current exceptions to consolidation of majority-owned investees are found in *ASC para. 810-10-15-10*:

Consolidate majority-owned subsidiaries unless the majority owner does not control the subsidiary. For example:

- The subsidiary is in legal reorganization.
- The subsidiary is in bankruptcy.
- Governmentally imposed restrictions, controls, or uncertainties cast significant doubt on the parent's ability to control the subsidiary.
- Approval or veto rights granted to the noncontrolling shareholders significantly limit the majority owner's ability to control the subsidiary.

Motivations for Off-Balance-Sheet Entities

Over the years companies have used many different tactics to avoid reporting bad news in their financial statements. Methods range from selective, but legal, application of generally accepted accounting principles to outright fraud.

LO2 Describe the motivations for off-balance-sheet financing.

A simple example illustrates the motivation to exclude certain subsidiaries. Before Manufacturing Company acquires the stock of Finance Corporation, a separate legal entity, their separate balance sheets are as follows:

	Manufacturing Co.	Finance Corp.
Total assets	$220,000,000	$110,000,000
Total liabilities...	$115,000,000	$100,000,000
Stockholders' equity	105,000,000	10,000,000
Total liabilities and equity.........................	$220,000,000	$110,000,000

Assume Finance Corporation's assets and liabilities are reported at fair value. Manufacturing Company pays $10,000,000 in cash for Finance Corporation's assets and liabilities, and then consolidates the assets and liabilities of Finance Corporation with its own assets and liabilities. Manufacturing Company's journal entry to acquire Finance Corporation, and its resulting balance sheet are:

Total assets	110,000,000	
Total liabilities		100,000,000
Cash		10,000,000
To record the acquisition of Finance Corporation.		

Consolidated Balance Sheet, Manufacturing Company and Subsidiary	
Total assets	$320,000,000
Total liabilities...	$215,000,000
Stockholders' equity	105,000,000
Total liabilities and equity................................	$320,000,000

If Manufacturing Company instead treats the transaction as an investment, accounted for by the equity method, its acquisition entry and resulting balance sheet are:

Investment in Finance Corporation	10,000,000	
Cash		10,000,000
To record the acquisition of Finance Corporation.		

Manufacturing Company with Equity Investment	
Other assets...	$210,000,000
Investment in Finance Corporation	10,000,000
Total assets	$220,000,000
Total liabilities...	$115,000,000
Stockholders' equity	105,000,000
Total liabilities and equity................................	$220,000,000

Notice the impact on leverage ratios:

	Manufacturing Co. prior to investment	Finance Corp. prior to investment	Manufacturing Co. plus equity method investment	Manufacturing Co. plus consolidated subsidiary
Total liabilities/Total assets	0.52	0.91	0.52	0.67
Total liabilities/Total equity.......	1.10	10.00	1.10	2.05

Finance Corporation is much more highly leveraged—has proportionally more liabilities—than Manufacturing Company. Use of the equity method to report the investment has virtually no impact on Manufacturing Company's leverage ratios. However, when Finance Corporation is consolidated with Manufacturing Company, its liabilities are included in the consolidated entity's financial results, significantly increasing both ratios. If investors and analysts use these ratios to evaluate the risk of a company, consolidating Finance Corporation could reduce the market valuation of Manufacturing Company.

Control and Consolidation of Equity Investments

When one company invests in the voting stock of another company, U.S. GAAP states that ownership of over 50 percent of the outstanding voting stock requires consolidation, unless there are unusual circumstances preventing control. However, the standards *do not prohibit* consolidation of subsidiaries where the investment is 50 percent or less, and a controlling interest exists. In U.S. practice, though, the principles evolved into rules, and today the vast majority of consolidated subsidiaries involving equity ownership have U.S. parents with majority ownership. Different outcomes occur internationally, where a more principles-based view prevails, as discussed in the last section of this chapter.

LO3 Apply the concept of control to equity investments.

BUSINESS APPLICATION   **2006 Deconsolidation of GMAC**

General Motors Acceptance Corporation (GMAC) was founded in 1919 as a wholly-owned finance subsidiary of GM Corporation, providing GM dealers and customers with financing for their car and truck purchases. Since then, it has expanded into banking, insurance, mortgages, and other commercial and retail financing. In 2010, it changed its name to Ally Financial.

On November 30, 2006, GM sold a 51 percent controlling interest in GMAC for $7.4 billion to FIM Holdings, a group of private investors that included Cerberus Capital Management, L.P., and Citigroup, Inc. GM retained a 49 percent interest in GMAC. Although GMAC's financial records had been consolidated with those of GM, after November 30, 2006, GM no longer consolidated GMAC, instead using the equity method to account for its investment. Chapter 1 in this text explains that rather than combining GMAC's assets, liabilities, revenues and expenses with those of GM in its financial statements, GM reported its investment in GMAC as one line in the assets section of its balance sheet, and reported its share of GMAC's earnings as one line in its income statement.

This scenario applies the guidelines of *FASB ASC Topic 810*, which require that majority-owned subsidiaries be consolidated in the financial statements of the parent. Since GM's ownership declined from 100 percent to 49 percent, it no longer was required to consolidate GMAC. One might wonder, however, how the change in ownership interest was decided, and whether the requirements of U.S. GAAP had any bearing on the choice. One might also wonder whether by changing its equity ownership to 49 percent, GM actually relinquished control over GMAC at the time.   *Source:* General Motors Corporation annual report, 2008.

A company can control another company *without* majority ownership of its voting stock. The next section discusses consolidation requirements when equity ownership does not determine the existence of control.

Control and Consolidation of Non-Equity Investments

Control over another company may be obtained without paying *any* consideration, or acquiring *any* of the company's stock. A company may form and control a separate entity, known as a **special purpose entity**, with little or no equity investment. The accounting standards discussed above deal with control achieved through majority equity ownership and therefore do not require consolidation of entities controlled by other means.

LO4 Apply the concept of control to non-equity investments (variable interest entities).

Motivations for Special Purpose Entities   Special purpose entities (SPEs) are legal structures formed for specific business activities. They frequently have no separate management or employees, are staffed by existing companies' personnel, typically obtain most of their financing from debt, and have a small outside equity interest that obtains a secure return with little or no risk. Common examples include:

- **Securitization:** A financial services company sets up an SPE to buy customer or loan receivables from its clients. The arrangement allows the clients to obtain immediate cash for their receivables, typically at a lower cost than factoring. The SPE issues debt securities backed (or collateralized) by the receivables, uses the money to buy the receivables, then uses the collection proceeds from the receivables to pay the interest and principal on the debt securities. A diagram of the securitization structure clarifies the relationships.

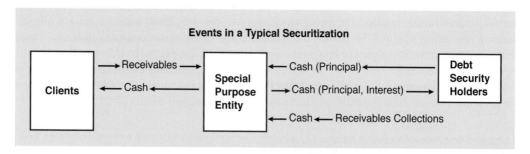

Events in a Typical Securitization

In recent years, large financial services entities such as **JP Morgan Chase** and **Citigroup** used SPEs to securitize billions of dollars of mortgages.

- **Leasing:** A company creates an SPE to purchase long-term assets. Funding for the purchases is obtained primarily through loans. The SPE then leases the assets to the company, and uses the lease payments to pay the interest and principal on the debt. The terms of the lease usually allow the lessee to report the lease as an operating lease.

- **Joint ventures:** An SPE is formed by two or more companies for specialized projects, often requiring large amounts of specialized skill and financing. The SPE structure legally separates the project's risk from that of the sponsors, therefore allowing financing to be obtained at a lower cost. If the companies have licensing agreements requiring them to share new technology with competitors, technology developed by the SPE is legally sheltered from these agreements.

Although many SPEs have legitimate business purposes, they provide the opportunity to hide debt and losses from investors. Because the companies creating the SPEs typically do not have significant equity ownership, the consolidation requirements of *ASC paras. 810-10-15-8* and *10* do not apply.

Applying the concept of control to SPEs is particularly challenging. Equity holders control most entities by holding voting shares. With SPEs, the equity investors provide little of the funding, and do not absorb the majority of the risks and rewards of the entity. Losses absorbed by the equity holders are usually limited, and they also often have limited voting power. SPE debt may be guaranteed by parties that do not have equity ownership.

The collapse of **Enron** in 2001 highlighted the limitation of consolidation standards that focused on equity ownership. Enron sponsored numerous legally separate "shadow entities," with limited purpose activities, that were not included in its consolidated financial statements. By not consolidating these entities, Enron understated its debt and overstated its income on "profitable" transactions with the SPEs. In one type of sham transaction, Enron issued its own stock to a nonconsolidated SPE that used the stock as collateral for a bank loan, paying Enron with the loan proceeds. When one views these transactions together, it is obvious that Enron increased its debt. However, because Enron did not consolidate the SPE, it reported the transaction as a stock issuance.

Consolidation Requirements To address the concept of control for off-balance-sheet entities, the FASB issued *Interpretation No. 46 (revised December 2003)*, Consolidation of Variable Interest Entities, commonly known as *FIN 46(R)*. These requirements are now found in *FASB ASC Topic 810*. To avoid the automatic assumption that the standard applies only to entities commonly known as SPEs, the Codification first defines the characteristics of entities to be considered for consolidation, and coins the term **variable interest entity** to describe an entity with these attributes. The Codification provides guidance for (1) identifying those SPEs that meet the definition of variable interest entities, and (2) determining whether such entities must be consolidated.

What is a Variable Interest Entity?   *ASC Topic 810* defines a variable interest entity (VIE) as one having the following characteristics (*paraphrased from ASC para. 810-10-15-14*):

- The total equity investment at risk does not allow the entity to finance its activities without additional subordinated financial support provided by other parties.

- The equity investment at risk lacks any one of the following characteristics of a controlling financial interest: (1) The power through voting rights or similar rights to make decisions about an entity's activities that most significantly impact the entity's economic performance, (2) The obligation to absorb the expected losses of the entity, or (3) The right to receive the expected residual returns of the entity.

- The equity investors as a group also are considered to lack characteristics of a controlling financial interest if the voting rights of some investors are not proportional to their obligations to absorb the expected losses of the entity, their rights to receive the expected residual returns of the entity, or both, and substantially all of the entity's activities, such as providing financing or buying assets, either involve or are conducted on behalf of an investor that has disproportionately few voting rights.

These characteristics focus on the equity investment. Even a company with a small equity investment in comparison with its debt is usually not considered to be a VIE because it can obtain regular debt financing based on the strength of its equity investment and future returns from its potential business operations. An entity is a VIE if it must obtain *guarantees from other parties* to obtain financing, or if the *equity holders do not have the usual rights and responsibilities* pertaining to equity ownership, such as voting rights and the right to residual returns. Instead, another entity holds the rights normally given to equity holders.

Guidelines help us decide whether the entity's equity investment is insufficient, thereby classifying it as a VIE. *ASC Section 810-10-25* states that an equity interest less than 10 percent of total assets indicates the entity is a VIE, absent evidence to the contrary. It also states that entities with an equity investment of more than 10 percent of assets *could* be VIEs. The question is whether the entity is able to finance its activities without additional support, such as guaranteed loans or future funding commitments, from affiliated entities. If the answer is no, the entity is a VIE *regardless of the level of equity investment*.

The sufficiency of an entity's equity investment may be evaluated using qualitative and/or quantitative analysis. Qualitative evidence that the entity is not a VIE includes the following:

- It can finance its activities without additional subordinated financial support.

- Its equity level is equal to or greater than similar entities that do not require subordinated financial support.

If qualitative analysis is not conclusive, quantitative analysis may be used to determine if the equity investment is high enough to absorb expected losses.

An example illustrates quantitative analysis of equity sufficiency. Suppose an SPE is formed with $15,000 in equity and $133,000 in debt, for a total investment of $148,000. All cash flows are expected to occur at the end of one year. Exhibit 3.1 shows expected cash flows and expected residual losses and gains, using a 5 percent discount rate and the computational technique provided in *ASC para. 810-10-55-53*.

EXHIBIT 3.1   Calculation of Expected Losses and Residual Gains

Expected Cash Flows	Present Value (@5%)	Probability	Expected Present Value	Investment Fair Value	Residual Returns	Expected Gains	Expected Losses
$189,000	$180,000	0.75	$135,000	$148,000	$ 32,000	$24,000	
63,000	60,000	0.15	9,000	148,000	(88,000)		$(13,200)
42,000	40,000	0.10	4,000	148,000	(108,000)		(10,800)
			$148,000			$24,000	$(24,000)

Although the $15,000 equity investment exceeds 10 percent of the total assets of $148,000, it is less than expected losses of $24,000 and cannot absorb these losses. This quantitative analysis indicates that the entity's equity investment is not sufficient to absorb the entity's risks. Therefore, the entity is likely to be classified as a VIE.

Who must consolidate a variable interest entity? The reporting entity with a *controlling* interest in a variable interest entity is the VIE's **primary beneficiary** and must consolidate the VIE. A reporting entity has a controlling interest if it possesses both of these attributes (*paraphrased from ASC para. 810-10-25-38A*):

- The power to direct the activities of the VIE that most significantly affect its economic performance, and
- The obligation to absorb the losses or the right to receive the benefits of the VIE that are potentially significant to the VIE.

Determining whether an entity is a VIE's primary beneficiary requires an understanding of the VIE's purpose and design, who makes the day-to-day operating and capital decisions, which decisions significantly affect performance, and how performance affects the VIE's shareholders, creditors, and providers of subordinated support.

BUSINESS APPLICATION   Dell Financial Services

In 2003, **Dell Computer Corporation** and **CIT Group, Inc.** had interests in **Dell Financial Services LP** (DFS), which provided leasing and customer financing services for Dell products. Dell owned 70 percent of the equity of DFS, but Dell and CIT had equal voting shares on DFS' board. DFS income was shared according to equity interests—70 percent to Dell and 30 percent to CIT, but CIT absorbed all losses. Dell and CIT both used the equity method to report their interests in DFS. In the months before *FIN 46* went into effect, Dell and CIT had opposite views on who should consolidate DFS under pending *FIN 46* requirements. Dell's view was that since CIT absorbed all losses, and losses dominate gains in deciding who is the primary beneficiary, CIT should consolidate DFS. CIT argued that it only shared in 30 percent of DFS' income, and that DFS was structured as a profitable operation, making the loss allocation irrelevant. What was the outcome? When *FIN 46* was implemented, Dell consolidated DFS in its financial statements. *Source:* J. Weil and G. McWilliams, "Dell-CIT Venture May Be an Orphan Under FASB's Rules," *The Wall Street Journal*, March 27, 2003.

Consolidation procedures for variable interest entities parallel those for controlling equity investments: the fair value of the VIE's assets and liabilities are consolidated with those of the primary beneficiary. If the primary beneficiary and the VIE are already under common control, however, the assets and liabilities of the VIE remain at book value. Because the primary beneficiary generally owns none of the VIE's equity, the difference between VIE assets and liabilities is reported as "noncontrolling interest" in the equity section of the primary beneficiary's consolidated balance sheet.

Reporting Perspective

Through 2009, the Codification provided an exception for so-called "qualified SPEs" (QSPEs), allowing primary beneficiaries to keep these entities off-balance-sheet even if they would otherwise qualify as VIEs. Certain financial structures used by banks to package and sell (securitize) various types of loans were called QSPEs. A major criterion for QSPE status was that the bank must relinquish control over the transferred assets. Because of this exception, banks and other financial institutions were able to remove loans from their balance sheets, hiding potential losses on these loans from investors, and in many cases reported gains on "sale" of these loans to the QSPE. Banks began incurring huge losses on subprime mortgages during the 2007 "credit crunch." At the end of 2007, **JP Morgan Chase** and **Citigroup** had securitized almost $1 trillion in loans in these QSPEs. Neither the loans nor their related losses were reported on the banks' balance sheets. In response to an SEC request, the FASB closed this loophole by abolishing special status for QSPEs. Management must uniformly apply the criteria outlined in *ASC Topic 810* to determine VIE status and identify the primary beneficiary for all entities, effective with 2010 financial statements.

As a result of this change in reporting standards, Citigroup added total assets of $137 billion and total liabilities of $146 billion to its 2010 consolidated balance sheet. *Source:* D. Reilly, "FASB Signals Stricter Rules for Banks' Loan Vehicles," *The Wall Street Journal*, May 2, 2007, and Citigroup Inc. 2010 annual report.

BUSINESS APPLICATION   GM's Variable Interest Entities

Footnote 17 of **General Motors'** 2010 annual report lists several consolidated VIEs related to GM's automotive operations:

(1) previously divested suppliers for which we provide or old GM provided guarantees or financial support;

(2) a program . . . to provide financial assistance to automotive suppliers (Receivables Program);

(3) vehicle sales and marketing joint ventures that manufacture, market and sell vehicles in certain markets;

(4) leasing SPEs which held real estate assets and related liabilities for which Old GM provided residual guarantees;

(5) an entity which manages certain private equity investments held by our and Old GM's defined benefit plans, along with seven associated general partner entities.

These VIEs are consolidated because GM could be liable for VIE obligations. In addition, GM consolidates 31-percent-owned GM Egypt because voting and other rights give GM the power to direct the activities that most significantly affect GM Egypt's financial performance. Consolidation of these VIEs adds $481 million in assets and $307 million in liabilities to GM's 2010 consolidated balance sheet, and $84 million to 2010 consolidated net income. *Source:* General Motors Company 2010 annual report

REVIEW 1 • Identifying Consolidated Entities

Assume that **General Motors** has the following relationships with other entities:

Entity	VIE	Relationship
A	No	Owns 45% of the voting stock
B	No	Owns 60% of the voting stock
C	No	Owns 60% of the nonvoting preferred stock
D	No	Owns 100% of the voting stock
E	Yes	Shares decision-making power, voting rights and board representation equally with another entity.
F	Yes	Has a small equity investment, but most funding is provided by GM-guaranteed debt. GM dictates the entity's strategies and manages its day-to-day activities.
G	Yes	Owns the entity's bonds (most of its financing) and receives fixed payments therefrom. An outside equity holder makes all operating and governance decisions.

Required: Which of the above entities are likely to be consolidated in GM's financial statements?

Solutions are located after the chapter assignments.

CONSOLIDATION AT DATE OF ACQUISITION

Once it is decided that separate legal entities should present consolidated financial statements, the challenge is to implement consolidation procedures. When the business combination takes the form of a statutory merger or consolidation, as in Chapter 2, the acquired company ceases to exist and the acquiring company records the assets and liabilities acquired on its books. However, when the two companies remain as separate legal entities they retain their separate financial records. The acquiring company

LO5 Prepare consolidated balance sheets using a consolidation working paper.

reports its investment as one line on its balance sheet, and does not report the individual assets and liabilities acquired. The acquired company makes *no entry at all*—the ownership of its outstanding shares has changed hands, but the cash, other assets paid, or stock issued by the acquiring company goes to the acquired company's *shareholders*, not to the acquired company itself. The only effect on the financial records of the acquired company is that any dividends paid will now go to the parent, rather than to the previous shareholders.

Consolidation of Financial Statements: Preliminary Issues

Some important issues must be resolved before considering procedures used to consolidate the financial statements of the separate companies.

Different Currencies   Suppose a U.S. parent consolidates a subsidiary whose records are maintained in another currency, such as the euro. This issue is common in our increasingly global economy. The accountant first *translates* the financial records of the subsidiary into U.S. dollars before consolidation. The translation process addresses the effects of changes in the foreign currency exchange rate over time, and how and where to report these effects, a topic covered in Chapter 7.

Different Accounting Principles   Suppose the financial records of the parent and the subsidiary follow different accounting standards. This often happens when the subsidiary is domiciled in another country. Although global standards are rapidly converging, many countries still require subsidiaries to follow country-specific accounting methods.

In many cases, the foreign subsidiary of a U.S. parent maintains its records using U.S. GAAP. If it does not, one must make adjustments during the consolidation process to convert the subsidiary's records to U.S. GAAP. For a variation on this theme, note that **HSBC Bank USA** is a subsidiary of **HSBC Holdings PLC**, a UK company headquartered in London. Although it is a U.S. operation, HSBC Bank USA uses the same international reporting standards (IFRS) to record its activities as its parent, HSBC Holdings PLC.

BUSINESS APPLICATION   GM's Non-U.S. Subsidiaries

General Motors consolidates hundreds of subsidiaries in its 2010 financial statements. Many of these subsidiaries are located in other countries, including:

- Adam Opel GmbH (Rüsselsheim, Germany)
- CAMI Automotive Inc. (Ingersoll, Ontario, Canada)
- GM Korea (Bupyeong-gu, Incheon, South Korea)
- Vauxhall Motors Limited (Luton, UK)

The financial records of these subsidiaries must be consolidated with those of General Motors itself to fairly present GM's financial statements. Consolidation procedures require adjusting the local numbers to U.S. GAAP and translating the financial records of these organizations to U.S. dollars.   *Source:* General Motors 10-K Filing, 2010.

Different Accounting Years   When the parent and subsidiary have different accounting year-ends, the subsidiary will typically adjust its year-end to conform with that of the parent. However, *ASC para. 810-10-45-12* allows consolidation of financial records with differing year-ends of up to three months.

When the fiscal year-ends of the parent and subsidiary differ, the consolidated financial statements should disclose material subsequent events that occurred. For example, if the parent's year-end is December 31, but the subsidiary's year-end is October 31, footnote disclosures should explain any material events affecting the subsidiary between October 31 and December 31.

Objectives of Consolidation

Consolidated statements stress *substance* over *form*. The fact that corporations remain as separate legal entities does not detract from the fact that they are under common control. Thus, these legally-separate affiliates constitute a single reporting entity.

The overriding objective in the preparation of consolidated statements is to report the affairs of a group of affiliated corporations *as a single economic entity*. Consolidation procedures are designed to *remove the effects of reported transactions and relationships between components of the reporting entity*. In this way, the financial statements for the consolidated entity are guided by the same accounting principles that guide any financial statement—namely, that information (revenues, expenses, gains, assets, liabilities, and so on) *reflects transactions with outside parties*. Just as a company's financial statements do not report transfers between different departments within the company, or obligations between segments of the company, consolidated financial statements do not report transactions or relationships between the parent and its subsidiaries.

Recall the procedures described in Chapter 2 to record an acquisition structured as a statutory merger or consolidation. The acquired assets and liabilities are identified, valued at fair value, recorded directly on the books of the acquirer, and the acquired company ceases to exist as a separate entity. When the acquired company remains as a separate legal entity, and continues to maintain its separate financial records, we must combine the records of the separate entities to create consolidated financial statements. At the date of acquisition, the final product after consolidation shows consolidated financial statements *as if the acquiring company had treated the acquisition as a statutory merger*. The consolidation process takes the assets and liabilities of the acquired company, revalues them to fair value, combines them with the assets and liabilities of the parent, and removes any intercompany transactions or account balances. This process must be performed *each time* financial statements are prepared.

Consolidation Working Paper

We use a simple illustration to explain procedures used to consolidate the separate balance sheets of the acquirer and the acquired company at the date of acquisition. Assume that **General Motors** pays $35,000,000 in cash for all of the stock of Automagic Parts, Inc., on January 1, 2013. Exhibit 3.2 shows the balance sheets of the two companies just prior to the acquisition and the fair values of Automagic's assets and liabilities.

EXHIBIT 3.2 Balance Sheets of GM and Automagic, January 1, 2013, Immediately Prior to Acquisition			
	General Motors	**Automagic Parts**	
	Book value Dr (Cr)	**Book value** Dr (Cr)	**Fair value** Dr (Cr)
Current assets	$100,000,000	$ 2,000,000	$ 1,800,000
Plant and equipment, net	400,000,000	50,000,000	80,000,000
Patents and copyrights	10,000,000	1,000,000	3,200,000
Current liabilities	(120,000,000)	(10,000,000)	(10,000,000)
Long-term debt	(300,000,000)	(38,000,000)	(40,000,000)
Common stock, $1 par	(10,000,000)	(500,000)	
Additional paid-in capital	(60,000,000)	(2,000,000)	
Retained earnings	(20,000,000)	(2,500,000)	

Because this is a stock acquisition, GM makes the following entry on its own books:

Investment in Automagic Parts	35,000,000	
Cash		35,000,000
To record investment in the stock of Automagic Parts.		

Automagic's balance sheet remains *exactly the same as before*, showing its assets and liabilities at book value, and including its stockholders' equity. Consolidation of the two balance sheets requires preparation of financial statements for a new reporting entity—the parent and subsidiary together. No financial records (books) exist for this consolidated entity; we have only separate books for the parent and subsidiary. To create financial records for the new reporting entity, we prepare a **consolidation working paper**. This working paper has the following elements:

● Accounts of the parent company, taken from the parent's books

● Accounts of the subsidiary company, taken from the subsidiary's books

● Eliminating entries necessary to consolidate the accounts of the parent and subsidiary

Exhibit 3.3 displays the general working paper format used to consolidate the balance sheets of GM and Automagic. GM's books now reflect the acquisition entry above. The goal is to show the consolidated balance sheet as if GM had reported the assets and liabilities of Automagic directly on its own books, valued at fair value, and Automagic had ceased to exist. Given that we are starting with the separate balance sheets of the two companies, the following adjustments must be made to those numbers:

● Eliminate the investment account on GM's books.

● Eliminate the stockholders' equity accounts on Automagic's books.

● Revalue Automagic's assets and liabilities from book value to fair value.

The following working paper **eliminating entries** achieve these goals:

(E)   Eliminate Automagic's Stockholders' **E**quity accounts against the investment account.

(R)   Eliminate the **r**emainder of the investment account, representing the difference between acquisition cost and Automagic's book value, and **R**evalue Automagic's assets and liabilities from book value to fair value at the acquisition date.

GM pays $35,000,000 for Automagic, but Automagic's net assets are reported on its own books at $5,000,000 (= $500,000 + $2,000,000 + $2,500,000). Therefore GM pays $30,000,000 more than Automagic's book value, which is explained as follows:

Acquisition cost		$35,000,000
Book value of Automagic		(5,000,000)
Cost in excess of Automagic's book value		30,000,000
Differences between fair value and book value:		
Current assets	$ (200,000)	
Plant and equipment, net	30,000,000	
Patents and copyrights	2,200,000	
Long-term debt	(2,000,000)	(30,000,000)
Goodwill		$ 0

GM pays $30,000,000 more than book value because the fair values of Automagic's current assets, plant and equipment, patents and copyrights and long-term debt differ from their book values. No goodwill arises in this illustration, because the differences between book and fair value for previously recorded assets and liabilities completely explain the $30,000,000 difference between the GM's cost and Automagic's book value.

The eliminating entries necessary to make these adjustments appear below, in journal entry form. Remember that the eliminations are labeled (E) and (R) to help you remember the purpose of each entry:

(E) **E**quity—eliminate the subsidiary's acquisition date equity balances.

(R) **R**evalue—recognize acquisition date fair value revaluations.

(E)	Common stock, $1 par.	500,000	
	Additional paid-in capital	2,000,000	
	Retained earnings	2,500,000	
	Investment in Automagic Parts		5,000,000
	To eliminate Automagic's equity accounts against the book value portion of the investment account.		
(R)	Plant and equipment, net.	30,000,000	
	Patents and copyrights	2,200,000	
	Current assets.		200,000
	Long-term debt		2,000,000
	Investment in Automagic Parts		30,000,000
	To eliminate the excess paid over book value from the investment account and revalue Automagic's assets and liabilities to fair value.		

The eliminating entries are shown in the "Eliminations" columns of the working paper, and the consolidated balance sheet appears in the last column. *The elimination debits always equal the credits.* Eliminations made on the working paper are *not* reported in the actual accounts of GM or Automagic. They appear *only on the working paper*.

Consolidation Illustration: Goodwill and Previously Unreported Intangibles   Unlike the illustration above, acquisition cost typically exceeds the fair values of identifiable net assets acquired, and new assets and/or liabilities not previously reported on the acquired company's balance sheet are recognized in consolidation. To illustrate these concepts, we reproduce in Exhibit 3.4 data for the acquisition of DataFile by IBM on July 1, 2012, described in Chapter 2, Exhibit 2.4.

EXHIBIT 3.3   Consolidation Working Paper for GM and Automagic, January 1, 2013

	Accounts Taken From Books		Eliminations		Consolidated Balances
	GM	**Automagic**	**Dr**	**Cr**	
Current assets	$ 65,000,000	$ 2,000,000		$ 200,000 (R)	$ 66,800,000
Plant and equipment, net.	400,000,000	50,000,000	(R)$30,000,000		480,000,000
Patents and copyrights	10,000,000	1,000,000	(R) 2,200,000		13,200,000
Investment in Automagic	35,000,000			5,000,000 (E)	
				30,000,000 (R)	
Total assets	$510,000,000	$53,000,000			$560,000,000
Current liabilities.	$120,000,000	$10,000,000			$130,000,000
Long-term debt	300,000,000	38,000,000		2,000,000 (R)	340,000,000
Common stock, $1 par.	10,000,000	500,000	(E) 500,000		10,000,000
Additional paid-in capital	60,000,000	2,000,000	(E) 2,000,000		60,000,000
Retained earnings	20,000,000	2,500,000	(E) 2,500,000		20,000,000
Total liabilities and equity.	$510,000,000	$53,000,000	$37,200,000	$37,200,000	$560,000,000

EXHIBIT 3.4   Consolidation Illustration with Identifiable Intangibles

IBM Corporation acquires all of the voting stock of DataFile Inc. on July 1, 2012 for $25,000,000 in cash.
Fair values of DataFile's reported assets and liabilities are as follows:

Account	Fair value
Current assets	$ 2,000,000
Plant and equipment, net.	60,000,000
Patents and copyrights	5,000,000
Current liabilities.	10,000,000
Long-term debt	40,000,000

In addition, IBM identified and valued DataFile's previously unreported intangible assets as follows:

Brand names	$ 1,000,000
Favorable lease agreements	600,000
Assembled workforce.	5,000,000
In-process contracts with potential customers	2,000,000
Contractual customer relationships	3,000,000

To consolidate the balance sheets of IBM and DataFile, we need their separate account balances. The balance sheets of IBM and DataFile *immediately prior to* the acquisition are shown in Exhibit 3.5.

EXHIBIT 3.5   Balance Sheets of IBM and DataFile, July 1, 2012, Immediately Prior to Acquisition

	IBM	DataFile
Current assets	$ 40,000,000	$ 2,300,000
Plant and equipment, net.	150,000,000	50,000,000
Patents and copyrights	3,000,000	1,000,000
Total assets	$193,000,000	$53,300,000
Current liabilities.	$ 15,000,000	$10,000,000
Long-term debt	100,000,000	38,000,000
Common stock, $0.50 par	2,000,000	500,000
Additional paid-in capital	60,000,000	2,000,000
Retained earnings	16,000,000	2,800,000
Total liabilities and equity.	$193,000,000	$53,300,000

IBM records the stock acquisition as follows on its own books:

Investment in DataFile	25,000,000	
Cash		25,000,000
To record the purchase of all of DataFile's stock.		

The consolidation working paper for this acquisition appears in Exhibit 3.6. IBM's balance sheet reflects the above acquisition entry.

Although IBM pays $25,000,000 for DataFile, DataFile's net assets are reported on its own books at $5,300,000. Therefore IBM pays $19,700,000 more than DataFile's book value, explained as follows:

Acquisition cost	$25,000,000
Book value of DataFile	(5,300,000)
Cost in excess of DataFile's book value	19,700,000

Differences between fair value and book value:		
Current assets	$ (300,000)	
Plant and equipment, net	10,000,000	
Patents and copyrights.	4,000,000	
Brand names	1,000,000	
Favorable lease agreements.	600,000	
Contractual customer relationships	3,000,000	
Long-term debt.	(2,000,000)	(16,300,000)
Goodwill		$ 3,400,000

Recall from Chapter 2 that the assembled workforce and in-process contracts listed in Exhibit 3.4 do not meet *ASC Topic 805*'s criteria for separate capitalization, and are therefore included in goodwill. The schedule above calculates the difference between the acquisition cost and the book value of Data-File—the sum of DataFile's equity accounts—and identifies why the acquisition price differs from DataFile's book value. The schedule tells the following story:

- IBM paid $19,700,000 more than the book value of DataFile's net assets.
- A comparison of book value to fair value for each of DataFile's identifiable assets and liabilities reveals that the fair value of DataFile's identifiable net assets exceeds book value by a total of $16,300,000.
- Since IBM's cost is $3,400,000 higher than the fair value of DataFile's identifiable net assets, this amount is reported as goodwill.

Working paper eliminations accomplish the tasks necessary to combine the two balance sheets:

- Eliminate Investment in DataFile, shown on IBM's books, against DataFile's stockholders' equity accounts.
- Revalue DataFile's assets and liabilities from book value to fair value. In this case, in addition to revaluing assets and liabilities currently on DataFile's balance sheet, new identifiable intangible assets and goodwill are created. These assets are reported at zero on DataFile's books.

The eliminating entries necessary to make these adjustments appear below, in journal entry form.

(E)	Common stock, $0.50 par	500,000	
	Additional paid-in capital	2,000,000	
	Retained earnings	2,800,000	
	Investment in DataFile.		5,300,000
	To eliminate DataFile's equity accounts against the book value portion of the investment account.		
(R)	Plant and equipment, net.	10,000,000	
	Patents and copyrights	4,000,000	
	Brand names	1,000,000	
	Favorable lease agreements	600,000	
	Contractual customer relationships	3,000,000	
	Goodwill	3,400,000	
	Current assets		300,000
	Long-term debt		2,000,000
	Investment in DataFile.		19,700,000
	To eliminate the excess paid over book value from the investment account and revalue DataFile's assets and liabilities to fair value.		

The eliminating entries are shown in the "Eliminations" columns of the working paper, Exhibit 3.6.

EXHIBIT 3.6 Consolidation Working Paper, July 1, 2012

	Accounts Taken From Books		Eliminations		Consolidated Balances
	IBM	**DataFile**	**Dr**	**Cr**	
Current assets	$ 15,000,000	$ 2,300,000		$ 300,000 (R)	$ 17,000,000
Plant and equipment, net.	150,000,000	50,000,000	(R)$10,000,000		210,000,000
Patents and copyrights	3,000,000	1,000,000	(R) 4,000,000		8,000,000
Investment in DataFile	25,000,000	—		5,300,000 (E)	—
				19,700,000 (R)	
Brand names	—	—	(R) 1,000,000		1,000,000
Favorable lease agreements	—	—	(R) 600,000		600,000
Contractual customer relationships	—	—	(R) 3,000,000		3,000,000
Goodwill	—	—	(R) 3,400,000		3,400,000
Total assets	$193,000,000	$53,300,000			$243,000,000
Current liabilities.	$ 15,000,000	$10,000,000			$ 25,000,000
Long-term debt	100,000,000	38,000,000		2,000,000 (R)	140,000,000
Common stock, $0.50 par	2,000,000	500,000	(E) 500,000		2,000,000
Additional paid-in capital	60,000,000	2,000,000	(E) 2,000,000		60,000,000
Retained earnings	16,000,000	2,800,000	(E) 2,800,000		16,000,000
Total liabilities and equity.	$193,000,000	$53,300,000	$27,300,000	$27,300,000	$243,000,000

The balances in the last column of Exhibit 3.6 display the consolidated balance sheet at the date of acquisition. If IBM had reported the acquisition as a **statutory merger**, the entry that IBM made on its own books is repeated from Chapter 2 below:

Current assets	2,000,000	
Plant and equipment, net.	60,000,000	
Patents and copyrights	5,000,000	
Brand names	1,000,000	
Favorable lease agreements	600,000	
Contractual customer relationships	3,000,000	
Goodwill	3,400,000	
Current liabilities		10,000,000
Long-term debt		40,000,000
Cash		25,000,000
To record the acquisition of DataFile Inc. as a statutory merger.		

If we combine this entry with IBM's balance sheet accounts immediately prior to the acquisition, shown in Exhibit 3.5, we see that IBM's balance sheet is *identical to* the consolidated balance sheet shown in the last column of the working paper in Exhibit 3.6.

Consolidation Illustration: Bargain Purchase
In a bargain purchase, the fair values of the identifiable net assets of the acquired company, including previously unrecorded intangibles, sum to more than the acquisition price. The parent reports the difference on its own books as a gain on acquisition, and reports no goodwill in consolidation. Repeat the illustration for IBM and DataFile, discussed above, but assume IBM pays only $20,000,000 in cash for all of the stock of DataFile. IBM makes the following entry to record the acquisition:

Investment in DataFile	21,600,000	
Cash		20,000,000
Gain on acquisition		1,600,000
To record the purchase of all of DataFile's stock; $21,600,000 = $5,300,000 book value + $16,300,000 revaluation of identifiable net assets.		

The consolidation working paper is shown in Exhibit 3.7. Because we are consolidating *balance sheets*, the $1,600,000 gain on acquisition enters IBM's retained earnings directly; $17,600,000 = $16,000,000 + $1,600,000.

EXHIBIT 3.7 Consolidation Working Paper, July 1, 2012, Bargain Purchase

	Accounts Taken From Books		Eliminations		Consolidated Balances
	IBM	DataFile	Dr	Cr	
Current assets	$ 20,000,000	$ 2,300,000		$ 300,000 (R)	$ 22,000,000
Plant and equipment, net.	150,000,000	50,000,000	(R)$10,000,000		210,000,000
Patents and copyrights	3,000,000	1,000,000	(R) 4,000,000		8,000,000
Investment in DataFile	21,600,000	—		5,300,000 (E)	—
				16,300,000 (R)	
Brand names	—	—	(R) 1,000,000		1,000,000
Favorable lease agreements	—	—	(R) 600,000		600,000
Contractual customer relationships	—	—	(R) 3,000,000		3,000,000
Total assets	$194,600,000	$53,300,000			$244,600,000
Current liabilities.	$ 15,000,000	$10,000,000			$ 25,000,000
Long-term debt	100,000,000	38,000,000		2,000,000 (R)	140,000,000
Common stock, $0.50 par	2,000,000	500,000	(E) 500,000		2,000,000
Additional paid-in capital	60,000,000	2,000,000	(E) 2,000,000		60,000,000
Retained earnings	17,600,000	2,800,000	(E) 2,800,000		17,600,000
Total liabilities and equity.	$194,600,000	$53,300,000	$23,900,000	$23,900,000	$244,600,000

Special Issues: Depreciable Assets and Previously Reported Goodwill

In the illustrations above, depreciable assets are shown net of accumulated depreciation. The books of the parent and subsidiary usually show depreciable assets in two accounts: original cost and accumulated depreciation. Also, if the subsidiary has previously acquired another company, it may report goodwill on its separate balance sheet. How do these items affect consolidation procedures?

When a company buys a **depreciable asset** from another company, the acquiring company reports the asset at fair value, which is the acquiring company's original cost. For example, assume Powerdown Inc., a manufacturer of auto parts, has equipment on its books at an original cost of $100,000 and accumulated depreciation of $40,000. It sells the equipment to General Motors for $50,000. General Motors reports the equipment at original cost of $50,000, and begins depreciating the equipment at the date it is acquired. The original cost and accumulated depreciation reported on Powerdown's books are irrelevant to General Motors. Similarly, when General Motors acquires Powerdown, Inc., it reports acquired equipment at fair value, which is original cost to the consolidated entity. The original cost and accumulated depreciation amounts reported on Powerdown's separate books are not reported on the consolidated balance sheet.

When consolidating a **subsidiary reporting goodwill** on its separate books, the previously reported goodwill is assigned a fair value of zero. The consolidation process assigns fair values to the subsidiary's identifiable assets and liabilities. The difference between acquisition cost and the fair value of net identifiable assets acquired is reported as goodwill on the consolidated balance sheet. Goodwill arising from a previous combination between the subsidiary and another company is *not* an identifiable asset and is not separately reported. For example, assume General Motors acquires Powerdown, Inc. for $40 million, and includes Powerdown on its consolidated balance sheet. Powerdown's separate balance sheet is as follows:

Powerdown, Inc., Balance Sheet	Book Value	Fair Value
Various identifiable assets	$50,000,000	$80,000,000
Goodwill	10,000,000	9,000,000
Total assets	$60,000,000	
Liabilities.	$55,000,000	$55,000,000
Stockholders' equity	5,000,000	
Total liabilities and equity.	$60,000,000	

The calculation of goodwill on the acquisition is as follows:

Acquisition cost		$40,000,000
Book value of Powerdown		(5,000,000)
Cost in excess of book value		35,000,000
Differences between fair value and book value:		
Various identifiable assets	$30,000,000	
Previously recorded goodwill	(10,000,000)	20,000,000
Goodwill		$15,000,000

REVIEW 2 • Consolidation with Identifiable Intangibles

Look at review problem #1 in Chapter 2, where **IBM** acquires Lotus for $1.2 billion in cash. Assume IBM acquires all of Lotus' stock in a stock investment. Information on book values for both companies and fair values of Lotus' assets and liabilities is below.

Balance Sheets of IBM and Lotus, Immediately *After* the Acquisition

(*in millions*)	IBM Book value Dr(Cr)	Lotus Book value Dr(Cr)	Fair value Dr(Cr)
Cash and receivables.	$ 800	$ 400	$ 400
Inventories	6,000	850	800
Property, plant and equipment, net	25,000	2,900	3,500
Investment in Lotus	1,200		
Accounts payable.	(7,000)	(300)	(300)
Long-term debt	(22,000)	(3,500)	(3,850)
Common stock, par value	(100)	(10)	
Additional paid-in capital	(2,500)	(200)	
Retained earnings	(1,300)	(260)	
Treasury stock		50	
Accumulated other comprehensive income.	(100)	70	

In addition, the following items are not currently reported on Lotus' balance sheet:

(*in millions*)	Fair value
Favorable lease agreements	$150
Skilled work force.	15
Favorable press reviews on products	5

Required: Prepare the consolidation working paper necessary to consolidate IBM and Lotus at the date of acquisition.

Solutions are located after the chapter assignments.

INTERNATIONAL FINANCIAL REPORTING STANDARDS FOR CONSOLIDATIONS

IFRS covering procedures to report acquisition cost and value and combine the assets and liabilities of the acquired company with that of the acquirer appears in *IFRS 3(R)*, Business Combinations, and is similar to U.S. GAAP. IFRS for determining *when* an entity should be consolidated is currently governed by *IAS 27*, Consolidated and Separate Financial Statements, and *SIC 12*, Consolidation—Special Purpose Entities, an interpretation of *IAS 27*. Both standards are superseded in 2013 by *IFRS 10*, Consolidated Financial Statements. *IFRS 12*, Disclosures of Involvement with Other Entities, also effective in 2013, specifies required disclosures of interests in other entities, such as subsidiaries and unconsolidated structured entities.

LO6 Explain IFRS for consolidations.

The Concept of Control

IFRS 10 clarifies that the *only* basis for consolidation of *all* entities is *control*. The investor must possess all three of these elements to conclude that it controls and therefore must consolidate the investee:

- power over the investee;
- exposure or rights to the investee's variable returns;
- ability to use power over the investee to influence the amount of returns to the investor.

"Power" is defined as the ability to direct the activities that significantly affect the investee's returns, and may be the result of equity voting rights, rights to appoint or remove key personnel, the ability to dominate nomination of members to the investee's governing body, or other contractual relationships. Decision-making power may exist with less than a majority ownership of voting rights. For example, an investor may hold a large minority of the voting rights, with the remaining rights spread among many small investors. Alternatively, a minority investor may have the potential to obtain majority ownership at any time, through convertible debt securities or call options.

"Exposure or rights to variable returns" includes economic exposure to both positive and negative returns. Examples include changes in the value of the investment, dividends or interest, service or management fees, and tax benefits. "Ability to use power to affect returns" requires that the controlling investor not only have the power to influence the investee's activities and exposure to the investee's returns, but also can use its power to affect those returns. An investor who directs the investee's major activities is likely to be the controlling investor, even though the investor has a small equity ownership.

IFRS 10 is viewed as an improvement over previous IFRS because it provides a consistent standard for consolidation of all types of entities that is based on the principle of control rather than using legalistic "bright lines" that can be circumvented. Control is based on the ability to direct significant activities of the investee, rather than just contractual exposure to the investee's risks and rewards. Assessment is qualitative, not quantitative, and involves considerable judgment. *IFRS 10* also offers specific guidance for determining whether control exists with less-than-majority equity ownership, which was lacking in *IAS 27*.

IFRS and U.S. GAAP Convergence

IFRS brings consolidation standards for variable interest entities closer to U.S. GAAP, as both standards use the same concepts of decision-making power and exposure to returns to determine whether an investor consolidates an entity—in U.S. GAAP, identification of the primary beneficiary. However, while IFRS applies these concepts to all entities, U.S. GAAP requires evaluation of each entity to determine if it meets the requirements of a variable interest entity—an entity whose equity interests are limited or insufficient. If the entity is a VIE, one searches for the primary beneficiary, applying the concepts of power and the obligation to absorb returns significant to the VIE.

For investments involving ownership of equity voting rights, in theory U.S. GAAP follows the concept of control, but in practice typically only majority-owned equity investments are consolidated. *IFRS 10* specifically identifies situations where control exists, and consolidation occurs, with less-than-majority ownership. As this edition goes to press, the FASB has not specifically addressed situations where control may exist with a minority equity ownership.

BUSINESS APPLICATION   **Consolidation Policy Under IFRS**

The financial statements and footnote disclosures of IFRS companies are often more detailed than those of U.S. companies. For example, many IFRS companies routinely list the names and ownership interests of their consolidated companies. An example is **France Telecom**, the major telecommunications provider in France. In its 2010 financial statements, France Telecom lists its fully consolidated companies. France Telecom owns 50 percent or less of many of these subsidiaries. Examples include:

- TP Group, Poland, 49.79% owned
- Orange Bissau, Guinea, 38.10% owned
- Sonatel and Subsidiaries, Senegal, 42.33% owned
- Orange Guinee, Guinea, 35.90% owned
- Orange Mali, 29.65% owned

France Telecom's footnote disclosures explain some of the reasons for consolidation. Sonatel is consolidated because "France Telecom controls Sonatel and its subsidiaries . . . under the terms of the shareholders' agreement . . . " TP Group is consolidated because France Telecom can appoint the majority of its supervisory board members.   *Source:* France Telecom annual report, 2010.

REVIEW OF KEY CONCEPTS

LO 1 **Explain the purpose of consolidated financial statements and how the concept of control determines when to consolidate. (p. 78)** When a business combination takes place as a stock acquisition, the acquired company remains as a separate legal entity. A **parent/subsidiary** relationship is established between these affiliated corporations. For reporting purposes, **consolidated statements** are prepared so that the financial affairs of two or more affiliated corporations will be reported as if they are a single unified economic entity. Consolidation is appropriate when **control over the subsidiary** exists.

LO 2 **Describe the motivations for off-balance-sheet financing. (p. 79)** Consolidation causes attributes of the subsidiary to affect the financial statements of the parent. Companies are motivated to avoid consolidating **highly leveraged** subsidiaries.

LO 3 **Apply the concept of control to equity investments. (p. 81)** For equity investments, current practice defines control as **majority ownership of voting shares**. All majority-owned subsidiaries are consolidated, unless control does not reside with the majority stockholder.

LO 4 **Apply the concept of control to non-equity investments (variable interest entities). (p. 81)** A company may have a relationship with a **variable interest entity** and own little or none of its equity. Even without equity ownership in this entity, if the company is the **primary beneficiary** of that entity, it must consolidate it.

LO 5 **Prepare consolidated balance sheets using a consolidation working paper. (p. 85)** **Preparation of consolidated financial statements** brings together the affiliated companies' separate statements for reporting purposes. The books of the individual affiliates are not affected by the consolidation process. This process removes all financial relationships between the affiliates to avoid overstating combined assets, liabilities, revenues and expenses. **Eliminating entries** that remove the various intercompany financial relationships are made on a **working paper** designed to facilitate the consolidation process. Eliminations remove the acquirer's investment account and the acquiree's equity accounts, and revalue the acquiree's assets and liabilities to fair value. **Consolidated statements** incorporating wholly-owned subsidiaries **are the same as if the subsidiaries had been merged** and their assets and liabilities recorded by the acquiring company as explained in Chapter 2. In parent/subsidiary relationships, combining the asset and liability balances and revaluing the subsidiary's assets and liabilities occurs on the working paper instead of on the books.

Explain IFRS for consolidations. (p. 95) Under IFRS, consolidation of any entities, whether equity investments or special purpose entities, relies on the concept of **control**. IFRS is more principles oriented, focusing on control over decision making rather than legalistically applying majority ownership or other "bright line" rules. As a result, companies following IFRS consolidate some affiliates in which they have less than majority ownership, when they have control over these entities. The decision to consolidate a special purpose entity is also based on the existence of control, while under U.S. GAAP an entity must first qualify as a VIE and then the primary beneficiary consolidates the VIE.

LO 6

MULTIPLE CHOICE QUESTIONS ·····························

1. Companies that invest in other companies often prefer using the equity method instead of consolidating their investments, because consolidating would

LO 2

   a.   reduce their stockholders' equity.
   b.   reduce their reported net income and earnings per share.
   c.   reduce their assets.
   d.   increase their leverage (debt to assets ratio).

2. A U.S. company consolidates a VIE with which it has a contractual relationship, but no equity investment. If the company and the entity were not previously under common control, at the date the company identifies the entity as a VIE that meets the requirements for consolidation, the U.S. company's consolidated balance sheet will report a noncontrolling interest valued at

LO 4

   a.   the VIE's book value.
   b.   the VIE's fair value.
   c.   zero.
   d.   the fair value of the VIE's assets.

3. A U.S. company performs a quantitative analysis of the sufficiency of a newly-formed special purpose entity's equity to absorb expected losses. The SPE was formed with $11,250 in equity and $99,750 in debt, for a total fair value of $111,000. Assume the SPE's expected net cash inflows all occur at the end of one year. Expected cash flows and probabilities are:

LO 4

Expected net cash flow	Probability
$156,000	0.65
46,800	0.20
31,200	0.15

The U.S. company uses a risk-adjusted discount rate of 4 percent to determine the present value of cash flows. The SPE's expected losses are

   a. $12,150
   b. $13,200
   c. $18,150
   d. $25,350

4. The consolidation working paper at the date of acquisition takes the book value balances of a parent and subsidiary and

LO 5

   a.   eliminates the parent's equity accounts and revalues the parent's assets and liabilities to fair value.
   b.   eliminates the subsidiary's equity accounts and revalues the subsidiary's assets and liabilities to fair value.
   c.   eliminates the parent's equity accounts and revalues the subsidiary's assets and liabilities to fair value.
   d.   eliminates the subsidiary's equity accounts and revalues the parent's assets and liabilities to fair value.

Use the following information to answer questions 5 – 8 below. All amounts are in thousands.

PR Company pays $10,000 in cash and issues stock with a fair value of $40,000 to acquire all of SX Corporation's stock. SX will be a subsidiary of PR. Balance sheets *just prior to the acquisition* are as follows:

	PR Company	SX Corporation	
	Book value	Book value	Fair value
Current assets	$ 14,000	$ 2,000	$ 4,200
Property, plant & equipment, net	110,000	10,000	6,000
Identifiable intangible assets	800	4,000	14,000
Total assets	$124,800	$16,000	
Current liabilities........................	$ 13,000	$ 1,600	$ 2,000
Long-term debt	60,000	12,000	11,600
Capital stock	44,400	5,000	
Retained earnings	8,000	8,000	
Accumulated other comprehensive income.....	200	(1,000)	
Treasury stock	(800)	(9,600)	
Total liabilities & equity...................	$124,800	$16,000	

PR's consultants find these items that are not reported on SX's balance sheet:

	Fair value
Potential contracts with new customers	$6,000
Advanced production technology	4,000
Future cost savings	2,000
Customer lists	1,000

Outside consultants are paid $200 in cash, and registration fees to issue PR's new stock are $400.

LO 5 **5.** Total acquisition cost reported by PR (the debit to Investment on PR's books) is

    a. $50,000
    b. $50,200
    c. $50,400
    d. $50,600

LO 5 **6.** On the consolidation working paper at the date of acquisition, elimination E credits the investment account by

    a. $ 2,400
    b. $ 3,400
    c. $ 5,000
    d. $13,000

LO 5 **7.** On the consolidation working paper at the date of acquisition, elimination R debits identifiable intangible assets by

    a. $10,000
    b. $13,000
    c. $15,000
    d. $23,000

LO 5 **8.** On the consolidated balance sheet at the date of acquisition, elimination R

    a. credits long-term debt by $400.
    b. debits long-term debt by $11,600.
    c. credits long-term debt by $11,600.
    d. debits long-term debt by $400.

9. ABC Corporation has a financial relationship with XYZ Company, but does not have an equity interest in XYZ. Should ABC consolidate XYZ? Which statement below is *true* concerning U.S. GAAP and IFRS on this question?   LO 6

   a. IFRS requires XYZ to be identified as a VIE, and then requires consolidation if ABC controls XYZ.

   b. There is no significant different in the standards; both require consolidation if XYZ is a VIE and ABC controls XYZ.

   c. There is no significant difference in the standards; both require consolidation if ABC controls XYZ.

   d. U.S. standards require XYZ to be identified as a VIE, and then require consolidation if ABC controls XYZ.

10. PX Company owns 40% of the equity of SC Corporation. Which statement is *true* concerning the choice of whether PX should consolidate SC, following IFRS?   LO 6

   a. PX should always consolidate SC.

   b. PX should never consolidate SC.

   c. PX should consolidate SC if the other 60% of SC's stock is held by thousands of shareholders with less than 1% ownership each.

   d. PX should consolidate SC if the other 60% of SC's stock is held by thousands of shareholders with less than 1% ownership each, decisions are made based on majority vote, and on average 85% of votes are cast at SC shareholders' meetings.

Assignments with the ✓ in the margin are available in an online homework system.
See the Preface of the book for details.

EXERCISES •

E3.1 **Combination and Consolidation**   Below are the condensed balance sheets of Princecraft and Sylvan Companies at December 31, 2012. On January 1, 2013, Princecraft acquired all of the voting shares of Sylvan by issuing 400,000 shares of its $1 par value common stock. Princecraft's stock is currently trading at $120 in an active market. The book values of Sylvan Company's net assets approximate fair value.   LO 5

Balance Sheets	Princecraft Company	Sylvan Company
Total assets	$150,000,000	$25,000,000
Total liabilities	$ 30,000,000	$ 8,000,000
Common stock	15,000,000	5,000,000
Additional paid-in capital	45,000,000	10,000,000
Retained earnings	60,000,000	2,000,000
Total liabilities and equity	$150,000,000	$25,000,000

Required

   a. Prepare the journal entry Princecraft makes to record the business combination as a stock acquisition.

   b. Prepare the eliminating entries necessary to consolidate the balance sheets of Princecraft Company and Sylvan Company on January 1, 2013.

   c. Present the consolidated balance sheet at January 1, 2013.

E3.2 **Eliminating Entries—Various Cases**   Pluto Company acquires all of the shares of Saturn Company's stock on January 1, 2013. At December 31, 2012, selected account balances of Saturn follow: LO 5

	Dr (Cr)
Common stock, par value $2.	$ (200,000)
Additional paid-in capital	(1,300,000)
Treasury stock	100,000
Accumulated other comprehensive income.	(150,000)
Retained earnings	(350,000)
Long-term debt	(800,000)

The book values of Saturn's reported assets and liabilities approximate fair value, and it has no unreported net assets that meet the criteria for recognition at acquisition.

Required

Prepare the consolidation working paper entries to consolidate the balance sheets of Pluto and Saturn on January 1, 2013 under each of the following conditions.

a. Pluto acquires all of Saturn's shares in the open market for $25 per share.
b. Pluto acquires all of Saturn's shares in the open market for $19 per share.
c. Pluto acquires all of Saturn's shares in the open market for $16 per share.

LO 5   E3.3   Simple Consolidation, Previously Unreported Intangibles   ProLock acquired all of the stock of Senyo for $10,000,000 on January 2, 2014. At that date, Senyo's $6,000,000 of reported net assets were fairly stated, except land was undervalued by $500,000 and unrecorded in-process R&D was valued at $1,000,000.

Required

Prepare the working paper eliminating entries needed to consolidate ProLock and Senyo on January 2, 2014.

LO 5   E3.4   Eliminating Entries, Acquisition Expenses   Pinnacle Corporation acquired all of Stengl Corporation's common stock in an exchange of common shares with a current market value of $10,000,000. Related accountants' and attorneys' fees were $300,000. The total book value of Stengl's stockholders' equity consists of capital stock of $200,000 and retained earnings of $1,800,000. Book values and fair values of Stengl's assets and liabilities are given below:

	Book Value	Fair Value
Cash and receivables.	$ 800,000	$ 800,000
Inventories	1,100,000	900,000
Plant assets, net.	1,600,000	1,000,000
Current liabilities.	(1,000,000)	(1,000,000)
Long-term debt	(500,000)	(475,000)
Totals	$2,000,000	$1,225,000

In addition, Stengl has previously unrecorded identifiable intangible assets with a fair value of $1,200,000 that meet *FASB ASC Topic 805* criteria for recognition.

Required

Prepare the working paper eliminating entries to consolidate the balance sheets of Pinnacle Corporation and Stengl Corporation at the date of acquisition.

LO 5   E3.5   Eliminating Entries—Bargain Purchase   Publix Company acquired all of Sherman Company's common stock for $2,750 million cash; fees paid to an outside firm to estimate the earning power of Sherman and the fair values of its properties amounted to $40 million. Book value of Sherman's net assets was $2,500 million. Book values of Sherman's identifiable assets and liabilities approximated their fair values except as noted below:

(in millions)	Book Value	Fair Value
Inventories	$1,500	$1,600
Land	100	200
Other plant assets, net.	800	1,050
Long-term debt	400	370

Required

a. Record Publix' acquisition entry.
b. Prepare the working paper eliminating entries necessary to prepare a consolidated balance sheet at the date of acquisition.

E3.6 Interpreting Eliminating Entries   The following two consolidation eliminating entries were made   LO 5 immediately following Plains' acquisition of a 100 percent ownership interest in Seaboard for $88,000,000 cash:

Stockholders' equity—Seaboard	?	
Investment in Seaboard		48,000,000
Goodwill.	?	
Noncurrent assets.		2,000,000
Investment in Seaboard		?

Required

Compute the following amounts:

a. Book value of Seaboard at the date of acquisition.
b. Excess paid over the book value of net assets acquired.
c. Goodwill.

E3.7 Acquisition Entry and Consolidation Working Paper   On January 31, 2014, Phoenix, Inc. ac-   LO 5 quired all of the outstanding common stock of Spark Corporation for $400 million cash plus 25 million shares of Phoenix' $10 par value common stock having a market value of $90 per share. Registration fees were $5 million and merger-related consultant and legal fees were $8 million, paid in cash. *Immediately prior* to the acquisition, the trial balances of the two companies were as follows:

	Dr (Cr)	
(in millions)	Phoenix	Spark
Current assets	$1,000	$200
Plant and equipment, net.	3,500	700
Current liabilities.	(500)	(150)
Long-term liabilities	(2,000)	(300)
Common stock.	(300)	(100)
Additional paid-in capital	(600)	(50)
Retained earnings	(1,100)	(300)
Totals	$ 0	$ 0

A review of the fair values of Spark's assets indicates that current assets are overvalued by $10 million, plant and equipment is undervalued by $200 million, and previously unreported brand names and trademarks have a fair value of $300 million.

Required

a. Prepare the entry Phoenix makes to record the acquisition of Spark.
b. Prepare a working paper to consolidate the balance sheets of Phoenix and Spark at January 31, 2014.

LO 4   **E3.8   Identifying and Analyzing Variable Interest Entities**   Corporations A and B are formed to purchase property and lease it to end users C and D.

Required

In each of these independent cases, indicate whether A and B are variable interest entities and, if so, whether C or D is the primary beneficiary that should consolidate it. If A or B are not variable interest entities and should be consolidated with C or D, explain why.

a.   C owns 30 percent of A's equity and other investors own 70 percent. Ninety-two percent of A's assets are funded by bank loans that C guarantees. A's board of directors makes all significant operating and capital decisions. C selects six of the ten board members.

b.   B reports total assets of $100 million and stockholders' equity of $2 million; D is the sole owner of B's stock.

c.   Outside investor E owns all the stock behind A's stockholders' equity, which amounts to 15 percent of A's total assets. C contracts with E to compensate E for any of A's losses and to cap its residual gains at 10 percent of A's average equity in any one year. Excess residual gains will be distributed to C, who also makes the day-to-day decisions that affect A's economic performance. After addressing the VIE and consolidation questions, suppose A earns $18 on average equity of $100, and explain how A should account for any net income that exceeds 10 percent of its average equity.

d.   B purchases property and leases 75 percent of it to C and 25 percent to D. Both C and D guarantee specific residual values for the property they leased and neither have any interest in the stockholders' equity amounting to 10 percent of B's total assets. The property that C leases is fairly generic and has an active aftermarket whereas the property leased by D is dedicated to D's special needs and has no alternative uses. D covers 60 percent of B's funding needs with an unsecured loan. Banks provide remaining funding that is secured by the leased property. B's operating decisions are made at the board level, and D controls the majority of the board.

LO 5   **E3.9   Reconstructing Eliminating Entries and Book Value**   Cove Corporation owns all of Bay Corporation's common stock, acquired for $1,600,000 cash. Immediately prior to the acquisition, Cove reported current assets of $5,200,000, noncurrent assets of $3,800,000, and liabilities of $3,500,000. The date-of-acquisition consolidated balance sheet reports consolidated total assets of $13,000,000, including goodwill of $340,000 related to the acquisition of Bay. The book values of Bay's identifiable assets and liabilities approximated their fair values, except for previously unreported identifiable intangibles with a fair value of $800,000.

Required

a.   Calculate the fair value of Bay's identifiable total assets at the date of acquisition.
b.   Calculate the fair value of Bay's liabilities at the date of acquisition.
c.   Calculate the book value of Bay's net assets at the date of acquisition.
d.   Prepare the working paper eliminating entries to consolidate Cove and Bay at the date of acquisition.

✔ LO 4   **E3.10   Identification of Variable Interest Entity and Primary Beneficiary**   Softek Corporation forms a separate legal entity, Startek, to develop new technology. The entity is funded by $4,000,000 in outside equity and $26,000,000 in debt. Softek guarantees Startek's debt. The entity is expected to generate the following cash flows at the end of one year:

Cash Flow	Probability
$11,000,000	0.40
33,000,000	0.20
55,000,000	0.40

A discount rate of 10 percent is appropriate.

Required

a.   Assume qualitative analysis of Startek's VIE status is inconclusive. Quantitatively analyze whether Startek is a variable interest entity.
b.   Assume Startek is a variable interest entity. Identify the factors that determine whether Softek is the primary beneficiary that must consolidate Startek.

LO 3, 5

THE COCA-COLA
COMPANY
[KO]

E3.11   Acquisition and Eliminating Entries   In October, 2010, the **Coca-Cola Company** owned 33 percent of the North American business of Coca-Cola Enterprises (CCE). That year, Coca-Cola acquired the other 67 percent of CCE's North American business. Acquisition cost of full ownership of CCE's North American business was the 33 percent interest previously held, plus cash consideration and replacement share-based compensation awarded to certain employees of CCE. Note 2 of Coca-Cola's annual report states that it remeasured its investment to its $5,373 million fair value at the date of acquisition, recognizing a gain of $4,978 million as other income on the 2010 consolidated income statement. Coca-Cola paid CCE's owners

$1,321 million in cash and $235 million in share-based payment awards to CCE employees. The share-based payments of $154 million associated with services performed prior to the acquisition were included in the acquisition cost. The remaining $81 million will be expensed over future periods.

Allocation of the purchase price is as follows (*in millions*):

Current assets	$2,690
Property, plant and equipment, net	5,385
Bottlers' franchise rights	6,393
Liabilities.	(15,366)
Net identifiable assets assumed	(898)
Goodwill.	7,746
Acquisition cost	$6,848

Required

a.   Why did Coca-Cola remeasure its 33 percent interest in CCE's North American business to fair value at the date of acquisition? How did Coca-Cola account for its investment previously?
b.   Total share-based payment awards connected with the acquisition were valued at $235 million. Why were $154 million of the share-based payment awards included in acquisition cost?
c.   Assume the acquisition was a statutory merger, and the net assets of CCE's North American business were recorded directly on Coca-Cola's books. Prepare the entry or entries Coca-Cola made on its own books to record the acquisition of CCE's North American net assets.
d.   Now assume the acquisition was a stock investment, and CCE's North American business remains a separate entity with separate books.

   1.   Prepare the entries Coca-Cola made on its own books to record the acquisition.
   2.   Assume the book value of current assets acquired was $2,000 million, the book value of property, plant and equipment acquired was $20,000 million, the franchise rights were previously unrecorded, and the book value of acquired liabilities approximated fair value. Prepare the consolidation eliminating entries necessary to consolidate Coca-Cola with CCE's North American business at the date of acquisition.

E3.12   Consolidation Policy: U.S. GAAP and IFRS   Marshall Corporation has 10,000,000 shares of Class   LO 3, 6
A common stock and 100,000,000 shares of Class B common stock outstanding. The Class A common stock has 60 percent of the voting rights and the Class B stock has the other 40 percent. All shares have equal dividend rights. Randolph Corporation owns 80 percent of the Class A shares and 40 percent of the Class B shares.

Required

a.   Following U.S. GAAP, should Randolph consolidate Marshall? Explain.
b.   Following IFRS, should Randolph consolidate Marshall? Explain.
c.   Repeat parts *a* and *b* assuming Randolph owns no Class B shares and a single investor owns them all.
d.   Repeat parts *a* and *b* assuming Randolph owns 70 percent of the Class A shares and ownership of all other shares is widely dispersed.

PROBLEMS ·

P3.1   Working Paper Eliminating Entries, Goodwill   On February 15, 2010, Pendragon Corporation ac-   LO 5 ✓
quired all of the stock of Sherwood, Inc. for $300 million in cash. Sherwood's stockholders' equity accounts at the date of acquisition were as follows:

(in millions)	
Common stock, par	$ 5
Additional paid-in capital	15
Retained earnings (deficit)	(30)
Accumulated other comprehensive income.	4
Treasury stock	(3)
Total stockholders' equity (deficit)	$ (9)

The following previously unreported assets of Sherwood were reported in the acquisition *(in millions)*:

Customer lists	$40
Brand names	60

Assume Sherwood's fixed assets are overstated by $10 million, its liabilities are overstated by $1 million, and its other assets and liabilities are fairly reported.

Required

a.   Calculate the goodwill for this acquisition.

b.   Present the working paper eliminating entries necessary to consolidate the balance sheets of Pendragon and Sherwood at the date of acquisition.

 LO 5   P3.2   Consolidated Balance Sheet Working Paper, Identifiable Intangibles, Goodwill   International Technology Inc. (ITI) acquires all of the voting stock of Global Outsourcing Corporation (GOC) on June 30, 2010. Amounts paid are as follows *(in millions)*:

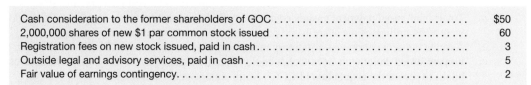

Cash consideration to the former shareholders of GOC	$50
2,000,000 shares of new $1 par common stock issued	60
Registration fees on new stock issued, paid in cash.	3
Outside legal and advisory services, paid in cash	5
Fair value of earnings contingency.	2

The earnings contingency provides for a potential payout to the former shareholders of GOC at the end of the third year following acquisition. The balance sheets of both companies *immediately prior to* the acquisition are as follows. Fair values of GOC's assets and liabilities at the date of acquisition are also provided.

	ITI	GOC	
Balance Sheets *(in millions)*	**Book Value**	**Book Value**	**Fair Value**
Current assets	$ 200	$ 10	$ 15
Property, plant and equipment, net	500	130	70
Intangible assets	1,300	20	30
Total assets	$2,000	$160	
Current liabilities.	$ 150	$ 20	$ 20
Long-term liabilities	1,200	100	103
Common stock, par	20	4	
Additional paid-in capital	550	60	
Retained earnings	100	(25)	
Accumulated other comprehensive income.	(15)	3	
Treasury stock	(5)	(2)	
Total liabilities and equity.	$2,000	$160	

The intangible assets reported above consist of patents and trademarks. GOC also has the following previously unreported intangible assets that meet *FASB ASC Topic 805* requirements for asset recognition:

	Fair Value
Advanced technology.	$ 5
Customer lists	25

Required

a.   Prepare the journal entry or entries ITI makes to record the acquisition on its own books.

b.   Prepare a working paper to consolidate the balance sheets of ITI and GOC at June 30, 2010.

LO 5   P3.3   Stock Acquisition and Consolidation Working Paper Eliminating Entries   **Pfizer** acquired
PFIZER   all of the stock of **Pharmacia** for 1,817 million shares of its $0.05 par value stock on April 16, 2003. The
[PFE]   fair value of the stock issued was $30.75/share. Merger-related cash costs were $101 million. Pharmacia's

PHARMACIA

stockholders' equity accounts at the date of acquisition totaled $7,236 million, and the fair values of its assets and liabilities differed from reported book values as follows:

(in millions)	Fair Value Less Book Value
Inventory..........	$ 2,939
Long-term investments	40
Property, plant and equipment..........	(317)
In-process research and development	5,052
Developed technology rights..........	37,066
Long-term debt (undervalued)	1,841
Other assets..........	(15,606)

Round all answers to the nearest million.

Required

a. Prepare the journal entry Pfizer made to record the acquisition on its own books, following current U.S. GAAP.
b. Calculate the goodwill purchased in this acquisition.
c. Prepare the consolidation working paper eliminating entries needed to consolidate the balance sheets of Pfizer and Pharmacia on April 16, 2003.

P3.4 **Consolidated Balance Sheet Working Paper, Bargain Purchase**   On December 31, 2012, Pax- LO 5 on Corporation acquired all of the outstanding common stock of Saxon Company for $1.8 billion cash. The balance sheets of Paxon and Saxon, *immediately prior* to the combination, are shown below:

Balance Sheets *(in millions)*	Paxon	Saxon
Assets		
Cash and receivables..........	$2,860	$ 720
Inventory..........	1,700	900
Long-term marketable securities	—	300
Land	650	175
Buildings and equipment $3,400		
Less accumulated depreciation .... (1,000)	2,400	600(net)
Total assets	$7,610	$2,695
Liabilities and Stockholders' Equity		
Current liabilities..........	$1,500	$1,000
Long-term debt	2,000	400
Common stock, par value	500	100
Additional paid-in capital	1,200	350
Retained earnings	2,410	845
Total liabilities and equity..........	$7,610	$2,695

Several of Saxon's assets and liabilities had fair values that were different from their book values. Estimates of the fair values of these items follow:

(in millions)	Estimated Fair Value
Inventory..........	$1,000
Long-term marketable securities (held-to-maturity portfolio)	250
Land	420
Buildings and equipment, net	900
Long-term debt	290

Required

a. Calculate the gain on acquisition in this bargain purchase.
b. Prepare a working paper to consolidate the balance sheets of Paxon and Saxon at December 31, 2012.

LO 5 **P3.5 Consolidated Balance Sheet Working Paper, Previously Reported Goodwill** Progressive Corporation acquired all of the outstanding stock of Static Company on June 30, 2013, by issuing 200,000 shares of its $1 par value common stock valued at $50 per share. Direct cash costs associated with the acquisition were $45,000, and the cost of registering and issuing the stock was $350,000. Condensed balance sheet data for the two companies *immediately prior* to the combination are given below.

| | Progressive | Static | |
Balance Sheets *(in thousands)*	Book Value	Book Value	Fair Value
Cash and receivables.........................	$ 8,000	$2,000	$1,500
Inventory......................................	7,000	2,400	1,000
Equity method investments	—	600	2,400
Plant assets, net...............................	10,000	3,600	2,500
Copyrights	1,000	200	5,000
Goodwill......................................	—	500	800
Total assets	$26,000	$9,300	
Current liabilities.............................	$ 6,000	$2,000	$2,000
Noncurrent liabilities..........................	4,000	3,300	3,500
Common stock, par	100	100	
Additional paid-in capital......................	900	400	
Retained earnings	15,000	3,500	
Total liabilities and equity.....................	$26,000	$9,300	

Required

a. Prepare the entry Progressive made to record the acquisition on its own books.
b. Prepare a schedule calculating the reported goodwill for this acquisition.
c. Prepare a working paper to consolidate the balance sheets of Progressive and Static at June 30, 2013.

LO 5 **P3.6 Consolidated Balances, Different Acquirers** Microtech Corporation and Webnet Solutions, Inc. have identical balance sheets, as follows *(in millions)*:

Assets	
Current assets	$10
Property, plant and equipment, net	50
Patents..	5
Total assets	$65
Liabilities and Stockholders' Equity	
Current liabilities...	$ 4
Long-term debt	20
Common stock, par value	2
Additional paid-in capital..	25
Retained earnings	14
Total liabilities and equity...	$65

Microtech's property, plant and equipment has a fair value of $70 million, and its patents have a fair value of $15 million. Microtech also has developed technology with a fair value of $100 million and client relationships worth $29 million. Both intangibles satisfy the Codification's criteria for capitalization. Webnet Solution's assets and liabilities are all fairly stated and it has no previously unrecorded intangibles. Assume that the two companies have the same stock price.

Microtech and Webnet Solutions are planning a business combination. One company will issue $200 million in stock, with a par value of $1 million, for the stock of the other company. They are not sure who will issue the stock, and therefore who will be the acquirer in this transaction.

Required

a. Prepare a consolidated balance sheet working paper, assuming Microtech is the acquiring company and issues $200 million in stock for all of the stock of Webnet Solutions.
b. Prepare a consolidated balance sheet working paper, assuming Webnet Solutions is the acquiring company, and issues $200 million in stock for all of the stock of Microtech.

c. What are the similarities and differences in the consolidated balances in parts *a* and *b*? Why are the balances different? Do you think management has a preference for one set of consolidated balances over the other?

P3.7 **Tangible and Intangible Asset Revaluations** During 2007, Motorola, Inc. made four significant acquisitions, paying a total of $4,286 million in cash. Following is a summary of information from Motorola's 2007 financial statement footnotes on these acquisitions. Each acquiree's preacquisition balance sheet reports only tangible assets and liabilities.

LO 5

MOTOROLA, INC.
[MOT]

Balance Sheets *(in millions)*	Symbol Technologies	Good Technology	Netopia	Terayon Communication Systems
Consideration paid	$3,528	$438	$183	$137
Previously unrecorded intangible assets acquired:				
Goodwill	2,300	301	122	102
In-process R&D	95	—	—	—
Other identifiable intangibles	1,000	158	100	52
Company book value (assumed)	100	30	10	15

Assume all of these transactions are stock acquisitions, and each subsidiary is consolidated following current U.S. GAAP.

Required

a. For each acquisition, calculate the fair value of net tangible assets acquired.

b. In three of the four acquisitions, the fair value of net tangible assets is negative, yet book value is positive in each case. Why do you think the fair value of net tangible assets is negative for these companies?

c. Prepare the eliminating entries required to consolidate each subsidiary in Motorola's balance sheet at its acquisition date.

d. The Symbol Technologies acquisition includes previously unrecorded in-process R&D. What is the nature of this asset? How is it measured?

P3.8 **Working Backwards—Eliminating Entries, Preparing Subsidiary's Balance Sheet** Proha Company acquired all of Sonara Company's voting stock on December 31, 2013 for $25 million cash. The book value of Sonara's net assets on that date was $5 million. The book values of Sonara's individual assets and liabilities approximated fair value, except for inventory, which was overvalued by $1 million, plant assets, which were undervalued by $0.6 million, and unreported identifiable intangibles valued at $4.5 million. Given below are condensed balance sheets for Proha Company before and after consolidation of Sonara Company. Inventory is included in current assets.

LO 5

	Proha Company Prior to Consolidation	Consolidated
Assets		
Current assets	$ 5,000,000	$ 6,000,000
Plant assets, net	25,000,000	35,000,000
Investment in Sonara	25,000,000	—
Identifiable intangible assets	—	4,500,000
Goodwill	—	15,900,000
Total assets	$55,000,000	$61,400,000
Liabilities and Stockholders' Equity		
Liabilities	$24,000,000	$30,400,000
Stockholders' equity	31,000,000	31,000,000
Total liabilities and equity	$55,000,000	$61,400,000

Required

a. Determine the working paper entries that were made in consolidation.

b. Prepare Sonara Company's separate condensed balance sheet at December 31, 2013.

LO 5

MOLSON COORS
BREWING
COMPANY
[TAP]

P3.9 Merger and Stock Acquisition, Merger-Related Costs On February 9, 2005, **Adolph Coors Company** merged with **Molson, Inc.**, in a transaction valued at approximately $3,556.5 million (the Merger). As the accounting acquirer, Adolph Coors Company became the parent of the merged companies and changed its name to **Molson Coors Brewing Company** (MCBC). The combined company was the world's fifth largest brewer at the time with combined annual volume of approximately 40 million barrels.

The Merger involved the exchange of 46.7 million equivalent shares of stock at a market price of $75.25 per share, the exchange of stock options valued at $4.0 million, and Merger-related costs incurred by Coors, of which $16 million was incurred prior to the Merger. The allocation of the purchase price according to the preliminary fair values of the assets acquired and liabilities assumed at the Merger date appears below.

(In millions)	February 9, 2005
Current assets	$ 486.7
Property, plant and equipment	1,011.6
Other assets	489.6
Intangible assets	3,734.9
Goodwill	1,837.6
Total assets acquired	7,560.4
Current liabilities	(688.3)
Noncurrent liabilities	(3,315.6)
Total liabilities assumed	(4,003.9)
Net assets acquired	$ 3,556.5

Required (Round all answers to the nearest thousand.)

a. Because this merger occurred before 2009, MCBC capitalized Merger-related costs. Compute the amount of Merger-related costs incurred and capitalized, excluding the $16 million that apparently was expensed before the Merger.

b. Based on the above information, and assuming the Merger-related costs calculated in part *a* were paid in cash, prepare the entry made by Adolph Coors Company to record the Merger following GAAP in effect in 2005.

c. Suppose instead that the Merger was accomplished as a stock acquisition. Assume that fair values approximated book values except for goodwill and the intangible assets, all of which were capitalized per GAAP. Prepare the working paper entries needed for a consolidated balance sheet as of February 9, 2005.

d. Had the Merger occurred pursuant to current U.S. GAAP, what item(s) in the entries in parts *b* and *c* above would be affected, and by how much?

LO 4

MOLSON COORS
BREWING
COMPANY
[TAP]

P3.10 Consolidation of Variable Interest Entities Excerpts from **Molson Coors Brewing Company** (MCBC)'s 2007 annual report indicates that it consolidates four joint ventures found to be VIEs, as follows:

> **Brewers' Retail Inc.**
>
> Brewers' Retail Inc. (BRI), a joint venture beer distribution and retail network for the Ontario region of Canada, owned by Molson, **Labatt** and **Sleeman** brewers, operates on a breakeven basis. The three owners guarantee BRI's debt of approximately $215 million and $184 million and pension liabilities of approximately $42 million and $49 million, respectively, at December 30, 2007 and December 31, 2006, respectively. MCBC owns about 52% of BRI and states that "ownership percentages fluctuate with sales volume."
>
> **Rocky Mountain Metal Container**
>
> RMMC, a Colorado limited liability company, is a joint venture with **Ball Corporation**. Under an agreement, RMMC supplies us with substantially all the can and end requirements for our Golden brewery. RMMC manufactures these cans and ends at our manufacturing facilities, which RMMC is operating under a use and license agreement. RMMC is a non-taxable entity. Accordingly, income tax expense on the accompanying statements of operations only includes taxes related to our share of the joint venture income or loss. The Company is the guarantor of approximately $27.3 million and $32.0 mil-

continued

continued from prior page

lion of RMMC debt at December 30, 2007 and December 31, 2006, respectively. MCBC owns a 50% interest in RMMC.

Rocky Mountain Bottle Company

RMBC, a Colorado limited liability company that is a joint venture with Owens-Brockway Glass Container, Inc. ("Owens"), produces glass bottles at our glass manufacturing facility for use at our Golden brewery. Under this agreement, RMBC supplies our bottle requirements, and Owens has a contract to supply the majority of our bottle requirements not met by RMBC. RMBC is a non-taxable entity. Accordingly, income tax expense in our consolidated statements of operations only includes taxes related to our share of the joint venture income or loss. MCBC owns 50% of RMBC.

Grolsch

Grolsch is a joint venture between CBL and Royal Grolsch N.V. that markets Grolsch branded beer in the United Kingdom and Ireland. Most of the Grolsch branded beer is produced by CBL under a contract brewing arrangement with the joint venture. CBL and Royal Grolsch N.V. sell beer to the joint venture, which sells the beer back to CBL (for onward sale to customers) for a price equal to what it paid, plus a marketing and overhead charge and a profit margin. Grolsch is a taxable entity in the United Kingdom. Accordingly, income tax expense in our Consolidated Statements of Operations includes taxes related to the entire income of the joint venture. MCBC owns a 49% interest in Grolsch.

These data summarize the total assets and results of operations of the above consolidated joint ventures:

	For years ended								
	December 30, 2007			December 31, 2006			December 25, 2005		
(In thousands)	Total Assets[1]	Revenues[2]	Pre-tax income	Total Assets[1]	Revenues[2]	Pre-tax income	Total Assets[1]	Revenues[2]	Pre-tax income
BRI	$442,704	$274,419	$ 2,212	$332,613	$263,570	$ 136	$324,160	$180,562	$ —
RMMC	66,498	295,114	5,809	66,427	245,371	12,346	54,411	219,365	8,925
RMBC	40,998	95,546	20,206	36,592	96,009	19,056	42,756	90,855	15,438
Grolsch	30,141	77,583	10,129	39,219	79,007	11,531	30,724	76,045	12,083

[1] Excludes receivables from the Company.
[2] Substantially all such sales are made to the Company (except for BRI), and as such, are eliminated in consolidation.

Required

a. Indicate the likely qualitative reasons that the four joint ventures were found to be VIEs.

b. MCBC reports the following amounts:

(in thousands)	Total Assets	Total Liabilities	Net Income
Year ended December 31, 2007	$13,451,566	$6,302,175	$497,192
Year ended December 31, 2006	11,603,413	5,786,057	361,031

Comment on the significance on MCBC'S financial results of consolidating the VIEs.

c. MCBC states: "Our share of the pre-tax joint venture profits for each of these investments was offset against cost of goods sold in our Consolidated Statements of Income." Comment on the propriety of this accounting treatment.

P3.11 Identifiable Intangibles and Goodwill (see related P2.5) Prince Corporation, a wholesale vehicle distributor, acquires all of the stock of Squire Service Corporation for one million shares of Prince stock, valued at $35 per share. Squire becomes a subsidiary of Prince. Professional fees connected with the acquisition are $1,200,000 and costs of registering and issuing the new shares are $600,000, both paid in cash.

Squire performs vehicle maintenance services for owners of auto, truck and bus fleets. The balance sheets of Prince and Squire *immediately prior* to the acquisition are shown next.

LO 5 ✔

Balance Sheets	Prince	Squire
Cash..	$ 2,800,000	$ 300,000
Accounts receivable.......................................	6,000,000	2,700,000
Parts inventory...	—	5,200,000
Vehicle inventory	15,000,000	—
Equipment, net..	40,000,000	17,600,000
Total assets	$63,800,000	$25,800,000
Current liabilities..	$ 5,000,000	$ 3,100,000
Long-term liabilities	25,000,000	8,600,000
Stockholders' equity	33,800,000	14,100,000
Total liabilities and equity................................	$63,800,000	$25,800,000

In reviewing Squire's assets and liabilities, you determine the following:

1. On a discounted present value basis, the accounts receivable have a fair value of $2,600,000, and the long-term liabilities have a fair value of $8,000,000.
2. The current replacement cost of the parts inventory is $6,000,000.
3. The current replacement cost of the equipment is $19,500,000.
4. Squire occupies its service facilities under an operating lease with ten years remaining. The rent is below current market levels, giving the lease an estimated fair value of $1,250,000.
5. Squire has long-term service contracts with several large fleet owners. These contracts have been profitable; the present value of expected profits over the remaining term of the contracts is estimated at $2,000,000.
6. Squire has a skilled and experienced work force. You estimate that the cost to hire and train replacements would be $750,000.
7. Squire's trade name is well-known among fleet owners and is estimated to have a fair value of $200,000.

Required

a. Prepare the acquisition entry and a working paper to consolidate the balance sheets of Prince and Squire as of the date of acquisition.
b. If the acquisition was a statutory merger, as in P2.5, Prince records Squire's assets and liabilities directly on its own books. Present Prince's entry to record the statutory merger, and compare Prince's balance sheet immediately after the entry is booked with the consolidated balance sheet prepared in part *a*.

LO 3, 6 **P3.12 Consolidation Policy: U.S. GAAP and IFRS** Andrews Company, a cement manufacturer, acquired all the voting common stock of Benson Company, a rug manufacturer, as part of a diversification program. As a result of a later decision to discontinue the diversification program and to concentrate on its primary line of business, Andrews divested all of its diversified businesses except for Benson. Andrews decided to retain an investment in Benson because it believed that Benson was well positioned for future growth and profitability. However, because of its current corporate strategy to commit capital resources only to its primary line of business, Andrews was unwilling to provide the capital needed to support the projected growth of Benson. Thus, Andrews caused Benson to issue additional shares of Benson's voting common stock in an initial public offering.

After Benson's initial public offering, Andrews' stockholding represented less than 50 percent of the total number of shares of Benson's voting common stock outstanding. But Andrews' shares were the largest block of Benson's voting common stock held by any single party, with the remainder widely held—no single party held more than 3 percent of the total number of shares of Benson's voting common stock outstanding. Benson had no other classes of equity securities or contingently issuable voting common stock.

Required

For each of the six cases below, indicate, with supporting reasons, what the consolidation conclusion would be under U.S. GAAP and under IFRS.

a. Andrews is able to elect a majority of Benson's board of directors solely as a result of exercising the voting rights of its large minority stockholding. Not all of Benson's stockholders exercise their right to vote, giving Andrews a majority of the votes cast. Following is information on votes cast in three separate cases (1), (2) and (3):

Case	Andrews' Percentage of Total Outstanding	Percentage of Total Outstanding That Voted	Andrews' Percentage of Votes Cast
(1)	49%	85%	58%
(2)	45%	85%	53%
(3)	40%	75%	53%

b.   Instead of the facts in part *a*, Andrews is able to dominate the election of the board of directors through nominating its choices for board members, obtaining proxies from other stockholders, and convincing still other stockholders to cast their votes for its nominees. While Andrews' ability to dominate the composition of Benson's board of directors is largely due to its large minority stockholding, Andrews itself is not able to cast a majority of the votes as a result of ownership of voting rights. Following is information on votes cast in three separate cases (4), (5) and (6):

Case	Andrews' Percentage of Total Outstanding	Percentage of Total Outstanding That Voted	Andrews' Percentage of Votes Cast
(4)	35%	65%	20%
(5)	30%	60%	25%
(6)	25%	55%	20%

REVIEW SOLUTIONS

Review 1 Solution   Non-VIEs: Entities B and D would be consolidated. GM has majority ownership of the voting shares of these entities.

VIEs: GM consolidates entity F because it has the power to make decisions significantly affecting the entity's economic performance and may realize significant losses or benefits from its equity investment and loan guarantee. GM is not the primary beneficiary of entity E, due to shared power and interests. GM does not have decision-making power in entity G.

Review 2 Solution

Consolidation Working Paper (in millions)	Accounts Taken From Books		Eliminations		Consolidated Balances
	IBM	Lotus	Dr	Cr	
Cash and receivables	$ 800	$ 400			$ 1,200
Inventories	6,000	850		$ 50 (R)	6,800
Property, plant and equipment, net	25,000	2,900	(R) $ 600		28,500
Investment in Lotus	1,200	—		350 (E)	—
				850 (R)	
Favorable lease agreements	—	—	(R) 150		150
Goodwill	—	—	(R) 500		500
Total assets	$33,000	$4,150			$37,150
Accounts payable	$ 7,000	$ 300			$ 7,300
Long-term debt	22,000	3,500		350 (R)	25,850
Common stock, par value	100	10	(E) 10		100
Additional paid-in capital	2,500	200	(E) 200		2,500
Retained earnings	1,300	260	(E) 260		1,300
Treasury stock	—	(50)		50 (E)	—
Accumulated other comprehensive income	100	(70)		70 (E)	100
Total liabilities and equity	$33,000	$4,150	$1,720	$1,720	$37,150

4

Consolidated Financial Statements Subsequent to Acquisition

LEARNING OBJECTIVES

LO1 Explain the general process of periodic consolidation. (p. 113)

LO2 Describe the relation between equity method and consolidated balances. (p. 118)

LO3 Report subsequent year write-offs of acquisition date revaluations of subsidiary identifiable assets and liabilities. (p. 118)

LO4 Measure and report goodwill impairment losses. (p. 121)

LO5 Discuss IFRS for intangibles reporting and impairment testing. (p. 136)

LO6 Explain consolidation when the parent uses the cost method. (p. 139, appendix)

TIME WARNER INC.
www.timewarner.com

Time Warner Inc. is one of the largest media and entertainment conglomerates in the world. Its more than 1,000 subsidiaries include Time Inc., Turner Broadcasting System, TW Ventures Inc., and Warner Communications Inc., providing cable, internet, filmed entertainment, digital on-demand, music, and other services. Its organizational structure is the product of many acquisitions through the years, highlighted by combination with Turner Broadcasting System in 1996 and America Online in 2001.

Time Warner's December 31, 2010, balance sheet reports $29,994,000,000 in goodwill, and specific intangible assets of $10,319,000,000. The goodwill and most of the specific intangibles were acquired in business combinations, and comprise almost 61 percent of Time Warner's total consolidated assets. Financial statement footnotes report 2010 amortization expense of $264,000,000 and $20,000,000 in impairment losses for the identifiable intangibles.

Time Warner acquired most of its subsidiaries in past years, sometimes many years ago. Each time they present financial statements, Time Warner's accountants must take the separate financial records of each subsidiary and consolidate them. How do their accountants perform this task? Does the passage of time since acquisition affect this process?

This chapter explains how a parent company, such as Time Warner, accounts for its investment in subsidiaries on its own books, the procedures needed to consolidate parent and subsidiary financial records, and methods used to measure appropriate amortization and impairment losses on acquired intangibles. *Source:* Time Warner Inc. annual report, 2010.

Consolidation procedures in subsequent years	Revaluations of acquired assets: subsequent years	Illustration of consolidation in subsequent years	IFRS for acquired intangibles	Appendix: Consolidation using the cost method
• Equity method on parent's books • Consolidation entries • Basic consolidation example • Presentation of consolidated financial statements • Complete equity method as one-line consolidation	• Depreciation and amortization of previously-reported assets • Amortization and impairment testing of previously-unreported specific intangible assets • Goodwill impairment • Illustration of amortization and impairment testing	• Consolidation after one year • Consolidation after two or more years	• Specific intangibles • Goodwill impairment testing	• Compare the cost and equity methods • Consolidation after one year • Consolidation after two or more years

INTRODUCTION

If a parent has a controlling interest in a legally separate subsidiary, it regularly presents consolidated financial statements that aggregate the financial records of the separate companies. Chapter 3 discussed procedures to consolidate financial statements at the *date of acquisition*. However, far more frequently accountants prepare consolidated statements for time periods *following* the date when the parent acquired the subsidiary. If consolidation is appropriate, the books of the parent and subsidiary must be consolidated at *every* financial reporting date.

Consolidating financial records of a parent and subsidiary at a date subsequent to acquisition raises many new challenges. How the parent reports its investment in the subsidiary on its own books over time affects consolidation procedures. On the acquisition date, consolidation working paper eliminations revalue the subsidiary's assets and liabilities to fair value. In subsequent years, revalued assets and liabilities change in reported value due to the passage of time, changing economic conditions, and transactions such as sales or other dispositions. The consolidated income statement includes results of the subsidiary's operations going forward from the acquisition date. Therefore, in subsequent years the accountant prepares a consolidated income statement and statement of cash flows, in addition to the consolidated balance sheet.

INTRODUCTION TO CONSOLIDATION PROCEDURES

We begin by describing and illustrating the general nature of the consolidation process at a date subsequent to the acquisition. The goal of this process, as discussed in Chapter 3, is to take the numbers reported on the books of the parent and the subsidiary, use a working paper to make changes necessary to remove intercompany relationships, and appropriately revalue the subsidiary's assets and liabilities.

In subsequent periods, the passage of time affects revaluations of subsidiary assets and liabilities. Suppose an acquisition occurs on January 1, 2012, when the subsidiary's equipment has a remaining life of ten years, a book value of $10,000,000, and a fair value of $15,000,000. On January 1, 2012, the consolidation process increases the plant and equipment account by $5,000,000. Now assume we are preparing consolidated financial statements at December 31, 2014, *three years later*. If the subsidiary still has the

LO1 Explain the general process of periodic consolidation.

equipment, it is three years older. Using straight-line depreciation, the consolidation process adds a net value of only $3,500,000 to the plant and equipment account [= $5,000,000 − 3 × ($5,000,000/10)]. The consolidation process also affects consolidated expenses. The subsidiary reports depreciation expense of $1,000,000 (= $10,000,000/10) for 2014. Because consolidated depreciation expense, based on fair value at the date of acquisition, is $1,500,000 (= $15,000,000/10), the consolidation process adds $500,000 (= $5,000,000/10) to depreciation expense for each year, 2012 through 2021, if the subsidiary still holds the equipment.

As time passes, the investment account reported on the parent's books also changes. If the parent reports its investment using the **equity method**, the parent reports the subsidiary's adjusted income on its own books by increasing the investment account. Subsidiary dividends received reduce the parent's investment account. The consolidation process removes these intercompany effects. Recall Chapter 1's discussion of the equity method, used for *external reporting* of significant influence stock investments, generally 20 to 50 percent ownership of the voting stock. When the investor controls the investee, consolidated financial statements are prepared. To simplify the consolidation process, this text assumes the parent uses the **complete (full) equity method** to report the investment on its own books. Calculation of equity in net income of the investee using the equity method for external reporting differs from the complete equity method used *internally* by a parent company in two major ways:

* **Impairment losses on previously unreported tangible and intangible assets,** including goodwill, do not adjust equity in net income using the equity method for external reporting; equity in net income is reduced by these impairment losses using the complete equity method.

* **Unconfirmed profits on downstream sales** are deducted to the extent of the investor's *ownership interest* in the investee when computing equity in net income for external reporting; the complete equity method subtracts *all* unconfirmed downstream intercompany profits when computing equity in net income as reported on the parent's separate books.

If the parent does not use the complete equity method internally, additional entries are necessary to convert the parent's account balances to the complete equity method before proceeding with the consolidation. Chapters 4 through 6 discuss consolidation procedures based on the parent using the complete equity method on its own books. The appendix to this chapter discusses how the consolidation process changes when the parent uses the cost method to account for the investment on its own books.

Consolidation Eliminating Entries

At reporting dates after the acquisition date, we consolidate the subsidiary's assets, liabilities and equity, and also its revenues, expenses, gains and losses. The consolidation process accomplishes the following goals:

* Eliminates equity method income reported on the parent's books and declared dividends on the subsidiary's books.
* Eliminates the stockholders' equity accounts reported on the subsidiary's books against the book value portion of the investment account reported on the parent's books.
* Adjusts the subsidiary's reported assets and liabilities for remaining acquisition date revaluations and eliminates the remainder of the investment balance.
* Adjusts reported expenses for current year revaluation write-offs.

We use a consolidation working paper to achieve these goals, with the following **eliminating entries**:

(C)   Eliminate the current year's equity method entries, restoring the investment account to its balance at the beginning of the current year.

(E)   Eliminate the subsidiary's beginning-of-year stockholders' equity account balances against the investment account.

(R)   Eliminate the rest of the investment account, representing the beginning-of-year revaluation balance, and revalue the subsidiary's assets and liabilities as of the beginning of the year.

(O)   Recognize current year write-offs of the subsidiary's asset and liability revaluations.

The acronym **CERO** may help you remember the four eliminating entries:

1. **C**urrent—eliminate the current year equity method entries.
2. **E**quity—eliminate the subsidiary's beginning-of-current-year equity balances.
3. **R**evalue—recognize the beginning-of-current-year fair value revaluations.
4. **W**rite-**O**ff—recognize current year revaluation write-offs.

Eliminating entries (E) and (R) parallel the entries introduced in Chapter 3, except that Chapter 3 uses *acquisition date* values to consolidate the financial statements at the date of acquisition. At any subsequent consolidation date, entries (E) and (R) eliminate the subsidiary's equity accounts and revalue its assets and liabilities as of the *beginning of the current year*.

Reporting Perspective

The parent company's use of the **complete equity method** facilitates the consolidation process by matching the parent's investment balance with the subsidiary's beginning-of-year equity and revaluations. Unless the investment account reflects the complete equity method, it will not be completely eliminated in eliminations C, E, and R. Further, we will see that use of the complete equity method results in the parent's net income and retained earnings equaling the consolidated amounts, maintaining consistency between the parent's books and the consolidated statements to the greatest extent possible. In practice, a parent company does not always use the complete equity method internally. If consolidated statements are prepared, the method used by the parent to account for its investments in subsidiaries does not affect the consolidated results. Details of the consolidation process differ, but the end result is the same. If the parent company uses a different method, such as the *cost method*, to report its investment internally, additional consolidation working paper entries, covered in the appendix to this chapter, are necessary to adjust the parent's accounts to the complete equity method before proceeding with the consolidation.

Illustration of Consolidation Process

Suppose Time Warner pays $75,000,000 for Midwest Cable on January 1, 2012. Midwest Cable's book value is $10,000,000. The book values of Midwest Cable's net assets equal their fair values, except equipment has a fair value $15,000,000 higher than its book value, and Midwest Cable has previously unreported identifiable intangible assets valued at $2,000,000. Midwest's plant and equipment has a remaining life of 20 years, and the identifiable intangibles have a remaining life of four years. Straight-line depreciation and amortization are appropriate for both assets. Analysis of the acquisition follows:

Acquisition cost		$75,000,000
Book value of Midwest Cable		(10,000,000)
Cost in excess of Midwest Cable's book value		65,000,000
Differences between fair value and book value:		
Equipment	$15,000,000	
Identifiable intangibles	2,000,000	(17,000,000)
Goodwill		$48,000,000

Goodwill is subject to impairment testing, discussed later in this chapter. Assume goodwill is not impaired in 2012. Midwest reports net income of $5,000,000 and pays cash dividends of $1,000,000 to Time Warner in 2012. Time Warner uses the complete equity method to report its investment in Midwest

Cable on its own books, and therefore reports Equity in Income of Midwest Cable of $3,750,000, calculated as follows:

Midwest Cable's reported income for 2012..	$5,000,000
Adjustments for revaluation write-offs:	
Equipment ($15,000,000/20)	(750,000)
Identifiable intangibles ($2,000,000/4)	(500,000)
Equity in Income of Midwest Cable	$3,750,000

In addition to the initial acquisition entry, Time Warner makes the following entries on its own books during 2012:

Investment in Midwest Cable...	3,750,000	
Equity in income of Midwest Cable...................................		3,750,000
To record equity in net income for 2012.		
Cash..	1,000,000	
Investment in Midwest Cable		1,000,000
To record dividends received in 2012.		

The investment account therefore has a December 31, 2012, balance of $77,750,000 (= $75,000,000 + 3,750,000 − 1,000,000).

On December 31, 2012, we prepare consolidated financial statements. The consolidation working paper in Exhibit 4.1 shows the preclosing accounts of Time Warner and Midwest Cable at December 31, 2012, in trial balance format. In journal entry form, the four eliminating entries needed to consolidate the 2012 financial statements of Time Warner and Midwest Cable are as follows:

(C)	Equity in income of Midwest Cable	3,750,000	
	Dividends..		1,000,000
	Investment in Midwest Cable		2,750,000
	To eliminate equity in net income on the parent's books, dividends on the subsidiary's books, and restore the investment account to its beginning-of-year value.		
(E)	Common stock, par	100,000	
	Additional paid-in capital	400,000	
	Retained earnings, January 1..	9,500,000	
	Investment in Midwest Cable		10,000,000
	To eliminate the subsidiary's beginning-of-year equity accounts against the investment account (see Exhibit 4.1 for balances).		
(R)	Plant and equipment, net...	15,000,000	
	Identifiable intangibles	2,000,000	
	Goodwill..	48,000,000	
	Investment in Midwest Cable...................................		65,000,000
	To recognize the beginning-of-year revaluations and eliminate the remainder of the investment account balance.		
(O)	Operating expenses...	1,250,000	
	Plant and equipment, net		750,000
	Identifiable intangibles..		500,000
	To write off the equipment and identifiable intangibles revaluations for the current year, by recognizing additional depreciation and amortization expense.		

Exhibit 4.1 displays these eliminating entries, and the consolidated balance for each account.

EXHIBIT 4.1 **Consolidation Working Paper for Time Warner and Midwest Cable**
At December 31, 2012, Trial Balance Format

	Accounts Taken From Books Dr (Cr)		Eliminations		Consolidated Balances Dr (Cr)
	Time Warner	Midwest Cable	Dr	Cr	
Current assets	$ 19,000,000	$ 4,000,000			$ 23,000,000
Plant and equipment, net	900,000,000	60,000,000	(R) $15,000,000	$ 750,000 (O)	974,250,000
Identifiable intangibles	—	—	(R) 2,000,000	500,000 (O)	1,500,000
Investment in Midwest Cable	77,750,000	—		2,750,000 (C)	—
				10,000,000 (E)	
				65,000,000 (R)	
Goodwill	—	—	(R) 48,000,000		48,000,000
Current liabilities	(10,000,000)	(10,000,000)			(20,000,000)
Long-term debt	(935,000,000)	(40,000,000)			(975,000,000)
Common stock, par	(500,000)	(100,000)	(E) 100,000		(500,000)
Additional paid-in capital	(19,500,000)	(400,000)	(E) 400,000		(19,500,000)
Retained earnings, January 1	(20,000,000)	(9,500,000)	(E) 9,500,000		(20,000,000)
Dividends	2,000,000	1,000,000		1,000,000 (C)	2,000,000
Sales revenue	(600,000,000)	(150,000,000)			(750,000,000)
Equity in income of Midwest Cable	(3,750,000)	—	(C) 3,750,000		—
Cost of goods sold	400,000,000	115,000,000			515,000,000
Operating expenses	190,000,000	30,000,000	(O) 1,250,000		221,250,000
Totals	$ 0	$ 0	$80,000,000	$80,000,000	$ 0

Consolidated Financial Statements

Using the working paper consolidated account balances in Exhibit 4.1, we prepare the following consolidated statement of income and retained earnings, and the consolidated balance sheet.

TIME WARNER and MIDWEST CABLE
Consolidated Statement of Income and Retained Earnings
For Year Ended December 31, 2012

Sales revenue	$750,000,000
Less: Cost of goods sold	515,000,000
Gross profit	235,000,000
Less: Operating expenses	221,250,000
Net income	**13,750,000**
Plus: Retained earnings, January 1	20,000,000
Less: Dividends	(2,000,000)
Retained earnings, December 31	$ 31,750,000

TIME WARNER and MIDWEST CABLE
Consolidated Balance Sheet
December 31, 2012

Assets		Liabilities and Stockholders' Equity	
Current assets	$ 23,000,000	Current liabilities	$ 20,000,000
Plant and equipment, net . . .	974,250,000	Long-term debt	975,000,000
Identifiable intangibles	1,500,000	Total liabilities	995,000,000
Goodwill	48,000,000	Stockholders' equity	
		Common stock, par	500,000
		Additional paid-in capital	19,500,000
		Retained earnings	31,750,000
		Total stockholders' equity	51,750,000
Total assets	$1,046,750,000	Total liabilities and stockholders' equity . . .	$1,046,750,000

Complete Equity Method as One-Line Consolidation

. . . .
LO2 Describe
the relation
between eq-
uity method and
consolidated
balances.

When Time Warner uses the complete equity method to report its investment in Midwest Cable, consolidated net income of $13,750,000 equals the net income Time Warner reports on its separate books ($13,750,000 = $600,000,000 + 3,750,000 − 400,000,000 − 190,000,000). Consolidated retained earnings at December 31, 2012 of $31,750,000 equals Time Warner's ending retained earnings reported on its own books ($31,750,000 = $20,000,000 + 13,750,000 − 2,000,000). This is *not* a coincidence. Exhibit 4.2 shows that consolidated net income and the parent's net income have exactly the same components, packaged in different ways.

EXHIBIT 4.2   Equivalence of Parent's Net Income and Consolidated Net Income

Parent's income statement	Consolidated income statement

Parent revenues
Less: Parent expenses
Plus: Equity in income of subsidiary: Subsidiary
    revenues less subsidiary expenses, adjusted
    for revaluation write-offs
	Parent revenues plus subsidiary revenues
	Less: Parent expenses plus subsidiary expenses,
	    adjusted for revaluation write-offs

Parent net income	**Consolidated net income**

The parent's retained earnings consist of its retained earnings balance at the date of acquisition plus its accumulated net income less its accumulated dividends after the acquisition. Consolidated retained earnings are the parent's retained earnings at the date of acquisition plus accumulated consolidated net income less accumulated consolidated dividends after the acquisition. Since consolidated net income and dividends are the same as the parent's income and dividends, the parent's retained earnings are equal to consolidated retained earnings.

The complete equity method is often called a **"one-line consolidation"** of the investee's financial results on the investor's books. The investment account is a one-line summary of the assets and liabilities of the investee, and the equity in income account is a one-line summary of the revenues and adjusted expenses of the investee.

REPORTING REVALUATIONS OF SUBSIDIARY ASSETS AND LIABILITIES IN SUBSEQUENT YEARS

. . . .
LO3 Report
subsequent year
write-offs of
acquisition date
revaluations of
subsidiary iden-
tifiable assets
and liabilities.

The acquisition date consolidation process included revaluation of the subsidiary's assets and liabilities at that date. Consolidation at a subsequent date requires recognition of write-offs of the reported revaluations over time. In the previous section's example, plant and equipment had a fair value $15,000,000 greater than book value at the acquisition date. When we prepare consolidated financial statements a year later, however, the equipment is a year older. At an estimated remaining life of 20 years and straight-line depreciation, the difference between fair and book value is now only $14,250,000 = [$15,000,000 − 1 × (15,000,000/20)]. Consolidated operating expenses increase by $750,000 (= $15,000,000/20) to reflect the year's write-off.

The consolidation process includes adjustments to revalue assets and liabilities already on the subsidiary's books, such as plant and equipment or inventories. Previously unreported identifiable intangible assets, such as trademarks, brand names, or favorable lease agreements are also recognized. Because the price paid generally exceeds the fair value of the identifiable net assets acquired, goodwill usually appears on consolidated balance sheets. Whether tangible or intangible, we must measure the appropriate balances and changes in the value of these assets and liabilities over time, and report them in the consolidated financial statements. The reported changes for the current year appear in eliminating entry **O**. This section describes the measurement and format of eliminating entry **O** for a variety of common revaluations.

Previously Reported Assets and Liabilities

Changes in revaluations of assets and liabilities already reported on the acquired company's books at the date of acquisition do not present new reporting challenges. As time passes, the revaluations are reported in the same way as the underlying assets or liabilities. Certain long-lived assets, such as land, inventories, and nonmarketable securities, remain at their reported values unless sold or impaired. Others, such as plant and equipment and finite-life intangibles, are systematically written off over their estimated lives. Below we discuss subsequent treatment of common revaluations of assets and liabilities reported on the subsidiary's books.

Inventories   Assume the fair value of a subsidiary's inventory is $1,000,000 and its book value is $800,000 when acquired on January 1, 2013. The subsidiary reports its inventory using the FIFO method, which assumes the beginning (oldest) inventory is sold first. Therefore the subsidiary likely reports on its own books its January 1, 2013, inventory as completely sold during 2013 as follows:

Cost of goods sold...	800,000	
Inventory		800,000
To record sale of beginning inventory during 2013.		

On the 2013 consolidated income statement, cost of goods sold reflects the $1,000,000 fair value of the beginning inventory, and is $200,000 higher than the subsidiary's recorded value. The consolidation working paper includes an eliminating entry that revalues the cost of goods sold to $1,000,000, as follows:

(O)	Cost of goods sold	200,000	
	Inventory		200,000
	Eliminating entry to revalue cost of sales to fair value at the date of acquisition.		

This entry is part of eliminating entry O on the working paper, and does *not* appear on the subsidiary's books. Consolidation eliminating entries related to the inventory revaluation are not necessary in 2014 and beyond, since the subsidiary no longer carries the original inventory on its books. If the subsidiary uses LIFO, the beginning inventory is likely not reported as sold, and no eliminating entry O is appropriate.

Depreciable Assets   Assume the subsidiary reports equipment at a net book value of $50,000,000 on January 1, 2013, when its fair value is $70,000,000. The subsidiary appropriately depreciates this equipment on a straight-line basis, with a remaining life of 10 years, no residual value, and records depreciation expense of $5,000,000 (= $50,000,000/10) for the year 2013. On the consolidation working paper for 2013 and the next 9 years, eliminating entry O adjusts recorded depreciation expense to reflect the fair value of the equipment at the date of acquisition, as follows:

(O)	Depreciation expense..	2,000,000	
	Plant and equipment (or accumulated depreciation)		2,000,000
	Eliminating entry to revalue depreciation to reflect fair value at the date of acquisition; $2,000,000 = ($70,000,000 − $50,000,000)/10.		

This eliminating entry is required each year the subsidiary depreciates the equipment.

Long-Term Debt   The fair value of debt may differ from its book value at the date of acquisition. On January 1, 2013, assume the subsidiary reports $100,000,000 in 5 percent bonds payable, issued in a previous year at par, and due on December 31, 2022. Market interest rates are higher than 5 percent on January 1, 2013, and the fair value of the bonds is $90,000,000, a discount of $10,000,000.

The subsidiary appropriately reports $5,000,000 of interest expense (= $100,000,000 × 5%) on its own books during 2013. Assuming for convenience straight-line amortization of the discount over the bonds' remaining 10-year life, the 2013 consolidation working paper eliminating entry follows:

(O)	Interest expense	1,000,000	
	Bonds payable (or bond discount)		1,000,000
	Eliminating entry to amortize bond discount for 2013;		
	$1,000,000 = $10,000,000/10.		

This eliminating entry is made each year the bonds remain outstanding.

Previously Unreported Intangibles Other Than Goodwill

The consolidated balance sheet reports a subsidiary's previously unreported intangible assets, if they meet the contractual or separability criteria of *FASB ASC Topic 805,* Business Combinations. Examples include use rights, brand names, customer lists, and noncompetition agreements. *ASC Topic 350,* Intangibles—Goodwill and Other, provides the reporting requirements for these intangibles in periods after the acquisition date.

Intangibles may have **limited** or **indefinite** lives. Intangibles with limited lives are amortized over their useful lives. *Both* types of intangibles are subject to periodic impairment testing.

Intangible Assets with Limited Lives   Limited life intangibles include favorable lease agreements and customer lists. Standards similar to those generally applicable to depreciable assets are relevant here:

- The intangible is amortized over its estimated (limited) useful life.
- The amount to be amortized is the recorded amount of the asset less estimated residual value. Residual value is generally zero unless there is compelling market evidence to the contrary.
- The method of amortization reflects the pattern in which the economic benefits of the intangible are consumed. If a pattern of consumption cannot be readily determined, the straight-line method is used. Any subsequent change in the estimate of life or residual value follows the usual rules for a change in estimate.

In estimating the life of a recognized intangible asset, the accountant examines a variety of economic, legal, regulatory, contractual, competitive, and other factors, including:

- How the intangible asset will be used.
- The expected useful life of other assets to which the intangible may relate.
- Legal, regulatory, or contractual provisions that limit the useful life of the intangible asset, or that enable renewal of the life without substantial additional cost.
- Economic factors that may impact the useful life, such as competition, demand, and obsolescence.
- The costs necessary to maintain the useful life of the asset; very high maintenance costs suggest a short useful life.

If the estimated life changes, the remaining book value is amortized over the newly estimated remaining life.

Intangible Assets with Indefinite Lives   If no factors appear to limit the intangible asset's life, then its life is deemed to be *indefinite.* To conclude that an intangible has an indefinite life does not mean it will last forever; it merely means that no life-limiting factors can be identified at this time. If circumstances change, the intangible should be reclassified as a limited life asset, subject to periodic amortization as explained above. Indefinite life intangibles can include brand names and franchises, and goodwill, discussed in a later section. Acquired in-process research and development costs are classified as indefinite-lived until the related projects are completed or abandoned.

Impairment Testing for Intangibles Other Than Goodwill   Accounting for impairments of **limited life intangibles** is guided by *ASC Section 350-30-35*. A two-step process determines the impairment loss:

Step 1 Compare the **undiscounted cash flows** expected from the future use of the asset and its subsequent disposition with the asset's book value. If the sum of the future undiscounted cash flows is less than the asset's book value, impairment has occurred and we go on to the second step. If the book value is lower than the sum of the future undiscounted cash flows, no impairment has occurred.

Step 2 If Step 1 indicates impairment, the amount of impairment loss is the difference between the intangible asset's book value and the **present value of the cash flows** expected from the future use of the asset and its subsequent disposition.

For **indefinite life intangible assets**, a company has the *option* to do a qualitative assessment of whether it is *more likely than not* (more than 50 percent likely) that the intangible asset's fair value is less than its book value. This assessment requires consideration of appropriate indicators of value, and is similar to the qualitative assessment of goodwill, discussed in greater detail in the next section. If qualitative assessment indicates impairment is likely, the intangible asset's fair value is determined. If fair value is less than book value, the loss is the difference between book and fair value. Note that the qualitative test is optional.

BUSINESS APPLICATION   **Time Warner's Identifiable Intangible Assets**

Time Warner's 2010 consolidated balance sheet reports acquired identifiable intangible assets totaling $10,319 million, of which $7,827 million have indefinite lives. Note 2 to the consolidated financial statements reports its December 31, 2010 identifiable intangibles as follows:

(in millions)	Gross	Accumulated Amortization	Net
Intangible assets subject to amortization:			
Film library	$3,534	$(2,036)	$1,498
Brands, tradenames and other intangible assets.	2,000	(1,006)	994
Total	$5,534	$(3,042)	$2,492
Intangible assets not subject to amortization:			
Brands, tradenames and other intangible assets.	$8,084	$ (257)	$7,827

Time Warner reported amortization expense of $264 million in 2010. It amortizes the film library using a "film forecast methodology," and other finite lived intangibles are straight-line amortized over an estimated average life of 18 years. Estimated useful lives are reassessed each reporting period.

Time Warner recorded intangibles impairment losses of $20 million in 2010, due to termination of a games licensing relationship and the decline in value of publishing intangibles. In 2009 it reported a $52 million impairment related to an interest in an entertainment network in India.

Due to the general economic decline in 2008, Time Warner recorded much larger impairment losses that year, including a $1.132 billion write-off of publishing tradenames.

The expenses reported above are very large. Think about the role that judgment plays in determining the asset values, classification of whether they have limited or indefinite lives, and reported amortization and impairment losses. *Source:* Time Warner Inc. annual report, 2010.

Goodwill

FASB ASC Section 350-20-35, previously *SFAS 142,* requires that goodwill—an indefinite life intangible—be regularly tested for **impairment**, using a unique process discussed below. This requirement applies to the goodwill of business combinations occurring after *SFAS 142* became effective in 2002 as well as goodwill arising in past combinations.

When companies first implemented *SFAS 142,* impairment losses related to prior years appeared "below the line" as a cumulative effect accounting principle change. However, goodwill impairment losses for years 2002 and beyond are reported in the *operating section* of the income statement. If goodwill impairment losses are material, they appear as a separate line.

LO4 Measure and report goodwill impairment losses.

BUSINESS APPLICATION   Time Warner's 2002 Goodwill Impairment

During 2002, the first year of *SFAS 142*'s implementation, many companies wrote off huge amounts of goodwill. Others did not report any goodwill write-offs at all. In either case, analysts and other financial statement readers had to adjust their comparative analysis of performance to reflect the change in goodwill reporting. 2002 followed a period of time when stock prices first rose and then dropped dramatically. Many acquisitions were undoubtedly overpriced, resulting in large amounts of goodwill. *SFAS 142* provided the opportunity to "clean up" the balance sheet by removing worthless assets. In addition, to the extent that the write-off pertained to prior years, *SFAS 142* allowed the loss to be reported on the income statement as a one-time cumulative change in accounting method, possibly reducing its importance in the eyes of investors. In 2002, Time Warner—then known as AOL Time Warner Inc.—reported a goodwill impairment loss of $54,235,000,000 as a cumulative change in accounting method, attributed to previous years' decline in the value of goodwill reported in the AOL merger. In addition, its 2002 income statement reported a $45,538,000,000 loss as a component of operating income, representing impairment of goodwill and other intangibles in 2002. This impairment included declines in goodwill allocated to its AOL segment ($33,489,000,000), its Cable segment ($10,550,000,000), and its Music segment ($646,000,000). *Source:* AOL Time Warner Inc. annual report, 2002.

The Reporting Unit Concept   Goodwill is not a free-standing asset, but has meaning only in the context of a business unit. It represents a variety of intangible benefits connected with that business, beyond its tangible and identifiable intangible net assets. **Goodwill** is the residual value remaining after the acquisition cost in a business combination is assigned to the fair values of tangible and identifiable intangible assets acquired net of liabilities assumed. For purposes of impairment testing, the fair value of goodwill must be assessed in terms of the *reporting unit* to which the goodwill belongs.

A **reporting unit** for this purpose is usually an operating segment of the business, as defined by *ASC Topic 280,* Segment Reporting. *ASC para. 280-10-50-1* defines an operating segment as follows:

An **operating segment** is a component of an enterprise:

    a. That engages in business activities from which it may earn revenues and incur expenses (including revenues and expenses relating to transactions with other components of the same enterprise),

    b. Whose operating results are regularly reviewed by the enterprise's chief operating decision maker to make decisions about resources to be allocated to the segment and assess its performance, and

    c. For which discrete financial information is available.

Assigning Goodwill to Reporting Units   Goodwill arising in a business combination is assigned to one or more reporting units, including **reporting units acquired** in the transaction and **existing reporting units** of the acquiring company.

Goodwill is assigned to *newly-acquired reporting units* the same way it is determined for the acquisition as a whole. The unit's goodwill is the difference between the fair value of the newly-acquired reporting unit and the fair values of specific assets and liabilities assigned to that unit.

When calculating the assignment of goodwill to *existing reporting units*, a "with and without" approach is used. The unit's fair value is estimated before (without) the business combination and again after (with) the business combination. The increase in fair value measures the goodwill assigned to that reporting unit, reflecting the expected benefits resulting from the combination.

The above procedures may not assign goodwill to individual reporting units in amounts that exactly equal the entire reported goodwill. If so, reasonable and consistent adjustments are made so that the exact amount of the total goodwill is assigned to various reporting units.

Assume that IBM acquires Softek Business Systems on January 1, 2013, at a cost of $840,000,000. Total goodwill from this acquisition is as follows:

Acquisition cost		$840,000,000
Fair value of identifiable net assets acquired:		
Previously reported assets.	$200,000,000	
Identifiable intangibles	800,000,000	
Liabilities.	(430,000,000)	570,000,000
Goodwill.		$270,000,000

IBM acquires two new reporting units, Tech Services and Tech Software, and the combination is also expected to benefit the operations of one of IBM's existing reporting units, Global Services. All identifiable assets acquired and liabilities assumed are assigned to the two new units as follows:

	Tech Services	Tech Software	Total
Identifiable assets acquired	$700,000,000	$300,000,000	$1,000,000,000
Liabilities assumed.	(260,000,000)	(170,000,000)	(430,000,000)
Identifiable net assets assigned.	$440,000,000	$130,000,000	$ 570,000,000

The fair value of the Tech Services unit is estimated to be $630,000,000 and the fair value of the Tech Software unit is $160,000,000. Management estimates that the acquisition of Softek will increase the fair value of IBM's Global Services unit by $80,000,000. The preliminary assignment of goodwill to reporting units is:

	Tech Services	Tech Software	Global Services
Fair value of unit.	$630,000,000	$160,000,000	
Identifiable net assets assigned.	440,000,000	130,000,000	
Initial goodwill assignment.	$190,000,000	$ 30,000,000	$ 80,000,000

Total assigned goodwill is $300,000,000 (= $190,000,000 + $30,000,000 + $80,000,000), which exceeds the $270,000,000 goodwill determined for the entire combination by $30,000,000, or ten percent of the total amount assigned [= ($300,000,000 − $270,000,000)/$300,000,000]. Although different adjustments may be defensible, one possibility is a ten percent reduction in the tentative allocation shown above. Implementing this adjustment results in the following assignment of goodwill, equaling the actual $270,000,000 goodwill for the combination:

	Tech Services	Tech Software	Global Services
Initial goodwill assignment.	$190,000,000	$30,000,000	$80,000,000
10 percent reduction	(19,000,000)	(3,000,000)	(8,000,000)
Final goodwill assignment	$171,000,000	$27,000,000	$72,000,000

Goodwill Impairment   Goodwill resulting from a business combination should be tested for impairment *at least annually*, unless circumstances indicate the likelihood of impairment is remote. More frequent testing may be indicated based on new events or changing circumstances, such as:

- Significant downturn in the business climate
- Adverse legal or regulatory outcomes
- Unanticipated new competition
- Loss of key personnel
- Expectation that a reporting unit will be sold

BUSINESS APPLICATION   **Time Warner's Reporting Units and Goodwill Impairment**

Time Warner reports $29,994 million in goodwill on its December 31, 2010 balance sheet, and assigns it to the following reporting units:

(in millions)	**December 31, 2010**
Filmed Entertainment	$ 5,618
Networks	21,232
Publishing.	3,144
Total	$29,994

In 2002 Time Warner reported a goodwill write-off of almost $100 billion. During 2003 through 2007, only $246 million of impairment losses were reported, most likely because of the large write-off in 2002. The economic difficulties experienced in 2008 resulted in over $8 billion in impairment losses. However, Time Warner reported no goodwill impairment losses in 2009 or 2010.

Time Warner chose Warner Bros., Home Box Office, Turner and Time Inc. as the reporting units used to evaluate its goodwill. It estimates the fair value of the reporting units using a combination of **discounted cash flow analysis** and a **market-based approach**. Time Warner exercises judgment in estimating discount rates, growth rates and future cash flows when calculating discounted cash flows. The market-based approach requires estimates of relevant earnings multiples.

Time Warner's 2010 annual report highlights these judgments by disclosing the estimates used, and implications if estimates of reporting unit fair values were lower. For example, it discloses that if the estimated fair values of the reporting units had been 20% lower, all reporting unit book values would have exceeded fair value. *Source:* Time Warner Inc. annual reports, 2003–2010.

Goodwill is tested for impairment at the reporting unit level. Effective in 2012, there are potentially *three steps* to the **goodwill impairment test**, as follows:

Step 0 A company has the *option* to qualitatively assess whether it is *more likely than not* (more than 50 percent likely) that a reporting unit's fair value is less than its book value. If not, the company is not required to test the reporting unit's goodwill for impairment. *ASC para. 350-20-35-3C* provides guidance on factors to consider in making this assessment, paraphrased below:

- **Macroeconomic conditions** such as general economic deterioration, limitations on accessing capital, fluctuations in foreign exchange rates, or other developments in equity and credit markets
- **Industry and market considerations** such as increased competition, a change in the market for the entity's products or services, or regulatory or political developments
- **Cost factors** such as increases in materials, labor, or other costs negatively affecting earnings and cash flows
- **Overall financial performance** such as negative or declining cash flows or declining performance relative to budgeted revenue or earnings
- **Changes in management**, key personnel, strategy, customers, or possible bankruptcy or litigation
- **Specific reporting unit issues**, such as a change in the composition of net assets, expectation of disposal, or recognition of goodwill impairment loss by a subsidiary that is part of the reporting unit.

Quantitative goodwill impairment testing is required only if the qualitative assessment reveals that it is more likely than not that the reporting unit's fair value is less than its book value. The quantitative test proceeds as follows:

Step 1 Estimate the **current fair value of the reporting unit** and compare it to its book value. If the fair value *exceeds* the book value, there is no impairment and the process stops. If the fair value is *less than* the book value, the reporting unit's goodwill *may be impaired*. We go to the second step to assess the amount of impairment of goodwill, if any.

Step 2 Estimate the **implied fair value of the reporting unit's goodwill** by repeating the process carried out at acquisition. Estimate the current fair values of identifiable net assets and subtract this total from the estimated fair value of the reporting unit to get the implied current fair value of the goodwill. If the implied fair value of goodwill is less than its book value, the goodwill is impaired and a write-off is made. Once made, *write-offs are not reversed* in the future, even if the fair value of goodwill increases.

For any reporting unit at any time, company has the "unconditional option" to skip Step 0 and go directly to Step 1 if desired. The company can subsequently resume using Step 0 at any time.

A reporting unit may have a zero or negative book value. Because fair value can never be negative, Step 1 assessment leads to no goodwill impairment. However, common sense suggests that a reporting unit with negative book value is *more* likely to have goodwill impairment. In *ASC para. 350-20-35-8A*, the FASB requires that when the reporting unit's book value is zero or negative, Step 2 must be performed when it is more likely than not that goodwill is impaired.

To illustrate goodwill impairment testing, return to the above example. It is now one year later, December 31, 2013, and we test for possible goodwill impairment in 2013. Assume the company either decided to skip step 0 or it concluded from its step 0 qualitative analysis that it is more likely than not that the fair values of all three reporting units are less than book value. The following information is available at December 31, 2013:

Step 1	Tech Services	Tech Software	Global Services
Fair value of unit...............	$700,000,000	$140,000,000	$1,000,000,000
Book value of unit.............	(500,000,000)	(160,000,000)	(1,200,000,000)
Difference...................	$200,000,000	$ (20,000,000)	$ (200,000,000)

Conclusion: Because the current fair values of Tech Software and Global Services are less than book value, goodwill assigned to these units may be impaired. Tech Services' goodwill is not impaired.

In Step 2, we compute the fair value of the goodwill at December 31, 2013, which we then compare to its current book value. Assume the December 31, 2013, fair values of the identifiable net assets of Tech Software and Global Services are $120,000,000 and $900,000,000, respectively. The Step 2 evaluation is as follows:

Step 2	Tech Software	Global Services
Fair value of unit.....................................	$140,000,000	$1,000,000,000
Fair value of identifiable net assets of unit..............	(120,000,000)	(900,000,000)
Current fair value of goodwill........................	20,000,000	100,000,000
Goodwill book value................................	27,000,000	72,000,000
Difference..	$ (7,000,000)	$ 28,000,000

Conclusion: Goodwill assigned to Tech Software is impaired by $7,000,000. Global Services' goodwill is not impaired.

We record an impairment loss of $7,000,000 for 2013 as part of eliminating entry O on the consolidation working paper, as follows:

(O)	Goodwill impairment loss	7,000,000	
	Goodwill...		7,000,000
	To record goodwill impairment loss for 2013.		

When goodwill is again tested for impairment in 2014, the book value of Tech Software's goodwill is $20,000,000 (= $27,000,000 − $7,000,000).

Amortization and Impairment of Specific Intangibles and Goodwill: An Illustration

The following example illustrates how acquired specific intangibles and goodwill are reported in years subsequent to acquisition. Primus Telecommunications Group acquires all of the voting stock of Matrix Internet on January 1, 2014. The following intangibles, previously unrecorded by Matrix, are reportable on the consolidated financial statements:

Intangible asset *(in millions)*	Fair Value	Useful life
Customer lists	$ 150	5 years
Brand names	240	4 years
Goodwill	3,200	Indefinite

The goodwill is appropriately allocated to two of Primus' reporting units, as follows *(in millions)*:

Broadband unit	$1,920
Wholesale carrier unit	1,280
Total goodwill	$3,200

Customer lists and brand names are straight-line amortized over their useful lives. It is now December 31, 2014, the end of the accounting year. We have the following information regarding these intangibles:

Intangible asset *(in millions)*	Total expected future cash inflows, undiscounted	Total expected future cash inflows, discounted
Customer lists	$100	$ 80
Brand names	200	125

(in millions)	Broadband	Wholesale Carrier
Fair value of unit	$17,600	$8,640
Book value of unit	15,040	8,960
Fair value of identifiable net assets	15,680	7,520

We must determine the 2014 amortization expense for the customer lists and brand names, and the appropriate impairment loss, if any, for all the intangibles.

Amortization expense on the customer lists and brand names is as follows *(in millions)*:

Customer lists	$150/5 = $30
Brand names	$240/4 = 60
Total amortization expense	$90

Because both customer lists and brand names have limited lives, we calculate impairment loss using the two-step process discussed on pp. 120–121:

Identifiable intangible *(in millions)*	Book value	Step 1: Book value greater than undiscounted cash flow?	Step 2: Impairment loss = book value less discounted cash flow
Customer lists	$150 − $30 = $120	Yes ($120 > $100)	$120 − $80 = $40
Brand names	$240 − $60 = $180	No ($180 < $200)	—

Primus reports an impairment loss of $40,000,000 on the customer lists.

Suppose Step 0 of the goodwill impairment test indicates that book value more likely than not exceeds fair value for both reporting units. Goodwill impairment testing follows the process discussed on pp. 124–125:

Step 1 *(in millions)*	Broadband	Wholesale Carrier
Fair value of unit..	$17,600	$8,640
Book value of unit.....................................	(15,040)	(8,960)
Difference..	$ 2,560	$ (320)

Conclusion: Because the current fair value of Wholesale Carrier is less than its book value, goodwill assigned to this unit may be impaired. Broadband's goodwill is not impaired.

Step 2 *(in millions)*	Wholesale Carrier
Fair value of unit..	$8,640
Fair value of identifiable net assets of unit..............	(7,520)
Current fair value of goodwill..........................	1,120
Book value of goodwill................................	1,280
Difference..	$ 160

Conclusion: Goodwill assigned to Wholesale Carrier is impaired by $160 million.

Consolidation eliminating entry O is as follows:

(O)	Amortization expense..	90,000,000	
	Impairment loss on identifiable intangibles	40,000,000	
	Goodwill impairment loss..................................	160,000,000	
	Customer lists...		70,000,000
	Brand names..		60,000,000
	Goodwill...		160,000,000
	To record amortization expense and impairment losses on previously unreported intangibles and goodwill for 2014.		

The $130,000,000 in amortization expense and impairment losses on customer lists and brand names can be combined with other operating items, such as general and administrative expenses, if desired. When the amount is material, the $160,000,000 goodwill impairment loss appears as a separate line in the operating section of the consolidated income statement.

Reporting Perspective

The FASB added the qualitative assessment option to make impairment testing less onerous. Prior to 2012, all companies were required to compare the fair value of each indefinite life intangible and reporting unit to its book value. Companies complained that estimating the fair value of each intangible asset and reporting unit was costly and time consuming, and unnecessary when fair value was obviously higher than book value.

Critics claim that this option weakens the impairment test, by giving managers additional earnings management opportunities. The subjective nature of the qualitative assessment increases the ability to delay recognition of impairment losses. Management can also choose to perform the quantitative test in good years, but take the qualitative option in bad years, thus increasing the likelihood of impairment recognition when earnings are high and avoiding it when earnings are low.

The new qualitative option may not result in time and cost savings. The subjective nature of this option can result in higher audit fees. Companies must develop a formal process for the qualitative assessment, and thoroughly document their reasons for not performing the quantitative test. When qualitative assessment reveals that fair value is only slightly above book value, the quantitative test may still be indicated.

REVIEW **1** • **Intangibles Impairment Testing**

FineChannel Media Corporation reports several acquired intangible assets on its consolidated financial statements. At the end of the 2014 reporting year, each intangible is tested for possible impairment loss. The intangible assets and their current balances are as follows *(all amounts below in millions)*:

Intangible asset	Book value at December 31, 2014
Customer lists (limited life)	$ 250
Television rights (limited life)	100
Brand names (indefinite life)	400
Goodwill	1,750

Information related to impairment testing is as follows:

Total expected future undiscounted cash flows, customer lists	$ 240
Total expected future discounted cash flows, customer lists	225
Total expected future undiscounted cash flows, television rights	105
Total expected future discounted cash flows, television rights	65
Total expected future undiscounted cash flows, brand names	500
Total expected future discounted cash flows, brand names	380
Goodwill is assigned to the following reporting units:	
Cable	$1,000
Filmed entertainment	200
Networks	550
Total	$1,750

FineChannel bypasses the qualitative assessment option for its indefinite life intangibles and goodwill impairment tests. Reporting unit information at December 31, 2014, is as follows:

	Cable	Filmed entertainment	Networks
Fair value of unit	$ 2,000	$ 2,800	$ 6,200
Fair value of identifiable assets	20,000	15,000	30,000
Fair value of liabilities	19,500	13,350	24,050
Book value of unit	2,300	2,000	6,500

Required

Calculate the 2014 impairment losses on identifiable intangibles and goodwill, and prepare the eliminating entry **O** to record these losses.

Solutions are located after the chapter assignments.

COMPREHENSIVE ILLUSTRATION: CONSOLIDATION IN SUBSEQUENT YEARS

We now apply consolidation procedures to a more complex acquisition in years beyond the first year. Return to IBM's acquisition of DataFile, found in Chapters 2 and 3. IBM Corporation buys all of the voting stock of DataFile Inc. on July 1, 2012, the beginning of the fiscal year for both companies, for

$25,000,000 cash. DataFile's book value on that date was $5,300,000. The analysis of the excess paid over book value from Chapter 3 appears below.

Acquisition cost		$25,000,000
Book value of DataFile		(5,300,000)
Cost in excess of DataFile's book value		19,700,000
Differences between fair value and book value:		
Current assets	$ (300,000)	
Plant and equipment, net	10,000,000	
Patents and copyrights.	4,000,000	
Brand names	1,000,000	
Lease agreements	600,000	
Customer relationships.	3,000,000	
Long-term debt.	(2,000,000)	(16,300,000)
Goodwill		$ 3,400,000

Exhibit 4.3 contains information on DataFile's assets and liabilities. Estimated lives and write-off policies, identification of limited life and indefinite life intangible assets, and calculated impairment losses for specific intangibles and goodwill follow the requirements of *FASB ASC Topic 350*, as discussed in the previous section.

EXHIBIT 4.3   Revaluation Write-Off Information for DataFile Acquisition

	Write-Off Policy	Write-Off for Fiscal 2013
Current assets	Revaluation pertains to inventory reported using FIFO	Full amount ($300,000), since beginning inventory is sold in 2013
Plant and equipment	25 years, straight-line	$10,000,000/25 = $400,000
Patents and copyrights	5 years, straight-line	$4,000,000/5 = $800,000
Brand names	Indefinite life	$100,000 impairment loss
Lease agreements	2 years, straight-line	$600,000/2 = $300,000
Customer relationships	3 years, straight-line	$3,000,000/3 = $1,000,000
Long-term debt	4 years, straight-line	$2,000,000/4 = $500,000
Goodwill	Impairment testing	No impairment loss

Consolidation After One Year

It is now June 30, 2013, one year after the acquisition. DataFile reports income of $3,000,000 for fiscal 2013 and paid dividends of $400,000 to IBM during the year. IBM uses the complete equity method to report its investment in DataFile on its own books. Calculation of equity in the income of DataFile for fiscal 2013 appears below.

DataFile's reported income for fiscal 2013	$3,000,000
Adjustments for revaluation write-offs of:	
Current assets (cost of goods sold)	300,000
Plant and equipment (depreciation expense).	(400,000)
Patents and copyrights (amortization expense)	(800,000)
Brand names (impairment loss)	(100,000)
Lease agreements (amortization expense).	(300,000)
Customer relationships (amortization expense)	(1,000,000)
Long-term debt (interest expense)	500,000
Equity in income of DataFile.	$1,200,000

After the initial acquisition entry, IBM makes the following entries on its own books during fiscal 2013:

Investment in DataFile	1,200,000	
Equity in income of DataFile		1,200,000
To record equity in net income for fiscal 2013.		
Cash	400,000	
Investment in DataFile		400,000
To record dividends received in fiscal 2013.		

After these entries, the investment account has a June 30, 2013, balance of $25,800,000 (= $25,000,000 + 1,200,000 − 400,000). The reported balances from the books of IBM and DataFile at June 30, 2013, appear in the consolidation working paper in Exhibit 4.4. The eliminating entries, in journal entry form, are as follows:

(C)	Equity in income of DataFile	1,200,000	
	Dividends		400,000
	Investment in DataFile		800,000
	To eliminate equity in net income on the parent's books, dividends on the subsidiary's books, and restore the investment account to its beginning-of-year value.		
(E)	Common stock, par	500,000	
	Additional paid-in capital	2,000,000	
	Retained earnings, July 1	2,800,000	
	Investment in DataFile		5,300,000
	To eliminate the subsidiary's beginning-of-year equity accounts against the investment account.		
(R)	Plant and equipment, net	10,000,000	
	Patents and copyrights	4,000,000	
	Brand names	1,000,000	
	Lease agreements	600,000	
	Customer relationships	3,000,000	
	Goodwill	3,400,000	
	Current assets		300,000
	Long-term debt		2,000,000
	Investment in DataFile		19,700,000
	To recognize the beginning-of-year revaluations and eliminate the remainder of the investment account balance.		
(O-1)	Current assets	300,000	
	Cost of goods sold		300,000
	To adjust current year cost of goods sold to reflect inventory revaluation.		
(O-2)	Operating expenses (depreciation)	400,000	
	Plant and equipment, net		400,000
	To adjust current year depreciation expense to reflect plant and equipment revaluation.		
(O-3)	Operating expenses (amortization)	2,100,000	
	Patents and copyrights		800,000
	Lease agreements		300,000
	Customer relationships		1,000,000
	To adjust current year amortization expense to reflect revaluations of limited life intangibles.		
(O-4)	Long-term debt	500,000	
	Operating expenses (interest)		500,000
	To adjust current year interest expense to reflect long-term debt revaluation.		

continued

(O-5)	Operating expenses (impairment loss).............................	100,000	
	Brand names..		100,000
	To record brand names impairment for the current year.		

EXHIBIT 4.4   Consolidation Working Paper for IBM and DataFile At June 30, 2013, Trial Balance Format

| | Accounts Taken From Books Dr (Cr) | | Eliminations | | Consolidated Balances Dr (Cr) |
	IBM	DataFile	Dr	Cr	
Current assets	$ 16,200,000	$ 3,000,000	(O-1) $ 300,000	$ 300,000 (R)	$ 19,200,000
Plant and equipment, net..........	145,200,000	55,000,000	(R) 10,000,000	400,000 (O-2)	209,800,000
Patents and copyrights	2,500,000	800,000	(R) 4,000,000	800,000 (O-3)	6,500,000
Investment in DataFile	25,800,000	—		800,000 (C)	—
				5,300,000 (E)	
				19,700,000 (R)	
Brand names	—	—	(R) 1,000,000	100,000 (O-5)	900,000
Lease agreements	—	—	(R) 600,000	300,000 (O-3)	300,000
Customer relationships	—	—	(R) 3,000,000	1,000,000 (O-3)	2,000,000
Goodwill	—	—	(R) 3,400,000		3,400,000
Current liabilities.................	(16,500,000)	(9,000,000)			(25,500,000)
Long-term debt	(90,000,000)	(41,900,000)	(O-4) 500,000	2,000,000 (R)	(133,400,000)
Common stock, par	(2,000,000)	(500,000)	(E) 500,000		(2,000,000)
Additional paid-in capital	(60,000,000)	(2,000,000)	(E) 2,000,000		(60,000,000)
Retained earnings, July 1..........	(16,000,000)	(2,800,000)	(E) 2,800,000		(16,000,000)
Dividends	1,000,000	400,000		400,000 (C)	1,000,000
Sales revenue..................	(500,000,000)	(100,000,000)			(600,000,000)
Equity in income of DataFile........	(1,200,000)	—	(C) 1,200,000		—
Cost of goods sold..............	420,000,000	65,000,000		300,000 (O-1)	484,700,000
Operating expenses.............	75,000,000	32,000,000	(O-2) 400,000	500,000 (O-4)	
			(O-3) 2,100,000		
			(O-5) 100,000		109,100,000
Totals	$ 0	$ 0	$31,900,000	$31,900,000	$ 0

Using the working paper consolidated account balances in Exhibit 4.4, we prepare the following consolidated statement of income and retained earnings, and the balance sheet.

IBM CORPORATION and DATAFILE, INC. Consolidated Statement of Income and Retained Earnings For Fiscal Year Ended June 30, 2013	
Sales revenue...	$600,000,000
Less: Cost of goods sold	(484,700,000)
Gross profit..	115,300,000
Less: Operating expenses	(109,100,000)
Net income	**6,200,000**
Plus: Retained earnings, July 1, 2012	16,000,000
Less: Dividends	(1,000,000)
Retained earnings, June 30, 2013	$ 21,200,000

IBM CORPORATION and DATAFILE, INC.
Consolidated Balance Sheet
June 30, 2013

Assets		Liabilities and Stockholders' Equity	
Current assets	$ 19,200,000	Current liabilities.	$ 25,500,000
Plant and equipment, net. . . .	209,800,000	Long-term debt	133,400,000
Patents and copyrights	6,500,000	Total liabilities.	158,900,000
Brand names	900,000	Stockholders' equity	
Lease agreements	300,000	Common stock, par	2,000,000
Customer relationships	2,000,000	Additional paid-in capital	60,000,000
Goodwill	3,400,000	Retained earnings	21,200,000
		Total stockholders' equity	83,200,000
Total assets	$242,100,000	Total liabilities and stockholders' equity	$242,100,000

Consolidation After Two Years

Now assume it is June 30, 2014, *two years* after the acquisition, and consolidated financial statements are again prepared. DataFile reports income of $3,500,000 for fiscal 2014 and paid dividends of $200,000 to IBM during the year. There are no changes in depreciation and amortization policy for DataFile's plant and equipment and limited life intangibles. Year-end impairment testing in 2014 reveals no impairment loss for brand names, whereas goodwill is impaired by $700,000. Calculation of equity in the income of DataFile for fiscal 2014 appears below.

DataFile's reported income for fiscal 2014	$3,500,000
Adjustments for revaluation write-offs:	
Plant and equipment (depreciation expense).	(400,000)
Patents and copyrights (amortization expense)	(800,000)
Lease agreements (amortization expense).	(300,000)
Customer relationships (amortization expense)	(1,000,000)
Long-term debt (interest expense).	500,000
Goodwill (impairment loss)	(700,000)
Equity in income of DataFile.	$ 800,000

IBM makes the following entries on its own books during fiscal 2014:

Investment in DataFile	800,000	
Equity in income of DataFile		800,000
To record equity in net income for fiscal 2014.		
Cash.	200,000	
Investment in DataFile.		200,000
To record dividends received in fiscal 2014.		

The investment account has a June 30, 2014, balance of $26,400,000 (= $25,800,000 + 800,000 − 200,000).

The reported balances from the books of IBM and DataFile at June 30, 2014 appear on the consolidation working paper in Exhibit 4.5. The reported retained earnings balance at July 1, 2013, for each company equals its reported July 1, 2012, balance plus 2013 income less 2013 dividends, as reported on the books of each separate company. Eliminating entries, in journal entry form, are as follows:

(C)	Equity in income of DataFile.	800,000	
	Dividends.		200,000
	Investment in DataFile.		600,000
	To eliminate equity in net income on the parent's books, dividends on the subsidiary's books, and restore the investment account to its beginning-of-year value.		
(E)	Common stock, par	500,000	
	Additional paid-in capital	2,000,000	
	Retained earnings, July 1.	5,400,000	
	Investment in DataFile.		7,900,000
	To eliminate the subsidiary's beginning-of-year equity accounts against the investment account.		
(R)	Plant and equipment, net.	9,600,000	
	Patents and copyrights	3,200,000	
	Brand names	900,000	
	Lease agreements	300,000	
	Customer relationships	2,000,000	
	Goodwill.	3,400,000	
	Long-term debt		1,500,000
	Investment in DataFile.		17,900,000
	To recognize the beginning-of-year revaluations and eliminate the remainder of the investment account balance.		
(O-1)	Operating expenses (depreciation)	400,000	
	Plant and equipment, net		400,000
	To adjust current year depreciation expense to reflect plant and equipment revaluation.		
(O-2)	Operating expenses (amortization).	2,100,000	
	Patents and copyrights		800,000
	Lease agreements.		300,000
	Customer relationships		1,000,000
	To adjust current year amortization expense to reflect revaluations of limited life intangibles.		
(O-3)	Long-term debt	500,000	
	Operating expenses (interest).		500,000
	To adjust current year interest expense to reflect long-term debt revaluation.		
(O-4)	Operating expenses (impairment loss).	700,000	
	Goodwill.		700,000
	To record goodwill impairment for the current year.		

Eliminating entry R reports revaluations as of the beginning of the second year, revaluations that are now one year old. For example, the original plant and equipment revaluation is an increase of $10,000,000. Because the equipment is straight-line depreciated over 25 years, one year later the remaining revaluation is $9,600,000 [= $10,000,000 − 1 × ($10,000,000/25)]. Eliminating entry O reports the write-off for the current year.

If consolidation occurs after the end of the life of the revaluated asset or liability, related eliminating entries are no longer necessary. For example, the consolidated balance sheet reports an identifiable intangible, lease agreements, at the date of acquisition and at the end of fiscal 2014. Consolidated operating expenses for fiscal 2013 and 2014 reflect amortization expense on lease agreements. Because the lease agreements have a two year life, consolidation working paper eliminations for fiscal 2015, the third year after acquisition, and any future years, do not recognize lease agreements in entry R or amortization of lease agreements in entry O.

EXHIBIT 4.5 Consolidation Working Paper for IBM and DataFile
At June 30, 2014, Trial Balance Format

	Accounts Taken From Books Dr (Cr)		Eliminations		Consolidated Balances Dr (Cr)
	IBM	DataFile	Dr	Cr	
Current assets	$ 17,000,000	$ 3,200,000			$ 20,200,000
Plant and equipment, net.	160,000,000	62,000,000	(R) $ 9,600,000	$ 400,000 (O-1)	231,200,000
Patents and copyrights	2,400,000	600,000	(R) 3,200,000	800,000 (O-2)	5,400,000
Investment in DataFile	26,400,000	—		600,000 (C)	—
				7,900,000 (E)	
				17,900,000 (R)	
Brand names	—	—	(R) 900,000		900,000
Lease agreements	—	—	(R) 300,000	300,000 (O-2)	
Customer relationships	—	—	(R) 2,000,000	1,000,000 (O-2)	1,000,000
Goodwill	—	—	(R) 3,400,000	700,000 (O-4)	2,700,000
Current liabilities.	(18,000,000)	(10,000,000)			(28,000,000)
Long-term debt	(95,000,000)	(44,600,000)	(O-3) 500,000	1,500,000 (R)	(140,600,000)
Common stock, par	(2,000,000)	(500,000)	(E) 500,000		(2,000,000)
Additional paid-in capital	(60,000,000)	(2,000,000)	(E) 2,000,000		(60,000,000)
Retained earnings, July 1	(21,200,000)	(5,400,000)	(E) 5,400,000		(21,200,000)
Dividends	1,200,000	200,000		200,000 (C)	1,200,000
Sales revenue.	(550,000,000)	(110,000,000)			(660,000,000)
Equity in income of DataFile.	(800,000)	—	(C) 800,000		—
Cost of goods sold.	450,000,000	68,000,000			518,000,000
Operating expenses	90,000,000	38,500,000	(O-1) 400,000	500,000 (O-3)	
			(O-2) 2,100,000		
			(O-4) 700,000		131,200,000
Totals	$ 0	$ 0	$31,800,000	$31,800,000	$ 0

Using the working paper consolidated account balances in Exhibit 4.5, we prepare the following consolidated statement of income and retained earnings, and balance sheet for fiscal 2014.

IBM CORPORATION and DATAFILE, INC.
Consolidated Statement of Income and Retained Earnings
For Fiscal Year Ended June 30, 2014

Sales revenue.	$660,000,000
Less: Cost of goods sold	(518,000,000)
Gross profit.	142,000,000
Less: Operating expenses	(131,200,000)
Net income	**10,800,000**
Plus: Retained earnings, July 1, 2013	21,200,000
Less: Dividends	(1,200,000)
Retained earnings, June 30, 2014	$ 30,800,000

IBM CORPORATION and DATAFILE, INC.
Consolidated Balance Sheet
June 30, 2014

Assets		Liabilities and Stockholders' Equity	
Current assets	$ 20,200,000	Current liabilities.	$ 28,000,000
Plant and equipment, net. . . .	231,200,000	Long-term debt	140,600,000
Patents and copyrights	5,400,000	Total liabilities.	168,600,000
Brand names	900,000	Stockholders' equity	
Customer relationships	1,000,000	Common stock, par	2,000,000
Goodwill	2,700,000	Additional paid-in capital	60,000,000
		Retained earnings	30,800,000
		Total stockholders' equity	92,800,000
Total assets	$261,400,000	Total liabilities and stockholders' equity	$261,400,000

REVIEW 2 • Consolidation in a Subsequent Year with Identifiable Intangibles

Time Warner acquired all of the stock of First Media for $1.2 billion in cash on January 1, 2012. First Media's book value was $350 million at the time, and the $850 million excess paid over book value is explained by the revaluations below. Information on reporting these items in subsequent years is also provided.

(in millions)	Book value	Fair value	Reporting policy
Inventories	$ 850	$ 800	LIFO; beginning inventory not reported as sold during 2012-2014.
Property, plant and equipment, net . . .	3,000	3,300	10 years, straight-line
Lease agreements	0	100	2 years, straight-line
Goodwill	0	500	Impairment calculated each year: 2012 and 2013: none; 2014: $100

During 2012 and 2013, First Media reported income of $200,000,000 and $240,000,000, respectively, and paid no dividends. In 2014, First Media reported income of $250,000,000 and paid dividends of $20,000,000. Time Warner uses the complete equity method to report its investment in First Media on its own books. The trial balances of Time Warner and First Media at December 31, 2014 (three years after the acquisition) appear in the consolidation working paper below.

Required

a. Calculate equity in income of First Media, reported on Time Warner's 2014 income statement.
b. Complete the working paper and present the December 31, 2014, consolidated balance sheet and the consolidated statement of income and retained earnings for 2014, in good form.

Consolidation Working Paper

	Accounts Taken From Books Dr (Cr)		Eliminations		
(in millions)	Time Warner	First Media	Dr	Cr	Consolidated Balances Dr (Cr)
Cash and receivables.	$ 1,200	$ 450			
Inventories	7,200	1,000			
Property, plant and equipment, net	38,860	4,540			
Investment in First Media.	1,580	—			
Lease agreements	—	—			
Goodwill	—	—			
Accounts payable.	(7,800)	(670)			
Long-term debt	(35,000)	(4,300)			
Common stock, par	(120)	(10)			
Additional paid-in capital	(3,000)	(130)			
Retained earnings, Jan. 1.	(2,550)	(700)			
Treasury stock	—	50			
Dividends	100	20			
Sales revenue.	(10,000)	(2,000)			
Equity in income of First Media	(120)	—			
Cost of goods sold.	8,500	1,600			
Operating expenses	1,150	150			
Totals	$ 0	$ 0			$ 0

Solutions are located after the chapter assignments.

IFRS FOR ACQUIRED INTANGIBLES

While IFRS procedures to consolidate financial statements in subsequent years are similar to U.S. GAAP, there are differences in subsequent reporting of acquired intangibles. IFRS for acquired specific intangibles and goodwill is found in *IAS 38*, Intangible Assets, and *IAS 36*, Impairment of Assets.

Specifically Identifiable Intangibles

Chapter 3 noted that *IAS 38*'s criteria for reporting specific intangibles acquired in a business combination are similar to U.S. GAAP: to be reportable, the intangible must be either separable or contractual. Although these intangibles are generally carried at cost less appropriate accumulated amortization and impairment loss, IFRS also allows them to be reported at *fair value* in limited circumstances.

Intangibles Reported Using the Cost Model   As with U.S. GAAP, intangibles reported using the cost model may have **limited** or **indefinite lives**. Those with limited lives are amortized over the period during which the intangible is expected to produce cash flows for the company, using the same methods used for tangible depreciable assets such as plant and equipment. Even though residual value is usually zero, a third party may commit to buy the intangible at the end of its useful life, or the residual value can be based on an active market value. Estimates used to report periodic amortization should be reviewed regularly and revised as necessary. Any changes in these estimates affect future amortization, not past amortization. Intangibles deemed to have indefinite lives are not systematically amortized. The assumptions and estimations behind this judgment must be reassessed each reporting period. For example, a change in consumer tastes or economic conditions may change an indefinite-life trademark to one with a limited life.

Like U.S. GAAP, all identifiable intangibles reported at cost are subject to **impairment testing** under IFRS, regardless of whether they have limited or indefinite lives. The IFRS impairment testing procedure, covered in *IAS 36*, differs from U.S. GAAP procedures. Recall that for limited life intangibles, U.S. GAAP requires a two-step impairment test, where the intangible's book value is first compared with the sum of its future expected *undiscounted* cash flows. Only when the book value is greater do we go to the second step and measure the actual impairment loss as the difference between the book value and the future expected *discounted* cash flows. U.S. GAAP also allows an optional qualitative test for indefinite life tangibles. IFRS uses a **one-step test** for **all** intangible assets: book value is compared with the *greater* of the asset's **"value-in-use"** (generally the present value of future expected cash flows) or **net market value**, defined as fair value less selling costs. Using the Primus illustration of U.S. GAAP impairment testing of identifiable intangibles, covered earlier in this chapter, we repeat the relevant information for December 31, 2014, below:

Intangible asset (in millions)	Book value	Total expected future cash inflows, undiscounted	Total expected future cash inflows, discounted
Customer lists	$120	$100	$ 80
Brand names	180	200	125

Assuming there is no active market for the customer lists and brand names, value-in-use is the relevant measure, calculated as discounted future expected cash flows. Following IFRS, Primus reports the following impairment loss for 2014:

Customer lists	$120,000,000 − $80,000,000 = $40,000,000
Brand names	$180,000,000 − $125,000,000 = 55,000,000
Total impairment loss.	$95,000,000

Compare this loss with the $40,000,000 impairment loss reported in U.S. GAAP. Under U.S. GAAP, limited life intangibles must pass the first stage, comparing book value with undiscounted cash flows, before any impairment loss is reported. Brand names do not pass the first stage in our example. IFRS will likely report *greater* impairment losses for the same factual situations than U.S. GAAP.

Intangibles Reported Using the Revaluation Model   Unlike U.S. GAAP, IFRS allows intangibles to be "marked to market" in specific circumstances. The *IAS 38* definition of fair value is **market value**, which limits fair value reporting to intangibles that are traded in an active market. Unique intangibles, such as most patents, trademarks and customer relationships, are not likely to be actively traded. Most intangibles do not have active markets and are reported using the cost model.

Intangibles that have active markets may be reported at fair value. Examples include generic software, taxi licenses and production quotas. Companies report increases in value directly in "revaluation surplus," a component of other comprehensive income, unless they are reversals of previously reported impairment losses. Decreases in value similarly reduce the revaluation surplus, with reductions exceeding previous increases reported in income.

For example, assume generic computer software with an active trading market is acquired in a business combination on January 1, 2013. Valued at $10,000,000 at the acquisition date, the software has a five-year estimated life, no residual value, and is reported using the revaluation model. Straight-line amortization is appropriate. On December 31, 2013, amortization expense of $2,000,000 is reported (= $10,000,000/5). If the software's fair value is now $12,000,000, it is revalued by $4,000,000 (= $12,000,000 − $8,000,000). The entries for 2013 are as follows:

Amortization expense.	2,000,000	
Computer software		2,000,000
To record amortization on the computer software for 2013.		
Computer software.	4,000,000	
Revaluation surplus (OCI)		4,000,000
To revalue the computer software to fair value as of December 31, 2013.		

Amortization expense in subsequent years is based on the revalued amount. If market value declines below carrying value, revaluation surplus is charged. Any value declines in excess of the surplus balance are charged to income. For example, amortization expense for 2014 is $3,000,000 (= $12,000,000/4). If the fair value of the software on December 31, 2014 is $8,000,000, we make the following additional entry:

Revaluation surplus (OCI).	1,000,000	
Computer software		1,000,000
To revalue the computer software to fair value as of December 31, 2014;		
$1,000,000 = ($12,000,000 − 3,000,000) − $8,000,000.		

If instead fair value declined to $3,000,000, we charge $4,000,000 against the revaluation surplus in other comprehensive income and $2,000,000 against income. Any remaining revaluation surplus is reclassified to retained earnings on sale or disposal of the software, and is never included in periodic net income.

Goodwill

IFRS goodwill impairment differs from U.S. GAAP goodwill impairment in two major ways:

- Goodwill is allocated to "cash generating units" (CGUs) rather than reporting units. A **CGU** is the smallest group of assets with independent cash inflows. Reporting units are generally operating segments that are regularly evaluated by top management. For a given firm, CGUs are likely to be smaller in size and greater in number than reporting units.

- Impairment loss is computed in one step, as the CGU's book value less its fair value. If Step 0 is bypassed, or it is more likely than not that the reporting unit's book value exceeds its fair value, U.S. GAAP requires a two-step process. Once it is determined that the reporting unit's book value exceeds its fair value, a second computation determines the amount of goodwill impairment loss, as the difference between the reporting unit's fair value and the fair value of its identifiable net assets.

IFRS allocates goodwill to the business units expected to benefit from the combination, as in U.S. GAAP. However, IFRS defines the appropriate business unit as a CGU, rather than an *ASC Topic 280* "reporting unit." Application of this concept involves much judgment and is specific to a particular company's business environment and organizational structure. However, there are likely to be *more* CGUs than *ASC Topic 280* reporting units.

After allocating the goodwill to CGUs, it is tested for impairment at least annually. Goodwill is impaired if the CGU's book value exceeds its fair value, typically measured as the present value of the CGU's expected future cash flows. Because IFRS assumes that the lower fair value resulted from a decline in goodwill value, the amount of the goodwill impairment loss equals the *difference between the CGU's book value and fair value*. The CGU's other assets are written down only when its goodwill is completely written off.

The differences in goodwill impairment testing between IFRS and U.S. GAAP make it likely that goodwill impairment loss under IFRS is *higher* than under U.S. GAAP, especially with U.S. GAAP's addition of the optional Step 0 qualitative assessment. To illustrate, look again at the Primus illustration. Goodwill was initially allocated on January 1, 2014, to reportable segments, per U.S. GAAP, as follows *(in millions)*:

Broadband unit.	$1,920
Wholesale carrier unit.	1,280
Total goodwill.	$3,200

Assume Primus uses IFRS, and allocates goodwill to the following CGUs *(in millions)*:

Broadband internet	$ 320
Broadband data.	1,600
Wholesale VoIP	960
Wholesale data services.	320
Total goodwill.	$3,200

On December 31, 2014, the following information is available:

(in millions)	Broadband internet	Broadband data	Wholesale VoIP	Wholesale data services
Fair value of unit.	$8,000	$ 9,600	$4,800	$3,840
Book value of unit.	4,800	10,240	5,440	3,520
Fair value of identifiable net assets	7,040	8,640	4,480	3,040

IFRS goodwill impairment loss for 2014 is calculated as follows:

(in millions)	Broadband internet	Broadband data	Wholesale VoIP	Wholesale data services
Fair value of CGU.	$8,000	$ 9,600	$4,800	$3,840
Book value of CGU.	4,800	10,240	5,440	3,520
Impairment.	No	Yes	Yes	No
Impairment loss	—	$ 640	$ 640	—

Total IFRS goodwill impairment loss is $1,280 million (= $640 million + $640 million). Compare this number with the U.S. GAAP impairment loss of $160 million, calculated earlier in this chapter.

BUSINESS APPLICATION   Nokia's Goodwill Impairment: IFRS versus U.S. GAAP

The SEC requires foreign companies listed on U.S. exchanges to file financial and other information using Form 20-F. For years ending after November 15, 2007, companies using official IFRS are not required to include a reconciliation of IFRS information to U.S. GAAP. Thus, the reconciliation does not appear in Nokia Corporation's 2007 or 2008 filing; however, there is an explanation of differences in goodwill impairment in its 2006 filing, as follows:

> **Impairment of goodwill**
>
> Under IFRS, goodwill is allocated to "cash-generating units", which are the smallest group of identifiable assets that include the goodwill under review for impairment and generate cash inflows from continuing use that are largely independent of the cash inflows from other assets. Under IFRS, the Group recorded an impairment of goodwill of EUR 151 million related to Amber Networks in 2003 as the carrying amount of the cash-generating unit exceeded the recoverable amount of the unit.
>
> Under US GAAP, goodwill is allocated to "reporting units", which are operating segments or one level below an operating segment (as defined in FAS 131, Disclosures about Segments of an Enterprise and Related Information). The goodwill impairment test under FAS 142 compares the carrying value for each reporting unit to its fair value based on discounted cash flows.
>
> The US GAAP impairment of goodwill adjustment reflects the cumulative reversal of impairments recorded under IFRS that did not qualify as impairments under US GAAP. Upon completion of the 2003 annual impairment test, the Group determined that the impairment recorded for Amber Networks should be reversed under US GAAP as the fair value of the reporting unit in which Amber Networks resides exceeded the book value of the reporting unit. The annual impairment tests performed subsequent to 2003 continue to support the reversal of this impairment. The Group recorded no goodwill impairments during 2006 and 2005.

In 2003, Nokia reports IFRS goodwill impairment of €151,000,000 for its CGU, Amber Networks, but this CGU is part of a larger reporting unit under U.S. GAAP. Since the reporting unit's fair value exceeds its book value, no goodwill impairment is reported under U.S. GAAP. *Source:* Nokia Corporation Form 20-F, 2006.

APPENDIX TO CHAPTER 4

Consolidation Eliminating Entries When the Parent Uses the Cost Method

Because the parent's investment account is eliminated in consolidation, the method the parent uses to account for the investment on its own books does not affect consolidated balances. In Chapter 4 and subsequently in Chapters 5 and 6, we assume that the parent uses the complete equity method on its own books. However some parent companies use the *cost method*, because it simplifies the accounting on their own books. In this appendix, we explain the consolidation eliminating entries when the parent uses the **cost method** on its own books. We use IBM's acquisition of DataFile Inc., discussed in Chapter 4 pp. 128–134, to illustrate the eliminating entries.

LO6 Explain consolidation when the parent uses the cost method.

Comparing the Cost and Complete Equity Methods

On July 1, 2012, the beginning of the fiscal year for both companies, IBM acquires all of the voting stock of DataFile Inc. for $25,000,000. DataFile's equity at the time is $5,300,000, consisting of $2,500,000 in capital stock and $2,800,000 in retained earnings. An analysis of the resulting revaluations of DataFile's assets and liabilities is repeated on the next page:

Acquisition cost		$25,000,000
Book value of DataFile		(5,300,000)
Cost in excess of DataFile's book value		19,700,000
Differences between fair value and book value:		
Current assets	$ (300,000)	
Plant and equipment, net	10,000,000	
Patents and copyrights	4,000,000	
Brand names	1,000,000	
Lease agreements	600,000	
Customer relationships	3,000,000	
Long-term debt	(2,000,000)	(16,300,000)
Goodwill		$ 3,400,000

Information on revaluation write-offs for fiscal 2013 is as follows:

	Write-Off Policy	Write-Off for Fiscal 2013
Current assets	Revaluation pertains to inventory reported using FIFO	Full amount ($300,000), since beginning inventory is sold in 2013
Plant and equipment	25 years, straight-line	$10,000,000/25 = $400,000
Patents and copyrights	5 years, straight-line	$4,000,000/5 = $800,000
Brand names	Indefinite life	$100,000 impairment loss
Lease agreements	2 years, straight-line	$600,000/2 = $300,000
Customer relationships	3 years, straight-line	$3,000,000/3 = $1,000,000
Long-term debt	4 years, straight-line	$2,000,000/4 = $500,000
Goodwill	Impairment testing	No impairment loss

During fiscal 2013, DataFile reports net income of $3,000,000, and declares and pays dividends of $400,000. If IBM uses the complete equity method, it computes fiscal 2013 equity in net income as follows:

DataFile's reported income for fiscal 2013	$3,000,000
Adjustments for revaluation write-offs of:	
Current assets (cost of goods sold)	300,000
Plant and equipment (depreciation expense)	(400,000)
Patents and copyrights (amortization expense)	(800,000)
Brand names (impairment loss)	(100,000)
Lease agreements (amortization expense)	(300,000)
Customer relationships (amortization expense)	(1,000,000)
Long-term debt (interest expense)	500,000
Equity in income of DataFile	$1,200,000

IBM records the equity in income of DataFile as an increase in its investment account, and the dividends as a decrease in the investment account.

In contrast, if IBM uses the cost method, it records the dividends as income, and the *investment account remains at original cost*. The following summarizes IBM's entries under the cost and complete equity methods, for fiscal 2013:

Books of IBM				
	Complete equity method		**Cost method**	
July 1, 2012				
Investment in DataFile	25,000,000		25,000,000	
Cash		25,000,000		25,000,000
Fiscal 2013				
Investment in DataFile	1,200,000		no entry	
Equity in income of DataFile		1,200,000		
Cash	400,000		400,000	
Investment in DataFile		400,000		—
Dividend income		—		400,000

Consolidation After One Year

The consolidated balances are the same whether IBM uses the complete equity method or the cost method to record its investment on its own books. However, if IBM uses the cost method, the consolidation eliminating entries illustrated on pp. 130-131 must be adjusted, because IBM's accounts are slightly different: IBM does not report equity in income of DataFile, reports dividend income, and maintains its investment account at original cost, $25,000,000. Under the complete equity method, IBM's fiscal 2013 year-end investment balance is $25,800,000.

    Consolidation eliminating entries for fiscal 2013, one year after the acquisition, are the same under the cost method as under the complete equity method, except for eliminating entry C.

Consolidation eliminating entry C				
	Complete equity method		**Cost method**	
(C) Equity in income of DataFile	1,200,000		—	
Dividend income		—	400,000	
Dividends		400,000		400,000
Investment in DataFile		800,000		—

Eliminating entries E, R, and O are identical to those illustrated in Chapter 4, pp. 130–131. Note that when IBM uses the cost method, entry C eliminates the current year's dividend income recorded on IBM's books against DataFile's dividends account. Entries E and R are the same under both methods, because after elimination C, the investment account is at its beginning-of-year balance, acquisition cost.

Consolidation After Two Years

In fiscal 2014, DataFile reports net income of $3,500,000 and declares and pays dividends of $200,000. There are no changes in depreciation and amortization policy for DataFile's plant and equipment and limited life intangibles. Year-end impairment testing in fiscal 2014 reveals no impairment loss for brand names, whereas goodwill is impaired by $700,000. Following the complete equity method, IBM calculates fiscal 2014 equity in income of DataFile as follows:

DataFile's reported income for fiscal 2014	$3,500,000
Adjustments for revaluation write-offs:	
Plant and equipment (depreciation expense)	(400,000)
Patents and copyrights (amortization expense)	(800,000)
Lease agreements (amortization expense)	(300,000)
Customer relationships (amortization expense)	(1,000,000)
Long-term debt (interest expense)	500,000
Goodwill (impairment loss)	(700,000)
Equity in income of DataFile	$ 800,000

The following summarizes IBM's fiscal 2014 entries under the cost and complete equity methods:

Books of IBM				
	Complete equity method		**Cost method**	
Investment in DataFile	800,000		no entry	
Equity in income of DataFile		800,000		
Cash	200,000		200,000	
Investment in DataFile		200,000		—
Dividend income		—		200,000

Under the complete equity method, IBM's investment account balance is $26,400,000. But the cost method maintains the investment balance at acquisition cost, $25,000,000. As done in the first year following acquisition, in eliminating entry C we eliminate IBM's dividend income account against DataFile's dividends account. To proceed with eliminating entries E and R, though, we must also adjust the investment account to its beginning-of-year balance under the complete equity method. Using the complete equity method, the investment account increases by the excess of last year's equity in income of DataFile over dividends received, or $1,200,000 − $400,000 = $800,000. IBM would have recorded $1,200,000 as income and included it in its beginning retained earnings balance. In contrast, using the cost method IBM recorded $400,000 in dividend income and included it in its beginning retained earnings balance. Eliminating entry A below adds $800,000 to IBM's investment account and its beginning retained earnings account. This entry converts IBM's investment and retained earnings accounts to the same beginning-of-year balances resulting under the complete equity method.

To summarize, IBM must make the following eliminating entries when using the cost method:

Eliminating entries at June 30, 2014		
(A) Investment in DataFile.	800,000	
Retained earnings, July 1		800,000
To adjust the investment account and IBM's beginning retained earnings to		
their beginning- of-year amounts under the complete equity method.		
(C) Dividend income.	200,000	
Dividends.		200,000
To eliminate DataFile's current year dividends.		

Eliminating entries A and C convert IBM's accounts to the same beginning balances resulting when IBM uses the complete equity method, and we can proceed with remaining eliminations E, R, and O.

The June 30, 2014, consolidation working paper showing IBM using the cost method appears below. Compare this working paper to Exhibit 4.5 on page 134, which shows the working paper when IBM uses the complete equity method. Note that the consolidated balances are identical, and that elimination A adjusts IBM's beginning retained earnings to the complete equity method amount shown in Exhibit 4.5. Elimination C does not change the investment account balance, and eliminations E, R, and O are identical to those required if IBM uses the complete equity method.

| | Accounts Taken From Books Dr (Cr) | | Eliminations | | Consolidated Balances |
	IBM	DataFile	Dr	Cr	Dr (Cr)
Current assets	$ 17,000,000	$ 3,200,000			$ 20,200,000
Plant and equipment, net.	160,000,000	62,000,000	(R) $ 9,600,000	$ 400,000 (O-1)	231,200,000
Patents and copyrights	2,400,000	600,000	(R) 3,200,000	800,000 (O-2)	5,400,000
Investment in DataFile	25,000,000	—	(A) 800,000	7,900,000 (E)	—
				17,900,000 (R)	
Brand names	—	—	(R) 900,000		900,000
Lease agreements	—	—	(R) 300,000	300,000 (O-2)	
Customer relationships	—	—	(R) 2,000,000	1,000,000 (O-2)	1,000,000
Goodwill	—	—	(R) 3,400,000	700,000 (O-4)	2,700,000
Current liabilities.	(18,000,000)	(10,000,000)			(28,000,000)
Long-term debt	(95,000,000)	(44,600,000)	(O-3) 500,000	1,500,000 (R)	(140,600,000)
Common stock, par	(2,000,000)	(500,000)	(E) 500,000		(2,000,000)
Additional paid-in capital	(60,000,000)	(2,000,000)	(E) 2,000,000		(60,000,000)
Retained earnings, July 1	(20,400,000)	(5,400,000)	(E) 5,400,000	800,000 (A)	(21,200,000)
Dividends	1,200,000	200,000		200,000 (C)	1,200,000
Sales revenue.	(550,000,000)	(110,000,000)			(660,000,000)
Dividend income.	(200,000)	—	(C) 200,000		—
Cost of goods sold.	450,000,000	68,000,000			518,000,000
Operating expenses	90,000,000	38,500,000	(O-1) 400,000	500,000 (O-3)	
			(O-2) 2,100,000		
			(O-4) 700,000		131,200,000
Totals	$ 0	$ 0	$32,000,000	$32,000,000	$ 0

In general, eliminating entry A converts the parent's cost method investment and retained earnings to their complete equity method beginning-of-year balances. The amount of the adjustment is the cumulative excess of (1) equity in net income over (2) dividends received from the date of acquisition to the beginning of the current year, computed as follows:

Change in the subsidiary's retained earnings from the date of acquisition
to the beginning of the current year (cumulative income less dividends)

+/− cumulative write-offs of revaluations from the date of acquisition
to the beginning of the current year
_____
Amount of adjustment (A)

To further illustrate eliminating entry A, assume it is now June 30, 2015, three years since acquisition. Recall that DataFile's retained earnings balance at the date of acquisition was $2,800,000. As of June 30, 2014, DataFile's retained earnings is $8,700,000 (= $2,800,000 + $3,000,000 − $400,000 + $3,500,000 − $200,000). Calculation of the adjustment amount in eliminating entry A is as follows:

Change in retained earnings, July 1, 2012 to June 30, 2014 ($8,700,000 − $2,800,000)	$5,900,000
Adjustments for revaluation write-offs for fiscal years 2013 and 2014:	
Plus FIFO inventory write-off to cost of goods sold.	300,000
Less plant and equipment depreciation ($400,000 × 2)	(800,000)
Less patents and copyrights amortization ($800,000 × 2).	(1,600,000)
Less brand names impairment loss($100,000 + $0)	(100,000)
Less lease agreement amortization ($300,000 × 2).	(600,000)
Less customer relationships amortization ($1,000,000 × 2)	(2,000,000)
Plus interest expense ($500,000 × 2).	1,000,000
Less goodwill impairment ($0 + $700,000)	(700,000)
Amount of eliminating adjustment A for fiscal 2015.	$1,400,000

Eliminating entry A appears on the June 30, 2015 consolidation working paper, as follows:

Eliminating entry A at June 30, 2015		
(A) Investment in DataFile.	1,400,000	
Retained earnings, July 1		1,400,000
To adjust the investment account and IBM's beginning retained earnings to their beginning-of-year amounts under the complete equity method.		

In summary, if the parent uses the cost method to account for the investment in a subsidiary on its own books, the most straightforward approach is to adjust the parent's accounts to the complete equity method as of the beginning of the year, and eliminate the subsidiary's current year dividends against the parent's dividend income in elimination C. The remaining eliminating entries are the same as if the parent used the complete equity method.

Reporting Perspective

The cost method may initially appear easier, as the parent only records dividends received from the subsidiary. As the discussion in this appendix shows, however, the need to calculate equity method income cannot be avoided. If the parent does not record equity method income on its own books, it must be incorporated, on a cumulative basis, into the consolidation eliminating entries, to arrive at the correct beginning balance for consolidated retained earnings.

REVIEW OF KEY CONCEPTS

LO 1 **Explain the general process of periodic consolidation. (p. 113)** When a business combination is recorded as a stock acquisition, it is carried on the parent's books as an intercorporate investment. If consolidation is appropriate, the accounts of the parent and subsidiary must be consolidated **whenever financial statements are presented**. At any point in time subsequent to acquisition, a working paper is used to consolidate the assets, liabilities, equity, revenue and expense accounts of the parent and subsidiary. The consolidation process requires **four eliminating entries**, represented by the acronym **CERO**, as follows: (**C**) elimination of the parent's Current year equity method income and the subsidiary's intercompany dividends, restoring the investment account to its beginning-of-year balance; (**E**) elimination of the subsidiary's beginning-of-year stockholders' Equity accounts against the investment account; (**R**) recognition of the beginning-of-year Revaluation balances for the subsidiary's assets and liabilities and elimination of the remaining investment balance, and (**O**) writing Off the revaluations for the current year.

LO 2 **Describe the relation between equity method and consolidated balances. (p. 118)** The method the parent uses to account for its investment in the subsidiary does not affect the consolidated statements, but does affect consolidation procedures. This text stresses the **complete equity method**, which reflects all consolidation adjustments and the parent's share of the subsidiary's net income and dividends, because use of this method simplifies the consolidation process. If the parent uses a different method, the consolidation process adjusts the parent's account balances to the complete equity method before proceeding.

LO 3 **Report subsequent year write-offs of acquisition date revaluations of subsidiary identifiable assets and liabilities. (p. 118)** Revaluations change in reported value as time passes. Revaluations of a subsidiary's previously reported net assets are accounted for in the same way as the underlying asset or liability. Previously unreported **identifiable intangibles** with **limited lives** are amortized over their useful lives, whereas those with **indefinite lives** are not amortized. Both types are periodically tested for impairment, following *FASB ASC Section 350-30-35*.

LO 4 **Measure and report goodwill impairment losses. (p. 121)** Goodwill is assigned to reporting units and is subject to **impairment testing** using the unique process described in *FASB ASC Section 350-20-35*. Goodwill impairment losses appear in the operating section of the consolidated income statement.

LO 5 **Discuss IFRS for intangibles reporting and impairment testing. (p. 136)** IFRS for intangibles reporting and impairment testing differs from U.S. GAAP. In limited circumstances, identifiable intangibles are reported at fair value and marked to market using a revaluation surplus account, reported in equity as a component of other comprehensive income. Impairment for identifiable intangibles is computed as the difference between reported carrying value and discounted future expected cash flows. Goodwill is allocated to cash generating units, and impairment is computed as the difference between the fair value of the unit and its book value.

Explain consolidation when the parent uses the cost method (p. 139, appendix) If the parent uses the cost   LO 6
method to account for the investment in a subsidiary, the consolidation eliminating entries differ; the consolidated
balances are not changed.

MULTIPLE CHOICE QUESTIONS ·······································

Use the following information to answer questions 1 – 4 below:

On January 1, 2011, Portland Company acquired all of Salem Company's voting stock for $16,000,000
in cash. Some of Salem's assets and liabilities at the date of purchase had fair values that differed from
reported values, as follows:

	Book value	Fair value
Buildings and equipment, net (20 years, straight-line)...............	$ 11,000,000	$ 3,000,000
Identifiable intangibles (5 years, straight-line)	0	10,000,000

Salem's total stockholders' equity at January 1, 2011, was $4,000,000. It is now December 31, 2014 (four
years later). Salem's retained earnings reflect the accumulation of income less dividends; there have been
no other changes in its retained earnings. Cumulative goodwill impairment to the beginning of 2014 is
$2,000,000. Goodwill impairment for 2014 is $500,000. Portland uses the complete equity method to account for its investment. The December 31, 2014, trial balance for Salem appears below.

	Salem Dr (Cr)
Current assets	$ 2,500,000
Plant assets, net...	28,000,000
Liabilities...	(10,000,000)
Capital stock	(2,000,000)
Retained earnings, January 1...	(16,000,000)
Sales revenue...	(14,000,000)
Cost of goods sold...	8,000,000
Operating expenses..	3,500,000
	-0-

1. On the 2014 consolidation working paper, eliminating entry R reduces Investment in Salem by   LO 1

    a. $3,100,000
    b. $5,200,000
    c. $6,400,000
    d. $8,000,000

2. On the 2014 consolidation working paper, eliminating entry O increases consolidated operating expenses by   LO 1

    a. $1,600,000
    b. $2,100,000
    c. $2,900,000
    d. $3,200,000

3. What is 2014 equity in net income of Salem, reported on Portland's books using the complete equity method?   LO 2

    a. $ 400,000
    b. $ 900,000
    c. $1,200,000
    d. $2,500,000

LO 2 **4.** On Portland's December 31, 2014 trial balance, what is the balance in its Investment in Salem account at December 31, 2014, using the complete equity method?

    a. $22,800,000
    b. $23,200,000
    c. $23,600,000
    d. $27,600,000

Use the following information to answer questions 5 – 8 below:

A company reports the following intangibles at December 31, 2013, ***prior to*** impairment testing:

	Book value
Customer lists	$1,500,000
Brand names	5,200,000
Goodwill	8,000,000

The customer lists have a limited life, and amortization expense has already been properly recorded, whereas the brand names have indefinite lives. The goodwill is allocated to Divisions 1 and 2 for both U.S. GAAP and IFRS.

Assume the company bypasses the Step 0 qualitative assessment. On December 31, 2013, the following information is available:

	Division 1	Division 2
Book value of goodwill	$ 1,600,000	$ 6,400,000
Fair value of division	14,000,000	20,000,000
Book value of division	16,000,000	24,000,000
Fair value of identifiable net assets of division	13,000,000	12,000,000

Intangible asset	Total expected future cash inflows, undiscounted	Total expected future cash inflows, discounted
Customer lists	$1,600,000	$1,200,000
Brand names	4,000,000	3,400,000

LO 3 **5.** Impairment loss for 2013 for the customer lists and brand names, following U.S. GAAP, is

    a. $ 0
    b. $ 300,000
    c. $1,800,000
    d. $2,100,000

LO 4 **6.** Goodwill impairment loss for 2013, following U.S. GAAP, is

    a. $6,000,000
    b. $5,600,000
    c. $2,200,000
    d. $ 600,000

LO 5 **7.** Goodwill impairment loss for 2013, following IFRS, is

    a. $ 600,000
    b. $2,200,000
    c. $5,600,000
    d. $6,000,000

8. Impairment loss for 2013 for the customer lists and brand names, following IFRS, is   LO 5

    a. $ 0
    b. $ 300,000
    c. $1,800,000
    d. $2,100,000

9. Which statement is ***true*** regarding the U.S. GAAP impairment test for limited life intangibles?   LO 4

    a. If the intangible passes step 1, there is always an impairment loss in step 2.
    b. If the fair value of the intangible is less than its book value, there is always an impairment loss.
    c. U.S. GAAP impairment is likely to be greater than IFRS impairment.
    d. The impairment test for limited life intangibles is the same as the impairment test for indefinite life intangibles.

10. A parent uses the cost method to report its investment in a wholly-owned subsidiary, acquired on January 1, 2013. If it had used the complete equity method, the parent would have reported 2013 equity in net income of $500,000 and 2014 equity in net income of $550,000. The subsidiary's 2013 and 2014 dividends were $100,000 and $120,000, respectively. On the 2014 consolidation working paper, an adjusting entry is necessary to increase the investment and the parent's beginning retained earnings balance by   LO 6 (APPENDIX)

    a. $ 400,000
    b. $ 500,000
    c. $ 830,000
    d. $1,050,000

**Assignments with the ✓ in the margin are available in an online homework system.
See the Preface of the book for details.**

EXERCISES ••

E4.1 Equity Method Accounting   George Corporation acquired all of the stock of Johnson Corporation on January 2, 2013. The book value of the net assets of Johnson on that date was $300,000,000 and the fair values of Johnson's identifiable net assets equaled the book values, except for plant assets undervalued by $50,000,000. The fair market value of the shares issued by George Corporation was $500,000,000. Revalued plant assets are to be straight-line depreciated over 25 years. For the year ended December 31, 2013, Johnson reported net income of $85,000,000 and paid dividends of $30,000,000.   LO 1, 3

Required

Prepare journal entries to record George's acquisition of Johnson and subsequent entries to the investment account for 2013, using the complete equity method. Assume goodwill impairment for 2013 is $20,000,000.

E4.2 Equity Method Income and Working Paper Eliminations   Pace acquired Saber on January 1, 2013, attributing its $200 million excess of acquisition cost over book value to plant assets (10-year life), $160 million and to goodwill, $40 million. At that time Saber's stockholders' equity was $2,000 million. It is now December 31, 2014, and consolidation entries are prepared. The investment account balance on January 1, 2014 was $2,286 million. Saber reported net income of $130 million and paid dividends of $40 million in 2014. Saber paid dividends of $60 million in 2013. Goodwill is not impaired in either year.   LO 1, 3

Required
    a. What was Saber's 2013 reported net income?
    b. What was Saber's stockholders' equity on January 1, 2014?
    c. Calculate Pace's equity income accrual for 2014, using the complete equity method.
    d. Prepare the eliminating entries needed to consolidate Pace and Saber at December 31, 2014.
    e. Assume it is now December 31, 2025. Total goodwill impairment as of January 1, 2025 is $30 million, and there is no impairment for 2025. Saber still owns the plant assets. Prepare consolidation eliminating entries (R) and (O) for 2025.

✓ LO 1, 3 **E4.3** **Consolidation at End of First Year** Peak Entertainment acquires its 100-percent-owned subsidiary Saddlestone Inc. on January 1, 2013. In preparing to consolidate Peak and Saddlestone at December 31, 2013, you assemble the following information:

> Value of stock given up to acquire Saddlestone: $10,000,000.
> Direct merger costs: $250,000.
> Saddlestone's stockholders' equity at acquisition: $7,200,000.
> Fair value of earnings contingency agreement to be paid in cash: $300,000.
> Fair value of previously unrecorded identifiable intangibles (5-year life): $2,000,000
> Goodwill and identifiable intangibles are not impaired in 2013.
> Saddlestone's net income in 2013: $3,000,000.
> Saddlestone's dividends paid in 2013: $1,000,000.

Required

a. Prepare the 2013 journal entries made by Peak to record the acquisition and calculate and record the equity method income accrual, using the complete equity method.
b. Prepare the consolidation eliminating entries made at December 31, 2013.

LO 1, 3 **E4.4** **Eliminating Entries after First and Second Years** During 2014, Peerless Company's wholly-owned subsidiary, Safeco Inc. reported net income of $1,600,000 and declared and paid dividends of $600,000. Peerless acquired Safeco on January 2, 2014, at a cash cost of $8,000,000, which was $1,000,000 in excess of the book value of net assets acquired. Safeco's equipment (five-year life) was undervalued by $500,000. Its inventory, reported using FIFO, was undervalued by $200,000. The remaining $300,000 could not be allocated to identifiable assets and liabilities. Impairment testing indicates that goodwill was impaired by $50,000 during 2014.

Required

a. Prepare the journal entries recorded by Peerless in 2014 to record the acquisition and apply the complete equity method. Prepare the necessary eliminating entries to consolidate the financial statements of Peerless and Safeco at December 31, 2014.
b. Safeco reported net income of $2,000,000 and paid dividends of $800,000 in 2015. There was no further goodwill impairment. Prepare the journal entries recorded by Peerless in 2015 to apply the complete equity method. Prepare the necessary eliminating entries to consolidate the financial statements of Peerless and Safeco at December 31, 2015.

LO 1, 3 **E4.5** **Equity Method, Eliminating Entries, Several Years after Acquisition** Data for Paris Corporation and its wholly-owned subsidiary, Oslo Corporation, are given below. Paris acquired Oslo on January 1, 2006. Paris uses the complete equity method to report its investment in Oslo, and its accounting year ends December 31.

Acquisition cost	$6,000,000
Oslo's stockholders' equity, January 1, 2006	2,500,000
Oslo's total reported income, 2006-2013	4,000,000
Oslo's total dividends paid, 2006-2013	1,200,000
Oslo's reported income, 2014	450,000
Dividends paid by Oslo, 2014	100,000
Allocation of excess of cost over book value to identifiable net assets, at acquisition date:	
Land	450,000
Buildings (20 year life, straight-line)	(400,000)
Identifiable intangibles (5 year life)	1,000,000
Long-term debt discount (10 years to maturity as of January 1, 2006)	250,000
Goodwill impairment loss, 2006-2013	300,000
Goodwill impairment loss, 2014	60,000

Required

a. Calculate the goodwill purchased in this acquisition.
b. Calculate the Equity in net income for 2014, reported on Paris's books, using the complete equity method.
c. Calculate the balance in the Investment in Oslo at December 31, 2014, reported on Paris's books.
d. Prepare the eliminating entries necessary to consolidate the financial statements of Paris and Oslo for 2014.

E4.6 Consolidation after Several Years Seven years ago, on December 31, 2006, Adams Corporation acquired all of the stock of Baker Company. The fair value of Adams' shares used in the exchange was $7,500,000. At the time of acquisition, the book value of Baker's stockholders' equity was $5,000,000, and the fair value of Baker's building (25-year life) exceeded its book value by $1,000,000. From the date of acquisition to December 31, 2012, Baker had cumulative net income of $1,300,000 and paid total dividends of $400,000. For 2013, Baker reported net income of $300,000 and paid cash dividends of $100,000. Adams uses the complete equity method to account for its investment in Baker. There is no goodwill impairment loss for the period 2007 through 2012, but there is impairment loss of $100,000 in 2013.

LO 1, 3

Required

Prepare the working paper eliminating entries necessary to consolidate the financial statements of Adams and Baker at December 31, 2013.

E4.7 Goodwill Impairment Losses CBS Corporation and Warner Bros., a subsidiary of Time Warner, Inc., each contributed assets for a 50 percent interest in a new national broadcasting network, The CW, in 2006. In September 2006, Warner Bros. shut down The WB Network and Time Warner recorded a $200 million goodwill impairment charge related to goodwill allocated to The WB Network. Although Time Warner's evaluation of goodwill occurred in 2006, use current GAAP for goodwill impairment to answer the questions below. Use the information above, as well as the information on Time Warner provided in Chapter 4.

LO 4

CBS CORPORATION
[CBS]

WARNER BROS.
TIME WARNER, INC.
[TWX]

Required

a. Why is goodwill assigned to business units? Was goodwill assigned to The WB Network as a business unit? Explain.
b. In general, how are goodwill impairment losses calculated? Why do you think Time Warner recorded the 2006 goodwill impairment loss of $200 million?
c. How does Time Warner account for its 50 percent investment in The CW in its consolidated financial statements?

E4.8 Projecting Consolidation Entries In the first consolidation following an acquisition that occurred at the beginning of the current year, you observe the following consolidation eliminating entries:

LO 1, 3

(R)	Inventory...	40,000	
	Land...	80,000	
	Equipment, net.....................................	30,000	
	Investment in Samson Company		150,000
(O)	Cost of goods sold..................................	40,000	
	Depreciation expense................................	6,000	
	Inventory		40,000
	Equipment, net		6,000

Required

For the above components of the consolidation process, what consolidation eliminating entries do you expect:

a. At the end of the third year, assuming that Samson had not sold any of its land or equipment?
b. At the end of the seventh year, assuming that Samson had not sold any of its land or equipment?
c. At the end of the seventh year, assuming that Samson sold its land two years earlier?

E4.9 Identifiable Intangibles and Goodwill, U.S. GAAP International Foods, a U.S. company, acquired two companies in 2013. As a result, its consolidated financial statements include the following acquired intangibles:

LO 3, 4 ✅

Intangible	Date of Acquisition	Fair Value at Date of Acquisition	Useful Life
Customer relationships	January 1, 2013	$ 4,000,000	4 years
Favorable leaseholds	June 30, 2013	8,000,000	5 years
Brand names	June 30, 2013	18,000,000	Indefinite
Goodwill.......................	January 1, 2013	500,000,000	Indefinite

Goodwill was assigned to the following reporting units:

Asia.	$100,000,000
South America	150,000,000
Europe	250,000,000
Total	$500,000,000

It is now December 31, 2014, the end of International Foods' accounting year. No impairment losses were reported on any intangibles in 2013. Assume that International Foods bypasses the qualitative option for impairment testing of goodwill and indefinite life intangibles.

Intangible	Sum of Future Expected Undiscounted Cash Flows	Sum of Future Expected Discounted Cash Flows
Customer relationships	$ 1,200,000	$ 900,000
Favorable leaseholds	6,000,000	4,400,000
Brand names	14,000,000	7,000,000

Reporting Unit	Unit Carrying Value	Unit Fair Value	Fair Value of Identifiable Net Assets
Asia.	$300,000,000	$400,000,000	$375,000,000
South America	200,000,000	350,000,000	280,000,000
Europe	600,000,000	500,000,000	385,000,000

Required

Compute 2014 amortization expense and impairment losses on the above intangibles, following U.S. GAAP.

✓ LO 5   **E4.10 Identifiable Intangibles and Goodwill, IFRS**   Assume the same information as in E4.9, except that International Foods reports using IFRS and allocated its goodwill to the following cash generating units (CGUs):

E. Asia	$ 40,000,000
Indonesia	60,000,000
Brazil.	150,000,000
Mediterranean	150,000,000
Scandinavia	100,000,000
Total	$500,000,000

The following information is available at December 31, 2014:

CGU	Unit Carrying Value	Unit Fair Value	Fair Value of Identifiable Net Assets
E. Asia	$200,000,000	$150,000,000	$300,000,000
Indonesia	100,000,000	120,000,000	75,000,000
Brazil.	130,000,000	140,000,000	100,000,000
Mediterranean	220,000,000	190,000,000	150,000,000
Scandinavia	300,000,000	230,000,000	200,000,000

Required

Compute 2014 amortization expense and impairment losses on the above intangibles, following IFRS.

LO 2, 3   **E4.11 Consolidated Income Statement**   When Parson Company acquired all of Soaper Company's stock on July 1, 2013, Soaper's inventory was undervalued by $160,000,000, plant assets with a ten-year life were overvalued by $200,000,000, and long-term debt which matures in five years was overvalued by $100,000,000. No goodwill arose in the combination. All of Soaper's depreciation and amortization charges are based on the straight-line method. The undervalued inventory was sold during the year ended June 30, 2014. The separate income statements of Parson and Soaper for the year ended June 30, 2014, are given below *(amounts in millions)*.

	Parson	Soaper
Sales.	$5,000	$2,000
Equity in net income of Soaper	140	—
Total revenue	5,140	2,000
Cost of goods sold.	3,000	800
Depreciation expense.	500	140
Interest expense.	100	60
Other expenses	600	700
Total expenses.	4,200	1,700
Net income.	$ 940	$ 300

Required
a. Prepare a consolidated income statement for Parson and Soaper for the year ended June 30, 2014.
b. Why is consolidated income the same as Parson's separately reported net income?

E4.12 Amortization and Impairment Testing of Identifiable Intangible Assets During the year ended July 31, 2007, **Cisco Systems, Inc.** acquired the following identifiable intangible assets through its purchase of two companies:

LO 3

CISCO SYSTEMS, INC.
[CSCO]

ARROYO VIDEO SOLUTIONS, INC.
WEBEX COMMU-NICATIONS, INC

	Technology		Customer Relationships	
Acquired Company (in thousands)	Useful life (in years)	Amount	Useful life (in years)	Amount
Arroyo Video Solutions, Inc.	5.0	$ 15,000	7.0	$ 14,000
WebEx Communications, Inc.	4.0	312,000	6.0	153,000

Cisco acquired Arroyo Video Solutions, Inc. on October 31, 2006, and WebEx Communications, Inc. on June 30, 2007. Assume that Cisco separately tests identifiable intangibles acquired from each company for impairment, and collects the following information to conduct impairment tests at the end of fiscal 2007:

	Technology		Customer Relationships	
Acquired Company (in thousands)	Sum of expected undiscounted cash flows	Sum of expected discounted cash flows	Sum of expected undiscounted cash flows	Sum of expected discounted cash flows
Arroyo Video Solutions, Inc.	$ 14,000	$ 10,000	$ 16,000	$ 12,000
WebEx Communications, Inc.	300,000	250,000	140,000	100,000

Required
a. Calculate amortization expense for the above identifiable intangibles for fiscal 2007. Intangibles are amortized on a straight-line basis starting in the month following acquisition.
b. Calculate impairment loss for fiscal 2007.
c. Determine the amounts reported on Cisco's July 31, 2007, balance sheet for technology and customer relationships.

E4.13 Consolidation Using Cost Method Assume the same information as in E4.6, except Adams uses the cost method to account for its investment in Baker.

LO 6
(APPENDIX)

Required

Prepare the working paper eliminating entries necessary to consolidate the financial statements of Adams and Baker at December 31, 2013.

PROLEMS ···

LO 1, 3 **P4.1** **Condensed Consolidated Financial Statements One Year after Acquisition**   Ponon Corporation acquired all of the stock of Santo Corporation on January 2, 2014, for $25,000,000 cash and debt. The book value of Santo's stockholders' equity was $10,000,000 and the resulting $15,000,000 excess of acquisition cost over book value was allocated as follows:

Account	Dr (Cr)	Amortization Period
Inventory.	$2,000,000	(1)
Plant assets, net.	8,000,000	8 years
Patents (previously unrecorded).	1,500,000	4 years
Long-term debt	(1,000,000)	10 years
Goodwill	4,500,000	(2)

(1) Santo uses the FIFO method of inventory valuation. Its inventory purchases in 2014 were $6,200,000.
(2) Goodwill is impaired by $400,000 during 2014.

Below are the condensed financial statements of Ponon and Santo at December 31, 2014. Neither company declared dividends in 2014. Ponon uses the complete equity method to report its investment in Santo on its own books.

Condensed Balance Sheets		
December 31, 2014	**Ponon**	**Santo**
Assets		
Cash and receivables.	$ 4,500,000	$ 3,100,000
Inventory.	5,000,000	5,200,000
Plant assets, net.	8,000,000	12,000,000
Investment in Santo	26,325,000	—
Total assets	$43,825,000	$20,300,000
Liabilities and Stockholders' Equity		
Current liabilities.	$ 5,100,000	$ 2,000,000
Long-term debt	20,000,000	3,300,000
Capital stock	8,000,000	6,000,000
Retained earnings	10,725,000	9,000,000
Total liabilities and stockholders' equity	$43,825,000	$20,300,000

Condensed Income Statements		
For Year Ended December 31, 2014	**Ponon**	**Santo**
Sales.	$30,000,000	$13,200,000
Equity in income of Santo	1,325,000	—
Total revenues	31,325,000	13,200,000
Cost of goods sold.	18,000,000	4,000,000
Depreciation and amortization expense.	2,000,000	3,200,000
Interest and other expenses.	5,400,000	1,000,000
Total expenses.	25,400,000	8,200,000
Net Income.	$ 5,925,000	$ 5,000,000

Required
a. Prepare a schedule to compute the 2014 equity method income accrual.
b. Use a working paper to consolidate the trial balances of Ponon and Santo at December 31, 2014.
c. Prepare the consolidated balance sheet and statement of income and retained earnings at December 31, 2014.

P4.2   Equity Method and Eliminating Entries Three Years after Acquisition   Puffin Industries ac-   LO 1, 2, 3
quired all of Sunset Coast Digital's stock on December 31, 2011, for $3,500,000, $2,100,000 in excess of book value. At that time, Sunset Coast's inventory (LIFO) was overvalued by $500,000 and its plant assets (10-year life) were overvalued by $1,000,000. The remaining excess of cost over book value is attributed to undervalued identifiable intangible assets being amortized over 20 years. Sunset Coast depreciates plant assets and amortizes intangibles by the straight-line method. During the next three years Sunset Coast reported total income of $850,000 and paid out 50 percent in dividends. Puffin carries its investment in Sunset Coast using the complete equity method. Sunset Coast's inventory increased each year since it was acquired by Puffin, and Sunset Coast's reported net income for 2014 was $200,000.

Required
a. Compute Puffin's 2014 equity method income accrual.
b. Compute the balance in the Investment in Sunset Coast account at December 31, 2014, after all equity method entries have been booked.
c. Prepare the working paper eliminating entries needed in consolidation at December 31, 2014.
d. If Puffin reports $600,000 income from its own operations in 2014, what is consolidated net income for 2014?

P4.3   Consolidation at End of First Year, Preacquisition Contingency   On January 2, 2013, Perkins   LO 1, 3
Company acquired all of Sanders Corporation's stock for $4,000,000 cash, when the book value of Sanders' stockholders' equity was $2,200,000. Sanders reported $500,000 of net income and paid dividends of $150,000 in 2013. Data related to the acquisition at January 2, 2013, appear below

Out-of-pocket merger costs paid in cash by Perkins	$ 50,000
Excess of fair value of Sanders' inventory over book value.	80,000
Excess of fair value of Sanders' equipment over book value (10-year life, straight-line). . . .	200,000
Fair value of Sanders' previously unrecorded lawsuit liability	70,000
Fair value of Sanders' previously unrecorded in-process research and development	300,000
Acquisition-related restructuring costs paid in cash by Perkins	100,000

Sanders' cost of goods sold for 2013 includes 60 percent of the undervalued inventory. The fair value of the previously unrecorded lawsuit liability increased to $85,000 by December 31, 2013, within the measurement period. Impairment tests of in-process R&D and goodwill showed no decline in value during 2013.

Required
a. Prepare a schedule to compute Perkins' equity method income accrual for 2013 using the complete equity method, and prepare all entries related to the investment made by Perkins during 2013.
b. Prepare the eliminating entries made in consolidation at December 31, 2013.

P4.4   Consolidated Balance Sheet Working Paper, Bargain Purchase (see related P3.4)   On De-   LO 1, 3
cember 31, 2012, Paxon Corporation acquired all of the outstanding common stock of Saxon Company for $1.8 billion cash. Paxon uses the complete equity method to report its investment. The trial balances of Paxon and Saxon at December 31, 2013, are shown below:

(in millions)	Dr (Cr)	
	Paxon	**Saxon**
Cash and receivables.	$ 3,100	$ 800
Inventory.	2,260	940
Marketable securities	—	—
Investment in Saxon.	2,158	—
Land	650	300
Buildings and equipment, net	3,600	1,150
Current liabilities.	(2,020)	(1,200)
Long-term debt	(5,000)	(450)
Common stock, par value	(500)	(100)
Additional paid-in capital	(1,200)	(350)
Retained earnings, January 1.	(2,610)	(845)
Dividends	500	100
Sales revenue.	(30,000)	(10,000)
Equity in net income of Saxon	(258)	—
Gain on sale of securities	—	(10)
Cost of goods sold.	26,000	8,000
Depreciation expense.	300	40
Interest expense.	250	25
Other operating expenses	2,770	1,600
Totals	$ 0	$ 0

Several of Saxon's assets and liabilities had fair values different from their book values at the acquisition date, as follows:

(in millions)	Fair Value – Book Value
Inventory (FIFO)	$100
Marketable securities (sold in 2013).	(50)
Land	245
Buildings and equipment, net (20 years, straight-line).	300
Long-term debt (overvalued) (5 years, straight-line)	(110)

Required

a. Prepare a schedule to compute equity in net income of Saxon for 2013, and the December 31, 2013, balance for the Investment in Saxon, as reported on Paxon's books.
b. Use a working paper to consolidate the trial balances of Paxon and Saxon at December 31, 2013.
c. Prepare the consolidated balance sheet and statement of income and retained earnings at December 31, 2013.

LO 4 **P4.5** **Goodwill Allocation and Impairment** Porter Corporation acquired Stewart Corporation on January 1, 2014, at a cost of $75 million. Stewart consisted of three identifiable reporting units, designated X, Y, and Z. Relevant data for the acquisition are as follows:

	Total	Unit X	Unit Y	Unit Z
Identifiable assets.	$60,000,000	$32,000,000	$20,000,000	$8,000,000
Liabilities.	25,000,000	18,000,000	6,000,000	1,000,000
Fair value of reporting unit		50,000,000	30,000,000	15,000,000

In addition, existing reporting unit J is expected to benefit from the acquisition, such that its fair value increases by $20,000,000. Unit J has a carrying value of $70,000,000.

Assume qualitative assessment at December 31, 2014, indicates it is more likely than not that book value exceeds fair value for all reporting units, and Porter proceeds with the quantitative test of goodwill impairment. On December 31, 2014, the following amounts were estimated for the four reporting units:

	Unit X	Unit Y	Unit Z	Unit J
Fair value of reporting unit	$30,000,000	$15,000,000	$12,000,000	$75,000,000
Fair value of identifiable net assets . . .	23,000,000	6,000,000	4,000,000	58,000,000
Book value	34,000,000	20,000,000	10,000,000	72,000,000

Required

a. Calculate the total goodwill and its allocation to business units at January 1, 2014.

b. Calculate any impairment of goodwill at December 31, 2014.

P4.6 **Intangible Assets and Goodwill: Amortization and Impairment** In early 2011, Bowen Company acquired a new business unit in a merger. Allocation of the acquisition cost resulted in fair values assigned as follows:

Intangible Asset	Fair Value	Estimated life
Customer lists	$ 500,000	5 years
Developed technology	800,000	10 years
Internet domain name	1,300,000	Indefinite
Goodwill[1]	6,200,000	Indefinite

[1] The goodwill is assigned entirely to the acquired business unit.

Impairment reviews at the end of 2011 and 2012 did not identify any impairment losses. After the business suffered a downturn during 2013, the year-end impairment review yielded the following information:

1. Customer lists are estimated to have undiscounted future cash flows of $250,000 and discounted future cash flows of $180,000.
2. Developed technology is estimated to have undiscounted future cash flows of $500,000 and discounted future cash flows of $420,000.
3. The internet domain name is estimated to have undiscounted future cash flows of $1,000,000 and discounted future cash flows of $750,000. Qualitative assessment indicates that it is more likely than not that the internet domain name is impaired.
4. Because of the economic downturn, Bowen bypassed qualitative assessment of the business unit (Step 0). The acquired business unit has a fair value of $17,000,000, a carrying amount of $18,500,000, and the fair value of its identifiable net assets is $14,200,000.

Required

Determine Bowen's amortization expense and impairment write-offs for 2013.

P4.7 **Consolidated Balance Sheet Working Paper, Three Years after Acquisition (see related P3.2)** International Technology Inc. (ITI) acquired all of the voting stock of Global Outsourcing Corporation (GOC) on June 30, 2010, for $110 million in cash and stock, plus an earnings contingency payable at the end of the third year with a fair value of $2 million at the date of acquisition. Within the measurement period, the earnings contingency declined to a fair value of zero and the acquisition price was appropriately adjusted. Both companies have a June 30 year-end. At June 30, 2010, GOC's total stockholders' equity was $40 million, as follows *(in millions)*:

Common stock, par	$ 4
Additional paid-in capital	60
Retained earnings (deficit)	(25)
Accumulated other comprehensive income.	3
Treasury stock	(2)
Total	$40

At the acquisition date, GOC's inventories were undervalued by $5 million, its property, plant and equipment was overvalued by $60 million, its reported patents and trademarks were undervalued by $10 million, and its long-term debt was undervalued by $3 million. GOC also had previously unreported identifiable intangibles: $5 million of advanced technology and $25 million of customer lists. GOC reports its inventory using the LIFO method, and purchases exceed sales every year. The acquisition date remaining lives of its assets and liabilities are as follows:

Property, plant and equipment, net	20 years
Patents and trademarks.	5 years
Advanced technology.	5 years
Customer lists	Indefinite
Long-term debt	3 years

The straight-line method is used for definite life assets. Impairment losses on the customer lists were $2 million in fiscal 2012 and $4 million in fiscal 2013. Goodwill impairment losses were $2 million in fiscal 2011, $3 million in fiscal 2012, and $2 million in fiscal 2013.

GOC reported net income of $15 million in fiscal 2011, and a net loss of $2 million in fiscal 2012. Neither company pays dividends. ITI uses the complete equity method to account for its investment in GOC on its own books. The trial balances of ITI and GOC at June 30, 2013, are as follows:

	Dr (Cr)	
(in millions)	**ITI**	**GOC**
Current assets	$ 232	$ 12
Property, plant and equipment, net	600	140
Identifiable intangible assets	1,100	30
Investment in GOC.	127	—
Current liabilities.	(175)	(10)
Long-term liabilities	(1,125)	(105)
Common stock, par	(22)	(4)
Additional paid-in capital	(580)	(60)
Retained earnings, July 1.	(118)	12
Accumulated other comprehensive income.	(20)	(5)
Treasury stock	8	2
Sales revenue.	(2,000)	(900)
Equity in net income of GOC	(7)	—
Cost of goods sold.	1,400	800
Operating expenses.	580	88
Totals	$ 0	$ 0

Required

a. Prepare a schedule that computes the June 30, 2013, investment in GOC balance and 2013 equity in net income on ITI's books.

b. Use a working paper to consolidate the trial balances of ITI and GOC at June 30, 2013.

c. Present the consolidated balance sheet at June 30, 2013, and the consolidated statement of income and retained earnings for 2013.

LO 1, 3 **P4.8** **Working Paper Eliminating Entries, Partial Year Consolidation (see related P3.3)** On April 16, 2003, **Pfizer** traded $55,873 million fair value of stock for all of the stock of **Pharmacia**, in a stock acquisition. Pharmacia's stockholders' equity accounts at the date of acquisition totaled $7,236 million, and the $48,637 million excess of acquisition cost over book value was allocated as follows *(in millions)*:

PFIZER
[PFE]

PHARMACIA

Inventory.	$ 2,939
Long-term investments	40
Property, plant and equipment.	(317)
In-process research and development	5,052
Developed technology rights	37,066
Long-term debt premium	(1,841)
Other assets	(15,606)
Goodwill.	21,304
Total	$48,637

Pfizer has a December 31 year-end, and Pharmacia's results of operations are included in the 2003 consolidated statements for the 8½ months following its acquisition. Reporting for the above revaluations during 2003 is as follows:

- Pharmacia's inventory was sold during 2003.
- Long-term investments remain on Pharmacia's books.
- Property, plant and equipment is depreciated over an average life of 20 years, straight-line.
- In-process research and development impairment for 2003 is $716 million.
- Finite-lived developed technology rights are valued at $31,596 million, and are amortized over an average life of 11 years, straight-line.
- Indefinite-lived developed technology rights are valued at $5,470 million, and no impairment loss is reported for 2003.
- Amortization of the long-term debt premium is $12 million.
- Other assets are written off over an average of 10 years, straight-line.
- Goodwill is not impaired during 2003.

Required (Round all numbers to the nearest million.)

a. Assume Pharmacia reports net income of $5,000 million for the period April 16 to December 31, 2003, and pays no dividends. Calculate 2003 Equity in Net Income of Pharmacia, recorded by Pfizer on its separate books using the complete equity method.
b. Prepare the eliminating entries necessary to consolidate Pharmacia's 2003 financial results with Pfizer.

P4.9 Goodwill Impairment Testing, IFRS and U.S. GAAP BP is an integrated global oil company operating in 100 countries. It is organized as two business segments: Exploration and Production, and Refining and Marketing. BP's financial statements are prepared using IFRS. Goodwill is first allocated to business segments (reporting units), and then to cash-generating units (CGUs) benefitting from the acquisition, within each segment. At the end of 2010, BP reported total goodwill of $8,598 million. Following are allocations of goodwill to CGUs *(in millions)*:

LO 4, 5

BP
[BP]

Exploration and Production	
UK.	$ 341
US.	3,479
Rest of world	630
Total	4,450
Refining and Marketing	
Rhine FVC	629
Lubricants.	3,285
Other	160
Total	4,074
Other.	74
Total goodwill	$8,598

BP uses "value in use" to measure the recoverable value of each CGU. A CGU's value at the end of 2007 is calculated as the present value of its expected future cash flows, discounted at 12 percent for the Exploration and Production segment and 14 percent for the Refining and Marketing segment. Exploration and Production segment cash flows are those expected to be generated from production of oil or natural gas for each producing field. Refining and Marketing segment cash flows come from the ten-year business segment plan. Assume the following end-of-2010 information on business segments and their CGUs:

	Value in use	Carrying value
Exploration and Production		
UK.	$ 9,000	$1,114
US.	35,000	6,144
Rest of world	2,500	2,840
Refining and Marketing		
Rhine FVC	13,000	1,557
Lubricants.	6,000	1,938
Other.	4,000	4,880

Required

a. What factors did BP consider when choosing the discount rates used to calculate value in use?
b. Calculate BP's 2010 goodwill impairment loss, following IFRS.
c. Assume the Rest of World CGU has a value in use of $2,140. How does your answer to *b* change?
d. If BP followed U.S. GAAP, would the 2010 impairment loss differ from the loss computed under IFRS? Explain.

LO 1, 3

NORTHROP GRUMMAN
[NOC]

ESSEX CORPORATION

P4.10 Consolidation One and Two Years after Acquisition **Northrop Grumman**, a global defense contractor and aircraft manufacturer headquartered in Los Angeles, CA, acquired **Essex Corporation** on January 25, 2007, for $590 million in cash, including transaction costs of $15 million, and assumed a further $23 million of debt on Essex's behalf. According to Northrop Grumman's annual report, "Essex provides signal processing services and products, and advanced optoelectronic imaging for U.S. government intelligence and defense customers."

Assume that Essex continued as a subsidiary of Northrop Grumman, its stockholders' equity at the date of acquisition was $350,000,000, and the excess of acquisition cost over book value was allocated to identifiable net assets as follows:

Inventories	$30,000,000
Identifiable intangibles (5-year life).	40,000,000
In-process research and development (IPRD)	60,000,000
Plant assets (20-year life, straight-line)	50,000,000

Inventories are accounted for under LIFO (60 percent) and FIFO (40 percent), and both pools increased in 2007 and 2008. The goodwill was impaired by $15,000,000 in 2007 and the IPRD was impaired by $20,000,000 in 2008. Essex reports the following net income and pays out 55 percent in dividends.

Year ended December 31, 2007 (post-acquisition)	$140,000,000
Year ended December 31, 2008	160,000,000

Required

a. Calculate the amount of goodwill recognized in the Essex acquisition, following current U.S. GAAP.
b. Use the complete equity method to compute the equity income accrual, and prepare all working paper eliminations in consolidation at December 31, 2007. A full year of revaluation write-offs is made in 2007.
c. Repeat part *b* at December 31, 2008.

LO 4, 5

ANHEUSER-BUSCH INBEV
[INTB]

SKOL
LABATT BLUE
SEDRIN

P4.11 Intangibles under IFRS **Anheuser-Busch InBev (InBev)** is the leading global brewer, headquartered in Belgium. Its major brands include **Skol** (Brazil), **Labatt Blue** (Canada), and **Sedrin** (China). Its 2008 combination with **Anheuser-Busch** added the Budweiser brand to its portfolio. InBev's financial statements are prepared following IFRS, with a December 31 year-end. The 2010 financial statements disclose €22,296 million in indefinite-lived intangibles and €1,063 million in finite-lived intangibles.

Required

Respond to each of the following assumed situations:

a. In a business combination on January 1, 2012, InBev acquires amortizable intangibles (10-year life) for €200 million. Calculate amortization expense for the year ended December 31, 2013, assuming the benefit pattern approximates 150 percent declining balance.
b. Assume that intangibles costing €40 million (10-year life), acquired on January 1, 2012, are traded in an active market. InBev amortizes them by the straight-line method. On December 31, 2012, the market value of these items is €45 million. One year later, new developments reduced the market value to €30 million. Prepare all journal entries related to these intangibles made under IFRS on December 31, 2012 and 2013. InBev uses the revaluation approach for qualifying intangibles.
c. On December 31, 2015, our impairment test produces the following information for distribution rights with indefinite lives acquired by InBev:

Carrying amount.	€2,000 million
Sum of undiscounted expected future cash flows.	2,500 million
Value-in-use	1,800 million
Present value of expected future cash flows (market value)	1,500 million

Calculate the impairment loss recognized under IFRS and U.S. GAAP, assuming InBev bypasses the qualitative assessment allowed under U.S. GAAP. What do you conclude about the relative impairment losses recognized under IFRS and U.S. GAAP?

P4.12 Consolidation in First Year, Intangible Asset Issues In March 2007, retail pharmacy giant **CVS** acquired all the shares of **Caremark Rx, Inc.** ("Caremark"), for about $26.9 billion. Caremark effectively became a newly formed subsidiary of CVS. Following the merger, the company changed its name to **CVS Caremark Corporation**. The company assigned $20.8 billion to goodwill and $9.4 billion to identifiable intangibles. Other assets amounted to about $4.8 billion. About $3 billion of the identifiable intangibles have average useful lives of 15 years; the $6.4 billion remaining are indefinite-lived intangibles (trade names).

Assume that the pre-acquisition book value of identifiable intangibles was $5 billion, of which $1 billion is limited-lived intangibles, and the remainder is indefinite-lived trade names acquired in previous business combinations. Limited-lived intangibles are straight-line amortized beginning in the month following acquisition. Also assume the goodwill relates to two reporting units (segments) within the new subsidiary and to the Pharmacy Services segment within CVS. The company reported no impairment of goodwill or the indefinite-lived intangibles. Assume also that the new subsidiary earned $1 billion in the nine months after the acquisition, and paid dividends of $550 million. The book values of all other assets acquired and liabilities assumed already approximated their fair values. In your answers below, present all dollar amounts in millions. CVS has a December 31 year-end.

Required
a. Calculate the apparent amount of liabilities assumed in the acquisition of Caremark.
b. Briefly describe management's considerations in deciding on the reported amounts of definite- and indefinite-lived intangibles.
c. Briefly explain whether the amounts of goodwill assigned to the three segments could have an effect on consolidated net income.
d. Compute the equity income accrual for the post-acquisition period in 2007 and prepare the December 31, 2007, consolidation working paper entries.

P4.13 Cost Method and Eliminating Entries Three Years after Acquisition Use the information provided in P4.2, but assume that Puffin Industries uses the cost method to account for its investment in Sunset Coast Digital.

Required
Prepare the working paper eliminating entries needed in consolidation at December 31, 2014.

REVIEW SOLUTIONS

Review 1 Solution
Impairment testing for identifiable intangibles:

Intangible asset (in millions)	Undiscounted cash flows < book value?	Impairment loss
Customer lists	$240 < $250? Yes	$250 − 225 = $25
Television rights	$105 < $100? No	NA
Brand names	NA	$400 − 380 = $20

Goodwill impairment testing:

(in millions)	Cable	Filmed entertainment	Networks
Fair value of unit..........................	$2,000	$2,800	$6,200
Book value of unit..........................	2,300	2,000	6,500
Fair value < Book value?....................	Yes	No	Yes
Fair value of unit..........................	2,000		6,200
Fair value of identifiable net assets	500		5,950
Fair value of goodwill	1,500		250
Book value of goodwill.....................	1,000		550
Goodwill impairment	$ 0		$ 300

In summary, the consolidated income statement reports $45 million in identifiable intangibles impairment loss and $300 million in goodwill impairment loss. The eliminating entry to record the impairment is *(in millions)*:

(O)	Impairment loss: identifiable intangibles	45	
	Impairment loss: goodwill	300	
	Identifiable intangibles: customer lists		25
	Identifiable intangibles: brand names		20
	Goodwill...		300

Review 2 Solution

a.

First Media reported income for 2014		$250,000,000
Revaluation write-offs:		
Property, plant and equipment ($300,000,000/10)...........................		(30,000,000)
Goodwill		(100,000,000)
Equity in income of First Media		$120,000,000

b.

Consolidation Working Paper

(in millions)	Accounts Taken From Books Dr (Cr) Time Warner	Accounts Taken From Books Dr (Cr) First Media	Eliminations Dr	Eliminations Cr	Consolidated Balances Dr (Cr)
Cash and receivables..........	$ 1,200	$ 450			$ 1,650
Inventories	7,200	1,000		$ 50 (R)	8,150
Property, plant and equipment, net	38,860	4,540	(R) $ 240	30 (O-1)	43,610
Investment in First Media.......	1,580	—		100 (C)	—
				790 (E)	
				690 (R)	
Lease agreements	—	—			—
Goodwill.....................	—	—	(R) 500	100 (O-2)	400
Accounts payable.............	(7,800)	(670)			(8,470)
Long-term debt	(35,000)	(4,300)			(39,300)
Common stock, par	(120)	(10)	(E) 10		(120)
Additional paid-in capital	(3,000)	(130)	(E) 130		(3,000)
Retained earnings, January 1....	(2,550)	(700)	(E) 700		(2,550)
Treasury stock	—	50		50 (E)	—
Dividends	100	20		20 (C)	100
Sales revenue................	(10,000)	(2,000)			(12,000)
Equity in income of First Media ..	(120)	—	(C) 120		
Cost of goods sold............	8,500	1,600			10,100
Operating expenses...........	1,150	150	(O-1) 30		1,430
			(O-2) 100		
Totals	$ 0	$ 0	$1,830	$1,830	$ 0

TIME WARNER and FIRST MEDIA
Consolidated Statement of Income and Retained Earnings
For Year Ended December 31, 2014 (*in millions*)

Sales revenue	$12,000
Less: Cost of goods sold	(10,100)
Gross profit	1,900
Less: Operating expenses	(1,430)
Net income	**470**
Plus: Retained earnings, January 1, 2014	2,550
Less: Dividends	(100)
Retained earnings, December 31, 2014	$ 2,920

TIME WARNER and FIRST MEDIA
Consolidated Balance Sheet
December 31, 2014 (*in millions*)

Assets		Liabilities and Stockholders' Equity	
Current assets		Accounts payable	$ 8,470
Cash and receivables	$ 1,650	Long-term debt	39,300
Inventories	8,150	Total liabilities	47,770
Total current assets	9,800		
Noncurrent assets		Stockholders' equity	
Property, plant and equipment, net	43,610	Common stock, par	120
Goodwill	400	Additional paid-in capital	3,000
Total noncurrent assets	44,010	Retained earnings	2,920
		Total stockholders' equity	6,040
Total assets	$53,810	Total liabilities and stockholders' equity	$53,810

5

Consolidated Financial Statements: Outside Interests

LAS VEGAS SANDS CORPORATION
www.lasvegassands.com

Las Vegas Sands Corporation (LVSC) owns and operates several entertainment destinations in Las Vegas, including The Venetian Las Vegas and the Palazzo Resort Hotel Casino. LVSC also owns several international properties, such as the Four Seasons Macao in Macau and the Marina Bay Sands in Singapore. LVSC incorporated in 2004 and lists its stock on the New York Stock Exchange.

LVSC presents financial statements that consolidate the parent company with more than ninety subsidiaries. One subsidiary, Sands China Ltd., owns and operates most of the Macau properties. In the equity section of LVSC's 2010 consolidated balance sheet, a "noncontrolling interest" of $1,268 million appears, comprising almost 16 percent of LVSC's total equity. The 2010 consolidated income statement reports "net income attributable to noncontrolling interests" of $182 million. Footnotes to the annual report reveal that LVSC owns 70.3 percent of Sands China Ltd.; other investors own the remaining 29.7 percent.

Because companies are required to consolidate companies they control, in the U.S. this almost always means consolidation of any majority-owned company. While most subsidiaries are wholly-owned, a substantial number are not. The "noncontrolling interest" lines on LVSC's consolidated financial statements reflect the portion of the consolidated subsidiary, Sands China Ltd., that is not owned by LVSC. "Noncontrolling interest" on the balance sheet represents the equity of the noncontrolling shareholders. "Noncontrolling interest" on the income statement reports the noncontrolling shareholders' share of consolidated income.

In this chapter you will learn how to consolidate financial statements of a parent and its subsidiaries that are not wholly-owned. The existence of outside ownership in a subsidiary affects valuation of goodwill and consolidated shareholders' equity, and impacts the display of information on the consolidated financial statements. *Source:* Las Vegas Sands Corporation annual report, 2010.

CHAPTER ORGANIZATION

Noncontrolling interests at acquisition date	Noncontrolling interests in subsequent periods	Bargain purchases with noncontrolling interests	IFRS for noncontrolling interests	Consolidated statement of cash flows
• Estimate fair value of noncontrolling interests • Value goodwill • Eliminating entries • Balance sheet • Consolidating variable interest entities	• Calculate equity in net income and noncontrolling interest in net income • Eliminating entries • Income statement presentation	• Date of acquisition • Subsequent periods	• Alternative valuation of noncontrolling interests • Impact of alternative IFRS valuation on financial statements	• Major items affecting calculation of cash from operations • Preparing the cash flow statement

INTRODUCTION

When a parent has a controlling interest in a legally separate subsidiary, it regularly presents consolidated financial statements that aggregate the financial records of the separate companies. Previous chapters considered valuation and consolidation procedures when the parent acquires *all* of the voting interests in a subsidiary. This chapter discusses consolidation of less-than-wholly-owned subsidiaries.

Recall that under U.S. GAAP, "controlling interest" generally means ownership of a majority of the voting shares of the subsidiary. Therefore, a parent owning any percentage of a subsidiary's stock exceeding 50 percent must consolidate the subsidiary's assets, liabilities, revenues and expenses in its financial statements. That portion of the subsidiary's stock held by other investors is called the **noncontrolling interest**.

In the sections below, we see that even when the parent owns less than 100 percent of the subsidiary, it consolidates 100 percent of the subsidiary's assets, liabilities, revenues and expenses with its own accounts. On the consolidated balance sheet, the noncontrolling interest in the net assets of the subsidiary appears as a separate line in the equity section. Similarly, on the consolidated income statement the noncontrolling interest's share of the subsidiary's income appears as a separate line, representing that portion of consolidated income attributable to the noncontrolling interest.

Companies acquire a less-than-100-percent interest in a subsidiary for many reasons, for example:

- The subsidiary's previous owners want to retain an interest in the company.
- The acquirer does not want to invest the resources necessary to buy all of the acquiree's stock.
- The acquirer cannot convince all the stockholders to sell.
- A smaller investment suffices to achieve the acquirer's goals.

A noncontrolling interest also appears on the consolidated financial statements when a company determines it is the **primary beneficiary** of a **variable interest entity**. Recall that *FASB ASC Topic 810* requires the primary beneficiary of a variable interest entity to consolidate that entity, even if the primary beneficiary holds little or no equity interest in the entity. The consolidated balance sheet then reports a noncontrolling interest equal to its share of the difference between the variable interest entity's assets and liabilities. If the primary beneficiary has no equity interest, the noncontrolling interest equals the variable interest's equity.

NONCONTROLLING INTERESTS AT ACQUISITION DATE

LO1 Consolidate a subsidiary with noncontrolling interests at the date of acquisition.

When the parent acquires a less-than-100-percent interest in a subsidiary, it reports its investment at acquisition cost. Acquisition cost includes the fair value of shares and debt issued, net of registration and issue costs, cash paid directly to the former shareholders of the acquired subsidiary, and any expected conditional payments. The consolidation working paper brings together the accounts of the parent and the subsidiary, and reports the noncontrolling interest in the subsidiary's equity as a component of consolidated equity.

Valuation of Noncontrolling Interests and Goodwill at Acquisition

U.S. GAAP initially reports noncontrolling interests at **fair value**. Revaluations of acquired identifiable net assets are attributed to both the controlling and noncontrolling interests in proportion to ownership interests. Goodwill is separately attributed to each interest, typically in different proportions. An example illustrates the valuations.

Assume Admiral Casino & Resort pays $42,600,000 in cash for 80 percent of the stock of Gold Road Motor Inn, Inc., on January 1, 2012. The book values of Gold Road's net assets equal their fair values, except for previously unrecorded intangibles: customer lists, with a four-year life, straight-line amortization, valued at $5,000,000. Gold Road's book value of $10,000,000 consists of $2,500,000 of capital stock and $7,500,000 in retained earnings. Admiral estimates the fair value of the 20 percent noncontrolling interest in Gold Road to be $8,400,000 at the acquisition date.

Total goodwill on this acquisition is $36,000,000, calculated as follows:

Acquisition cost	$42,600,000
Fair value of noncontrolling interest	8,400,000
Total fair value	51,000,000
Book value of Gold Road	(10,000,000)
Fair value in excess of Gold Road's book value	41,000,000
Difference between fair value and book value:	
Customer lists	(5,000,000)
Goodwill	$36,000,000

We allocate goodwill between the controlling and noncontrolling interest by first calculating goodwill attributed to the controlling interest, and then attributing the remainder to the noncontrolling interest.

Goodwill to controlling interest	
Acquisition cost	$42,600,000
Less controlling interest in the fair value of Gold Road's identifiable net assets:	
80% × ($10,000,000 + $5,000,000)	(12,000,000)
Controlling interest's share	$30,600,000
Goodwill to noncontrolling interest	
Total goodwill	$36,000,000
Less goodwill to controlling interest	(30,600,000)
Noncontrolling interest's share	$ 5,400,000

These goodwill allocations of 85 percent (= $30,600,000/$36,000,000) and 15 percent (= $5,400,000/$36,000,000) attribute goodwill to the controlling and noncontrolling interests when consolidating the financial statements in future years. Thus the percentage ownership interests do not govern the goodwill allocation.

Measuring the Fair Value of Noncontrolling Interests

ASC para. 805-20-30-1 requires the acquiring company to value the noncontrolling interest in the subsidiary at its fair value at the acquisition date. The example above sets the estimated fair value of the noncontrolling interest at $8,400,000. How is this value determined? If there is an active market for the subsidiary's stock, the stock price at the acquisition date may be appropriate. If not, alternative valuation methods are used. *ASC paras. 805-20-30-7* and *8* provide some guidance, as follows:

> An acquirer sometimes will be able to measure the acquisition-date fair value of a noncontrolling interest on the basis of active market prices for the equity shares not held by the acquirer. In other situations, however, the active market price for the equity shares will not be available. In those situations, the acquirer would measure the fair value of the noncontrolling interest using other valuation techniques.
>
> The fair values of the acquirer's interest in the acquiree and the noncontrolling interest on a per-share basis might differ. The main difference is likely to be the inclusion of a control premium in the per-share fair value of the acquirer's interest in the acquiree or, conversely, the inclusion of a discount for lack of control (also referred to as a noncontrolling interest discount) in the per-share fair value of the noncontrolling interest if market participants would take into account such a premium or discount when pricing the noncontrolling interest.

When public companies are involved, the current share price reflects transactions among noncontrolling shareholders. Such stockholders tend to be passive investors, earning a return from dividends and any future growth in the market price. Controlling owners, on the other hand, can direct business operations, set compensation and benefits, change capital structure, sell or merge the company, or even liquidate it. Because of all the powers a controlling owner has, a controlling ownership interest is worth more than a noncontrolling interest. The premium offered when a public company acquisition is proposed reflects, in part at least, the value the buyer assigns to acquiring control.

Because the stock of the company to be acquired is usually widely held by individual and institutional investors, the prospective buyer must offer a control premium large enough to induce sufficient numbers of existing noncontrolling holders to sell their stock. In the case of a nonpublic business, the seller may be the controlling owner, perhaps the sole owner. Such a seller is in a better position to capture the value of the control premium than the dispersed noncontrolling interests in most public companies.

Thus the **current stock price** of a publicly-traded company reflects transactions among noncontrolling shareholders, and **is appropriate for valuing the noncontrolling interest**. Including a control premium in the acquirer's cost is reasonable, but deducting a discount for lack of control is not. If a valuation method such as capitalization of future returns is used to estimate the value of the company as a whole, it may be reasonable to deduct a discount for lack of control when valuing the noncontrolling interest.

Suppose an acquiree's current market price is $30 per share. The acquirer is willing to pay a 6.67 percent control premium, or $2 (= 6.67% × $30) per share to obtain the shares, and therefore pays $32 per share for 90 percent of the acquiree. The acquirer could logically value the noncontrolling interest at the acquiree's $30 per share market price. If the acquiree is not publicly traded, the acquirer may use one or more valuation techniques to estimate the value of the acquiree. If a business valuation method values the company at $32 per share, a discount of 6.25 percent [= 1 − (1/(1 + .067))] may be applied to value the noncontrolling interest at $30 [= $32 × (1 − .0625)] per share.

In the illustration above, Admiral pays $42,600,000 for 80 percent of Gold Road. The 20 percent noncontrolling interest's fair value is $8,400,000. If Gold Road has 1,000,000 outstanding shares, the noncontrolling interest is valued at $42 per share (= $8,400,000/200,000). The controlling interest's cost of $53.25 per share (= $42,600,000/800,000) reflects a control premium of about 27 percent [= ($53.25 − $42)/$42].

When an active market price is not available, acquirers use other valuation methods to estimate the fair value of both the controlling and noncontrolling interests in the acquiree. Business valuation methods include the following:

* Capitalization of expected future earnings or cash flows, where estimated future returns are discounted using an appropriate discount rate.
* Capitalization of excess earnings, where firm value is estimated as the fair value of tangible net assets plus capitalized earnings in excess of earnings attributable to the tangible assets.
* Direct comparison approach, using the terms of a similar acquisition, such as a multiple of book value, billings, or other appropriate measures.

ASC para. 805-20-50-1 requires disclosure of the following information for each business combination during the reporting period, in which the acquirer obtained less than 100 percent of the acquiree's equity interests:

* The fair value of the noncontrolling interest in the acquiree at the acquisition date.
* The valuation technique(s) and significant inputs used to measure the fair value of the noncontrolling interest.

Consolidation Eliminating Entries at Acquisition Date

Chapter 3 explained the eliminating entries required to consolidate a wholly-owned subsidiary at the date of acquisition:

(E)   Eliminate the subsidiary's stockholders' equity accounts against the investment account.

(R)   Eliminate the remainder of the investment account, representing the difference between acquisition price and the subsidiary's book value, and revalue the subsidiary's assets and liabilities from book value to fair value at the acquisition date.

When a noncontrolling interest is present, the eliminating entries accomplish the same goals as when the subsidiary is wholly-owned: eliminate the investment account and the subsidiary's equity accounts, and revalue the subsidiary's assets and liabilities to fair value at the date of acquisition. In addition, the eliminations create the noncontrolling interest in equity to be reported on the consolidated balance sheet. The date-of-acquisition noncontrolling interest in the subsidiary's net assets consists of its interest in the book value of the subsidiary, plus its interest in the revaluations that occur at the date of acquisition. We modify eliminating entries E and R to allow for noncontrolling interests, as follows:

> **(E)**   Eliminate the subsidiary's stockholders' equity accounts, reducing the investment account and increasing the noncontrolling interest account according to each ownership interest's share of the subsidiary's equity.
>
> **(R)**   Revalue the subsidiary's assets and liabilities from book value to fair value at the acquisition date, reducing the investment account and increasing the noncontrolling interest account according to each ownership interest's share of the revaluations.

Eliminating entry E allocates the subsidiary's book value (equity) between the controlling interest—the investment account—and the noncontrolling interest, in proportion to their ownership interests. For example, if the parent owns 90 percent of the subsidiary, 10 percent of the subsidiary's equity is added to the noncontrolling interest. Eliminating entry R revalues the subsidiary's identifiable net assets, such as plant and equipment, previously unrecorded intangibles or liabilities, and acquired goodwill. The controlling and noncontrolling interests share revaluations in identifiable net assets in proportion to their ownership interests.

However, goodwill is allocated according to each interest's share in the goodwill. Goodwill is shared in proportion to ownership interests only when the acquisition price and the fair value of the noncontrolling interest are equal on a per share basis, which is unlikely. When there is a noncontrolling interest valuation discount, the goodwill allocation to the noncontrolling interest will be, on a percentage basis, *less* than the ownership interest. In our illustration above, the noncontrolling interest in Gold Road is 20 percent, but it is allocated only 15 percent of the goodwill.

The acquisition date eliminating entries necessary to consolidate the balance sheets of Admiral and Gold Road appear below, in journal entry form.

(E)	Capital stock	2,500,000	
	Retained earnings	7,500,000	
	Investment in Gold Road (80%)		8,000,000
	Noncontrolling interest in Gold Road (20%)		2,000,000
	To eliminate Gold Road's equity accounts against the book value portion of the investment account and recognize the book value of the noncontrolling interest.		
(R)	Customer lists	5,000,000	
	Goodwill	36,000,000	
	Investment in Gold Road		34,600,000
	Noncontrolling interest in Gold Road		6,400,000
	To revalue Gold Road's net assets to fair value and allocate the revaluations to the controlling and noncontrolling interest.		
	$34,600,000 = (80% x $5,000,000) + $30,600,000.		
	$6,400,000 = (20% x $5,000,000) + $5,400,000.		

The consolidation working paper appears in Exhibit 5.1. Account balances other than the investment on Admiral's books and the equity accounts on Gold Road's books are assumed.

EXHIBIT 5.1   Consolidation Working Paper for Admiral and Gold Road, January 1, 2012

	Accounts Taken From Books		Eliminations		Consolidated Balances
	Admiral	**Gold Road**	**Dr**	**Cr**	
Current assets	$ 10,000,000	$ 4,000,000			$ 14,000,000
Equity investments	35,000,000	4,200,000			39,200,000
Plant and equipment, net	250,000,000	60,000,000			310,000,000
Investment in Gold Road	42,600,000	—		$ 8,000,000 (E)	—
				34,600,000 (R)	
Identifiable intangible assets	620,000,000	—	(R) $ 5,000,000		625,000,000
Goodwill	—	—	(R) 36,000,000		36,000,000
Totals	$957,600,000	$68,200,000			$1,024,200,000
Current liabilities	$ 12,000,000	$10,000,000			$ 22,000,000
Long-term debt	920,600,000	48,200,000			968,800,000
Capital stock	5,000,000	2,500,000	(E) 2,500,000		5,000,000
Retained earnings	20,000,000	7,500,000	(E) 7,500,000		20,000,000
Noncontrolling interest	—	—		2,000,000 (E)	
				6,400,000 (R)	8,400,000
Totals	$957,600,000	$68,200,000	$51,000,000	$51,000,000	$1,024,200,000

Noncontrolling Interests in the Consolidated Balance Sheet

ASC Sections 810-10-45 and *55* provide authoritative guidance on presentation of noncontrolling interests in consolidated financial statements. On the **consolidated balance sheet**, the noncontrolling interest in the equity of a subsidiary appears as a **separate component of consolidated equity**. The equity section is divided between the controlling and noncontrolling interests. Controlling interests include separate lines for the parent's capital stock, retained earnings, accumulated other comprehensive income, and other equity accounts. *Noncontrolling interests appear on one line*. If there are multiple subsidiaries, noncontrolling interests may be presented in aggregate.

Admiral's consolidated balance sheet at January 1, 2012, the date of acquisition, appears below.

ADMIRAL CASINO & RESORT
Consolidated Balance Sheet
January 1, 2012

Assets		Liabilities and Stockholders' Equity	
Current assets	$ 14,000,000	Current liabilities	$ 22,000,000
Equity investments	39,200,000	Long-term debt	968,800,000
Plant and equipment, net . . .	310,000,000	Total liabilities	990,800,000
Identifiable intangibles	625,000,000	Stockholders' equity	
Goodwill	36,000,000	Admiral stockholders' equity:	
		Capital stock	5,000,000
		Retained earnings	20,000,000
		Total Admiral stockholders' equity	25,000,000
		Noncontrolling interest	8,400,000
		Total stockholders' equity	33,400,000
Total assets	$1,024,200,000	Total liabilities and stockholders' equity	$1,024,200,000

Consolidating Variable Interest Entities

Recall that a company must consolidate an entity even if it has little or no equity ownership, when it is the entity's primary beneficiary. Companies that are primary beneficiaries of VIEs follow consolidation procedures outlined in *ASC paras. 810-10-30-1 and 2*. These procedures feature two valuation alternatives, depending on the prior relationship between the primary beneficiary (PB) and the VIE.

If the PB and the VIE are under *common control*, the assets and liabilities of the VIE are included on the consolidated balance sheet at **book value**. Entities under common control have common ownership and management. In that case, the VIE was not really "acquired" as it is already part of the corporate family, and there is no transaction to justify revaluation of the VIE's assets and liabilities. The book value of the VIE's net assets appears as noncontrolling interest. Consolidation eliminations delete the VIE's equity accounts and reclassify them as noncontrolling interests.

More typically, the primary beneficiary and the VIE do *not* have common ownership, although the PB must have some financial relationship with the VIE. Absent common ownership, the assets and liabilities of the VIE, as well as the noncontrolling interest, are consolidated at **fair value** as of the date it is determined that the PB should consolidate the VIE. The consolidation working paper entries eliminate the VIE's equity accounts, revalue its identifiable assets and liabilities as appropriate, and establish the noncontrolling interest. Goodwill valuation follows *ASC Topic 805*, defined as the excess of acquisition cost and the fair value of noncontrolling interests over the fair value of identifiable net assets of the VIE. Consolidation of the VIE in subsequent years follows the requirements of *ASC Topic 810*, with no additional issues.

NONCONTROLLING INTERESTS IN SUBSEQUENT YEARS

LO2 Consolidate a subsidiary with noncontrolling interests in subsequent years.

Consolidating the accounts of the parent and subsidiary in periods after the acquisition requires that we consider the effect of the noncontrolling interest on consolidated income and changes in the equity value of the noncontrolling interest over time. The noncontrolling interest in income is its share of subsidiary's reported net income, adjusted for the noncontrolling interest's share of revaluation write-offs. Noncontrolling interest on the balance sheet is its initial fair value, updated for its share of accumulated income and dividends during the post-acquisition period.

Assume the parent uses the complete equity method in reporting the investment on its own books. Equity in net income is the controlling interest's share of the subsidiary's reported net income, adjusted for its share of revaluation write-offs. Equity in net income on the parent's books and noncontrolling interest in net income on the consolidated income statement involve parallel calculations, so we calculate both balances in one schedule. We continue with Admiral's 80 percent ownership of Gold Road.

Consolidation at End of the First Year

Suppose Gold Road reports net income of $5,000,000 and pays cash dividends of $600,000 in 2012, the first year following acquisition. Admiral uses the complete equity method to report its investment in Gold Road on its own books. Impairment testing reveals that the goodwill recognized in this acquisition is impaired by $500,000 during 2012.

Under the complete equity method, Admiral reports its share of Gold Road's 2012 income on its own books. The schedule below simultaneously calculates the parent's equity in net income of the subsidiary reported on the parent's books, and the noncontrolling interest in the net income of the subsidiary reported on the consolidated income statement. The calculations are as follows:

	Total	Equity in net income	Noncontrolling interest in net income
Gold Road's reported income for 2012	$5,000,000	$4,000,000	$1,000,000
Adjustment for revaluation write-offs:			
Customer lists ($5,000,000/4).	(1,250,000)	(1,000,000)	(250,000)
Goodwill (85:15 ratio)	(500,000)	(425,000)	(75,000)
Totals	$3,250,000	$2,575,000	$ 675,000

There is no specific authoritative guidance on how to allocate revaluation write-offs between the controlling and noncontrolling interests. This text assumes that write-offs of the subsidiary's asset and liability revaluations are shared *in the same proportions* used to assign the original revaluations. Because revaluations of identifiable net assets are attributed according to ownership interests, the write-off of customer lists is distributed in an 80:20 ratio. With 85 percent of the goodwill assigned to the controlling interest in our illustration, we allocate goodwill impairment losses in an 85:15 ratio.

In addition to the initial acquisition entry, Admiral makes the following entries on its own books during 2012:

Investment in Gold Road	2,575,000	
Equity in income of Gold Road		2,575,000
To record equity in net income for 2012.		
Cash	480,000	
Investment in Gold Road		480,000
To record dividends declared and received in 2012		
($480,000 = 80% × $600,000).		

Given the $42,600,000 acquisition cost, the investment account has a December 31, 2012, balance of $44,695,000 (= $42,600,000 + $2,575,000 − $480,000).

The consolidation eliminating entries are similar to the **CERO** entries used to consolidate wholly-owned subsidiaries in subsequent years, covered in Chapter 4. However, we now add entry **N** to update the **N**oncontrolling interest for its share of the subsidiary's income and dividends for the current year. The eliminating entries are as follows:

(C) Eliminate the current year's equity method entries, restoring the investment account to its balance at the beginning of the current year.

(E) Eliminate the subsidiary's beginning-of-year stockholders' equity account balances, reducing the investment account and increasing the noncontrolling interest account according to each ownership interest's share of the subsidiary's beginning equity.

(R) Revalue the subsidiary's assets and liabilities as of the beginning of the year. Eliminate the remainder of the investment account, representing the controlling interest's beginning-of-year revaluation balance, and attribute the beginning-of-year net asset revaluations to the noncontrolling interest.

(O) Recognize current year write-offs of the subsidiary's asset and liability revaluations.

(N) Recognize the noncontrolling interest in net income. Update the noncontrolling interest in equity for its share of income and dividends.

The consolidation working paper in Exhibit 5.2 shows the preclosing accounts of Admiral and Gold Road at December 31, 2012, in trial balance format. Here are the five eliminating entries needed to consolidate the 2012 financial statements of Admiral and Gold Road, in journal entry form:

(C)	Equity in income of Gold Road	2,575,000	
	Dividends		480,000
	Investment in Gold Road		2,095,000

To eliminate equity in net income on the parent's books, the parent's share of the subsidiary's dividends, and restore the investment account to its beginning-of-year value.

(E)	Capital stock	2,500,000	
	Retained earnings, January 1	7,500,000	
	Investment in Gold Road (80%)		8,000,000
	Noncontrolling interest in Gold Road (20%)		2,000,000

To eliminate the subsidiary's beginning-of-year equity accounts against the beginning-of-year book value portion of the investment account and recognize the beginning-of-year book value of the noncontrolling interest.

(R)	Customer lists	5,000,000	
	Goodwill	36,000,000	
	Investment in Gold Road		34,600,000
	Noncontrolling interest in Gold Road		6,400,000

To revalue Gold Road's net assets to fair value and allocate the revaluations to the controlling and noncontrolling interest.
$34,600,000 = (80% x $5,000,000) + $30,600,000.
$6,400,000 = (20% x $5,000,000) + $5,400,000.

(O)	Goodwill impairment loss	500,000	
	Other operating expenses	1,250,000	
	Goodwill		500,000
	Customer lists		1,250,000

To write off the revaluations for the current year.

(N)	Noncontrolling interest in net income	675,000	
	Dividends		120,000
	Noncontrolling interest in Gold Road		555,000

To recognize the noncontrolling interest in the subsidiary's income and dividends for the current year.

Exhibit 5.2 displays these eliminating entries and the consolidated account balances. Account balances unrelated to the discussion above are assumed.

EXHIBIT 5.2   Consolidation Working Paper for Admiral and Gold Road, December 31, 2012

	Accounts Taken From Books Dr (Cr)		Eliminations		Consolidated Balances Dr (Cr)
	Admiral	Gold Road	Dr	Cr	
Current assets	$ 10,880,000	$ 4,400,000			$ 15,280,000
Equity investments.	40,000,000	5,000,000			45,000,000
Plant and equipment, net.	260,000,000	55,000,000			315,000,000
Investment in Gold Road	44,695,000	—		$ 2,095,000 (C)	—
				8,000,000 (E)	
				34,600,000 (R)	
Identifiable intangible assets	600,000,000	—	(R) $ 5,000,000	1,250,000 (O)	603,750,000
Goodwill	—	—	(R) 36,000,000	500,000 (O)	35,500,000
Current liabilities.	(10,000,000)	(10,000,000)			(20,000,000)
Long-term debt	(910,000,000)	(40,000,000)			(950,000,000)
Capital stock	(5,000,000)	(2,500,000)	(E) 2,500,000		(5,000,000)
Retained earnings, January 1.	(20,000,000)	(7,500,000)	(E) 7,500,000		(20,000,000)
Noncontrolling interest.	—	—		2,000,000 (E)	
				6,400,000 (R)	
				555,000 (N)	(8,955,000)
Dividends	2,000,000	600,000		480,000 (C)	
				120,000 (N)	2,000,000
Sales and other revenue.	(600,000,000)	(150,000,000)			(750,000,000)
Equity in income of Gold Road	(2,575,000)	—	(C) 2,575,000		—
Cost of goods sold.	400,000,000	115,000,000			515,000,000
Goodwill impairment loss.	—	—	(O) 500,000		500,000
Other operating expenses	190,000,000	30,000,000	(O) 1,250,000		221,250,000
Noncontrolling interest in net income	—	—	(N) 675,000		675,000
Totals	$ 0	$ 0	$56,000,000	$56,000,000	$ 0

Noncontrolling Interests in the Consolidated Income Statement

Following the requirements of *ASC Sections 810-10-45* and *55*, the consolidated income statement reports consolidated net income in total and the portions attributable to the controlling and noncontrolling interest. Either on the face of the income statement or in the notes, amounts of income from continuing operations, discontinued operations, and extraordinary items attributable to the controlling and noncontrolling interests are disclosed. However, earnings per share are shown *only for the controlling interest*. Using the consolidated account balances in Exhibit 5.2, the consolidated statement of income and retained earnings for 2012 and the consolidated balance sheet as of December 31, 2012 appear below.

ADMIRAL CASINO & RESORT Consolidated Statement of Income and Retained Earnings For Year Ended December 31, 2012	
Sales and other revenue.	$750,000,000
Less: Cost of goods sold	(515,000,000)
Goodwill impairment loss	(500,000)
Other operating expenses.	(221,250,000)
Consolidated net income.	**13,250,000**
Less: Noncontrolling interest in net income.	(675,000)
Net income attributable to Admiral	12,575,000
Plus: Retained earnings, Admiral, January 1	20,000,000
Less: Dividends	(2,000,000)
Retained earnings, Admiral, December 31.	$ 30,575,000

ADMIRAL CASINO & RESORT
Consolidated Balance Sheet
December 31, 2012

Assets		Liabilities and Stockholders' Equity	
Current assets	$ 15,280,000	Current liabilities.	$ 20,000,000
Equity investments.	45,000,000	Long-term debt	950,000,000
Plant and equipment, net. . .	315,000,000	Total liabilities.	970,000,000
Identifiable intangibles	603,750,000	Stockholders' equity	
Goodwill	35,500,000	Admiral stockholders' equity:	
		Capital stock.	5,000,000
		Retained earnings.	30,575,000
		Total Admiral stockholders' equity	35,575,000
		Noncontrolling interest	8,955,000
		Total stockholders' equity	44,530,000
Total assets	$1,014,530,000	Total liabilities and stockholders' equity	$1,014,530,000

Consolidation at End of the Second Year

Now it is December 31, 2013, and we again consolidate the trial balances of Admiral and Gold Road. The December 31, 2013, preclosing trial balances appear on the consolidation working paper in Exhibit 5.3. Gold Road reports net income of $6,000,000 and pays cash dividends of $500,000 in 2013, the second year following acquisition. Goodwill is impaired by $200,000 during 2013.

Calculation of the parent's equity in net income of subsidiary, reported on the parent's books, and the noncontrolling interest in the net income of the subsidiary, reported on the consolidated income statement, proceeds as follows:

	Total	Equity in net income	Noncontrolling interest in net income
Gold Road's reported income for 2013	$6,000,000	$4,800,000	$1,200,000
Adjustment for revaluation write-offs:			
Customer lists ($5,000,000/4).	(1,250,000)	(1,000,000)	(250,000)
Goodwill (85:15 ratio)	(200,000)	(170,000)	(30,000)
Totals	$4,550,000	$3,630,000	$ 920,000

Admiral makes the following entries on its own books during 2013:

Investment in Gold Road	3,630,000	
Equity in income of Gold Road		3,630,000
To record equity in net income for 2013.		
Cash.	400,000	
Investment in Gold Road.		400,000
To record dividends declared and received in 2013		
($400,000 = 80% x $500,000).		

The investment account therefore has a December 31, 2013, balance of $47,925,000 (= $44,695,000 + $3,630,000 − $400,000).

On December 31, 2013, we prepare consolidated financial statements using these five eliminating entries to consolidate the 2013 financial statements of Admiral and Gold Road:

(C)	Equity in income of Gold Road	3,630,000	
	Dividends.		400,000
	Investment in Gold Road.		3,230,000
	To eliminate equity in net income on the parent's books, the parent's		
	share of the subsidiary's dividends, and restore the investment account		
	to its beginning-of-year value.		

continued

continued from prior page

(E)	Capital stock	2,500,000	
	Retained earnings, January 1.	11,900,000	
	Investment in Gold Road (80%)		11,520,000
	Noncontrolling interest in Gold Road (20%)		2,880,000
	To eliminate the subsidiary's beginning-of-year equity accounts against the beginning-of-year book value portion of the investment account and recognize the beginning-of-year book value of the noncontrolling interest.		
(R)	Customer lists	3,750,000	
	Goodwill	35,500,000	
	Investment in Gold Road.		33,175,000
	Noncontrolling interest in Gold Road		6,075,000
	To revalue Gold Road's net assets to fair value and allocate the revaluations to the controlling and noncontrolling interest. *$33,175,000 = (80% x $3,750,000) + (85% x $35,500,000).* *$6,075,000 = (20% x $3,750,000) + (15% x $35,500,000).*		
(O)	Goodwill impairment loss.	200,000	
	Other operating expenses	1,250,000	
	Goodwill.		200,000
	Customer lists		1,250,000
	To write off the revaluations for the current year.		
(N)	Noncontrolling interest in net income	920,000	
	Dividends.		100,000
	Noncontrolling interest in Gold Road		820,000
	To recognize the noncontrolling interest in the subsidiary's income and dividends for the current year.		

Exhibit 5.3 displays these eliminating entries, and each account's consolidated balance.

EXHIBIT 5.3 Consolidation Working Paper for Admiral and Gold Road at December 31, 2013

	Accounts Taken From Books Dr (Cr)		Eliminations		Consolidated Balances
	Admiral	**Gold Road**	**Dr**	**Cr**	**Dr (Cr)**
Current assets	$ 12,280,000	$ 8,900,000			$ 21,180,000
Equity investments.	50,000,000	4,000,000			54,000,000
Plant and equipment, net.	235,000,000	64,000,000			299,000,000
Investment in Gold Road	47,925,000	—		$ 3,230,000 (C)	—
				11,520,000 (E)	
				33,175,000 (R)	
Identifiable intangible assets	580,000,000	—	(R) $ 3,750,000	1,250,000 (O)	582,500,000
Goodwill	—	—	(R) 35,500,000	200,000 (O)	35,300,000
Current liabilities.	(13,000,000)	(12,000,000)			(25,000,000)
Long-term debt	(870,000,000)	(45,000,000)			(915,000,000)
Capital stock	(5,000,000)	(2,500,000)	(E) 2,500,000		(5,000,000)
Retained earnings, January 1.	(30,575,000)	(11,900,000)	(E) 11,900,000		(30,575,000)
Noncontrolling interest.	—	—		2,880,000 (E)	
				6,075,000 (R)	
				820,000 (N)	(9,775,000)
Dividends	2,000,000	500,000		400,000 (C)	
				100,000 (N)	2,000,000
Sales and other revenue.	(620,000,000)	(160,000,000)			(780,000,000)
Equity in income of Gold Road	(3,630,000)	—	(C) 3,630,000		—
Cost of goods sold.	410,000,000	120,000,000			530,000,000
Goodwill impairment loss.	—	—	(O) 200,000		200,000
Other operating expenses	205,000,000	34,000,000	(O) 1,250,000		240,250,000
Noncontrolling interest in net income	—	—	(N) 920,000		920,000
Totals	$ 0	$ 0	$59,650,000	$59,650,000	$ 0

Using the consolidated account balances in Exhibit 5.3, the consolidated statement of income and retained earnings for 2013 and the consolidated balance sheet at December 31, 2013 appear next.

ADMIRAL CASINO & RESORT
Consolidated Statement of Income and Retained Earnings
For Year Ended December 31, 2013

Sales and other revenue.	$780,000,000
Less: Cost of goods sold	(530,000,000)
Goodwill impairment loss	(200,000)
Other operating expenses.	(240,250,000)
Consolidated net income.	**9,550,000**
Less: Noncontrolling interest in net income.	(920,000)
Net income attributable to Admiral	8,630,000
Plus: Retained earnings, Admiral, January 1	30,575,000
Less: Dividends	(2,000,000)
Retained earnings, Admiral, December 31.	$ 37,205,000

ADMIRAL CASINO & RESORT
Consolidated Balance Sheet
December 31, 2013

Assets		**Liabilities and Stockholders' Equity**	
Current assets	$ 21,180,000	Current liabilities.	$ 25,000,000
Equity investments.	54,000,000	Long-term debt	915,000,000
Plant and equipment, net.	299,000,000	Total liabilities.	940,000,000
Identifiable intangibles	582,500,000	Stockholders' equity	
Goodwill	35,300,000	Admiral stockholders' equity:	
		Capital stock.	5,000,000
		Retained earnings.	37,205,000
		Total Admiral stockholders' equity	42,205,000
		Noncontrolling interest	9,775,000
		Total stockholders' equity	51,980,000
Total assets	$991,980,000	Total liabilities and stockholders' equity	$991,980,000

Admiral Casino & Resort does not report other comprehensive income. However, many less-than-wholly-controlled subsidiaries have investments with unrealized gains and losses reported in OCI—as covered in Chapters 1, 8, and 9 of this text, or currency translation adjustments reported in OCI—as covered in Chapter 7. There are also other income items reported in OCI. FASB *ASC Section 220-10-45* requires that the components of yearly net income and other comprehensive income be reported either in a single statement of net income and OCI, or in two separate statements—a statement of net income, followed immediately by a separate statement of other comprehensive income that displays a total for comprehensive income, equal to net income plus other comprehensive income.

If a consolidated subsidiary reports OCI and has a noncontrolling interest, *ASC Section 810-10-50* requires that the amounts of comprehensive income attributable to the parent and to the noncontrolling interest be separately disclosed. Thus for a less-than-wholly-owned subsidiary that reports OCI in a particular year, eliminating entry N includes the noncontrolling interest's share of OCI. For example, if Gold Road reported a net OCI gain of $200,000 for 2013, we use this revised eliminating entry N:

(N)	Noncontrolling interest in net income	920,000	
	Noncontrolling interest in OCI	40,000	
	Dividends.		100,000
	Noncontrolling interest in Gold Road		860,000
	To recognize the noncontrolling interest in the subsidiary's net income, other comprehensive income, and dividends for the current year.		

Eliminating entry C eliminates the parent's share of the subsidiary's current year OCI, and if the subsidiary has a beginning accumulated OCI balance, eliminating entry E allocates the beginning AOCI balance between the investment and the noncontrolling interest.

Chevron Corporation's 2009 Consolidated Statement of Comprehensive Income illustrates the display of the noncontrolling interest in OCI using the two separate statements approach.

	Year ended December 31		
Millions of dollars	**2009**	**2008**	**2007**
Net income	**$10,563**	$24,031	$18,795
Currency translation adjustment			
Unrealized net change arising during period	**60**	(112)	31
Unrealized holding gain (loss) on securities.	**2**	(6)	19
Derivatives			
Net derivatives loss (gain) on hedge transactions	**(69)**	139	(10)
Reclassification to net income of net realized (gain) loss.	**(23)**	32	7
Income taxes on derivatives transactions	**32**	(61)	(3)
Total	**(60)**	110	(6)
Defined benefit plans	**(399)**	(1,901)	685
Other Comprehensive (Loss) Gain, Net of Tax	**(397)**	(1,909)	729
Comprehensive Income.	**10,166**	22,122	19,524
Comprehensive income attributable to noncontrolling interests	**(80)**	(100)	(107)
Comprehensive Income Attributable to Chevron Corporation	**$10,086**	$22,022	$19,417

Chevron's Statement of Comprehensive Income also appears in Chapter 7, illustrating the currency translation adjustment.

Reporting Perspective

Previous standards in effect until December 2008 did not provide specific guidance on placement of noncontrolling interests in subsidiaries—commonly labeled "minority interests"—on the consolidated balance sheet. In practice, companies reported noncontrolling interests as a component of liabilities or equity, but most companies chose to present these interests in the unlabeled "mezzanine section" between liabilities and equity. Noncontrolling interest in subsidiary income was treated as an expense, so consolidated net income reflected earnings to the parent only. Current U.S. GAAP, effective in 2009, requires noncontrolling interests to be reported in equity, and consolidated net income to include the noncontrolling interest's share of subsidiary income.

The *valuation* of noncontrolling interests and acquired assets and liabilities also changed in 2009. Noncontrolling interests previously did not share in the revaluations of identifiable net assets or goodwill. Instead, noncontrolling interests were valued at their share of book value reported in the subsidiaries' accounts, and identifiable assets and liabilities were only revalued to the extent of the parent's percentage ownership.

To see this, suppose an acquired company's previously unrecorded intangible asset, such as developed technology, had a fair value of $10 million. If the parent acquired only 60 percent of the voting interests, the consolidated financial statements reported the developed technology at $6 million. Similarly, if the acquired company reported equipment with a fair value of $8 million at $5 million, the equipment appeared on the consolidated balance sheet at the date of acquisition at $6.8 million [= $5,000,000 + (60% × $3,000,000)]. Acquired asset and liability values therefore reflected a confusing mix of book and fair values. Current U.S. GAAP values the developed technology, equipment, and similar items at full fair value at the date of acquisition, providing a consistent measurement basis.

Changes in reported goodwill follow the same pattern. Previous standards reported only the parent's share of goodwill. Current standards require recognition of full goodwill, based on the full fair value of the company: the controlling interest's acquisition price plus the fair value of the noncontrolling interest. Goodwill is then allocated between the parent and noncontrolling interests.

continued

continued from prior page

The impacts of these reporting changes depend on the acquisition price and the relationship between the fair and book values of the acquired company's assets and liabilities. On average, the fair value of the acquired company exceeds its book value, and the reporting changes *increase* consolidated net assets when acquired assets are reported at full fair value, even when a noncontrolling interest exists.

For the majority of companies that reported noncontrolling interests in liabilities or in the mezzanine section of the balance sheet, the 2009 change *reduces* liabilities and *increases* equity. The debt-to-equity and debt-to-assets ratios therefore *decrease*. In computing ratios that use earnings measures, analysts must specify the earnings number that is appropriate: consolidated net income, or consolidated net income to the controlling interest. Implementation of the new standards will likely *reduce* consolidated return on assets, since assets are fully revalued and related write-offs increase. A comparative analysis of company performance that includes years before and after 2009 must take these effects into account.

BUSINESS APPLICATION Vail Resorts, Inc., Balance Sheet

Vail Resorts, Inc. is a public holding company that operates ski resorts, hotels and related services through its subsidiaries. Its resort properties include Breckenridge Mountain, Vail Mountain and Beaver Creek Resort in the Colorado Rocky Mountains, and Heavenly Mountain Resort at Lake Tahoe.

Prior to fiscal year 2010, Vail Resorts reported the noncontrolling interests (previously called "minority" interests) in its subsidiaries in the "mezzanine" section of its balance sheet, between liabilities and equity, leaving the reader to decide its actual classification. We observe the effect of Vail's 2010 adoption of the requirements of *ASC Section 810-10-45* by comparing the fiscal 2009 balance sheet as presented in the fiscal 2009 annual report with the fiscal 2009 comparative data shown in the fiscal 2010 report (*all amounts in thousands*).

Fiscal 2009 balance sheet, presented in the fiscal 2009 annual report

Total assets	$1,884,480
Current liabilities	$ 251,348
Long-term debt	491,608
Other long-term liabilities	233,169
Deferred income taxes	112,234
Minority interest in net assets of consolidated subsidiaries	30,826
Stockholders' equity	
Common stock	400
Additional paid-in capital	555,728
Retained earnings	356,995
Treasury stock	(147,828)
Total stockholders' equity	765,295
Total liabilities and stockholders' equity	$1,884,480

Fiscal 2009 balance sheet, presented in the fiscal 2010 annual report

Total assets	$1,884,480
Current liabilities	$ 251,348
Long-term debt	491,608
Other long-term liabilities	233,169
Deferred income taxes	112,234
Redeemable noncontrolling interest	15,415
Stockholders' equity	
Common stock	400
Additional paid-in capital	555,728
Retained earnings	356,995
Treasury stock	(147,828)
Total Vail Resorts, Inc. stockholders' equity	765,295
Noncontrolling interests	15,411
Total stockholders' equity	780,706
Total liabilities and stockholders' equity	$1,884,480

continued

continued from prior page

About half of Vail's 2009 noncontrolling interests are "redeemable" interests, where the holder can require Vail to repurchase the interests whenever the holder decides to do so. These interests are still classified in the "mezzanine" section between liabilities and equity. The remainder of the noncontrolling interests ($15,411 = $30,826 − $15,415) is included in stockholders' equity. The current classification requirements clarify the nature of the noncontrolling interests and do not leave the reader guessing.
Source: Vail Resorts, Inc. annual reports, 2009 and 2010.

REVIEW 1 • Consolidation with noncontrolling interest at end of third year, U.S. GAAP

The trial balances of Admiral and Gold Road at December 31, 2014, *three* years after acquisition, appear in the consolidation working paper below.

	Accounts Taken From Books Dr (Cr)		Eliminations		Consolidated Balances
	Admiral	Gold Road	Dr	Cr	Dr (Cr)
Current assets	$ 14,000,000	$ 9,200,000			
Equity investments.	55,000,000	5,000,000			
Plant and equipment, net.	235,000,000	80,000,000			
Investment in Gold Road	54,285,000	—			
Identifiable intangible assets	550,000,000	—			
Goodwill	—	—			
Current liabilities.	(16,000,000)	(11,000,000)			
Long-term debt	(837,580,000)	(54,100,000)			
Capital stock	(5,000,000)	(2,500,000)			
Retained earnings, January 1.	(37,205,000)	(17,400,000)			
Noncontrolling interest.	—	—			
Dividends	2,500,000	800,000			
Sales and other revenue.	(700,000,000)	(200,000,000)			
Equity in income of Gold Road	(7,000,000)	—			
Cost of goods sold.	480,000,000	140,000,000			
Operating expenses.	212,000,000	50,000,000			
Noncontrolling interest in net income . . .	—	—			
Totals	$ 0	$ 0			$ 0

There is no goodwill impairment during 2014.

Required

Prepare a consolidation working paper to consolidate the trial balances of Admiral and Gold Road, and present the 2014 financial statements in proper format.

Solutions are located after the chapter assignments.

NONCONTROLLING INTERESTS AND BARGAIN PURCHASES

LO3 Consolidate a subsidiary with noncontrolling interests when the acquisition is a bargain purchase.

In unusual cases an acquirer's acquisition cost is less than the fair value of the identifiable net assets acquired. Chapters 3 and 4 cover consolidation involving bargain purchases of wholly-owned subsidiaries. In the case of a partially owned subsidiary, the "bargain gain" or **gain on acquisition** is the difference between total firm value—acquisition cost plus the fair value of the noncontrolling interest—and the fair value of the acquiree's identifiable net assets, as follows:

Fair value of identifiable net assets	
Less acquisition cost	
Less fair value of noncontrolling interest	
Gain on acquisition	

ASC para. 805-30-25-2 requires that the bargain gain be *attributed entirely to the controlling interest.* In the year of acquisition, the parent reports the gain and closes it to retained earnings. In future years the gain remains as part of the parent's retained earnings, which are not eliminated in consolidation.

Bargain Purchase Consolidation at Date of Acquisition

Return to our earlier illustration, where Admiral Casino & Resort acquires an 80 percent interest in Gold Road Motor Inn, Inc. on January 1, 2012. Admiral pays $11,000,000 for its investment, and the fair value of the 20 percent noncontrolling interest in Gold Road is $2,500,000. All other information remains the same, including the fair values of all of Gold Road's identifiable net assets, which were carefully checked for accuracy.

    The gain on acquisition is calculated below.

Book value	$10,000,000
Revaluation of identifiable net assets:	
Customer lists	5,000,000
Fair value of identifiable net assets	15,000,000
Less acquisition cost	(11,000,000)
Less fair value of noncontrolling interest	(2,500,000)
Gain on acquisition.	$ 1,500,000

Admiral makes the following entry on its own books to record the acquisition:

Investment in Gold Road	12,500,000	
Cash		11,000,000
Gain on acquisition of Gold Road		1,500,000
To record 80 percent acquisition of Gold Road.		

The date-of-acquisition eliminating entries are as follows:

(E)	Capital stock	2,500,000	
	Retained earnings	7,500,000	
	Investment in Gold Road (80%)		8,000,000
	Noncontrolling interest in Gold Road (20%)		2,000,000
	To eliminate Gold Road's equity accounts against the book value portion of the investment account and recognize the book value of the noncontrolling interest.		
(R)	Customer lists	5,000,000	
	Investment in Gold Road.		4,500,000
	Noncontrolling interest in Gold Road		500,000
	To revalue Gold Road's identifiable net assets to fair value, eliminate the remaining investment balance and bring the noncontrolling interest to fair value. $4,500,000 = $12,500,000 − $8,000,000. $500,000 = $2,500,000 − $2,000,000.		

In a bargain purchase, the investment account and noncontrolling interest do not reflect the total revaluation of the identifiable net assets because a bargain price was paid. We therefore set the amount credited to the investment in entry (R) equal to the amount necessary to eliminate its remaining balance. The amount credited to the noncontrolling interest in entry (R) is the amount needed to establish its fair value.

Bargain Purchase Consolidation at End of the First Year

Because the noncontrolling interest does not share in the gain, it also does not fully share in the revaluations of the acquired company's assets and liabilities. The most straightforward way to value the noncontrolling interest on the consolidated balance sheet in years subsequent to acquisition is to keep track of its value at the end of the previous year, and use elimination (R) to set the beginning-of-year value. At the end of the first year, the beginning-of-year value of the noncontrolling interest is of course its original estimated fair value. As before, Gold Road reports net income of $5,000,000 and pays cash dividends of $600,000 in 2012, the first year following acquisition.

Calculation of equity in net income and noncontrolling interest in net income for 2012 follows:

	Total	Equity in net income	Noncontrolling interest in net income
Gold Road's reported income for 2012	$5,000,000	$4,000,000	$1,000,000
Adjustment for revaluation write-offs:			
Customer lists ($5,000,000/4).	(1,250,000)	(1,000,000)	(250,000)
Totals	$3,750,000	$3,000,000	$ 750,000

Because the gain on acquisition is attributed only to the parent, it is unlikely that the original revaluations of identifiable net assets are allocated between the controlling and noncontrolling interests in ownership proportions. However, for simplicity we assume that amortization of the customer lists is allocated according to ownership interests.

Admiral records equity in net income of $3,000,000, and its share of Gold Road's dividends for 2012, $480,000. The investment account therefore has a December 31, 2012, balance of $15,020,000 (= $12,500,000 + $3,000,000 − $480,000).

The consolidation working paper in Exhibit 5.4 shows the preclosing accounts of Admiral and Gold Road at December 31, 2012, in trial balance format, for our bargain gain illustration. Following are the five eliminating entries needed to consolidate the 2012 financial statements of Admiral and Gold Road, in journal entry form:

(C)	Equity in income of Gold Road	3,000,000	
	Dividends.		480,000
	Investment in Gold Road.		2,520,000

To eliminate equity in net income on the parent's books, the parent's share of the subsidiary's dividends, and restore the investment account to its beginning-of-year value.

(E)	Capital stock	2,500,000	
	Retained earnings, January 1.	7,500,000	
	Investment in Gold Road (80%)		8,000,000
	Noncontrolling interest in Gold Road (20%)		2,000,000

To eliminate the subsidiary's beginning-of-year equity accounts against the beginning-of-year book value portion of the investment account and recognize the beginning-of-year book value of the noncontrolling interest.

continued

continued from prior page

(R)	Customer lists	5,000,000	
	Investment in Gold Road..		4,500,000
	Noncontrolling interest in Gold Road		500,000
	To revalue Gold Road's identifiable net assets to fair value, eliminate the remainder of the investment balance, and bring the noncontrolling interest to its beginning-of-year value of $2,500,000.		
(O)	Operating expenses..	1,250,000	
	Customer lists		1,250,000
	To record the current year's amortization for customer lists.		
(N)	Noncontrolling interest in net income	750,000	
	Dividends..		120,000
	Noncontrolling interest in Gold Road		630,000
	To recognize the noncontrolling interest in the subsidiary's income and dividends for the current year.		

Exhibit 5.4 displays these eliminating entries, and each account's consolidated balance.

EXHIBIT 5.4   Consolidation Working Paper for Admiral and Gold Road at December 31, 2012, Bargain Purchase

	Accounts Taken From Books Dr (Cr)		Eliminations		Consolidated Balances Dr (Cr)
	Admiral	**Gold Road**	**Dr**	**Cr**	
Current assets	$ 42,480,000	$ 4,400,000			$ 46,880,000
Equity investments...................	40,000,000	5,000,000			45,000,000
Plant and equipment, net..............	260,000,000	55,000,000			315,000,000
Investment in Gold Road	15,020,000	—		$ 2,520,000 (C)	—
				8,000,000 (E)	
				4,500,000 (R)	
Identifiable intangible assets	600,000,000	—	(R) $ 5,000,000	1,250,000 (O)	603,750,000
Current liabilities.....................	(10,000,000)	(10,000,000)			(20,000,000)
Long-term debt	(910,000,000)	(40,000,000)			(950,000,000)
Capital stock	(5,000,000)	(2,500,000)	(E) 2,500,000		(5,000,000)
Retained earnings, January 1.............	(20,000,000)	(7,500,000)	(E) 7,500,000		(20,000,000)
Noncontrolling interest.................	—	—		2,000,000 (E)	
				500,000 (R)	
				630,000 (N)	(3,130,000)
Dividends	2,000,000	600,000		480,000 (C)	
				120,000 (N)	2,000,000
Sales and other revenue................	(600,000,000)	(150,000,000)			(750,000,000)
Equity in income of Gold Road	(3,000,000)	—	(C) 3,000,000		—
Cost of goods sold....................	400,000,000	115,000,000			515,000,000
Operating expenses...................	190,000,000	30,000,000	(O) 1,250,000		221,250,000
Gain on acquisition....................	(1,500,000)	—			(1,500,000)
Noncontrolling interest in net income	—	—	(N) 750,000		750,000
Totals	$ 0	$ 0	$20,000,000	$20,000,000	$ 0

Bargain Purchase Consolidation at End of the Second Year

December 31, 2013, preclosing trial balances of Admiral and Gold Road appear in the consolidation working paper in Exhibit 5.5. Gold Road reports net income of $6,000,000 and pays cash dividends of $500,000 in 2013.

Calculation of the parent's equity in net income of subsidiary, reported on the parent's books, and the noncontrolling interest in the net income of the subsidiary, reported on the consolidated income statement, is as follows:

	Total	Equity in net income	Noncontrolling interest in net income
Gold Road's reported income for 2013	$6,000,000	$4,800,000	$1,200,000
Adjustment for revaluation write-offs:			
Customer lists ($5,000,000/4).	(1,250,000)	(1,000,000)	(250,000)
Totals	$4,750,000	$3,800,000	$ 950,000

After Admiral records equity in net income of Gold Road and its share of Gold Road's dividends for 2013, the investment balance at December 31, 2013, is $18,420,000 (= $15,020,000 + $3,800,000 − $400,000). The five eliminating entries needed to consolidate the 2013 financial statements of Admiral and Gold Road, in journal entry form, follow:

(C)	Equity in income of Gold Road	3,800,000	
	Dividends.		400,000
	Investment in Gold Road.		3,400,000
	To eliminate equity in net income on the parent's books, the parent's share of the subsidiary's dividends, and restore the investment account to its beginning-of-year value.		
(E)	Capital stock	2,500,000	
	Retained earnings, January 1.	11,900,000	
	Investment in Gold Road (80%)		11,520,000
	Noncontrolling interest in Gold Road (20%)		2,880,000
	To eliminate the subsidiary's beginning-of-year equity accounts against the beginning-of-year book value portion of the investment account and recognize the beginning-of-year book value of the noncontrolling interest.		
(R)	Customer lists	3,750,000	
	Investment in Gold Road.		3,500,000
	Noncontrolling interest in Gold Road		250,000
	To revalue Gold Road's net assets to fair value, eliminate the remaining investment balance, and bring the noncontrolling interest balance to its beginning-of-year value of $3,130,000.		
(O)	Operating expenses.	1,250,000	
	Customer lists		1,250,000
	To record the current year's amortization for customer lists.		
(N)	Noncontrolling interest in net income	950,000	
	Dividends.		100,000
	Noncontrolling interest in Gold Road		850,000
	To recognize the noncontrolling interest in the subsidiary's income and dividends for the current year.		

EXHIBIT 5.5 Consolidation Working Paper for Admiral and Gold Road at December 31, 2013, Bargain Purchase

	Accounts Taken From Books Dr (Cr)		Eliminations		Consolidated Balances Dr (Cr)
	Admiral	**Gold Road**	**Dr**	**Cr**	**Dr (Cr)**
Current assets	$ 43,880,000	$ 8,900,000			$ 52,780,000
Equity investments	50,000,000	4,000,000			54,000,000
Plant and equipment, net	235,000,000	64,000,000			299,000,000
Investment in Gold Road	18,420,000	—		$ 3,400,000 (C)	—
				11,520,000 (E)	
				3,500,000 (R)	
Identifiable intangible assets	580,000,000	—	(R) $ 3,750,000	1,250,000 (O)	582,500,000
Current liabilities	(13,000,000)	(12,000,000)			(25,000,000)
Long-term debt	(870,000,000)	(45,000,000)			(915,000,000)
Capital stock	(5,000,000)	(2,500,000)	(E) 2,500,000		(5,000,000)
Retained earnings, January 1	(32,500,000)	(11,900,000)	(E) 11,900,000		(32,500,000)
Noncontrolling interest	—	—		2,880,000 (E)	
				250,000 (R)	
				850,000 (N)	(3,980,000)
Dividends	2,000,000	500,000		400,000 (C)	
				100,000 (N)	2,000,000
Sales and other revenue	(620,000,000)	(160,000,000)			(780,000,000)
Equity in income of Gold Road	(3,800,000)	—	(C) 3,800,000		—
Cost of goods sold	410,000,000	120,000,000			530,000,000
Operating expenses	205,000,000	34,000,000	(O) 1,250,000		240,250,000
Noncontrolling interest in net income	—	—	(N) 950,000		950,000
Totals	$ 0	$ 0	$24,150,000	$24,150,000	$ 0

INTERNATIONAL FINANCIAL REPORTING STANDARDS FOR NONCONTROLLING INTERESTS

LO4 Explain IFRS for noncontrolling interests.

IFRS 3(R) presents IFRS for valuing and reporting noncontrolling interests in consolidated financial statements. Although IFRS agrees with U.S. GAAP that the noncontrolling interest should be reported at acquisition-date fair value, *IFRS 3(R)* actually allows the acquirer to choose between **two different valuation methods**:

1. Value the noncontrolling interest at **full fair value** at the acquisition date, as in U.S. GAAP.

2. Value the noncontrolling interest at its share of the **fair value of the subsidiary's identifiable net assets** at the acquisition date.

Using valuation method #2, the noncontrolling interest is not allocated any goodwill: only the controlling interest's share of goodwill is recognized. Therefore the IFRS alternative reports goodwill and noncontrolling interests at *lower amounts* on the consolidated balance sheet than under U.S. GAAP. When goodwill is impaired, IFRS noncontrolling interest in net income is *higher* than U.S. GAAP, since no goodwill impairment loss is charged against the noncontrolling interest.

Return to Admiral's acquisition of 80 percent of Gold Road's stock for $42,600,000. The alternative valuation method allowed by IFRS (#2) leads to this initial value of the noncontrolling interest:

Gold Road book value	$10,000,000
Revaluation of identifiable net assets:	
Customer lists	5,000,000
Fair value of identifiable net assets	15,000,000
Noncontrolling interest %	× 20%
Noncontrolling interest	$ 3,000,000

Goodwill is attributed only to the parent, giving us the same goodwill amount attributed to the parent under U.S. GAAP:

Acquisition cost	$42,600,000
80% book value	(8,000,000)
80% revaluation: customer lists	(4,000,000)
Goodwill	$30,600,000

To further illustrate the IFRS alternative valuation of noncontrolling interests, we consolidate the financial statements of Admiral and Gold Road at December 31, 2012, one year after acquisition. Assuming $425,000 goodwill impairment on the $30,600,000 in goodwill, as in the previous illustration, we calculate equity in net income and noncontrolling interest in net income as follows:

	Total	Equity in net income	Noncontrolling interest in net income
Gold Road's reported income for 2012	$5,000,000	$4,000,000	$1,000,000
Adjustment for revaluation write-offs:			
Customer lists ($5,000,000/4)	(1,250,000)	(1,000,000)	(250,000)
Goodwill	(425,000)	(425,000)	—
Totals	$3,325,000	$2,575,000	$ 750,000

Here are the five eliminating entries needed to consolidate the 2012 financial statements of Admiral and Gold Road, in journal entry form:

(C)	Equity in income of Gold Road	2,575,000	
	Dividends.		480,000
	Investment in Gold Road.		2,095,000
	To eliminate equity in net income on the parent's books, the parent's share of the subsidiary's dividends, and restore the investment account to its beginning-of-year value.		
(E)	Capital stock	2,500,000	
	Retained earnings, January 1	7,500,000	
	Investment in Gold Road (80%)		8,000,000
	Noncontrolling interest in Gold Road (20%)		2,000,000
	To eliminate the subsidiary's beginning-of-year equity accounts against the beginning-of-year book value portion of the investment account and recognize the beginning-of-year book value of the noncontrolling interest.		
(R)	Customer lists	5,000,000	
	Goodwill	30,600,000	
	Investment in Gold Road.		34,600,000
	Noncontrolling interest in Gold Road		1,000,000
	To revalue Gold Road's net assets to fair value and allocate the revaluations to the controlling and noncontrolling interest. *$34,600,000 = (80% x $5,000,000) + $30,600,000.* *$1,000,000 = (20% x $5,000,000).*		
(O)	Goodwill impairment loss.	425,000	
	Other operating expenses	1,250,000	
	Goodwill.		425,000
	Customer lists		1,250,000
	To write off the revaluations for the current year.		
(N)	Noncontrolling interest in net income	750,000	
	Dividends.		120,000
	Noncontrolling interest in Gold Road		630,000
	To recognize the noncontrolling interest in the subsidiary's income and dividends for the current year.		

Exhibit 5.6 displays these eliminating entries, and each account's consolidated balance.

EXHIBIT 5.6 Consolidation Working Paper for Admiral and Gold Road at December 31, 2012, IFRS Alternative

	Accounts Taken From Books Dr (Cr)		Eliminations		Consolidated Balances Dr (Cr)
	Admiral	Gold Road	Dr	Cr	
Current assets	$ 10,880,000	$ 4,400,000			$ 15,280,000
Equity investments.	40,000,000	5,000,000			45,000,000
Plant and equipment, net.	260,000,000	55,000,000			315,000,000
Investment in Gold Road	44,695,000	—		$ 2,095,000 (C)	—
				8,000,000 (E)	
				34,600,000 (R)	
Identifiable intangible assets	600,000,000	—	(R) $ 5,000,000	1,250,000 (O)	603,750,000
Goodwill	—	—	(R) 30,600,000	425,000 (O)	30,175,000
Current liabilities.	(10,000,000)	(10,000,000)			(20,000,000)
Long-term debt	(910,000,000)	(40,000,000)			(950,000,000)
Capital stock	(5,000,000)	(2,500,000)	(E) 2,500,000		(5,000,000)
Retained earnings, January 1.	(20,000,000)	(7,500,000)	(E) 7,500,000		(20,000,000)
Noncontrolling interest.	—	—		2,000,000 (E)	
				1,000,000 (R)	
				630,000 (N)	(3,630,000)
				480,000 (C)	
Dividends	2,000,000	600,000		120,000 (N)	2,000,000
Sales and other revenue.	(600,000,000)	(150,000,000)			(750,000,000)
Equity in income of Gold Road	(2,575,000)	—	(C) 2,575,000		—
Cost of goods sold.	400,000,000	115,000,000			515,000,000
Goodwill impairment loss.	—	—	(O) 425,000		425,000
Other operating expenses	190,000,000	30,000,000	(O) 1,250,000		221,250,000
Noncontrolling interest in net income	—	—	(N) 750,000		750,000
Totals	$ 0	$ 0	$50,600,000	$50,600,000	$ 0

Compare the IFRS consolidated balances with the U.S. GAAP balances on the 2012 consolidated financial statements.

	IFRS	U.S. GAAP
Goodwill	$30,175,000	$35,500,000
Noncontrolling interest (balance sheet)	3,630,000	8,955,000
Noncontrolling interest in net income (income statement).	750,000	675,000

Goodwill is *lower* under IFRS because only the controlling interest's share is recognized. Noncontrolling interest in the equity section of the consolidated balance sheet is *lower* for the same reason. The difference in reported goodwill, $5,325,000 (= $35,500,000 − $30,175,000), is the noncontrolling interest's share of the ending goodwill balance under U.S. GAAP ($5,325,000 = 15% × $35,500,000). Noncontrolling interest in net income is *higher* under IFRS if there is any goodwill impairment during the year; the difference, $75,000 (= $750,000 − $675,000) is the noncontrolling interest's share of 2012 goodwill impairment under U.S. GAAP ($75,000 = 15% × $500,000). If there is no goodwill impairment, noncontrolling interest in net income based on the IFRS alternative equals U.S. GAAP.

Valuation of the noncontrolling interest using the IFRS alternative is more conservative. Rather than inferring the noncontrolling interest's share of goodwill from its acquisition-date fair value, the IFRS alternative reports only the parent's share of goodwill as revealed by its acquisition cost.

BUSINESS APPLICATION **IFRS and Nokia Corporation**

Nokia Corporation uses IFRS to present its financial statements. In 2007, Nokia and **Siemens AG** formed **Nokia Siemens Networks (NSN)** to combine the mobile and fixed-line telecommunications network equipment businesses of the two companies. Each corporation owns 50 percent of the new company, but Nokia consolidates NSN, because Nokia can appoint key officers and a majority of the Board of Directors. The €5,551 million reported cost of the acquisition is attributed to identifiable net assets of €3,995 million, and €1,556 million total goodwill. However, Nokia subtracts €753 "non-controlling interest in goodwill" to arrive at the €803 million goodwill reported on the consolidated balance sheet. Two major differences between IFRS and U.S. GAAP are illustrated.

- First, Nokia consolidates Nokia Siemens Networks. Under U.S. GAAP, the investment would probably not be consolidated since even though Nokia has effective control, it does not own the majority of the shares. The investment would instead be reported as an equity investment.

- Second, Nokia reports only the controlling interest in goodwill. If Nokia followed current U.S. GAAP, total goodwill would be reported and attributed to the controlling and noncontrolling interests. *Source:* Nokia Corporation, Form 20-F, December 31, 2007.

REVIEW 2 • Consolidation with noncontrolling interest at end of the third year, IFRS

Refer to the information in review problem #1, and now assume Admiral follows IFRS and uses the alternative method for valuing noncontrolling interests and goodwill. The consolidation working paper for 2014 is again presented below.

	Accounts Taken From Books Dr (Cr)		Eliminations		Consolidated Balances Dr (Cr)
	Admiral	**Gold Road**	**Dr**	**Cr**	
Current assets	$ 14,000,000	$ 9,200,000			
Equity investments	55,000,000	5,000,000			
Plant and equipment, net	235,000,000	80,000,000			
Investment in Gold Road	54,285,000	—			
Identifiable intangible assets	550,000,000	—			
Goodwill	—	—			
Current liabilities	(16,000,000)	(11,000,000)			
Long-term debt	(837,580,000)	(54,100,000)			
Capital stock	(5,000,000)	(2,500,000)			
Retained earnings, January 1	(37,205,000)	(17,400,000)			
Noncontrolling interest					
Dividends	2,500,000	800,000			
Sales and other revenue	(700,000,000)	(200,000,000)			
Equity in income of Gold Road	(7,000,000)	—			
Cost of goods sold	480,000,000	140,000,000			
Goodwill impairment loss	—	—			
Other operating expenses	212,000,000	50,000,000			
Noncontrolling interest in net income . . .	—	—			
Totals	$ 0	$ 0			$ 0

Assume that accumulated goodwill impairment to the beginning of 2014 is $595,000. There is no goodwill impairment during 2014.

Required

Prepare a consolidation working paper to consolidate the trial balances of Admiral and Gold Road, and present the 2014 financial statements in proper format.

Solutions are located after the chapter assignments.

CONSOLIDATED STATEMENT OF CASH FLOWS

LO5 Prepare the consolidated statement of cash flows.

Although not directly related to the topic of noncontrolling interests, we now discuss preparation of the **consolidated statement of cash flows**, one of a firm's required financial statements. At this point in the text you have encountered the consolidation issues related to preparing this statement.

ASC Topic 230, Statement of Cash Flows, specifies the content and format of the statement, organized in sections showing the cash effect of *operating activities*, *investing activities*, and *financing activities*, and disclosure of material noncash transactions affecting investing or financing activities or both. Companies may use either the direct or indirect method to report cash flows from operating activities. The **direct method** converts each line on the income statement from accrual to cash basis: cash received from customers, cash paid for purchases, and so forth. When the direct method is used, a reconciliation of net income to cash flow from operations is also required. The **indirect method** focuses on that reconciliation. It begins with net income, adds or subtracts those income statement items that did not affect operating cash, and adjusts for operating cash flows not reflected in net income by considering operating changes in current asset and current liability accounts. Because the indirect method is almost always found in practice, we use it to illustrate preparation of the statement of cash flows.

We do not duplicate the more complete discussions of the statement of cash flows found in intermediate accounting textbooks. Rather, we highlight particular items related to the consolidation process that affect the consolidated statement of cash flows.

Preparation of Consolidated Statement of Cash Flows

The consolidated statement of cash flows is most efficiently prepared from comparative consolidated balance sheets, consolidated statements of income and retained earnings, and supplementary information. Attempts to prepare a consolidated statement of cash flows from the unconsolidated accounts of the parent and subsidiary are more difficult and require duplicative eliminating entries. The following items are frequently encountered in a consolidated statement of cash flows.

- When presenting cash provided by operations using the indirect method, start with **consolidated net income**, rather than consolidated income attributed to the parent, and adjust this balance for noncash and nonoperating items. If you start with consolidated income attributable to the parent, you must add (subtract) the noncontrolling interest in net income (loss), because it is a noncash deduction. Using consolidated net income avoids this adjustment.
- In determining cash provided by operations, we add back **goodwill impairment charges** arising in consolidation to consolidated net income. This deduction from net income does not use cash—it decreases a noncurrent asset, goodwill. Similarly, we add back amortization of previously unrecorded identifiable intangibles arising in consolidation to consolidated net income.
- **Dividends paid to noncontrolling shareholders**, as well as dividends paid to the parent's shareholders, are shown as cash used for financing activities.
- **Undistributed equity method income (loss)** from equity method investments is subtracted from (added to) net income in computing cash provided by operations. The accrual of equity method income increases long-term equity investments—noncurrent assets—and does not itself provide cash. Dividends received from such investments, however, represent a realization of the equity method income and do increase cash. Because these dividends are included in cash provided by operations, we subtract from net income the *undistributed* equity method income (not received in dividends) in arriving at cash provided by operations.

Consolidated Statement of Cash Flows: An Illustration

The following illustration is based on the data previously developed for Admiral Casino & Resort and its 80-percent-owned subsidiary, Gold Road Motor Inn, Inc., in Exhibits 5.2 and 5.3. Exhibit 5.7 shows comparative consolidated balance sheets for Admiral and Gold Road at December 31, 2013, and 2012, and a consolidated statement of income and retained earnings for 2013. Exhibit 5.7 also provides supplementary information necessary to prepare the consolidated statement of cash flows for 2013, which appears in Exhibit 5.8.

EXHIBIT 5.7 Admiral and Gold Road Consolidated Financial Statements

ADMIRAL CASINO & RESORT
Comparative Consolidated Balance Sheets
December 31

	2013	2012
Assets		
Cash	$ 3,400,000	$ 3,150,000
Receivables	8,800,000	9,300,000
Inventory	8,980,000	2,830,000
Total current assets	21,180,000	15,280,000
Equity investments	54,000,000	45,000,000
Plant and equipment, net	299,000,000	315,000,000
Identifiable intangibles	582,500,000	603,750,000
Goodwill	35,300,000	35,500,000
Total noncurrent assets	970,800,000	999,250,000
Total assets	$991,980,000	$1,014,530,000
Liabilities and Stockholders' Equity		
Liabilities		
Current liabilities	$ 25,000,000	$ 20,000,000
Long-term debt	915,000,000	950,000,000
Total liabilities	940,000,000	970,000,000
Stockholders' equity		
Admiral stockholders' equity:		
Capital stock	5,000,000	5,000,000
Retained earnings	37,205,000	30,575,000
Total Admiral stockholders' equity	42,205,000	35,575,000
Noncontrolling interest	9,775,000	8,955,000
Total stockholders' equity	51,980,000	44,530,000
Total liabilities and stockholders' equity	$991,980,000	$1,014,530,000

ADMIRAL CASINO & RESORT
Consolidated Statement of Income and Retained Earnings
For Year Ended December 31, 2013

Sales and other revenue	$780,000,000
Less: Cost of goods sold	(530,000,000)
Goodwill impairment loss	(200,000)
Other operating expenses	(240,250,000)
Consolidated net income	**9,550,000**
Less: Noncontrolling interest in net income	(920,000)
Net income attributable to Admiral	8,630,000
Plus: Retained earnings, Admiral, January 1	30,575,000
Less: Dividends	(2,000,000)
Retained earnings, Admiral, December 31	$ 37,205,000

Supplementary information

1. Other operating expenses include $30,000,000 depreciation expense on plant and equipment and $21,250,000 amortization expense on intangibles. Consolidated accumulated depreciation on plant and equipment for 2013 and 2012 is $175,000,000 and $160,000,000, respectively.
2. Sales and other income includes $3,000,000 gain on cash sales of plant and equipment.
3. Cash acquisitions of plant and equipment for 2013 were $40,000,000.
4. Sales and other revenue includes $10,000,000 income from equity method investments; $1,000,000 in cash dividends was received from those investments.
5. Cash dividends paid by Gold Road during 2013 totaled $500,000.

EXHIBIT 5.8   Admiral and Gold Road Consolidated Statement of Cash Flows

ADMIRAL CASINO & RESORT
Consolidated Statement of Cash Flows
For Year Ended December 31, 2013

Cash from operating activities		
Consolidated net income		$ 9,550,000
Add (subtract) items not affecting cash:		
Depreciation expense	$ 30,000,000	
Amortization expense	21,250,000	
Goodwill impairment loss	200,000	
Undistributed equity method income	(9,000,000)	42,450,000
Changes in current assets and liabilities:		
Decrease in receivables	500,000	
Increase in inventory	(6,150,000)	
Increase in current liabilities	5,000,000	(650,000)
Nonoperating item:		
Gain on sale of plant and equipment		(3,000,000)
Net cash flows from operating activities		48,350,000
Cash from investing activities		
Acquisition of plant and equipment	(40,000,000)	
Sale of plant and equipment[1]	29,000,000	(11,000,000)
Cash from financing activities		
Net decrease in long-term debt	(35,000,000)	
Dividends paid to controlling shareholders	(2,000,000)	
Dividends paid to noncontrolling shareholders	(100,000)	(37,100,000)
Net increase in cash.		250,000
Cash balance, January 1		3,150,000
Cash balance, December 31		$ 3,400,000

[1] Cost of plant and equipment sold = $41,000,000 = ($315,000,000 + $160,000,000) + $40,000,000 − ($299,000,000 + $175,000,000). Accumulated depreciation on plant and equipment sold = $15,000,000 = $160,000,000 + $30,000,000 − $175,000,000. Thus, book value of plant and equipment sold = $41,000,000 − $15,000,000 = $26,000,000. Book value + gain on sale = cash received; $26,000,000 + $3,000,000 = $29,000,000.

REVIEW OF KEY CONCEPTS • • • • • • • • • • • • • • • •

LO 1   **Consolidate a subsidiary with noncontrolling interests at the date of acquisition. (p. 164)** Whenever an acquirer purchases less than 100 percent but more than 50 percent of an acquiree's stock, the acquirer consolidates the accounts of the acquiree in its financial statements. That portion of the acquiree's equity not owned by the acquirer is the **noncontrolling interest**. *ASC Topic 805* outlines procedures for valuing noncontrolling interests, while *ASC Topic 810* provides the requirements for presenting these interests in the consolidated financial statements. Consolidated assets and liabilities include the subsidiary's balances, in full. The noncontrolling interest in the acquiree's accounts appears on a **noncontrolling interest line in the equity section of the consolidated balance sheet**—the portion of consolidated net assets attributable to noncontrolling interests. **Acquired goodwill** is the controlling interest's acquisition cost plus the fair value of the noncontrolling interest less the fair value of identifiable net assets acquired, and goodwill is attributed to the controlling and noncontrolling interests. The **fair value of the noncontrolling interest** may be the acquisition-date market price per share, if there is an active market for the stock. Alternative valuation methods such as discounted cash flow models and earnings multiples may be used. Generally the per-share acquisition price exceeds the per-share value of the noncontrolling interest due to a **control premium**. **Variable interest entities** (VIEs) commonly have noncontrolling interests. *ASC Topic 810* requires the VIE's primary beneficiary to consolidate the VIE's assets and liabilities at book value if the primary beneficiary and the VIE are under common control, and to report the noncontrolling interest at book value. More typically, if the two entities are not under common control, the VIE's assets, liabilities, and noncontrolling interest are initially reported at fair value.

LO 2   **Consolidate a subsidiary with noncontrolling interests in subsequent years. (p. 168)** Consolidated revenues, expenses and other income-related accounts include the subsidiary's balances, in full. **A noncontrolling interest**

in income line on the consolidated income statement—the portion of consolidated net income attributed to noncontrolling interests—appears as a distribution of consolidated net income. It is calculated as the noncontrolling interest's share of the subsidiary's reported income, adjusted for the noncontrolling interest's share of write-offs of revalued assets and liabilities. Consolidation eliminating entries are represented by the acronym **CERON**, as follows: **(C)** elimination of the parent's **C**urrent year equity method income and the subsidiary's intercompany dividends; **(E)** elimination of the subsidiary's beginning-of-year stockholders' **E**quity accounts, reducing the investment account and increasing the noncontrolling interest in equity account in proportion to ownership interests; **(R)** recognition of the beginning-of-year **R**evaluation balances for the subsidiary's assets and liabilities, with revaluations attributed to the controlling interest eliminating the remainder of the investment balance and revaluations attributed to the noncontrolling interest increasing the noncontrolling interest account; **(O)** writing **O**ff the revaluations for the current year; and **(N)** updating the **N**oncontrolling interest for its share of current year income and dividends.

Consolidate a subsidiary with noncontrolling interests when the acquisition is a bargain purchase. (p. 177) **Gains on bargain purchases are attributed entirely to the controlling interest.** Because the subsidiary's net asset revaluations are not shared according to ownership interests, elimination entry R removes the remaining investment balance and adjusts the noncontrolling interest to its value as of the end of the previous year. **LO 3**

Explain IFRS for noncontrolling interests. (p. 182) **IFRS** may differ from U.S. GAAP in the valuation of the noncontrolling interest and goodwill. Although IFRS allows valuation according to U.S. GAAP, companies may choose an alternative method that initially values the noncontrolling interest at its share of the fair value of the subsidiary's identifiable net assets, and reports only the controlling interest's share of goodwill. **LO 4**

Prepare the consolidated statement of cash flows. (p. 186) The **consolidated statement of cash flows** is most efficiently prepared from comparative consolidated balance sheets and the current consolidated income statement, plus supplementary information. The operating activities section starts with consolidated net income. Noncash items such as amortization expense on previously unrecorded intangibles and undistributed equity method income adjust consolidated income to arrive at cash from operating activities. The financing section reports cash dividends paid by the subsidiary to the noncontrolling interest as well as cash dividends paid by the parent. **LO 5**

MULTIPLE CHOICE QUESTIONS ••••••••••••••••••••••••••••

Use the following information to answer questions 1 – 7 below:

> On January 1, 2012, Pomegranate Company acquired 90% of the voting stock of Starfruit Company for $91,700,000 in cash. The fair value of the noncontrolling interest in Starfruit at the date of acquisition was $6,300,000. Starfruit's book value was $13,000,000 at the date of acquisition. Starfruit's assets and liabilities were reported on its books at values approximating fair value, except its plant and equipment (10-year life, straight-line) was overvalued by $25,000,000. Starfruit Company had previously unreported intangible assets, with a market value of $40,000,000 and 5-year life, straight-line, which were capitalized following GAAP.

1. At the date of acquisition, consolidation eliminating entry R credits the noncontrolling interest in Starfruit Company in the amount of **LO 1**

   a. $1,500,000
   b. $5,000,000
   c. $6,300,000
   d. $8,500,000

Use the following additional information to answer questions 2 and 3 below:

> Pomegranate uses the complete equity method to account for its investment in Starfruit on its own books. Goodwill recognized in this acquisition was impaired by a total of $2,000,000 in 2012 and 2013, and by $500,000 in 2014. It is now December 31, 2014, the accounting year-end. Here is Starfruit Company's trial balance at December 31, 2014:

	Dr (Cr)
Current assets	$ 28,100,000
Plant & equipment, net.	188,000,000
Intangibles	2,000,000
Liabilities.	(180,000,000)
Capital stock	(1,000,000)
Retained earnings, January 1.	(30,000,000)
Dividends	400,000
Sales revenue.	(24,000,000)
Cost of goods sold.	10,000,000
Operating expenses.	6,500,000
	$ 0

LO 2 **2.** On the 2014 consolidation working paper, eliminating entry R reduces the Investment in Starfruit by

    a. $ 3,600,000
    b. $64,800,000
    c. $68,200,000
    d. $81,000,000

LO 2 **3.** On the 2014 consolidated income statement, the noncontrolling interest in net income of Starfruit is

    a. $150,000
    b. $175,000
    c. $200,000
    d. $750,000

LO 4 **4.** If Pomegranate follows IFRS and uses the alternative method of valuing the noncontrolling interest, at the date of acquisition the noncontrolling interest in Starfruit appears in the equity section of the consolidated balance sheet in the amount of

    a. $7,800,000
    b. $6,300,000
    c. $2,800,000
    d. $1,300,000

LO 4 **5.** If Pomegranate follows IFRS and uses the alternative method of valuing the noncontrolling interest, the 2014 noncontrolling interest in net income of Starfruit is

    a. $150,000
    b. $175,000
    c. $200,000
    d. $750,000

Use the following information to answer questions 6 and 7 below:

Now assume Pomegranate paid only $20,000,000 to acquire 90% of Starfruit. The fair value of the noncontrolling interest at the date of acquisition was $2,000,000.

LO 3 **6.** At the date of acquisition, consolidation elimination entry R credits the noncontrolling interest in Starfruit in the amount of

    a. $6,700,000
    b. $4,900,000
    c. $2,000,000
    d. $ 700,000

LO 3 **7.** On the 2014 consolidation working paper, eliminating entry R debits goodwill in the amount of

    a. $ 0
    b. $11,300,000
    c. $53,700,000
    d. $68,000,000

8. Which is the *best* way to measure the fair value per share of a subsidiary's noncontrolling interest?   LO 1

   a. The per share market value of the subsidiary's stock, in an active market, less a discount for lack of control

   b. The price per share that the parent paid for the subsidiary's stock

   c. The price per share that the parent paid for the subsidiary's stock, plus a premium for lack of control

   d. The per share market value of the subsidiary's stock, in an active market

9. If the operating section of the consolidated statement of cash flows is displayed using the indirect method, which of the following is *not* an adjustment to consolidated net income?   LO 5

   a. Goodwill impairment loss

   b. Noncontrolling interest in net income

   c. Undistributed equity method income

   d. Amortization expense on previously unreported identifiable intangibles

10. On the consolidated statement of cash flows, cash dividends paid to noncontrolling shareholders are   LO 5

   a. a cash outflow in the financing section.

   b. an adjustment to income when the indirect method is used for the operating section.

   c. a cash outflow in the investing section.

   d. not reported.

Assignments with the ⊘ in the margin are available in an online homework system.
See the Preface of the book for details.

EXERCISES

E5.1 **Combination and Consolidation, Date of Acquisition (see related E3.1)**   Below are the pre-combination condensed balance sheets of Princecraft and Sylvan Companies at December 31, 2012. On January 1, 2013, Princecraft acquired 90 percent of the voting shares of Sylvan by issuing 360,000 shares of its $1 par value common stock. Princecraft's stock is currently trading at $120 in an active market. Sylvan Company's net assets are carried at fair value. The noncontrolling interest in Sylvan has a fair value of $4,250,000.   LO 1

	Princecraft Company	Sylvan Company
Total assets	$150,000,000	$25,000,000
Total liabilities.	$ 30,000,000	$ 8,000,000
Common stock.	15,000,000	5,000,000
Additional paid-in capital	45,000,000	10,000,000
Retained earnings	60,000,000	2,000,000
Total liabilities and equity.	$150,000,000	$25,000,000

Required

   a. Calculate total goodwill and its allocation to the controlling and noncontrolling interests.

   b. Prepare a working paper to consolidate the balance sheets of Princecraft and Sylvan at January 1, 2013.

   c. Present, in good form, the consolidated balance sheet at January 1, 2013.

E5.2 **Date of Acquisition Consolidation with In-Process R&D**   Pennant Corporation acquired 80 percent of Saylor Company's common stock for $10,000,000 in cash on January 2, 2013. At that date, Saylor's $6,000,000 of reported net assets were fairly stated, except land was undervalued by $500,000 and unrecorded in-process R&D was valued at $1,000,000. The estimated fair value of the noncontrolling interest is $2,000,000 at the acquisition date.   LO 1 ⊘

Required

   a. Calculate total goodwill and its allocation to the controlling and noncontrolling interests.

   b. Prepare the working paper eliminating entries needed to consolidate Pennant and Saylor on January 2, 2013.

LO 3   **E5.3**   **Date of Acquisition Consolidation, Bargain Purchase**   Peregrine Company acquired 80 percent of Sparrow Company's common stock on June 30, 2014, for $22,000,000 in cash; fees paid to an outside firm to estimate the earning power of Sparrow and the fair values of its properties amounted to $3,000,000. Book value of Sparrow's net assets was $25,000,000. Book values of Sparrow's identifiable assets and liabilities approximated their fair values except as noted below:

	Book Value	Fair Value
Land	$1,000,000	$ 200,000
Other plant assets, net	6,000,000	8,000,000
Investments	2,000,000	3,500,000
Long-term debt	4,000,000	4,700,000

Assume that the fair values above have been carefully evaluated for accuracy. The fair value of the noncontrolling interest is estimated to be $4,000,000 at the date of acquisition.

Required

a.   Calculate the gain on acquisition and prepare Peregrine's acquisition entry.
b.   Prepare the working paper eliminating entries needed to consolidate Peregrine and Sparrow on June 30, 2014.

LO 1, 4   **E5.4**   **Consolidated Balance Sheet, Date of Acquisition: U.S. GAAP and IFRS**   Assume that on January 31, 2014, **Microsoft Corporation** acquired 90 percent of the outstanding common stock of Powerline Technologies for $3,000,000 cash plus 200,000 shares of Microsoft's $10 par value common stock having a market value of $80 per share. Immediately prior to the acquisition, the trial balances of the two companies were as follows:

MICROSOFT CORPORATION
[MSFT]

	Dr (Cr)	
	Microsoft	**Powerline**
Current assets	$ 10,000,000	$ 2,000,000
Plant and equipment, net	35,000,000	7,000,000
Current liabilities	(5,000,000)	(1,500,000)
Long-term liabilities	(20,000,000)	(3,000,000)
Common stock	(3,000,000)	(100,000)
Additional paid-in capital	(6,000,000)	(1,400,000)
Retained earnings	(11,000,000)	(3,000,000)

A review of the fair values of Powerline's assets indicates that current assets are undervalued by $500,000, plant and equipment is undervalued by $6,000,000, and previously unrecorded brand names have a fair value of $2,000,000. The fair value of the noncontrolling interest is $1,800,000.

Required

a.   Calculate total goodwill and its allocation to the controlling and noncontrolling interests, following U.S. GAAP.
b.   Prepare a working paper to consolidate the balance sheets of Microsoft and Powerline at January 31, 2014, following U.S. GAAP.
c.   Assume Microsoft uses IFRS and the alternative valuation method for noncontrolling interests. Calculate total goodwill and repeat part *b* following IFRS.

✅ **LO 1, 4**   **E5.5**   **Consolidation Eliminating Entries, Date of Acquisition: U.S. GAAP and IFRS**   Plummer Corporation acquired 90 percent of Softek Technologies' voting stock on June 15, 2014, by issuing 2,000,000 shares of $2 par common stock with a fair value of $25,000,000. In addition, Plummer paid $500,000 in cash to the consultants and accountants who advised in the acquisition. Softek's stockholders' equity at the date of acquisition is as follows:

	Book Value	Fair Value
Common stock..		$ 200,000
Additional paid-in capital		8,000,000
Retained earnings		5,000,000
Accumulated other comprehensive income.............................		(800,000)
Treasury stock		(400,000)
Total		$12,000,000

Softek's assets and liabilities were carried at fair value except as noted below:

	Book Value	Fair Value
Plant assets, net..	$12,000,000	$9,000,000
Trademarks	—	1,500,000
Customer lists	—	1,000,000
Long-term debt	2,000,000	2,100,000

The fair value of the noncontrolling interest is estimated to be $2,500,000 at the date of acquisition.

Required

a.   Prepare the acquisition entry on Plummer's books and the working paper consolidation eliminating entries on June 15, 2014, following U.S. GAAP.

b.   Prepare the working paper consolidation eliminating entries on June 15, 2014, following IFRS and the alternative valuation method for noncontrolling interests.

E5.6 Consolidation at End of First Year (see related E4.3)   Peak Entertainment acquires 60 percent   LO 2 of its subsidiary Saddlestone Inc. on January 1, 2013. In preparing to consolidate Peak and Saddlestone at December 31, 2013, we assemble the following information:

* Value of stock given up to acquire Saddlestone: $10,000,000.
* Direct merger costs: $250,000.
* Saddlestone's stockholders' equity at acquisition: $7,200,000.
* Fair value of earnings contingency agreement to be paid in cash: $300,000.
* Fair value of previously unrecorded identifiable intangibles (5-year life): $2,000,000
* Goodwill and identifiable intangibles are not impaired in 2013.
* Fair value of the 40 percent noncontrolling interest at acquisition: $6,500,000.
* Saddlestone's net income in 2013: $3,000,000.
* Saddlestone's dividends paid in 2013: $1,000,000.
* Peak uses the complete equity method to report the investment on its own books.

Required

a.   Calculate total goodwill and its allocation to the controlling and noncontrolling interests.

b.   Calculate equity in net income for 2013, as reported on Peak's books, and the noncontrolling interest in net income, as reported on the consolidated income statement for 2013.

c.   Prepare the consolidation eliminating entries made at December 31, 2013.

E5.7 Consolidation Two Years after Acquisition   Mirror Resorts, Inc., a U.S. company, acquires an 80   LO 2 percent interest in Silver Nugget Company on January 1, 2013, for $80 million cash. The estimated fair value of the 20 percent noncontrolling interest in Silver Nugget is $18 million. Silver Nugget's book value at the date of acquisition is $10 million. Silver Nugget's recorded assets and liabilities are carried at fair value, but it has previously unrecorded intangibles valued at $20 million that are capitalizable under the requirements of *ASC Topic 805*. These intangibles have an estimated life of five years, straight-line. There are no identifiable intangible or goodwill impairments in either 2013 or 2014. Mirror Resorts uses the complete equity method to account for its investment in Silver Nugget. It is now December 31, 2014, and the trial balances of the two companies are as follows:

	Dr (Cr)	
(in thousands)	**Mirror Resorts**	**Silver Nugget**
Current assets	$ 35,000	$ 5,000
Plant and equipment, net.	215,700	140,000
Intangibles	350,000	51,000
Investment in Silver Nugget	86,400	—
Current liabilities.	(50,000)	(20,000)
Long-term debt	(600,000)	(150,000)
Common stock, par value	(500)	(100)
Additional paid-in capital	(6,000)	(5,500)
Retained earnings, January 1.	(25,000)	(17,500)
Treasury stock	4,000	1,600
Dividends	2,000	1,500
Sales revenue.	(800,000)	(100,000)
Equity in net income of Silver Nugget	(1,600)	—
Cost of goods sold.	650,000	80,000
Operating expenses.	140,000	14,000
Totals	$ 0	$ 0

Required

a.   Calculate equity in net income of Silver Nugget for 2014, as reported on Mirror Resorts' books, and the noncontrolling interest in net income of Silver Nugget, as reported on the consolidated income statement for 2014.

b.   Prepare a working paper to consolidate the 2014 financial statements of Mirror Resorts and Silver Nugget.

✔ **LO 2**   **E5.8**   **Consolidation after Several Years**   Paramount Corporation acquired its 75 percent investment in Sun Corporation in January 2009, for $2,910,000, and accounts for its investment internally using the complete equity method. At the acquisition date, total book value of Sun was $1,500,000, including $800,000 of retained earnings, and the estimated fair value of the 25 percent noncontrolling interest was $790,000. The fair values of Sun's assets and liabilities were equal to their carrying values, except for the following items:

	Fair value less book value
Accounts receivable.	$ (100,000)
Inventory.	(200,000)
Equipment (10 years, straight-line).	(400,000)
Patents (5 years, straight-line)	200,000

The receivables were collected and the inventory sold during the first three years following the acquisition. An impairment test made at the end of 2014 indicates a remaining value of $2,000,000 for the goodwill recognized as a result of the acquisition. Sun's stockholders' equity is $2,500,000, including $1,800,000 of retained earnings, at the end of 2014.

Required

a.   Calculate the amount of goodwill initially recognized as a result of the acquisition, and its allocation to the controlling and noncontrolling interests.

b.   Calculate the balance in the investment account, carried on Paramount's books, and the value of the noncontrolling interest, reported in the equity section of the consolidated balance sheet, as of the end of 2014.

c.   Assume eliminating entry (C), to reverse Paramount's equity method entries for 2015, has been made. Prepare 2015 eliminating entries (E) and (R) to adjust Sun's assets to the correct values as of the beginning of 2015, eliminate the remainder of the investment, and recognize the beginning-of-2015 value of the noncontrolling interest.

E5.9 Consolidated Cash Flow from Operations Consider the following data: LO 5

Controlling interest's share of consolidated net income	$15,000,000
Noncontrolling interest's share of consolidated net income	5,000,000
Consolidated depreciation expense	3,000,000
Amortization of asset and liability revaluations:	
Previously unrecognized identifiable intangibles	1,400,000
Premium on long-term debt	(80,000)
Net income reported by the 75 percent-owned subsidiary	8,000,000
(Net income − Dividends) reported by a 40-percent-owned equity investment	1,700,000
Decrease in noncash current operating assets	2,800,000
Decrease in current operating liabilities	2,100,000

Required

Use the above data to prepare the operating cash flow section of a consolidated statement of cash flows.

E5.10 Consolidated Cash Flow from Operations Consider the following data reported in the accounts of LO 5 a parent company and its 80-percent-owned subsidiary:

(in thousands)	**Parent**	**Subsidiary**
Net income.	$1,000,000[1]	$240,000
Depreciation expense.	175,000	38,000
Amortization expense.	50,000	—
Dividends paid in cash	250,000	75,000
Income from equity method investments.	60,000	—
Cash dividends received from equity investments	35,000	—
Items appearing in eliminating entries:		
Revaluation write-offs:		
Depreciation expense	$ 3,000	
Amortization expense	15,000	
Goodwill impairment loss [2]	40,000	

[1] Includes equity in net income of the subsidiary.
[2] Goodwill impairment losses are shared with the noncontrolling interest in proportion to ownership interests.

Required

Prepare the cash flow from operating activities section of the consolidated statement of cash flows, in proper form, using the indirect method. Assume no adjustment is required for changes in consolidated current asset and current liability accounts.

E5.11 Consolidation at Date of Acquisition, IFRS In June 2007, **Deutsche Post World Net** acquired 49 LO 4 percent of the shares of U.S. airline **ASTAR Air Cargo Holdings** for €67 million. ASTAR is consolidated by Deutsche Post. Following is information on ASTAR's identifiable net assets at the date of acquisition:

DEUTSCHE POST
WORLD NET
[DPW]

ASTAR AIR
CARGO
HOLDINGS

	Dr (Cr)	
(in millions)	**Fair value**	**Book value**
Intangible assets	€ 6.0	€ 10.0
Aircraft	65.0	65.0
Other property, plant and equipment.	5.0	5.0
Noncurrent financial assets	14.5	12.5
Current assets	68.0	68.0
Noncurrent liabilities.	(94.0)	(94.0)
Current liabilities.	(87.0)	(87.0)
Totals	€(22.5)	€(20.5)

Required

a. Calculate total goodwill and the reported amount of noncontrolling interests at the date of acquisition, assuming Deutsche Post uses the IFRS alternative valuation method for noncontrolling interests.

b. Prepare the consolidation eliminating entries at the date of acquisition.

LO 4

CANAL+FRANCE
VIVENDI
[VIVDY]

TPS CINEMA

E5.12 Consolidation Worksheet, Date of Acquisition and One Year Later, IFRS   **Canal+France**, a subsidiary of **Vivendi**, acquired 85 percent of **TPS Cinema** in January 2007 for €787 million fair value of Canal+France shares. Information on the acquisition is as follows *(in millions)*:

Net carrying value of TPS before business combination:	
Long-lived assets.	€ 112
Cash and cash equivalents	81
Net non-cash working capital	(210)
Liabilities.	(101)
Carrying value of TPS' assets and liabilities.	€(118)
Fair value adjustments of TPS' assets acquired and liabilities assumed at combination date:	
Customer lists	€ 150
TPS trade name	25
Assumed liabilities related to broadcasting rights and	
fair value adjustments to other long-term contracts	(484)
Deferred tax assets, net.	123
Total fair value adjustments of TPS' assets acquired and liabilities assumed.	€(186)

Required

a. Calculate total goodwill and the reported amount of noncontrolling interests at the date of acquisition, assuming Vivendi uses the IFRS alternative valuation method for noncontrolling interests.

b. Prepare the consolidation eliminating entries at the date of acquisition.

c. Prepare the consolidation eliminating entries at December 31, 2007, assuming the following information for 2007 *(in millions)*:

   i.   TPS reports net income of €80 and pays no dividends.

   ii. The customer lists have a five-year life, straight-line; the TPS trade name has an indefinite life, and impairment is €5; goodwill impairment is €100.

   iii. There are no write-offs of assumed liabilities, fair value adjustments, or deferred tax assets.

   iv. Vivendi uses the complete equity method to report its investment in TPS on its own books.

LO 1, 4

VIVENDI
[VIVDY]

MAROC
TELECOM
[MSPA]

SOTELMA

E5.13 Consolidation at Acquisition Date, IFRS   **Vivendi**, headquartered in Paris, is a worldwide leader in digital entertainment. In 2009, **Maroc Telecom**, a subsidiary of Vivendi, acquired a 51 percent controlling interest in **Sotelma**, a Malian telecoms operator, for €278 million. The book value of Sotelma at the date of acquisition was €35 million. The estimated fair value of Sotelma's noncontrolling interests was €208 million. Fair value adjustments to Sotelma's identifiable net assets were *(in millions)*:

License, depreciated over 8 years.	€24
Customer bases, depreciated over 8 years.	2
Deferred tax, net.	(3)
Total fair value adjustments	€23

Vivendi and its subsidiaries follow IFRS, and choose to value noncontrolling interests at fair value. Round all answers below to the nearest million.

Required

a. Calculate total goodwill for this acquisition, and its allocation to the controlling and noncontrolling interests.

b. Does the purchase price include a control premium? Explain.

c. Prepare eliminating entries E and R required to consolidate Sotelma with Maroc Telecom at the date of acquisition.

d. If Maroc Telecom had used the alternative method for valuing the noncontrolling interest, at what value would the noncontrolling interest be reported at the date of acquisition?

PROBLEMS ••

P5.1 **Consolidation Working Paper, Date of Acquisition**   On July 1, 2013, **The Hershey Company** acquired 75 percent of the common stock of Bagota Organic Chocolates. The $1.2 billion purchase price was paid in cash and newly-issued debt securities. The acquisition entry is reflected below in the two companies' balance sheets just after the acquisition.

LO 1

THE HERSHEY COMPANY [HSY]

Balance Sheets at July 1, 2013		
(in millions)	**Hershey**	**Bagota**
Assets		
Current assets	$1,500	$ 325
Property, plant and equipment, net	1,600	600
Investment in Bagota	1,200	—
Patents and trademarks.	1,300	75
Total assets	$5,600	$1,000
Liabilities and Stockholders' Equity		
Current liabilities.	$1,600	$ 100
Long-term liabilities	1,900	400
Common stock, par value	300	10
Additional paid-in capital	1,950	200
Retained earnings	3,900	300
Treasury stock	(4,000)	—
Accumulated other comprehensive income (loss)	(50)	(10)
Total liabilities and stockholders' equity	$5,600	$1,000

Independent appraisals produced the following fair value estimates for certain of Bagota's previously recorded assets and liabilities. In addition, previously unreported customer-related intangibles have an estimated fair value of $30 million. Bagota's noncontrolling interest has an estimated fair value of $375 million.

(in millions)	**Fair Value**	**Book Value**
Property, plant and equipment, net	$400	$600
Patents and trademarks.	120	75
Long-term liabilities	375	400

Required

a.   Prepare a schedule to compute the total goodwill and its allocation to the controlling and noncontrolling interest.

b.   Prepare a working paper to consolidate the balance sheets of Hershey and Bagota at July 1, 2013.

c.   Prepare a formal consolidated balance sheet for Hershey and Bagota at July 1, 2013.

P5.2 **Consolidated Balance Sheet Working Paper, Date of Acquisition, Bargain Purchase (see related P3.4)**   On December 31, 2012, Paxon Corporation acquired 80 percent of the outstanding common stock of the Saxon Company for $1 billion cash. The balance sheets of Paxon and Saxon, *immediately prior* to the combination, are shown below:

LO 3

(in millions)	**Paxon**		**Saxon**
Assets			
Cash and receivables.		$2,860	$ 720
Inventory.		1,700	900
Long-term marketable securities		—	300
Land		650	175
Buildings and equipment	$3,400		
Less Accumulated depreciation.	(1,000)	2,400	600 (net)
Total assets		$7,610	$2,695

continued

continued from prior page

(in millions)	Paxon	Saxon
Liabilities and Stockholders' Equity		
Current liabilities.	$1,500	$1,000
Long-term debt	2,000	400
Common stock, par value	500	100
Additional paid-in capital	1,200	350
Retained earnings	2,410	845
Total liabilities and stockholders' equity	$7,610	$2,695

Several of Saxon's assets and liabilities had fair values that were different from their book values. Estimates of the fair values of these items follow:

(in millions)	Estimated Fair Value
Inventory.	$1,000
Long-term marketable securities (held-to-maturity portfolio)	250
Land.	420
Buildings and equipment, net	900
Long-term debt	290

The estimated fair value of the noncontrolling interest in Saxon is $200 million.

Required

a.   Calculate the gain on acquisition and prepare Paxon's entry to record the acquisition.
b.   Prepare a working paper to consolidate the balance sheets of Paxon and Saxon at December 31, 2012.
c.   Prepare a formal consolidated balance sheet for Paxon and Saxon at December 31, 2012.

LO 1   P5.3   Consolidation Eliminating Entries, Date of Acquisition   On January 2, 2014, Placer Company acquired a 75 percent interest in Summer Company for $8,000,000 in cash. The condensed balance sheets *immediately prior* to the acquisition are below:

	Placer	Summer	
(in thousands)	Book Value	Book Value	Fair Value
Cash and receivables.	$10,000	$ 2,000	$1,800
Inventories	8,000	3,000	2,500
Plant assets, net.	12,000	5,000	4,000
Intangibles	2,000	1,000	0
Total assets	$32,000	$11,000	
Current liabilities.	$ 6,000	$ 2,500	$2,500
Noncurrent liabilities.	8,000	5,000	4,900
Common stock	5,000	500	
Retained earnings	13,000	3,000	
Total liabilities and stockholders' equity	$32,000	$11,000	

Additional information:

1.   In addition to the above cash cost, out-of-pocket merger-related costs of $300,000 were paid in cash.
2.   The merger agreement includes an earnings contingency agreement to be settled in cash; its fair value is $800,000.
3.   It is determined that Summer has an unreported preacquisition contingency, consisting of a liability with an estimated present value of $400,000.
4.   In-process research and development owned by Summer is worth $1,500,000.
5.   The fair value of the 25 percent noncontrolling interest in Summer is $2,500,000.

Required

a. Prepare the acquisition entry made by Placer on January 2, 2014.

b. Prepare the working paper eliminating entries made in consolidation on January 2, 2014.

P5.4 **Consolidation Working Paper One Year after Acquisition, Bargain Purchase (see related** LO 3
P4.4) On December 31, 2012, Paxon Corporation acquired 90 percent of the outstanding common
stock of Saxon Company for $1,620 million cash. The fair value of the 10 percent noncontrolling inter-
est in Saxon was estimated to be $180 million at the date of acquisition. Paxon uses the complete equity
method to report its investment. The trial balances of Paxon and Saxon at December 31, 2013, appear
below:

(in millions)	Dr (Cr)	
	Paxon	Saxon
Cash and receivables...	$ 3,270	$ 800
Inventory..	2,260	940
Marketable securities...	—	—
Investment in Saxon..	1,962.2	—
Land..	650	300
Buildings and equipment, net	3,600	1,150
Current liabilities..	(2,020)	(1,200)
Long-term debt	(5,000)	(450)
Common stock, par value	(500)	(100)
Additional paid-in capital	(1,200)	(350)
Retained earnings, January 1...................................	(2,610)	(845)
Dividends	500	100
Sales revenue..	(30,000)	(10,000)
Equity in net income of Saxon	(232.2)	—
Gain on sale of securities......................................	—	(10)
Cost of goods sold...	26,000	8,000
Depreciation expense..	300	40
Interest expense...	250	25
Other operating expenses	2,770	1,600
Totals	$ 0	$ 0

Several of Saxon's assets and liabilities had fair values different from their book values at the acquisition
date, as follows:

(in millions)	Fair Value – Book Value
Inventory (FIFO)	$100
Marketable securities (sold in 2013)............................	(50)
Land...	245
Buildings and equipment, net (20 years, straight-line)...........	300
Long-term debt (5 years, straight-line)..........................	(110)

Required

a. Prepare a schedule computing the gain on acquisition.

b. Prepare a schedule calculating the equity in net income of Saxon for 2013, reported on Paxon's books,
and the noncontrolling interest in income for 2013, to be reported on the consolidated income statement for 2013.

c. Prepare a working paper to consolidate the trial balances of Paxon and Saxon at December 31, 2013.

LO 3   **P5.5**   **Consolidation Working Paper Two Years after Acquisition, Bargain Purchase (see related P5.4)**   Refer to the information in P5.4. Now assume it is December 31, 2014, *two years* after the acquisition. The trial balances of Paxon and Saxon at December 31, 2014, appear below:

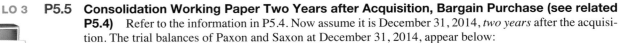

	Dr (Cr)	
(in millions)	**Paxon**	**Saxon**
Cash and receivables.	$ 3,000	$ 850
Inventory.	2,500	950
Investment in Saxon.	2,063.9	—
Land	650	250
Buildings and equipment, net	5,905	1,440
Current liabilities.	(2,500)	(1,000)
Long-term debt	(6,000)	(800)
Common stock, par value	(500)	(100)
Additional paid-in capital	(1,200)	(350)
Retained earnings, January 1.	(3,022.2)	(1,090)
Dividends	500	50
Sales revenue.	(35,000)	(12,000)
Equity in net income of Saxon	(146.7)	—
Cost of goods sold.	30,000	9,500
Depreciation expense.	450	60
Interest expense.	300	40
Other operating expenses	3,000	2,200
Totals	$ 0	$ 0

Required

a.   Prepare a schedule computing equity in net income of Saxon for 2014, reported on Paxon's books, and the noncontrolling interest in income for 2014, to be reported on the consolidated income statement for 2014.

b.   Prepare a working paper to consolidate the trial balances of Paxon and Saxon at December 31, 2014.

LO 2   **P5.6**   **Consolidation Working Paper, Second Year Following Acquisition**   On January 1, 2007, **Harrah's Entertainment, Inc.** acquired a 70 percent interest in the company that owns **Emerald Safari Resort** for $600 million in cash and stock. Assume the following information at the date of acquisition *(in millions)*:

HARRAH'S ENTERTAINMENT, INC.
[HET]

EMERALD SAFARI RESORT

Book value of Emerald Safari Resort	$580
Fair value of noncontrolling interest in Emerald Safari Resort	225
Fair value of previously unrecorded identifiable intangibles	100

The previously unrecorded identifiable intangibles have indefinite lives. In 2007 and 2008, intense competition and a declining economic outlook led to reduced projected performance for this property. Testing indicated impairment of the identifiable intangibles by $5 million in 2007 and $8 million in 2008. Although the goodwill was not impaired in 2007, the entire goodwill balance associated with this property was impaired in 2008. The December 31, 2008, trial balances of Harrah's and Emerald Safari Resort appear below. Harrah's uses the complete equity method to report the investment on its own books.

(in millions)	Dr (Cr) Harrah's	Emerald Safari Resort
Current assets	$ 1,400	$ 200
Land, buildings, riverboats and equipment, net.	17,696.2	2,549
Intangible assets	2,500	800
Investment in Emerald Safari Resort	515.2	—
Current liabilities.	(1,500)	(300)
Long-term liabilities	(14,000)	(2,600)
Common stock.	(20)	(4)
Capital surplus	(5,500)	(320)
Retained earnings, January 1.	(900)	(300)
Dividends	100	5
Casino revenues.	(6,600)	(2,200)
Food and beverage revenues.	(1,400)	(300)
Rooms revenues	(1,000)	(200)
Equity in net loss of Emerald Safari Resort	108.6	—
Direct casino, food and beverage, rooms expenses	7,200	1,670
General and administrative expenses	1,400	1,000
Totals	$ 0	$ 0

Required

a. Calculate total goodwill for this acquisition and its allocation to the controlling and noncontrolling interests.
b. Prepare a schedule to calculate the 2008 equity in net loss and the noncontrolling interest in the net loss of Emerald Safari Resort.
c. Prepare a consolidation worksheet to consolidate the trial balances of Harrah's and Emerald Safari Resort.

P5.7 **Equity Method and Eliminating Entries Three Years after Acquisition (see related P4.2)** LO 2

Puffin Industries acquired 90 percent of Sunset Coast Digital's stock on December 31, 2011, for $3,150,000. At that time, Sunset Coast's stockholders' equity totaled $1,400,000, and the estimated fair value of the noncontrolling interest was $350,000. Sunset Coast's inventory (LIFO) was overvalued by $500,000 and its plant assets (10-year life) were overvalued by $1,000,000. The remaining excess of fair value over book value is attributed to undervalued identifiable intangible assets being amortized over 20 years. Sunset Coast depreciates plant assets and amortizes intangibles by the straight-line method. During the next three years Sunset Coast reported total income of $850,000 and paid out 50% in dividends. Puffin carries its investment in Sunset Coast using the complete equity method. Sunset Coast's inventory increased each year since it was acquired by Puffin, and Sunset Coast's reported net income for 2014 was $200,000.

Required

a. Compute Puffin's 2014 equity method income accrual and the noncontrolling interest in net income for 2014.
b. Compute the balance in the investment in Sunset Coast account at December 31, 2014, after all equity method entries have been booked.
c. Compute the balance of noncontrolling interest, reported on the December 31, 2014, consolidated balance sheet.
d. Prepare the working paper eliminating entries needed in consolidation at December 31, 2014.

LO 2

COCA-COLA
BOTTLING
CONSOLIDATED
[COKE]

PIEDMONT
COCA-COLA
BOTTLING
PARTNERSHIP

THE COCA-COLA
COMPANY
[KO]

P5.8 **Consolidation Working Paper after Several Years**   Coca-Cola Bottling Consolidated acquired a 75 percent interest in **Piedmont Coca-Cola Bottling Partnership** on January 1, 2003. The other 25 percent interest was held by **The Coca-Cola Company**. Assume the following information related to this acquisition:

Acquisition price, paid by Coca-Cola Bottling Consolidated, in cash..................	$70,000,000
Fair value of the 25 percent interest held by The Coca-Cola Company	15,000,000
Book value of Piedmont at date of acquisition	25,000,000

The excess of fair value over book value at the acquisition date is attributed to previously unreported franchise rights valued at $5,000,000, and to goodwill.

Piedmont has not engaged in any stock transactions since it was acquired. The franchise rights have indefinite lives, and total impairment losses for 2003 through 2011 are $1,000,000. There are no goodwill impairment losses for this period. Piedmont's business prospects declined during 2012, resulting in franchise rights impairment of $2,500,000 and goodwill impairment of $6,000,000. Coca-Cola Consolidated uses the complete equity method to report its investment in Piedmont on its own books.

The trial balances of Coca-Cola Consolidated and Piedmont at December 31, 2012, appear below:

	Dr (Cr)	
(in thousands)	**Coca-Cola Consolidated**	**Piedmont**
Current assets	$ 160,000	$ 30,000
Property, plant and equipment, net	250,000	233,800
Franchise rights, net.......................................	466,400	—
Investment in Piedmont	68,793	—
Current liabilities.......................................	(120,000)	(20,000)
Long-term debt	(700,000)	(210,000)
Common stock..	(12,000)	(1,000)
Additional paid-in capital	(100,000)	(12,000)
Retained earnings, January 1...........................	(50,500)	(18,000)
Accumulated other comprehensive loss	12,000	—
Treasury stock	30,000	200
Dividends	2,000	—
Net sales..	(1,200,000)	(300,000)
Equity in net loss of Piedmont	4,807	—
Cost of sales..	760,000	175,000
Selling, delivery and administrative expenses	400,000	114,000
Amortization expense...................................	500	—
Interest expense.......................................	28,000	8,000
Totals	$ 0	$ 0

Required

a.   Calculate goodwill for this acquisition, and its allocation to controlling and noncontrolling interests.

b.   Prepare a schedule calculating the 2012 equity in net loss of Piedmont on Coca-Cola Consolidated's books ($4,807,000) and the noncontrolling interest in the 2012 net loss to be reported on the consolidated income statement.

c.   Prepare a schedule showing how the December 31, 2012, investment balance on Coca-Cola Consolidated's books ($68,793,000) was calculated.

d.   Prepare a consolidation working paper for December 31, 2012.

e.   Present the consolidated financial statements, in good form, for 2012.

LO 5   **P5.9**   **Consolidated Statement of Cash Flows**   Sunny Valley Resort has owned 80 percent of Mountain Lodging, Inc. since Mountain Lodging's inception. The condensed consolidated balance sheets of Sunny Valley Resort at December 31, 2012 and 2011 and other relevant information are presented below:

SUNNY VALLEY RESORT AND SUBSIDIARY Condensed Consolidated Balance Sheets December 31		
(in thousands)	**2012**	**2011**
Assets		
Cash..	$ 600,000	$ 700,000
Other current assets...	1,400,000	1,000,000
Plant assets	4,000,000	4,200,000
Accumulated depreciation.....................................	(1,500,000)	(1,600,000)
Goodwill...	300,000	330,000
Total assets	$4,800,000	$4,630,000
Liabilities and Stockholders' Equity		
Current liabilities..	$1,282,000	$1,550,000
Noncurrent liabilities...	1,800,000	1,700,000
Stockholders' equity—controlling interest......................	1,430,000	1,100,000
Noncontrolling interest..	288,000	280,000
Total liabilities and stockholders' equity	$4,800,000	$4,630,000

Additional information for 2012 *(in thousands)*:

1. Consolidated net income to the controlling interest is $400,000.
2. Mountain Lodging reported net income of $120,000 on its own books, and paid $80,000 in dividends.
3. Consolidated depreciation expense was $350,000.
4. Plant assets with an original cost of $500,000 were retired from service and scrapped. Goodwill was impaired by $30,000.
5. Sunny Valley paid $70,000 in dividends.

Required

Prepare, in good form, a consolidated statement of cash flows for 2012.

P5.10 Consolidated Statement of Cash Flows   Comparative consolidated balance sheets and the interven-   LO 5
ing income statement for Prime Casinos and its subsidiary Saratoga International Hotels are shown below:

PRIME CASINOS and SARATOGA INTERNATIONAL HOTELS Comparative Consolidated Balance Sheets December 31		
(in millions)	**2013**	**2012**
Assets		
Cash..	$ 500	$ 200
Other current assets...	900	800
Property, plant and equipment.................................	3,100	2,500
Accumulated depreciation.....................................	(1,000)	(800)
Goodwill...	275	300
Total assets	$3,775	$3,000
Liabilities and Stockholders' Equity		
Current liabilities..	$ 900	$ 650
Long-term liabilities	950	800
Capital stock	700	500
Retained earnings	1,065	900
Noncontrolling interest..	160	150
Total liabilities and stockholders' equity	$3,775	$3,000

PRIME CASINOS and SARATOGA INTERNATIONAL HOTELS Consolidated Statement of Income and Retained Earnings For Year Ended December 31, 2013	
Sales and other revenue.	$3,555
Cost of goods sold.	(1,700)
Operating expenses.	(1,243)
Consolidated net income.	612
Noncontrolling interest in net income	(12)
Controlling interest in net income	600
Retained earnings, January 1, 2013.	900
Dividends paid.	(435)
Retained earnings, December 31, 2013.	$1,065

Additional information *(in millions)*:

1. Consolidated depreciation expense was $250.
2. During the year, plant assets of $675 were acquired for cash.
3. Operating expenses include $10 in losses on sale of plant assets for cash.

Required

Prepare, in good form, the consolidated statement of cash flows for the year ended December 31, 2013.

LO 4   **P5.11 Consolidation Two Years after Acquisition, IFRS**   Rendezvous Resorts is a Swiss company with an 80 percent interest in Monaco Hotels, located in France. Rendezvous acquired its interest in Monaco on January 1, 2012, for €4 billion. Monaco's book value at the date of acquisition was €1 billion. Monaco's balance sheet reported its assets and liabilities at fair value, except for these items:

- Inventories (FIFO) were overvalued by €100 million.
- Property, plant and equipment (10 year life, straight-line) was undervalued by €400 million.
- Previously unreported identifiable intangibles (3 year life, straight-line) had a fair value of €300 million. These intangibles meet the IFRS criteria for capitalization.

It is now December 31, 2013. Rendezvous uses the complete equity method to account for its investment in Monaco on its own books and prepares consolidated financial statements using IFRS. Goodwill impairment losses were €100 million in 2012 and €200 million in 2013. The trial balances of Rendezvous and Monaco at December 31, 2013, are as follows:

	Dr (Cr)	
(in millions)	**Rendezvous Resorts**	**Monaco Hotels**
Current assets	€ 500	€ 900
Property, plant and equipment, net	3,000	2,000
Investment in Monaco	4,316	—
Identifiable intangibles	—	200
Liabilities.	(4,648)	(1,150)
Capital stock	(1,500)	(800)
Retained earnings, January 1.	(1,000)	(600)
Dividends	—	50
Sales revenue.	(5,000)	(3,500)
Equity in net income of Monaco.	(168)	—
Cost of sales.	4,200	2,500
Administrative and other operating expenses	300	400
Totals	€ 0	€ 0

Required

a. Calculate the total goodwill initially arising from this acquisition, using the IFRS alternative method of valuation.

b. Prepare a schedule calculating Rendezvous' equity in net income of Monaco and the noncontrolling interest in Monaco's net income for 2013.

c. Prepare a working paper consolidating the trial balances of Rendezvous and Monaco at December 31, 2013.

P5.12 Consolidation Several Years after Acquisition, IFRS Lily Bakeries, located in Belgium, specializes in biscuit and cake products. Lily owns 75 percent of Hearty Foods, a French company acquired on January 1, 2010, for cash and stock totaling €150 million. Hearty's book value at the date of acquisition was €70 million. Its assets and liabilities were fairly reported at the date of acquisition, except for these items:

LO 4

(in thousands)	Book value	Fair value
Plant and equipment, net (10-year life, straight-line)...............	€150,000	€100,000
Secret recipes (10-year life, straight-line)........................	—	40,000
Long-term debt (4-year life, straight-line)......................	30,000	28,000

It is now December 31, 2014. Impairment testing on the acquired goodwill reveals that total impairment during the years 2010-2013 was €2.5 million, and impairment in 2014 is €0.75 million. Lily uses the complete equity method to account for its investment internally. The December 31, 2014, trial balances of Lily and Hearty follow:

(in thousands)	Dr (Cr) Lily Bakeries	Hearty Foods
Current assets	€ 35,000	€ 20,000
Plant and equipment, net.....................................	226,500	202,000
Investment in Hearty	176,750	—
Identifiable intangibles......................................	100,000	10,000
Current liabilities	(30,000)	(25,000)
Long-term debt	(350,000)	(100,000)
Capital stock	(80,000)	(54,000)
Retained earnings, January 1................................	(60,000)	(38,000)
Sales revenue..	(400,000)	(140,000)
Equity in net income of Hearty...............................	(11,250)	—
Cost of goods sold..	250,000	80,000
Operating expenses.......................................	143,000	45,000
Totals	€ 0	€ 0

Lily follows IFRS and uses the IFRS alternative valuation for goodwill and noncontrolling interests.

Required

a. Calculate the total goodwill arising from this acquisition.

b. Prepare a schedule calculating Lily's equity in net income of Hearty and the noncontrolling interest in Hearty's net income for 2014.

c. Prepare a working paper consolidating the trial balances of Lily and Hearty at December 31, 2014.

P5.13 Noncontrolling Interest in Comprehensive Income Below is selected financial statement information for **Verizon Communications Inc.**, taken from its 2010 annual report. Verizon's noncontrolling interest is comprised primarily of **Vodafone's** 45 percent interest in **Verizon Wireless**, which Verizon consolidates due to its 55 percent controlling interest. All amounts are in millions, except per share amounts.

LO 2

VERIZON COM-
MUNICATIONS
INC
[VZ]

VODAFONE
[VOD]

VERIZON
WIRELESS

Income statement, year ended December 31, 2010:	
Operating Revenues	$106,565
Operating Expenses	
Cost of services and sales (exclusive of items shown below)	44,149
Selling, general and administrative expense	31,366
Depreciation and amortization expense	16,405
Total Operating Expenses	91,920
Operating Income	14,645
Equity in earnings of unconsolidated businesses	508
Other income and (expense), net	54
Interest expense	(2,523)
Income Before (Provision) Benefit for Income Taxes	12,684
(Provision) benefit for income taxes	(2,467)
Net Income	$ 10,217
Net income attributable to noncontrolling interest	$7,668
Net income (loss) attributable to Verizon	2,549
Net Income	$ 10,217
Basic Earnings (Loss) Per Common Share	
Net income (loss) attributable to Verizon	$ .90
Weighted-average shares outstanding (in millions)	2,830
Diluted Earnings (Loss) Per Common Share	
Net income (loss) attributable to Verizon	$ .90
Weighted-average shares outstanding (in millions)	2,833

Equity section of balance sheet, December 31, 2010 and 2009:	2010	2009
Common stock ($.10 par value; 2,967,610,119 shares issued in both periods)	$ 297	$ 297
Contributed capital	37,922	40,108
Reinvested earnings	4,368	7,260
Accumulated other comprehensive income (loss)	1,049	(1,372)
Common stock in treasury, at cost	(5,267)	(5,000)
Deferred compensation - employee stock ownership plans and other	200	89
Noncontrolling interest	48,343	42,761
Total equity	$86,912	$84,143

Excerpts from statement of changes in equity for 2010:

Noncontrolling Interest	
Balance at beginning of year	$42,761
Net income attributable to noncontrolling interest	7,668
Other comprehensive income (loss)	(35)
Total comprehensive income	7,633
Distributions and other	(2,051)
Balance at end of year	48,343
Total Equity	$86,912
Comprehensive Income	
Net income	$10,217
Other comprehensive income (loss)	2,363
Total comprehensive income	12,580
Comprehensive income attributable to noncontrolling interest	7,633
Comprehensive income (loss) attributable to Verizon	4,947
Total comprehensive income	$12,580

Required

a. Assume the noncontrolling interest consists *entirely* of Vodafone's 45 percent interest in Verizon Wireless. What was Verizon Wireless' separate net income for 2010? What was Verizon Communications' separate net income for 2010?

b. The noncontrolling interest in other comprehensive income is a *loss* of $35. Total consolidated other comprehensive income is a *gain* of $2,363. Explain this result.

c. Prepare consolidation eliminating entry N for 2010, assuming "distributions and other" are cash dividends declared.

REVIEW SOLUTIONS •••••••••••••••••••••••••••••••••••

Review 1 Solution

	Accounts Taken From Books Dr (Cr)		Eliminations		Consolidated Balances Dr (Cr)
	Admiral	**Gold Road**	**Dr**	**Cr**	
Current assets	$ 14,000,000	$ 9,200,000			$ 23,200,000
Equity investments	55,000,000	5,000,000			60,000,000
Plant and equipment, net	235,000,000	80,000,000			315,000,000
Investment in Gold Road	54,285,000	—		$ 6,360,000 (C)	—
				15,920,000 (E)	
				32,005,000 (R)	
Identifiable intangible assets	550,000,000	—	(R) $ 2,500,000	1,250,000 (O)	551,250,000
Goodwill	—	—	(R) 35,300,000		35,300,000
Current liabilities	(16,000,000)	(11,000,000)			(27,000,000)
Long-term debt	(837,580,000)	(54,100,000)			(891,680,000)
Capital stock	(5,000,000)	(2,500,000)	(E) 2,500,000		(5,000,000)
Retained earnings, January 1	(37,205,000)	(17,400,000)	(E) 17,400,000		(37,205,000)
Noncontrolling interest	—	—		3,980,000 (E)	
				5,795,000 (R)	
				1,590,000 (N)	(11,365,000)
Dividends	2,500,000	800,000		640,000 (C)	
				160,000 (N)	2,500,000
Sales and other revenue	(700,000,000)	(200,000,000)			(900,000,000)
Equity in income of Gold Road	(7,000,000)		(C) 7,000,000		—
Cost of goods sold	480,000,000	140,000,000			620,000,000
Operating expenses	212,000,000	50,000,000	(O) 1,250,000		263,250,000
Noncontrolling interest in net income	—	—	(N) 1,750,000[1]		1,750,000
Totals	$ 0	$ 0	$67,700,000	$67,700,000	$ 0

[1] $1,750,000 = 20% × ($200,000,000 − $140,000,000 − $50,000,000 − $1,250,000).

ADMIRAL CASINO & RESORT
Consolidated Statement of Income and Retained Earnings
For Year Ended December 31, 2014

Sales and other revenue	$900,000,000
Less: Cost of goods sold	(620,000,000)
Operating expenses	(263,250,000)
Consolidated net income	**16,750,000**
Less: Noncontrolling interest in net income	(1,750,000)
Net income attributable to Admiral	15,000,000
Plus: Retained earnings, Admiral, January 1	37,205,000
Less: Dividends	(2,500,000)
Retained earnings, Admiral, December 31	$ 49,705,000

ADMIRAL CASINO & RESORT
Consolidated Balance Sheet
December 31, 2014

Assets		Liabilities and Stockholders' Equity	
Current assets	$ 23,200,000	Current liabilities...................	$ 27,000,000
Equity investments......	60,000,000	Long-term debt	891,680,000
Plant and equipment, net	315,000,000		
Identifiable intangibles ...	551,250,000	Total liabilities.....................	918,680,000
Goodwill	35,300,000	Stockholders' equity	
		Admiral stockholders' equity:	
		Capital stock....................	5,000,000
		Retained earnings................	49,705,000
		Total Admiral stockholders' equity	54,705,000
		Noncontrolling interest..............	11,365,000
		Total stockholders' equity	66,070,000
Total assets	$984,750,000	Total liabilities and stockholders' equity ...	$984,750,000

Review 2 Solution

	Accounts Taken From Books Dr (Cr)		Eliminations		Consolidated Balances
	Admiral	**Gold Road**	**Dr**	**Cr**	**Dr (Cr)**
Current assets	$ 14,000,000	$ 9,200,000			$ 23,200,000
Equity investments.................	55,000,000	5,000,000			60,000,000
Plant and equipment, net............	235,000,000	80,000,000			315,000,000
Investment in Gold Road	54,285,000	—		$ 6,360,000 (C)	—
				15,920,000 (E)	
				32,005,000 (R)	
Identifiable intangible assets	550,000,000	—	(R) $ 2,500,000	1,250,000 (O)	551,250,000
Goodwill	—	—	(R) 30,005,000		30,005,000
Current liabilities...................	(16,000,000)	(11,000,000)			(27,000,000)
Long-term debt	(837,580,000)	(54,100,000)			(891,680,000)
Capital stock	(5,000,000)	(2,500,000)	(E) 2,500,000		(5,000,000)
Retained earnings, January 1..........	(37,205,000)	(17,400,000)	(E) 17,400,000		(37,205,000)
Noncontrolling interest..............	—	—		3,980,000 (E)	
				500,000 (R)	
				1,590,000 (N)	(6,070,000)
Dividends	2,500,000	800,000		640,000 (C)	
				160,000 (N)	2,500,000
Sales and other revenue.............	(700,000,000)	(200,000,000)			(900,000,000)
Equity in income of Gold Road	(7,000,000)	—	(C) 7,000,000		—
Cost of goods sold.................	480,000,000	140,000,000			620,000,000
Goodwill impairment loss.............	—	—			—
Other operating expenses	212,000,000	50,000,000	(O) 1,250,000		263,250,000
Noncontrolling interest in net income ...	—	—	(N) 1,750,000		1,750,000
Totals	$ 0	$ 0	$62,405,000	$62,405,000	$ 0

ADMIRAL CASINO & RESORT
Consolidated Statement of Income and Retained Earnings
For Year Ended December 31, 2014

Sales and other revenue.	$900,000,000
Less: Cost of goods sold	(620,000,000)
Operating expenses	(263,250,000)
Consolidated net income.	**16,750,000**
Less: Noncontrolling interest in net income.	(1,750,000)
Net income attributable to Admiral	15,000,000
Plus: Retained earnings, Admiral, January 1	37,205,000
Less: Dividends	(2,500,000)
Retained earnings, Admiral, December 31.	$ 49,705,000

ADMIRAL CASINO & RESORT
Consolidated Balance Sheet
December 31, 2014

Assets		**Liabilities and Stockholders' Equity**	
Current assets	$ 23,200,000	Current liabilities.	$ 27,000,000
Equity investments.	60,000,000	Long-term debt	891,680,000
Plant and equipment, net. . .	315,000,000	Total liabilities.	918,680,000
Identifiable intangibles	551,250,000	Stockholders' equity	
Goodwill	30,005,000	Admiral stockholders' equity:	
		Capital stock.	5,000,000
		Retained earnings.	49,705,000
		Total Admiral stockholders' equity	54,705,000
		Noncontrolling interest.	6,070,000
		Total stockholders' equity	60,775,000
Total assets	$979,455,000	Total liabilities and stockholders' equity . . .	$979,455,000

6

Consolidated Financial Statements: Intercompany Transactions

LEARNING OBJECTIVES

LO1   Prepare eliminating entries for intercompany service and financing transactions. (p. 212)

LO2   Describe elimination of unconfirmed profits and their effect on equity in net income and noncontrolling interest in net income. (p. 213)

LO3   Prepare eliminating entries for intercompany transfers of land. (p. 215)

LO4   Prepare eliminating entries for intercompany transfers of inventory. (p. 218)

LO5   Prepare eliminating entries for intercompany transfers of depreciable assets. (p. 223)

NIKE, INC.
www.nike.com

Nike, Inc. is a leading worldwide supplier of athletic clothing, footwear and equipment, headquartered in Portland, Oregon. As of 2010, Nike's major subsidiaries are Cole Haan, Converse, Inc., Hurley International and Umbro. Cole Haan produces upscale footwear, leather goods, outerwear and sunglasses. Converse is known for the Chuck Taylor All Star basketball shoe. Hurley International produces and markets action sports clothing and accessories. Umbro, located in the United Kingdom, makes football (soccer) clothing and equipment.

Note 1 to Nike's 2010 consolidated financial statements includes the following statement:

The consolidated financial statements include the accounts of NIKE, Inc. and its subsidiaries (the "Company"). All significant intercompany transactions and balances have been eliminated.

Nike's consolidated financial statements present the results of transactions and events for Nike, Inc. and its subsidiaries as *one entity*. The financial statements do not report transactions *between* the parent company and its subsidiaries. Nike's subsidiaries are in similar businesses, and they may transact business with each other and with Nike. For example, Converse may sell materials used in producing athletic shoes to Nike, and Nike may provide financing to its subsidiaries. To avoid creating additional complexities in the accounting system, the separate books of each company record these transactions the same way they record transactions with outside suppliers, customers, and other entities. When consolidating the financial statements of the parent and its subsidiaries, the accountant uses eliminating entries to remove the effects of these **intercompany transactions**.

In this chapter you will learn how to prepare consolidation eliminating entries that remove the effects of common intercompany relationships and transactions. Source: Nike, Inc. annual report, 2010.

Intercompany service and financing transactions	Intercompany profits	Intercompany land sales	Intercompany merchandise sales	Intercompany sales of depreciable assets	Comprehensive illustration
• Intercompany revenues and expenses • Intercompany receivables and payables	• Unconfirmed profits • Effect on equity income accrual and noncontrolling interest in net income	• Year of transfer • Subsequent years • Year of sale to outside party	• Unconfirmed profit in ending inventory • Unconfirmed profit in beginning inventory • Cost flow assumptions • Shipping and installation	• Year of transfer • Subsequent years • Year of sale to outside party	• Goodwill, equity in income, noncontrolling interest in income • Eliminations CIERON • Consolidation working paper and consolidated statements

INTRODUCTION

Affiliated companies often transact business with each other. Some companies acquire their suppliers or customers to create supply chain efficiencies. A parent and its subsidiaries may sell each other fixed assets, such as land or equipment, occasionally or in the normal course of business. The consolidated financial statements present the financial performance and status of the consolidated companies as a **single economic entity**. Consolidated statements do not reflect the effects of these intercompany transactions, just as transactions between divisions or segments of a company are not reported externally.

In the discussion below, we use the terminology introduced in Chapter 1 to distinguish between intercompany sales or transfers *from parent to subsidiary* and *from subsidiary to parent*, as follows:

- A **downstream** sale or transfer occurs when the parent sells to a subsidiary.
- An **upstream** sale or transfer indicates that a subsidiary is selling to the parent.

When goods or services are sold between affiliated companies, the consolidation process eliminates intercompany revenues and expenses. Neither arose out of transactions with outside parties, and both must be eliminated to avoid overstatement of consolidated revenues and expenses. Any related intercompany receivables and payables must also be eliminated.

Assets may be transferred among affiliates at a gain or loss to the selling company. If the buying company still holds these assets at the end of an accounting period, the asset balances include intercompany gains and losses. Since such gains and losses are not yet **confirmed** by transactions with outside parties, they must be eliminated and the asset balances adjusted in consolidation.

The consolidation elimination entries discussed in this chapter add to the consolidation process in Chapters 3, 4 and 5. We add step **I** to include all necessary **I**ntercompany eliminations. Because intercompany eliminations can affect the subsidiary's beginning retained earnings balance and the parent's beginning investment balance, step I appears *between steps C and E*, as follows:

(C) Eliminate the current year's equity method entries, restoring the investment account to its balance at the beginning of the current year.

(I) Eliminate the effects of upstream and downstream intercompany transactions.

(E) Eliminate the remainder of the subsidiary's beginning-of-year stockholders' equity account balances, reducing the investment account and increasing the noncontrolling interest according to each ownership interest's share of the subsidiary's remaining beginning equity.

(R) Revalue the subsidiary's assets and liabilities as of the beginning of the year. Eliminate the remainder of the investment account, representing the controlling interest's beginning-of-year revaluation balance, and attribute the appropriate beginning-of-year net asset revaluations to the noncontrolling interest.

(O) Recognize current year write-offs of the subsidiary's asset and liability revaluations.

(N) Recognize the noncontrolling interest in net income. Update the noncontrolling interest in equity for its share of income and dividends.

The acronym **CIERON** may help you to remember the six elimination steps used in the consolidation process.

This chapter examines consolidation issues related to balances overstated or understated by intercompany transactions, and unconfirmed profits and losses arising out of intercompany services, financing, and transfers of land, inventory, and depreciable assets. Unconfirmed profits and losses also affect the calculation of the parent's equity method income accrual and, where appropriate, the noncontrolling interest in net income. We begin with service and financing transactions that do not result in unconfirmed profits.

INTERCOMPANY SERVICE AND FINANCING TRANSACTIONS

LO1 Prepare eliminating entries for intercompany service and financing transactions.

In a strategic acquisition, a parent and subsidiary typically have complementary resources that lead to intercompany business transactions. **VF Corporation** acquired **The Timberland Company** in 2011. The merger augments VF's outdoor line and global market share, and Timberland's apparel offerings. VF and Timberland likely engage in significant supply chain transactions. **Brown Shoe Company**, known for its Famous Footwear retail outlets, has wholesale, retail, and development subsidiaries that support its supply chain. Transactions between these affiliates likely include borrowing and lending activities.

Intercompany service and financing transactions between a parent and a subsidiary require entries to eliminate them in consolidation. Suppose Parrish Shoe Factory is a subsidiary of Jordan Athleticwear. During 2013 Jordan provides design services costing $650,000 to Parrish and bills Parrish $900,000 for these services. At year-end, Parrish still owes Jordan $100,000 for these services. In addition, Jordan loans $1,000,000 to Parrish. Interest on this loan, accrued and paid during 2013, is $50,000. The separate books of the two companies report the following accounts related to these transactions:

	Jordan	Parrish
Balance Sheet		
Accounts receivable...	$ 100,000	—
Loan receivable	1,000,000	—
Accounts payable..	—	$ 100,000
Loan payable	—	1,000,000
Income Statement		
Design revenue..	900,000	—
Interest revenue	50,000	—
Design expense..	650,000	900,000
Interest expense...	—	50,000

The consolidated entity incurred design costs of $650,000 in developing its products. There are no other transactions with outside parties. Therefore only the $650,000 in design expenses should appear on the current consolidated financial statements. The step **I** eliminating entries needed to achieve this result are:

(I-1)	Accounts payable.	100,000	
	Accounts receivable		100,000
	To eliminate the intercompany receivable/payable.		
(I-2)	Loan payable	1,000,000	
	Loan receivable		1,000,000
	To eliminate the intercompany loan principal.		
(I-3)	Design revenue.	900,000	
	Design expense.		900,000
	To eliminate the intercompany service revenue/expense.		
(I-4)	Interest revenue	50,000	
	Interest expense		50,000
	To eliminate the intercompany interest revenue/expense.		

These eliminating entries are necessary to avoid overstating revenues, expenses, receivables and payables related to intercompany service and financing transactions.

INTERCOMPANY PROFITS

Elimination of intercompany profits on asset transfers within an affiliated group reflects the fundamental argument that, *since the parent and the subsidiary are under common control, transactions between them are not the result of arm's-length bargaining*. Therefore, any profits or losses recorded in such transactions are *tentative*, subject to **confirmation** via arm's-length transactions with external parties. *FASB ASC Section 810-10-45* clarifies that unconfirmed gains and losses on *all* intercompany transactions must be eliminated, whether they are upstream or downstream:

> As consolidated financial statements are based on the assumption that they represent the financial position and operating results of a single economic entity, such statements shall not include gain or loss on transactions among the entities in the consolidated group. *(para. 1)*

LO2 Describe elimination of unconfirmed profits and their effect on equity in net income and noncontrolling interest in net income.

Intercompany profits that require elimination relate only to transferred assets remaining **inside the affiliated group** at the end of the reporting period. These profits or losses are **not yet confirmed** by further sale to outside parties; confirmed profits require no elimination. Suppose Jordan acquired land sometime in the past at a cost of $1,000,000. During the current year, it sells the land to Parrish for $1,400,000. Prior to consolidation, a gain of $400,000 (= $1,400,000 − $1,000,000) appears on Jordan's books, and Parrish's books carry the land at $1,400,000. From a single-entity perspective, *no gain occurred*—the land was merely transferred internally, and should continue to be carried at its original cost of $1,000,000. The necessary eliminating entry made in consolidation for the year of sale is:

(I)	Gain on sale of land	400,000	
	Land.		400,000
	To eliminate the unconfirmed intercompany profit and reduce the land to		
	original acquisition cost.		

The land is reported in the consolidated balance sheet at $1,000,000, the original acquisition cost to the group, and the unconfirmed gain of $400,000 is eliminated. From a consolidated point of view, *the transaction is treated as if it never occurred*. However, since consolidation eliminating entries appear only on a working paper and are not booked, the $400,000 gain remains in Jordan's retained earnings, and the land remains at $1,400,000 on Parrish's books. Thus, the $400,000 intercompany gain must be eliminated in consolidation *each year* until it is *confirmed* through sale to an outside party.

Remember that only *unconfirmed* profits at year-end require elimination. In the above example, Parrish held the land at year-end. If Parrish sold the land to a third party for $1,600,000 during the current year, no elimination is required: Jordan reports a gain of $400,000 and Parrish reports a gain of $200,000. From a single-entity perspective, land costing $1,000,000 was sold for $1,600,000, a gain of $600,000. The consolidation process adds the parent and subsidiary gain accounts to arrive at the correct gain on sale of land without any eliminating entries.

If the subsidiary has a noncontrolling interest, we must consider to what extent elimination of unconfirmed profits affects the noncontrolling interest. Elimination of intercompany profits arising in *downstream* sales affects *only the controlling interest's share of consolidated income*. Because the parent is the seller in the transaction, and records profit on a downstream sale, there is no effect on the subsidiary's net income and therefore no effect on any noncontrolling interest in net income. If the parent does not own 100 percent of the subsidiary, elimination of intercompany profits arising in *upstream* sales affects both the controlling and noncontrolling interests in consolidated net income. The subsidiary is the seller in upstream sales, and records the intercompany profit, so elimination of that profit is shared between the controlling and noncontrolling interests.

Equity in Net Income and Noncontrolling Interest in Net Income

Recall from Chapter 4 that the complete equity method results in a **one-line consolidation**—if the parent uses the complete equity method, its separate net income equals consolidated net income attributed to the parent. Any adjustments made in consolidation that affect consolidated net income must also affect the parent's equity method income accrual. Therefore, unconfirmed intercompany gains and losses on upstream and downstream sales affect the equity method income accrual. Specifically, the parent's share of any unconfirmed intercompany gains (losses) is deducted from (added to) its share of the subsidiary's reported net income in computing the equity method income accrual.

The parent's unconfirmed intercompany profit on downstream sales seems to have nothing to do with the income the parent accrues from its subsidiary. However, because these unconfirmed profits are eliminated in consolidation, they are also removed in determining the equity method income accrual. If a consolidation eliminating entry affects consolidated net income, it must also affect equity in net income the same way. Otherwise the parent's separate net income, which includes the equity method income accrual, will not equal the controlling interest's share of consolidated net income.

When the equity method is used for external reporting of unconsolidated investments, unconfirmed profits on downstream and upstream sales are deducted to the extent of the investor's ownership interests. In contrast, when the parent reports its controlling interest in a subsidiary *internally* using the complete equity method, the *entire* unconfirmed profit on **downstream transactions** is removed from equity in net income reported by the parent. If the subsidiary is not wholly owned, the *parent's share* of the unconfirmed profit on **upstream transactions** is removed from equity in net income. The noncontrolling interest in the subsidiary is affected only by *upstream* intercompany transactions because the subsidiary reports unconfirmed profits on upstream sales on its own books. With the noncontrolling interest sharing in the subsidiary's profits, removal of unconfirmed upstream profits affects the noncontrolling interest in net income.

To illustrate the above concepts, assume Jordan acquires 80 percent of Parrish on January 1, 2013. During 2013, Jordan sells merchandise costing $380,000 to Parrish for $400,000. Parrish still holds the merchandise in its inventory at year-end. The $20,000 profit on the intercompany transfer is *unconfirmed* until Parrish sells the merchandise to an outside customer. When computing Jordan's equity in the income of Parrish, we make the adjustments for revaluation write-offs, and deduct an additional $20,000 to remove the downstream intercompany profit.

Suppose Parrish instead sells the merchandise to Jordan, recording a profit of $20,000, and Jordan still holds the merchandise in its inventory at year-end. Now the unconfirmed upstream profit is removed from both Jordan's equity in net income *and* the noncontrolling interest in net income reported on the consolidated income statement. We subtract Jordan's share of the unconfirmed profit, $16,000 (= 80% × $20,000), from equity in net income, and $4,000 from the noncontrolling interest in net income. The following chart summarizes the effects of intercompany transactions on equity in net income and the noncontrolling interest in net income.

Effects of Unconfirmed Intercompany Profits		
Transaction Type	**Equity in Net Income**	**Noncontrolling Interest in Net Income**
Downstream...............	Remove all unconfirmed profit	No effect
Upstream.................	Remove parent's share of unconfirmed profit	Remove noncontrolling interest's share of unconfirmed profit

INTERCOMPANY TRANSFERS OF LAND

Transfers of land between affiliated companies represent the most straightforward application of the concepts inherent in accounting for unconfirmed intercompany profits. Because land does not depreciate or affect accounts such as cost of sales, intercompany eliminations that remove the effects of land sales between parent and subsidiary are less complex than eliminations for intercompany merchandise and depreciable asset sales.

LO3 Prepare eliminating entries for intercompany transfers of land.

Eliminations in the Year of Transfer

In the year of transfer, the purchasing affiliate records the purchase of land at the price paid, and the selling affiliate recognizes a gain or loss on the intercompany sale. This gain or loss is included in the net income and ultimately in the retained earnings of the selling affiliate.

Since an unconfirmed intercompany gain or loss affects consolidated net income and is eliminated in consolidation, an equivalent elimination must be reflected in the parent's equity method income accrual. If the sale is downstream, all of the unconfirmed gain is deducted from the equity accrual, thereby offsetting the gain reported in the parent's separate income statement. In the case of an upstream sale, the parent's share of the subsidiary's unconfirmed gain is deducted from the equity accrual. This deduction offsets the parent's share of the gain reported in the subsidiary's separate income statement.

Assume that in 2013 Jordan sells land costing $2,000,000 to Parrish for $2,300,000. Parrish holds the land at year-end. The consolidation eliminating entry for this downstream transfer is:

Consolidation eliminating entry, year of transfer		
(I) Gain on sale of land	300,000	
Land...		300,000
To eliminate the unconfirmed intercompany profit and reduce the land to original acquisition cost.		

We make the same eliminating entry whether the transfer is upstream or downstream. However, the 20 percent noncontrolling interest in Parrish makes the upstream/downstream distinction important. Equity in net income, reported on Jordan's books, and noncontrolling interest in net income, reported on the consolidated income statement, are affected differently if Jordan sold the land to Parrish or Parrish sold the land to Jordan.

Effect of $300,000 Unconfirmed Intercompany Profit in Year of Transfer		
Transaction Type	**Equity in Net Income**	**20% Noncontrolling Interest in Net Income**
Downstream..............	Subtract $300,000	No effect
Upstream	Subtract $240,000	Subtract $60,000

Because consolidation elimination entries are not posted to the books, the gain remains on the seller's books, as part of retained earnings, and the land remains overvalued on the purchaser's books. When we prepare the consolidated statements each year, working paper entries must be made to eliminate this transaction. We now consider these subsequent year eliminations for both upstream and downstream sales.

Eliminations in Subsequent Years

Elimination entries for intercompany land transfers in subsequent years differ depending on whether the transfers are upstream or downstream.

Upstream Transfers   If the land was sold *upstream* in a prior period, we eliminate the unconfirmed gain from the *beginning retained earnings of the subsidiary*. Although we eliminated the gain on the prior period working paper, it remained intact on the subsidiary's books and was closed to its retained earnings in the year of sale. If Jordan still holds the land at the end of 2014, the consolidation eliminating entry is:

December 31, 2014, consolidation eliminating entry, upstream			
(I)	Retained earnings, beginning—Parrish	300,000	
	Land.		300,000
	To eliminate the unconfirmed upstream intercompany profit from a previous year and reduce the land to original acquisition cost.		

Eliminating the intercompany profit from Parrish's beginning retained earnings balance facilitates eliminating the investment account against Jordan's share of Parrish's stockholders' equity in step E, and automatically charges the noncontrolling interest for its proportional share of the unconfirmed profit.

To understand why Parrish's retained earnings are reduced in the above eliminating entry, suppose Jordan paid $80 million to acquire an 80 percent interest in Parrish on January 1, 2013. Parrish's book value was $100 million: capital stock of $75 million and retained earnings of $25 million. Because $80 million is 80 percent of $100 million, the acquisition is at book value and no revaluations are necessary. During 2013, Parrish reported net income of $5 million, including the gain of $300,000 on the intercompany sale of land, and paid no dividends. Jordan's December 31, 2013 investment balance is:

January 1, 2013 balance	$80,000,000
Equity in net income, 2013:	
80% × ($5,000,000 − $300,000)	3,760,000
December 31, 2013 balance	$83,760,000

Thus, the investment account has been *reduced* by Jordan's share of the unconfirmed gain, $240,000 (= 80% × $300,000) via the equity method income accrual, but Parrish's December 31, 2013 retained earnings balance, $30,000,000 (= $25,000,000 + $5,000,000), *includes* the $300,000 unconfirmed gain.

Step E of the consolidation process calls for eliminating the investment balance against the subsidiary's stockholders' equity *as of the beginning of the year*, and recognizing the noncontrolling interest's share of the subsidiary's beginning equity:

• Debit beginning balance of stockholders' equity—subsidiary

• Credit beginning balance of investment (parent's share of subsidiary's equity)

• Credit noncontrolling interest in subsidiary (noncontrolling interest's share of subsidiary's equity)

We computed the beginning investment balance for 2014 to be $83,760,000. The beginning noncontrolling interest balance for 2014 is:

January 1, 2013 balance	
$100,000,000 × 20%	$20,000,000
Noncontrolling interest in net income, 2013:	
20% × ($5,000,000 − $300,000)	940,000
December 31, 2013 noncontrolling interest	
balance	$20,940,000

Using the subsidiary's beginning-of-year book retained earnings balance, we do *not* have a balanced elimination for step E:

- Beginning balance of stockholders' equity—subsidiary = $105,000,000
     = $100,000,000 + $5,000,000 in 2013 net income
- Beginning balance of investment = $83,760,000
- Beginning balance of noncontrolling interest = $20,940,000

Elimination entry I above reduces Parrish's beginning retained earnings by $300,000, leaving a remaining balance of $104,700,000, which balances elimination entry E; $83,760,000 = 80% × $104,700,000.

Downstream Transfers   When *downstream* sales occur, in subsequent years we add the unconfirmed gain to the *investment account*. In this case, the total intercompany gain was originally charged against the equity income accrual and reduced the investment account. But there was no corresponding effect on the subsidiary's net income at the time of consolidation. As in the case of upstream sales, a discrepancy exists between the investment account and the subsidiary's stockholders' equity. We cannot adjust the subsidiary's retained earnings, because downstream transfers do not affect the subsidiary's income and are not charged against the noncontrolling interest. For a balanced elimination in step E, the following eliminating entry I is made:

December 31, 2014, consolidation eliminating entry, downstream

(I)	Investment in Parrish	300,000	
	Land.		300,000
	To eliminate the unconfirmed downstream intercompany profit from a previous year and reduce the land to original acquisition cost.		

Continuing the above example, if Jordan sold the land to Parrish in 2013 at a profit of $300,000, the 2014 beginning investment balance is:

January 1, 2013 balance	$80,000,000
Equity in net income, 2013:	
(80% x $5,000,000) - $300,000	3,700,000
December 31, 2013 balance	$83,700,000

The beginning noncontrolling interest balance for 2014 is:

January 1, 2013 balance	
$100,000,000 x 20%	$20,000,000
Noncontrolling interest in net income, 2013:	
20% x $5,000,000	1,000,000
December 31, 2013 balance	$21,000,000

Using the parent's beginning-of-year book investment balance, we do not have a balanced elimination for step E:

- Beginning balance of stockholders' equity—subsidiary = $105,000,000
- Beginning balance of investment = $83,700,000
- Beginning balance of noncontrolling interest = $21,000,000

Eliminating entry I above increases Jordan's investment balance to $84,000,000, which balances elimination entry E; $84,000,000 = 80% × $105,000,000.

We continue to make elimination I in subsequent years' consolidations as long as the land remains in the consolidated entity, but intercompany land sales in previous years do not affect the parent company's equity income accrual or the noncontrolling interest in consolidated net income.

Eliminations in Year of Sale to Outside Party

Sale of the land to an outside party in a subsequent year requires that the original intercompany gain be recognized in consolidated net income in that subsequent year. If the original intercompany gain was upstream, the working paper entry transfers the original intercompany gain out of the subsidiary's retained earnings and into current income. In the downstream case, the entry adds the gain back to the investment account from which it was previously deducted via the equity method income accrual, and recognizes it as current income.

The parent's equity method income accrual in the year of external sale includes all of the now-confirmed downstream intercompany gain, or the parent's share of the now-confirmed upstream gain. If the intercompany sale was upstream, the noncontrolling interest in net income is increased by the noncontrolling interest's share of the now-confirmed intercompany gain.

Continuing our example, suppose the land was sold in 2015 for $3,000,000. Given that the original cost of the land to the consolidated entity was $2,000,000, a consolidated gain of $1,000,000 should be reported. The selling entity carries the land at $2,300,000, and reports a gain of $700,000. Recognizing the $300,000 intercompany gain in elimination step I brings the total consolidated gain to its correct amount.

December 31, 2015, consolidation eliminating entry, upstream

(I)	Retained earnings, beginning – Parrish	300,000	
	Gain on sale of land.		300,000
	To include in current consolidated net income the previously recorded		
	upstream gain now confirmed through external sale.		

December 31, 2015, consolidation eliminating entry, downstream

(I)	Investment in Parrish	300,000	
	Gain on sale of land.		300,000
	To include in current consolidated net income the previously recorded		
	downstream gain now confirmed through external sale.		

These eliminations affect consolidated income, thereby affecting Jordan's equity income accrual and the noncontrolling interest in net income. These effects are summarized as follows:

Effect of $300,000 Intercompany Profit Confirmed in Year of Sale to Outside Party		
Transaction Type	**Equity in Net Income**	**20% Noncontrolling Interest in Net Income**
Downstream.	Add $300,000	No effect
Upstream	Add $240,000	Add $60,000

Confirmation of the intercompany sale and removal of the land from the books mean that no further consolidation eliminating entries related to the land are needed.

INTERCOMPANY TRANSFERS OF INVENTORY

LO4 Prepare eliminating entries for intercompany transfers of inventory.

Transfers of inventory between affiliated corporations are quite common. Component parts are often manufactured by one affiliate and assembled by another. Or finished goods may be produced by one affiliate and marketed by another. In all such cases, preparation of consolidated statements requires elimination of intercompany revenues and expenses. If the intercompany transfer price differs from cost, and the goods remain in the affiliated entity at year-end, an unconfirmed gain or loss results.

To see the intuition behind required eliminations for intercompany inventory transfers, consider this example. During 2013, Jordan sells merchandise costing $1,000,000 to Parrish for $1,500,000. At the end of 2013, all of the merchandise remains in Parrish's inventory. This information is reported in the companies' separate books as follows:

	Jordan	Parrish
Balance sheet		
Inventory.	—	$1,500,000
Income statement		
Sales revenue.	$1,500,000	—
Cost of goods sold.	1,000,000	—

From a consolidated perspective, no transaction is reported unless it is with an outside party. Therefore the consolidated balance sheet must report Parrish's inventory at cost, $1,000,000, and no sales revenue or cost of goods sold appear on the consolidated income statement. The eliminating entries necessary to achieve this result are:

(I-1)	Sales.	1,500,000	
	Cost of goods sold		1,500,000
	To eliminate intercompany merchandise sales and purchases.		
(I-2)	Cost of goods sold.	500,000	
	Inventory		500,000
	To eliminate unconfirmed profit from Parrish's ending inventory.		

Although the two eliminating entries above could be combined, separating them clarifies the two steps—elimination of gross intercompany sales and purchases, and elimination of unconfirmed profits in ending inventory.

Had Parrish sold all merchandise purchased from Jordan to outside customers by year-end, we only eliminate gross intercompany sales and purchases. If Parrish sold the inventory for $1,800,000 during 2013, the companies' separate books report the following:

	Jordan	Parrish
Balance sheet		
Inventory.	$ —	$ —
Income statement		
Sales revenue.	1,500,000	1,800,000
Cost of goods sold.	1,000,000	1,500,000

Because the consolidated financial statements report $1,800,000 in sales to outside customers, and cost of goods sold of $1,000,000, the following elimination entry achieves this result:

(I)	Sales.	1,500,000	
	Cost of goods sold		1,500,000
	To eliminate intercompany merchandise sales and purchases.		

The principles involved in intercompany inventory profit eliminations parallel those encountered in eliminations arising from land transfers among affiliates. Nevertheless, the procedures may seem more complex because inventory is reflected in the income statement through cost of goods sold. There is no separate gain on sale of inventory on the income statement. Rather, the unconfirmed gain is part of the ending or beginning inventory balance, and is eliminated by adjusting cost of goods sold. Recall this familiar calculation:

Cost of goods sold = Beginning inventory + Purchases − Ending inventory

Eliminating intercompany profit in *ending* inventory *increases* cost of goods sold, whereas eliminating intercompany profit in *beginning* inventory *decreases* cost of goods sold. In addition, the total dollar amount of inventory transfers must be eliminated to avoid overstating consolidated sales revenue and cost of goods sold.

Unconfirmed Profit in Ending Inventory

The eliminating entry to remove unconfirmed profit in ending inventory is the same whether the parent or the subsidiary holds the inventory—in other words, whether the transaction was *upstream* or *downstream*. Unconfirmed profit is removed from the purchaser's ending inventory, increasing cost of goods sold. Suppose Jordan sold merchandise priced at $5,000,000 to Parrish during 2013, and at December 31, 2013, Parrish's ending inventory includes $840,000 purchased from Jordan. Jordan's markup is 20 percent of cost. The eliminating entries are:

December 31, 2013 consolidation eliminating entries		
(I-1) Sales.	5,000,000	
Cost of goods sold		5,000,000
To eliminate intercompany merchandise sale and purchases.		
(I-2) Cost of goods sold.	140,000	
Inventory		140,000
To eliminate unconfirmed intercompany profit in ending inventory;		
$140,000 = $840,000 - $840,000/1.2.		

If Jordan's markup was 20 percent on *selling price*, the unconfirmed intercompany profit in elimination (I-2) is $168,000 (= 20% × $840,000). The entry to eliminate the unconfirmed profit in ending inventory is the same for upstream sales, in which Parrish sold the merchandise and it is now held in Jordan's year-end inventory.

Because the increase in cost of goods sold reduces consolidated income, adjustments must be made to Jordan's equity income accrual and the 20 percent noncontrolling interest in net income:

Effect of $140,000 Unconfirmed Profit in Ending Inventory		
Transaction Type	**Equity in Net Income**	**20% Noncontrolling Interest in Net Income**
Downstream.	Subtract $140,000	No effect
Upstream	Subtract $112,000	Subtract $28,000

Unconfirmed Profit in Beginning Inventory

Unconfirmed profits in the *ending* inventory of one period means that next period's *beginning* inventory also reflects those profits. Working paper eliminations do not affect the companies' books, so at the next consolidation point cost of goods sold is *overstated by the previous year's unconfirmed profits*. A working paper elimination transfers these gains into current year income by reducing cost of goods sold. In effect, this procedure assumes that the profits are confirmed in the second year by virtue of the sale of the inventory to outside customers. Any such profits not actually confirmed during the current year are included in unconfirmed profits removed from the ending inventory. As in the earlier discussions concerning upstream and downstream sales of land, the offsetting debit is to beginning retained earnings of the subsidiary for upstream sales and to the parent's investment account for downstream sales. These adjustments are necessary for a balanced elimination.

The need to transfer unconfirmed intercompany profits in beginning inventory into current year income also extends to the parent's equity method income accrual. Whereas unconfirmed intercompany profits in *ending* inventory were *deducted* from the equity accrual, unconfirmed intercompany profits in *beginning* inventory, assumed confirmed in the current year, are *added* to the equity accrual. As before, such adjustments are for the total amount of the profit in downstream sales, and for a proportional amount in upstream sales.

Continuing our illustration above, if Parrish's beginning inventory includes $840,000 purchased from Jordan—a *downstream* sale—the eliminating entry is:

December 31, 2014, consolidation eliminating entry, downstream		
(I) Investment in Parrish	140,000	
Cost of goods sold		140,000
To eliminate unconfirmed downstream intercompany profit in beginning inventory.		

If *Jordan's* beginning inventory includes $840,000 purchased from *Parrish*—an *upstream* sale—the eliminating entry is:

December 31, 2014, consolidation eliminating entry, upstream		
(I) Retained earnings, beginning—Parrish	140,000	
Cost of goods sold		140,000
To eliminate unconfirmed upstream intercompany profit in beginning inventory.		

Because the decrease in cost of goods sold increases consolidated income, adjustments must be made to Jordan's equity income accrual and the 20 percent noncontrolling interest in net income, as follows:

Effect of $140,000 Unconfirmed Profit in Beginning Inventory		
Transaction Type	Equity in Net Income	20% Noncontrolling Interest in Net Income
Downstream	Add $140,000	No effect
Upstream	Add $112,000	Add $28,000

Intercompany Profits and Inventory Cost Flow Assumptions

Most companies employ a cost flow assumption such as LIFO (last-in, first-out) or FIFO (first-in, first-out). The intercompany profit elimination techniques discussed here are compatible with *any* cost-flow assumption. Our eliminations seem to imply a FIFO cost flow because any intercompany profit in beginning inventory is assumed confirmed and is added to current income.

Suppose, however, that LIFO was being used and, to simplify matters, that the ending LIFO inventory was unchanged from the beginning LIFO inventory. Following our procedure, we *add* the beginning intercompany profit to current income, and *subtract* the ending intercompany profit. What is the effect on current income? Absolutely zero! Since the LIFO inventory is assumed constant, so is the unconfirmed intercompany profit, and its elimination from beginning and ending inventories on the income statement has *no net effect* on current period income. Moreover, in making the elimination from ending inventory on the income statement, we also remove the unconfirmed profit from the overstated inventory on the balance sheet. Under FIFO, of course, our procedure shows as confirmed the beginning intercompany profit and eliminates as unconfirmed any ending intercompany profit—precisely what is needed.

Shipping and Installation Costs

Intercompany transfers of inventory and equipment frequently result in shipping or installation costs paid to third parties. When the *purchasing* affiliate pays these costs, they represent valid costs to the affiliated group, with no impact on the profit eliminated. In contrast, payment of such costs by the *selling* affiliate indicates a concession in the intercompany transfer price, and the intercompany profit is reduced accordingly. In both cases the resulting consolidated asset reflects original acquisition cost plus any shipping and installation costs paid to outside parties, regardless of which company actually pays for the costs. As an example, consider the following data:

Intercompany inventory transfer price	$100
Cost to selling affiliate	80
Shipping cost	5

When the *purchasing affiliate pays the shipping cost*, it records the inventory at $105. Assuming the product is unsold at consolidation, unconfirmed intercompany profit of $20 (= $100 − $80) is eliminated, reducing consolidated inventory to $85 (= $105 − $20).

In contrast, *payment of the shipping cost by the selling affiliate* indicates that the transfer price is actually $95 (= $100 − $5), and the intercompany profit is $15 (= $95 − $80). The purchasing affiliate records the inventory at $100. If the product is unsold at consolidation, we eliminate unconfirmed intercompany profit of $15, and reduce consolidated inventory to $85 (= $100 − $15), as in the previous case.

Reporting Perspective

Recall from Chapter 1 that when used for external reporting, the equity method eliminates the investor's share of unconfirmed profits on intercompany merchandise sales. Intercompany revenues and cost of sales are *not* eliminated. Analysis of sales volume and gross margin can therefore be misleading, as the numbers used for analysis include the results of non-market transactions between affiliates. But when affiliates are consolidated, intercompany revenues and cost of sales reflect only transactions with outside customers. To illustrate, suppose an investor sells merchandise for $1 million to outside customers. Cost of sales is $800,000. The investor also sells merchandise costing $600,000 to its affiliate for $1 million. Suppose for simplicity that the affiliate makes no sales during the year. Using the equity method for an unconsolidated affiliate, the investor adjusts its equity in net income of the affiliate for the unconfirmed profit on merchandise sales, but does *not* adjust its sales or cost of sales numbers. Its gross margin on sales is 30 percent [= ($2,000,000 − $800,000 − $600,000)/$2,000,000]. If the investor controls and consolidates its affiliate, the intercompany sales and unconfirmed profits are eliminated. Gross margin on sales drops to 20 percent [= ($1,000,000 − $800,000)/$1,000,000]. The consolidation process removes the effect of non-market sales from reported performance.

BUSINESS APPLICATION   Crocs, Inc.

Crocs, Inc. designs and sells footwear, apparel, and related accessories. Its footwear comes in a variety of colors and is made from Croslite, a unique resin producing casual shoes that are lightweight, soft and recyclable. Crocs' wholly-owned subsidiaries include **Jibbitz, LLC**, which makes charms that decorate Crocs shoes, **EXO Italia**, which develops ethylene vinyl acetate footwear products, and **Ocean Minded, LLC**, which designs, manufactures, markets and distributes beach and sport sandals. Because Jibbitz, EXO Italia, and Ocean Minded are subsidiaries, they maintain separate books that reflect all their transactions, including transactions with Crocs, Inc. These subsidiaries likely do business with Crocs on a regular basis, through merchandise and raw materials transfers and marketing services. For example, Crocs provides the foot beds necessary for production of Ocean Minded sandals, creating intercompany revenues, expenses, receivables and payables, and unconfirmed profits in the subsidiaries' beginning and ending inventories of foot beds. In preparing consolidated financial statements, the accountants at Crocs, Inc. must eliminate the effects of these intercompany transactions.

REVIEW 1   •   Intercompany eliminations: land and merchandise transfers

Protective Workshoes, Inc. owns 90 percent of the voting stock of Sandalite, Inc., acquired at book value several years ago. The fair value of the noncontrolling interest equaled 10 percent of Sandalite's book value. It is now December 31, 2014, and you are preparing the consolidated financial statements of Protective. The following information relates to its intercompany transactions with Sandalite.

1.   Protective sold land costing $3,000,000 to Sandalite during 2012 for $3,500,000. Sandalite sold the land to an outside party for $3,300,000 in 2014.
2.   Sandalite sells merchandise to Protective at a markup of 30 percent on cost. Protective sells raw materials to Sandalite at a markup of 20 percent on sales. Information on 2014 intercompany merchandise transactions is:

	Protective	Sandalite
Sales to affiliate	$14,000,000	$26,000,000
Beginning inventory balance purchased from affiliate	1,235,000	1,500,000
Ending inventory balance purchased from affiliate	1,378,000	1,125,000

Sandalite reported net income of $1,700,000 in 2014. Protective uses the complete equity method to report its investment in Sandalite on its separate books.

Required

a. Prepare the step **I** eliminating entries at December 31, 2014, in journal entry form.

b. Calculate Protective's equity income accrual for 2014, and the consolidated noncontrolling interest in net income for 2014.

Solutions are located after the chapter assignments.

INTERCOMPANY TRANSFERS OF DEPRECIABLE ASSETS

Though less common than intercompany inventory sales, transfers of depreciable assets between affiliates also require eliminating entries when preparing consolidated statements. The complication results from the way in which intercompany gains on depreciable assets are assumed confirmed. Recall that gains and profits arising on intercompany transfers of land and inventory *are confirmed when the items are sold to outsiders*. In contrast, *confirmation of intercompany gains on depreciable assets normally is linked to their depreciation*. As the book values of depreciable assets are written down, their services are assumed to be included in the goods and services sold externally by the purchasing affiliate. Because depreciation represents the expiration of assets' services, it also represents the "sale" of the assets' services to outsiders.

LO5 Prepare eliminating entries for intercompany transfers of depreciable assets.

For reasons of simplicity and materiality, we typically assume that *all* of the annual depreciation is "sold" outside and the portion of the gain equal to the excess depreciation is confirmed. This is, of course, not strictly true. If the purchasing affiliate is a manufacturing concern, a part of its annual depreciation is included in manufactured goods under full absorption costing, which may still be retained in ending inventory. Some of the manufactured goods may be sold to other affiliates and not to outsiders at all. These cost flows are generally not traced to their ultimate external disposition because the amounts involved are not material and the costs of tracing them would exceed the benefits. For this reason, we assume that recorded depreciation adequately measures the expiration of assets' services and their "sale" to outsiders, and we attempt no further investigation of actual cost flows.

Objectives of the Eliminations

When one affiliate transfers a depreciable asset to another affiliate, the amount recorded by the purchasing affiliate typically differs from the asset's net book value (original acquisition cost less accumulated depreciation) to the selling affiliate. If the selling affiliate records a gain (loss) on the transfer, the resulting asset balance on the books of the purchaser is greater (less) than the net book value of the asset. The general objective in consolidation is to remove the effects of the intercompany transaction, treating it as if it had never occurred. From this general objective, we derive three specific objectives for our working paper eliminations:

• Eliminate the unconfirmed intercompany gain or loss.

• Eliminate the *excess* depreciation—the difference between the annual depreciation expense recorded by the purchasing affiliate and the amount based on original acquisition cost.

• Restate the balances in the asset and accumulated depreciation accounts so that they are based on original acquisition cost.

Eliminations in Year of Transfer

Suppose that on January 2, 2013, Jordan sells equipment with a 10-year remaining life to Parrish for $4,500,000. The equipment originally cost Jordan $5,000,000 several years ago, and at the date of transfer total reported depreciation was $2,000,000. Jordan records a gain of $1,500,000 [= $4,500,000 − ($5,000,000 − $2,000,000)]. Assuming the equipment remains on Parrish's books at year-end and that Parrish uses straight-line depreciation, the separate companies report the following on their 2013 financial statements:

	Jordan	Parrish
Balance sheet, December 31, 2013		
Equipment	$ —	$4,500,000
Accumulated depreciation	—	450,000
2013 Income statement		
Depreciation expense.		450,000
Gain on sale of equipment	1,500,000	—

From a consolidated viewpoint, depreciation expense for 2013 based on original cost is $300,000 [= ($5,000,000 − $2,000,000)/10]. On December 31, 2013, the equipment is reported in consolidation at its original cost of $5,000,000, with accumulated depreciation of $2,300,000 [= $2,000,000 + $300,000]. The following eliminating entries accomplish these goals:

December 31, 2013, consolidation eliminating entries		
(I-1) Gain on sale of equipment	1,500,000	
Equipment		1,500,000
To eliminate unconfirmed gain on intercompany transfer of equipment.		
(I-2) Accumulated depreciation	150,000	
Depreciation expense		150,000
To eliminate the excess annual depreciation expense recorded by the purchasing affiliate; $150,000 = $1,500,000/10.		
(I-3) Equipment	2,000,000	
Accumulated depreciation.		2,000,000
To restate the asset and accumulated depreciation accounts to their original acquisition cost basis. The amount of adjustment equals the accumulated depreciation at the date of transfer.		

Taken together, the above entries restate the asset, accumulated depreciation, and depreciation expense accounts so that they reflect *original acquisition cost*. At the date of transfer, January 2, 2013, the unconfirmed gain is $1,500,000. As time passes, this gain is *confirmed* by *reducing depreciation expense* in the second entry above. Although the discussion above illustrates a downstream transfer of equipment, Parrish may also sell depreciable assets to Jordan. In the year of transfer, the eliminating entries are the same whether the transfer is downstream or upstream.

Because the eliminating entries affect consolidated income, they also affect Jordan's equity income accrual and, if upstream, the 20 percent noncontrolling interest in net income. The intercompany gain on *downstream* transfers is *attributed to the parent*, affecting only the parent's equity income accrual. On *upstream* transfers, the *gain belongs to the subsidiary*, affecting both the parent's equity income accrual and the noncontrolling interest in consolidated income. Using the example above, the equity income accrual and noncontrolling interest in net income for 2013 are affected as follows:

Effect of $1,500,000 Unconfirmed Gain on Intercompany Transfers of Depreciable Assets (10-year life) Year of Transfer		
Transaction Type	Equity in Net Income	20% Noncontrolling Interest in Net Income
Downstream..............	Subtract $1,500,000 Add $150,000	No effect
Upstream	Subtract $1,200,000 Add $120,000	Subtract $300,000 Add $30,000

Eliminations in Subsequent Years

At consolidation points subsequent to the year of sale, we make eliminations to achieve the three consolidation objectives previously discussed. Fortunately, only the entry made to eliminate the unconfirmed intercompany gain as of the beginning of the year differs from elimination entries made in the year of intercompany sale. The same entries made in the year of sale to eliminate the excess annual depreciation expense and accumulated depreciation and to restate the asset and accumulated depreciation accounts to their original cost basis are made at each subsequent consolidation point. Of course, the amount of excess depreciation expense eliminated each year is different when accelerated depreciation is used.

In the year of sale we first eliminated the entire gain and then recognized the amount confirmed by reducing depreciation expense. As with land and inventory transfers, in subsequent years the beginning-of-year unconfirmed gains on *upstream* sales are removed by *reducing the subsidiary's beginning retained earnings*. Beginning-of-year unconfirmed gains on *downstream* sales are eliminated by *increasing the investment account*.

Continuing our illustration, on December 31, 2014, suppose the purchasing affiliate still holds the equipment. If Jordan sold the equipment downstream to Parrish, the eliminating entries required in step **I** of the consolidation process are:

December 31, 2014, consolidation eliminating entries, downstream		
(I-1) Investment in Parrish	1,350,000	
Accumulated depreciation	150,000	
Equipment...		1,500,000
To eliminate beginning-of-year unconfirmed gain on downstream intercompany transfer of equipment.		
(I-2) Accumulated depreciation	150,000	
Depreciation expense		150,000
To eliminate the excess annual depreciation expense recorded by the purchasing affiliate.		
(I-3) Equipment	2,000,000	
Accumulated depreciation.....................................		2,000,000
To restate the asset and accumulated depreciation accounts to their original acquisition cost basis.		

If Parrish transferred the equipment to Jordan, the eliminating entries are:

December 31, 2014, consolidation eliminating entries, upstream		
(I-1) Retained earnings, beginning—Parrish	1,350,000	
Accumulated depreciation	150,000	
Equipment...		1,500,000
To eliminate beginning-of-year unconfirmed gain on upstream intercompany transfer of equipment.		

continued

continued from prior page

(I-2)	Accumulated depreciation.		150,000	
	Depreciation expense			150,000
	To eliminate the excess annual depreciation expense recorded by the purchasing affiliate.			
(I-3)	Equipment		2,000,000	
	Accumulated depreciation.			2,000,000
	To restate the asset and accumulated depreciation accounts to their original acquisition cost basis.			

Only the first upstream eliminating entry differs from the downstream eliminations. Whereas the upstream beginning-of-year unconfirmed gain reduces the subsidiary's beginning retained earnings, the downstream beginning-of-year unconfirmed gain increases the investment account.

The equity income accrual and noncontrolling interest in net income for 2014 are affected by the reduction in depreciation expense as follows:

Effect of $1,500,000 Unconfirmed Gain on Intercompany Transfers of Depreciable Assets (10-year life) Subsequent Year		
Transaction Type	**Equity in Net Income**	**20% Noncontrolling Interest in Net Income**
Downstream.	Add $150,000	No effect
Upstream	Add $120,000	Add $30,000

We repeat this consolidation procedure as long as the equipment remains within the consolidated entity. The unconfirmed gain eliminated from the investment account or the subsidiary's beginning retained earnings on a downstream or upstream transfer, respectively, equals the original gain less the confirmed portion of the gain as of the beginning of the year. For example, at December 31, 2015, the beginning-of-year unconfirmed gain is $1,200,000, or the original gain of $1,500,000 less the amounts confirmed through reduction in depreciation expense in 2013 and 2014, $150,000 + $150,000.

Eliminations in Year of Sale to Outside Party

Sale of the depreciable asset to an outside party in a subsequent year requires that the remaining unconfirmed intercompany gain be recognized in consolidated net income in that subsequent year. If the original intercompany gain was *upstream*, the working paper entry transfers the beginning-of-year unconfirmed intercompany gain *out of the subsidiary's retained earnings* and into current income. In the *downstream* case, the unconfirmed gain is *added back to the investment account* from which it had been previously deducted via the equity method income accrual, and is recognized in current income.

The parent's equity method income accrual in the year of external sale includes all of the now-confirmed downstream intercompany gain, or the parent's share of the now-confirmed upstream gain. If the intercompany sale was upstream, the noncontrolling interest in net income is increased by the noncontrolling interest's share of the now-confirmed intercompany gain.

Suppose Jordan originally sold the equipment to Parrish on January 2, 2013, and on January 2, 2015, two years later, Parrish sells the equipment to an outside party for $3,800,000. Parrish's books report a $200,000 gain on sale of equipment [= $3,800,000 − ($4,500,000 − 2 × ($4,500,000/10))]. *From the viewpoint of the consolidated entity*, the book value of the equipment on January 2, 2015 is $2,400,000 [= $3,000,000 − (2 × ($3,000,000/10)], and the 2015 gain on the sale is $1,400,000 (= $3,800,000 − $2,400,000). This eliminating entry corrects the $200,000 gain already reported on Parrish's books:

2015 consolidation eliminating entry, downstream			
(I)	Investment in Parrish	1,200,000	
	Gain on sale of equipment.		1,200,000
	To recognize the remaining unconfirmed gain as confirmed.		

If Parrish originally sold the equipment to Jordan, this elimination corrects the $200,000 gain already reported on Jordan's books in 2015:

2015 consolidation eliminating entry, upstream		
(I) Retained earnings, beginning—Parrish	1,200,000	
Gain on sale of equipment		1,200,000
To recognize the remaining unconfirmed gain as confirmed.		

This eliminating entry affects consolidated income, so the parent's equity income accrual and noncontrolling interest in consolidated net income are adjusted as follows:

Effect of Remaining Unconfirmed $1,200,000 Gain on Intercompany Transfers of Depreciable Assets Year of Sale to Outside Party		
Transaction Type	**Equity in Net Income**	**20% Noncontrolling Interest in Net Income**
Downstream	Add $1,200,000	No effect
Upstream	Add $960,000	Add $240,000

Once the equipment is sold to an outside party, no eliminations are required in subsequent years.

REVIEW 2 ● Intercompany eliminations: depreciable asset transfers

Refer to the information in review problem #1. Add the following additional information:

1. On January 2, 2011, Protective sold equipment with $10,000,000 original cost and accumulated depreciation of $3,000,000 to Sandalite for $9,000,000. On that date the equipment had a remaining life of five years, straight-line. Sandalite still holds the equipment at December 31, 2014.
2. On June 30, 2013, Sandalite sold a building costing $15,000,000, with accumulated depreciation of $2,000,000, to Protective for $10,500,000. On that date the building had a remaining life of 20 years, straight-line. Protective still holds the building at December 31, 2014.

Required

a. Prepare the step **I** eliminating entries at December 31, 2014, in journal entry form.
b. Calculate Protective's equity income accrual for 2014, and the consolidated noncontrolling interest in net income for 2014.

Solutions are located after the chapter assignments.

INTERNATIONAL FINANCIAL REPORTING STANDARDS FOR INTERCOMPANY TRANSACTIONS

IFRS for consolidating the financial statements of a parent and its subsidiaries are found in *IFRS 10*, Consolidated Financial Statements. Although *IFRS 10* is effective in 2013, the previous guidance for intercompany eliminations, found in *IAS 27*, does not change.

Like U.S. GAAP, financial statements consolidated under IFRS present the results as if the affiliated group is a single economic entity. Intergroup balances and transactions and unconfirmed profits in assets such as land, inventory and depreciable assets are eliminated in full. Therefore the procedures described in this chapter apply also to companies reporting using IFRS.

● ●

BUSINESS APPLICATION **Reconciling intercompany transactions**

To perform intercompany eliminations, the records of the related parties must agree. If the parent reports a €500,000 receivable from its subsidiary, the subsidiary must report a €500,000 payable to the parent. Downstream merchandise sales recorded by the parent at €1,000,000 must initially be valued at €1,000,000 in the subsidiary's inventory account. However, in many cases errors, timing issues or differences in information systems cause parent and subsidiary records to disagree. Before eliminations can be made, intercompany transactions must be reconciled. A 2005 article in CFO Magazine provides a humorous comment on this process.

> "Mention intercompany transactions to finance managers, and most get a peculiar look on their faces—a look most readily compared to the soulless expression seen on prospective root-canal patients just before they disappear down the long hallway and into the dentist's lair. Admittedly, this may be something of an exaggeration (dentists don't have lairs). But reconciling intercompany transactions has never been a favorite pastime of finance department employees. While most accounting and financial consolidation packages include some capabilities for intercompany elimination or transaction monitoring, many programs track figures only at an aggregate level, requiring extensive analysis to resolve variances."

The article describes the situation at **Ferrero International Group**, headquartered in Luxembourg, and known for its Ferrero Rocher chocolates, Nutella chocolate hazelnut spread, and Tic Tac mints.

> In the past, workers at Ferrero's 50 subsidiaries manually input transaction data, with the balances keyed separately into the company's reporting system. This created a double loading of data (the preferred method for guaranteeing that mistakes make their way into a ledger).

Financial software and centralized systems can facilitate reconciliation of intercompany transactions. In Ferrero's case, the consolidation department now has web access to detailed integrated information on intercompany transactions, allowing it to analyze the causes of discrepancies on a timely basis. (Source: Esther Shein, "Other Invoices, Other Rooms," *CFO Magazine*, July 1, 2005.)

● ●

COMPREHENSIVE ILLUSTRATION

We complete this chapter—and the mergers and acquisitions section of this text—with a comprehensive example illustrating many of the consolidation reporting concepts discussed in Chapters 3 through 6.

Adonis Corporation, a producer of sportswear, acquired 90 percent of the voting stock of Reelock Company, an athletic footwear manufacturer, on January 2, 2010, at an acquisition cost of $27,830,000. Reelock's book value was $2 million at the date of acquisition, and the estimated fair value of the noncontrolling interest was $2,170,000. Reelock's assets and liabilities were fairly reported except plant and equipment with a 10-year remaining life was undervalued by $7 million, long-term debt with a 4-year remaining term was overvalued by $400,000, and two previously unreported identifiable intangibles met the criteria for capitalization under *ASC Topic 805*: an order backlog with a 2-year life, valued at $1 million, and favorable leaseholds with a 5-year life, valued at $3 million. All revaluations are written off on a straight-line basis.

Goodwill arising from this acquisition is tested annually for impairment. Accumulated impairment for 2010–2012 was $1 million. Impairment for 2013 is $200,000.

Intercompany transactions between Adonis and Reelock are as follows:

● In 2011, Reelock sold land costing $5 million to Adonis for $5.5 million. In 2013, Adonis sold the land to a real estate investment firm for $6.5 million.

● Total 2013 retail merchandise sales by Reelock to Adonis (upstream) were $3 million. Adonis' January 1, 2013 inventory balance includes $400,000 in merchandise purchased from Reelock. Its December 31, 2013 inventory balance includes $450,000 purchased from Reelock. Reelock sells to Adonis at a 20 percent markup on sales. At year-end, Adonis owes Reelock $100,000 related to merchandise sales.

- Total 2013 retail merchandise sales by Adonis to Reelock (downstream) were $2 million. Reelock's January 1, 2013 inventory balance includes $300,000 in merchandise purchased from Adonis. Its December 31, 2013 inventory balance includes $240,000 purchased from Adonis. Adonis sells to Reelock at a 20 percent markup on cost. At year-end, Reelock owes Adonis $85,000 related to merchandise sales.

- On January 2, 2010 Adonis sold equipment costing $5 million with $3 million accumulated depreciation, and a 10-year remaining life, straight-line, to Reelock for $3.5 million. Reelock still holds the equipment.

- In 2013 Adonis charged Reelock $500,000 for marketing services costing $400,000. At year-end, Reelock owes Adonis $25,000 related to these services.

Exhibit 6.1 shows the consolidation working paper at December 31, 2013, with the separate account balances for Adonis and Reelock.

Total acquired goodwill and its allocation between the parent and noncontrolling interests is as follows:

Acquisition cost		$27,830,000
Fair value of noncontrolling interest		2,170,000
Total fair value		30,000,000
Book value of Reelock	$2,000,000	
Difference between fair value and book value:		
Plant and equipment.	7,000,000	
Identifiable intangible: order backlog	1,000,000	
Identifiable intangible: favorable leaseholds.	3,000,000	
Long-term debt.	400,000	13,400,000
Total goodwill.		$16,600,000
Goodwill to controlling interest		
Acquisition cost		$27,830,000
Less controlling interest in the fair value of Reelock's identifiable net assets:		
90% × $13,400,000		(12,060,000)
Controlling interest's share.		$15,770,000
Goodwill to noncontrolling interest		
Total goodwill		$16,600,000
Less goodwill to controlling interest.		(15,770,000)
Noncontrolling interest's share.		$ 830,000

Adonis is therefore allocated 95 percent of the goodwill (= $15,770,000/$16,600,000).

We calculate 2013 equity in net income and noncontrolling interest in net income as follows:

	Total	Equity in net income	Noncontrolling interest in net income
Reelok's reported income for 2013[1].	$2,000,000	$1,800,000	$200,000
Adjustments for revaluation write-offs:			
Plant and equipment ($7,000,000/10)	(700,000)	(630,000)	(70,000)
Favorable leaseholds ($3,000,000/5)	(600,000)	(540,000)	(60,000)
Long-term debt ($400,000/4)	(100,000)	(90,000)	(10,000)
Goodwill (95:5 ratio)	(200,000)	(190,000)	(10,000)
Adjustments for intercompany transactions:			
Upstream confirmed gain on land sale.	500,000	450,000	50,000
Upstream confirmed profit in beginning inventory	80,000	72,000	8,000
Downstream confirmed profit in beginning inventory.	50,000	50,000	—
Upstream unconfirmed profit in ending inventory	(90,000)	(81,000)	(9,000)
Downstream unconfirmed profit in ending inventory	(40,000)	(40,000)	—
Downstream confirmed gain on sale of equipment	150,000	150,000	—
	$1,050,000	$ 951,000	$ 99,000

[1] Reelock's 2013 reported income is $2,000,000 = $35,000,000 − $25,000,000 − $8,000,000; see Exhibit 6.1.

Based on the account balances reported in Exhibit 6.1, here are the eliminating entries needed to consolidate the 2013 financial statements of Adonis and Reelock, in journal entry form:

(C)	Equity in income of Reelock..	951,000	
	Investment in Reelock..		951,000
	To eliminate equity in net income on the parent's books and restore the investment account to its beginning-of-year value.		
(I-1)	Retained earnings, January 1.......................................	500,000	
	Gain on sale of land..		500,000
	To recognize the confirmed gain on the upstream land sale.		
(I-2)	Sales revenue..	5,000,000	
	Cost of goods sold		5,000,000
	To eliminate intercompany sales and purchases ($5,000,000 = $3,000,000 + $2,000,000).		
(I-3)	Retained earnings, January 1.......................................	80,000	
	Cost of goods sold		80,000
	To recognize the confirmed upstream profit in beginning inventory.		
(I-4)	Investment in Reelock	50,000	
	Cost of goods sold		50,000
	To recognize the confirmed downstream profit in beginning inventory.		
(I-5)	Cost of goods sold...	130,000	
	Current assets		130,000
	To eliminate the unconfirmed upstream and downstream profit in ending inventory ($130,000 = $90,000 + $40,000).		
(I-6)	Investment in Reelock	1,050,000	
	Accumulated depreciation.......................................	450,000	
	Plant and equipment..		1,500,000
	To remove the unconfirmed beginning-of-year profit on downstream sale of equipment [$1,050,000 = $1,500,000 − (($1,500,000/10) × 3)].		
(I-7)	Accumulated depreciation..	150,000	
	Operating expenses		150,000
	To recognize the confirmed profit (excess depreciation) on downstream sale of equipment ($150,000 = $1,500,000/10).		
(I-8)	Plant and equipment	3,000,000	
	Accumulated depreciation.....................................		3,000,000
	To restate the asset and accumulated depreciation accounts to their original acquisition cost basis.		
(I-9)	Sales revenue..	500,000	
	Operating expenses		500,000
	To eliminate the intercompany sale of marketing services.		
(I-10)	Current liabilities...	210,000	
	Current assets		210,000
	To eliminate intercompany receivables/payables ($210,000 = $100,000 + $85,000 + $25,000).		
(E)	Capital stock	1,400,000	
	Retained earnings, January 1......................................	8,020,000	
	Investment in Reelock (90%)...................................		8,478,000
	Noncontrolling interest in Reelock (10%)		942,000
	To eliminate the subsidiary's beginning-of-year capital stock account and the remainder of its beginning retained earnings account against the beginning-of-year book value portion of the investment account, and recognize the beginning-of-year book value of the noncontrolling interest. [$8,020,000 = $8,600,000 − $500,000 (I-1) − $80,000 (I-3)].		

continued

continued from prior page

(R)	Plant and equipment	7,000,000	
	Identifiable intangibles	1,200,000	
	Long-term debt	100,000	
	Goodwill	15,600,000	
	Accumulated depreciation		2,100,000
	Investment in Reelock		20,400,000
	Noncontrolling interest in Reelock		1,400,000

To revalue Reelock's net assets as of the beginning of the year and allocate the revaluations to the controlling and noncontrolling interest.
$20,400,000 = (90\% \times \$6,200,000) + (95\% \times \$15,600,000);$
$1,400,000 = (10\% \times \$6,200,000) + (5\% \times \$15,600,000);$
$6,200,000 = (\$7,000,000 + \$1,200,000 + \$100,000 - \$2,100,000).$

(O)	Operating expenses	1,600,000	
	Accumulated depreciation		700,000
	Identifiable intangibles		600,000
	Long-term debt		100,000
	Goodwill		200,000

To write off the revaluations for the current year.

(N)	Noncontrolling interest in net income	99,000	
	Noncontrolling interest in Reelock		99,000

To recognize the noncontrolling interest in the subsidiary's income.

Exhibit 6.1 displays these eliminating entries, and each account's consolidated balance.

Using the consolidated account balances in Exhibit 6.1, we prepare the consolidated statement of income and retained earnings for 2013 and the consolidated balance sheet at December 31, 2013.

ADONIS CORPORATION AND SUBSIDIARY Consolidated Statement of Income and Retained Earnings For Year Ended December 31, 2013	
Sales revenue and gains	$85,000,000
Less: Cost of goods sold	(58,000,000)
Operating expenses	(24,950,000)
Consolidated net income	**2,050,000**
Less: Noncontrolling interest in net income	(99,000)
Net income attributable to Adonis	1,951,000
Plus: Retained earnings, Adonis, January 1	25,000,000
Less: Dividends	(500,000)
Retained earnings attributable to Adonis, December 31	$26,451,000

EXHIBIT 6.1   Consolidation Working Paper for Adonis and Reelock, December 31, 2013

| | Accounts Taken From Books Dr (Cr) | | Eliminations | | Consolidated Balances Dr (Cr) |
	Adonis	Reelock	Dr	Cr	
Current assets	$ 8,000,000	$ 2,000,000		$ 130,000 (I-5) 210,000 (I-10)	$ 9,660,000
Plant and equipment	100,000,000	30,000,000	(I-8) $ 3,000,000 (R) 7,000,000	1,500,000 (I-6)	138,500,000
Accumulated depreciation	(25,000,000)	(13,000,000)	(I-6) 450,000 (I-7) 150,000	3,000,000 (I-8) 2,100,000 (R) 700,000 (O)	(43,200,000)
Investment in Reelock (90%)	28,729,000	—	(I-4) 50,000 (I-6) 1,050,000	951,000 (C) 8,478,000 (E) 20,400,000 (R)	—
Identifiable intangible assets	—	—	(R) 1,200,000	600,000 (O)	600,000
Goodwill	—	—	(R) 15,600,000	200,000 (O)	15,400,000
Current liabilities.	(17,000,000)	(2,500,000)	(I-10) 210,000		(19,290,000)
Long-term debt	(66,278,000)	(4,500,000)	(R) 100,000	100,000 (O)	(70,778,000)
Capital stock	(2,000,000)	(1,400,000)	(E) 1,400,000		(2,000,000)
Retained earnings, January 1	(25,000,000)	(8,600,000)	(I-1) 500,000 (I-3) 80,000 (E) 8,020,000		(25,000,000)
Noncontrolling interest	—	—		942,000 (E) 1,400,000 (R) 99,000 (N)	(2,441,000)
Dividends	500,000	—			500,000
Sales revenue and gains	(55,000,000)	(35,000,000)	(I-2) 5,000,000 (I-9) 500,000	500,000 (I-1)	(85,000,000)
Equity in income of Reelock.	(951,000)	—	(C) 951,000		—
Cost of goods sold.	38,000,000	25,000,000	(I-5) 130,000	5,000,000 (I-2) 80,000 (I-3) 50,000 (I-4)	58,000,000
Operating expenses	16,000,000	8,000,000	(O) 1,600,000	150,000 (I-7) 500,000 (I-9)	24,950,000
Noncontrolling interest in net income . .	—	—	(N) 99,000		99,000
	$ 0	$ 0	$47,090,000	$47,090,000	$ 0

ADONIS CORPORATION AND SUBSIDIARY
Consolidated Balance Sheet
December 31, 2013

Assets		Liabilities and Stockholders' Equity	
Current assets	$ 9,660,000	Current liabilities.	$ 19,290,000
Plant and equipment, net of $43,200,000 accumulated depreciation	95,300,000	Long-term debt	70,778,000
Identifiable intangibles	600,000	Total liabilities.	90,068,000
Goodwill	15,400,000	Stockholders' equity	
		Adonis stockholders' equity:	
		Capital stock.	2,000,000
		Retained earnings.	26,451,000
		Total Adonis stockholders' equity	28,451,000
		Noncontrolling interest	2,441,000
		Total stockholders' equity	30,892,000
Total assets	$120,960,000	Total liabilities and stockholders' equity	$120,960,000

REVIEW OF KEY CONCEPTS ••••••••••••••••••••••••••••••••

Prepare eliminating entries for intercompany service and financing transactions. (p. 212) Service and financing transactions between the parent and subsidiary require elimination of related receivables and payables, revenues and expenses. These eliminations are necessary to avoid duplicating balances, and involve no unconfirmed profits.

LO 1

Describe elimination of unconfirmed profits and their effect on equity in net income and noncontrolling interest in net income. (p. 213) Intercompany profit refers to the difference between the intercompany transfer price and the net book value to the selling affiliate. In consolidation, the entire amount of the unconfirmed intercompany profit is eliminated on the working paper. Elimination of unconfirmed intercompany profits on upstream sales—from subsidiary to parent—is proportionate between the controlling and noncontrolling interests, and the noncontrolling interest in net income is affected. Elimination of unconfirmed intercompany profit on downstream sales—from parent to subsidiary—is entirely against the parent's net income. Following the one-line consolidation concept, the equity method income accrual reflects the same eliminations of unconfirmed intercompany profits as those made in computing consolidated net income. The parent's share of the subsidiary's reported net income is reduced by the total unconfirmed intercompany profits on downstream sales and by the parent's share of the unconfirmed intercompany profits on upstream sales.

LO 2

Prepare eliminating entries for intercompany transfers of land. (p. 215) Eliminating entries for intercompany profits or losses on transfers of land remaining within the consolidated entity restore the land balance to its original cost and remove the unconfirmed gain or loss. When the intercompany gain or loss is confirmed through sale to a third party, an eliminating entry reclassifies the gain or loss to consolidated income.

LO 3

Prepare eliminating entries for intercompany transfers of inventory. (p. 218) Three eliminating entries for inventory sales between the parent and subsidiary are necessary to (1) remove duplication in sales and cost of sales, (2) confirm the intercompany markup on beginning inventory, and (3) remove the unconfirmed markup on ending inventory.

LO 4

Prepare eliminating entries for intercompany transfers of depreciable assets. (p. 223) Intercompany profit on transfers of depreciable assets is confirmed as the assets depreciate. Eliminating entries restore the asset, accumulated depreciation and depreciation expense balances to amounts shown if no intercompany transfer occurred.

LO 5

MULTIPLE CHOICE QUESTIONS ••••••••••••••••••••••••••••••

1. Suzlon, a subsidiary of Patni, provides services to Patni. During 2013, Suzlon charged $3,000,000 for services provided to Patni. Cost of the services provided was $2,100,000. How should the consolidated income statement report these services?

   LO 1

	Service revenue	Service expense
a.	$3,000,000	$0
b.	$3,000,000	$2,100,000
c.	$0	$2,100,000
d.	$0	$3,000,000

2. A parent makes an interest-bearing loan to its 90%-owned subsidiary in 2012, which is still outstanding in 2013. The elimination entries I on the consolidation working paper for 2013, related to this loan,

   LO 1

   a. reduce investment in subsidiary by the amount of 2012's interest revenue.
   b. reduce the subsidiary's beginning retained earnings by the amount of 2012's interest revenue.
   c. reduce investment in subsidiary by the amount of interest owing at the end of 2013.
   d. have no effect on investment in subsidiary or the subsidiary's beginning retained earnings.

3. Petronet sells merchandise to its 80-percent-owned subsidiary Sonata at a markup of 20 percent on cost. During 2013, Petronet charges Sonata $4,000,000 for merchandise sales. Sonata's 2013 beginning inventory contains $540,000 in merchandise purchased from Petronet. Sonata's 2013 ending inventory contains $480,000 in merchandise purchased from Petronet. Petronet uses the complete equity method to record its investment in Sonata. How are Petronet's 2013 equity in net income of Sonata and 2013 consolidated income to the noncontrolling interest affected by intercompany merchandise transactions?

   LO 2

	Equity in net income	Noncontrolling interest in net income
a.	$10,000 increase	$0
b.	$ 8,000 increase	$2,000 increase
c.	$12,000 increase	$0
d.	$ 9,600 increase	$2,400 increase

LO 2

4. Pentamedia owns 90 percent of Sesa. At the start of 2012, Sesa sold buildings carried at $4,000,000, net, to Pentamedia for $6,000,000. The buildings had a remaining life of 10 years and straight-line depreciation is used. Pentamedia uses the complete equity method to record its investment in Sesa. Pentamedia still owns the buildings. How are Pentamedia's 2013 equity in net income of Sesa and 2013 consolidated income to the noncontrolling interest affected by the intercompany sale of buildings?

	Equity in net income	Noncontrolling interest in net income
a.	$200,000 increase	$0
b.	$360,000 increase	$40,000 increase
c.	$400,000 increase	$0
d.	$180,000 increase	$20,000 increase

LO 3

5. A parent sells land costing $35,000 to a subsidiary in 2012 for $55,000. The subsidiary sells the land in 2014 to a third party for $85,000. On the consolidated income statement for 2014, the gain on sale of land should be reported at:

a. $20,000
b. $50,000
c. $30,000
d. $ 0

LO 3

6. A subsidiary sells land costing $1,000,000 to its parent in 2010 for $1,400,000. The parent owns 80 percent of the subsidiary's stock. In 2013, the parent sells the land to an outside party for $550,000. What elimination entry I is required on the 2013 consolidation working paper?

a. Debit the subsidiary's beginning retained earnings and credit the loss on sale of land for $400,000.
b. Debit investment in subsidiary and credit the loss on sale of land for $400,000.
c. Debit the subsidiary's beginning retained earnings and credit the loss on sale of land for $450,000.
d. Debit investment in subsidiary and credit the loss on sale of land for $450,000.

LO 4

7. A subsidiary sells merchandise to its parent at a markup of 25% on cost. In 2013, the parent paid $500,000 for merchandise received from the subsidiary. By year-end 2013, the parent has sold $400,000 of the merchandise to outside customers for $450,000, but still holds the other $100,000 in its ending inventory. Which statement is **true** concerning how this information should be reported on the 2013 consolidated financial statements?

a. Consolidated sales should be $450,000.
b. The consolidated ending inventory balance should be $100,000.
c. Consolidated cost of goods sold should be $400,000.
d. Consolidated cost of goods sold should be $720,000.

LO 4

8. A parent sells $30,000,000 retail value of merchandise to its subsidiary during 2012. The subsidiary's beginning inventory for 2012 contains $1,000,000 in merchandise purchased from the parent, including a markup of $200,000. The subsidiary's ending inventory for 2012 contains $1,500,000 in merchandise purchased from the parent. The markup included in the ending inventory balance is $225,000. On the 2012 consolidation working paper, eliminations I:

a. reduce ending inventory by $200,000.
b. reduce beginning retained earnings by $225,000.
c. reduce cost of goods sold by $225,000.
d. increase the parent's investment account by $200,000.

LO 5

9. At the beginning of 2011, a parent company sold a patent, carried on its books at $4,000,000, to its subsidiary for $3,000,000. The patent had a remaining life of five years and straight-line amortization is used. It is now the end of 2013, and the subsidiary still owns the patent. On the 2013 consolidation working paper, eliminations I:

a. increase the patent by $800,000.
b. reduce the parent's investment account by $600,000.
c. increase the subsidiary's beginning retained earnings by $200,000.
d. reduce amortization expense by $400,000.

10. At the beginning of 2009, a subsidiary sold equipment, carried on its books at $3,000,000, net, to its parent for $5,000,000. The equipment had a remaining life of 20 years and straight-line depreciation is used. It is now the end of 2012, and the parent still owns the equipment. On the 2012 consolidation working paper, eliminations I:

LO 5

   a. reduce the parent's investment account by $1,700,000.
   b. reduce the subsidiary's beginning retained earnings account by $1,600,000.
   c. reduce depreciation expense by $100,000.
   d. reduce net equipment by $2,000,000.

**Assignments with the ✅ in the margin are available in an online homework system.
See the Preface of the book for details.**

EXERCISES •

E6.1 **Intercompany Land Transactions** Sunnyvale Company, a wholly-owned subsidiary of Pickford Company, purchased a tract of land from Pickford in 2012 for $200,000. Pickford originally acquired the land for $50,000 and accounts for its investment in Sunnyvale using the complete equity method.

LO 3 ✅

Required
   a. Assuming that Sunnyvale still owns the land, give the working paper eliminations needed for the intercompany land sale when consolidated statements are prepared at the end of 2012 and 2013.
   b. If Sunnyvale sells the land to a third party for $240,000 in 2014, prepare the eliminations needed for the intercompany land sale when consolidated statements are prepared at the end of 2014.

E6.2 **Intercompany Land Transactions** We observe the following eliminating entries relating to intercompany transactions, made in consolidation at December 31, 2012. Assume that each eliminating entry relates to a distinct transaction.

LO 3

1.	Retained earnings—Subsidiary	20,000	
	Land.		20,000

2.	Land	14,000	
	Loss on sale of land.		14,000

3.	Investment in Subsidiary	30,000	
	Land.		30,000

4.	Retained earnings—Subsidiary	18,000	
	Gain on sale of land.		18,000

Required
Describe, as completely as possible, what occurred during 2012 and, where relevant, what occurred in prior years.

E6.3 **Intercompany Merchandise Transactions** **Nike, Inc.** sells merchandise to its wholly-owned subsidiary, **Converse**, at a 30 percent markup on cost and Converse sells to Nike at a markup of 20 percent on selling price. Transactions between the affiliates during the year ended December 31, 2013, are given below *(in thousands)*:

LO 4 ✅

NIKE, INC.
[NKE]

CONVERSE

	Nike	Converse
Inventories at January 1, 2013, acquired from affiliate	$ 75,000	$117,000
Sales made to affiliate during 2013	600,000	550,000
Inventories at December 31, 2013, acquired from affiliate	80,000	110,500

Required
Prepare the working paper eliminations related to these intercompany transactions at December 31, 2013.

LO 4, 5 **E6.4** **Analysis of Land Sale Alternatives** You are the 20 percent noncontrolling shareholder in Sawyer Corporation. Under an agreement at the time of acquisition, Sawyer distributes half of the noncontrolling interest in net income as dividends each year. Sawyer holds a valuable tract of land, carried on its books at $100,000. This land is in great demand as a site for a shopping mall in a rapidly growing community. An outside developer offered $4 million for the site. Sawyer's parent company is considering buying the land from Sawyer for $5 million, then leasing it under a 75-year lease to the developer. The annual lease payment to the parent company would be $750,000.

Required

As the noncontrolling shareholder in Sawyer, which transaction provides the most dividends? Explain.

LO 5 **E6.5** **Intercompany Equipment Transactions** Plato Company sold equipment to its wholly owned subsidiary, Sawyer Company, on January 2, 2013. At time of sale, Plato's books showed the equipment at cost of $750,000 and accumulated depreciation of $200,000. Sawyer bought the equipment for $800,000 and depreciated it over its remaining five-year life (straight-line, no salvage value).

Required

a. Prepare the necessary consolidation eliminating entries at December 31, 2013.
b. Prepare the necessary consolidation eliminating entries at December 31, 2014.

LO 3, 4, 5 **E6.6** **Various Intercompany Transactions** In consolidation of Perpetual Industries and Sand Hill Company at December 31, 2012, you assemble the following data related to unconfirmed intercompany profits:

	January 1, 2012	December 31, 2012
Land (one parcel)	$2,500,000	$2,500,000
Merchandise inventory.	1,400,000	3,200,000
Equipment (one item)	800,000	600,000

The equipment is carried on the purchasing affiliate's books at $7,200,000 with accumulated depreciation of $3,600,000 (straight-line, no salvage value) at December 31, 2012. Accumulated depreciation at the date of intercompany sale was $2,000,000; the original intercompany gain was $1,200,000. Perpetual owns 80 percent of Sand Hill.

Required

a. Assume that all of the above unconfirmed intercompany profits arose from *upstream* sales. Prepare the eliminating entries related to these intercompany transactions when consolidating the financial statements of Perpetual Industries and Sand Hill Company at December 31, 2012.
b. Repeat part *a* assuming that all of the above unconfirmed intercompany profits arose from *downstream* sales.

LO 2, 3, 4, 5 **E6.7** **Intercompany Transactions, Equity Method Income and Noncontrolling Interest** Putnam Company owns 80 percent of Swaraj Company. The excess of acquisition cost over book value was attributed entirely to previously unrecorded identifiable intangibles. For 2014, Swaraj Company reported net income of $7,000,000 and paid dividends of $2,000,000. Appropriate amortization of the previously unrecorded identifiable intangibles for 2014 is $1,750,000. The following information is available regarding intercompany transactions:

1. During 2014, Swaraj sold land to Putnam at a loss of $300,000.
2. Putnam's ending inventory at December 31, 2014, included merchandise acquired from Swaraj; the unconfirmed profit on this inventory was $600,000.
3. Putnam's ending inventory at December 31, 2013, included merchandise acquired from Swaraj; the unconfirmed profit was $350,000.
4. On January 3, 2011, Putnam sold equipment to Swaraj at a gain of $1,000,000; at the time of sale, the remaining life of this equipment was 10 years, straight-line.

Required

a. Calculate Putnam Company's equity method income accrual for 2014 and the noncontrolling interest in net income for 2014.
b. Prepare the working paper eliminations made in consolidation at December 31, 2014, related to the intercompany transactions.

E6.8 Income Effects of Unconfirmed Intercompany Profits Petra purchased 80 percent of Sage's stock at the beginning of 2013. At the end of 2013, the following intercompany profits are unconfirmed: LO 2, 3, 4

1. Petra sold land to Sage at a gain of $200,000; Sage still holds the land.
2. Sage sold land to Petra at a gain of $300,000; Petra still holds the land.
3. Petra sold inventory to Sage; intercompany profits in Sage's ending inventory total $800,000.
4. Sage sold inventory to Petra; intercompany profits in Petra's ending inventory total $650,000.

Required

Calculate the effect of eliminating these items on consolidated net income to the controlling interest and the noncontrolling interest in net income for 2013.

E6.9 Consolidated Income Statement—Intercompany Transactions Condensed income statements for PCO and its 75-percent-owned subsidiary, SCO, appear below: LO 2, 4

(in thousands)	PCO	SCO
Sales.	$2,000,000	$1,200,000
Equity in income of SCO	43,000	—
Total revenue	2,043,000	1,200,000
Cost of goods sold.	1,000,000	700,000
Other expenses	600,000	300,000
Total expenses.	1,600,000	1,000,000
Net income.	$ 443,000	$ 200,000

Intercompany sales amounted to $400,000, unconfirmed intercompany profits in ending inventory are $50,000 (downstream) and $40,000 (upstream). The difference between acquisition cost and SCO's book value was allocated to previously unreported identifiable intangibles. The current year write-off of these intangibles is $36,000.

Required

a. Prepare a schedule to compute PCO's equity method income accrual and the noncontrolling interest in net income.
b. Prepare a condensed consolidated income statement for PCO and SCO.

E6.10 Consolidated Income Statement, Intercompany Transactions Condensed income statements for Pon and its 80 percent-owned subsidiary, Star, appear below. LO 2, 4

Condensed Income Statements	Pon	Star
Sales.	$9,000,000	$4,000,000
Equity in income of Star.	508,000	—
Cost of goods sold.	(6,000,000)	(2,500,000)
Other expenses	(2,000,000)	(600,000)
Net income.	$1,508,000	$ 900,000

Intercompany sales are $1,000,000, unconfirmed intercompany profit in Pon's beginning inventory is $110,000 and unconfirmed intercompany profit in Star's ending inventory is $60,000. At the date of combination four years ago, previously unrecorded identifiable intangibles (8-year life, straight-line) of $800,000 were recognized. The total goodwill recognized at date of business combination is shared with the noncontrolling interest according to ownership interests. This year's goodwill impairment test indicates a $200,000 reduction in value.

Required

a. Prepare a schedule to compute Pon's equity method income accrual and the noncontrolling interest in net income.
b. Prepare a condensed consolidated income statement for Pon and Star.

LO 1, 4 **E6.11 Ratio Analysis of Enron-Type Intercompany Transactions** The financial effects of intercompany transactions are eliminated in consolidated financial statements. This helps insure that the statements reflect only assets, liabilities, revenues and expenses arising from transactions with outside parties. Criticisms of **Enron**'s accounting include (1) gains recognized on asset transfers to controlled special purpose entities (SPEs) that escaped consolidation and, hence, elimination; (2) borrowings by unconsolidated controlled SPEs; and (3) using SPEs to enable recognition of gains on one's own stock. To demonstrate these phenomena we consider the following data from Sponsor and Sponsoree, an SPE, *before any intercompany transactions*. Except as noted, Sponsor has no equity interest in Sponsoree but may qualify as Sponsoree's primary beneficiary.

ENRON

(in millions)	Sponsor	Sponsoree
Assets.	$10,000	$4,000
Liabilities.	6,000	3,600
Revenues	9,000	2,000
Expenses	8,000	1,900

Required

For each independent situation below, present the required calculations assuming (1) Sponsor and Sponsoree are *not* consolidated, and (2) Sponsor and Sponsoree *are* consolidated.

a.   Sponsor sells inventory to Sponsoree for $3,000 million and recognizes $500 million profit. The inventory is on hand at year end. Compute Sponsor's return on assets (ROA) and return on sales (ROS).

b.   Sponsoree borrows $3,500 million from a bank, uses it to purchase Sponsor's stock directly from Sponsor, and Sponsor reports stock issued for cash. Compute Sponsor's total liabilities/total assets.

c.   Sponsoree's stock investment in part *b* was assigned to its trading portfolio. The stock investment's value is $4,300 million at year end. Compute Sponsor's ROA. For (1), assume that Sponsor owns 25% of Sponsoree's stock and that Sponsor's revenues include the equity accrual, except for the value change in the stock investment made in part *b*.

LO 2, 4, 5 **E6.12 Comprehensive Consolidated Net Income** The following information relates to **Brown Shoe Company** and its 90 percent-owned subsidiary, **Shoes.com**, for 2013 *(in thousands)*.

BROWN SHOE COMPANY
[BWS]

SHOES.COM

Brown Shoe Company's net income from its own operations.	$50,000
Shoes.com's net income from its own operations.	20,000
Dividends paid by Shoes.com	8,000
Acquisition date overvaluation of inventory sold in 2013.	900
Reduction in depreciation expense on equipment overvalued at acquisition date	300
Increase in fair value of contingent consideration liability outside of measurement period	200
Amortization of discount on long-term debt created at acquisition date	100
Impairment loss on in-process R&D capitalized at acquisition date	600
Unconfirmed upstream inventory profit in Brown Shoe Company's ending inventory	400
Downstream loss on January 2 sale of patent to Shoes.com; 5-year life	500

Required

Prepare a schedule to determine consolidated net income for 2013 and the amounts attributed to the controlling and noncontrolling interests.

PROBLEMS •

LO 2, 4 **P6.1 Consolidation Working Paper, Noncontrolling Interest, Intercompany Inventory Transactions** Peninsula Industries and Seaport Company, a 90 percent owned subsidiary, engage in extensive intercompany transactions involving raw materials, component parts, and completed products. Peninsula acquired its interest in Seaport several years ago, at a cost of $3,000,000. At that time, Seaport's book value was $2,000,000 and the fair value of the noncontrolling interest in Seaport was $275,000. The excess of acquisition cost over book value was attributed to previously unrecorded indefinite-lived intangibles, valued at $500,000, and to goodwill. As of January 1, 2013, the intangibles were impaired by $200,000 and the goodwill was impaired by $300,000. Impairment testing reveals no additional impairment of either asset in

2013. Intercompany sales for 2013 and the unconfirmed intercompany profits in the beginning and ending inventories of both companies are summarized below:

(in thousands)	Peninsula Industries	Seaport Company
Intercompany profit in inventory, January 1, 2013..................	$ 100,000	$ 60,000
Intercompany sales to affiliate.....................................	2,200,000	3,700,000
Intercompany profit in inventory, December 31, 2013..............	80,000	75,000

Prior to consolidation at December 31, 2013, the separate condensed trial balances of the two companies are shown below:

	Dr (Cr)	
(in thousands)	Peninsula Industries	Seaport Company
Current assets	$ 1,950,000	$ 980,000
Investment in Seaport	4,183,000	—
Property, plant and equipment, net	5,810,000	5,120,000
Intangibles	4,270,000	—
Liabilities...	(4,900,000)	(2,100,000)
Capital stock	(3,000,000)	(1,200,000)
Retained earnings, January 1...............................	(6,700,000)	(2,300,000)
Dividends	1,000,000	400,000
Sales...	(15,000,000)	(6,000,000)
Equity in net income of Seaport............................	(813,000)	—
Cost of goods sold.......................................	9,050,000	3,170,000
Operating expenses......................................	4,150,000	1,930,000
Totals	$ 0	$ 0

Required

a. Prepare a schedule to calculate total goodwill for this acquisition and its allocation to the controlling and noncontrolling interests.

b. Prepare a schedule to show how the equity method income accrual for 2013 was computed, and to compute noncontrolling interest in net income for 2013.

c. Prepare a working paper consolidating the trial balances of Peninsula and Seaport for 2013.

P6.2 Consolidation Working Paper, Noncontrolling Interest, Intercompany Merchandise Transactions Kellogg Company (Kellogg's) acquired 75% of the outstanding stock of Wholesome & Hearty Foods ("Wholesome") at the end of 2007, for cash and stock totaling $120 million. Assume that Wholesome's assets and liabilities were fairly reported at the date of acquisition, except for these items:

LO 2, 4

KELLOGG COMPANY [K]

WHOLESOME & HEARTY FOODS

(in thousands)	Book value	Fair value
Plant & equipment, net (10-year life, straight-line).................	$150,000	$135,000
Veggie burger recipe (10-year life, straight-line)	0	25,000
Long-term debt (4-year life, straight-line).......................	30,000	34,000

Wholesome's book value at the date of acquisition was $74 million, and the fair value of the 25% noncontrolling interest was $35 million. It is now December 31, 2013 (the end of the sixth year since acquisition). Impairment testing on the goodwill arising in this acquisition reveals that total impairment during 2008-2012 is $2 million, and impairment in 2013 is $1 million.

Wholesome sells merchandise and raw materials to Kellogg's at a markup of 30% on cost. Here is information on these intercompany sales *(in thousands)*:

Inventory, January 1, 2013, reported on Kellogg's books	$10,400
Inventory, December 31, 2013, reported on Kellogg's books	13,000
Transfer price for 2013 sales from Wholesome to Kellogg's.........................	60,000

Below are the separate trial balances of Kellogg's and Wholesome at December 31, 2013.

	Dr (Cr)	
(in thousands)	**Kellogg's**	**Wholesome**
Current assets	$ 35,000	$ 20,000
Plant and equipment, net.	262,650	192,000
Investment in Wholesome	131,100	—
Identifiable intangibles	100,000	10,000
Current liabilities.	(30,000)	(25,000)
Long-term debt	(350,000)	(100,000)
Capital stock	(80,000)	(54,000)
Retained earnings, January 1.	(60,000)	(38,000)
Sales revenue.	(400,000)	(140,000)
Equity in net income of Wholesome.	(1,750)	—
Cost of sales.	250,000	65,000
Operating expenses	143,000	70,000
Totals	$ 0	$ 0

Required (In your answers below, present all numbers in thousands.)

a. Calculate the initial goodwill arising from this acquisition, and its allocation to the controlling and noncontrolling interests.

b. Prepare a schedule computing Kellogg's equity in net income of Wholesome and noncontrolling interest in net income for 2013.

c. Prepare a working paper to consolidate the trial balances of Kellogg's and Wholesome at December 31, 2013.

✓ **LO 5** **P6.3** **Intercompany Transfers of Depreciable Assets** Pert Corporation acquired 80 percent of the Smart Company ten years ago. In the intervening years, Pert and Smart made several intercompany transfers of depreciable assets. Pert's controller is beginning to prepare consolidated financial statements for the current year ended December 31, 2012. As the new assistant controller, you are asked to develop the working paper eliminations for the following group of intercompany transactions. Pert uses the equity method to account for its investment in Smart. All depreciation is straight-line.

Transaction No.	Date	Original Cost	Accumulated Depreciation	Transfer Price	Remaining Life	Upstream (U) Downstream (D)
1.	6/30/06	$100,000	$ 20,000	$160,000	8 years	D
2.	1/2/08	450,000	300,000	200,000	10 years	U
3.	1/1/11	600,000	360,000	200,000	5 years	D

Required

a. Prepare the necessary working paper eliminations related to the above intercompany transactions at December 31, 2012.

b. Assume that the item in transaction 2 was sold externally on January 1, 2012, for $400,000. Prepare the working paper eliminations needed for transaction 2 at December 31, 2012, reflecting the sale to the outside party during 2012.

LO 2, 3, 4, 5 **P6.4** **Consolidated Income Statement—Intercompany Transactions** Several years ago Pow Company exchanged its own shares for 95 percent of the outstanding stock of Sow Company. At that time, Sow's assets and liabilities were fairly stated and the acquisition cost and fair value of the noncontrolling interest reflected Sow's book value. Condensed income statements for the two companies appear below. Pow uses the equity method to account for its investment in Sow.

Pow Company and Sow Company **Statements of Income and Retained Earnings**		
	Pow	**Sow**
Sales.	$25,000,000	$10,000,000
Other income	1,200,000	500,000
Equity in income of Sow.	895,000	—
Total revenue	27,095,000	10,500,000
Cost of goods sold.	19,000,000	7,600,000
Operating expenses	4,100,000	1,800,000
Other expenses	800,000	300,000
Total expenses.	23,900,000	9,700,000
Net income.	3,195,000	800,000
Retained earnings, January 1.	15,700,000	6,200,000
Dividends	(1,000,000)	(400,000)
Retained earnings, December 31.	$17,895,000	$ 6,600,000

Additional information:

1. Pow's beginning inventory includes $400,000 of intercompany profit on goods purchased from Sow, and made no intercompany purchases during the current year. Sow's ending inventory includes $200,000 of intercompany profit on purchases of $3,000,000 from Pow.
2. Sow's other expenses include a loss of $100,000 on an intercompany sale of land to Pow.
3. Pow's other income reflects a $250,000 gain on the sale of machinery to Sow at the beginning of the year. At date of sale, the machinery had a remaining life of five years; it is being depreciated by the straight-line method.
4. Several years ago, Pow recorded a gain of $60,000 on land sold to Sow for $280,000. Sow sold the land externally during the year for $390,000. The current gain is reflected in Sow's other income account.

Required

a. Prepare a schedule to calculate Pow's equity method income accrual and noncontrolling interest in consolidated net income for the year.
b. Prepare a consolidated statement of income and retained earnings for Pow and Sow.

P6.5 Equity Accrual and Eliminating Entries—Intercompany Asset Transfers and Services On January 2, 2011, Pohang Company acquired 80 percent of Suro Corporation's voting common stock for $1.25 billion. The fair value of the noncontrolling interest at the date of acquisition was $300 million. The $50 million excess of acquisition cost and noncontrolling interest over the book value of Suro was attributed entirely to goodwill. Suro reported net income of $150 million and $200 million in 2011 and 2012, respectively, paying out 40 percent of each period's earnings in dividends. Pohang reports its investment in Suro at equity. There is no goodwill impairment in 2011 or 2012. Information on intercompany transactions follows: *LO 1, 2, 3, 4, 5,* ✅

1. On March 5, 2011, Suro sold a parcel of land to Pohang for $60 million; the land originally cost $45 million. Pohang continues to hold the land.
2. During 2012, Pohang and Suro recorded intercompany merchandise sales of $350 million, an amount equal to cost plus 25 percent. Suro's beginning inventory included $50 million of merchandise purchased from Pohang in prior years, while Pohang's ending inventory included $80 million of merchandise purchased from Suro.
3. On January 2, 2012, Suro sold a piece of machinery to Pohang for $60 million and recorded a gain of $25 million. Accumulated depreciation on the machinery amounted to $40 million at January 2. The machinery is being depreciated by the straight-line method over its remaining life of five years.
4. Pohang billed Suro $20 million for computer services during the year. The costs incurred by Pohang in supplying these services amounted to $15 million. On December 31, 2012, the unpaid portion of these intercompany services amounted to $3 million.

Required

a.   Prepare a schedule to compute Pohang's equity method income accrual and the noncontrolling interest in consolidated net income for 2012.

b.   Prepare the working paper eliminations to consolidate the accounts of Pohang and Suro at December 31, 2012.

LO 2, 4, 5   **P6.6   Comprehensive Problem: Consolidation Working Paper and Financial Statements**   Pierre Corporation acquired 75 percent of Selene Corporation's common stock for $20,100,000 on January 2, 2011. The estimated fair value of the noncontrolling interest was $5,900,000. Selene's book value at date of acquisition was $10,000,000, and its identifiable net assets were fairly stated except for previously unreported completed technology, valued at $4,000,000, with a remaining life of 5 years, straight-line. It is now December 31, 2014, and you are preparing consolidated financial statements for Pierre and Selene. Following is information on intercompany transactions:

1.   On January 2, 2012, Pierre sold equipment to Selene for $6 million and recorded a gain of $2 million. The equipment had a remaining life of 10 years at that time.

2.   Selene supplies Pierre with component parts for its products, at a markup of 20 percent on cost. During 2014, Selene made sales totaling $20 million to Pierre. Pierre had parts purchased for $1.8 million and $2.4 million in its 2014 beginning and ending inventory balances, respectively.

3.   Pierre sells materials to Selene for use in its manufacturing processes, at a markup of 20 percent on selling price. During 2014, Pierre made sales totaling $15 million to Selene. Selene had materials purchased for $3 million and $2.8 million in its 2014 beginning and ending inventory balances, respectively.

Goodwill arising from this acquisition was impaired by $3 million during the years 2011-2013, and no further goodwill impairment occurred in 2014. Pierre uses the complete equity method to report the investment in Selene on its own books. The separate December 31, 2014 trial balances of Pierre and Selene appear below, *before* Pierre's end-of-year adjustment to record its equity in Selene's income for 2014.

(in thousands)	Dr (Cr)	
	Pierre	**Selene**
Cash	$ 1,000	$ 2,500
Receivables	5,600	10,000
Inventories	70,000	30,000
Plant and equipment, net	460,000	150,000
Investment in Selene	20,225	—
Current liabilities	(4,000)	(2,800)
Long-term debt	(489,825)	(163,700)
Capital stock	(5,000)	(2,000)
Retained earnings, January 1	(90,000)	(20,000)
Dividends	40,000	3,000
Sales revenue	(150,000)	(50,000)
Cost of sales	100,000	35,000
Operating expenses	42,000	8,000
Totals	$ 0	$ 0

Required

a.   Calculate the total goodwill arising from this acquisition and its percentage allocation to the controlling and noncontrolling interests.

b.   Prepare a schedule calculating Pierre's equity in the income of Selene for 2014, and the noncontrolling interest in Selene's income for 2014.

c.   Update Pierre's trial balance for its 2014 equity in Selene's income and prepare a working paper consolidating the 2014 trial balances of Pierre and Selene.

d.   Present the consolidated financial statements of Pierre and Selene, in proper format.

LO 2, 3, 4, 5   **P6.7   Calculation of Investment and Consolidated Accounts Several Years After Acquisition**   Pentland Shoe Company acquired 75 percent of Sketchers Inc.'s common stock on January 2, 2011, for $180 million. The fair value of the 25 percent noncontrolling interest was $50 million at the date of acquisition, and Sketchers' book value was $20 million. Sketchers' assets and liabilities were fairly stated, except for previously unreported customer-related intangible assets (five year life, straight-line), capitalized under U.S. GAAP, and valued at $60 million. During the four years following the acquisition, Sketchers reported total net income of $140 million, paid $12 million in dividends, and goodwill was impaired by $5 million. In addition, the following intercompany transactions occurred:

1. During 2011, Sketchers sold land carried on its books at $50 million to Pentland for $80 million. Pentland still holds the land.
2. Early in 2012, Pentland sold a patent recorded at $15 million to Sketchers for $25 million. Sketchers currently holds the patent and is amortizing it over a ten-year period.
3. Over the years since acquisition, total intercompany merchandise sales amounted to $400 million, reflecting an average markup of 40 percent over cost. Unconfirmed intercompany profits in the ending inventories of Pentland and Sketchers at December 31, 2014, are $20 million and $17 million, respectively.

Required

a. Prepare a schedule calculating consolidated retained earnings at December 31, 2014. Pentland's retained earnings from its own operations is $55 million.
b. Pentland uses the complete equity method to account for its investment on its own books. Calculate the balance in the investment account at December 31, 2014.
c. Calculate the balance in the noncontrolling interest, appearing in the equity section of the December 31, 2014, consolidated balance sheet.

P6.8 Bonus Based on Adjusted Subsidiary Income McDeer Equipment Company manufactures farm equipment. It has fifty co-owned dealership subsidiaries. McDeer owns 75 percent of each, and the local operator has a 25 percent equity interest. McDeer sells merchandise to the dealerships at a transfer price that reflects a 35 percent gross margin on sales, and finances dealership inventories at 80 percent of the purchase price. Financing bears 10 percent interest, and must be settled within 30 days of the dealer's sale of the merchandise. **LO 1, 4**

Western Nebraska Farm Supply, one of McDeer's dealer subsidiaries, acquires 80 percent of its merchandise from McDeer and 20 percent from other vendors, at markups similar to those charged by McDeer. For the year ended December 31, 2013, Western Nebraska Farm Supply presents the following income statement:

Sales revenue.	$3,400,000
Cost of goods sold.	2,500,000
Gross margin	900,000
Operating expenses.	750,000
Income before taxes.	$ 150,000

The dealership's balance sheet shows ending inventory of $680,000 and inventory financing due to McDeer of $720,000. Beginning-of-year balances were inventory of $300,000 and financing due of $380,000. Average financing indebtedness during the year was $600,000; interest expense is included in cost of goods sold.

Wendy Carr, the manager and 25 percent stockholder in Western Nebraska Farm Supply, receives a salary (included in operating expenses) and a bonus based on income. McDeer retains 40 percent for income taxes and corporate costs, and distributes 15 percent of the remainder to the local dealer as a bonus. Accordingly, Wendy expects a bonus of $13,500 (= $150,000 × 60% × 15%). However, McDeer bases the bonus on the dealership's income after adjustments to remove unconfirmed intercompany profits in the dealership inventory and interest paid to the parent company.

Required

Prepare a report computing Wendy Carr's bonus for 2013.

P6.9 Consolidated Income Statement—Intercompany Transactions Condensed income statements from their own operations for Portland Company and its 80 percent-owned subsidiary, Salem Company, appear below. **LO 2, 3, 4, 5**

	Portland	Salem
Sales.	$40,000,000	$25,000,000
Other income	6,000,000	2,000,000
Total revenue	46,000,000	27,000,000
Cost of goods sold.	28,000,000	15,000,000
Operating expenses.	7,000,000	5,000,000
Other expenses	1,000,000	800,000
Total expenses	36,000,000	20,800,000
Net income (from own operations).	$10,000,000	$ 6,200,000

Additional information:

1. Salem's beginning inventory includes $650,000 of profit on goods purchased from Portland, and Portland's ending inventory includes $500,000 of profit on purchases of $4,000,000 from Salem.
2. Portland's other expenses include a $360,000 loss on a sale of depreciable assets to Salem at the beginning of the year. These assets have a 6-year remaining life at the date of intercompany sale and are depreciated by the straight-line method.
3. Salem's other income includes a $190,000 gain on sale of land to Portland.
4. Salem previously recorded a gain of $250,000 on a patent sold to Portland for $500,000. At that time the patent had a remaining life of 5 years. At the end of this year (three years later) Portland sold the patent externally for $420,000, reporting the gain in Portland's other income account.

Required

a. Prepare a schedule to compute Portland Company's equity method income accrual and the noncontrolling interest in consolidated income for the current year.
b. Prepare a consolidated income statement for Portland Company and Salem Company.

LO 1, 4, 5 **P6.10 Comprehensive Intercompany Transactions** MC Enterprises began business some years ago as a franchiser of fast food restaurants known as The Mighty Chicken. Initially, all franchises were independently owned, but eventually the company began to buy individual franchises from owners who wanted to sell. MC Enterprises formed a wholly-owned subsidiary, Mighty Chicken Shops, to own and operate these repurchased franchises. Currently, there are 46 independently owned franchises, and 33 company-owned franchises held by the subsidiary. Following are condensed trial balances for MC Enterprises (the parent) and Mighty Chicken Shops (the subsidiary) at December 31, 2012:

	Dr (Cr)	
	MC Enterprises	**Mighty Chicken Shops**
Investment in Mighty Chicken Shops.	$ 5,000,000	$ —
Other assets.	78,000,000	56,000,000
Liabilities.	(23,000,000)	(43,000,000)
Stockholders' equity, January 1.	(46,000,000)	(7,000,000)
Sales revenue.	(140,000,000)	(89,000,000)
Franchise fee revenue	(15,000,000)	—
Interest revenue	(6,000,000)	—
Cost of goods sold.	98,000,000	57,000,000
Franchise fee expense	—	8,000,000
Interest expense.	3,000,000	4,000,000
Operating expenses (including depreciation).	46,000,000	14,000,000
Totals	$ 0	$ 0

Mighty Chicken Shops' cost of goods sold consisted of beginning inventory of $10,000,000, purchases of $60,000,000, and ending inventory of $13,000,000. The subsidiary makes all of its purchases from the parent; the transfer price includes a 20 percent gross margin on sales for MC Enterprises. The gross margin percentage has been constant for several years. All of Mighty Chicken Shops' franchise fees and interest expense were paid to MC Enterprises and all of the subsidiary's debt is owed to the parent. MC Enterprises provides equipment at cost to all its franchisees, including those owned by Mighty Chicken Shops. The subsidiary currently has such equipment originally costing $20,000,000. On average, the equipment has a ten-year life and is currently half depreciated.

Required

Prepare appropriate consolidation eliminating entries at December 31, 2012. There is no need to reverse the equity method income accrual, as the parent did not record it. MC Enterprises paid dividends of $5,000,000 (debited directly to stockholders' equity); Mighty Chicken Shops paid no dividends in 2012.

P6.11 Consolidation of Equity Method Investments The annual report of **Starbucks Corporation** for the year ended October 3, 2010, included information on seven investments in which Starbucks generally held a 50 percent ownership interest. Thus these investments were not consolidated, but were reported as unconsolidated equity method investments. Summary data for Starbucks and for its equity method investments is as follows:

LO 1, 4

STARBUCKS CORPORATION
[SBUX]

Income Statement Data		
(in thousands)	Starbucks Corporation	Equity Method Investments
Revenues	$10,707,400	$2,128,000
Cost of sales and other operating expenses	(9,396,600)	(1,882,700)
Equity method income	108,600	—
Operating income.	1,419,400	245,300
Other expenses, net.	(471,100)	(40,200)
Net earnings.	$ 948,300	$ 205,100

Balance Sheet Data		
(in thousands)	Starbucks Corporation	Equity Method Investments
Current assets	$2,756,400	$390,100
Noncurrent assets	3,629,500	570,300
Total assets	$6,385,900	$960,400
Current liabilities.	$1,779,100	$260,600
Noncurrent liabilities.	924,500	70,500
Total liabilities.	2,703,600	331,100
Shareholders' equity	3,682,300	629,300
Total liabilities and shareholders' equity	$6,385,900	$960,400

Equity method investments are carried as noncurrent assets on Starbucks' balance sheet at $308,100 on October 3, 2010 *(all amounts in thousands)*. The notes to the financial statements also disclose the following (edited to reflect fiscal year 2010 data only):

> Also included (in the income from equity investees account) is our proportionate share of gross margin resulting from coffee and other product sales to, and royalty and license fee revenues generated from, equity investees. Revenues generated from these related parties, net of eliminations, were $125.7 million. Related costs of sales, net of eliminations, were $65.3 million. As of October 3, 2010, there were $31.4 million of accounts receivable on Starbucks' balance sheet from equity investees, primarily related to product sales and store license fees.

Required

a. Using the data above, but assuming that Starbucks owns 51 percent of each of the seven companies, prepare a working paper to consolidate Starbucks' income statement and balance sheet with those of the seven companies. Assume that any excess of carrying value of equity investees over net book value is attributable to goodwill, which is shared with the noncontrolling interest in proportion to ownership interests. There is no goodwill impairment in 2010. The statement of cash flows reports that Starbucks received $91,400 (thousand) in dividends from the seven companies. Assume Starbucks paid no dividends in 2010.

b. What percentage increase in total assets and in revenues would be reported by Starbucks had these seven companies been 51 percent-owned and hence consolidated?

LO 1

CATERPILLAR INC. [CAT]

P6.12 Evaluation of Eliminations Disclosures **Caterpillar Inc.** is a major producer and supplier of construction equipment, industrial machinery, and related financial services. Its annual report shows consolidating information for its two major business units, Machinery & Engines, and Financial Products. Each of these business units may in turn be composed of multiple companies. These data appear in Caterpillar's 2007 annual report:

Results of Operations				
(in millions)	**Consolidated**	**Machinery & Engines**	**Financial Products**	**Consolidating Adjustments**
Sales and revenues:				
Sales of Machinery & Engines	$41,962	$41,962	$ —	
Revenues of Financial Products.	2,996	—	3,396	$(400)
Total	44,958	41,962	3,396	
(in millions)	**Consolidated**	**Machinery & Engines**	**Financial Products**	**Consolidating Adjustments**
Operating costs:				
Cost of goods sold.	32,626	32,626	—	
SG&A expenses	3,821	3,356	480	(15)
Research & development.	1,404	1,404	—	
Interest expense of Financial Products	1,132	—	1,137	(5)
Other operating	1,054	(8)	1,089	(27)
Total	40,037	37,378	2,706	
Operating profit	4,921	4,584	690	
Other interest expense.	(288)	(294)	—	(6)
Other income (expense)	320	(104)	77	347
Profit before tax	4,953	4,186	767	
Income taxes	1,485	1,220	265	
Profit of consolidated companies.	3,468	2,966	502	
Equity in profit of unconsolidated companies	73	69	4	
Equity in profit of Financial Products	—	506	—	(506)
Profit	$ 3,541	$ 3,541	$ 506	

		Machinery	**Financial**	**Consolidating**
(in millions)	**Consolidated**	**& Engines**	**Products**	**Adjustments**

Financial Position

Assets
Current assets:

Cash & investments	$ 1,122	$ 862	$ 260	
Receivables, trade	8,249	4,715	525	$3,009
Receivables, finance	7,503	—	10,961	(3,458)
Deferred taxes	816	746	70	
Prepaid expenses.	583	565	39	(21)
Inventories	7,204	7,204	—	
Total current assets	25,477	14,092	11,855	
Property, plant & equipment, net	9,997	6,782	3,215	
Long-term receivables, trade.	685	90	30	565
Long-term finance receivables.	13,462	—	14,057	(595)
Investment in unconsolidated companies	598	610	12	(24)
Investment in Financial Products	—	3,948	—	(3,948)
Noncurrent deferred taxes	1,553	1,803	68	(318)
Intangible assets	475	471	4	
Goodwill	1,963	1,963	—	
Other assets	1,922	293	1,629	
Total assets.	**$56,132**	**$30,052**	**$30,870**	

Liabilities
Current liabilities:

Short-term borrowings.	$ 5,468	$ 187	$ 5,556	$ (275)
Accounts payable.	4,723	4,518	373	(168)
Accrued expenses	3,178	1,932	1,273	(27)
Accrued salaries, wages & benefits	1,126	1,108	18	
Customer advances	1,442	1,442	—	
Dividends payable	225	225	—	
Other current liabilities	6,083	1,047	5,057	(21)
Total current liabilities.	22,245	10,459	12,277	
Long-term debt due after one year	17,829	3,669	14,190	(30)
Liability for postemployment benefits	5,059	5,058	1	
Other liabilities	2,116	1,983	454	(321)
Total liabilities	47,249	21,169	26,922	

Stockholders' Equity

Common stock.	2,744	2,744	860	(860)
Treasury stock	(9,451)	(9,451)	—	
Profit employed in the business.	17,398	17,398	2,566	(2,566)
Accumulated other comprehensive income.	(1,808)	(1,808)	522	(522)
Total stockholders' equity	8,883	8,883	3,948	
Total liabilities and stockholders' equity	**$56,132**	**$30,052**	**$30,870**	

Required

a. Which business unit is the parent company? How do you know?

b. No goodwill arises in the consolidation of Machinery & Engines with Financial Products. What is a likely explanation?

c. Why is consolidated goodwill already on the books of Machinery & Engines?

d. How much intercompany revenue was earned, and by which entity?

e. Using the data in the Consolidating Adjustments column, reconstruct the entry necessary to eliminate the Investment in Financial Products.

f. Describe the apparent main intercompany activity between Machinery & Engines and Financial Products.

REVIEW SOLUTIONS ••

Review 1 Solution

a.

(I-1)	Investment in Sandalite	500,000	
	Gain on sale of land.		500,000
	To transfer unconfirmed downstream intercompany land sale gain to year of sale to outside party.		
(I-2)	Sales.	40,000,000	
	Cost of goods sold		40,000,000
	To eliminate upstream and downstream merchandise sales; $40,000,000 = $14,000,000 + $26,000,000.		
(I-3)	Retained earnings, beginning—Sandalite	285,000	
	Investment in Sandalite	300,000	
	Cost of goods sold		585,000
	To remove intercompany profit from beginning inventory; $285,000 = $1,235,000 − $1,235,000/1.3; $300,000 = $1,500,000 × 20%.		
(I-4)	Cost of goods sold.	543,000	
	Inventory		543,000
	To remove intercompany profit from ending inventory; $543,000 = $318,000 + $225,000; $318,000 = $1,378,000 − $1,378,000/1.3; $225,000 = $1,125,000 × 20%.		

b. Protective acquired its 90% investment at book value, and the noncontrolling interest's fair value equaled book value at the date of acquisition. Therefore no revaluations appear, and no revaluation write-offs are necessary. The only items affecting the equity accrual are intercompany transactions.

	Equity in net income	Noncontrolling interest in net income
Sandalite reported net income.	$1,530,000	$170,000
Confirmed gain on downstream sale of land	500,000	
Confirmed profit on downstream beginning inventory.	300,000	
Confirmed profit on upstream beginning inventory	256,500	28,500
Unconfirmed profit on downstream ending inventory	(225,000)	
Unconfirmed profit on upstream ending inventory	(286,200)	(31,800)
	$2,075,300	$166,700

Review 2 Solution

a. Add the following eliminations to those prepared for review problem #1:

Downstream equipment sale:

(I-1)	Investment in Sandalite	800,000	
	Accumulated depreciation.	1,200,000	
	Equipment.		2,000,000
	To eliminate beginning-of-year unconfirmed profit on intercompany transfer of equipment.		
(I-2)	Accumulated depreciation	400,000	
	Depreciation expense		400,000
	To eliminate the excess annual depreciation expense recorded by the purchasing affiliate; $400,000 = $2,000,000/5.		

continued

continued from prior page

(I-3)	Equipment	3,000,000	
	Accumulated depreciation.		3,000,000

To restate the asset and accumulated depreciation accounts to their original acquisition cost basis.

Upstream building sale:

(I-4)	Building	2,500,000	
	Retained earnings—Sandalite, January 1		2,437,500
	Accumulated depreciation.		62,500

To eliminate beginning-of-year unconfirmed loss on intercompany transfer of building (½ year depreciation in 2013); $62,500 = ($2,500,000/20) × ½.

(I-5)	Depreciation expense.	125,000	
	Accumulated depreciation.		125,000

To adjust to cost the annual depreciation expense recorded by the purchasing affiliate; $125,000 = $2,500,000/20.

(I-6)	Building	2,000,000	
	Accumulated depreciation.		2,000,000

To restate the asset and accumulated depreciation accounts to their original acquisition cost basis.

b.

	Equity in net income	Noncontrolling interest in net income
Sandalite reported net income.	$1,530,000	$170,000
Downstream confirmed gain on sale of land	500,000	—
Downstream confirmed profit on beginning inventory. . . .	300,000	—
Upstream confirmed profit on beginning inventory	256,500	28,500
Downstream unconfirmed profit on ending inventory	(225,000)	—
Upstream unconfirmed profit on ending inventory	(286,200)	(31,800)
Downstream confirmed profit on equipment sale	400,000	—
Upstream confirmed loss on building sale.	(112,500)	(12,500)
	$2,362,800	$154,200

7

Consolidating Foreign Currency Financial Statements

WAL-MART STORES, INC.
www.walmart.com

Wal-Mart Stores, Inc. successfully operates retail stores in the U.S. and many other countries. Wal-Mart's international subsidiaries are consolidated in its financial statements. An excerpt from its 2011 annual report describes the extent of Wal-Mart's international holdings:

> The Company's operations in Argentina, Brazil, Chile, China, Costa Rica, El Salvador, Guatemala, Honduras, India, Japan, Mexico, Nicaragua and the United Kingdom are consolidated using a December 31 fiscal year-end, generally due to statutory reporting requirements . . . The Company's operations in the United States, Canada and Puerto Rico are consolidated using a January 31 fiscal year-end.

Typically the accounts of an international subsidiary are measured in its local currency. For example, Wal-Mart's United Kingdom operations are reported in pounds sterling. How does Wal-Mart convert its subsidiaries' accounts into U.S. dollars? Are consolidation procedures for an international subsidiary different from the procedures for consolidating a U.S. subsidiary?

This chapter explains conversion and consolidation of the accounts of international subsidiaries. This chapter also explains how changing exchange rates and translation methodologies affect financial analysis of international subsidiaries.   *Source: Wal-Mart Stores, Inc. 2011 annual report.*

CHAPTER ORGANIZATION

Converting foreign currency accounts	Translation and remeasurement procedures	Financial statement analysis	Consolidation of international subsidiaries	Currency Conversion under IFRS
• The conversion process • The functional currency	• Translation procedures • Remeasurement procedures • Translation and remeasurement gains and losses • Highly inflationary economies • Illustration for an existing subsidiary • Statement of cash flows • Disclosures	• Profitability analysis • Short-term liquidity and long-term solvency • Interperiod comparisons	• Equity method entries • Consolidation at date of acquisition • Consolidation in subsequent years	• Translation and remeasurement • Hyperinflationary economies

INTRODUCTION

The global character of business presents challenges for corporate managers, professional accountants, and financial analysts. For a diversified corporation headquartered in the United States, two major problems faced by management are (1) controlling wide-ranging, geographically dispersed operations and (2) measuring the financial position and performance of its various divisions or subsidiaries. Several other difficulties are also common to multinational operations:

- Corporate headquarters located great distances from international operations.
- Books of account maintained in units of various currencies.
- Interest rates, inflation rates, and growth rates that vary widely across countries.
- Political conditions and economic institutions that differ among nations.
- Language and other cultural barriers to effective communication.
- Alternative accounting and reporting procedures.

When a U.S. company invests in a non-U.S. entity, the familiar concept of control determines the reporting for its investment. A multinational corporation with a controlling interest in an international subsidiary consolidates the subsidiary's financial results. The subsidiary usually prepares its financial statements in its local currency. Before consolidating its accounts with those of the U.S. parent, the subsidiary's financial information must be converted into U.S. dollars. Then the subsidiary's accounts are consolidated with those of the parent.

CONVERTING A SUBSIDIARY'S FOREIGN CURRENCY ACCOUNTS TO THE PARENT'S CURRENCY

This section discusses conversion of an international subsidiary's accounts to U.S. dollars, the currency in which its U.S. parent reports financial information. However, the concepts and procedures are equally applicable to a non-U.S. company desiring to change its reporting currency to U.S. dollars, an equity method investment in a non-U.S. company that is held by a U.S. investor, or non-U.S. branch operations of a U.S. company.

The financial statements of international subsidiaries owned by U.S. companies report the assets, liabilities, revenues, and expenses of these entities in their local currency. **Asda Stores Ltd.**, a British supermarket chain, has been a subsidiary of Wal-Mart since 1999. Asda reports its financial statements in pounds sterling. To consolidate Asda in Wal-Mart's financial statements, Wal-Mart must first convert Asda's financial statements to U.S. dollars, using **foreign exchange rates**.

A foreign exchange rate is the price of a unit of one country's currency expressed in units of another country's currency. Exchange rates are expressed in two ways: the amount of foreign currency that can be acquired per unit of domestic currency (the **indirect rate**), or the amount of domestic currency needed to acquire one unit of foreign currency (the **direct rate**). In the case of a U.S. company, the indirect rate is the foreign currency value per dollar, such as the number of yen per dollar, or the number of pounds sterling per dollar. An indirect rate of £0.64/dollar means that 0.64 pounds can purchase one dollar. The direct rate is the number of dollars needed to purchase one yen or pound. When the direct rate is $1.56/pound, $1.56 will buy one pound. Notice that the direct rate is the reciprocal of the indirect rate ($1.56 = $1/0.64). For an international subsidiary of a U.S. company, the direct rate is used to change the subsidiary's accounts into U.S. dollars.

Foreign currencies are traded on both **spot markets** and **forward markets** or **futures markets**. Transactions involving *immediate delivery* of the foreign currency are executed at **spot rates**. Transactions involving delivery of the foreign currency at some *later date* are executed at **forward rates**. Standardized contracts for future delivery trade at **futures rates**. When *more* U.S. dollars are required to buy one unit of foreign currency (the direct rate rises), the U.S. dollar is said to have **weakened** with respect to that currency. When *fewer* U.S. dollars are required (the direct rate falls), the U.S. dollar **strengthens**.

The Conversion Process

Generally accepted accounting principles for converting a subsidiary's financial information for consolidation with its parent are found in *ASC Topic 830*. First, we must identify the subsidiary's *reporting currency*, *local currency*, and *functional currency*. The **reporting currency** is the currency in which a parent reports its consolidated financial statements. Wal-Mart's reporting currency is the U.S. dollar. The **local currency** is the currency in which the subsidiary reports its accounts. Asda's local currency is the British pound. The subsidiary's **functional currency** is the currency in which the subsidiary conducts most of its transactions. In most cases, a subsidiary's functional currency is its local currency. Asda conducts business primarily with British customers and suppliers, and therefore its functional currency is its local currency, the British pound.

Sometimes a subsidiary does not record transactions in its functional currency. A subsidiary of a U.S. parent may be located in Hong Kong, but conducts most of its business with U.S. customers and suppliers. In that case its functional currency is the U.S. dollar, even though its accounts are measured in Hong Kong dollars. The Hong Kong subsidiary's functional currency is the same as the reporting currency, the U.S. dollar. Occasionally a subsidiary of a U.S. parent may report its accounts in one currency and conduct business in another currency other than the U.S. dollar. Suppose a Swiss subsidiary of a U.S. parent records its accounts in Swiss francs and conducts business primarily in euros. Its local currency is the Swiss franc, its functional currency is the euro, and the reporting currency is the U.S. dollar.

The subsidiary's accounts expressed in its functional currency reflect the performance and financial health of the subsidiary, reported in its revenues, expenses, assets, liabilities, and equity, and the relationships between these accounts. Converting the subsidiary's accounts to U.S. dollars, the parent's currency, should not change the subsidiary's financial picture. The process of converting functional currency accounts to the reporting currency is known as **translation**. The FASB states the objectives of translation as follows:

a. Provide information that is generally compatible with the expected economic effects of a rate change on a reporting entity's cash flows and equity

b. Reflect in consolidated statements the financial results and relationships of the individual consolidated entities as measured in their functional currencies in conformity with U.S. generally accepted accounting principles. *(ASC para. 830-10-10-2)*

As we will see in subsequent sections, translation generally converts the subsidiary's functional currency accounts to U.S. dollars using the same or similar exchange rates, maintaining the functional currency relationships.

If the subsidiary's accounts are not expressed in its functional currency, before translation can occur the accounts must be converted into the subsidiary's functional currency. Because it conducts business primarily in a different currency, the local currency accounts do not adequately reflect the subsidiary's financial health and how it is affected by exchange rate changes. The process of converting local currency accounts to the functional currency is known as **remeasurement**. The FASB states the objective of remeasurement as follows:

> The remeasurement procedure is intended to produce the same result as if the entity's books of record had been maintained in the functional currency. *(ASC para. 830-10-45-17)*

The Swiss subsidiary of a U.S. parent conducts business in euros but maintains its accounts in Swiss francs. Remeasurement converts the subsidiary's accounts to their balances as if the Swiss subsidiary had actually recorded its transactions and adjustments in euros.

The process of converting an international subsidiary's accounts to dollars, the U.S. parent's reporting currency, occurs in one of three scenarios:

- **The subsidiary's functional currency is its local currency.** The subsidiary's accounts are *translated* to U.S. dollars. No remeasurement is needed.

- **The subsidiary's functional currency is the U.S. dollar.** The subsidiary's accounts are *remeasured* to U.S. dollars. No translation is needed.

- **The subsidiary's functional currency is another foreign currency.** The subsidiary's accounts are remeasured into the other currency. Then the accounts are translated into U.S. dollars.

A diagram of the conversion process follows:

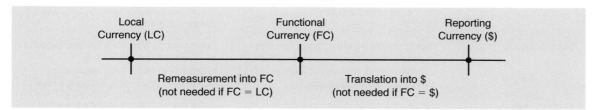

Codification requirements follow from this basic objective: **preservation of the international entity's financial results and relationships expressed in its functional currency**. An international subsidiary that functions as a branch of a U.S. company, and regularly converts its cash flows to U.S. dollars, should report data equivalent to those reported had the U.S. parent entered into those foreign currency transactions directly. *Remeasurement*, which simulates the international entity's transactions as if they had all taken place in dollars, accomplishes this objective.

Alternatively, an international subsidiary of a U.S. company functioning primarily as a self-contained business unit, buying, selling, investing and financing in its own country and rarely converting these cash flows into U.S. dollars, should report data equivalent to those reported in the local currency. By multiplying all accounts by similar rates, *translation* largely accomplishes this goal by preserving local currency financial results and relationships.

Suppose Wal-Mart has a subsidiary, Euro-Mart, located in Germany. The subsidiary's accounts are maintained in euros, its local currency. If Euro-Mart's transactions are mostly *denominated* in euros — it does most of its business with customers and suppliers in euro countries, borrows and repays loans using euros, etc.—then Euro-Mart's functional currency is also the euro. When Wal-Mart consolidates Euro-Mart's accounts at the end of its reporting period, it *translates* Euro-Mart's local currency accounts into U.S. dollars. No remeasurement is required. If Euro-Mart's transactions are mostly denominated in U.S. dollars—it does most of its business with U.S. customers and suppliers and most transactions take place in U.S. dollars—then Euro-Mart's local currency accounts are *remeasured* into U.S. dollars. No translation is required. If Euro-Mart is located in Germany but most of its transactions are denominated in British pounds—it does most of its business with customers, suppliers, banks, etc. in the U.K.—then at the end of Wal-Mart's reporting period Euro-Mart's local currency accounts are first *remeasured* into British pounds, and then *translated* into U.S. dollars.

Before we discuss the mechanics of translation and remeasurement, we must determine the appropriate conversion process. This requires identifying the subsidiary's functional currency.

The Functional Currency

The Codification defines the functional currency as follows:

> An entity's **functional currency** is the currency of the primary economic environment in which the entity operates; normally, that is the currency of the environment in which an entity primarily generates and expends cash. *(ASC para. 830-10-45-2)*

The functional currency may be the international entity's **local currency**, **another foreign currency**, or the **U.S. dollar**. Exhibit 7.1 summarizes the economic indicators identified in *ASC Section 830-10-55* to be considered when determining an entity's functional currency. These indicators assess the extent to which the international entity is relatively self-contained or is an extension of the U.S. parent. In the end, determination of the functional currency is essentially a matter of *fact*.

EXHIBIT 7.1 Economic Indicators Influencing Determination of the Functional Currency

Economic Indicator	Functional Currency Probably is:	
	Local or Other Foreign Currency	**Parent's Currency ($)**
Cash flow	Cash flows are primarily in the foreign currency and do not have a direct impact on the parent's cash flows.	Cash flows have an impact on parent's cash flows on a current basis and are readily available for remittance to the parent company.
Sales price	Selling prices are determined primarily by local competition or governmental regulation, and not by short-term changes in exchange rates.	Selling prices are primarily determined by worldwide competition or international prices and respond to short-term changes in exchange rates.
Sales market	Active sales market for the entity's products is primarily local.	Sales market for the entity's products is primarily in the parent's country or sales contracts are denominated in the parent's currency.
Expenses	Costs of labor, materials, and so forth are primarily local costs.	Costs of labor, materials, and so forth are primarily costs for components obtained from the parent's country.
Financing	Financing is primarily denominated in the local currency and is serviced by foreign currency cash flows generated in the entity's country.	Financing is primarily from dollar-denominated obligations or parent company funds are needed to service debt obligations.
Intercompany	Volume of intercompany transactions and transactions is low, resulting in minimal relationship between the operations of the international entity and the parent.	Volume of intercompany transactions is high, resulting in substantial relationship between the operations of the international entity and the parent.

Source: *ASC para. 830-10-55-5*

Determination of the functional currency can generally be summarized as follows:

- An international entity whose operations are relatively self-contained and integrated within the country in which it is located normally uses the **local currency** of that country as its functional currency.

- An international entity whose operations are a direct and integral component or extension of a U.S. parent company's operations normally uses the **U.S. dollar** as its functional currency.

- An international entity located in one country but generating most of its cash flows in the currency of another country normally uses the **currency of the other country** as its functional currency.

TRANSLATION AND REMEASUREMENT PROCEDURES

This section summarizes the procedures used to remeasure a subsidiary's local currency accounts into its functional currency, and to translate the subsidiary's functional currency accounts to the U.S. parent's reporting currency, the U.S. dollar. Recall that when the subsidiary does business mostly in its local currency, its local currency is its functional currency and we only need to translate the subsidiary's accounts into U.S. dollars. When the subsidiary does business primarily in the U.S. parent's currency, its functional currency is the reporting currency and we only need to remeasure the subsidiary's accounts into U.S. dollars.

LO1 Apply translation and remeasurement procedures.

Conversion of the subsidiary's accounts to another currency requires the use of *current exchange rates* and *historical exchange rates*. The **current exchange rate** is the spot rate at the end of the current reporting period—the rate in existence on the balance sheet date. A **historical exchange rate** is a past spot rate, in existence when a particular transaction occurred. For recurring transactions, such as salaries and utilities, an **average exchange rate** may approximate historical rates.

Translation Procedures

Translating the subsidiary's functional currency accounts into the parent's reporting currency, the U.S. dollar, is necessary because the subsidiary's accounts must be consolidated with those of the parent. However, the functional currency accounts best represent the financial health of the subsidiary.

The **objective of translation** is to **maintain the financial statement results and relationships** as they exist in the functional currency statements.

All of the subsidiary's **assets and liabilities** are translated to U.S. dollars using the exchange rate at the balance sheet date, the **current rate**. **Historical rates** are used to translate **contributed capital accounts** such as capital stock and additional paid-in capital. All **income statement accounts** are translated using the **exchange rate at the dates when these items are reported in income** as revenues, expenses, gains and losses.

Literal application of the requirement for translating income items requires identifying the exact date on which each income item is reported. It would be necessary to identify when each sale was made and when each expense was recognized during the year and use the exchange rate on that day to translate the revenue and expense balances to dollars. This level of detail is usually not cost effective, and therefore approximations are allowed. If a subsidiary's sales and expenses are recognized relatively evenly over the year, the **average exchange rate** for the year may be used to translate all income accounts. Average rates should be weighted according to the level of transactions. If a subsidiary's revenues and expenses are not recognized evenly, quarterly or monthly items may be translated at the average rate for the quarter or month, as appropriate.

Translating all asset and liability balances at the same (current) rate and income items at the same (average) rate generally achieves the objective of maintaining the relationships between accounts as measured in the subsidiary's functional currency. Income statement profitability ratios such as the gross profit percentage are similar whether based on functional currency balances or translated U.S. dollar balances. Liquidity ratios such as the current ratio are the same in the functional currency as in U.S. dollars. However, measures that combine balance sheet and income statement numbers, such as return on assets (income divided by average total assets) can be somewhat distorted by translation.

Remeasurement Procedures

Remeasuring the subsidiary's local currency accounts into its functional currency occurs when the subsidiary records its accounts in one currency but does most of its business in another currency. Therefore the functional currency accounts reflect the financial health of the subsidiary.

> The **objective of remeasurement** is to show the financial statements **as if all transactions occurred in the functional currency**

Balance sheet accounts measured at current money prices, also called **monetary assets and liabilities**, are remeasured using the exchange rate at the balance sheet date, the **current rate**. Monetary assets and liabilities include cash, receivables, held-to-maturity investments, inventories carried at fair value and most liabilities. **Balance sheet accounts measured at historical prices**, such as plant and equipment, intangibles, inventories carried at cost, and capital accounts are remeasured at historical rates. Dividends are remeasured at the declaration rate. The remeasured retained earnings balance is an accumulation of remeasured income and dividend flows.

Revenues and expenses are remeasured at **historical rates**, reflecting how these items would be recorded in the functional currency. For example, salary expenses are remeasured at the rates in effect when the salaries are accrued. Similar to translation, revenues and recurring out-of-pocket expenses such as salaries, utilities, and taxes may be remeasured using appropriate average rates if these accounts represent multiple inflows and outflows occurring fairly evenly. For example, if sales occur evenly throughout the year, a yearly average may be used. However, if most sales occur in December, the average rate for December should be used to remeasure most of the sales revenues. **Depreciation and amortization expenses, cost of goods sold**, and other write-offs of assets carried at cost are remeasured at the **rate in effect when the related asset was acquired**. For example, if Euro-Mart acquired a building for €5,000,000 in 2011, when the exchange rate was $1.25, and in 2013 reports €100,000 in depreciation expense on the building, the remeasured depreciation expense is $125,000, regardless of changes in the exchange rate over time.

Matching current rates to current prices and historical rates to historical prices achieves the remeasurement objective. Suppose Euro-Mart's functional currency is the U.S. dollar but its accounts are reported in euros. It acquires land when the exchange rate is $1.30, and records the land at €1,000,000. If its functional currency is the dollar, it probably used U.S. dollars to buy the land, and paid $1,300,000. Using the historical rate of $1.30 to remeasure the land account at any future date reports the account as if Euro-Mart had actually used U.S. dollars to acquire the land.

Comparing Translation and Remeasurement

Exhibit 7.2 identifies the exchange rates used to translate or remeasure various major balance sheet and income statement accounts. To summarize the major differences between remeasurement and translation, we *remeasure* assets carried at cost using historical rates, but *translate* them using the current rate. Expenses related to assets carried at cost, such as cost of goods sold, depreciation and amortization expense, are *remeasured* using the rate when the asset was acquired. Expenses are *translated* at the rate when each income item appears in income, and therefore expenses related to using assets carried at cost are translated at the rate in effect when these items are included in expenses, *not* the rates when the assets were acquired.

Translation and Remeasurement Gains and Losses

From the above sections we know that an international subsidiary's local currency accounts are remeasured into its functional currency, if necessary, and then translated into the parent's reporting currency. Current and historical exchange rates are used, as appropriate, to convert local currency accounts to the appropriate currency. **Gains and losses** result from both processes, due to changes over time in the rate used to convert an account.

EXHIBIT 7.2   Exchange Rates Used to Convert Financial Statement Items

	Remeasurement	Translation
Balance Sheet		
Cash and receivables.	C	C
Prepaid expenses.	H	C
Inventory at cost.	H	C
Inventory at market	C	C
Investments at cost	H	C
Investments at market	C	C
Property, plant and equipment.	H	C
Intangible assets	H	C
Accounts payable.	C	C
Long-term debt	C	C
Capital stock	H	H
Retained earnings	Note 1	Note 1
Dividends	H	H
Income Statement		
Sales revenue.	Note 2	Note 4
Cost of goods sold.	H	Note 4
Out-of-pocket expenses	Note 2	Note 4
Amortization of prepaid expenses or deferred income	Note 3	Note 4
Depreciation, amortization, impairment losses	Note 3	Note 4

Notes:
C = Current rate; H = Historical rate
Note 1: Retained earnings is an accumulation of previous periods' translated or remeasured income less dividends.
Note 2: Remeasurement requires conversion of sales revenue and out-of-pocket expenses at the rates when incurred—the historical rates. However, these rates can generally be approximated by average rates.
Note 3: These accounts are remeasured at the same historical rates as the related assets or liabilities.
Note 4: Translation requires conversion of all revenues, expenses, gains and losses at the exchange rate when these items are recognized on the income statement. Theses rates can generally be approximated by average rates.

   Suppose Wal-Mart establishes its German subsidiary, Euro-Mart, with the following initial balance sheet, measured in thousands of euros (€).

Cash.	€ 10,000	Debt	€ 40,000
Other assets.	90,000	Equity	60,000
Total assets	€100,000	Total liabilities and equity.	€100,000

If the direct exchange rate is $1.20/€, all initial account balances are multiplied by $1.20, and Euro-Mart's balance sheet in dollars (*in thousands*) is:

Cash.	$ 12,000	Debt	$ 48,000
Other assets.	108,000	Equity	72,000
Total assets	$120,000	Total liabilities and equity.	$120,000

As time passes and the exchange rate used to convert an account changes, a *gain or loss* occurs. In Euro-Mart's case, assume the U.S. dollar weakens against the euro, and the exchange rate rises to $1.30/€. If Euro-Mart's assets and liabilities continue to be converted to dollars using the current exchange rate, total assets, in dollars, are now $130,000 (= €100,000 × $1.30), an increase of $10,000 (= $130,000 − $120,000). Total assets increased in U.S. dollar equivalent, creating a *gain*. Total debt, in dollars, is now $52,000 (= €40,000 × $1.30), an increase of $4,000 (= $52,000 − $48,000). The debt increased in U.S. dollar amount, creating a *loss*.

The process of translation and remeasurement requires the use of both current and historical exchange rates. Those accounts converted using the *current rate* change in dollar equivalents, whereas those converted at *historical rates* remain fixed in dollar equivalents. Therefore a company's **exposure to translation and remeasurement gains and losses** comes from *those accounts converted at the current exchange rate*. In the example above, total assets of €100,000 are multiplied by the current rate, which increases from $1.20 to $1.30, causing a $10,000 gain. If the assets were acquired when the exchange rate was $1.20, and they are converted to dollars using the historical rate, the balance in dollars stays at $120,000 (= €100,000 × $1.20), with no gain or loss. Therefore, the gain or loss is caused by a combination of the **exposed position**—those items converted using the current exchange rate—and **changes in the current exchange rate during the period.**

To calculate the gain or loss, the exposed position at the *beginning* balance sheet date is multiplied by the beginning-of-period current rate. The exposed position at the *ending* balance sheet date, which reflects increases and decreases during the period, is multiplied by the end-of-period current rate. Changes in the exposed position are converted at the rates in effect when the changes occur.

> **Translation and remeasurement gains and losses** arise because the *ending exposed position* is converted at the *current rate*, while the *beginning exposed position* is converted at the beginning-of-period rate and *all changes* during the current year are converted at *historical rates*.

Suppose Euro-Mart has a cash position of €1,000,000 on January 1, 2013, when the exchange rate is $1.25/€. Its cash position is unchanged at year-end, when the exchange rate is $1.35/€. If cash is converted using the current rate, Euro-Mart's gain on conversion of euros to dollars is:

	€	rate	$
Beginning exposed position (cash)	€1,000,000	$1.25	$1,250,000
Change in exposed position	—		—
			1,250,000
Ending exposed position (cash)	€1,000,000	$1.35	−1,350,000
Gain			$ (100,000)

A **gain** arises because the exposed position is an *asset*, which *increased* in U.S. dollar terms. If the exposed position is a *liability*, a **loss** occurs.

Now assume Euro-Mart starts with a cash balance of €1,000,000, and receives €500,000 in cash on August 1, 2013, when the exchange rate is $1.32/€. Its ending cash balance is €1,500,000. Its gain on conversion of euros to dollars is:

	€	rate	$
Beginning exposed position (cash)	€1,000,000	$1.25	$1,250,000
Change in exposed position	500,000	1.32	660,000
			1,910,000
Ending exposed position (cash)	€1,500,000	$1.35	−2,025,000
Gain			$ (115,000)

Euro-Mart's €1,000,000 is the equivalent of $1,250,000 at the beginning of the year, and $1,350,000 at the end of the year, a $100,000 gain. Similarly, €500,000 received during the year was originally worth $660,000. At the end of the year these euros are worth $675,000 (= €500,000 × $1.35), another $15,000 gain.

Companies usually have many more accounts than cash that are converted using the current rate. Remember that when the rate *increases*, a company *gains* from holding *assets* converted using the current rate, and *loses* from holding *liabilities* converted using the current rate. The opposite effects occur when the rate declines. Translation and remeasurement gains and losses derive from the overall exposed position.

Exposed position =	Assets converted at the current rate less liabilities converted at the current rate

Changes in the exposed position include *any transactions affecting the exposed position*. For example, if the exposed position is cash less all liabilities, the purchase of land for cash reduces the exposed position— cash decreases. But borrowing cash from the bank has no effect—the transaction increases cash and liabilities, with no change in *overall* exposed position.

Suppose Euro-Mart has the following account balances at January 1, 2013, converted using the current rate:

Cash...	€1,000,000
Accounts receivable............................	3,000,000
Liabilities.....................................	6,000,000

Euro-Mart's exposed position at January 1, 2013, is a €2,000,000 *net liability position* (= €1,000,000 + €3,000,000 − €6,000,000). During 2013, the following transactions affect Euro-Mart's exposed position:

1. Sales revenues of €5,000,000 occur when the rate is $1.27.
2. Inventory is purchased for €3,800,000 when the rate is $1.25.
3. Salaries of €1,600,000 are paid when the rate is $1.31.

Euro-Mart's exposed position at December 31, 2013, is a €2,400,000 net liability position (= − €2,000,000 + €5,000,000 sales revenues − €3,800,000 inventory purchases − €1,600,000 salaries paid). The loss on conversion of euros to dollars is calculated as:

	€	rate	$
Beginning exposed position..........................	€(2,000,000)	$1.25	$(2,500,000)
Change in exposed position:			
Sales revenues.....................................	5,000,000	1.27	6,350,000
Inventory purchases................................	(3,800,000)	1.25	(4,750,000)
Salaries paid......................................	(1,600,000)	1.31	(2,096,000)
			(2,996,000)
Ending exposed position............................	€(2,400,000)	1.35	−(3,240,000)
Loss...			$ 244,000

How do you know if the conversion process results in a gain or a loss? Although there are mechanical methods for answering this question, the best approach is an intuitive one: Compare the exposed position converted using historical rates with the exposed position converted using the current rate. If the current dollar amount of an exposed *liability* position is higher (lower), it is a loss (gain). If the current dollar amount of an exposed *asset* position is higher (lower), it is a gain (loss). In the above illustration, Euro-Mart's net liability position converted using historical rates is $2,996,000, while the same position converted using the current rate is $3,240,000. Therefore Euro-Mart's exposed net *liability* position is *higher*, creating a *loss*. The following table summarizes these relationships:

Exposed Position in Foreign Currency (FC)	Change in Value of U.S. Dollar	Adjustment
Asset.......................................	Strengthens ($/FC falls)	Loss
Liability....................................	Strengthens ($/FC falls)	Gain
Asset.......................................	Weakens ($/FC rises)	Gain
Liability....................................	Weakens ($/FC rises)	Loss

These gains and losses may have little economic significance. For example, suppose a British subsidiary of a U.S. company purchases merchandise from a U.K. supplier on credit and liquidates the payable with £10,000 generated from customers in the United Kingdom. Assuming that the direct exchange rate ($/£) *increases* by $.05, the dollar equivalent of the payable rises by $500, but the quantity of pounds sterling required to discharge it does not change. Has the U.S. firm incurred a loss when this happens? No economic loss has occurred.

A similar situation occurs when the subsidiary acquires plant assets in the U.K. using debt of £100,000. The debt is to be retired with pounds sterling generated in normal business operations. If the direct exchange rate ($/£) *falls* by, say, $.08, then $8,000 less is required to retire the debt. Has the U.S. firm realized a gain? As long as management intends to use pounds to retire the debt, there is no economic gain.

In cases such as these, there are neither actual nor intended conversions of dollars into foreign currency, and the changes in exchange rates are not relevant to performance. Such situations result in paper gains and losses with no immediate economic consequences. By contrast, when the U.S. firm uses dollars to liquidate foreign currency obligations, and purchases foreign currency to do so, the gain or loss measures the actual change in the number of dollars to be paid, a real economic effect. The difference in the actual economic impact of gains and losses resulting from converting a subsidiary's accounts to U.S. dollars is embodied in the translation and remeasurement reporting requirements for these gains and losses. We now discuss the specific calculation and reporting of translation and remeasurement gains and losses.

Translation   When we translate a subsidiary's functional currency accounts to the U.S. parent's reporting currency, we convert all of the subsidiary's assets and liabilities to dollars using the current rate. Therefore the subsidiary's **exposure to translation gains and losses is its net assets, or equity**. Changes in equity, such as net income, dividends, and stock issuances, affect the subsidiary's exposed position. If a subsidiary has a positive net asset position—the most likely situation for solvent firms—and the direct rate increases, translation produces a gain due to the increased U.S. dollar equivalent of the subsidiary's net assets. Translation of an international subsidiary's accounts generally results in a gain when the U.S. dollar weakens with respect to the subsidiary's functional currency, and a loss when the U.S. dollar strengthens.

Recall that the subsidiary's financial health is best represented by its functional currency financial statements. Translation to the parent's reporting currency is necessary to consolidate the subsidiary's accounts with the parent, but has no economic implications for the subsidiary. Therefore the *translation gain or loss* is reported as a component of **other comprehensive income** and does not affect consolidated net income.

Remeasurement   When we remeasure a subsidiary's local currency accounts to its functional currency, we convert the subsidiary's assets measured at current money prices, such as cash, receivables, held-to-maturity investments and investments and inventories carried at fair value, to dollars using the current rate. We also remeasure the subsidiary's liabilities using the current rate. Therefore the subsidiary's **exposure to remeasurement gains and losses is its net assets carried at current money prices**. Revenues, out-of-pocket expenses, inventory and long-term asset purchases, dividends, and stock issuances affect the subsidiary's exposed position. Often a subsidiary has more liabilities than it has assets carried at current money prices, and it therefore has a negative exposed position. If the direct rate increases, remeasurement produces a loss due to the increased functional currency equivalent of the subsidiary's net exposed liability position. If the subsidiary's functional currency is the U.S. dollar, remeasurement of its accounts to dollars generally results in a loss when the U.S. dollar weakens with respect to the subsidiary's local currency, and a gain when the U.S. dollar strengthens.

Remeasurement converts the subsidiary's accounts to its functional currency, the currency in which it does most of its business. If a British subsidiary's functional currency is the U.S. dollar, for example, the subsidiary reports its liabilities in pounds but pays them in U.S. dollars. If the U.S. dollar strengthens against the pound, fewer U.S. dollars are needed to pay the liability, and the subsidiary has a real economic benefit. The *remeasurement gain or loss* has a real impact on the subsidiary's financial health, and is therefore **reported in income**, on the consolidated income statement.

BUSINESS APPLICATION   **Wal-Mart's International Subsidiaries**

Wal-Mart consolidates its operations in several different countries, including China, Japan and Mexico. Footnotes to its 2011 annual report describe the method used to convert the accounts of its non-U.S. subsidiaries to U.S. dollars.

> The assets and liabilities of all international subsidiaries are translated from the respective local currency to the U.S. dollar using exchange rates at the balance sheet date. The income statements of international subsidiaries are translated from the respective local currency to the U.S. dollar using average exchange rates for the period covered by the income statements. Related translation adjustments are recorded as a component of accumulated other comprehensive income (loss).

It is clear from this description that the functional currencies of all of Wal-Mart's international subsidiaries are their local currencies. The Consolidated Statement of Shareholders' Equity reveals that Wal-Mart reported foreign currency translation *gains* of $2,854 million and $1,137 million in fiscal 2010 and 2011 respectively, but a translation *loss* of $6,860 million in fiscal 2009. We conclude that in fiscal 2010 and 2011, the U.S. dollar *weakened*, on average, against the currencies of Wal-Mart's subsidiaries, but significantly *strengthened* in fiscal 2009. *Source:* Wal-Mart Stores, Inc. 2011 annual report.

BUSINESS APPLICATION   **Walt Disney's International Subsidiaries**

The footnotes to Walt Disney Company and Subsidiaries' consolidated financial statements for 2010 describe its translation policy:

> The U.S. dollar is the functional currency for the majority of our international operations… For U.S. dollar functional currency locations, foreign currency assets and liabilities are remeasured into U.S. dollars at end-of period exchange rates, except for nonmonetary balance sheet accounts, which are remeasured at historical exchange rates. Revenue and expenses are remeasured at average exchange rates in effect during each period, except for those expenses related to the non-monetary balance sheet amounts, which are remeasured at historical exchange rates. Gains or losses from foreign currency remeasurement are included in income.

The accounts of Euro Disney, Hong Kong Disneyland, and international locations of The Disney Stores are *translated*, but the accounts of most of Disney's subsidiaries are *remeasured*. It is interesting to note that although translation adjustments for subsidiaries whose functional currency is the local currency are separately disclosed in other comprehensive income, remeasurement gains and losses on the majority of Disney's subsidiaries whose functional currency is the U.S. dollar are combined with other items on its income statement, and are not separately disclosed. *Source:* Walt Disney Company and Subsidiaries, 2010 annual report.

Translation and Remeasurement Illustrated

To illustrate remeasurement and translation, we work through a simple example using the data in Exhibit 7.3. To clearly show the differing accounting results for each method, this example contains few transactions. Exhibit 7.4 shows the entries that Multiple Methods, Inc., a U.K. company, makes to record the events of 2013, and the resulting balance sheet and income statement. Remember that these entries are denominated in pounds sterling.

EXHIBIT 7.3   Data for Multiple Methods

MULTIPLE METHODS, INC.

Balance Sheet, January 1, 2013	June 30, 2013	December 31, 2013
Cash. . . . . £ 50	1. Sell 1 unit for £120.	1. Record depreciation on
Inventory (2 units @ £50) 100	2. Replace unit for £80.	furniture, £10.
Furniture (5-year life). 50	3. Pay other expenses of £30.	2. Close books and prepare
────	4. Accrue other expenses of	financial statements.
£200	£20.	Assume FIFO for inventory.
Contributed capital. £200		

Exchange rates ($/£)
January 1, 2013 . . . . $2.00
Average for 2013 . . . . 1.60
December 31, 2013 . . . . 1.44

EXHIBIT 7.4   Entries and End-of-Year Financial Statements for Multiple Methods

MULTIPLE METHODS, INC.

Entries (in £)
June 30, 2013:

| Cash. . . . . | 120 | |
| Sales. . . . . | | 120 |

| Cost of goods sold. . . . . | 50 | |
| Inventory. . . . . | | 50 |

| Inventory. . . . . | 80 | |
| Cash . . . . | | 80 |

| Other expenses . . . . | 30 | |
| Cash . . . . | | 30 |

| Other expenses . . . . | 20 | |
| Accounts payable. . . . . | | 20 |

December 31, 2013:

| Depreciation expense. . . . . | 10 | |
| Furniture . . . . | | 10 |

Balance Sheet at December 31, 2013

Cash.	£ 60
Inventory (1 unit @ £50, 1 unit @ £80) . . .	130
Furniture, net	40
Total assets	£230

Accounts payable.	£ 20
Contributed capital.	200
Retained earnings	10
Total liabilities and equity.	£230

Income Statement for year ended December 31, 2013

Sales.	£120
Cost of goods sold.	(50)
Other expenses	(50)
Depreciation expense.	(10)
Net income.	£ 10

Remeasurement   Assume Multiple Methods' functional currency is the U.S. dollar, and it therefore **remeasures** its accounts to U.S. dollars. Calculation of Multiple Methods' remeasurement gain or loss requires the beginning and ending net assets carried at current money prices, and the transactions that affected these net assets during the year. In Multiple Methods' case, balances carried at current money prices are cash and accounts payable. Use the balance sheets for the beginning and end of the year to calculate beginning and ending exposure. To determine the changes in exposure during the year, consider the transactions that occurred and how they affected cash and accounts payable.

Calculation of Multiple Methods, Inc.'s remeasurement gain or loss for the year appears in Exhibit 7.5, panel A. In deciding whether the adjustment is a gain or loss, think clearly about the relationship between the ending exposed position remeasured at historical rates, $84.0, and the ending exposed position remeasured at the current rate, $57.6. Since the current equivalent is less than the historical amount, the company incurred a loss. Note that if the company's net assets carried at current money prices are a net *liability*, the same numbers produce a *gain*—a reduction in a net liability position.

EXHIBIT 7.5   Remeasurement and Translation Adjustments for Multiple Methods

MULTIPLE METHODS, INC.

Panel A. Calculation of Remeasurement Gain or Loss

	£	rate	$
Exposed position, January 1 (Cash, £50)...............................	£ 50	$2.00	$100.0
Changes in exposed position:			
Sales...	120	1.60	192.0
Inventory purchase...	(80)	1.60	(128.0)
Other expenses..	(50)	1.60	(80.0)
			84.0
Exposed position, December 31 (Cash, £60 less accounts payable, £20)	£ 40	1.44	−57.6
Remeasurement loss (reported in income).............................			$ 26.4

Panel B. Calculation of Translation Gain or Loss

	£	rate	$
Exposed position, January 1 (Assets, £200 less liabilities, £0)	£200	$2.00	$400.0
Changes in exposed position:			
Net income...	10	1.60	16.0
			416.0
Exposed position, December 31 (Assets, £230 less liabilities, £20)	£210	1.44	−302.4
Translation loss (reported in OCI).....................................			$113.6

The year-end remeasured financial statements of Multiple Methods, Inc., appear in Exhibit 7.6, panel A. Note that the remeasurement loss calculated in Exhibit 7.5, panel A is shown on the remeasured income statement. Although the remeasured retained earnings balance is normally taken from the remeasured statement of retained earnings, this illustration has no beginning balance of retained earnings and no dividends were declared. Thus the ending retained earnings balance is the net income for the year.

Translation   Assume Multiple Methods' functional currency is its local currency, the pound, and therefore **translation** of its accounts to U.S. dollars is appropriate. Calculation of Multiple Methods' translation adjustment requires the beginning and ending net assets position (assets less liabilities = equity), and the transactions that affected net assets during the year. Use the balance sheets for the beginning and end of the year to calculate beginning and ending net assets. To determine the changes in net asset position during the year, consider the events that affected equity. For Multiple Methods, the only change is net income. Other companies may have additional effects on equity during the year, such as dividends and capital stock transactions.

Calculation of Multiple Methods, Inc.'s translation adjustment for the year appears in Exhibit 7.5, panel B. In deciding whether the translation adjustment is a gain or loss, think clearly about the relationship between the ending exposed position translated at historical rates, $416.0, and the ending exposed position translated at the current rate, $302.4. Since the current dollar equivalent for net assets is less than its historical amount, the company reports a translation loss.

Translation of the year-end financial statements of Multiple Methods, Inc. appears in Exhibit 7.6, panel B. The translation adjustment calculated in Exhibit 7.5, panel B is part of 2013 other comprehensive income and reported in AOCI in the equity section of the translated balance sheet. This example has no beginning balance for AOCI, and no other items affecting this balance. In an actual company, there are likely to be other items affecting AOCI, such as unrealized gains and losses on AFS investments. As with remeasurement, the ending translated retained earnings balance is derived from translated income.

EXHIBIT 7.6   Financial Statements for Multiple Methods

MULTIPLE METHODS, INC.

Panel A. Remeasurement	£	rate	$
Balance Sheet			
Cash.	£ 60	$1.44	$ 86.4
Inventory, unit 2	50	2.00	100.0
Inventory, unit 3	80	1.60	128.0
Furniture, net	40	2.00	80.0
Total assets	£230		$394.4
Accounts payable.	£ 20	1.44	$ 28.8
Contributed capital.	200	2.00	400.0
Retained earnings	10	see I/S	(34.4)
Total liabilities and equity.	£230		$394.4
Income Statement			
Sales.	£120	1.60	$192.0
Cost of goods sold.	(50)	2.00	(100.0)
Other expenses	(50)	1.60	(80.0)
Depreciation expense.	(10)	2.00	(20.0)
Remeasurement loss		see Exh. 7.5	(26.4)
Net income (loss)	£ 10		$ (34.4)

Panel B. Translation	£	rate	$
Balance Sheet			
Cash	£ 60	$1.44	$ 86.4
Inventory, unit 2	50	1.44	72.0
Inventory, unit 3	80	1.44	115.2
Furniture, net	40	1.44	57.6
Total assets	£230		$331.2
Accounts payable.	£ 20	1.44	$ 28.8
Contributed capital.	200	2.00	400.0
Retained earnings	10	see I/S	16.0
Accumulated other comprehensive income.		see Exh. 7.5	(113.6)
Total liabilities and equity.	£230		$331.2
Income Statement			
Sales.	£120	1.60	$192.0
Cost of goods sold.	(50)	1.60	(80.0)
Other expenses	(50)	1.60	(80.0)
Depreciation expense.	(10)	1.60	(16.0)
Net income.	£ 10		$ 16.0

REVIEW 1 • Calculation of Remeasurement and Translation Gain or Loss

Seaco, Inc., is a Canadian subsidiary of Guardian Marine, a U.S. company. Seaco began operations on January 1, 2014, with assets consisting of a cash balance of C$411,200, obtained by issuing stock. Financial statements of Seaco as of December 31, 2014, are as follows, in Canadian dollars:

Balance Sheet, December 31, 2014		Income Statement For Year 2014	
Cash.	C$ 30,000	Sales.	C$404,000
Receivables	23,500	Beginning inventory	0
Inventories	42,500	Purchases.	375,500
Equipment	369,500	Ending inventory.	(42,500)
Accumulated depreciation	(27,500)	Cost of goods sold.	333,000
Total assets	C$438,000	Gross margin	71,000
		Depreciation expense.	(27,500)
Liabilities.	C$ 2,000	Other expenses	(18,700)
Capital stock	411,200	Net income.	C$ 24,800
Retained earnings	24,800		
Total liabilities and equity.	C$438,000		

Seaco acquired the equipment for cash when the exchange rate was $1.03. Merchandise purchases, sales and other expenses occurred evenly over the year. Exchange rates are as follows:

Date	Spot rate ($/C$)
January 1, 2014	$1.05
2014 average	0.98
December 31, 2014	0.93

Required

a. Assume Seaco's functional currency is the Canadian dollar. Calculate Seaco's 2014 translation gain or loss.
b. Assume Seaco's functional currency is the U.S. dollar. Calculate Seaco's 2014 remeasurement gain or loss.

Solutions are located after the chapter assignments.

REVIEW 2 • Translation and Remeasurement of Foreign Currency Financial Statements

Greco-Mart is a Greek subsidiary of United Stores, Inc., a U.S. company. Greco-Mart began operations on January 1, 2015. Its balance sheets for January 1, and December 31, 2015, are presented below, in euros:

Balance Sheets	January 1, 2015	December 31, 2015
Cash and receivables.	€ 10,000	€ 20,000
Inventories, at cost.	40,000	90,000
Noncurrent assets, net.	700,000	530,000
Total assets	€750,000	€640,000
Liabilities.	€550,000	€420,000
Capital stock	200,000	200,000
Retained earnings	0	20,000
Total liabilities and equity.	€750,000	€640,000

During 2015, the following events occurred:
1. Sales revenue was €2,000,000, earned evenly over the year.
2. Inventory purchases were €1,200,000, made evenly over the year.
3. Cost of goods sold was €1,150,000.
4. Out-of-pocket operating expenses were €650,000, incurred evenly over the year.
5. Depreciation expense on the equipment was €170,000.
6. Dividends of €10,000 were declared and paid when the exchange rate was $1.52/€.

Exchange rates are as follows:

Date	$/€
January 1, 2015	$1.40
2015 average	1.50
December 31, 2015	1.55

Required

a. Assume Greco-Mart's functional currency is the euro. Calculate the translation gain or loss for 2015, and prepare Greco-Mart's translated income statement for 2015 and balance sheet at December 31, 2015.
b. Assume Greco-Mart's functional currency is the U.S. dollar. Calculate the remeasurement gain or loss for 2015, and prepare Greco-Mart's remeasured income statement for 2015 and balance sheet at December 31, 2015.

Solutions are located after the chapter assignments.

Highly Inflationary Economies

International inflation rates significantly higher than U.S. inflation rates can cause the U.S. dollar value of the currency to fall dramatically, severely distorting translated financial results and relationships. Highly inflationary economies are frequently found in certain countries in South America, Africa and Asia.

When an international entity is located in a highly inflationary economy, and its functional currency is the local currency, translation causes the dollar value of assets, liabilities, revenues and expenses to significantly shrink over time, as the current and average exchange rates fall sharply. Thus local currency relationships are not preserved, as translation intends.

> The Codification requires that an international entity located in a country with a **highly inflationary economy**, defined as **cumulative inflation of 100 percent or more over a three-year period**, use the U.S. dollar as its functional currency and **remeasure** its local currency accounts to the reporting currency. *(ASC para. 830-10-45-11)*

The Board stated that this decision was based on its belief that a local currency that "has largely lost its utility as a store of value cannot be a functional measuring unit." The FASB's pragmatic decision to require remeasurement to the reporting currency for international entities located in highly inflationary economies was also intended to preserve local currency results and relationships. When the local currency is more inflationary than the dollar, the dollar strengthens and the direct rate falls. Use of a highly inflationary local currency as the functional currency produces translated international asset balances that dwindle to nominal amounts. Of particular concern is the **disappearing plant phenomenon** in which land, factories and other plant assets seem to disappear in translation. Assuming the local currency account balances and the plant assets themselves remain unimpaired, the translated balances are meaningless.

Suppose the Brazilian real lost much of its value in U.S. dollars due to high inflation. A Brazilian subsidiary has plant assets of R100,000,000 acquired when the exchange rate was $0.60/R. With much lower inflation in the United States, the dollar strengthens and the direct exchange rate drops to $0.15/R. Plant assets translated at the current rate shrink to $15,000,000 from $60,000,000, suggesting that only 25 percent of the assets remain when in fact 100 percent of the physical assets are still intact. In contrast, continued remeasurement at $0.60/R, the historical rate, preserves the reported plant assets at $60,000,000.

Changing the Functional Currency

The Codification intends that determination of an entity's functional currency be a matter of *fact* and not a choice between accounting alternatives. Thus the functional currency is changed only when significant new economic facts and circumstances clearly justify a different functional currency.

BUSINESS APPLICATION   Mattel Inc.'s Venezuelan Subsidiary

Mattel, Inc., headquartered in the U.S., has the highest revenue among toy manufacturers worldwide. Mattel has many subsidiaries worldwide, including one in Venezuela. In 2010, Venezuela was classified as a highly inflationary economy. This affected Mattel's reporting of this subsidiary in its 2010 consolidated financial statements. The following appears in its annual report footnotes:

> Effective January 1, 2010, and as required by US GAAP, Mattel will account for Venezuela as a highly inflationary economy as the three-year cumulative inflation rate for Venezuela using the blended Consumer Price Index (which is associated with the city of Caracas) and the National Consumer Price Index (developed commencing in 2008 and covering the entire country of Venezuela) exceeded 100%. Accordingly, Mattel's Venezuelan subsidiary will use the US dollar as its functional currency effective January 1, 2010. As of December 31, 2009, Mattel's Venezuelan subsidiary had approximately $20 million of net monetary assets denominated in bolivar fuertes. As a result of the change to a US dollar functional currency, monetary assets and liabilities denominated in bolivar fuertes will generate income or expense in 2010 for changes in value associated with parallel exchange rate fluctuations against the US dollar. For every $10 million of net monetary assets denominated in bolivar fuertes, a 1% increase/(decrease) in the parallel rate would decrease/(increase) Mattel's pre-tax income by approximately $100 thousand.

Note that in addition to explaining the change in reporting for its Venezuelan subsidiary, Mattel also provides risk analysis of the future effect of rate changes on its income.

Because a change in an entity's functional currency is caused by changes in facts and circumstances, a change in conversion method is not a change in accounting principle. Thus, the change does not call for retrospective application to prior periods, as is otherwise required under *ASC Topic 250*. All changes are reported *prospectively*.

Change from Local Currency to U.S. Dollar   When the functional currency changes from the local currency to the U.S. dollar, translated assets and liabilities at the end of the prior period are the beginning remeasured book values. Last period's closing rate becomes the historical rate attached to items such as inventories, and property, plant and equipment. The cumulative translation adjustment balance as of the date of change remains in AOCI. This procedure applies if a subsidiary's functional currency is normally its local currency, but its economy becomes highly inflationary.

Change from U.S. Dollar to Local Currency   When the functional currency changes from the U.S. dollar to local currency, assets and liabilities are translated at the current rate. The **opening balance in the cumulative translation adjustment** equals the **difference between translated net assets and remeasured net assets**. This procedure applies if a subsidiary's economy becomes no longer highly inflationary, and translation is now appropriate.

Translation and Remeasurement of an Existing Entity

We now illustrate translation and remeasurement procedures when a U.S. parent acquires an international subsidiary at some point after it came into existence.

Domestic Corporation acquired all of the stock of International Company on January 1, 2013. International's comparative balance sheets for December 31 and January 1, 2013 and its income statement for 2013 appear below. International Company has been in existence for several years, and reports in its local currency, the euro.

INTERNATIONAL COMPANY
Balance Sheet

	December 31, 2013	January 1, 2013
Assets		
Cash...	€ 600,000	€ 300,000
Receivables	600,000	700,000
Inventory...	800,000	1,000,000
Plant assets, net	2,300,000	2,000,000
Total assets	€4,300,000	€4,000,000
Liabilities and stockholders' equity		
Accounts payable	€ 840,000	€ 660,000
Long-term debt	1,260,000	1,340,000
Capital stock	800,000	800,000
Retained earnings	1,400,000	1,200,000
Total liabilities and stockholders' equity	€4,300,000	€4,000,000

INTERNATIONAL COMPANY
Statement of Income and Retained Earnings
For Year Ended December 31, 2013

Sales...	€5,000,000
Cost of sales..	(2,250,000)
Depreciation...	(350,000)
Current operating expenses..........................	(1,700,000)
Net income..	700,000
Retained earnings, January 1........................	1,200,000
Dividends	(500,000)
Retained earnings, December 31.....................	€1,400,000

Relevant exchange rates are:

	$/€
January 1, 2013	$1.50
Average for 2013	1.55
December 31, 2013	1.60

International declared and paid 2013 dividends when the exchange rate was $1.58. It purchased inventory of €2,050,000 evenly throughout 2013, and acquired plant assets of €650,000 when the exchange rate was $1.57. International reports inventory using FIFO, and purchased its December 31, 2013, inventory balance when the exchange rate was $1.58. Depreciation expense for 2013 consists of €300,000 related to plant assets acquired prior to January 1, 2013, and €50,000 related to plant assets acquired in 2013.

Exhibit 7.7 shows translation of International's 2013 income statement and comparative balance sheets at December 31 and January 1, 2013, when its functional currency is the euro. Exhibit 7.8 displays remeasured financial information when International's functional currency is the U.S. dollar. Because Domestic acquired International on January 1, 2013, *the appropriate historical rate for any balances relating to transactions occurring prior to January 1, 2013, is the acquisition date exchange rate,* $1.50.

EXHIBIT 7.7   International Company: Translation for the Year Ended December 31, 2013

Statement of Income and Retained Earnings

	€	rate	$
Sales.	€5,000,000	$1.55	$7,750,000
Cost of sales.	(2,250,000)	1.55	(3,487,500)
Depreciation.	(350,000)	1.55	(542,500)
Current operating expenses.	(1,700,000)	1.55	(2,635,000)
Net income.	700,000		1,085,000
Retained earnings, January 1.	1,200,000	1.50	1,800,000
Dividends.	(500,000)	1.58	(790,000)
Retained earnings, December 31.	€1,400,000		$2,095,000

Calculation of Translation Adjustment

	€	rate	$
Exposed position, January 1 (€4,000,000 − €660,000 − €1,340,000).	€2,000,000	$1.50	$3,000,000
Changes in exposed position:			
Net income.	700,000	1.55	1,085,000
Dividends.	(500,000)	1.58	(790,000)
			3,295,000
Exposed position, December 31 (€4,300,000 − €840,000 − €1,260,000).	€2,200,000	1.60	−3,520,000
Translation gain.			(225,000)
Accumulated other comprehensive income, January 1.			0
Accumulated other comprehensive income, December 31.			$(225,000)

Balance Sheet

	December 31, 2013			January 1, 2013[1]
	€	rate	$	$
Assets				
Cash.	€ 600,000	$1.60	$ 960,000	$ 450,000
Receivables.	600,000	1.60	960,000	1,050,000
Inventory.	800,000	1.60	1,280,000	1,500,000
Plant assets, net.	2,300,000	1.60	3,680,000	3,000,000
Total assets.	€4,300,000		$6,880,000	$6,000,000
Liabilities and stockholders' equity				
Accounts payable.	€ 840,000	1.60	$1,344,000	$ 990,000
Long-term debt.	1,260,000	1.60	2,016,000	2,010,000
Capital stock.	800,000	1.50	1,200,000	1,200,000
Retained earnings.	1,400,000	see above	2,095,000	1,800,000
Accumulated other comprehensive income.	—	see above	225,000	—
Total liabilities and stockholders' equity.	€4,300,000		$6,880,000	$6,000,000

[1] All January 1, 2013, accounts are translated at the exchange rate at acquisition date, $1.50.

The International illustration highlights the differences between translation and remeasurement. Because the euro strengthened relative to the U.S. dollar during 2013,

- Translated total assets are higher, since the current rate is higher than historical rates.
- Translated cost of sales and depreciation expense are higher, since the average rate exceeds historical rates.
- Translation produces a *gain* on a net *asset* exposed position, reported as a component of OCI. But remeasurement produces a *loss* on a net *liability* position, reported in income.

EXHIBIT 7.8   International Company: Remeasurement for Year Ended December 31, 2013

Statement of Income and Retained Earnings

	€	rate	$
Sales.	€5,000,000	$1.55	$7,750,000
Cost of sales.	(2,250,000)	see below	(3,413,500)
Depreciation	(350,000)	see below	(528,500)
Current operating expenses.	(1,700,000)	1.55	(2,635,000)
Remeasurement loss		see below	(67,000)
Net income.	700,000		1,106,000
Retained earnings, January 1.	1,200,000	1.50	1,800,000
Dividends	(500,000)	1.58	(790,000)
Retained earnings, December 31.	€1,400,000		$2,116,000

Calculation of Remeasurement Adjustment

	€	rate	$
Exposed position, January 1			
(€300,000 + €700,000 − €660,000 − €1,340,000)	€(1,000,000)	$1.50	$(1,500,000)
Changes in exposed position:			
Sales.	5,000,000	1.55	7,750,000
Inventory purchases	(2,050,000)	1.55	(3,177,500)
Plant assets purchases.	(650,000)	1.57	(1,020,500)
Current operating expenses	(1,700,000)	1.55	(2,635,000)
Dividends	(500,000)	1.58	(790,000)
			(1,373,000)
Exposed position, December 31			
(€600,000 + €600,000 − €840,000 − €1,260,000)	€ (900,000)	1.60	−(1,440,000)
Remeasurement loss			$ 67,000

Balance Sheet

	December 31, 2013			January 1, 2013[1]
	€	rate	$	$
Assets				
Cash	€ 600,000	$1.60	$ 960,000	$ 450,000
Receivables	600,000	1.60	960,000	1,050,000
Inventory.	800,000	1.58	1,264,000	1,500,000
Plant assets, net.	2,300,000	see below	3,492,000	3,000,000
Total assets	€4,300,000		$6,676,000	$6,000,000
Liabilities and stockholders' equity				
Accounts payable.	€ 840,000	1.60	$1,344,000	$ 990,000
Long-term debt	1,260,000	1.60	2,016,000	2,010,000
Capital stock	800,000	1.50	1,200,000	1,200,000
Retained earnings.	1,400,000	see above	2,116,000	1,800,000
Total liabilities and stockholders' equity	€4,300,000		$6,676,000	$6,000,000

Remeasurement of Inventory and Plant Assets

	€	rate	$
Inventory, January 1, 2013.	€1,000,000	$1.50	$1,500,000
Purchases.	2,050,000	1.55	3,177,500
Inventory, December 31, 2013.	(800,000)	1.58	(1,264,000)
Cost of sales.	€2,250,000		$3,413,500
Plant assets, net, January 1, 2013.	€2,000,000	1.50	$3,000,000
Purchases.	650,000	1.57	1,020,500
Depreciation expense.	(350,000)	See Note 2	(528,500)
Plant assets, net, December 31, 2013.	€2,300,000		$3,492,000

[1] All January 1, 2013 accounts are remeasured at the exchange rate at acquisition date, $1.50.
[2] $528,500 = (€300,000 × $1.50) + (€50,000 × $1.57)

Because the exchange rate rose to $1.60/€ from $1.50/€ during 2013, the dollar equivalents of euro balances increased. Remeasured net income is $21,000 higher due to (1) $74,000 (= $3,487,500 - $3,413,500) less in cost of sales and $14,000 (= $542,500 - $528,500) less in depreciation expense from applying lower historical rates for those items, offset by (2) a $67,000 remeasurement loss on the net liability exposed position.

Converting the Statement of Cash Flows to the Reporting Currency

ASC para. 830-230-45-1 requires conversion of the statement of cash flows to the parent's currency to display "the reporting currency equivalent of foreign currency cash flows using the exchange rates in effect at the time of the cash flows." The objective is to **change foreign currency cash flows into dollars at the exchange rate(s) in effect when the cash flows occurred**, a result *not* affected by the company's choice of functional currency.

Although gains and losses accrue to all accounts that are translated or remeasured at the current rate, *only the portion of the gain or loss affecting cash is disclosed separately in the statement of cash flows.* Converting the foreign cash transactions to the reporting currency proceeds as follows:

- *Repetitive cash transactions*, such as payments for salaries and utilities, are converted at the *average rate*.
- *Large, discrete cash transactions*, such as dividend payments or proceeds from issuing securities, are converted at the *rate(s) in effect when they occurred*.

International Company's statement of cash flows for the year ended December 31, 2013, in euros and dollars, appears in Exhibit 7.9. Operating cash flows occur evenly throughout the year, and we assume retirement of long-term debt also occurs evenly. The $73,000 conversion gain accruing to cash appears in a separate schedule. *Cash flow from operations* is displayed using the direct method. We illustrate the indirect method reconciliation assuming International's functional currency is the euro.

Disclosures

ASC Section 830-30-50 requires companies to provide an analysis of changes in the cumulative translation adjustment during the year. In the past, companies generally disclosed each year's translation adjustment in their statement of changes in shareholders' equity, as a component of accumulated other comprehensive income. This option was eliminated in 2012. Currently *FASB ASC Section 220-10-45* requires that the components of yearly net income and other comprehensive income be reported either in a single statement of net income and OCI, or in two separate statements, a statement of net income, followed immediately by a separate statement of other comprehensive income.

Chevron Corporation's 2009 Consolidated Statement of Comprehensive Income illustrates the dual statement approach. Chevron reports a translation *gain* of $60 million in 2009, implying that the U.S. dollar *weakened* against the functional currencies of its international subsidiaries in 2009.

| | Year ended December 31 | | |
Millions of dollars	2009	2008	2007
Net income	$10,563	$24,031	$18,795
Currency translation adjustment			
Unrealized net change arising during period.	60	(112)	31
Unrealized holding gain (loss) on securities	2	(6)	19
Derivatives			
Net derivatives loss (gain) on hedge transactions.	(69)	139	(10)
Reclassification to net income of net realized (gain) loss	(23)	32	7
Income taxes on derivatives transactions.	32	(61)	(3)
Total.	(60)	110	(6)
Defined benefit plans	(399)	(1,901)	685
Other Comprehensive (Loss) Gain, Net of Tax	(397)	(1,909)	729
Comprehensive Income.	10,166	22,122	19,524
Comprehensive income attributable to noncontrolling interests	(80)	(100)	(107)
Comprehensive Income Attributable to Chevron Corporation	$10,086	$22,022	$19,417

EXHIBIT 7.9   International Company: Converted Statement of Cash Flows

INTERNATIONAL COMPANY
Statement of Cash Flows
For Year Ended December 31, 2013

	€	rate	$
Operating Activities			
Cash received from customers[1]	€5,100,000	$1.55	$ 7,905,000
Cash paid to suppliers[2]	(1,870,000)	1.55	(2,898,500)
Cash paid for operating expenses	(1,700,000)	1.55	(2,635,000)
Cash provided by operating activities	1,530,000		2,371,500
Investing Activities			
Acquisition of plant assets	(650,000)	1.57	(1,020,500)
Cash used by investing activities	(650,000)		(1,020,500)
Financing Activities			
Retirement of long-term debt	(80,000)	1.55	(124,000)
Dividends paid	(500,000)	1.58	(790,000)
Cash used by financing activities	(580,000)		(914,000)
Change in cash.	300,000		437,000
Effect of exchange rate changes on cash		see below	73,000
Cash balance, January 1, 2013	300,000	1.50	450,000
Cash balance, December 31, 2013	€ 600,000	1.60	$ 960,000

Effect of Exchange Rate Changes on Cash

	€	rate	$
Beginning cash balance	€ 300,000	$1.50	$ 450,000
Plus cash provided by operating activities.	1,530,000	1.55	2,371,500
Less cash used for investing activities.	(650,000)	1.57	(1,020,500)
Less retirement of long-term debt	(80,000)	1.55	(124,000)
Less dividends paid	(500,000)	1.58	(790,000)
			887,000
Ending cash balance	€ 600,000	1.60	−960,000
Effect of exchange rate changes on cash			$ (73,000)

Reconciliation of Net Income to Cash Provided by Operating Activities

	€	rate	$
Net income	€ 700,000	$1.55	$1,085,000
Depreciation expense.	350,000	1.55	542,500
Decrease in accounts receivable	100,000	1.55	155,000
Decrease in inventory.	200,000	1.55	310,000
Increase in accounts payable.	180,000	1.55	279,000
Cash provided by operating activities	€1,530,000		$2,371,500

[1] €5,100,000 = €5,000,000 + (€700,000 − €600,000)
[2] €1,870,000 = €2,250,000 − (€1,000,000 − €800,000) − (€840,000 − €660,000)

FINANCIAL ANALYSIS USING TRANSLATED AND REMEASURED INFORMATION

LO2 Describe how changing exchange rates affect financial analysis of international entities.

Translation and remeasurement of local currency accounts affect analysis and interpretation of an international subsidiary's financial picture in pervasive ways. This section discusses effects on ratio analysis and addresses the problem of interperiod comparisons. We focus on how a subsidiary's reported performance is affected by the way its accounts are converted to U.S. dollars.

Notice how translation and remeasurement impact components of financial statement data and influence ratios calculated with these data.

- Translated total assets are larger (smaller) than remeasured total assets when the exchange rate has been rising (falling) over time. This effect occurs because assets carried at historical cost are remeasured at historical rates, but are translated at the current rate.
- Disregarding the gain or loss from converting local currency accounts to U.S. dollars, translated income is larger (smaller) than remeasured income when the exchange rate has been falling (rising) over time. This effect occurs because depreciation, amortization and cost of sales are remeasured at historical rates, but are usually translated at the average rate.
- Remeasurement creates a gain or loss that affects income, while the translation gain or loss appears in equity.

Measures of profitability, short-term liquidity and long-term solvency are all affected by the foreign currency conversion process. We first examine the DuPont Analysis, a common approach to assessing profitability.

Effects on Profitability: The "DuPont Analysis"

The basic **DuPont Analysis** disaggregates the *Return on Assets* ratio into *Return on Sales* and *Total Assets Turnover* ratios as follows.

$$\text{Return on Assets} = \text{Return on Sales} \times \text{Total Assets Turnover}$$

$$\frac{\text{Income}}{\text{Average Total Assets}} = \frac{\text{Income}}{\text{Sales}} \times \frac{\text{Sales}}{\text{Average Total Assets}}$$

Return on assets measures the profitability of the firm's asset portfolio, **return on sales** measures the profitability of sales, and **total assets turnover** measures efficiency—the ability of the firm's asset portfolio to generate sales.

Although various measures of income are used by financial analysts, we prefer either after-tax operating income, approximated by: net income + (1 − tax rate) (interest expense), or earnings before interest and taxes (EBIT). Use of income measures before interest expense rather than net income enables measurement of profitability before considering interest payments to suppliers of capital. In this way, the firm's operating and investing decisions are separated from its financing decisions. Using similar reasoning, remeasured *operating income* is calculated *before the remeasurement gain or loss*.

Relevant data from the International Company example for 2013 in Exhibits 7.7 through 7.9 are summarized below, followed by the profitability analysis calculations.

	€	$: Translation	$: Remeasurement
Sales.	€5,000,000	$7,750,000	$7,750,000
Operating income.	700,000	1,085,000	1,173,000[1]
Average total assets.	4,150,000[2]	6,440,000[3]	6,338,000[4]

[1] $1,173,000 = $1,106,000 (net income) + $67,000 (translation loss) [see Exhibit 7.8]
[2] €4,150,000 = (€4,000,000 + €4,300,000)/2 [see balance sheets p. 268]
[3] $6,440,000 = ($6,000,000 + $6,880,000)/2 [see Exhibit 7.7]
[4] $6,338,000 = ($6,000,000 + $6,676,000)/2 [see Exhibit 7.8]

Currency	Profitability Analysis				
	Return on Assets	=	Return on Sales	×	Total Assets Turnover
Euro	$\frac{700,000}{4,150,000}$	=	$\frac{700,000}{5,000,000}$	×	$\frac{5,000,000}{4,150,000}$
	0.17	=	0.14	×	1.20
$ (translation)	$\frac{1,085,000}{6,440,000}$	=	$\frac{1,085,000}{7,750,000}$	×	$\frac{7,750,000}{6,440,000}$
	0.17	=	0.14	×	1.20
$ (remeasurement)	$\frac{1,173,000}{6,338,000}$	=	$\frac{1,173,000}{7,750,000}$	×	$\frac{7,750,000}{6,338,000}$
	0.19	=	0.15	×	1.22

When the international subsidiary's functional currency is the U.S. dollar, required remeasurement of local accounts into U.S. dollars presents a different picture of the subsidiary's profitability than that provided by the local currency accounts. However, when the subsidiary's functional currency is its local currency, the euro, translation of local currency accounts to U.S. dollars does not significantly change the profitability picture depicted by the local currency amounts.

In the International Company illustration, the U.S. dollar steadily weakens against the local currency, the euro. Historical rates are therefore lower than the average rate for the year, and the average rate is lower than the ending rate. Lower historical rates are used to remeasure some assets, cost of sales, and depreciation expense, causing remeasured operating income to be higher than translated operating income. Remeasured assets are lower than translated assets. Assuming the average rate approximates historical rates for revenues and out-of-pocket expenses, remeasured return on sales is higher than translated return on sales and remeasured assets turnover is higher than translated assets turnover.

Translated and remeasured ratios differ from local currency ratios if the local currency amounts in the numerator and denominator are multiplied by different rates. In remeasuring return on sales, operating income accounts are converted using average and historical rates, while sales is converted using the average rate. In remeasuring assets turnover, the numerator, sales, is multiplied by the average rate, but the denominator, assets, is multiplied by appropriate historical rates. For International Company, with the U.S. dollar steadily weakening against the euro, remeasured return on sales is greater than local currency return on sales, and remeasured assets turnover is greater than local currency assets turnover.

In contrast, translated ratios maintain local currency relationships. Translation of return on sales multiplies both the numerator and denominator local currency amounts by the average rate, so the ratio is unchanged by the translation process. In translating assets turnover, the numerator, sales, is multiplied by the average rate, and the denominator, assets, is an average of beginning and ending assets, converted using the beginning and ending rates respectively. Translated assets turnover differs from local currency assets turnover only to the extent that the average rate used to translate sales in the numerator differs from the average of the beginning and ending rates used to translate average total assets in the denominator.

Effects on Analysis of Short-Term Liquidity and Long-Term Solvency

Because translation and remeasurement generally lead to different U.S. dollar asset balances, income, and stockholders' equity accounts, other ratios employing those U.S. dollar amounts are also affected. For example, referring back to International Company's December 31, 2013, data in Exhibits 7.7 and 7.8, we make the following calculations:

Currency	Current Ratio	Total Liabilities/ Total Assets	Long-Term Debt/ Stockholders' Equity
Euro	$\frac{2,000,000}{840,000} = 2.38$	$\frac{2,100,000}{4,300,000} = 0.488$	$\frac{1,260,000}{2,200,000} = 0.573$
$ (translation)	$\frac{3,200,000}{1,344,000} = 2.38$	$\frac{3,360,000}{6,880,000} = 0.488$	$\frac{2,016,000}{3,520,000} = 0.573$
$ (remeasurement)	$\frac{3,184,000}{1,344,000} = 2.37$	$\frac{3,360,000}{6,676,000} = 0.503$	$\frac{2,016,000}{3,316,000} = 0.608$

In this example, remeasured ratios portray liquidity and solvency less favorably than the euro data suggest; the lower historical rates used to remeasure inventory and plant assets raise the ratio of current and total liabilities to current and total assets. Translated ratios preserve the local currency relationships exactly — *both numerator and denominator in local currency are multiplied by the same year-end current rate.*

The Codification justifies translation of local currency accounts to U.S. dollars when the subsidiary is relatively self-contained and independent by explaining that translation better preserves the financial results and relationships expressed in the subsidiary's local currency. Translation is required when the subsidiary's local currency is its functional currency. The above ratio analyses indicate that translation preserves these local currency relationships better than remeasurement.

Not all translated ratios, however, are identical to their functional currency counterparts. Significant changes in exchange rates and total assets cause ratios such as return on assets to diverge. Nevertheless, translated ratios avoid the potential large distortions that can occur when drastically different historical rates are used during remeasurement.

In contrast, remeasurement seeks to report the transactions of the subsidiary, recorded in its local currency, as if they were undertaken in the subsidiary's functional currency. If the subsidiary's functional currency is the parent's currency, the U.S. dollar, remeasuring local currency accounts into U.S. dollars at the exchange rates in effect when the transactions occurred produces ratio values equal to those resulting if the parent transacted directly with international suppliers and customers. The functional currency concept indicates that preserving local currency results and relationships are relatively unimportant when the subsidiary's functional currency is the dollar.

Interperiod Comparisons

Assessing changes in performance over time using translated or remeasured data is complicated by a factor over which the international entity has no control—*changes in exchange rates*. Comparative local currency data, desired by some financial analysts, are often not available to users of financial statements. Moreover, users of *consolidated statements* are not able to factor out an *individual international entity's* influence on those statements. Sufficient disaggregated data in dollars, either in the form of supplementary disclosures or internal breakdowns, are needed if an assessment is to be attempted.

One approach to judging year-to-year changes in an international entity's performance involves factoring out exchange rate changes and calculating data translated or remeasured with constant exchange rates. For example, suppose the following condensed income statement data and exchange rates pertain to an international entity.

	2014	2013
Sales.	£1,000	£ 800
Costs and expenses.	(800)	(700)
Operating income.	£ 200	£ 100
Change in income (%)	100%	—

The average exchange rate is $1.45/£ for 2014 and $1.55/£ for 2013. Composite historical rates relating to costs and expenses are $1.50/£ for 2014 and $1.60/£ for 2013. Comparative translated/remeasured data based on the above exchange rates are:

	Translation		Remeasurement	
	2014	2013	2014	2013
Sales.	$1,450	$1,240	$1,450	$1,240
Costs and expenses.	(1,160)	(1,085)	(1,200)	(1,120)
Operating income.	$ 290	$ 155	$ 250	$ 120
Change in income (%)	87%	—	108%	—

Translation *understates* the percentage change in local currency income by 13% (= 87% − 100%) and remeasurement *overstates* the percentage change in local currency income by 8% (= 108% − 100%). Now we recalculate translated/remeasured income using *the same 2013 exchange rates* in both 2013 and 2014.

	Translation		Remeasurement	
	2014	2013	2014	2013
Sales.	$1,550	$1,240	$1,550	$1,240
Costs and expenses.	(1,240)	(1,085)	(1,280)	(1,120)
Operating income.	$ 310	$ 155	$ 270	$ 120
Change in income (%)	100%	—	125%	—

2014 local currency data are translated at the same rate used in 2013—$1.55/£—and the 100% change in translated income agrees with the 100% change in local currency income.

Unfortunately, the same cannot be said for remeasurement. Although the 2013 rates of $1.55/£ and $1.60/£ were used to remeasure 2014 local currency sales, and costs and expenses, respectively, the 125% change in remeasured income is greater than the 108% change observed when the 2014 data were remeasured at 2014 exchange rates. This occurs because local currency sales increased by 25% whereas local currency costs and expenses increased by only 14%. The effect on income of remeasuring the £200 increase in 2014 sales at $1.55/£ is much greater than the effect of remeasuring the £100 increase in costs and expenses at $1.60/£. Thus, whether use of 2013 rates to remeasure 2014 local currency data parallels changes in local currency results depends on both changes in the local currency data and in exchange rates.

· ·

Reporting Perspective

The FASB approved the reporting standards for converting a subsidiary's accounts to the parent's currency in 1981, and these requirements are essentially the same today. This commentary identifies some of the reasons why these standards have stood the test of time.

The FASB's conceptual framework provides a structure to guide board decisions on specific accounting issues. *SFAC 1* concludes that the principal objective of financial reporting is *usefulness to decision makers*, with particular emphasis on the role of financial information in assessing the amounts, timing, and uncertainty of future cash flows. In setting standards for converting an international subsidiary's financial information to the parent's reporting currency, the board focused on decision usefulness, not on an abstract theory that might be at odds with events' real economic impact. The *functional currency approach* seeks to match an entity's *economic exposure* to exchange rate movements with the *accounting exposure* that produces translation and remeasurement gains and losses. When a subsidiary's economic exposure is best measured by the viability of its operations, the exposed position of translation (net assets) applies. In contrast, when the subsidiary's economic exposure relates to specific monetary assets and liabilities, an exposed position focusing on those items leads to remeasurement gains and losses.

Prior to 1981, only remeasurement was allowed, requiring parent companies to report gains and losses on their subsidiaries' net monetary exposure in income. It is alleged that although the exposure had no economic effect, U.S. parent companies used resources to neutralize the income effect of this accounting exposure. Companies with relatively independent, self-contained international subsidiaries no longer need to waste resources in this way. Translation provides a more accurate depiction of international subsidiaries' exposure to exchange rate changes, and translation gains and losses bypass earnings and are carried directly to stockholders' equity via OCI.

Although financial statement users may applaud the decision usefulness of the standards, they may have some difficulty working with the translated or remeasured data. Ratios such as return on assets can produce inappropriate signals when based on translated data. And when nonmonetary assets are translated at the current rate, their meaning in U.S. dollars becomes unclear. They are neither historical dollar measures of historical cost nor current dollar measures of current value.

· ·

CONSOLIDATION OF INTERNATIONAL SUBSIDIARIES

LO3 Explain procedures for consolidating international subsidiaries.

This section explains the process for consolidating international subsidiaries. Although the procedures generally parallel those discussed in Chapters 3 through 5, additional issues related to changing exchange rates must be addressed. In the discussion below, we assume the subsidiary's financial information has already been remeasured to its functional currency, if necessary.

Equity Method Reporting

Under the complete equity method explained in Chapter 4, a parent company adjusts its investment account on its own books for its share of changes in the subsidiary's stockholders' equity. As part of that process, the parent records its share of the subsidiary's annual net income. The subsidiary's functional currency financial statements must therefore be translated into dollars before the U.S. parent books the equity method income accrual.

The parent books its share of any dividend payment as a reduction of its investment account; dividends are translated at historical rates. The parent also adjusts its investment account for its share of the year's translation adjustment, which affects the subsidiary's OCI. The parent includes this amount as a component of its own OCI. These concepts are illustrated below.

The Consolidation Process

Translation of foreign currency financial statements occurs when the operations of international subsidiaries are to be included in the U.S. financial statements of the parent company. There are two major steps: (1) translate the subsidiary's functional currency accounts into U.S. dollars, and (2) consolidate the subsidiary using a consolidation working paper.

We illustrate the consolidation process for a subsidiary whose *functional currency is the local currency*, using the International Company illustration from earlier in the chapter. When the exchange rate is $1.50/€, Domestic Corporation pays $3,900,000, or equivalently €2,600,000, for all of the common stock of International Company on January 1, 2013. The balance sheet of International Company on January 1, 2013, is repeated below.

INTERNATIONAL COMPANY Balance Sheet at January 1, 2013	
Assets	
Cash	€ 300,000
Receivables	700,000
Inventory	1,000,000
Plant assets, net	2,000,000
Total assets	€4,000,000
Liabilities and stockholders' equity	
Accounts payable	€ 660,000
Long-term debt	1,340,000
Capital stock	800,000
Retained earnings	1,200,000
Total liabilities and stockholders' equity	€4,000,000

International Company's reported assets and liabilities approximate fair values. However, we discover previously unreported identifiable intangibles meeting the asset-recognition requirements of *ASC Topic 805*, with a fair value of €400,000. Analysis of the acquisition cost is:

	€	rate	$
Acquisition cost	€2,600,000	$1.50	$3,900,000
Book value of International	(2,000,000)	1.50	3,000,000
Cost in excess of International's book value	600,000		900,000
Difference between fair value and book value:			
Identifiable intangibles	400,000	1.50	600,000
Goodwill	€ 200,000		$ 300,000

Consolidation at Date of Acquisition We translate International Company's assets, liabilities, and stockholders' equity using the spot rate at the acquisition date. Domestic Corporation's assumed balance sheet and International Company's translated balance sheet are shown in the consolidated working paper in Exhibit 7.10 below. In consolidation at the date of acquisition, we eliminate the translated stockholders' equity of International Company against the investment account in elimination E, and revalue International's assets per the above schedule in elimination R.

EXHIBIT 7.10   Consolidation Working Paper, Domestic Corporation and International Company, January 1, 2013

	Domestic Corporation	International Company	Eliminations Dr.	Eliminations Cr.	Consolidated Balance Sheet
Assets					
Cash	$ 800,000	$ 450,000			$ 1,250,000
Receivables	1,200,000	1,050,000			2,250,000
Inventory	4,000,000	1,500,000			5,500,000
Plant assets, net	8,000,000	3,000,000			11,000,000
Investment in International Company	3,900,000	—		$3,000,000 (E)	—
				900,000 (R)	
Identifiable intangible assets	—	—	(R) $ 600,000		600,000
Goodwill	—	—	(R) 300,000		300,000
Total assets	$17,900,000	$6,000,000			$20,900,000
Liabilities and stockholders' equity					
Accounts payable	$ 600,000	$ 990,000			$ 1,590,000
Long-term debt	1,400,000	2,010,000			3,410,000
Capital stock	8,000,000	1,200,000	(E) 1,200,000		8,000,000
Retained earnings	7,900,000	1,800,000	(E) 1,800,000		7,900,000
Total liabilities and stockholders' equity	$17,900,000	$6,000,000	$3,900,000	$3,900,000	$20,900,000

Consolidation Subsequent to Acquisition   At December 31, 2013, we again prepare consolidated statements. Domestic Corporation uses the complete equity method to account for its investment in International Company. The exchange rate is $1.60/€ at December 31, 2013. The average exchange rate for 2013 is $1.55/€. International Company declared and paid dividends when the exchange rate was $1.58/€.

The first step is to translate International's December 31, 2013, trial balance into U.S. dollars. Exhibit 7.11 shows the translation, using data from Exhibit 7.7.

EXHIBIT 7.11   Translation of International Company's Trial Balance, December 31, 2013

Trial Balances	€ Dr (Cr)	$/€	$ Dr (Cr)
Cash	€ 600,000	1.60	$ 960,000
Receivables	600,000	1.60	960,000
Inventory	800,000	1.60	1,280,000
Plant assets, net	2,300,000	1.60	3,680,000
Accounts payable	(840,000)	1.60	(1,344,000)
Long-term debt	(1,260,000)	1.60	(2,016,000)
Capital stock	(800,000)	1.50	(1,200,000)
Retained earnings, January 1	(1,200,000)	1.50	(1,800,000)
Accumulated other comprehensive income	—	See note1	(225,000)
Dividends	500,000	1.58	790,000
Sales	(5,000,000)	1.55	(7,750,000)
Cost of sales	2,250,000	1.55	3,487,500
Depreciation expense	350,000	1.55	542,500
Current operating expenses	1,700,000	1.55	2,635,000
Totals	€ 0		$ 0

[1] See calculation in Exhibit 7.7.

The next step is to enter the account balances of the two companies in the consolidation working paper and make the required eliminating entries. Before continuing, however, examine how Domestic reports its investment in International on its own books.

Because Domestic uses the equity method to report the investment on its own books, the investment account is updated each year to reflect Domestic's share of International's income, with necessary adjustments, and dividends. Assume that the previously unreported intangibles have an estimated life of four years, and that goodwill impairment is €20,000 during 2013. Domestic's equity method income accrual is calculated as follows:

International's reported net income ($1.55 × 700,000)	$1,085,000
Less revaluation write-offs:	
Amortization expense [$1.55 × (400,000/4)]	(155,000)
Goodwill impairment loss ($1.55 × 20,000)	(31,000)
Equity method income accrual for 2013	$ 899,000

The investment account is reduced by dividends of $790,000 (= $1.58 × 500,000). There is an additional change in International's stockholders' equity for 2013—the translation adjustment shown in OCI. The equity method reports Domestic's share of International's OCI as well as net income, and therefore increases the investment account by another $225,000. Domestic's entries appear below.

Investment in International Company	899,000	
Equity in income of International Company		899,000
To record equity in net income for 2013.		
Cash	790,000	
Investment in International Company		790,000
To record dividends received in 2013.		
Investment in International Company	225,000	
Other comprehensive income		225,000
To record translation adjustment for 2013.		

Domestic's investment account now has a balance of $4,234,000 (= $3,900,000 + $899,000 − $790,000 + $225,000).

Working paper eliminations in journal entry format at December 31, 2013, are shown below, and the consolidation working paper is in Exhibit 7.12. Assets are translated at the current rate ($1.60), expenses are translated at the average rate ($1.55), and capital stock is translated at the acquisition date rate ($1.50).

(C)	Equity in net income of International Company	899,000	
	Dividends—International Company		790,000
	Investment in International Company		109,000
(E)	Capital stock—International Company	1,200,000	
	Retained earnings, January 1—International Company	1,800,000	
	Accumulated other comprehensive income—International Company	225,000	
	Investment in International Company		3,225,000
(R)	Intangible assets (a)	640,000	
	Goodwill (b)	320,000	
	Investment in International Company (c)		900,000
	Other comprehensive income		60,000
(O)	Amortization expense (d)	155,000	
	Goodwill impairment loss (e)	31,000	
	Other comprehensive income	6,000	
	Intangible assets (f)		160,000
	Goodwill (g)		32,000

(a) $640,000 = €400,000 × $1.60
(b) $320,000 = €200,000 × $1.60
(c) $900,000 = Remaining Investment balance after eliminating entries (C) and (E).
(d) $155,000 = €100,000 × $1.55
(e) $31,000 = €20,000 × $1.55
(f) $160,000 = €100,000 × $1.60
(g) $32,000 = €20,000 × $1.60

EXHIBIT 7.12   Consolidation Working Paper, Domestic Corporation and International Company, December 31, 2013

	Domestic Corporation Dr (Cr)	International Company Dr (Cr)	Eliminations Dr	Eliminations Cr	Consolidated
Cash.	$ 1,000,000	$ 960,000			$ 1,960,000
Receivables	3,208,000	960,000			4,168,000
Inventory.	5,000,000	1,280,000			6,280,000
Plant assets, net.	9,000,000	3,680,000			12,680,000
Investment in International Company.	4,234,000	—		$ 109,000 (C)	—
				3,225,000 (E)	
				900,000 (R)	
Intangible assets	—	—	(R) $ 640,000	160,000 (O)	480,000
Goodwill	—	—	(R) 320,000	32,000 (O)	288,000
Accounts payable.	(700,000)	(1,344,000)			(2,044,000)
Long-term debt	(2,100,000)	(2,016,000)			(4,116,000)
Capital stock	(8,000,000)	(1,200,000)	(E) 1,200,000		(8,000,000)
Retained earnings, January 1.	(7,900,000)	(1,800,000)	(E) 1,800,000		(7,900,000)
Accumulated other comprehensive income.	(225,000)	(225,000)	(E) 225,000	60,000 (R)	(279,000)
			(O) 6,000		
Dividends	—	790,000		790,000 (C)	—
Sales.	(25,000,000)	(7,750,000)			(32,750,000)
Equity in net income–International Company.	(899,000)	—	(C) 899,000		—
Cost of sales.	15,000,000	3,487,500			18,487,500
Depreciation expense.	—	542,500			542,500
Goodwill impairment loss.	—	—	(O) 31,000		31,000
Other operating expenses	7,382,000	2,635,000	(O) 155,000		10,172,000
Totals	$ 0	$ 0	$5,276,000	$5,276,000	$ 0

The adjustments to OCI in elimination entries (R) and (O) are caused by additional exposure to translation gains and losses through the consolidation process. The translation adjustment reflects exposure of the net asset position to changes in the exchange rate. When the net assets of International Company are *revalued and written off* in the eliminating entries, its *net asset position changes*, creating *additional translation gains or losses*. As can be seen from elimination entries (R) and (O), the net translation gain caused by recognizing and writing off the revaluations is $54,000 (= $60,000 − 6,000), and is independently calculated as follows:

	€	rate	$
Revaluation (net assets), January 1, 2013	€600,000	$1.50	$900,000
Less revaluation write-offs:			
Amortization expense.	(100,000)	1.55	(155,000)
Goodwill impairment loss	(20,000)	1.55	(31,000)
			714,000
Revaluation (net assets), December 31, 2013	€480,000	1.60	−768,000
Translation gain attributed to revaluations.			$ (54,000)

The International illustration demonstrates that consolidation of international subsidiaries changes exposure to translation gains and losses. The resulting additional translation adjustments are reported in OCI.

REVIEW 3   •   Consolidation of an International Subsidiary

Alti, a U.S. international discount supermarket chain, acquired all of the voting stock of Lodl, a German grocery chain, on January 2, 2014, for $14,000,000, when Lodl's book value was €3,000,000 and the spot rate was $1.40/ €. The excess of acquisition cost over book value was attributed to goodwill.

It is now December 31, 2014, and the spot rate is $1.30/€. The average rate for 2014 was $1.36/€. Lodl's December 31, 2014, trial balance, in euros, is shown below. There is no goodwill impairment in 2014. Lodl's functional currency is the euro.

	Dr (Cr)
Current assets	€ 1,500,000
Plant and equipment, net	50,000,000
Liabilities	(48,300,000)
Capital stock	(1,000,000)
Retained earnings, January 1	(2,000,000)
Sales revenue	(25,000,000)
Cost of goods sold	12,000,000
Operating expenses	12,800,000
Total	€ 0

Required

a. Translate Lodl's December 31, 2014, trial balance into dollars.
b. Prepare Alti's journal entries for 2014, related to its investment in Lodl, using the complete equity method.
c. Prepare the elimination entries necessary to consolidate Lodl with Alti at December 31, 2014.

Solutions are located after the chapter assignments.

IFRS FOR TRANSLATING AND CONSOLIDATING FOREIGN CURRENCY FINANCIAL STATEMENTS

IFRS for translating and consolidating the financial statements of international branches and subsidiaries is found in the following standards:

LO4 Apply IFRS translation requirements.

- *IAS 21*, The Effects of Changes in Foreign Exchange Rates
- *IAS 29*, Financial Reporting in Hyperinflationary Economies

Translation and Remeasurement

Similar to U.S. GAAP, *IAS 21* requires that an international subsidiary's accounts be remeasured to its functional currency before they are translated into the parent's currency, known as the **presentation currency**. IFRS remeasurement computes account balances as if all transactions had occurred in the functional currency.

If the subsidiary's functional currency is *not* hyperinflationary, translation of functional currency accounts into the presentation currency follows the translation procedures required in U.S. GAAP—assets and liabilities are translated at the end of year spot rate and capital accounts are translated at the rate when the shares were issued. Income accounts are translated at the rate on the date of each transaction; however if rates do not change significantly the average rate for the period may be used. Translation gains and losses caused by exchange differences are recognized in other comprehensive income.

Subsidiaries in Hyperinflationary Economies

A difference between IFRS and U.S. GAAP occurs when the subsidiary reports in the currency of a hyperinflationary economy. U.S. GAAP defines a "highly inflationary" economy in terms of the *inflation rate*, a cumulative inflation of about 100 percent or more over three years. In contrast, IFRS offers

BUSINESS APPLICATION   Foreign Currency Translation at Bayer Group

Bayer AG is a large global pharmaceutical company headquartered in Germany, with operations in the areas of health care, nutrition, and high-tech materials. Its consolidated financial statements are presented in euros and prepared using IFRS. In the footnotes to its 2010 financial statements, Bayer Group describes the translation process:

> The financial statements of the individual companies for inclusion in the consolidated financial statements are prepared in their respective functional currencies. . . . The majority of consolidated companies carry out their activities autonomously from a financial, economic and organizational point of view, and their functional currencies are therefore the respective local currencies. . . . In the consolidated financial statements, the assets and liabilities of companies outside the eurozone at the start and end of the year are translated into euros at closing rates. All changes occurring during the year and all income and expense items and cash flows are translated into euros at average monthly rates. Components of stockholders' equity are translated at the historical exchange rates prevailing at the respective dates of their first-time recognition in Group equity.
>
> The exchange differences arising between the resulting amounts and those obtained by translating at closing rates are reported separately as "Exchange differences on translation of operations outside the eurozone" or as "Exchange differences."

Note that Bayer uses "average monthly rates" to translate revenues and expenses, implying that there is sufficient variation in monthly volume to warrant using individual monthly rates instead of a simple yearly average.

Bayer has consolidated entities whose functional currency is not the euro located in countries all over the world, including the U.K, Switzerland, North America, and Asia/Pacific. To help in analysis, Bayer also discloses the variation in exchange rates against the euro, for major currencies:

Exchange Rates for Major Currencies		**Closing rate**		**Average rate**	
€/1/		**2009**	**2010**	**2009**	**2010**
ARS	Argentina	5.47	5.31	5.20	5.18
BRL	Brazil.	2.51	2.23	2.77	2.33
CAD	Canada.	1.51	1.33	1.59	1.36
CHF	Switzerland.	1.48	1.25	1.51	1.38
CNY	China	9.84	8.82	9.52	8.96
GBP	United Kingdom	0.89	0.86	0.89	0.86
JPY	Japan	133.16	108.65	130.31	116.04
MXN	Mexico	18.92	16.55	18.79	16.72
USD	United States	1.44	1.34	1.39	1.32

Bayer reports 2010 "exchange differences on translation of operations outside the euro zone" of €627 million, as an increase in other comprehensive income. The 2010 ending balance in exchange differences is a €1,827 million reduction in accumulated other comprehensive income. In 2010, the euro on average *weakened* with respect to the functional currencies of Bayer's consolidated international subsidiaries. The cumulative effect, however, shows that the euro has generally *strengthened* over the years against these currencies. *Source:* Bayer Group Annual Report 2010.

characteristics indicating hyperinflation, which can be used to decide whether hyperinflation exists. *IAS 29* provides these characteristics:

- Local currency amounts held by the general population are immediately invested in non-monetary assets or in a more stable currency.
- Prices may be quoted in a different, more stable currency.

- Prices for credit sales and purchases reflect the expected loss in purchasing power during the credit period, even for short-term credit transactions.
- Prices, wage and interest rates are linked to a price index.
- The cumulative inflation rate over three years is near 100 percent.

If the subsidiary's functional currency *is* hyperinflationary, *IAS 29* requires that the subsidiary's accounts be *price-level adjusted* using a general price index such as a consumer or wholesale price index, before translation to the presentation currency. Suppose the price index was 100 on January 1, 2012, when a Venezuelan subsidiary purchased land for VEF100,000,000. On December 31, 2014, the price index is 350. The price-level-adjusted land balance is 100,000,000 × 350/100 = VEF350,000,000. Monetary accounts—generally cash, receivables and liabilities, whose value is fixed in currency units—are not adjusted, as they are already expressed in units of current purchasing power. Purchasing power gains and losses on monetary accounts are reported in income.

Once the subsidiary's accounts are remeasured in currency units of the same (current) purchasing power, they are translated to the presentation currency. When the presentation currency is the euro, and the December 31, 2014, exchange rate is €0.0004/VEF, the translated land balance is €140,000 (= VEF350,000,000 × €0.0004).

IFRS for subsidiaries with hyperinflationary functional currencies differs from U.S. GAAP. Instead of adjusting the subsidiary's functional currency accounts to units of current purchasing power and then translating to the presentation currency, U.S. GAAP requires the subsidiary's functional currency accounts to be remeasured to the parent's currency. In the example above, a Venezuelan subsidiary acquired land for VEF100,000,000 on January 1, 2012. Suppose that on January 1, 2012, the exchange rate was €0.0008/VEF. U.S. GAAP remeasures the land balance at €80,000 (= VEF100,000,000 × €0.0008). The difference between the IFRS translated land amount, €140,000, and the U.S. GAAP remeasured land amount, €80,000, is due to the relation between changes in the general purchasing power of the Venezuelan bolivar, and changes in the exchange rate between bolivars and U.S. dollars. To the extent that changes in the general purchasing power of the subsidiary's currency are *not* reflected in changes in the presentation currency exchange rate, IFRS balances differ from U.S. GAAP balances.

REVIEW OF KEY CONCEPTS ••••••••••••••••••••••••••••••••

Apply translation and remeasurement procedures. (p. 255) U.S. companies with subsidiaries in other countries must convert the accounts of those business units into U.S. dollars for inclusion in the consolidated financial statements. The subsidiary's local currency accounts are **remeasured** into its **functional currency**, and then **translated** into the parent's reporting currency, the U.S. dollar. Both procedures result in gains and losses from accounts converted using the **current rate**, which changes over time. Remeasurement presents the accounts as if the subsidiary's transactions were recorded in the functional currency. **Remeasurement gains and losses** have real economic effects, and are reported in income. Translation converts the functional currency accounts to the parent's reporting currency, the U.S. dollar, with the objective of maintaining the functional currency relationships between accounts. **Translation gains and losses** have little or no economic effect, and are reported in OCI. If a subsidiary's functional currency is **highly inflationary**, its accounts are remeasured into U.S. dollars to avoid distortions caused by extreme changes in exchange rates.

LO 1

Describe how changing exchange rates affect financial analysis of international entities. (p. 272) The subsidiary's financial picture is affected by the procedure used to convert its local currency accounts to dollars. **Profitability, liquidity, and solvency ratios** calculated using functional currency and translated information are generally the same, while ratios calculated using remeasured accounts will differ from the local currency ratios.

LO 2

Explain procedures for consolidating international subsidiaries. (p. 276) **Consolidation** of an international subsidiary's accounts with those of its parent requires (1) translation of the subsidiary's functional currency accounts into U.S. dollars, and (2) preparation of a consolidation working paper. Because the consolidation process typically requires **revaluation of a subsidiary's assets and liabilities** and subsequent write-offs, **additional translation gains and losses** occur.

LO 3

Apply IFRS translation requirements. (p. 281) **IFRS for remeasuring and translating the accounts of international subsidiaries** are similar to U.S. GAAP. A subsidiary's accounts are **remeasured into its functional currency**, and then **translated into the parent's presentation currency**. However, IFRS treatment in **hyperinflationary**

LO 4

economies uses **price-level adjustments** to remeasure the subsidiary's accounts to the functional currency before translation into the presentation currency.

MULTIPLE CHOICE QUESTIONS •••••••••••••••••••••••••••••••••••••••

LO 1 **1.** A German subsidiary of a U.S. parent reports its accounts in euros. Its functional currency, however, is the Swedish krona. You are responsible for changing the subsidiary's accounts into U.S. dollars in preparation for consolidation. Which statement is *true* regarding this procedure?

    a. Remeasure the subsidiary's euro accounts into krona and then translate the krona accounts into U.S. dollars.

    b. Translate the subsidiary's euro accounts into krona and then remeasure the krona accounts into U.S. dollars.

    c. Remeasure the subsidiary's euro accounts into U.S. dollars.

    d. Translate the subsidiary's euro accounts into U.S. dollars.

LO 1 **2.** At the end of 2014, an Italian subsidiary of a U.S. parent reports €1,000,000 in equipment purchased when the exchange rate was $1.40, and €3,000,000 in equipment purchased when the exchange rate was $1.50. The average exchange rate for 2014 is $1.35, and the beginning and ending rates for 2014 are $1.42 and $1.31, respectively. If the Italian subsidiary's functional currency is the U.S. dollar, the equipment account, in U.S. dollars, is

    a. $5,240,000
    b. $5,350,000
    c. $5,400,000
    d. $5,900,000

Use the following information to answer questions 3 and 4:

A U.S. parent owns all of the stock of an Italian subsidiary. The subsidiary's January 1 and December 31, 2014 trial balances are as follows, in euros:

	January 1, 2014 Dr (Cr)	December 31, 2014 Dr (Cr)
Cash, receivables.	€ 200,000	€ 180,000
Inventories, at FIFO cost	400,000	500,000
Plant & equipment, net.	1,600,000	1,300,000
Liabilities.	(1,400,000)	(1,080,000)
Capital stock	(200,000)	(200,000)
Retained earnings, beginning.	(600,000)	(600,000)
Dividends		100,000
Sales revenue.		(4,000,000)
Cost of goods sold.		2,300,000
Depreciation expense.		300,000
Out of pocket expenses.		1,200,000
	€ 0	€ 0

Sales, purchases, and recurring out of pocket expenses occurred evenly throughout the year. Exchange rates ($/€) are:

January 1, 2014	$1.45
Average for 2014	1.35
Rate when dividends declared.	1.32
December 31, 2014	1.30

3. Assume the subsidiary's functional currency is the euro. What is the translation gain or loss for 2014?   LO 1

   a. $128,000 loss
   b. $134,000 loss
   c. $128,000 gain
   d. $134,000 gain

4. Assume the subsidiary's functional currency is the U.S. dollar. What is the remeasurement gain or loss for 2014?   LO 1

   a. $162,000 loss
   b. $ 30,000 loss
   c. $162,000 gain
   d. $ 30,000 gain

5. A subsidiary's accounts are measured in euros. Assume the leverage ratio is ending total liabilities divided   LO 2
by ending total assets. The current ratio is ending current assets divided by ending current liabilities. The
subsidiary's accounts must be converted to U.S. dollars for consolidation. If the U.S. dollar has been steadily
strengthening against the euro, which statement is *true* concerning the subsidiary's financial ratios?

   a. Leverage in euros equals leverage remeasured from euros to dollars.
   b. Current ratio in euros equals current ratio translated from euros to dollars.
   c. Current ratio translated from euros to dollars is higher than current ratio remeasured from euros to dollars.
   d. Leverage remeasured from euros to dollars is higher than leverage translated from euros to dollars.

6. Assume the U.S. dollar has been steadily *weakening* with respect to the euro. Your client, a U.S. company   LO 2
with a subsidiary in Germany, wants to know the **effect of the weakening dollar** on its consolidated financial statements. The subsidiary's functional currency is the euro. Which statement below is *false*?

   a. Sales revenue will increase.
   b. Translated net income will increase.
   c. Translated assets will be lower.
   d. Translated liabilities will be higher.

7. A U.S. parent acquired its Singapore subsidiary for a price that is S$10,000,000 in excess of the subsidiary's   LO 3
book value. The excess paid was attributable to goodwill, which has not been impaired in the past, but is
impaired by S$1,000,000 in 2014. The subsidiary's functional currency is the Singapore dollar. In 2014, the
U.S. dollar has *strengthened* against the Singapore dollar. When doing eliminating entries R and O to consolidate the subsidiary with the parent at the end of 2014,

   a. there will be a credit to OCI in elimination R and a debit to OCI in elimination O.
   b. there will be a debit to OCI in elimination R and a credit to OCI in elimination O.
   c. there will be debits to OCI in both eliminations R and O.
   d. there will be credits to OCI in both eliminations R and O.

8. A U.S. parent acquired all of the stock of its British subsidiary at the beginning of 2010, when the exchange   LO 3
rate was $1.50/£. The acquisition price exceeded the subsidiary's book value, and this excess was attributed
to intangibles with a life of 5 years, valued at £400,000, and goodwill. The subsidiary's functional currency
is the pound. In 2015, the subsidiary reports income of £500,000 and pays no dividends. Goodwill impairment is £20,000. The beginning and ending exchange rates for 2015 are $1.60 and $1.70, respectively, and
the average rate for 2015 is $1.65. The U.S. parent uses the equity method to account for its investment on
its own books. The parent's equity method income accrual for 2015 is

   a. $660,000.
   b. $720,000.
   c. $792,000.
   d. $825,000.

9. A U.K.parent has a wholly owned subsidiary in Mexico, whose functional currency is the Mexican peso.   LO 4
The subsidiary reports plant and equipment of 10,000,000 pesos at the end of 2014. The Mexican economy
is determined to be hyperinflationary at the beginning of 2014. The peso is worth £0.01 at the end of 2014.
The plant and equipment was acquired when the exchange rate was £0.05. The general price-level index for
Mexico rose from 100 to 400 during the time the subsidiary held the plant and equipment. The translated
plant and equipment, following IFRS and U.S. GAAP, is

a. £500,000 under IFRS and £500,000 under U.S. GAAP.
b. £400,000 under IFRS and £500,000 under U.S. GAAP.
c. £500,000 under IFRS and £100,000 under U.S. GAAP.
d. £400,000 under IFRS and £100,000 under U.S. GAAP.

LO 4   **10.** IFRS conversion of an international subsidiary's accounts to the parent's presentation currency is the same as U.S. GAAP for *non*-hyperinflationary functional currencies,

a. with the exception that remeasurement gains and losses are reported in OCI.
b. with the exception that translation gains and losses are reported in income.
c. with the exception that translation is the only option; remeasurement is not allowed.
d. with no differences.

Assignments with the ⊘ in the margin are available in an online homework system. See the Preface of the book for details.

EXERCISES ···

LO 1   **E7.1 Translation and Remeasurement of Inventory, Cost of Sales, Plant Assets and Depreciation**   Consider the following independent situations:

1. On January 1, 2013, Ben Company formed a subsidiary in Brazil. On February 15, 2013, Ben's subsidiary purchased inventory for 100,000 real (R). On August 23, 2013, the subsidiary purchased more inventory for R75,000. The subsidiary's inventory balance on December 31, 2013, consists of R20,000 purchased on August 23. The exchange rates were $0.45/R from January 1 to June 30, 2013, $0.50/R from July 1 to October 31, and $0.52/R on December 31, 2013. The average rate for 2013 was $0.475.

2. France Company owns a subsidiary in Singapore with property, plant and equipment acquired at a cost of 2,400,000 Singapore dollars (S$). Of this amount, plant costing S$1,500,000 was acquired on January 1, 2011, when the exchange rate was $0.675/S$, and S$900,000 was acquired on January 1, 2012, when the exchange rate was $0.625/S$. The exchange rate on December 31, 2013, was $0.525/S$, and the average rate for 2013 was $0.55/S$.

Required

a. Assume the Brazilian subsidiary's functional currency is the real. Calculate (1) the translated inventory balance of the Brazilian subsidiary at December 31, 2013, and (2) the Brazilian subsidiary's translated 2013 cost of sales.
b. Now assume the Brazilian subsidiary's functional currency is the U.S. dollar. Calculate the remeasured values of the accounts described in *a*.
c. Assume the Singapore subsidiary's functional currency is the Singapore dollar, and that the Singapore subsidiary's property, plant and equipment are depreciated using the straight-line method over a ten-year period with no salvage value. Calculate (1) the translated balances of property, plant and equipment, and accumulated depreciation at December 31, 2013, and (2) translated 2013 depreciation expense.
d. Now assume the Singapore subsidiary's functional currency is the U.S. dollar. Calculate the remeasured values of the accounts described in *c*.

LO 2, 3   **E7.2 Translation and Remeasurement Gain or Loss Calculations and Consolidation**   On September 10, 2014, the Globe Trading Company invested $3,000,000 to establish a small sales subsidiary in Lima, Peru. The subsidiary converted $3,000,000 into 10,000,000 new sols (S/) and opened a bank account in Lima. At December 31, 2014, the subsidiary reports the following trial balance:

Trial Balance	Dr (Cr)
Cash.	S/ 4,400,000
Equipment, purchased on September 10	2,700,000
Operating expenses.	2,900,000
Capital	(10,000,000)
Total	S/ 0

The subsidiary reports no depreciation on the equipment in 2014. The exchange rate was $0.33/S/ on December 31, 2014, and averaged $0.31/S/ during the period from September 10 to December 31, 2014. Other than the equipment purchase, all other payments occurred evenly over the period.

Required

a. Assuming the functional currency of the sales subsidiary is the U.S. dollar, prepare a schedule to compute the remeasurement gain or loss in 2014.
b. Assuming the functional currency of the subsidiary is the new sol, prepare a schedule to compute the translation gain or loss in 2014.
c. For each functional currency alternative, give the entry or entries made by Globe at year-end, assuming Globe uses the complete equity method to report its investment in the sales subsidiary.
d. Globe's trial balance at December 31, 2014, before year-end adjustments for its investment in the Lima subsidiary, is below. Prepare a working paper to consolidate the subsidiary, for each functional currency alternative.

	Dr (Cr)
Cash.	$ 500,000
Property, plant and equipment, net.	22,000,000
Investment in subsidiary.	3,000,000
Liabilities.	(16,000,000)
Capital	(5,000,000)
Retained earnings, January 1.	(2,000,000)
Revenues.	(15,000,000)
Expenses	12,500,000
Total.	$ 0

E7.3 Translation and Remeasurement of Account Balances U.S. Industries has a subsidiary in Switzerland. The subsidiary's financial statements are maintained in Swiss francs (CHF). Exchange rates ($/CHF) for selected dates are as follows:

LO 1

January 1, 2012	$0.85	January 1, 2014	$0.78
January 1, 2013	0.80	December 31, 2014	0.75
		Average for 2014	0.76

The following items appear in the subsidiary's trial balance at December 31, 2014:

1. Cash in bank, CHF4,000,000.
2. Inventory on LIFO basis, CHF3,000,000. The inventory cost consists of CHF1,000,000 acquired in January 2012 and CHF2,000,000 acquired in January 2014.
3. Machinery and equipment, CHF11,000,000. A review of the records indicates that the company bought equipment costing CHF5,000,000 in January 2012 (20 percent of this was sold in January 2014) and additional equipment costing CHF7,000,000 in January 2013. Ignore accumulated depreciation.
4. Depreciation expense on machinery and equipment, CHF1,100,000 (depreciated over ten years, straight-line basis).

Required

Calculate the dollar amount for each of the above items, assuming the functional currency of the Swiss subsidiary is (a) the U.S. dollar and (b) the Swiss franc.

E7.4 Translation and Remeasurement Gain and Loss Asda is a British supermarket chain owned by Wal-Mart Stores, Inc., and headquartered in Leeds, West Yorkshire, England. Assume that the following data relate to Asda's activities for 2014 *(in millions)*.

LO 1 ✓

ASDA
WAL-MART
STORES, INC.
[WMT]

Net assets (liabilities) reported at fair value, January 1, 2014	£ 700
Acquisition of plant assets for debt, February 15, 2014	1,000
Purchase of inventory made evenly during 2014.	3,500
Collection of receivables outstanding at January 1, 2014.	2,700
Sales made evenly during 2014.	6,000
Cost of goods sold.	3,300
Depreciation of assets acquired when the exchange rate was $1.80/£	400
Current operating expenses (excluding depreciation and amortization), incurred evenly during 2014.	1,200
Refinancing or "rollover" of commercial paper	800

Exchange rates ($/£) during 2014 are:

January 1, 2014	$1.90	Average for 2014	$1.97
February 15, 2014	1.95	December 31, 2014	2.01

Required

a. Assuming Asda's functional currency is the U.S. dollar, prepare a schedule to compute the remeasurement gain or loss during 2014.
b. Assuming Asda's functional currency is the pound, prepare a schedule to compute the translation gain or loss for 2014. Assume net assets on January 1, 2014, amounted to £1,200 million.

LO 1 **E7.5** **Translation and Remeasurement Gains and Losses** The following transactions were recorded by Larson Company's subsidiary in Finland during 2014. The exchange rate at January 1, 2014, was $1.13/€; at December 31, 2014, it was $1.10/€.

	€	$/€
Purchase of inventory.	€8,000,000	$1.10
Proceeds from sale of land	1,000,000	1.11
Book value of land sold	700,000	1.15[1]
Sales.	10,000,000	1.12[2]
Cost of sales.	6,000,000	1.16[1]
Cash operating expenses.	1,800,000	1.12[2]
Issue of bonds payable for cash	2,000,000	1.14
Amortization of prepayments.	200,000	1.13[1]

[1] Exchange rates when assets sold or amortized were acquired by the Finnish subsidiary.
[2] The weighted average exchange rate during 2014.

Required

a. Assuming the functional currency of the subsidiary is the U.S. dollar, prepare a schedule to compute the 2014 remeasurement gain or loss. Net assets (liabilities) reported at fair value (current money prices) amounted to (€12,000,000) at January 1, 2014.
b. Assuming the functional currency of the subsidiary is the euro, prepare a schedule to compute the translation gain or loss for 2014. Net assets were €9,000,000 at January 1, 2014.

LO 2 **E7.6** **Effect of Translation and Remeasurement on Ratios** The following data relate to the Bainbridge Company's South African subsidiary, which maintains its records in the South African Rand (R), its local currency.

		Translated amounts in $ when functional currency is	
	R	**$**	**R**
Sales.	R5,000,000	$ 750,000	$ 750,000
Operating income.	1,000,000	130,000	150,000
Average total assets.	8,000,000	2,000,000	1,400,000

Required

a. Using the "DuPont Analysis," compute and disaggregate the subsidiary's return on assets into its return on sales and total asset turnover components under the three alternatives shown.

b. Explain whether the exchange rate ($/R) has been increasing or decreasing and how that change might affect the usefulness of these ratios. Assume that remeasured operating income does not include the remeasurement gain or loss.

E7.7 Remeasured Financial Statements   On January 2, 2013, Maddox Corporation, headquartered in the U.S., established a wholly-owned subsidiary in Mexico City. An initial investment of $1,000,000 was made on that date; the exchange rate was $0.10/peso. During 2013, the following cash transactions occurred at the Mexico City subsidiary. All amounts are in pesos (P).   **LO 1**

Legal expenses of organizing the subsidiary (January 2; 5-year life).................	P 300,000
Purchase of office equipment (April 1; 10-year life)................................	1,000,000
Sales..	12,000,000
Merchandise purchases...	9,000,000
Operating expenses..	3,000,000

The exchange rate was $0.11/P in April when the office equipment and P2,000,000 of merchandise were purchased. Sales, other merchandise purchases, and operating expenses were assumed to have been made or incurred at an average exchange rate of $0.12/P. At year-end, the exchange rate was $0.15/P and the ending inventory (LIFO) amounted to P2,000,000. All depreciation and amortization is straight-line.

Required

Prepare the balance sheet and income statement for the Mexico City subsidiary as of December 31, 2013, in dollars, the subsidiary's functional currency. Show all calculations.

E7.8 Change in Functional Currency   Oliver Corporation decided on January 1, 2014, that its Canadian subsidiary's functional currency is the Canadian dollar rather than the U.S. dollar. On that date, the net assets of its Canadian subsidiary amounted to C$20,000,000 and to $15,000,000 when remeasured; the exchange rate was $1.05/C$. During 2014, the Canadian subsidiary reported net income of $C2,500,000 and paid dividends of $C1,000,000. No other changes in owners' equity occurred.   **LO 1**

Required

Prepare an analysis of the cumulative translation gain or loss for 2014. Relevant exchange rates were $1.03/$C (average); $1.02/$C (dividend declaration date); $1.01/$C (December 31, 2014).

E7.9 Translated/Remeasured Financial Statements   The Thode Company established a wholly-owned subsidiary in Saudi Arabia on January 1, 2013, when the exchange rate was $0.30/riyal (SAR). Of Thode's initial $60,000,000 investment, $30,000,000 was used to acquire plant assets (ten-year life) and $15,000,000 was used to acquire inventory. The remaining amount was initially held as cash by the subsidiary.   **LO 1** ⊘

During 2013, the subsidiary reported net income of SAR20,000,000. Inventory purchases of SAR15,000,000 were made evenly during the year. It paid dividends of SAR10,000,000 on September 30, when the exchange rate was $0.255/SAR. No other transactions occurred between the subsidiary and the parent. The subsidiary's condensed income statement appears below:

Sales...	SAR85,000,000
Cost of goods sold..	(40,000,000)[1]
Depreciation expense.......................................	(10,000,000)[2]
Other cash expenses..	(15,000,000)
Net income..	SAR20,000,000

[1] Assume a FIFO inventory flow assumption.
[2] Relates solely to plant assets acquired on January 1, 2013.

The average rate during the year was $0.265/SAR. On the balance sheet date, it was $0.25/SAR.

Required

a. Assuming the functional currency is the riyal, translate the subsidiary's 2013 income statement and December 31, 2013, balance sheet into dollars and prepare an analysis of the subsidiary's translation gain or loss for 2013.

b. Repeat the requirements of part *a*, assuming the subsidiary's functional currency is the U.S. dollar.

LO 2   **E7.10 Exchange Rate Changes and Return on Assets**   Murdock Company has a Spanish subsidiary whose functional currency is the euro. Relevant translated data for the subsidiary appear below.

Date or Annual Period	Total Assets	Operating Income	Exchange Rate
January 1, 2014	$112,000,000	—	$1.40/€
2014	—	$12,000,000	1.20/€[1]
December 31, 2014	95,000,000	—	1.00/€
2015	—	10,890,000	0.90/€[1]
December 31, 2015	95,000,000	—	1.00/€

[1] Average rate

Required

a.   Calculate return on assets for 2014 and 2015 using both translated ($) and euro data.
b.   Explain whether translation has distorted the Spanish subsidiary's performance in 2015 compared with 2014. If so, explain how changes in the exchange rate contributed to the distortion.

LO 2   **E7.11 Comparison of Translation and Remeasurement**   **Sears Holdings Corporation** has a subsidiary in Canada. Assume that **Sears Canada Inc.** has a positive equity balance, and its assets carried at fair value exceed its debt. Assume the U.S. dollar has steadily weakened against the Canadian dollar in the past few years.

SEARS HOLDING CORPORATION
[SHLD]

SEARS CANADA
[SCC]

Required

a.   Is Sears Canada's remeasured net income greater than or less than its translated net income? Give reasons for your answer. How would your answer change if the subsidiary's debt exceeded its assets carried at fair value?
b.   How does Sears Canada's remeasured return on assets compare with its translated return on assets? Why?
c.   Repeat part *b* for the subsidiary's current ratio and debt to assets ratio.

LO 1   **E7.12 Cash Flow Statement Conversion**   The Luh Company's 2014 cash flow statement appears below, in its functional currency, New Taiwan dollars (NT$).

THE LUH COMPANY Statement of Cash Flows For Year Ended December 31, 2014 *(in thousands)*	
Operating Activities	
Net income..	NT$100,000
Depreciation and amortization expense...........................	45,000
Gain on sale of long-term investments............................	(4,000)
Decrease in other current operating assets......................	24,000
Decrease in current operating liabilities.........................	(32,000)
Cash provided by operating activities	133,000
Investing Activities	
Acquisition of plant assets.......................................	(85,000)
Sale of long-term investments....................................	50,000
Cash used in investing activities................................	(35,000)
Financing Activities	
Retirement of long-term debt....................................	(98,000)
Issuance of common stock	170,000
Dividends paid	(65,000)
Cash provided by financing activities...........................	7,000
Increase in cash	105,000
Cash balance, January 1, 2014	210,000
Cash balance, December 31, 2014	NT$315,000

Additional information:

1. Exchange rates: January 1, 2014: $0.042/NT$; December 31, 2014: $0.039/NT$; 2014 average: $0.04/NT$.
2. Changes in current operating assets and liabilities and dividend payments occurred at the average rate.
3. Common stock was issued and plant assets were acquired when the rate was $0.0423/NT$.
4. The long-term investments were sold and the long-term debt was retired when the rate was $0.0394/NT$.

Required

Convert the above statement of cash flows into dollars. Include a computation of the effect of exchange rate changes on cash.

E7.13 Consolidation of an International Subsidiary at Date of Acquisition   Fairview Corporation, a U.S. company, has a wholly-owned subsidiary in Mexico. The subsidiary's functional currency is the Mexican peso, and translation to U.S. dollars is appropriate. The subsidiary was acquired on January 2, 2014, for $18,000,000. The balance sheet of the subsidiary on the date of acquisition is as follows:

Mexican Subsidiary Balance Sheet at January 2, 2014	
Assets	
Cash and receivables.	P 15,000,000
Inventories	35,000,000
Noncurrent assets, net.	75,000,000
Total assets	P125,000,000
Liabilities and stockholders' equity	
Liabilities.	P 25,000,000
Capital stock	80,000,000
Retained earnings	20,000,000
Total liabilities and stockholders' equity	P125,000,000

The fair values of the subsidiary's inventories are P50,000,000, and the fair values of the subsidiary's noncurrent assets are P70,000,000. All other amounts are reported at approximate fair value. The exchange rate on January 2, 2014, is $0.10/peso.

Required

Present a schedule showing the calculation of goodwill for the acquisition, in U.S. dollars, and the entries necessary to consolidate the balance sheets of Fairview and its subsidiary on January 2, 2014.

PROBLEMS ●

P7.1 Translating and Remeasuring Selected Accounts   On January 2, 2012, the Franklin Company   LO 1 formed a Swiss subsidiary, TEurope AG. The subsidiary issued all of its currently outstanding common stock on that date. Selected accounts from its balance sheets on December 31, 2012 and 2013, all of which are shown in Swiss francs (CHF), are as follows:

(in millions)	December 31	
	2013	**2012**
Accounts receivable, net	CHF 40,000	CHF 35,000
Inventories, at cost.	80,000	75,000
Property, plant and equipment, net of accumulated depreciation of CHF31,000 at December 31, 2013 and CHF14,000 at December 31, 2012	163,000	150,000
Long-term debt	100,000	120,000
Common stock, 10,000 shares authorized, issued and outstanding 5,000 shares at December 31, 2013 and December 31, 2012	50,000	50,000

Additional information:

1. Exchange rates are as follows:

	$/CHF
January 1, 2012 – July 31, 2012.	0.50
August 1, 2012 – October 31, 2012.	0.55
November 1, 2012 – June 30, 2013.	0.58
July 1, 2013 – December 31, 2013.	0.67
Average rate for 2012.	0.53
Average rate for 2013.	0.63

2. An analysis of inventories, for which the FIFO inventory method is used, is as follows:

	2013	2012
Inventory at beginning of year	CHF 75,000	—
Purchases (June 2013 and June 2012)	335,000	CHF375,000
Goods available for sale.	410,000	375,000
Inventory at end of year	(80,000)	(75,000)
Cost of goods sold.	CHF330,000	CHF300,000

3. On January 2, 2012, Europe purchased land for CHF24,000 and plant and equipment for CHF140,000. On July 4, 2013, additional equipment was purchased for CHF30,000. Plant and equipment is depreciated on a straight-line basis over a ten-year period with no salvage value. A full year's depreciation is taken in the year of purchase.

Required

a. Prepare a schedule remeasuring the selected accounts above into dollars (the functional currency) at December 31, 2013, and December 31, 2012, respectively. Show supporting computations in good form.

b. Prepare a schedule translating the selected accounts above into dollars at December 31, 2013, and December 31, 2012, assuming the Swiss franc is the functional currency.

LO 1 **P7.2** **Existing Subsidiary—Remeasurement** Domestic Corporation, a U.S. firm, acquired Valiant AB on January 1, 2013. Valiant is a Swedish company that has been in existence for several years, and whose functional currency is the U.S. dollar. Comparative account balances for January 1 and December 31, 2013, appear below, measured in krona (kr), the Swedish currency.

	Dr (Cr)	
Account Balances	**January 1**	**December 31**
Cash.	kr 175,000	kr 240,000
Accounts receivable, net	400,000	360,000
Plant and equipment, net.	2,320,000	2,000,000
Accounts payable.	(535,000)	(200,000)
Notes payable	(800,000)	(600,000)
Capital stock	(400,000)	(400,000)
Retained earnings, January 1.	(1,160,000)	(1,160,000)
Sales.	—	(1,200,000)
Depreciation expense.	—	320,000
Other expenses	—	640,000
Totals.	kr 0	kr 0

Exchange rates in 2013 were:

Date	$/kr
January 1, 2013	$0.16
Average for 2013	0.17
December 31, 2013	0.19

Required
a. Remeasure Valiant's 2013 beginning and ending trial balances into dollars.
b. Prepare a remeasured income statement and balance sheet for Valiant, plus a schedule calculating the 2013 remeasurement gain or loss.

P7.3 Existing Subsidiary—Translation   Refer to the information in problem P7.2.   LO 1

Required
Repeat the requirements of problem P7.2, assuming the krona (kr) is the functional currency of the subsidiary. As part of part *b*, prepare a schedule calculating the 2013 translation adjustment and the December 31, 2013, balance for accumulated other comprehensive income.

P7.4 Translation and Performance Evaluation   Management compensation is often based on reported   LO 2
profits. What profit measurement is appropriate for top management to use in judging the performance of a U.S. company's international subsidiary? Consider a Finnish subsidiary that reported the following results in euros for 2015 and 2014.

(in thousands)	2015	2014
Sales.	€2,400	€2,000
Cost of sales.	1,320	1,200
Gross margin	1,080	800
Other operating expenses	230	200
Profit before taxes	850	600
Income tax expense.	255	180
Net income.	€ 595	€ 420

Average exchange rate: $1.35/€ for 2015, $1.45/€ for 2014. Composite historical rates relating to cost of sales and other operating expenses (including depreciation): $1.37/€ for 2015, $1.48/€ for 2014.

Required
a. Prepare a schedule showing the Finnish subsidiary's income statement for 2014 and 2015 in euros and in dollars, assuming the subsidiary's functional currency is the euro. Compute the percentage change in income in each case.
b. Repeat the requirements of *a*. assuming the subsidiary's functional currency is the dollar.
c. Comment on the comparability of the income statements in *a*. and *b*., focusing on the impact of the change in dollar value of the euro. How could you adjust the translated and remeasured statements to enhance comparability? Show computations and comment on the results.

P7.5 Translation and Ratio Analysis   Suppose that on January 1, 2014, **La-Z-Boy Inc.** established a sub-   LO 1, 2
sidiary in Ireland, La-Z-Boy Ireland, to design, manufacture and distribute specialized furniture in the European market. Its condensed balance sheet at January 1, 2014, in euros, is below *(in thousands)*.   **LA-Z-BOY INC.**
[LZB]

Assets		Liabilities and equity	
Cash.	€100,000	Liabilities.	€200,000
Plant assets, net.	300,000	Capital stock	200,000
Total assets	€400,000	Total liabilities and equity.	€400,000

At December 31, 2014, La-Z-Boy Ireland reported the following condensed trial balance:

	Dr (Cr)
Cash...	€ 10,000
Merchandise inventory..	200,000
Plant assets, net...	250,000
Liabilities..	(220,000)
Capital stock	(200,000)
Sales...	(500,000)
Cost of sales..	320,000
Operating expenses...	140,000
Total	€ 0

No dividends were declared or paid. Relevant exchange rates are as follows:

	$/€
January 2, 2014	$1.50
Average for 2014	1.30
December 31, 2014	1.10

Required

a. Prepare a translated income statement and balance sheet for La-Z-Boy Ireland as of December 31, 2014, assuming the subsidiary's functional currency is the euro. Include an analysis of the 2014 translation adjustment.

b. Assume that operating expenses include €50,000 of depreciation on the original plant assets, the merchandise inventory on hand at December 31 was acquired when the exchange rate was $1.15, and merchandise purchases and cash operating expenses were incurred evenly during 2014. Repeat the requirements of part *a*, assuming the subsidiary's functional currency is the U.S. dollar. Include a separate calculation of the remeasurement gain or loss for the year.

c. Compute the ratios of net income/sales and net income/total assets at December 31, 2014, using the euro financial statements and the translated and remeasured financial statements. Comment on the results.

d. Suppose the euro continues to weaken ($/€ continues to decline) in subsequent years. What will happen to the ratios computed in part *c*? Do the signals they provide indicate improving or deteriorating performance? Should La-Z-Boy's management use the ratios as justification for additional investments in La-Z-Boy Ireland?

 **P7.6 Translation and Remeasurement of Financial Statements** Loring Company owns a subsidiary in Switzerland. The subsidiary was acquired on January 1, 2013. Subsidiary trial balances for January 1 and December 31, 2013, in Swiss francs (CHF) appear below.

	Dr (Cr)	
(in thousands)	**January 1**	**December 31**
Cash and receivables...........................	CHF 25,000	CHF 30,000
Inventories	60,000	55,000
Plant and equipment, net.......................	150,000	175,000
Accounts and notes payable	(125,000)	(120,000)
Common stock.................................	(30,000)	(30,000)
Retained earnings, January 1...................	(80,000)	(80,000)
Sales..	—	(500,000)
Cost of sales..................................	—	375,000
Operating expenses............................	—	75,000
Dividends.....................................	—	20,000
Totals	CHF 0	CHF 0

Additional information:

1. Included in operating expenses is depreciation expense of CHF5,000.
2. Plant and equipment of CHF30,000 was purchased for cash during 2013, when the exchange rate was $0.50. Depreciation of CHF2,000 was taken on this purchase during 2013.
3. The ending inventory was purchased during the month of December.
4. Revenues, purchases, and operating expenses other than depreciation occurred evenly during the year.
5. Dividends were declared and paid on December 31, 2013.
6. Exchange rates for 2013 were as follows ($/CHF):

January 1, 2013	$0.49
Average for 2013	0.52
Average for December, 2013	0.54
December 31, 2013	0.55

Required

a. Assume the functional currency of the subsidiary is the dollar. Prepare remeasured financial statements for the subsidiary, including a schedule showing the computation of the remeasurement gain or loss for 2013.
b. Repeat the requirements of part *a*, assuming the functional currency of the subsidiary is the Swiss franc.

P7.7 **Converting the Cash Flow Statement** Comparative balance sheets and the intervening statement of income and retained earnings for **Sears Canada Inc.** appear below. Sears Canada is a subsidiary of Sears Holdings Corporation, a U.S. corporation. All amounts are in Canadian dollars.

LO 1

SEARS CANADA
[SCC]

SEARS CANADA INC. Comparative Balance Sheets		
(in millions)	**January 29, 2011** **C$**	**January 30, 2010** **C$**
Assets		
Cash	426	1,382
Other current operating assets.	1,209	1,110
Plant assets, net.	875	913
Total assets	2,510	3,405
Liabilities and equity		
Accounts payable and accruals	957	1,304
Income taxes payable	67	73
Long-term debt	485	370
Total liabilities.	1,509	1,747
Capital stock	15	15
Retained earnings	986	1,643
Accumulated other comprehensive income.	—	—
Total stockholders' equity	1,001	1,658
Total liabilities and stockholders' equity	2,510	3,405

SEARS CANADA INC. Statement of Income and Retained Earnings For Year Ended January 29, 2011	
	C$
Sales...	4,958
Cost of goods sold..............................	(3,800)
Operating expenses.............................	(833)
Depreciation expense...........................	(105)
Income tax expense.............................	(70)
Net income.....................................	150
Retained earnings, January 30, 2010.............	1,643
Dividends paid..................................	(807)
Retained earnings, January 29, 2011.............	986

Exchange rates (U.S.$/C$) are as follows:

January 30, 2010	$0.94
Average, January 30, 2010 to January 29, 2011	$0.97
January 29, 2011	$1.02

Required

a. Prepare a statement of cash flows (indirect format) in Canadian dollars and U.S. dollars for the year ended January 29, 2011, and a computation of the effect of exchange rate changes on cash. Assume all investing and financing activities took place evenly throughout the year and that Sears Canada's functional currency is the Canadian dollar.

b. Prepare a schedule computing the January 29, 2011, cumulative translation adjustment balance (the only component of AOCI), including computation of the translation adjustment for the year ended January 29, 2011. Assume that the beginning balance in AOCI was a gain of $60.

c. How would the converted cash flow statement differ if Sears Canada's functional currency was the U.S. dollar? Explain.

LO 1, 2 **P7.8** **Analysis of Translation Adjustment Disclosure** **Asiamart, Inc.** was a U.S. company that operated shopping centers in Hong Kong. The shopping centers offered discounted international brands, to
ASIAMART, INC. Chinese tourists brought to the shopping centers by travel companies and tour operators. Asiamart had five
[AAMAE] wholly-owned subsidiaries in Hong Kong. Asiamart's 2008 annual report includes the following excerpt
from the Consolidated Statement of Changes in Shareholders' Equity.

ASIAMART, INC AND SUBSIDIARIES Consolidated Statement of Changes in Stockholders' Equity For Years Ended December 31, 2008, 2007, and 2006	
(Currency expressed in United States Dollars)	**Accumulated Other Comprehensive Income**
Balance, December 31, 2005.........................	$18,611
2006 foreign currency translation adjustment	28,947
Balance, December 31, 2006.........................	47,558
2007 foreign currency translation adjustment	18,563
Balance, December 31, 2007.........................	66,121
2008 foreign currency translation adjustment	(4,374)
Balance, December 31, 2008.........................	$61,747

Required

a. Is the Hong Kong dollar or the U.S. dollar the functional currency of Asiamart's subsidiaries? Explain your answer.

b. For each of the years 2006, 2007, and 2008, on average was the U.S. dollar strengthening or weakening with respect to the Hong Kong dollar? How do you know?

c. Prior to 2006, on average was the U.S. dollar strengthening or weakening with respect to the Hong Kong dollar? How do you know?

d. If Asiamart had used the alternative approach allowed under U.S. GAAP to report the operations of its Hong Kong subsidiaries, would Asiamart's 2008 net income have been higher or lower than income reported in Hong Kong dollars? Clearly state your reasoning and any assumptions made.

P7.9 Translated/Remeasured Trial Balances   On January 1, 2013, the U.K. subsidiary of U.S. International Corporation had the following condensed balance sheet, in pounds sterling (*in millions*):

LO 1

Assets		Liabilities and equity	
Cash and receivables............	£2,000	Accounts payable..............	£2,100
Inventory (LIFO)	2,200	Long-term debt	1,200
Plant assets	1,600	Equity.......................	2,100
Accumulated depreciation	(400)		
Total assets	£5,400	Total liabilities and equity........	£5,400

The exchange rate on January 1, 2013, was $2/£. Inventory and plant assets at January 1 were acquired when the exchange rate was $1.80/£. Plant assets costing £200 million were purchased when the exchange rate was $2.15/£. No depreciation was taken on these assets in 2013, and no transactions between the parent and the subsidiary occurred during 2013. At the end of 2013, the subsidiary reported the following trial balance:

(in millions)	Dr (Cr)
Cash and receivables..	£2,660
Inventory (LIFO)	2,500
Plant assets	1,800
Accumulated depreciation	(560)
Accounts payable...	(2,200)
Long-term debt	(1,100)
Equity, January 1	(2,100)
Sales...	(4,000)
Cost of goods sold..	2,000
Depreciation expense..	160
Other operating expenses	840
Total...	£ 0

The exchange rate when the new LIFO layer arose was $2.05/£ and the subsidiary purchased merchandise sold at an average exchange rate of $2.12/£. Sales and other operating expenses occurred evenly over the year. At year-end, the exchange rate was $2.20/£; the average for the year was $2.10/£.

Required

a. Prepare the remeasured December 31, 2013, trial balance of the U.K. subsidiary, assuming the dollar is the functional currency of the subsidiary. Assume the remeasured balance of equity on January 1, 2013, was $3,520 million. Prepare a schedule to calculate the remeasurement gain or loss.

b. Repeat part *a*, assuming the pound is the functional currency of the subsidiary. Assume the translated balance of equity on January 1, 2013, is $4,200 million. Prepare a schedule to calculate the translation gain or loss.

P7.10 Translating and Remeasuring Financial Statements   The SA Company was organized in Mexico on January 1, 2014, with a capital stock issue that yielded 1,000,000 pesos (P). The exchange rate was $0.10/P. Transactions for 2014 and the relevant exchange rates are shown below. The average exchange rate for 2014 was $0.12/P.

LO 1

Date	Transaction	Exchange rate
January 5	Bought 2,000 wood carvings at P200 each. Purchased office equipment (ten-year life) for P200,000.	$0.10/P
June 30.	Sold 1,000 carvings for P300,000. Bought 1,500 carvings for P360,000. Paid rent of P30,000.	0.12/P
December 31	Recorded straight-line depreciation on office equipment. Closed books and prepared financial statements.	0.15/P

Required

Prepare the SA Company's balance sheet and income statement in U.S. dollars, assuming SA Company's functional currency is (*a*) the U.S. dollar, and (*b*) the peso. Show the calculation of the remeasurement/translation gain or loss. Assume FIFO for inventory.

LO 3 **P7.11 Consolidated Financial Statements with an International Subsidiary** On January 1, 2014, the Phillips Company acquired all of the outstanding shares of Standard, Ltd., a U.K. firm, for £8,000,000 in cash. At the end of 2014, the two companies presented the condensed financial statements below.

Balance Sheets December 31, 2014		
	Phillips	**Standard**
Assets		
Cash and receivables.	$ 2,100,000	£ 3,000,000
Inventory.	4,000,000	3,000,000
Property, plant and equipment, net	12,000,000	5,000,000
Investment in Standard	13,900,000	—
Total assets	$32,000,000	£11,000,000
Liabilities and Stockholders' Equity		
Current liabilities.	$ 8,000,000	£ 4,000,000
Long-term debt	4,000,000	1,000,000
Capital stock	10,000,000	2,000,000
Retained earnings	10,000,000	4,000,000
Total liabilities and stockholders' equity	$32,000,000	£11,000,000

Statements of Income and Retained Earnings For Year Ended December 31, 2014		
	Phillips	**Standard**
Sales.	$30,000,000	£10,000,000
Cost of goods sold.	20,000,000	6,000,000
Depreciation.	1,000,000	500,000
Other operating expenses	5,000,000	2,000,000
Total expenses.	26,000,000	8,500,000
Net income.	4,000,000	1,500,000
Dividends	(2,000,000)	(1,000,000)
Retained earnings, beginning.	8,000,000	3,500,000
Retained earnings, ending	$10,000,000	£ 4,000,000

At date of acquisition, the exchange rate was $2/£. Standard's inventory and buildings were undervalued by £100,000 and £500,000, respectively. All of the undervalued inventory was sold during the year, and the buildings are depreciated over a 20-year life, straight-line. Other relevant information is as follows:

1. The exchange rate at the end of 2014 was $2.30/£. The average exchange rate for 2014 was $2.15/£.
2. Goodwill impairment during 2014 was £200,000.
3. Phillips reports its Investment in Standard using the complete equity method. However, neither the equity method income accrual nor Phillips' share of the translation gain for 2014 have been booked. Intercompany dividends, paid when the exchange rate was $2.10/£, were credited to the investment account.

Required

Assuming the pound is Standard's functional currency, prepare a consolidated balance sheet and a consolidated statement of income and retained earnings for Phillips and Standard. All supporting schedules and computations should be in good form.

P7.12 Hyperinflationary Economy, U.S. GAAP and IFRS   A subsidiary of a U.S. company began   LO 1, 4 operations on January 1, 2014, in a country whose currency is identified as hyperinflationary. The subsidiary's local currency (LC) is its functional currency. The subsidiary's trial balances as of the beginning and end of 2014, in LC, are as follows *(in millions)*:

	January 1, 2014 Dr (Cr)	December 31, 2014 Dr (Cr)
Cash..	10,000	125,000
Plant assets, net..............................	40,000	35,000
Liabilities......................................	—	(50,000)
Capital stock	(50,000)	(50,000)
Sales revenue.................................	—	(200,000)
Out of pocket operating expenses..................	—	135,000
Depreciation expense..........................	—	5,000
	0	0

Sales and out of pocket operating expenses were incurred evenly throughout the year.

The general price-level index for the country in which the subsidiary operates is:

Date	Price-level index
January 1, 2014	100
2014 average	400
December 31, 2014	600

Exchange rates (U.S. $/LC) are:

Date	Exchange rate
January 1, 2014	$0.65
2014 average	0.15
December 31, 2014	0.10

Required

Present the subsidiary's balance sheet at December 31, 2014 and income statement for 2014, in U.S. dollars, following *(a)* U.S. GAAP, and *(b)* IFRS. Include schedules of any gain or loss on conversion.

REVIEW SOLUTIONS

Review 1 Solution

a. Schedule of translation gain or loss

	C$	rate	$
Beginning exposed position..............	C$411,200	$1.05	$431,760
Change in exposed position:			
Net income	24,800	0.98	24,304
			456,064
Ending exposed position	C$436,000	0.93	−405,480
Translation loss (OCI)...................			$ 50,584

b. Schedule of remeasurement gain or loss

	C$	rate	$
Beginning exposed position..............	C$411,200	$1.05	$431,760
Change in exposed position:			
Sales................................	404,000	0.98	395,920
Purchases...........................	(375,500)	0.98	(367,990)
Other expenses......................	(18,700)	0.98	(18,326)
Equipment purchase..................	(369,500)	1.03	(380,585)
			60,779
Ending exposed position	C$ 51,500	0.93	−47,895
Remeasurement loss (earnings).............			$ 12,884

Review 2 Solution

a. Schedule of translation gain or loss

	€	rate	$
Beginning exposed position..............	€200,000	$1.40	$280,000
Change in exposed position:			
Net income	30,000	1.50	45,000
Dividends	(10,000)	1.52	(15,200)
			309,800
Ending exposed position	€220,000	1.55	−341,000
Translation gain (OCI)...................			$ (31,200)

Income Statement for 2015

	€	rate	$
Sales revenue..........................	€2,000,000	$1.50	$3,000,000
Cost of goods sold......................	(1,150,000)	1.50	(1,725,000)
Out of pocket operating expenses............	(650,000)	1.50	(975,000)
Depreciation expense....................	(170,000)	1.50	(255,000)
Net income............................	30,000		45,000
Retained earnings, January 1...............	0	given	0
Dividends	(10,000)	1.52	(15,200)
Retained earnings, December 31.............	€ 20,000		$ 29,800

Balance Sheet, December 31, 2015

	€	rate	$
Cash and receivables.	€ 20,000	$1.55	$ 31,000
Inventories	90,000	1.55	139,500
Noncurrent assets, net.	530,000	1.55	821,500
Total assets	€640,000		$ 992,000
Liabilities.	€420,000	$1.55	$ 651,000
Capital stock	200,000	1.40	280,000
Retained earnings	20,000	See income stmt.	29,800
Accumulated other comprehensive income. . .	—	See schedule	31,200
Total liabilities and equity.	€640,000		$ 992,000

b. Schedule of remeasurement gain or loss

	€	rate	$
Beginning exposed position.	€ (540,000)	$1.40	$ (756,000)
Change in exposed position:			
Sales revenue	2,000,000	1.50	3,000,000
Purchases.	(1,200,000)	1.50	(1,800,000)
Out of pocket operating expenses	(650,000)	1.50	(975,000)
Dividends	(10,000)	1.52	(15,200)
			(546,200)
Ending exposed position	€ (400,000)	1.55	−(620,000)
Remeasurement loss (earnings).			$ 73,800

Income Statement for 2015

	€	rate	$
Sales revenue.	€2,000,000	$1.50	$3,000,000
Cost of goods sold.	(1,150,000)	See schedule	(1,716,500)
Out of pocket operating expenses.	(650,000)	1.50	(975,000)
Depreciation expense.	(170,000)	1.40	(238,000)
Remeasurement loss		See schedule	(73,800)
Net gain (loss).	€ 30,000		$ (3,300)
Retained earnings, 1/1	0	given	0
Dividends	(10,000)	1.52	(15,200)
Retained earnings, 12/31	€ 20,000		$ (18,500)

Calculation of cost of goods sold

	€	rate	$
Beginning inventory	€ 40,000	$1.40	$ 56,000
Purchases.	1,200,000	1.50	1,800,000
Ending inventory.	(90,000)	1.55	(139,500)
Cost of goods sold.	€1,150,000		$1,716,500

Balance Sheet, December 31, 2015

	€	rate	$
Cash and receivables....................	€ 20,000	$1.55	$ 31,000
Inventories	90,000	1.55	139,500
Noncurrent assets, net..................	530,000	1.40	742,000
Total assets	€640,000		$912,500
Liabilities.............................	€420,000	$1.55	$651,000
Capital stock	200,000	1.40	280,000
Retained earnings	20,000	See income stmt.	(18,500)
Total liabilities and equity..............	€640,000		$912,500

Review 3 Solution

a. Trial balance, December 31, 2014

	€	Rate	$
Current assets	€ 1,500,000	$1.30	$ 1,950,000
Plant and equipment, net.................	50,000,000	1.30	65,000,000
Liabilities.............................	(48,300,000)	1.30	(62,790,000)
Capital stock	(1,000,000)	1.40	(1,400,000)
Retained earnings, January 1..............	(2,000,000)	1.40	(2,800,000)
Accumulated other comprehensive income.....	—	See schedule	312,000
Sales revenue.........................	(25,000,000)	1.36	(34,000,000)
Cost of goods sold......................	12,000,000	1.36	16,320,000
Operating expenses.....................	12,800,000	1.36	17,408,000
Totals	€ 0		$ 0

Schedule of translation gain or loss

	€	rate	$
Beginning exposed position................	€3,000,000	$1.40	$4,200,000
Change in exposed position:			
Net income	200,000	1.36	272,000
			4,472,000
Ending exposed position	€3,200,000	1.30	−4,160,000
Translation loss			$ 312,000

b.

Investment in Lodl	14,000,000	
Cash		14,000,000
To record the acquisition of Lodl's stock for $14,000,000.		
Investment in Lodl	272,000	
Equity in income of Lodl		272,000
To record Lodl's 2014 income.		
Accumulated other comprehensive income........................	312,000	
Investment in Lodl		312,000
To record Lodl's translation loss.		

The December 31, 2014, Investment balance is $13,960,000 (= $14,000,000 + $272,000 − $312,000).

c. Consolidation eliminating entries are:

(C)	Equity in income of Lodl.....................................	272,000	
	Investment in Lodl.		272,000
(E)	Capital stock...	1,400,000	
	Retained earnings, January 1.................................	2,800,000	
	Accumulated other comprehensive income.................		312,000
	Investment in Lodl		3,888,000
(R)	Goodwill[1]	9,100,000	
	Accumulated other comprehensive income.....................	700,000	
	Investment in Lodl[2]...................................		9,800,000

[1] $9,100,000 = €7,000,000 × $1.30
[2] $9,800,000 = $13,960,000 − $272,000 − $3,888,000.

8 Foreign Currency Transactions and Hedging

LEARNING OBJECTIVES

LO1 Report import and export transactions and borrowing and lending denominated in foreign currency. (p. 306)

LO2 Report hedges of foreign-currency-denominated receivables and payables. (p. 317)

LO3 Report hedges of foreign-currency-denominated firm commitments. (p. 320)

LO4 Report hedges of foreign-currency-denominated forecasted transactions. (p. 325)

LO5 Report hedges of net investments in international operations. (p. 329)

LO6 Report speculative investments in foreign currency financial derivatives. (p. 330)

LO7 Describe IFRS for foreign currency transactions and hedging activities. (p. 332)

MCDONALD'S CORPORATION
www.mcdonalds.com

McDonald's Corporation is well-known for its Big Macs, Chicken McNuggets and Egg McMuffins. At the end of 2010, it had a presence in 117 countries, mainly through franchised restaurants. As a result, McDonald's transacts business in many different currencies. Revenues include sales by company-operated restaurants and rent and royalties paid by franchisees, with more than half coming from Europe, Asia/Pacific, the Middle East, and Africa.

McDonald's is a U.S. company, and it must report its activities in U.S. dollars. But a substantial amount of its revenues and expenses are denominated in other currencies, as described in this excerpt from its 2010 annual report:

> A significant part of the Company's operating income is generated outside the U.S., and about 40% of its total debt is denominated in foreign currencies. Accordingly, earnings are affected by changes in foreign currency exchange rates, particularly the Euro, British Pound, Australian Dollar and Canadian Dollar. Collectively, these currencies represent approximately 65% of the Company's operating income outside the U.S. In 2010, foreign currency translation had a positive impact on consolidated operating results driven by stronger global currencies, primarily the Australian Dollar and Canadian Dollar, partly offset by the weaker Euro.

Foreign currency-denominated transactions also expose McDonald's to financial risk. As exchange rates change, the U.S. dollar values of its foreign currency-denominated revenues, expenses, receivables and payables also change. To reduce foreign currency risk and stabilize U.S. dollar values, McDonald's invests in various financial derivatives.

McDonald's represents one example of the global nature of business activities. The related reporting issues are relevant to virtually all U.S. companies. In this chapter, you learn about the nature of global transactions and related foreign currency risk, how companies manage this risk through investments in financial derivatives, and how companies report these activities in the financial statements. *Source:* McDonald's Corporation annual report 2010.

CHAPTER ORGANIZATION

Foreign currency transactions	Foreign currency risk and hedge investments	IFRS for foreign currency transactions and hedging
• Import and export transactions • Borrowing and lending transactions	• Types of risk and analysis of risk management investments • Reporting derivative investments under *FASB ASC Topic 815* • Hedges of receivables and payables • Hedges of firm commitments • Hedges of forecasted transactions • Hedges of net investments in international operations • Speculative investments • Footnote disclosures	• Criteria for hedge accounting • Differences between IFRS and U.S. GAAP • Footnote disclosures • FASB and IASB hedge accounting projects

FOREIGN CURRENCY TRANSACTIONS AND RISK

This chapter examines transactions between U.S. companies and international suppliers or customers, and ways to manage the resulting foreign exchange risk caused by changes in exchange rates. A U.S. company may be an exporter, selling its products to customers in other countries, or an importer, purchasing products from suppliers in other countries. When payments from international customers to the U.S. exporter are in dollars, we account for the export sale in the same way as domestic sales. Similarly, when the U.S. company pays international suppliers in dollars, the accounting for import purchases is identical to domestic purchases. But when the amount received from a international customer or paid to a international supplier is denominated in a foreign currency, there are new risks and accounting issues involved.

Chapter 7 explains that foreign currencies are traded on both **spot markets** and **forward markets** or **futures markets**. Transactions *involving immediate delivery* of the foreign currency are executed at **spot rates**. Transactions involving delivery of the foreign currency at some *later date* are executed at **forward rates**. Standardized contracts for future delivery trade at **futures rates**.

This chapter addresses issues involved when a U.S. company engages in transactions that are **denominated** (settled) in a foreign currency. When a U.S. exporter sells goods to a customer in Japan, and payment will be received in yen, how should the sale be recorded on the books of the exporter? If the customer is extended credit, and pays the exporter at a later date, how is the dollar equivalent of the sale affected if the foreign exchange rate changes between the time the sale is made and the payment is received in yen?

When a U.S. exporter sells to an international customer on credit, the U.S. company expects to receive the foreign currency at a future date. The U.S. company is exposed to *foreign exchange risk*, because the dollar equivalent of this future cash receipt likely will change due to changes in the foreign exchange rate. Similarly, a U.S. importer may purchase goods from an international supplier on credit. The U.S. importer is exposed to foreign exchange risk because the dollar equivalent of this future cash payment varies as the foreign exchange rate changes.

Changing exchange rates can be an advantage or a disadvantage. The dollar equivalent of foreign currency received from a customer or paid to a supplier may either increase or decrease. The U.S. importer or exporter can utilize financial instruments designed to *neutralize* the risks caused by changing exchange rates. Subsequent sections of this chapter discuss the accounting for import purchases and export sales, and the accounting for investments that neutralize, or **hedge**, foreign exchange risk.

Financial risk due to changing exchange rates can significantly impact the stability of a multinational company's financial results. Exhibit 8.1 shows how the value of the U.S. dollar changed in relation to other currencies in recent years. The numbers indicate how many U.S. dollars were needed to purchase one unit of foreign currency for immediate delivery (spot rates). When *more* U.S. dollars are required to buy one unit of foreign currency, the U.S. dollar is said to have **weakened** with respect to that currency. When *fewer* U.S. dollars are required, the U.S. dollar **strengthens**. Thus, in 2010, the dollar strengthened with respect to the euro, and weakened with respect to the Canadian dollar and the Brazilian real. In 2009, the dollar weakened against all three currencies, and in 2008 it strengthened against all three currencies.

EXHIBIT 8.1 Foreign exchange rates (U.S. dollars per unit of foreign currency)							
December 31	**2004**	**2005**	**2006**	**2007**	**2008**	**2009**	**2010**
$ price of a euro	$1.36	$1.18	$1.32	$1.47	$1.41	$1.44	$1.32
$ price of a Canadian dollar	0.83	0.86	0.86	1.02	0.82	0.95	1.00
$ price of a Brazilian real	0.38	0.43	0.47	0.57	0.43	0.57	0.59

FOREIGN CURRENCY TRANSACTIONS

LO1 Report import and export transactions and borrowing and lending denominated in foreign currency.

Import and export transactions and borrowing and lending in another currency have very similar characteristics. When importers and borrowers pay their obligations in foreign currency, they benefit when their currency strengthens against the other currency. When exporters and lenders receive payments in foreign currency, they benefit when their currency weakens against the other currency.

Import and Export Transactions

Import/export transactions—purchases from international suppliers and sales to international customers—present no particular accounting problem *if* all sales, purchases, payments, and receipts are denominated in dollars. In that case our international customers and suppliers do business in terms of the dollar, a currency foreign to *them*, and they accept the exchange rate risk. In any international transaction, at least one of the parties deals in a foreign currency. If a third currency is involved—for example if a U.S. company and a Japanese company specify that their transactions are settled in euros—then both parties deal in a foreign currency.

When a U.S. company makes a credit sale abroad and states the transaction price in foreign currency units, the dollar value of the account receivable may change before the foreign currency payment is received and converted into dollars. Similarly, when a U.S. company purchases goods from abroad on account at a price denominated in foreign currency units, the dollar amount owed may change before the U.S. company converts dollars into foreign currency and makes payment. These changes in the dollar value of receivables and payables generate *exchange gains and losses* to the U.S. firm that must be recognized at settlement and at intervening balance sheet dates.

Generally accepted accounting principles for import and export transactions denominated in a foreign currency are found in *ASC Topic 830,* Foreign Currency Matters. The initial sale or purchase transaction is recorded at its dollar equivalent, based on the foreign exchange spot rate in effect at the time of the transaction. Any *changes* in the dollar equivalent of the resulting receivable or payable are treated separately as **exchange gains or losses**, and do not affect the original dollar value of the sale or purchase. Exchange gains and losses are reported on the income statement. A summary of the accounting procedures for import or export transactions follows:

Reporting Import and Export Transactions Denominated in Foreign Currency

1. Restate the foreign currency invoice price into dollars using the appropriate foreign exchange spot rate and record the transaction in dollars.
2. Record an exchange gain or loss when the transaction is settled if exchange rate changes cause the number of dollars received or paid to differ from that originally recorded.
3. If the transaction is not settled at a balance sheet date, record an exchange gain or loss on the existing receivable or payable by adjusting it to the dollar equivalent implied by the spot rate at the balance sheet date.

Observe two objectives of these procedures. *First*, the accounting recognizes changes in the value of receivables and payables attributable to movements in the exchange rate. *Second*, fair value accounting applies, and the recognized value change is not deferred until eventual settlement if a balance sheet date occurs prior to settlement.

The following example illustrates the accounting for import and export transactions.

1. On October 16, 2013, **Gap Inc.**, a U.S. clothing company, purchased woolen sweaters at an invoice price of 17,000 New Zealand dollars (NZ$) from a New Zealand clothing manufacturer. The exchange rate was $0.82/ NZ$. Payment was to be made on December 16, 2013.

2013			
Oct. 16	Inventories	13,940	
	Accounts payable		13,940
	To record the purchase of sweaters from New Zealand;		
	$13,940 = $0.82 × 17,000.		

2. On December 16, 2013, Gap purchased NZ$17,000 at an exchange rate of $.83/NZ$ and transmitted them to the clothing manufacturer's bank in New Zealand.

2013			
Dec. 16	Exchange loss	170	
	Accounts payable		170
	To revalue the account payable to the current exchange rate;		
	$170 = ($0.83 − $0.82) × 17,000.		
	Foreign currency	14,110	
	Cash		14,110
	To purchase sufficient foreign currency to pay the New		
	Zealand manufacturer; $14,110 = $0.83 × 17,000.		
	Accounts payable....................................	14,110	
	Foreign currency		14,110
	To record payment of the liability to the New Zealand		
	manufacturer; $14,110 = $13,940 + $170.		

Consider the exchange loss recorded on December 16. Gap's liability to the New Zealand manufacturer was denominated in New Zealand dollars. Because the exchange rate *rose*, it took more U.S. dollars to purchase NZ$17,000, the dollar value of the liability *increased*, and Gap incurred a loss.

3. On December 20, 2013, Gap purchased wool scarves from a British mill for £40,000, when the exchange rate was $1.65/£. Payment is due on February 20, 2014.

2013			
Dec. 20	Inventories	66,000	
	Accounts payable		66,000
	To record the purchase of wool scarves from the U.K.;		
	$66,000 = $1.65 × 40,000.		

4. On December 22, 2013, Gap sold a quantity of deluxe wool coats to a Canadian concern for 9,800 Canadian dollars (C$). The exchange rate was $0.99/C$. Gap's terms are 90 days, net.

2013			
Dec. 22	Accounts receivable..	9,702	
	Sales		9,702
	To record the sale of coats to Canada;		
	$9,702 = $0.99 × 9,800.		

5. On December 29, 2013, Gap purchased buttons costing 10,000 pesos (P) from a Mexican supplier. The exchange rate was $0.05/P; a check was mailed immediately.

2013			
Dec. 29	Inventories	500	
	Cash		500
	To record the cash purchase of buttons from Mexico;		
	$500 = $0.05 × 10,000.		

Because no time lapsed between the recording of the transaction and time of payment on December 29, there can be *no exchange gain or loss*.

6. Gap prepared financial statements at January 31, 2014, its fiscal year-end, and made the following adjusting entries. Exchange rates were $1.61/£ and $1.005/C$ at January 31, 2014.

2014			
Jan. 31	Accounts payable..	1,600	
	Exchange gain..		1,600
	To revalue the liability to the British mill to the current		
	exchange rate; $1,600 = ($1.65 − $1.61) × 40,000.		
	The dollar value of this liability decreased to $64,400		
	(= $1.61 × 40,000).		
	Accounts receivable.....................................	147	
	Exchange gain..		147
	To revalue the receivable from Canada to the current		
	exchange rate; $147 = ($1.005 − $0.99) × 9,800. The dollar		
	value of this asset increased to $9,849 (= $1.005 × 9,800).		

Contrast the two exchange gains accrued on January 31, 2014. Because the dollar *strengthened*, the direct exchange rate for pounds (£) *declined*, the dollar value of Gap's liability declined, and a gain resulted. The exchange rate for Canadian dollars *rose* by year-end (U.S. dollar *weakened*), also producing a gain. As the value of Canadian dollars rose, so did the U.S. dollar value of Gap's C$9,800 receivable from the Canadian firm.

7. Gap paid its obligation to the British mill on February 20, 2014. The exchange rate was $1.58/£.

2014			
Feb. 20	Accounts payable..	1,200	
	Exchange gain..		1,200
	To revalue the account payable to the current exchange rate;		
	$1,200 = ($1.61 − $1.58) × 40,000.		
	Foreign currency	63,200	
	Cash		63,200
	To record the purchase of foreign currency to pay the British		
	mill; $63,200 = $1.58 × 40,000.		
	Accounts payable..	63,200	
	Foreign currency		63,200
	To record payment of the liability to the British mill;		
	$63,200 = $66,000 − $1,600 − $1,200.		

8. On March 20, 2014, payment was received from the Canadian customer on the sale of the coats. The exchange rate was $.97/C$.

2014			
Mar. 20	Exchange loss	343	
	Accounts receivable		343
	To revalue the receivable to the current exchange rate;		
	$343 = ($1.005 − $0.97) × 9,800.		
	Foreign currency	9,506	
	Accounts receivable		9,506
	To record receipt of foreign currency from Canada in		
	payment of the receivable; $9,506 = $0.97 × 9,800 =		
	$9,702 (original value) + $147 (exchange gain in fiscal 2014)		
	− $343 (exchange loss in fiscal 2015).		
	Cash..	9,506	
	Foreign currency		9,506
	To record exchange of the Canadian currency for U.S. dollars.		

To summarize, accounts receivable and accounts payable arising in international transactions are often denominated in a foreign currency and are recorded at the dollar equivalent of a fixed quantity of foreign currency. The specified foreign currency amount does not change. Because these receivables and payables are exposed to exchange rate risk, as the exchange rate changes their dollar equivalents also change. The display below summarizes the effects of changing exchange rates on the dollar equivalents of these exposed accounts and the resulting transaction gains and losses:

Effects of Changing Exchange Rates on Exposed Receivables and Payables Denominated in Foreign Currencies		
	Exchange Gains and Losses Due to Changes in Direct Exchange Rate	
Exposed Account	**Increase ($ Weakens)**	**Decrease ($ Strengthens)**
Accounts Receivable (AR)	AR increases; gain	AR decreases; loss
Accounts Payable (AP)...................	AP increases; loss	AP decreases; gain

The accounting for import and export transactions reflects the **two-transaction approach**. Under this approach, the dollar valuation of the inventories purchased from international suppliers or the revenue on sales made to international customers is unaffected by changes in the foreign exchange rate between the time the purchase or sale is made and the foreign currency is paid or collected. For example, Gap's purchase of sweaters on October 16, 2013, is valued at $13,940, even though Gap ends up paying $14,110 to settle the transaction. The exchange loss of $170 appears separately on the income statement.

The alternative **single-transaction approach** views a sale or purchase denominated in a foreign currency as incomplete until settled. Under this alternative, any intervening gain or loss adjusts the dollar basis of the initial transaction. The single-transaction approach initially states the cost of Gap's sweater purchase on October 16, 2013, at $13,940. Because Gap pays $170 more to settle the debt, this additional payment would be added to the cost of the inventory purchased.

The FASB's position on this issue illustrates the traditional separation of operating transactions from financing transactions. When purchase of a building is financed by a mortgage, the cost of the building does not include interest on the mortgage. Similarly, the manner in which the import purchase is financed does not affect the cost of the inventory.

REVIEW 1 ● Foreign-Currency-Denominated Import and Export Transactions

Fine Foods, Inc., a U.S. wholesaler, buys merchandise from suppliers in Germany, and pays the suppliers in euros. It also sells merchandise to customers in Italy, and receives payment in euros. Fine Foods' accounting year ends June 30. Exchange rates are as follows:

Date	Spot rate ($/€)
March 1, 2013	$1.35
April 1, 2013	1.40
June 30, 2013	1.42
July 15, 2013	1.43
August 15, 2013	1.45
August 31, 2013	1.48

Purchases of €1,000,000 are made on March 1, 2013. Fine Foods pays its German suppliers on August 15, 2013, and sells the merchandise to its U.S. customers on August 31, 2013. Sales of €100,000 are made on April 1, 2013. Fine Foods receives payment from its Italian customers on July 15, 2013.

Required
a. Accounts payable, on the June 30, 2013, balance sheet?
b. Accounts receivable, on the June 30, 2013, balance sheet?
c. Exchange gain or loss, on the fiscal 2013 income statement?
d. Exchange gain or loss, on the fiscal 2014 income statement?
e. Sales revenue, on the fiscal 2013 income statement?
f. Cost of goods sold, on the fiscal 2014 income statement?

Solutions are located after the chapter assignments.

Foreign Borrowing and Lending Transactions

Growth in the volume of international capital flows indicates that substantial investment funds move across national boundaries. U.S. companies engage in these and other investment transactions requiring foreign currency conversions:

● Investment in securities of international companies, banks, and governments.

● Borrowing from international lenders.

● Direct investment in international branches and subsidiaries.

Investments in securities of international entities often require the U.S. firm to convert dollars into foreign currency to acquire the security and then to convert the foreign currency into dollars when investment income is received and when the security matures or is sold. Similarly, borrowing internationally may mean that the U.S. firm borrows a quantity of foreign currency, converts it into dollars for use domestically, and later purchases sufficient foreign currency to repay the interest and principal. Direct investment in international branches and subsidiaries involves setting up a business operation, acquiring assets, and incurring debts in the country. Chapter 7 addresses the problems associated with converting these items for inclusion in U.S. company financial statements.

When an interest-bearing investment or note payable is denominated in another currency, what exchange rate should the U.S. firm use to translate the interest income or expense? Theoretically, the average exchange rate in effect while the interest is accruing should be used. Yet the receivable, payable, or collection or disbursement of cash when the accrued interest is recorded is translated at the current exchange rate. Taken together, these practices result in a discrepancy between the revenue or expense and the asset or liability when exchange rates fluctuate. We avoid this by translating interest income and expense at the current spot rate when the interest is accrued. After recording interest receivable and interest payable, exchange gains or losses can result from subsequent movements in the exchange rate.

Consider a U.S. investment in an international bank certificate of deposit (CD). On August 15, 2013, Gap Inc. purchases a 90-day CD from a Swiss bank. The certificate has a face value of 1,000,000 Swiss francs (CHF), costs $1,250,000 (the spot rate is $1.25/CHF), and pays interest at an annual rate of 5 percent. The entry to record purchase of the CD is:

2013			
Aug. 15	Temporary investments	1,250,000	
	Cash		1,250,000
	To record purchase of a Swiss CD with face value of		
	CHF1,000,000; $1,250,000 = 1,000,000 × $1.25.		

On November 13, 2013, the certificate of deposit matures and Gap receives principal and interest of CHF1,012,500 [= CHF1,000,000 + 0.05(CHF1,000,000)/4] when the spot rate is $1.24/CHF. The following three entries record the exchange adjustment on the certificate, receipt of the foreign currency from the Swiss bank (including interest earned) and conversion of the Swiss francs into dollars.

2013			
Nov. 13	Exchange loss	10,000	
	Temporary investments.		10,000
	To recognize the exchange loss accrued on the certificate of		
	deposit; $10,000 = ($1.25 − $1.24) × 1,000,000.		
	Foreign currency ($1.24 × 1,012,500)	1,255,500	
	Temporary investments ($1,250,000 − $10,000)		1,240,000
	Interest income ($1.24 × 12,500)		15,500
	To record foreign currency received at maturity of the CD and		
	record the interest income translated at the current spot rate.		
	Cash.	1,255,500	
	Foreign currency		1,255,500
	To record the exchange of CHF1,012,500 for $1,255,500.		

Note that the interest accrued over ninety days, possibly at various exchange rates. However, because there was no previous accrual, we convert the interest income into dollars as of the date it is received by the U.S. company.

HEDGING FOREIGN EXCHANGE EXPOSURES

Importers and exporters, as well as borrowers and lenders in foreign currency, are exposed to *foreign exchange risk*. An importer or borrower faces the danger that the direct exchange rate will *rise* between the time the purchase or loan is made and the time the foreign currency obligation is paid, requiring the importer or borrower to use more dollars to purchase the foreign currency necessary to pay the obligation. An exporter or lender faces the risk that the direct exchange rate will *fall* between the time the exporter makes the sale or the lender lends the money, and the time the foreign currency is received, causing the exporter or lender to receive fewer dollars on conversion of the foreign currency received. There is also the chance in either case that rates will move in the U.S. company's favor.

Types of Foreign Exchange Risk

So far this chapter has concentrated on the risk associated with holding a receivable or payable denominated in a foreign currency. Here are several other situations that expose companies to foreign exchange risk.

- A company enters into a *firm agreement* to buy merchandise from an international supplier or sell merchandise to an international customer. Known as a **firm commitment**, in this situation the exposure to foreign exchange risk is in the future.

- A company buys regularly from international suppliers or sells to international customers and expects to do so in the future. Although such anticipated transactions are not in the form of firm commitments, the risk of expense or revenue streams denominated in a foreign currency is just as real. These expected events are known as **forecasted transactions**.

- A company invests in an international subsidiary. When the subsidiary's accounts are translated or remeasured for consolidation with the parent, a gain or loss results. A **net investment in international operations** exposes the parent to foreign exchange risk.

- When a company believes it can predict the future movement of exchange rates, it may deliberately expose itself to exchange risk using **speculative investments**. For example, if a U.S. company believes the exchange rate for a particular currency will increase, it can invest in a CD denominated in the currency. If the exchange rate rises, it receives more U.S. dollars in principal and interest when the CD matures. If the rate falls, it receives fewer dollars.

Derivative Instruments Used in Hedging

Importers and exporters can **hedge**, or neutralize, foreign exchange risks by trading in the forward, futures or options markets. Hedging involves covering a foreign currency exposure by contracting in the forward market to purchase or sell foreign currency at a specified time in the future for a fixed price. In this way, managers neutralize the impact of changing exchange rates on the exposure by removing the uncertainty involved in not knowing how many U.S. dollars will be paid or received.

Forward and Futures Contracts Contracting for future delivery of a foreign currency can involve either **forward contracts**—individual contracts negotiated with dealers—or **futures contracts**—standardized contracts traded on organized exchanges that generally require margin deposits. Both forwards and futures are examples of *derivatives*. In general, a **derivative** is a financial instrument that derives its value from some other financial item, such as a foreign currency rate, an interest rate, or a security price. For example, a forward contract that specifies the future purchase price of yen derives its value from the current market price of yen. The contract becomes more valuable as the market price of yen increases.

We concentrate here on forward contracts, the most basic derivative instruments commonly used to hedge foreign exchange risk. Other foreign-currency-denominated instruments, such as futures, option contracts, international loans and investments in international debt securities, can also function as hedges. Accounting for exchange gains or losses on such transactions parallels the forward contract case.

Refer to the **Gap Inc.** illustration discussed earlier in the chapter. On October 16, 2013, Gap agreed to pay a New Zealand manufacturer NZ$17,000 on December 16, 2013 for a purchase of sweaters. The October 16 exchange rate is $0.82/NZ$, but there is the risk that the exchange rate will increase or decrease by the time payment is to be made. Gap can remove this uncertainty by contracting with a foreign exchange broker on October 16, 2013, to buy NZ$17,000 in 60 days at a fixed price. This contract is called a **forward contract**, and prices for future delivery of currency are called **forward rates**.

If the forward rate for delivery of New Zealand dollars in 60 days is $0.81, Gap is no longer affected by the uncertainty of the future exchange rate. Gap now knows with certainty that it will pay $13,770 (= $0.81 × 17,000) for the merchandise. In hindsight this arrangement was beneficial for Gap, because without the forward contract $14,110 would be paid on December 16, 2013.

Note carefully, however, that hedging with forwards neutralizes both the potential *losses* and the potential *gains* from changes in the exchange rate. If the spot rate *falls* to $0.78 on December 16, Gap is still required to fulfill the forward contract and pay $13,770 for the NZ$17,000 necessary to pay the obligation, even though without the forward contract only $13,260 (= $0.78 × 17,000) would be paid for the needed currency on the spot market. By removing the uncertainty of decreases as well as increases in the exchange rate, the forward contract neutralizes both potential gains and potential losses.

Option Contracts Foreign exchange **options** provide a hedge against the "downside risk" of foreign exchange losses, but without losing the chance to experience foreign exchange gains. The option holder has the right—but not the obligation—to buy or sell the contracted amount of foreign currency at a specified exchange rate called the **exercise price** or **strike price**. **Call options** give the holder the right to *buy* currency at a fixed price. **Put options** give the holder the right to *sell* currency at a fixed price. Option "holders" acquire options directly from option "writers," or indirectly from exchanges that facilitate options trading.

The option writer must follow through with selling or buying the currency if the option is exercised by the option holder. However, when it is not favorable to the option holder to exercise the option, the holder can let the option expire. Notice that the option writer incurs all of the risk of potential loss on the contract. For this reason, the option writer charges the holder a fee or **premium** as compensation for the risk undertaken.

To illustrate hedging with an option contract, look again at Gap Inc.'s purchase of sweaters on October 16, 2013, calling for payment of NZ$17,000 to be made on December 16, 2013. Gap can hedge the risk that the exchange rate will increase during this time interval by purchasing a 60-day call option giving Gap the right to buy NZ$ at a fixed price. Assume the option's strike price is $0.81, and the option costs Gap $400.

Call Option for NZ$17,000 with $0.81 Strike Price		
December 16, 2013, Spot Rate	Exercise?	Gap Pays
> $0.81	Yes	$13,770 = $0.81 × 17,000
< 0.81	No	Spot rate

Thus Gap neutralizes the risk that the exchange rate will increase above $0.81. The cost of the currency needed to pay the NZ$17,000 debt will be $13,770 or less. If Gap used a forward contract with a forward rate of $0.81, the cost of the currency would be $13,770 exactly. By hedging with an option contract, the cost could be less if the spot rate goes below $0.81. Gap pays $400 to hedge the downside risk while retaining the opportunity for an upside gain.

Currency Swaps   In a **currency swap**, the parties to the agreement initially exchange currencies, or agree on a **notional** or **contractual** amount to be "exchanged," and then reverse the "exchange" at some future point in time. The parties agree on the exchange rates to be used at inception and completion of the swap. Payments in the foreign currency are also made at intermediate points during the swap, based on agreed-upon exchange rates. Although gross amounts are sometimes exchanged, usually only net cash flows actually change hands, based on exchange rate differentials, net of fees.

A typical currency swap occurs when a U.S. firm has international investments or recurring sales to international customers that generate periodic foreign currency cash inflows, and an international firm has U.S. investments or recurring sales to U.S. customers that generate periodic U.S. currency cash inflows. The U.S. firm wants to swap foreign currency for U.S. dollars on a periodic basis, and the international firm wants to swap U.S. dollars for foreign currency. The two firms agree to the terms of the swap. When the exchange and re-exchange of principal amounts at the beginning and end of the swap do not take place, the principal amount is referred to as *notional*. If they do occur, each firm has the option of immediately converting the unwanted foreign currency into its home currency. Because currency swaps are very similar to a series of forward contracts, the reporting requirements are the same as for forward contracts.

Decisions Involving Hedging   Even when hedges are effective, firms still must decide whether hedging is the best way to neutralize exchange rate risk. If the forward rate in a purchase contract is $1.40/€ and the spot rate is $1.50/€ when the firm liquidates its payable, the firm gained $0.10/€ by hedging while neutralizing the exchange rate risk. But if the spot rate is $1.35/€ at settlement, the firm lost $0.05/€ by hedging. A firm can avoid exchange rate risk by purchasing the foreign currency up front and either paying immediately or holding the currency until payment is due. In the latter case, the foreign currency could be temporarily placed in a foreign short-term interest-bearing investment until needed.

Suppose McDonald's Corporation has a €1,000,000 payable due in 60 days; the current spot rate is $1.40/€ and the 60-day forward rate is $1.41/€.

Case 1: Forward Contract. If McDonald's enters a 60-day forward purchase contract, $1,410,000 (= $1.41 × 1,000,000) is required when the contract matures to purchase €1,000,000 from the broker and liquidate the payable.

Case 2: Purchase € Now. By purchasing €1,000,000 now and holding the currency for 60 days (or paying now), McDonald's liquidates the payable for $1,400,000, a saving of $10,000 over the forward contract. However, interest is a relevant cost or benefit in this analysis. Although McDonald's can earn interest on the €1,000,000 by investing it in an international short-term interest-bearing instrument, by investing $1,400,000 in foreign currency now McDonald's gives up interest on possible alternative investments of the $1,400,000. If McDonald's must borrow to acquire the foreign currency, the interest expense on the loan must be taken into account.

Thus, the $10,000 savings on acquiring the €1,000,000 now represents only one part of the larger economic picture. McDonald's must consider all effects—additional interest revenue, interest expense, or interest lost—in evaluating the choice between a forward contract and purchasing the foreign currency now. A firm may also be able to neutralize exchange rate risk with a strategy that does not involve hedging. Be sure to consider all relevant costs when analyzing such situations.

BUSINESS APPLICATION   **Natural Hedging**

Investing in financial derivatives is not the only way a company can hedge against foreign exchange risk. Consider this excerpt from **McDonald's** 2010 annual report:

> . . . where practical, the Company's restaurants purchase goods and services in local currencies resulting in natural hedges.

Companies can avoid the effects of changing currency rates by doing business in the local currency and reducing the need to exchange currency. For example, McDonald's may receive euros from customers, and use these euros to pay suppliers. This type of activity is known as **natural hedging**. *Source:* McDonald's Corporation 2010 annual report.

Reporting Investments in Foreign Currency Derivatives

Generally accepted accounting principles for foreign currency forward, futures, swaps and option contracts, as well as other derivative financial instruments, are found in *ASC Topic 815,* Derivatives and Hedging *(originally issued as SFAS 133)*.

Reporting Goals   The provisions in *ASC Topic 815* have the following general features, as applied to foreign exchange hedges:

- All investments in foreign currency forward or option contracts are shown on the balance sheet at their current *fair value*.

- If the contract is a qualifying hedge instrument, gains and losses due to changes in the fair value of the contract are recognized in the income statement *at the same time* the losses and gains on the exposure the contract is hedging are recognized. Thus the neutralizing effect of the hedge is properly represented in the income statement by offsetting gains and losses.

- **Hedge accounting** changes the timing of gain and loss recognition so hedge and hedged item gains and losses appear on the same income statement.

- Hedges of firm commitments, such as contractual purchase or sale orders denominated in a foreign currency, are called **fair value hedges**. Hedges of forecasted transactions, such as anticipated purchases or sales denominated in a foreign currency, are called **cash flow hedges**.

- If the company does not completely hedge its foreign exchange risk, gains and losses due to its net (unhedged) exposure are shown in the income statement as foreign currency rates change.

- If a company invests in **speculative** derivatives, changes in their fair value are reported in the income statement as foreign currency rates change.

This and subsequent sections illustrate accounting for forward contracts in detail. The accounting for foreign exchange option contracts parallels the accounting for option contracts in the commodities and financial markets. Accounting for option contracts is analyzed in Chapter 9. Currency swaps are equivalent to a series of foreign currency forward contracts, and therefore are not separately discussed.

Calculating Fair Value of a Foreign Currency Forward Contract   A **forward purchase contract** requires its holder to purchase foreign currency at a specified time in the future for a known price. An **importer** enters into a forward purchase contract so that, when an obligation to an international supplier comes due, the needed amount of foreign currency is available at a price agreed upon in advance. The fair market value of a forward purchase contract at any point in time derives from the **difference between the contracted forward rate and the current forward rate for delivery on the contracted date**.

For example, suppose that on February 1 McDonald's enters into a forward contract to purchase C$100,000 for $0.97/C$ on April 1. Valuation of the forward contract follows:

	Forward rate for April 1 delivery	Value of forward contract asset (liability)
Date		
February 1	$0.97	$ 0 = [($0.97 − $0.97) × 100,000]
March 1	0.99	2,000 = [($0.99 − $0.97) × 100,000]
March 15	0.96	(1,000) = [($0.96 − $0.97) × 100,000]

Forward Purchase Contract—C$100,000 for Delivery April 1 at $0.97/C$

The value of the forward contract changes as the current forward rate for the contracted delivery date changes. Note that the forward purchase contract has a negative fair value when the forward rate for delivery of C$ on April 1 goes below $0.97 because the contract requires purchase of C$ at a higher cost than that now available on the market. To be completely accurate, since the forward contract involves cash flows that will occur in the future, the difference between the current forward rate and the contracted rate should be discounted to its present value. This chapter assumes that the effect of discounting is immaterial and ignores it.

The value changes that occur in forward contracts can be visualized with the help of familiar T-accounts. Think of a forward contract as having two sides: (1) *the current value of the currency involved*—a variable amount equal to the current forward rate multiplied by the currency amount, and (2) *the contract value of the currency*—the fixed obligation equal to the forward rate at inception (the contract rate) multiplied by the currency amount. In the case of forward currency purchases, the debit/asset side of the T-account is the current value of the currency to be received. The credit/liability side of the T-account is the fixed contract value that must be paid to the dealer for the currency. We can make the following observations about the forward contract T-account:

- At inception the two sides are equal—the current value of the currency equals its contract value and the contract itself has no net value.
- As time passes, the *current value side changes* but the contract value side does not.
- With a *forward purchase contract*, the *debit side* is the current value of the currency to be received; it changes with the current forward rate.
- The *credit side* is the fixed obligation to pay for the currency—the contract value—that *does not change*.
- When the forward rate increases, the value of the currency to be received rises above the contract value, and the contract has a net debit balance, which is an asset.
- When the forward rate decreases, the value of the currency to be received falls below the contract value, and the contract has a net credit balance, which is a liability.

The above value changes correspond with our intuition. An *increase* in the forward rate gives us the ability to buy the currency for less than its current value, an advantage (asset). A *decrease* in the forward rate means that we must buy the currency for more than its current value, a disadvantage (liability).

Recall that on February 1 McDonald's entered into a forward contract to purchase C$100,000 for $0.97/C$, with delivery to take place April 1. On March 1, the forward rate for delivery April 1 is $0.99. We depict these events in T-account format as follows:

Investment in Forward Purchase Contract		
	Current Value	**Contract Value**
February 1	$97,000 (= $0.97 × 100,000)	$97,000 (= $0.97 × 100,000)
Value change	2,000 [=($0.99 − $0.97) × 100,000]	—
Balance March 1	$ 2,000	

Because the current dollar value of the currency to be received is higher than the contract obligation to be paid, the investment in forward contract is an asset.

A **forward sale contract** requires the holder to sell foreign currency at a specified time in the future for a known price. An **exporter** can hedge exposure to exchange rate changes by entering into a *forward sale contract* so that when international customers remit payments in foreign currency to the exporter, the foreign currency can be sold for a prearranged dollar amount. As with a forward purchase contract, the fair market value of a forward sale contract derives from the difference between the contracted forward rate and the current forward rate for delivery on the contracted date.

Suppose that on June 1 McDonald's enters into a forward contract to sell C$100,000 for $0.97/C$ on August 1. On July 1, the forward rate for delivery of C$ on August 1 is $0.955, and the fair value of the forward contract is $1,500 [= ($0.97 − $0.955) × 100,000]. The contract has value because it allows McDonald's to sell C$ on August 1 for $0.97, when the market price for delivery on August 1 is now $0.955. In contrast, the forward sale contract has a negative fair value when the forward rate for delivery of C$ rises above $0.97.

As with the forward purchase contract, the above discussion on forward sales contracts can be visualized using a T-account. The forward sale contract has two sides: the current value is the obligation to deliver the foreign currency, and the contract value is the fixed amount to be received from the dealer in U.S. dollars. We can make the following observations:

- With a *forward sale contract*, the *credit side* is the *current value of the obligation to deliver the currency to the dealer*, which *changes with the current forward rate*. The debit side is the receivable from the dealer, which is the *fixed contract value*.

- When the forward rate increases, the current value of the obligation to deliver the currency rises above the contract value and the contract has a net credit balance, a liability.

- When the forward rate decreases, the current value of the obligation to deliver the currency falls below the contract value and the contract has a net debit balance, an asset.

The above value changes also correspond with our intuition. An increase in the forward rate means that we must sell the currency for less than its current value, a disadvantage (liability). A decrease in the forward rate gives us the ability to sell the currency for more than its current value, an advantage (asset).

Recall that on June 1 McDonald's entered into a forward contract to sell C$100,000 for $0.97/C$, with delivery to take place August 1. On July 1, the forward rate for delivery on August 1 is $0.955. We depict these events in T-account format as follows:

	Investment in Forward Sale Contract	
	Contract Value	**Current Value**
June 1	$97,000 (= $0.97 × 100,000)	$97,000 (= $0.97 × 100,000)
Value change	—	(1,500) [= ($0.955 − $0.97) × 100,000]
Balance July 1	$ 1,500	

Because the dollar contract value to be received is higher than the current value of the currency to be paid for and delivered, the investment in forward contract is an asset.

Reporting Gains and Losses on Forward Contracts

Reporting requirements for changes in the fair value of a forward contract depend on whether it qualifies as a hedge investment. According to *ASC Section 815-20-25*, qualified hedges must be **documented as hedging a specific and recognized financial risk**, and must also be **highly effective** in neutralizing that risk. Effectiveness is first evaluated when the hedge is initiated, and periodically over time.

Hedge effectiveness is the extent to which the hedge instrument neutralizes the financial risk. A common measure of hedge effectiveness is to divide the change in fair value of the hedge instrument by the change in fair value of the hedged item.

$$\text{Hedge effectiveness ratio} = \frac{\text{Change in fair value of hedge instrument}}{\text{Change in fair value of hedged item}}$$

Because the two value changes move in opposite directions, the hedge effectiveness ratio is negative. Although there is no official ratio level that must be met, in practice a range of -80% to -125% is generally viewed as sufficiently effective.

If the investment is an effective hedge, it qualifies for **hedge accounting**, which allows the company to deviate from normal accounting for the investment and the hedged item. By so doing, hedge gains and losses and hedged item losses and gains are reported on the same income statement. The reporting for changes in its value depends on whether the investment is a *fair value* or *cash flow* hedge. Changes in the value of **fair value hedges** are reported on the income statement, along with corresponding changes in the value of the hedged item—a contractual purchase or sale order denominated in a foreign currency (firm commitment).

Changes in the value of **cash flow hedges**—hedges of forecasted future foreign currency-denominated purchases or sales—are initially reported in shareholders' equity, as a component of **other comprehensive income**. When the forecasted transaction is reported in the income statement, such as when the forecasted purchases enter into cost of goods sold (the merchandise is sold), the value changes are reclassified to income to match against the hedged item.

Using Forward Contracts to Hedge Import and Export Transactions   U.S. importers and exporters whose payables and receivables are denominated in foreign currency face the risk that the U.S. dollar value of the payables and receivables will change as foreign currency rates change. Hedge investments lock in the U.S. dollar amounts paid or received.

Hedge accounting does not apply when the hedged item is a foreign-currency-denominated receivable or payable. Receivables, payables and hedge investments are normally marked to market; therefore offsetting gains and losses automatically appear on the same income statement.

LO2 Report hedges of foreign-currency-denominated receivables and payables.

Forward Purchase Contract: Hedge of Foreign-Currency-Denominated Payable   Suppose that Gap Inc. purchases goods costing £1,000 from a British supplier on October 1, 2013, when the spot rate is $1.60/£. Payment in pounds is due on March 1, 2014. Because Gap's account payable is denominated in pounds, it exposes Gap to risk of exchange rate movements. To hedge this liability to the British supplier, a *forward purchase contract* calling for a foreign exchange broker to deliver £1,000 on March 1 is entered on October 1. If the forward rate for delivery on March 1 is $1.61/£, Gap "locks in" the dollar equivalent of the obligation to the British supplier at $1,610 (= $1.61 × 1,000) and is not affected by subsequent movements in the exchange rate.

An entry is required on October 1 to record the purchase of the goods. Gap makes *no entry* to record the forward purchase contract; it has a fair value of zero on October 1 because the contract price for delivery on March 1 equals the current forward rate for delivery on March 1. The entry on October 1 is:

2013			
Oct. 1	Inventories	1,600	
	Accounts payable		1,600
	To record the purchase of goods from the U.K.;		
	$1,600 = $1.60 × 1,000.		

On January 31, 2014, Gap's accounting year-end, entries are needed to record the change in fair value of both the account payable and the forward contract. If the spot rate on January 31, 2014 is $1.65 and the forward rate for delivery on March 1 is $1.66, Gap makes these entries:

2014			
Jan. 31	Exchange loss	50	
	Accounts payable		50
	To revalue the account payable to the current exchange rate;		
	$50 = ($1.65 − $1.60) × 1,000.		
	Investment in forward contract	50	
	Exchange gain...		50
	To record the change in fair value of the forward purchase		
	contract; $50 = ($1.66 − $1.61) × 1,000.		

Gap's income statement reflects the exchange *gain* on the forward purchase contract offsetting the exchange *loss* on the account payable exposure, because the forward purchase contract completely neutralizes the exchange risk caused by the import transaction. To the extent that forward rates and spot rates move together, the gains and losses will exactly offset. Otherwise, the hedge is partially ineffective and net income is affected. On the balance sheet date, the forward purchase contract appears on the balance sheet as a *current asset* at its fair value of $50.

On March 1, the forward purchase contract is settled and the supplier is paid. The spot rate and, equivalently, the forward rate for delivery on March 1 are $1.68. First, Gap makes entries to "mark to market" both the account payable and the forward purchase contract:

2014			
Mar. 1	Exchange loss	30	
	Accounts payable		30
	To revalue the account payable to the current exchange rate;		
	$30 = ($1.68 − $1.65) × 1,000.		
	Investment in forward contract	20	
	Exchange gain..		20
	To record the gain in fair value on the forward purchase contract;		
	$20 = ($1.68 − $1.66) × 1,000.		

Thus for the period January 31 to March 1, forward rates and spot rates do not move exactly together, so the gain on the forward contract does not exactly offset the loss on the account payable. The net exchange loss of $10 for the period October 1 to March 1 can also be calculated as the difference between the spot and forward rates at the inception of the contract; $10 = ($1.61 − $1.60) × 1,000, since spot and forward rates must be equal on the delivery date.

At this point, we make entries to settle the forward contract and pay the British supplier:

2014			
Mar. 1	Foreign currency	1,680	
	Investment in forward contract		70
	Cash		1,610
	To record payment of $1,610 to the dealer, receipt of £1,000		
	valued at the current spot rate of $1.68, and fulfillment of the		
	forward purchase contract.		
	Accounts payable..	1,680	
	Foreign currency		1,680
	To record payment to the British supplier; $1,680 =		
	$1,600 + $50 + $30.		

In retrospect, this hedge was beneficial to Gap. Rather than paying $1,680 on the spot market on March 1, Gap paid $1,610 under the forward contract. Even if Gap purchased the currency on the spot market on October 1 for $1,600, the forward contract cost only $10 more. Thus Gap paid an additional $10 on a $1,600 obligation for the privilege of delaying payment for five months from October 1 to March 1, an annual interest rate of only 1.5 percent [= ($10/$1,600) × 12/5].

Forward Sale Contract: Hedge of Foreign-Currency-Denominated Receivable Suppose that Gap Inc. sold goods to a British customer on October 1, 2013, at a price of £2,000, when the spot rate was $1.60/£. Payment in pounds will be received on March 1, 2014. Because the account receivable is denominated in pounds, Gap is exposed to risk of exchange rate movements. To hedge this receivable from the British customer, a *forward sale contract* calling for delivery of £2,000 to a broker on March 1 is entered on October 1. If the forward rate for delivery on March 1 is $1.61/£, Gap "locks in" the dollar equivalent value of the receivable from the British customer at $3,220 (= $1.61 × 2,000), and is not affected by subsequent movements in the exchange rate.

Gap makes an entry on October 1 to record the sale of the goods, but no entry to record the forward sale contract, since it has a fair value of zero. The entry on October 1 is:

2013			
Oct. 1	Accounts receivable..	3,200	
	Sales revenue		3,200
	To record the sale of goods to the British customer;		
	$3,200 = $1.60 × 2,000.		

On January 31, 2014, Gap's accounting year-end, we record the change in fair value of both the account receivable and the forward contract. Assume the spot rate is $1.65 and the forward rate for delivery on March 1 is $1.66. Entries are as follows:

2014			
Jan. 31	Accounts receivable..	100	
	Exchange gain..		100
	To revalue the account receivable to the current exchange rate;		
	$100 = ($1.65 − $1.60) × 2,000.		
	Exchange loss	100	
	Investment in forward contract		100
	To record the loss in fair value on the forward sale contract;		
	($100) = ($1.61 − $1.66) × 2,000.		

Unlike the forward purchase contract discussed earlier in this section, the forward sale contract has a positive value when the current forward rate is *less than* the contracted rate. In the Gap example, the current forward rate is *greater than* the contracted rate. On the balance sheet date the forward sale contract appears on the balance sheet as a *current liability* at its fair value of $100.

On March 1, the British customer pays Gap and the forward sale contract is settled. Assume the spot rate and, equivalently, the forward rate for delivery on March 1 is $1.68. First, entries are made to mark to market both the account receivable and the forward sale contract:

2014			
Mar. 1	Accounts receivable..	60	
	Exchange gain..		60
	To revalue the account receivable to the current exchange rate;		
	$60 = ($1.68 − $1.65) × 2,000.		
	Exchange loss	40	
	Investment in forward contract		40
	To record the loss in fair value on the forward sale contract;		
	$(40) = ($1.66 − $1.68) × 2,000.		

At this point, the customer submits payment and Gap settles the forward contract with these entries:

2014			
Mar. 1	Foreign currency	3,360	
	Accounts receivable		3,360
	To record the payment by the British customer; $3,360 =		
	$3,200 + $100 + $60.		
	Cash..	3,220	
	Investment in forward contract	140	
	Foreign currency		3,360
	To record the delivery of the foreign currency to the dealer,		
	receipt of $3,220 as specified in the contract, and settlement of		
	the forward contract.		

In retrospect, the hedge was *not* beneficial to Gap. It could have sold the foreign currency in the spot market on March 1 for $3,360 rather than at the contracted price of $3,220. However, if spot prices had instead decreased over this period, the forward contract protects Gap from the resulting decline in the value of the receivable.

The following table summarizes the implications of changing exchange rates for the fair value of forward contracts.

	Fair Value of Forward Contracts		
Type of Contract	Contract Rate (CR) vs Current Forward Rate (FR)	Net Income Statement Effect	Balance Sheet Disclosure
Forward purchase	FR > CR	Gain	Current Asset
Forward purchase	FR < CR	Loss	Current Liability
Forward sale.....................	FR > CR	Loss	Current Liability
Forward sale.....................	FR < CR	Gain	Current Asset

REVIEW 2 • Using Forward Contracts to Hedge Foreign-Currency-Denominated Import Transactions

Fine Foods, Inc., a U.S. wholesaler, buys merchandise from suppliers in Germany, and pays the suppliers in euros. Fine Foods' accounting year ends June 30. Exchange rates are as follows:

Date	Spot rate ($/€)	Forward rate for delivery August 15, 2013
March 1, 2013	$1.35	$1.37
June 30, 2013..................	1.42	1.44
August 15, 2013...............	1.45	1.45
August 31, 2013...............	1.48	NA

On March 1, 2013, Fine Foods makes inventory purchases of €1,000,000, and enters into a forward purchase for delivery of €1,000,000 on August 15, 2013 to hedge its foreign currency risk. Fine Foods pays its suppliers on August 15, 2013, and sells the merchandise to its U.S. customers on August 31, 2013.

Required

a. Accounts payable, on the June 30, 2013, balance sheet?
b. Investment in forward contract, on the June 30, 2013, balance sheet?
c. Exchange gain or loss, on the fiscal 2013 income statement?
d. Exchange gain or loss, on the fiscal 2014 income statement?
e. Cost of goods sold, on the fiscal 2014 income statement?

Solutions are located after the chapter assignments.

LO3 Report hedges of foreign-currency-denominated firm commitments.

Using Forward Contracts to Hedge Firm Foreign Currency Commitments Many purchase or sale transactions are preceded by contractual agreements where both parties to the transaction commit to perform. For example, an exporter agrees to ship a specified quantity of goods on a preset future date, at a preset price. If the price is denominated in foreign currency, the exporter has the risk that the dollar equivalent value of the sale will decline between the time the commitment to ship is made and the time the payment is received. The exporter can hedge this risk by entering into a forward sale contract to lock in the dollar value of the sale, even before the shipment date.

An importer issues a purchase order obligating it to purchase goods from an international supplier at a contracted price denominated in foreign currency. The importer incurs a loss if the dollar equivalent of the purchase cost increases prior to payment. To hedge this risk, the importer can enter into a forward purchase contract to lock in the dollar cost of the purchase at the time the purchase order is issued.

Accounting for the above situations is simplified when one separates the commitment period from the period when the recorded account payable or account receivable exposure exists. The *commitment period* begins when the purchase or sale agreement occurs and the forward contract begins. The *exposed asset or liability period* begins when the goods are received or delivered and the company records the purchase or sale. The time line below depicts the events for a *forward purchase contract*.

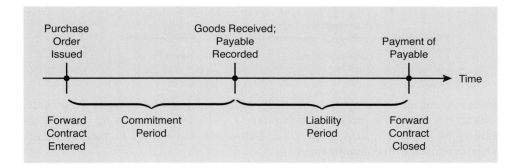

For hedges of firm commitments, normal accounting reports changes in hedge investment value on the income statement, but there is no offsetting change in value of the purchase or sale order. As explained below, during the commitment period, hedge accounting enables matching of hedge gains and losses with hedged item losses and gains.

ASC Section 815-20-35 specifies the accounting for forward contracts used as hedges of *firm foreign currency commitments*. The *ASC* glossary defines the commitments that qualify for hedge accounting.

> A **firm commitment** is defined as an agreement with an unrelated party, binding on both parties and usually legally enforceable, with the following characteristics:
>
> a.   The agreement specifies all significant terms, including the quantity to be exchanged, the fixed price, and the timing of the transaction. The fixed price may be expressed as a specified amount of an entity's local currency or of a foreign currency.
>
> b.   The agreement includes a disincentive for nonperformance that is sufficiently large to make performance probable.

The Codification requires that the gain or loss on a forward contract used to hedge a firm foreign currency commitment be recognized *currently in earnings*. The offsetting loss or gain on the firm purchase or sale commitment must also be recognized in earnings. But the commitment itself has not yet been recorded on the books because generally accepted accounting principles do not recognize purchase or sale orders as accounting events. Instead, a balance sheet account accumulates the losses or gains on the commitment, which is then *closed against the related sales revenue or inventory account* when the sale or purchase and related account receivable or payable are eventually booked. Because a firm commitment relates to a future transaction, valuation using forward rates is appropriate.

Forward Purchase Contract: Fair Value Hedge of a Foreign Currency Purchase Commitment   A firm foreign currency commitment exists when an importer issues a **purchase order** prior to actual receipt of the goods. Assume that on November 10, 2013, Gap Inc. issues a purchase order to Queens, Ltd., a U.K. exporter, to purchase apparel for £100,000. Delivery of the clothing to Gap is expected on February 20, 2014, and payment is due on March 10, 2014. This future payment of £100,000 is a firm foreign currency purchase commitment that Gap elects to hedge by purchasing £100,000 for delivery on

March 10, 2014, at a forward rate of $1.605/£. The commitment period runs from November 10, 2013, to February 20, 2014. The time line for this sequence of events is shown below:

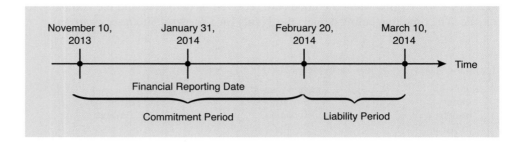

Gap makes no entries on November 10, 2013, because the purchase order is not recorded and the forward contract has no value at this time. On January 31, 2014, Gap's accounting year-end, the forward rate for delivery on March 10, 2014, is $1.625/£. Entries are now needed to mark to market both the forward contract and the firm commitment:

2014
Jan. 31

Investment in forward contract		2,000	
Exchange gain			2,000
To record the gain in fair value on the forward contract;			
$2,000 = ($1.625 − $1.605) × 100,000.			
Exchange loss		2,000	
Firm commitment			2,000
To record the loss on the firm commitment.			

The "firm commitment" account appears on the balance sheet as a current liability, representing the increased cost of the purchase commitment caused by the rising forward rate.

On February 20, the apparel is delivered to Gap. If the spot rate is $1.64/£ and the forward rate for delivery on March 10 is $1.645/£, Gap makes these entries:

2014
Feb. 20

Investment in forward contract		2,000	
Exchange gain			2,000
To record the gain in fair value on the forward contract;			
$2,000 = ($1.645 − $1.625) × 100,000.			
Exchange loss		2,000	
Firm commitment			2,000
To record the loss on the firm commitment.			
Inventories		164,000	
Accounts payable			164,000
To record delivery of the apparel at the current spot rate of $1.64.			
Firm commitment		4,000	
Inventories			4,000
To adjust the carrying value of apparel for the accumulated			
loss on the firm commitment during the commitment period.			

With the firm commitment gone, the forward contract hedges the recorded account payable. Now Gap accounts for the forward contract as a hedge of a foreign-currency-denominated liability, as discussed in the previous section on hedges of import and export transactions. If the spot rate on March 10 and, equivalently, the forward rate for delivery on March 10 is $1.635, Gap's entries to mark to market the account payable and the forward contract are:

2014			
Mar. 10	Accounts payable.	500	
	Exchange gain.		500
	To revalue the liability to Queens, Ltd. to the current exchange rate; $500 = ($1.64 − $1.635) × 100,000.		
	Exchange loss	1,000	
	Investment in forward contract		1,000
	To record the loss in fair value on the forward contract; $(1,000) = ($1.635 − $1.645) × 100,000.		

Gap records settlement of the forward contract and payment to Queens, Ltd. as follows:

2014			
Mar. 10	Foreign currency	163,500	
	Investment in forward contract		3,000
	Cash		160,500
	To record the payment of $160,500 to the broker, receipt of £100,000 valued at the current spot rate of $1.635, and settlement of the forward purchase contract; $3,000 = $2,000 + $2,000 − $1,000.		
	Accounts payable	163,500	
	Foreign currency		163,500
	To record the payment to the supplier.		

To summarize, Gap uses the hedging process to fix the dollar amount of the liability to Queens, Ltd. at $160,500. Income is unaffected during the commitment period because the forward contract perfectly hedges the loss on the firm commitment. After the goods are delivered, a net loss of $500 on hedge activity arises because the change in the value of the forward contract, measured by the change in the forward rate, does not exactly match the change in the value of the account payable, measured by the change in the spot rate. The change in value of the purchase commitment during the hedging period reduces the inventory balance from $164,000 to $160,000, and is therefore recognized in earnings at a higher gross margin when the inventory is sold. If the commitment is for the purchase of a depreciable asset such as equipment, the change in value impacts earnings as the asset is depreciated.

Forward Sale Contract: Fair Value Hedge of a Foreign Currency Sale Commitment An exporter may contract to sell goods at a specified time in the future at a fixed price denominated in foreign currency. The exporter can hedge the risk that the dollar value of the sale will decline by entering a forward contract to sell the currency when received. If the contract begins prior to the time delivery of the goods is made, the forward contract hedges a firm commitment. The time line below depicts the events for a *forward sale contract*:

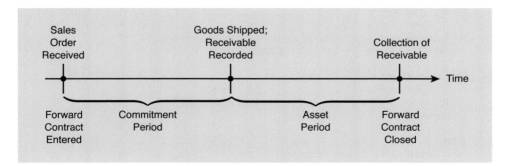

We illustrate the accounting with an example in which the sale transaction, collection, and settlement of the forward contract take place simultaneously. Therefore, the forward sale contract hedges only the foreign currency commitment; there is no asset to be hedged following the sale.

Suppose that Gap Inc. negotiated a cash sale of wool coats at a price of C$50,000 to Corsin, a Canadian retailer, on October 21, 2013. Payment is expected on March 19, 2014, at the same time the coats are delivered and the sale is recorded by Gap. The time line for this example appears below:

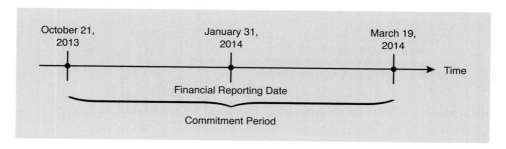

On October 21, 2013, the forward rate for delivery on March 19, 2014, is $0.98/C$. On January 31, 2014, the balance sheet date, the forward rate for delivery on March 19, 2014, is $0.975/C$, and on March 19, 2014, the spot rate is $0.96. No entries are required on October 21, 2013, because the forward contract has a fair value of zero and Gap does not record Corsin's order. Year-end adjusting entries are:

2014			
Jan. 31	Investment in forward contract	250	
	Exchange gain.		250
	To record the gain in fair value on the forward contract;		
	$250 = ($0.98 − $0.975) × 50,000.		
	Exchange loss	250	
	Firm commitment		250
	To record the offsetting change in fair value of the firm		
	commitment.		

On March 19, 2014, Gap delivers the coats, receives payment from Corsin, and closes the forward contract.

2014			
Mar. 19	Investment in forward contract	750	
	Exchange gain.		750
	To record the gain in fair value on the forward contract;		
	$750 = ($0.975 − $0.96) × 50,000.		
	Exchange loss	750	
	Firm commitment		750
	To record the offsetting loss in fair value on the firm commitment.		
	Foreign currency	48,000	
	Sales revenue		48,000
	To record the receipt of foreign currency and the sales revenue,		
	valued at the spot rate; $48,000 = $0.96 × 50,000.		
	Firm commitment.	1,000	
	Sales revenue		1,000
	To adjust the sales revenue for the change in value of the firm		
	commitment.		
	Cash.	49,000	
	Investment in forward contract		1,000
	Foreign currency		48,000
	To record delivery of the foreign currency to the broker, and		
	settlement of the forward contract.		

REVIEW 3 • Using Forward Contracts to Hedge Foreign-Currency-Denominated Firm Commitments

Fine Foods, Inc., a U.S. wholesaler, buys merchandise from German suppliers, paying the suppliers in euros. Fine Foods' accounting year ends June 30. Here are the relevant exchange rates:

Date	Spot rate ($/€)	Forward rate for delivery August 15, 2013
March 1, 2013	$1.35	$1.37
June 30, 2013	1.42	1.44
August 15, 2013	1.45	1.45
August 31, 2013	1.48	NA

On March 1, 2013, Fine Foods sends a purchase order to a German supplier for €1,000,000 in merchandise, payable in euros, delivery to take place August 15, 2013. Also on March 1, Fine Foods enters into a forward contract for delivery of €1,000,000 on August 15. The forward qualifies as a hedge of a firm commitment. On August 15, Fine Foods closes the forward contract, takes delivery of the merchandise, and pays the supplier. The merchandise is sold to a U.S. customer on August 31.

Required

a. Firm commitment, on the June 30, 2013, balance sheet?
b. Exchange gain or loss, on the fiscal 2013 income statement?
c. Exchange gain or loss, on the fiscal 2014 income statement?
d. Reported inventory amount, August 15, 2013?
e. Cost of goods sold, on the fiscal 2014 income statement?

Solutions are located after the chapter assignments.

Using Forward Contracts to Hedge Forecasted Transactions   It is common practice for companies to invest in forward contracts to hedge planned purchase or sale transactions denominated in foreign currencies, even though there is no firm commitment involved. Normal accounting for hedges of forecasted transactions does not match hedge gains and losses against losses and gains on the forecasted transaction, because forecasted transactions are not recorded.

LO4 Report hedges of foreign-currency-denominated forecasted transactions.

If the forward contract qualifies as a cash flow hedge of the forecasted transaction, *ASC Section 815-20-35* allows gains and losses due to changes in the fair value of such forward contracts to be reported in **other comprehensive income**, outside of earnings. These gains and losses are removed from other comprehensive income and recognized in earnings when the hedged forecasted transaction impacts earnings. This process matches the income effect of the hedge instrument against the income effect of the hedged item.

It is not possible to accurately recognize in the financial statements the changes in the fair value of the forecasted transaction as exchange rates change, as is the case with firm commitments, since the actual terms of the forecasted transaction are not yet known. Therefore, changes in the value of forward contracts used to hedge forecasted transactions are held in other comprehensive income to allow gains and losses on the hedge instrument to be matched against subsequent losses and gains on the hedged transaction.

Because hedge accounting delays income statement recognition of gains and losses on the hedge instrument, hedges of forecasted transactions must meet stringent criteria. These criteria include:

• The forecasted transaction must be identified, probable, part of an established business activity, and expose the company to exchange risk.

• There is formal documentation of the hedging relationship and the entity's risk management strategy for undertaking the hedge.

• The hedging relationship is expected to be highly effective and is assessed on a regular basis.

• The forecasted transaction involves an exchange with a third party external to the reporting entity, unless it is a forecasted intercompany foreign-currency-denominated transaction.

When these criteria are satisfied, the forward contract used to hedge the forecasted transaction qualifies as a *cash flow hedge*, and changes in its value are reported in other comprehensive income until the hedged transaction affects income. When these criteria are not satisfied, changes in the value of the forward contract are recognized currently in earnings.

Suppose Gap Inc. plans to purchase merchandise for €1,000,000 at the end of March, 2014, from a supplier in France. To hedge against a possible weakening of the dollar against the euro, Gap enters a forward purchase contract on December 2, 2013, for delivery of €1,000,000 on March 31, 2014, at a forward rate of $1.47/€. Because no cash changes hands initially, and the contract has no value at inception, no entry is made on December 2. On January 31, 2014, Gap's balance sheet date, the forward rate for delivery on March 31, 2014, is $1.472/€. The following entry marks to market the forward contract:

2014			
Jan. 31	Investment in forward contract	2,000	
	Other comprehensive income............................		2,000
	To record the gain in the fair value of the forward contract;		
	$2,000 = ($1.472 − $1.47) × 1,000,000.		

On March 31, 2014, Gap buys the foreign currency using the forward purchase contract and completes the forecasted transaction. If the spot rate is $1.482, these entries are made:

2014			
Mar. 31	Investment in forward contract	10,000	
	Other comprehensive income............................		10,000
	To record the gain in the fair value of the forward contract;		
	$10,000 = ($1.482 − $1.472) × 1,000,000.		
	Foreign currency	1,482,000	
	Investment in forward contract..........................		12,000
	Cash		1,470,000
	To record the settlement of the forward contract.		
	Inventories	1,482,000	
	Foreign currency		1,482,000
	To record the merchandise purchase.		

The gain on the forward purchase contract remains in other comprehensive income until the forecasted transaction impacts earnings. In this case, the forecasted transaction affects earnings when the inventory is sold. Assume the inventory is sold on June 21, 2014, for $2,482,000. In addition to the usual entries to record sales revenue of $2,482,000 and cost of goods sold of $1,482,000, this entry recognizes the gain on the forward contract, increasing the gross margin from $1,000,000 to $1,012,000:

2014			
June 21	Other comprehensive income	12,000	
	Cost of goods sold		12,000
	To reclassify as a component of current earnings the increase		
	in fair value of the forward contract used to hedge the now-		
	completed forecasted transaction.		

When the forward contract hedges a forecasted *sale* transaction, the gain or loss on the forward contract remains in other comprehensive income until the forecasted sale is made. At that point, it is reclassified out of other comprehensive income as an adjustment to sales revenue.

REVIEW 4 • Using Forward Contracts to Hedge Foreign-Currency-Denominated Forecasted Transactions

Fine Foods, Inc., a U.S. wholesaler, buys merchandise from German suppliers on a regular basis, and pays the suppliers in euros. Fine Foods' accounting year ends June 30. Exchange rates are as follows:

Date	Spot rate ($/€)	Forward rate for delivery August 15, 2013
March 1, 2013	$1.35	$1.37
June 30, 2013.	1.42	1.44
August 15, 2013	1.45	1.45
August 31, 2013	1.48	NA

Fine Foods plans to buy merchandise from the supplier in mid-August, 2013. On March 1, it enters into a forward contract for delivery of €1,000,000 on August 15. The forward qualifies as a cash flow hedge of a forecasted transaction. On August 15, Fine Foods closes the forward contract, takes delivery of the merchandise, and pays the supplier. The merchandise is sold to a U.S. customer on August 31 for $2,000,000.

Required Prepare the journal entries to record the above events.

Solutions are located after the chapter assignments.

BUSINESS APPLICATION   McDonald's Cash Flow hedges

McDonald's regularly receives payments from franchise operations in other countries which it can designate as forecasted transactions. These payments are denominated in the franchisees' local currencies. McDonald's uses cash flow hedges to reduce its exposure to changes in the value of these forecasted transactions. Footnotes to its 2010 financial statements describe the hedging relationships:

> To protect against the reduction in value of forecasted foreign currency cash flows (such as royalties denominated in foreign currencies), the Company uses forward foreign currency exchange agreements and foreign currency options to hedge a portion of anticipated exposures.
>
> When the U.S. dollar strengthens against foreign currencies, the decline in present value of future foreign denominated royalties is offset by gains in the fair value of the forward foreign currency exchange agreements and/or foreign currency options. Conversely, when the U.S. dollar weakens, the increase in the present value of future foreign denominated royalties is offset by losses in the fair value of the forward foreign currency exchange agreements and/or foreign currency options.

In 2010, McDonald's reported a net decrease of $1.5 million in OCI related to its cash flow hedges, compared with a net decrease of $31.5 million in 2009. Possible reasons for this much lower 2010 effect on OCI include the following: McDonald's did not engage in as much cash flow hedging, exchange rates did not fluctuate as much, or the investments did not qualify for hedge accounting. *Source:* McDonald's Corporation 2010 annual report.

Forward Contracts as Both Cash Flow and Fair Value Hedges   An importer or exporter may use the same forward contract to hedge a forecasted transaction through its cash settlement date. Such a forward contract starts as a cash flow hedge, and becomes a fair value hedge of a firm commitment or a recorded foreign-currency-denominated receivable or payable as time passes. The Codification requires that changes in the value of the forward contract be reported in other comprehensive income *throughout the hedging period*, even though the forward contract later becomes a fair value hedge. As changing exchange rates lead to gains and losses reported in earnings on the hedged item, a portion of other comprehensive income is reclassified to earnings as an offset.

Refer to the example just before Review 4, in which Gap hedges a €1,000,000 forecasted purchase from a supplier in France. Instead of paying for the merchandise on delivery, assume Gap expects to make payment on May 15, 2014. Assume also a May 15 delivery date for the forward contract, at a forward rate of $1.47. This forward contract hedges a forecasted transaction through March 31, and an exposed payable from March 31 to May 15.

The adjusting entry to mark the forward contract to market on January 31, the company's balance sheet date, is the same as shown previously, with the $2,000 unrealized gain reported in other comprehensive income. On March 31, the company records delivery of the merchandise as before:

2014			
Mar. 31	Inventories	1,482,000	
	Accounts payable		1,482,000
	To record the purchase of the merchandise at the $1.482 spot rate.		

On May 15, when the spot rate is $1.485, the forward contract is settled and the supplier is paid, Gap makes these entries:

2014			
May 15	Investment in forward contract	13,000	
	Other comprehensive income		13,000
	To record the gain in fair value on the forward contract;		
	$13,000 = ($1.485 − $1.472) × 1,000,000.		
	Exchange loss	3,000	
	Accounts payable		3,000
	To revalue the payable to the current exchange rate;		
	$3,000 = ($1.485 − $1.482) × 1,000,000.		
	Foreign currency	1,485,000	
	Investment in forward contract		15,000
	Cash		1,470,000
	To record the settlement of the forward contract.		
	Accounts payable.	1,485,000	
	Foreign currency		1,485,000
	To record payment to the supplier.		

Because the forward contract became a hedge of the exposed payable on March 31, the Codification provides that an amount exactly offsetting the reported loss on the accounts payable be reclassified from other comprehensive income to earnings, as follows:

2014			
May 15	Other comprehensive income	3,000	
	Exchange gain.		3,000
	To reclassify a portion of the gain on the forward contract to		
	earnings, as an offset to the loss on the accounts payable.		

When Gap sells the merchandise on June 21, it reclassifies the remainder of the gain on the forward contract to earnings, as an adjustment to cost of goods sold:

2014			
June 21	Cost of goods sold.	1,470,000	
	Other comprehensive income	12,000	
	Inventory		1,482,000
	To recognize the cost of merchandise sold, and reclassify the		
	unrealized gain on the forward contract to earnings.		

Reporting Perspective

ASC Topic 815 allows hedging gains and losses to be reported in many locations on the financial statements, including other comprehensive income, sales revenue, cost of sales, other operating expenses and various asset and liability accounts. As a result, it is difficult to develop a cohesive picture of a company's financial risks and the effectiveness of its hedge investments in neutralizing that risk. *ASC Topic 815* addresses this problem by requiring footnote disclosures that separate out and summarize the effects of hedging activities. These requirements are discussed later in the chapter.

Hedge of Net Investment in an International Company A U.S. company that invests in an international subsidiary is exposed to the risk that the value of its investment will change as exchange rates change. The company may hedge this foreign exchange risk with derivative investments or financial instruments denominated in the currency.

LO5 Report hedges of net investments in international operations.

As studied in Chapter 7, exposure of a net investment in an international entity to exchange rate changes consists of the account balances that are converted to U.S. dollars using the current exchange rate. As the current exchange rate changes, the U.S. dollar value of these accounts changes, generating gains and losses. If an international subsidiary's functional currency is the local currency, the U.S. parent *translates* the accounts of the international subsidiary into U.S. dollars. All assets and liabilities are translated at the current rate. If the international subsidiary's functional currency is the U.S. dollar, the U.S. parent *remeasures* the accounts of the subsidiary into U.S. dollars. Monetary assets and liabilities are remeasured at the current rate.

The parent of an international subsidiary whose functional currency is the local currency is exposed to foreign exchange risk through the *net* assets—assets less liabilities—of the subsidiary. Since net assets are usually positive—total assets are greater than total liabilities—the parent's exposure is similar to that of an exporter, with a net "receivable" denominated in the foreign currency. Effective hedges of this currency risk include forward sale contracts, put options, and debt denominated in the same currency.

The parent of an international subsidiary whose functional currency is the U.S. dollar is exposed to foreign exchange risk through monetary assets less total liabilities. Since this exposure is usually negative—total liabilities are greater than monetary assets—the parent's exposure is similar to that of an importer, with a net "payable" denominated in the foreign currency. Effective hedges of this currency risk include forward purchase contracts, call options, and other investments, such as loans receivable, denominated in the same currency. These concepts are summarized below.

	Foreign Currency Risk and Hedges	
Conversion Process	**Typical Exposure**	**Hedge Investments**
Translation	Assets − Liabilities > 0	Forward sale contracts Put options Foreign-currency-denominated debt
Remeasurement	Monetary assets − Liabilities < 0	Forward purchase contracts Call options Foreign-currency-denominated investments

ASC Topic 815 recognizes as hedges those forward contracts or other foreign currency investments or liabilities undertaken to neutralize the effect of exchange rate movements on a U.S. firm's investment in an international branch, an equity investee, or a subsidiary. If a hedge is so designated and is effective, it is viewed as an **economic hedge of a net investment in an international entity**.

Recall that a major goal of hedge accounting is to match gains and losses on the hedge investment with losses and gains on the hedged item in the same reporting period. When the international subsidiary's functional currency is its local currency, the gain or loss on a hedge of the net investment in the subsidiary is netted against the translation adjustment in AOCI. When the international subsidiary's functional currency is the U.S. dollar, the gain or loss on a hedge of the net investment in the subsidiary offsets the remeasurement gain or loss in income.

BUSINESS APPLICATION   McDonald's Net Investment Hedges

The functional currencies of **McDonald's** subsidiaries in Europe and Asia are generally their local currencies. Therefore McDonald's translates its subsidiaries' accounts into U.S. dollars, and the subsidiaries' net assets expose McDonald's to exchange risk. The footnotes to McDonald's 2010 annual report describe hedges of this exposure:

> Certain foreign currency denominated debt is used, in part, to protect the value of the Company's investments in certain foreign subsidiaries and affiliates from changes in foreign currency exchange rates.

Net investment hedges generated losses of $148.6 million in 2010, reported in OCI. We can conclude that the U.S. dollar *weakened*, on average, against the currencies of McDonald's subsidiaries, resulting in *translation gains* and offsetting *hedge losses*. Translation gains or losses, net of hedging losses and gains, are reported in McDonald's consolidated statement of shareholders' equity. For 2010, the net translation loss reduced OCI by $3 million. *Source:* McDonald's Corporation 2010 annual report.

LO6 Report speculative investments in foreign currency financial derivatives.

Use of Forward Contracts for Speculation   Forward contracts entered for hedging purposes represent defensive measures to protect against adverse effects of exchange rate movements. In contrast, some firms sell or purchase foreign currency forward for **speculative purposes**—to gain from anticipated changes in the exchange rate.

Because speculative forward contracts are by definition not hedge instruments, any gains and losses due to changes in their fair value are recognized currently in earnings. Having no offsetting loss or gain, speculative contracts increase earnings volatility.

Suppose a company expects the Canadian dollar (C$) to strengthen relative to the U.S. dollar, and decides to speculate by purchasing, on November 1, 2013, C$8,000,000 for delivery on March 29, 2014. The company will cover the contract by selling these Canadian dollars in the spot market when the forward contract matures on March 29, gaining if the rate increases, and losing if it falls. Assume that the company's accounting year ends on December 31. Relevant direct exchange rates ($/C$) are as follows:

Date	Spot Rate	Forward Rate for Delivery On March 29, 2014
November 1, 2013	$0.970	$0.940
December 31, 2013	0.965	0.935
March 29, 2014	0.932	0.932

The company records the events relating to this speculative forward contract, including sale of the Canadian dollars received from the forward contract, as follows:

2013			
Nov. 1	No entry at inception; the forward contract has no value.		
Dec. 31	Exchange loss	40,000	
	Investment in forward contract		40,000
	To record the loss in the fair value on the forward contract;		
	$40,000 = ($0.94 − $0.935) × 8,000,000.		

The company's December 31, 2013, balance sheet reports the $40,000 balance in the investment as a *current liability*.

2014			
Mar. 29	Exchange loss	24,000	
	Investment in forward contract		24,000
	To record the loss in fair value on the forward contract;		
	$24,000 = ($0.935 − $0.932) × 8,000,000.		
	Foreign currency	7,456,000	
	Investment in forward contract	64,000	
	Cash		7,520,000
	To record settlement of the forward contract and receipt of		
	Canadian dollars valued at the spot rate of $0.932/C$.		
	Cash	7,456,000	
	Foreign currency		7,456,000
	To record sale of Canadian dollars in the spot market at $0.932/C$.		

The total exchange loss recognized in the accounts, $64,000 (= $40,000 + $24,000), equals the net cash loss of $64,000 (= $7,520,000 − $7,456,000) from the speculative activity. The speculative contract results in a loss of $64,000 because the company must purchase C$8,000,000 under the contract for $0.94, and then sell that foreign currency on the spot market for $0.932. This company obviously did not possess sufficient insight on the future direction of exchange rates in this case.

Summary of Accounting for Foreign Currency Forward Contracts   The accounting for forward contracts requires reporting the contracts at fair market value in the financial statements. If the contract is a qualifying hedge, gains and losses on the contract and losses and gains on the hedged item are reported on the same period's income statement.

Hedges of accounts receivable or payable denominated in foreign currency do not require hedge accounting to achieve this result. The offsetting effects appear on the same income statement using normal accounting.

Hedge accounting is used for fair value hedges of firm foreign currency commitments and cash flow hedges of forecasted transactions. Fair value hedges of firm foreign currency commitments require concurrent recognition of commitment assets or liabilities. Gains and losses on forward contracts used as cash flow hedges of forecasted transactions accumulate in other comprehensive income until the forecasted transactions impact income. Gains and losses on speculative contracts are recognized currently in earnings as exchange rates change.

Derivatives Disclosure Requirements   The use of derivatives has grown dramatically over the years, and the instruments used can significantly affect financial performance. As we have seen in this chapter, the financial effects of foreign currency derivatives used for hedging and speculation are complex and not easily extracted from the financial statements. These effects are not separated out but are included in various accounts, such as sales revenue, cost of sales, administrative expenses and various asset and liability accounts. The related assets and liabilities are typically not separately listed on the balance sheet. As a result, financial statement readers rely on footnote disclosures to evaluate a company's performance with respect to derivatives activities and hedging.

Disclosures required by *ASC Topic 815* are designed to give financial statement readers a better view of the extent of a company's exposure to financial risk, its hedging activities, and the degree to which its financial risk is neutralized.

An entity with derivative instruments shall disclose information to enable users of the financial statements to understand:

a.   How and why an entity uses derivative instruments

b.   How derivative instruments and related hedged items are accounted for under *Topic 815*

c.   How derivative instruments and related hedged items affect an entity's financial position, financial performance, and cash flows.

Source: *ASC para. 815-10-50-1*

Specific required disclosures include the following:

- Discussion of hedging activities organized by risk exposure, such as foreign currency risk, interest rate risk, and price risk
- Volume of derivative activity
- Location and fair value amounts of derivative instruments reported in the balance sheet
- Location and amount of gains and losses reported in the income statement

Chapter 9 provides further discussion of these disclosure requirements.

BUSINESS APPLICATION   **Reporting Effects of Hedging Activities**

McDonald's financial statements illustrate how the effects of hedging activities are scattered throughout the financial statements. The footnotes to its 2010 annual report disclose the fair values of its foreign currency derivative investments and where they are reported on its 2010 balance sheet:

(in millions)	
Derivatives designated as hedging instruments	
Prepaid expenses and other current assets.	$7.5
Accrued payroll and other liabilities	4.6
Derivatives not designated as hedging instruments	
Prepaid expenses and other current assets.	$6.0
Miscellaneous other assets	2.7
Accrued payroll and other liabilities	3.8

Gains and losses on derivative investments are reported on McDonald's 2010 income statement in selling, general and administrative expenses, interest expense, and nonoperating (income) expense.

ASC Topic 815 requires footnote disclosure of the amount of gain or loss reported in income and in OCI for both the hedge instrument and the hedged item, by hedge type, to aid users in evaluating hedge performance. For 2010, McDonald's reports a $11.2 million gain in OCI from foreign currency cash flow hedges and $13.4 million in gains reclassified from AOCI to income. OCI also includes a loss of $148.6 million on net investment hedges.

Although they meet *ASC Topic 815* requirements, McDonald's footnote disclosures for cash flow hedges are not particularly helpful in evaluating hedge performance. To what extent do the gains of $13.4 million offset foreign currency losses on related hedged forecasted transactions? What gains on hedged net investments did the $148.6 million loss on net investment hedges offset? *Source:* McDonald's Corporation 2010 annual report.

The FASB and IASB recognize that current disclosure requirements for hedging activities need improvement. Both have proposals outstanding addressing this issue, but as of 2011, no conclusions have been reached.

INTERNATIONAL FINANCIAL REPORTING STANDARDS FOR FOREIGN CURRENCY TRANSACTIONS AND HEDGING

LO7 Describe IFRS for foreign currency transactions and hedging activities.

IFRS for reporting foreign currency transactions and investments in financial instruments appears in the following standards:

- *IAS 21*, The Effects of Changes in Foreign Exchange Rates
- *IAS 39*, Financial Instruments: Recognition and Measurement
- *IFRS 7*, Financial Instruments: Disclosures

IFRS for import and export transactions, as well as borrowing and lending in foreign currency, is the same as U.S. GAAP. IFRS for derivatives and hedging have the same goals as U.S. GAAP, requiring all financial derivatives to be reported at fair value on the balance sheet. Changes in value are reported in income, unless the derivative is a cash flow hedge of a forecasted transaction. Changes in the value of cash flow hedges are reported in a separate component of equity, and released to income in the same time period in which the hedged item impacts income.

Qualifications for Hedge Accounting

Because hedge accounting allows companies to determine when gains and losses are recognized on the income statement, *IAS 39* limits its use. Conditions to be met parallel those required under U.S. GAAP:

- There is formal designation and documentation of the hedging relationship and the company's risk management objective and strategy.
- The hedging relationship is effective.
- For cash flow hedges of forecasted transactions, the hedged forecasted transaction is highly probable and exposes the company to financial risk.

The IFRS hedge effectiveness measure is the same as under U.S. GAAP, calculated as the change in the value of the hedge divided by the change in the value of the hedged item. Although the FASB Codification does not provide specific numerical values indicating hedge effectiveness, *IAS 39* specifically states that the general range is -80% to -125%, the informal range in U.S. GAAP.

Differences Between IFRS and U.S. GAAP

The overall structure of derivatives reporting under IFRS, including categorization of investments as fair value or cash flow hedges and their reporting implications, is generally the same as under U.S. GAAP. However, we discuss below some differences that can have significant impacts on financial results.

Basis Adjustments   Changes in the value of cash flow hedges are reported in equity under both IFRS and U.S. GAAP. IFRS accumulates these gains and losses in an "equity reserve" account. If the hedge of a forecasted transaction results in the recognition of a nonfinancial asset, companies reporting under IFRS have the option to reclassify the hedge gains and losses as a **basis adjustment** to the asset. Although total reported income is the same, assets and equity are different when the basis adjustment is used, as illustrated next.

   Fiat Group is headquartered in Turin, Italy, and reports its financial statements in euros. It plans to purchase equipment for $1,000,000 on June 30, 2014. On November 1, 2013, the Group enters a forward contract to purchase $1,000,000 for €700,000 on June 30, 2014, and designates the contract as a cash flow hedge of the equipment purchase. By December 31, 2013, the Group's year-end, the U.S. dollar has appreciated and the forward price for delivery of $1,000,000 is €750,000. The year-end adjusting entry, in euros, is:

2013			
Dec. 31	Investment in forward contract	50,000	
	Equity reserve		50,000
	To record the change in the fair value of the forward contract.		

On June 30, 2014, the U.S. dollar has appreciated further, and $1,000,000 can be purchased in the spot market for €820,000. The Group settles the forward contract and purchases the equipment.

2014			
June 30	Investment in forward contract	70,000	
	Equity reserve		70,000
	To record the gain in the fair value of the forward contract.		
	Equipment	820,000	
	Investment in forward contract		120,000
	Cash		700,000
	To settle the forward contract and acquire the equipment.		

If Fiat Group chooses the basis adjustment option, the following entry is made:

2014			
June 30	Equity reserve.	120,000	
	Equipment		120,000
	To reclassify the gain on the cash flow hedge as a basis adjustment.		

Because U.S. GAAP does not permit the basis adjustment option, the equipment is initially reported at €820,000. U.S. companies retain the gain or loss on cash flow hedges in accumulated other comprehensive income until the hedged item impacts income. In this case, the gain is reclassified to income over time as an adjustment to periodic depreciation expense on the equipment.

If the equipment has a two-year life, straight-line, entries to record depreciation for the six months ending December 31, 2014, under IFRS and U.S. GAAP, respectively, are:

2014			
Dec. 31			
IFRS	Depreciation expense.	175,000	
	Equipment		175,000
	To record six months of depreciation on equipment;		
	$175,000 = $700,000/2 × ½.		

2014			
Dec. 31			
U.S. GAAP	Depreciation expense.	175,000	
	Other comprehensive income	30,000	
	Equipment		205,000
	To record six months of depreciation on equipment;		
	$205,000 = $820,000/2 × ½ and $30,000 = $120,000/2 × ½.		

The table below summarizes financial statement disclosure for the above example.

Fiat Group Selected Financial Statement Disclosures		
December 31, 2014	**IFRS**	**U.S. GAAP**
Depreciation expense.	€175,000	€175,000
Equipment, net.	525,000	615,000
Equity reserve/AOCI.	—	(90,000)

The income effect in the above example is the *same* whether the cash flow hedge gain remains in equity and adjusts depreciation, or is reclassified as an adjustment to the equipment. However, reported assets and equity are *lower* if Fiat Group chooses the basis adjustment option.

Requirements for Hedge Accounting   As in the U.S., companies subject to IFRS requirements need to know whether they can elect hedge accounting for their derivative investments. Hedge accounting generally results in smoother earnings recognition by matching hedge gains and losses against losses and gains on hedged items. Do IFRS companies have more opportunities to elect hedge accounting than U.S. companies? A comparison of the standards does not lead to an obvious conclusion. U.S. GAAP allows a hedging relationship to automatically qualify for hedge accounting if the critical terms of the hedge match those of the hedged item ("shortcut method"); IFRS does not. On the other hand, IFRS allows portfolio or "macro" hedges and partial hedges to qualify for hedge accounting, while U.S. GAAP does not.

BUSINESS APPLICATION   **Effects of IFRS Adoption for Hedging**

Ernst & Young examined reconciliations of IFRS to U.S. GAAP filed by 130 SEC foreign private issuers in 2006, and found that 85 companies had IFRS/U.S. GAAP reporting differences for derivatives and hedge accounting. Many international issuers did not meet the requirements for hedge accounting under U.S. GAAP, but this was usually because the company decided not to meet the documentation requirements. In addition, when companies adopted IFRS, many abandoned the hedge accounting practices previously allowed under their own country GAAP. **Rolls Royce Group**, a U.K. company, is an example. Below is an excerpt from its annual report for 2005. *Source:* Rolls Royce Group annual report 2005.

A large element of the Group's trading is denominated in US dollars and a significant portion of its costs is incurred in Sterling and Euros. In order to protect itself from the associated currency volatility, the Group takes significant levels of forward cover relating to its net exposure. Under UK GAAP, gains or losses on this cover are not recognised in the income statement until realised, matching them with the underlying transactions. Contracts may be signed several years in advance of delivery and forecasts of aftermarket sales have to be made. As contracts may be signed several years in advance of delivery, delivery dates may change and meeting the strict criteria for hedge accounting in IAS 39 is not considered to be practicable within the current risk management practices. Rolls-Royce believes that its current risk management practices are in the best economic interests of shareholders and should not be amended purely to achieve a particular accounting treatment. Accordingly, Rolls-Royce has decided not to adopt hedge accounting for forecast foreign exchange transactions. Rolls-Royce will continue to hedge its future forecast US dollar income on a portfolio basis, which it considers is the most efficient economic basis for doing so.

As a result of not hedge accounting for forecast foreign exchange transactions, the movements on the fair value of derivative contracts held for the purpose of hedging these transactions will be recognised in the income statement. The size of this movement in fair values will be largely dependent on movements in spot exchange rates as is indicated by the disclosures required by FRS 13 and included in the notes to accounts under UK GAAP.

Financial Instruments Disclosures

IFRS 7 disclosure requirements seek to provide financial statement users with the information necessary to evaluate the risks resulting from the use of financial instruments, how these risks are managed, and how these instruments affect financial performance.

For *each designated hedge type*—fair value hedges and cash flow hedges—the following information is required:

- Description of each hedge type
- Description of the financial instruments designated as hedges and their fair values
- Nature of the risks being hedged

Financial information on hedge activity is also required, as follows:

- For fair value hedges, the amount of gains or losses on the hedge instrument and the hedged item
- For cash flow hedges,
    - the amount of hedge ineffectiveness recognized in income
    - the amount of gains and losses recognized in equity during the period
    - the amount reclassified from equity to income during the period
    - the amount reclassified from equity as a basis adjustment

IFRS and U.S. GAAP disclosure standards have limitations that are currently being addressed. The next section briefly discusses current proposals.

FASB and IASB Hedge Accounting Projects

The FASB and IASB are currently considering changes to current hedge accounting standards to make hedging activities more transparent to financial statement users and to simplify the reporting requirements. Chapter 9 discusses these proposals in more detail. Here we briefly summarize the status of this effort as of 2012.

In 2010 the FASB and IASB made proposals that significantly change current hedge accounting standards. The FASB issued a proposed Accounting Standards Update covering reporting for all financial instruments, including derivatives used for hedging. The IASB issued an exposure draft of proposed hedge accounting standards as the third phase of their project to replace *IAS 39*'s financial instruments standards with *IFRS 9*. As of 2012, the IASB proposal is in Draft Review form.

The current IASB proposal differs in many ways from the FASB proposal. In general, the IASB proposal:

* broadens the definition of hedged item
* bases qualification for hedge accounting on how entities use hedges to manage risk
* makes hedge effectiveness criteria and evaluation more flexible
* focuses on disclosure of the risks being hedged, hedging activities, and hedging outcomes

The IASB's principles-based approach allows companies to apply hedge accounting when it is warranted by their particular activities. Current IFRS permits hedge accounting under limited circumstances, and companies cannot use hedge accounting for some hedging situations. The focus on disclosure of risks and how they are addressed provides more useful information for assessment of risk management performance.

The 2010 FASB proposal also makes hedge effectiveness criteria and evaluation more flexible, but puts more limitations on the definition of hedged item and qualification for hedge accounting. The IASB and FASB are working together to achieve convergence. Updates may be found on the IASB and FASB websites.

REVIEW OF KEY CONCEPTS

LO 1 **Report import and export transactions and borrowing and lending denominated in foreign currency. (p. 306)** Import and export transactions and borrowing and lending abroad by domestic companies often generate **receivables and payables denominated in a foreign currency**. As the direct exchange rate—$/foreign currency—rises (falls), the number of dollars ultimately to be received or paid increases (decreases). Such changes in the dollar equivalents of receivables and payables generate **exchange gains and losses** reported in earnings by the domestic company as exchange rates change.

LO 2 **Report hedges of foreign-currency-denominated receivables and payables. (p. 317)** **Changes in the value of forward contracts** used to hedge foreign-currency-denominated receivables or payables are **reported in earnings as forward rates change**. To the extent that spot and forward rates move together, gains and losses on the forward contracts completely offset the losses and gains on the receivables and payables.

LO 3 **Report hedges of foreign-currency-denominated firm commitments. (p. 320)** Forward contracts can hedge firm commitments, such as purchase or sales orders denominated in foreign currency. Changes in the value of these forwards are reported in earnings, offsetting changes in the value of the firm commitments recognized for this purpose. The hedging gains or losses eventually **adjust the inventory balance or sales revenue**.

LO 4 **Report hedges of foreign-currency-denominated forecasted transactions. (p. 325)** Changes in the value of forward contracts used to hedge forecasted purchases or sales denominated in foreign currency are initially recognized in **other comprehensive income**. When the hedged purchase or sale is reported in earnings, the hedging gain or loss is reclassified out of AOCI and **adjusts cost of sales or sales revenue**.

Report hedges of net investments in international operations (p. 329). Gains and losses on qualifying hedges **LO 5**
of a company's net investment in an international subsidiary are matched with the related loss or gain on conversion of the subsidiary's accounts to the parent's currency. When the subsidiary's functional currency is the local
currency, the translation gain or loss and the hedge loss or gain are both reported in other comprehensive income.
When the subsidiary's functional currency is the parent's currency, the remeasurement gain or loss and the hedge
loss or gain are both reported in income.

Report speculative investments in foreign currency financial derivatives. (p. 330) Changes in the value of **LO 6**
forward contracts not qualifying as hedges are **reported in earnings** as forward rates change.

Describe international financial reporting standards for foreign currency transactions and hedging activi- **LO 7**
ties. (p. 332) **IFRS** for foreign currency denominated import and export transactions, borrowing and lending,
financial instruments and hedging activities are similar to U.S. GAAP, although some differences in application
include allowing **basis adjustments** for cash flow hedges.

MULTIPLE CHOICE QUESTIONS ·····················

1. On May 20, 2013, when the spot rate is $1.28/€, a U.S. company buys merchandise from a supplier in Italy, **LO 1**
at a cost of €100,000. The spot rate is $1.25/€ on June 30, the company's year-end. Payment of €100,000
is made on July 30, 2013, when the spot rate is $1.32/€. What is the effect on fiscal 2013 and fiscal 2014
income?

	fiscal 2013	fiscal 2014
a.	No effect	$4,000 exchange loss
b.	$3,000 exchange loss	$7,000 exchange gain
c.	No effect	$4,000 exchange gain
d.	$3,000 exchange gain	$7,000 exchange loss

2. On April 10, 2013, when the spot rate is $1.30/€, a U.S. company sells merchandise to a customer in Italy. **LO 1**
The spot rate is $1.31/€ on June 30, the company's year-end. Payment of €100,000 is received on August
10, 2013, when the spot rate is $1.28/€. What is the effect on fiscal 2013 and 2014 income?

	fiscal 2013	fiscal 2014
a.	$1,000 exchange loss	$3,000 exchange gain
b.	No effect	$2,000 exchange loss
c.	No effect	$2,000 exchange gain
d.	$1,000 exchange gain	$3,000 exchange loss

Use the following forward and spot prices for Canadian dollars (C$) to answer questions 3 – 8 below. The prices
are in U.S. dollars ($/C$).

	Spot rate	Forward rate for 4/15/14 delivery of Canadian dollars
November 15, 2013	$0.905	$0.895
December 31, 2013	0.965	0.950
March 1, 2014	0.920	0.915
April 15, 2014	0.940	0.940

3. On November 15, 2013, a U.S. company takes delivery of merchandise costing C$1,000,000 from a Cana- **LO 2**
dian supplier and records an account payable. On the same date, the company enters a forward contract locking in the U.S. dollar purchase price of C$1,000,000, for delivery on April 15, 2014. The forward contract
is closed and payment is made to the supplier on April 15, 2014. The company's accounting year ends on

December 31. Assuming the company still holds the merchandise at December 31, 2013, at what amount is the merchandise reported?

   a. $895,000
   b. $905,000
   c. $950,000
   d. $965,000

LO 2   **4.** Use the information from question 3. What is the net exchange gain or loss for 2014?

   a. $15,000 gain
   b. $25,000 loss
   c. $10,000 loss
   d. $25,000 gain

LO 3   **5.** On November 15, 2013, a U.S. company issues a purchase order to a Canadian supplier for merchandise costing C$1,000,000. On the same date, the company enters a forward contract locking in the U.S. dollar purchase price of C$1,000,000, for delivery on April 15, 2014. The forward qualifies as a hedge of the firm commitment. Delivery of the merchandise takes place on March 1, 2014, and the forward contract is closed and payment is made to the supplier on April 15, 2014. How is the forward contract reported on the company's December 31, 2013, balance sheet?

   a. $60,000 asset
   b. $60,000 liability
   c. $55,000 liability
   d. $55,000 asset

LO 3   **6.** Use the information from question 5. After delivery, at what amount is the merchandise carried on the U.S. company's books?

   a. $895,000
   b. $900,000
   c. $905,000
   d. $915,000

LO 4   **7.** A U.S. company expects to buy merchandise from a Canadian supplier for approximately C$1,000,000, in the middle of April. On November 15, 2013, the company enters a forward contract locking in the U.S. dollar purchase price of C$1,000,000, for delivery on April 15, 2014. The forward qualifies as a hedge of the forecasted transaction. Delivery of the merchandise takes place on April 15, 2014, and the forward contract is closed and payment is made to the supplier. At what amount is the merchandise reported on delivery on April 15, 2014?

   a. $895,000
   b. $905,000
   c. $940,000
   d. $950,000

LO 4   **8.** Use the information from question 7. When the merchandise is sold, at what amount will the company report cost of goods sold?

   a. $895,000
   b. $905,000
   c. $940,000
   d. $950,000

LO 6   **9.** On March 1, 2014, a U.S. company enters a forward contract locking in the selling price of C$1,000,000, for delivery on April 15, 2014. The contract does not qualify for hedge accounting. What is the gain or loss on the forward contract that is reported on the company's 2014 income statement?

   a. $ 5,000 loss
   b. $20,000 gain
   c. $25,000 loss
   d. $ 5,000 gain

LO 7 **10.** A UK company hedges its U.S. dollar purchase of equipment from a U.S. supplier using a forward contract exchanging pounds for U.S. dollars at a fixed rate. The forward qualifies as a hedge of a forecasted transaction. The company reports gains on the forward, and then closes the forward and buys the equipment. The company follows IFRS, and it uses the gain as a basis adjustment to the reported cost of the equipment. Which statement is **true**?

a. The IFRS company will report a lower equipment value on its balance sheet than if it followed U.S. GAAP.
b. The IFRS company will report less total depreciation expense on the equipment than if it followed U.S. GAAP.
c. The IFRS company will report a higher equipment value on its balance sheet than if it followed U.S. GAAP.
d. The IFRS company will report more total depreciation expense on the equipment than if it followed U.S. GAAP.

Assignments with the ✓ in the margin are available in an online homework system.
See the Preface of the book for details.

EXERCISES ••

E8.1 **Recording Import Transactions** Northern Merchandise Company imports a variety of items for re- **LO 1** sale to U.S. retailers. Following is a description of purchases and foreign-currency-denominated payments made in the last accounting period, plus the direct exchange rates for each date:

Country	Amount	Currency	Spot Rate at Purchase	Spot Rate at Payment
Australia	200,000	Australian Dollar	$1.02000	$1.05000
Thailand	800,000	Baht	0.03500	0.03300
Indonesia	5,000,000	Rupiah	0.00015	0.00014
Jordan	500,000	Dinar	1.42000	1.42000

Required

Prepare the journal entries made by Northern, a U.S. company, to record the above purchase and payment transactions.

E8.2 **Recording Export Transactions** Southern Exports, a U.S. company, sells items abroad. Southern **LO 1** prices many of these transactions in the currency of the customer. Following are four such transactions made in the last accounting period, plus the direct exchange rates for each date:

Country	Amount	Currency	Spot Rate at Sale	Spot Rate at Collection
Argentina	250,000	Peso	$0.239	$0.251
Canada	400,000	Dollar	1.010	1.025
India	300,000	Rupee	0.024	0.022
South Africa	100,000	Rand	0.141	0.137

Required

Prepare the journal entries made by Southern to record the above sale and collection transactions.

E8.3 **Recording Import and Export Transactions** Walsh Corporation imports raw materials from other **LO 1** ✓ countries and exports finished goods to customers throughout the world. Information regarding four such transactions occurring in the last accounting period, all denominated in units of foreign currency, is given below:

Country	Amount	Spot Rate at Transaction Date	Spot Rate at Payment Date
1. Import from Taiwan	100,000 T dollars	$0.033	$0.038
2. Import from Poland	600,000 zloty	0.300	0.285
3. Export to Brazil	400,000 real	0.296	0.263
4. Export to Switzerland	950,000 francs	0.750	0.786

Required

Prepare the journal entries made by Walsh to record the above events on the transaction date and on the payment date.

LO 1

YUM! BRANDS, INC.
[YUM]

E8.4   Adjusting Entry at Balance Sheet Date   Yum! Brands, Inc. has the following receivables and payables denominated in foreign currencies, prior to closing on December 31. The spot rates at December 31 are also given.

Item	$ Balance	FC Balance	Spot rate
1. Receivable	$ 75,000	1,000,000 Mexican pesos	$0.08
2. Receivable	240,000	225,000 Canadian dollars	1.02
3. Payable.	550,000	400,000 Jordan dinar	1.35
4. Payable.	50,000	200,000 Saudi Arabian riyal	0.26

Required

Prepare the adjusting entry recorded by Yum! Brands at December 31. Show all calculations.

LO 2   E8.5   Hedging Foreign-Currency-Denominated Liability   On March 15, 2014, Schaeffer Corporation purchased goods from a South Korean company at an invoice price of 20,000,000 won (W); payment is due on April 14, 2014. To hedge its exposed position, Schaeffer purchased W20,000,000 on March 15 for delivery on April 14 at a forward rate of $.00090/W. The spot rate was $.000905/W on March 15 and rose to $.000908/W on April 14.

Required

a.   Prepare the journal entries made by Schaeffer on March 15 and April 14, 2014.
b.   Calculate the cash gain or loss realized by Schaeffer by hedging compared with not hedging.

LO 2   E8.6   Hedging Foreign-Currency-Denominated Asset   Ruhf Company, a U.S. firm, manufactures culinary equipment for sale to customers worldwide. On September 1, 2013, Ruhf Company sold coffee-roasting equipment to a Brazilian customer at an invoice price of 40,000,000 real; the customer paid on September 30, 2013. Ruhf hedged its risk exposure by selling forward 40,000,000 real on September 1 for delivery on September 30, at a forward rate of $0.652/real. The spot rate was $0.65/real on September 1 and fell to $0.64 on September 30.

Required

a.   Prepare the journal entries made by Ruhf on September 1 and September 30.
b.   Calculate the cash gain or loss realized by Ruhf by hedging compared with not hedging.

LO 2, 3   E8.7   Hedged Purchase Commitment and Foreign-Currency-Denominated Liability   On September 15, 2014, the Hawkins Corporation, a U.S. company, agreed to purchase 10,000 PDAs from a Mexican supplier for a total invoice price of 15,000,000 pesos. The PDAs are received on November 15 and payment is made on January 15, 2015. Concurrently, on September 15, 2014, Hawkins purchased 15,000,000 pesos for delivery on January 15, 2015, for payment of the invoice price. Hawkins Corporation closes its books on December 31. Relevant exchange rates ($/peso) are as follows:

	Spot Rate	Forward Rate for Delivery on January 15, 2015
September 15, 2014.	$0.102	$0.104
November 15, 2014	0.103	0.105
December 31, 2014	0.105	0.107
January 15, 2015	0.108	0.108

Required

Prepare the journal entries made by Hawkins to record the above events, including any required year-end adjusting entries.

LO 2, 3   E8.8   Hedged Sale Commitment and Foreign-Currency-Denominated Asset   The Stanley Company, a calendar-year U.S. corporation, manufactures various filter materials. On April 15, 2013, Stanley received an order from a diamond-mining company in South Africa for a large quantity of reusable filters to be used in the dust masks of diamond miners. The total price in rands (R) was R1,000,000. Stanley shipped the filters on April 30, 2013, and payment was received in rands on May 15, 2013. Upon receipt of the sales order, Stanley immediately sold R1,000,000 for delivery in 30 days. Relevant exchange rates ($/R) are shown below:

	Spot Rate	Forward Rate for Delivery on May 15, 2013
April 15, 2013	$0.138	$0.140
April 30, 2013	0.146	0.148
May 15, 2013	0.149	0.149

Required

Prepare the journal entries made by Stanley to record the above events.

E8.9 Hedged Forecasted Purchase Mansfield Corporation purchases merchandise from a German supplier on a regular basis. On April 1, 2013, Mansfield purchased €14,000 for delivery on June 30, 2013, in anticipation of an expected purchase of merchandise for €14,000 at the end of June. The forward contract was a qualified hedge of a forecasted transaction. Mansfield took delivery of the merchandise, settled the forward contract, and paid the German supplier €14,000 on June 30, 2013. The merchandise was subsequently sold in the U.S. on July 12, 2013, for $19,000 in cash. Relevant exchange rates ($/€) are as follows: **LO 4**

	April 1, 2013	June 30, 2013
Spot rate	$1.40	$1.44
Forward rate for delivery on June 30, 2013	1.38	1.44

Required

Prepare the journal entries made by Mansfield on June 30 and July 12 concerning the above events. Assume Mansfield is a calendar-year company.

E8.10 Hedged Forecasted Sale Bectel, Inc. expects to sell merchandise for C$1,000,000 to a Canadian customer at the end of November, 2014. In anticipation of this forecasted transaction, on August 30, 2014, Bectel sold C$1,000,000 forward for delivery on November 30, 2014. Bectel made the sale as expected on November 30, and settled the forward contract. Relevant exchange rates ($/C$) are as follows: **LO 4**

	August 30	November 30
Spot rate	$0.98	$1.03
Forward rate for delivery on November 30, 2014	1.02	1.03

Required

Prepare the journal entries made by Bectel on November 30 concerning the above events. Assume Bectel is a calendar-year company.

E8.11 Recording International Investment To take advantage of high short-term interest rates, **Chipotle Mexican Grill** purchased a 1,000,000 krona six-month certificate of deposit from a Swedish bank for $124,500 on October 1, 2012. The annual interest rate is 15 percent. Chipotle received the full principal and interest, in krona, on March 31, 2013, and immediately exchanged the krona for U.S. dollars at the current spot rate. Spot rates ($/krona) at December 31, 2012, and March 31, 2013, were $0.1445 and $0.1228, respectively. Chipotle is a calendar-year company. **LO 1**

CHIPOTLE MEXICAN GRILL [CMG]

Required

a. Prepare the journal entries recorded by Chipotle on October 1, 2012, December 31, 2012, and March 31, 2013.

b. Was this a good investment? Explain with calculations.

KRISPY KREME DOUGHNUTS, INC.
[KKD]

✓ LO 6   **E8.12 Speculative Foreign Contracts**   **Krispy Kreme Doughnuts, Inc.** has franchises operating outside the U.S. and invests in derivatives to hedge its foreign currency risk. Although it tries to hedge its various positions, on December 16, 2013, Krispy Kreme finds itself with the following unhedged forward contracts:

• Agreement to purchase 10,000,000 Hong Kong dollars ($H) in 30 days at $0.13/$H.
• Agreement to sell 10,000,000 Singapore dollars ($S) in 30 days at $0.84/$S.

Relevant exchange rates are:

30-day forward rates at December 16, 2013	$0.128/$H	$0.834/$S
15-day forward rates at December 31, 2013	0.125/$H	0.842/$S
Spot rates at January 15, 2014	0.131/$H	0.836/$S

Required
a. What are the correct balances for the above contracts at December 16, 2013?
b. Prepare the journal entries made by Krispy Kreme on December 31, 2013, and January 15, 2014, assuming that the balances of the forward contracts are properly stated at December 16, 2013, and that the company closes its books on December 31.

PROBLEMS ●

LO 1, 2   **P8.1**   **Computation of Exchange Gain or Loss**   Wheelstick Corporation, incorporated in the state of Delaware, is active in the import/export business. An analysis of Wheelstick's receivables, payables, and other assets (liabilities) prior to adjustment at December 31, 2012, disclosed the following:

Receivables	
U.S. customers	$ 100,000
Belgian customers (300,000 euros)	428,200
Indian customers (1,200,000 rupees)	23,950
Saudi Arabian customers (90,000 riyal)	24,000
Total receivables	$ 576,150
Payables	
U.S. suppliers	$ (60,000)
Japanese suppliers (1,000,000 yen)	(12,000)
Mexican suppliers (500,000 pesos)	(39,550)
Total payables	$(111,550)
Other current assets (liabilities)	
Investment in forward purchase contract (for delivery of 500,000 pesos in 30 days at $0.0816)	$ (1,125)
Investment in forward sale contract (for delivery of 300,000 euros in 60 days at $1.40)	(10,000)
Total other current assets (liabilities)	$ (11,125)

Relevant exchange rates ($/FC) for the above currencies at December 31, 2012, are:

Currency	
Euro (spot rate)	$1.43800
Euro (60-day forward rate)	1.44400
Rupee (spot rate)	0.02350
Riyal (spot rate)	0.26660
Yen (spot rate)	0.01303
Mexican peso (spot rate)	0.08140
Mexican peso (30-day forward rate)	0.08165

Required

a. Prepare a schedule to compute the exchange gain or loss recognized by Wheelstick in 2012. Record the needed adjusting entries.

b. Comment on the hedge effectiveness of the two forward contracts.

P8.2 **Import/Export Transactions and Hedged Commitment**   The following international transactions were entered into during 2013 by **Sysco Corporation**, the largest foodservice distributor in North America:

LO 1, 3 ✓

SYSCO CORPORATION [SYY]

1. June 15, 2013: Entered into a firm commitment to purchase frozen pasta entrees from Italy which will be resold in the United States. The invoice price was €4,000,000, and delivery and payment were to be made in 60 days. Concurrently, €4,000,000 was purchased in the forward market for delivery in 60 days at the forward rate of $1.45. The goods were received, payment was made, and the forward contract was settled on August 14, 2013, when the spot rate was $1.43.

2. September 1, 2013: Canned products priced at 3,000,000 zloty were sold to a food distributor in Poland when the spot rate was $0.38. Payment was received on November 3, 2013, when the spot rate was $0.36, and the zloty were immediately converted to dollars.

Required

Prepare the 2013 journal entries made by Sysco Corporation relating to the above transactions. Sysco is a calendar year company.

P8.3 **Accounting for Forward Contracts—Hedging and Speculation**   Futura Corporation, a calendar-year corporation, is an active trader in foreign exchange, to hedge its international activities and for outright speculation. In particular, it is active in the forward market for krone (kr), the currency of Denmark. On November 1, 2012, Futura entered into the following forward contracts. The contracts were settled on January 29, 2013.

LO 2, 3, ✓ 4, 6

1. Sold kr2,000,000 forward to hedge a forthcoming kr2,000,000 sale to a Danish firm; the sale price and January 29, 2013 delivery date have been negotiated and the customer will pay upon delivery.

2. Purchased kr3,000,000 forward to hedge a forecasted purchase from a Danish supplier. Delivery and payment on the forecasted purchase takes place on January 29, 2013.

3. Sold kr1,000,000 forward in anticipation of a fall in the spot rate.

Relevant exchange rates ($/kr) are as follows:

	November 1, 2012	**December 31, 2012**	**January 29, 2013**
Spot rate.	$0.162	$0.172	$0.192
Thirty-day forward rate. . . .	0.145	0.165	0.185
Sixty-day forward rate	0.125	0.145	0.190
Ninety-day forward rate . . .	0.105	0.132	0.195

Required

a. Prepare the journal entries made by Futura on December 31, 2012, and January 29, 2013, regarding the above transactions.

b. Indicate how the above transactions would be disclosed on Futura's December 31, 2012, balance sheet and income statement.

c. Comment on the specific use of the forward market by Futura.

P8.4 **Hedging, Leverage, Return on Assets**   The Cheesecake Factory Inc.'s December 31, 2012, balance sheet shows total liabilities of $700 million and total assets of $1 billion; measured financial leverage is therefore 0.70. Included in current liabilities is $400 million (C$500 million) payable on April 1, 2013, to a Canadian supplier. Cheesecake Factory's management expects exchange rates to converge to $0.83/C$ on March 31, 2013, and April 1, 2013.

LO 2

THE CHEESECAKE FACTORY INC. [CAKE]

Required

Assuming that Cheesecake Factory's management always seeks to portray the most positive financial picture possible, assess the effects of the following actions. Disregard income taxes.

a. On January 1, 2013, management enters into a 90-day forward purchase contract for C$500 million, costing $440 million. Compute the expected gain or loss from hedging compared with not hedging. Assuming total assets and liabilities are unchanged except as indicated by exchange rate movements, analyze how the hedge affects Cheesecake Factory's financial leverage when first quarter 2013 interim financial statements are issued.

b.   If Cheesecake Factory can borrow domestically at 12% per annum, evaluate the wisdom of using the forward contract described in part *a* above to neutralize the exchange rate risk.

c.   Cheesecake Factory's operating income for 2012 was $152 million; its annual return on average total assets (ROA) in 2012 was 16 percent. Cheesecake Factory projects the same relationship for 2013 at current exchange rates. Management considers purchasing C$500 million on January 1, 2013, for delivery in 90 days for $405 million to hedge the payable to the Canadian supplier. Cheesecake Factory projects total assets at $1.2 billion at March 31, 2013. Holding March 31, 2013, assets at $1.2 billion, analyze how hedging the payable, compared with not hedging, affects the first quarter ROA. Assume that foreign exchange gains and losses are part of operating income.

LO 1   **P8.5**   **Transaction Exposure and Credit Analysis**   You were recently hired as a credit analyst at a large financial institution. You have assembled the following information for Poole Corporation.

Poole Corporation Balance Sheet *(in millions)* December 31, 2013	
Cash and receivables.	$ 450
Inventory.	300
Plant assets, net.	500
Total assets	$1,250
Current liabilities.	$ 400
Long-term liabilities	475
Stockholders' equity	375
Total liabilities and stockholders' equity	$1,250

Additional information:

1.   Net income reported for 2013 was $150 million.
2.   Depreciation expense was $50 million.
3.   Noncash working capital increased by $40 million, including $25 million of unrealized exchange gains accruing on foreign currency denominated current assets ($11 million) and liabilities ($14 million).
4.   Unrealized exchange gains on long-term debt, $22 million.
5.   Inventory includes $100 million in items normally sold to customers in Argentina for 500 million Argentina pesos; estimated sales value at the current spot rate of $.35/peso is $175 million.
6.   Poole's various disclosures indicate no hedging of foreign currency exposures.

Required

a.   One dimension of earnings quality is nearness to cash. Using the information given, calculate cash flow from operations to assess this dimension of earnings quality.

b.   Sales to international customers are denominated in a highly volatile foreign currency. The dollar is forecast to strengthen relative to this currency during 2014, with the spot rate possibly falling to $0.20/peso. Discuss the likely effect of this development on Poole's cash flow.

c.   Describe the measures you would like to see Poole undertake to raise your level of comfort before making a loan to the company.

LO 3   **P8.6**   **Hedging a Foreign Currency Commitment—Effects on Income**   On October 1, 2013, Ellis Corporation agreed to sell 50,000 electric motors to a Swiss customer for 500,000 swiss francs (CHF). Delivery is to be made on November 30, 2013, and payment is to be received on January 31, 2014. Concurrently, Ellis sold CHF500,000 forward for delivery on January 31, 2014, for a total contract price of $634,000. Ellis closes its books annually on December 31. Current spot rates and forward rates ($/CHF) for delivery on January 31, 2014, are as follows:

	Spot Rate ($/CHF)	Forward Rate ($/CHF)
October 1, 2013	$1.220	$1.268
November 30, 2013	1.250	1.310
December 31, 2013	1.240	1.290
January 31, 2014	1.280	1.280

Required

a. Prepare all journal entries relative to the sale and the forward contract during 2013 and 2014.
b. Prepare a schedule showing the income statement effects of the above events in each of the two years.
c. Did Ellis gain or lose from hedging the foreign currency commitment? Explain.

P8.7 **Hedging a Forecasted Transaction** On September 1, 2013, Morton Industries, a calendar-year company, decided to purchase merchandise from a supplier in Jordan for 1,000,000 dinar at the end of January, 2014. Morton plans to submit payment to the supplier on March 1, 2014. Concurrently, Morton purchased 1,000,000 dinar forward for delivery on March 1, 2014, for a total price of $1,420,000. This forward contract qualifies as a hedge of a forecasted transaction. On January 29, 2014, Morton took delivery of the merchandise. On March 1, 2014, the forward contract was settled and payment was made to the supplier. On April 8, 2014, the merchandise was sold to a U.S. customer for $1,600,000. Relevant exchange rates ($/dinar) are as follows: **LO 4**

	Spot Rate	Forward Rate for Delivery on March 1, 2014
September 1, 2013	$1.410	$1.420
December 31, 2013	1.431	1.441
January 29, 2014	1.450	1.458
March 1, 2014	1.460	1.460

Required

Prepare the required journal entries to record the above events, including December 31, 2013 adjusting entries.

P8.8 **Analyzing the Performance of an Import/Export Department** William Johnston manages the import/export department of Bush Specialty Products. Because of the complexities of foreign currency transactions and the continual changes in exchange rates, Bush's management is having difficulty determining exactly how Johnston's operation is performing. You have been called in as a consultant to give advice on this performance-evaluation task. **LO 1, 2, 6**

After you discuss the problem with Mr. Johnston, he produces the summary of his department's activities shown below. The letters FC identify foreign currency units, and exchange rates are defined as $/FC.

	Import Transactions			
Quantity—Part No.	Unit Cost (FC)	Spot Rate When Purchased	Spot Rate When Paid	Unit Selling Price
2,000—K14	6.4	$0.83	$0.80	$ 7.75
17,000—KR08	10.0	0.49	0.58	6.00
5,000—L16	8.2	1.13	1.22	10.00
10,000—M29Q	25.2	0.37	0.32	9.20

	Export Transactions			
Quantity—Part No.	Unit Selling Price (FC)	Spot Rate When Sold	Spot Rate When Collected	Unit Cost
14,000—A24...............	8.4	$0.27	$0.29	$ 1.98
6,000—DD2	12.5	2.00	1.92	24.00
20,000—A27...............	10.0	1.10	1.16	8.90
1,000—B23	14.6	0.63	0.58	8.50

	Forward Contracts			
Quantity of FC Purchased (Sold)	Spot Rate at Inception	Forward Rate at Inception	Spot Rate at Maturity	Purpose of Contract
210,000................	$0.57	$0.62	$0.59	Hedge
(300,000)	0.88	0.90	0.87	Hedge
1,000,000................	0.28	0.25	0.22	Speculation
(1,000,000)	0.75	0.74	0.85	Speculation

Required

a. Prepare, in good form, schedules to calculate the profit contribution or loss realized by the import/export department.

b. Write a short memorandum to top management regarding your findings. Should Mr. Johnston be fired? Explain.

LO 1, 2 **P8.9 Recording a Hedged International Loan** The Roderick Company borrowed £50 million from a London bank on December 16, 2014. The £50 million were immediately converted to dollars for use in the United States and were scheduled to be repaid with interest of £500,000 on January 15, 2015. To hedge the risk of an unfavorable change in the exchange rate, Roderick purchased £50.5 million for delivery on January 15, 2015. Roderick's accounting period ends on December 31. Exchange rates on various dates follows:

	December 16, 2014	December 31, 2014	January 15, 2015
Spot rate................................	$1.68	$1.66	$1.63
Forward rate for delivery on January 15, 2015...	1.71	1.69	1.63

Required

Prepare the journal entries made by Roderick on December 16, 2014, December 31, 2014, and January 15, 2015.

LO 4 **P8.10 Interpretation of Financial Statement Disclosures** Following are excerpts from the footnotes to **IBM Corporation**'s 2010 financial statements:

IBM CORPORATION [IBM]

The company's operations generate significant nonfunctional currency, third-party vendor payments and intercompany payments for royalties and goods and services among the company's non-U.S. subsidiaries and with the parent company. In anticipation of these foreign currency cash flows and in view of the volatility of the currency markets, the company selectively employs foreign exchange forward contracts to manage its currency risk.

At December 31, 2010 and 2009, in connection with cash flow hedges of anticipated royalties and cost transactions, the company recorded net losses of $147 million and of $718 million (before taxes), respectively, in accumulated other comprehensive income/(loss). Within these amounts $249 million and $427 million of losses, respectively, are expected to be reclassified to net income within the next 12 months, providing an offsetting economic impact against the underlying anticipated transactions.

Required

a. Explain how IBM uses forward contracts to reduce currency risk related to anticipated royalties and cost transactions.
b. If the hedges described above are **net forward sale contracts**, does IBM anticipate a net inflow or outflow of foreign currency related to its hedged royalty and cost transactions? Explain.
c. Again assuming the hedges are net forward sale contracts, on average did the U.S. dollar strengthen or weaken with respect to the currencies hedged in 2010 and 2009? How do you know?
d. For these cash flow hedges, where and when will the reclassification to income be recorded?

P8.11 **Hedge of Forecasted Transaction, Firm Commitment, and Foreign-Currency-Denominated** **LO 4**
Liability   Willson Leather Company, a calendar-year company, purchases merchandise from an Italian supplier on a regular basis. On November 1, 2013, Willson purchased €10,000,000 for delivery on March 1, 2014, in anticipation of an expected purchase of merchandise. The forward purchase qualifies as a cash flow hedge. On January 15, 2014, Willson issued a purchase order for €10,000,000 in merchandise, establishing a firm commitment. The merchandise was received on February 1, 2014. On March 1, 2014, Willson closed the forward and paid the supplier. On March 15, the merchandise was sold to a U.S. customer for $25,000,000. Exchange rates ($/€) are as follows:

	Spot Rate	Forward Rate for Delivery on March 1, 2014
November 1, 2013	$1.38	$1.41
December 31, 2013	1.39	1.42
January 15, 2014	1.40	1.43
February 1, 2014	1.43	1.45
March 1, 2014.	1.45	1.45

Required

Prepare the journal entries to record the above events.

P8.12 **Evaluation of Domestic and International Investments**   The treasurer of Enormo Corporation is   **LO 1** always on the lookout for short-term, high-yielding investments. Six-month low-risk domestic investments currently yield 6 percent per annum. Two international investments of comparable risk are also being considered.

1. A six-month certificate of deposit issued by the Bank of England has a coupon rate of 7 percent per annum. Spot and six-month forward exchange rates are $1.60 and $1.63, respectively ($/£).
2. A six-month certificate of deposit issued by the Bundesbank in Germany carries a coupon rate of 5 percent per annum. Spot and six-month forward rates are $1.45 and $1.50, respectively ($/€).

Required

Assuming that Enormo has $1,000,000 to invest, cannot tolerate exchange rate risk, and wants to maximize the number of dollars at the end of six months, analyze the three alternative investments and make a recommendation. Support your analysis with calculations.

P8.13 **Hedge of Net Investment in an International Subsidiary**   PriceSmart, Inc. is a U.S. company   **LO 5** that operates international membership shopping warehouse clubs. Its subsidiaries are located in 13 countries, including Panama, Guatemala, Jamaica, and Nicaragua, and one U.S. territory, the U.S. Virgin Islands. Suppose PriceSmart hedges its net investment in its three Guatemalan subsidiaries. The quetzal is the Guatemalan currency.

PRICESMART, INC. [PSMT]

Required

a. If the functional currency of the Guatemalan subsidiaries is the U.S. dollar,
    1. What kinds of hedge investments are effective hedges of PriceSmart's foreign currency risk?
    2. If the value of the quetzal, in U.S. dollars, increases from $0.125 to $0.15, will PriceSmart report a gain or a loss on the hedges?
    3. Where in its financial statements will PriceSmart report gains and losses on hedges of its net investments?
b. If the functional currency of the Guatemalan subsidiaries is the quetzal,
    1. What kinds of hedge investments are effective hedges of PriceSmart's foreign currency risk?
    2. If the value of the quetzal, in U.S. dollars, increases from $0.125 to $0.15, will PriceSmart report a gain or a loss on the hedges?
    3. Where in its financial statements will PriceSmart report gains and losses on hedges of its net investments?

REVIEW SOLUTIONS ···

Review 1 Solution

a. Accounts payable, June 30, 2013 = €1,000,000 × $1.42 = $1,420,000
b. Accounts receivable, June 30, 2013 = €100,000 × $1.42 = $142,000
c. Exchange gain or loss for fiscal 2013:
Accounts payable: ($1.42 − $1.35) × €1,000,000 = $70,000 loss
Accounts receivable: ($1.42 − $1.40) × €100,000 = $2,000 gain
d. Exchange gain or loss for fiscal 2014:
Accounts payable: ($1.45 − $1.42) × €1,000,000 = $30,000 loss
Accounts receivable: ($1.43 − $1.42) × €100,000 = $1,000 gain
e. Sales revenue, fiscal 2013 = €100,000 × $1.40 = $140,000
f. Cost of goods sold, fiscal 2014 = €1,000,000 × $1.35 = $1,350,000

Review 2 Solution

a. Accounts payable, June 30, 2013 = €1,000,000 × $1.42 = $1,420,000
b. Investment in forward contract, June 30, 2013 = €1,000,000 × ($1.44 − $1.37)
    = $70,000 current asset
c. Exchange gain or loss for fiscal 2013:
Accounts payable: ($1.42 − $1.35) × €1,000,000 = $70,000 loss
Forward contract: ($1.44 − $1.37) × €1,000,000 = $70,000 gain
Net gain or loss is zero.
d. Exchange gain or loss for fiscal 2014:
Accounts payable: ($1.45 − $1.42) × €1,000,000 = $30,000 loss
Forward contract: ($1.45 − $1.44) × €1,000,000 = $10,000 gain
    = Net loss of $20,000.
e. Cost of goods sold, fiscal 2014 = €1,000,000 × $1.35 = $1,350,000

Note that cost of goods sold is valued at the spot rate at the time the inventory was purchased ($1.35), although it actually pays $1,370,000, through the forward contract, for the inventory.

Review 3 Solution

a. Firm commitment, June 30, 2013 = €1,000,000 × ($1.44 − $1.37) = $70,000 current liability
b. Exchange gain or loss for fiscal 2013:
Firm commitment: ($1.44 − $1.37) × €1,000,000 = $70,000 loss
Forward contract: ($1.44 − $1.37) × €1,000,000 = $70,000 gain
Net gain or loss is zero.
c. Exchange gain or loss for fiscal 2014:
Firm commitment: ($1.45 − $1.44) × €1,000,000 = $10,000 loss
Forward contract: ($1.45 − $1.44) × €1,000,000 = $10,000 gain
Net gain or loss is zero.
d. Reported inventory value, August 15 = currency paid adjusted for the firm commitment
    = [€1,000,000 × $1.45] − ($70,000 + $10,000) = $1,370,000
e. Cost of goods sold, fiscal 2014 = $1,370,000

Review 4 Solution

2013			
June 30	Investment in forward contract	70,000	
	Other comprehensive income		70,000
	To adjust the forward contract to the June 30 rate for delivery on August 15; $70,000 = ($1.44 − $1.37) × 1,000,000.		
2013			
Aug. 15	Investment in forward contract	10,000	
	Other comprehensive income		10,000
	To adjust the forward contract to the August 15 spot rate; $10,000 = ($1.45 − $1.44) × 1,000,000.		
	Foreign currency	1,450,000	
	Investment in forward contract		80,000
	Cash		1,370,000
	To close the forward contract.		
	Inventory	1,450,000	
	Foreign currency		1,450,000
	To purchase the inventory.		
2013			
Aug. 31	Accounts receivable.	2,000,000	
	Sales revenue		2,000,000
	To record the sale of inventory to the U.S. customer.		
	Cost of goods sold.	1,370,000	
	Accumulated other comprehensive income.	80,000	
	Inventory		1,450,000
	To record cost of goods sold on the sale of inventory, including adjustment for gains on forward contract used to hedge the purchase.		

Futures, Options and Interest Rate Swaps

LEARNING OBJECTIVES

LO1 Describe futures contracts and account for common futures transactions. (p. 353)

LO2 Explain options contracts and account for common options transactions. (p. 360)

LO3 Describe and account for interest rate swaps. (p. 366)

LO4 Discuss disclosure requirements for derivatives and hedging. (p. 371)

LO5 Discuss IFRS for derivatives and hedging. (p. 373)

THE KELLOGG COMPANY
www.kelloggs.com

Giant breakfast and snack foods manufacturer **The Kellogg Company** uses derivatives extensively to reduce the risks inherent in its everyday business. In the footnotes to its 2010 annual report, Kellogg's identifies these risks and describes its hedging strategy:

> The Company is exposed to certain market risks such as changes in interest rates, foreign currency exchange rates, and commodity prices, which exist as part of its ongoing business operations. Management uses derivative financial and commodity instruments, including futures, options, and swaps, where appropriate, to manage these risks. Instruments used as hedges must be effective at reducing the risk associated with the exposure being hedged and must be designated as a hedge at the inception of the contract.

In addition to hedges of foreign currency risk, Kellogg's uses commodity futures and options to lock in the costs of forecasted purchases of materials it uses in manufacturing its products:

> The Company is exposed to price fluctuations primarily as a result of anticipated purchases of raw and packaging materials, fuel, and energy. The Company has historically used the combination of long-term contracts with suppliers, and exchange-traded futures and option contracts to reduce price fluctuations in a desired percentage of forecasted raw material purchases over a duration of generally less than 18 months.

Kellogg's uses interest rate swaps to hedge its interest rate risk:

> The Company is exposed to interest rate volatility with regard to future issuances of fixed rate debt. The Company periodically uses interest rate swaps, including forward-starting swaps, to reduce interest rate volatility and funding costs associated with certain debt issues, and to achieve a desired proportion of variable versus fixed rate debt, based on current and projected market conditions.

This chapter discusses various types of risk encountered by companies, the use of futures, options and swaps as hedging instruments to neutralize this risk, and the requirements for reporting hedging activities.

Source: The Kellogg Company 2010 annual report.

CHAPTER ORGANIZATION

Derivatives and hedge accounting	Futures contracts	Option contracts	Interest rate swaps	Disclosure requirements	IFRS for derivatives and hedging
• Characteristics of derivatives • Accounting for derivatives and hedging transactions • Assessing hedge effectiveness	• Description and accounting events • T-account analysis • Illustrations of hedging transactions	• Definitions • Price changes and "multiplier" effects • Illustrations of hedging transactions	• Definitions and motivations • Accounting events • Illustrations of hedging transactions	• Required derivatives and hedging disclosures	• IFRS provisions • 2010 hedge accounting proposal

DERIVATIVES AND HEDGE ACCOUNTING

Chapter 8 studied the use of forward contracts to hedge foreign exchange risk. This chapter discusses other types of risk and the derivative investments used to hedge this risk. *ASC para. 815-10-15-83* identifies four critical characteristics of derivatives:

1. Derivative values are tied to one or more **underlyings**—an interest rate, share price, foreign exchange rate, commodity price or other variable—that is subject to price changes. Kellogg's may purchase derivatives to lock in the future cost of oats used in its cereals.
2. A derivative specifies a face or **notional amount**. The notional amount is the number of bushels, pounds, shares, or other units specified in the contract. When Kellogg's uses a derivative contract to lock in the future price of a million bushels of oats, the notional amount is a million bushels.
3. Derivatives require **no initial net investment**, or a very small investment in relation to the total commitment. When Kellogg's agrees to buy a million bushels of oats in six months at a price of $3.50 per bushel, the total value of the contract is $3.5 million. However, Kellogg's typically pays nothing to enter the agreement.
4. Derivatives provide for a **net settlement** based on the interaction between the change in the underlying value and the notional amount. Suppose Kellogg's agrees to buy a million bushels of oats at $3.50 per bushel, and settles the contract by selling a million bushels when the per-bushel price is $3.75. Kellogg's receives a net cash payment of $250,000 [= ($3.75 - $3.50) x 1,000,000]; no delivery of oats takes place.

Futures, options and interest rate swaps possess these four characteristics. A **futures contract** "locks in" the purchase or sale of a specific amount of a commodity at a fixed price at a future delivery date. If Kellogg's enters a futures contract to *sell* 1,000,000 bushels of wheat at the fixed price of $8 per bushel, the contract gains value when the price of wheat falls below $8; a futures contract to *buy* wheat at a fixed price of $8 per bushel gains value when the price of wheat rises above $8.

Like a futures contract, an **option contract** locks in the future purchase or sale of a commodity at a fixed price. The option holder has the ability but not the obligation to buy or sell the commodity at the option price. If Kellogg's holds an option to buy wheat at $8 per bushel, and the price of wheat rises above $8, there is opportunity for gain and the option's value usually increases. Because options have no downside risk—Kellogg's can let the option expire if the price falls below $8—Kellogg's pays a premium to invest in the option.

A third common derivative is a "plain vanilla" **interest rate swap**, a contract in which Kellogg's may "swap" or exchange variable interest rate payments on its debt for fixed interest rate payments, or vice versa. When Kellogg's swaps variable payments for fixed payments, the swap gains value if interest rates rise because Kellogg's avoids payments at the higher variable rate.

With the foreign currency forward contracts discussed in Chapter 8, delivery is intended and occurs when settling the contract. A U.S. exporter settles a forward sale of euros by selling the euros acquired from customer sales and receiving dollars at the contract price. A U.S. importer settles a forward purchase of euros by using dollars to buy the euros necessary to pay its suppliers.

In contrast, futures, options and swap derivatives are typically settled with net cash payments, even when a delivery mechanism exists. A futures contract that locks in a purchase or sale is settled when the holder takes an opposite position. When Kellogg's enters a futures contract to sell wheat at $8 per bushel, and the price of wheat increases to $8.50, it can enter a contract to buy wheat at $8.50, paying $0.50 per bushel to settle the contract. When Kellogg's has an option to sell wheat at $8 per bushel, and the price of wheat increases to $8.50, it can let the option expire with no cash effect. When Kellogg's swaps variable payments at 4 percent for fixed payments at 4.5 percent, it makes a net cash payment of 0.5 percent of the debt principal at the interest payment date to settle the contract.

Accounting for Derivatives and Hedging Transactions

Generally accepted accounting principles for all derivatives and hedging activities are found in *ASC Topic 815*, Derivatives and Hedging. Chapter 8 discusses the general principles for reporting derivative investments and hedging activities, summarized below:

- All derivatives appear on the balance sheet at their current *fair value*. Unless the derivative is a qualifying hedge instrument, changes in value are reported on the income statement as they occur.

- A derivative is a qualifying hedge instrument if it hedges a specific risk and is *effective* in hedging that risk.

- If the contract is a qualifying hedge instrument, gains and losses due to changes in the fair value of the contract are recognized in the income statement *at the same time* the losses and gains on the exposure the contract is hedging are recognized. When the applicable accounting standards do not automatically match hedge gains and losses with hedged item losses and gains, *hedge accounting* changes the timing of gain and loss recognition.

- Derivatives qualifying as hedges of *exposed positions*, such as inventories and investments, and *firm commitments* to buy and sell these items, are *fair value hedges*. Changes in the value of fair value hedges and related hedged items are reported in the income statement as they occur.

- Derivatives qualifying as hedges of *forecasted transactions*, such as planned purchases and sales of commodities, are *cash flow hedges*. Changes in the value of cash flow hedges are reported in other comprehensive income and reclassified to the income statement when the hedged item is reported in the income statement. Any portion of the derivative's gain or loss that is *not effective* in hedging the forecasted transaction is reported directly in earnings.

Assessing Hedge Effectiveness

Because a derivative must qualify as a hedging instrument to use hedge accounting, *ASC Section 815-20-25* requires management to explicitly assess the derivative's *hedge effectiveness*. When management documents its risk management strategy, identifies risks being hedged and designates hedging instruments, it tests the effectiveness of the hedging instrument in neutralizing the hedged risk.

> Because **hedge accounting moves gains and losses between accounting periods**, such that the timing of realization and recognition differs, unwarranted use of hedge accounting creates opportunities for earnings management.

Management must identify how it intends to assess hedge effectiveness and must conclude that a derivative will be *highly effective* (not *perfectly* effective) for that derivative to qualify as a hedging instrument. The portion of a hedging derivative's gain or loss due to hedge *ineffectiveness* always goes to earnings, creating earnings volatility. Effectiveness must be gauged initially and, for hedge accounting to continue, when earnings are reported and at least every three months thereafter. However, a detailed analysis of hedge effectiveness is not needed when management documents that the terms of the hedging instrument—term, notional amount and underlying(s)—are the same as the hedged item.

High effectiveness occurs when the derivative neutralizes or offsets between 80% and 125% of the fair value or cash flow changes that represent the risk being hedged; 100% offset is not required. These limits do not depend on the arbitrary choice of numerator and denominator: 80% = 4/5 and 125% = 5/4. If the hedging relation becomes less than highly effective, hedge accounting terminates as of the last date that management documented high effectiveness.

A common *measure of hedge effectiveness* divides the change in fair value of the hedging instrument by the change in fair value or cash flows of the hedged item, as follows:

$$\text{Hedge Effectiveness Measure} = \frac{\textbf{Change in fair value of hedge instrument}}{\textbf{Change in fair value of hedged item}}$$

Because one value change is a gain and the other is a loss, the *hedge effectiveness measure is negative.*

Suppose **ConAgra** has an inventory of 100,000 bushels of soybeans to be sold in three months on a local market. The current local market price of soybeans is $15.50 per bushel. ConAgra protects the eventual sales value of the inventory against a fall in soybean prices by entering a futures contract to sell 100,000 bushels in three months at $15.60 per bushel. When acquiring the futures contract, management documents that prices in the derivative's standardized market generally match 90 percent of the price movements on ConAgra's local market. Therefore the derivative is classified as highly effective at inception. If the local market price subsequently falls by $0.20 to $15.30 and the futures price falls by $0.17 to $15.43, these results occur:

- The local value of the soybean inventory declines by $20,000 (= $0.20 × 100,000).
- Concurrently, the futures contract that provides for selling the soybeans at $15.60 rises in value by $17,000 (= $0.17 × 100,000).
- ConAgra assesses ongoing hedge effectiveness by dividing the change in the fair value of the futures contract—$17,000 increase—by the change in the fair value of the inventory due to the hedged risk—$20,000 decrease—and obtains a hedge effectiveness measure of −85 percent [= $17,000/($20,000)].
- ConAgra concludes that the futures contract continues to qualify as a highly effective hedge.

FUTURES CONTRACTS

Discussion in Chapter 8 focused on hedging with foreign currency *forward contracts. Futures contracts*—standardized contracts for future delivery—can also be used to lock in future foreign exchange rates, prices of commodities, interest rates and stock indexes. Most futures contracts are traded on the Chicago Board of Trade, the New York Mercantile Exchange and the London International Financial Futures Exchange.

LO1 Describe futures contracts and account for common futures transactions.

Introduction to Futures Contracts

A **futures contract** is a legally-enforceable agreement between an investor and the clearinghouse of a futures exchange that:

- Obligates the investor to accept or make delivery of a standardized quantity of a commodity or financial instrument at a specified date, during a specified time period or to settle in cash.
- Requires daily cash settlement of changes in the contract's value.
- Can be canceled prior to the delivery date by entering into an identical but offsetting contract; e.g., cancel a purchased futures contract by selling an identical futures contract.

To illustrate these points, recall that in the hedge effectiveness illustration above, ConAgra sold futures for 100,000 bushels of soybeans and obligated itself to deliver 100,000 bushels in three months for $15.60 per bushel. When the futures price fell to $15.43, the clearinghouse deposited $17,000 in ConAgra's account because ConAgra's $15.60 selling price exceeds the current $15.43 price. At any time ConAgra could cancel its sales contract by purchasing futures for 100,000 bushels of soybeans. If ConAgra decided to cancel its contract by purchasing for $15.43 the futures it sold for $15.60, a $17,000 gain results.

Commodity futures, which involve contracting for future delivery of commodities such as agricultural products, precious metals and oil, have existed for well over 125 years. **Interest rate futures,** however, developed within the last 30 years. Prices of interest rate futures are normally stated as a percentage of 100 or face value and reflect the annual discount yield. Thus if the futures price is 96, the designated securities will be delivered at a discount yield of 4 percent ($= 100 - 96$). Among the most common interest rate futures are futures contracts on *U.S. Treasury securities* and *Eurodollar deposits* of varying maturities.

Principal Differences between *Forward Contracts* and *Futures Contracts*.

- Futures are standardized exchange-traded contracts whereas forwards are tailored to specific needs and handled through dealers.

- Futures are normally closed out prior to maturity by entering an offsetting contract (without delivery) whereas forwards usually result in delivery.

- Because futures contracts are transacted with a clearinghouse and involve daily cash settlement, there is no credit or nonperformance risk; those risks exist with forwards.

Whether a given futures price change means an increase in value (gain) or decrease in value (loss), depends on whether futures are purchased (go **long** and *accept* future delivery) or sold (go **short** and *make* future delivery), as follows:

Changes in Fair Value of Futures Contracts

Type of Contract	Change in Futures Price	Effect on Income	Balance Sheet Disclosure
Purchase (go long)	Increase	Gain	Current asset
Purchase (go long)	Decrease	Loss	Current liability
Sell (go short)	Increase	Loss	Current liability
Sell (go short)	Decrease	Gain	Current asset

Transacting in Futures Contracts

Actual sale and delivery of commodities or securities for which futures contracts exist occurs in cash or spot markets. As spot prices and futures prices usually move together, any gain or loss realized on the futures contract usually offsets the loss or gain caused by changes in spot prices of the commodities or securities of concern. Even though spot prices and futures prices tend to move together, they differ by an amount called *basis*.

Basis refers to the difference between an item's spot price and the corresponding futures price.

For example, when the cash (spot) price of a ton of soybean meal in Decatur, Illinois, is $377 in June and the futures price for July delivery is $384, the July basis is "$7 under." Or when the spot price of crude oil is $90 per barrel (bbl.) and the September futures price is $88 per bbl., the September basis is "$2 over." Basis fluctuates over time as supply and demand conditions change in futures and spot markets. Because spot and futures prices may not move in perfect tandem, changes in basis mean that hedging may not produce a "perfect wash."

Accounting Events in Futures Trading

An entity using futures contracts traded on an organized exchange encounters two types of accounting events prior to settlement of the contract:

1. An **initial margin deposit**—cash or government securities—is paid to the clearinghouse upon inception of the contract. The margin deposit ranges from less than 1 percent of face value on some interest rate futures contracts to over 10 percent on some commodity futures. Not a commission or transaction cost, margin deposits are intended to guarantee performance, similar to a security deposit on an apartment.

2. At the end of each trading day, the clearinghouse values each outstanding contract at the closing price; i.e., **marks the contract to market.** The entity must either deposit additional funds with the broker—a realized loss—or receive cash or a credit to its account from the broker—a realized gain—for the change in the value of the contract.

The *initial margin deposit* is recorded as an asset—*Investment in Futures*. Subsequent changes in the amount deposited cannot fall below the *maintenance margin* required by the clearinghouse, which may be lower than the initial margin deposit. Thus if the initial margin deposit is 5 percent and the maintenance margin is 3 percent, the entity can incur losses without depositing additional collateral as long as the amount on deposit is at least 3 percent of the contract's value. The gain or loss arising when the contract is *marked to market* is added to or deducted from Investment in Futures. The next two numerical examples illustrate the effects of price changes on long and short positions:

'Long' Example. Suppose Kellogg's purchases 100,000 bushels of oat futures (goes *long*) at $4.50 per bushel. When the oat futures close at $4.60 on the next day, Kellogg's realizes a *gain* of $10,000 [= ($4.60 − $4.50) × 100,000]—it would receive an additional $0.10 per bushel if it sold the futures for $4.60 to close out its long position.

'Short' Example. Suppose **General Mills, Inc.** sells (goes *short*) $1,000,000 face value interest rate futures (one-year Treasury bills) at 97. At the end of the next trading day, when the interest rate futures close at 97.5, General Mills realizes a *loss* of $5,000 [= (0.97 − 0.975) × $1,000,000]—it would pay $0.005 per dollar more if it purchased long futures contracts at 97.5 to close out its short position.

T-Account Analysis of Futures Contracts

T-accounts help us visualize the value changes that occur in futures contracts. Like forward contracts, a futures contract has two sides: (1) *the current value*—a variable amount equal to the current futures price multiplied by the notional amount—and (2) *the contract value*—the fixed obligation to the clearinghouse equal to the futures price at inception (contract price) multiplied by the notional amount. When long in futures, the debit side is the current value and the credit side is the contract value. When short in futures the sides are reversed. A futures contract account with a debit balance is an asset; a credit balance is a liability. We observe that:

- At inception the two sides are equal and the contract itself has no net value—the current value of the item to be delivered equals its contract value

- As time passes the current value side changes but the contract value side remains constant

- The *change* in the current value is posted to the current value side at reporting dates or when contracts are closed

- A *long contract's* debit side—the current value of the item to be received—changes as the futures price changes. The credit side is the fixed contract value (obligation to the clearinghouse)

- A *short contract's* credit side—the current value of the item to be delivered—changes as the futures price changes. The debit side is the fixed contract value (amount due from the clearinghouse)

- Changes in the net balance represent the reported gains and losses

In the 'long' example just discussed, Kellogg's bought 100,000 bushels of oat futures at $4.50 per bushel. At the end of the next trading day the futures price closed at $4.60, producing a gain of $10,000 [= ($4.60 − $4.50) × 100,000]. These events are depicted as follows:

	Investment in Futures (Long)	
	Current Value	Contract Value
At inception	$450,000 (= 4.50 × 100,000)	$450,000 (= 4.50 × 100,000)
Value change	10,000 [= (4.60 − 4.50) × 100,000]	—
Balance, next day.	$ 10,000	

In the 'short' example just discussed, General Mills sold $1,000,000 face value of interest rate futures at 97. The futures price closed at 97.5 on the next trading day and produced a loss of $5,000 [= (0.975 − 97) × $1,000,000]. We post these events to our T-account as follows:

	Investment in Futures (Short)	
	Contract Value	Current Value
At inception	$970,000 (= 0.97 × 1,000,000)	$970,000 (= 0.97 × 1,000,000)
Value change	—	5,000 [= (0.975 − 0.97) × 1,000,000]
Balance, next day.		$ 5,000

To summarize, at inception the futures contract T-account has a zero balance. As the current futures price varies after inception, value changes that debit the account arise from gains whereas value changes that credit the account arise from losses.

Illustrations of Accounting for Futures Contracts

In the examples below, the futures contract is closed out prior to delivery. We ignore daily mark-to-market for convenience and recognize total realized gain or loss when each futures contract is closed. We also ignore brokerage commissions and other transaction costs.

Fair Value Hedge of an Exposed Asset.   **Del Monte Corporation** owns 100,000 bushels of corn carried in inventory at cost, $600,000, to be sold in the normal course of business in 90 days. Seeking to guarantee the current 90-day futures price of $700,000, Del Monte sells corn futures (goes *short*) for delivery in 90 days for $700,000 and designates the sale of corn futures as a *fair value hedge* of its corn inventory. The hedging derivative has the same terms as the hedged inventory and high effectiveness is assumed. We begin by recording a $60,000 margin deposit.

Investment in futures	60,000	
Cash		60,000
To record the initial margin deposit on the sale of $700,000 in commodity futures.		

By the end of the next accounting period, the futures price decreases to $650,000. At current prices, the fair value of the corn inventory also declines by $50,000. Del Monte closes out its short position by purchasing a corn futures contract at the then-current price of $650,000. This action locks in Del Monte's realized gain of $50,000 (= $700,000 − $650,000) and adds it to the deposit account at the brokerage. The next entries record the gain and closing of the futures contract.

Investment in futures	50,000	
Gain on hedging		50,000
To record in earnings the gain on the futures contract hedging existing inventory.		
Cash.	110,000	
Investment in futures.		110,000
To record receipt of cash from the broker, including the $60,000 initial margin, when the futures contract is closed out.		

Normally Del Monte carries the corn inventory at cost. Because the futures contract is a qualified fair value hedge, Del Monte uses *hedge accounting* to match the loss on its corn inventory with the gain on the futures contract, with the following entry:

Loss on hedging..	50,000	
Inventory		50,000
To record in earnings the decrease in fair value of the hedged inventory.		

The $50,000 realized gain on this fair value hedge enters current earnings. Moreover, because the futures are hedging an existing asset, Del Monte reports the $50,000 loss from the decline in the corn inventory's market value in earnings and reduces inventory: the gain on the hedging instrument and the loss on the hedged inventory offset. When sold, Del Monte charges the reduced carrying value of the inventory to cost of goods sold and recognizes the gain as part of the gross profit on the sale.

In this example, Del Monte wished to lock in profit of $100,000 (= $700,000 − $600,000). If the corn is sold for $650,000, Del Monte achieves the anticipated profit. The $50,000 gain on the futures contract reduces the carrying value of the inventory to $550,000, and profit of $100,000 (= $650,000 − $550,000) results. Without hedging, profit on the sale of the inventory is only $50,000 (= $650,000 − $600,000).

Suppose the futures price does not exactly track the spot price because the basis changed. The futures price fell to $656,000 when the spot price fell to $650,000 and the $44,000 gain (= $700,000 − $656,000) on the short futures contract does not fully offset the $50,000 loss on the inventory. The hedge effectiveness measure (= change in fair value of the hedge instrument/change in fair value of the hedged item) is − 0.88 [= $44,000/($50,000)], high enough for hedge accounting to continue. But the net $6,000 loss (= $44,000 gain on futures − $50,000 loss on inventory) due to hedge ineffectiveness reduces earnings with no offset.

If basis changes cause the futures contract to no longer be effective, hedge accounting is discontinued. Gains and losses on the futures contract continue to be recorded in income, but no entries are made to record the offsetting changes in the value of the inventory.

Fair Value Hedge of a Firm Liability Commitment. **Lafayette Ambassador Bank** contracts with a financing syndicate to roll over a $1,000,000 floating rate term loan payable every 91 days, at the then-current Treasury bill rate plus 1.5 percent, and designates the contract as a *firm commitment*. The current annual interest rate on such loans is 6 percent; on U.S. Treasury bills it is 4.5 percent.

To hedge against the possibility that interest rates will rise in 91 days, thereby increasing the interest cost on its new loan, Lafayette Bank sells (goes *short*) $1,000,000 face value of 91-day Treasury bill (interest rate) futures at 95.5 (= 100 − annual discount yield of 4.5 percent). Because Treasury bills sell at a discount from par that represents the interest to be earned at maturity, no separate interest payment or coupon exists. Selling Treasury bill futures benefits the bank when interest rates rise and the futures price falls: the short contract can be covered by purchasing futures (going long) for a lower price. This gain will offset the higher interest rate on the new loan. When Lafayette Bank enters the futures contract it makes a $2,500 margin deposit.

Investment in futures	2,500	
Cash		2,500
To record the initial margin deposit on the sale of $1,000,000 face value 91-day Treasury bill futures.		

By the end of the 91-day period, the U.S. Treasury bill rate declined to 1.7 percent and the futures price rose to 98.3. Although these are 91-day Treasury bills, the futures price reflects annual yields, not 91-day yields, and the value change must be divided by 4. Thus Lafayette realized a loss of $7,000 [= (0.955 − 0.983) × $1,000,000/4] on the short position, $4,500 more than the margin deposit. The bank now closes out its short futures position by paying $4,500 to the clearinghouse.

Loss on hedging..	7,000	
Investment in futures..		2,500
Cash		4,500
To record the realized loss on the futures contract and close the futures contract.		

Concurrently, Lafayette uses hedge accounting to recognize the increase in the fair value of the firm commitment to roll over the term loan as a gain, because the bank can now borrow at 3.2 percent (= 1.7 percent + 1.5 percent spread), not 6 percent.

Firm commitment	7,000	
Gain on hedging		7,000
To record the gain due to decline in borrowing cost of new loan.		

At this point Lafayette Bank rolls over the loan and closes the firm commitment asset against the new loan payable, creating a $7,000 discount on the new loan.

Short-term loan payable (old).	1,000,000	
Short-term loan payable (new)		1,000,000
To roll over the floating rate term loan.		
Discount on short-term loan payable (new).	7,000	
Firm commitment		7,000
To reclassify the firm commitment asset resulting from the hedge as a discount		
on the new loan payable.		

Lafayette Bank amortizes the $7,000 discount on the new loan to interest expense over the 91-day term of the new loan. Assuming the 1.5 percent spread between the bank's short-term rate and the Treasury bill rate still holds, the bank reports interest expense on the new loan at the rate of 3.2 percent (= 1.7 percent + 1.5 percent) . The $7,000 loss on the futures contract exactly offsets the reduced interest on the new loan, $7,000 [= (0.06 − 0.032) × $1,000,000/4]. Thus the bank maintains the old 6 percent rate for another 91-day period. Had the hedge not been undertaken, the interest cost on the loan is only 3.2 percent.

Although the hedge could be criticized, it was effective because it locked in and extended the previous interest cost to the new financing period. Had interest rates risen instead, the resulting decline in the futures price produces a gain on the short futures contract. This gain offsets the increased interest the bank must pay on the new loan, an economic loss that creates a firm commitment liability. Lafayette Bank was hedging against a rise in rates but an effective hedge works whether the price of the hedged item rises or falls, and neutralizes both loss *and* gain.

Cash Flow Hedge of an Anticipated Purchase.　In planning its silver requirements over the next several months, jewelry manufacturer **Zale Corporation** anticipates a higher price of silver. To guarantee a supply of silver at relatively favorable prices, Zales purchases 20,000 ounces of silver bullion (goes *long*) for delivery in 90 days at $42/ounce. The long futures position qualifies as a *cash flow hedge* of the forecasted purchase of silver. Zales makes a $25,000 margin deposit.

Investment in futures	25,000	
Cash		25,000
To record the initial margin deposit of $25,000 on the purchase of		
$840,000 (= $42 × 20,000) of silver futures.		

As predicted, over the next three months the futures price rises to $45/ounce, and Zales realizes a gain of $60,000 [= ($45 − $42) × 20,000] on the long position. Zales closes out its long position and purchases silver on the spot market for $44/ounce.

Because the silver futures qualify as a cash flow hedge of the forecasted purchase of silver, Zales reports the gain on the futures contract in OCI until the hedged silver appears in its income statement. However, only the effective gain on the hedge enters OCI. If the spot price of silver equaled the $42 futures price when the futures were purchased, the hedge was overeffective. The $60,000 gain on the hedge exceeded the $40,000 [= ($44 − $42) × 20,000] loss on the forecasted purchase. Hence only $40,000 of the gain on the hedge enters OCI and Zales reports the other $20,000 (the ineffective portion of the hedge) in current earnings. Zales records these events as follows:

Investment in futures	60,000	
Other comprehensive income		40,000
Gain on futures contract (earnings)		20,000
To record the effective portion of the gain on the futures contract in OCI and the non-effective portion in current earnings.		
Cash	85,000	
Investment in futures		85,000
To record the receipt of cash from the broker, including the initial $25,000 deposit, when the futures contract is closed out.		
Silver inventory	880,000	
Cash		880,000
To record the purchase of 20,000 ounces of silver bullion at $44/ounce on the spot market.		

This hedge effectively locked in the original silver futures price of $42 per ounce. Even though Zales realized a $40,000 gain on the effective portion of the hedge, the gain was offset by the higher price of silver on the spot market. When Zales acquired the silver on the spot market for $44 per ounce, its net cost, considering the effective portion of the hedge, was $42 [= ($880,000 − $40,000)/20,000] per ounce. The $40,000 gain will be released to earnings when products manufactured with this silver purchase are sold. At that time, the following entry reclassifies the $40,000 from AOCI to cost of goods sold to reflect the net silver purchase cost of $840,000.

Other comprehensive income	40,000	
Cost of goods sold		40,000

BUSINESS APPLICATION   General Mills Hedge Accounting

Requirements for hedge accounting are rigorous and involve substantial cost. Companies must document their hedges and monitor effectiveness. The reporting standards and the financial terms of the hedges are often extremely complex. As a result, hedging activities often do not qualify for hedge accounting. An example is **General Mills, Inc.**'s hedges of commodity risk. Below is an excerpt from its 2011 annual report.

> We utilize derivatives to manage price risk for our principal ingredients and energy costs, including grains (oats, wheat, and corn), oils (principally soybean), non-fat dry milk, natural gas, and diesel fuel. Our primary objective when entering into these derivative contracts is to achieve certainty with regard to the future price of commodities purchased for use in our supply chain. We manage our exposures through a combination of purchase orders, long-term contracts with suppliers, exchange-traded futures and options, and over-the-counter options and swaps.
>
> We use derivatives to manage our exposure to changes in commodity prices. We do not perform the assessments required to achieve hedge accounting for commodity derivative positions. Accordingly, the changes in the values of these derivatives are recorded currently in cost of sales in our Consolidated Statements of Earnings.
>
> Although we do not meet the criteria for cash flow hedge accounting, we nonetheless believe that these instruments are effective in achieving our objective of providing certainty in the future price of commodities purchased for use in our supply chain.

Because General Mills does not use hedge accounting for its hedges of commodity price risk, changes in the fair values of its hedge investments may not appear in the same income statement as changes in the fair values of related hedged commodities, increasing income volatility. *Source:* General Mills, Inc. 2011 annual report.

REVIEW 1 ● Accounting for Futures Contracts

Suppose on March 1, 2013, Kellogg's goes long in commodity futures and makes a $50,000 margin deposit. These contracts decline in value by $200,000 on March 31 when quarterly reports are prepared and increase in value by $300,000 on April 15 when the contracts are closed. Kellogg's then buys the commodity on the spot market for $10,180,000. On June 1 Kellogg's sells the commodity as part of its finished products.

Required

a. Suppose the commodity futures hedge a firm commitment to buy the commodity. Prepare the journal entries Kellogg's makes on March 1, March 31, April 15, and June 1.

b. Suppose the commodity futures hedge a forecasted purchase of the commodity. Repeat part *a*.

Solutions are located after the chapter assignments.

OPTION CONTRACTS

LO2 Explain options contracts and account for common options transactions

Options can lock in a future price, but unlike futures contracts, **option contracts** are *one-sided* and require performance only when exercised. Options on individual securities and indexes, such as the S&P 500, ValueLine, and Gold/Silver indexes, are traded on the Chicago Board Options Exchange, the American Stock Exchange and the Philadelphia Stock Exchange. Traders of most options execute agreements with the clearinghouses of those exchanges, not with each other as individuals.

> An **option contract** *allows,* but *does not require,* its holder to buy (*call*) or sell (*put*) a commodity, security or other financial instrument at an *agreed-upon price* during an *agreed-upon time period* or on a *specific date*.

Definitions

The two basic types of options are *puts* and *calls*. A **put**, or *option to sell,* allows the *holder* to *sell* the optioned item to the *writer,* who is obligated to pay the agreed-upon price during the agreed-upon time period. In contrast, a **call**, or *option to buy*, allows the *holder* to *purchase* the optioned item from the *writer,* who is obligated to accept the agreed-upon price during the agreed-upon time period.

Suppose **Smith Barney** writes and sells to **Del Monte Corporation** for $120 a *call option* for 100 shares of **TreeHouse Foods, Inc.** stock, exercisable at the stock's current market price of $60 per share and expiring in 90 days. If the stock price stays at or below $60 during the 90 days, Del Monte does not exercise the right to buy, allows the call to expire and loses the $120. But if the stock rises above $60, say to $65, Del Monte can *exercise the call* by paying $6,000 to Smith Barney for 100 shares of stock worth $6,500 or *sell the call*. The call is worth at least $500 [= $($65 − $60) × 100], because the stock's price is $5 *above* $60.

Suppose Smith Barney had instead written and sold to Del Monte a *put option* with the above terms. Del Monte will exercise or sell the put only if the stock's price falls below $60. If the stock's price falls to $57, Del Monte can *exercise the put* by selling 100 shares of TreeHouse stock worth $5,700 to Smith Barney for $6,000, or *sell the put*. The put is worth at least $300 [= ($60 − $57) × 100], because the stock's price is $3 *below* $60.

The *agreed-upon price* is referred to as the **strike price** or **exercise price**, and the *agreed-upon time period* is bounded by the *expiration date*. An **American option** can be exercised at any time during the agreed-upon time period, whereas a **European option** can be exercised only on the *expiration date*. Only American options are discussed in this text.

An option is **in the money** when it is more profitable for the holder to exercise the option than to transact directly in the optioned item. Otherwise the option is **out of the money** or, when the optioned item's current market price equals the strike price, the option is **at the money**. A *put* is in the money when the strike price *exceeds* the current market price of the optioned item; a *call* is in the money when the strike price is *less than* the current market price of the optioned item.

For example, suppose the price of **J.M. Smucker Company** stock is $75 per share. A *call option* on Smucker stock with a strike price of $80 is *out of the money* because the holder could purchase the stock in the stock market for $75, less than the strike price of $80 to exercise the call and buy the stock from the option writer. But a *put option* at $80 is *in the money*, because the holder could sell the stock to the writer for $80, more than the $75 it would bring from sale in the stock market. These relations are summarized below.

Price Relation	In, Out or At the Money	
	Puts	Calls
Strike price > Price of optioned Item.	In	Out
Strike price < Price of optioned Item.	Out	In
Strike price = Price of optioned Item.	At	At

The option's price, or **premium,** includes the option's **intrinsic value**—the amount that the option is *in the money,* if any—and its **time value**—the excess of the premium over the option's intrinsic value. Because the probability that the option will be in the money increases as the expiration date grows more distant, the time value component of the premium is positively related to the time remaining to expiration. When options are used in hedging, the time value is the *cost of protection* and is a type of insurance cost.

Returning to the above options on Smucker stock with an $80 strike price, suppose the stock is currently priced at $75. On the Chicago Board Options Exchange (CBOE) web site, we see that a *call option* on one share of Smucker stock expiring in 30 days, even though out of the money, is priced at $1.00. A *put option* with an $80 strike price, expiring in 45 days, is priced at $6.20. Because it has no intrinsic value, the call option's time value is its full price, $1.00. The put option is in the money, with an intrinsic value of $5 (= $80 - $75), and its time value is $1.20 (= $6.20 - $5.00). In general, the time value cannot be negative and reflects market participants' expectations about anticipated movements in the market price of the optioned item.

"Multiplier Effect" of Call Options

Options are used for hedging and speculative purposes. An advantage to the option holder is the ability to benefit from constructive ownership of large quantities of stock with a small investment. Suppose that one standard call contract for 100 shares of Smucker stock with a $80 exercise price that expires in 90 days costs $100. This $100 premium compares with $7,500 to buy 100 shares of Smucker at $75. If Smucker stock rises to $85 before expiration, the option goes in the money by $5, a total increase of $500 that provides a return of $400 (= $500 − $100). Investment in 100 shares increases by $1,000 [= ($85 − $75) x 100]. Computations below compare the return on the options versus direct investment in the stock.

	$ Return	Cost	% Return
Option Purchase.	$ 400	$ 100	400%
Stock Purchase	1,000	7,500	13%

Note: Any Smucker dividends during the option period are paid to the owner of the stock, not the option holder. The option premium is a loss when the option expires without being exercised.

Effects of Price Changes of Optioned Items

The *holder* of a call bets that the price of the optioned item will rise, and the call *writer* bets against a price increase and takes the time value component of the premium to compensate for the risk. Although some option writers are net speculators, many take offsetting speculative positions to hedge their aggregate risk. Changes in the optioned item's price affect the option's intrinsic value only when the option is *at* or *in* the money. We summarize below how such changes affect the holder and writer when the option initially is in a neutral position—*at the money.*

	Holder		Writer	
Price of Optioned Item	**Puts**	**Calls**	**Puts**	**Calls**
Increases	—*	Gain	—*	Loss
Decreases..	Gain	—*	Loss	—*
* Holder's potential loss and writer's potential gain are limited to the initial premium.				

Accounting Events in Options Trading

Transacting in options contracts involves two types of accounting events prior to exercising the option or selling it.

1. Payment of the **initial premium** to the broker when purchasing the option. Not a margin deposit, this payment is for the option to buy (call) or sell (put) the optioned item.
2. The option is **marked to market** when exercised, sold and at financial statement dates. There is no daily cash settlement; until sold or exercised, gains and losses on options are *unrealized*.

The *premium paid* is recorded as an asset—*Investment in Options*. Mark-to-market gains and losses change the Investment in Options account.

Illustrations of Accounting for Options

Fair Value Hedge of an AFS Debt Security. On January 30, 2013, **H.J. Heinz Company** owns $3,000,000 face value 2.725 percent U.S. Treasury bonds due in 2023. Purchased at face value, Heinz classifies the bonds as *available for sale*. The bonds currently sell for 97 and yield about 3 percent. Concerned about rising interest rates and concurrent decreases in Treasury bond prices, Heinz purchases July 2013 *put options* on the bonds with a strike price of 100, designating them as an effective hedge of the bonds owned. Management designates the *intrinsic value component of the option as the hedging instrument*.

The premium is $3.04 per $100 of bonds, $91,200 [= $3.04 × ($3,000,000/$100)] for the 30,000 puts on $3,000,000 in bonds. Because the 100 strike price exceeds the bonds' current price of 97, the puts are *in the money* by $3.00. Thus the $3.04 option premium includes $3.00 of intrinsic value and $0.04 of time value. This entry records purchase of the Treasury bond puts.

2013			
Jan. 30	Investment in options..	91,200	
	Cash		91,200
	To record the purchase of put options to hedge Treasury bonds owned; $91,200 = 30,000 × $3.04.		

When Heinz closes its books on April 30, 2013, the bonds are at 98 and the puts at $2.26 (= $2.00 of intrinsic value and $0.26 of time value). The options' $23,400 loss [= ($2.26 − $3.04) × 30,000] is reported in earnings. Concurrently, the bonds' fair value increased by $30,000 [= ($98 − $97) × 30,000]. Because the bonds are designated as AFS, Heinz normally reports this increase in OCI. However, the put options qualify as a fair value hedge of the bonds. Because Heinz uses *hedge accounting* to match the options' loss with the bonds' gain, it reports the increase in the value of the bonds in earnings, not OCI. The $6,600 excess of the gain on the bonds over the loss on the options represents the increase in the time value of $6,600 [= ($0.26 − $0.04) × 30,000]. This net amount is recognized in earnings with no offset.

2013			
April 30	Loss on hedging......................................	23,400	
	Investment in options		23,400
	To recognize the decline in the puts' value; $23,400 = ($2.26 − $3.04) × 30,000.		

continued

2013			
April 30	Investment in bonds..	30,000	
	Gain on hedging		30,000
	To recognize the increase in fair value of the AFS bonds		
	attributable to the hedged risk. (Had the bonds not been hedged,		
	Heinz records the $30,000 gain in OCI.)		

Because management designated only the intrinsic value component of the option as the hedging instrument, the hedge was fully effective, with a hedge effectiveness measure of −1 [= ($30,000)/$30,000]. If the total option premium was designated as the hedging instrument, the hedge would no longer be highly effective: the hedge effectiveness measure would be −0.78 [= ($23,400)/$30,000], below the lower cutoff point of −0.8.

Now suppose that on July 1, 2013, Heinz' Treasury bonds are at 95 and the firm closes the hedge by selling the put options for their current premium of $5.19. Because each put is in the money by $5.00, the total proceeds include time value of $5,700 [= ($5.19 − $5.00) × 30,000]. We now record the gain on the options, the loss on the bonds, and sale of the puts.

2013			
July 1	Investment in options	87,900	
	Gain on hedging		87,900
	To record the increase in the options' fair value;		
	$87,900 = ($5.19 − $2.26) x 30,000.		
	Loss on hedging	90,000	
	Investment in bonds		90,000
	To record the decline in the fair value of the AFS bonds		
	attributable to the hedged risk; $90,000 [= (0.95 − 0.98) ×		
	$3,000,000]. (Had the bonds not been hedged, the loss enters		
	OCI).		
	Cash..	155,700	
	Investment in options		155,700
	To record sale of the options; $155,700 = ($5.19 × 30,000)		
	= $91,200 − $23,400 + $87,900.		

The overall *gain* of $60,000 on the 30,000 puts due to an increase in their intrinsic value from $3 to $5 offsets the decline in current value of the bonds by $60,000 [= (0.97 − 0.95) × 3,000,000]. After the puts are sold, the company netted a $64,500 cash gain (= $155,700 proceeds − $91,200 cost). Of this, $60,000 (= $90,000 increase in intrinsic value on July 1 − $30,000 premium paid on April 30) offsets the loss in carrying value of the bond investment to $2,850,000 (= 0.95 × $3,000,000) from $2,910,000 (= 0.97 × $3,000,000). The other $4,500—the increase in the time value from $1,200 to $5,700 when the options are sold—is recognized in earnings through its inclusion in the $64,500 net gain on the options.

Fair Value Hedge of a Foreign Currency Firm Commitment. Chapter 8 discusses forward contracts used to hedge foreign exchange risk. Here we illustrate hedging with foreign currency *options*. On September 1, 2014, when the spot rate is $1.05/A$ and the 120-day forward rate is $1.052/A$, **Winesellers, Ltd.** in the U.S. issued an A$5,000,000 purchase order to an Australian company for 10,000 cases of Australian wine. To protect itself against a weakening U.S. dollar, Winesellers pays $0.0105 each for December 2014 *call options* on A$5,000,000 with a strike price of $1.05—the entire premium is time value. Management designates the intrinsic value of the calls as a fair value hedge of a firm commitment, and records the purchase of the calls.

2014			
Sep. 1	Investment in options......................................	52,500	
	Cash		52,500
	To record the purchase of call options to hedge a firm commitment		
	denominated in A$; $52,500 = $0.0105 × 5,000,000.		

When the books are closed on September 30, the spot rate is $1.06/A\$ and the 90-day forward rate is $1.062/A\$, indicating a weakening U.S. dollar. Now $0.01 in the money, the calls sell for $0.017 and the time value component is $0.007. Winesellers marks the calls to market and recognizes $32,500 [= ($0.0170 − $0.0105) × 5,000,000] in earnings.

2014			
Sep. 30	Investment in options...	32,500	
	Gain on hedging		32,500
	To revalue the call options to market.		

Concurrently, a firm commitment liability valued at the change in forward rate is established for the increase in the U.S. dollar cost of the wine purchase. The loss on the firm commitment due to the increase in the forward rate more than offsets the gain on the options.

2014			
Sep. 30	Loss on hedging..	50,000	
	Firm commitment		50,000
	To record the liability for the increased $ cost of settling the firm		
	commitment; $50,000 = ($1.062 − $1.052) × 5,000,000.		

Suppose that on December 30, Winesellers takes delivery of the wine, sells the options, and pays for the wine by buying Australian dollars in the spot market at $1.08/A\$. The calls sell for their intrinsic value of $0.03. Winesellers marks the calls to market, recognizing $65,000 [= ($0.03 − $0.017) × 5,000,000] in earnings, and sells the options.

2014			
Dec. 30	Investment in options	65,000	
	Gain on hedging		65,000
	To revalue the call options to market.		
	Cash..	150,000	
	Investment in options		150,000
	To record the sale of the options; $150,000 = $0.03 × 5,000,000.		

Winesellers also adjusts the firm commitment for the additional loss due to the increase in the forward rate. At December 30, 120 days have passed and the spot rate equals the forward rate for delivery that day.

2014			
Dec. 30	Loss on hedging..	90,000	
	Firm commitment		90,000
	To record the increased $ cost of settling the firm commitment;		
	$90,000 = ($1.08 − $1.062) × 5,000,000.		

Winesellers takes delivery of the wine, pays for it by buying Australian dollars at the $1.08 spot rate, and closes the firm commitment against the inventory balance.

2014			
Dec. 30	Inventory..	5,260,000	
	Firm commitment..	140,000	
	Cash		5,400,000
	To record delivery of the inventory, $5,400,000 payment to suppliers		
	(= $1.08 × 5,000,000) and closing of the firm commitment.		

Because Winesellers gained on its hedge of the purchase order, the inventory balance is $140,000 lower. This gain impacts earnings when the wine is sold.

Note that although the options increased in value by only $97,500, their intrinsic value, designated as the hedge, gained $150,000 [= ($.03 − $0.00) × 5,000,000]. The intrinsic value qualifies for hedge accounting through the firm commitment account. Because spot and forward rates do not change by exactly the same amount each period, there is a $10,000 difference (= $150,000 − $140,000) between the loss in the firm commitment value, valued according to changes in forward rates, and the gain in the options' intrinsic value, valued according to changes in spot rates. However, the options were still a highly effective hedge, as $150,000/$(140,000) = 107%.

Cash Flow Hedge with an Interest Rate Cap. Companies can purchase an *interest rate cap* to protect against rising interest rates on their variable rate loans. Effectively a call option, an **interest rate cap** goes in the money when the variable rate rises above the cap's strike price—the rate specified in the cap agreement. Once in the money, the writer of the cap pays the holder the difference between the holder's variable rate interest and the cap rate. An interest rate cap is a *cash flow hedge:* it hedges against increased cash interest cost on the loans due to rising interest rates. The cap cannot hedge a firm commitment because future interest rates are unknown. Management normally designates the cap's intrinsic value as the hedging instrument. The cost of the cap itself, if it is not in the money when purchased, is time value.

Suppose that on January 2, 2013, **Seneca Foods Corporation** borrows $10 million from its bank for five years at prime plus 2 percent, a variable rate adjusted quarterly. Currently at 1.5 percent, Seneca Foods believes prime will rise during the life of its loan, and it buys a five-year, 4.5 percent interest rate cap from another bank for 0.5 percent per year to be paid in full immediately. This cap prevents the interest cost on the loan from going above 4.5 percent. The cap is out of the money and the entire premium is time value.

2013			
Jan. 2	Investment in interest rate cap..............................	250,000	
	Cash		250,000
	To record premium paid on a five-year 12 percent interest rate cap;		
	$250,000 = 0.005 × $10,000,000 × 5.		

Nine months later, prime increased to 3.5 percent, forcing Seneca Foods' variable rate to 5.5 percent during the last quarter of 2013, and the interest rate cap is now in the money. Suppose the cap's fair value decreased by $30,000 to $220,000: an increase in intrinsic value of $25,000 [= (0.055 − 0.045) × $10,000,000/4] and a $55,000 decrease in time value. The rise in intrinsic value hedges the higher interest cost on the loan whereas Seneca Foods reports the $55,000 decrease in time value in earnings as a loss on options. On December 31, 2013, Seneca Foods makes these end-of-period entries:

2013			
Dec. 31	Interest expense...	137,500	
	Cash		137,500
	To record interest paid to the bank for the last quarter of 2013;		
	$137,500 = 0.055 × $10,000,000/4.		
	Loss on options	55,000	
	Investment in interest rate cap		30,000
	Interest expense		25,000
	To record the loss in time value and the net decrease in the cap's		
	fair value, and reduce interest expense by the increase in the cap's		
	intrinsic value.		

Note that the net interest expense recorded above, $112,500 (= $137,500 - $25,000), allows Seneca Foods to report interest on the loan at 4.5 percent, the cap amount [= $112,500/($10,000,000/4)]. Later, the writer of the cap reimburses Seneca Foods for the excess interest it paid in the fourth quarter.

	Cash..	25,000	
	Investment in interest rate cap		25,000
	To record receipt of excess interest from the interest rate cap.		

REVIEW 2 • Accounting for Option Contracts

On August 10, 2013, **TreeHouse Foods** invests in equity securities costing $3,000,000 and classifies them as AFS investments. On September 30, 2013, the value of the equity securities falls to $2,910,000, and TreeHouse pays $100,000 for March 2014 put options with a strike price of $3,000,000, as a fair value hedge of its equity investments. The intrinsic value of the options is designated as the hedging instrument. On January 2, 2014, TreeHouse's accounting year-end, the options have a fair value of $76,600 and the securities have a fair value of $2,940,000. TreeHouse sells the options on March 1, 2014, for $159,800, when the fair value of the securities is $2,850,000, and sells the securities for $2,900,000 on March 30, 2014.

Required

Prepare the journal entries made by TreeHouse on August 10, 2013, September 30, 2013, January 2, 2014, March 1, 2014, and March 30, 2014.

Solutions are located after the chapter assignments.

INTEREST RATE SWAPS

LO3 Describe and account for interest rate swaps.

Interest rate swaps are derivative financial instruments used primarily to lower financing costs, hedge interest rate risk, and for speculative purposes. They are a type of *financial swap,* in which two **counterparties** exchange cash flows over time. A swap's value is *derived* from the net present value of the swapped cash flows. Interest rate swaps have fixed and variable cash flow components—one cash flow component changes in value and the other does not. When the variable cash flow component is an asset (liability), a gain (loss) results when that component increases in value.

In a **financial swap,** two end-users, or counterparties, negotiate a contract to exchange a series of cash flows at specified times and at specified prices. The counterparties may deal with each other directly or through an intermediary, such as a bank. The **principal amount** is the basis for calculating the swapped flows and often consists of assets or liabilities of the counterparties. Because the principal amount is normally not exchanged, it is called the **notional amount.**

An **interest rate swap** has the counterparties agree to exchange a fixed-rate interest obligation for a floating rate obligation, or the reverse, on existing or new debt typically denominated in the same currency. Only the net payment between the counterparties usually changes hands. In this way swap users can effectively convert floating rate debt to fixed rate debt, and vice versa. Other versions include **basis** (or **basis rate**) **swaps** and **currency coupon swaps** (also known as a **circus**—combined interest rate and currency swap).

We discuss here the simplest "plain vanilla" interest rate swap, where a company swaps fixed interest payments on its debt for variable payments, or it swaps variable payments for fixed payments. The reasons for entering these swaps include:

- If a company wishes to avoid the risk of rising interest rates it may swap its floating rate interest obligations for fixed rate interest obligations.

- A bank with fixed rate investments, such as mortgages, may convert its floating rate interest payments to fixed payments to reduce its financial risk.

- A company that can borrow only at high fixed rates may swap its floating rate obligations to a counterparty able to borrow at low fixed rates.

- A company expects a decline in interest rates and swaps fixed for variable payments in anticipation of lower interest costs.

ASC Topic 815 treats *plain vanilla swaps that* **qualify as hedges** as follows:

- **Swap of fixed interest payments on fixed-rate debt for variable interest payments** (receive fixed/pay variable) is a **fair value hedge** because the fair value of the fixed-rate debt changes as market interest rates change. When market interest rates fall, the present value of all payments due on the debt increases, the fair value of the debt rises, and a loss occurs on the debt. This decline in interest rates also produces an increase in the present value of the fixed payments received in the swap, a gain that offsets the loss on the debt.

- **Swap of variable interest payments on variable-rate debt for fixed interest payments** (receive variable/pay fixed) is a **cash flow hedge** because, as interest rates change, the floating payments received in the swap hedge against unfavorable unknown future interest payments on the variable rate debt. When market interest rates rise, the present value of the fixed payments made in the swap falls, and a gain occurs on the swap. This gain will be offset by the larger floating interest payments on the floating rate debt when they occur.

The floating rate is typically tied to an interest rate index. Common rate indexes include the **London Interbank Offered Rate (LIBOR)**—a fluctuating free-market rate for Eurodollar deposits—or a Treasury bill rate. The positions of the counterparties and the movements of the swapped cash flows in a plain vanilla interest rate swap are described below and shown in Figure 9.1.

FIGURE 9.1   Details of AA/BB Interest Rate Swap

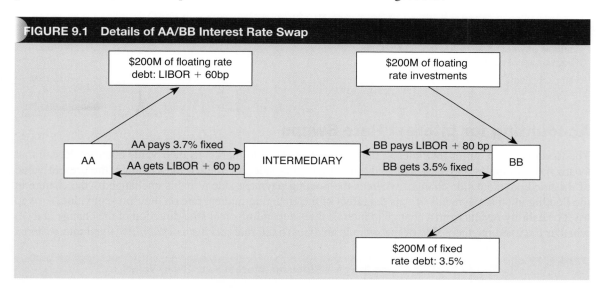

Assume that when the swap is entered, LIBOR stands at 2 percent or 200 *basis points*. A **basis point (bp)** is 1/100 of a percent in interest or .0001.

- AA has $200 million of existing debt with a floating rate equal to LIBOR + 60 bp (currently 2.6 percent). It wants to protect against increases in interest rates but cannot borrow directly at a fixed rate of less than 4 percent.

- BB also has $200 million of debt, but its debt carries a fixed coupon of 3.5 percent. Moreover, BB has $200 million of floating rate investments. It seeks to protect against decreases in interest rates which would cause its floating rate revenues to decline and its fixed rate expenses to become more onerous.

- Intermediary proposes this swap: it offers AA floating rate payments at LIBOR + 60 bp in exchange for fixed rate payments from AA at 3.7 percent; it offers BB fixed rate payments at 3.5 percent in exchange for floating payments from BB at LIBOR + 80 bp.

All payments are to be calculated on a notional amount of $200 million.

> **AA:** Because AA pays LIBOR + 60 bp on its debt and receives LIBOR + 60 bp from intermediary, its net outflow is the 3.7 percent fixed payment to intermediary. AA becomes the *fixed rate payer* and the *floating rate receiver* in the swap. AA has an annual opportunity gain of $600,000 [= (0.04 − 0.037) × $200M] because the swap enables it to borrow fixed at 3.7 percent—30 bp or 0.3 percent below its best direct fixed borrowing opportunity. By locking in this 3.7 percent rate, AA benefits directly if LIBOR goes above 3.1 percent (3.1 percent + 60 bp = 3.7 percent) but forgoes interest savings if LIBOR stays below 3.1 percent.

continued

> **BB:** The 3.5 percent fixed rate payment from intermediary offsets the 3.5 percent fixed rate payment BB makes on its debt. BB has *unlocked* its fixed rate and now pays LIBOR + 80 bp to intermediary. BB becomes the *floating rate payer* and the *fixed rate receiver* in the swap. Although BB directly benefits when LIBOR does not go above 2.7 percent (2.7 percent + 80 bp = 3.5 percent), it achieved its goal of stabilizing the relation between its floating rate revenues and its borrowing costs.

The swap produces a net spread of 40 basis points to intermediary. This spread's annual net cash inflow of $800,000 compensates intermediary for arranging the swap and for accepting the risk of default by either counterparty. The following display summarizes intermediary's cash inflows and outflows when LIBOR is 2 percent.

Fixed payment received from AA, 0.037 × $200M	$7.4M
Variable payment received from BB, 0.028 × $200M	5.6
Variable payment paid to AA, 0.026 × $200M	(5.2)
Fixed payment paid to BB, 0.035 × $200M	(7.0)
Net cash inflow to intermediary	$0.8M

Accounting for Interest Rate Swaps

The Codification requires that interest rate swaps be marked to market as their value changes. Recall that swaps have a floating payment side and a fixed payment side. As interest rates change, the present value of the fixed payment side changes whereas the floating payment side remains unchanged—the change in the floating interest payments offsets the effect of the changing interest rate on their present value. A swap asset or liability results from a change in interest rates depending on (1) the direction of the change and (2) whether the fixed payment side of the swap is an *asset* (fixed rate *receiver*) or *liability* (fixed rate *payer*):

	Effect of Changing Interest Rates on Interest Rate Swap Value			
	Interest Rates Rise		**Interest Rates Fall**	
Fixed Payment Side	**Gain/ Loss**	**Change in Swap Asset/Liability**	**Gain/ Loss**	**Change in Swap Asset/Liability**
Fixed rate receiver	Loss	Asset down or liability up	Gain	Asset up or liability down
Fixed rate payer	Gain	Liability down or asset up	Loss	Liability up or asset down

To summarize, the *fixed rate receiver* hedging with a plain vanilla swap has a *fair value hedge* and reports a gain (loss) on the hedged fixed rate debt's fair value as interest rates rise (fall) that offsets the loss (gain) on the swap. The *fixed rate payer* hedging with a plain vanilla swap has a *cash flow hedge* and reports the gain (loss) on the swap when interest rates rise (fall).

Assessing Hedge Effectiveness

In principle, assessing the effectiveness of interest rate swaps that qualify as hedges involves dividing the change in the present value of the cash flows from the swap (the hedge) by the change in the present value of the cash flows from the hedged item. *ASC Topic 815* provides a **short-cut method** for interest rate swaps—when certain conditions are satisfied, full hedge effectiveness is assumed. Although the conditions for fair value and cash flow hedges differ somewhat (*paras. 815-20-25-102* through *111*), this short-cut method generally applies when the:

- notional amount of the swap matches the principal amount of the debt
- fair value of the swap is zero at inception
- expiration date of the swap matches the maturity date of the debt (*fair value hedges*)

hedge applies only to all interest payments during the term of the swap and not to interest payments beyond the term of the swap (*cash flow hedges*)

BUSINESS APPLICATION   Del Monte's Use of Interest Rate Swaps

Del Monte Corporation uses interest rate swaps to change its payments on variable rate term loans to fixed payments. This excerpt from its 2011 annual report provides specific details concerning its swaps.

> The Company from time to time manages a portion of its interest rate risk related to floating rate debt by entering into interest rate swaps in which the Company receives floating rate payments and makes fixed rate payments. On April 12, 2011, DMFC [Del Monte Foods Company] entered into interest rate swaps with a total notional amount of $900.0 million, as the fixed rate payer. The interest rate swaps fix LIBOR at 3.029% for the term of the swaps. The swaps have an effective date of September 4, 2012 and a maturity date of September 1, 2015. On August 13, 2010, the Company entered into an interest rate swap, with a notional amount of $300.0 million, as the fixed rate payer. The interest rate swap fixes LIBOR at 1.368% for the term of the swap. The swap has an effective date of February 1, 2011 and a maturity date of February 3, 2014. The fair value of the Company's interest rate swaps was recorded as a current liability of $3.2 million and a non-current liability of $14.0 million at May 1, 2011.

Del Monte's variable debt requires interest payments based on a constant spread over LIBOR. By "fixing" LIBOR at a specific value, the swaps turn variable payments into fixed payments. Del Monte reports the swaps as current and non-current liabilities at May 1, 2011, leading to the conclusion that interest rates *fell* during the time Del Monte held these swaps. *Source:* Del Monte Corporation 2011 annual report.

Accounting Events and Entries for Interest Rate Swaps

The accounting at **settlement** and **balance sheet dates** involves journalizing these events:

1. Interest expense on the hedged debt
2. Adjustment to interest expense—increase when making net payments to intermediary, decrease when receiving net payments from intermediary
3. Change in fair value of the swap hedge
4. Change in fair value of the hedged debt attributable to the hedged risk (fair value hedges)

We illustrate the entries using the swaps described above.

BB swap.   BB has fixed rate debt and swaps its fixed payments for variable payments. This receive fixed/pay variable swap is a *fair value hedge.* When market interest rates fall, the present value of the future payments on the debt increases, creating a loss on the fixed debt. This is offset by the gain from swapping its 3.5 percent fixed interest payments for lower variable interest payments. The gain and the loss are both reported in income.

BB's first entry records interest expense on the hedged debt.

Interest expense.	7,000,000	
Cash		7,000,000
To record periodic interest expense on BB's fixed rate debt; *$7,000,000 = 0.035 × $200,000,000.*		

BB then receives $1,400,000 [= (0.035 − 0.028) × $200M] net cash from intermediary to settle the swap.

Cash...	1,400,000	
Interest expense		1,400,000
To record cash received from intermediary to reduce interest expense under		
the terms of the swap.		

Suppose interest rates decline by 0.5 percent. Applying a lower discount rate to the future fixed debt payments results in a *higher* fair value for the fixed debt. Similarly, applying a lower discount rate to the future fixed payments received from intermediary increases their present value and results in a *higher* fair value for the swap. We assume the decline in interest rates results a $920,000 increase in the fair value of the debt and the swap.

Investment in swaps..	920,000	
Gain on hedging		920,000
To mark interest rate swap to market and record the gain produced by the		
decrease in interest rates.		
Loss on hedging..	920,000	
Long-term debt		920,000
To mark hedged fixed-rate debt to market and record the loss produced by the		
decrease in interest rates.		

AA swap. AA has variable rate debt and swaps its variable payments for fixed payments. This receive variable/pay fixed swap is a *cash flow hedge*. When market interest rates fall, the loss on swapping variable payments for fixed payments is reported in OCI. This loss is reclassified from AOCI to interest expense in the next period, to offset the lower variable interest expense.

AA's first entry records interest expense on the hedged debt at the 2.6 percent variable rate.

Interest expense..	5,200,000	
Cash		5,200,000
To record periodic interest expense on AA's floating rate debt;		
$5,200,000 = 0.026 × $200,000,000.		

AA then pays $2,200,000 [= (0.037 − 0.026) x $200M] net cash to intermediary to settle the swap.

Interest expense..	2,200,000	
Cash		2,200,000
To record cash paid to intermediary to settle additional interest under the terms		
of the swap.		

Suppose interest rates decline 0.5 percent. Applying a lower discount rate to the future fixed payments to intermediary increases their present value and results in a *lower* fair value for the swap. Assume the decline in the fair value of the swap is $900,000. The variable rate debt is not revalued, since the decline in interest rates affects both the interest payments and the discount rate, with no effect on the present value of the debt.

Other comprehensive income	900,000	
Investment in swaps		900,000
To mark interest rate swap to market and record the loss produced by the		
decrease in interest rates.		

Next year, AA makes a $4,200,000 (= .021 × $200M) interest payment on its variable rate debt, down from $5,200,000. We reclassify the $900,000 loss out of AOCI to offset the lower interest expense.

Interest expense..	5,100,000	
Other comprehensive income		900,000
Cash		4,200,000
To record cash paid to intermediary to settle additional interest under the terms		
of the swap.		

REVIEW 3 • Accounting for Interest Rate Swaps

On May 1, 2014, **H.J. Heinz Company** issues $100 million in 4 percent fixed rate debt, with interest payments due annually. On the same day, it enters into a 2-year $100 million notional amount receive fixed/pay variable interest rate swap, with settlement annually. The swap provides that the company receive payments at 4 percent and pay LIBOR + 60 bp. LIBOR is 2.2 percent at inception of the swap. On April 30, 2015, the market interest rate attributable to the debt increases, reducing the fair value of the debt by $450,000. The fair value of the swap also declines by $450,000 due to increasing interest rates. LIBOR increases to 2.3 percent for 2015.

Required

a. Prepare the journal entries to record the debt issuance on May 1, 2014 and all necessary entries at April 30, 2015. Heinz' accounting year ends April 30.

b. Suppose Heinz issues variable rate debt and entered into a receive variable/pay fixed interest rate swap. Explain how the entries at April 30, 2015, would differ from those you recorded in part *a*.

Solutions are located after the chapter assignments.

Reporting Perspective

The choice of whether to use hedge accounting for hedging activities involves a clear cost-benefit tradeoff:

*   The substantial **cost** of documentation and monitoring complex monitoring relationships, and the risk that a company will misapply the standards and be required to restate its financial statements

*   The **benefit** of smoother earnings, as the effects of the hedge and the hedged item appear in the same income statement

Broader application of the **fair value option** for financial instruments and other assets reduces the need for hedge accounting to achieve matching of gains and losses on hedges and hedged items. Using normal accounting for derivatives, realized and unrealized fair value changes appear on the income statement as they occur. When hedged items are also reported at fair value, realized and unrealized gains and losses also appear on the income statement as they occur. Matching is achieved without using hedge accounting to change the timing of income recognition.

DISCLOSURE REQUIREMENTS

ASC Section 815-10-50 prescribes disclosures specifically for *derivatives and hedging activities*.

LO4 Discuss disclosure requirements for derivatives and hedging.

Derivatives and Hedging Disclosures

To set the overall context, entities must explain how and why they use derivatives, how they account for them, how derivatives and hedging activities affect financial position, performance and cash flows, and the risk exposure(s)—interest rate, credit, exchange rate, price, and the like. Some specific disclosure requirements are:

*   For derivatives used for hedging, descriptions of risk management policies governing fair value, cash flow and foreign currency hedges, including the types of risks hedged, objectives of hedging activities and strategies for achieving those objectives.

*   For derivatives not used for hedging, the objectives of such usage of derivatives.

*   Net gain or loss recognized in earnings from (1) fair value and (2) cash flow hedges, including the amounts arising from hedge ineffectiveness and any derivative components excluded from hedge effectiveness assessment.

- Descriptions of transactions and events that will cause reclassification of gains and losses from other comprehensive income into earnings, and the estimated amount of such reclassifications over the next year.
- Maximum length of time covered by cash flow hedges of forecasted transactions.
- Amounts of gains and losses reclassified into earnings when cash flow hedges are discontinued.
- Net gain or loss on foreign currency hedges reported in accumulated other comprehensive income (AOCI).
- Analysis of the derivatives component of AOCI related to cash flow hedges, including beginning balance of accumulated gain or loss, current period net gain or loss, net amount reclassified into earnings, and ending balance of accumulated gain or loss.

These disclosures seek to inform the reader about a company's use of derivatives, the effectiveness of those used for hedging, and their impact on current earnings. They also seek to highlight derivatives' impact on OCI, and their likely effect on future earnings. How companies comply with these requirements affects their usefulness. For example, because quantitative information presented in tabular rather than narrative form can be more useful, and companies had not been providing enough of it, the Codification now requires tabular disclosures of the following kinds of quantitative information.

- Fair values of the different derivative types as assets and liabilities, hedges and non-hedges, and the balance sheet line items that include these values.
- Amounts of gains and losses and where reported—in income statement line items or OCI—presented separately for fair value and cash flow hedges and by type of derivative contract.

ASC para. 815-10-50-4E also requires tabular presentation of this information:

- Fair values of derivative contracts reported as assets and liabilities, separated by qualifying hedges and non-hedges, and by types of derivative contracts, and the balance sheet line items in which they are reported.
- Gains and losses on derivative contracts, separated by qualifying fair value and cash flow hedges and non-hedges, by types of derivative contracts, and by effective and ineffective portions on qualifying hedges.

As one might imagine, the resulting tables can be complex, possibly to the point where their complexity outweighs the well-meaning transparency goals motivating such presentations.

BUSINESS APPLICATION   J.M. Smucker Company Derivatives Disclosures

The **J.M. Smucker Company**'s tabular disclosure of derivatives clearly provides the information required by the Codification. The following table discloses the amounts and accounts where derivatives appear on Smucker's balance sheet, separated by hedges and non-hedges and by type of hedge. Dollar amounts are in thousands.

	April 30, 2011		
	Other Current Assets	Other Current Liabilities	Other Noncurrent Liabilities
Derivatives designated as hedging instruments:			
Commodity contracts................................	$ 3,408	$ —	$ —
Interest rate contract	5,423	—	1,384
Total derivatives designated as hedging instruments	$ 8,831	$ —	$1,384
Derivatives not designated as hedging instruments:			
Commodity contracts................................	$ 9,887	$5,432	$ —
Foreign currency exchange contracts	317	3,204	—
Total derivatives not designated as hedging instruments	$10,204	$8,636	$ —
Total derivative instruments.............................	$19,035	$8,636	$1,384

continued

Gains on cash flow hedges of commodity price risk, and where they are reported, appear next.

	2011
Gains recognized in other comprehensive income (effective portion)...................	$21,082
Gains reclassized from accumulated other comprehensive income (loss) to cost of products sold (effective portion)......................................	14,780
Change in accumulated other comprehensive income (loss)	6,302
Gains recognized in cost of products sold (ineffective portion)......................	611

This table discloses realized and unrealized losses on derivatives *not* designated as hedges. These losses are reported in cost of products sold.

	2011
Losses on commodity contracts	$3,994
Losses on foreign currency exchange contracts	3,290
Losses recognized in cost of products sold (derivatives not designated as hedging instruments)....	$7,284

Although Smucker's follows the Codification requirements for its derivatives disclosures, readers may still have difficulty evaluating the effectiveness of its hedging strategy. The FASB and IASB propose major changes in reporting and disclosure requirements for hedging activities. We discuss these changes in the next section. *Source:* J.M. Smucker Company 2011 annual report.

DERIVATIVES AND HEDGING UNDER IFRS

Because reporting requirements for derivatives and hedging activities are the same whether a company invests in foreign currency forward contracts or futures, options and swaps, Chapter 8's discussion of IFRS for derivatives and hedging applies to this chapter as well. IFRS for derivatives and hedging activities are found in *IAS 39*, Financial Instruments: Recognition and Measurement, and *IFRS 7*, Financial Instruments: Disclosures. Requirements for qualifying hedges and the mechanics of hedge accounting are similar to U.S. GAAP, except that IFRS allows use of the **basis adjustment** method for cash flow hedges of nonfinancial assets. Required disclosures are also similar.

LO5 Discuss IFRS for derivatives and hedging.

IASB Hedge Accounting Project

As briefly summarized in Chapter 8, as of 2012 the FASB and IASB are considering changes to current hedge accounting standards, to make hedging activities more transparent to financial statement users, but also to simplify the reporting requirements.

In 2010 the IASB issued an exposure draft of proposed hedge accounting standards as the third phase of their project to replace *IAS 39* financial instruments standards with *IFRS 9*. This proposal is in Draft Review form in 2012. The IASB's goal is to accurately report the effects a company's risk management activities have on its financial performance. Investors view *IAS 39*'s current standards as arbitrary and rules-based, preventing the use of hedge accounting for many hedging activities. The difference between the accounting for fair value and cash flow hedges also reduces investors' ability to evaluate hedging performance.

Chapter 8 provides an overview of the IASB's proposal. Here we elaborate on major specific items pertaining to Chapter 9 topics.

Qualification for hedge accounting. The rigorous and complex rules governing whether a derivative investment qualifies for hedge accounting prevent many companies from using hedge accounting for legitimate and effective hedging practices. The IASB proposal expands the types of investments that can be designated as hedges and expands the types of items that can be hedged. Risk components of assets and liabilities and groups of items can be designated as hedged items.

Evaluation of hedge effectiveness. Currently a hedge must be "highly effective" initially and in subsequent periods to qualify for hedge accounting. Under the IASB proposal, an effective hedge must meet the company's objective concerning hedge effectiveness and generally offset the hedged risk. Historical evaluation of whether the hedge was actually effective is no longer required, but prospective assessment continues.

Accounting for the time value of options. While the intrinsic value of options is an effective hedge, the time value is not. Because management generally designates intrinsic value as the hedging instrument, changes in time value affect income as they occur. Accounting treatment for options used as hedges has long been a source of frustration for companies: the accounting for time value creates income volatility. The IASB proposes that the initial time value, usually the premium paid for the option, be recognized in income either over the duration of the hedge or, similar to intrinsic value, when the hedged item affects income.

As of 2012, the FASB has not issued a new hedge accounting standard. Changes in its 2010 proposal are expected as it works with the IASB to develop a converged hedge accounting standard.

REVIEW OF KEY CONCEPTS •••••••••••••••••••••••••••

LO 1 **Describe futures contracts and account for common futures transactions. (p. 353)** Similar to foreign currency forward contracts, **futures contracts** lock in the future purchase or sale price of a commodity or financial instrument. Companies use futures to avoid price risk on the expected future sale of inventories and forecasted purchases of commodities. Futures positions are normally settled by taking an opposite position; delivery rarely occurs. Changes in the value of futures used to hedge exposed positions or firm commitments are reported in income. Changes in the value of futures used to hedge forecasted transactions are reported in OCI and reclassified to income when the hedged transaction affects income.

LO 2 **Explain options contracts and account for common options transactions. (p. 360)** An **option contract** allows the holder to buy (call) or sell (put) the optioned commodity or financial instrument at a specified price (strike price) during a specified time period. The holder exercises or sells the option when it profits the holder by being in the money, and lets it expire when it is out of the money. Option value is composed of intrinsic value that measures the amount by which the option is in the money, and time value based on expectations of future prices. When hedging with options, option holders generally specify the intrinsic value as the hedge instrument; changes in time value are reported in income as they occur.

LO 3 **Describe and account for interest rate swaps. (p. 366)** Companies use **interest rate swaps** to change payments on variable rate debt into fixed payments, and vice versa. Receive fixed/pay variable interest rate swaps are fair value hedges; changes in the fair value of the swap and the hedged fixed rate debt are reported in income. Receive variable/pay fixed interest rate swaps are cash flow hedges; changes in the fair value of the swap are reported in OCI and reclassified as adjustments to future interest expense.

LO 4 **Discuss disclosure requirements for derivatives and hedging. (p. 371)** Companies are required to disclose the objectives of derivatives investments, where they are reported in the financial statements, and the expected impact on future income of reclassifications from AOCI. Information is categorized by hedge type and risk hedged.

LO 5 **Discuss IFRS for derivatives and hedging. (p. 373)** IFRS for derivatives and hedging is similar but not identical to U.S. GAAP. IFRS sometimes allows hedge accounting when U.S. GAAP does not, and vice versa. Unlike U.S. GAAP, in limited circumstances IFRS allows hedge gains and losses reported in AOCI to be reclassified as a **basis adjustment**. In 2010 the IASB proposed many changes to hedge accounting requirements, designed to increase transparency to investors and more accurately reflect companies' actual hedging activities.

MULTIPLE CHOICE QUESTIONS ·····································

Use the following information to answer questions 1-3 below:

On December 1, 2014, Metallic Wonders Corporation has an inventory of metals carried at a cost of $1,000,000. The company plans to sell the inventory in about 60 days, and wishes to guarantee the current 60-day futures price of $1,400,000. On December 1, 2014, it takes a $1,400,000 short position in metal futures for delivery in 60 days. No margin deposit is required. The futures position is a qualified fair value hedge of the inventory, and the company elects to use hedge accounting. The company closes its futures position on January 31, 2015, and sells the metals on the spot market on February 5, 2015. The company's accounting year ends December 31.

Spot and futures prices for the inventory are:

	spot price	January 31, 2015 futures price
December 1, 2014	$1,340,000	$1,400,000
December 31, 2014	1,245,000	1,310,000
January 31, 2015	1,200,000	1,200,000
February 5, 2015	1,290,000	N/A

1. At what amount is the inventory reported on Metallic Wonders' December 31, 2014, balance sheet? LO 1

   a. $ 905,000
   b. $ 910,000
   c. $1,000,000
   d. $1,250,000

2. At what amount is the investment in futures reported on Metallic Wonders' December 31, 2014, balance sheet? LO 1

   a. $90,000 liability
   b. $95,000 asset
   c. $95,000 liability
   d. $90,000 asset

3. What is the gross margin on the February 5, 2015, sale of inventory? LO 1

   a. $290,000
   b. $340,000
   c $430,000
   d. $490,000

4. GE stock has a current market value of $15. A call option in GE stock has a strike price of $11 and sells for $6. Which statement is *false*? LO 2

   a. The time value of the option is $2.
   b. The call option could be hedging a company's investment in GE stock.
   c. The intrinsic value of the option is $4.
   d. If the market price of GE stock falls, the option will be less valuable.

Use the following information to answer questions 5–6 below.

Golden Corporation invests in an interest rate cap to hedge $4,000,000 in variable rate debt, whose rate is set at LIBOR plus 20 bp. The cap fixes LIBOR at 4.7%. For the 6-month period ending December 31, 2013, LIBOR is 5%. For this same period, the cap's market value increases by $5,000.

LO 2   **5.** How much does Golden receive in cash to settle the swap for the 6-month period ending December 31, 2013?

    a. $ 6,000
    b. $ 12,000
    c. $ 94,000
    d. $100,000

LO 2   **6.** What is Golden's gain or loss on the cap (the change in time value) for the 6-month period ending December 31, 2013?

    a. $5,000 gain
    b. $6,000 loss
    c. $1,000 loss
    d. $5,000 loss

Use the following information to answer questions 7–10 below:

Sunny Corporation has $1,000,000 in fixed rate debt, with an annual interest rate of 4%, and interest payments due June 30 and December 31 of each year. On January 1, 2013, it entered a receive fixed/pay variable interest rate swap, where the variable rate is LIBOR. On January 1, 2013, LIBOR is 3.8%. On June 30, 2013, LIBOR declines to 3.5% and causes the variable rate to be reset at that time. The swap qualifies for hedge accounting.

LO 3   **7.** How much does Sunny pay or receive to settle the swap for the 6-month period ending June 30, 2013?

    a. $ 1,000 paid
    b. $20,000 received
    c. $19,000 paid
    d. $ 1,000 received

LO 3   **8.** Suppose the fixed rate debt changed in value by $80,000 as of June 30, 2013. How does Sunny record this change in value?

    a. Gain reported in income
    b. Loss reported in income
    c. Loss reported in OCI
    d. Not recorded

LO 3   **9.** Suppose the swap contract changed in value by $80,000 as of June 30, 2013. How does Sunny record this change in value?

    a. Gain reported in income
    b. Loss reported in income
    c. Loss reported in OCI
    d. Not recorded

LO 3   **10.** Suppose the same facts as above, except Sunny Corporation has variable rate debt, with interest payments at LIBOR, and enters a receive variable/pay fixed interest rate swap, with the annual fixed rate set at 4%. The swap changed in value by $80,000 as of June 30, 2013. How does Sunny record this change in value?

    a. Gain reported in income
    b. Loss reported in income
    c. Loss reported in OCI
    d. Not recorded

**Assignments with the ✓ in the margin are available in an online homework system.
See the Preface of the book for details.**

EXERCISES ••

LO 1   **E9.1 Fair Value Hedge: Short in Commodity Futures** American Italian Pasta Company (AIPC) manufactures several varieties of pasta. The price of pasta is very sensitive to the cost of certain commodities. On January 1, 2013, AIPC had excess commodity inventories carried at acquisition cost of $150,000. These commodities could be sold or manufactured into pasta later in the year. To hedge against possible declines in the value of its commodities inventory, on January 6 AIPC sold commodity futures, obligat-

AMERICAN
ITALIAN PASTA
COMPANY
[AIPC]

ing the company to deliver the commodities in February for $160,000. The futures exchange requires a $10,000 margin deposit. On February 19, the futures price increased to $171,000 and the company closed out its futures contract. Spot prices continued to rise and AIPC sold its inventory for $173,500 on March 2.

Required

a. Prepare the journal entries related to AIPC's futures contract and sale of commodities inventory. Assume a perpetual inventory system and that spot and futures prices move in tandem.
b. By how much would AIPC's profit increase if the hedge was *not* undertaken?

E9.2 **Fair Value Hedge: Long in Commodity Futures**   Daley, Inc., engages in futures trading on a regular basis. Its books are closed on June 30 of each year. On June 1, 2014, Daley enters a futures contract and makes an initial margin deposit of $10,000. The contract requires Daley to purchase 10,000 units of commodity futures at $10 per unit for delivery in 90 days. Daley has a liability, recorded as Deferred Revenue, to supply the commodity (which it plans to purchase on the spot market) in 90 days to a customer. The futures are hedging the fair value of the liability even though the customer has already paid the full $150,000 selling price.   **LO 1** ✓

Required

a. Prepare the journal entries made on June 1, on June 30 when the futures are selling at $11 per unit, and on August 29 when the long position is closed out at $11.50 per unit.
b. Explain why Daley purchased commodity futures when it intends to purchase the commodity on the spot market. How much did Daley save by hedging as opposed to not hedging?

E9.3 **Hedge of Firm Commitment: Short in Commodity Futures**   On May 1, 2014, Keister, Inc., sells 100,000 units of commodity futures at $5/unit for delivery in 120 days and makes an initial margin deposit of $10,000. Spot and futures prices move in tandem. Keister will buy the commodity from a supplier in 90 days and, pursuant to a firm sale commitment, will sell it 30 days later at the prevailing spot price. Keister designates the futures contracts to protect the proceeds to be received when the sale commitment is fulfilled and has a May 30 fiscal year-end.   **LO 1**

Required

Prepare the journal entries made on May 1, on May 30 when the futures are selling at $4.80 per unit, on July 29 when the futures are selling for $4.75 per unit and the commodity is purchased at a total cost of $460,000, and on August 28 when the short position is closed out at $4.77 per unit.

E9.4 **Economics of Hedging with Futures; Propriety of Hedge Accounting**   McVeigh Company buys 100,000 units of commodity futures at $5.50 per unit to cover a firm commitment to deliver 100,000 units (which McVeigh does not own) to a customer at a fixed price. Spot and futures prices for this commodity are equal and fluctuate between $4 and $6 per unit.   **LO 1**

Required

a. Use calculations to show that, regardless of whether McVeigh eventually purchases the commodity for as little as $4 or as much as $6, hedging with futures fixes the net cost to McVeigh at $5.50 per unit.
b. Suppose McVeigh grows the commodity on its own farms and will not need to purchase it on the spot market. Explain whether *ASC Topic 815* permits hedge accounting treatment for the 100,000 units of commodity futures purchased by McVeigh.

E9.5 **Interest Rate Cap**   On July 1, 2013, **Molson Coors Brewing Company** borrowed $3 million for two years with interest paid semi-annually based on LIBOR adjusted semiannually. On that date, LIBOR is 4 percent per annum and is set at 4 percent for the first six months. To hedge against a possible rise in interest rates, on July 2 Molson Coors bought a two-year 4.1 percent interest rate cap for 0.15 percent per year, payable in full immediately. The intrinsic value of the cap is designated as the hedge instrument and the hedge is fully effective. LIBOR increased during the second half of 2013 and is reset to 4.3 percent for the first half of 2014. Molson Coors closes its books on December 31 and June 30. The cap's fair value is $7,000 on December 31, 2013, before the rate adjustment, and is $8,000 on June 30, 2014, when the time value component is $5,000.   **LO 2**

MOLSON COORS BREWING COMPANY [TAP]

Required

Prepare all journal entries related to the loan interest and the interest rate cap on July 2, 2013, December 31, 2013, and June 30, 2014.

E9.6 **Fair Value Hedge with Put Options**   In January, 2014, Combo Corporation purchased $200,000 of 5 percent government bonds at par for its trading portfolio, carried at market pursuant to *ASC Topic 320*. By late February, the bonds were selling at 98. To hedge against a further price decrease on these bonds, on   **LO 2**

March 1, 2014, Combo purchased March 2015 put options on these bonds at 101 for a premium of $3.10 per $100 of bonds. The intrinsic value of the puts is designated as the hedge instrument. By June 30, 2014, the company's fiscal year-end, the bonds were selling at 100 and the puts for $1.30. On December 31, 2014, when the bonds were selling at 97, Combo closed out its position by selling the puts for $4.30.

Required

Prepare Combo Corporation's journal entries during 2014 related to the puts and the hedged bonds.

LO 2 **E9.7** **Call Options Hedging Foreign Currency Debt** Taking advantage of lower interest rates in the United Kingdom, Carlton Inc., a U.S. firm, borrowed £2,000,000 on July 1, 2012, to be repaid in one year. When the transaction occurred, the exchange rate was $1.50/£. To hedge against possible appreciation of the British pound, Carlton paid a premium of $0.014/£ for July 2013 call options on £2,000,000, with a strike price of $1.49/£. Because the calls are hedging a foreign-currency-denominated obligation, hedge accounting does not apply and there is no need to designate all or part of the option premium as the hedge instrument. On December 31, 2012, when Carlton's books are closed, the exchange rate is $1.55/£, and the calls are selling for $0.069/£. On June 30, 2013, Carlton sells the calls for $0.12/£. The exchange rate at that time is $1.61/£.

Required

Prepare Carlton's journal entries made on July 1, 2012, December 31, 2012, and June 30, 2013, to recognize the calls' value changes and the exchange rate adjustments on the debt. Ignore interest on and repayment of the debt.

LO 3 **E9.8** **Interest Rate Swap: Profit and Default** On July 1, 2014, Queen Corp. and Prince, Inc. entered into an interest rate swap on a notional amount of $1 million. With T representing the Treasury bill rate, they accepted the following offer of Intermediary:

To Intermediary from Queen	LIBOR + 30 (floating)
To Intermediary from Prince	T + 40 (fixed)
To Queen from Intermediary	T + 30 (fixed)
To Prince from Intermediary	LIBOR + 20 (floating)

At inception of the swap, T = 3 percent and LIBOR = 3.3 percent. Due to an increase of 20 bp in the floating interest rate at the end of September, Queen Corp. defaulted and Intermediary honored its commitment to Prince, Inc. by continuing with the swap.

Required

a. What monthly profit, if any, was Intermediary making on the swap before default?
b. Is Intermediary losing money after the default? If so, how much?

LO 3 **E9.9** **Interest Rate Swap: Journal Entries** Refer to the data in E9.8. Assume that the floating rate is adjusted on October 1 and that default did *not* occur. Assume also that on September 30, 2014, the swap's fair value is a $75,000 liability to Queen and a $33,000 asset to Prince.

Required

Prepare the journal entries made by Queen and Prince on September 30, 2014, when the first payments pursuant to the swap are made. Do not record the interest on the underlying debt or mark it to market.

LO 3 **E9.10** **Interest Rate Swap** On January 1, 2013, Marshall Corp. issues $10,000,000 in 4 percent fixed rate debt with interest payments due every six months. Concurrently, Marshall enters into a plain vanilla interest rate swap in which it receives 4 percent fixed and pays variable at *average* LIBOR + 60 bp on a notional amount of $10,000,000. On June 30, 2013 the market interest rate on comparable fixed rate debt is 3 percent and LIBOR declined to 2.2 percent. LIBOR averaged 2.7 percent during the six-month period. The estimated fair value of the swap to Marshall is $275,000 on June 30, 2013, and the fair value of the debt is $10,275,000.

Required

a. Prepare the journal entries made by Marshall on January 1 and June 30 in connection with the debt issuance, the periodic interest, and value changes in the swap and debt.
b. Suppose instead that Marshall issued variable rate debt and entered a swap in which it receives variable and pays fixed. If the market rate of interest on comparable fixed-rate debt declines on June 30,

does Marshall record the fair value of the swap as an asset or a liability? Does Marshall recognize a gain or loss on the swap and what is its accounting treatment?

E9.11 Interpreting Interest Rate Swap Disclosures Note 7 to **General Mills'** fiscal 2011 consolidated financial statements includes the following:

LO 3

GENERAL MILLS
[GIS]

(in millions)	**May 29, 2011**	**May 30, 2010**
Pay-floating swaps – notional amount...................	$838.0	$2,155.6
Average receive rate.................................	1.8%	4.8%
Average pay rate.....................................	0.2%	0.3%
Pay-fixed swaps – notional amount.....................	—	$1,600.0
Average receive rate.................................	—	0.3%
Average pay rate.....................................	—	7.3%

Required

a. Based on the data above, explain whether the overall swap position seems more or less beneficial to General Mills in fiscal 2011 compared with fiscal 2010. Which are the fair value hedges? The cash flow hedges?

b. General Mills states that the amount of hedge ineffectiveness in each year and on each type of swap was less than $1 million. It also states that "effective gains and losses on these derivatives [fair value hedges] and the underlying hedged items are recorded as net interest. Comment on the propriety of General Mills' "net interest" treatment.

c. Elsewhere in Note 7 General Mills states that a total of $29.4 million of aftertax unrealized losses from interest rate cash flow hedges are recorded in AOCI at the end of fiscal 2011. Explain the effect of the eventual reclassification of these amounts from AOCI to earnings.

E9.12 Futures and Options as Hedging Alternatives Companies seeking to hedge future purchases or revenue flows can often choose between futures contracts and option contracts. Sami Corp. projects purchasing 100 tons of a commodity in three months; its current spot price is $700/ton and the six-month futures price is $710/ton. Ninety-one day call options on the commodity at the money sell for $50.

LO 1, 2 ✓

Assume that Sami subsequently signs purchase orders for 100 tons to be delivered in three months at the then-current spot price, and hedges those firm commitments with six-month futures contracts requiring a $20,000 margin deposit. At the end of the three-month period, when the futures price is $690/ton, Sami closes its futures position and takes delivery of the 100 tons at the spot price of $682/ton.

Required

a. What factors should Sami consider when deciding between hedging with futures and options?

b. Prepare summary journal entries to record all the events surrounding the firm commitment, the futures hedge and the eventual purchase of the 100 tons at the $682/ton spot price.

c. Suppose that Sami does not sign purchase orders and instead uses option contracts to hedge its anticipated purchases, designating the options' intrinsic values as the hedge instrument. The option contracts remain out of the money and expire when Sami makes the spot market purchase at $682/ton. Prepare summary journal entries to record these events.

d. Compute the cash gain or loss from hedging versus not hedging in parts *b* and *c*.

PROBLEMS •••

P9.1 Commodity Futures The Davis Company grows soybeans and processes them into soybean meal for eventual sale to food companies. Davis currently owns 10,000 tons of soybean meal, carried in inventory at cost of $3,400,000. Soybean meal trades on the spot markets for $350 per ton; three-month futures are selling for $363 per ton. Davis expects to sell the 10,000 tons in 90 days. On August 1, 2014, Davis sells 10,000 tons of soybean meal futures to be delivered on October 30, 2014, at the $363 price. The price of Davis' futures contracts has advanced to $367 and the spot price is $354 on September 30, when the books are closed for interim reporting purposes. Davis closes out its short position on October 28, 2014, when the futures price is $361 per ton and the spot price is $348.

LO 1

Required

a. Assuming that Davis deposits $75,000 margin with the broker on August 1, prepare the journal entries it makes on August 1, on September 30, and on October 28.

    b.   If Davis sells the soybean meal in the spot market on November 2, 2014, for $348.50 per ton, calculate its net cash gain or loss from the sale, taking into account the hedging transaction.

    c.   Suppose instead that Davis *purchased* the 10,000 tons of soybean futures on August 1, 2014, closing the long position on October 28, 2014. Calculate the net cash gain or loss on the long futures position and compare its accounting treatment with the gain or loss on the short futures position in part *a* above at October 28, 2014.

LO 1 **P9.2** **Interest Rate Futures** As part of its cash management activities, Greenstein Corp. regularly invests in 91-day Treasury bills. It purchased $1,000,000 face value of these bills on June 1 and, fearing lower interest rates when it rolls over these short-term investments, Greenstein purchases $1,000,000 face value Treasury bill futures at 96 to be delivered in 91 days and makes a $10,000 margin deposit.

    Required

    a.   Prepare the journal entries made on June 1, on the June 30 reporting date when the Treasury bill futures are selling at 97, and on August 30 when the old Treasury bills mature and the new ones are delivered. On August 30, Greenstein's futures contract is selling at 97.5.

    b.   Assume the new Treasury bills cost $993,750. Use calculations to show how the hedge enables Greenstein to report a 4 percent annualized return on the new Treasury bills even though they currently yield 2.5 percent annually.

LO 1 **P9.3** **Interest Rate Futures: Fair Value Hedge** Fabric retailer Petren Corp. buys 300,000 yards of cloth each quarter at an average price of $3.00/yard. To finance these purchases, Petren sells $1,000 face value Treasury bonds from its available-for-sale investment portfolio. The bonds are presently carried at 90, their current market value.

    Required

    a.   Petren sells Treasury bond futures at 90 on enough bonds to finance next quarter's purchases and settles the contracts at 92 in three months. Management designates the futures as a perfectly effective hedge. Considering both the futures contracts and the sale of the company's own Treasury bonds to finance the fabric purchase, compute the net effect on earnings.

    b.   Suppose a balance sheet date occurs in 45 days when the futures and the bonds are selling at 91.5. Prepare the related journal entries at this balance sheet date.

    c.   Suppose instead that Petren buys Treasury bond futures at 90 on enough bonds to finance the next quarter's purchases and closes out the contract at 93 in three months. Is this use of futures likely to be a qualifying hedge?

    d.   Considering both the futures contracts in part *c* and sale of the company's own Treasury bonds to finance the purchases, calculate the effect on earnings.

✅ LO 1 **P9.4** **Evaluating Hedging With Futures Contracts** A large farming company likes to firm up prices for its agricultural products. It anticipates harvesting and selling 1,000,000 bushels of a particular commodity in six months. Constant news reports and changes in forecasts cause fluctuations in the spot price for the commodity. The current spot price is $5.00 per bushel. Futures contracts are available at $4.75 per bushel and six-month put option contracts with an exercise price of $5.00 per bushel are available for $0.35. A noninterest-bearing margin deposit of $200,000 is required if futures contracts covering the entire 1,000,000 bushels are sold. The company's current cost of money is 4 percent per annum.

    Required

    a.   Explain the advantages and disadvantages of hedging the harvest's value with futures contracts.

    b.   Calculate the spot price six months hence at which the company is indifferent between not hedging and hedging with futures contracts.

    c.   Assume the spot price stands at $5.25 per bushel when 1,000,000 bushels of the commodity are harvested (not sold) and that commodity inventories are carried at market. Explain, using calculations as needed, how the company's financial statements will differ without hedging compared to hedging with futures contracts.

LO 2 **P9.5** **Evaluating Hedging With Option Contracts** Refer to the data in P9.4.

    Required

    a.   Explain the advantages and disadvantages of hedging the harvest's value with option contracts.

    b.   Calculate the spot price 6 months hence at which the company is indifferent between not hedging and hedging with option contracts.

    c.   Assume the spot price stands at $4.75 per bushel when 1,000,000 bushels of the commodity are harvested (not sold) and that commodity inventories are carried at market. Explain, using calculations as needed, how the company's financial statements will differ without hedging compared to hedging with option contracts.

P9.6 Currency Options: Short Answer Questions The following short answer questions ask you to explain specific uses of currency options. LO 2

Required

a. The **Footlocker** retail chain in the U.S. imports soccer shoes from the U.K. based on prices in British pounds and makes payments one month after delivery. To hedge against potential losses caused by a weakening dollar, Footlocker could buy call options to purchase pounds with dollars or buy put options to sell dollars for pounds. Explain whether these alternatives are likely to have the same economic effect on Footlocker. **FOOTLOCKER** [FL]

b. Another strategy for Footlocker in part *a* involves both buying call options to purchase pounds with dollars and writing put options to sell dollars for pounds at the same exercise price. Explain whether this strategy is likely to have the same economic effect on Footlocker.

c. **KBR, Inc.**, a U.S construction firm, is building a stadium in Italy. Costs are incurred in euros (€) but Italian suppliers require payment in U.S. dollars at the prevailing exchange rate. Explain whether KBR, Inc. can hedge against exchange rate risk by purchasing call options to purchase euros with dollars. **KBR, INC.** [KBR]

d. Higher interest rates in Europe led Citibank, a subsidiary of **Citigroup,** to purchase and invest €20,000,000 in a euro-denominated certificate of deposit paying 4 percent per annum. The bank's financial wizard wants to write 12-month calls at the money to protect the dollar equivalent of the €800,000 of interest due in 12 months. If the premium is $0.1111/€ and the dollar strengthens by 7 percent in 12 months, use calculations to explain whether writing the calls will increase Citibank's return. **CITIGROUP** [C]

e. **IBM** borrowed €2,000,000 from a German bank, taking advantage of the low 3.5 percent interest rate in Germany, and converted the euros to dollars when the exchange rate was $1.40/€. Because the euro may strengthen over the next year, IBM hedges the first year's interest payment by purchasing at-the-money calls for €70,000 when the exchange rate is $1.43/€; the premium is $0.03125/€. If at the end of the first year the exchange rate is $1.45/€, explain whether purchasing the calls increased IBM's financing cost compared with not hedging. **IBM** [IBM]

P9.7 Present Value Analysis of Interest Rate Cap and Journal Entries At July 1, 2013, Comiskey Company has $10,000,000 of debt due in four years with interest floating at prime. The rate is adjusted annually each July 1 and interest for the preceding year is payable on June 30. Comiskey closes its books on June 30 and December 31 of each year. Prime currently stands at 4 percent annually and is expected to fluctuate between 2 percent and 8 percent over the next four years. On July 1, 2013, Atlanta National Bank offers Comiskey a 4-year interest rate cap with a strike price of 5 percent for $400,000 payable immediately. LO 2

Required

a. Suppose the prime rate is expected to be 6 percent on July 1, 2014, 8 percent on July 1, 2015, and stay at 8 percent for the remaining two years. Use a present value analysis to determine whether purchasing the cap is a good economic decision in this set of circumstances. *Hint:* Let the applicable prime rate(s) when the interest changes occur be the discount rate(s).

b. Suppose instead that the prime rate drops to 2 percent on July 1, 2014, and stays at 2 percent for the remaining three years. Use a present value analysis to determine whether the savings in interest cost (2 percent versus the original 4 percent) will offset the cost of the cap.

c. Assume the cap is purchased and prime rises to 6 percent on July 1, 2014. Prepare the journal entries made by Comiskey to account for the periodic interest expense and the cap at December 31, 2014, and June 30, 2015. Assume that the fair value of the cap declines by $50,000 in each 6-month period.

P9.8 Fair Value Hedge: Put Options **Overhill Farms Inc.** has a large portfolio of marketable equity securities held as short-term investments. To protect against declines in the value of 10,000 shares of ABC Corp. common stock, on November 1, 2013, Overhill Farms purchased 90-day put options for $35,000 on the 10,000 ABC shares it had purchased at $40. The exercise price is $40 and the shares are selling for $38 each. Overhill Farms designates the intrinsic value of the puts as the hedge instrument. Assume the fair value of the time value component of the premium declines on a straight-line basis. Overhill Farms classifies the ABC Corp. shares as available-for-sale securities. LO 2 **OVERHILL FARMS INC.** [OFI]

Required

a. Prepare journal entries to record purchase of the puts and relevant events on November 1, 2013, and when the books are closed at December 31, 2013, and the stock is selling for $35.50.

b. Thirty days after the closing in part *a*, Overhill Farms decides to sell the 10,000 ABC shares for $32 each and to sell the put options. Calculate the net cash gain or loss realized on these sale transactions.

c. How much of this net cash gain or loss is recognized in 2013 income? In 2014 income?

LO 2 **P9.9** **Speculative Straddle: Journal Entries and Profit Calculation** Fastbuck, Inc. trades put and call options on common stock. Acting on a tip, on January 31, 2014, Fastbuck wrote both calls and puts expiring on March 31—known as a **"straddle"**—on 5,000 shares of Montclair Corporation stock that was selling for $42 a share. March 2014 calls with a strike price of $45 closed at $2; puts with the same terms closed at $3.10. On February 28, when the price of Montclair stock rose to $49 and the puts were selling at $0.80, Fastbuck sold the calls at $4.20. On March 31, Montclair stock fell to $47 and the puts expired without being exercised.

Required

a. Prepare journal entries to record writing the puts and calls and any other related accounting events including expiration of the puts. The books are closed monthly.
b. Calculate Fastbuck's cash gain or loss on the straddle.

LO 3

APPLE COMPUTER [AAPL]

P9.10 **Evaluate Strategies to Hedge Against Rising Interest Rates** Suppose **Apple Computer** has $100 million of two-year floating rate debt outstanding at LIBOR + 80 bp. In a swap, Apple can get LIBOR + 80 bp from intermediary in return for fixed payments to intermediary at 4 percent. Alternatively, Apple could purchase a 4 percent interest rate cap for the two years remaining until the debt matures. LIBOR is currently 3 percent.

Required

a. Assume LIBOR remains at 3 percent for the next two years. Compute the maximum amount Apple would pay for the cap and be indifferent between the swap and the cap. Ignore discounting.
b. Assume LIBOR does not remain at 3 percent for the next two years, and could go up or down. Explain the factors you would evaluate in deciding whether to make the swap or purchase the cap.
c. Suppose Apple also could transact in $100 million notional amount of interest rate futures at 96; the discount yield on the futures closely tracks movements in LIBOR. If Apple decides on the futures, should they be bought or sold? What other factors would you consider?

LO 3

JOHNSON & JOHNSON [JNJ]

P9.11 **Interest Rate Swap: Journal Entries and Valuation** **Johnson & Johnson** (J&J) has $10,000,000 of floating rate debt, with interest at LIBOR + 120 bp adjusted quarterly, and an equivalent amount of 2-year fixed-rate investments yielding 5 percent annually. To match fixed rate financing with its fixed-rate investments, J&J swaps 4 percent fixed payments to intermediary in exchange for LIBOR + 120 bp on the notional amount of $10,000,000 for 2 years. LIBOR is 2.8 percent.

Required

a. After the swap is in effect one quarter, LIBOR rises to 3.3 percent and the discount rate applicable to the fixed payments rises to 4.5 percent. Prepare the entries made by J&J at the end of the *second quarter* to record net interest expense under the swap.
b. Prepare the entries to revalue the swap and the hedged investments at the end of the second quarter. Assume a value change of $65,000 relates to the swap and the hedged investments.
c. Suppose the swap is not hedging fixed-rate investments and is a receive variable/pay fixed cash flow hedge. Record the $65,000 change in the swap's value assumed in part *b* above.

LO 3 **P9.12** **Critique Proposed Currency/Interest Rate Swap Arrangement** On June 25, 2016, Reno Company, a U.S. firm, will be taking out a £10,000,000 loan, due in three years and carrying an annual interest rate of LIBOR + 80 bp. In anticipation of the loan, a spot rate of $1.60/£ and LIBOR of 5 percent, Reno negotiates a currency swap and interest rate swap with Sterling Benteen, Ltd. (SB), a British firm. SB recently negotiated a fixed-rate dollar denominated loan. Proceeds from both loans will be converted into the home currency and used to finance projects in each company's home country. The two counterparties propose the following:

1. On June 25, 2016, Reno will receive £10,000,000 from SB in exchange for $16,000,000.
2. On June 24, 2019, Reno will receive $16,000,000 from SB in exchange for £10,000,000.
3. On June 24, 2017, 2018 and 2019, SB will pay Reno $960,000 (fixed at 6 percent annually) in exchange for sufficient £ to cover the annual interest on Reno's £10,000,000 floating rate loan.

Despite hours of staff work and pages of elegant computer printouts, you sense that this deal does not pass the "smell test." You wonder whether you are becoming a harbinger of doom. Surely the fate of George Armstrong Custer at the Little Bighorn, so vividly depicted by Errol Flynn in the classic film, "They Died with Their Boots On," can easily make one skeptical of forecasts and analyses of conditions that seem at first glance to be quite correct.

Required

a. What is wrong with the above arrangements? Recast them into swaps sensible for Reno and SB.

b. After you recast the arrangements into sensible swaps, suppose throughout the year ended June 24, 2019, LIBOR is 7 percent and the spot rate is $1.50. For that year only, calculate the undiscounted number of dollars that Reno saved (lost) by entering these swaps as opposed to not entering them.

REVIEW SOLUTIONS •••

Review 1 Solution

a. Fair value hedge

March 1	Investment in futures		50,000	
	Cash			50,000
	To record margin deposit on long futures position in fair value hedge.			
March 31	Loss on hedging		200,000	
	Cash			200,000
	To record decline in value of futures contracts and pay clearinghouse.			
	Commitment asset/liability		200,000	
	Gain on hedging			200,000
	To record the commitment asset resulting from the reduced cost to buy the commodity when it is eventually purchased.			
April 15	Cash		300,000	
	Gain on hedging			300,000
	To record gain and concurrent settlement for clearinghouse.			
	Loss on hedging		300,000	
	Commitment asset/liability			300,000
	To record the commitment liability resulting from increased cost to buy the commodity when it is eventually purchased.			
	Cash		50,000	
	Investment in futures			50,000
	To record refund of margin deposit from clearinghouse.			
	Commodities inventory		10,180,000	
	Cash			10,180,000
	To record purchase of commodities on a cash market.			
	Commitment asset/liability		100,000	
	Commodities inventory			100,000
	To adjust inventory balance for commitment liability.			
June 1	Cost of goods sold		10,080,000	
	Commodities inventory			10,080,000
	To record the sale of products containing the commodity.			

b.   Cash flow hedge

March 1	Investment in futures	50,000	
	Cash		50,000
	To record margin deposit on long futures position in cash flow hedge.		
March 31	Other comprehensive income (loss on hedging)	200,000	
	Cash		200,000
	To record decline in value of futures contracts and pay clearinghouse.		
April 15	Cash	300,000	
	Other comprehensive income		300,000
	To record gain and concurrent settlement for clearinghouse.		
	Cash	50,000	
	Investment in futures		50,000
	To record refund of margin deposit from clearinghouse.		
	Commodities inventory	10,180,000	
	Cash		10,180,000
	To record purchase of commodities on a cash market.		
June 1	Cost of goods sold	10,080,000	
	Other comprehensive income	100,000	
	Commodities inventory		10,180,000
	To record the sale of products containing the commodity.		

Review 2 Solution

2013			
Aug. 10	Investment in AFS securities	3,000,000	
	Cash		3,000,000
	To record purchase of AFS securities.		
Sept. 30	OCI	90,000	
	Investment in AFS securities		90,000
	To record decline in value to $2,910,000.		
	Investment in options	100,000	
	Cash		100,000
	To record purchase of options.		
2014			
Jan. 2	Loss on hedging	23,400	
	Investment in options		23,400
	To record decline in value to $76,600.		
	Investment in AFS securities	30,000	
	Gain on hedging		30,000
	To record increase in value to $2,940,000, using hedge accounting.		
Mar. 1	Investment in options	83,200	
	Gain on hedging		83,200
	To record increase in value to $159,800.		
	Loss on hedging	90,000	
	Investment in AFS securities		90,000
	To record decline in value to $2,850,000, using hedge accounting.		

Cash..		159,800	
Investment in options			159,800
To record sale of options.			

Mar. 30	Investment in AFS securities	50,000	
	OCI		50,000
	To record increase in value to $2,900,000.		

Cash..		2,900,000	
Realized loss on sale of securities		40,000	
OCI			40,000
Investment in AFS securities....................			2,900,000
To record sale of securities and release of unrealized loss			
from AOCI to income.			

Review 3 Solution

a. *(in thousands)*

2014			
May 1	Cash..	100,000	
	Long-term debt		100,000
	To record debt issuance.		
2015			
April 30	Interest expense....................................	4,000	
	Cash		4,000
	To record periodic interest expense on fixed rate debt;		
	$4,000 = 0.04 × $100,000.		
	Cash..	1,200	
	Interest expense		1,200
	To record net cash payment from intermediary to settle the		
	swap; $1,200 = (.040 − .028) × $100,000.		
	Long-term debt	450	
	Gain on hedging activity		450
	To record decline in fair value of the fixed rate debt.		
	Loss on hedging activity............................	450	
	Investment in swap		450
	To record decline in fair value of the swap.		

b. If Heinz issues variable rate debt and enters a receive variable/pay fixed interest rate swap, the swap is a cash flow hedge. At the end of the year, if interest rates increase, the swap increases in value and the gain is credited to OCI. When Heinz makes next year's variable rate interest payment at the higher rate, the swap gain is reclassified from AOCI to offset the higher interest expense.

10 State and Local Governments: Introduction and General Fund Transactions

LEARNING OBJECTIVES

LO1 Describe the reporting environment for state and local governments. (p. 387)

LO2 Identify the fund types and reporting methods for state and local governments. (p. 393)

LO3 Prepare entries and financial statements for the general fund. (p. 398)

MECKLENBURG COUNTY, NORTH CAROLINA
www.charmeck.org

Mecklenburg County, North Carolina is the sixth largest urban region and the second largest financial center in the U.S. The county's largest city is Charlotte. Bank of America's headquarters are located in Mecklenburg County. Johnson & Wales University and the University of North Carolina both have campuses here. The County is also home to the NFL's Carolina Panthers and the NBA's Charlotte Bobcats.

Main funding sources for the County are property taxes and sales taxes. Major expenditures include the Charlotte-Mecklenburg Schools, Central Piedmont Community College, public television station WTVI and the Mecklenburg Emergency Medical Services Agency.

Each year Mecklenburg County issues a Comprehensive Annual Financial Report (CAFR), detailing its financial status and activities. The County's 2010 CAFR reports a total net asset deficit of over $688 million. However, the year's revenues exceeded expenses by $62 million, a significant improvement over 2009's $170 million deficit. Property tax revenues increased 2%, and sales tax revenues declined 6.5%, due to lower consumer spending in the County. Revenue from County services declined 3%, primarily because of a continuing reduction in construction permits. Interest revenue on investments fell 75%, a result of lower interest rates.

Who reads governmental financial statements? What kinds of information are provided? How do the financial statements differ from those of for-profit businesses? What accounting standards apply?

This chapter and the two that follow provide the answers to these questions.

CHAPTER ORGANIZATION

Reporting for state and local governments	Fund structure	Accounting for the general fund	Illustration of general fund accounting
• External users of financial information • Sources of GAAP • GAAP hierarchy • Objectives of financial reporting • Reporting entity	• Governmental, proprietary and fiduciary activities • Fund types and financial statements • Basis of reporting	• Budgetary accounts • Property tax revenue • Purchase of goods and services • Supplies inventories • Interfund transactions • Capital assets and long-term debt • Closing entries • Encumbrances	• Record budget, transactions, and closing entries • Prepare financial statements

Chapters 10-12 explain reporting practices and requirements for *state and local governments*. A **government** can be a state, county, city, town, village, or school district, or a separate revenue-generating organization such as a toll road. When the term *municipality* is used to describe a government, **municipality** means a local government, such as a city, town or village. This chapter provides an overview of government reporting and discusses the accounting for day-to-day operating activities of state and local governments.

NATURE OF GOVERNMENT ACTIVITIES

Government at all levels is an increasingly important segment of the economy. As the scope and diversity of governmental services and programs expand, so too does the importance of governmental accounting and reporting. The internal and external structure of accounting and reporting for state and local governments reflects the operating environment, legal constraints, and goals of these governments. Because a government differs from a business on all these dimensions, the accounting and reporting policies are in many ways very different, although changes in external reporting requirements in the last decade moved the government reporting model closer to that of business reporting.

LO1 Describe the reporting environment for state and local governments.

Major factors differentiating a state or local government from a business include:

* Resources come from such sources as taxes, fees, and fines. The government has a legal right to collect taxes, which provide most governmental resources.

* There are no ownership interests in a government.

* A government must adhere to a legal budget. Expenditures cannot exceed amounts provided in the budget.

* Financial inflows are often legally required to be used in a particular way. For example, a bond issue for construction of a building must be used for that purpose. Citizens may be assessed a special tax to finance a street light project. A federal grant to operate a community center must be used for that purpose.

* The main objective of government is to provide services to citizens, usually on a nonprofit basis. The notion of "matching" governmental expenditures with revenues does not apply, since revenue does not come from services provided. Profit is not a valid measure of performance for most governmental activities.

* Users of governmental financial statements are:
    ○ credit market representatives, who determine bond ratings, provide bond insurance guaranteeing bond payments, and provide investment banking services

○ elected and appointed officials of the government

○ citizens, typically from budget advisory groups and "watchdog" organizations

○ supervisory levels of government, such as a state controller monitoring county government financial performance

○ public sector labor unions

• The **Governmental Accounting Standards Board** (GASB) sets accounting requirements for governmental external reporting. Many governments are legally required to follow GAAP and issue audited financial statements.

Activities of a government can be divided into three major categories: *governmental*, *proprietary*, and *fiduciary*. **Governmental activities** benefit the government or its citizens, and for the most part consist of primary services such as health and safety, economic assistance, education, culture and recreation, and legislative services. These activities typically do not generate significant inflows of resources, and are funded by income, sales, and property tax levies, and state and federal aid.

Proprietary activities are similar to the activities of a business, in that goods and services are primarily financed by user fees, paid either by citizens or other departments within the government. User fees are usually set to approximate the cost of the goods or services provided. Examples are parking and recreational facilities, utilities, and motor pools.

Fiduciary activities are those where the government holds resources in a custodial capacity for entities or individuals outside the governmental unit. For example, a local government collects sales taxes as an agent for the state, or a municipality funds and manages a pension plan for its employees.

Reporting Perspective

Credit market representatives use municipal financial statements to evaluate the credit-worthiness of the governmental unit. The major forms of municipal debt obligations are bonds, notes, and leases. There are legal restrictions on the amount and types of debt a municipality can issue. Two basic types of bonds are *general obligation* and *revenue bonds*. **General obligation bonds** are secured by the full faith, credit, and general taxing powers of the municipality. Investors generally consider this form of debt to be the most secure. **Revenue bonds** are secured by the pledge of specific revenues and, unlike general obligation bonds, usually contain bond covenants or restrictions. As an example, water revenue bonds may be issued to finance the construction of a water treatment plant. A portion of the connection fees and charges paid by users of the water system is pledged to pay the principal and interest on the bonds. Bond restrictions may require that the construction be completed, and that rates be sufficient to pay all costs, including bond debt service.

Hybrid bond securities have characteristics of both general obligation and revenue debt, or possess other unique features. A common example is **guaranteed revenue bonds**, revenue bonds also backed by the full faith and credit of the municipality. If pledged revenues are insufficient to repay the debt, it is repaid with the municipality's general revenues. Municipalities may also issue **notes**, typically outstanding for periods of less than three years. Examples are tax, revenue, grant, and bond anticipation notes, and tax-exempt commercial paper. These notes are issued in *anticipation* of collecting expected taxes, revenue, grant revenue, or bond proceeds. **Bond anticipation notes** finance the start-up costs of a project for which the bonds cannot be issued immediately and are repaid from the subsequent bond issue proceeds.

In general, the classification of debt is important because it determines which regulations and limitations apply. Both federal and state laws regulate the issuance and trading of municipal debt securities. Although nontaxable municipal bonds are exempt from most federal regulatory requirements of the 1933 and 1934 securities acts, they are not exempt from the antifraud provisions. State laws often limit the amounts and/or types of debt financing allowed by local governments. Some states only allow the issuance of revenue bonds, whereas others allow only general obligation bonds. Other states limit the amount of debt issued, and limits can vary depending on the type of debt.

External Users of Governmental Financial Statements

External users of governmental financial statements include credit market representatives, elected officials, and citizens. Each group has different information needs.

Credit Market Representatives Organizations that provide financing to the government, in the form of bonds and loans, are interested in its ability to generate resources for required interest and principal payments. Important factors in this assessment include:

* sources of revenues and expenditures by function and program
* funding information on pensions and related liabilities
* changes in all liabilities, including pending litigation and contingent liabilities
* future financing plans
* extent to which revenues from one program subsidize costs of another program
* individual program or activity surpluses or deficits
* material departures from GAAP
* whether financial statements are audited on a timely basis
* liquidity and flexibility of the governmental unit
* evidence of management's performance
* economic factors

Elected Officials and Citizens Citizens, legislators, unions and oversight officials focus on how much money a government has available to spend, how tax dollars are used, how much governmental services cost, sources of financing for various programs, and how current activities and plans affect future taxes and future ability to provide services. Financial information related to these concerns includes:

* where a government's money comes from and goes
* how much resources a government has available to spend
* budget allocations for major programs
* comparison of actual results to the original budget
* detailed capital improvement plans
* costs of services in detail
* percentage of total expenditures financed by taxes
* impact of current performance on future tax rates and services

SOURCES OF GAAP FOR STATE AND LOCAL GOVERNMENTS

Current governmental accounting principles developed from several sources and in response to user needs. Although many principles and procedures evolved from practice over the years, formal pronouncements now play the dominant role. A sense of how GAAP developed is valuable background for understanding current requirements.

In the late 1800s, when misuse of funds was prevalent in many large cities, the National Municipal League recommended accounting and financial reporting methods, which some cities adopted. In 1904, New York was the first state to require cities to use standardized financial reporting. In the depression years of the 1930s, new demands for services were placed on governments while resources diminished. The Municipal Finance Officers Association (MFOA) published accounting and financial reporting standards during this time. Although the MFOA was the first of several organizations that issued standards, none of these had the status of "authoritative pronouncements."

In the 1970s, many cities were near bankruptcy, due largely to high interest rates and large expenditures on social and economic programs. Popular sentiment held that governmental accounting and reporting methods were at least partly to blame by hiding the true financial condition of troubled governments. The National Council on Governmental Accounting (NCGA), the organization that issued prevailing standards, did not adequately address these deficiencies. Lack of confidence in this organization led to formation of the Governmental Accounting Standards Board (GASB) in 1984. Appointed by the Financial Accounting Foundation, which also oversees the FASB, the GASB follows the same due process in establishing standards as the FASB. The GASB establishes current GAAP for state and local governments.

Governmental Accounting Standards Board

The GASB issues authoritative standards on accounting and financial reporting by state and local governmental entities, including not-for-profit entities owned by or related to the government, such as state colleges and universities and public hospitals. The GASB issues *Statements of Governmental Accounting Standards* (*SGAS*), *Statements of Governmental Accounting Concepts* (*SGAC*), *Interpretations*, and *Technical Bulletins*. Current accounting principles deemed authoritative by the GASB are organized into a publication entitled *Codification and Original Pronouncements*.

The GASB does *not* establish GAAP for the *federal government*. Standards for federal government units are developed by the Office of Management and Budget (OMB), the Government Accountability Office (GAO), the Treasury Department, and the Federal Accounting Standards Advisory Board.

GAAP Hierarchy in Government Accounting

Although the GASB is *the* source of authoritative governmental accounting principles today, pronouncements of other standard-setting bodies and guidance of professional organizations remain relevant. Certain publications by the NCGA and the American Institute of Certified Public Accountants (AICPA) were embraced by the GASB in *SGAS 1*. The Government Finance Officers Association (GFOA), formerly the MFOA, publishes a widely used source of nonauthoritative guidance: the GAAFR—*Governmental Accounting, Auditing and Financial Reporting*. Moreover, the FASB has standards on issues not addressed by the GASB.

To advise governmental reporting entities of the authoritative ranking of accounting principles sources, *SGAS 55* establishes the following **GAAP hierarchy**.

Level 1 GASB *Statements* and *Interpretations*, including FASB and AICPA pronouncements adopted by the GASB.

Level 2 GASB *Technical Bulletins* and applicable AICPA *Industry Audit and Accounting Guides* and *Statements of Position* approved by the GASB.

Level 3 AICPA *Practice Bulletins* approved by the GASB and GASB Emerging Issues Task Force consensus positions.

Level 4 GASB *Implementation Guides* and practices commonly found in state and local government.

Level 5 Other accounting literature, such as GASB *Concepts Statements*, FASB pronouncements not specifically dealing with state and local governmental accounting, and accounting texts and articles.

Levels 1 and 5 above indicate that the FASB plays a role in governmental accounting. The FASB determines GAAP for private organizations and the GASB determines GAAP for public organizations. In the past the reporting standards for similar organizations, such as a public versus a private hospital or university, were not comparable. In 1989 the Committee to Review Structure for Governmental Accounting Standards made the GASB responsible for evaluating the need for comparability with private-sector not-for-profits subject to FASB standards. In 1999, the GASB issued *SGAS 34*, outlining the external reporting model for state and local governments, and *SGAS 35*, amending *SGAS 34* to include public colleges and universities. This reporting model is similar to that required by the FASB for private not-for-profit organizations, indicating increasing convergence in reporting the activities of public and private organizations.

OBJECTIVES OF FINANCIAL REPORTING

The GASB formalized the objectives of financial reporting by state and local governments in *SGAC 1*, Objectives of Financial Reporting. *SGAC 1* states that governmental financial reports should respond to the needs of the citizenry, their representatives (either elected or appointed members of oversight boards), and investors and creditors involved in the lending process. Paragraph 32 lists four specific **uses of financial reports** in making economic, social and political decisions, and in evaluating accountability:

> 1. Comparing actual financial results with the legally adopted budget.
> 2. Assessing financial condition and results of operations.
> 3. Determining compliance with finance-related laws, rules and regulations.
> 4. Evaluating efficiency and effectiveness. *(SGAC 1, para. 32)*

Note the stress on **accountability** in Items 1 and 3, in terms of fulfilling the budgetary plan and in complying with relevant laws, such as those specifying taxing and debt limits. Indeed, the GASB states that:

> Accountability is the cornerstone of all financial reporting in government . . . Accountability requires governments to answer to the citizenry—to justify the raising of public resources and the purposes for which they are to be used. *(SGAC 1, para. 56)*

Another key GASB concept is **interperiod equity**, a balanced budget notion stressing the need for users of governmental financial reports to "assess whether current-year revenues are sufficient to pay for the services provided that year and whether future taxpayers will be required to assume burdens for services previously provided." *(para. 60)*

Identifying the Reporting Entity

Financial information is to be presented for a **reporting entity**. For state or local governments, this entity could be a state, town, city, county, school district, water district, or fire protection district. Although a city or town may appear to be the reporting entity, additional legal entities often exist within a governmental unit or overlap it. For example, a school district may be a legally separate entity from the city or town in which it operates. A municipality may contain **special districts**—legally separate entities that provide a particular service such as sewers, sidewalks, street lighting, or fire protection to particular areas. Each entity likely has its own taxing authority, ability to issue debt, and other powers.

For state and local governments, the GASB concluded in *SGAS 14* that:

> The concept underlying the definition of the financial reporting entity is that elected officials are **accountable** to their constituents for their actions. *(para. 10)*

The financial statements should enable readers to assess the performance of elected officials, by including information on all activities for which these officials are accountable.

SGAS 14 defines the financial reporting entity as follows:

> The financial reporting entity consists of (a) the **primary government** and (b) its **component units**: organizations for which the primary government is **financially accountable**, and **other organizations** for which the nature and significance of their relationship with the primary government are such that exclusion would cause the reporting entity's financial statements to be misleading or incomplete. *(para. 12)*

The nucleus of a governmental financial reporting entity is the **primary government**, with a separate governing body elected by the citizenry. The primary government is a state government, municipality, township or county, or another entity such as a school district, if it satisfies all three conditions in paragraph 13 of *SGAS 14*.

1. It has a **separately elected** governing body.
2. It is **legally separate**.
3. It is **fiscally independent** of other state and local governments.

An organization is a **component unit** of a primary government when the primary government is financially accountable for it. According to *SGAS 14*, a primary government is financially accountable when it controls appointment of a voting majority of the organization's governing body and can **impose its will** on the organization's operations. Financial accountability also exists when the primary government can **derive financial benefits or financial obligations** from the organization.

Professional judgment is required to determine whether an organization is a component unit of a primary government. The decision is particularly difficult for financially independent *affiliated organizations* created to support the primary government's activities. *SGAS 39* provides additional guidance for these organizations. An **affiliated organization** is a component unit if it uses all or most of its resources to directly benefit the primary government or its component units, if the primary government has access to these resources, and the resources are significant to the primary government *(para. 5)*. A library foundation entirely benefitting and providing significant support to the library is a component unit of the library. A university alumni association that provides tuition and fee scholarships to students is a component unit of the university.

Presentation of Component Units   For financial reporting purposes, a component unit's information is either *blended* with that of the primary government, or *discretely presented* in the financial statements, depending on its relationship with the primary government. If the component unit's financial information is **blended** with the results of the primary government, it is not separately distinguishable. If a component unit's financial results are **discretely presented**, its results appear separately from the primary government, but are included in account totals.

Blended component units either have the same governing body as the primary government, or exist to provide services to the primary government *(SGAS 14, para. 53)*. Suppose a legally separate building authority issues tax-exempt bonds to finance a city's capital assets, and has a governing board appointed by the mayor, subject to city council approval. If the city funds the bond payments, the capital assets and the debt become the responsibility of the city, and the building authority is a blended component unit.

BUSINESS APPLICATION   Reporting Entity for Mecklenburg County

Mecklenburg County's CAFR reports the activities of its primary government, the County, and several component units. A county manager and elected Board of Commissioners govern the County. The County's three component units are all separate legal entities and discretely presented:

-   The Public Library of Charlotte and Mecklenburg County is funded by general obligation bonds, for which the County is responsible. The County appoints six of the seven Library Board members.
-   The Mecklenburg Emergency Medical Services Agency (Medic Agency) provides emergency medical services to County residents. Its Board consists of seven members; the County recommends one member, and health care agencies recommend the others. The County approves the Medic Agency's budget allocation.
-   The Mecklenburg County Alcoholic Beverage Control Board (ABC Board) operates retail liquor stores in the County and investigates beverage control law violations. The County appoints its five-member Board. The ABC Board supports itself with retail operations, uses its resources to support educational and rehabilitation programs related to alcohol use, and is obligated to distribute resources to the general fund.

Discretely presented component units are relatively autonomous. Consider a public housing authority that provides subsidized housing. Its board is approved by the city council, but the city does not control the board's decisions. The board adopts its own budget, makes hiring decisions, sets rents, selects tenants, and issues bonds for which it is financially obligated. However, the city is obligated to provide significant funding as well. Because the city appoints the board and is a major source of funding, the housing authority is a discretely presented component unit.

SGAS 61, effective in 2012, clarifies when an organization is a component unit and when it should be blended. Organizations are currently presented as component units when they are fiscally dependent on the primary government; new guidance requires that this relationship include a financial benefit or burden.

Component units are currently blended if they have the same governing body as the primary government; new guidance also requires either a financial relationship or that primary government management is operationally responsible for the component unit's activities.

FUND STRUCTURE

A key aspect of accounting and reporting for state and local governments is the use of different reporting entities to account for resources subject to different restrictions. This structure often requires multiple journal entries to record a single transaction.

LO2 Identify the fund types and reporting methods for state and local governments.

A typical governmental unit engages in most or all of the three types of activities discussed earlier in the chapter: *governmental*, *proprietary*, and *fiduciary*. Legislation and regulations often specify how resources are used. It may be stipulated that resources derived from local property taxes be spent in certain ways, resources derived from a bond issue in other ways, and resources received from federal programs in yet other ways. State and local government management is responsible for ensuring that resources are spent in the legally prescribed manner. This is the concept of **accountability** or **stewardship**—the community entrusts management with resources, and management must carry out certain specified responsibilities with respect to their use.

Typical activities of a state or local government are:

Governmental activities:

- Collection of taxes, fees and fines
- Issuance of bonds and repayment of bond principal and interest
- Provision of primary services for which no user fees are collected, such as education, public safety, social and judicial services, administration
- Acquisition, construction, and disposition of long-lived assets, financed either by general resources, special assessments or long-term debt
- Special projects benefitting the public, funded by grants or other restricted resources

Proprietary activities:

- Provision of goods and services for which a cost-based fee is collected from the public, such as utilities, public transportation, parking facilities, recreational facilities, hospitals and colleges
- Provision of goods and services to other governmental units at cost by a central motor pool, central supplies activity, or similar activity

Fiduciary activities:

- Financial resources held in trust for those outside the governmental unit, such as pensions
- Financial resources collected for and eventually disbursed to another governmental unit, such as state sales taxes collected by the county

Because of the need to adhere to legal requirements affecting the source and use of resources, and the large number and diversity of governmental activities, the financial reporting system of a single governmental entity is organized into several accounting entities, called *funds*.

> A **fund** is defined as a fiscal and accounting entity with a self-balancing set of accounts recording cash and other financial resources, together with all related liabilities and residual equities or balances, and changes therein, which are segregated for the purpose of carrying on specific activities or attaining certain objectives in accordance with special regulations, restrictions, or limitations. *(GASB, Codification, Section 1100.102)*

Instead of a single entity with one set of books, a typical government contains several entities, or funds, that have their own sets of books and issue financial statements. For external reporting purposes, however, the government presents financial statements on both a *fund basis*, and a *government-wide basis* that combines the activities of the various funds. Chapter 12 examines the external reporting requirements for state and local governments.

As **accounting segregations of financial resources**, funds become accountable for and exercise stewardship over resources. **Fund equity** measures the difference between a fund's assets and liabilities. Portions of fund equity are often designated for particular purposes. Total fund equity therefore consists of (1) an *unassigned portion*, indicating financial resources available for general spending, and (2) one or more *designated portions*, signifying amounts not available for expenditure or legally segregated for specific future uses.

An important focus of governmental financial reporting is demonstrating fiscal compliance. Operating statements report on whether financial resources received during a period cover expenditures, and whether spending complies with approved budgets. Division of resources into funds dedicated to spending for particular purposes is a control technique. Each fund keeps track of the flows of financial resources restricted to its specific activities. Financial reporting on fund activities reveals whether financial resources used complied with restrictions imposed by law or by third parties.

Fund Types

The financial affairs of a government are organized into fund groups used for the governmental activities mentioned above. Individual funds belong to one of the following groups:

- **Governmental funds** account for most traditional governmental functions, and report on resources available to finance activities benefitting the government or its citizens.
- **Proprietary funds** account for a government's ongoing businesslike activities similar to those found in the private sector, where fees are charged for goods provided or services performed.
- **Fiduciary funds** account for resources held by the governmental unit in a trustee or agency capacity on behalf of individuals or other organizations outside the governmental unit, and which cannot be used to support the government or its programs.

A typical city government uses many or all of these fund types to account for its resources and activities, as described below.

Governmental Funds

General fund—Accounts for the basic services provided by city government, financed by general revenue, that are not required to be accounted for in another fund.

    a. Resources come from property taxes, sales taxes, general state aid, fees, fines, and other general revenues.

    b. Resources are used for city administration, police, fire protection, courts, streets, parks, sanitation, and other general services.

Special revenue funds—Account for specified activities of the city that benefit the public using revenue legally restricted to those activities.

    a. Resources come from state or federal aid for specific purposes (for example, resources from federal programs used in public safety activities), taxes levied for certain purposes, grants, and public-purpose trusts. All resources are expendable.

    b. Resources are used for the particular operations specified by the revenue source.

Capital projects funds—Account for the construction or acquisition of major capital assets used for governmental activities, including those financed by special assessments on property owners.

  a. Resources come primarily from proceeds of bond issues. Other sources include state or federal aid, allocation of general fund revenues, or special tax assessments on property owners.

  b. Resources are used for construction or acquisition of buildings, major equipment, and public improvements—commonly known as **infrastructure**—such as roads, bridges, and sewer systems.

Debt service funds—Account for the accumulation and payment of resources for principal and interest on the general long-term debt of the city.

  a. Resources come from transfers from other funds, such as the general fund or the capital projects fund, from certain special assessment levies and from interest earned on investments.

  b. Resources are used for payment of interest and principal; in some cases, resources are accumulated and invested to provide for future debt service payments.

Permanent funds—Account for activities and resources that are legally restricted—perhaps by trust agreement—to the expenditure of earnings for a specific purpose, with the principal remaining intact. *The specific purpose must benefit the government or its citizens.* Examples include a library fund that provides resources for the acquisition of public library materials, and a park fund that consists of resources held in trust for the maintenance of city parks.

  a. Resources are derived from trusts or other legal agreements set up by individuals or private organizations. In contrast to special revenue funds, only the earnings may be used.

  b. Resources are used for the particular activities specified by the trust agreement.

Proprietary Funds

Enterprise funds—Account for business-type activities, such as a city water department or a municipal golf course, that sell goods or services on a continuing basis to the public.

  a. Resources come from amounts charged to customers on a cost recovery basis, and from financing sources.

  b. Resources are used for the activity's operating expenses, capital expenditures and financing payments.

Internal service funds—Account for central services provided to other departments of the city on a cost-reimbursement basis; for example, a central supply unit that buys supplies in large quantities for distribution to various departments, or a central vehicle maintenance shop.

  a. Resources come from charges to and support from other city departments.

  b. Resources are used for operating expenses, capital expenditures and financing payments.

Fiduciary Funds

Pension trust funds—Account for resources held in trust for individuals enrolled in pension plans or other employee benefit plans.

  a. Resources come from employer and plan participant contributions, and investment income.

  b. Resources are used for pension benefits and administrative costs.

Investment trust funds—Account for the net assets of investors outside the governmental reporting entity, typically other governments, held in governmental investment pools.

  a. Resources come from investments and investment income.

  b. Resources are used for administrative costs, investment losses, and payments to investors.

Private-purpose trust funds—Account for the activities of all other trust agreements that benefit individuals, private organizations, or other governments, such as a fund holding resources from abandoned bank accounts and undeliverable amounts owed to individuals.

    a. Resources come from assets put in trust and from income on investment of assets.

    b. Resources are used for activities specified by the trust agreement, and for administrative costs and distributions.

Agency funds—Account for resources collected for and remitted to individuals, private organizations, or other governments, where the collecting government acts in a custodial capacity only. For example, a county may collect taxes for the town.

    a. Resources come from collections on behalf of other entities, such as income taxes withheld from employees and certain special assessment levies.

    b. Resources are used for transmittal of amounts collected to other entities and for service of certain special assessment bond issues using collections from property owners.

A comparison of the fund types with the activities of a state or local government reveals that these funds encompass all the activities of those governments. Although **a government always has one and only one general fund**, none, one, or several of each of the other fund types may exist. If a city has no construction projects underway, there are no capital projects funds. If three projects are currently under construction, the city may use three capital projects funds or combine all three projects in one capital projects fund.

REVIEW 1 • Fund Types

Required For each of the following transactions of a county government, identify which fund(s) is affected.

a. Construction begins on a new double-span bridge across the river that bisects the county, and $200,000 is paid to contractors.

b. The county collects sales taxes to be remitted to the state.

c. The municipal swimming pool collects $40,000 in user fees.

d. A new snowplow is purchased for road maintenance. The snowplow is expected to last 15 years.

e. General tax revenues are collected from taxpayers. Some of these revenues are set aside for future payment of general obligation debt principal.

f. Principal and interest on general obligation debt is paid.

g. The municipal swimming pool purchases a new cover for its baby pool. The cover is expected to last 8 years.

h. A state grant, legally restricted to the development of a new preschool program, is received in cash.

i. An endowment is received in cash from a wealthy citizen. The principal of the endowment is not expendable, and income on the principal must be used to landscape one of the county parks.

Solutions are located after the chapter assignments.

ACCOUNTING AND REPORTING BY FUNDS

We now consider the general accounting principles applicable to the fund entities discussed above, and introduce the typical fund financial statements issued by the reporting government.

Accounting for Governmental Funds

Governmental funds—**general fund, special revenue funds, capital projects funds, debt service funds, and permanent funds**—use the *modified accrual basis* of accounting. The measurement focus is on accountability for the flow of financial resources. The GASB defines the flow of resources as **the flow of current financial resources**—cash, receivables, prepaid items, consumable goods such as supplies, and related current liabilities. Any transaction affecting current financial resources appears on the operating statement of a governmental fund. This statement is called the **Statement of Revenues, Expenditures, and Changes in Fund Balances**. Fund equity on the balance sheet of a governmental fund is called **fund balance**.

The **modified accrual basis of accounting** reflects the following reporting principles:

- **Revenues** are defined as *inflows of current financial resources*. Revenues are recognized when they are **measurable** and **available to finance expenditures of the current period**. Property taxes and intergovernmental grants are accrued as receivables and revenue before the cash is collected, if the uncollectible portion can be reasonably estimated, and amounts collected are expected to be available to liquidate current period obligations.

- Borrowings, and receipts of current financial resources from the sale of long-lived assets, are shown on the Statement of Revenues, Expenditures and Changes in Fund Balances, as **other financing sources**. Resources received from long-term borrowings are *not* shown as liabilities in the fund statements. Receipts from the sale of long-lived assets are reported in total without recognizing gain or loss.

- **Expenditures** are defined as *outflows of current financial resources*, and can be significantly different from full accrual expenses.

  ○ Payments of current financial resources for long-lived assets are treated as expenditures. Governmental funds do not capitalize long-lived assets or recognize depreciation.

  ○ Payments of current financial resources for long-term debt principal or interest are expenditures. Long-term debt does *not* appear as a liability and no liability is reduced when principal payments are made.

- Interest on long-term debt is accrued only in the period when it is expected to be paid.

- An excess of revenues over expenditures may reduce the taxes levied next year. Expenditures in excess of revenues burden taxpayers or reduce services in future years.

- **Interfund transactions** occur when governmental units engage in transactions between funds. These include, but are not limited to, **loans** and **transfers**. The general fund may loan money to the special revenue fund, with repayment expected within a few months. Or the general fund may transfer resources to an internal service fund to finance its expenditures. The balance sheet reports interfund loans as receivables and payables, typically labeled "due from" or "due to" a specific fund. Interfund transfers appear in the Statement of Revenues, Expenditures, and Changes in Fund Balances, as **other financing sources or uses**.

Fund statements for governmental funds are the **Statement of Revenues, Expenditures and Changes in Fund Balances**, the **Balance Sheet**, and the **Budgetary Comparison Schedule**, which compares budgeted and actual revenues, expenditures and other changes in fund balances for the general fund and any other fund that has a legally adopted budget.

Accounting for Proprietary Funds

For the proprietary funds—**enterprise and internal service funds**—the business concepts of revenue recognition and matching of expenses against revenues are appropriate, as these funds' operations are similar to those of private sector businesses. It is important to know the costs of services, because the fees charged to users—whether citizens or other departments within the government—are expected to cover those costs. Therefore *full accrual accounting* is used.

Revenues are recognized when earned and measurable, and expenses are matched with revenues as product costs or recognized with the passage of time as period costs. Outlays for buildings and equipment are capitalized as assets and depreciated over their useful lives. Amounts borrowed through loans or bond issues are shown as liabilities and interest expense is accrued as owed.

Proprietary fund statements are the **Statement of Net Position**, the **Statement of Revenues, Expenses and Changes in Net Position**, and the **Statement of Cash Flows**. Revenues and expenses are classified as operating or nonoperating items. Fund net position on the balance sheet consists of three components: **net investment in capital assets**, **restricted**, and **unrestricted**.

Accounting for Fiduciary Funds

Fiduciary funds—**pension trust funds, investment trust funds, private-purpose trust funds, and agency funds**—account for governmental activities where resources are held in a trust or agency capacity for individuals or organizations outside the reporting government.

The *full accrual basis of accounting* is used to account for the activities of fiduciary funds. For example, *SGAS 45* requires full accrual of postemployment benefits. Agency funds accumulate resources held for disbursement to other entities. Assets are the resources accumulated in an agency capacity, and liabilities are the amounts owed to individuals or organizations. Agency fund assets equal liabilities. Standard financial statements for fiduciary funds are the **Statement of Fiduciary Net Position** and the **Statement of Changes in Fiduciary Net Position**. Agency funds do not report a net position and do not prepare a Statement of Changes in Fiduciary Net Position.

ACCOUNTING FOR THE GENERAL FUND

LO3 Prepare entries and financial statements for the general fund.

The general fund accounts for the government's routine operating activities. This section explains accounting procedures for the major activities of the general fund that are reported using the *modified accrual basis* of accounting.

The 2010 general fund balance sheet and statement of revenues, expenditures, and changes in fund balances for Mecklenburg County, appearing in Exhibits 10.1 and 10.2, illustrate the format of general fund financial statements. Because the general fund uses the modified accrual basis of reporting, its balance sheet has no long-term assets or liabilities. Assets include cash and investments, accounts receivable—mostly accrued state and federal aid—and taxes receivable. Liabilities include current payables and deferred revenue, representing taxes collected in advance of the fiscal year in which they are available to spend.

Fund balance is the difference between assets and liabilities, and represents net resources available to spend. Mecklenburg County's general fund balance sheet illustrates that prior to 2011, fund balance was divided between reserved and unreserved, separating the portion of fund balance set

---

EXHIBIT 10.1   Mecklenburg County Balance Sheet—General Fund

MECKLENBURG COUNTY, NORTH CAROLINA
General Fund Balance Sheet
June 30, 2010

Assets

Cash and investments	$302,338,278
Interest receivable	1,592,630
Accounts receivable	86,333,194
Accounts receivable—clinics	818,137
Less allowance for uncollectible claims	(793,593)
Taxes receivable	50,082,090
Less allowance for uncollectible taxes	(15,600,000)
Advances to other governmental agencies	59,513
Due from other governments	54,669
Deferred charges	42,485
Inventory	4,960
Total assets	**$424,932,363**

Liabilities and fund balances

Liabilities

Accounts payable and accrued liabilities	$ 58,613,067
Deferred revenue	36,850,371
Total liabilities	**95,463,438**

Fund balances

Reserved for encumbrances	20,538,100
Reserved by state statute	87,950,368
Unreserved	220,980,457
Total fund balances	**329,468,925**
Total liabilities and fund balances	**$424,932,363**

EXHIBIT 10.2 Mecklenburg County Operating Statement—General Fund

MECKLENBURG COUNTY, NORTH CAROLINA
Statement of Revenues, Expenditures, and Changes in Fund Balances
General Fund
For Year Ended June 30, 2010

Revenues

Taxes	$ 996,823,542
Licenses and permits	12,440,081
Intergovernmental	193,977,052
Charges for services	60,637,111
Interest earned on investments	3,861,305
Administrative charges	2,744,287
Other	7,006,874
Total revenues	1,277,490,252

Expenditures

Current

Customer satisfaction and management	10,436,098
Administrative services	61,936,299
Financial services	9,284,883
Land use and environmental services	41,387,536
Community services	77,281,017
Detention and court support services	114,936,695
Health and human services	304,143,599
Business partners	381,590,920

Debt service

Principal payments	171,604,097
Interest and fiscal charges	86,043,667
Total expenditures	1,258,644,811
Excess (deficiency) of revenues over (under) expenditures	18,845,441

Other financing sources (uses)

Transfers in	1,814,507
Transfers out	(60,567,978)
Premium on bonds issued	58,708,355
Refunding bonds issued	589,310,000
Payment to escrow agent for refunding bonds	(638,141,957)
Total other financing sources (uses)	(48,877,073)
Net change in fund balances	(30,031,632)
Fund balances—beginning of year	359,548,852
Closeout fund	(48,295)
Fund balances—end of year	$ 329,468,925

aside for specific purposes. Starting in 2011, *SGAS 54* requires five standard categories of fund balance, as follows:

- **Nonspendable** fund balance indicates amounts, such as inventories, that are not spendable.
- **Restricted** fund balance reports amounts that can only be spent consistent with stipulations of external resource providers.
- **Committed** fund balance reports amounts that can only be spent for purposes stipulated by formal action of the government's highest level of decision-making authority.
- **Assigned** fund balance indicates amounts intended to be used in specific ways. For funds other than the general fund, assigned fund balance is that portion of the fund balance available to that fund, and is not nonspendable, restricted or committed.
- **Unassigned** fund balance equals the portion of the *general fund's* fund balance that is not nonspendable, restricted, committed or assigned.

The first four categories replace the "reserved" balances found in prior practice, while the fifth category is "unreserved" fund balance. We discuss these fund balance categories in more detail in Chapters 11 and 12, and use these standard categories throughout Chapters 10-12.

The County's operating statement displays revenues and expenditures, and other financing sources and uses. Most of Mecklenburg County's general fund revenues come from taxes. The largest expenditure line is Business Partners, which include the Charlotte-Mecklenburg Schools, Central Piedmont Community College, the public television station, and the Mecklenburg Emergency Medical Services Agency. The County also reports large expenditures for health and human resources, principal payments on debt, and detention and court support services. All items reported on the general fund operating statement represent inflows and outflows of current financial resources and are closed to fund balance at year-end.

Budgetary Accounts

Accounting serves an important control function in state and local government, helping to ensure that resources are spent in compliance with legal requirements. Legal restrictions on spending are usually expressed in the form of a **budget** that prescribes both the total amount of spending allowed and the amounts in each expense category. A budget may be adopted by legislative/executive action or by popular vote, as in many school districts. Typically, any change in the total budget must be approved in the same way, whereas changes within the budget—transfers among budget components—usually require less formal approval. For example, a school board may approve budget transfers without voter approval.

At the beginning of the year, the general fund's budgeted revenues and budgeted expenditures are entered in **budgetary accounts** to aid in controlling revenues and expenditures. As actual revenues come in and resources are spent during the year, management compares these amounts with the budget to help ensure that, in each category of the budget, actual spending does not exceed the authorized amount. Recording budget data in the accounts is a key aspect of accounting for funds with legal budgets, and a major difference between governmental accounting and business accounting. In business, the budget is a managerial plan; in government, it is a legal constraint. The budget establishes legal spending limits that must not be exceeded.

Budget Entry   A budget has two elements: budgeted revenues and budgeted expenditures. In state and local government, **Estimated Revenues** accounts for the former and **Appropriations** accounts for the latter. The budget entry debits Estimated Revenues because it represents the expected inflow of resources to the fund, roughly analogous to receivables. Similarly, the budget entry credits Appropriations because it represents the expected outflow of resources from the fund, roughly analogous to payables.

Some general fund inflows, such as proceeds from bond issues and sale of capital assets and transfers in from other funds, are reported not as revenues, but as **other financing sources**. Similarly, some general fund outflows, such as transfers to other funds, are reported not as expenditures, but as **other financing uses**. The budget entry reports the budgeted amounts for these expected inflows and outflows as **Estimated Other Financing Sources and Uses**.

To illustrate, suppose that for 2014 Mecklenburg County budgets expenditures of $1,500,000,000 and other financing uses of $50,000,000. It budgets revenues of $1,520,000,000 and other financing sources of $30,000,000. Since budgeted outflows equal budgeted inflows, the budget is **balanced**. The budget entry is:

Estimated revenues	1,520,000,000	
Estimated other financing sources.	30,000,000	
Appropriations.		1,500,000,000
Estimated other financing uses		50,000,000
To record the 2014 (balanced) budget.		

The budget need not be balanced in a particular fiscal period. When a government plans to spend less than its anticipated revenue, the budget entry credits the unassigned fund balance.

Suppose Mecklenburg County expects revenues of $1,530,000,000, and all other budgeted amounts are as indicated above. Now the general fund plans to spend less than it receives and the budget entry increases its unassigned fund balance by $10,000,000.

Estimated revenues	1,530,000,000	
Estimated other financing sources	30,000,000	
Appropriations		1,500,000,000
Estimated other financing uses		50,000,000
Fund balance—unassigned		10,000,000
To record the 2014 (surplus) budget.		

Alternatively, suppose Mecklenburg County plans to spend more than its anticipated revenue, using resources accumulated in previous periods. If expected revenues are only $1,505,000,000, and all other budgeted amounts are as originally stated, the budget entry decreases unassigned fund balance.

Estimated revenues	1,505,000,000	
Estimated other financing sources	30,000,000	
Fund balance—unassigned	15,000,000	
Appropriations		1,500,000,000
Estimated other financing uses		50,000,000
To record the 2014 (deficit) budget.		

After recording the budget, the unassigned fund balance account shows the **expected year-end balance**. In the last entry, showing total budgeted inflows of $1,535,000,000 and total budgeted outflows of $1,550,000,000, assume that the beginning fund balance was $105,000,000. After recording the budget, the fund balance is $90,000,000 (= $105,000,000 − $15,000,000). If the budgeted amounts are achieved, the actual year-end fund balance will also be $90,000,000.

Recording Property Tax Revenue

The modified accrual basis is used to account for property tax revenue. Because the government levies specific property tax amounts, the amount of revenue to be collected can be estimated with a reasonable degree of accuracy, and the probability of collection on a timely basis is very high. Thus the government records property taxes as revenue when the taxes are levied, as long as the tax revenue is to be used in the same period that it is levied. Under the modified accrual basis, revenue is recognized in the period when the taxes are *available to be used*. "Available" means either collected during the period or expected to be collected soon enough after the period ends that the revenues can be used to pay liabilities incurred during the period.

When taxes levied in 2013 are expected to be collected and used in 2013, they are reported as property tax revenue on the date levied. However, if taxes levied in 2013 are for use in 2014, the government reports the levied amount as **deferred revenue** until 2014, when the money becomes available to spend. Mecklenburg County's June 30, 2010, general fund balance sheet in Exhibit 10.1 reports deferred revenue of $36,850,371, representing taxes collected in 2010 for use in 2011.

The amount recorded as revenue is the gross amount of the tax levy, less an appropriate allowance for uncollectibles. Even though the gross amount of the levy is recorded as Taxes Receivable, the amount credited to revenues is the **net** amount the government expects to collect. This amount reflects the financial resources expected to be available for expenditure during the current period. Note the difference from business accounting that records gross revenue and accounts for bad debt expense separately. Because modified accrual accounting treats expenditures as outflows of current financial resources, bad debt "expense" is not an expenditure.

After a period of time, often by the end of the fiscal period, any uncollected taxes become delinquent. These taxes receivable should be reclassified to a Taxes Receivable—Delinquent account with a corresponding Allowance for Uncollectible Taxes—Delinquent. An adjusting entry sets the allowance equal to the amount expected to be uncollectible.

Suppose that Mecklenburg County levies a property tax of $950,000,000 that is expected to be 95 percent collectible. We first record the property tax levy:

Taxes receivable—current	950,000,000	
Allowance for uncollectible taxes—current		47,500,000
Tax revenues		902,500,000
To record tax levy.		

Subsequent collection of $900,000,000 and declaration of uncollected amounts as delinquent are recorded as follows:

Cash	900,000,000	
Taxes receivable—current		900,000,000
To record collection of property taxes.		
Taxes receivable—delinquent	50,000,000	
Taxes receivable—current		50,000,000
To reclassify unpaid taxes as delinquent.		

The modified accrual basis provides that assessed but uncollected tax revenues be reported in the current year when they are measurable and expected to be collected early enough in the next year to be used to pay the current year's liabilities. The time limit for recognition of uncollected taxes as revenue is expected collection 60 days after the end of the year. Suppose Mecklenburg County estimates at year-end that $15,000,000 of the $50,000,000 in uncollected taxes will be collected within 60 days. Tax revenues are therefore $915,000,000 (= $900,000,000 collected in cash and $15,000,000 expected to be collected within 60 days), and the allowance balance is $35,000,000. The following entry reclassifies the original allowance and adjusts the accounts accordingly:

Allowance for uncollectible taxes—current	47,500,000	
Tax revenues		12,500,000
Allowance for uncollectible taxes—delinquent		35,000,000
To recognize additional tax revenues, reclassify allowance for uncollectible taxes and reduce it to $35,000,000.		

In the next year, suppose Mecklenburg County collects $20,000,000 of the delinquent taxes and writes off the remainder. These entries record this activity:

Cash	20,000,000	
Taxes receivable—delinquent		20,000,000
To record collection of delinquent taxes.		
Allowance for uncollectible taxes—delinquent	35,000,000	
Taxes receivable—delinquent		30,000,000
Tax revenues		5,000,000
To write off uncollected delinquent taxes.		

The County records tax revenues of $5,000,000 related to last year's property taxes, because $5,000,000 more was collected than was estimated at the end of last year.

Following the modified accrual basis, if year-end uncollected taxes will be collected more than 60 days after the end of the fiscal year, they are not considered revenue of the current period, but are reported as deferred revenues, a liability. Continuing the example above, suppose at year-end Mecklenburg County determines that of the $15,000,000 in collectible assessed taxes, $14,000,000 will be collected within 60 days and $1,000,000 will be collected more than 60 days later. It makes the following adjusting entry at year-end:

Allowance for uncollectible taxes—current	47,500,000	
Tax revenues		11,500,000
Deferred property tax revenues		1,000,000
Allowance for uncollectible taxes—delinquent		35,000,000
To recognize additional tax revenues and unavailable revenues, reclassify the allowance for uncollectible taxes and reduce it to $35,000,000.		

In this case, tax revenues for the year are $914,000,000 (= $900,000,000 collected in cash + $14,000,000 expected to be collected early next year and available to pay this year's obligations). When the $1,000,000 is collected the following year, an adjusting entry reclassifies deferred revenues as revenues of the period in which they are collected.

After additional time passes, delinquent taxes become **tax liens**—legal claims against the taxed property—which may be satisfied by forcing sale of the property. The delinquent taxes are reclassified to a tax liens receivable account, with a corresponding allowance for uncollectibles. It is common practice to "fully reserve" tax liens by setting up an allowance equal to the amount of the receivable.

BUSINESS APPLICATION   Mecklenburg County's Property Tax

Most counties receive significant funding from property taxes, based on the assessed valuation of property. Commonly, the property upon which taxes are based consists of real estate, such as vacant land, homes and business establishments. Mecklenburg County, however, also assesses property taxes on registered motor vehicles, boats, trailers, and income-producing personal property. In 2010, the total fair value of assessed property was $99,763 million and the total amount needed to be collected (the tax levy) was $837 million, resulting in a tax rate of $0.839 per $100 of assessed valuation [= ($837 million/$99,763 million) × $100]. For purposes of property tax assessment, the market value of real property in Mecklenburg County is updated (reassessed) every four years. In the reassessment year, the tax rate drops when the market value of assessed property increases. The tax rate then increases during the years between reassessments, as the budget increases faster than the dollar value of assessed property. In Mecklenburg County, a reassessment occurred in 2007, and the tax rate dropped from $0.837 to $0.819 per $100 of assessed valuation.

Purchase of Goods and Services

Acquisition of goods and services by a government typically involves three steps: (1) issuance of a purchase order or contract, (2) receipt of the goods or services, and (3) payment. In business accounting, only steps (2) and (3) are formally recorded in the accounting records. Unlike a business, a governmental unit has legal limits on its spending authority. Because of these legal restrictions, it is important to know not only the amount actually spent to date and the amount of unpaid bills, but also the amount of outstanding spending commitments. If no formal record is kept of purchase orders, the danger exists that the government will overcommit itself and exceed the legal spending authority. To aid in the control of expenditures, spending commitments, known as **encumbrances**, are recorded in the accounts.

Recording Purchase Orders   Accounting for issuance of a purchase order requires the following:

- A debit to *Encumbrances* representing the charge against the fund's limited spending authority; encumbrances become expenditures when the goods or services ordered are delivered.

- A credit to *Fund Balance—Assigned* signifying restriction of a portion of the fund balance for the items ordered: these financial resources are set aside for a specific future use. The fund balance category used for encumbrances can be restricted, committed or assigned, depending on who authorized the expenditure. In this chapter we assume outstanding encumbrances are appropriately reported in *Fund Balance—Assigned*.

Recording encumbrances does not create liabilities because the goods and services have not been delivered. Encumbrance entries are temporary, and are reversed when the goods or services are delivered.

Assume Mecklenburg County places an order for repair services on March 18, at an expected cost of $1,850,000. To formally record this commitment, an encumbrance entry is made on March 18, signifying that $1,850,000 of the repair services budget is no longer available for other purposes.

Encumbrances	1,850,000	
Fund balance—assigned		1,850,000
To record purchase order for repair services.		

Suppose that the repair services budget is $4,200,000 and that $800,000 was previously spent. Recording the $1,850,000 encumbrance tells county management that only $1,550,000 of the repair services budget remains available for use during the current period. This balance is often referred to as **available funds**.

Appropriations for repair services	$4,200,000
Expended to date.	(800,000)
Unexpended balance.	3,400,000
March 18 purchase order.	(1,850,000)
Available funds.	$1,550,000

Recording Receipt of Goods and Services   When the government receives goods or services and acknowledges liability for payment, it records *expenditures,* following the modified accrual approach. If an encumbrance was previously recorded, we reverse the amount originally encumbered, indicating that the purchase order is no longer outstanding, and then record the expenditure.

Recall that *expenditures* in modified accrual accounting signify *outflows of current financial resources*, unlike the recognition of *expenses* in business accounting, which measure consumption of resources in the process of earning revenue. To illustrate the difference, modified accrual accounting records an expenditure when financial resources are used to acquire office equipment; periodic depreciation expense is not recorded. Business accounting requires capitalization of resources used to acquire the office equipment, and recognizes consumption of that equipment over time through periodic depreciation expense.

Continuing the example above, assume that by April 3 the repair services ordered on March 18 are received, accompanied by an invoice for $1,865,000. The two journal entries (1) reverse the previously recorded encumbrance, and (2) record the expenditure.

Fund balance—assigned	1,850,000	
Encumbrances.		1,850,000
To reverse encumbrance entry.		
Expenditures	1,865,000	
Accounts payable		1,865,000
To record cost of repair services.		

The amount of the encumbrance and the amount of the expenditure need not be equal because the purchase order reflected an estimated cost of the goods or services. The reversing entry removes the *amount previously encumbered*, $1,850,000, and the expenditure entry records the *actual* cost of $1,865,000.

Supplies Inventories

The two acceptable methods of accounting for supplies inventories in the general fund and other governmental funds are the *consumption method*, which treats inventories as expenditures when *used*, and the *purchases method*, which treats them as expenditures when *purchased*.

The **consumption method** treats inventories as a financial resource, available to provide public service when "spent" or consumed, similar to cash. This method debits inventory when supplies are purchased, and debits expenditures when supplies are used, as in business accounting. Suppose that Mecklenburg County acquires supplies costing $21,000,000 during the year. The encumbrances recorded when the supplies were ordered are reversed upon delivery. Receipt of the supplies is recorded as follows:

Supplies inventory	21,000,000	
Accounts payable		21,000,000
To record purchase of supplies under the consumption method.		

If supplies costing $17,700,000 were consumed during the year, this entry summarizes the year's expenditures for the supplies consumed:

Expenditures	17,700,000	
Supplies inventory.		17,700,000
To record supplies used under the consumption method.		

Recall that expenditures are closed at year-end, reducing unassigned fund balance. Because expenditures only include $17,700,000 in supplies used, an additional year-end adjusting entry signifies that $3,300,000 of fund balance is in the form of nonspendable inventories:

Fund balance—unassigned	3,300,000	
Fund balance—nonspendable		3,300,000
To adjust nonspendable fund balance for change in supplies inventory balance.		

In subsequent years, an adjusting entry records *changes* in the amount of supplies on hand at year-end. Suppose that in the following year, supplies are acquired for $24,000,000 and supplies costing $24,500,000 are consumed, reducing the supplies inventory to $2,800,000. Mecklenburg Country records expenditures of $24,500,000 during the year, and at year-end the following adjusting entry reduces the nonspendable fund balance to $2,800,000.

Fund balance— nonspendable	500,000	
Fund balance— unassigned		500,000
To adjust nonspendable fund balance for change in supplies inventory balance.		

Under the **purchases method**, the cost of materials, supplies and other prepayments is charged to expenditures as the items are purchased. The method reflects the use of financial resources when these items are purchased, regardless of whether the materials or supplies are currently consumed. The purchases method itself recognizes no inventories of materials and supplies in the accounts. But when significant physical levels of inventory remain at year-end, this inventory must be reported on the balance sheet, increasing total fund balance by adding a nonspendable account.

To illustrate the *purchases method*, the supplies acquired at a cost of $21,000,000 in the previous example are recorded as expenditures when delivered:

Expenditures	21,000,000	
Accounts payable		21,000,000
To record purchase of supplies under the purchases method.		

The following year-end entry reports the supplies of $3,300,000 remaining in inventory:

Supplies inventory	3,300,000	
Fund balance—nonspendable		3,300,000
To record inventory of supplies at year-end under the purchases method.		

In subsequent years, changes in the amount of supplies on hand are recognized by making or reversing the above entry to record the changes. Using the same information as above for subsequent year supplies acquisition and consumption, Mecklenburg County records expenditures of $24,000,000 during the year for the supplies purchased, and at year-end the following adjusting entry reduces the inventory balance and the nonspendable fund balance to $2,800,000.

Fund balance—nonspendable	500,000	
Supplies inventory		500,000
To adjust inventory to current year-end balance of $2,800,000 under the		
purchases method.		

The **consumption method** follows regular business accounting—inventory is an asset when purchased and an expenditure when consumed. Since modified accrual accounting defines expenditures as *outflows of current financial resources*—cash, receivables and payables—under the consumption method inventories must be defined as current financial resources. Accordingly, purchase of inventories does not involve outflows of net current financial resources—instead, we exchange one current financial resource for another. Under the **purchases method**, current financial resources do **not** include inventories. Purchases of inventory are therefore a use of current financial resources and are recorded as expenditures.

Either the consumption or purchases method can currently be used in a governmental unit's external financial statements. However, the purchases method is typically used in general fund reporting because it is more consistent with modified accrual accounting.

Interfund Transactions

Transactions among funds—**interfund transactions**—are common in state and local government. These transactions are of two general types: loans and advances, and transfers.

Loans and Advances **Loans and advances** are temporary transfers from one fund to another, with authorization by statute or ordinance often required and repayment expected. These transfers are recorded as receivables or payables by the funds involved, with special account titles: *Due from Fund* and *Due to Fund*. Suppose a federal grant is awarded to a city to support a project to be accounted for in a special revenue fund. To cover project costs incurred prior to the actual receipt of the grant, the city might advance $800,000 from the general fund to the special revenue fund. This transaction is recorded in the *general fund* as follows:

Books of General Fund

Due from special revenue fund	800,000	
Cash		800,000
To record advance to special revenue fund.		

A parallel entry is required on the books of the *special revenue fund*:

Books of Special Revenue Fund

Cash	800,000	
Due to general fund		800,000
To record advance from general fund.		

Repayment of the advance triggers opposite entries by the general and special revenue funds.

Transfers **Transfers** involve legally authorized payments of resources from the fund receiving the revenues (frequently the general fund) to the fund that will make the expenditures. Transfers may be recurring or capital contributions of a permanent equity nature. Transfers are reported in the statement of revenues, expenditures, and changes in fund balances as **other financing sources (uses)**. A proprietary fund reports an incoming permanent equity transfer in its statement of revenues, expenses and changes in net position as a capital contribution, shown as a separate item below nonoperating revenues and expenses. Examples of transfers include:

- Principal and interest payments on long-term debt originally issued by the general or capital projects funds are commonly made using general fund resources. Money is transferred from the general fund (*transfer out*) to the debt service fund (*transfer in*) that makes the debt-related expenditures.
- When a business activity such as the water department is partially subsidized by general fund resources, the general fund records a *transfer out*. The water department enterprise fund records receipt of the resources as a *transfer in*.
- A construction project is financed in part by a bond issue and in part by general fund resources transferred (*transfer out*) to the capital projects fund (*transfer in*).
- A city establishes an internal service fund and transfers general fund resources (*transfer out*) to provide the initial capital of the internal service fund (*capital contribution*).
- A construction project funded by a bond issue is completed and the related capital projects fund is closed. Cash remaining in the terminated capital projects fund is transferred (*transfer out*) to the debt service fund (*transfer in*).

Capital Assets and Long-Term Debt

Like all governmental funds, the general fund uses the modified accrual basis of accounting to report its transactions. A major difference between the modified accrual basis and business accounting is in the treatment of capital assets and long-term debt. Because the modified accrual basis emphasizes the *flow of current financial resources*, the balance sheet of the general fund reports unexpended financial assets and financial liabilities to be paid during the reporting period, but does *not* report capital assets or long-term debt. Capital assets cannot be expended, and long-term debt due beyond the current year does not require the use of current financial resources.

Accounting for Capital Assets   When acquiring a capital asset with general fund resources, the general fund reports the cost of the asset as an *expenditure*. Purchased and self-constructed assets are recorded at acquisition cost. If Mecklenburg County's general fund purchases highway equipment costing $4,000,000, this entry is made:

Capital outlay	4,000,000	
Accounts payable or cash		4,000,000
To record the purchase of highway equipment.		

Capital outlay is reported as one of the *expenditures* in the Statement of Revenues, Expenditures, and Changes in Fund Balances.

Because the equipment is not recorded as an asset, the general fund does not report periodic depreciation on the equipment. When the equipment is sold by the general fund, the gross proceeds increase fund balance. If the equipment is sold at some future date for $1,500,000 in cash, this entry is made:

Cash	1,500,000	
Proceeds from sale of capital assets		1,500,000
To record proceeds from sale of highway equipment.		

The fact that the capital assets have no book value in the general fund precludes recognizing a gain or loss on the sale. Instead, the gross proceeds are reported on the general fund's Statement of Revenues, Expenditures, and Changes in Fund Balances as part of *other financing sources*.

Accounting for Long-Term Debt   The general fund may incur long-term debt in the form of bonds of various types or long-term notes payable. As long as the government is liable for the general fund debt, inflows of current financial resources from debt issuances are recorded as *other financing sources* by the general fund. Outflows to pay principal and interest on the debt are recorded as expenditures. The following example uses long-term bonds to illustrate the accounting; similar procedures apply to other types of long-term debt.

Suppose Mecklenburg County's general fund issues $30,000,000 of long-term bonds to finance a service project. This event is recorded as follows:

Cash	30,000,000	
Bond proceeds		30,000,000
To record proceeds of bond issue.		

The general fund reports bond proceeds on its Statement of Revenues, Expenditures, and Changes in Fund Balances as *other financing sources*.

Rather than transferring resources to a debt service fund, suppose the general fund pays principal and interest on the bonds directly. The general fund payments are $1,000,000 for principal and $400,000 for interest. The payments are recorded as follows:

Debt service: principal	1,000,000	
Debt service: interest	400,000	
Cash		1,400,000
To record payment of principal and interest on bonds.		

Outlays for both principal and interest appear as separate *expenditures* on the general fund's Statement of Revenues, Expenditures, and Changes in Fund Balances.

BUSINESS APPLICATION   **Bond Refunding**

In periods of falling interest rates, municipalities often find it cost effective to buy back outstanding debt before its maturity date and issue new debt at lower rates. This process is called **advance refunding**. Refer to Mecklenburg County's General Fund Statement of Revenues, Expenditures and Changes in Fund Balances in Exhibit 10.2. The other financing sources (uses) section reveals that in fiscal 2010, Mecklenburg County issued new bonds, collecting $648,018,355 (= refunding bonds issued $589,310,000 + premium on bonds issued $58,708,355) of advance funding. The County then placed $638,141,957 of the amount collected in escrow for payment of outstanding debt.

In this case, Mecklenburg County used the proceeds from sale of new bonds to finance the advance refunding of the old bonds. Both activities are reported in the *other financing sources (uses) section* of the general fund operating statement. If the resources for advanced refunding of debt come from the general fund's resources and not from issuing new debt, the payment is reported as an *expenditure for debt service*, rather than other financing uses.

Closing Entries

Entries are prepared at the end of the reporting period to close all temporary accounts, *including the budgetary accounts*, to the fund balance. A single combined closing entry is possible, but use of two closing entries—one for revenues and other financing sources, and the other for expenditures and other financing uses—aids in understanding the process. These closing entries affect only the *unassigned* fund balance.

To illustrate the closing process, assume Mecklenburg County's budgeted revenues for 2014 are $1,505,000,000, estimated other financing sources are $30,000,000, budgeted expenditures are $1,500,000,000, and estimated other financing uses are $50,000,000. Actual revenues for the year are $1,507,000,000, actual expenditures amount to $1,488,300,000, outstanding encumbrances are $2,700,000 and actual other financing sources and uses are as budgeted. The following closing entries are made:

Revenues	1,507,000,000	
Other financing sources	30,000,000	
Estimated revenues		1,505,000,000
Estimated other financing sources		30,000,000
Fund balance—unassigned		2,000,000
To close revenues and estimated revenues to fund balance.		
Appropriations	1,500,000,000	
Estimated other financing uses	50,000,000	
Expenditures		1,488,300,000
Encumbrances.		2,700,000
Other financing uses		50,000,000
Fund balance—unassigned.		9,000,000
To close expenditures, encumbrances and appropriations to fund balance.		

These entries increase the unassigned fund balance by $11,000,000, because actual revenues exceeded the budget by $2,000,000, and actual expenditures and outstanding encumbrances were $9,000,000 less than planned. Recall the beginning-of-year budget entry:

Estimated revenues	1,505,000,000	
Estimated other financing sources.	30,000,000	
Fund balance—unassigned	15,000,000	
Appropriations.		1,500,000,000
Estimated other financing uses		50,000,000
To record the 2014 (deficit) budget.		

Whereas the fund balance was originally expected to decrease by $15,000,000, it actually decreased by only $4,000,000, as shown in this condensed budgetary comparison schedule:

	Budget	Actual	Variance—Favorable (Unfavorable)
Revenues and other financing sources	$1,535,000,000	$1,537,000,000	$ 2,000,000
Expenditures, encumbrances and other financing uses . . .	(1,550,000,000)	(1,541,000,000)	9,000,000
Change in fund balance—unassigned	$ (15,000,000)	$ (4,000,000)	$11,000,000

The $15,000,000 debit to the fund balance in the budget entry and the $11,000,000 total credits to the fund balance in the closing entries account for the actual $4,000,000 decrease during the year.

Outstanding Encumbrances at Year-End

Outstanding encumbrances at year-end are closed, even though the goods were not received as of year-end. Most jurisdictions honor outstanding purchase orders in the next period. Therefore, the amount reported as fund balance—assigned for outstanding encumbrances is *not closed* and remains as part of total assigned fund balance.

Mecklenburg County's general fund issued purchase orders amounting to $2,700,000 late in 2014 that are still outstanding at year-end. When the orders were issued, the encumbrance entry was:

Encumbrances	2,700,000	
Fund balance—assigned		2,700,000
To record purchase orders.		

As shown in the closing entries above, outstanding encumbrances are closed to unassigned fund balance along with expenditures and other financing uses, while the related Fund Balance—Assigned remains. The net effect reports $2,700,000 of the total fund balance as set aside for future payment of outstanding purchase orders. The accounting in the following year depends on how the government treats outstanding encumbrances in its budgetary accounts.

GAAP Budgetary Basis When the government uses the *GAAP budgetary basis*, outstanding encumbrances are *not* equivalent to expenditures of that year. A GAAP budgetary comparison schedule shows actual expenditures only, and appropriations are reduced by outstanding encumbrances. Next year, expenditures include the actual expenditure associated with last year's encumbrance, and appropriations include the outstanding encumbrance from last year, moving the appropriation and the expenditure to the year when the goods are received and the resources spent. The $2,700,000 encumbrances for purchase orders outstanding at the end of 2014 do not appear in the 2014 budgetary comparison schedule. At the beginning of 2015, the previously closed encumbrances are restored to the accounts, and the unassigned fund balance is increased, effectively reversing part of the 2014 closing entry:

Encumbrances	2,700,000	
Fund balance—unassigned		2,700,000
To restore encumbrances carried over from 2014.		

The expenditure signifying receipt in 2015 of the goods and services ordered in 2014 is recorded in the same manner as all other 2015 expenditures. Assume the actual expenditure related to the carryover encumbrance is $2,660,000. The $2,700,000 encumbrances are reversed, and the expenditure is recorded at the actual amount owed.

Fund balance—assigned	2,700,000	
Encumbrances		2,700,000
To reverse encumbrance entry.		

Expenditures	2,660,000	
Accounts payable		2,660,000
To record delivery of orders.		

In the GAAP budgetary comparison schedule, total 2015 expenditures include the actual $2,660,000 expenditure related to the carryover encumbrance, and total 2015 appropriations include the $2,700,000 carryover encumbrance.

Legal Budgetary Basis   When the government uses the *legal budgetary basis*, outstanding encumbrances are equivalent to expenditures, since the obligation arises at the time of the purchase order. A budgetary comparison schedule at year-end compares actual expenditures *and* encumbrances to appropriations, including the portion for the outstanding encumbrance. The expenditure from the carryover encumbrance does not appear on the following year's budgetary comparison schedule.

The legal budgetary basis includes the $2,700,000 in encumbrances outstanding at the end of 2014 with expenditures in the 2014 budgetary comparison schedule. In the next year, the $2,660,000 expenditure related to the prior year outstanding encumbrance is recorded separately and closed against the portion of the prior year's fund balance assigned for encumbrances, not against the 2015 budget. When the goods and services ordered in 2014 are received in 2015 at a cost of $2,660,000, a separate expenditures account records completion of the transaction initiated in 2014:

Expenditures—prior year encumbrances.	2,660,000	
Accounts payable		2,660,000
To record invoices for goods and services ordered in 2014.		

At the end of 2015 an additional closing entry is required to close the prior year encumbrances:

Fund balance—assigned	2,700,000	
Expenditures—prior year encumbrances		2,660,000
Fund balance—unassigned.		40,000
To close encumbrances carried over from 2014 and related expenditures.		

The $40,000 credit to the unassigned fund balance effectively corrects the 2014 closing entry. Even though that entry charged $2,700,000 of 2014 encumbrances against the unassigned fund balance, the actual expenditure for these goods and services was $2,660,000.

Accounting for carryover encumbrances under these two alternative budgetary bases may be summarized as follows, using an encumbrance outstanding at the end of 2014. *Under both budgetary bases, outstanding encumbrances (the "encumbrances" account) are closed against the unassigned fund balance at year-end.*

1. The *GAAP budgetary basis* carries the encumbered amount into 2015:
    a. It is temporarily closed to the unassigned fund balance at the end of 2014, and reversed in 2015.
    b. It is not included in comparing budget to actual for 2014.
    c. The actual expenditure that occurs in 2015 is recorded as a regular 2015 expenditure.
    d. In comparing budget to actual for 2015, the 2015 budget includes the carryover encumbered appropriation from 2014.

2. The *legal budgetary basis* treats the encumbered amount in the budgetary comparison schedule as if it were an expenditure in 2014:
    a. It is closed to the unassigned fund balance in 2014.
    b. It is included in comparing budget to actual for 2014.
    c. The actual expenditure that occurs in 2015 is recorded separately from 2015 expenditures as "prior year," and is closed against the carried-over assigned fund balance; any difference is closed to the unassigned fund balance.
    d. It does not affect the 2015 comparison of budget to actual.

The general fund should report on the budgetary basis prescribed by the applicable laws and regulations in its jurisdiction to demonstrate legal compliance with those laws and regulations. However, GAAP-based financial statements **cannot** include encumbrances as expenditures. Therefore, if the legal budgetary basis is used, a **reconciliation to the GAAP basis** must be shown on the budgetary comparison schedule. See Chapter 12 for further explanation of this schedule.

COMPREHENSIVE ILLUSTRATION OF GENERAL FUND ACCOUNTING AND REPORTING

The following illustrates a county government's accounting for general fund activities, and presentation of year-end financial statements. Ranford County follows the *GAAP budgetary basis*, uses the *purchases method* for supplies inventory and does *not* recognize supplies inventory. Assume that the fiscal year for the Ranford County general fund is the calendar year. On January 1, 2013, the accounts of the general fund had the following balances:

RANFORD COUNTY Trial Balance—General Fund January 1, 2013		
Accounts	**Debit**	**Credit**
Cash.	$ 80,000,000	
Taxes receivable—delinquent	15,000,000	
Allowance for uncollectible taxes—delinquent		$ 12,000,000
Due from special revenue fund	10,000,000	
Accounts payable.		8,000,000
Fund balance—unassigned		83,000,000
Fund balance—assigned		2,000,000
Totals	$105,000,000	$105,000,000

Assigned fund balance consists entirely of outstanding encumbrances. The 2013 general fund budget included revenues from the following sources:

Property taxes ($200,000,000 levied; 5% deemed uncollectible)	$190,000,000
State aid	30,000,000
Fees and licenses.	8,000,000
Charges for services.	12,000,000
Total estimated revenues	$240,000,000

Appropriations for 2013 included estimated expenditures for:

General services.	$180,000,000
Maintenance.	14,000,000
Supplies	18,000,000
Capital outlay	6,000,000
Total appropriations	$218,000,000

The general fund planned to transfer $28,000,000 to the debt service fund for payment of principal and interest on general obligation debt, and sell property for $7,000,000 during 2013.

Transactions During the Year

Ranford County records the events and transactions occurring during 2013 as follows:

1. The budget was recorded on January 2.

Estimated revenues	240,000,000	
Estimated other financing sources	7,000,000	
Appropriations		218,000,000
Estimated other financing uses		28,000,000
Fund balance—unassigned		1,000,000
To record 2013 budget.		

2. Taxes were levied.

Taxes receivable—current	200,000,000	
Allowance for uncollectible taxes—current		10,000,000
Tax revenues		190,000,000
To record property tax levy, estimated to be 95 percent collectible.		

3. The county received $30,000,000 in state aid.

Cash	30,000,000	
State aid revenues		30,000,000
To record aid received from state government.		

4. Delinquent taxes of $4,000,000 were received; the remainder of 2012 taxes were reclassified as tax liens and fully reserved.

Cash	4,000,000	
Taxes receivable—delinquent		4,000,000
To record collection of delinquent taxes.		
Tax liens receivable	11,000,000	
Taxes receivable—delinquent		11,000,000
To reclassify uncollected delinquent taxes as tax liens.		
Allowance for uncollectible taxes—delinquent	12,000,000	
Allowance for uncollectible tax liens		11,000,000
Tax revenues		1,000,000
To reclassify allowance for uncollectible taxes and fully reserve tax liens.		

5. The $28,000,000 authorized was transferred to the debt service fund.

Transfers out	28,000,000	
Cash		28,000,000
To record transfers to the debt service fund.		

6. Old equipment was sold for $7,300,000, and new equipment was purchased for $5,900,000.

Cash	7,300,000	
Proceeds from sale of capital assets		7,300,000
To record sale of old equipment.		
Capital outlay	5,900,000	
Cash		5,900,000
To record purchase of new equipment.		

7. Ranford County follows the GAAP budgetary basis for year-end encumbrances. Encumbrances outstanding at the end of 2012 were for general services, $2,000,000. The bill received in 2013 was $1,800,000, paid in cash.

Encumbrances..	2,000,000	
Fund balance—unassigned.......................................		2,000,000
To restore encumbrances carried over from 2012.		
Fund balance—assigned...	2,000,000	
Encumbrances...		2,000,000
To reverse encumbrances.		
General service expenditures....................................	1,800,000	
Cash..		1,800,000
To record expenditures.		

8. Revenues of $21,300,000 were received as follows: $9,500,000 from fees and licenses, and $11,800,000 from charges for services.

Cash..	21,300,000	
Fee and license revenues......................................		9,500,000
Service revenues..		11,800,000
To record revenues.		

9. Supplies of $18,000,000 were ordered.

Encumbrances..	18,000,000	
Fund balance—assigned.......................................		18,000,000
To record supplies ordered.		

10. Cash expenditures were $40,300,000 for general services. Orders were issued for maintenance services, $14,000,000; for general services, $135,000,000.

General services expenditures....................................	40,300,000	
Cash..		40,300,000
To record cash expenditures.		
Encumbrances..	149,000,000	
Fund balance—assigned.......................................		149,000,000
To record encumbrances for goods and services ordered.		

11. Supplies ordered in transaction *9* were received and $18,000,000 in cash was paid to suppliers. Ranford County follows the *purchases method* of accounting for inventory expenditures.

Fund balance—assigned...	18,000,000	
Encumbrances...		18,000,000
To reverse encumbrances.		
Supplies expenditures...	18,000,000	
Cash..		18,000,000
To record payment for supplies.		

12. Current taxes of $183,000,000 were collected.

Cash..	183,000,000	
Taxes receivable—current.....................................		183,000,000
To record collection of current taxes.		

13. Invoices for goods and services ordered in transaction *10* and received were maintenance, $14,000,000, and general services, $136,000,000. Ranford paid a total of $152,000,000 on its 2013 accounts payable.

Fund balance—assigned...	149,000,000	
Encumbrances...		149,000,000
To reverse encumbrances.		

continued

continued from prior page

Maintenance expenditures.	14,000,000	
General services expenditures.	136,000,000	
Accounts payable		150,000,000
To record expenditures.		
Accounts payable.	152,000,000	
Cash		152,000,000
To record payment of accounts payable.		

14. Goods to be used in providing general services were ordered late in December for $1,300,000 but were not received in 2013.

Encumbrances	1,300,000	
Fund balance—assigned.		1,300,000
To record encumbrances for goods ordered.		

15. Cash of $10,000,000 was received from the special revenue fund as repayment of a loan made in 2012.

Cash	10,000,000	
Due from special revenue fund		10,000,000
To record repayment of loan.		

16. Taxes uncollected at year-end were classified as delinquent. $2,000,000 of uncollected amounts are expected to be collected early in 2014.

Tax revenues	5,000,000	
Taxes receivable—delinquent	17,000,000	
Allowance for uncollectible taxes—current	10,000,000	
Taxes receivable—current.		17,000,000
Allowance for uncollectible taxes—delinquent		15,000,000
To reclassify uncollected taxes as delinquent, adjust the related allowance account, and adjust tax revenues.		

The preclosing trial balance for Ranford County at December 31, 2013, appears as follows:

RANFORD COUNTY
Trial Balance—General Fund
December 31, 2013

Accounts	Debit	Credit
Cash.	$ 89,600,000	
Taxes receivable—delinquent	17,000,000	
Tax liens receivable	11,000,000	
Encumbrances	1,300,000	
General services expenditures.	178,100,000	
Maintenance expenditures.	14,000,000	
Supplies expenditures	18,000,000	
Capital outlay	5,900,000	
Transfers out	28,000,000	
Estimated revenues	240,000,000	
Estimated other financing sources.	7,000,000	
Allowance for uncollectible taxes—delinquent		$ 15,000,000
Allowance for uncollectible tax liens		11,000,000
Accounts payable.		6,000,000
Tax revenues		186,000,000
State aid revenues		30,000,000
Fee and license revenues.		9,500,000
Service revenues		11,800,000
Proceeds from sale of capital assets		7,300,000
Appropriations		218,000,000
Estimated other financing uses		28,000,000
Fund balance—unassigned		86,000,000
Fund balance—assigned		1,300,000
Totals	$609,900,000	$609,900,000

Closing Entries

Closing entries at December 31, 2013, are as follows:

Tax revenues	186,000,000	
State aid revenues	30,000,000	
Fee and license revenues	9,500,000	
Service revenues	11,800,000	
Proceeds from sale of capital assets	7,300,000	
Fund balance—unassigned	2,400,000	
Estimated revenues		240,000,000
Estimated other financing sources		7,000,000
To close revenues and other financing sources.		
Appropriations	218,000,000	
Estimated other financing uses	28,000,000	
General services expenditures		178,100,000
Maintenance expenditures		14,000,000
Supplies expenditures		18,000,000
Capital outlay		5,900,000
Encumbrances		1,300,000
Transfers out		28,000,000
Fund balance—unassigned		700,000
To close expenditures, other financing uses, and encumbrances.		

Financial Statements

The financial statements for the general fund of Ranford County can now be prepared. Ranford's **balance sheet** appears in Exhibit 10.3.

EXHIBIT 10.3   Ranford County Balance Sheet—General Fund

RANFORD COUNTY
Balance Sheet—General Fund
December 31, 2013

(in thousands)

Assets

Cash	$89,600
Taxes receivable—delinquent (net of $15,000,000 allowance for uncollectible taxes)	2,000
Tax liens receivable (net of $11,000,000 allowance for uncollectible tax liens)	—
Total assets	$91,600

Liabilities and fund balances

Liabilities:

Accounts payable	$ 6,000
Total liabilities	6,000

Fund balances:

Assigned	1,300
Unassigned	84,300
Total fund balances	85,600
Total liabilities and fund balances	$91,600

The general fund balance sheet is unclassified because modified accrual accounting excludes fixed assets and long-term debt. Thus the assets of the general fund include only those able to be spent or otherwise consumed during the next fiscal period in carrying on the fund's activities. Similarly, the liabilities of the general fund are limited to claims to be paid during the next fiscal year. The total fund balance includes an assigned balance that signifies outstanding encumbrances at year-end.

Ranford's **statement of revenues, expenditures, and changes in fund balances** explains changes in the *total fund balance* and appears in Exhibit 10.4. Use of the *purchases method* for the supplies inventory includes supplies purchased during the year in expenditures. Reported fund balance does *not* include resources invested in supplies on hand at year-end because Ranford County does not recognize supplies inventory.

EXHIBIT 10.4 Ranford County Statement of Revenues, Expenditures, and Changes in Fund Balances—General Fund

RANFORD COUNTY
Statement of Revenues, Expenditures, and Changes in Fund Balances
General Fund
For Year Ended December 31, 2013

(in thousands)

Revenues	
Property taxes	$186,000
State aid	30,000
Fees and licenses	9,500
Services	11,800
Total revenues	237,300
Expenditures	
General services	178,100
Maintenance	14,000
Supplies	18,000
Capital outlay	5,900
Total expenditures	216,000
Excess of revenues over expenditures	21,300
Other financing sources (uses)	
Proceeds from sale of capital assets	7,300
Transfers out	(28,000)
Total other financing sources (uses)	(20,700)
Excess of revenues and other financing sources over expenditures and other financing uses	600
Fund balances—January 1	85,000*
Fund balances—December 31	$85,600

* Unassigned fund balance	$83,000
Assigned fund balance	2,000
	$85,000

Revenues are classified by *source*. For the general fund, major sources of revenue include taxes, state aid, fees and licenses, and charges for services. *Expenditures* are often classified by character and function. Classification by *character* hinges on the time period (or periods) that the expenditures benefit. Common character classifications are *current expenditures*, *capital outlays*, and *debt service*. Classification by *function* identifies groups of related activities designed to accomplish a particular service or regulatory responsibility, such as general government, public safety, education, highways, sanitation, health, and recreation. Classification of expenditures by *object classes*—types of goods and services acquired—such as personnel compensation, supplies, and utilities is also common. Other financing sources and uses may include proceeds of long-term debt issues, proceeds from sales of capital assets, and transfers to or from the general fund.

The operating statement reconciles the beginning and ending *total* fund balances of the general fund. This reconciliation may not be as straightforward as the reconciliation of beginning and ending retained earnings in a business, for the following reasons:

- If the *purchases method* is used to account for a government's inventories and inventories are significant, the change in the Fund Balance—Nonspendable is included as part of the reconciliation, because this change in fund balance is not reported in the Statement of Revenues, Expenditures, and Changes in Fund Balances.

- If the *legal budgetary basis* is used to account for encumbrances, prior year expenditures are subtracted as part of the reconciliation, because they are not reported in the Statement of Revenues, Expenditures, and Changes in Fund Balances.

In addition to the Statement of Revenues, Expenditures, and Changes in Fund Balances, a parallel statement showing the comparison between budget and actual data is required. The format of this **budgetary comparison schedule** is similar to the format of the Statement of Revenues, Expenditures, and Changes in Fund Balances. For each item on the operating statement, the budgetary comparison schedule presents: (1) the original budgeted amount, (2) the final budgeted amount, after adjustment for legally authorized changes, and (3) the actual amount. An additional column reporting the variance between the final budget and actual amounts is encouraged but not required.

In the event the government uses a non-GAAP budgetary basis, "expenditures" likely include outstanding encumbrances. Because those "expenditure" amounts differ from the corresponding amounts in the Statement of Revenues, Expenditures, and Changes in Fund Balances, a reconciliation with GAAP is also required, as discussed in Chapter 12.

The budgetary comparison schedule for Ranford County, assuming the original budget was not changed during the year, appears in Exhibit 10.5. Because expenditures are legally limited by the budget, actual expenditures are less than or equal to budgeted expenditures.

EXHIBIT 10.5   Budgetary Comparison Schedule—General Fund

RANFORD COUNTY
Budgetary Comparison Schedule—General Fund
For Year Ended December 31, 2013

(in thousands)	Budget	Actual	Variance— Favorable (Unfavorable)
Revenues			
Property taxes	$190,000	$186,000	$(4,000)
State aid	30,000	30,000	
Fees and licenses	8,000	9,500	1,500
Services	12,000	11,800	(200)
Total revenues	240,000	237,300	(2,700)
Expenditures			
General services	180,000	178,100	1,900
Maintenance	14,000	14,000	—
Supplies	18,000	18,000	—
Capital outlay	6,000	5,900	100
Total expenditures	218,000	216,000	2,000
Excess of revenues over expenditures	22,000	21,300	(700)
Other financing sources (uses)			
Proceeds from sale of capital assets	7,000	7,300	300
Transfers out	(28,000)	(28,000)	—
Total other financing sources (uses)	(21,000)	(20,700)	300
Excess of revenues and other financing sources over expenditures and other financing uses	1,000	600	(400)
Fund balances—January 1	85,000	85,000	—
Fund balances—December 31	$ 86,000	$ 85,600	$ (400)

REVIEW 2 ● General Fund Budget and Closing Entries, Financial Statements

Here is the December 31, 2013, pre-closing trial balance for the general fund of Eerie County, NY. The county uses the GAAP budgetary basis for encumbrances, of which $1,200 were outstanding at December 31, 2012.

	Debit	Credit
Cash	$ 11,400	
Property taxes receivable.	64,000	
Allowance for uncollectible property taxes		$ 12,000
Due from other funds	3,000	
Accounts payable.		20,000
Due to other funds		4,000
Fund balance-assigned		1,000
Fund balance-unassigned		50,000
Estimated revenues	700,000	
Estimated other financing sources.	30,000	
Appropriations		708,000
Estimated other financing uses		8,000
Revenues – property taxes.		300,000
Revenues – sales taxes		380,000
Expenditures	698,000	
Proceeds of general obligation debt		12,000
Proceeds from sale of capital assets		16,000
Transfers out	7,600	
Transfers in.		4,000
Encumbrances	1,000	
Totals	$1,515,000	$1,515,000

Assigned fund balance consists entirely of outstanding encumbrances.

Required
a. Prepare the budget entry made at January 1, 2013.
b. Compute the balance in fund balance—unassigned on December 31, 2012.
c. Prepare the required closing entries at December 31, 2013.
d. Prepare the statement of revenues, expenditures, and changes in fund balances for 2013.
e. Prepare the balance sheet at December 31, 2013.

Solutions are located after the chapter assignments.

REVIEW OF KEY CONCEPTS ●●●●●●●●●●●●●●●●●●●●●●●●●●●

LO 1 **Describe the reporting environment for state and local governments. (p. 387)** State and local governments differ in many ways from for-profit enterprises. Resources are derived from taxes, fees, fines and debt financing. A **legal budget** limits expenditures. The main purpose of the government is to provide services to the citizenry. External users of governmental financial statements include **credit market representatives**, **elected officials**, **public sector labor unions**, and **citizens**. Credit market representatives use the financial statements to judge the governmental unit's ability to generate resources to fund required interest and principal payments. Citizens and legislators are concerned with services provided, and how current activities and plans affect future taxes and ability to provide services. The **Governmental Accounting Standards Board (GASB)** sets accounting requirements for state and local governmental external reporting. The emphasis in external reporting is on **stewardship** and **interperiod equity**. Financial statements are prepared for the governmental **reporting entity**, which consists of the **primary government** (usually a state or local government) and its **component units**. Deciding which organizations comprise the reporting entity is primarily based on whether **financial accountability** exists.

Identify the fund types and reporting methods for state and local governments. (p. 393) The government LO 2 consists of several accounting entities known as **funds**, which correspond to the major activities of the government. Although there is always one general fund, a particular government uses some or all of the other fund types, depending on its activities. The general, special revenue, capital projects, debt service, and permanent funds are known as **governmental funds**. These funds focus on sources, uses, and balances of **current financial resources** available to fund current expenditures, and use **modified accrual accounting**. Encumbrance and budgetary accounts aid in the control of resources. Required financial statements of governmental funds are the **statement of revenues, expenditures, and changes in fund balances**, the **balance sheet**, and the **budgetary comparison schedule**. Under the modified accrual basis of accounting, revenues represent **inflows of current financial resources**, excluding borrowings and transfers from other funds. Revenues are recognized when they are **measurable** and **available to finance expenditures in the current period**. Expenditures—outflows of current financial resources—are recognized when they are **measurable** and the **related liability is incurred**. The enterprise and internal service funds are known as **proprietary funds** because they are used to conduct business-type activities. Proprietary funds focus on determination of net income, financial position, and cash flows, and follow **full accrual accounting** as used in business. Required financial statements of proprietary funds are the **statement of revenues, expenses and changes in net position**, the **statement of net position**, and the **statement of cash flows**. **Fiduciary funds** account for resources held by the government in a custodial capacity for individuals or organizations outside the reporting government. These resources are not available to support government programs. Fiduciary funds are classified as **pension trust funds, investment trust funds, private-purpose trust funds**, and **agency funds**. All use accrual accounting. Agency funds record only assets and liabilities, and have no net position.

Prepare entries and financial statements for the general fund. (p. 398) The general fund's legal budget is recorded LO 3 directly in the accounts using a **budget entry**. Property taxes are accrued when billed; **tax revenue** is reported net of estimated uncollectible amounts. Purchase orders are recorded as **encumbrances**, reducing available funds. **Interfund transactions** appear as temporary advances on the balance sheet or as transfers on the operating statement. Inventories of supplies can be accounted for by the **consumption method**, which recognizes expenditures when the supplies are used, or by the **purchases method**, which recognizes expenditures when the supplies are purchased. Alternative treatments also exist for **encumbrances outstanding at year-end**, depending on the budgetary basis used by the governmental unit. Under the **GAAP budgetary basis**, expenditures—including those related to carryover encumbrances—are charged against the budget for the year the *expenditures* are made. However, the budget is increased by the amount of the carryover encumbrance. Under the **legal budgetary basis**, expenditures are charged against the budget for the year the *encumbrances* are made. **Capital assets** acquired by the general fund and by other governmental funds are capital outlays, classified as *expenditures*. Depreciation is not recorded in governmental funds. Proceeds from the sale of capital assets are *other financing sources*. Proceeds from the issuance of **long-term debt** are *other financing sources*. Resources used to pay principal and interest on long-term debt are *expenditures*.

MULTIPLE CHOICE QUESTIONS •

1. A county government annual report includes the activities of the primary government and its component LO 1 units. Component units can be presented in the financial statements as blended or *discrete*. A discrete component unit is most likely to

   a. have the same governing body as the primary government.
   b. exist to provide services to the primary government.
   c. issue bonds for which the component unit is financially obligated.
   d. receive funding mostly from endowments from county citizens.

2. What is the highest authoritative source of generally accepted accounting principles for state and local LO 1 governments?

   a. FASB
   b. AICPA
   c. GASB
   d. NCGA

3. The governmental funds operating statement will *never* report LO 2

   a. accrued pension costs.
   b. interest revenue.
   c. proceeds from sale of property.
   d. property tax revenue.

LO 2   **4.** Which of the following funds is *not* a governmental fund?

     a.   Internal service fund

     b.   Debt service fund

     c.   Special revenue fund

     d.   Permanent fund

LO 3   **5.** Some of a county government's account balances at November 30, 2013 appear below. The government's fiscal year ends June 30, 2014.

Cash in bank	$ 100,000
Estimated revenues	20,000,000
Budgetary deficit	500,000
Revenues	8,000,000
Expenditures	7,600,000
Fund balance–assigned	75,000
Fund balance–unassigned	300,000

The assigned fund balance relates entirely to outstanding encumbrances. How much does the government have available to spend for the remainder of fiscal 2014?

     a. $ 300,000

     b. $ 325,000

     c. $12,325,000

     d. $12,825,000

Use the following information to answer questions 6 – 9 below. All numbers are in thousands.

Here is the preclosing December 31, 2014 trial balance for the general fund of Lancaster County:

	Debit	Credit
Cash	$ 371,000	
Taxes receivable	113,000	
Estimated revenues	1,290,000	
Estimated other financing sources	60,000	
General expenditures	1,015,000	
Capital outlay	25,000	
Debt service: principal payments	2,000	
Debt service: interest payments	8,000	
Transfers out	20,000	
Due from other funds	12,000	
Allowance for uncollectible taxes		$ 45,000
Accounts payable		50,000
Due to other funds		21,000
Property tax revenues		950,000
Speeding ticket revenues		400,000
Transfers in		8,000
Bond proceeds		50,000
Appropriations		1,085,000
Estimated other financing uses		22,000
Fund balance—unassigned		285,000
Totals	$2,916,000	$2,916,000

LO 3   **6.** What was the amount of fund balance—unassigned at the beginning of the year, before the budget entry?

     a. $ 20,000

     b. $ 42,000

     c. $ 80,000

     d. $102,000

LO 3   **7.** By how much do the *closing entries* at the end of 2014 increase fund balance—unassigned?

     a. $37,000

     b. $40,000

     c. $73,000

     d. $95,000

8. Total expenditures reported on Lancaster County's 2014 statement of revenues, expenditures and changes in   **LO 3**
   fund balance are

   a. $1,015,000.
   b. $1,025,000.
   c. $1,048,000.
   d. $1,050,000.

9. Total assets reported on Lancaster County's December 31, 2014 balance sheet are   **LO 3**

   a. $439,000.
   b. $451,000.
   c. $472,000.
   d. $476,000.

10. The Town of Pavilion's July 1, 2012, balance sheet reports the following property tax accounts: **LO 3**

Taxes receivable.	$70,000
Allowance for uncollectible taxes.	(49,000)
Taxes receivable, net	$21,000

    During fiscal 2013, $30,000 in cash is collected on fiscal 2012 taxes and the remainder are written off. The
    Town levies fiscal 2013 property taxes in the amount of $1,000,000. It estimates that uncollectible property
    taxes for 2013 are $25,000. Cash collected for 2013 property taxes is $940,000. $15,000 of the remaining
    uncollected 2013 taxes are expected to be collected early in fiscal 2014. What are property tax revenues for
    fiscal 2013?

    a. $955,000
    b. $964,000
    c. $966,000
    d. $970,000

**Assignments with the ✓ in the margin are available in an online homework system.
See the Preface of the book for details.**

EXERCISES •

E10.1 Identify Appropriate Fund   Following are some common activities or transactions of a state or local   **LO 2** ✓
government.

1. Public safety programs financed by state and federal grants.
2. Proceeds of a state grant to be used to finance construction of a community center.
3. Operations of a municipal swimming pool, financed by user fees.
4. Accumulation of payroll deductions from local employees for health insurance premiums, to be
   remitted to various insurance companies.
5. Activities of a central printing operation that provides services to various government agencies.
6. Transactions of a state employee retirement plan.
7. A town collects property taxes to be used for county services, and periodically remits these taxes to
   the county.
8. Purchase of materials for the construction of a county courthouse.
9. Payment of interest on general obligation bonds.
10. Payment of salaries to municipal employees.
11. Acquisition of books by a local public library, where the library is funded by a special property tax.
12. Accumulation of money to be used to pay interest on general obligation bonds.
13. Activities of a park trust, where income from non-spendable trust investments is restricted to the
    funding of maintenance costs for public parks.
14. Accumulation of abandoned bank balances that have reverted to the town.

Required

Indicate the type of fund in which each activity or transaction should be recorded by a state or local
government.

LO 2 **E10.2** **Identify Appropriate Funds** Each of the following transactions relates to a city government:

1. A sinking fund is set up to accumulate and invest resources for the retirement of a general bond issue maturing in ten years.
2. The city receives a $50,000 grant from the federal government to institute a meal delivery program for senior citizens.
3. New curbing is being installed on the south side of the city, with resources initially provided by the general fund. No debt is issued. Residents of the south side will pay for the cost of the curbing with an additional charge on their property tax bill during each of the next ten years.
4. Same as 3., except that initial financing is provided by issuing bonds for which the city is (a) liable or (b) not liable.
5. To remedy a flooding problem, the city plans a new drainage system in the northern part of the city, financed with a general bond issue.
6. The city establishes a retirement fund for its fire fighters, and sets aside 8 percent of the fire fighters' wages each year. The city administers the investment of funds and the payment of benefits.
7. Same as 6., except that the city pays a premium to an insurance company fully responsible for investment of funds and benefit payments.
8. The city set up a computer services division to handle payroll and other functions for all city agencies, for a fee.
9. Fifteen new police cars are purchased, as provided in the general budget.
10. Received state aid funds to be used for any of the city's general operations.
11. The city deducts federal income taxes from its employees' wages and periodically remits them to the federal government.
12. The city receives a $3,000,000 trust from a citizen. Income from trust investments must be used to maintain the public museum.
13. The city invests money received from other governments that pool their investments to increase return on excess funds invested.

Required

Identify the fund(s) affected by each of the above transactions.

LO 1 **E10.3** **Property Tax Rate and Revenues** Steuben County anticipates appropriations of $9,500,000 and revenue from the state and other sources of $855,000. During the last fiscal year, the tax rate was $0.88 per $100 of assessed valuation, applied to property assessed at $900 million. Uncollectible property taxes are negligible. In the current year, the county's reassessment program increased the aggregate assessed value of property to $950 million.

Required

a. Compute the property tax revenue raised during the last fiscal year.
b. Compute the tax rate needed to balance the current budget.
c. Assume that the Steuben County charter requires a balanced budget and that increasing the tax rate is politically unacceptable. Compute the maximum amount of appropriations that can be funded by property taxes given the increase in assessed valuation.

⊘ LO 3 **E10.4** **Computing Available Funds** As the newly-hired assistant controller for the **City of Columbia, Mis-**
CITY OF **souri,** you are working diligently to unravel the mysteries of governmental accounting. On your desk this
COLUMBIA, morning is a memorandum from the controller asking you to advise her of the amount of available funds.
MISSOURI After consulting your assistant and the city treasurer, you begin to analyze the following information.

(in thousands)		Dr (Cr)
Cash in bank		$ 40,000
Estimated revenue		4,000,000
Budgetary surplus		(200,000)
Revenue		(3,700,000)
Expenditures		2,500,000
Accounts payable		(300,000)
Fund balance—assigned		(225,000)
Fund balance—unassigned		(800,000)

Assigned fund balance consists of outstanding encumbrances.

Required

a. Calculate the funds available to be encumbered.
b. Suppose it is now August 31, close to the September 30 fiscal year-end. Operating costs occur evenly throughout the year. Do you expect to see an effort to cut next period's budget? Why?

E10.5 Reconstruct Budget Entry, Compute Fund Balance The following information relates to ac- **LO 3** tual revenues and expenditures for the general fund of the **City of Greenwood, Mississippi**:

CITY OF GREENWOOD, MISSISSIPPI

	Actual	Over (under) Budget
Revenues		
Property taxes	$2,975,000	$125,000
Fines	6,000	6,000
Intergovernmental revenue	12,000	—
Fees and service charges	500,000	(75,000)
Miscellaneous	4,000	(1,000)
Expenditures		
Administration	500,000	(1,000)
Public safety	2,050,000	(6,000)
Health and environment	950,000	(4,000)

Required

a. What budget entry was made at the beginning of the year?
b. If the fund balance *before* the budget entry was $2,100,000, what is the fund balance after year-end closing entries?

E10.6 Transactions, Closing Entries, and Budgetary Comparison Schedule The January 1, 2013, **LO 3** balance sheet for the general fund of the village of Owen, Texas is:

VILLAGE OF OWEN
General Fund Balance Sheet
January 1, 2013

(in thousands)

Cash	$30,000	Accounts payable	$13,000
Taxes receivable	20,000	Fund balance	37,000
Total assets	$50,000	Total liabilities and fund balance	$50,000

Transactions for the village during 2013 were *(in thousands)*:

1. The village council approved a budget estimating revenues of $41,000 in property taxes and $10,000 in fees and service charges. The budget authorized expenditures of $51,000.
2. Collected receivables of $18,500 from last year and $26,500 of the 2013 tax levy.
3. Recorded encumbrances of $50,300. On December 31, 2013, purchase orders of $13,000 were outstanding.
4. Bills received exceeded the amounts encumbered by $200.
5. Mailed checks for $44,000 in payment of accounts payable.
6. Collected fees and service charges of $11,000.

Required

a. Prepare the journal entries to record the transactions during 2013.
b. Prepare closing entries at December 31, 2013.
c. Compute the unassigned fund balance at December 31, 2013.
d. Prepare a budgetary comparison schedule for 2013. Use the GAAP budgetary basis.

LO 3 **E10.7** **Property Tax Transactions** On July 10, the town of Salt Flats, Utah levied property taxes of $30,000,000. Based on past experience, town management estimated that the town will not collect 4 percent of the taxes. Taxes were due September 30, but $9,009,000 was received before that date from taxpayers taking advantage of the 1 percent discount for early payment. Salt Flats treats discounts given as a reduction of revenues. On January 1, outstanding taxes due of $2,000,000 were declared delinquent; Salt Flats estimates that $200,000 of delinquent taxes will be collected early next year. By the end of the fiscal year, $300,000 of the delinquent taxes were collected and the rest were written off. No taxes receivable, either current or delinquent, existed at the beginning of the fiscal year. Actual expenditures of $25,000,000 equaled appropriations. All expenditures were cash transactions. The budget entry included $29,000,000 of estimated revenues. After the budget entry, the general fund balance was $5,200,000.

Required

a. Prepare the journal entries to record the property tax transactions and the expenditures.
b. State the balance sheet accounts and their respective balances relating to the property tax levy and collections as of the end of the fiscal year. Assume an $850,000 cash balance at the beginning of the fiscal year.

LO 3 **E10.8** **Inventory Accounting** General City's general fund reported a supplies inventory costing $1,000,000 at the beginning of the fiscal year. During the year, General City purchased materials and supplies on account for $18,000,000; $2,500,000 remains unpaid at year-end. Materials and supplies costing $1,100,000 are on hand at the end of the fiscal year.

Required

Prepare the summary journal entries made this year under the two allowable methods used by governmental funds to account for inventories.

LO 3 **E10.9** **Closing Entries** The Newberry County budget for the 2014 fiscal year included estimated revenues of $3,501,000 and appropriations of $3,449,000.

Required

Prepare the closing entries for 2014 under each of the following independent assumptions:

a. Actual revenues and expenditures equaled estimates.
b. Actual revenues were as expected, but appropriations exceeded actual expenditures by $22,000.
c. Actual revenues of $3,440,000 equaled actual expenditures.
d. The net effect of the closing entries on the fund balance was zero. Actual revenues were $3,495,000.

LO 3 **E10.10** **Carryover Encumbrances** The December 31, 2012, balance sheet for the general fund of Burnville showed an assigned fund balance of $1,900,000 for outstanding encumbrances. This figure represented $1,100,000 encumbered for office equipment and $800,000 for supplies. Early in 2013, the equipment and supplies were delivered and bills received for $1,170,000 and $795,000, respectively.

Required

Prepare the journal entries for 2013 relating to these events, using the

a. Legal budgetary basis.
b. GAAP budgetary basis.

LO 3 **E10.11** **Interfund Transactions** Interfund transfers of the general fund of **Contra Costa County** for 2014 were as follows:

CONTRA COSTA COUNTY, CALIFORNIA

1. $1,800,000 advance to the Land Development special revenue fund, to permit initial expenditures under a project to be fully supported by a federal grant.
2. $2,500,000 to the Contra Costa County Fire Protection District (a special revenue fund) as the county's contribution to fire and emergency medical service activities for the year.
3. $700,000 from the Roads capital projects fund, unspent proceeds of a bond issue.
4. $1,200,000 to the County Hospital (enterprise fund), as the city's cost of services provided.
5. $3,500,000 to the Airport Fund (enterprise fund) to temporarily finance the maintenance of runways.
6. $1,800,000 from the Land Development special revenue fund, to repay the advance.

Required

For each of the above interfund transfers, state how the transaction is reported on the general fund's balance sheet and/or statement of revenues, expenditures, and changes in fund balances.

E10.12 Adjusting and Closing Entries, Balance Sheet The preclosing trial balance for the general fund **LO 3**
of Graystone County is given below:

	Dr (Cr)
Cash.	$ 3,500,000
Taxes receivable—current	800,000
Allowance for uncollectible taxes—current	(450,000)
Supplies	280,000
Estimated revenues	13,000,000
Expenditures	10,500,000
Expenditures—prior year	420,000
Encumbrances	300,000
Due from other funds	120,000
Accounts payable.	(1,800,000)
Due to other funds	(210,000)
Revenues	(14,000,000)
Appropriations	(11,000,000)
Fund balance—nonspendable.	(280,000)
Fund balance—assigned	(750,000)
Fund balance—unassigned	(430,000)
Total	$ 0

Additional information:

1. At year-end, all uncollected taxes are deemed delinquent and are fully reserved.
2. A physical count of inventory revealed $250,000 of supplies on hand.
3. Assigned fund balance consists of $300,000 in outstanding encumbrances at year-end, and $450,000
    in prior year encumbrances.

Required

a. Prepare all year-end adjusting and closing entries for Graystone County's general fund.
b. Prepare a year-end balance sheet for Graystone County's general fund.

E10.13 General Fund Capital Asset and Long-Term Debt Transactions During the current year, the **LO 3**
following transactions were recorded by the general fund of the City of Margate:

1. Acquired new fire-fighting equipment costing $2,250,000.
2. Sold for $370,000 old fire-fighting equipment acquired ten years ago for $1,500,000.
3. Paid interest and principal on long-term capital debt of $2,000,000 and $500,000, respectively.

Required

a. Prepare all journal entries made by the City of Margate's general fund for the above transactions.
b. State how each transaction is reported in the general fund financial statements.
c. Compute the effect of the foregoing on the general fund unassigned fund balance.

E10.14 Identifying the Reporting Entity These descriptions of organizations relate to a city government. **LO 1**

1. The public school district is a legally separate entity responsible for the administration of city schools
    and has a separate board elected by the public. The city council approves the school district's budget,
    levies taxes and issues debt on behalf of the school district. The city is legally liable for school dis-
    trict debt. The city also provides significant funding to the school district.
2. The housing authority is a legally separate entity that manages public housing in the city. The au-
    thority issues its own debt, payment on which is financed by housing rents. The city has no financial
    liability for the housing authority's debt. The city has input in choosing the authority's board, but
    does not appoint the board or control its decisions.
3. The waste disposal authority is a legally separate entity that operates the city landfill; its board is
    appointed and landfill rates are approved by the city council.
4. The sewer district provides sewage treatment services to several surrounding local governments, in-
    cluding the city. The city appoints a minority of the sewer district's board members. The district sets
    service rates and makes all decisions regarding its operations. Its operations are funded by property
    tax levies and user charges, and by debt for which it is legally liable.
5. The building authority is a separate legal entity whose board is appointed by the city. The authority
    issues bonds to finance construction of city capital assets. The city is legally liable for the bonds.

Required

For each organization described above, indicate whether it should be reported as a component unit of the city. If it is a component unit, should its financial information be blended with that of the city, or discretely presented? Justify your answers.

PROBLEMS ••

LO 1 **P10.1** **Determining the Reporting Entity** The governmental reporting entity consists of a primary government and its component units. Various governmental structures are described below.

1. By a vote of 9-6, the Megalopolis city council voted to establish a Convention Authority (CA). Megalopolis's mayor appoints the CA's governing board with the approval of city council. City council's direct financial commitment to the CA is limited to a $100,000 appropriation of seed money to be repaid from the CA's permanent financing as soon as possible. The CA's initial responsibility is to obtain the funding for a downtown convention center. Funding will likely come from a combination of federal development grant money, tax-exempt bonds issued and backed by the city, and corporate contributions.

2. Consider the same facts as in 1. except that the CA is authorized to issue its own bonds without city backing and may levy a small sales tax to support its activities. The CA's bond issues and sales taxes need not be approved by the city council but, as a matter of courtesy, council is advised of the CA's plans.

3. Many local communities in Gigantic County are served by volunteer fire departments. Each such fire department is a separate not-for-profit corporation governed by a board elected by and from its own membership. The county has a three-year contract with each fire department to pay for the department's fire-fighting services. Also, the county has historically paid for fire trucks and similar equipment used and owned by the fire departments.

4. The Winitville Board of Education is elected by the voters. This Board governs the Winitville school district and obtains an annual appropriation from the city to fund school district activities. The City of Winitville levies whatever taxes and issues whatever bonds it needs to fund its expenditures, including those attributable to the school district, and has no authority over the individual line items in the school district's budget.

STATE OF MICHIGAN

5. The **State of Michigan**, along with seven other states, participates in a joint venture to examine the water quality of the Great Lakes. Michigan is the largest contributor, and contributions to the **Great Lakes Protection Fund** (GLPF) are permanently restricted and are not available for disbursement. Each participating state is represented by two members on the GLPF's board of directors. The GLPF's financing and budgeting operations are controlled by the directors within requirements established by its own Articles of Incorporation.

STATE OF GEORGIA

6. The **Georgia Public Telecommunications Commission** is a legally separate entity within the **State of Georgia**. This commission is a public charitable organization created for the purpose of providing educational, instructional and public broadcasting services to the citizens of Georgia. The budget of the commission must be approved by the State. The Board consists of three State officials designated by statute and six members appointed by the Governor.

Required

For each of the above independent situations, identify the primary government and explain whether the other governmental enterprise is part of the primary government's financial reporting entity.

LO 3 **P10.2** **General Fund Entries and Financial Statements** The **Town of Amherst, NY** finances its operations from revenues collected from property taxes, waste management fees, municipal court fines, and interest on investments. Amherst maintains only a general fund. The following information is available for the year ended December 31, 2013:

TOWN OF AMHERST, NY

1. Following is the general fund trial balance on January 1, 2013:

	Dr (Cr)
Investments	$ 6,000,000
Cash	3,500,000
Waste management supplies	380,000
Accounts receivable—waste management	400,000
Fund balance—nonspendable	(380,000)
Fund balance—unassigned	(9,900,000)
Total	$ 0

2. The budget for 2013, adopted by the town board, follows:

Property taxes	$2,700,000
Waste management costs	6,700,000
Court costs	1,150,000
Waste management revenues	3,500,000
Court fines	1,000,000
Salaries and operating expenditures	750,000
Investment income	250,000
Supplies expenditures	350,000
Miscellaneous expenditures	150,000

3. All property taxes were collected in cash. Waste management costs, all paid in cash, were $6,680,000. Court costs, all paid in cash, were $1,120,000.
4. Waste management revenues of $3,600,000 were billed during the year. All outstanding waste management bills on January 1, 2013, were collected during 2013. All 2013 billings were paid with the exception of $210,000, which were mailed to customers the last week of the year.
5. Court fines of $920,000 were collected in cash. Salaries and operating expenditures, all paid in cash, were $745,000. Investment income of $235,000 accumulates in the investments account until the investments mature. No investments matured in 2013.
6. Miscellaneous expenditures, all paid in cash, were $149,000.
7. Waste management supplies on hand at year-end were $40,000. The town uses the consumption method to report supplies.

Required

a. Prepare 2013 journal entries to record the above events and to close the books for the year.
b. Prepare a statement of revenues, expenditures, and changes in fund balances and the balance sheet for 2013.

P10.3 General Fund Adjustments and Financial Statements The books for the Town of Fountain   LO 3
Inn are maintained by an inexperienced bookkeeper. All transactions were recorded in the town's general fund for the fiscal year ended June 30, 2014. The bookkeeper prepared the following trial balance:

TOWN OF FOUNTAIN INN
General Fund Trial Balance
June 30, 2014

	Debit	Credit
Cash	$ 28,000,000	
Accounts receivable	2,000,000	
Taxes receivable, current	10,000,000	
Accounts payable		$ 18,000,000
Appropriations		380,000,000
Expenditures	315,000,000	
Estimated revenues	460,000,000	
Revenues		440,000,000
Town property	19,000,000	
Bonds payable	40,000,000	
Fund balance		36,000,000
Totals	$874,000,000	$874,000,000

Additional information:

1. The accounts receivable balance was due from the town's golf course, representing an advance made by the general fund. Accounts for the municipal golf course operated by the town are maintained in a separate enterprise fund.
2. The total tax levy for the year was $300,000,000. The town's tax collection experience in recent years indicates an average loss of 5 percent of the net tax levy for uncollectible taxes. At year-end, all taxes receivable are considered delinquent and are fully reserved.
3. On June 30, 2014, the town retired at face value 4-percent general obligation serial bonds totaling $35,000,000. The bonds were issued on July 1, 2012, in the total amount of $150,000,000. Interest paid during the year was also recorded in the Bonds Payable account.

4. At the beginning of the year, the town council authorized a supply room with an inventory not to exceed $10,000,000. During the year, supplies totaling $14,000,000 were purchased and charged to Expenditures. The physical inventory taken at June 30, 2014, disclosed that supplies totaling $10,500,000 were used. The town uses the purchases method to report supplies, and supplies are reported in the balance sheet.

5. Expenditures for 2014 included $2,600,000 applicable to purchase orders issued in the prior year. Outstanding purchase orders at June 30, 2014, not recorded in the accounts, amounted to $4,500,000. The GAAP budgetary basis is used.

6. The amount of $9,000,000, due from the state for the town's share of state gasoline taxes, was not recorded in the accounts.

7. Equipment costing $8,000,000 was removed from service and sold for $1,000,000 during the year, and new equipment costing $20,000,000 was purchased. These transactions were recorded in the Town Property account.

Required

a. Prepare the adjusting and closing entries for the general fund of Fountain Inn.

b. Prepare a statement of revenues, expenditures and changes in fund balances and balance sheet for Fountain Inn's general fund.

LO 3   P10.4   Reconstructing General Fund Journal Entries   General fund balance sheets for the **City of Golden, Colorado**, appear as follows:

CITY OF GOLDEN, COLORADO

CITY OF GOLDEN **General Fund** **Balance Sheets at June 30**		
(in thousands)	**2014**	**2013**
Assets		
Cash..	$ 31,000	$ 12,000
Investments..	30,000	53,000
Due from state government................................	49,000	—
Due from federal government..............................	—	105,000
Totals...	$110,000	$170,000
Liabilities and fund balances		
Accounts payable..	$ 32,000	$ 42,000
Fund balance—assigned...................................	—	8,000
Fund balance—unassigned................................	78,000	120,000
Totals...	$110,000	$170,000

All numbers below are in thousands. Assigned fund balance consists of outstanding encumbrances. The following budget entry was made on July 1, 2013:

Estimated revenues..	65,000	
Fund balance—unassigned................................	30,000	
Appropriations..		95,000
To record budget for fiscal 2014.		

Bills for the June 30, 2013, encumbrances were $1,000 less than the amount encumbered. Actual revenues were $16,000 less than budgeted. The legal budgetary basis is used for outstanding encumbrances. Investments were liquidated at book value.

Required

Reconstruct the journal entries, including closing entries, for the year ended June 30, 2014, for Golden's general fund.

LO 3   P10.5   General Fund—Corrections, Adjustments, and Financial Statements   During the fiscal year ending June 30, 2013, all transactions of Salleytown were recorded in the general fund due to the inexperience of the town's bookkeeper. The trial balance of Salleytown's general fund is as follows:

SALLEYTOWN
General Fund Trial Balance
June 30, 2013

(in thousands)	Debit	Credit
Cash.	$ 16,800	
Short-term investments	40,000	
Accounts receivable.	11,500	
Taxes receivable—current	30,000	
Accounts payable.		$ 50,000
Appropriations		520,000
Expenditures	382,000	
Estimated revenues	520,000	
Revenues		560,000
General property	85,400	
Bonds payable	52,000	
Fund balance—unassigned		7,700
Totals	$1,137,700	$1,137,700

The following information is also available *(in thousands)*:

1. The accounts receivable of $11,500 includes $1,500 due from the town's water utility. Accounts for the municipal water utility operated by the town are maintained in a separate fund.
2. The balance in Taxes receivable—current is now considered delinquent, and the town estimates that $24,000 will be uncollectible.
3. On June 30, 2013, the town retired, at face value, 6-percent general obligation serial bonds totaling $40,000. The bonds were issued on July 1, 2008, at face value of $200,000. Interest and principal paid during the year ended June 30, 2013, were charged to bonds payable.
4. During the year, supplies totaling $128,000 were purchased and charged to expenditures. The town conducted a physical inventory of supplies on hand at June 30, 2013, and this physical count disclosed that supplies of $84,000 were used. The purchases method is used and ending inventory is recognized.
5. Expenditures for the year ended June 30, 2013, included $11,200 applicable to purchase orders issued in the prior year. Outstanding purchase orders at June 30, 2013, not recorded in the accounts, amounted to $5,000. The legal budgetary basis is used.
6. On June 28, 2013, the state revenue department informed the town that its share of a state-collected, locally shared tax would be $34,000.
7. During the year, equipment with a book value of $7,900 was removed from service and sold for $4,600. In addition, new equipment costing $90,000 was purchased. The transactions were recorded in general property.
8. During the year, 100 acres of land were donated to the town for use as an industrial park. The land had a value of $125,000. This donation was not recorded.

Required

a. Prepare the formal reclassification, adjusting, and closing journal entries for the general fund as of June 30, 2013.
b. Present, in good form, the general fund's statement of revenues, expenditures, and changes in fund balances for the fiscal year ended June 30, 2013.
c. Present, in good form, the general fund's balance sheet for the fiscal year ended June 30, 2013.

P10.6 **Comprehensive General Fund Review** The Wayne City Council approved and adopted its general fund budget for 2013. The budget contained the following amounts: LO 3 ✓

Estimated revenues	$70,000,000
Appropriations	66,000,000
Authorized transfer to the Library debt service fund	3,000,000

During 2013, various transactions and events occurred which affected the general fund. The legal budgetary basis is used.

Required

For items 1–39, indicate whether the item should be **debited (D)**, **credited (C)**, or is **not affected (N)** in the general fund.

a. Items 1–5 involve recording the adopted budget
  1. Estimated revenues
  2. Fund balance—unassigned
  3. Appropriations
  4. Estimated other financing uses
  5. Expenditures

b. Items 6–10 involve recording the 2013 property tax levy. It was estimated that $500,000 would be uncollectible.
  6. Property taxes receivable—current
  7. Bad debt expense
  8. Allowance for uncollectibles—current
  9. Revenues
  10. Estimated revenues

c. Items 11–15 involve recording encumbrances at the time purchase orders are issued.
  11. Encumbrances
  12. Fund balance—assigned
  13. Expenditures
  14. Accounts payable
  15. Purchases

d. Items 16–20 involve recording expenditures which had been previously encumbered in the current year.
  16. Encumbrances
  17. Fund balance—assigned
  18. Expenditures
  19. Accounts payable
  20. Purchases

e. Items 21–25 involve recording the transfer made to the Library debt service fund. No previous entries were made regarding this transaction.
  21. Fund balance—assigned
  22. Due from Library debt service fund
  23. Cash
  24. Other financing uses
  25. Encumbrances

f. Items 26–36 involve recording the closing entries (other than encumbrances) for 2013.
  26. Estimated revenues
  27. Due to special revenue fund
  28. Appropriations
  29. Estimated other financing uses
  30. Expenditures
  31. Revenues
  32. Other financing uses
  33. Bonds payable
  34. Bad debt expense
  35. Depreciation expense
  36. Fund balance—assigned

g. Items 37–39 involve recording the closing entry related to $1,200,000 of outstanding encumbrances at the end of 2013.
  37. Encumbrances
  38. Fund balance—assigned
  39. Fund balance—unassigned

LO 3 **P10.7 Comprehensive General Fund—Entries and Statements** Data relating to the general fund of the Quarryville School District are:

QUARRYVILLE SCHOOL DISTRICT			
(in thousands)	General Fund Balance Sheet June 30, 2013		
Assets		**Liabilities and fund balances**	
Cash..........................	$ 4,000	Accounts payable.................	$3,000
Taxes receivable—current		Fund balances	
(net of $1,250 allowance for		Nonspendable	2,000
uncollectible taxes)..............	5,000	Assigned.......................	500
Inventory.......................	2,000	Unassigned	5,500
Total	$11,000	Total	$11,000

Additional information for fiscal 2014 *(in thousands)*:

1. The fiscal 2014 budget included $30,000 in expected revenue, all from property taxes, estimated other financing uses of $800, and a $2,000 planned decrease in the fund balance. The tax levy was for $37,000.

2. Tax collections during fiscal 2014 were as follows:

Fiscal 2013 taxes..	$ 5,500
Fiscal 2014 taxes..	25,000

3. Taxes due at year-end are not considered delinquent but are 20-percent reserved. Unpaid 2013 taxes are written off as uncollectible.
4. Old school desks were sold for $100 in cash.
5. New desks were purchased for $300 in cash.
6. Vandalism to the schools resulted in $400 of unexpected repair and cleanup costs.
7. Additional expenditures by the general fund were $28,000.
8. Supplies on hand at year-end totaled $1,500, per annual physical inventory. Quarryville uses the consumption method.
9. Although no accounts payable were outstanding at the end of fiscal 2014, $600 was encumbered for goods ordered but not yet received. The GAAP budgetary basis is used.
10. The 2013 encumbrance for $500 was canceled when the goods ordered were found to be defective.
11. Cash of $750 was paid to the enterprise fund, as the school district's support for its operating costs.

Required
a. Prepare all the fiscal 2014 journal entries and closing entries for the school district's general fund.
b. Prepare a fiscal 2014 statement of revenues, expenditures, and changes in fund balances and balance sheet for the general fund.

P10.8 Employee Compensated Absences Like most employees, governmental employees receive an- LO 2 nual compensated sick leave, family leave, and vacation days. Often, employees are compensated for unused accumulated annual leave upon retirement or termination. Following is supplementary footnote information concerning governmental funds' compensated absences for the **State of South Carolina** for fiscal year 2010:

STATE OF SOUTH CAROLINA

Unpaid compensated absences as of July 1, 2009............................	$219,949,000
Unpaid compensated absences as of June 30, 2010	214,113,000

Required
Suppose that compensated absences are recorded in the general fund, and the general fund paid $25,000,000 to employees during fiscal 2010 for compensated absences.

a. Present the journal entry or entries necessary to record the above events in the general fund.
b. How would the above events be recorded if the general fund used full accrual accounting?
c. Comment on the value of the general fund balance sheet in evaluating South Carolina's future obligation for compensated absences.

P10.9 General Fund Reporting The following information is available concerning general fund activities LO 3 of the City of Middletown for the year 2014. Middletown uses the GAAP budgetary basis to account for encumbrances.

1. The general fund budget for 2014 consisted of the following items:

Estimated property tax revenues	$8,500,000
Appropriations	8,800,000
Transfers to capital projects fund	200,000
Transfers to enterprise fund	50,000
Estimated bond proceeds	500,000

2. $78,000 in encumbrances were outstanding at the end of 2013.
3. Current property tax revenues of $8,500,000 were accrued at the beginning of the year, along with a current uncollectible portion of $100,000. The general fund reported equal balances of $25,000 in its delinquent property taxes receivable and uncollectible allowance accounts at the beginning of the year.
4. At the end of the year, current property tax receivables of $120,000 remained uncollected. The current uncollectible accounts balance was $40,000. Delinquent property taxes of $15,000 were collected during the year. The remaining delinquent balances were written off at the end of the year. The general fund's policy is to fully reserve any remaining current property taxes receivable and reclassify them as delinquent.
5. General obligation bonds with a face value of $500,000 were issued at par. Interest at 4% of principal and $20,000 of principal are due annually in 2015. These bonds will be used to finance a community project, which is reported in the general fund. Principal payments will be handled through the debt service fund, but interest payments will be paid through the general fund.
6. The general fund sold equipment with an original cost of $40,000 for $6,000, and purchased a building for $200,000 during 2014. Equipment with an original cost of $30,000 was retired during the year.
7. The transfers to the capital projects and enterprise funds were made as budgeted.
8. Actual expenditures (including the building purchase) for the year were $8,720,000, of which $80,000 related to encumbrances outstanding at the beginning of the year. Encumbrances outstanding at year-end were $130,000.

Required

Answer the following questions related to Middletown's general fund activities for 2014.

a. Present the beginning of 2014 budget and encumbrance entries. What is their net impact on fund balance—unassigned?
b. What is total property tax revenue for 2014? How much cash was collected from property taxes in 2014?
c. How much in bond interest payable should be shown on the general fund's year-end balance sheet?
d. Prepare the end of 2014 closing entries for the general fund.
e. Present a general fund budgetary comparison schedule for 2014.

LO 3 **P10.10 General Fund—Entries and Financial Statements** The general fund trial balance for the City of Los Alvos at December 31, 2013, follows:

CITY OF LOS ALVOS General Fund Trial Balance December 31, 2013		
	Debit	**Credit**
Cash	$ 30,000	
Due from other funds	2,000	
Due From federal government	10,000	
Property taxes receivable—delinquent	65,000	
Allowance for uncollectible taxes—delinquent		$ 40,000
Inventories	15,000	
Accounts payable		30,000
Fund balance—nonspendable		15,000
Fund balance—assigned		6,000
Fund balance—unassigned		31,000
Totals	$122,000	$122,000

Assigned fund balance consists of outstanding encumbrances.

The following information is available for the year 2014:

1. The general fund adopted the following budget for 2014:

Property tax revenues	$500,000
Licenses and fines	35,000
Federal grants	100,000
General government expenditures	250,000
Human services expenditures	402,000
Transfers to other funds	14,000

2. Property taxes totaling $500,000 were levied. Of this amount, $50,000 was estimated to be uncollectible. Collections during the year were $430,000 on currently levied taxes and $60,000 related to taxes declared delinquent in 2013. Delinquent taxes uncollected as of the end of 2014 were written off. All uncollected 2014 property taxes were classified as delinquent and $15,000 of these taxes are expected to be collected early in 2015.

3. The $10,000 federal grant accrued in 2013 was received in cash in early 2014. Of the $100,000 in federal grants expected and accrued in 2014, $85,000 was received in cash.

4. Cash received for licenses and fines totaled $34,000.

5. Cash payments for general government and human services activities were $234,000 and $400,000, respectively. At the end of the year, the accounts payable balance was $15,000 and inventories totaled $18,000. Accounts payable and inventories relate only to general government activities. Inventories costing $6,000, relating to encumbrances outstanding at the beginning of the year, were received during 2014. $4,000 in inventory purchase orders were outstanding at the end of the year.

6. Transfers of $14,000 were made to the city's debt service fund. The city's community center enterprise fund paid back a $2,000 cash advance provided by the general fund in 2013. The general fund provided $5,000 to the capital projects fund for temporary financing of a project; this amount is expected to be paid back in 2015.

7. The general fund received a $25,000 cash advance from the city nursing home (an enterprise fund) to cover its cash deficit. It is expected to be paid back next year.

The general fund uses the consumption method for inventory reporting, and the GAAP budgetary basis for year-end encumbrances.

Required

a. Prepare 2014 journal entries to record the above events in the general fund, and to close the books for the year.

b. Prepare the following financial statements for the City of Los Alvos general fund:
   (1) Statement of revenues, expenditures, and changes in fund balances for the year 2014
   (2) Balance sheet for the year ended December 31, 2014
   (3) Budgetary comparison schedule for the year 2014.

P10.11 General Fund—Budget and Closing Entries, Financial Statements Here is the December 31, 2014 pre-closing trial balance for the general fund of the **City of Akron, Ohio**. The city uses the GAAP budgetary basis for encumbrances, and $800 in encumbrances were outstanding at January 1, 2014.

LO 3

CITY OF AKRON, OHIO

(in thousands)	Debit	Credit
Cash.	$ 5,000	
Investments	14,000	
Property taxes receivable.	63,000	
Allowance for uncollectible property taxes		$ 27,000
Due from special revenue fund	9,000	
Accounts payable.		33,200
Due to internal service fund		7,600
Fund balance—assigned		500
Fund balance—unassigned		23,000
Estimated revenues	260,000	
Estimated other financing sources.	2,000	
Appropriations		257,000
Estimated other financing uses		4,800
Revenues—property taxes.		55,000
Revenues—income taxes.		180,000
Revenues—fines and licenses		18,000
Revenues—state grants.		6,000
Encumbrances	500	
Expenditures—general government.	130,400	
Capital outlay	11,000	
Transfers out	4,500	
Proceeds from sale of capital assets		2,300
Debt service—interest	35,000	
Debt service—principal	80,000	
Totals	$614,400	$614,400

Assigned fund balance consists of outstanding encumbrances.

Required

a.   Prepare the budget entry that was made at January 1, 2014.
b.   Calculate the balance in fund balance—unassigned on December 31, 2013.
c.   Prepare the required closing entries at year-end.
d.   Prepare the general fund statement of revenues, expenditures, and changes in fund balances for 2014.
e.   Prepare the general fund balance sheet at December 31, 2014.

✅ **LO 3**   **P10.12 General Fund—Entries and Financial Statements**   Below are the July 1, 2012, balances for the general fund of Montana County. The county's fiscal year ends June 30.

	Debit	Credit
Cash.	$120,000	
Taxes receivable—delinquent	22,500	
Allowance for uncollectible taxes—delinquent		$ 22,500
Due from special revenue fund	15,000	
Inventories	7,500	
Accounts payable.		7,500
Fund balance—assigned		3,000
Fund balance—nonspendable.		7,500
Fund balance—unassigned		124,500
Totals	$165,000	$165,000

Montana County uses the purchases method for inventories, and the GAAP budgetary basis for encumbrances outstanding at year-end. Assigned fund balance consists of outstanding encumbrances.

The following events occurred in fiscal 2013:

1. Passed the 2013 budget, consisting of expected revenues from property taxes, fees and licenses of $370,500, expected state grants of $40,000, estimated expenditures of $370,000, and expected transfers out of $50,000. Accrued the state grants.
2. Levied property taxes of $300,000, of which 5 percent are estimated to be uncollectible. Collected $280,000 of these taxes.
3. Received $25,000 in state grants.
4. Collected $10,000 in fully reserved delinquent taxes; wrote off the remainder.
5. Transferred $50,000 to the special revenue fund.
6. Received $65,000 in cash for fees and licenses.
7. Received the inventories connected with purchase orders outstanding as of the end of fiscal 2012. The bill was $3,200.
8. Paid $8,000 to the capital projects fund, as a temporary loan.
9. Received $12,000 from the special revenue fund as partial repayment of a loan made in fiscal 2012.
10. Purchased inventories of $45,000 on account.
11. Made expenditures of $320,000 during the year. Purchase orders outstanding at year-end total $4,000.
12. Total accounts payable paid in fiscal 2012 amounted to $367,000. Included are amounts related to expenditures and inventory purchases.
13. Inventories on hand at year-end total $6,000.
14. Taxes uncollected at year-end are to be classified as delinquent and fully reserved.

Required

a. Prepare entries necessary at the beginning of the year to record the budget and make any other necessary adjustments or accruals.
b. Prepare entries necessary to record the events of the year and any year-end adjustments.
c. Prepare the necessary closing entries for June 30, 2013.
d. Present, in good form, the statement of revenues, expenditures and changes in fund balances for Montana County for fiscal 2013. Include a reconciliation of beginning and ending fund balances.
e. Present, in good form, the balance sheet for the general fund of Montana County for June 30, 2013.

REVIEW SOLUTIONS

Review 1 Solution
a. Capital projects fund
b. Agency fund
c. Enterprise fund
d. General fund, unless a designated capital projects fund makes such purchases
e. General fund for the revenues and transfer to the debt service fund; debt service fund for resources set aside for debt service
f. Debt service fund or general fund
g. Enterprise fund
h. Special revenue fund
i. Permanent fund

Review 2 Solution
a.

Estimated revenues	700,000	
Estimated other financing sources.	30,000	
Appropriations.		708,000
Estimated other financing uses		8,000
Fund balance—unassigned.		14,000

b. In addition to the above budget entry, the following entry made in 2013 to reverse last year's closing of outstanding encumbrances is also included in the $50,000 trial balance amount:

Encumbrances	1,200	
Fund balance—unassigned		1,200

December 31, 2012, fund balance—unassigned = $50,000 − $14,000 − $1,200 = $34,800

c.

Revenues—property taxes	300,000	
Revenues—sales taxes	380,000	
Proceeds of general obligation debt	12,000	
Proceeds from sale of capital assets	16,000	
Transfers in	4,000	
Fund balance—unassigned	18,000	
Estimated revenues		700,000
Estimated other financing sources		30,000
Appropriations	708,000	
Estimated other financing uses	8,000	
Expenditures		698,000
Transfers out		7,600
Encumbrances		1,000
Fund balance—unassigned		9,400

d.

EERIE COUNTY GENERAL FUND
Statement of Revenues, Expenditures, and Changes in Fund Balances
For Year Ended December 31, 2013

Revenues:		
Property taxes		$300,000
Sales taxes		380,000
Total revenues		680,000
Expenditures		(698,000)
Excess of revenues over (under) expenditures		(18,000)
Other financing sources (uses):		
Proceeds from general obligation debt	$12,000	
Proceeds from sale of capital assets	16,000	
Transfers in	4,000	
Transfers out	(7,600)	
Total other financing sources (uses)		24,400
Excess of revenues and other financing sources over expenditures and other financing uses		6,400
Fund balances, January 1, 2013		36,000*
Fund balances, December 31, 2013		$ 42,400**

* Fund balance—assigned	$ 1,200	
Fund balance—unassigned (from part *b*)	34,800	
Total fund balances, January 1, 2013	$ 36,000	
** Fund balance—assigned	$ 1,000	
Fund balance—unassigned	41,400	
Total fund balances, December 31, 2013	$ 42,400	

e.

EERIE COUNTY GENERAL FUND
Balance Sheet
December 31, 2013

Assets

Cash	$11,400
Property taxes receivable, net of $12,000 allowance	52,000
Due from other funds	3,000
Total assets	$66,400

Liabilities and fund balances

Liabilities

Accounts payable	$20,000
Due to other funds	4,000
Total liabilities	24,000

Fund balances

Assigned	1,000
Unassigned	41,400
Total fund balances	42,400
Total liabilities and fund balances	$66,400

11

State and Local Governments: Other Transactions

ALAMEDA COUNTY, CALIFORNIA
www.acgov.org

Alameda County, California is located on the east side of San Francisco Bay, and includes the cities of Oakland, Berkeley, Albany, Fremont, Livermore, Hayward and San Leandro. The University of California at Berkeley and California State University of the East Bay are located in the county, as well as the Oakland International Airport, Bay Area Rapid Transit System (BART), and the O.co Coliseum and Oracle Arena, home to Major League Baseball's Oakland Athletics, the NBA Golden State Warriors and the NFL Oakland Raiders.

Alameda County's 2010 CAFR reveals that the county completed and opened a new Castro Valley Library. It was awarded $16.9 million in stimulus funds for public protection and community development and $11 million to assist run-down neighborhoods and abandoned and foreclosed homes. It manages the Alameda County Medical Center, and provides flood control services. It also services general obligation and revenue bonds, has central transportation and printing facilities for county business, and runs an investment fund that consolidates investments on behalf of school and community college districts, courts, and other special districts.

How does Alameda County account for these activities? Do they use full or modified accrual accounting? What do the financial statements for these activities look like? This chapter answers these questions and others concerning transactions of state and local governments in other funds besides the general fund.

CHAPTER ORGANIZATION

Special purpose activities	Capital projects	Debt service	Proprietary activities	Fiduciary activities	Investments and other liabilities
• Special revenue funds • Permanent funds	• Basic transactions • Interactions with other funds • Financial statements	• Basic transactions • Interactions with other funds • Financial statements	• Enterprise funds • Internal service funds • Financial statements	• Trust funds • Agency funds • Financial statements	• Investments • Compensated absences • Landfills • Leases

Whereas Chapter 10 explained the accounting for general fund operating activities, this chapter discusses accounting and reporting for governmental funds other than the general fund, i.e. special revenue, capital projects, debt service, and permanent funds. The chapter also discusses activities reported in proprietary funds and fiduciary funds. Funds other than the general fund report specific government activities, such as construction of roads and buildings, services provided to citizens for a fee, and external funding of specific projects.

The first sections of this chapter cover reporting for governmental funds other than the general fund. Recall from Chapter 10 that *SGAS 54* specifies five standardized categories of fund balance for governmental funds: *nonspendable*, *restricted*, *committed*, *assigned*, and *unassigned*. Unassigned fund balance is usually only reported by the general fund. The fund balance of other governmental funds is divided between four categories, as appropriate.

- The **nonspendable** category includes inventories, prepaid expenses, and resources legally or contractually required to remain intact, such as endowment principal.

- The **restricted** category contains amounts that can only be used for specific purposes, as specified by *external grant providers, contributors, creditors, or by laws and regulations of the other governments* providing the funds.

- **Committed** fund balance includes resources that can only be used for specific purposes, as authorized by the *highest level of the reporting government*. For a school district, for example, this authority might come from the district board of directors. Committed fund balance also includes resources intended to fulfill contractual obligations.

- **Assigned** fund balance contains residual resources not designated as nonspendable, restricted or committed. These amounts are *intended* for the specific purpose, expressed by the government or its delegate, such as a finance committee. But if the residual is negative, it appears as **unassigned** fund deficit.

To determine the balances in each category, first identify the nonspendable amounts. When restricted and unrestricted resources are available for expenditure, apply the government's spending priority policy, specifying the order in which resources are used, to calculate restricted fund balance. For the remainder of fund balance, apply the government's spending priority policy for use of committed or assigned resources.

ACCOUNTING FOR SPECIAL PURPOSE ACTIVITIES

State and local governments often obtain resources *restricted* by external resource providers or *committed* by the highest authority in the government, to be used for specified purposes other than capital projects and debt service. Examples include a state gasoline tax raised to fund repairs and improvements in

LO1 Describe reporting for special purpose activities.

the state transportation system, a property tax levy to finance refuse collection, and federal grants given to states to pay for particular social services programs. Alameda County has a Property Development Fund for the sale and development of surplus County land, a Flood Control Fund for resources received and used for provision of flood control services, and a Fish and Game Fund to account for fines received and used for fish and wildlife conservation.

Special Revenue Funds

When restricted or committed resources must be used for *activities that benefit the government and/ or its citizens*, these resources are the *major ongoing revenue source* for these activities, and all the resources are *expendable*—available for expenditure—**special revenue funds** account for the collection and expenditure of these resources. The accounting for special revenue funds parallels that of the general fund, except that fund balance is restricted or committed, while the fund balance of the general fund can also be assigned and unassigned.

Suppose a county has a special revenue fund for flood control. The fund starts the year as follows:

Cash	$5,000,000	Fund balance—restricted	$2,000,000
		Fund balance—committed	3,000,000
Total assets	$5,000,000	Total fund balances	$5,000,000

Restricted fund balance is a state grant for flood control, and committed fund balance is amounts authorized by the highest level of county government for flood control.

During the year, expenditures for flood control are $4,000,000, and bills of $100,000 are unpaid at year-end. The county's policy is to spend restricted resources first. The flood control fund's year-end balance sheet appears below:

Cash	$1,100,000	Accounts payable	$100,000
		Fund balance—committed	1,000,000
Total assets	$1,100,000	Total liabilities and fund balance	$1,100,000

Permanent Funds

When resources are *nonexpendable*—expenditures are limited to investment income, and the principal remains intact—permanent funds account for the collection and expenditure of these resources. Permanent funds report income transactions separately from principal transactions. The principal part of the fund balance is *nonspendable*, and the income portion is *restricted* by the grantor or donor.

To illustrate the accounting for permanent funds, suppose that in fiscal 2013 a resident of Alameda County puts $1,000,000 in trust to support public library acquisitions. The trust specifies that income from trust investments be used to purchase books. A permanent fund is created to account for the activities of the trust, and the $1,000,000 is immediately invested. The Library Fund's entries follow:

Cash—principal	1,000,000	
Fund balance—nonspendable		1,000,000
To record receipt of library gift.		
Investments—principal	1,000,000	
Cash—principal		1,000,000
To record investment of library gift.		

During the year, investments earn $30,000 in cash interest, and the fund spends $25,000 for library acquisitions. Entries are:

Cash—income	30,000	
Investment income		30,000
To record earnings on investments.		
Expenditures	25,000	
Cash—income		25,000
To record library acquisitions.		

The closing entry for the Library Fund follows:

Investment income	30,000	
Expenditures		25,000
Fund balance—restricted		5,000
To close expenditures and income.		

In the permanent funds balance sheet, the fund balance distinguishes between nonspendable resources held in trust, and resources that are spendable but are restricted by the external resource provider for library acquisitions. Similarly, assets are reported as principal and income assets. The Library Fund's balance sheet appears in Exhibit 11.1.

EXHIBIT 11.1 Permanent Fund Balance Sheet

ALAMEDA COUNTY
Balance Sheet—Library Fund
June 30, 2013

Assets

Cash—income	$ 5,000
Investments—principal	1,000,000
Total assets	$1,005,000

Fund balances

Nonspendable	$1,000,000
Restricted	5,000
Total fund balances	$1,005,000

BUSINESS APPLICATION   Special Purpose Activities in State CAFRs

State and local governments report a wide array of funds for special purpose activities, reflecting their diverse environments and public concerns. Following is a sampling of the funds encountered in state Comprehensive Annual Financial Reports (CAFRs).

Special Revenue Funds

The **State of Louisiana** has a Video Draw Poker Device Fund which collects revenue from owner licenses and net device revenue. The fund supports district attorneys, governing authorities, and the Department of Public Safety and Corrections. Louisiana's Transportation Trust Fund collects money from fuel taxes to be used exclusively for highway construction and maintenance, flood control, state police traffic control, and other transportation-related programs. The **State of Mississippi**'s Rice and Soybean Promotion

continued

continued from prior page

Fund collects fees charged for the sale of rice and soybeans. Revenue is used to promote the rice and soybean industries, through research, education and advertising. The **State of Alaska**'s Exxon Valdez Oil Spill Restoration Fund reports on how the $50 million restitution received by the state has been used for restoration projects related to the oil spill. Alaska also has a Fishermen's Fund that uses commercial fishing license fees to pay for emergency medical treatment of commercial fishermen.

Permanent Funds

The **State of Michigan**'s Children's Trust Fund uses investment earnings to support programs for the prevention of child abuse and neglect in the state. The Michigan Natural Resources Trust Fund uses interest income to acquire land and develop public recreational facilities. The **Texas** Commission on the Arts Trust Funds support art education, economic development, and the well-being of communities. Texas also has a Permanent Health Fund for Higher Education that uses earnings on tobacco settlement monies for health care, tobacco education and enforcement. The **State of Alaska**'s Alaska Permanent Fund receives at least 25 percent of state mineral-related revenues. Resources are invested, and the income is distributed each year to qualified Alaskan citizens as their share of Alaska's natural resources. In 2011, the dividend was $1,174 per person.

ACCOUNTING FOR CAPITAL PROJECTS

LO2 Explain reporting for capital projects.

When a government acquires or constructs capital assets—land, buildings, equipment, or infrastructure such as sidewalks, sewers, roads, and bridges—reporting for these activities depends on the fund financing the asset.

The budget of a general or special revenue fund often includes appropriations for acquisitions of property and equipment, such as police cars and office equipment. Chapter 10 indicates that these funds report capital acquisitions as **capital outlays**, part of **expenditures.** For example, the entry to record the general fund's purchase of equipment costing $50,000 in cash is:

Books of General Fund

Capital outlay	50,000	
Cash		50,000
To record purchase of equipment.		

Acquisitions by a proprietary fund—enterprise or internal service fund—are recorded using normal business accounting. A cash acquisition of $350,000 in new golf carts by a municipal golf course is recorded as follows:

Books of Enterprise Fund

Equipment	350,000	
Cash		350,000
To record purchase of golf carts.		

If the golf carts are straight-line depreciated over five years with no salvage value, the entry to record yearly depreciation is:

Depreciation expense.	70,000	
Accumulated depreciation.		70,000
To record annual depreciation on golf carts.		

Capital Projects

A government often engages in large capital projects involving construction of buildings or infrastructure. The projects can be financed by general obligation or revenue bonds issued to fund the construction, tax assessments on benefitted property owners, federal or state capital grants, or by transfers from other funds. Unless the project relates to an enterprise or internal service fund, a **capital projects fund** accounts for resources restricted, committed or assigned for capital outlay expenditures.

A separate capital projects fund may be established for each project or each type of asset. In some cases the fund is temporary, originating when the project begins, and ending when the capital asset is completed. However, governments commonly establish continuing capital projects funds for ongoing construction of particular types of assets such as roads or bridges.

Because the budget for a capital project typically requires formal approval, budgetary accounts are often used. If the project is to be financed by general obligation bonds, cost of initial work may be covered by a temporary advance from another fund or by short-term financing known as **bond anticipation notes**—short-term loans from a bank or other financial institution. Issuance of the long-term bonds produces the resources to repay these temporary loans. Any bond proceeds not used for the project are used to pay principal and interest on the bonds. Even if the project is financed by multi-year property tax assessments, bonds typically provide up-front money to finance the project. Cash eventually collected from these assessments repays bond principal and interest. The chart below lists major sources and uses of cash for capital projects funds.

Capital Projects Fund Cash Flows	
Sources of Cash	**Uses of Cash**
Bond anticipation notes	Construction costs
Bond proceeds	Repayment of advances
Grants	Repayment of bond anticipation notes
Advances or transfers from other funds	Investments
Investment proceeds	Transfers to other funds

Accounting for the Capital Projects Fund

Assume that in fiscal 2014 Alameda County decides to build a new addition to its main library, and accounts for the project in its Library Facilities capital projects fund. The expected $15,000,000 total cost of the project is to be funded by a $10,000,000 state grant and general obligation bonds of $5,000,000. The state grant and the bonds represent external restrictions on Library Facilities resources, and therefore the entire fund balance of this capital projects fund is *restricted*.

Budget Entry   Whether a budget entry is recorded depends on applicable local laws and regulations. If a budget entry is recorded, it appears as:

Books of Capital Projects Fund

Bonds authorized—unissued.	5,000,000	
Estimated revenues—state grant.	10,000,000	
Appropriations.		15,000,000
To record approval of library addition project.		

Bonds authorized—unissued and *estimated revenues—state grant* signify the resources budgeted for the project, similar to estimated revenues in the general fund.

Revenue Recognition   Capital projects funds typically recognize awarded grants as revenue, since collection is reasonably assured. The entry to record the grant revenue is:

Books of Capital Projects Fund

State grant receivable	10,000,000	
State grant revenue		10,000,000
To record state grant awarded but not yet received.		

Temporary Financing   Initial resources for the project might be temporarily advanced from another fund to allow work to begin before issuing the bonds. We record a $500,000 advance from the general fund as follows:

Books of Capital Projects Fund

Cash	500,000	
Due to general fund		500,000
To record temporary advance from the general fund.		

Books of General Fund

Due from capital projects fund	500,000	
Cash		500,000
To record temporary advance to the capital projects fund.		

Issuance of Bonds   When bonds finance a construction project, the proceeds must at least equal the amount budgeted. Therefore, the coupon rate on the bonds is typically at or above the interest rate demanded by investors, to ensure that the bond issue provides enough financing for the project. Legal provisions prescribe the use of any premium on a bond issue. The premium cannot be used on project construction costs, since the total cost of construction was previously authorized and cannot be increased unless approved by the same level of authority. The premium is typically applied toward paying the principal and interest on the bonds, and is therefore transferred to the debt service fund.

    Assume bonds used to finance the library addition have a coupon rate of 5 percent and are issued at 102. The premium is to be transferred to the debt service fund for future payment of principal and interest.

Books of Capital Projects Fund

Cash	5,100,000	
Bond proceeds		5,000,000
Due to debt service fund		100,000
To record issuance of $5,000,000 face value bonds for $5,100,000.		

Bond proceeds appear as *other financing sources* on the capital project fund's statement of revenues, expenditures, and changes in fund balances. The following entries record transfer of the premium to the debt service fund.

Books of Capital Projects Fund

Due to debt service fund	100,000	
Cash		100,000
To record transfer of premium to the debt service fund.		

Books of Debt Service Fund

Cash...	100,000	
Transfers in		100,000
To record receipt of bond premium from capital projects fund.		

The capital projects fund could also record the premium as *other financing sources*, and its transmittal to the debt service fund as *transfers out*.

Partial Collection of Grant; Repayment of Advance The County receives half of the $10,000,000 state grant, and repays the advance from the general fund, as follows:

Books of Capital Projects Fund

Cash...	5,000,000	
State grant receivable		5,000,000
To record receipt of half of the state grant.		
Due to general fund	500,000	
Cash		500,000
To record repayment of advance from general fund.		

Books of General Fund

Cash...	500,000	
Due from capital projects fund		500,000
To record repayment of advance to capital projects fund.		

Investment of Excess Cash Governments often temporarily invest bond proceeds and other resources not yet needed to fund construction. State laws typically restrict investments to U.S. Treasury or similar low-risk instruments. Laws also restrict the use of interest earned on such investments. Interest earned on temporary investments is typically used to offset future debt service payments.

Suppose that $2,000,000 is invested, and $60,000 of interest is earned and received for the year. State law requires such interest to be used for future debt service.

Books of Capital Projects Fund

Investments	2,000,000	
Cash		2,000,000
To record investment of excess cash.		
Cash...	60,000	
Interest income		60,000
To record interest on investments.		
Transfers out	60,000	
Cash		60,000
To record transfer of interest to debt service fund.		

Books of Debt Service Fund

Cash...	60,000	
Transfers in		60,000
To record transfer from capital projects fund.		

Awarding the Contract After the County receives bids for construction of the library addition, it awards a contract for $13,000,000 to the qualified low bidder. This constitutes an encumbrance, recorded as:

Books of Capital Projects Fund

Encumbrances	13,000,000	
Fund balance—restricted		13,000,000
To record award of contract for construction of library addition.		

Expenditure Recognition; Partial Payment Construction contracts are usually paid as stages of construction are completed, and often provide for withholding a portion of each billing until the entire project is completed and passes inspection. Known as **retainage**, this provision helps protect against failure of the contractor to complete the project or against deficiencies that need to be remedied.

Assume receipt of $4,000,000 in invoices, representing partial completion of the encumbered construction contract, and that the contract provides for a 10 percent retainage. Entries for payment are:

Books of Capital Projects Fund

Fund balance—restricted.	4,000,000	
Encumbrances.		4,000,000
To reverse encumbrances for amount billed by contractor.		
Expenditures	4,000,000	
Contracts payable.		3,600,000
Contracts payable—retainage.		400,000
To record billing from contractor.		
Contracts payable	3,600,000	
Cash		3,600,000
To record payment to the contractor.		

Year-End Closing Entries When the fiscal year ends on June 30, 2014, the County makes these closing entries:

Books of Capital Projects Fund

State grant revenue	10,000,000	
Bond proceeds.	5,000,000	
Interest income.	60,000	
Bonds authorized—unissued		5,000,000
Estimated revenues—state grant		10,000,000
Fund balance—restricted		60,000
To close actual against budgeted revenues and other financing sources.		
Appropriations	15,000,000	
Expenditures		4,000,000
Encumbrances.		9,000,000
Transfers out		60,000
Fund balance—restricted		1,940,000
To close actual expenditures, encumbrances and transfers against appropriations.		

Financial statements of the Library Facilities capital projects fund at June 30, 2014, appear in Exhibit 11.2. There are no other library facilities projects currently in process.

EXHIBIT 11.2   Financial Statements of Alameda County Capital Projects Fund

ALAMEDA COUNTY
Capital Projects Fund—Library Facilities
Statement of Revenues, Expenditures, and Changes in Fund Balances
For Year Ended June 30, 2014

Revenues	
State grant revenue	$10,000,000
Interest income	60,000
Total revenues	10,060,000
Expenditures	
Contract expenditures	(4,000,000)
Excess of revenues over expenditures	6,060,000
Other financing sources (uses)	
Bond proceeds	5,000,000
Transfers out	(60,000)
Total other financing sources (uses)	4,940,000
Excess of revenues and other financing sources over expenditures and other financing uses	11,000,000
Fund balance, June 30, 2013	0
Fund balance, June 30, 2014	$11,000,000

ALAMEDA COUNTY
Capital Projects Fund—Library Facilities
Balance Sheet
June 30, 2014

Assets		Liabilities and fund balances	
Cash	$ 4,400,000	Contracts payable—retainage	$ 400,000
Investments	2,000,000	Fund balance—restricted	11,000,000
State grant receivable	5,000,000		
Total assets	$11,400,000	Total liabilities and fund balances	$11,400,000

Completion of the Project
Because the budget for the entire project is usually established at the outset, at the beginning of fiscal 2015 we reestablish any carryover encumbrances and appropriations:

Books of Capital Projects Fund

Encumbrances	9,000,000	
Fund balance—restricted		9,000,000
To restore encumbrances closed at prior year-end.		
Fund balance—restricted	11,000,000	
Appropriations		11,000,000
To restore unspent appropriations for the year.		

Assume the contractor completes the library addition and it passes inspection. The County makes all contracted payments and receives the remainder of the state grant. An additional $1,500,000 is paid for items not previously encumbered. Investments are liquidated without earning additional interest. The following entries record these events:

Books of Capital Projects Fund

Cash.	5,000,000	
State grant receivable		5,000,000
To record receipt of remainder of the state grant.		
Cash.	2,000,000	
Investments.		2,000,000
To record liquidation of investments.		
Fund balance—restricted.	9,000,000	
Encumbrances.		9,000,000
To record reversal of encumbrances.		
Expenditures	10,500,000	
Contracts payable—retainage	400,000	
Cash		10,900,000
To record remaining expenditures and payments under contract, plus additional expenditures.		

The $500,000 cash balance remaining after completion of the project represents unspent bond proceeds. State law requires transfer of that balance to the debt service fund to pay principal and interest on the bonds:

Books of Capital Projects Fund

Transfers out	500,000	
Cash		500,000
To record transfer of unspent bond proceeds to debt service fund.		

Books of Debt Service Fund

Cash.	500,000	
Transfers in		500,000
To record receipt of unspent bond proceeds from capital projects fund.		

The following entry closes the Library Facilities fund:

Appropriations	11,000,000	
Expenditures		10,500,000
Transfers out		500,000
To close expenditures and transfers out against appropriations.		

ACCOUNTING FOR GENERAL OBLIGATION DEBT

LO3 Describe reporting for debt service.

Treatment of long-term debt in the fund financial statements depends on the source of cash used for repayment, the fund making the payment, and the fund incurring the debt. Debt of *proprietary funds* is reported as a *liability of the fund itself*, and interest and principal payments follow business accounting procedures. Fiduciary funds typically do not issue long-term debt. Transactions involving general obligation debt—debt for which the government is liable and which is used to finance general operations or capital projects—are usually reported in two funds: the fund that receives the proceeds, and a *debt service fund* that services the debt. Debt proceeds increase the fund balance of the fund receiving the proceeds—usually the capital projects fund or the general fund. A **debt service fund** accounts for resources that are restricted, committed or assigned for payment of principal and interest on general obligation debt.

When *special assessment* construction activities are financed by debt for which only the affected property owners are liable, the periodic assessments are recorded as both assets and liabilities in an *agency fund*. The asset represents current amounts receivable from the property owners, and the liability represents current amounts due to the bondholders. Collection of assessments is recorded as a debit to cash and a credit to receivables. Payment to the bondholders is recorded as a debit to the liability and a credit to cash. A summary of the treatment of debt in the various funds statements appears below.

Long-term debt incurred by	Where liability is recorded	Source of resources to repay debt	Debt payment made from
General, special revenue, capital projects funds	Not recorded	General fund budget Special tax levies Bond premium Unspent bond proceeds	Debt service fund
Enterprise, internal service funds	Specific enterprise or internal service fund	Revenues from operations	Specific fund
Special assessment construction activities:			
Government liable for debt	Not recorded	Assessments on property owners	Debt service fund
Government not liable for debt	Not recorded	Assessments on property owners	Agency fund

General Obligation Debt

Funding for interest and principal payments on general obligation debt comes primarily from the general fund, or from special tax levies for debt payment. We saw earlier that some resources for general obligation debt payment are provided by bond premiums and unspent appropriations on capital projects. The chart below lists major sources and uses of cash in the debt service fund.

Debt Service Fund Cash Flows	
Sources of Cash	**Uses of Cash**
Budgeted transfers from general fund	Current payments of interest and principal on general
Transfers from special revenue fund (special tax levies for debt service)	obligation debt
Transfers from capital projects fund (bond premium, unspent bond proceeds, investment earnings)	Investment for future principal and interest payments
Special assessments	
Investment earnings	
Liquidation of investments	

Accounting for the Debt Service Fund

Governments often record a budget for estimated revenues and appropriations in the accounts of the debt service fund, even though the budget usually results from managerial design rather than from a legal approval process. The modified accrual basis of accounting precludes accounting and budgeting for accrued interest on long-term debt. Instead, appropriations include only interest due in the current year. A debt service fund may be used for either *serial bonds* or *term bonds*.

Serial bonds generally mature in equal annual installments over the life of the bond issue so that interest payments, and some principal payments, are made annually according to a predetermined schedule. Budgeted resource inflows are recorded as **estimated revenues** or **estimated financing sources**.

Because these budgeted resource inflows normally equal the appropriations for interest and principal payments, the annual budget is typically balanced.

In contrast, **term bonds** mature at the end of the bond issue. Although only interest on term bonds is paid currently, sufficient resources must be available in the debt service fund to repay the principal of the bonds on their maturity date. When the debt service fund serves as a *sinking fund* for term bonds, the annual budget calls for the periodic inflows needed to fund current interest payments and future principal retirement. We use two estimated revenue accounts: **required additions** indicate the transfers needed from the appropriate funds; **required earnings** reflect the estimated income from debt service fund investments.

When the debt service fund accumulates resources for future repayment of term bonds, annual appropriations differ from annual estimated revenues. During years in which resources are accumulated toward future principal payments, appropriations are less than estimated revenues. When an accumulation is expended in later years, appropriations exceed estimated revenues.

Illustration of Accounting for Term Bonds   Suppose that in fiscal 2014 Alameda County establishes a debt service fund to make annual interest payments on the 5 percent, $5,000,000 general obligation bond issue to finance the library addition, and to accumulate resources for the future retirement of principal. The highest level of County government has authorized that all resources in the debt service fund be used for principal and interest payments. Therefore the entire debt service fund balance is *committed*. Although the annual amount needed to fund principal retirement is frequently determined actuarially, we assume that an annual general fund transfer of $500,000 to the debt service fund suffices. Investment income for the year is estimated at $27,000. With the only planned expenditure being the $250,000 interest payment on the bonds, here is the budget entry for the debt service fund:

Required additions.	500,000	
Required earnings	27,000	
Appropriations.		250,000
Fund balance—committed		277,000
To record debt service fund budget.		

Assume that early in the year the debt service fund receives the $500,000 transfer from the general fund and immediately invests the cash received in interest-bearing securities.

Cash.	500,000	
Transfers in		500,000
To record transfer from general fund.		
Investments	500,000	
Cash		500,000
To record investments.		

Later in the year, the bond interest payment is made. To get the needed cash, securities that cost $240,000 are sold for $250,000:

Cash.	250,000	
Investments.		240,000
Gains on investments		10,000
To record sale of securities.		
Debt service—interest	250,000	
Cash		250,000
To record payment of bond interest.		

At year-end, interest income accrued on the investments is $15,000, and $160,000 is transferred in from the capital projects fund:

Investments	15,000	
Interest income		15,000
To record earnings accrued on investments.		
Cash	160,000	
Transfers in		160,000
To record cash transferred from capital projects fund.		

Because the modified accrual method precludes the debt service fund from accruing interest on long-term debt, there is no year-end adjusting entry for the bond interest accrued since the last payment date. Assuming that the fair values of investments equal their cost at year-end, closing entries for the debt service fund at June 30, 2014, are:

Transfers in	660,000	
Gains on investments	10,000	
Interest income	15,000	
Required additions		500,000
Required earnings		27,000
Fund balance—committed		158,000
To close actual against budgeted revenues and other financing sources.		
Appropriations	250,000	
Debt service—interest		250,000
To close actual expenditures against appropriations.		

The financial statements for the debt service fund appear in Exhibit 11.3.

EXHIBIT 11.3 Financial Statements of Alameda County's Debt Service Fund

ALAMEDA COUNTY
Debt Service Fund
Statement of Revenues, Expenditures, and Changes in Fund Balances
For Year Ended June 30, 2014

Revenues	
Gains on investments	$ 10,000
Interest income	15,000
Total revenues	25,000
Expenditures	
Debt service—interest	(250,000)
Excess of revenues over (under) expenditures	(225,000)
Other financing sources (uses)	
Transfers in	660,000
Excess of revenues and other financing sources over (under) expenditures	435,000
Fund balance, June 30, 2013	0
Fund balance, June 30, 2014	$435,000

ALAMEDA COUNTY
Debt Service Fund
Balance Sheet
June 30, 2014

Assets		Fund balance	
Cash	$160,000	Fund balance—committed	$435,000
Investments	275,000		
Total assets	$435,000	Total fund balance	$435,000

Had *serial bonds* been issued instead of term bonds, the annual budget provides only for interest due and principal amount to be retired this fiscal year. Unless the bond indenture requires that the debt service fund also have a cash reserve to protect the bondholders, the budget is balanced. Account titles such as required additions and required earnings are not used, and no investments are purchased.

Interaction with Other Funds   Below are the entries made by other funds to record the above events.

Books of General Fund

Transfers out	500,000	
Cash		500,000
To record transfer of appropriated contribution to debt service fund.		

Books of Capital Projects Fund

Due to debt service fund	100,000	
Cash		100,000
To transfer premium on bonds issued to debt service fund.		
Transfers out	60,000	
Cash		60,000
To record transfer of interest income on investments to debt service fund.		

Special Assessment Debt   A government may finance some projects, such as water or sewer improvements, by assessing only those property owners that directly benefit. The project is financed by *special assessment debt*, and assessments on the property owners provide resources for debt service. When the government has no liability for the debt, an agency fund accounts for debt service transactions.

When the government is obligated for special assessment debt in case of default by the property owners, the debt is reported like any other general obligation debt. A capital projects fund reports proceeds from debt issuance, and a debt service fund accounts for the assessments and debt payments.

Reporting Perspective

When interest rates decline, governments find they can reduce interest costs by refunding their outstanding debt. If the existing debt cannot be immediately called, governments issue new debt at the lower interest rate and invest the proceeds until the old debt can be called. Under federal law, if the interest on these investments exceeds the interest paid on the new debt, the tax exempt status of the debt may be revoked. Governments may use the lower cost debt to pay off the old high-cost debt, but not to earn a higher market return. Any excess must be remitted to the U.S. Treasury. So if the new bonds carry an interest rate of 4 percent, temporary investment of bond money can only yield 4 percent or less. In the last two decades the IRS and SEC have charged some investment bankers with using a tactic called **yield burning** to inflate their profits at the expense of the government. Yield burning occurs when investment bankers purchase higher yield investments and resell them to governments at inflated prices, thereby reducing their yield to the level restricted by law. The higher price "burns away" the excess yield, and the investment banker pockets the difference. The IRS, SEC, and other governmental agencies investigated several large Wall Street firms, including **Merrill Lynch** (now part of **Bank of America**), **Lehman Brothers Inc.** (now no longer in existence), **Morgan Stanley Co. Inc.** and **Credit Suisse First Boston Corp.** for alleged yield-burning activities, resulting in millions of dollars in fines.

BUSINESS APPLICATION Tobacco Settlement Reporting

In the late 1990s, the major tobacco companies agreed to pay each of the states billions of dollars in compensation for tobacco-related health care costs. The annual payments vary with industry sales and profitability, and are made in perpetuity. Counties within each state receive a share of this settlement. The states and municipalities were expected to use these resources for medical care and health education. Because most governments could not wait for the yearly payments, they issued bonds to generate immediate resources, secured by revenues generated from the tobacco companies. This financial arrangement is another form of **securitization**, discussed in Chapter 3. Although many governments use their tobacco settlement money for health-related expenditures or for educating citizens about the dangers of smoking, others use these resources for unrelated purposes, such as closing budget deficits and building roads.

Tobacco settlement money is generally reported in special revenue, capital projects, and debt service funds. For example, **Alameda County, CA** uses a capital projects fund to report settlement money that finances construction of health care facilities. **Erie County, NY** reports activities funded with tobacco settlement money in both special revenue and capital projects funds. Both counties have separate debt service funds for the debt service connected with tobacco settlement bonds.

REVIEW 1 ● Capital Projects and Debt Service Fund Transactions and Financial Statements

Following are selected transactions of the **Town of Letchworth, NY**, during 2013 (its accounting year ends December 31):

1. A capital projects fund is established for the construction of a new garage for the highway department at an estimated cost of $5,000,000. The following sources provide funding: general obligation bond issue, $4,000,000, and state government grant, $1,000,000.
2. The general obligation bond issue yields a total of $4,100,000. The premium is transferred to the debt service fund for eventual payment of bond principal and interest.
3. The state government pays $900,000 on the grant.
4. A contract for $4,750,000 is awarded to the qualified low bidder.
5. Invoices of $2,300,000 are paid, less a 20% retainage.
6. The town makes $100,000 in interest and $40,000 in principal payments on the bonds, using a general fund transfer of $140,000.

Assume that capital project and debt service fund resources are *restricted*.

Required

For both the capital projects fund and the debt service fund,

a. Prepare journal entries to record the above events. Include the budget entry, entries made during the year, and closing entries.
b. Prepare the statement of revenues, expenditures, and changes in fund balances for 2013.
c. Prepare the balance sheet as of December 31, 2013.

Solutions are located after the chapter assignments.

ACCOUNTING FOR PROPRIETARY ACTIVITIES

Proprietary funds report government activities that provide goods or services in return for a fee. Like business reporting, the emphasis in proprietary funds is on measuring income, financial position, and cash flows.

LO4 Account for proprietary activities.

Enterprise funds account for provision of goods or services *to the general public*, including:

- Utilities—municipal water, gas, and electricity
- Sanitation—sewer systems and landfills
- Recreational facilities—golf courses, marinas, swimming pools, stadiums
- Lotteries
- Commercial facilities—airports, ports, and farmers' markets
- Transportation facilities—buses, rapid transit, parking and toll bridges
- Public hospitals and health clinics
- Public housing projects
- Public colleges

In addition to user charges, these activities are often subsidized by general governmental revenues. The principal source of revenue usually determines whether an enterprise fund or the general fund is used. If user charges provide most of the activity's revenue, the activity is accounted for in an enterprise fund; otherwise, the general fund is used.

Internal service funds account for provision of goods or services by *one department or agency of the government to another*, on a cost reimbursement basis. Centralized service functions are the most common examples, including such activities as:

- Maintenance and repair services
- Vehicle pool and transportation services
- Supply facilities
- Print shop
- Computing and information services

Centralizing such activities enables cost savings to be realized through more efficient use of equipment, volume purchasing, and other economies of scale. The internal service fund pays the cost of operating the central service facility and sets user charges to produce sufficient revenues to recover costs and to perpetuate the facility's activities.

Accounting for Enterprise and Internal Service Funds

Because enterprise and internal service funds use business accounting, revenues and expenses (*not* expenditures), including depreciation, are recognized using the full accrual basis. Enterprise and internal service funds account for their own capital assets and long-term debt, and often issue **revenue bonds** secured by the enterprise fund's operating revenues.

Statement of Net Position   The fund financial statements of enterprise and internal service funds follow those of business firms. The balance sheet, also called the **statement of net position**, has the same accounts and structure as a business balance sheet. Because proprietary funds have no capital stock and no stockholders, "equity" becomes "net position" that is displayed in three categories:

- Net investment in capital assets
- Restricted
- Unrestricted

The balance for "net investment in capital assets" is derived this way:

Cost of capital assets
Less accumulated depreciation—capital assets
Less outstanding principal of related debt
Net investment in capital assets

The *related debt* includes only those debt proceeds invested in capital assets. Suppose a county parking division issued $10 million in bonds for a construction project, but only spent $2 million to date for construction. Net investment in capital assets includes only the $2 million invested in capital assets, net of $2 million in debt, or a net amount of zero.

Restricted net position is subject to external or governmental restrictions. Suppose a state government provides resources to a county recreation facility, for development of exercise programs. The county itself may impose legal spending restrictions on the fund's assets. For example, **Mecklenburg County, NC**'s Solid Waste enterprise fund reports net position restricted for landfill development and postclosure care.

Statement of Revenues, Expenses and Changes in Net Position Proprietary funds prepare the operating statement using full accrual accounting. The statement has the following categories:

- Operating revenues and expenses
- Nonoperating revenues and expenses
- Capital contributions and transfers

The **State of Missouri** reports the activities of its state lottery in an enterprise fund. Its operating statement for fiscal 2010 appears in Exhibit 11.4. Prior to 2012, a proprietary fund's net position was called "net assets."

EXHIBIT 11.4 Missouri State Lottery Enterprise Fund Operating Statement

STATE OF MISSOURI
Statement of Revenues, Expenses, and Changes in Net Assets
State Lottery
For Fiscal Year Ended June 30, 2010

(in thousands)

Operating revenues:	
Sales	$971,915
Operating expenses:	
Cost of goods sold	16,107
Personal service	9,946
Operations	61,750
Prizes expense	628,058
Depreciation and other charges	9,013
Total operating expenses	724,874
Operating income	247,041
Non-operating revenues (expenses):	
Net increase in the fair value of investments	1,113
Interest	310
Disposal of capital assets and miscellaneous	12,276
Total non-operating revenues (expenses)	13,699
Income (loss) before transfers	260,740
Transfers in	46
Transfers out	(259,722)
Change in net assets	1,064
Total net assets—beginning	10,033
Total net assets—ending	$ 11,097

Similar to many state lotteries, Missouri's state lottery transfers to the State's general fund a large portion of its excess of revenues over expenses—almost $260 million in 2010—to support elementary and secondary education.

Statement of Cash Flows Per *SGAS 9* and *SGAS 34*, the proprietary funds statement of cash flows reports the following categories:

- Cash flows from operating activities, presented using the direct method
- Cash flows from noncapital financing activities
- Cash flows from capital and related financing activities
- Cash flows from investing activities

The investing and financing cash flow classifications differ considerably from the classifications found on a statement of cash flows for a business. The items included in each category are summarized below.

> **Cash flows from operating activities**
>   Cash received from sales of goods and services
>   Cash paid to suppliers, employees, etc. to provide goods and services
>   Cash paid for other operating costs
> **Cash flows from noncapital financing activities**
>   Borrowings, repayment of borrowings and interest, and operating grants or transfers
>   from other funds, for *other than* acquisition or improvement of capital assets
> **Cash flows from capital and related financing activities**
>   Borrowings, grants, special assessment levies, and other inflows, and repayment
>   of debt and interest, related to acquisition of capital assets
>   Payments to acquire capital assets
> **Cash flows from investing activities**
>   Purchase and sale of investments in equity and debt instruments
>   Interest and dividends received in cash

Similar to requirements for businesses, a reconciliation of operating income to cash from operating activities is required. However, *SGAS 34* requires the direct method of reporting operating cash flows, whereas businesses can use either the indirect or direct method, and most businesses use the indirect approach.

Alameda County reports the activities of its motor pool in an internal service fund. Its statement of cash flows for fiscal 2010 appears in Exhibit 11.5.

EXHIBIT 11.5   Alameda County Internal Service Fund Statement of Cash Flows

COUNTY OF ALAMEDA, CALIFORNIA
Statement of Cash Flows
Motor Pool
For Year Ended June 30, 2010

(in thousands)

Cash flows from operating activities	
Receipts from customers (including other funds)	$8,841
Payments to suppliers	(4,687)
Payments to employees	(1,648)
Payments to other funds	(755)
Net cash provided by operating activities	1,751
Cash flows from noncapital financing activities	
Transfers in	43
Cash flows from capital and related financing activities	
Acquisition of capital assets	(1,990)
Proceeds from sale of capital assets	166
Net cash used in capital and related financing activities	(1,824)
Cash flows from investing activities	
Interest on investments	39
Net increase (decrease) in cash and cash equivalents	9
Cash and cash equivalents—beginning	7,215
Cash and cash equivalents—ending	$7,224
Reconciliation of operating income (loss) to net cash provided by operating activities:	
Operating income (loss)	$ (303)
Depreciation	2,010
Change in receivables	(78)
Change in accounts payable	114
Change in compensated employee absences payable	8
Total adjustments	2,054
Net cash provided by operating activities	$1,751

BUSINESS APPLICATION   Proprietary Activities in State CAFRs

A sampling of enterprise and internal service funds reported in state CAFRs provides insight into the variety of business-type activities among the states.

Enterprise Funds

The **State of Hawaii** reports the following enterprise funds: the Department of Transportation-Airports Division, and the Department of Transportation-Harbors Division. The airports fund accounts for the operation of the state airports. The harbors fund supports water transportation, harbor operations, preservation of ocean shores and navigational safety. The **State of Texas** has a Texas Prepaid Tuition Plans enterprise fund which allows Texas families to lock in college costs at today's prices. **Alaska**'s Commercial Fishing Revolving Loan Fund supports the development and continued maintenance of commercial fishing gear and vessels. The Historical District Revolving Loan Fund supports restoration of buildings within an historical district. **California**'s State University Dormitory Building Maintenance and Equipment Fund accounts for student charges for housing, parking, and health services, and for revenue bond proceeds used to construct or acquire dormitories. The **State of Maine** has a State Ferry Service Fund that accounts for the operation of ferry services between the mainland and various islands.

Internal Service Funds

The **State of Georgia** has an internal service fund to account for management of state office buildings and maintenance of the Governor's Mansion and State Capitol grounds. **Michigan**'s Correctional Industries Revolving Fund reports on manufacturing and processing activities employing inmates of the State's correctional institutions. **Maine** has a Statewide Radio & Network System Fund that reports the activities of a radio and network system used by state agencies.

REVIEW 2   •   Enterprise Fund Transactions and Financial Statements

A county water utility has the following post-closing trial balance at December 31, 2013 (its accounting year ends each December 31):

	Debit	Credit
Cash.	$ 40,000	
Accounts receivable, net	75,000	
Supplies	3,500	
Capital assets.	120,000	
Accumulated depreciation		$ 62,000
Accounts payable.		10,000
Bonds payable		80,000
Net investment in capital assets		38,000
Unrestricted net position		48,500
Totals	$238,500	$238,500

Information for 2014:

1. The utility sent out water bills of $450,000 and collected $460,000.
2. Purchased supplies of $50,000; the ending inventory of supplies is $3,000.
3. Acquired capital assets of $25,000 for cash; depreciation expense was $4,000.
4. Incurred out-of-pocket operating expenses of $395,000.
5. The ending accounts payable balance was $15,000.
6. Bond interest of $3,200 and principal of $5,000 were paid in cash.

Required

a. Prepare journal entries to record the events of 2014, including adjusting and closing entries.
b. Prepare the operating statement and statement of cash flows for 2014, in good form.
c. Prepare the statement of net position at December 31, 2014.

Solutions are located after the chapter assignments.

ACCOUNTING FOR FIDUCIARY ACTIVITIES

LO5 Account for fiduciary activities.

Fiduciary funds report financial activities where the government acts as a trustee or agent for others. Assets may *not* be used to support the government's programs. Fiduciary funds consist of two distinct elements: *trust funds* and *agency funds*. Although both involve resources collected, held, paid out, and/or managed by the government acting as a fiduciary for individuals and organizations outside the reporting government, the purpose and duration of fiduciary responsibility of the two fund types differ. Trust and agency funds use full accrual accounting, with some exceptions.

SGAS 34 specifies the following three types of **trust funds**:

- **Pension and other employee benefit trust funds** account for health insurance, pension, and other benefits to government employees.

- **Investment trust funds** account for investment pools where other governments invest excess cash on a short-term basis to earn additional income.

- **Private-purpose trust funds** account for all other trusts not benefitting the public in general. A common private-purpose trust fund reports unclaimed assets from abandoned bank accounts.

Agency funds report activities where the government acts in an *agency* capacity, collecting resources and remitting them to individuals or organizations outside the government. The two most common situations involving agency funds are employee deductions and tax collections. Deductions for federal and state taxes, health insurance, retirement contributions, union dues, and payroll savings are withheld from employees and periodically remitted to appropriate entities. Some states collect income taxes or sales taxes on behalf of a city or county. A county may collect property taxes on behalf of other legal entities—cities, towns, or special districts—within its jurisdiction.

Agency funds are also used to account for the *financing of special assessment activities* when the government itself has no liability for related debt. For example, a township issues bonds to finance the building of a road in a rural area. The property owners are liable for principal and interest payments on the bonds. The county collects assessments from the property owners and remits them to the bondholders, using an agency fund to report the collections and payments.

Accounting for Trust and Agency Funds

Accounting for the three types of trust funds is similar to the accounting for permanent funds, discussed earlier in this chapter. Full accrual accounting is used. The most common form of trust fund is the **pension trust fund**; its revenues include resources from the government, employees, and earnings on investments, and the majority of its expenses are in the form of retirement benefits.

Transactions in most agency funds fall into two categories: *collection* and *payment*. A **collection transaction** entry requires a debit to cash and a credit to an appropriate liability account; a **payment transaction** entry requires a debit to the liability and a credit to cash. Because these transactions use cash to create or settle liabilities, an agency fund has no revenues and expenses, and no net asset balance. Instead, it has offsetting assets and liabilities. Even fees charged by an agency fund as a collector of taxes for several jurisdictions are not revenue to the agency fund. Such fees are deducted from amounts due to the other jurisdictions and are recorded as liabilities due to the general fund of the government operating the agency fund.

Special Assessment Financing in an Agency Fund

Special assessment construction activities often require bonds to be issued to provide up-front cash needed for construction. The bonds are then serviced and retired over time as the special assessment money is collected periodically from the property owners.

Suppose a township decides to install new streetlights in a certain area. A ten-year 6 percent serial bond issue totaling $1,000,000 provides cash for construction. Residents in the affected area will be assessed $1,318,000 over ten years to retire the bonds and pay interest on the outstanding bonds, for which the government has no liability. The bonds are secured by commercial and residential buildings where the streetlights are located.

The serial bonds mature at the rate of $100,000 per year. Each year the assessments collected will be used to pay the $100,000 principal of the bonds maturing and the current year's interest on the outstanding bonds. Because the township has no liability for the bonds, an agency fund accounts for transactions related to the financing and the assessments. If the township has primary or residual liability for the bonds, a debt service fund accounts for the financing and assessment transactions.

The first year's assessments levied on the property owners are $160,000, which the township records in an agency fund. We assume uncollectible assessments are negligible; if estimated uncollectible amounts are significant, they are netted against the recorded asset and liability.

Assessments receivable—current	160,000	
Due to special assessment creditors		160,000
To record levy of special assessments.		

The year's assessments are collected, and used to pay the $100,000 of principal and $60,000 (= 0.06 × $1,000,000) of interest.

Cash	160,000	
Assessments receivable—current		160,000
To record collection of current assessments.		
Due to special assessment creditors	160,000	
Cash		160,000
To record payment of $100,000 of principal and $60,000 of interest.		

At the beginning of the next year, the second year's assessments are recorded. In this year, $154,000 is needed to retire $100,000 in bond principal and pay interest of $54,000 [= 0.06 × ($1,000,000 − $100,000)] on the $900,000 of bonds still outstanding.

Assessments receivable—current	154,000	
Due to special assessment creditors		154,000
To record the second year's assessments.		

The township makes similar sets of entries each year until all assessments are collected and all bondholders are paid. The agency fund records only the *current* portion of assessments receivable each period. Recording future assessments would create a reported liability for the full amount of the debt, which contradicts the fact that the government is not liable for any of the debt.

Financial Statements for Fiduciary Funds   *SGAS 34* as amended by *SGAS 63* requires that fiduciary fund activities be reported in a **statement of changes in fiduciary net position** and a **statement of fiduciary net position**. Because agency funds have no revenue and expenditure transactions, and no net position, agency fund activities are not reported in the statement of changes in fiduciary net position; only trust fund activities are reported in this statement. Trust fund net position is generally reported in total for each fund type.

If assets are held in an agency capacity pending distribution to *other funds within the government*, those assets are reported in the funds for which the assets are held, and not in a separate agency fund. Fiduciary funds only report on resources held for individuals or organizations *outside the reporting government*.

Alameda County reports each of the four fiduciary fund types—pension trust, investment trust, private purpose trust, and agency funds. Its investment trust fund accounts for investments made on behalf of external school and community college districts, courts, and other special districts. The private purpose trust fund reports management of assets belonging to conservatees of the County. Agency funds account for resources held in custody for others, including disputed property taxes receivable, payroll deductions, and federal and state funds to be distributed to local agencies. Summarized financial statements for Alameda County's fiduciary funds are in Exhibits 11.6 and 11.7. Prior to 2012, fiduciary fund net position was called "net assets."

EXHIBIT 11.6   Alameda County Statement of Changes in Fiduciary Net Assets

COUNTY OF ALAMEDA, CALIFORNIA
Statement of Changes in Fiduciary Net Assets
For Year Ended June 30, 2010

(in thousands)	Pension and Other Employee Benefit Trust Funds	Investment Trust Fund	Private Purpose Trust Fund
Additions:			
Employer and employee contributions.	$ 213,670	$ —	$ —
Contributions to pooled investments	—	7,610,471	3,465
Total contributions	213,670	7,610,471	3,465
Investment income:			
Interest and dividends	111,881	10,109	104
Net change in fair value of investments	852,129	(361)	(6)
Real estate, securities lending income.	33,613	—	—
Total investment income	997,623	9,658	98
Less investment expenses	33,961	—	—
Net investment income.	963,662	9,658	98
Miscellaneous income	2,272	—	—
Total additions, net	1,179,604	7,620,129	3,563
Deductions:			
Benefit payments	288,773	—	—
Refunds of contributions	7,718	—	—
Administration expenses	12,255	—	—
Distribution of pooled investments.	—	7,386,008	3,679
Total deductions.	308,746	7,386,008	3,679
Change in net assets	870,858	234,121	(116)
Net assets—beginning.	3,807,447	1,338,271	15,829
Net assets—ending	$4,678,305	$1,572,392	$15,713

EXHIBIT 11.7   Alameda County Statement of Fiduciary Net Assets

COUNTY OF ALAMEDA, CALIFORNIA
Statement of Fiduciary Net Assets
June 30, 2010

(in thousands)	Pension and Other Employee Benefit Trust Funds	Investment Trust Fund	Private Purpose Trust Fund	Agency Funds
Assets:				
Cash and investments	$5,248,168	$1,617,803	$15,701	$246,786
Taxes receivable.	—	—	—	277,499
Interest and other receivable	33,357	2,304	23	161
Prepaid expenses.	—	3,661	—	—
Capital assets, net of depreciation.	3,222	—	—	—
Total assets	5,284,747	1,623,768	15,724	524,446
Liabilities:				
Accounts payable, accrued expenses	18,451	51,376	11	689
Securities lending obligation	587,991	—	—	—
Due to other governmental units	—	—	—	523,757
Total liabilities.	606,442	51,376	11	524,446
Net assets:				
Held in trust for pension.	4,006,823	—	—	
Held in trust for postemployment medical benefits.	596,576	—	—	
Held in trust for other postemployment benefits.	73,481	—	—	
Held in trust for other employee benefit trust . . .	1,425	—	—	
Held in trust for other purposes	—	1,572,392	15,713	
Total net assets held in trust	$4,678,305	$1,572,392	$15,713	

ACCOUNTING FOR INVESTMENTS

A government typically invests liquid assets on either a short-term or long-term basis. Amounts accumulated in the debt service fund for payment of term bond principal can be invested for several years. Bond proceeds for construction of capital assets can be temporarily invested by the capital projects fund. Permanent funds invest principal and use the income for specified activities benefitting the public. Trust funds, especially pension trust funds, typically invest in a variety of low-risk investments. The government can invest individually, or may combine resources with other governments in the form of an investment pool. State and local governments place legal restrictions on the types of investments made with governmental resources. Usually investments are restricted to low-risk securities such as obligations of the U.S. or state government, and highly rated commercial paper.

LO6 Explain reporting for investments, compensated absences, land-fills, and leases.

SGAS 31, Accounting and Financial Reporting for Certain Investments and for External Investment Pools, specifies that investments in debt or equity securities, mutual funds, external investment pools, options, warrants, and stock rights be reported at *fair value*. If a market price is not available, discounted cash flow or other estimation methods are used to determine fair value. *SGAS 31* applies to governmental, proprietary, and fiduciary funds. Investments appear on the fund's balance sheet or statement of net position.

Investment income and changes in the fair value of investments appear as revenue in the fund's operating statement—the statement of revenues, expenditures, and changes in fund balances for governmental funds, the statement of revenues, expenses, and changes in net position for proprietary funds, or the statement of changes in net position for fiduciary funds. Alameda County's operating statement for fiduciary funds, Exhibit 11.6, reports that in fiscal 2010, the fair value of investments increased for the pension and other employee benefit trust funds, but decreased for the investment and private purpose trust funds.

Cases of poor investment management by governments have unfortunately been too common in the past. For example, in the early 1990s, **Orange County, California** ran a $20 billion investment pool which invested on behalf of 187 California municipalities. The County and its investment pool filed for bankruptcy court protection when the pool lost $1.7 billion on risky derivatives investments. In 2002, the Florida state pension system lost $335 million on its investment in **Enron** stock. From 2008 to 2011 **Jefferson County, Alabama** was on the brink of bankruptcy in part due to ill-conceived investments in interest rate swaps. Jefferson County finally declared bankruptcy in late 2011. *SGAS 31*'s fair value requirements allow more timely assessment of the financial condition of a government, since the financial effects of poor investment decisions are reported as values decline.

Derivatives Investments

Governments are subject to many of the same financial risks as businesses. A government that plans to purchase a commodity in the future takes the risk that commodity prices will increase. A government that issues variable rate debt takes the risk that interest rates will increase. Governments may hedge these risks using derivative instruments such as forwards, futures, options or swaps. We discuss the reporting for derivative instruments used by businesses in Chapter 9. *SGAS 53*, Accounting and Financial Reporting for Derivative Instruments, provides the reporting standards for derivatives used by governments. This section focuses on reporting investments in derivatives in the fund statements. Chapter 12 discusses reporting for investments in derivative instruments in the Comprehensive Annual Financial Report.

Derivatives differ from other investments because governments enter a derivatives agreement with little or no investment, and they can be settled early. A government may enter a futures contract fixing the price of wheat purchased in 120 days at $6 per bushel. The contract requires no initial investment, and the government may settle the contract at any time within the next 60 days by selling wheat at the current futures price. Suppose that after 30 days the government decides to settle the contract, when the 90-day futures price is $6.50 per bushel. The government receives a net payment of $0.50 per bushel by buying at $6.00 per bushel, per the futures contract, and selling at the market price of $6.50 per bushel.

SGAS 53 requires that derivatives be reported at *fair value* in a fund's *accrual-based* statement of net position. Unlike other investments, *this standard does not apply to governmental funds*, which use the modified accrual basis. *SGAS 53* divides derivatives into two types:

- A derivative used to generate income is reported using *SGAS 31* standards. Changes in fair value are reported on the fund's operating statement.

- Changes in the fair value of a derivative used as a *hedge investment* must be *deferred* on the fund's statement of net position.

In order to qualify as a hedge investment, the derivative's terms must match the terms of the hedged item and be effective in hedging the risk. A government issues 3-year variable rate bonds with a par value of $100 million. To hedge the risk that interest rates will rise, the government enters a 3-year receive variable/pay fixed interest rate swap with a notional value of $100 million, where a counterparty pays the government the variable interest it needs to pay its bondholders, and the government pays the counterparty a fixed rate. The swap hedges the government's interest rate risk by changing the variable rate to a fixed rate, and its terms match the terms of the government's debt.

Because governments commonly use interest rate swaps to hedge their interest rate risk on variable rate debt, we illustrate the hedge accounting requirements of *SGAS 53* using a receive variable/pay fixed interest rate swap. On July 1, 2012, Orleans County's enterprise fund issues 3-year $100,000,000 face value variable rate bonds, with interest paid annually on June 30, the end of the accounting year. The variable rate for fiscal 2013 is 5 percent. The County enters an interest rate swap, where the counterparty pays the County the variable interest it requires to pay its bondholders, and the County pays the counterparty 4 percent on a notional amount of $100,000,000. There is no initial investment and the swap has no value at inception. Orleans County's enterprise fund records the events of fiscal 2013 as follows:

2012			
July 1	Cash..	100,000,000	
	Bonds payable......................................		100,000,000
	To record issuance of variable rate bonds.		
2013			
June 30	Interest expense—bonds...................................	5,000,000	
	Interest expense—counterparty		1,000,000
	Cash		4,000,000
	To record interest payments.		

Suppose the fair value of the swap rises from zero on July 1, 2012 to $2,800,000 on June 30, 2013. Because the swap qualifies as a hedge, the change in fair value is *deferred* on the proprietary fund's statement of net position:

2013			
June 30	Investment in swap	2,800,000	
	Deferred gain/loss on swap..............................		2,800,000
	To report the change in swap fair value and report the swap at fair value.		

The variable rate falls to 3 percent for fiscal 2014, and the fair value of the swap falls to $1,200,000. These entries report the events of fiscal 2014:

2014			
June 30	Interest expense—bonds...................................	3,000,000	
	Interest expense—counterparty...............................	1,000,000	
	Cash		4,000,000
	To record interest payments.		
	Deferred gain/loss on swap	1,600,000	
	Investment in swap		1,600,000
	To report the change in swap fair value.		

The variable rate falls to 2.5 percent for fiscal 2015, and the swap expires and has no value on June 30, 2015:

2015			
June 30	Interest expense—bonds...................................	2,500,000	
	Interest expense—counterparty.............................	1,500,000	
	Cash		4,000,000
	To record interest payments.		
	Deferred gain/loss on swap.................................	1,200,000	
	Investment in swap.....................................		1,200,000
	To report the change in swap fair value.		

If the swap is settled early or no longer qualifies for hedge accounting, any deferred gains or losses are reclassified as investment income or loss in the operating statement.

Hedge accounting provides current year-end information by reporting derivative investments at fair value on the fund's statement of net position. However, the unrealized changes in fair value do not impact the fund's bottom line. Businesses report these value changes in other comprehensive income, and therefore avoid impacting income. Governments do not report other comprehensive income, but the deferred accounts on the statement of net position achieve the same result.

Because *SGAS 53* and other recent standards and proposals require the use of "deferred" accounts, the GASB issued *SGAS 63* to address proper display of these balances. Chapter 12 discusses the requirements of this standard.

ACCOUNTING FOR OTHER LIABILITIES

Like most organizations, governments engage in transactions and activities resulting in future payment obligations. Reporting for these activities differs significantly depending on whether the affected fund uses full or modified accrual accounting. We describe here the accounting and reporting for three common examples: compensated absences, landfill operations, and leases.

Compensated Absences

Governments offer various benefits to employees, such as vacation pay, paid holidays, and sick pay. When these costs are paid in the period earned, no particular reporting issues arise. In many cases, however, the benefits are paid in future periods. *SGAS 16* provides the reporting requirements for compensated absences.

Accounting and Reporting in Proprietary Funds *SGAS 16* requires that proprietary funds recognize the liability for compensated absences as incurred, when employees perform the services on which the benefits are based. However, if the benefit depends on a future event, or on future services provided by the employee, no liability is recognized. Most sick leave is therefore not accrued, since payment of this benefit depends on the health of the employee, an unknown future event. Assume that for proprietary funds administrative employees, the year's estimated liability for compensated absences is $2,500,000. This entry accrues the expense and liability:

Administrative expense	2,500,000	
Liability—compensated absences		2,500,000
To record estimated compensated absences related to employee services performed this year.		

Subsequent benefit payments reduce the liability.

Accounting and Reporting in Governmental Funds Because governmental funds use modified accrual accounting, only compensated absences expected to be paid with current financial resources are accrued in the current period. Although the entry is the same as for proprietary funds, the amount is likely much lower because the amount accrued is only that portion of the total benefits earned to be paid with current resources. Remaining benefits are reported as expenditures when actually paid.

Landfill Operations

Governments often operate landfill sites for the disposal of refuse. Although current operating activities pose no particular reporting issues, the U.S. Environmental Protection Agency established specific closure requirements for landfills that carry significant future costs. *SGAS 18* contains the reporting requirements for landfills.

Landfill costs include current operating costs and estimated costs of closure and postclosure care. Costs of closure include equipment and facilities acquired at or near the date of closure, plus costs of capping the landfill. Postclosure care includes mandated monitoring and maintenance costs.

Accounting and Reporting in Proprietary Funds When a proprietary fund accounts for the landfill, it allocates the estimated current cost of future closure and postclosure care to each period of landfill operation, based on usage. This approach is similar to the "units of production" depreciation method. Suppose the estimated current cost of closure and postclosure care is $20,000,000, $3,000,000 was reported in previous periods, and the landfill is 40% filled. Closure and postclosure costs recognized this period are $5,000,000 [= ($20,000,000 × 0.4) − $3,000,000], as follows:

Expense—landfill closure and postclosure care	5,000,000	
Liability—landfill closure and postclosure care.		5,000,000
To record the current year's allocation of future closure and postclosure		
care costs.		

As actual closure and postclosure care costs are incurred, they are charged against the estimated liability. Proprietary funds also report expenditures for capital assets acquired for this purpose as reductions in the liability—which includes their estimated cost—and do not capitalize the assets.

Changes in estimates of future costs are handled prospectively as just described if the landfill is still in operation. Changes in estimates occurring after the landfill has closed are reported as current year costs, as they cannot be allocated over future periods.

Accounting and Reporting in Governmental Funds When a governmental fund accounts for the landfill, it reports only costs requiring current financial resources in the current year. Since estimated closure and postclosure care costs are not incurred until the landfill closes, governmental funds do not report these costs while the landfill is in operation. The estimated future liability connected with the landfill does not appear in the governmental funds financial statements.

• •

BUSINESS APPLICATION **Compensated Absences and Landfill Liabilities**

Mecklenburg County, NC accounts for the operations of its landfill in a proprietary fund. The liabilities section of the fund's 2010 balance sheet reports $129,598 in current and $390,802 in long-term compensated absence liabilities related to landfill employees. Landfill development and postclosure care costs of $8,374,290 are listed as long-term liabilities. Current expenses include $40,088 in final closure and postclosure costs. There is no separate listing for compensated absences on the balance sheet or operating statement of Mecklenburg County's governmental funds. The County reports a liability for vacation pay/sick leave in the governmental funds balance sheet "only if the benefit has matured, for example, as a result of employee resignations and retirements." Mecklenburg County pays terminated employees one fourth of their unused sick leave. *Source:* Mecklenburg County June 30, 2010, CAFR.

• •

Accounting for Leased Assets

Governments often enter into lease agreements for the use of long-term assets such as buildings and equipment. The proper accounting for leases depends on whether the lease is a *capital* or *operating lease* and whether the affected fund uses full or modified accrual accounting. State and local governments follow the provisions of *ASC Topic 840* concerning lease classification, which consider the lease agreement to be a capital lease when its terms transfer substantially all of the risks and benefits of ownership to the lessee. Proprietary funds use full accrual accounting for capital leases.

The following example illustrates general fund reporting for leases, using modified accrual accounting. Suppose that on January 1, 2014, Alameda County's general fund agrees to lease equipment for five years under these terms: $500,000 is due at the lease signing, and payments of $500,000 per year are due at the end of each of the next four years. The lease agreement reflects an implicit interest rate of 5 percent.

If the lease qualifies as a **capital lease**, the general fund records the lease as follows:

2014			
Jan. 1	Expenditures—capitalized leases	2,273,000	
	Other financing sources—capitalized leases		2,273,000
	To record the signing of the lease; $2,273,000 is the present value of the lease payments at 5 percent.		
	Expenditures—principal	500,000	
	Cash		500,000
	To record initial payment on the capital lease.		

The first entry records both expenditures and other financing sources at the present value of the lease payments. The rationale is that if the lease is a capital lease, it should be recorded as the purchase of a capital asset financed with debt. Thus, the government reports the amount borrowed as an other financing source, and the asset purchase as an expenditure. The payment at the end of 2014 is recorded as follows:

2014			
Dec. 31	Expenditures—principal	411,350	
	Expenditures—interest	88,650	
	Cash		500,000
	To record the lease payment. The outstanding debt during 2012 is $1,773,000 (= $2,273,000 − $500,000) and the interest portion of the payment is $88,650 (= 5% × $1,773,000).		

If the lease qualifies as an **operating lease**, the general fund treats the lease payments as rent. Each $500,000 lease payment is recorded as follows:

Expenditures—rent	500,000	
Cash		500,000
To record the operating lease payment.		

REVIEW OF KEY CONCEPTS

Describe reporting for special purpose activities. (p. 439) Resources collected and legally restricted for a particular purpose that benefits the public are reported in **special revenue** or **permanent funds**. A special revenue fund is used if the resources are **expendable**, and a permanent fund is used if the collected resources are **nonexpendable** but the income is expendable.   **LO 1**

Explain reporting for capital projects. (p. 442) **Construction activities** or major asset acquisitions are accounted for in the **capital projects fund**. Typical transactions include temporary financing, collection of debt proceeds, expenditures for construction, temporary investments, and transfers to other funds. Capital projects funds use modified accrual accounting.   **LO 2**

Describe reporting for debt service. (p. 448) The **debt service fund** accumulates resources and uses them for payment of principal and interest on **general obligation debt**. The debt service fund for **term bonds** typically also engages in investment activities. Debt service funds use modified accrual accounting.   **LO 3**

LO 4   **Account for proprietary activities. (p. 453)** **Enterprise funds** account for the provision of goods or services to the public, in return for a fee. **Internal service funds** are used when the goods or services are provided to other departments or agencies within the government. Proprietary funds use full accrual accounting.

LO 5   **Account for fiduciary activities. (p. 458)** **Fiduciary funds** consist of **pension and other employee benefit trusts, investment trusts, private purpose trusts,** and **agency funds,** and report on activities related to individuals and entities outside the government.

LO 6   **Explain reporting for investments, compensated absences, landfills, and leases. (p. 463)** **Investments** by state or local governments are reported at **fair market value,** with income and realized and unrealized gains and losses reported in the fund's operating statement. Changes in the value of derivative investments used by proprietary or fiduciary funds to hedge financial risk appear as deferred gains and losses on the fund's statement of net position. Estimated liabilities for **compensated absences** and **future closure and postclosure costs of landfills** are recognized in proprietary funds statements. These liabilities are recognized in governmental funds only if they will be paid with current financial resources. **Leases** are classified as **capital** or **operating** leases following the requirements of *ASC Topic 840*. At inception, governmental funds report capital leases as expenditures and other financing sources, at the present value of the lease payments. Subsequent capital lease payments are reported as principal and interest expenditures.

MULTIPLE CHOICE QUESTIONS ···

LO 1   **1.** A county receives $10,000,000 from a private foundation. The foundation requires that the county maintain the principal of this endowment, and income from its investment must be used to maintain county parks. The county reports activities related to this endowment in a permanent fund. During the year, the county invests the $10,000,000, earns investment income of $300,000, and spends $280,000 on park maintenance. At year-end, how does the permanent fund report fund balance?

   a. Nonspendable $10,000,000 and restricted $20,000
   b. Restricted $10,000,000 and committed $20,000
   c. Restricted $10,000,000 and assigned $20,000
   d. Nonspendable $10,000,000 and assigned $20,000

LO 1   **2.** A county receives $10,000,000 from a private foundation. The foundation specifies that the $10,000,000 must be used for county park maintenance. The county reports activities related to this contribution in a special revenue fund. During the year, the county spends $1,000,000 on park maintenance. At year-end, how does the special revenue fund report fund balance?

   a. Nonspendable $10,000,000 and restricted $(1,000,000)
   b. Restricted $10,000,000 and assigned $(1,000,000)
   c. Restricted $9,000,000
   d. Committed $9,000,000

LO 2   **3.** A county capital projects fund receives resources of $8,000,000 from a bond issue and a state grant of $15,000,000, to build an administration building. Both funding sources are externally restricted to the capital project. During the year contracts are signed for $20,000,000. Contractors submit bills for $5,000,000 and the county pays $4,000,000. At year-end, how does the capital projects fund report fund balance?

   a. Restricted $4,000,000, committed $15,000,000
   b. Restricted 3,000,000, committed $15,000,000
   c. Restricted $18,000,000
   d. Restricted $19,000,000

LO 2   **4.** A capital projects fund buys equipment for $4,000,000. The equipment has a 4-year estimated life, straight-line, no residual value. The equipment is sold after 3 years for $200,000. Which statement is *true* regarding the effect on the capital project fund's operating statement in the year the equipment is sold?

   a. $800,000 loss is reported in the nonoperating section.
   b. $200,000 proceeds are reported as other financing sources.
   c. $800,000 loss is reported as other financing uses.
   d. $200,000 proceeds are reported in the revenues section.

5. Which statement below is *false* concerning the reporting for bond issues in the fund statements of a   **LO 3**
    government?

    a. Proceeds from bonds issued to finance capital projects are reported as other financing sources in the capital projects fund operating statement.
    b. Payments of principal and interest on bonds issued by an enterprise fund are accounted for using a debt service fund.
    c. Payments of principal on general obligation bonds are reported as expenditures in the debt service fund operating statement.
    d. The principal of bonds issued to finance capital projects of an internal service fund is reported as a liability on the internal service fund's balance sheet.

6. The debt service fund makes a $10,000,000 payment on the principal of general obligation long-term debt.   **LO 3**
    How is this reported on the financial statements of the debt service fund?

    a. Expenditure on the statement of revenues, expenditures and changes in fund balances
    b. Expenditure on the statement of revenues, expenditures and changes in fund balances, and long-term debt on the balance sheet will be lower
    c. Long-term debt on the balance sheet will be lower
    d. Outflow of cash for financing on the statement of cash flows, and long-term debt on the balance sheet will be lower

7. An enterprise fund buys equipment for $4,000,000. The equipment has a 4-year estimated life, straight-line,   **LO 4**
    no residual value. The equipment is sold after 3 years for $200,000. Which statement is *true* regarding the reporting for the sale in the enterprise fund's operating statement?

    a. $800,000 loss is reported in the nonoperating section.
    b. $200,000 proceeds are reported as other financing sources.
    c. $800,000 loss is reported as other financing uses.
    d. $200,000 proceeds are reported in the revenues section.

8. The net position section of the proprietary funds statement of net position is divided into which three   **LO 4**
    categories?

    a. Unrestricted; temporarily restricted; permanently restricted
    b. Operating; nonoperating; restricted
    c. Reserved; assigned; unreserved
    d. Net investment in capital assets; restricted; unrestricted

9. Agency funds do not appear in the statement of changes in fiduciary net position because   **LO 5**

    a. agency funds are not fiduciary funds.
    b. they do not report on activities related to services to regular citizens.
    c. they are not major funds.
    d. agency funds have no net position.

10. A sales tax is shared 50-50 between the county and the state. Businesses pay the county the full amount of the   **LO 5**
    tax, and the county distributes half of the tax to the state. The county reports activities regarding the state's share of the sales tax in an agency fund. During 2013, the county collects $2,750,000 in sales taxes that belong to the state, and distributes $2,500,000 to the state. How are these activities reported by the county's agency fund?

    a. Revenues of $2,750,000 and expenditures of $2,500,000
    b. Net liability decrease of $250,000
    c. Liability increase of $2,750,000 and expenditures of $2,500,000
    d. Net liability increase of $250,000

11. At the beginning of the fiscal year, a general fund leases property. The lease qualifies as a capital lease. At the   **LO 6**
    time the lease is initiated, the present value of the future lease payments is $3,000,000. The lease agreement reflects an implicit interest rate of 4 percent. The first payment of $500,000 is made at the end of the fiscal year. On its operating statement for the year, the general fund reports

    a. other financing sources of $3,000,000 and a capital outlay expenditure of $500,000.
    b. a capital outlay expenditure of $500,000.
    c. a capital outlay expenditure of $3,000,000 and other financing sources of $3,000,000, an expenditure for interest of $120,000, and an expenditure for principal of $380,000.
    d. an expenditure for interest of $120,000.

LO 6 **12.** Landfill operations may be reported in a governmental fund or a proprietary fund. Assume an operating land-fill is estimated to be 40% filled. Total expected future costs of closure and postclosure care are estimated at $5,000,000. Which statement below is *true*?

a. If the landfill is reported in a governmental fund, the total liability for future closure and postclosure costs is reported at $2,000,000.

b. If the landfill is reported in a governmental fund, the total liability for future closure and postclosure costs is reported at zero.

c. If the landfill is reported in a proprietary fund, and previously reported closure and postclosure costs are $1,000,000, the total liability for future closure and postclosure costs is reported at $3,000,000.

d. If the landfill is reported in a proprietary fund, the total liability for future closure and postclosure costs is reported at zero.

**Assignments with the ⊘ in the margin are available in an online homework system.
See the Preface of the book for details.**

EXERCISES ••

⊘ LO 1 **E11.1** **Permanent Fund Transactions** In March 2013, a resident of Randall City died, leaving her entire estate to the Randall City School District. The will specified that proceeds from the liquidation of her estate are to be invested, and investment income used to provide scholarships for needy high school students. Three students were to be selected each year by the school superintendent. At the date of the donor's death, the fair market value of the estate was estimated to be $1,030,000. When liquidated in December, the estate realized $1,050,000. Administrative costs of the estate in 2013 were $40,000. The net proceeds were then transferred to the school district and were invested in appropriate securities. In 2014, income from investments was $70,000. Administrative costs (all related to income) were $2,500. The first scholarships were awarded in 2014 for a total of $50,000. The investments are worth $1,040,000 at the end of 2014.

Required
Record the events described above in a permanent fund. Include closing entries.

LO 2 **E11.2** **Capital Project Transactions** On January 14, 2014, the city of Westport authorized a $900,000 bond issue for the purchase of a building to be used as a community center. On May 3, the bonds were issued at par, and on June 1, the building was purchased and paid for. On November 1, the general fund paid the semiannual interest of $18,000 on the bonds.

Required
Record all necessary entries in the capital projects fund and the general fund for the above information. State where each account is reported in the fund financial statements.

⊘ LO 2 **E11.3** **Capital Project Transactions** The **City of Portsmouth, VA** authorized construction of a new po-lice station on February 1, 2014. The $15,000,000 project will be financed by a bond issue to be sold in March 2014. The City's fiscal year ends June 30. The following events occurred in fiscal 2014:

**CITY OF
PORTSMOUTH, VA**

• February 10: The general fund advanced $100,000 to the capital projects fund to finance initial project planning.

• March 1: $80,000 was paid for initial planning.

• March 15: The bonds were issued at 101. The excess cash received was remitted to the debt service fund. The advance from the general fund was paid.

• March 20: The contract was awarded for $14,000,000.

• June 10: The contractors submitted bills for $8,000,000. The city applied its 10% retainage policy, and paid the net amount owed.

Assume all capital projects resources are restricted.

Required

a. Record all necessary entries in the capital projects fund for the above information, including closing entries.

b. Assuming this is the only project reported in the capital projects fund, prepare its statement of revenues, expenditures, and changes in fund balances and ending balance sheet for fiscal 2014.

E11.4 **Capital Project Calculations** The town of Kaley recently completed construction of a recreational   LO 2
facility which was accounted for in a capital projects fund. Bonds were issued at the onset of the project
to finance construction. Legal constraints prevented use of the $800,000 premium on the bonds toward
construction costs. The premium has not yet been transferred to the debt service fund. Temporary investments of bond proceeds yielded a 3% return, or $2,424,000. Kaley awarded the construction contract for
the facility to the lowest bidder. The contract called for a 15% retainage. Kaley's books show $11,550,000
due the contractor pending final inspection. All other amounts due the contractor have been remitted. Assume interest on temporary investments remains in the capital projects fund.

Required

a. What was the face value of the bonds issued?
b. What was the amount of the contract awarded?
c. What was the original authorization for the project?
d. What is the total fund balance of the capital projects fund after closing entries?

E11.5 **Adequacy of Capital Project Authorization** The Board of Supervisors of Hanover Township   LO 2
authorized construction of a $10,000,000 community center. The township will contribute $1,000,000
from general fund revenues and bonds will be issued for the rest. Construction activities will last about
eighteen months. The project is reviewed after six months when the construction manager indicates that
the project is 41% complete and the township's $1,000,000 contribution was made. At that time, the fol-
lowing data from the capital projects fund are presented.

Cash—construction	$1,500,000
Short-term investments	5,000,000
Cash—debt service	150,000
Construction in progress	4,500,000
Bonds payable	9,000,000
Bond anticipation notes payable	1,000,000
Encumbrances (balance of construction contract)	6,500,000

Required

a. At what amount were the bonds apparently issued?
b. Calculate the apparent potential cost overrun.
c. Identify the items above that are improperly reported in the capital projects fund.

E11.6 **Debt Service Fund Transactions** The Town of Canterbury accounts for debt service related to   LO 3 ✅
its $25,000,000 face value, 5% general obligation term bonds, issued October 1, 2013, in a debt service
fund. The Town's accounting year ends on September 30. Interest on the bonds is due each March 31 and
September 30. The following events occur in fiscal 2014:

1. The debt service fund budget called for $3,250,000 in transfers from the general fund, $65,000 in
income on investments, and appropriations for the two semiannual interest payments.
2. The general fund transferred $3,250,000 to the debt service fund on November 15. The debt service
fund invested the cash.
3. The debt service fund liquidated investments costing $580,000 and made the March 31 interest pay-
ment.
4. The debt service fund liquidated investments costing $600,000 and made the September 30 interest
payment.
5. Investment income for the year, received in cash, was $68,000.
6. At September 30, 2014, the debt service fund's investments had a fair value of $2,060,000.

Assume that all debt service fund resources are committed.

Required

a. Prepare the journal entries to record the above events in the debt service fund. Include necessary
closing entries.
b. Prepare the debt service fund's statement of revenues, expenditures, and changes in fund balances
and the year-end balance sheet for fiscal 2014.

E11.7 **Debt Service Fund Irregularities** A debt service fund's condensed trial balance at December 31,   LO 3
2014 shows the following:

	Dr (Cr)
Cash.	$1,000,000
Due from water utility (an enterprise fund).	200,000
Short-term investments	9,000,000
Estimated revenues	8,000,000
Expenditures	200,000
Interest payable	(200,000)
Water utility bonds payable	(8,000,000)
Appropriations	(200,000)
Fund balance—committed.	(7,800,000)
Contributions from property owners	(2,200,000)
Total	$ 0

The water utility bonds were issued on July 1, 2014, and pay 5 percent interest annually on June 30. The contributions from property owners represent the proceeds from special assessment debt for which the government has no liability.

Required

Identify the apparent irregularities in the above debt service fund trial balance and suggest corrective action for them.

✔ LO 4 **E11.8** **Internal Service Fund Financial Statements** At the beginning of fiscal year 2014, the City of Wooster established a central supplies storehouse to service its several funds. The general fund contributed $25,000,000 (nonrefundable) to aid in the establishment of the supplies storehouse. It was agreed that the storehouse would charge other funds for the purchase price of supplies plus 20 percent. During the year, the storehouse purchased $20,000,000 of supplies, paid operating expenses of $2,000,000, and billed other funds for $19,200,000. All accounts are settled except $1,500,000 remaining to be collected from the general fund for supplies billed.

Required

a. Prepare the statement of revenues, expenses, and changes in net position for fiscal 2014, and the statement of net position at the end of fiscal 2014 for the central supplies storehouse.

b. State any effects of the transactions on the financial statements of the general fund of Wooster. Assume the general fund bought supplies for $12,000,000, consumed $11,700,000 of supplies, uses the purchases method, and supplies balances are significant.

LO 4 **E11.9** **Enterprise Fund Profitability Analysis** Below are summary data for the first two years of operation of an enterprise fund prepared under modified accrual accounting and business (accrual) accounting.

(in thousands)	Modified Accrual Accounting		Business Accounting	
	Year 2	**Year 1**	**Year 2**	**Year 1**
Revenues	$1,100	$1,000	$1,300	$1,150
Expenditures/Expenses	4,000	3,500	1,000	900
Total assets	320	300	3,550	3,050
Fund balance/Net position.	(3,400)	(500)	2,550	2,250

Required

a. For both the modified accrual and accrual accounting data, perform a basic profitability analysis for Year 2 using the "DuPont Analysis" shown below.

$$\text{Return on assets} = \text{Return on sales} \times \text{Total assets turnover}$$

$$\frac{\text{Income}}{\text{Average total assets}} = \frac{\text{Income}}{\text{Sales}} \times \frac{\text{Revenue}}{\text{Average total assets}}$$

b. Which basis of accounting better reflects the profitability of the enterprise fund during Year 2? To what do you attribute the differences?

E11.10 Special Assessment Project   After discussions with property owners in **San Antonio's King William Historic District**, City Council authorized installation of a large number of particularly elegant and tasteful street lights in the district. Total cost of the project is $3,300,000. Council will contribute $300,000 and ten-year term bonds will be issued to fund construction of the project. San Antonio can issue bonds paying 6 percent annually at par. The principal and interest will be repaid in ten equal annual assessments paid by the property owners in the historic district. Because each annual assessment exceeds the interest due on the bonds, the excess is invested at 6 percent to retire the principal.

LO 3

SAN ANTONIO'S KING WILLIAM HISTORIC DISTRICT

Required

a.   Calculate the amount of the total annual assessment needed to pay the annual interest for ten years and retire the bonds.
b.   Assume the government is liable for the bonds. Prepare the fund journal entries and identify the funds affected when the bonds are issued, the assessments are levied, the first assessment is collected, and the first interest payment is made.
c.   Repeat b. assuming the government has *no* liability for the bonds.

E11.11 Capital Asset Transactions   The city of Jeffersonville acquired the following capital assets in 2013:

LO 2

1.   Snow removal equipment was purchased by the general fund at a cost of $1,000,000.
2.   A used delivery van was purchased by the internal service fund at a cost of $25,000.
3.   A building was purchased for $2,000,000 by the capital projects fund to serve as a youth center. The purchase was financed by a 20-year bond issue.
4.   Pool equipment was purchased for $800,000 by the community center enterprise fund. The purchase was financed by a bank loan.

Required

Prepare the entries needed to record the above transactions. For each entry, indicate the fund in which the entry is recorded, and how the asset, and liability if appropriate, are reported in the fund's balance sheet.

E11.12 Lease Transactions   On July 1, 2013, **Alameda County** leased equipment, agreeing to pay $400,000 at the start of the lease, and make five annual payments of $400,000 per year on June 30 of each subsequent year. The lease carries an interest rate of 4%. The county's fiscal year ends June 30, and the equipment is reported in the general fund.

LO 6 ✅

ALAMEDA COUNTY, CALIFORNIA

Required

a.   Assume the lease qualifies as a capital lease. Prepare the entries to record the lease agreement and payments on July 1, 2013, June 30, 2014, and June 30, 2015.
b.   Assume the lease qualifies as an operating lease. Repeat the requirements in part a.
c.   Comment on the difference in total expenditures recognized under the two lease accounting methods.

PROGRAMS ••

PROBLEMS ••

P11.1 Special Revenue Fund   In 2013, Grand City established a special revenue fund to account for acquisitions of wildlife by the city zoo. Financing for the project includes:

LO 1

Federal grant	$ 900,000
General fund transfers	900,000
Total	$1,800,000

During 2013, the following occurred:
1.   Cash from the general fund and federal grant was received as scheduled.
2.   Investments are purchased for $320,000 in cash.
3.   Contracts for $1,750,000 for the acquisition of wildlife were signed. Animals, reptiles, and birds were delivered, and Grand City was billed for $1,750,000.
4.   Investments yielded $18,000 in revenues. The investments were liquidated at cost.
5.   Bills remaining to be paid at year-end totaled $80,000.
6.   Any remaining resources were reclassified for future transfer to the general fund.

The federal grant resources are restricted, while the general fund transfers and investment income are committed resources. City policy is to spend restricted resources first. The special revenue fund does not use budgetary accounts.

Required

a. Prepare all 2013 journal entries and closing entries for the special revenue fund.
b. Prepare the balance sheet for the special revenue fund as of December 31, 2013.

LO 1 **P11.2** **Reporting for Endowment** Warren County, Ohio maintains the Scheurer-Smith Trust Fund to report restricted private contributions where the earnings are earmarked to provide education to residents of the Mary Haven Center, a county-run residential treatment center for delinquent youth. Suppose that on January 1, 2012, the initial bequest was received from a wealthy citizen, consisting of the following:

WARREN COUNTY, OHIO

Cash.	$ 25,000
Corporate bonds, $500,000 par value, 5 percent coupon paid semiannually, due on December 31 of each year, 6 percent yield to maturity, at current value	485,000

The cash was immediately invested in certificates of deposit yielding 3 percent, payable semiannually on July 1 and January 1 of each year. The county board also authorized a transfer of $30,000 to support the education fund during 2012. Education-related expenses in 2012 totaled $55,000, of which $50,000 was paid in cash. Assume that increases in the reported value of the investment represent spendable income.

Required

a. Identify the fund type used to report the Scheurer-Smith Trust Fund.
b. Assume income is received as expected. Prepare the fund's 2012 operating statement and December 31, 2012, balance sheet. Assume the fund accrues interest as earned and uses the effective interest method for the bond investment.

LO 2, 3 **P11.3** **Capital Projects and Debt Service Activities** In fiscal 2013, the City of Allen, Texas plans to issue $100,000,000 face value of 5 percent general obligation bonds to finance the construction of a new state-of-the-art fire station plus equipment. Additional financing will be obtained from a federal grant. A capital projects fund will account for the activities relating to this project, and a debt service fund will account for resources used to make payments on the debt. The general fund will provide the resources to pay the annual interest payments. The following transactions occurred in each of the two years beginning October 1, 2012, and ending September 30, 2014.

CITY OF ALLEN, TEXAS

Fiscal 2013

1. October 2: A budget was established for the fire station project, as follows:

General obligation bonds.	$100,000,000
Federal grant	200,000,000

2. October 10: The general fund advanced $1,000,000 to cover planning activities.
3. October 15: $950,000 was spent for engineering and architectural work. The amount was not previously encumbered.
4. October 30: The general obligation bonds were issued at a total price of $100,500,000. The bonds mature on October 30, 2022, and interest is paid yearly. The bond premium is legally restricted to be used for bond payments, and is accordingly transferred to the debt service fund.
5. November 9: $65,000,000 of the federal grant proceeds was received.
6. December 1: Contracts were signed with several construction and fire equipment companies who will be responsible for various aspects of the project. All contracts provide for a 20 percent retainage. The contracts totaled $285,000,000.
7. May 15: The advance from the general fund was repaid.
8. September 30: Extensive work was done on the fire station during fiscal 2013, and the construction and equipment companies have submitted invoices in the amount of $180,000,000. $120,000,000 in cash has been paid as of year-end.

Fiscal 2014

1. October 2: $5,000,000 was transferred from the general fund to the debt service fund to cover its interest expenditure for the year.

2. October 30: Interest was paid on the bonds.
3. January 12: The remainder of the federal grant was received by the capital projects fund.
4. June 15: Additional invoices totaling $115,000,000 were received, representing the final billings of the contractors. $116,000,000 in cash was paid to contractors.
5. July 25: The fire station was accepted by the city. All contractors were paid in full, and the remaining balance was transferred to the debt service fund to finance future payments on the bonds.

Assume all resources of the capital project fund are restricted. Debt service fund resources are committed.

Required

a. Prepare the journal entries, including closing entries, for the capital projects and debt service funds for fiscal 2013 and 2014.
b. Prepare the balance sheet for the capital projects fund on September 30, 2013.
c. Prepare the balance sheet for the debt service fund on September 30, 2014.

P11.4 **Capital Projects and Debt Service Activities** The information below relates to the construction of a new recreation building in the City of Lander. Lander's fiscal year ends on June 30. LO 2, 3

Fiscal 2013 transactions

1. A bond issue in the amount of $10,000,000 was authorized to provide funds for the construction. The bonds are to be repaid, in 20 annual installments, from a debt service fund, with the first installment due on June 30, 2013. Interest at 4 percent of face value is to be paid yearly on June 30.
2. An advance of $800,000 was received from the general fund to make a deposit on the land contract of $1,200,000. The deposit was made.
3. On July 1, 2012, bonds having a face value of $10,000,000 were sold for cash at 102, for an effective interest rate of 3.8 percent.
4. Contracts amounting to $7,800,000 were awarded to the lowest bidder for the construction of the recreation center.
5. The temporary advance from the general fund was repaid, and the balance on the land contract was paid.
6. The architect certified that work in the amount of $6,400,000 was completed, and submitted bills for that amount. $200,000 is to be held as retainage.
7. Bills paid by the treasurer relative to the completed work amounted to $6,200,000.
8. The bond premium was transferred to the debt service fund.

Fiscal 2014 transactions

9. Due to engineering modifications in the construction plans, the contract was revised to $8,800,000.
10. The recreation center was completed and billed at a further cost of $2,300,000. The building passed final inspection.
11. The treasurer paid all bills.
12. The cash balance remaining was transferred to the debt service fund.

Additional information:

1. Interest on the bond issue is paid directly from the general fund.
2. Budgeted and actual transfers from the general fund to the debt service fund are $450,000 in fiscal 2013 and $550,000 in fiscal 2014.
3. Cash accumulated in the debt service fund through transfers from the capital projects fund and the general fund was invested in certificates of deposit which yielded interest income of $5,000 in fiscal 2013 and $4,000 in fiscal 2014. Expected investment income on these investments was $5,000 in each year.
4. To meet the yearly bond principal payment, the debt service fund liquidated investments of $500,000 during each of the fiscal years 2013 and 2014. It paid installments on the bonds when due on June 30 of each year.

Assume recreation fund resources are restricted. Debt service fund resources are committed.

Required

a. Prepare the journal entries, including closing entries, for the recreation center capital projects fund for fiscal years 2013 and 2014.
b. Prepare the balance sheet for the recreation center fund on June 30, 2013.
c. Prepare the journal entries, including closing entries, for the debt service fund for fiscal years 2013 and 2014.

LO 2 **P11.5** **Evaluating Municipality Financial Condition** Well-known examples of current municipal finan-

JEFFERSON
COUNTY, AL
HARRISBURG,
PA

cial problems, such as **Jefferson County, Alabama** and **Harrisburg, Pennsylvania,** may have sur-
prised capital market participants and other observers. Perhaps the modified accrual basis of accounting
and the use of separate funds to report financial results complicate analysis of the relations between a
government's sources and uses of financial resources and changes in its levels of fixed assets and debt.
Governmental funds financial statements use modified accrual accounting. Modestly inappropriate uses
of fungible financial resources in these funds can mask impending financial difficulties. Consider the five
years of selected data for a hypothetical municipality shown below.

(in thousands)	2010	2011	2012	2013	2014
Estimated revenue— general fund..........	$3,400	$3,650	$3,800	$4,000	$4,100
Actual revenue—general fund	3,360	3,570	3,700	3,820	3,900
Short-term borrowings....................	200	250	310	370	500
Change in long-term debt—					
capital projects funds...................	440	600	620	550	580
Expenditures—capital projects funds	300	480	510	470	430
Fund balance (all governmental funds)	810	830	845	815	795

Required

a. Explain what is meant by "fungible financial resources."
b. Identify and explain any signals these data provide regarding the evolving financial condition of this
municipality.
c. Discuss how the use of modified accrual accounting, rather than full accrual accounting, reduces the
ability to evaluate the financial condition of a municipality.

LO 1 **P11.6** **Evaluating Status of Capital Project** As a newly elected member of the Wannabe Area School
Board, you are exhausted after listening to two hours of discussion on an obscure and inconsequential
administrative issue. Now, at 11 PM, as part of the Business Manager's monthly report, a post-closing
trial balance at the end of the first year of a two-year school construction project is circulated to update
the Board. All financing authorized for the project has been recorded.

Because of your technical accounting background, you look sharply at the trial balance displayed below. While doing so, you recall that the Board just passed its largest budget ever, requiring a tax increase
opposed by several citizens taxpayer groups.

WANNABE AREA SCHOOL DISTRICT
Middle School Extension Capital Projects Fund
Trial Balance at June 30, 2013

(in thousands)	Dr (Cr)
Cash in bank	$ 1,400
Supplies	750
Interest receivable	200
Temporary investments	9,700
Due from general fund	1,000
Accounts payable...	(960)
Contracts payable	(1,340)
Fund balance—nonspendable..	(750)
Fund balance—restricted..	(12,600)
Fund balance—unassigned	2,600
Total	$ 0

Required

a. Another Board member wants to move on to the next item of business. You object. Why?
b. Prepare an analysis designed to get the attention of your colleagues, citing specific items in the trial
balance. Be sure to discuss the status of the project in relation to its budget.

P11.7 Internal Service Fund The **County of Alameda, California** operates a motor pool through an internal service fund to maintain all County-owned motor vehicles, including cars, trucks, and heavy equipment. Revenues come from fees charged for services provided. Suppose the post-closing trial balance for the motor pool at June 30, 2012, was as follows:

(in thousands)	Debit	Credit
Cash	$18,000	
Receivable from general fund	4,000	
Materials and supplies	10,000	
Capital assets, net of $3,200 accumulated depreciation	34,800	
Accounts payable		$ 5,000
Net investment in capital assets		34,800
Unrestricted net position		27,000
Totals	$66,800	$66,800

The following information applies to the fiscal year ending June 30, 2013 (in thousands):

1. Materials and supplies were purchased on account for $9,500.
2. The inventory of materials and supplies at June 30, 2013, was $8,400, which agreed with the physical count taken.
3. Salaries and wages paid to employees totaled $35,000, including fringe benefit costs.
4. A billing was received from an enterprise fund for utility charges totaling $4,000, and was paid.
5. Depreciation on the building, machinery and equipment was recorded in the amount of $1,900.
6. Machinery with an original cost of $800 and book value of $250 was sold for $90.
7. Transfers from the general fund, to support motor pool activities, were $125.
8. Billings to other departments for services rendered to them were:

General fund	$30,000
Water and sewer fund	12,000
Special revenue fund	7,000

9. Unpaid interfund receivable balances at June 30, 2013, were:

General fund	$ 900
Special revenue fund	2,000

10. Accounts payable at June 30, 2013, were $2,300.

Required

a. For the period July 1, 2012 through June 30, 2013, prepare journal entries to record all of the transactions in the motor pool fund accounts.
b. Prepare the closing entries for the motor pool fund at June 30, 2013.
c. Present, in good form, the June 30, 2013, balance sheet for the motor pool fund.

P11.8 Critique Enterprise Fund Accounting Two years ago, Mightyfine Township took over the swimming pool of a defunct private swim club and converted it into a community pool financed by user charges. Most user charges are in the form of low-cost family season passes sold to Township residents; the fee charged to nonresidents is five times the fee charged to residents.

The township manager boasts about how he can provide such fine swimming facilities at a low cost to residents. He dismisses last year's dismal financial results—the first year the Township ran the pool—as an aberration. During that year, a diving board and baby pool were added to the facilities. In his report to the Board of Supervisors, the manager presents the following schedule, taken from a subsidiary ledger in the township's general fund without adjustment.

MIGHTYFINE TOWNSHIP COMMUNITY SWIMMING POOL Operating Statement	
Season passes—residents.	$ 224,000
Season passes—nonresidents.	50,000
Daily admission fees.	13,000
Concessions, net	37,000
Total revenues	324,000
Salaries—pool manager and lifeguards.	228,000
Maintenance and repairs	67,000
Total expenditures	295,000
Excess of revenues over expenditures	$ 29,000
Notes:	
1. Fair value of original pool (20-year life)	$3,000,000
2. Cost of baby pool addition (25-year life)	500,000
3. Cost of diving board (10-year life)	150,000
4. Cost of rider to Township's liability insurance (paid by the Township)	42,000

Required

a. Discuss the basis of accounting used in the above report.
b. What deficiencies in the report cause it to depart from GAAP?
c. Evaluate whether the township manager is justified in boasting. Support your evaluation with a numerical analysis.
d. A township resident who teaches accounting at Superfine University states that the pool is never crowded and that more revenue could be generated by reducing the cost of nonresident season passes from $200 per family to $120 per family. She estimates that the price elasticity of demand $[= - (\Delta q/q)/(\Delta p/p)]$ for a nonresident season pass is 2.5. Using the professor's numbers, calculate the additional revenue generated from lowering the cost of nonresident season passes.

LO 4   **P11.9   Enterprise Fund Statement of Cash Flows**

MISSOURI STATE LOTTERY

Below are the summarized financial statements of the **Missouri State Lottery** for the year ended June 30, 2014.

Statement of Revenues, Expenses and Changes in Net Position For Year Ended June 30, 2014 *(in thousands)*	
Ticket sales.	$900,000
Prize expenses.	(450,000)
Operating expenses.	(180,000)
Operating income.	270,000
Nonoperating items:	
Unrealized losses on investments	(2,000)
Loss on sale of capital assets	(5,000)
Transfers to State of Missouri	(258,000)
Nonoperating expense	(265,000)
Change in net position.	$ 5,000

MISSOURI STATE LOTTERY
Statement of Net Position
June 30, 2014 and 2013

(in thousands)	2014	2013
Cash and cash equivalents	$ 14,000	$ 21,000
Accounts receivable, net	39,000	25,000
Investments	42,000	38,000
Capital assets	51,000	60,000
Less accumulated depreciation	(13,000)	(12,000)
Totals	$133,000	$132,000
Current operating liabilities	$ 35,000	$ 40,000
Prize liabilities	86,000	85,000
Net position	12,000	7,000
Totals	$133,000	$132,000

Additional information (in thousands):

1. Accounts receivable are related to ticket sales.
2. Current liabilities relate to operating expenses.
3. Additional investments of $15,000 were made in 2014.
4. Depreciation expense on capital assets, included in operating expenses, was $3,000.
5. Capital assets of $14,000 were acquired in 2014.
6. Investments that matured in 2014 were liquidated at book value.

Required

Present the fiscal 2014 statement of cash flows for the Missouri State Lottery. Include a reconciliation schedule.

P11.10 Agency Fund In compliance with a newly enacted state law, Dial County assumed the responsibility of collecting all property taxes for the county, as well as Eton City and Bart Township within the county, as of July 1, 2012. A composite property tax rate per $1,000 of assessed valuation was developed for the fiscal year ending June 30, 2013:

Dial County general fund	$ 60
Eton City general fund	30
Bart Township general fund	10
Composite tax rate	$100

When collected, the property taxes are distributed to the governmental units. Dial County established a tax agency fund to administer collection and distribution of taxes.

Additional information:

1. To reimburse Dial County for administrative costs of operating the agency fund, 2 percent of all tax collections are remitted to the Dial County general fund.
2. Tax bills sent out on July 1, 2012, for fiscal 2013, and estimated amounts to be collected are:

	Gross Levy	Estimated Amount to be Collected
Dial County	$36,000,000	$35,000,000
Eton City	18,000,000	17,400,000
Bart Township	6,000,000	5,600,000
Totals	$60,000,000	$58,000,000

3. As of September 30, 2012, the tax agency fund received $14,400,000 in tax payments. On October 1, the tax agency fund distributed the payments to the three governmental units.

Required

a. Prepare the journal entries made in the tax agency fund and in each of the three general funds to record the tax bills sent out July 1, 2012.
b. Calculate the amounts to be distributed to each of the three general funds on October 1, 2012.
c. Prepare the journal entries made in the tax agency fund to record the tax collection, and in the tax agency fund and each of the three general funds to record the distribution made on October 1, 2012.

LO 6

MECKLENBURG COUNTY, NORTH CAROLINA

P11.11 Reporting for Landfills Mecklenburg County, North Carolina's landfill is reported in a proprietary fund. On the county's 2010 CAFR, the liabilities section of the landfill's balance sheet reports landfill development and postclosure care costs in the amount of $8,374,290. Current expenses shown on the landfill's operating statement include $40,088 in development and postclosure costs.

Required

a. The financial statement footnotes state that the landfill is at 72 percent of capacity at the end of fiscal 2010. What is the current cost estimate of total closure and postclosure costs for the landfill? What total expense was reported in previous financial statements for closure and postclosure costs?
b. If the landfill had been reported in a governmental fund, what amounts would appear in the financial statements of governmental funds, related to the landfill?
c. The landfill is expected to close in 2025. The landfill was at 66 percent of capacity at the end of 2008. Comment on the reasonableness of the expected closing date.
d. Based on the analysis above, what average expense must be accrued each year from 2011 to 2025? Comment on the adequacy of the expense reported in 2010.

LO 1, 2, 3, 4, 5

P11.12 Budgeting for Various Funds The Laurens city council passed a resolution requiring a yearly cash budget by fund for the city beginning with its fiscal year ending September 30, 2014. The city's financial director prepared a list of expected cash receipts and disbursements, shown in Exhibit 11.8, which follows. The financial director is having trouble subdividing the receipts and disbursements by fund.

Additional information:

1. A bond issue was authorized for the construction of a civic center. Future civic center revenues are to account for 20 percent of the repayment of the debt. The remainder is to come from general property taxes.
2. A bond issue was authorized for additions to the library. The debt is to be paid from general property taxes.
3. General obligation bonds are paid from general property taxes collected by the general fund.
4. Ten percent of the total annual school taxes represents an individually voted tax for payment of bonds, the proceeds of which were used for school construction. School operations are accounted for in the general fund.
5. In 2011, a wealthy citizen donated rental property to the city. Net income from the property is to be used to assist in operating the library. The net cash increase attributable to the property is transferred to the library on September 30 of each year.
6. All sales taxes are collected by the city; the state receives 85 percent of these taxes. The state's portion is remitted at the end of each month.
7. Payment of the street construction bonds, for which the city has no liability, is to be made from assessments previously collected from the respective property owners. The proceeds from the assessments were invested and the principal of $312,000 is expected to earn $15,000 interest during the coming year.
8. In 2013, a special assessment in the amount of $203,000 was made on certain property owners for sewer construction. During fiscal 2014, $50,000 of this assessment is expected to be collected. The remainder of the sewer cost is to be paid from a $153,000 bond issue to be sold in fiscal 2014. Future special assessment collections will be used to pay principal and interest on the bonds, for which the city has residual liability.
9. All sewer and sanitation services are provided by a separate enterprise fund.
10. The federal grant is for fiscal 2014 school operations.
11. The proceeds remaining at the end of the year from the sale of civic center and library bonds are to be invested.
12. The state motor vehicle tax, state gasoline tax, and state alcoholic beverage license revenue represent the city's share of state revenues.

Required

Prepare a budget of cash receipts and disbursements by fund for the year ending September 30, 2014. Include all interfund cash transfers. Set up your solution in the following format:

Description	General Fund	Capital Projects Fund	Debt Service Fund	Permanent Fund	Agency Fund	Enterprise Fund
Cash receipts						
Cash disbursements						
Interfund transfers						
Net cash flow						

EXHIBIT 11.8 List of Cash Receipts and Disbursements for P11.12

Cash Receipts

Taxes:

General Property.	$ 685,000
School.	421,000
Franchise	223,000
	1,329,000

Licenses and Permits:

Business Licenses	41,000
Automobile Inspection Permits.	24,000
Building Permits	18,000
	83,000

Intergovernmental Revenue:

Sales Tax	1,012,000
Federal Grants	128,000
State Motor Vehicle Tax	83,500
State Gasoline Tax	52,000
State Alcoholic Beverage Licenses . . .	16,000
	1,291,500

Charges for Services:

Sanitation Fees.	121,000
Sewer Connection Fees	71,000
Library Revenues	13,000
Park Revenues	2,500
	207,500

Bond Issues:

Civic Center	347,000
General Obligation	200,000
Sewer	153,000
Library.	120,000
	820,000

Other:

Proceeds from Sale of Investments . . .	312,000
Sewer Assessments	50,000
Rental Revenue.	48,000
Interest Revenue.	15,000
	425,000

Total Receipts	$4,156,000

Cash Disbursements

Public Services:

General Government.	$ 671,000
Public Safety.	516,000
School	458,000
Sanitation	131,000
Library.	28,000
Rental Property.	17,500
Parks.	17,000
	1,838,500

Debt Service:

General Obligation Bonds.	618,000
Street Construction Bonds.	327,000
School Bonds	119,000
Sewage Disposal Plant Bonds	37,200
	1,101,200

Investments	358,000
State Portion of Sales Tax	860,200

Capital Expenditures:

Sewer Connection (Assessed Area) . . .	114,100
Civic Center Construction.	73,000
Library Construction	36,000
	223,100

Total Disbursements	$4,381,000

REVIEW SOLUTIONS ••

Review 1 Solution

a.   **Journal entries for capital projects fund:**

Bonds authorized—uninssued	4,000,000	
Estimated revenues—state grant	1,000,000	
Appropriations		5,000,000
To record the budget entry.		
State grant receivable	1,000,000	
State grant revenue		1,000,000
To accrue state grant.		
Cash	4,100,000	
Bond proceeds		4,000,000
Due to debt service fund		100,000
To record bond issuance.		
Due to debt service fund	100,000	
Cash		100,000
To record remittance of bond premium to debt service fund.		
Cash	900,000	
State grant receivable		900,000
To record partial receipt of state grant.		
Encumbrances	4,750,000	
Fund balance—restricted		4,750,000
To record awarding of contract.		
Fund balance—restricted	2,300,000	
Encumbrances		2,300,000
To record reversal of encumbrances on bills received.		
Expenditures	2,300,000	
Contracts payable—retainage		460,000
Cash		1,840,000
To record expenditures.		
Appropriations	5,000,000	
State grant revenue	1,000,000	
Bond proceeds	4,000,000	
Expenditures		2,300,000
Encumbrances		2,450,000
Bonds authorized—unissued		4,000,000
Estimated revenues—state grant		1,000,000
Fund balance—restricted		250,000
To close the books.		

Journal entries for debt service fund:

Required additions	140,000	
Appropriations		140,000
To record budget entry.		
Cash	100,000	
Transfer in		100,000
To record transfer of bond premium from capital projects fund.		

continued

Cash..	140,000	
Transfer in..		140,000
To record transfer from general fund.		
Debt service: interest..	100,000	
Debt service: principal...	40,000	
Cash		140,000
To record payment of principal and interest.		
Appropriations...	140,000	
Transfers in...	240,000	
Debt service: interest....................................		100,000
Debt service: principal...................................		40,000
Required additions		140,000
Fund balance—restricted		100,000
To close the books.		

b.

TOWN OF LETCHWORTH
Capital Projects Fund
Statement of Revenues, Expenditures, and Changes in Fund Balances
For Year Ended December 31, 2013

State grant revenue	$1,000,000
Expenditures	(2,300,000)
Excess of revenues over (under) expenditures	(1,300,000)
Other financing sources (uses):	
Bond proceeds..	4,000,000
Total other financing sources (uses)...	4,000,000
Excess of revenues and other financing sources over (under)	
expenditures and other financing uses..................................	2,700,000
Fund balance—beginning	0
Fund balance—ending..	$2,700,000

Debt Service Fund
Statement of Revenues, Expenditures, and Changes in Fund Balances
For Year Ended December 31, 2013

Expenditures:	
Debt service: interest	$(100,000)
Debt service: principal	(40,000)
Total expenditures	(140,000)
Other financing sources (uses):	
Transfers in..	240,000
Excess of revenues and other financing sources over	
expenditures and other financing uses..................................	100,000
Fund balance—beginning	0
Fund balance—ending..	$ 100,000

c.

TOWN OF LETCHWORTH
Capital Projects Fund—Balance Sheet
December 31, 2013

Cash..........................	$3,060,000	Contracts payable—retainage	$ 460,000
State grant receivable	100,000	Fund balance—restricted.........	2,700,000
Total........................	$3,160,000	Total........................	$3,160,000

Debt Service Fund—Balance Sheet
December 31, 2013

Cash..........................	$100,000	Fund balance—restricted.........	$100,000
Total........................	$100,000	Total........................	$100,000

Review 2 Solution

a.

Cash..	460,000	
Accounts receivable		10,000
Water revenues		450,000
To record revenues and collection.		
Supplies expense...	50,500	
Supplies...		500
Cash		50,000
To record supplies purchased and used.		
Capital assets..	25,000	
Cash		25,000
To record acquisition of capital assets.		
Depreciation expense...	4,000	
Accumulated depreciation.................................		4,000
To record depreciation on capital assets.		
Operating expenses...	395,000	
Accounts payable		5,000
Cash		390,000
To record out-of-pocket operating expenses.		
Interest expense..	3,200	
Bonds payable	5,000	
Cash		8,200
To record payment of bond principal and interest.		
Water revenues	450,000	
Unrestricted net position	2,700	
Supplies expense		50,500
Depreciation expense		4,000
Operating expenses		395,000
Interest expense		3,200
To close the books.		
Unrestricted net position	21,000	
Net investment in capital assets		21,000
To reclassify unrestricted net position to net investment in		
capital assets; $21,000 = $25,000 − $4,000.		

b.

WATER UTILITY
Statement of Revenues, Expenses, and Changes in Net Position
For Year Ended December 31, 2014

Water revenues		$450,000
Less operating expenses:		
Supplies	$ 50,500	
Depreciation	4,000	
Other operating expenses	395,000	(449,500)
Operating income		500
Nonoperating expense:		
Interest expense		(3,200)
Change in net position		(2,700)
Net position—beginning		86,500
Net position—ending		$ 83,800

WATER UTILITY
Statement of Cash Flows
For Year Ended December 31, 2014

Cash flows from operating activities	
Receipts from customers	$460,000
Payments to suppliers	(50,000)
Payments for operating expenses	(390,000)
Net cash from operating activities	20,000
Cash flows from noncapital financing activities	
Payments for interest	(3,200)
Payments for principal	(5,000)
Net cash used for noncapital financing activities	(8,200)
Cash flows from capital and related financing activities	
Acquisition of capital assets	(25,000)
Net decrease in cash	(13,200)
Cash—beginning	40,000
Cash—ending	$ 26,800

c.

WATER UTILITY
Statement of Net Position
December 31, 2014

Cash	$ 26,800		Accounts payable	$ 15,000
Accounts receivable	65,000		Bonds payable	75,000
Supplies	3,000		Net position:	
Capital assets	145,000		Net investment in capital assets	59,000
Accum. depreciation	(66,000)		Unrestricted	24,800
Total	$173,800		Total	$173,800

12

State and Local Governments: External Financial Reporting

CITY OF ST. LOUIS, MISSOURI
stlouis.missouri.org

The **City of St. Louis**, Missouri, known for its Gateway Arch, is located at the confluence of the Mississippi and Missouri Rivers, and borders the state of Illinois. Home to Saint Louis University and Washington University, St. Louis also has a campus of the University of Missouri. Corporations headquartered in St. Louis include Energizer, Monsanto, Enterprise Rent-a-Car, and Hardee's. The city is famous for the Anheuser-Busch Breweries, now owned by InBev, and the St. Louis Cardinals.

The City of St. Louis issues an audited Comprehensive Annual Financial Report (CAFR), containing a full accrual-based balance sheet and operating statement, and separate financial statements for its various governmental, proprietary, and fiduciary activities. Each year the City receives the GFOA's Certificate of Achievement for Excellence in Financial Reporting, for publishing a reader-friendly CAFR that meets all professional and legal requirements. The CAFR is audited by KPMG LLP, following generally accepted auditing standards.

The 2010 CAFR for the City of St. Louis reveals that it has over $3.6 billion in assets and over $2.2 billion in liabilities, government-wide. Total revenues were $966 million, of which 50 percent came from taxes. But the cost of programs and services was $1 billion, resulting in a 32 percent decrease in net assets.

A government's CAFR presents financial statements for its governmental funds, proprietary funds, and fiduciary funds. Government-wide financial statements are also presented, on a full accrual basis. This chapter explains the GASB's requirements for the CAFR.

CHAPTER ORGANIZATION

External reporting model	Government-wide statements	Fund Statements	Analysis and supplementary information	Accounting for infrastructure and investments
• MD&A • Government-wide statements • Fund statements • Notes and required supplementary information	• Statement of net position • Statement of activities	• Major funds • Governmental fund statements • Reconciliations to government-wide statements • Proprietary fund statements • Fiduciary fund statements	• Modified accrual versus full accrual information • Budgetary comparison schedules	• Capitalization requirements • Modified approach for depreciation • Income and hedge investments

The external financial report of a state or local government is known as the **Comprehensive Annual Financial Report**, or **CAFR**, and is equivalent to a corporation's annual report to shareholders. *SGAS 34* prescribes the external reporting requirements for state and local governments, emphasizing readability and the use of accrual accounting to report the full cost of governmental services. The GASB subsequently issued *SGAS 35*, requiring public colleges and universities to follow *SGAS 34*. Subsequent GASB statements clarify and extend the provisions of *SGAS 34*.

EXTERNAL REPORTING MODEL

Chapter 10 explains the three major users of governmental financial reports: investors and creditors, citizens, and legislative and oversight bodies. Traditionally, credit market representatives have the greatest interest in governmental financial reports, being concerned with the government's ability to meet obligations as they come due. Citizens, legislative and oversight bodies want to know how much money the government has available to spend, where tax dollars are going, costs of services, sources of funding for various programs, and the implications of the current level of services for future tax obligations.

LO1 Discuss the components of the Comprehensive Annual Financial Report.

Prior to 2001, The CAFR included only fund financial statements focused entirely on **accountability**. Governments are expected to use resources for their intended purpose and to comply with legally enacted budgets. Fund financial statements report how current activities are financed, the amount of current financial resources available for future expenditures, how the period's budget compares with actual revenues and expenditures, and any significant changes in current financial position during the year.

The **measurement focus** in the governmental fund financial statements is on the **flow of current financial resources**, defined as cash, cash equivalents and receivables, net of payables and short-term debt. Revenues and other financing sources are inflows of current financial resources, and expenditures and other financing uses are outflows of current financial resources. Revenues earned but not yet available to finance expenditures in the current period are not recognized. Expenses accrued but not requiring current resources, such as depreciation, or interest to be paid in future years, are also not recognized.

This measurement focus underlies **modified accrual accounting**, and matches resources available to finance current period expenditures with outflows of current period resources. The difference between current assets and current liabilities, or fund balance, represents financial resources available for future expenditure. The measurement focus of the **full accrual basis of accounting** is based on the **flow of economic resources**; it is used for proprietary funds, where fee-for-service activities make it essential to know the *full cost* of services, not just those costs using current financial resources. Fiduciary funds also use the full accrual basis, with some exceptions.

SGAS 34 revolutionized external reporting for state and local governments by diverting attention away from exclusive focus on current financial resource flows.

> *SGAS 34's* most significant change in reporting standards is that **full accrual financial statements** be provided for the **government as a whole**. These full accrual statements, called **government-wide statements**, are *in addition to* the fund financial statements for governmental, proprietary, and fiduciary funds.

The GASB believes full accrual government-wide financial statements provide more accurate and complete information about the full cost of services, results of operations, and financial position. Accrual basis reporting conveys more accurately the government's ability to maintain current service levels and the impact of current activities on future financial condition. Accrual-based statements report on the overall financial health of the primary government and its component units, and the government's ability to provide services now and in the future. The reporting requirements of *SGAS 34* parallel the changes in reporting for not-for-profit organizations that occurred in the mid-1990s, discussed in Chapter 13.

SGAS 34 requires, at a minimum, the following disclosures in the governmental unit's CAFR:

- Management's discussion and analysis (MD&A)
- Basic financial statements
  - ○ Government-wide financial statements
  - ○ Fund financial statements
  - ○ Notes to financial statements
- Required supplementary information (RSI) other than MD&A

Figure 12.1 shows the minimum requirements, per *SGAS 34, paragraph 7*.

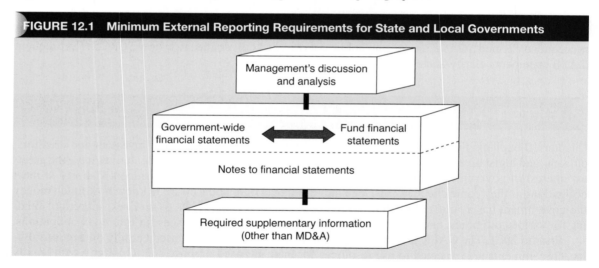

FIGURE 12.1 Minimum External Reporting Requirements for State and Local Governments

MANAGEMENT'S DISCUSSION AND ANALYSIS

MD&A provides an objective and readable overview and analysis of the government's financial performance for the year. Charts and graphs are encouraged. The discussion focuses on the short- and long-term financial performance of the primary government. MD&A introduces the basic financial statements, and is similar in content to that required by the SEC for public companies.

Minimum requirements include:

- Overview of the information provided by the basic financial statements, including an explanation and comparison of the government-wide and fund statements.

- Condensed government-wide financial statements that compare the current year to the prior year, with analysis of the reasons for significant changes.

- Discussion of changes in the government's overall financial position and analysis of significant changes in the financial position of specific funds.

- Analysis of significant differences between original and final budget amounts and between budget and actual amounts for the general fund, and how those differences affect future services and liquidity.

- A description of capital expenditure commitments, changes in credit ratings, and the effect of debt limitations on the ability to finance future services or asset acquisitions.

GOVERNMENT-WIDE FINANCIAL STATEMENTS

The two required government-wide financial statements are the *statement of net position* and *statement of activities*. These statements report financial performance overall, and focus on *activities benefitting the government or its citizens*. Like a corporate balance sheet, the **statement of net position** reports the assets, liabilities, and net position of the government. The **statement of activities** reports revenues and expenses.

LO2 Prepare government-wide financial statements.

Both statements separately disclose resources and activities pertaining to *governmental activities* and *business-type activities*. **Governmental activities** are those primarily financed by taxes and inter-governmental transfers, and include the activities of governmental funds—general, special revenue, capital projects, debt service, and permanent funds—and internal service funds. **Business-type activities** are those financed at least partially by user fees and include only the activities of enterprise funds.

Although internal service funds use business accounting, they are included with governmental activities because their activities support other government departments. Fiduciary funds are **not** included in the government-wide statements, because the resources of fiduciary activities reported in agency and trust funds are not available to finance government programs and do not benefit citizens in general.

Unlike most of the fund financial statements discussed in Chapters 10 and 11, the government-wide financial statements use **full accrual accounting,** reflecting the GASB's *economic resources measurement focus*. Revenues, expenses, gains, losses, assets, and liabilities are reported using business accounting principles.

Land, buildings, equipment, infrastructure and similar items—termed **capital assets** by *SGAS 34*—are reported on the statement of net position at historical cost, net of accumulated depreciation. Depreciation expense on depreciable capital assets is reported in the statement of activities. **Infrastructure assets** are long-term stationary capital assets that can be maintained for a longer period than most capital assets. Examples include roads, bridges, and water and lighting systems. Governments may or may not depreciate infrastructure assets; see discussion later in the chapter.

All liabilities, including accrued interest and other obligations not requiring current financial resources, as well as bonds and other forms of long-term debt, are recognized in the statement of net position. Accrued interest expense is reported in the statement of activities.

Government-Wide Financial Statements

Statements:
  Statement of net position (balance sheet)
  Statement of activities (operating statement)
Basis of reporting:
  Full accrual basis
Activities reported:
  Governmental activities
    Activities of governmental funds and internal service funds
  Business-type activities
    Activities of enterprise funds

Governmental funds report on a modified accrual basis, and do not report revenues, expenses, assets or liabilities unless they involve current flows of financial resources. These funds account for acquisition and disposition of capital assets and issuance and payment of long-term debt as changes in fund balance. Therefore, *major adjustments must be made to governmental fund financial information* so that governments can accurately report their activities in the full accrual government-wide financial statements.

Statement of Net Position

SGAS 63, effective in 2012, changed the name and format of government balance sheets prepared using full accrual accounting. The balance sheet, formerly called the Statement of Net Assets, is now the Statement of Net **Position**. This standard applies to proprietary and fiduciary fund balance sheets as well as to the government-wide balance sheet discussed below. Further discussion of *SGAS 63* appears later in this chapter.

The **statement of net position** reports the assets and liabilities of the primary government and its component units, both in total and separately by governmental and business-type activities. Presentation in order of liquidity, or in a classified format, is encouraged. Net position is presented in three categories:

- **Net investment in capital assets**: Capital assets net of depreciation, less debt incurred to acquire or improve the capital assets.
- **Restricted**: Unspent contributions, grants and loans subject to *external constraints* imposed by creditors, donors, or legislators.
- **Unrestricted**: Amounts not included in the other two categories. This category includes net position affected by internal restrictions imposed by management.

Internal transactions are common within and between the governmental, internal service, and enterprise funds, and lead to interfund receivables and payables or other "duplicate" balances. *SGAS 34* strives to minimize overstatement of assets and liabilities in the statement of net position, by requiring elimination of interfund receivables and payables in the governmental and business-type activities columns. However, the statement shows the net amounts owing *between the governmental and business-type activities* as offsetting internal balances. Because the government-wide statements do not include fiduciary funds, a*mounts due from or to fiduciary funds* are reported as external balances.

Statement of Activities

The **statement of activities** reports all **changes in net position** during the year. Gross expenses are shown by function or program within the governmental or business-type categories. Specific revenues received for program services and/or grants and contracts are deducted from gross expenses. The net balance shows *how much each function or program uses or contributes to general revenues*, such as property taxes and other broad-based tax levies, unrestricted grants, and investment income. After adding general revenues, the "bottom line" reports the change in net position. Because program expenses are reported using full accrual accounting, they reflect full costs, not just amounts paid during the current period. Therefore the change in net position reflects the *degree to which the total costs of current services and activities are financed by total revenues for the period*.

Duplicate balances also may exist within the statement of activities. For example, when overhead expenses incurred by one function are allocated to other functions, the allocated overhead expenses should be reported only by the function to which they are allocated. To accurately report expenses and revenues by function, costs of goods and services provided between functions are reported as revenues by the selling function and expenses by the buying function.

Discussion of Government-Wide Statements

Exhibits 12.1 and 12.2 present the 2010 statement of net assets (net position effective in 2012) and statement of activities, respectively, for the City of St. Louis, Missouri. Component units are combined in one column for brevity.

The primary government is the City. Blended component units are the Public Facilities Protection Corporation (PFPC), a self-insurance program; the St. Louis Municipal Finance Corporation (SLMFC), which acquires and finances city property; the St. Louis Parking Commission Finance Corporation (SLPCFC), which acquires and finances assets for the Parking Commission; and the Grand Center Municipal Parking Finance Corporation (MPFC), which manages parking services for Grand Center, the downtown arts and entertainment district. The activities of these blended units are reported in the primary government accounts.

Discretely presented component units are the St. Louis Development Corporation (SLDC), in charge of economic development in the city; the Metropolitan Police Department (SLPD), which funds police department activities; and the Solid Waste Management and Development Corporation (SWM-DC), which owns and leases a system of underground pipes providing pressurized steam to downtown municipal buildings.

Governmental activities reported in St. Louis' government-wide statements include general government operations, federal grants and other revenues legally restricted to specific purposes, capital projects, and debt service. These internal service activities are also included in governmental activities: the self insurance program, mail-handling services, and employee health insurance claims. St. Louis' business-type activities include its airport, water division, and parking division.

St. Louis' statement of activities in Exhibit 12.2 reports the 2010 cost of governmental programs and functions, net of related program revenues, at $547,173,000, funded by $490,957,000 in general revenues, primarily earnings and payroll, sales, and property taxes. The resulting shortfall is $56,216,000. Expenses of business-type activities were $238,768,000, but charges for services and other revenue sources totaled $257,219,000 (= $223,789,000 + $1,615,000 + 31,815,000). The resulting surplus of $18,451,000 is primarily due to airport charges, grants and contributions in excess of expenses. After unrestricted investment earnings and transfers, the surplus for business-type activities is $15,976,000. The net effect is to decrease primary government net position by $40,240,000 (= $56,216,000 − $15,976,000).

The end-of-year total net position for the primary government, reported on the statement of activities as $1,379,810,000, is also reported on the statement of net position in Exhibit 12.1. Restricted and

EXHIBIT 12.1 2010 Statement of Net Assets, City of St. Louis, Missouri

CITY OF ST. LOUIS, MISSOURI
Statement of Net Assets
June 30, 2010

(in thousands)	Primary Government Governmental Activities	Primary Government Business-type Activities	Total	Component Units Total
Assets				
Cash and cash equivalents	$ 59,354	$ 29,079	$ 88,433	$ 12,080
Investments	9,474	—	9,474	1,433
Receivables, net	160,745	29,056	189,801	17,989
Inventories	—	4,415	4,415	1,257
Restricted assets	161,795	399,454	561,249	7,540
Deferred charges	17,839	31,443	49,282	—
Internal balances	8,948	(8,948)	—	—
Other assets	48	659	707	555
Receivable from primary government	—	—	—	6,790
Receivable from component unit	1,258	—	1,258	—
Net pension asset	36,420	—	36,420	—
Property held for development, net	—	—	—	17,483
Capital assets, net:				
Non-depreciable	116,281	813,663	929,944	6,888
Depreciable	692,019	1,060,228	1,752,247	42,477
Total assets	1,264,181	2,359,049	3,623,230	114,492
Liabilities				
Accounts payable and accrued liabilities	22,838	16,869	39,707	4,228
Accrued salaries and other benefits	7,513	12,303	19,816	3,014
Accrued interest payable	60,607	24,484	85,091	256
Unearned revenue	7,473	4,818	12,291	—
Other liabilities	6,288	—	6,288	—
Notes payable	9,068	—	9,068	—
Payable to primary government	—	—	—	1,258
Payable to component units	6,790	—	6,790	—
Payable to other government agencies	38	212	250	—
Long-term liabilities:				
Due within one year	80,929	35,528	116,457	41,885
Due in more than one year	941,550	1,006,112	1,947,662	99,210
Total liabilities	1,143,094	1,100,326	2,243,420	149,851
Net assets				
Invested in capital assets, net of related debt	483,812	1,071,899	1,555,711	38,246
Restricted:				
Debt service	1,490	124,456	125,946	1,986
Airport improvement program	—	4,662	4,662	—
Capital projects	—	4,043	4,043	—
Passenger facility charges	—	30,288	30,288	—
Statutory restrictions	27,900	—	27,900	5,766
Unrestricted (deficit)	(392,115)	23,375	(368,740)	(81,357)
Total net assets	$ 121,087	$1,258,723	$1,379,810	$ (35,359)

unrestricted net position of governmental activities is a deficit of $(362,725,000) (= $121,087,000 − 483,812,000). This means that for these activities, reported liabilities exceed reported assets.

EXHIBIT 12.2 2010 Statement of Activities, City of St. Louis, Missouri

CITY OF ST. LOUIS, MISSOURI
Statement of Activities
For Year Ended June 30, 2010

(in thousands)	Expenses	Charges for Services	Operating Grants and Contributions	Capital Grants and Contributions	Governmental Activities	Business-type Activities	Total	Component Units
Primary Government								
Governmental activities								
General government	$ 84,330	$ 39,340	$13,920	$ —	$ (31,070)	$ —	$ (31,070)	$ —
Convention and tourism	4,507	18	—	—	(4,489)	—	(4,489)	—
Parks and recreation.	32,778	4,419	9	—	(28,350)	—	(28,350)	—
Judicial	54,880	20,791	3,419	—	(30,670)	—	(30,670)	—
Streets	66,263	17,644	147	—	(48,472)	—	(48,472)	—
Public safety	280,021	26,699	405	—	(252,917)	—	(252,917)	—
Health and welfare	51,552	591	29,540	—	(21,421)	—	(21,421)	—
Public service	59,980	1,487	2,597	7,548	(48,348)	—	(48,348)	—
Community development . . .	76,264	4,528	48,233	—	(23,503)	—	(23,503)	—
Interest and fiscal charges . .	57,933	—	—	—	(57,933)	—	(57,933)	—
Total governmental activities.	768,508	115,517	98,270	7,548	(547,173)	—	(547,173)	—
Business-type activities								
Airport.	181,775	160,378	1,615	31,815	—	12,033	12,033	—
Water Division.	43,479	50,983	—	—	—	7,504	7,504	—
Parking Division	13,514	12,428	—	—	—	(1,086)	(1,086)	—
Total business-type activities.	238,768	223,789	1,615	31,815	—	18,451	(18,451)	—
Total primary government.	$1,007,276	$339,306	$99,885	$39,363	$(547,173)	$ 18,451	$ (528,722)	$ —
Component Units	$ 203,171	$ 13,551	$31,781	$ 1,133	$ —	$ —	$ —	$(156,706)
General revenues								
Taxes:								
Property taxes.					$ 73,754	$ —	$ 73,754	$ —
Sales taxes					142,295	—	142,295	—
Earnings/payroll taxes					172,450	—	172,450	—
Other taxes					94,193	—	94,193	—
Unrestricted investment earnings.					886	3,878	4,764	187
Support provided by the City					—	—	—	141,805
Gain on sale of capital assets					62	553	615	—
Transfers.					7,317	(6,906)	411	(411)
Total general revenues, transfers					490,957	(2,475)	488,482	141,581
Change in net assets.					(56,216)	15,976	(40,240)	(15,125)
Net assets—beginning of year					177,303	1,242,747	1,420,050	(20,234)
Net assets—end of year					$121,087	$1,258,723	$1,379,810	$ (35,359)

Program Revenues columns: Charges for Services, Operating Grants and Contributions, Capital Grants and Contributions.
Primary Government columns: Governmental Activities, Business-type Activities, Total.

REVIEW 1 • Prepare a Statement of Activities

We obtain the following information from the financial records of the Town of Scottsville for the year ended December 31, 2013 *(in thousands)*.

Expenses—water utility (enterprise fund)..	$ 700
Expenses—general government	3,500
Expenses—public safety	27,000
Expenses—education	45,600
General property taxes..	58,000
Grants and contributions—education	9,000
Interest on general long-term debt...	340
Charges for general government services	100
Charges for water services...	715
Charges for public safety services...	2,500
Charges for education services	1,100
State grants for public safety...	4,000
Gain on sale of general capital assets	50
Investment income—governmental activities	300
Beginning of year net position—governmental activities..............................	90,000
Beginning of year net position—business-type activities	12,000

Required

Prepare, in good form, the government-wide statement of activities for the Town of Scottsville for the year 2013.

Solutions are located after the chapter assignments.

FUND FINANCIAL STATEMENTS

In addition to the government-wide statements, the CAFR includes financial statements for each of the government's fund types—governmental, proprietary, and fiduciary. Chapters 10 and 11 discuss in detail the preparation of these statements. This section summarizes the CAFR format requirements, including reconciliation of funds statement information to government-wide information. Recall from Chapters 10 and 11 that the fund statements differ in format and method of reporting, as follows:

LO3 Present the fund statements.

Fund Financial Statements

Governmental Funds: modified accrual basis
   Balance sheet
   Statement of revenues, expenditures, and changes in fund balances
Proprietary Funds: full accrual basis
   Statement of net position
   Statement of revenues, expenses, and changes in net position
   Statement of cash flows
Fiduciary Funds: full accrual basis
   Statement of fiduciary net position
   Statement of changes in fiduciary net position

Major Funds

In the fund financial statements, *the general fund is always reported separately*. However, other individual **governmental** and **enterprise** funds are separately disclosed in columnar format only if they are *major funds*. The GASB specifies two tests for determining **major funds**:

- The fund's total assets, liabilities, revenues *or* expenditures (expenses) are *at least ten percent* of the corresponding total for funds of that type—either governmental or enterprise, *and*
- The fund's total assets, liabilities, revenues, *or* expenditures (expenses) are *at least five percent* of the corresponding total for all governmental and enterprise funds.

Suppose total assets of all governmental funds of a local government are $30,000,000, and total assets of all governmental and enterprise funds are $70,000,000. If a specific governmental fund's total assets are $3,500,000 or more, it is separately disclosed, since total assets of $3,500,000 or more meet the $3,000,000 ($= 10\% \times \$30,000,000$) threshold *and* the $3,500,000 ($= 5\% \times \$70,000,000$) threshold. A fund must meet both thresholds; a fund meeting the 10 percent test for assets and the 5 percent test for assets is a major fund. Any governmental or enterprise fund may be reported as a major fund without meeting these criteria, if separate reporting of its activities is judged to be *relevant to financial statement readers*.

The financial results of **nonmajor** funds are combined in a separate column. Except for the general fund, fund information for governmental and enterprise funds is not disclosed by fund type unless there is only one fund within the fund type, *and* it is a major fund. *SGAS 34* requires that only *individual major funds* within a fund type be separately disclosed. Thus if a county has two of six special revenue funds meeting the major funds criteria, two columns appear on the fund financial statements to separately report the two major special revenue funds. The rest are combined in one column as nonmajor funds. If none of the county's capital projects funds meet the criteria for major funds, no separate information on capital projects funds is reported.

Separate reporting of major funds applies to governmental and enterprise funds, but *not* internal service funds or fiduciary funds. Internal service funds are reported *in total* on the proprietary funds financial statements. The fiduciary funds are separately reported *by fund type*—pension trusts, investment trusts, private-purpose trusts, and agency funds.

Governmental Funds Financial Statements

The governmental funds financial statements reflect modified accrual accounting, and report on the activities of the general, special revenue, capital projects, debt service, and permanent funds.

- The **balance sheet** shows current assets, current liabilities, and fund balances for the general fund and each major governmental fund and the total balances of the non-major funds. A separate column reports the total assets, liabilities, and fund balances for all governmental funds. Per *SGAS 54*, fund balances are categorized as nonspendable, restricted, committed, assigned and unassigned.
- The **statement of revenues, expenditures, and changes in fund balances** shows operating results for each major governmental fund and totals for the non-major funds and for all governmental funds. Revenues are shown by source, and expenditures are categorized by program or function. Other financing sources and uses are separately listed.

The governmental funds financial statements for the City of St. Louis appear in Exhibits 12.3 and 12.4. The City has two major governmental funds other than the general fund—the capital projects fund and the grants special revenue fund. Most revenues come from taxes. Expenditures for public safety comprise about 34 percent of total governmental fund expenditures.

Because governmental funds use modified accrual accounting, they report capital asset acquisitions as *expenditures* (capital outlay), and long-term debt issuance as *other financing sources*. Expenditures exceeded revenues by $131,289,000, partially offset by $116,620,000 in net other financing sources, primarily long-term debt proceeds. Governmental fund balances therefore declined by $14,669,000.

EXHIBIT 12.3 **2010 Governmental Funds Balance Sheet, City of St. Louis, Missouri**

CITY OF ST. LOUIS, MISSOURI
Balance Sheet
Governmental Funds
June 30, 2010

(in thousands)	Major Funds			Nonmajor Funds	
	General Fund	Capital Projects Fund	Grants Fund	Other Governmental Funds	Total Governmental Funds
Assets					
Cash and cash equivalents:					
Restricted.................................	$ 16,293	$ 12,113	$ —	$ 7,260	$ 35,666
Unrestricted.............................	16,444	7,857	—	32,328	56,629
Investments:					
Restricted.................................	13,468	105,447	—	7,214	126,129
Unrestricted.............................	905	843	2,897	4,736	9,381
Receivables, net of allowances:					
Taxes	89,904	2,833	—	37,816	130,553
Licenses and permits	2,528	—	—	215	2,743
Intergovernmental	3,841	1,505	18,771	197	24,314
Charges for services	492	55	—	1,346	1,893
Notes and loans	—	—	—	50	50
Other......................................	592	1	1	68	662
Due from component units...................	708	—	—	—	708
Due from other funds	18,462	—	—	2,366	20,828
Total assets...............................	$163,637	$130,654	$21,669	$93,596	$409,556
Liabilities and fund balances					
Liabilities:					
Accounts payable and accrued liabilities	$ 4,536	$ 6,180	$ 8,853	$ 1,798	$ 21,367
Accrued salaries and other benefits	6,083	89	585	756	7,513
Due to component units...................	4,749	—	—	2,041	6,790
Due to other funds........................	1,403	240	12,293	1,599	15,535
Due to other government agencies	38	—	—	—	38
Advance from other funds	19,036	—	—	—	19,036
Deferred revenue	68,577	—	—	24,205	92,782
Other liabilities	5,799	—	—	489	6,288
Total liabilities...............................	110,221	6,509	21,731	30,888	169,349
Fund balances:					
Reserved:					
Encumbrances	1,600	29,470	—	6,087	37,157
Debt service	29,684	1,374	—	15,404	46,462
Special revenues	—	—	—	21,813	21,813
Capital projects...........................	—	107,262	—	—	107,262
Unreserved, reported in:					
General fund	22,132	—	—	—	22,132
Special revenue funds.....................	—	—	(62)	19,404	19,342
Capital projects fund......................	—	(13,961)	—	—	(13,961)
Total fund balances.......................	53,416	124,145	(62)	62,708	240,207
Total liabilities and fund balances	$163,637	$130,654	$21,669	$93,596	$409,556

CITY OF ST. LOUIS, MISSOURI
Statement of Revenues, Expenditures, and Changes in Fund Balances
Governmental Funds
For Year Ended June 30, 2010

	Major Funds			Nonmajor Funds	
(in thousands)	General Fund	Capital Projects Fund	Grants Fund	Other Governmental Funds	Total Governmental Funds
Revenues					
Taxes	$319,556	$ 18,234	$ —	$142,292	$480,082
Licenses and permits	18,990	—	—	5,224	24,214
Intergovernmental	23,311	8,178	80,264	5,331	117,084
Charges for services, net	16,586	241	—	14,079	30,906
Court fines and forfeitures	11,558	—	—	—	11,558
Investment income	563	240	—	83	886
Interfund services provided	3,043	—	—	—	3,043
Miscellaneous	5,692	1,476	—	8,819	15,987
Total revenues	399,299	28,369	80,264	175,828	683,760
Expenditures					
Current:					
General government	47,687	7	11,938	18,274	77,906
Convention and tourism	159	—	—	17	176
Parks and recreation	18,544	4,041	29	4,743	27,357
Judicial	46,700	—	3,430	3,855	53,985
Streets	29,424	5,274	155	2,503	37,356
Public Safety:					
Fire	65,402	—	—	1,188	66,590
Police	122,393	1,274	—	18,138	141,805
Police-Pension	11,785	—	—	2,998	14,783
Other	45,493	—	362	8,798	54,653
Health and welfare	2,994	—	30,121	18,115	51,230
Public services	23,828	3,436	2,143	29,908	59,315
Community development	—	—	30,288	45,976	76,264
Capital outlay	—	49,678	—	1,497	51,175
Debt service:					
Principal	17,924	12,656	895	15,246	46,721
Interest and fiscal charges	19,512	8,929	903	25,211	54,555
Payment to bond escrow agent	1,178	—	—	—	1,178
Total expenditures	453,023	85,295	80,264	196,467	815,049
Deficiency of revenues over expenditures	(53,724)	(56,926)	—	(20,639)	(131,289)
Other financing sources (uses)					
Sale of capital assets	—	62	—	—	62
Issuance of leasehold revenue bonds	27,078	47,113	—	—	74,191
Issuance of contractual obligation with component unit	—	—	—	16,960	16,960
Bond premium on debt issuances	96	—	—	300	396
Bond discount on debt issuances	(85)	—	—	(299)	(384)
Issuance of capital lease–Rolling Stock	—	704	—	—	704
Issuance of tax increment financing notes	—	—	—	28,352	28,352
Payment to refunded escrow agent-leasehold revenue bonds	(12,391)	—	—	—	(12,391)
Payment to refunded escrow agent-capital lease	—	(341)	—	—	(341)
Payment to redeem tax increment financing note	—	—	—	(16,961)	(16,961)
Receipt of redevelopment lease proceeds from component unit	—	—	—	18,006	18,006
Transfers in	36,013	20,430	—	2,132	58,575
Transfers out	(5,625)	(820)	—	(44,104)	(50,549)
Total other financing sources (uses), net	45,086	67,148	—	4,386	116,620
Net change in fund balances	(8,638)	10,222	—	(16,253)	(14,669)
Fund balances:					
Beginning of year	62,054	113,923	(62)	78,961	254,876
End of year	$ 53,416	$124,145	$ (62)	$ 62,708	$240,207

The 2010 governmental funds balance sheet for the City of St. Louis displays fund balance in pre-*SGAS 54* format, because *SGAS 54* is not effective until 2011. Therefore the City displays the fund balances of its governmental funds in "reserved" and "unreserved" classifications. Without additional information on fund balance restrictions, it is not possible to accurately recast the 2010 balance sheet in the new format. However, the City's 2010 governmental funds fund balances might appear as follows, under these assumptions:

● Restricted assets are nonspendable.

● General fund unreserved fund balance and deficits in unreserved fund balances of other funds are unassigned.

● Positive (surplus) unreserved fund balances in funds other than the general fund are assigned.

● All other fund balances are externally restricted.

CITY OF ST. LOUIS, MISSOURI
Balance Sheet
Governmental Funds
June 30, 2010

	Major Funds			Nonmajor Funds	
(in thousands)	General Fund	Capital Projects Fund	Grants Fund	Other Governmental Funds	Total Governmental Funds
Fund balances:					
Nonspendable	$29,761	$117,560	$ —	$14,474	$161,795
Restricted	1,523	20,546	—	28,830	50,899
Assigned...........	—	—	—	19,404	19,404
Unassigned.........	22,132	(13,961)	(62)	—	8,109
Total fund balances ...	$53,416	$124,145	$(62)	$62,708	$240,207

Required Reconciliations Because the governmental funds statements reflect modified accrual accounting, they do not agree with the government-wide statements that follow full accrual accounting. *SGAS 34* requires (1) a *reconciliation of total governmental fund balances to the total net position of governmental activities*, and (2) a *reconciliation of the change in governmental fund balances to the change in total net position of governmental activities.*

Recall the major differences between modified accrual and full accrual accounting.

● Acquisitions of capital assets increase assets in the government-wide statements, but reduce fund balance—as expenditures—in the fund statements.

● Depreciation of general capital assets reduces net position in the government-wide statements, but is not reported in the fund statements.

● When capital assets of governmental funds are sold, the difference between the proceeds and the book value of the assets is reported as a change in net position—a gain or a loss—in the government-wide statements, but the total proceeds increase fund balance in the governmental fund statements.

● Issuance of long-term general obligation debt increases liabilities in the government-wide statements, but increases fund balance—as other financing sources—in the fund statements.

● Payments on long-term debt reduce liabilities in the government-wide statements, but reduce fund balance—as expenditures—in the fund statements.

● Governmental funds do not accrue any revenues or expenditures not involving flows of current financial resources, so accrued interest, compensated absences, pension and OPEB costs not currently using financial resources are not reported.

In addition to differences between modified and full accrual accounting, recall that *"governmental activities" on the government-wide statements include internal service funds, whereas "governmental funds" do not*. Therefore, reconciliation of governmental funds to governmental activities requires the addition of internal service funds information. Because internal service funds report on the full accrual basis, their data need not be adjusted.

Reconciliation of the Governmental Funds Balance Sheet to the Statement of Net Position   This schedule appears with the governmental funds balance sheet. It reconciles the total fund balances on that statement with the balance reported for net position of governmental activities in the government-wide statement of net position. The general format of the reconciliation is:

Total fund balances, governmental funds	$XXX
+ Capital and other long-term assets used in governmental activities, net of accumulated depreciation ..	XXX
+ Receivables producing financial resources in future periods	XXX
− Long-term liabilities used to finance governmental activities.	(XXX)
− Other payables not requiring current financial resources.	(XXX)
+ Internal service fund net position included in the government-wide statement of net position but not included in the governmental funds balance sheet.	XXX
Net position of governmental activities.	$XXX

The 2010 reconciliation of governmental fund balances to net position of governmental activities for the City of St. Louis appears in Exhibit 12.5. Total fund balances—governmental funds, $240,207,000, is found on the governmental funds balance sheet in Exhibit 12.3. Total net position (net assets)—governmental activities, $121,087,000, is on the government-wide statement of net position in Exhibit 12.1. The major reconciliation items are additions for net capital assets of $808,276,000 that were deducted from governmental fund balances but not from net position of governmental activities, and deductions for bonds and notes payable of $898,020,000 that were added to governmental fund balances but not net position of governmental activities. The City adds $71,556,000 in tax receivables to be collected in future periods, recognized as assets on the full accrual basis but not reported using modified accrual accounting. Accrued compensated absences of $27,814,000 and interest payable of $60,607,000 are deducted because they are reported as liabilities on the statement of net position but not on the governmental funds balance sheet.

Reconciliation of the Governmental Funds Statement of Revenues, Expenditures, and Changes in Fund Balances to the Government-Wide Statement of Activities   This schedule appears with the governmental funds operating statement. It reconciles the total change in fund balances on that statement with the change in net position of governmental activities in the government-wide statement of net position. The general format of the reconciliation is:

Change in total fund balances, governmental funds	$XXX
+ Outlays for general capital assets	XXX
− Depreciation expense for general capital assets	(XXX)
+ Accrued revenues of governmental funds producing resources in future periods.	XXX
− Long-term debt proceeds used to finance governmental activities.	(XXX)
+ Repayments of long-term debt principal	XXX
− Accrued expenses of governmental funds using resources in future periods	(XXX)
+ Increase (- decrease) in internal service fund net position not included in the governmental funds operating statement but included in the government-wide statement of activities	XXX
Change in net position of governmental activities	$XXX

The 2010 reconciliation of the change in governmental fund balances to the change in net position (net assets) of governmental activities for the City of St. Louis appears in Exhibit 12.6. The

$(14,669,000) change in total fund balances—governmental funds, is found on the governmental funds statement of revenues, expenditures, and changes in fund balances in Exhibit 12.4. The $(56,216,000) change in total net position (assets)—governmental activities, is on the government-wide statement of activities in Exhibit 12.2. The major reconciliation items are capital outlay of $51,175,000, depreciation of $45,618,000, and total debt proceeds, net of principal repayments, of $42,783,000.

EXHIBIT 12.5   2010 Reconciliation, Governmental Funds Balance Sheet to Statement of Net Assets, City of St. Louis, Missouri

CITY OF ST. LOUIS, MISSOURI
Reconciliation of the Balance Sheet of Governmental Funds to the Statement of Net Assets
June 30, 2010

(in thousands)

Total fund balances—governmental funds—balance sheet..	$240,207
Amounts reported for governmental activities in the statement of net assets are different because:	
Capital assets and certain other assets used in governmental activities (excluding internal service fund capital assets) are not financial resources and, therefore, are not reported in the fund financial statements.	808,276
The City reports a net pension asset on the statement of net assets to the extent actual contributions to the City's retirement plans exceed the annual actuarial required contribution. This asset is not reported in the fund financial statements. Fluctuations in net pension assets are reported in the statement of activities.	36,420
Various taxes related to fiscal year 2010 will be collected beyond the 60-day period used to record revenue in the fund financial statements. Revenue for this amount is recognized in the government-wide financial statements.	13,753
Property taxes are assessed by the City on January 1st of each calendar year, but are not due until December 31st. Taxes assessed on January 1, 2010, and payable on December 31, 2010, are deferred within the fund financial statements. However, revenue for this amount is recognized in the government-wide financial statements.	71,556
Internal service funds are used by management to change the cost of risk management and mailroom services to the individual funds, generally on a cost reimbursement basis. The assets and liabilities of internal service funds are included in governmental activities in the statement of net assets, net of amounts due from enterprise funds....	2,554
Bond issuance costs are reported in the governmental funds financial statements as expenditures when debt is issued, whereas the amounts are deferred and amortized over the life of the debt on the government-wide financial statements.	17,839
Short-term promissory notes payable applicable to the City's governmental activities are not due and payable using current financial resources and, accordingly, are not reported as liabilities within the fund financial statements.	(9,068)
Long-term liabilities applicable to the City's governmental activities are not due and payable in the current period and, accordingly, are not reported as liabilities within the fund financial statements. Interest on long-term debt is not accrued in governmental funds, but rather is recognized as an expenditure when due. All liabilities—both current and long-term—are reported on the government-wide statement of net assets. Also, during the year, the City issued new debt and refunded some of its existing debt. Discounts, premiums, bond issuance costs, and deferred amounts on refunding are reported in the governmental fund financial statements when the debt was issued, whereas these amounts are deferred and amortized over the life of the debt on the government-wide financial statements. Balances as of June 30. 2010. are:	
Accrued compensated absences..	(27,814)
Net pension obligation	(25,123)
Accrued interest payable	(60,607)
Joint venture financing agreement..	(53,873)
Bonds and notes payable and other long-term debt..	(898,020)
Unamortized discounts...	5,394
Unamortized premiums...	(11,286)
Unamortized deferred amounts on refunding	10,879
Total net assets—governmental activities—statement of net assets...................................	$121,087

EXHIBIT 12.6 2010 Reconciliation, Governmental Funds Operating Statement to Statement of Activities, City of St. Louis, Missouri

CITY OF ST LOUIS. MISSOURI
Reconciliation of the Statement of Revenues, Expenditures, and Changes in Fund Balances
of Governmental Funds to the Statement of Activities
For Year Ended June 30, 2010

(in thousands)

Net change in fund balances—governmental funds—statement of revenues, expenditures, and changes in fund balances		$ (14,669)
Amounts reported for governmental activities in the statement of activities are different because:		
Governmental funds report capital outlays as expenditures. However, in the statement of activities. The cost of those assets, meeting the capitalization threshold, is allocated over their estimated useful lives and recorded as depreciation expense. Additionally, contributions of capital assets to the City are recorded as capital contributions on the statement of activities. This is the amount by which capital outlays and capital contributions, meeting the capitalization threshold, exceeded depreciation expense in the current year. Details of the reported amounts are as follows:		
Capital outlay	$ 51,175	
Capital contribution	407	
Loss on disposal of capital assets	(5,265)	
Depreciation expense.	(45,618)	699
Revenues in the statement of activities that do not provide current financial resources are not reported as revenues in the fund financial statements. These amounts represent the extent to which revenues not providing current financial resources in the current fiscal year exceeded revenues not providing current financial resources in the prior fiscal year (which are recognized in the fund financial statements in the current year). Such amounts are attributable to the following factors:		
Change in revenues received after the 60-day accrual period	186	
Property taxes due in the fiscal year following the fiscal year in which they were assessed	2,554	2,740
Internal service funds are used by management to charge the cost of risk management and mailroom services to the individual funds. The net income of internal service funds attributable to governmental activities is reported on the statement of activities..		1,082
Adjustment to record effect of internal service activities adjustment within business-type activities		(1,120)
The City reports a net pension obligation/asset on the statement of net assets to the extent actual contributions to the City's retirement plan fall below/exceed the annual required contribution. This obligation/asset is not reported in the fund financial statements. Fluctuations in net pension obligations/assets are reported in the statement of activities..		409
Bond proceeds are reported as financing sources in governmental funds financial statements and thus contribute to the net change in fund balance. In the statement of net assets, however, issuing debt increases long-term liabilities and does not affect the statement of activities. Similarly, repayments of principal is an expenditure in the governmental funds financial statements, but reduces the liability in the statement of net assets.		
Debt issued during the current year:		
Leasehold revenue bonds:		
Series 2009A Convention Center Compound Interest Leasehold Revenue Bonds	(7,762)	
Series 2009B Convention Center Current Interest Junior Lien Leasehold Revenue Bonds.	(23,255)	
Series 2010A Convention Center Compound Interest Leasehold Revenue Bonds	(24,736)	
Series 2010B Convention Center Compound Interest Leasehold Revenue Refunding Bonds	(8,518)	
Series 2009 Justice Center Leasehold Revenue Refunding Bonds	(9,920)	
Obligation with component unit—Series 2010 LCRA Recovery Zone Facility Special Obligation Redevelopment Bonds. . . .	(16,960)	
Capital Lease-Rolling Stock	(705)	
Tax increment financing notes payable	(28,352)	
Repayments during the current year:		
Advance refunding of Series 1996B Justice Center Leasehold Revenue Bonds.	10,835	
Advance refunding of Series 1993A Convention Center Leasehold Revenue Bonds	2,567	
Advance refunding of Series 2006 Capital Lease-Rolling Stock	341	
Advance refunding of 600 Washington-One City Centre TIF notes	16,961	
Annual principal payments on bonds and notes payable.	39,832	
Annual principal payments on joint venture financing agreement	3,643	
Annual principal payments on capital leases	2,676	
Annual principal payments on SLMFC Lease Certificates of Participation	570	
		(42,783)
Under the modified accrual basis of accounting used in the governmental funds financial statements, expenditures are not recognized for transactions that are not normally paid with expendable available financial resources. In the statement of activities, however, which is presented on the accrual basis of accounting, expenses and liabilities are reported regardless of when financial resources are available. In addition, interest on long-term debt is not recognized under the modified accrual basis of accounting until due, rather than as it accrues. This adjustment combines the net changes of the following:		
Accrued compensated absences.	398	
Accrued interest payable	(5,307)	
Landfill closure liability	250	
Discounts on debt issuances, net of amortization	175	
Premiums on debt issuances, net of amortization	1,300	
Deferred bond issuance costs. net of amortization	2,144	
Deferred amounts on refundings	(1,534)	(2,574)
Change in net assets—governmental activities—statement of activities		$ (56,216)

Reporting Perspective

When reconciling the governmental funds financial statements, prepared on a modified accrual basis, to the government-wide statements, prepared using full accrual accounting, do you expect the fund balances to always be larger than the full accrual net position balances? A significant shortcoming of the modified accrual basis is that a government can improve its financial health by issuing long-term debt. This was a major motivation for requiring presentation of government activities on the full accrual basis. Long-term debt proceeds add to fund balances, but not to net position. Borrowing to improve financial position is not a long-term solution to deficit spending. Governments that engage in this practice will likely report higher fund balances than net position. The City of St. Louis reconciliations are a case in point. In 2010, the fund balances of governmental funds declined by $14,669,000, while net position of governmental activities declined by $56,216,000, almost four times as much. The City covered much of its net deficit by issuing long-term debt. We should not, however, assume that all governments report the same pattern. For example, for the year ended April 30, 2010, the **City of Kansas City, Missouri** reports a net *negative* change in governmental fund balances of $(2,461,000), and a *positive* change in net position of governmental activities of $3,598,000. In 2010, Kansas City's net capital outlays and debt principal repayments exceeded proceeds from debt issuance.

REVIEW 2 ● Reconcile the Change in Fund Balances to Change in Net Position

We obtain the following information from Shasta County's financial records for 2014 *(in thousands)*:

1.	Net change in fund balances—governmental funds.	$(2,200)
2.	Principal repayments—general obligation debt.	5,600
3.	Accrued OPEB expense.	100
4.	Cost of general capital assets acquired	14,000
5.	Proceeds from sale of general capital assets.	300
6.	Loss on sale of general capital assets.	10
7.	Accrued interest expense on general obligation debt.	192
8.	Depreciation expense on general capital assets.	3,800
9.	Proceeds from issuance of general obligation debt.	9,300

Required

Prepare a reconciliation of change in fund balances—governmental funds, to change in net position—governmental activities. Shasta County has no internal service funds.

Solutions are located after the chapter assignments.

Proprietary Funds Financial Statements

Proprietary funds consist of enterprise and internal service funds. As with governmental funds, each major enterprise fund is shown separately and an aggregate total is reported for non-major enterprise funds. However, *only a single total for all internal service funds is shown*. The GASB believes that this reporting format allows readers to more easily reconcile the proprietary fund financial statements with the government-wide statements. Separate reporting of each fund type in the fund statements allows readers to relate the totals to those in the government-wide statements, since governmental activities on the government-wide statements include both governmental and internal service funds, and business-type activities report the results of enterprise funds. These financial statements are required for proprietary funds:

- **Statement of net position**, with individual assets and liabilities classified according to liquidity, and net position reported in three categories as in the government-wide statements. Since proprietary funds use full accrual accounting, *no* reconciliation to the government-wide statements is needed. The total net position of all enterprise funds equals the total net position of business-type activities on the government-wide statement of net position.

- **Statement of revenues, expenses, and changes in net position**, with operating and nonoperating items separately categorized. Reporting a revenue or expense as operating or nonoperating depends on the government's policy, disclosed in the notes to the financial statements. Capital contributions received from other funds are reported separately, below nonoperating items. A reconciliation of the change in net position of proprietary funds to the change in net position shown on the government-wide statements is *not* needed, because both statements use full accrual accounting. The change in net position of enterprise funds on the statement of revenues, expenses, and changes in net position equals the change in net position of business-type activities on the government-wide statement of activities.

- **Statement of cash flows**, using the *direct* method to present cash from operating activities, and reconciliation of operating income to cash flow from operating activities, as in business reporting. Statement categories are: cash flows from operating activities, cash flows from noncapital financing activities, cash flows from capital and related financing activities, and cash flows from investing activities. Chapter 11 discusses these categories in detail.

Because proprietary funds use full accrual accounting, any differences between the government-wide statements and proprietary funds statements should be due to differences in classification, not valuation.

The three required statements for the proprietary funds of the City of St. Louis, Missouri appear in Exhibits 12.7, 12.8, and 12.9. The City has three enterprise funds, all major funds—the Lambert-St. Louis International Airport, the Water Division, and the Parking Division. The proprietary funds operating statement in Exhibit 12.8 reports the 2010 change in enterprise fund net position (net assets) as $14,856,000. The change in net position (net assets) of business-type activities reported in the government-wide statement of activities in Exhibit 12.2 is $15,976,000. The $1,120,000 discrepancy is attributed to an adjustment to reclassify internal service fund activities. Enterprise fund net position, reported in the proprietary funds balance sheet in Exhibit 12.7, is $1,258,723,000. The government-wide statement of net position in Exhibit 12.1 reports business-type net position at the same amount.

CITY OF ST. LOUIS, MISSOURI
Statement of Fund Net Assets
Proprietary Funds
June 30, 2010

(in thousands)	Major Funds—Enterprise Funds				Internal Service Funds
	Lambert— St. Louis International Airport	Water Division	Parking Division	Total Enterprise Funds	
Assets					
Current assets					
Cash and cash equivalents:					
Restricted cash and cash equivalents	$ 65,955	$ 5,101	$ 661	$ 71,717	$ —
Unrestricted cash and cash equivalents	9,346	9,888	9,845	29,079	2,725
Investments—unrestricted	—	—	—	—	93
Receivables, net of allowances:					
Intergovernmental	7,422	—	—	7,422	530
Charges for services	11,147	6,802	67	18,016	—
Passenger facility charges	3,193	—	—	3,193	—
Accrued interest	425	—	—	425	—
Prepaid assets	—	—	—	—	48
Due from other funds and component unit	—	—	—	—	4,469
Advance to other funds	—	—	—	—	19,036
Inventories	2,219	2,196	—	4,415	—
Other current assets	636	3	20	659	—
Total current assets	100,343	23,990	10,593	134,926	26,901
Noncurrent assets					
Investments—restricted	311,662	5,744	10,331	327,737	—
Capital assets:					
Property, plant and equipment	1,511,274	276,227	80,353	1,867,854	137
Less accumulated depreciation	(659,174)	(127,451)	(21,001)	(807,626)	(113)
Net property, plant and equipment	852,100	148,776	59,352	1,060,228	24
Land and easements	754,343	1,238	21,319	776,900	—
Construction-in-progress	32,872	3,891	—	36,763	—
Capital assets, net	1,639,315	153,905	80,671	1,873,891	24
Deferred charges and other assets	29,594	121	1,728	31,443	—
Total noncurrent assets	1,980,571	159,770	92,730	2,233,071	24
Total assets	2,080,914	183,760	103,323	2,367,997	26,925
Liabilities					
Current liabilities					
Accounts payable and accrued liabilities	5,519	1,008	479	7,006	1,471
Accrued salaries and other benefits	5,123	1,242	149	6,514	—
Accrued vacation and compensatory time benefits	3,949	1,691	149	5,789	—
Contracts and retainage payable	9,863	—	—	9,863	—
Accrued interest payable	23,851	501	132	24,484	—
Current portion of revenue bonds	29,970	3,585	1,973	35,528	—
Due to other funds	3,547	4,641	760	8,948	264
Due to other government agencies	—	—	212	212	—
Claims payable	—	—	—	—	22,636
Deferred revenue	725	2,215	1,878	4,818	—
Total current liabilities	82,547	14,883	5,732	103,162	24,371
Noncurrent liabilities					
Revenue bonds payable, net	894,248	15,666	69,403	979,317	—
Customer deposits	—	1,851	—	1,851	—
Other liabilities	16,575	6,613	1,756	24,944	—
Total noncurrent liabilities	910,370	24,130	71,159	1,006,112	—
Total liabilities	993,370	39,013	76,891	1,109,274	24,371
Net assets					
Invested in capital assets, net of related debt	926,576	134,654	10,669	1,071,899	24
Restricted:					
Debt service	108,514	4,951	10,991	124,456	—
Capital projects	—	4,043	—	4,043	—
Airport improvement program	4,662	—	—	4,662	—
Passenger facility charges	30,288	—	—	30,288	—
Unrestricted	17,504	1,099	4,772	23,375	2,530
Total net assets	$1,087,544	$144,747	$ 26,432	$1,258,723	$ 2,554

EXHIBIT 12.8 2010 Proprietary Funds Statement of Revenues, Expenses, and Changes in Fund Net Assets, City of St. Louis, Missouri

CITY OF ST. LOUIS, MISSOURI
Statement of Revenues, Expenses, and Changes in Fund Net Assets
Proprietary Funds
For Year Ended June 30, 2010

Major Funds—Enterprise Funds

(in thousands)	Lambert— St. Louis International Airport	Water Division	Parking Division	Total Enterprise Funds	Internal Service Funds
Operating revenues					
Aviation revenues	$ 93,211	$ —	$ —	$ 93,211	$ —
Concessions	21,329	—	—	21,329	—
Water sales	—	47,994	—	47,994	—
Lease revenue	3,751	—	—	3,751	—
Parking, net	17,147	—	12,018	29,165	—
Charges for services	—	—	—	—	21,416
Intergovernmental revenue	—	—	—	—	695
Miscellaneous	—	2,365	410	2,775	—
Total operating revenues	135,438	50,359	12,428	198,225	22,111
Operating expenses					
Claims incurred	—	—	—	—	18,936
Premiums	—	—	—	—	1,464
Personal services	41,169	15,425	5,174	61,768	267
Material and supplies	5,698	9,741	238	15,677	352
Purchased power	—	2,421	—	2,421	—
Contractual services	38,034	5,936	978	44,948	—
Miscellaneous	—	1,893	826	2,719	—
Depreciation and amortization	46,937	4,964	2,452	54,353	13
Interfund services used	2,484	1,807	75	4,366	—
Total operating expenses	134,322	47,187	9,743	186,252	21,032
Operating income	1,116	8,172	2,685	11,973	1,079
Nonoperating revenues (expenses)					
Intergovernmental revenue	1,615	—	—	1,615	—
Investment income	3,247	312	319	3,878	3
Interest expense	(45,854)	(1,261)	(3,771)	(50,886)	—
Passenger facility charges	24,848	—	—	24,848	—
Amortization of bond issue costs	(1,599)	(31)	—	(1,630)	—
Loss on disposal of capital assets	423	—	130	553	—
Miscellaneous. net	92	624	—	716	—
Total nonoperating revenues (expenses), net	(17,228)	(356)	(3,322)	(20,906)	3
Income (loss) before transfers and capital contributions	(16,112)	7,816	(637)	(8,933)	1,082
Transfers in	—	—	676	676	—
Transfers out	(5,813)	(2,889)	—	(8,702)	—
Capital contributions	31,815	—	—	31,815	—
Change in net assets	9,890	4,927	39	14,856	1,082
Total net assets-beginning of year	1,077,654	139,820	26,393	1,243,867	1,472
Total net assets-end of year	$1,087,544	$144,747	$26,432	$1,258,723	$ 2,554

CITY OF ST. LOUIS, MISSOURI
Statement of Cash Flows
Proprietary Funds
For Year Ended June 30, 2010

(in thousands)	Major Funds—Enterprise Funds			Total Enterprise Funds	Internal Service Funds
	Lambert—St. Louis International Airport	Water Division	Parking Division		
Cash flows from operating activities					
Receipts from customers and users..........................	$ 137,763	$49,820	$12,384	$ 199,967	$19,061
Other operating cash receipts	—	—	36	36	—
Payments to suppliers of goods and services	(48,546)	(18,768)	(1,980)	(69,294)	(17,684)
Payments to employees..................................	(41,341)	(15,264)	(4,893)	(61,498)	(264)
Payments for interfund services used	(3,113)	(1,967)	—	(5,080)	
Net cash provided by operating activities...................	44,763	13,821	5,547	64,131	1,113
Cash flows from noncapital financing activities					
Interest paid on share of bond pension liability	—	(238)	—	(238)	—
Transfers from other funds...............................	—	—	676	676	—
Transfers to other funds	(5,813)	(2,846)	—	(8,659)	—
Net cash used in noncapital financing activities..............	(5,813)	(3,084)	676	(8,221)	
Cash flows from capital and related financing activities					
Cash collections from passenger facility charges	24,903	—	—	24,903	—
Receipts from federal financing assistance	41,923	—	—	41,923	—
Acquisition and construction of capital assets.................	(34,770)	(3,691)	(4,164)	(42,625)	—
Insurance recoveries....................................	(2,479)	—	12	(2,467)	—
Proceeds from sale of surplus property	535	—	137	672	—
Proceeds from issuance of bond	128,430	—	—	128,430	—
Principal paid on commercial paper.........................	(25,000)	—	—	(25,000)	—
Principal paid on revenue bond maturities....................	(21,670)	(3,440)	(1,929)	(27,039)	—
Cash paid for interest	(44,528)	(959)	(3,505)	(48,992)	—
Proceeds from lease termination and other	—	677	—	677	—
Net cash provided by (used in) capital and related financing activities................................	67,334	(7,413)	(9,449)	50,482	
Cash flows from investing activities					
Purchase of investments	(549,989)	(26,790)	(21,291)	(598,070)	—
Proceeds from sales and maturities of investments.............	440,528	28,921	24,310	493,759	—
Investment income	2,689	312	344	3,345	—
Net cash provided by (used in) investing activities.............	(106,772)	2,443	3,363	(100,966)	—
Net increase (decrease) in cash and cash equivalents..........	(478)	5,767	137	5,426	1,113
Cash and cash equivalents:					
Beginning of year:					
Unrestricted..	5,336	3,927	1,612	10,875	1,705
Restricted	70,443	5,295	8,757	84,495	—
	75,779	9,222	10,369	95,370	1,705
End of year:					
Unrestricted..	9,346	9,888	9,845	29,079	2,818
Restricted	65,955	5,101	661	71,717	—
	$ 75,301	$14,989	$10,506	$100,796	$ 2,818
Reconciliation of operating income (loss) to net cash provided by operating activities:					
Operating income......................................	$ 1,116	$ 8,172	$ 2,685	$ 11,973	$ 1,079
Adjustments to reconcile operating income (loss) to net cash provided by operating activities:					
Depreciation and amortization	46,937	4,964	2,452	54,353	13
Changes in assets and liabilities:					
Receivables, net	3,501	(652)	17	2,866	(406)
Inventories.......................................	(318)	262	—	(56)	—
Other assets, net..................................	25	—	20	45	(33)
Accounts payable, accrued liabilities, accrued salaries and other benefits........................	(890)	(344)	51	(1,183)	365
Claims payable	—	—	—	—	2,270
Deferred revenue..................................	(576)	363	(25)	(238)	—
Due to/from other funds	(629)	810	98	279	771
Advance to other funds.............................	—	—	—	—	(2,946)
Advance from other funds...........................	—	—	—	—	—
Customer deposits	—	241	—	241	—
Other long term liabilities...........................	(4,403)	5	249	(4,149)	—
Total adjustments	43,647	5,649	2,862	52,158	34
Net cash provided by operating activities................	$ 44,763	$13,821	$ 5,547	$ 64,131	$ 1,113
Supplemental disclosure for noncash activities:					
Gain on disposal of surplus property........................	$ 423	$ —	—	$ 423	
Unrealized (loss) gain on investments	$ (174)	$ —	114	$ (60)	

Fiduciary Funds Financial Statements

Fiduciary funds use full accrual accounting to report the resources and activities related to assets held in trust or in an agency capacity for entities or individuals outside the governmental unit. Separate columns appear for each of the four fiduciary fund types. No reconciliations to the government-wide statements exist, because those statements do not include fiduciary activities. Required financial statements are:

- **Statement of fiduciary net position.** The net position category generally shows only the balance of net position held in trust for others. Agency funds have no net position balance, because assets equal liabilities.

- **Statement of changes in fiduciary net position.** Only trust fund activities are reported, since agency funds do not report net position.

The City of St. Louis has pension trust funds and agency funds; their financial statements are in Exhibits 12.10 and 12.11. The pension trust funds report the activities of the City's activities as trustee of the three public employee retirement systems—the Firemen's Retirement System, the Police Retirement System, and the Employees' Retirement System. As expected, various investments comprise the majority of pension trust fund assets. Agency funds account for assets held on behalf of others, including taxes to be remitted to other governmental agencies, payroll withholdings for insurance premiums, and bail bonds received from court defendants. Agency fund assets, consisting of cash, investments and accrued taxes receivable, equal agency fund liabilities, consisting of amounts due to or deposits held for others.

EXHIBIT 12.10   2010 Statement of Fiduciary Net Assets, City of St. Louis, Missouri

CITY OF ST. LOUIS, MISSOURI
Statement of Fiduciary Net Assets
Fiduciary Funds
June 30, 2010

(in thousands)	Pension Trust Funds	Agency Funds
Assets		
Cash and cash equivalents-unrestricted	$ 20,279	$26,651
Cash and cash equivalents-restricted	—	5,971
Investments-unrestricted	—	3,400
Pension trust investments-unrestricted:		
Bonds	209,325	—
Domestic bond funds	49,290	—
Stocks	615,896	—
Mortgage-backed securities	31,774	—
Collective investment funds	288,227	—
Guaranteed fixed income securities	1,641	—
Real estate equities and investment trust	105,249	—
Investment property	1,375	—
Hedge funds	18,658	—
Money market mutual funds and other short -term investments	65,972	—
Managed international equity funds	134,652	—
Total investments	1,522,059	—
Securities lending collateral	61,898	—
Receivables, net of allowances:		
Taxes	—	28,421
Contributions	154	—
Accrued interest	2,283	—
Other	8,219	925
Capital assets, net	424	—
Total assets	1,615,316	65,368
Liabilities		
Accounts payable and accrued liabilities	1,515	2,186
Deposits held for others	406	27,833
Due to other governmental agencies	—	35,349
Securities lending collateral liability	61,898	—
Other liabilities	4,843	—
Total liabilities	68,662	65,368
Net assets		
Net assets held in trust for pension benefits	$1,546,654	$ —

EXHIBIT 12.11   2010 Statement of Changes in Fiduciary Net Assets, City of St. Louis, Missouri

CITY OF ST. LOUIS, MISSOURI
Statement of Changes in Fiduciary Net Assets
Fiduciary Funds
For Year Ended June 30, 2010

(in thousands)	Pension Trust Funds
Additions	
Contributions:	
Members	$ 7,416
Employers	54,058
Investment income:	
Interest and dividends	31,994
Net decline in fair value of investments	(56,378)
Investment income (loss)	(24,384)
Less investment expense	(5,529)
Net investment income (loss)	(29,913)
Total additions	31,561
Deductions	
Benefits	143,922
Refunds of contributions	7,586
Administrative expense	2,661
Total deductions	154,169
Net decrease	(122,608)
Net assets held in trust for pension benefits:	
Beginning of year	1,669,262
End of year	$1,546,654

COMPARISON OF GOVERNMENT-WIDE AND FUNDS INFORMATION

How do the balances in the government-wide statements correspond with those reported in the funds statements? This section compares the governmental activities and business-type activities information reported on the government-wide financial statements with the information reported on the governmental funds and proprietary funds financial statements. Figure 12.2 summarizes the required fund financial statements and their relation to the government-wide financial statements.

LO4 Describe the relation between government-wide and fund statements

Governmental Activities

The government-wide statements report the assets and liabilities, revenues and expenses of governmental funds and internal service funds on a full accrual basis, as governmental activities. The funds statements report similar information, but governmental funds activities use modified accrual accounting, and internal service funds use full accrual accounting.

Compare some of the numbers reported for governmental activities on the statement of net position, Exhibit 12.1, with those reported for governmental funds and internal service funds in their respective fund balance sheets, Exhibits 12.3 and 12.7. Unrestricted cash and cash equivalents in the funds statements are $56,629,000 and $2,725,000 for governmental and internal service funds, respectively. The total, $59,354,000, matches the cash and cash equivalents reported in the government-wide statement of net position for governmental activities.

However, in the funds statements total assets are $409,556,000 for governmental funds and $26,925,000 for internal service funds, much lower than total assets of governmental activities, $1,264,181,000. The difference of $827,700,000 can be mostly explained by the net capital assets of $116,281,000 and $692,019,000 reported on the government-wide statement of net position. Internal service fund capital assets are very small, so most relate to governmental funds, which do not report capital assets on the funds balance sheet.

FIGURE 12.2 Relation Between Fund and Government-Wide Financial Statements

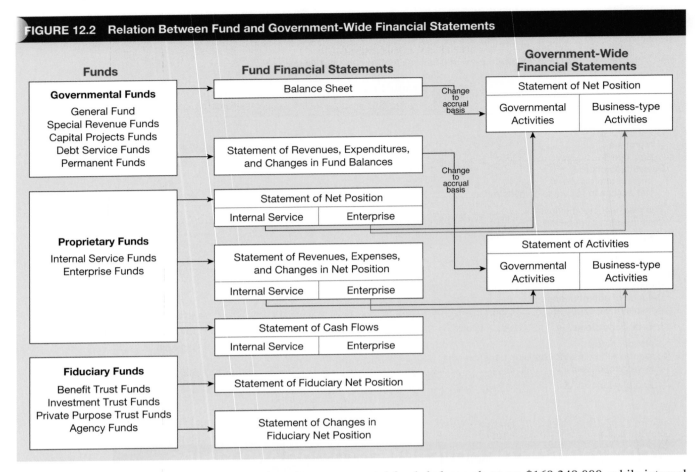

Total liabilities reported on the governmental funds balance sheet are $169,349,000, while internal service fund liabilities reported on the proprietary funds balance sheet are $24,371,000. These amounts are much lower than $1,143,094,000 in total liabilities of governmental activities on the government-wide statement of net position, due to the fact that governmental funds do not report long-term liabilities.

On the government-wide statement of activities, the functional expense categories are similar to those listed on the statement of revenues, expenditures, and changes in fund balances for governmental funds. Functional expenses are typically greater than expenditures, since expenditures exclude such items as depreciation and accrued pension and OPEB costs not requiring current financial resources. For example, general government *expenses* are $84,330,000 but general government *expenditures* are $77,906,000. Convention and tourism *expenses* are $4,507,000, but convention and tourism *expenditures* are only $176,000.

Business-Type Activities

The government-wide statements report the assets and liabilities, revenues and expenses of enterprise funds as business-type activities, and proprietary funds statements also report the activities of enterprise funds. Because both statements use full accrual accounting, the same information should appear in both sets of statements.

Compare some of the numbers reported for business-type activities on the statement of net position, Exhibit 12.1, with those reported for enterprise funds in the proprietary funds statement of net position, Exhibit 12.7. Total assets of business-type activities are $2,359,049,000, while total assets of enterprise funds are $2,367,997,000. Total liabilities of business-type activities are $1,100,326,000, and total liabilities of enterprise funds are $1,109,274,000. Remember that the government-wide financial statements eliminate interfund receivables and payables, and the funds statements do not. We therefore expect the government-wide totals for assets and liabilities for business-type activities to be slightly lower than the enterprise funds totals reported on the funds statement of net position. The proprietary funds statement of net position reports $8,948,000 of enterprise fund liabilities due to other funds, an item not reported on the government-wide statement of net position. This amount explains the discrepancy between government-wide liabilities for business-type activities and enterprise fund liabilities (= \$1,100,326,000 − \$1,109,274,000).

The government-wide statement of activities reports total expenses of business-type activities as \$238,768,000. On the proprietary funds statement of revenues, expenses, and changes in net position, total expenses of enterprise funds are also \$238,768,000, after combining operating and nonoperating expenses (= \$186,252,000 + \$50,886,000 + \$1,630,000).

NOTES AND REQUIRED SUPPLEMENTARY INFORMATION

Both the government-wide and fund financial statements use the same set of accompanying notes. The notes explain the information presented, including the measurement focus, asset capitalization policy, and details on capital assets, long-term debt, and endowment activities. Required supplementary information (RSI) includes the MD&A, presented before the basic financial statements, and information that follows the financial statements and notes.

Budgetary Comparison Schedules

Information presented after the basic financial statements includes **budgetary comparison schedules** for the general fund and each major fund with a legally adopted budget. These schedules report the original and final budgets, reflecting legislative and executive changes during the year, actual results, and a **reconciliation** of budget information to GAAP information.

The budgetary comparison schedule compares the legally budgeted revenues and expenditures for the government, based on applicable laws and regulations, with "actual" balances calculated on the same basis. If budgetary reporting methods differ from GAAP reporting requirements used to measure revenues and expenditures on the funds statements, another schedule reconciles the actual fund balances on the budgetary comparison schedule with the fund balances on the governmental funds balance sheet. Reconciling items include any or all of the following:

- **Entity differences.** Component unit results that appear in the fund financial statements but are not part of the legal budget.

- **Perspective differences.** The legal budget may include programs not reported in the governmental funds.

- **Basis differences.** Budget numbers may use the cash basis while the fund financial statements use the modified accrual basis of accounting.

- **Timing differences.** Year-end outstanding encumbrances are treated as expenditures for budget purposes, but not in GAAP-based fund financial statements.

The City of St. Louis has an annual budget for the general fund, debt service fund, capital projects fund, and several special revenue funds. The summarized 2010 budgetary comparison schedule for St. Louis' general fund appears in Exhibit 12.12. Overall, the final budgeted deficiency of revenues and other financing sources over expenditures and other financing uses was \$(2,605,000), while the actual deficiency of revenues and other financing sources over expenditures and other financing uses was \$(2,706,000), for a negative variance of \$(101,000). Because the actual reported deficiency of \$(2,706,000) does not match the actual change in general fund balance of \$(8,638,000) on the governmental funds operating statement in Exhibit 12.4, the footnotes provide the following reconciliation of the difference *(in thousands)*:

Budget basis	\$(2,706)
Increase (decrease) due to:	
Revenue accruals	(4,761)
Expenditure accruals	(6,241)
Unbudgeted activities and funds	5,070
GAAP basis	\$(8,638)

For the City of St. Louis, the difference between the budget basis and GAAP basis of reporting is due to two factors:

- **Basis differences**—some revenues and expenditures are accrued prior to the cash receipt or payment under the GAAP modified accrual basis, while the budget uses the cash basis.

- **Perspective differences**—the budget does not include certain activities of the general, special revenue and capital projects funds, reported in the general fund financial statements.

EXHIBIT 12.12   Summarized 2010 Budgetary Comparison Schedule, General Fund, City of St. Louis, Missouri

CITY OF ST. LOUIS, MISSOURI
Schedule of Revenues, Expenditures, and Changes in Fund Balances—Budget and Actual
General Fund
For Year Ended June 30, 2010

(in thousands)	Original Budget	Final Revised Budget	Actual	Variance with Final Budget Favorable (Unfavorable)
Revenues				
Taxes	$353,129	$353,129	$332,555	$(20,574)
Licenses and permits	18,259	18,259	18,998	739
Intergovernmental	18,880	18,880	18,140	(740)
Charges for services	20,089	20,089	17,601	(2,488)
Court fines and forfeitures	7,086	7,086	8,236	1,150
Interest	732	732	269	(463)
Miscellaneous	3,525	3,525	4,745	1,220
Total revenues	421,700	421,700	400,544	(21,156)
Expenditures				
General government	43,194	43,149	42,930	219
Convention and tourism	161	161	159	2
Parks and recreation	18,922	18,922	18,649	273
Judicial	47,276	47,382	44,693	2,689
Streets	30,610	30,586	29,537	1,049
Public safety	120,784	120,748	122,442	(1,694)
Health and welfare	3,147	3,147	3,010	137
Public services	26,497	26,496	23,872	2,624
Debt service	24,174	24,174	24,479	(305)
Total expenditures	314,765	314,765	309,771	4,994
Excess of revenues over expenditures	106,935	106,935	90,773	(16,162)
Other financing sources (uses)				
Transfers in	32,200	32,200	33,255	1,055
Transfers to component units	(131,418)	(131,418)	(122,545)	8,873
Transfers out	(10,322)	(10,322)	(4,189)	6,133
Total other financing sources (uses)	(109,540)	(109,540)	(93,479)	16,061
Excess (deficiency) of revenues and other financing sources over expenditures and other financing uses	$ (2,605)	$ (2,605)	$ (2,706)	$ (101)

Another common reconciliation addresses outstanding year-end encumbrances, treated as expenditures in the legal budget at time of encumbrance, but not reported as expenditures until the goods or services are delivered in the following year. Chapter 10 introduced this reconciliation in its discussion of carryover encumbrances.

Suppose the budget basis excess of revenues and other financing sources over expenditures and other financing uses is $400,000, the beginning encumbrances balance was $12,000, and the ending encumbrances balance is $15,000. The reconciliation is as follows:

Budget basis (expenditures and encumbrances)	$400,000
Less beginning encumbrances	(12,000)
Plus ending encumbrances	15,000
GAAP basis (expenditures only)	$403,000

CAPITAL ASSETS, INFRASTRUCTURE AND INVESTMENTS

Capital assets and investments typically comprise a significant part of a government's total assets. The modified accrual basis of reporting in the governmental funds leads to significant differences in how these items appear in the funds statements versus the government-wide statements.

LO5 Explain the external reporting for infrastructure and investments.

Capital Assets and Infrastructure

SGAS 34 requires that the government-wide statements report **all capital assets** using full accrual accounting, including periodic recognition of depreciation expense. Gains and losses on sale or disposition of capital assets are reported in the statement of activities and equal the difference between proceeds and book value.

While proprietary funds always followed the above reporting requirements, governmental funds report purchases and sales of capital assets in the funds statements using modified accrual accounting. Purchases of capital assets are expenditures, and proceeds from sale of capital assets are other financing sources. Prior to *SGAS 34*, governments disclosed the costs of capital assets such as land, buildings and equipment in a separate schedule, but recorded no depreciation. Disclosing the costs of infrastructure assets, such as roads, sidewalks, and sewer systems, was optional. Therefore, when governmental fund capital assets had to be included in the government-wide financial statements, **major implementation issues** arose in **determining depreciation on capital assets used by governmental funds**, and in **measuring the cost of infrastructure assets**. The GASB realized that governments needed extra time and may not have enough information to fully implement the new requirements.

Although current acquisitions of governmental funds' **infrastructure assets** must be reported by all governments using full accrual accounting, retroactive reporting of existing infrastructure assets was not required until 2005 for governments with revenues of $100 million or more, 2006 for governments with revenues of $10 to $100 million, and is optional for remaining governments. If information on the cost of existing infrastructure assets is lacking, governments need only estimate the cost of infrastructure acquired after 1980.

Depreciation on capital assets other than infrastructure follows usual business accounting methods, but the GASB also allows use of the **modified approach** for *infrastructure*—it need not be depreciated when preserved in good condition. The cost of *maintaining* the infrastructure—preserving its useful life—is instead reported as an expense. This modified approach for well-maintained infrastructure makes sense, because infrastructure is usually very long-lived. Bridges, roads, and water and sewer systems can last a hundred years or more. The traditional approach to allocating asset cost over an estimated useful life is therefore not as meaningful. Costs of increasing infrastructure capacity or efficiency are capitalized. Information on how the government accounts for infrastructure assets is reported in the required supplementary information.

Investments

Chapter 11 discussed reporting for investments in the fund statements. Following *SGAS 31*, all fund types, including governmental funds, report investments held for income at fair value on their balance sheet or statement of net position. Unrealized changes in investment value appear on the appropriate operating statement.

Governments increasingly invest in derivative instruments, such as futures, options and swaps, both for income and to hedge their financial risk. *SGAS 53* requires that derivatives be reported at fair value in the government's proprietary and fiduciary accrual-based fund statements. *SGAS 53* also applies to the accrual-based government-wide financial statements. The government-wide statement of activities reports changes in fair value of derivatives held for income. Changes in fair value of derivatives used as qualified hedges are reported as *deferred inflows/outflows* on the government-wide statement of net position. If the derivative no longer qualifies as a hedge investment, all deferred amounts are reclassified to the statement of activities.

SGAS 53 does not apply to governmental funds. Therefore the information reported in the government-wide statements for governmental funds' hedge investments will likely differ from the information reported in the governmental funds statements.

New and proposed standards increasingly require balances for "deferred inflows/outflows" to be reported in fund and government-wide balance sheets prepared on a full accrual basis. The GASB issued *SGAS 63*, Financial Reporting of Deferred Outflows of Resources, Deferred Inflows of Resources, and Net Position, to address financial statement format for these deferred inflows/outflows. The major provisions of this standard, effective in 2012, are as follows:

- The Statement of Net Assets is now called the Statement of Net Position.
- The "net assets" section of the Statement of Net Position is now called "net position."
- Deferred outflows appear in a separate section following assets, and deferred inflows appear in a separate section following liabilities, on the Statement of Net Position.
- Net position equals total assets plus deferred outflows less total liabilities less deferred inflows.

The provisions of *SGAS 63* apply to the government-wide financial statements, and also to the financial statements of proprietary and fiduciary funds.

BUSINESS APPLICATION   **City of New York Hedge Accounting**

The City of New York uses derivative instruments for investment income and for hedging. On its June 30, 2010, government-wide statement of net position, the City reports $89 million fair value of derivative instruments held as investments. The City also uses interest rate swaps to hedge the interest rate risk associated with its outstanding variable interest bonds. At June 30, 2010, pay fixed/receive variable interest rate swaps hedged variable rate bonds with a notional amount of almost $1.5 billion. In the assets section of its government-wide statement of net position, the City reports almost $92 million in "Deferred outflows of resources," representing the fair value of these swaps. The fair values of the swaps are determined by estimating the future net settlement cash flows (net cash received from or paid to the counterparty at each interest date) and discounting these cash flows to the present, using estimates of future variable interest rates as the discount rates.

At the end of fiscal 2010, the City determined that one of its swaps was no longer effective in hedging its interest rate risk. The swap's fair value at the time was a net liability of over $5 million, implying that the City would be required to pay $5 million to settle the swap at that date. The corresponding deferred outflow asset was reclassified as a reduction of investment income on the City's fiscal 2010 statement of activities. *Source:* City of New York 2010 CAFR.

BENEFITS OF GOVERNMENT-WIDE FULL ACCRUAL INFORMATION

SGAS 34 requires full accrual accounting for governmental activities in the government-wide statements, whereas governmental funds encompassing most governmental activities affecting the public were previously reported only on separate funds statements using the modified accrual basis. Because of this change, more accurate and timely information on the total costs of services and programs benefitting the public appears on one set of financial statements with these characteristics:

- **Government-wide financial statements use full accrual accounting** for all activities. Required schedules reconcile balances in the fund statements with those in the government-wide statements.

The government-wide statements focus on the primary government as one economic entity, and exclude fiduciary activities.

- **Capital assets, including infrastructure assets, are reported in the government-wide financial statements**, and depreciation expense is shown as an expense of providing services and programs.

- **Long-term debts are reported as liabilities on the government-wide statements**, and interest expense is accrued as incurred.

- The **statement of activities discloses the extent to which each of the various government programs and services use or contribute to general revenues**.

The financial reporting model for state and local governments is designed to make the financial statements readable and informative to users. Its principal benefits are discussed below.

- **Use of full accrual accounting in the government-wide financial statements allows a more precise measure of** *interperiod equity*—a comparison of resources obtained versus claims incurred during a period. Expenses are recorded when a transaction or event results in a claim on a financial resource, regardless of when that claim is due. Accrual accounting allows a better evaluation of whether services provided this year create a burden of payment in future years—for example, in the form of future tax increases—since the full costs of current services are more accurately measured.

- Accrual-based **government-wide statements present a clearer picture of financial performance**. From a long-term perspective, balancing the budget with a bond issue or by reducing the funding of pension liabilities does not improve the government's financial position. The accrual basis reports *no* improvement in financial position for such strategies, but the modified accrual basis reports an *increase in fund balance* for both. Recording capital asset acquisitions as expenditures and ignoring wear and tear on these assets over time obscures costs and declines in productivity, encouraging governments to delay necessary upkeep and replacement.

- **Financial performance is measured from both current and long-term perspectives**. Those interested in the current financial status of the government and its ability to meet short-term claims look to the fund statements to assess short-term financial position, inflows and outflows of current financial resources, amounts available for immediate use, and compliance with legal and budgetary restrictions. Readers interested in the government's longer-term financial position, its ability to provide services and the impact of current activities on future tax levels, look to the government-wide, full accrual statements.

- **Information is presented in a readable format**. MD&A, government-wide and fund statements, and other RSI offer both summaries and details. A reader may look to the MD&A and government-wide statements for an overall view of the government's performance and financial position, and to the funds statements for Information on compliance with legal restrictions, and details on specific fund activities.

Reporting Perspective

State and local governments are labor-intensive, and governments typically provide their employees with defined benefit pension plans involving significant commitments of future benefit payments. However, unlike businesses, current accounting standards for pensions do not require accurate recognition of pension expense and liabilities. The reconciliation in Exhibit 12.6 illustrates the current funding orientation in accounting for pensions. In its government-wide financial statements, the City of St. Louis recognizes a liability or asset equal to "the extent actual contributions to the City's retirement plans fall below/exceed the annual required contribution."

The GASB and users of financial statements agree that although the government-wide statements and proprietary and fiduciary fund statements are supposed to reflect full accrual accounting, current standards do not measure on a timely basis the actual expense and liability for pension benefits promised to employees. *SGAS 68*, effective in 2014, eliminates the current funding orientation and instead bases expense and liability recognition on the present value of future expected pension cash flows, regardless of how funded. This new standard is expected to add billions in unfunded pension liabilities to the government-wide statement of net position. It also standardizes the way governments calculate pension liabilities. Note that these requirements do *not* apply to the governmental fund statements. The major requirements of *SGAS 68* are as follows:

continued

- Use one actuarial method to compute pension expense and liability. Currently governments may choose from six different methods.

- Use the expected rate of return on pension investments to discount *funded* pension liabilities, but use a lower municipal bond rate to discount *unfunded* liabilities. Currently governments generally use an optimistic estimate of the expected rate of return on pension investments to discount all estimated future pension payments. The higher rate understates the liability, and a lower rate is more appropriate for unfunded pension liabilities, especially considering the low uncertainty of future pension payments.

- Recognize pension expense for each employee over the period in which the employee actually earns pension benefits. Currently many governments spread the expense over 30 years, representing the average length of a career in public service.

- Include most changes in net pension liability in current pension expense in the period of change. Effects of changes in certain economic and demographic assumptions may be spread over future years. Currently governments have more flexibility in deferring expense recognition.

The provisions of *SGAS 68* are designed to more accurately measure state and local government pension obligations. However, they will also require state and local governments to address how these liabilities will be funded.

REVIEW OF KEY CONCEPTS

LO 1 **Discuss the components of the Comprehensive Annual Financial Report. (p. 485)** The **external financial statements** of a state or local government are presented in the **Comprehensive Annual Financial Report**, or **CAFR**. *SGAS 34* requires **full accrual financial statements for the government as a whole**. These government-wide statements report on activities of the primary government and component units that provide services and programs to the public. Minimum financial disclosures are **management's discussion and analysis** (MD&A), the **basic financial statements**, and other **required supplementary information** (RSI). The MD&A introduces the financial statements and provides a readable overview and analysis of financial performance. The basic financial statements consist of government-wide statements, fund financial statements, and explanatory notes. RSI includes budgetary comparison schedules for governmental funds with legally-approved budgets, and additional information on accounting for infrastructure assets.

LO 2 **Prepare government-wide financial statements. (p. 487)** The **government-wide statements** use full accrual accounting, report on the resources and activities benefitting the public, and report **governmental** activities and **business-type** activities separately. Governmental activities include governmental and internal service fund activities. Business-type activities consist of enterprise fund activities. Fiduciary fund activities are not included. The government-wide **statement of net position** shows assets, liabilities, and net position, including long-term assets and liabilities. The **statement of activities** shows the full costs of the government's various programs and activities. Specific revenues related to these programs, such as user fees and grants, are deducted to produce a net balance that indicates **how much each activity uses or contributes to general revenues**. General revenues, such as property taxes, are added to obtain the change in net position for the year.

LO 3 **Present the fund statements. (p. 491)** **Fund financial statements** are presented for governmental, proprietary, and fiduciary funds. **Governmental fund financial statements** include a balance sheet and a statement of revenues, expenditures, and changes in fund balances, based on modified accrual accounting. **Proprietary fund financial statements** consist of a balance sheet, a statement of revenues, expenses, and changes in net position, and a statement of cash flows, using the direct method. **Fiduciary fund financial statements** include a statement of fiduciary net position and a statement of changes in fiduciary net position. Proprietary and fiduciary fund statements reflect full accrual accounting. Governmental and proprietary fund financial statements separately report only **major funds**, defined as the general fund, plus other individual governmental and enterprise funds that meet certain significance tests. Internal service funds are reported in total, and fiduciary funds are reported by fund type. Financial information on non-major funds is combined.

LO 4 **Describe the relation between government-wide and fund statements. (p. 505)** The relation between government-wide and fund financial statements is disclosed to readers through **reconciliations** of (1) the total governmental fund balances to the total net position of governmental activities, and (2) the change in governmental fund balances to the change in net position of governmental activities. These reconciliations are needed to understand how the governmental funds use of modified accrual accounting differs from the government-wide statements use of full accrual accounting. The government-wide financial statements provide readers with new information on the **long-term financial health** of the government, and the **full cost** of its programs and services. This information allows readers to better assess the future financial implications of current activities.

Explain the external reporting for infrastructure and investments. (p. 509) Governmental funds' current acquisitions of infrastructure are reported in the government-wide statements using full accrual accounting. However, pre-1980 infrastructure need not be reported. Infrastructure depreciation can be measured using the **modified approach**, as the cost of **maintaining** infrastructure. Investments are reported at fair value. Unrealized gains and losses generally appear on the statement of activities. However, unrealized gains and losses on hedge investments are reported as deferred inflows and outflows on the statement of net position. **LO 5**

MULTIPLE CHOICE QUESTIONS ·····································

Use the following information to answer questions 1-4 below:

Here are some of the financial statements required in the **State of New York** CAFR:

1. Government-wide statement: Statement of net position
2. Government-wide statement: Statement of activities
3. Fund statement: Balance sheet–Governmental funds
4. Fund statement: Statement of revenues, expenditures and changes in fund balances—Governmental funds
5. Fund statement: Statement of net position–Proprietary funds
6. Fund statement: Statement of revenues, expenses and changes in net position–Proprietary funds

For each of the following balances related to the financial performance of the State of New York, indicate the number(s) of the statements on which the balance is reported.

1. Personal income tax revenue **LO 1, 2**

   a. 6 only
   b. 2 only
   c. 4 only
   d. 2 and 4

2. Accrued postemployment benefit liability, governmental fund employees **LO 1, 2**

   a. 1 and 3
   b. 1 only
   c. 3 only
   d. 5 only

3. Bonds payable, enterprise funds **LO 1, 2**

   a. 1 and 3
   b. 5 only
   c. 1 only
   d. 1 and 5

4. Depreciation expense on general fund assets **LO 1, 2**

   a. 2 and 4
   b. 2 only
   c. 2, 4 and 6
   d. 4 only

5. Following is information for a county (*numbers are in millions*): **LO 3**

Total governmental fund balances.	$138
Bonds payable—governmental funds	690
Accrued other postemployment benefit liabilities—governmental funds	130
Capital assets—governmental funds	790
Accrued other liabilities—governmental funds.	128
Other long-term assets—governmental funds.	48

The net position of governmental activities is *(in millions)*

a. $ 28
b. $ 248
c. $1,568
d. $ 172

LO 3 **6.** The following information is available concerning the financial activities of the **State of New York** for fiscal 2010 *(all amounts are in millions)*:

Net change in fund balances–governmental funds	$ 123
Depreciation expense on general capital assets	300
Net losses on disposal of capital assets of governmental funds	14
Revenues of governmental funds that do not provide current financial resources	80
Repayments of principal on general long-term debt	5,020
Proceeds from disposal of capital assets of governmental funds	306
Proceeds from issuance of general long-term debt	7,287
Expenses of governmental funds, other than depreciation, not requiring current financial resources	1,871
Capital outlays—governmental funds	1,637

The fiscal 2010 change in net position—governmental activities is *(in millions)*

a. $(8,588)
b. $(2,918)
c. $ 2,228
d. $ 3,164

LO 4 **7.** A county uses the legal budgetary basis to report encumbrances. Information for its latest fiscal year is as follows:

Encumbrances outstanding at the beginning of the year	$ 50,000
Encumbrances outstanding at the end of the year	75,000
Excess of revenues and other financing sources over expenditures and other financing uses, legal budgetary basis	860,000

What is the excess of revenues and other financing sources over expenditures and other financing uses, using the GAAP budgetary basis?

a. $810,000
b. $835,000
c. $885,000
d. $935,000

LO 4 **8.** A county's 2013 operating statement for governmental funds reports transportation expenditures of $19,000,000. The government-wide statement of activities reports transportation expenses of $55,000,000. Which one of the following items would *not* explain why the government-wide statement reports a higher number than the governmental funds statement?

a. The $19,000,000 does not include depreciation on transportation-related equipment.
b. The $55,000,000 includes accrued pension costs earned this year by transportation-related employees.
c. The $19,000,000 does not include expenses not paid in cash this year.
d. The $55,000,000 includes temporary loans made by the transportation-related funds.

LO 5 **9.** A governmental fund reports derivative investments that qualify for hedge accounting. How are unrealized gains and losses on these investments reported in the government-wide financial statements?

a. They are not reported.
b. They appear on the governmental funds balance sheet as part of fund balance—nonspendable.
c. Unrealized gains appear on the statement of net position as deferred liabilities and unrealized losses appear as deferred assets.
d. Unrealized gains appear on the statement of net position as deferred assets and unrealized losses appear as deferred liabilities.

10. A county's general fund bought equipment for $50,000. The equipment was estimated to have a 10-year life, **LO 5** straight-line, no salvage value. Four years later, it sold the equipment for $18,000. In the year of the sale, the government-wide statement of activities will report

    a. Loss on sale of capital assets of $12,000
    b. Proceeds from sale of capital assets of $18,000
    c. Loss on sale of capital assets of $32,000
    d. Proceeds from sale of capital assets of $32,000

Assignments with the ⊘ in the margin are available in an online homework system.
See the Preface of the book for details.

EXERCISES ••

E12.1 **Fund and Government-Wide Reporting** Consider the following transactions of Dillingham **LO 2, 3** County:

1. General obligation bonds of $8,000,000 are issued at par to finance the cost of a new fire station. The fire station is built for $7,850,000, and remaining cash of $150,000 is transferred for future payment of the debt principal.
2. An old fire truck with a book value of $10,000 is sold for $7,000. A new fire truck is purchased using general revenues of $350,000. Fire station activities are reported as part of general operations.
3. A municipal golf course issues $500,000 in bonds to finance its activities. The bonds are expected to be paid using golf course revenues.
4. A central printing shop, which services municipal agencies on a fee-for-service basis, purchases printing equipment for $200,000.
5. Equipment is purchased by a fund dedicated to enhanced 911 service, at a cost of $400,000. This service is funded by a property tax levy for that purpose.
6. Books costing $10,000 are purchased by a local public library. The acquisition is financed by a trust fund set up by a wealthy citizen, using income from investments. The principal of the trust must remain intact. Public library activities are reported in the general fund.
7. Same as 6., but there is no restriction on spending the principal of the trust.

Required

For each of the above transactions, prepare journal entries necessary to record the transactions in both the fund financial statements and the government-wide financial statements for Dillingham County. For the government-wide entries, indicate whether the item is reported in governmental or business-type activities. For the fund entries, indicate which fund is affected.

E12.2 **Fund and Government-Wide Reporting** Consider these transactions of the City of Somerville: **LO 2, 3**

1. An investment pool that accumulates and invests money contributed by other governments invests $30,000 in securities.
2. Interest totaling $100,000 is paid on bonds used to finance sewer construction, where the bonds are the liability of the affected property owners, and the interest payment is financed by a special assessment on the property owners.
3. Property tax bills of $3,500,000 are sent out, to be used to finance primary government services. All bills are considered collectible.
4. Payment of $15,000 is made for the costs of public park programs, where the resources are provided by income from a grant provided by a private philanthropic institution. The principal of the grant must remain intact.
5. $80,000 in benefits are paid by an unemployment compensation benefit plan, funded by employers and required to cover its costs. Benefits are paid to all eligible citizens.
6. Interest of $20,000, due next year, is accrued on bonds used to finance a city parking garage that charges parking fees to the public.
7. Interest of $20,000, due next year, is accrued on bonds that finance general government activities.

Required

For each of the above transactions, prepare entries necessary to record the transactions in both the fund financial statements and the government-wide financial statements of the City of Somerville. For the government-wide entries, indicate whether the item is reported in governmental or business-type activities. For the fund entries, indicate which fund is affected.

✅ **LO 2, 3** **E12.3** **Fund and Government-Wide Financial Statements** Below is information on the financial performance of the City of Leland:

1. Depreciation expense on municipal parking garage assets
2. Gains on the sale of general fund county snowplowing equipment
3. Payroll deductions to be paid to tax authorities
4. Depreciation expense on general fund assets
5. Payments for general obligation debt principal

Required

Indicate on which of the City's financial statement(s) we would report each item of information. Choose from the following list of financial statements:

a. Government-wide statement of net position
b. Government-wide statement of activities
c. Statement of revenues, expenditures and changes in fund balances–governmental funds
d. Statement of revenues, expenses and changes in net position–proprietary funds
e. Statement of net position—fiduciary funds

LO 2, 3 **E12.4** **Transaction Reporting in Fund and Government-Wide Statements** Each transaction relates to the activities of Lancaster County.

1. General obligation bonds, due in 10 years, are issued for $5,000,000 in cash. The bonds are used to finance the building of a new community center. The total cost of the community center is $6,000,000.
2. Principal of $300,000 and interest of $50,000 are paid on general obligation debt. This debt was not used to finance capital assets.
3. Snow removal equipment is purchased by the general fund at a cost of $90,000.
4. Equipment with original cost of $400,000 is sold for $50,000. The equipment had a 5-year life when purchased, and was sold after 4 years. Straight-line depreciation is appropriate. The equipment was used in general government operations.
5. A county government collects $35,000 in property taxes to be remitted to the town.
6. Investments are made using $600,000 withheld from paychecks of county workers to finance their pension plan.
7. The investments in transaction 6 increase in value by $40,000 during the year, although the investments are not liquidated.
8. Cash of $50,000 is received from a citizen, to be held in trust and used for scholarships for local citizens to attend local universities. All amounts received are spendable.

Required

Indicate how each transaction is reported in Lancaster County's (a) fund statements, and (b) government-wide statements. Identify (i) the statement affected, (ii) the account where the item appears, and (iii) its classification if necessary. For example, assets purchased by the general fund appear as capital assets (governmental activities) on the statement of net position, and as general fund expenditures on the governmental funds statement of revenues, expenditures, and changes in fund balances. For the fund statements, assume whenever necessary that the relevant fund qualifies as a major fund.

LO 2, 3 **E12.5** **Transaction Reporting in Fund and Government-Wide Statements** Consider the following transactions of Daley County:

1. General property taxes of $50,000,000 are levied and collected.
2. Grants of $1,000,000 are received from the state to finance public safety programs.
3. Investment income of $40,000 is earned on investments of a debt service fund.
4. Investment income of $25,000 is earned on investments made using money received from a wealthy citizen. The money is held in trust to finance acquisitions of the public art gallery, outlays are limited to earnings and the original contribution cannot be spent.
5. User fees of $50,000 are received from operations of the community pool.
6. Depreciation on public safety equipment is $2,000 for the year.
7. Investment income of $35,000 is earned on government investments of excess cash. The income is not restricted.
8. The data processing unit submits $65,000 in charges for services to other units in the government.
9. Current year accrued interest on general long-term debt is $27,000, and is not due for several years.

Required

Indicate how each transaction is reported in Daley County's (a) fund statements, and (b) government-wide statements. Identify (i) the statement affected, (ii) the account where the item appears, and (iii) its classification if necessary. For example, assets purchased by the general fund appear as capital assets (governmental activities) on the statement of net position, and as general fund expenditures on the governmental funds statement of revenues, expenditures, and changes in fund balances. For the fund statements, assume whenever necessary that the relevant fund qualifies as a major fund.

E12.6 **Choice of Fund Type**   Following are descriptions of actual funds found in state CAFRs.   LO 1 ✓

1. The **Financial Institutions Deposits Fund** is used to account for security deposits held by the Michigan State Treasurer on behalf of banks which operate trust departments. Deposits are in the form of securities or other acceptable assets.
2. Michigan's **Second Injury Fund** insures carriers and self-insured employers against certain workers' compensation losses. The fund is supervised by the administrator who is appointed by the fund's Board of Trustees. Revenue consists of assessments on insurance carriers and self-insured employers.

   STATE OF MICHIGAN
3. The **Iowa Infrastructure Fund** accounts for resources directed by the General Assembly for public infrastructure related expenditures.
4. Iowa's **Scholarship and Tuition Grant Reserve Fund** receives surplus monies for scholarships and grants at the end of each fiscal year to cover over-expenditures in the scholarship and grant accounts.

   STATE OF IOWA
5. The **Alcoholic Beverage Control Board** operates facilities in Alabama for the distribution and sale of alcoholic beverages to the public.

   STATE OF ALABAMA
6. **Alabama's Air Transportation Fund** provides air transportation for state personnel and maintenance facilities for state aircraft, on a cost-reimbursement basis.

Required

For each item, identify the type of fund, and the method of accounting.

E12.7 **Reporting Capital Assets in the Government-Wide and Fund Statements**   Landon County   LO 3, 4, 5
reports all capital asset activities used in general government operations in its general fund. The following changes related to capital assets occurred during 2013:

	Beginning	Increases	Decreases	Ending
Capital assets, original cost	$3,200,000	$450,000	$(382,000)	$3,268,000
Accumulated depreciation	(1,300,000)	(225,000)	250,000	(1,275,000)
Capital assets, net	$1,900,000	$225,000	$(132,000)	$1,993,000

Capital assets were acquired for cash, and $150,000 in cash was received from the sale of capital assets during 2013.

Required

How will the above information be reported in the government-wide and governmental funds financial statements?

E12.8 **Major Funds**   Olean County uses the following capital projects funds for acquisition or construction   LO 3
of capital facilities:

Capital Projects Fund	Assets	Liabilities	Revenues	Expenditures
Buildings, equipment and improvements. . . .	$40,000	$25,000	$190,000	$180,000
Highways, roads, bridges and equipment . . .	55,000	40,000	220,000	150,000
Olean County Medical Center	30,000	32,000	260,000	240,000

Total balances for governmental, enterprise, internal service, and fiduciary funds are:

Governmental funds.	$500,000	$460,000	$2,000,000	$1,890,000
Enterprise funds	200,000	120,000	3,500,000	2,710,000
Internal service funds	45,000	42,000	320,000	300,000
Fiduciary funds.	410,000	390,000	1,200,000	1,050,000

Required

Which of the capital projects funds, if any, are reported as major funds in Olean County's CAFR?

LO 3 **E12.9** **Reconciliation of Governmental Funds Balance Sheet to Government-Wide Statement of Net Position** Below is the June 30, 2014, governmental funds balance sheet for Collins County *(in thousands)*:

Assets	
Cash	$200,000
Property taxes receivable, net	128,000
State grant receivable	100,000
Investments	150,000
Total	$578,000
Liabilities and fund balances	
Accounts payable	$175,000
Fund balance—restricted	20,000
Fund balance—assigned for capital projects	200,000
Fund balance—assigned for debt service	80,000
Fund balance—unassigned	103,000
Total	$578,000

Additional information (in thousands):

1. The county owns capital assets with original cost of $430,000 and accumulated depreciation of $150,000.
2. Total accrued compensated absences and OPEB costs are $65,000.
3. Total bonds payable outstanding is $250,000.
4. Accrued interest payable on bonds is $3,000.
5. Internal service fund net position is $5,000.

Required

Prepare a reconciliation of governmental funds fund balances to governmental activities net position as of June 30, 2014.

LO 3 **E12.10** **Reconciliation of Governmental Funds Statement of Revenues, Expenditures, and Changes in Fund Balances to Government-Wide Statement of Activities** Below is the June 30, 2014, governmental funds statement of revenues, expenditures, and changes in fund balances for Collins County *(in thousands)*:

Revenues	
Property taxes	$ 650,000
Fines and licenses	100,000
Investment revenue	4,000
Grants	230,000
Total	984,000
Expenditures	
General government	320,000
Health and safety	330,000
Education	260,000
Capital outlay	70,000
Debt service: interest	10,000
Debt service: principal	90,000
Total	1,080,000
Excess of revenues over (under) expenditures	(96,000)
Other financing sources (uses)	
Bond proceeds	125,000
Proceeds from sale of capital assets	15,000
Total	140,000
Excess of revenues and other financing sources over expenditures and other financing uses	$ 44,000

Additional information (in thousands):

1. Depreciation for 2014 on governmental funds' capital assets is $40,000.
2. Pension and OPEB costs incurred during 2014 total $95,000.
3. Accrued interest expense for 2014 is $3,000.

4. Change in internal service fund net position for 2014 is $800.
5. The book value of capital assets sold was $20,000.

Required

Prepare a reconciliation of governmental funds change in fund balances to governmental activities change in net position for the year ended June 30, 2014.

E12.11 Reconciliation of Budgetary Basis to GAAP Basis Erie County, New York uses the legal budgetary basis to report the change in fund balances in its budgetary comparison schedule. It reports the following information for the year ended December 31, 2010 *(in thousands)*:

LO 4

ERIE COUNTY, NEW YORK

Excess of revenues and other financing sources over expenditures and other financing uses—budgetary basis	$24,335
Encumbrances, January 1, 2010	4,722
Encumbrances, December 31, 2010	3,862

Required

Present a reconciliation of the budgetary basis to the GAAP basis of operating results.

E12.12 Reporting Compensated Absences in Government-Wide and Fund Statements Dare County, NC reports the following information about its compensated absence liabilities for fiscal 2010:

LO 4

DARE COUNTY, NORTH CAROLINA

(in thousands)	Governmental Activities	Business-type Activities
July 1, 2009, balance	$2,696	$240
Additions	1,065	103
Reductions	(1,093)	(116)
June 30, 2010, balance	$2,668	$227

Assume that liability reductions were cash payments to employees, and that internal service fund compensated absences included in governmental activities are as follows:

(in thousands)	Internal Service Fund
July 1, 2009, balance	$59
Additions	80
Reductions	(85)
June 30, 2010, balance	$54

Required

How is the above information reported in the government-wide and fund financial statements?

PROBLEMS

P12.1 Reconcile Fund Statements to Statement of Net Position The following information is taken from the financial records of Jackson City at December 31, 2014:

LO 3

Total fund balances—governmental funds	$ 51,000,000
Total net position—enterprise funds	12,000,000
Total net position—internal service funds	3,000,000
Total net position—fiduciary funds	6,000,000
Total capital assets, net of depreciation—governmental funds	135,500,000
Total capital assets, net of depreciation—enterprise funds	71,000,000
Total capital assets, net of depreciation—internal service funds	9,000,000
Total long-term debt—governmental funds	75,000,000
Total long-term debt—enterprise funds	35,000,000
Total long-term debt—internal service funds	8,400,000

Required

Prepare a reconciliation of total fund balances—governmental funds, as reported on the governmental funds balance sheet, to net position—governmental activities, as reported on the government-wide statement of net position.

✓ LO 3   **P12.2**   **Reconcile Fund Statements to Statement of Activities**   The following information is taken from the financial records of Bretton City for the year 2014:

Change in total fund balances—governmental funds	$ 90,000
Change in net position—enterprise funds	50,000
Change in net position—internal service funds	4,000
Change in net position—fiduciary funds	25,000
Total capital assets, net of depreciation—governmental funds	1,065,000
Total capital assets, net of depreciation—enterprise funds	500,000
Total capital assets, net of depreciation—internal service funds	175,000
Capital outlays—governmental funds	85,000
Capital outlays—enterprise funds	30,000
Capital outlays—internal service funds	26,000
Depreciation expense on general capital assets	45,000
Book value of general capital assets sold	110,000
Proceeds on sale of general capital assets	35,000
Revenues of governmental funds not providing current financial resources	21,000
Revenues of enterprise funds not providing current financial resources	6,000
Revenues of internal service funds not providing current financial resources	3,000
Expenses of governmental funds not requiring current financial resources, other than depreciation	15,000
General long-term debt balance	260,000
Proceeds from issuance of general long-term debt	73,000
Repayments of general long-term debt	116,000

Required

Prepare a reconciliation of the change in total fund balances—governmental funds, as reported on the governmental funds operating statement, to the change in net position—governmental activities, as reported on the government-wide statement of activities.

LO 2   **P12.3**   **Government-Wide Statement of Activities**   Consider the following information for the City of Daysville for the year ended December 31, 2014.

Expenses—parking garage (enterprise fund)	$ 1,200,000
Expenses—general government	52,000,000
Expenses—public safety	36,000,000
Expenses—health and sanitation	15,000,000
General property taxes	62,000,000
Unrestricted grants and contributions	6,000,000
Interest on general long-term debt	420,000
Charges for general government services	20,000,000
Charges for parking services	1,300,000
Charges for public safety services	2,500,000
Charges for health services	8,100,000
State grants for public safety	4,000,000
Gain on sale of general capital assets	200,000
Investment income—governmental activities	210,000
Beginning of year net position—governmental activities	120,000,000
Beginning of year net position—business-type activities	40,000,000

Required

Prepare, in good form, the government-wide statement of activities of Daysville for the year 2014.

P12.4 **Government-Wide Statement of Net Position** The City of Gardenvale records financial activi- LO 2
ties in a general fund and a community center (enterprise) fund. Consider the following information for
the City for the year ended December 31, 2013:

General property taxes levied	$15,000,000
General property taxes collected	14,900,000
Community center user fees, collected in cash	1,200,000
Investment income earned—general fund, received in cash	230,000
Capital assets purchased with cash—general fund	540,000
Capital assets purchased using loans—general fund	410,000
Capital assets purchased with cash—community center	25,000
Fair value of investments—general fund, December 31, 2013	14,090,000
General long-term debt principal payments, in cash[1]	300,000
General long-term debt interest payments, in cash	50,000
Total expenses of governmental programs[2]	15,500,000
Total expenses of community center programs[3]	1,205,000
Governmental program expenses paid in cash	14,920,000
Community center program expenses paid in cash	1,178,000
State grant received in cash, restricted for use in community center programs	20,000
Sales taxes collected in cash, to be remitted to state	1,700,000
Sales taxes remitted to state	1,692,000

[1] Payments reduce debt used to finance capital assets.
[2] Includes $500,000 of depreciation expense on capital assets.
[3] Includes $30,000 of depreciation expense on capital assets.

The December 31, 2012, statement of net position for the City of Gardenvale is as follows:

	Governmental Activities	Business-type Activities	Total
Assets			
Cash	$ 1,500,000	$ 40,000	$ 1,540,000
Taxes receivable	1,000,000	—	1,000,000
Investments	14,000,000	—	14,000,000
Capital assets, net	85,000,000	560,000	85,560,000
Total assets	101,500,000	600,000	102,100,000
Liabilities			
Accounts payable	1,000,000	25,000	1,025,000
Long-term debt	40,000,000	200,000	40,200,000
Total liabilities	41,000,000	225,000	41,225,000
Net position			
Net investment in capital assets	50,000,000	380,000	50,380,000
Restricted for community center projects	—	6,000	6,000
Unrestricted	10,500,000	(11,000)	10,489,000
Total net position	$ 60,500,000	$375,000	$ 60,875,000

Required
Prepare, in good form, the 2013 government-wide statement of net position for the City of Gardenvale.

P12.5 **Budgetary Comparison Schedule Reconciliation** Dare County, North Carolina's Water Fund LO 4
is an enterprise fund. The County presents a budgetary comparison schedule for the Water Fund, using
the modified accrual basis to report actual expenditures in excess of revenues and other financing sources
of $(775,089). The following information is available for fiscal 2010:

DARE COUNTY,
NORTH
CAROLINA

1. Water Fund asset depreciation: $2,123,592.
2. Compensated absences payable decreased by $12,882.
3. Inventory increased by $63,587.
4. Water Fund asset amortization: $147,916.
5. Debt principal payment: $1,285,000.
6. Capital outlay: $2,222,558.

7. Accrued interest payable decreased by $10,487.
8. OPEB payable increased by $454,385.

Required

Prepare a schedule reconciling the $(775,089) expenditures in excess of revenues and other financing sources, prepared on a modified accrual basis, to the change in net position, as reported on the Water Fund's operating statement.

LO 2 **P12.6 Government-Wide Statement of Net Position** Central City reports the following balances at September 30, 2014, its fiscal year-end, using full accrual accounting:

(in thousands)	Governmental Activities	Business-Type Activities
Assets		
Cash and cash equivalents.	$150,000	$ 40,000
Property taxes receivable, net	130,000	—
Due from business-type activities	12,000	—
Supplies	35,000	2,000
Capital assets:		
Depreciable, net	300,000	120,000
Nondepreciable.	62,000	19,000
Liabilities		
Accounts payable.	34,000	21,000
Accrued current liabilities	8,000	4,000
Due to governmental activities.	—	12,000
Bonds payable	200,000	56,000

Additional information (in thousands):

1. All bonds were used to acquire capital assets.
2. Governmental activities consist of the general fund, a special revenue fund for grants, a capital projects fund, and a debt service fund. At September 30, 2014, the special revenue fund has $35,000 in net position restricted to grant-related activities, the capital projects fund has $220,000 in net position restricted to capital projects, and the debt service fund has $140,000 in net position restricted to debt service, all calculated on a full accrual basis.
3. Business-type activities consist of the parking garage and community center. $1,000 in parking garage net position is restricted to specific facility improvements.

Required

Prepare a government-wide statement of net position for Central City as of September 30, 2014, in good form.

LO 2 **P12.7 Statement of Activities** Dare County, North Carolina reports the following information for the fiscal year ended June 30, 2010 *(in thousands)*:

DARE COUNTY, NORTH CAROLINA

Property tax revenues	$49,431
Sales tax revenues.	14,397
Collections on property and sales taxes	60,987
Hotel occupancy, alcoholic beverage, and other general tax revenues	12,099
Unrestricted investment earnings—general.	1,528
Unrestricted investment earnings—business-type activities.	278
Proceeds from sale of capital assets	1,825
Transfers from water department to general government	432
General government expenses	11,640
Public safety expenses.	23,690
Economic development, human services, cultural and recreational expenses.	23,444
Environmental protection expenses.	8,989
Education and transportation expenses	19,458
Interest on general long-term debt.	6,682
Proceeds from issuance of general long-term debt.	3,245
Water department expenses	9,362

continued

Charges for services—general government.	1,825
Charges for services—public safety	3,171
Charges for services—economic development, human services, cultural and recreational.	2,838
Charges for services—environmental protection.	1,873
Charges for services—water department	9,808
Grants and contributions—general government	154
Grants and contributions—public safety	289
Grants and contributions—economic development, human services, cultural and recreational . . .	5,792
Grants and contributions—environmental protection	51
Grants and contributions—water department	2,386

Dare County has one enterprise fund, its water department.

Required

Prepare, in good form, the government-wide statement of activities for Dare County for the fiscal year ending June 30, 2010.

P12.8 Major Funds Lenox County provides the following information on its governmental and enterprise funds: LO 3 ✓

Fund	Assets	Liabilities	Revenues	Expenditures/ Expenses
General fund.	$80,000	$72,000	$680,000	$783,000
Grants special revenue fund	55,000	43,500	200,000	97,000
Parks and recreation special revenue fund .	2,000	1,300	40,000	42,000
Licensed gaming special revenue fund	8,000	7,000	65,000	62,000
Roads capital projects fund	14,000	12,000	200,000	203,000
Bridges capital projects fund	35,000	30,000	120,000	115,000
Buildings capital projects fund.	40,000	30,000	100,000	98,000
Water enterprise fund.	210,000	200,000	890,000	780,000
Airport enterprise fund	650,000	620,000	950,000	953,000

Required

In the *governmental funds* financial statements, which of these funds are reported separately as major funds? Show calculations.

P12.9 Long-Term Liabilities in the Government-Wide and Fund Statements The City of Fremont's fiscal year ends June 30. The City issued the following general obligation bonds: LO 4 ✓

1. On July 1, 2011, the City issued 5 percent, $100,000 face value, 10-year bonds for $92,640, to yield 6 percent. Interest is payable on June 30 of each year.
2. On January 1, 2013, the City issued 5 percent, $100,000 face value, 10-year bonds for $108,115, to yield 4 percent. Interest is payable on December 31 of each year.

Required

a. Determine the amounts reported in the government-wide statement of activities and statement of net position for fiscal year 2014, related to the bonds.
b. Determine the amounts reported in the governmental funds statement of revenues, expenditures, and changes in fund balances and balance sheet for fiscal year 2014, related to the bonds.

P12.10 Fund and Government-Wide Financial Statements Below are various types of information on the financial performance of the Town of Granville: LO 2, 3

1. General property taxes collected.
2. Depreciation expense on general long-term assets.
3. Amount of general long-term debt outstanding.
4. Costs of providing public service programs.
5. Amounts on hand for future payment of general obligation debt.
6. Payroll deductions collected for health insurance, to be remitted to a private insurance carrier.
7. Amounts collected as user fees that fully fund community center day-care programs for the public.

8. Cost of general long-term assets purchased this year.
9. Investments held by a pension trust fund.
10. Gain on sale of public park land.

Required

Indicate which of Granville's financial statement(s) would report each item of information, according to *SGAS 34*. Choose from the following list of financial statements:

a. Government-wide statement of net position
b. Government-wide statement of activities
c. Governmental funds balance sheet
d. Governmental funds statement of revenues, expenditures, and changes in fund balances
e. Proprietary funds statement of net position
f. Proprietary funds statement of revenues, expenses, and changes in net position
g. Proprietary funds statement of cash flows
h. Fiduciary funds statement of fiduciary net position
i. Fiduciary funds statement of changes in fiduciary net position

LO 4   **P12.11 Analysis of the City of St. Louis CAFR**   Refer to the 2010 financial statements of the **City of St. Louis**, appearing in Exhibits 12.1 through 12.12.

**CITY OF
ST. LOUIS,
MISSOURI**

Required

a. The statement of net position (assets) (Exhibit 12.1) and the statement of activities (Exhibit 12.2) divide financial information into governmental and business-type activities. The activities of which fund(s) are included in each category?
b. Compare the statement of net position (assets) (Exhibit 12.1) with the balance sheet for governmental funds (Exhibit 12.3). Explain the major differences in assets and liabilities reported.
c. Compare the statement of activities (Exhibit 12.2) and the statement of revenues, expenditures, and changes in fund balances for governmental funds (Exhibit 12.4).
   1. Explain differences in the categorization of revenues on each statement.
   2. The statement of revenues, expenditures, and changes in fund balances lists two expenditures that do not appear as expenses of governmental activities on the statement of activities. Identify the two items, and explain why they are not reported on the statement of activities.
   3. The statement of revenues, expenditures, and changes in fund balances reports several items as "other financing sources (uses)." Where is each of the items reported on the government-wide financial statements?
   4. The statement of activities lists streets expenses at $66,263,000, while the statement of revenues, expenditures, and changes in fund balances lists streets expenditures at $37,356,000. Why are these two numbers different?
d. Where are the amounts reported in the proprietary fund statement of revenues, expenses, and changes in fund net position (assets) (Exhibit 12.8) shown in the statement of activities?
e. Where are the amounts reported in the statement of fiduciary net position (assets) (Exhibit 12.10) shown in the government-wide financial statements?

LO 3   **P12.12 Capital Leases in Government-Wide and Fund Statements**   Oceanside County's fiscal year ends June 30. The county leased equipment during fiscal 2014, as follows:

1. The general fund signed a 4-year lease on July 1, 2013, with payments of $15,000 to be made each June 30.
2. The water department enterprise fund signed a 5-year lease on July 1, 2013, with payments of $10,000 to be made each June 30.

Both leases qualify as capital leases, at an interest rate of 4 percent. When appropriate, the equipment is straight-line depreciated with no residual value.

Required

a. How is each lease reported in the fund statements for fiscal 2014?
b. How is each lease reported in the government-wide statements for fiscal 2014?

REVIEW SOLUTIONS

Review 1 Solution

TOWN OF SCOTTSVILLE
Statement of Activities
For Year Ended December 31, 2013

(in thousands) Functions/Programs	Expenses	Program Revenues		Net (Expense) Revenue and Changes in Net Position		
		Charges for Services	Grants & Contributions	Governmental Activities	Business-type Activities	Total
Governmental activities:						
General government	$ 3,500	$ 100	$ —	$ (3,400)	$ —	$ (3,400)
Public safety	27,000	2,500	4,000	(20,500)	—	(20,500)
Education...........................	45,600	1,100	9,000	(35,500)	—	(35,500)
Interest on long-term debt	340	—	—	(340)	—	(340)
Total governmental activities...........	76,440	3,700	13,000	(59,740)	—	(59,740)
Business-type activities:						
Water utility	700	715	—	—	15	15
Total primary government	$77,140	$4,415	$13,000	$(59,740)	$ 15	$ (59,725)

General revenues			
Property taxes....................................	58,000	—	58,000
Investment income................................	300	—	300
Gain on sale of assets............................	50	—	50
Total	58,350	—	58,350
Excess (deficiency) of revenues over expenses	(1,390)	15	(1,375)
Net position—beginning............................	90,000	12,000	102,000
Net position—ending.............................	$88,610	$12,015	$100,625

Review 2 Solution

Net change in fund balances—governmental funds	$(2,200)
Plus cost of general capital assets acquired	14,000
Less depreciation expense on general capital assets....................................	(3,800)
Less proceeds on sale of general capital assets	(300)
Less loss on sale of general capital assets	(10)
Plus principal repayments—general obligation debt	5,600
Less proceeds from issuance of general obligation debt................................	(9,300)
Less accrued OPEB expense	(100)
Less accrued interest expense	(192)
Change in net position—governmental activities	$ 3,698

13 Private Not-For-Profit Organizations

BETA ALPHA PSI
www.bap.org

Beta Alpha Psi is an honors organization, recognizing and promoting academic excellence and achievement in accounting, finance and information systems. Beta Alpha Psi's activities include regional and annual meetings, and case and chapter competitions supporting professionalism, service, and public responsibility. Founded in 1919, there are almost 300 Beta Alpha Psi chapters on college and university campuses in the U.S., New Zealand and Australia, with over 300,000 members initiated since its inception.

Although not-for-profit organizations are not subject to the reporting requirements of the stock exchanges, their donors and other funding sources generally expect financial disclosure in the form of audited financial statements, following GAAP. Each year Beta Alpha Psi provides an audited annual report, consisting of a statement of activities, a statement of financial position, and a statement of cash flows.

The goals and activities of private NFP organizations differ in many ways from those of for-profit entities. How do the reporting requirements for private NFP organizations compare with the standards you learned in your principles and intermediate accounting courses? How do the financial statements differ? This chapter discusses the accounting and reporting by private not-for-profit organizations.

CHAPTER ORGANIZATION

Financial reporting display model	Accounting for contributions received	Accounting for investments	Comprehensive illustration	Reporting for specific NFPs	Evaluate financial information
• Statement of financial position	• Unconditional and unrestricted cash contributions	• Gains and losses	• Record transactions	• Voluntary health and welfare organizations	• Strengths and weaknesses of reporting requirements
• Statement of activities	• Contributions of goods and services	• Investment income	• Prepare financial statements	• Colleges and universities	
• Statement of cash flows	• Temporarily restricted contributions	• Endowments		• Health care organizations	
	• Conditional contributions				
	• Permanently restricted contributions				
	• Contributions of long-lived assets				
	• Annuity and life income contributions				
	• Contributions received on behalf of others				

CHARACTERISTICS OF PRIVATE NOT-FOR-PROFIT (NFP) ORGANIZATIONS

Private (nongovernmental) NFP organizations share the following characteristics:

• Significant amounts of the organization's resources come from providers who expect no payment or economic benefits proportionate to the resources provided.

• The organization's primary mission is to contribute to society, *not* to generate a profit.

• There are no ownership interests that can be sold, transferred, or redeemed, or that convey entitlement to a share of resources in the event the organization is liquidated. The NFP is owned by its members or the public, and is run by a board of directors or trustees.

Private NFP organizations generally fall into these categories:

Voluntary health and welfare organizations (VHWOs).   These organizations generate the majority of their support from voluntary contributions and grants, and offer their services to the general public. Services include social welfare, health, or community activities. Examples include the **American Heart Association,** the **Salvation Army**, the **YMCA**, and **Habitat for Humanity**.

Colleges and universities.   This category includes private not-for-profit two- and four-year colleges and universities. Support comes mainly from student tuition and fees, alumni contributions, grants and private endowments, and state and federal funding.

Hospitals and other health care organizations.   These organizations include private not-for-profit hospitals, nursing homes, health maintenance organizations, medical groups, ambulatory care facilities, and clinics. Major support comes from patient charges, including third party payments, contributions, endowments and grants.

Other private NFP organizations.   These include private NFP elementary and secondary schools, social and political groups, churches, museums, and civic and fraternal organizations. The **American Automobile Association, Beta Alpha Psi,** and the **American Institute of Certified Public Accountants** are examples.

This chapter covers the reporting requirements for *private* NFP organizations. Private NFPs may receive a significant amount of public funding, but they are run by a nongovernmental group. The FASB issues reporting standards for these organizations. *Public* NFPs must follow the accounting requirements of the GASB, covered in Chapters 10, 11 and 12.

When deciding whether the FASB requirements for NFP reporting apply to a particular organization, one must consider two important issues: Is the organization under the jurisdiction of a private group, or is it a governmental entity? If private, is it a not-for-profit or a for-profit organization? The latter question cannot be answered merely by identifying the nature of the services rendered and the funding sources. For-profit forms of voluntary health and welfare organizations, elementary and secondary schools, and health care organizations also exist.

NFP REPORTING ENVIRONMENT

FASB reporting standards apply to private NFPs; public NFPs follow GASB standards. Differing reporting requirements have been troubling in the past, since it does not seem reasonable that similar public and private NFPs should report different types of information. Why should the reporting requirements for **The Ohio State University** differ from the requirements for the **University of Dayton**? In recent years the GASB has worked to bring the reporting requirements for public NFPs and state and local governments closer to the requirements for private NFP entities. *SGAS 34* outlines the external reporting requirements for state and local governments, studied in Chapter 12 of this text. *SGAS 35* applies the same requirements to public colleges and universities. These requirements are similar to the external reporting requirements for private NFPs studied in this chapter.

Most major FASB reporting requirements for private NFP organizations emerged in the 1990s. These standards are now part of *FASB ASC Topic 958*, Not-For-Profit Entities. FASB *Statement of Financial Accounting Concepts No. 4*, Objectives of Financial Reporting by Nonbusiness Organizations, and sections of *FASB Statement of Financial Accounting Concepts No. 6*, Elements of Financial Statements provide the reporting framework.

External Financial Reporting Requirements: General Concepts

Years ago, much like the governmental funds statements studied in Chapters 10–12, NFPs provided their stakeholders with segregated financial information by funds—pools of resources segregated by purpose—that focused on stewardship over these resources. The financial data allowed readers to track resources received and expended for particular functions and activities.

The financial climate and information demands on NFPs changed over the last few decades. NFPs now look to external financial markets to finance escalating costs, and solicit contributions from corporations and foundations, as well as individuals. As the number of NFPs grows, there is greater competition for limited resources, and donors demand accurate and complete information to support their own resource allocation decisions. This demand for financial accountability encouraged the FASB to develop accounting and reporting requirements that provide external readers with useful and readable financial statements for the NFP organization as a complete entity. As a result, external financial statements report on the organization as a whole and provide more understandable and user-friendly information on the entire organization's performance and financial condition.

Goals of Financial Reporting by NFPs   Unlike for-profit businesses, NFPs are not expected to generate a net profit from their activities. However, they are expected to use contributions for their intended purposes, choose activities that effectively further the organization's goals, and operate efficiently. Users of an NFP's financial statements should be able to find evidence on these dimensions of performance. Contributors, lenders, organization members, charity watchdog groups, managers, and the general public are potential users.

Contributors and watchdog groups are interested in what part of each dollar contributed is spent on administration and fund-raising, and how much the organization spends on its prime mission. Charity watchdog groups monitor spending, and evaluate organizations on various dimensions of financial performance.

Lenders are concerned with the organization's ability to meet obligations as they come due. An NFP's bond ratings are affected by management, governance, debt structure and history, as well as its revenue and expense base and financial condition. To assess credit-worthiness, lenders need information on the amount of the organization's assets available to meet debt payments and planned and unplanned expenditures. Lenders also assess the stability and expected future level of revenue sources.

External users want to know whether the organization's activities are above-board and within its mission, whether the organization is fiscally responsible, and whether it can continue to provide services and pay its bills in the future. These concepts form the basis for current GAAP for NFPs.

BUSINESS APPLICATION   Charity Watchdog Groups

The standards developed by two watchdog groups—the Council of Better Business Bureaus and the American Institute of Philanthropy—provide insight into the financial information demanded by external readers. The **Council of Better Business Bureaus**—www.give.org—publishes standards for charity accountability, divided into standards of governance, finances, and disclosure. The "finances" section lists these standards:

- Spend at least 65% of total expenses on program activities.

- Spend no more than 35% of "related contributions" on fund-raising. Related contributions are those received as a result of fund-raising efforts.

- Avoid accumulating resources that could be used for current program activities. Unrestricted net assets available for use should not be more than three times the size of the past year's expenses or three times the size of the current year's budget, whichever is higher.

- Make available to all, on request, complete annual financial statements prepared in accordance with generally accepted accounting principles.

- Include in the financial statements a breakdown of expenses that shows the portions of these expenses allocated to program, fund-raising and administrative activities.

- Accurately report expenses, including joint cost allocations, in the financial statements.

- Have a board-approved annual budget for the current fiscal year that outlines projected expenses for major program activities, including fund-raising and administration.

The **American Institute of Philanthropy** (AIP)—www.charitywatch.org—publishes a Charity Rating Guide, which rates charitable organizations using the following statistics:

- Percent of total expenses spent on charitable programs: In AIP's view, 60% or greater is reasonable for most charities.

- Cost to raise $100 in related contributions: $35 or less is considered reasonable in most cases.

- Years of available assets, measuring how long a charity could continue to operate at current levels without additional fund-raising: Organizations having available assets of over three years of operating expenses receive a negative rating.

Overall Reporting Concepts
FASB Concepts Statement No. 4 presents the basic principles and objectives of NFP reporting. The three broad objectives are:

- Financial information should be useful to contributors, lenders, suppliers, organization members, oversight bodies, and managers in making resource allocation decisions—either how much to give to the organization, or how much to allocate to alternative activities within the organization.

- Financial information should be useful in evaluating the services provided by the organization and in determining its ability to continue to provide these services.

- Financial information should be useful in assessing the performance of management.

FASB *Concepts Statement No. 6* partitions the **net assets** ("equity") section of an NFP's balance sheet into **three classes**:

- **Permanently restricted net assets.** Contributions or other net inflows where donor-imposed restrictions limit use indefinitely.

- **Temporarily restricted net assets.** Contributions or other net inflows subject to donor-imposed restrictions that expire either through the passage of time or by actions of the organization.
- **Unrestricted net assets.** All other net assets.

These principles and objectives were implemented in the contributions and financial statement requirements of *ASC Topic 958*. The financial statements must include information on the organization's assets, liabilities, and net assets, transactions affecting net assets, how the organization obtains and uses cash, and its service efforts.

FINANCIAL REPORTING DISPLAY MODEL

LO1 Prepare financial statements of private not-for-profit (NFP) organizations in proper format.

The FASB Codification calls for a common structure in financial reporting that provides financial results for the entity as a whole. Accordingly, an NFP organization's required financial statements are a **statement of financial position**, a **statement of activities**, and a **statement of cash flows**.

Statement of Financial Position

The statement of financial position presents the assets, liabilities, and net assets of the organization. Important features are:

- Assets and liabilities are classified in order of liquidity.
- **Basic concepts of business accounting** are followed in **valuing assets and liabilities**, except for investments in debt and equity securities, where *ASC Subtopic 958-320* requires that fair values be used for *all* investments in debt and equity securities with determinable fair values.
- **Cash or other assets donor-restricted** in a way that **limits their use** over the long-term, such as for construction of long-term assets or as permanent endowments, should be **reported separately** from unrestricted cash and other assets that are available for current use.
- Net assets must be presented in the **three net asset categories** discussed above.

Beta Alpha Psi's 2011 statement of financial position in Exhibit 13.1 reports unrestricted and temporarily restricted net assets, but has no endowments. Most assets and all liabilities are current; the organization does not own property, plant or equipment or engage in any long-term borrowing.

Statement of Activities

The statement of activities shows **changes in each of the net asset categories** during the year. Important features are:

Contributions and Other Inflows

- **Inflows**—from contributions, sales, and so forth—**are revenues, reported as increases in the appropriate net asset category**. For example, unrestricted donations increase unrestricted net assets; contributions restricted by the donor for use in a particular time period or for a particular purpose increase temporarily restricted net assets; contributions where the donor stipulates that the principal is to be kept intact and only the income earned on the contribution is to be used, increase permanently restricted net assets.
- As **donor-imposed temporary restrictions** are met, either because the stipulated time passed or the contributions were used for the intended purpose, temporarily restricted net assets decrease and unrestricted net assets increase. These items appear separately on the statement of activities as **net assets released from restrictions** with equal amounts shown as reductions in temporarily restricted net assets and increases in unrestricted net assets. By definition, there can be no release of permanently restricted net assets, unless donor-imposed restrictions change.

Expenses

- **Expenses are reported as reductions in the unrestricted net assets category only**. Use of restricted resources is reported first as **net assets released from restrictions**—moved from the

EXHIBIT 13.1 Beta Alpha Psi 2011 Statements of Financial Position

BETA ALPHA PSI
Statements of Financial Position

For Years Ended	April 30, 2011	April 30, 2010
Current assets		
Cash and cash equivalents	$1,662,800	$1,037,837
Investments	50,000	304,213
Accounts receivable.	97,336	58,410
Prepaid expenses and other assets.	24,401	35,611
Total current assets	1,834,537	1,436,071
Investments	100,000	115,839
Web site development, net of accumulated amortization of $162,687 and $156,523	7,705	25,569
Total assets	$1,942,242	$1,577,479
Liabilities		
Accounts payable.	$ 193,053	$ 88,621
Unearned revenue	34,820	41,052
Total liabilities.	227,873	129,673
Net assets		
Unrestricted	1,635,219	1,350,506
Temporarily restricted	79,150	97,300
Total net assets	1,714,369	1,447,806
Total liabilities and net assets	$1,942,242	$1,577,479

temporarily restricted category to the unrestricted category—with the related expense then shown as a reduction in unrestricted net assets. *No expenses appear in the other net asset categories.*

- **Expenses are classified functionally**, separating out expenses of each major program or service, and **showing support costs**—administrative, membership development, and fund-raising—**separately**.

- **Administrative costs** are those not specifically related to a particular program, fund-raising activity, or membership development activity, but are required for the organization's continued operations. Administrative costs include accounting, financing, and business management costs.

- **Membership development costs** include costs of soliciting prospective members, collection of dues, and membership relations.

- **Fund-raising costs** are costs incurred to persuade potential donors to make contributions, such as the costs of fund-raising campaigns, including the cost of preparing and distributing printed material. It is important to provide readers with an accurate breakdown of fund-raising costs, since donors have an avid interest in the proportion of their contributions spent on programs versus fund-raising.

- Organizations often use an activity for both mission-related and fund-raising purposes. Those organizations incurring such *joint costs* must disclose the fact that costs have been allocated between functional categories, and the amounts allocated to each classification.

- For **voluntary health and welfare organizations**, a **natural** or object **classification of expenses**—for example, salaries, rent, depreciation—**is required** in addition to the functional classification. These organizations must show expenses separately by functional *and* natural classification in matrix format. Other organizations are encouraged but not required to show a natural classification of expenses. Exhibit 13.7, presented later in the chapter, illustrates this disclosure.

Investments in Securities

- The FASB Codification requires that **investments in debt and equity securities** be valued at **fair market value**. Changes in investment values are shown in the statement of activities. Unless they are donor-restricted, value changes are reported as changes in unrestricted net assets. Similarly, investment income is unrestricted unless the donor specifically says otherwise.

Format

- The general format of the statement of activities shows **changes in each of the three classifications of net assets**, with the change in net assets as the "bottom line." However, **NFPs are encouraged to include additional classifications** within their operating statement, which provide better disclosure of the organization's performance. For example, changes in net assets may be classified as operating and nonoperating, recurring and nonrecurring, or realized and unrealized.

Beta Alpha Psi's 2011 statement of activities in Exhibit 13.2 reports changes in unrestricted and temporarily restricted net assets. Most unrestricted revenues come from initiation fees and charges for

EXHIBIT 13.2 Beta Alpha Psi 2011 Statements of Activities

BETA ALPHA PSI
Statement of Activities

For Years Ended	April 30, 2011	April 30, 2010
Changes in unrestricted net assets		
Revenue and support:		
Initiation fees.	$ 667,370	$ 642,818
Associates program contributions	189,000	181,000
Chapter maintenance fees	82,505	53,905
Annual student convention.	237,354	217,862
Charter and petition fees	12,000	8,000
Regional meetings	129,220	135,188
Interest income.	4,087	6,652
Contributed services.	170,349	149,639
Net assets released from restrictions.	161,175	149,341
Miscellaneous.	10,874	16,167
Total unrestricted revenue and support.	1,663,934	1,560,572
Expenses		
Annual student convention.	380,652	384,905
Board of directors meetings.	35,158	37,357
Chapter installations and visitations.	3,087	9,498
Banners and gavels	212	4,367
Regional meetings	213,914	306,176
Superior chapter awards	34,925	31,125
Best practice awards	28,250	27,250
Diversity awards.	15,500	10,000
Faculty advisor awards.	25,000	25,000
Gold Challenge awards	37,500	35,966
Project Run With It awards.	12,000	10,000
Miscellaneous.	8,996	6,655
Total program expenses.	795,194	888,299
General and administrative.	584,027	503,590
Total expenses.	1,379,221	1,391,889
Change in unrestricted net assets	284,713	168,683
Change in temporarily restricted net assets		
Contributions	143,025	184,241
Net assets released from restrictions.	(161,175)	(149,341)
Change in temporarily restricted net assets.	(18,150)	34,900
Change in net assets	266,563	203,583
Net assets, beginning of year.	1,447,806	1,244,223
Net assets, end of year	$1,714,369	$1,447,806

the national conference and regional meetings. Expenses are categorized functionally, with amounts spent for superior chapter awards, faculty advisor awards, the national conference and regional meetings clearly displayed. The statement of activities reports 2011 temporarily restricted contributions of $143,025 and net assets released from restrictions of $161,175. Footnotes indicate that temporarily restricted net assets received and released from restrictions relate to contributions received to finance chapter awards. Temporarily restricted net assets were released from restrictions in 2011 and 2010 when spent on the following donor-restricted chapter awards:

	2011	2010
Best practice awards	$ 28,250	$ 27,250
Faculty advisor awards	25,000	25,000
Superior chapter awards	34,925	31,125
Diversity awards	15,500	10,000
Project Run With It awards and program expenses	20,000	20,000
Gold Challenge awards	37,500	35,966
Totals	$161,175	$149,341

These awards are financed by various accounting firms, including Deloitte, McGladrey, KPMG, Ernst & Young and Moss Adams LLP.

Unspent temporarily restricted net assets at year-end appear on the Statement of Financial Position in Exhibit 13.1. For 2011 and 2010 these amounts are $79,150 and $97,300, respectively, in the following awards categories:

	2011	2010
Best practice awards	$11,100	$39,350
Faculty advisor awards	38,800	13,800
Superior chapter awards	2,150	2,150
Diversity awards	6,500	22,000
Project Run With It awards and program expenses	20,600	20,000
Totals	$79,150	$97,300

Statement of Cash Flows

The statement of cash flows follows the usual business format for reporting cash flows from operations, investing, and financing, except for the following special features for NFPs:

- Contributions and income that are **donor restricted for long-term purposes**, such as plant assets and endowment, are reported as **financing cash flows**.

- Proceeds from the **sale of donated financial assets**, such as securities, are reported as **operating cash flows**, if they are sold immediately after they are received and the donor did not restrict their use to long-term purposes.

- The **reconciliation** of income to operating cash flows appears as a reconciliation of the **change in total net assets**—the bottom line of the statement of activities—to **cash from operations**.

Either the direct or indirect method of reporting cash from operating activities is allowed. The comprehensive illustration later in the chapter uses the direct method, and the required reconciliation of the change in assets to cash from operations illustrates the indirect method.

Beta Alpha Psi's statement of cash flows in Exhibit 13.3 reports operating and investing activities. Like most businesses, it presents operating cash flow via the indirect method that reconciles the change in net assets to cash from operations.

EXHIBIT 13.3   Beta Alpha Psi 2011 Statements of Cash Flows

BETA ALPHA PSI
Statements of Cash Flows

For Years Ended	April 30, 2011	April 30, 2010
Operating activities		
Change in net assets	$ 266,563	$ 203,583
Adjustments to reconcile change in net assets to net cash provided by operating activities:		
Amortization	6,164	4,623
Loss on disposition of website development costs	11,700	—
Changes in operating assets and liabilities:		
Accounts receivable	(38.926)	(10,474)
Prepaid expenses and other assets	11,210	(25,493)
Accounts payable	104,432	(26,189)
Unearned revenue.	(6,232)	6,390
Net cash provided by operating activities	354,911	152,440
Investing activities		
Capital expenditures	—	(25,280)
Proceeds from maturation of investments.	270,052	—
Purchase of investments	—	(4,996)
Net cash provided by (used in) investing activities	270,052	(30,276)
Net increase in cash and cash equivalents	624,963	122,164
Cash and cash equivalents, beginning of year	1,037,837	915,673
Cash and cash equivalents, end of year	$1,662,800	$1,037,837

ACCOUNTING FOR CONTRIBUTIONS RECEIVED

LO2 Report all types of contributions received.

NFPs measure contributions at *fair value* and recognize them as increases in **unrestricted, temporarily restricted**, or **permanently restricted net assets**, as described above. Contributions received may be in cash, other assets, forgiveness of liabilities, and qualified volunteer services. According to the ASC glossary, a contribution is "an **unconditional transfer** of cash or other assets to an entity or a settlement or cancellation of its liabilities in a voluntary *nonreciprocal transfer* by another entity acting other than as an owner." **Unconditional** implies that there are no circumstances under which the contribution would be returned. A **nonreciprocal transfer** signifies that the donor receives nothing of significant value in return. Therefore if a donor receives goods or services, other than a minor thank-you item, the "contribution" is *payment for goods or services*, and normal business accounting is appropriate.

Unconditional and Unrestricted Cash Contributions

Unconditional and unrestricted cash contributions have no donor-imposed conditions or restrictions. An example is the cash deposited in Salvation Army kettles at the holiday season. Conditions or restrictions of contributions are *donor-imposed* conditions or restrictions *only*. If the Board of the NFP organization decides to set aside unrestricted contributions for a designated purpose, such as funding a particular program or accumulating a sinking fund for repayment of debt, the contributions are still unrestricted.

    Unconditional contributions of cash not subject to donors' restrictions are recorded as increases in *unrestricted net assets* on the statement of activities. Suppose Beta Alpha Psi receives a contribution of $1,000, for general use, from a recent accounting graduate. The journal entry to record this unconditional contribution of cash is:

Cash.	1,000	
Contribution revenue—unrestricted		1,000
To record unconditional cash contribution of $1,000.		

Unconditional and Unrestricted Contributions of Goods and Services

Unconditional contributions of goods not subject to donors' restrictions are reported as increases in unrestricted net assets, at fair market value on the date contributed. The contributor's book value or basis in the goods is irrelevant. An NFP organization is required to make good faith estimates of the value of goods received. This may require independent appraisal information.

Organizations such as the **Salvation Army** and **Goodwill Industries** receive a significant amount of contributions in the form of used clothing, furniture and appliances. These items are sold either in thrift stores or to brokers. The Salvation Army and Goodwill Industries must value these contributions at fair value when received. Of course, this does not require estimation of the value of all contributions when received. Most contributions are received and liquidated in the same accounting period, and fair value is the amount received on liquidation. Only those contributions received in one period and sold in another period require appraisal.

Revenue from contributed goods not subject to donors' restrictions increases unrestricted net assets on the statement of activities. Suppose a company donates office supplies with a fair value of $5,000 to Beta Alpha Psi, with no restrictions as to use. The entry to record this unconditional contribution of goods is:

Office supplies	5,000	
Contribution revenue—unrestricted		5,000
To record an unconditional contribution of office supplies with a		
fair market value of $5,000.		

Unconditional contributions of services increase unrestricted net assets when the services:

- Create or enhance nonfinancial assets or
- Require specialized skills, are provided by individuals possessing those skills, and are typically purchased if not provided by donation. Services requiring specialized skills are provided by accountants, architects, carpenters, doctors, electricians, lawyers, nurses, plumbers, teachers, and other professionals.

Contributed services that do not meet the above criteria are not recognized. Specialized services that do not create or enhance nonfinancial assets, and would otherwise be purchased, are valued at the *fair value of the services rendered*. Services that create or enhance nonfinancial assets, such as services donated by a contractor to build an addition to the organization's community center, are valued at the *fair value of the asset created*.

Unless the service creates or enhances a nonfinancial asset, the entry to record unconditional contributions of services typically involves both an increase *and* a decrease in unrestricted net assets, as it simultaneously recognizes revenue and expense. Suppose Beta Alpha Psi receives organizational support from the AICPA for its annual conference, in the form of professional consulting services, valued at $3,000. The entry to record this unconditional contribution of services is:

Annual convention expenses	3,000	
Revenues from contributed services—unrestricted		3,000
To record the donation of consulting services valued at $3,000.		

Annual convention expenses reduce unrestricted net assets, while revenues from contributed services increase unrestricted net assets on the statement of activities.

Beta Alpha Psi records services that create or enhance nonfinancial assets, such as donated services of a contractor in building a new conference facility, in this way:

Building	800,000	
Revenue from contributed services—unrestricted		800,000
To record services donated to construct a new conference facility,		
estimated to add $800,000 to the fair value of the facility.		

BUSINESS APPLICATION   Contributions of Services

Most NFPs rely on volunteers for everyday operations and delivery of services. Here are two examples of the reporting for these contributions:

Habitat for Humanity International's 2010 consolidated financial statements reveal the following:

> A substantial number of volunteers have made significant contributions of their time to Habitat's program and supporting services. The value of this contributed time is not reflected in the consolidated financial statements since it does not require a specialized skill. However, certain other contributed services that require specialized skills, where provided by individuals possessing those skills and otherwise needing to be purchased if not provided by donation, are recognized as revenue and expense.

Beta Alpha Psi's 2011 financial statements recognize the efforts of students and faculty, but do not report these contributions:

> The Organization recognizes contribution revenue for certain contributed services received at the fair value of those services. Those services include facilities and organizational support...furnished by the American Institute of Certified Public Accountants. In addition, a significant amount of time, for which no value has been assigned because it does not meet the criteria for recognition, was volunteered by professors and students to the activities of the Organization.

Donor-Imposed Temporary Restrictions

Donors may impose two types of **temporary restrictions** on their contributions: *time restrictions* and *use restrictions*. The most common **time-restricted contributions** are unconditional **promises**, discussed below. Future payments in multi-year pledges are automatically time-restricted. With a **use-restricted contribution**, the donor specifies that the contribution be used for a particular purpose. This restriction may be explicitly stated by the donor or inferred because of the way the contribution was solicited. For example, a donor makes a donation to a university, stipulating that the donation be used to finance scholarships for accounting students. Alternatively, the accounting department solicits contributions in a scholarship fund drive. Although the donor may not specifically state the restriction, donations to the fund drive are implicitly restricted to scholarship use.

Both time and use restrictions are **temporary restrictions** since the restrictions disappear either with the passage of time or by using the contributions for the intended purpose. Temporarily restricted contributions initially increase temporarily restricted net assets. When the restriction is met, net assets are released from temporarily restricted to unrestricted net assets. Suppose Beta Alpha Psi receives $20,000 donor-designated to fund best practice awards to the chapters, and then makes the awards. Entries are:

Cash	20,000	
Contribution revenue—temporarily restricted		20,000
To record the cash contribution.		
Net assets released from restrictions—temporarily restricted	20,000	
Net assets released from restrictions—unrestricted		20,000
To record the release of net assets.		
Best practice awards (expense)	20,000	
Cash		20,000
To record distribution of cash awards.		

Contribution revenue increases temporarily restricted net assets on the statement of activities. The "net assets released" accounts reduce temporarily restricted net assets and increase unrestricted net assets, respectively. If the expenditure of restricted funds is an expense, it reduces unrestricted net assets. The expenditure is capitalized as an asset if the contribution was donor-restricted to a building fund and the expenditure was a payment to a contractor.

As a practical matter, when donations restricted to a particular use are used for this purpose in the same accounting period, we need not first classify the donations as temporarily restricted and then release them from restrictions when the expenditures are made. Although the reporting is technically not as accurate, such donations may be included with unrestricted net assets in the period received.

Unconditional Promises   An **unconditional promise** to give in the future, having **verifiable documentation**, is reported in the period the promise is given, as an increase in unrestricted, temporarily restricted, or permanently restricted net assets. The promise appears as a receivable, valued at *realizable value, net of estimated uncollectible amounts*. Contributions expected to be collected over more than one year are measured at present value.

Most promises to contribute over more than one year are recorded as *time-restricted contributions*. Because the organization does not receive the payments immediately, their use is automatically restricted to the period(s) in which payment is received. Thus if the promise has the documentation allowing it to be recorded in the period the promise is made, the contribution revenue is temporarily restricted.

As an example of an unconditional promise that qualifies for recognition in the year the promise is made, suppose a donor agrees in writing to contribute $5,000 per year to Beta Alpha Psi for the next five years. Using a discount rate of 10 percent, when the agreement is signed Beta Alpha Psi makes the following entry:

Contributions receivable	18,954	
Contribution revenue—temporarily restricted		18,954
To record the present value of the written agreement. At a 10% discount rate,		
$18,954 is the present value of an annuity of $5,000 per year for five years. The		
promise is assumed to be 100% collectible.		

Each year, Beta Alpha Psi recognizes interest on the receivable and the $5,000 cash donation. The interest is included in *contribution revenue*, not interest income, and accumulates in temporarily restricted net assets until the donation becomes available for use (*ASC para. 958-310-45-2*). Entries for the first year are:

Contributions receivable	1,895	
Contribution revenue—temporarily restricted		1,895
To record interest earned on outstanding contributions receivable;		
$1,895 = 10% × $18,954.		
Cash	5,000	
Contributions receivable		5,000
To record the donor's cash contribution for the year.		
Net assets released from restrictions—temporarily restricted	5,000	
Net assets released from restrictions—unrestricted		5,000
To record satisfaction of the time restriction.		

NFP organizations must keep careful records of promises and payments, and make judgments as to their collectibility and whether the promise is backed by verifiable documentation. Clearly a donor's written agreement to contribute $5,000 per year for the next five years is recognized as revenue in the year the agreement is signed. Just as clearly, a phone pledge during a telethon, where the potential donor asks to "think it over" before making the donation, is not immediately recognized. However, other situations may not be as clear.

Sufficient verifiable documentation supporting recognition of contribution revenue includes written agreements, pledge cards, or follow-up written confirmations of oral agreements. It is important to distinguish an intention from a promise. Even though an individual indicates that the organization is a beneficiary in his or her will, the will may be legally modified before death. Thus this intention to give is not recognized as revenue by the organization. However, if the individual dies without modifying the will, the organization recognizes the contribution as revenue after probate, prior to receiving the bequest.

Donor-Imposed Conditions

A donor-imposed **condition** refers to an uncertain future event that could void the contribution. Conditional and documented *promises* to give are recognized as receivables and contribution revenue *in the period the condition is met*. When a donor makes the contribution *before* the condition is met, the organization recognizes a liability. Suppose a donor promises in writing to contribute $1,000,000 to Beta Alpha Psi if contributions by others total $1,000,000. When that condition is met, Beta Alpha Psi records the $1,000,000 promise as revenue. If the donor pays $1,000,000 to the organization *before* the condition is met, entries are:

Cash...	1,000,000	
Refundable contributions		1,000,000
To record the receipt of a conditional contribution as a liability because the		
required condition has not been met.		
Refundable contributions..	1,000,000	
Contribution revenue—unrestricted		1,000,000
To record contribution revenue when the condition is met, assuming the		
contribution has no donor-imposed restrictions.		

Donations made *after* the condition is met are immediately recognized as contribution revenue.

Donor-Imposed Permanent Restrictions

Donors of permanently restricted contributions generally stipulate that the principal of the donation be maintained, and any income earned on investment of the principal may be unrestricted, or restricted to a particular purpose or time period. The amount donated is a **permanent endowment** and increases permanently restricted net assets. Income on the endowment is either unrestricted or temporarily restricted, depending on the donor's wishes.

Suppose a large CPA firm gives $1,000,000 to Beta Alpha Psi in 2012. The $1,000,000 principal is to be left intact, and income earned on the principal must be used to fund annual faculty advisor awards. Beta Alpha Psi invests the $1,000,000 in securities that generate income of $50,000 in 2013. This $50,000 is paid out in faculty advisor awards in 2014. The entries are:

2012			
	Restricted cash	1,000,000	
	Contribution revenue—permanently restricted		1,000,000
	To record receipt of the permanent endowment.		
	Investment in securities	1,000,000	
	Restricted cash		1,000,000
	To record investment in securities.		
2013			
	Cash...	50,000	
	Investment income—temporarily restricted		50,000
	To record the investment income.		
2014			
	Net assets released from restrictions—temporarily restricted.........	50,000	
	Net assets released from restrictions—unrestricted		50,000
	To record release of funds from temporary restrictions.		
	Faculty advisor awards (expense)	50,000	
	Cash		50,000
	To record use of the funds for the donor-specified purpose.		

The faculty advisor award expense reduces unrestricted net assets on the statement of activities.

BUSINESS APPLICATION   Net Assets of The American National Red Cross

The American National Red Cross provides support in national and international emergency situations. Programs include armed forces emergency services, biomedical services, community, domestic disaster, and international relief and development services. Biomedical services include collection and distribution of blood and blood products, and related testing and research facilities. The Red Cross' June 30, 2010, balance sheet reports the following net assets for 2009 and 2010:

(in thousands)	2010	2009
Unrestricted net assets	$448,142	$459,983
Temporarily restricted net assets.	884,910	620,214
Permanently restricted net assets	625,835	592,269

Included in temporarily restricted net assets are contributions to support recovery from specific natural disasters. In the fiscal year ended June 30, 2010, these natural disasters included floods and tornadoes in the United States, an 8.8 magnitude earthquake and tsunami in Chile, a 7.0 magnitude earthquake in Haiti, and an 8.1 magnitude earthquake and tsunami in American Samoa. When an NFP organization collects contributions that are donor-specified to support a particular program or activity, the unspent balance of contributions is reported in temporarily restricted net assets. The footnotes to its 2010 financial statements report that $425,374,000 of the Red Cross' temporarily restricted net assets at June 30, 2010, are designated for international relief and development services. Of this amount, contributions of approximately $320,000,000 are unspent contributions related to the Haiti earthquake.

Contributions of Long-Lived Assets

Donations of long-lived assets, valued at fair market value at the date of donation, may increase unrestricted net assets or temporarily restricted net assets. When the *asset's use is donor-restricted*, either by use or time, the donation increases *temporarily restricted net assets*. If the *organization intends to liquidate the assets*, the donation is most likely an increase in *unrestricted net assets*.

When the donor does not stipulate how long or in what capacity the organization must use the donated asset, reporting procedures depend on whether the organization has a consistent policy with respect to donations of long-lived assets. Organizations that have a policy of treating such contributions as *time restricted* meet that restriction over time as the asset depreciates. *ASC para. 958-605-45-6* also requires organizations to follow the same policy with respect to cash contributions donor-restricted to the acquisition of long-lived assets. In the absence of a policy, donations of long-lived assets without donor restrictions increase unrestricted net assets.

Suppose a former Beta Alpha Psi chapter president, now a successful partner in a large CPA firm, donates a building with a fair market value of $1,500,000 to Beta Alpha Psi, with no restrictions on use. Beta Alpha Psi has a policy of recognizing such contributions as time restricted. Straight-line depreciation is based on the building's estimated 15-year life, with no salvage value. Entries are:

Building	1,500,000	
Contribution revenue—temporarily restricted		1,500,000
To record receipt of the building.		
Net assets released from restrictions—temporarily restricted.	100,000	
Net assets released from restrictions—unrestricted		100,000
To record release of restrictions as the building depreciates.		
Depreciation expense.	100,000	
Accumulated depreciation—building		100,000
To record depreciation expense on the building.		

Organizations that initially record the contribution as unrestricted do not need the entry to release net assets in connection with depreciation recognition.

Organizations also receive donations of nondepreciable assets, such as land or artworks. Contributions of land are recorded at fair value as increases in permanently restricted, temporarily restricted, or unrestricted net assets, depending on donor stipulations and organization policy. Organizations are *not* required to report revenue for donations of works of art or items of historical value that meet these criteria:

- They are held for public exhibition, education, or research in furtherance of public service rather than financial gain
- They are protected, not used as collateral for loans, cared for, and preserved
- They are subject to an organizational policy that requires the proceeds from sales of collection items to be used to acquire other items for collections. (ASC glossary definition of "collection," and *ASC para. 958-605-25-19*)

Contributions not reported as revenue are also not capitalized as assets.

Annuity and Life Income Contributions

NFPs often use *annuity or life income agreements* to raise funds. A donor makes a contribution of money or other resources that is recorded at fair market value. In exchange, the organization agrees to make periodic payments, either to the donor or to other specified individuals, over several time periods. When the periodic payment is a fixed amount, we have an *annuity agreement*; when the payment is defined as the amount of income earned on the contributed assets, we have a *life income agreement*.

In an **annuity agreement**, the present value of the annuity payments is recorded as a liability. The difference between the amount contributed and the present value of the annuity payments is the value of the agreement to the organization, and increases net assets. If this amount becomes part of a permanent endowment when the agreement terminates, the increase is to permanently restricted net assets. If it is available for restricted purposes, or available for unrestricted use when the agreement terminates, it initially increases temporarily restricted net assets.

In a **life income agreement**, future payments to beneficiaries equal future income, and the present value of the liability is zero. Thus the entire contribution initially increases either temporarily or permanently restricted net assets, depending on the donor's intent.

Annuity Agreement Illustration   Suppose that a retired accounting professional with a remaining life expectancy of nine years donates $500,000 to Beta Alpha Psi under an annuity agreement. She is to receive $70,000 annually for life, with the first payment occurring in one year. Using a 6 percent discount rate, the present value of the liability equals $70,000 × present value of an ordinary annuity of nine years at 6% = $70,000 × 6.8017 = $476,119. Once the agreement terminates, Beta Alpha Psi has unrestricted access to the value of the annuity in excess of the present value of the related obligation. The initial entry is:

Cash	500,000	
Annuity payable		476,119
Contribution revenue—temporarily restricted		23,881
To record the contribution and corresponding annuity agreement.		

Suppose further that the $500,000 was invested and earned 8 percent. Entries for the first year are:

Investments	500,000	
Cash		500,000
To record investment of the $500,000.		
Cash	40,000	
Investment income		40,000
To record income for the year from investments; $40,000 = $500,000 × 8%.		

Interest expense for the year of $28,567 (= $476,119 × 6%) is recognized on the annuity payable. Since expenses can only be reported in unrestricted net assets, an entry releases the restricted net assets before the expense can be recognized.

Net assets released from restrictions—temporarily restricted......................	28,567	
Net assets released from restrictions—unrestricted........................		28,567
To record release of net assets.		
Interest expense..	28,567	
Annuity payable..	41,433	
Cash..		70,000
To record interest expense on the annuity obligation and		
reduction in the annuity liability.		

Life Income Agreement Illustration   Assume the $500,000 contribution described above is made under a *life income agreement*. Beta Alpha Psi has no initial liability, because the donor will receive whatever income is generated each year. The entries for a life income agreement are:

Cash..	500,000	
Contribution revenue—temporarily restricted........................		500,000
To record contribution under a life income agreement.		
Investments..	500,000	
Cash..		500,000
To record investment of the $500,000.		
Cash..	40,000	
Life income payable...		40,000
To record the 8% income for the year from investments, and related		
obligation to donor.		
Life income payable..	40,000	
Cash..		40,000
To record payment of current income to donor per agreement.		

Contributions Received on Behalf of Others

An NFP organization may collect contributions for distribution to other NFP organizations. For example, the **United Way** encourages donors to designate their contributions for specific unaffiliated organizations. A church collects contributions from members to support an unaffiliated missionary organization.

Accounting for such transactions hinges on whether the recipient organization is a **donee** or end user that benefits from the contribution or merely an **intermediary** that accepts the contribution on behalf of another organization. If a recipient organization is a donee, the contribution is recorded as **contribution revenue**. But when the recipient organization serves as an agent that collects assets for distribution to specified unaffiliated organizations, the amount received is recorded as a **liability**, not a contribution. The specified beneficiaries record the contribution as revenue.

Suppose you make a contribution to the United Way, and specify that your donation is to support the **American Cancer Society**. The United Way records your donation as a liability, and, when informed, the American Cancer Society records a receivable and contribution revenue. When the cash is transferred to the American Cancer Society, the liability on the United Way's books and the receivable on the American Cancer Society's books are extinguished. However, if you give United Way the *right* to redirect your money to other beneficiaries, or if you do not specify a particular beneficiary, United Way becomes a donee and treats your donation as contribution revenue. When the money is eventually distributed, United Way records it as *contributions made* (expense) and the organization receiving the contribution records the revenue.

If you make a contribution to an organization, and specify that the money is to be used by an **affiliated organization**, the recipient organization treats your contribution as temporarily restricted revenue. Perhaps you make a cash contribution to a private foundation that controls two organizations. One organization provides scholarships to college students interested in accounting careers. The other organization supports programs to encourage high school students to pursue accounting careers. If you specify that your contribution is to be used to support college scholarships, the foundation records your contribution as temporarily restricted revenue.

REVIEW 1   ●   Accounting for Contributions

Contribution-related information for **Make-A-Wish Foundation** during 2014 is described below.

1. On January 2, a donor promises, in writing, to contribute $1,000 each year for the next five years, starting on December 31, 2014. The appropriate discount rate is 5%. On December 31, the Foundation receives the first payment.
2. A donor contributed $50,000 in cash in 2013, to fund wishes related to baseball. During 2014, three baseball-related wishes are granted, costing $35,000.
3. A donor contributes equipment with a fair value of $100,000 and useful life of 5 years. Make-A-Wish's policy is to report donations of long-lived assets as temporarily restricted. One year of depreciation is recorded in 2014.
4. Donations of services are as follows: Legal services performed by a lawyer, valued at $40,000; development of architectural plans for a new administrative facility by an architect, $25,000; fund-raising activities by families of wish recipients, $10,000.

Required

Prepare entries to record the above events occurring in 2014. Specify how each category of net assets is affected.

Solutions are located after the chapter assignments.

ACCOUNTING FOR INVESTMENTS

LO3 Report investments in financial securities.

NFP organizations frequently invest endowment and other restricted resources on a long-term basis, and invest unrestricted resources on a temporary basis. *Purchased investments* are recorded at *cost* and *donated investments* at *fair value when received*. *ASC Subtopic 958-320* specifies the post-acquisition accounting for investments held by NFP organizations.

All investments in *equity securities with determinable fair values* and *all debt securities* are reported at **fair (market) value**. Unrealized gains and losses are reported in the statement of activities. Note that no distinction is made between securities held for trading, available-for-sale, and held-to-maturity, as specified for investments held by business entities. Realized and unrealized gains and losses on purchased investments are categorized as changes in unrestricted, temporarily restricted, or permanently restricted net assets, depending on the existence of donor restrictions or applicable laws. In many cases, a donor specifies a restriction on investment *gains* but not investment *losses*. If no donor-specified restrictions exist, all value changes are changes in unrestricted net assets, even if the NFP Board's policy is to restrict such value changes to a particular use.

Reporting Perspective

Business accounting for financial investments uses a three-portfolio approach: such investments are assigned to the trading, available-for-sale or held-to-maturity portfolios based on management's intent. The trading and available-for-sale portfolios are carried at market with value changes recognized in earnings or carried directly to stockholders' equity and reported in accumulated other comprehensive income, respectively. In contrast, the held-to-maturity portfolio, reserved for investments in debt securities that management intends and has the ability to hold to maturity, is carried at amortized cost. This controversial provision is strongly favored by financial institutions. When determining the standards for NFP investments, the FASB decided that not-for-profits do not need a "held-to-maturity" portfolio in the same way as financial institutions subject to *ASC Topic 320*.

> [Financial institutions]. . . manage their interest rate risk by coordinating the maturity and repricing characteristics of their investments and their liabilities. Reporting unrealized holding gains and losses on only the investments, and not the related liabilities, could cause volatility in earnings that is not representative of how financial institutions are affected by economic events (*SFAS 124*, para 43).

When the donation is a **specific investment**, such as 5,000 shares of AT&T common stock, and the donor specifies that the shares be held as a permanent endowment, any change in their value is a change in permanent net assets. Because the shares themselves are the permanent endowment, their value is permanently restricted, regardless of how that value changes. Changes in the value of the securities do not impact unrestricted net assets.

If the donation is $40,000 in **cash**, donor-restricted as a permanent endowment, and the organization invests the cash in equity securities, gains and losses on the securities increase or reduce unrestricted or temporarily restricted net assets, depending on the donor's wishes, leaving the value of the permanent endowment unchanged at $40,000.

BUSINESS APPLICATION   Securitizations of The American National Red Cross

The American National Red Cross engages in financing arrangements that parallel the activities of for-profit businesses. Note 11 to its 2010 financial statements reveals a securitization arrangement where receivables were sold to a "third party conduit."

> In August 2005, the Organization initiated a $100 million program to sell (securitize), on a revolving basis, certain biomedical hospital accounts receivable, while retaining a subordinated interest in a portion of the receivables. In August 2007, the securitized receivable amount was increased to $150 million. The eligible receivables are sold, without legal recourse, to a third party conduit through a wholly owned bankruptcy-remote special purpose entity that is consolidated for financial reporting purposes. The Organization continues servicing the sold receivables.

Note that the Red Cross consolidates the special purpose entity through which it sells its receivables. Since the conduit is wholly owned by the Red Cross, the consolidation decision is based on majority ownership rather than primary beneficiary status. NFP organizations must follow the same consolidation policies as for-profit companies, including consolidation of variable interest entities.

BUSINESS APPLICATION   Hedging Activities of The American National Red Cross

The American National Red Cross uses interest rate swap agreements to hedge its interest rate risk. Note 5 to its 2010 financial statements describes the hedge.

> The Organization held variable rate debt of approximately $289 million and $461 million at June 30, 2010 and 2009, respectively. Interest rate swap agreements are used by the Organization to mitigate the risk of changes in interest rates associated with variable interest rate indebtedness. Under such arrangements, a portion of variable rate indebtedness is converted to fixed rates based on a notional principal amount. The interest rate swap agreements are derivative instruments that are required to be marked to fair value and recorded on the statement of financial position. The change in fair value on these interest rate swap agreements was a loss of approximately $0.5 million and $2.4 million for the years ended June 30, 2010 and June 30, 2009, respectively, and is included as nonoperating gains/(losses) in the consolidated statement of activities.

The Red Cross follows the provisions of *ASC Topic 815* and marks its interest rate swaps to market. Note that unlike for-profit entities, NFPs cannot use hedge accounting to match hedge and hedged item gains and losses. A business can defer changes in the fair value of "cash flow hedge" swaps in other comprehensive income and reclassify them as adjustments to future variable rate interest expense. Because an NFP organization's statement of activities reports all changes in net assets, gains and losses on hedges and hedged items are not matched in the same reporting period. For more information on hedge accounting for businesses, see Chapters 8 and 9.

REVIEW 2 • Reporting for Investments

On January 1, 2013, the Gatehouse Foundation has the following equity investments, reported at fair value:

1. Securities valued at $100,000. The securities are investments of excess cash. At year-end, the securities have a fair value of $65,000. Dividend income for 2013 is $4,000.
2. Securities valued at $48,000. The securities were purchased several years ago with $55,000 in cash permanently restricted by the donor. Income must be used to fund the Foundation's publications and brochures. At year-end, the securities have a fair value of $42,000. Dividend income for 2013 is $2,500.
3. Securities valued at $75,000. The securities were contributed in 2012; fair value at the time of donation was $70,000. The donor specified that the securities were to be held by the Foundation. There is no restriction on income. At year-end, the securities have a fair value of $78,000. Dividend income for 2013 is $6,000.

Required

Prepare a schedule showing how the dividend income and unrealized gains and losses on these securities are reported on the Foundation's statement of activities. Indicate the effect on each category of net assets.

Solutions are located after the chapter assignments.

COMPREHENSIVE ILLUSTRATION OF NFP ACCOUNTING: NORTHEASTERN HEART SOCIETY

This section illustrates many of the accounting and reporting requirements for NFP organizations. It records typical transactions for the year and prepares the financial statements in good form.

The Northeastern Heart Society supports research, education, and public awareness programs on the prevention of heart disease. The Society's resources are generated from contributions, bequests, and grants. A trial balance at December 31, 2013, appears below.

	Dr (Cr)
Cash.	$11,700,000
Pledges receivable, net of $1,600,000 allowance for uncollectibles	6,400,000
Investments	72,000,000
Land	2,000,000
Equipment, net of accumulated depreciation	2,400,000
Accounts payable.	(3,300,000)
Net assets—unrestricted	(19,200,000)
Net assets—permanently restricted.	(72,000,000)
Total	$ 0

The following events occur during 2014:

1. Contributions pledged by the public during 2014 amounted to $130,000,000, of which $115,000,000 was collected during the year. In addition, $6,700,000 of the $8,000,000 in gross pledges outstanding at January 1 were collected; the balance was written off. The Society records pledges at gross and provides an allowance for uncollectibles equal to 20 percent of pledges outstanding at year-end. Pledges are recorded at full value because collection usually occurs within one year. Revenue of $4,600,000 was earned from programs which the Society conducted for employees of various corporations.

Cash.	115,000,000	
Pledges receivable.	15,000,000	
Contributions—unrestricted		130,000,000
To record contributions and cash collections for 2014.		

continued

continued from prior page

Cash.	6,700,000	
Pledges receivable		6,700,000
To record collection of receivables outstanding on January 1, 2014.		
Allowance for uncollectible pledges.	1,300,000	
Pledges receivable		1,300,000
To write off the remaining January 1, 2014 pledges receivable balance.		
Bad debt expense (general administration)	2,700,000	
Allowance for uncollectible pledges		2,700,000
To adjust the allowance for uncollectible pledges account to its correct		
ending balance of $3,000,000 (= 20% × $15,000,000); prior to adjustment		
the allowance stood at $300,000 (= $1,600,000 beginning balance −		
$1,300,000 write-offs).		
Cash.	4,600,000	
Educational program revenue—unrestricted.		4,600,000
To record revenue from educational programs.		

2. Cash disbursements amounted to $115,500,000 in 2014, as follows:

Research	$ 40,000,000
Public awareness programs.	35,000,000
Corporate programs.	3,500,000
General administration	19,500,000
Fund-raising	17,500,000
Total	$115,500,000

Accounts payable increased from $3,300,000 to $4,800,000; all unpaid invoices at beginning and end of year relate to general administration costs.

Expenses—research	40,000,000	
Expenses—public awareness programs	35,000,000	
Expenses—corporate programs	3,500,000	
Expenses—general administration.	21,000,000	
Expenses—fund-raising.	17,500,000	
Cash		115,500,000
Accounts payable		1,500,000
To record expenses for 2014.		

3. Early in 2014 the Society received a federal grant of $20,000,000 to expand its public awareness programs into smaller communities where it had not been active. The grant period expires on March 31, 2015. During the last half of 2014, $14,300,000 was spent on the project under the terms of the grant; the balance of $5,700,000 is designated by the grantor for expenditure in 2015 and remains temporarily restricted.

Cash.	20,000,000	
Federal grant support—temporarily restricted		20,000,000
To record receipt of the federal grant.		
Net assets released from restrictions—temporarily restricted.	14,300,000	
Net assets released from restrictions—unrestricted.		14,300,000
To record release of assets from temporary restrictions.		
Expenses—public awareness programs	14,300,000	
Cash		14,300,000
To record expenditures for designated programs.		

4. The Society's permanent endowment contains donor-restricted money to be used for research scholarships. Several years ago, the Society received a $50,000,000 bequest to establish this fund.

The donor stipulated that the principal be maintained intact, with income used for research scholarships. Subsequent bequests and contributions increased the principal of the fund to $72,000,000 at the beginning of 2014. During 2014, contributions of $350,000 and a bequest of $1,000,000 added to principal. Investment income of $8,000,000 was earned. At year-end, all but $500,000 of principal was invested in certificates of deposit. Endowment cash held at year-end is separately categorized.

Restricted cash	1,350,000	
Contributions—permanently restricted		1,350,000
To record support designated for endowment.		
Investments	850,000	
Restricted cash		850,000
To record purchase of investments; $850,000 = $1,350,000 − $500,000.		
Cash	8,000,000	
Investment income—temporarily restricted		8,000,000
To record income from investments.		

5. In 2014, $7,500,000 was spent for research scholarships, pursuant to the fund restrictions.

Net assets released from restrictions—temporarily restricted	7,500,000	
Net assets released from restrictions—unrestricted		7,500,000
To record release of assets from temporary restrictions.		
Expenses—research scholarships	7,500,000	
Cash		7,500,000
To record disbursement of scholarship funds.		

6. During 2014, construction began on an office building estimated to cost the Society $40,000,000. The Society borrowed $30,000,000 from the bank on a short-term building loan. During 2014, construction costs were $24,000,000, and $2,800,000 in interest was paid on the loan. Investment of excess cash balances in time deposits yielded $770,000 in interest revenue; the Society's board of directors authorized the use of this money for unanticipated construction costs. Office equipment depreciation of $300,000 was charged to general administration.

Cash	30,000,000	
Loan payable		30,000,000
To record financing for the building.		
Construction in progress	24,000,000	
Cash		24,000,000
To record construction activity during 2014.		
Interest expense—general administration	2,800,000	
Cash		2,800,000
To record interest expense on the loan (assumed not capitalized).		
Cash	770,000	
Investment income—unrestricted		770,000
To record interest revenue on investments of excess cash.		
Expenses—general administration	300,000	
Accumulated depreciation		300,000
To record depreciation on the office equipment.		

The statement of activities for Northeastern Heart Society for the year ended December 31, 2014, the statement of financial position at December 31, 2014, and the statement of cash flows for the year ended December 31, 2014, appear in Exhibits 13.4, 13.5, and 13.6. An analysis of expenses, by natural and functional classification, appears in Exhibit 13.7.

EXHIBIT 13.4 Northeastern Heart Society Statement of Activities

NORTHEASTERN HEART SOCIETY
Statement of Activities
For Year Ended December 31, 2014

Change in unrestricted net assets:
Revenues and support:

Contributions	$130,000,000
Educational programs	4,600,000
Investment income	770,000
Net assets released from program restrictions	21,800,000
Total unrestricted revenues and support	157,170,000

Expenses:

Research programs	47,500,000
Public awareness programs	49,300,000
Corporate programs	3,500,000
General administration	26,800,000
Fund-raising	17,500,000
Total expenses	144,600,000
Increase in unrestricted net assets	12,570,000

Change in temporarily restricted net assets:

Grants	20,000,000
Investment income	8,000,000
Net assets released from program restrictions	(21,800,000)
Increase in temporarily restricted net assets	6,200,000

Change in permanently restricted net assets:

Contributions	1,350,000
Increase in net assets	20,120,000
Net assets, January 1, 2014	91,200,000
Net assets, December 31, 2014	$111,320,000

EXHIBIT 13.5 Northeastern Heart Society Statement of Financial Position

NORTHEASTERN HEART SOCIETY
Statements of Financial Position
December 31, 2014 and 2013

Assets	2014	2013
Cash	$ 32,670,000	$11,700,000
Pledges receivable, net	12,000,000	6,400,000
Restricted cash	500,000	—
Investments	72,850,000	72,000,000
Land	2,000,000	2,000,000
Equipment, net	2,100,000	2,400,000
Construction in progress	24,000,000	—
Total assets	$146,120,000	$94,500,000

Liabilities and net assets
Liabilities

	2014	2013
Accounts payable	$ 4,800,000	$ 3,300,000
Loan payable	30,000,000	—
Total liabilities	34,800,000	3,300,000

Net assets

	2014	2013
Unrestricted	31,770,000	19,200,000
Temporarily restricted	6,200,000	—
Permanently restricted	73,350,000	72,000,000
Total net assets	111,320,000	91,200,000
Total liabilities and net assets	$146,120,000	$94,500,000

EXHIBIT 13.6 Northeastern Heart Society Statement of Cash Flows

NORTHEASTERN HEART SOCIETY
Statement of Cash Flows
For Year Ended December 31, 2014

Cash flows from operating activities	
Contributions	$121,700,000
Investment income	8,000,000
Program revenue	4,600,000
Grant support	20,000,000
Interest revenue	770,000
Interest expense	(2,800,000)
Program expenditures	(137,300,000)
Net cash from operating activities	14,970,000
Cash flows from investing activities	
Investments	(850,000)
Construction	(24,000,000)
Net cash used for investing activities	(24,850,000)
Cash flows from financing activities	
Loan proceeds	30,000,000
Endowments	1,350,000
Net cash from financing activities	31,350,000
Increase in cash	21,470,000
Cash balance, January 1, 2014	11,700,000
Cash balance, December 31, 2014	$ 33,170,000

Reconciliation of Change in Net Assets
To Net Cash from Operating Activities

Increase in net assets	$ 20,120,000
Adjustments:	
Depreciation expense	300,000
Endowment contributions	(1,350,000)
Increase in pledges receivable, net	(5,600,000)
Increase in accounts payable	1,500,000
Net cash from operating activities	$ 14,970,000

REPORTING ISSUES FOR SPECIFIC NOT-FOR-PROFIT ORGANIZATIONS

LO4 Describe major reporting issues for specific NFPs.

This section discusses reporting issues specific to each of the three specific types of NFP organizations. Detailed guidelines may be found in such publications as the AICPA Audit and Accounting Guide—*Not-for-Profit Entities*, which is updated regularly, and in *ASC Topic 954*, Health Care Entities.

Voluntary Health and Welfare Organizations

VHWOs, such as **Habitat for Humanity International**, generate most of their resources from **public support**—contributions, bequests, and grants—and revenues from providing goods and services. Donors to VHWOs take a strong interest in the distinction between program service expenses, and administrative and fund-raising expenses. The discussion earlier in the chapter on the functional classification of expenses and treatment of joint educational and fund-raising costs is particularly applicable to VHWOs.

Accounting for revenues and expenses related to providing goods and services should be carefully separated from activities related to contributions. VHWOs follow revenue recognition principles from regular business accounting in accounting for the sale of goods or services. For example, the **YWCA**

EXHIBIT 13.7 Northeastern Heart Society Statement of Functional Expenses

NORTHEASTERN HEART SOCIETY
Statement of Functional Expenses
For Year Ended December 31, 2014

	Program Services			Supporting Services		
	Research	Public Programs	Corporate Programs	General Administration	Fund-Raising	Total Expenses
Salaries.........................	$ 8,700,000	$20,500,000	$2,800,000	$14,000,000	$ 2,700,000	$ 48,700,000
Fees	—	—	—	—	7,000,000	7,000,000
Supplies	4,500,000	2,300,000	—	1,000,000	1,000,000	8,800,000
Utilities	2,000,000	8,000,000	—	1,500,000	3,000,000	14,500,000
Occupancy.....................	1,500,000	1,500,000	500,000	2,000,000	500,000	6,000,000
Maintenance....................	3,500,000	2,000,000	—	1,500,000	—	7,000,000
Printing........................	2,000,000	9,000,000	—	—	3,000,000	14,000,000
Travel	4,000,000	4,000,000	200,000	—	300,000	8,500,000
Conferences....................	3,500,000	2,000,000	—	1,000,000	—	6,500,000
Research grants.................	10,300,000	—	—	—	—	10,300,000
Scholarships....................	7,500,000	—	—	—	—	7,500,000
Interest........................	—	—	—	2,800,000	—	2,800,000
Bad debts......................	—	—	—	2,700,000	—	2,700,000
Depreciation....................	—	—	—	300,000	—	300,000
Totals.........................	$47,500,000	$49,300,000	$3,500,000	$26,800,000	$17,500,000	$144,600,000

provides childcare services to the public, and **Goodwill Industries** does contract work for local businesses. Revenue on such services and contracts is recognized when earned, and expenses are recognized when resources are consumed, using business accounting principles. All such activities are changes in unrestricted net assets.

Colleges and Universities

Private colleges and universities derive much of their resources from student tuition and fees, contributions, contracts, endowment income and grants. Tuition revenue is typically shown gross, with adjustments such as scholarships and waivers shown as either revenue deductions or as expenses. If the tuition adjustments are in return for services provided, such as tuition waivers for graduate teaching assistantships, the adjustments are shown as expenses. If the tuition adjustments do not involve any services, as with scholarships, the adjustments are revenue deductions. Functional classifications of expenses include the following: **education costs**, such as faculty salaries, supplies, and classroom facility costs, **support costs**, such as student services and maintenance, and **self-supporting services**, such as dormitories, food service, and health service.

Colleges and universities must be especially diligent in tracking donations restricted to particular uses. They usually have a **permanent endowment** consisting of funds that are donor-restricted indefinitely, with the income either unrestricted or donor-restricted for particular purposes. For example, a business school endowment may restrict endowment income to expenditures for upgrading the accounting curriculum. Donors often establish an **annuity fund**, where the university must pay a specified amount each year to the donor, with any excess remaining when the agreement terminates going to the university. A **life income fund** pays the donor the income on fund investments for life, with the remainder going to the university upon the donor's death.

Health Care Organizations

The business environment for health care organizations has changed substantially over the years, causing changes in the information required to make decisions. These organizations face significant pressure from escalating operating costs and competition. Most hospital bills are paid by third parties such as Medicare, Medicaid, and insurance carriers. Third-party payers reimburse providers using flat rates for many services based on the patient's diagnosis, not the actual treatment cost incurred. These third-party payers require detailed analyses of costs incurred to develop reasonable reimbursement rates by diagnosis. Cost information is also used to rank health care providers. These rankings help determine whether a particular health care facility qualifies for reimbursement, and can strongly influence its ability to attract patients.

Operating revenues consist of **patient service revenue**, generated from patient charges, and **revenue from research grants and auxiliary services** such as the cafeteria and gift shop. Amounts realizable from third-party payers are typically less than gross revenues. On the statement of activities, gross patient service revenue appears first, with provisions for contractual and other adjustments deducted from gross revenue to determine net patient service revenue.

Charity care must be distinguished from *bad debt expense*. **Charity care** represents services performed with no expectation that payment will be received, and is separately reported at *cost*; no revenue or profit is recognized on charity care. Services provided to patients, with the expectation that payment will be received, are recorded as patient service revenue. Uncollectible portions of this patient service revenue are typically shown separately as **bad debt expense** and not netted against revenue, unless revenue is recognized at the time service is rendered, before assessing ability to pay.

Medical malpractice claims and similar liabilities are reported at the gross amount expected to be paid. Amounts expected to be reimbursed through insurance are reported as receivables and are not netted against the liability.

Health care expenses fall into the following major classifications: nursing services, other professional services, general services, administrative services, uncollectible accounts, and depreciation. The AICPA Audit and Accounting Guide—*Health Care Entities,* updated annually, provides detailed guidance.

Reporting Perspective

NFPs merge with or acquire other NFPs with about the same frequency as for-profit businesses. NFPs combine to improve the quality and efficiency of services, expand the types of services offered, gain access to better funding opportunities, or enter new geographic areas.

Prior to 2010, combinations of NFP organizations were exempted from the guidance in *ASC Topic 805*, Business Combinations, and instead followed the old requirements of *APB Opinion 16* (1970) which allowed either purchase or pooling accounting. An Accounting Standards Update, effective in 2010, recognizes the unique features of NFPs, and provides specific guidance for NFP mergers and acquisitions in *ASC Topic 958*, Not-for-Profit Entities. This guidance differs from business accounting for mergers and acquisitions as follows:

- If an NFP organization obtains control of another entity, the combination is an **acquisition**, and the valuation requirements of *ASC Topic 805* apply. The acquiring NFP reports the acquired NFP's assets and liabilities at fair value, including previously unreported intangibles. However, the accounting treatment of the excess of acquisition cost over the fair value of identifiable net assets acquired depends on the nature of the acquired NFP. If the acquiree operates like a business, charging fees to cover costs, the acquirer recognizes this difference as *goodwill*. If the acquiree is primarily supported by contributions, the acquirer reports the excess as a *separate charge* in its statement of activities. Although a business records a bargain purchase gain on its income statement when the fair value of identifiable net assets acquired exceeds the acquisition cost, an acquiring NFP records an *inherent contribution received*, as a credit in its statement of activities.

  Valuation of the acquired organization's assets and liabilities at fair value is appropriate if the acquirer takes control. Because goodwill is not as relevant to donors' assessment of organizations funded primarily by contributions, acquisition cost in excess of the fair value of identifiable net assets acquired is immediately expensed.

- If two or more NFP organizations give up control to create a new entity with a new governing board, the combination is a **merger**. The new entity accounts for the merger using the *carryover method*— the assets and liabilities of the merging organizations are combined at the amounts reported on their separate financial statements at the merger date, and are not recorded at fair value. No "goodwill" or "bargain purchase" issues arise. The carryover method is essentially the same as the pooling-of-interests method allowed for businesses prior to 2001.

NFP organizations often combine to improve services to the public or to otherwise further their mission. An NFP acquirer frequently pays nothing for the acquired NFP's net assets. Because of the unique nature of NFP combinations, the FASB decided to retain the pooling-of-interests method for mergers.

EVALUATION OF EXTERNAL REPORTING FOR NFP ORGANIZATIONS

The FASB requirements for NFPs are supported by some and criticized by others. This section discusses both sides of the major issues, in terms of the impact of the requirements on the external reader's ability to evaluate the financial performance of NFPs.

LO5 Evaluate financial information provided by NFPs.

Strengths of External Reporting Requirements

The strengths of the external reporting model for NFPs include standardization, completeness and comparability between types of NFP organizations.

* The requirements provide a **standardized presentation** of financial performance and condition by all NFP organizations. Prior to these standards, each type of NFP organization had its own presentation methodology. In addition, disclosures were often omitted, such as the statement of cash flows and a functional classification of expenses.

* The external reporting model does not preclude an NFP from **tailoring its financial statements** to meet readers' needs. For example, although the "bottom line" on the statement of activities is the change in net assets, the NFP may include a measure of operating performance that it feels best reflects its activities.

* The presentation requirements focus on the **entity as a whole**. Creditors, donors, members, and other interested readers prefer to evaluate the performance of the entire organization.

* Restricted contributions and changes in the value of investments appear on the financial statements on a more **timely basis**, providing full information to financial statement users.

Criticisms of External Reporting Requirements

Criticism of the FASB requirements generally follows one major theme—that the required reporting of changes in net assets can cause readers of the financial statements to *overestimate resources available for organization activities*.

* Investments in debt and equity securities are reported at fair value rather than at cost. Unrealized gains can be misinterpreted as funds available for the organization's activities.

* Contributions are reported as revenue in the period they are promised, not when received. Critics contend that financial statements are misleading to the extent that promised contributions not yet available are shown as increases in net assets, especially when multi-year pledges are involved.

* Recognition of contributions in the period received has special complications for those organizations receiving large amounts of contributions in the form of goods, such as used clothing. The Codification requires that these organizations estimate the market value of contributions when received, which may be subject to a high degree of error.

* Restricted contributions are recognized as increases in net assets in the period received. Critics say that these contributions are not revenues until the period the restrictions are met and they become available for use. Showing them as increases in net assets can be misleading, even though they are segregated under temporarily restricted net assets.

* Donations of long-lived assets are recognized as increases in net assets in the period received. The full fair value of the asset is shown as revenue in the period received, but the asset will benefit many periods in the future. Even though the organization may treat such donations as temporarily restricted, critics feel that this causes a mismatching of revenues with expenses, and overstates the resources available to fund program services.

* Net assets are classified according to donor restrictions, not internal organization restrictions. Critics feel that classification by management intention provides a more meaningful presentation of resources available for future use. In practice, income on restricted funds is often used for the same purpose as the original restricted funds, but unless the income is donor-restricted, it appears as an increase in unrestricted assets.

- Assets are not classified according to intended use. Critics feel that assets to be used as a part of operations should be clearly separated from those assets which are held as part of a restricted endowment.

- Organizations find it difficult to distinguish between restrictions and conditions. Restricted contributions are shown as increases in net assets, while conditional contributions are shown as increases in liabilities. A contribution to a building fund may be considered restricted, in the sense that the donor intends that it be used to finance building construction. On the other hand, the contribution is conditional in the sense that if total contributions are too low, plans to build may be scrapped and the money returned.

Many of the criticisms of FASB reporting requirements for NFPs are mitigated by additional disclosures. Although it is true that GAAP requires that the statement of activities present the change in each of the categories of net assets and the change in total net assets, organizations are encouraged to show other measures of performance. If an organization feels that its "bottom line" change in net assets is not an accurate reflection of the change in resources available for future activities, it can show a subtotal in the statement of activities, such as "increase in net assets from operations," or provide a more detailed presentation of changes in unrestricted net assets.

BUSINESS APPLICATION   The American National Red Cross Statement of Activities

A summarized excerpt of its 2010 statement of activities illustrates how **The American National Red Cross** presents changes in unrestricted net assets:

(in thousands)	**Unrestricted**
Operating revenues and gains	$3,362,054
Operating expenses:	
Program services	3,102,170
Supporting services	268,665
Total operating expenses.	3,370,835
Change in net assets from operations	(8,781)
Nonoperating gains	82,616
Pension-related changes other than net periodic benefit cost	(85,676)
Change in net assets	$ (11,841)

Although the net decrease in unrestricted net assets is $(11,841,000), the Red Cross reports $3,060,000 (= $85,676,000 − $82,616,000) of this decline as "nonoperating." Nonoperating items include gains on investments and changes in pension and postretirement benefit liabilities, primarily due to actuarial losses and prior service cost.

REVIEW OF KEY CONCEPTS

LO 1 **Prepare financial statements of private not-for-profit (NFP) organizations in proper format. (p. 530)** Three financial statements are required: a **statement of financial position**, a **statement of activities**, and a **statement of cash flows**. The **statement of financial position** reports the organization's net assets classified as **unrestricted**, **temporarily restricted**, or **permanently restricted**. The **statement of activities** reports **changes in each of the three net asset categories. Expenses** are reductions in **unrestricted net assets** only, whereas **revenues** can appear in each category. The **statement of cash flows** reconciles the change in total net assets to cash flow from operating activities. Cash flows from investing and financing activities complete the analysis of the change in cash and cash equivalents during the period.

Report all types of contributions received. (p. 534) Contributions increase unrestricted net assets unless donor-restricted. **Temporary restrictions** take the form of **time** or **use restrictions**. When donor restrictions on contributions expire, **net assets are released** by reducing temporarily restricted net assets and increasing unrestricted net assets. If the donor stipulates that the principal of the donation be maintained, it is added to permanently restricted net assets. **Promises to contribute** are recognized when they are **supported by verifiable documentation**. **Contributions of services** are recognized when they meet conditions prescribed in the Codification. When an organization acts as an **agent** in collecting contributions intended for other unaffiliated organizations, the contributions increase **liabilities** and not contribution revenue.   LO 2

Report investments in financial securities. (p. 542) **Investments** held by NFP organizations are reported at **fair market value**. Value changes and investment income are reported in the statement of activities as changes in unrestricted net assets unless subject to donor restrictions.   LO 3

Describe major reporting issues for specific NFPs. (p. 548) All NFP organizations follow FASB requirements for financial statement presentation. Donors to **VHWOs** take particular interest in the distinction between program service and administrative and fund-raising expenses. Revenues and expenses related to providing goods and services are reported separately. **Colleges and universities** report gross tuition revenue, with scholarships as revenue adjustments. Expenses include tuition waivers as compensation for student work assignments. **Health care organizations** typically show patient service revenue gross, with contractual adjustments as revenue deductions. Estimated uncollectibles appear as bad debt expense, and charity care is reported at cost.   LO 4

Evaluate financial information provided by NFPs. (p. 551) The NFP reporting model **standardizes** reporting for the **entity as a whole**, while allowing flexibility in categorizing revenues and expenses. Critics claim that the requirements **overstate reported revenue**. They believe that unrealized increases in investment value, documented promises, donated services, restricted contributions and contributions of long-lived assets should not be considered revenue because such items are not available to fund current programs.   LO 5

MULTIPLE CHOICE QUESTIONS ··························

Use the following information to answer questions 1 – 5 below.

Geneva Preschool provides free instruction for children from low-income families. Its January 1, 2013, trial balance is as follows:

	Debit	Credit
Cash.	$ 100,000	
Equipment & furnishings, net	1,500,000	
Building, net	3,500,000	
Accounts payable.		$ 200,000
Net assets—unrestricted		3,400,000
Net assets—temporarily restricted.		1,500,000
	$5,100,000	$5,100,000

Activities for 2013:

a.   Unrestricted cash contributions were $4,500,000.

b.   On January 1, 2013, a donor made a documented promise of $500,000, to be paid at the end of 2015 (3 years later). Using a 5 percent discount rate, the present value of this promise is $431,918.

c.   Each year, Geneva collects donor-restricted contributions to purchase technology for educational programs. During 2013, $200,000 was received and $500,000 was spent. Geneva expenses technology purchases.

d.   Out-of-pocket operating expenses for the year were $4,200,000. The year-end accounts payable balance, all related to operating expenses, was $150,000.

e.   A licensed CPA did all of Geneva's required financial statements and IRS forms for free. Fair value of these services is $25,000. Parents of students donated their time to lead preschool classes in safety and nutrition. The fair value of their time is $5,000.

f.   Depreciation for the year on equipment and furnishings was $250,000. Depreciation on the building was $600,000.

LO 1 **1.** How do Geneva's 2013 financial statements report the out-of-pocket operating expenses described in item *d.* above?

	Statement of Activities	**Statement of Cash Flows**
a.	$4,250,000 reduction in unrestricted net assets	$4,250,000 cash for operating activities
b.	$4,200,000 reduction in unrestricted net assets	$4,250,000 cash for operating activities
c.	$4,200,000 reduction in temporarily restricted net assets	$4,200,000 cash for operating activities
d.	$4,250,000 reduction in temporarily restricted net assets	$4,200,000 cash for operating activities

LO 1 **2.** On Geneva's 2013 statement of cash flows, a reconciliation of the change in net assets to cash from operating activities requires *adding* which of the following adjustments to change in net assets?

a. $50,000 change in accounts payable
b. $25,000 contribution of services
c. $850,000 depreciation expense
d. $431,918 promises to contribute

LO 2 **3.** Geneva's 2013 statement of activities reports item e. as follows:

a. $25,000 increase in unrestricted net assets (contributions) and $25,000 decrease in unrestricted net assets (expenses)
b. $30,000 increase in unrestricted net assets (contributions) and $30,000 decrease in unrestricted net assets (expenses)
c. $25,000 increase in temporarily restricted net assets (contributions)
d. Not reported

LO 2 **4.** Geneva's 2013 statement of activities reports item *b.* as follows:

a. $431,918 increase in temporarily restricted net assets
b. $431,918 increase in temporarily restricted net assets and $21,596 increase in unrestricted net assets
c. $453,514 increase in temporarily restricted net assets
d. This promise is not reported until the contribution is received

LO 2 **5.** Item *c.* affects Geneva's net assets in 2013 as follows:

a. $500,000 net decrease in unrestricted net assets, $300,000 net decrease in temporarily restricted net assets
b. $500,000 net decrease in unrestricted net assets, $500,000 net decrease in unrestricted net assets
c. No change in unrestricted net assets, $200,000 net increase in temporarily restricted net assets
d. No change in unrestricted net assets, $300,000 net decrease in temporarily restricted net assets

LO 3 **6.** At the beginning of 2014, a private not-for-profit museum receives a donation of equity securities valued at $10,000,000. The donor specifies that the securities be held as a permanent endowment, and income from the securities is restricted to the purchase of Native American artifacts. The securities have a fair value of $9,500,000 at the end of 2014. The museum reports the $500,000 decline in the value of the securities as

a. a reduction in permanently restricted net assets.
b. a reduction in temporarily restricted net assets.
c. a reduction in unrestricted net assets.
d. not reported.

LO 3 **7.** At the beginning of 2014, a private not-for-profit museum receives a donation of $10,000,000. The donor specifies that the donation be held as a permanent endowment, and income from its investment can be used for any purpose. The museum invests the $10,000,000 in equity securities. The securities have a fair value of $9,500,000 at the end of 2014. The museum reports the $500,000 decline in the value of the securities as

a. a reduction in permanently restricted net assets.
b. a reduction in temporarily restricted net assets.
c. a reduction in unrestricted net assets.
d. not reported.

LO 4 **8.** On its statement of activities, a private NFP hospital reports charity care

a. at cost.
b. at the fair value of services rendered.
c. at fair value net of cost to provide services.
d. in the footnotes to its financial statements, not on the statement of activities itself.

9. Critics of the FASB's reporting requirements for NFPs have a common concern, that current GAAP for not-for-profit organizations   LO 5

    a. does not accurately recognize pledges of contributions.
    b. misreports the actual value of investments.
    c. does not recognize all donations of services.
    d. overstates resources available for spending.

10. Which of the following is *most likely* your major concern when auditing an NFP?   LO 5

    a. The NFP is overstating pledges receivable.
    b. The NFP is understating fund-raising expenses.
    c. The NFP is overstating investment income.
    d. The NFP is understating cash contributions.

Assignments with the ✓ in the margin are available in an online homework system.
See the Preface of the book for details.

EXERCISES ••

E13.1 **Reporting Donations** The **Orange County Rescue Mission, Inc.**, receives the following donations: LO 2

    1. A donor contributes cash, with no restrictions or conditions.
    2. An accountant provides services in maintaining organization records.
    3. Volunteers provide services in staffing the local soup kitchen.
    4. A donor signs an agreement promising to contribute cash next year.
    5. A donor contributes land. The Mission has no accounting policy regarding donations of long-lived assets.
    6. A donor contributes cash, specifying that it be used to support a program to teach life skills to battered women.

ORANGE COUNTY RESCUE MISSION, INC.

Required

For each of the above donations, identify the effect on net assets. Use the following alternatives:
    UR affects unrestricted net assets
    TR affects temporarily restricted net assets
    PR affects permanently restricted net assets
    N   does not affect net assets

E13.2 **Reporting Donations** Dunning College, a private college in northern Idaho, receives the following donations: LO 2

    1. A parent of a current accounting student contributes $1,000,000, with the stipulation that the donation be used to fund a new building for the business school. The college does not know whether it can accumulate enough additional resources to go ahead with the project.
    2. An accounting alumnus contributes $100,000 to the accounting department. The alumnus stipulates that the principal of the contribution remain intact, and any investment income be used to fund a speaker series on current accounting issues. The college invests the $100,000 in securities, and earns income of $5,000. The $5,000 is used to pay transportation costs and speaker fees.
    3. A retired recruiter from a local CPA firm notifies the college that her will states that $2,000,000 of her estate be paid to the accounting department of the college.
    4. An alumnus promises to contribute $100,000 if the college can raise $100,000 from other sources. The college raises the $100,000 and the alumnus contributes the additional $100,000.
    5. A student donates a car valued at $5,000, specifying that the car be used to transport disabled students from their dorms to class.
    6. The car in item 5. depreciates by $1,000.
    7. Cash contributions to the college total $5,000,000. The college's Board sets aside $300,000 for repairs to the administration building.

Required

For each of the above items, prepare the appropriate journal entry or entries. If the item affects net assets, specify which category of net assets is affected.

LO 2

YWCA

E13.3   Donated Building   On January 1, 2013, the **YWCA** receives a donated building with a fair market value of $30,000,000. The donor specifies that the building is to be used to house international families until they obtain permanent housing. The YWCA estimates that the building has a remaining useful life of 25 years, uses straight-line depreciation, and is a calendar year organization.

Required

Prepare the journal entries necessary in 2013 and 2014 to account for this donation and subsequent depreciation. If the entry affects net assets, indicate which category of net assets is affected.

⊘ LO 3

E13.4   Accounting for Investments   In 2013, Western Community Hospital, a private facility, receives donated debt securities with a fair market value and face value of $350,000. The donor specifies that the debt securities be held as a permanent endowment, and investment income earned on these securities can be used for any purpose. The securities have a fair market value of $320,000 at the end of 2013, and $360,000 at the end of 2014. Interest income earned on the securities is $14,000 in each of the two years.

Required

a.   Prepare the journal entries to record the above events in 2013 and 2014. Indicate the balance in each account and its placement in the financial statements.

b.   Assume the same facts as above, except the donation was $350,000 in cash, and the hospital invested the $350,000 in debt securities. How do the entries in *a.* change?

⊘ LO 2

E13.5   Reporting Pledged and Restricted Contributions   Consider the following contributions to private not-for-profit organizations:

1.   Pledge cards signed by church members pledge $3,000,000 to a facilities improvement campaign. Church officials expect that 90 percent of the pledges will be collected.
2.   A university phone-a-thon produces $75,000 of "intentions to give;" respondents have 30 days to think it over.
3.   A prominent alumnus pledges $5,000,000 to support the MS in accounting program in a local university, conditional on the program becoming separately accredited by the AACSB.
4.   Contributors sign pledge cards for $150,000 to support ongoing programs at a local teaching hospital. Past experience indicates that 75 percent will be collected.
5.   A college receives cash gifts of $250,000 restricted by the donors to a new graduate program in mathematical finance. College officials believe $1,000,000 is needed before the new program can begin.

Required

State whether each of the above items is recognized as a contribution. If recognized, give the amount of revenue and whether it is unrestricted or temporarily restricted. If it is not recognized, explain why.

LO 2

E13.6   Recognition of Donations   Hopeville Retreat is a private not-for-profit organization that counsels former drug addicts in readjusting to productive community life. Donations provide the major support for Hopeville Retreat. During 2013, the following gifts were received:

1.   Cash from the semiannual fund-raising campaign, $4,000,000.
2.   Cash from rehabilitated clients, $100,000.
3.   Clothing donated by a department store. Cost to the store was $5,000; market value was $7,000.
4.   A flat-screen television, valued at $800, donated by a friend of the Retreat.
5.   Medication, donated by a pharmaceutical company. Cost of the medication was $3,000; market value was $5,000.
6.   Accounting services for necessary paperwork and record-keeping performed by a CPA, valued at $7,000.
7.   Door-to-door fund solicitation time donated by high school students, as part of their school community service requirement. Their time is estimated to be worth $2,800 when valued using minimum wage rates.
8.   Free radio announcements of the fund-raising campaign given by a local radio station. The normal charge for advertisements of comparable length is $1,000.

Required

For each item, indicate at what amount the donation is recorded on the books of Hopeville Retreat, and where it would appear in its statement of activities.

LO 1, 2

INSTITUTE OF MANAGEMENT ACCOUNTANTS

E13.7   Effect of Transactions on Net Assets   The **Institute of Management Accountants** (IMA) incurs the following transactions:

1.   A gift of cash is received with no stipulations as to use.

2. The IMA borrows money to finance construction of a new office building.
3. Money is collected from participants for the future annual conference.
4. The Board of Directors sets aside money for distribution to universities as awards for best management accounting doctoral dissertations.
5. An automobile is donated; the donor specifies that the automobile is to be used in transporting staff on official organization business.
6. Depreciation is computed on the automobile in 5.
7. General revenues are set aside to repay the loan in 2.
8. Gently used accounting textbooks are collected for distribution to inner city high schools.

Required

For each item, indicate the category of net assets affected, if any.

E13.8 **Promises of Future Gifts** On July 1, 2012, Rajeev Gupta, a wealthy alumnus of Clearwater University, promises in writing to contribute $150,000 at the beginning of each of the next ten fiscal years to help offset the expenses of operating the Greek Affairs Office in those years. The first $150,000 payment is received on July 1, 2013. The university's fiscal year runs from July 1 to June 30. **LO 2**

Required

Prepare journal entries to report this donation on the following dates: July 1, 2012, June 30, 2013, July 1, 2013, and June 30, 2014. A 6 percent discount rate is appropriate. If the entry affects net assets, indicate the net asset category affected.

E13.9 **Temporary Investments** The National Leukemia Society maintains a portfolio of temporary equity investments. At December 31, 2013, the Society holds the following securities: **LO 3**

Security	Cost	Fair Value
300 shares of Alpha Corporation	$ 20,000	$ 21,000
1,000 shares of Beta, Inc	300,000	298,000
200 shares of Sigma Company	42,000	49,000

Quarterly dividends paid in 2014 on each investment were as follows:

Alpha Corporation	$1.50/share
Beta, Inc.	0.40/share
Sigma Company.	1.60/share

At December 31, 2014, fair values of the above securities are as follows. No securities were bought or sold during 2014.

	Fair Value
300 shares of Alpha Corporation	$ 19,700
1,000 shares of Beta, Inc	304,000
200 shares of Sigma Company	46,800

Required

Prepare a schedule showing the investment income recognized on the Society's 2014 statement of activities, including any unrealized gains or losses.

E13.10 **College Transactions** San Rafael College's transactions include the following: **LO 1, 2, 4**

1. An alumna donates cash for the purchase of accounting research software.
2. An alumna donates cash, stipulating that income generated by investment of the cash be paid to the donor during her lifetime. At the donor's death, the gift and all future income belong to the college.
3. An alumna donates cash, stipulating that income generated by investment of the cash be used for accounting student scholarships. The principal is to remain intact.
4. A student center is constructed.
5. Salaries to faculty are paid.
6. Tuition loans are made to students.

7. Student activity fees for student organizations are collected with tuition payments.
8. Depreciation on college facilities is recognized.

Required

For each item, identify the accounts affected and for all changes in net assets, their placement on the college's statement of activities.

LO 1, 2, 4 **E13.11 College Journal Entries** Following are transactions of Canton College:

1. The college's general fund-raising campaign generates written pledges of $800,000. Past history shows pledges to be 90 percent collectible. Cash collection is expected within one year.
2. A previously recorded unrestricted pledge is received, $7,000.
3. A staff member borrows $1,000 from the college and signs a note for repayment within one year.
4. Previously collected student activity fees of $6,000 are transferred to student organizations.
5. Salaries of $500,000 are paid to employees. An accrual had not been recorded.
6. A loan of $100,000 is taken to buy audiovisual equipment.
7. An $800 scholarship is awarded from funds donor-restricted to scholarships.

Required

For each of the above transactions, record the journal entry and, if appropriate, indicate where each item appears on the college's statement of activities.

LO 2 **E13.12 Annuity/Life Income Transactions** On January 1, 2013, Pauline Doyle gave Rocky Mountain College $400,000 in cash with the provision that the cash be invested in income-producing securities. Actuarial estimates set Doyle's life expectancy at 15 years from the date of the gift. The annual discount rate is 4 percent. Rocky Mountain College invested the $400,000 in securities earning 5 percent in cash dividends in 2013.

Required

Record all 2013 events relating to Pauline Doyle's gift, under each of the following *independent* arrangements.

a. The college is to pay Pauline Doyle $14,000 every December 31 of her remaining life. Upon Doyle's death, remaining resources become available to the college with no restrictions as to use.
b. The college is to pay Pauline Doyle all earnings of the principal for life. Upon Doyle's death, remaining resources become available to the college with no restrictions as to use.

LO 1 **E13.13 Critique of Statement of Activities Format** Your accounting firm audits the financial statements of the Sioux Falls Society for the Preservation of Prairie Dogs, a private not-for-profit organization. Your job is to review the format of the Society's operating statement for the year. Here is the statement:

SIOUX FALLS SOCIETY FOR THE PRESERVATION OF PRAIRIE DOGS Statement of Activities For Fiscal Year Ended June 30, 2014			
	Unrestricted net assets	Temporarily restricted net assets	Permanently restricted net assets
Revenues, gains and other support:			
Contributions	$215,000	$180,000	$350,000
Fees	150,000	—	—
Investment income	1,500	25,000	—
Gains on investments	2,000	1,000	5,000
Net assets released from restrictions	150,000	(45,000)	(85,000)
Total revenues, gains, and other support	518,500	161,000	270,000
Expenses:			
Salaries	130,000	25,000	—
Supplies	75,000	10,000	—
Rent	290,000	—	—
Total expenses	495,000	35,000	—
Net profit	23,500	126,000	270,000
Beginning net assets	102,000	140,000	460,000
Ending net assets	$125,500	$266,000	$730,000

Required

There are five different reporting errors in this statement. Identify each error. Assume the numbers are correct.

PROBLEMS •••

P13.1 **Journal Entries and Financial Statements** The Southside Counseling Center was established on January 10, 2013, to provide a variety of counseling services to community residents, including marital and family counseling and treatment for alcoholism and drug abuse. The center's initial resources were provided by a private foundation in the form of a $1,000,000 capital grant. Of this sum, the foundation designated $500,000 for building and equipment and $250,000 for the establishment of a special program for counseling parolees. The following transactions occurred during 2013:

LO 1, 2, 3 ✓

1. Contributions of $800,000 were received through the local United Way campaign, and an additional $130,000 was received in direct contributions. Of the direct contributions, $10,000 was for the parolees' program and $30,000 was for the building fund; the remaining $90,000, of which $40,000 was in the form of pledges, expected to be 75 percent collectible, was unrestricted.
2. Operating expenses for the year were $930,000, of which $850,000 had been paid by year-end.
3. The special parolees' program had not yet begun as of December 31, 2013. All resources dedicated to this program were invested in short-term securities. Investment income for the year, which was reinvested, was $20,000.
4. The center purchased a building for $2,200,000 ($1,800,000 is owed on the mortgage at year-end) and equipment for $240,000, of which $140,000 is owed on a three-year note. The initial $500,000 capital grant was used.

Required

a. Prepare journal entries to record the transactions for 2013.
b. Prepare Southside's statement of activities for 2013 and its statement of financial position at December 31, 2013.

P13.2 **Recognition of Contributions** The following events relate to **Habitat for Humanity International**'s activities. If appropriate, assume a discount rate of 6 percent per annum.

LO 2 ✓

HABITAT FOR HUMANITY INTERNATIONAL

1. In a telephone solicitation, a potential donor says he will contribute $500 in 30 days.
2. In a telephone solicitation, a potential donor requests that a pledge card be mailed, suggesting that a $250 contribution may be forthcoming.
3. A potential donor makes a documented promise to contribute $100,000 when Habitat for Humanity has raised $100,000 in matching funds; $40,000 in matching funds has been raised to date.
4. Same as 3. except that the potential donor promises to contribute up to $100,000 by giving $1 for each $1 of matching funds raised.
5. A group of college students helps build a house for Habitat for Humanity in inner city Los Angeles; Habitat for Humanity estimates the value of the group's services at $10,000.
6. A potential donor signs an agreement to contribute $15,000 now and $15,000 at the beginning of each of the next four years, to help pay for general operating expenses.
7. A donor contributes $200,000, stating that half is to be used to restore and build houses in upstate New York this year, and half is to be used for the same purpose next year.
8. At the beginning of the year, a donor contributes a building worth $4,000,000 and requires that it be used to house Habitat for Humanity's administrative offices over the building's 20-year remaining estimated useful life.
9. A registered plumber volunteers her services to install plumbing in several Habitat for Humanity houses. The plumber's services are valued at $5,000.
10. A donor contributes $1,000,000 face value of 4 percent bonds as an endowment to Habitat for Humanity. Income generated from the bonds is to be used to buy appliances for new houses. Donated between interest payment dates, the bonds' $1,060,000 value includes accrued interest of $25,000.

Required

In each case, identify (a) whether the item should be recorded as a contribution and (b) if recorded, the dollar amount of the item to be reported as unrestricted, temporarily restricted, or permanently restricted.

LO 1, 2   **P13.3**   **Journal Entries and Financial Statements**   The Learning Circle is a private organization that provides after-school and summer tutoring and educational activities to children from low-income families. The organization is funded by member dues and contributions. Following is Learning Circle's trial balance at July 1, 2012:

	Debit	Credit
Cash..	$ 50,000	
Dues receivable..	4,000	
Supplies..	30,000	
Land..	150,000	
Building, net...	530,000	
Equipment, net..	240,000	
Accounts payable...		$ 25,000
Unrestricted net assets...................................		729,000
Temporarily restricted net assets.......................		250,000
Totals..	$1,004,000	$1,004,000

Cash receipts and payments for fiscal 2013 are:

Receipts:	
Collection of dues...	$ 98,000
Contributions..	180,000
Grants...	320,000
Disbursements:	
Tutoring programs...	250,000
After-school programs......................................	340,000
Fund-raising...	15,000

Additional information:

1. Depreciation for the year is $20,000 for the building and $30,000 for the equipment; depreciation is allocated equally between tutoring and after-school programs.
2. The grants were restricted to a new tutoring program for inner city teens. Of the amount received in fiscal 2013, $140,000 was spent for the specified program (included in expenditures above).
3. Supplies of $20,000 were on hand at the end of fiscal 2013. All supplies relate to the tutoring programs.
4. Dues of $6,000 were uncollected as of June 30, 2013.
5. The July 1, 2012, balance in temporarily restricted net assets consists of grants restricted to after-school programs. These grants were spent for the specified programs in fiscal 2013 (included in expenditures above).
6. The July 1, 2012, accounts payable balance was paid during fiscal 2013, and consisted of bills related to tutoring programs. Accounts payable at year-end total $80,000, of which $30,000 are bills related to tutoring program activities, and the remainder relates to after-school program activities.

Required

a.   Record the transactions and adjustments for the fiscal year ended June 30, 2013.
b.   Prepare The Learning Circle's statement of activities for fiscal year 2013, and its statement of financial position as of June 30, 2013.

LO 1, 2, 3   **P13.4**   **Presentation of Corrected Financial Statements**   The Chicago History Museum is a privately funded institution that promotes the history of Chicago and Illinois. It receives support from memberships, fees, grants and investment income. Suppose that the Museum's unadjusted trial balance at June 30, 2013, is as follows:

THE CHICAGO HISTORY MUSEUM

	Debit	Credit
Cash.	$ 2,800,000	
Assets restricted to investment in plant assets	40,000,000	
Pledges receivable, net	53,000,000	
Supplies	4,500,000	
Land, buildings, and equipment, net	65,000,000	
Investments	12,500,000	
Accounts payable.		$ 2,200,000
Notes payable		80,000,000
Net assets—unrestricted, July 1, 2012		17,600,000
Net assets—temporarily restricted, July 1, 2012.		35,000,000
Contributions—unrestricted.		60,000,000
Contributions—temporarily restricted		44,700,000
Investment income—unrestricted		300,000
Expenses—exhibitions and programs	39,000,000	
Expenses—membership and development.	1,000,000	
Expenses—administrative	8,000,000	
Expenses—building operations	14,000,000	
Totals	$239,800,000	$239,800,000

Additional information:

1. At the end of fiscal 2013, documented pledges were received in the amount of $5,000,000 per year for the next 10 years. These pledges have not been recorded. The appropriate discount rate is 4%, and no amounts are estimated to be uncollectible.
2. In fiscal 2012, the Museum received and properly recorded as restricted contributions a documented pledge in the amount of $10,000,000 per year for five years, to cover operating expenses. In fiscal 2013, the Museum recorded receipt of the first $10,000,000 installment as an unrestricted contribution. The appropriate discount rate is 4%.
3. The Museum recorded a $2,500,000 conditional contribution received in 2013 as an unrestricted contribution. The condition has not been met as of the fiscal year-end.
4. The Museum used $27,500,000 in donations restricted to the building fund for construction activities. This was recorded as an increase in land, buildings and equipment. The Museum also spent $4,000,000 in donations restricted to specific program activities, recorded as an increase in expenses for exhibitions and programs. Both expenditures reduced cash.
5. The following donated services were not recorded. Estimated fair values are in parenthesis.
    *   Tax and other financial services performed by CPAs ($500,000)
    *   Maintenance services provided by neighborhood volunteers ($800,000)
    *   Contractor services for construction of the building ($10,000,000)
6. The investments held at year-end have a fair value of $15,000,000. Investment gains are donor-restricted to specific program activities.

Required

a. Record the entries necessary to correct The Chicago History Museum's June 30, 2013 trial balance.
b. Prepare, in good form, The Chicago History Museum's fiscal 2013 statement of activities and its June 30, 2013, statement of financial position.

P13.5 Hospital Transactions The following information was taken from the books of Garden Court Hospital for the year ended December 31, 2014: LO 1, 2, 3, 4

1. The hospital received $60,000,000 in cash from patients it cared for during the year. Another $30,000,000 is due from patients, and $15,000,000 is due from various insurance companies, all at standard charge rates. Revenues from other nursing services amounted to $2,500,000 and revenues from other professional services were $6,000,000. Only $4,000,000 of those revenues were collected in cash during the year; half of these cash collections related to nursing services. Other revenue, mostly from cafeteria sales, amounted to $2,000,000. Except for cafeteria sales, all revenues flowed through accounts receivable.
2. Garden Court has certain agreements with various insurance companies under which standard rates were adjusted downward by $2,100,000. Garden Court is also involved in a community assistance program; the hospital provided $1,600,000 of charity and other free services. An allowance for

uncollectible accounts was established based on one percent of all revenue flowing through accounts receivable in 2014. Receivables written off in 2014 were $800,000.

3. Supplies costing $5,100,000 were ordered and received in 2014; however, only half have been paid for as of the end of 2014. A pharmaceutical company donated medicinal supplies with a fair value of $2,000,000. In addition, an appliance company donated a large refrigeration unit; its book value to the appliance company was $4,000,000 and its fair market value was $6,000,000.

4. Garden Court's principal expense categories are salaries and wages, supplies, and other operating expenses. An allocation of these expenses among the principal service categories shows the following:

	Wages and Salaries	Supplies	Other Expenses
Nursing services....................	$2,000,000	$1,800,000	$1,700,000
General health care services	1,900,000	1,600,000	1,300,000
Professional services	1,400,000	1,200,000	1,500,000
Auxiliary services	2,400,000	800,000	1,100,000
Totals	$7,700,000	$5,400,000	$5,600,000

Of these expenses, $1,000,000 of wages and $1,200,000 of other operating expenses remain unpaid at year-end.

5. Early in 2014, Garden Court received a gift to be used for conducting research on a deadly and intractable disease. Of the $4,000,000 received, $1,800,000 was expended on the research. Another $2,000,000 was invested in bonds and earned interest of $300,000. The donor specified that investment income is restricted for the designated research purposes.

6. A friend of the hospital donated marketable securities worth $20,000,000. These securities cost the donor $15,000,000 in 2010. The principal is to be maintained and 75 percent of the income is restricted for research on brain diseases; the balance is available for current operating expenses. During 2014, $1,600,000 in dividends were received and $1,000,000 was expended on the designated research.

7. The hospital is replacing its scanning equipment. Volunteers conducted a fund-raising campaign to finance the new equipment and raised $15,000,000 in cash. In order to cover the $40,000,000 cost of the equipment, a $25,000,000 loan was obtained. The hospital purchased the new equipment in late November. Sale of the old equipment (book value, $2,000,000) yielded $2,500,000 in proceeds.

Required

Prepare journal entries to record the transactions of Garden Court Hospital for 2014.

⊘ LO 1, 2, 3, 4 **P13.6 Hospital Statement of Activities** The following information pertains to the activities of Montclair Hospital for the year ended December 31, 2014.

1.

Gross patient service revenue	$80,000,000
Charity allowances..	15,000,000
Contractual discounts to third party payers................................	5,000,000

The hospital calculates a provision for uncollectibles at 5 percent of net patient service revenue.

2. Fair market value of noncash donations:

Volunteer workers in public-relations campaign	$200,000
Medical supplies donated by a pharmaceutical firm	800,000

3. Operating expenses, of which $3,000,000 are unpaid at year-end:

Professional patient care	$33,000,000
General services...	9,500,000
Nursing services...	10,000,000
Administrative services...	3,500,000

4. The hospital conducts various educational programs for which it received fees of $500,000 during 2014.

5. The cafeteria and gift shop reported profit of $120,000 on sales of $1,320,000; operating costs are recorded as administrative expenses.

6. A retired doctor provided $1,000,000 to be used in validating the accuracy of a new cholesterol testing procedure. The funds were spent this year. In addition, $2,800,000 was spent for health education programs, using donor-restricted funds donated last year. Both expenditures were recorded as general services expenses.

7. In July, a donor established a trust in the amount of $6,000,000. Income from the trust is to be paid to the hospital until the donor's death. At that time, the principal is to be given to a local university. A local bank is appointed as trustee. Income received by the trust, and due to be distributed in 2014, amounted to $100,000. As of December 31, the bank had remitted only $60,000 to the hospital.

8. A donor's will provided for a bequest to the hospital of common stock of a public company. The donor had inherited the stock four years ago, when it was worth $1,000,000, from a decedent who purchased it for $500,000. When the donor died on March 15, the stock was worth $1,500,000; at year-end it was worth $1,270,000.

9. A new X-ray machine was purchased for $4,000,000, using unrestricted cash.

Required

Prepare Montclair Hospital's 2014 statement of activities. Ignore beginning and ending net asset balances.

P13.7 Transactions and Financial Statements   Irvine Services is a private organization that provides   **LO 1, 2** community services for the prevention of substance abuse. The following events occur in 2013:

1. Cash contributions of $550,000 are received. Of this amount, $350,000 is donor-designated for educational program activities. The rest is unrestricted.

2. Contributions of $375,000 are promised to the organization during the year. Irvine has signed agreements from the donors that payment will be received in early 2014. It is estimated that 70 percent of these promises are collectible. Due to the short collection period, it is not necessary to report these promises at present value.

3. A donor contributes marketable securities valued at $200,000, with the stipulation that the securities be held intact. The income is unrestricted. The value of the securities at year-end is $215,000. Income earned on the securities during 2013 is $12,000.

4. Cash expenses for the year are:

General services.	$ 25,000
Program services	490,000
Fund-raising.	65,000

Included in the program services expenses above are $225,000 from contributions made last year which were donor-designated for educational program activities, and $140,000 from contributions made this year (see 1. above) which were donor-designated for educational program activities.

5. Volunteers contributed services as follows:
   - A local CPA provided accounting and payroll services valued at $8,000.
   - A contractor donated his services to finish the upper floor in the organization's office building. The fair value of these services is $35,000.

Required

Prepare Irvine Services' statement of activities for 2013.

P13.8 Accounting for Investments   The American Hereditary Disease Association, a private organization   **LO 3** supporting research and education related to hereditary diseases, holds the following long-term investments at December 31, 2012:

December 31, 2012	Market Value
Investment in mortgage bonds	$ 800,000
Investment in debentures.	1,600,000
Investment in equity securities.	7,000,000

All debt investments were purchased at par value.

Notes:

1. The mortgage bonds were donated several years ago; the donor stipulated that the securities be held as a permanent endowment, and income on the securities be used for research projects relating to sickle cell disease. The market value of these securities was $750,000 when donated.

2. The debentures are a recent investment of permanently restricted cash contributions of $1,600,000. There are no donor restrictions on investment income, gains or losses.

3. The equity securities are investments of permanently restricted cash contributions of $8,500,000. The donor specified that income and gains be restricted to community education programs on Crabbe's Disease. The decline in value to $7,000,000 was properly recorded.

4. Income on investments during 2013 was:

Interest on bonds.	$ 60,000
Interest on debentures.	80,000
Dividends on equity securities	420,000

5. Market values at December 31, 2013 are:

Investment in bonds.	$ 850,000
Investment in debentures.	1,700,000
Investment in equity securities.	7,200,000

Required

Show how the events of 2013 are reported in the American Hereditary Disease Association's statement of activities. Identify the effect on each category of net assets.

LO 1, 2, 3 **P13.9** **Statement of Activities** The information below was taken from the records of the **Milwaukee Art Museum, Inc.** All information pertains to activities for the year 2013.

MILWAUKEE ART MUSEUM, INC.

Restricted contributions.	$ 9,200,000
Unrestricted contributions	56,000,000
Investment income.	4,000,000
Expenses—administrative	3,900,000
Expenses—membership development	6,000,000
Expenses—fund-raising.	1,500,000
Expenses—educational programs.	40,000,000
Expenses—research	15,000,000

Additional information:

1. The Museum holds investments in debt and equity securities. The investment income listed above represents cash receipts of interest and dividends on these investments. $2,500,000 of this amount is donor-restricted to educational programs. The rest is unrestricted. In addition, $500,000 of interest and dividends has accrued as of year-end. All accrued investment income is unrestricted.

2. The investments in debt and equity securities held by the Museum increased in value by $900,000 during 2013. Of this amount, $400,000 relates to shares of stock donated several years ago, where the donor specified that the shares be held as a permanent endowment. $200,000 relates to permanently restricted cash that was invested in securities, with gains and income restricted to research activities, and $300,000 was unrestricted. The value of all these securities at the beginning of 2013 was significantly above their cost or donated value.

3. Included in educational programs expenses is $3,500,000 funded by contributions in past years that were restricted to educational programs. The Museum has just completed a capital campaign to raise money for a new wing to house the works of Wisconsin native Georgia O'Keeffe. During 2013, $4,000,000 was spent to begin construction on the new wing. All funds used were donor-restricted to the capital campaign.

4. All cash received from contributions was recorded as restricted or unrestricted contributions. Restricted contributions include $600,000 in permanently restricted contributions; the rest are temporarily restricted. In addition, documented unrestricted pledges of $2,200,000 were received in 2013, estimated to be 100 percent collectible. Of the cash contributions received in 2013, $1,200,000 recorded as unrestricted contributions relate to pledges made in 2012.

5. The beginning balances of net assets are as follows: Unrestricted, $22,000,000; temporarily restricted, $24,000,000; permanently restricted, $6,000,000.

Required

Prepare Milwaukee Art Museum's 2013 statement of activities.

P13.10 Complete Financial Statements The information below was taken from the records of Greenvale LO 1, 2
Community Day Care Center, a private not-for-profit organization, for the year 2013. The Center provides free day care to low-income families.

1. Trial balance as of January 1, 2013:

Cash.	$ 100,000
Contributions receivable, net of $8,000 in uncollectibles	152,000
Equipment and furnishings, net	2,500,000
Building, net	3,500,000
Accounts payable.	(220,000)
Salaries and wages payable.	(42,000)
Net assets—unrestricted	(5,020,000)
Net assets—temporarily restricted.	(970,000)
Total	$ 0

2. Unrestricted pledges of $4,250,000 were made during 2013, of which $4,200,000 was collected. In addition, $140,000 of the $160,000 in gross pledges outstanding on January 1, 2013, were collected in cash. The remaining balance was written off. The Center records pledges at gross and provides an allowance for uncollectibles equal to 5 percent of pledges outstanding at year-end.
3. The Center won a state grant of $1,000,000 to support a new preschool program. To date, $600,000 of the grant has been received, and $300,000 has been spent on the program. Of the $300,000 spent, $100,000 was for salaries and wages and $200,000 was for equipment.
4. Donor-restricted resources are accumulated to purchase computers and software for child development programs. During the year, $350,000 was received for child development programs, and $400,000 was spent; $350,000 on computers and $50,000 for software. The Center capitalizes the computers and expenses the software.
5. Cash paid for salaries and wages during the year totaled $3,300,000. The balance of accrued salaries and wages as of year-end is $72,000. Salaries and wages are attributed as 20 percent administrative and 80 percent program services.
6. Expenses for utilities, food, and supplies totaled $750,000 for the year, all for program services. The year-end balance for accounts payable, all related to utilities, food, and supplies, is $170,000.
7. Depreciation for the year on equipment and furnishings, including the computers in 4. above, was $240,000. Depreciation on the building was $550,000. All depreciation is 25 percent administrative and 75 percent program services.
8. $250,000 in state grant money was temporarily invested in short-term debt securities near the end of the year. No interest revenue was earned on these investments in 2013, and their fair value at year-end equaled cost.

Required

Prepare, in good form, a statement of activities, statement of financial position, and statement of cash flows, using the direct method, for Greenvale Community Day Care Center for the year 2013. In the statement of cash flows, include a reconciliation of change in net assets to net cash provided by operating activities.

P13.11 Statement of Activities for a University Buena Vista University is a small private liberal arts LO 1, 2, 3, 4
university in Iowa. Below are transactions and events for 2013.

**BUENA VISTA
UNIVERSITY**

1. $180,000,000 in tuition was charged to students.
2. $24,000,000 in scholarships were awarded. In addition, tuition waivers for teaching assistantships totaled $12,000,000.
3. Securities were donated to the university. At the time of donation, the securities had a fair value of $15,000,000. The donor specified that the university must retain the securities, but any income is unrestricted. The securities increased in value by $3,000,000 at year-end.
4. Salaries and overhead for the year was as follows:

Instruction.	$120,000,000
Research programs	24,000,000
Student services.	6,000,000
Administration	12,000,000

5. Research grants received from outside agencies totaled $2,000,000, and are unrestricted.
6. Cash gifts were received as follows: restricted to programs: $6,000,000, and restricted to the capital fund: $3,600,000.
7. The university spent $650,000 for building construction, financed by the capital fund. Program spending financed by restricted gifts totaled $5,200,000.
8. Investment income totaled $420,000. Of that amount, $280,000 is donor-restricted to programs, and $60,000 is restricted by the Board of Trustees to research programs.

Required

Prepare, in good form, the 2013 statement of activities for Buena Vista University. Assume beginning balances of net assets are $3,800,000 unrestricted, $4,000,000 temporarily restricted, and $22,000,000 permanently restricted.

LO 1, 2, 3

MAKE-A-WISH
FOUNDATION

P13.12 Prepare Complete Financial Statements The **Make-A-Wish Foundation** is a privately funded VHWO that grants wishes to children with life-threatening illnesses. Since 1980, it has reached over 165,000 children worldwide through a network of thousands of volunteers. Suppose the Foundation's trial balance as of January 1, 2014, follows:

MAKE-A-WISH FOUNDATION
Trial Balance
January 1, 2014

(in thousands)	Dr (Cr)
Cash.	$ 40,000
Contributions receivable, net.	20,000
Property and equipment, net	12,000
Investments	120,000
Accounts payable.	(8,000)
Notes payable	(1,000)
Unrestricted net assets	(135,000)
Temporarily restricted net assets.	(30,000)
Permanently restricted net assets	(18,000)
Total.	$ 0

Transactions and events for 2014 are as follows *(dollars in thousands)*:

1. Cash contributions of $157,500 were received. They consist of:
   (a) $150,000 received from the public as general contributions, either through the mail or at special fund-raising events.
   (b) $6,000 in grants, of which $5,000 is designated for purchase of property and equipment, $50 is a permanent endowment, and $950 is unrestricted.
   (c) $1,500 in permanent endowments received from the public.
2. The contributions receivable outstanding on January 2, 2014, represent the present value of promises to contribute, discounted at 5 percent. On December 31, 2014, $15,000 was received related to these promises. These promises are undesignated.
3. Additional promises to contribute $8,000 were made on January 2, 2014, to be received over the next five years. The present value of these contributions at January 2, 2014, discounted at 5 percent is $6,000. These promises were properly recorded as contributions receivable. At the end of 2014, $2,000 was received in cash on these promises. These contributions are undesignated.
4. The investments on hand at January 1, 2014 are:
   (a) A donor contributed securities several years ago; fair value at January 1, 2014, is $15,000. The securities are permanently restricted. The fair value of the securities at December 31, 2014, is $12,000.
   (b) $2,000 fair value of securities represent investment of permanently restricted cash contributions of $2,000 at the end of 2013. The fair value of these securities at December 31, 2014, is $1,500.
   (c) The remainder of $103,000 fair value of securities are investments of excess cash and have a fair value of $98,000 at December 31, 2014.
   (d) No securities were sold in 2014.
5. Undesignated endowments of $4,000 were donated during 2014, and the cash was invested in securities. There are no unrealized gains or losses on these investments in 2014.

6. Property and equipment of $12,000 was purchased in 2014. The $5,000 grant in 1. above was used to buy some of the property.
7. Investment income, received in cash, totaled $7,000. Of this amount, $2,000 is income restricted to specific wish fulfillment.
8. Expenses for 2014 were:

Wish granting	$150,000
Chapter support	10,000
Fund-raising	30,000
Management and general	16,000
Total	$206,000

$20,000 of this total represents spending for donor-specified activities. Also included is $1,500 depreciation on Foundation property. Accounts payable increased by $800 during 2014.

9. Volunteers supplied the following services to the Foundation:
(a) $6,000 fair value of management and general services, meeting the criteria for recognition.
(b) Public service announcements with a fair value of $32,000, that don't meet the criteria for recognition.

Required

a. Present Make-A-Wish Foundation's 2014 statement of activities and December 31, 2014, statement of financial position, in good form.

b. Present Make-A-Wish Foundation's 2014 statement of cash flows, in good form. Use the direct approach for the operating section, and provide a reconciliation of change in net assets to cash from operating activities.

REVIEW SOLUTIONS •

Review 1 Solution

1.

Contributions receivable	4,330	
Contribution revenue—temporarily restricted		4,330
To record a documented pledge, discounted at 5%; $4,330 =		
$1,000 × 4.33, the present value of a 5-period ordinary annuity		
of $1 discounted at 5% per period.		
Contributions receivable	217	
Contribution revenue—temporarily restricted		217
To record increase in value of pledge; $217 = 5% × $4,330.		
Cash	1,000	
Contributions receivable		1,000
To record receipt of pledge payment.		
Net assets released from time restriction—temporarily restricted	1,000	
Net assets released from time restriction—unrestricted		1,000
To record release of time restriction for pledge payment.		

2.

Net assets released from use restriction—temporarily restricted	35,000	
Net assets released from use restriction—unrestricted		35,000
To record release of use restriction.		
Wish-granting expenses (reduces unrestricted net assets)	35,000	
Cash		35,000
To record cash expenditures for wishes.		

3.	Equipment	100,000	
	Contributions revenue—temporarily restricted		100,000
	To record contribution of equipment.		
	Net assets released from time restriction—temporarily restricted..........	20,000	
	Net assets released from time restriction—unrestricted...........		20,000
	To record release of restriction for donated equipment depreciation.		
	Depreciation expense (reduces unrestricted net assets)................	20,000	
	Accumulated depreciation.....................................		20,000
	To record depreciation on donated equipment.		
4.	Administrative expenses (reduces unrestricted net assets)...............	40,000	
	Property (asset)	25,000	
	Contributed services (increases unrestricted net assets)		65,000
	To record contributed services. Volunteer services for fund-raising do not meet recognition criteria.		

Review 2 Solution

GATEHOUSE FOUNDATION
Statement of Activities
For Year Ended December 31, 2013

		Unrestricted	Temporarily Restricted	Permanently Restricted
1.	Unrealized loss.....................	$(35,000)	—	—
	Dividend income....................	4,000	—	—
2.	Unrealized loss.....................	(6,000)	—	—
	Dividend income....................	—	$2,500	—
3.	Unrealized gain.....................	—	—	$3,000
	Dividend income....................	6,000	—	—

Note: In part 2, the Foundation invested the donor's permanently restricted cash donation. The original donation amount is permanently restricted and the Foundation accepts the risk of value changes, affecting its unrestricted net assets.

14 Partnership Accounting and Reporting

LEARNING OBJECTIVES

LO1   Distinguish between the characteristics of a partnership and a corporation. (p. 571)

LO2   Record the formation of a partnership. (p. 576)

LO3   Allocate partnership income to partners. (p. 578)

LO4   Record the admission of a partner. (p. 582)

LO5   Record the retirement of a partner. (p. 588)

LO6   Determine appropriate cash distributions in partnership liquidations. (p. 592)

SUBURBAN PROPANE PARTNERS, L.P.
www.suburbanpropane.com

Suburban Propane Partners is a publicly traded limited partnership; its limited partnership interests trade like shares on the New York Stock Exchange under the symbol SPH. The company is engaged in the nationwide marketing and distribution of propane, fuel oils and refined fuel. It is the fifth largest retail marketer of propane in the U.S., serving more than 800,000 active residential, commercial, industrial, and agricultural customers from approximately 300 locations in 30 states. Suburban Propane markets and distributes fuel oil, kerosene, diesel fuel and gasoline to residential and commercial customers in the Northeast. It also markets natural gas and electricity in the deregulated markets of New York and Pennsylvania, primarily to residential and small commercial customers.

Although most publicly-traded companies are organized as corporations, some are structured as partnerships. Most of these are limited partnerships, with a general partner (which itself may be a corporation) and a large number of limited partners. Suburban Propane has 35 million units (shares) outstanding.

In this chapter you will learn how accounting for partnerships differs from corporations. The primary differences are in the accounting for equity interests. *Source:* Suburban Propane Partners, L.P. annual report, 2010.

CHAPTER ORGANIZATION

Distinguish between the characteristics of a partnership and a corporation	Record the formation of a partnership	Allocate partnership income to partners	Record the admission of a partner and the retirement of a partner	Determine appropriate cash distributions in partnership liquidations
• Characteristics of a partnership • Relations of partners to others • Partners' property rights • Limited partnerships • Partnership accounting issues	• Bonus approach • Goodwill approach • Investment of an existing business	• Measuring partnership net income • Salaries and bonus to partners • Interest on capital accounts • Percentage allocation	• Admission by purchase of existing interest and by investment of new capital • Bonus and goodwill methods for admission • Retirement using personal assets and partnership assets • Bonus and goodwill methods for retirement	• Priorities for payments and rights of creditors • Simple liquidations • Installment liquidations • Calculation of safe payments • Preparing a cash distribution plan

INTRODUCTION

Despite the popularity of the corporate form of business organization, most businesses in the United States are sole proprietorships or partnerships. These business forms are easier and less costly to establish than forming a corporation. In addition, while a corporation is a separate taxable entity, the income from a sole proprietorship or a partnership is taxed directly to the owners. Relatively few partnerships are public entities like Suburban Propane; most are small, non-public entities. Financial information is still important to creditors and to the partners themselves. This chapter examines the partnership form of business organization and the applicable accounting procedures.

CHARACTERISTICS OF A PARTNERSHIP

The organizational and operational rules for partnerships derive from two sources: *law*—the **Revised Uniform Partnership Act**, and *contract*—the **partnership agreement**. Partnerships are subject to the laws of the particular state in which they are organized. Many states adopted the provisions of the Revised Uniform Partnership Act of 1994 (the Act) that deal with:

LO1 Distinguish between the characteristics of a partnership and a corporation.

- The nature of a partnership.
- Relations of partners to others.
- Relations among partners.
- Partners' property rights.
- Termination and dissolution of the partnership.

The Revised Uniform Partnership Act defines a **partnership** as "an association of two or more persons to carry on as co-owners a business for profit."

Some implications of this definition are:

- The **actions** of individuals as they jointly conduct a business activity and share profits and losses **legally create a partnership** even if no formal agreement among the individuals exists.

- A partnership is considered to be an **entity distinct from the individual partners**.

- **Co-ownership of property**, even if that property is income-producing, **does not necessarily create a partnership**. For example, three individuals who jointly own a rental property do not constitute a partnership. The rental property is deemed a passive investment, not an ongoing business activity. However, the greater the activity by the owners, the more likely the entity becomes a partnership.

The term *persons* in this definition is not limited to individuals. Corporations or other legal entities may be partners.

Relations of Partners to Others

Each partner is considered an agent of the partnership. For most transactions, any one partner can act for the entire partnership and can legally enter into contracts that also bind the other partners. Only a few transactions, such as disposing of the goodwill of the business or confessing a judgment in court, require authorization of all the partners. Known as **mutual agency**, this characteristic is of great convenience to partners in transacting business. Because one partner may act for the entire partnership, outsiders know that any partner they deal with legally represents the entire partnership. Mutual agency also imposes a risk on individual partners, as they are bound by the actions of fellow partners.

Another significant aspect of this section of the Act states that although any one partner may enter into transactions on behalf of the partnership, all partners are liable for the partnership's obligations. Partners are **liable jointly and severally**; the partnership group is liable for the partnership obligations and each partner has personal liability which could extend to the entire partnership obligation. Creditors of the partnership can seek to collect the full amount of the partnership debt from a single partner. Because partners' obligations are not limited to their investments in the partnership—personal assets are also at risk—partners assume **unlimited liability**. To reduce personal liability, many partnerships are now organized under limited liability company (LLC) or limited liability partnership (LLP) laws, not under the partnership laws.

Relations among Partners

The Act provides that the rights and duties of the partners in relation to the partnership shall be determined, subject to any agreement between them, by the following rules:

- **Each partner shall be repaid all contributions**, whether capital or advances (loans) to the partnership, and **share equally in the profits and surplus** remaining after all liabilities, including those to partners, are satisfied. Each partner must contribute toward the losses sustained by the partnership according to each partner's share in the profits.

- **The partnership must indemnify every partner** for payments made and personal liabilities reasonably incurred by a partner in the ordinary and proper conduct of its business, or for the preservation of its business or property.

- A partner who makes any payment or advance beyond the amount of capital which the partner agreed to contribute, **shall be paid interest** from the date of payment or advance.

- A partner shall **receive interest** on the capital contributed only from the date when repayment should be made.

- All partners have **equal rights** in the management and conduct of the partnership business.

- **No partner is entitled to compensation** for conducting partnership business, except that a surviving partner is entitled to reasonable compensation for services in winding up the partnership affairs.

- **No person can become a member** of a partnership **without the consent** of all the partners.

- Any difference arising as to ordinary matters connected with the partnership business may be decided by a **majority of the partners**; but no act in contravention of any agreement between the partners may be done rightfully without the consent of all the partners.

The partnership agreement may modify the above statutory rules. For example, the partners could agree to divide profits and losses in unequal shares. When no specific agreement exists, however, the provision of the Act regarding equal sharing applies.

Partners' Property Rights

The Act defines two specific property rights which a partner possesses:

1. The partner possesses a **partnership interest**—a right to a share of the capital and profits. This right to a share of profits and to receipt of distributions is transferable by the partner to another party. Such a transfer does not confer partner status on the recipient, give the recipient any managerial rights in the partnership, or entitle the recipient to financial or business information from the partnership.
2. The partner has a **right to participate in managing the partnership**. However, a partner is not a co-owner of partnership property, and has no transferable interest in such property.

Contractual Provisions: The Partnership Agreement

The **partnership agreement**, sometimes referred to as the **articles of partnership**, is a contract among the partners. On certain matters, such as the allocation of income among partners, the contractual agreement takes precedence over the provisions of the Revised Uniform Partnership Act. On other matters, such as the rights of outside parties, the agreement cannot be at variance with the law. In general, the partnership agreement deals with the following matters:

- Characteristics of the partnership, such as its name, nature of its business activity, location, duration, and fiscal year.
- Methods of allocating partnership income to the partners.
- Procedures for admitting new partners and for settling a partner's interest upon withdrawal or death, including life insurance to be carried on partners and buy-sell agreements.

Limited Partnerships

The discussion thus far focuses on **general partnerships** in which all partners can participate in the management of the firm and all are liable for the partnership's obligations. Another type of partnership, the **limited partnership**, has both general partners (at least one) and limited partners. The general partner(s) manage the firm and have all the rights and obligations previously discussed. The limited partners invest capital and have the right to a specified share of income or loss but have no right to participate in management. Their liability for the partnership's obligations is limited to their investment in the partnership.

Limited partnerships are often used when large amounts of investment capital are needed and tax treatment as a partnership is desired. A general partner initiates the project, such as real estate development or natural resource exploration, and finances it by selling limited partnership interests to investors. The general partner acquires the needed capital without relinquishing management control, and investors acquire a right to share in income without bearing any personal responsibility for partnership liabilities.

Limited Liability Companies and Partnerships

The **limited liability company (LLC)** combines many of the organizational and tax treatments of a noncorporate entity—a partnership or proprietorship—with the limited liability protection of a corporation. An LLC has an underlying structure similar to a corporation, including articles of organization (similar to a corporate charter) and, in many states, a governing board. This form of organization is taxed as a partnership rather than as a corporation. This feature created a great interest in the LLC form of organization, and all states have now adopted LLC statutes.

As an alternative to the LLC, the **limited liability partnership (LLP)** has an underlying partnership structure. The LLP form is widely used by professional firms that have a long history of organizing as partnerships.

LLCs and LLPs are typically considered to be superior forms of organization to the general partnership, because they retain most of the latter's desirable characteristics but largely eliminate the unlimited liability facing individual partners. Most LLC/LLP laws limit liability to a partner's investment; personal liability exists only for personal involvement in, or supervision of, a specific wrongful act. Thus if a CPA firm is organized as a limited liability partnership, an individual partner involved in a negligent audit is personally liable, but a partner not involved in the engagement in any way is not personally liable.

In recent years, most general partnerships converted their legal status to an LLC or LLP. Virtually all the large CPA firms and partnerships in other professions are LLPs. Most characteristics of partnership operation and the accounting procedures for an LLP follow those of the general partnership.

Reporting Perspective

Many partnerships are small local businesses with few partners. In such cases, mutual agency and joint and several liability may be manageable characteristics; each partner is likely to be aware of the actions of the other partners. But some partnerships, such as international CPA firms, are large national or international enterprises with hundreds or thousands of partners. Mutual agency and joint and several liability may cause major problems in these firms. For example, suppose a partner in the Los Angeles office of a CPA firm presides over an audit failure that leads to a large liability judgment against the firm. Under general partnership law, every partner in the firm, whether in New York or Grand Rapids, Michigan, has potential personal liability for the judgment, even though he or she had absolutely no involvement with the failed audit.

Historically, professionals such as CPAs, attorneys and physicians were not allowed to limit personal liability by organizing their affairs as corporations. Professional corporations, allowed in many jurisdictions, provide corporate income tax treatment, but do not offer limited liability. Creation of the LLC and LLP forms of organization largely remedies the problem of joint and several liability for professionals. Under these newer organizational arrangements, partners involved in a particular engagement are personally liable for damages arising out of that engagement but their liability does not extend to their partners who are not involved in the engagement.

Comparison of Corporate and Partnership Forms of Organization

Each form of partnership organization possesses advantages and disadvantages. A general partnership ceases to exist legally when a new partner enters or an existing partner retires or dies, but the partnership agreement can provide for continued business operations seemingly unaffected by changes in partnership personnel. All partners must consent to transfers of ownership interests. In a limited partnership, the entity ceases to exist when a general partner is no longer present. Interests of the limited partners are freely transferable whereas changes in the general partner's interest are subject to consent of all other partners. The tax law treats all qualified partnerships as **conduits**. Transactions with tax effects pass through to the partners; no income tax is levied on the partnership itself. This feature may or may not be a benefit, depending on the tax status of the partners.

A corporation is formed under a charter granted by a governmental entity. Shareholders have no personal liability for the corporation's debts, and have no right to participate in management, although they do elect the corporation's governing board of directors. The life of a corporation is generally unlimited and shares are freely transferable. Most corporations are taxable entities, as are those partnerships that possess corporate characteristics. Because income taxes are levied on the corporation and on certain distributions to shareholders, "double taxation" can result.

PARTNERSHIP ACCOUNTING ISSUES

Being a business entity, a partnership uses many corporate accounting principles. For example, revenue and expense recognition and asset and liability valuation generally receive the same treatment. There are, however, a few important areas where partnership accounting differs from corporate accounting.

Like a corporation, a partnership is a separate accounting entity distinct from the individual partners. However, the partners typically are actively involved in the firm; they are not absentee owners.

This fact influences the concept of net income for a partnership as well as the treatment of owners' equity. Corporate owners' equity is reflected in several accounts—common stock, additional paid-in capital, and retained earnings—but a corporation does not maintain separate equity accounts for each stockholder. Partnership equity, on the other hand, is recorded in **capital accounts** that reflect the partners' shares of invested capital and undistributed earnings. A separate capital account is maintained for each partner. These accounting considerations also apply to sole proprietorships, with only a single capital account for the sole proprietor.

Income Allocations versus Payments to Partners

When discussing the distribution of partnership income to the individual partners, one must distinguish between:

1. **Allocations to partners**, which are *credits* to the partners' capital accounts for their respective shares of partnership income (or debits for their shares of partnership loss).
2. **Payments to partners**, which are *debits* to their capital accounts reflecting the transfer of resources from the partnership to the partners. Also called **drawings**, these payments create no special accounting problems, except in cases where the partnership is being liquidated.

Measuring Partnership Income

Although partnerships employ the same revenue and expense recognition criteria as corporations, net income has a special meaning in a partnership. In corporate accounting, net income signifies the *return to the corporation*; the return to the owners/shareholders comes in dividends and capital gains. In partnership accounting, however, net income signifies the *return to the owners/partners*. In addition to being investors, partners may also render personal services in the day-to-day conduct of business and may loan money to the partnership. It can be difficult to separate these roles. Stockholders of a corporation may also be employees of, or lenders to, that corporation, but these roles are more distinct; salaries and interest paid to them are subtracted from revenue in computing corporate net income.

Accounting and tax requirements necessitate a careful distinction between the corporate entity and the individual, along with a distinction among the individual's possible roles as stockholder, employee, and lender. These distinctions are not particularly useful in a partnership because a partnership does not have the formal legal status of a corporation and is not a taxable entity.

When partners have multiple involvement in the financial affairs of the partnership—as investors, employees, and lenders—it can be difficult to distinguish among: (1) compensation for services performed, (2) interest on loans, and (3) return on capital invested. Certain income allocations may be called *salaries*, other allocations *interest*, and still others *shares of profit*. The lack of arm's-length transactions in valuing these allocations causes the various role distinctions to be disregarded—all income allocations to partners are considered to be divisions of partnership net income. In other words, net income of a partnership is determined *before* any allocations are made to partners; allocations such as *salaries and interest to partners are not treated as expenses*. Similarly, net income of a sole proprietorship is the return to the proprietor; *no compensation to the proprietor is subtracted*.

A second area of difference between corporation and partnership net income is the treatment of income taxes. As noted earlier, a corporation is a taxable entity, but a partnership is a conduit through which income flows to the individual partners. The individual partners include their share of partnership income—their allocations—and any special tax-treatment items on their personal income tax returns. *The income statement of the partnership does not report income tax expense*.

Partnership Income Allocations

Once the partnership's net income is determined, it must be allocated among the individual partners. Because all allocations to partners are viewed as divisions of partnership net income, partnership agreements frequently consider the various roles—investor, employee, lender—that partners hold. The partnership agreement should specify the income allocation rules. These rules may be simple or complex, sometimes calling for salary, interest, and bonus allocations. If the partnership agreement is silent, the law requires income to be divided equally among all partners.

Capital Changes

Another important issue in accounting for partnerships involves changes in the capital structure. Such changes include initial formation of partnerships, investments and withdrawals by the partners, subsequent entry and exit of individual partners, and eventual liquidation of partnerships. Partnerships frequently report these events in a schedule of changes in capital accounts, similar to the corporate statement of changes in stockholders' equity.

Summary of Accounting for Partnership Operations

Corporate accounting standards for revenue and expense recognition and asset and liability valuation generally apply to partnerships. As a result, accounting matters specific to partnerships focus on events affecting the capital accounts that represent the owners' equity accounts. These accounts combine invested capital and undistributed income and are impacted by:

1. **Investment of capital.** An individual partner's capital account is affected not only by the partner's own investment, but also by the investments of new partners and retirements of existing partners.
2. **Allocation of net income.** As stated, partnership net income—the return to the partners—is determined before subtracting any compensation to the partners. Then the partnership's net income is allocated to the partners in accordance with the partnership agreement, or in equal shares if the partners have not agreed otherwise. The income shares are credited to the partners' capital accounts. When a loss occurs, the partners' loss shares are debited to their capital accounts.
3. **Withdrawal of capital.** Amounts withdrawn by partners from invested capital or undistributed income allocations are debited to each partner's capital account. When withdrawals are made in anticipation of income allocations, they are debited to separate **drawing accounts** for each partner that are closed at year-end to the capital accounts. For example, if partner Burns draws $500 per month to help with living expenses, the following entry is made monthly:

Drawing—Burns	500	
Cash		500
To record monthly drawing.		

At year-end, the balance in the drawing account is closed, as follows:

Capital—Burns	6,000	
Drawing—Burns		6,000
To close drawing account to capital; $6,000 = $500 × 12.		

Use of drawing accounts is optional; withdrawals may be directly debited to the capital accounts.

FORMATION OF THE PARTNERSHIP

LO2 Record the formation of a partnership.

Accounting for the formation of a partnership requires setting values for assets contributed by the partners and establishing the initial capital account balances. Assets contributed to a partnership in exchange for a capital interest are recorded at fair market value.

Bonus and Goodwill Approaches

Establishing the opening balance in each partner's capital account can be complicated even though fair market values of the contributed assets are known. The simplest approach sets each partner's capital account equal to the fair market value of net assets invested. Suppose Prince and Quinn form a partnership. Prince invests $30,000 cash, and Quinn invests land and a building having a combined fair market value of $75,000, subject to a $35,000 mortgage that the partnership assumes. Thus Quinn invested net assets with fair market value of $40,000 (= $75,000 − $35,000). When each partner's capital account is set equal to net assets invested at fair market value, we have:

Cash..	30,000	
Land and building..	75,000	
Mortgage payable..		35,000
Capital—Prince...		30,000
Capital—Quinn...		40,000
To record formation of partnership.		

Alternatively, the partners could specify a capital percentage for each partner that provides each partner with an agreed-upon percentage interest in initial total partnership capital. This approach could generate several different entries to record the partnership's formation, depending on the agreement between Prince and Quinn. One approach assigns the total capital based on the agreed-upon capital percentages of the respective partners. Suppose that Prince and Quinn decide that each will have a 50 percent interest in the partnership's initial capital. Perhaps the reason the partners agreed on equal capital balances while making unequal tangible investments is that one partner, Prince in this case, brings certain talents, contacts, or other intangible benefits to the partnership.

Because Prince invested $30,000 and Quinn invested $40,000, they must decide how to apply their capital percentages to determine their opening capital balances. Two approaches are possible:

1. **Bonus approach**: divide the total capital of $70,000 according to the capital percentages, in this case equally, and credit each partner with $35,000. This situation implies a capital transfer, or *bonus*, of $5,000 from Quinn to Prince. Under the **bonus approach to partnership formation,** the entry is:

Cash..	30,000	
Land and building..	75,000	
Mortgage payable..		35,000
Capital—Prince...		35,000
Capital—Quinn...		35,000
To record formation of partnership under the bonus approach.		

2. **Goodwill approach**: assume that Prince contributes enough intangible assets in the form of talents and contacts to bring the investments, and the capital balances, into the desired relation. We record this intangible asset, called **goodwill**, in an amount sufficient to achieve the desired relation among the capital accounts. Quinn's contribution of $40,000 of tangible net assets establishes the amount that Prince's investment must meet. In the current example, we need to record $10,000 (= $40,000 − $30,000) of goodwill to make Prince's investment equal to Quinn's. Under the **goodwill approach to partnership formation**, the entry is:

Cash..	30,000	
Land and building..	75,000	
Goodwill...	10,000	
Mortgage payable..		35,000
Capital—Prince...		40,000
Capital—Quinn...		40,000
To record formation of partnership.		

When forming a partnership, the partners must specify which accounting approach is to be used.

When an existing business entity, currently operated as a proprietorship, becomes that partner's investment in the partnership, revaluation of proprietorship assets may be necessary to reflect the fair market value of assets being transferred to the partnership, and intangible assets may be recognized. After settling these matters, the partners record their investments in an entry signifying formation of the partnership.

REVIEW 1 ● Formation of a partnership

Abel, Baker and Cahn form an insurance agency, as equal partners. Abel invests $100,000 cash; Baker invests $30,000 cash and has extensive experience in the insurance industry. Cahn invests a building worth $200,000, subject to a mortgage of $125,000, and office equipment having a fair value of $17,000.

Required
a. Record the formation of the partnership under the bonus method.
b. Record the formation under the goodwill method.

Solutions are located after the chapter assignments.

ALLOCATION OF NET INCOME TO PARTNERS

LO3 Allocate partnership income to partners.

As previously discussed, partnership net income does not reflect expenses for partners' salaries or interest. Because such provisions are considered in allocating partnership net income among the individual partners, a multifactor allocation procedure may be used. Although partners may agree to use any factors, three common ones are:

1. A **salary factor**, representing compensation for the personal services a partner provides to the operations of the partnership.
2. An **interest factor**, a return on the capital each partner has invested.
3. A **percentage factor**, the agreed income-sharing ratio to allocate income or loss remaining after providing for any salaries and interest.

An income-sharing ratio must exist in all cases; salary and interest provisions may or may not exist.

Salaries to Partners

Allocations of net income in the form of salary allowances are typically established by the partnership agreement. This agreement usually specifies (1) each partner's amount or (2) a formula, such as a bonus formula, based on the time, effort, or experience that each partner contributes to the business. For example, the DEF partnership might agree that D's annual salary is $200,000, E's is $60,000, F receives no salary, and any remaining income or loss is to be divided equally among the partners. Suppose partnership net income for the year is $380,000. The allocation first provides for the $260,000 in salaries and then divides the remaining $120,000 in the income-sharing ratio, yielding the following allocation of partnership net income:

	D	E	F	Total
Salaries	$200,000	$ 60,000	$ 0	$260,000
Balance	40,000	40,000	40,000	120,000
Net allocation	$240,000	$100,000	$40,000	$380,000

The partnership agreement should specify whether salary and other allocations are to be **fully implemented**, even if they exceed partnership net income. *We assume full implementation unless otherwise stated*. In the DEF example, assume that net income is $170,000 and that salaries are to be fully implemented. Because the $260,000 salary allocation exceeds net income; the $90,000 "loss" is then allocated by the income-sharing ratio, as follows:

	D	E	F	Total
Salaries	$200,000	$ 60,000	$ 0	$260,000
Balance	(30,000)	(30,000)	(30,000)	(90,000)
Net allocation	$170,000	$ 30,000	$(30,000)	$170,000

When partners' salaries or other income allocation devices are not fully implemented, the partnership agreement must specify the order for applying the various devices. The partners could agree to first implement salaries, followed by interest on capital balances, and so forth. Moreover, the partners must agree on a procedure for partial implementation of any income-sharing device. In the above example, income of $170,000 is not enough to implement even the salaries, let alone any other income allocation device. Two of the many possible approaches are (1) allocate D's salary first or (2) allocate using D's $200,000 salary and E's $60,000 salary in the proportion that the salary of each bears to total salaries of $260,000. Using the proportional basis in (2), the $170,000 of income is allocated as follows:

	D	E	F	Total
Net allocation	$130,769*	$ 39,231**	$ 0	$170,000

* $130,769 = ($200,000/$260,000) × $170,000
** $ 39,231 = ($60,000/$260,000) × $170,000

Bonus to Partners

Allocation of net income to partners for services rendered may reflect a bonus based on profit, perhaps in addition to a fixed salary. In discussing various bonus relationships, we use the following symbols:

    X = Net income before bonus
    B = Amount of bonus
    Y = Net income after bonus ($= X - B$)
    R = Percentage rate of bonus

When we define the bonus as a percentage of net income before the bonus, we have:

    $B = RX$

When the bonus is defined as a percentage of the net income that remains *after* the bonus, we have a somewhat more complex formula:

    $B = RY$
    $B = R(X - B)$
    $B = RX - RB$
    $B + RB = RX$
    $B = RX/(1 + R)$

For example, assume net income before the bonus is $300,000 and the bonus rate is 25 percent of net income after the bonus, an amount currently unknown. Using the above formula, we calculate the bonus as follows:

    $B = RX/(1 + R)$
    $B = (0.25 \times 300,000)/1.25$
    $B = 75,000/1.25$
    $B = 60,000$

We can verify that the $60,000 bonus is 25 percent of Y, the $240,000 of net income after the bonus ($Y = \$300,000 - \$60,000$).

Many other bonus possibilities exist, including different percentages based on different levels of income. Or the bonus could be determined after implementing one income-sharing device, such as salaries, but before implementing another, such as interest on capital accounts.

Interest on Partners' Capital Accounts

Allocations of net income may also reflect interest allowances on partners' capital accounts. A specified interest rate is usually applied to weighted average capital balances. We calculate the weighted average capital balance by multiplying each different amount of a partner's capital balance by the fraction of the year during which that amount existed. Suppose a partner's capital account has a balance of $60,000 on January 1, additional capital of $200,000 is invested on March 1, and $20,000 is withdrawn on September 1. The *weighted average capital balance* for the year is:

Period	Capital Balance	Fraction of Year	Weighted Average
January 1–February 28............	$ 60,000	2/12	$ 10,000
March 1–August 31	260,000	6/12	130,000
September 1–December 31	240,000	4/12	80,000
Total........................			$220,000

If the specified interest rate is 8 percent, $17,600 ($= 0.08 \times \$220,000$) of the partnership net income is allocated to this partner for interest on the average capital balance.

As with salary allocations to partners, any interest-based allocation of net income may be fully implemented, even if it exceeds total net income. Any remaining income or loss created by previous allocations is divided according to the percentages in the income-sharing ratio.

Percentage Allocation by Income-Sharing Ratio

A percentage allocation formula, or **income-sharing ratio**, always exists for a partnership. Although the entire net income of the partnership can be allocated by this percentage formula, some income may be allocated by salaries, by interest, or both. In the latter case, the amount of partnership net income remaining after full implementation of salaries and interest, whether positive or negative, is allocated by the income-sharing ratio.

The partnership agreement sets forth the income-sharing ratio. Although a single set of percentages is typically applied to all forms of income, the partners may agree to divide different types of income, or expense, in different ways. When the partnership agreement fails to specify an income-sharing ratio, the Uniform Partnership Act provides that all partners share equally.

Comprehensive Illustration of Partnership Net Income Allocation

Thomas, Underwood, and Vickers are partners in a printing firm. Their partnership agreement contains the following income allocation provisions:

- Thomas devotes two days per week to partnership business and receives an annual salary of $150,000. Underwood and Vickers work full time and receive annual salaries of $350,000 and $300,000, respectively.
- Vickers, who is responsible for sales, receives a bonus equal to 10% of any net income, before allocations, in excess of $1,000,000.
- The partners receive 10% interest on their weighted average capital balances, before considering allocations of salaries and bonus.
- After implementing these three allocations, allocate any remaining income or loss 50% to Thomas, 30% to Underwood, and 20% to Vickers.

Suppose that partnership net income for 2013 was $1,500,000. The partners' capital balances at the beginning of the year were: Thomas, $690,000; Underwood, $400,000; and Vickers, $400,000. Underwood invested another $100,000 on March 31, 2013. At the end of each quarter, the partners withdrew a total of $60,000, divided according to the income-sharing percentages—Thomas withdrew $30,000, Underwood $18,000, and Vickers $12,000. Thomas withdrew an additional $180,000 on October 31, 2013. Exhibit 14.1 shows the allocation of 2013 income.

Schedule of Changes in Capital Accounts

Partnerships frequently summarize the events affecting the partners' capital accounts during an accounting period in a **schedule of changes in capital accounts**. Exhibit 14.2 illustrates this schedule using the information for the year ended December 31, 2013, for Thomas, Underwood, and Vickers.

When the schedule of changes in capital accounts is included with the formal financial statements prepared by a partnership, items such as Drawings appear in total on a single line.

EXHIBIT 14.1   Illustration of Income Allocation

	Thomas	Underwood	Vickers	Total
Salaries......................	$150,000	$350,000	$300,000	$ 800,000
Bonus*	—	—	50,000	50,000
Interest**....................	61,500	44,800	38,200	144,500
				994,500
Balance***..................	252,750	151,650	101,100	505,500
Totals	$464,250	$546,450	$489,300	$1,500,000

*Bonus is 10 percent of $500,000 (=$1,500,000 − $1,000,000)

**Weighted average capital is calculated as follows. 10% of the weighted average capital is the amount of interest.

	Thomas		Underwood		Vickers	
January 1–March 31............	$690,000 × 3/12 =	$172,500	$400,000 × 3/12 =	$100,000	$400,000 × 3/12 =	$100,000
April 1–June 30...............	660,000 × 3/12 =	165,000	482,000 × 3/12 =	120,500	388,000 × 3/12 =	97,000
July 1–September 30	630,000 × 3/12 =	157,500	464,000 × 3/12 =	116,000	376,000 × 3/12 =	94,000
October 1–October 31	600,000 × 1/12 =	50,000	446,000 × 1/12 =	37,167	364,000 × 1/12 =	30,333
November 1–December 31	420,000 × 2/12 =	70,000	446,000 × 2/12 =	74,333	364,000 × 2/12 =	60,667
Weighted average		$615,000		$448,000		$382,000

***The balance of $505,500 is allocated 50% to Thomas, 30% to Underwood, and 20% to Vickers.

EXHIBIT 14.2   Schedule of Changes in Capital Accounts

	Capital Accounts			
Event	Thomas	Underwood	Vickers	Total
Beginning balance, January 1	$690,000	$400,000	$400,000	$1,490,000
Investment, March 31......................	—	100,000	—	100,000
Drawings, March 31.......................	(30,000)	(18,000)	(12,000)	(60,000)
Drawings, June 30	(30,000)	(18,000)	(12,000)	(60,000)
Drawings, September 30	(30,000)	(18,000)	(12,000)	(60,000)
Withdrawal, October 31	(180,000)	—	—	(180,000)
Income allocation, December 31*	464,250	546,450	489,300	1,500,000
Drawings, December 31....................	(30,000)	(18,000)	(12,000)	(60,000)
Ending balance, December 31...............	$854,250	$974,450	$841,300	$2,670,000

*From Exhibit 14.1.

REVIEW 2   •   Income allocation

The Abel, Baker & Cahn Insurance Agency completed its first year of operations, earning a net income of $177,000. Assume the bonus method was used to record the formation of the partnership (see Review Problem 1). Abel is Baker's father-in-law; Abel is not active in the business, but agreed to invest to help get the agency under way. Baker is the manager of the agency and the primary salesperson. Cahn also sells insurance, but he is less experienced than Baker. The partnership agreement provides that Abel receives 15 percent interest on his beginning-of-year capital balance. Baker receives an annual salary of $80,000 and a 10 percent bonus on partnership income above $100,000. Cahn receives 8 percent interest on beginning-of-year capital and a $40,000 salary. Remaining profits are divided equally. All salary, bonus, and interest provisions are to be fully implemented.

Required
a.   Determine the allocation of the partnership's net income.
b.   Assume that salaries and the bonus were distributed in cash to the appropriate partners. Calculate the capital balances at year end.

Solutions are located after the chapter assignments.

ADMISSION OF A NEW PARTNER

Admission of a new partner gives rise to another important accounting problem for partnerships. Technically, there is no such thing as "admission of a new partner." When a new partner is admitted, the old partnership legally ends, and a new partnership is created. For practical purposes, however, business operations are likely to continue without interruption. As is often the case in accounting, the economic substance—the continuing business activity—takes precedence over the legal form—termination of the old partnership and the creation of a new one. It is in this economic sense that we speak of admission of a new partner.

In the illustrations that follow, assume the partnership of Arthur Associates has this balance sheet at June 30, 2014:

		ARTHUR ASSOCIATES **Balance Sheet** **June 30, 2014**			
Various assets	$140,000	Liabilities.			$ 50,000
		Capital			
		Arthur	$31,000		
		Bradley	26,000		
		Crowe	33,000		90,000
Total assets	$140,000	Total liabilities and capital			$140,000

Assume further that the partners' income-sharing ratio is as follows: Arthur, 50%; Bradley, 20%; and Crowe 30%.

Admission by Purchase of an Existing Partnership Interest

A new partner may enter an existing partnership by purchasing the interest of one or more existing partners. Such a transaction occurs between the old and new partners as individuals and usually has no direct effect on the partnership accounts. This parallels the case in which one individual sells shares of stock in a corporation to another individual. Only the two individuals are involved in the transaction; the corporation makes no entry other than to update its stockholder records. In a similar manner, when one individual buys an existing partnership interest, the only partnership entry usually needed transfers the capital account from the old partner to the new.

Transfer of Capital Interests   The usual method of accounting for a purchase of an existing partnership interest is to transfer the capital balance of the selling partner to a new capital account established for the entering partner. The amount of the entry is the existing capital balance of the selling partner, which may be different from the selling price.

Purchase from One Partner   Suppose that on July 1, 2014, Findley purchases Crowe's entire partnership interest for $45,000. The partnership records the transfer of Crowe's capital balance to Findley as follows:

Capital—Crowe	33,000	
Capital—Findley		33,000
To record transfer of partnership interest from Crowe to Findley.		

The $45,000 purchase price has no bearing on the partnership entry. Crowe realized a gain of $12,000 on the sale of the partnership interest, assuming Crowe's basis is $33,000. The cost (and tax basis) of Findley's partnership interest is $45,000, despite the fact that the partnership books show the capital account as $33,000. Findley's cost of $45,000 has no effect on any capital-based distributions the partnership makes. However, the $45,000 cost affects the amount of taxable gain or loss recognized by Findley when that partnership interest is sold.

Purchase from Several Partners   A new partner may purchase a portion of the interest of several partners. Suppose that Grogan buys a 25 percent interest in Arthur Associates by purchasing 25 percent of each partner's interest for $28,000. We could simply record the transfer of 25 percent of each partner's capital interests to Grogan.

Capital—Arthur.	7,750	
Capital—Bradley	6,500	
Capital—Crowe	8,250	
Capital—Grogan		22,500
To record transfer of 25% interest to Grogan.		

The debits to the capital accounts of the three existing partners represent 25 percent of their respective capital balances. As before, the $28,000 purchase price has no bearing on the entry. The three existing partners recognize gains or losses as individuals on the sale of part of their partnership interests.

A new income-sharing ratio must be established for the four partners. We typically assume that the contract for the new partnership specifies that (1) the new partner's percentages of income and of the initial capital balance are equal and (2) the old partners maintain their income-sharing relationship. After Grogan joins the firm, therefore, the partners share income as follows: Arthur, 37.5%; Bradley, 15%; Crowe, 22.5%; and Grogan, 25%. These percentages are based on the fact that the old partners now own 75% of the partnership: Arthur has 50% of 75%, or 37.5%; Bradley has 20% of 75%; and Crowe has 30% of 75%.

Recognition of Implied Goodwill   Admission of a new partner by purchase of an existing partnership interest is usually recorded by transferring capital accounts as described above. Another approach involves recognizing implied goodwill. Under this approach, we use the purchase price to infer the value of the entire partnership. To illustrate, again consider the case where Grogan buys 25 percent of each partner's interest for $28,000.

If Grogan is willing to pay $28,000 for a 25 percent interest in the partnership, the entire partnership must be worth $112,000 (= $28,000/0.25). But the partnership books show only $90,000, the total capital of Arthur, Bradley, and Crowe. This implies that $22,000 (= $112,000 implied total value − $90,000 recorded capital) of unrecorded assets exist. We call these unrecorded assets *goodwill*, unless we have evidence that other identifiable assets are undervalued. We first record the goodwill, apportioning a share to each existing partner according to the established income-sharing ratio of 50% for Arthur, 20% for Bradley, and 30% for Crowe. The entry to record the **implied goodwill** is as follows:

Goodwill	22,000	
Capital—Arthur		11,000
Capital—Bradley		4,400
Capital—Crowe		6,600
To record implied goodwill.		

We now make the entry transferring 25 percent of each partner's capital to Grogan:

Capital—Arthur (25% × 42,000)	10,500	
Capital—Bradley (25% × 30,400)	7,600	
Capital—Crowe (25% × 39,600)	9,900	
Capital—Grogan		28,000
To record transfer of 25% interest to Grogan.		

Under the implied goodwill approach, the credit to the new partner's capital account equals the amount paid to acquire the interest. Unless the agreement covering the purchase of partners' interests specifically provides for recognizing implied goodwill on the partnership books, the transfer of capital accounts method should be used.

Admission by Investment of New Capital

A new partner may enter an existing partnership by investing directly in the partnership: the new partner contributes an agreed-upon amount of assets—cash, property, or services to the partnership. In return, the new partner receives an agreed-upon share of capital at date of entry and a specified share of subsequent income and loss. This agreed-upon capital percentage is used to establish the new partner's initial capital balance. Thereafter, the income percentage guides the division of subsequent profits and losses among the partners. In many cases, the capital percentage and income percentage are equal. When they are not equal, their use is guided by the following rule:

> **Capital percentage** (capital-sharing ratio) is used to establish the value of the firm and the total amount of goodwill.
>
> **Income percentage** (income-sharing ratio) is used to allocate goodwill or bonus to partners and to allocate income.

The partnership records the investment of assets by the new partner, the capital account of the new partner, and any adjustments needed to reconcile the two. When the investment by the new partner equals the new partner's capital percentage times the new capital—old capital plus assets invested—no accounting problem exists. For example, suppose that on July 1, 2014, Edwards invests $10,000 in Arthur Associates in exchange for a 10 percent interest in capital and income (hereafter referred to as a 10 percent interest). We have the following:

1. Investment by Edwards = $10,000.
2. Edwards' share of new capital = 10% × ($90,000 old capital + $10,000 invested by Edwards) = 10% × $100,000 = $10,000.

Since Items 1 and 2 are equal, we make the following entry:

Assets.	10,000	
Capital—Edwards		10,000
To record investment by Edwards.		

When the new partner does not invest an amount equal to the capital share, there are two possibilities:

Case A

Edwards invests $9,000 for the 10% interest:

1. Investment by Edwards = $9,000.
2. Edwards' share of new capital = 10% × ($90,000 + $9,000) = $9,900.

Case B

Delano invests $12,000 for a 10% interest:

1. Investment by Delano = $12,000.
2. Delano's share of new capital = 10% × ($90,000 + $12,000) = $10,200.

In Cases A and B above, the investment differs from the computed share of capital. When this situation occurs, the disparity must be reconciled in one of two ways before the entry recording the investment can be made.

1. Consider the share of capital amount (item 2 in Cases A and B) to be the correct amount credited to the new partner's capital account. The difference between this amount and the amount invested is treated as an adjustment of the existing partners' capital accounts. This is known as the **bonus method of admission**.
2. Consider the invested amount (item 1 in Cases A and B) to be the correct amount credited to the new partner's capital account. Bring the investment and the share of capital (item 2) amounts into agreement by inferring the existence of intangible assets and adding these either to the capital of the new partner or to the capital of the existing partners. This is known as the **goodwill method of admission**.

The partnership agreement should specify the methods to be used when admitting a new partner to the partnership. The following sections discuss and illustrate both methods.

Bonus Method of Admission   The bonus method of admission avoids revaluing assets and recognizing goodwill when a new partner enters.

Under the **bonus method of admission**, the total capital of the new partnership after admission of the new partner equals the capital before admission plus the investment of the new partner. The new partner's capital account is credited with the agreed-upon share of the total capital.

Suppose that the new partner's investment is less than the computed share of capital, as in Case A above, where Edwards invests $9,000 but receives a $9,900 share in capital. In such a situation, the existing partners have some reason for admitting Edwards at this less-than-fair-share price. Perhaps Edwards brings some important talents or resources to the firm, and to obtain these the existing partners subsidize Edwards' admission by giving a $9,900 share for only $9,000. The $900 difference is charged against the existing partners' capital accounts in their income-sharing percentages. Here is the entry to record Edwards' admission for a 10 percent interest with an investment of $9,000:

Cash	9,000	
Capital—Arthur	450	
Capital—Bradley	180	
Capital—Crowe	270	
Capital—Edwards		9,900
To record Edwards' admission under the bonus method.		

The Edwards admission, in which the new partner's investment is less than the computed capital balance, results in a **bonus to the new partner**.

Suppose the new partner's investment is more than the computed share of capital, as in Case B above, where Delano invests $12,000 for a $10,200 share in total capital. Here the existing partners are able to command a premium when admitting a new partner. Perhaps the assets of the partnership are worth more than their book value. Perhaps the partnership has above-average earning potential. Or perhaps the existing partners wish to be compensated for the risk and effort they incurred in establishing the firm. In any event, to gain admittance Delano must contribute not only a fair share of assets, $10,200, but another $1,800 that is credited to the capital accounts of the existing partners in their income-sharing percentages. The entry to record Delano's admission for an investment of $12,000 in exchange for a 10% interest, is as follows:

Cash	12,000	
Capital—Arthur		900
Capital—Bradley		360
Capital—Crowe		540
Capital—Delano		10,200
To record Delano's admission under the bonus method.		

The Delano admission, in which the new partner's investment is more than the computed capital balance, results in a **bonus to the existing partners**.

Goodwill Method of Admission   The goodwill method of admission specifically provides for asset revaluation and goodwill recognition supported by the amount of the new partner's investment.

The **goodwill method of admission** attributes the difference between the amount invested by the new partner and the share of capital initially calculated to the presence of unrecorded intangible assets or other undervalued assets. This method reconciles the difference by recording these unrecorded or undervalued assets.

Any goodwill recorded in admitting a new partner is not amortized; *ASC Section 350-20-35* requires that goodwill should be evaluated periodically for impairment of its value.

Goodwill to the New Partner   Suppose the new partner's investment of tangible assets is less than the initially computed share of capital, as in Case A above, where Edwards invests $9,000 cash for a $9,900 share in net assets. To explain this imbalance, we infer that Edwards brings something more to the firm than $9,000 cash—perhaps some special skills or talents—such that the existing partners will admit Edwards as a 10 percent partner for $9,000. Calculation of the goodwill proceeds as follows:

1. Calculate the total value of the new firm implied by the capital of the existing partners. In the current example, existing capital amounts to $90,000. Because the existing partners will have a 90 percent interest in the new partnership, the total value of the new partnership must be $100,000 (= $90,000/0.9).
2. Calculate the new partner's share of this total value. In the current example, Edwards' share is $10,000 (10 percent of $100,000).
3. The goodwill invested by the new partner is the difference between the share of the firm's calculated value and the amount of tangible assets invested. In this example, Edwards invested $1,000 of goodwill (= $10,000 share of firm's value − $9,000 cash invested).

The entry to record Edwards' admission follows:

Cash...	9,000	
Goodwill...	1,000	
Capital—Edwards...		10,000
To record Edwards' admission under the goodwill method with goodwill to new partner.		

Goodwill to the Existing Partners   Suppose again that the new partner's investment of tangible assets is more than the initially computed share of capital, as in Case B above, where Delano invests $12,000 cash for a $10,200 share in net assets. Perhaps this imbalance results from the net assets of the existing partnership being understated. Some of the firm's tangible assets may have market values in excess of their book values. Or the firm may have unrecorded goodwill in the form of established customers, product recognition, and skillful management. The fact that a new partner will pay more than book value for a partnership interest supports the notion that undervalued or unrecorded assets exist. We bring the new partner's investment into balance with the share of net assets, acknowledging these unrecorded asset amounts, calculated as follows:

1. Calculate the total value of the new firm implied by the new partner's investment. In the current example, the fact that Delano invests $12,000 for a 10 percent interest implies a total value of the new partnership of $120,000 (= $12,000/0.10).
2. Calculate the amount by which assets are understated. In this example, net assets are recorded at $90,000. Delano's investment of $12,000 brings the total to $102,000. Because we calculated the value of the new firm to be $120,000, assets are understated by $18,000 (= $120,000 − $102,000).
3. Correct the understatement of assets by recognizing the presence of goodwill with offsetting credits to the capital accounts of the existing partners in their income-sharing percentages. This procedure attributes the past unrecorded increase in net assets to the existing partners. Revaluation of tangible assets to remove the understatement is generally not proper unless objective evidence, such as quoted market prices of securities, substantiates the revaluation.

The following entry is used to record Delano's admission:

Cash...	12,000	
Goodwill...	18,000	
Capital—Arthur...		9,000
Capital—Bradley..		3,600
Capital—Crowe..		5,400
Capital—Delano...		12,000
To record Delano's admission under the goodwill method with goodwill to existing partners.		

Effects of Bonus and Goodwill Methods on Partners' Capital

In general, the bonus and goodwill methods do not yield the same capital balances for the individual partners or the same total capital for the partnership.

Total Partnership Capital after Admission of New Partner	
Bonus Method	**Goodwill Method**
Total capital before admission + Amount invested by new partner	Total capital before admission + Amount invested by new partner + Goodwill recorded

Compare the bonus and goodwill results obtained in the illustrations for Arthur Associates. The total capital before admission was $90,000. New partner Edwards invested $9,000. Under the goodwill method, $1,000 of goodwill was attributed to Edwards. The capital balances after admission follow:

	Bonus Method	Goodwill Method
Arthur	$30,550	$ 31,000
Bradley	25,820	26,000
Crowe	32,730	33,000
Edwards	9,900	10,000
Totals	$99,000	$100,000

In the other illustration, new partner Delano invested $12,000. Under the goodwill method, $18,000 of goodwill was attributed to the existing partners. The capital balances after admission follow:

	Bonus Method	Goodwill Method
Arthur	$31,900	$ 40,000
Bradley	26,360	29,600
Crowe	33,540	38,400
Delano	10,200	12,000
Totals	$102,000	$120,000

Evaluation of Bonus and Goodwill Methods

In comparing the bonus and goodwill methods, we find the rationales for the discrepancy between investment and share of net assets to be similar, but the accounting conclusions are quite different. An investment *smaller* than the computed share of net assets—Case A in the preceding illustrations—is explained in terms of the intangible benefits the new partner brings to the firm. The goodwill method recognizes these intangibles as an asset. The bonus method transfers capital from the existing partners to the new partner, to obtain these intangible benefits for the firm.

An investment *larger* than the computed share of net assets—Case B in the preceding illustrations—is explained in terms of understated or unrecorded asset values presently existing in the partnership. The goodwill method records these increases in asset values and the bonus method transfers capital from the new partner to the existing partners, to obtain an interest in these assets.

In sum, both the bonus and goodwill methods deal with the presence of unrecorded assets signaled by the amount invested by an incoming partner. The bonus method is conservative in that it avoids recording intangible assets whose presence and value are difficult to verify and which may have no realizable value upon liquidation. However, we believe that the goodwill approach has a better theoretical foundation. Because admission of a new partner creates a new legal entity, and probably a new economic entity, a new basis of asset accountability is appropriate. The transaction that occurs—investment by an outsider, the new partner—provides the basis for revaluing the assets.

Reporting Perspective

Admission to a partnership is conceptually similar to the acquisition of one corporation by another in a business combination. The bonus approach to admission of new partners is roughly comparable to the pooling-of-interests method allowed for corporate business combinations prior to 2001. The assets of the combining entities—the acquiring and acquired corporations or the existing partnership and new partner—are simply added together. No revaluation of assets occurred in a pooling; the bonus method recognizes no goodwill. The goodwill approach to admission of new partners shares some similarities with the *acquisition method* for corporate business combinations. Under both methods, the amount of investment may cause assets to be revalued.

The purchase-goodwill analogy is not perfect, however. When the acquisition method is used in corporate acquisitions, goodwill is recorded only with respect to the *acquired firm's* assets—comparable to goodwill to the new partner. Yet in partnership accounting, goodwill may be recognized on the *existing* firm's assets, a method referred to earlier as goodwill to the existing partners. But there is an important difference in circumstances. In the corporate case, the acquiring corporation usually continues to exist, while in the partnership case, the old partnership is terminated legally and a new one created. Even if both the acquiring and acquired corporations are absorbed into a new entity, we still revalue only the net assets of the acquired company.

RETIREMENT OF A PARTNER

LO5 Record the retirement of a partner.

A partnership terminates legally whenever the composition of the partnership changes through admission of a new partner or the retirement or death of an existing partner. Because accounting is concerned with the economic entity rather than the legal entity, we now consider legal dissolution of a partnership and examine two economic interpretations: the partnership may continue as an economic entity or it may cease to exist.

When a partnership terminates legally but continues the business activities by a successor partnership, the economic entity is intact. This occurs when a partner leaves the business due to retirement, resignation, death, situations of physical or mental incapacity, or the partner's personal bankruptcy.

Ownership composition of a partnership changes when a partner withdraws. Accounting for such changes depends on whether the withdrawing partner's interest is purchased by one or more remaining partners with their personal assets or by the partnership with partnership assets. Similar accounting treatment regardless of the reason for withdrawal—resignation, retirement, or death—leads us to discuss only the case of retirement.

Purchase with Personal Assets

Suppose the remaining partners, as individuals, purchase the interest of the retiring partner with their personal assets. This transaction, between the retiring partner and the remaining partners, occurs outside the partnership; the partnership need only transfer the capital balances. To illustrate, the partners in KLM Associates have capital balances and income-sharing percentages as follows:

Partner	Capital Balance	Income Share
Keenan	$ 75,000	45%
Ludlow	60,000	30%
Morris	30,000	25%
Totals	$165,000	100%

If Keenan and Ludlow buy Morris' interest for $60,000, Morris' $30,000 capital balance must be transferred to Keenan and Ludlow. If the purchasers retain their relative income-sharing ratio (45:30, or 3:2), $18,000 is credited to Keenan and $12,000 to Ludlow, as follows:

Capital—Morris	30,000	
Capital—Keenan		18,000
Capital—Ludlow		12,000
To record Morris' retirement and purchase of her interest by Keenan and Ludlow.		

This treatment is similar to procedures discussed earlier for admitting a new partner by purchase of an existing interest. In that case, however, the purchase transaction with an outside party could lead to recognition of implied goodwill on the partnership books. No outside party is involved in this retirement case; all participants are partners. Without an arm's-length transaction, the existence of credible market value to support goodwill recognition is unlikely.

Purchase with Partnership Assets

Now suppose the retiring partner receives assets directly from the partnership in settlement of that individual's capital interest.

Determination of Payment to Retiring Partner   Settlement with a retiring partner should reflect the fair value of the partner's interest, but one cannot expect this value to equal the balance in the retiring partner's capital account. The partnership agreement should prescribe an equitable approach for setting the payment to the retiring partner. When forming the partnership, the partners should agree upon a method of valuing a partner's interest in the event of resignation, retirement, or death. They could use a formula, such as "five times the partner's average share of income over the preceding three years, plus the balance in the capital account." Or they could base the value on an outside appraisal of the partnership's net assets. When the partnership agreement does not address these issues, the parties must agree on valuation procedures at the time of retirement.

Accounting for Retirement   The retiring partner's capital account must be removed from the partnership books, and any differences between the payment and the capital balance accounted for. We first assume that the retiring partner is paid with partnership cash. When the payment includes other partnership assets, those assets are adjusted to fair market value before recording their distribution to the retiring partner. Any difference between fair market value and book value is entered in the partners' capital accounts according to their income-sharing percentages.

Accounting for a partner's retirement via distribution of partnership assets is similar to accounting for admission of a new partner via direct investment in the partnership. Where payment to the retiring partner equals that partner's capital balance, the entry is as follows:

Capital—Retiring Partner	XXX	
Cash (or other assets)		XXX
To record retirement of partner.		

When the payment does not equal the capital balance, we account for the difference by either the bonus or goodwill method.

Bonus Method   Suppose the partners agree to pay Morris $55,000. Under the bonus method, the $25,000 difference between the $55,000 payment and the $30,000 balance in Morris' capital account is transferred from Keenan and Ludlow to Morris. This entry records the bonus.

Capital—Keenan	15,000	
Capital—Ludlow...	10,000	
Capital—Morris		25,000
To record retirement bonus to Morris.		

The bonus is charged against Keenan and Ludlow in their respective income shares (45:30, or 3:2). The next entry records the payment to Morris and removes Morris' capital account.

Capital—Morris	55,000	
Cash		55,000
To record retirement payment to Morris.		

When Morris receives *less* than the $30,000 capital balance, the difference is transferred from Morris to Keenan and Ludlow. For example, if Morris is paid $22,000, we record the retirement as follows:

Capital—Morris	30,000	
Capital—Keenan		4,800
Capital—Ludlow		3,200
Cash		22,000
To record Morris' retirement under the bonus method.		

Now the bonus of $8,000 (= $30,000 − $22,000) is credited to the remaining partners in their 3:2 income-sharing ratio, with $4,800 credited to Keenan and $3,200 to Ludlow.

Goodwill Method   The goodwill method calls for asset revaluations when a positive or negative difference exists between the settlement amount and the retiring partner's capital balance. A positive difference means that existing assets are written up, intangible assets—goodwill—are recorded, or both. Alternatively, a negative difference means that existing assets are written down.

Two interpretations of the goodwill method exist: the *partial goodwill approach* and the *total goodwill approach*. Either can be applied to upward or downward asset revaluations. Use of the retirement payment to justify asset revaluations is less supportable in the retirement case than in the admission case because the retirement transaction is with one of the partners and is not arm's-length. Moreover, if the retirement payment includes an inducement to buy out an unproductive or dissident partner, it may not be evidence of undervalued assets or goodwill at all.

The **partial goodwill approach** limits revaluations of assets triggered by a partner's retirement to the difference between the settlement price and the retiring partner's capital account. When the payment exceeds the capital balance, we first revalue any existing undervalued assets and attribute any remaining difference to goodwill. When the payment is less than the capital balance, we first write down overvalued assets to the extent of the difference. Asset revaluations under the partial goodwill approach are charged or credited only to the retiring partner's capital account. In contrast, the **total goodwill approach** calls for *all* asset revaluations apparent at the time of retirement to be charged or credited to the capital accounts of all partners according to their income-sharing ratio.

Illustration of Goodwill Approaches   Returning to the example of Morris' retirement from KLM Associates, assume that Morris receives $55,000, that Morris' capital account balance is $30,000, and that the partners determine that existing assets are appropriately valued. The *partial goodwill approach* calls for recognizing $25,000 of goodwill—the difference between the settlement price and the capital balance. The *total goodwill approach* follows the logic that if $25,000 of goodwill is attributable to Morris' 25 percent interest, then total goodwill of the firm is $100,000 (= $25,000/0.25) This entire amount should be recognized and allocated to the partners according to their income-sharing percentages. The *total goodwill approach* yields total partnership capital, before Morris' retirement, of $265,000, the original $165,000 capital plus $100,000 of goodwill.

Calculation of total goodwill when partners retire does *not* parallel the earlier calculation of goodwill when new partners are admitted. In the retirement case, payment to a retiring partner includes the retiree's existing capital balance plus any goodwill. If that payment is capitalized, and goodwill is calculated by subtracting existing capital from the capitalized payment, the goodwill depends directly on the retiree's capital balance. Thus, the retiree could influence the amount of goodwill simply by making investments to, or withdrawals from, the capital account. To avoid this type of manipulation, total goodwill in retirement situations is based on the goodwill attributable to the retiring partner rather than the payment made to the retiring partner.

Exhibit 14.3 illustrates application of these two variations of the goodwill method under three independent assumptions regarding Morris' retirement from KLM Associates.

EXHIBIT 14.3 Comparison of Partial and Total Goodwill Approaches: KLM Associates

Assumption	Partial Goodwill Approach		Total Goodwill Approach		
Excess payment is attributed to goodwill					
Morris' retirement payment is $55,000	Goodwill 25,000		Goodwill 100,000		
	Capital—Morris. . . .	25,000	Capital—Keenan. . .		45,000
			Capital—Ludlow . . .		30,000
			Capital—Morris. . . .		25.000
	Capital—Morris 55,000		Capital—Morris 55,000		
	Cash	55,000	Cash		55,000
Excess payment is attributed to undervalued existing assets $15,000 and to goodwill					
Morris' retirement payment is $55,000	Other assets 15,000		Other assets 15,000		
	Capital—Morris. . . .	15,000	Capital—Keenan. . .		6,750
			Capital—Ludlow . . .		4,500
			Capital – Morris. . . .		3,750
	Goodwill 10,000		Goodwill 85,000		
	Capital – Morris. . . .	10,000	Capital—Keenan. . .		38,250
			Capital—Ludlow . . .		25,500
			Capital—Morris. . . .		21,250
	Capital—Morris 55,000		Capital—Morris 55,000		
	Cash	55,000	Cash		55,000
Difference is attributed to overvalued assets $32,000					
Morris' retirement payment is $22,000	Capital—Morris 8,000		Capital—Keenan 14,400		
	Other assets	8,000	Capital—Ludlow. 9,600		
			Capital—Morris 8,000		
			Other assets		32,000
	Capital—Morris 22,000		Capital—Morris 22,000		
	Cash	22,000	Cash		22,000

Accountants should evaluate the propriety of revaluing assets and recognizing goodwill upon retirement on a case-by-case basis. The lack of an arm's-length transaction and the presence of motives for "excess" payments that do not signify the presence of asset revaluations and goodwill must be kept in mind. Accountants should insist that other evidence supporting the amounts of revaluations and goodwill recognized be provided to substantiate amounts recorded.

REVIEW 3 ● Retirement of a partner and admission of a new partner

The Abel, Baker and Cahn Agency is established and has a successful first year. Abel wishes to resign from the partnership. It is agreed that he will receive his original $100,000 investment, plus 20 percent of the partnership's net income to date. (See Review Problem 2 for information on the partners' income-sharing and capital balances.)

Required
a. Record Abel's resignation using the bonus approach.
b. Record Abel's resignation using the partial goodwill approach.
c. Record Abel's resignation using the total goodwill approach.

Subsequent to Abel's resignation, which was recorded by the total goodwill approach, the remaining partners admit Dexter as a 20 percent partner in exchange for a cash investment of $38,000. Dexter brings skills in insurance fields different from those of Baker and Cahn.

d. Record Dexter's admission using the bonus approach.
e. Record Dexter's admission using the goodwill approach.

Solutions are located after the chapter assignments.

PARTNERSHIP LIQUIDATIONS

LO6
Determine appropriate cash distributions in partnership liquidations.

Our discussion thus far addressed situations in which a partnership continued as an economic entity despite legal dissolution through retirement of a partner. When the assets of a partnership are liquidated and distributed, the partnership ceases to exist as an economic entity. Reasons for this type of termination include:

- Bankruptcy of the partnership.
- Partners agreed that the partnership would exist for a limited time or until a certain purpose was accomplished. For example, a partnership is created to buy a tract of land and to develop and sell subdivision lots; when all lots are sold and paid for, the partnership is dissolved.
- Desire to terminate an unsuccessful partnership.
- Partners wish to pursue other activities.
- Conversion to a sole proprietorship by the remaining partner.
- Reorganization as a corporation.

Accounting for partnership liquidations emphasizes the proper sequence of distributions to the partners when the liquidation extends over a period of time. The proper sequence preserves equity among the partners, particularly when the proceeds do not cover all partners' investments.

Priorities for Payments

The sequence of liquidating distributions must consider: (1) outside creditors' claims against partnership assets, and (2) partners' claims on partnership assets resulting from loans of personal assets to the partnership, investments in the partnership, and the right to share in undistributed income of the partnership.

Liquidation distributions go first to outside creditors and then to partners. When considering partners' claims, the sequence of liquidation distributions can be more complicated. The law identifies three subcategories of partners' claims: partners' loans, partners' invested capital, and partners' undistributed income. However, there is little difference between partners' invested capital and the undistributed income, closed annually to the capital accounts. Partners' drawings typically do not specify whether they are withdrawals of capital or income. There is also little practical difference between partners' loans or partners' invested capital, even though loans to the partnership are to be paid off before invested capital.

Partnership law requires partners to contribute sufficient capital to cover a **capital deficiency**—a debit balance in the capital account. If a partner with a capital deficiency made loans from personal assets to the partnership, then the **right of offset** applies the loan payable balance to the deficiency. Thus if the partner has insufficient invested capital, the loan payable to the partner, instead of being paid off first, becomes another component of invested capital and increases the capital balance. Similarly, a loan receivable from a partner decreases the capital balance.

Suppose Partner A has a capital deficiency—an amount due to the partnership—of $8,000 and also made a loan to the partnership—an amount due to Partner A—of $10,000. The *right of offset* enables Partner A to receive $2,000 of the liquidation proceeds. Similarly, if the partnership has a loan receivable from a partner—an amount due to the partnership from that partner—the right of offset calls for the loan to increase the capital deficiency.

> Although more complexity may exist in particular cases, we use the **following two-step priority sequence for distribution of cash in a partnership liquidation**:
>
> 1. Outside creditors
> 2. Partners' combined loans and capital

In partnership liquidations, therefore, the first concern is to meet obligations to outside creditors. After providing for payment of outside creditors, we focus on the proper sequence for distributing, to the partners, any remaining cash arising during the liquidation process.

Rights of Creditors

Both partnership creditors and individual partners' creditors have legal rights to available resources during a partnership liquidation. *Creditors of the partnership* must first seek payment of their claims from partnership assets. If the partnership is technically insolvent, the partnership creditors may seek payment from any partner; therefore, the partnership is technically solvent so long as any individual partner is solvent. Thus a partner can be individually liable for any and all claims against the partnership. The first priority of distribution to outside creditors is subdivided among *fully secured*, *partially secured*, and *unsecured* creditors, categories discussed in Chapter 15. For purposes of illustrating partnership liquidation, this chapter treats all outside creditors as a single category.

Creditors of an individual partner must first seek payment of their claims from the individual. If the individual is insolvent, creditors have a claim against all of that partner's assets, including the partnership interest. Such claims are not limited to the individual's insolvency. The creditor that obtains a judgment against the individual may petition the court for a *charging order*. A **charging order** specifies that any partnership payments to which the individual partner becomes entitled shall be made to the creditor. These payments include distributions of profits and withdrawals of capital. The debtor remains as a partner and the creditor does not assume any of the rights of partnership. A charging order amounts to a lien on the partner's interest until the judgment is repaid.

When a creditor's claim is so large that there is no prospect that the partnership distributions will repay it within a reasonable time, the court may order **foreclosure**, sale of the partnership interest for the benefit of the creditor. As previously discussed, a partnership interest is transferable property. The purchaser of that interest does not automatically become a partner, but does acquire the rights to distributions held by the previous partner.

When the partnership and all partners are insolvent, the relative rights of partnership creditors and individual creditors to the assets of the various parties become important. The Revised Uniform Partnership Act and recent changes in federal bankruptcy law provide that partnership creditors and individual creditors have equal standing with respect to the assets of an insolvent partner. Partnership creditors retain their priority over individual creditors with respect to *partnership assets*, but all unsecured parties have equal claim to an individual's assets.

The *right of offset*, mentioned earlier, nets loans payable to a partner against a capital deficiency. When all parties are insolvent, the provisions of the Revised Uniform Partnership Act and federal bankruptcy law may override the right of offset. This chapter assumes that the right of offset is operable.

Simple versus Installment Liquidations

Liquidation of a partnership may be carried out in several ways.

- One possibility is for all assets to be sold in a single transaction, at a going-business price.
- Another is for the assets to be sold in a single transaction at distress prices, perhaps at a bankruptcy auction.
- Or some assets might be sold individually over a period of time, as buyers for specific items are found, while other assets, such as receivables and prepayments, are collected or otherwise consumed
- Sometimes the partners seek distribution of cash as it becomes available, before all assets are liquidated.

The timing of cash distributions to partners influences the accounting procedures. In a **simple liquidation** or **lump-sum liquidation**, all assets are sold before any cash distributions to partners. When cash distributions to partners occur before the sale of assets is complete, an **installment liquidation** exists. Some assets are sold and some cash is distributed, then additional assets are sold and more cash is distributed, and so on, producing a series of payments to the partners.

Simple Liquidations

Determining the proper distribution of cash to partners of a liquidating partnership can be straightforward or complex. Even in the *simple liquidation* situation, any partners that have initial capital deficiencies or develop them during the liquidation complicate settlement.

Successful Liquidating Partnerships One views a liquidating partnership as *successful* when all partners receive a return of capital. This means that the sale of partnership assets produces either a net gain, or a net loss small enough that no capital deficiencies result. In this case, proper distribution of cash to outside creditors and to partners is easily accomplished.

Suppose that the JKL partnership has the following balance sheet immediately prior to liquidation.

JKL PARTNERSHIP			
Balance Sheet			
Cash.............................	$12,000	Liabilities.............................	$17,000
Other assets........................	48,000	Capital—J...........................	21,000
		Capital—K...........................	6,000
		Capital—L...........................	16,000
Total assets	$60,000	Total liabilities and capital	$60,000

The three partners share income in a 2:1:1 ratio. If the other assets are sold for $64,000 and the resulting $16,000 gain is allocated to the partners, the accounts show the following:

Cash.............................	$76,000	Liabilities.............................	$17,000
		Capital—J [$21,000 + (0.5 × $16,000)]....	29,000
		Capital—K [$6,000 + (0.25 × $16,000)]....	10,000
		Capital—L [$16,000 + (0.25 × $16,000)]...	20,000
Total assets	$76,000	Total liabilities and capital	$76,000

With sufficient cash to pay off the outside creditors, and no capital deficiencies, the $76,000 can be distributed in amounts equal to the liability and capital balances: $17,000 to the outside creditors, $29,000 to J, $10,000 to K, and $20,000 to L.

Unsuccessful Liquidating Partnerships   An unsuccessful liquidating partnership occurs when losses from the sale of assets result in one or more capital deficiencies. Suppose a partner has a capital deficiency, after offsetting any loans payable to that partner against the debit balance in the capital account. The partner may invest resources sufficient to remedy the deficiency such that enough assets are then available to pay the creditors and the other partners. If the deficient partner cannot invest enough to eliminate the deficiency, the deficiency is allocated to the other partners before assets are distributed.

Suppose that the pre-liquidation balance sheet of the XYZ partnership is:

XYZ PARTNERSHIP			
Balance Sheet			
Cash.............................	$ 10,000	Liabilities.............................	$ 20,000
Loan receivable—Z	8,000	Loan payable—X	6,000
Other assets........................	100,000	Loan payable—Y	4,000
		Capital—X	41,000
		Capital—Y	10,000
		Capital—Z	37,000
Total assets	$118,000	Total liabilities and capital	$118,000

The partners share income and loss in a 5:3:2 ratio, respectively. If the other assets are sold for $30,000, we allocate the $70,000 (= $100,000 − $30,000) loss on the sale as follows:

	Capital Accounts before Loss	Loss Allocation		Capital Accounts after Loss
Partner X................	$41,000	(0.5 × $70,000) =	$(35,000)	$ 6,000
Partner Y	10,000	(0.3 × $70,000) =	(21,000)	(11,000)
Partner Z................	37,000	(0.2 × $70,000) =	(14,000)	23,000
Totals	$88,000		$ 70,000	$18,000

Thus Y has a capital deficiency of $11,000, before considering the loan payable to Y of $4,000.

Since the partnership owes $4,000 to Y, $7,000 is Y's net deficiency. If Y invests $7,000, and we offset Y's loan against the capital account, the accounts appear as follows. The cash balance of $47,000 equals the original $10,000 plus the $30,000 sale proceeds and Y's $7,000 investment.

Cash.	$47,000	Liabilities.	$20,000
Loan receivable—Z	8,000	Loan payable—X	6,000
		Capital—X	6,000
		Capital—Y	0
		Capital—Z	23,000
Total assets	$55,000	Total liabilities and capital	$55,000

After offsetting the loan receivable from Z against Z's capital account, the cash is distributed as follows:

Outside creditors	$20,000
Partner X.	12,000
Partner Y	0
Partner Z ($23,000 − $8,000).	15,000
Total cash distributed.	$47,000

Now suppose that Y is personally insolvent. Because Y cannot invest any resources to remedy the deficiency, after the $4,000 owed to Y is offset against Y's capital account the accounts show the following:

Cash.	$40,000	Liabilities.	$20,000
Loan receivable—Z	8,000	Loan payable—X	6,000
		Capital—X	6,000
		Capital—Y	(7,000)
		Capital—Z	23,000
Total assets	$48,000	Total liabilities and capital	$48,000

Because Y is unable to invest further, X and Z must absorb Y's deficiency. We allocate Y's $7,000 deficiency to X and Z in the 5:2 income-sharing ratio, charging X with $5,000 and Z with $2,000, producing these new account balances:

Cash.	$40,000	Liabilities.	$20,000
Loan receivable—Z	8,000	Loan payable—X	6,000
		Capital—X	1,000
		Capital—Y	0
		Capital—Z	21,000
Total assets	$48,000	Total liabilities and capital	$48,000

Again, after offsetting the $8,000 loan receivable against Z's capital account and adding the $6,000 loan payable to X's capital account, the $40,000 cash is distributed as follows:

Outside creditors	$20,000
Partner X	7,000
Partner Y	0
Partner Z ($21,000 − $8,000)	13,000
Total cash distributed.	$40,000

In summary, **simple partnership liquidations** use the following sequence of accounting procedures:

1. Determine the gain or loss on the sale of assets.
2. Allocate the gain or loss to the partners' capital accounts according to the income-sharing ratio.
3. Subtract loans receivable from capital accounts.
4. Add loans payable to capital accounts.
5. Record any investments by partners in response to capital deficiencies.
6. Allocate any remaining deficiencies to partners with positive capital account balances. If this step produces new capital deficiencies, repeat Steps 4 through 6.
7. Distribute the cash.

Installment Liquidations

The preceding sections focused on simple liquidations characterized by sale of all assets before distributing any cash to the partners. All gains and losses were realized and allocated to the partners' capital accounts. Suppose, however, that the partners request cash distributions before all assets are sold. Because the net gain or loss on future asset sales is unknown, how to distribute cash to the partners as it becomes available is not immediately evident. Outside creditors have the first claim and they must be paid before distributing any cash to the partners. Once the creditors are paid, we need a method for determining an equitable distribution of available cash to the partners. The two general approaches—determination of *safe payments* and preparation of a *cash distribution plan*—yield the same ultimate results.

Safe Payment Approach   The **safe payment approach** determines how the cash available in a single installment is to be distributed. The calculation, repeated prior to distribution of each installment, relies on two simple and highly conservative assumptions:

1. All *remaining assets will be a total loss*: no more cash will be realized.
2. *Deficient partners will not invest any additional resources:* other partners will be charged with those deficiencies.

To illustrate the safe payment approach, assume that the ABC partnership decided to terminate business and liquidate its assets. Assets will be sold or otherwise converted into cash over a period of time, and the partners intend to distribute cash as it becomes available. The partners share income and loss in a 4:4:2 ratio and the pre-liquidation balance sheet is:

ABC PARTNERSHIP Balance Sheet			
Cash	$ 3,000	Liabilities	$ 30,000
Receivables	30,000	Loan payable—A	20,000
Inventory	47,000	Capital—A	86,000
Land	25,000	Capital—B	140,000
Building, net	72,000	Capital—C	41,000
Equipment, net	140,000		
Total assets	$317,000	Total liabilities and capital	$317,000

Suppose that half of the receivables are collected and that the entire inventory is sold for $35,000. After distributing the realized loss of $12,000 (= $47,000 − $35,000) on the inventory to the capital accounts ($4,800 to A, $4,800 to B, and $2,400 to C), the accounts show the following:

Cash ($3,000 + $15,000 + $35,000)	$ 53,000	Liabilities	$ 30,000
Receivables	15,000	Loan payable—A	20,000
Land	25,000	Capital—A	81,200
Building, net	72,000	Capital—B	135,200
Equipment, net	140,000	Capital—C	38,600
Total assets	$305,000	Total liabilities and capital	$305,000

If the partners distribute the $53,000, the outside creditors get the first $30,000. How is the remaining $23,000 to be distributed?

First, we combine the partners' loans with the partners' capital accounts. In this example, the $20,000 loan payable to A is combined with A's capital balance of $81,200. *Second,* we assume that all remaining noncash assets will result in a total loss, which is allocated by the income-sharing ratio. When additional expenses are anticipated as part of the liquidation process, these should also be included in the loss allocation. Book values of these remaining assets—receivables, land, building, and equipment—total $252,000. If these produce a total loss, the partners' capital accounts are affected as follows:

	Capital Accounts before Loss	Loss Allocation		Capital Accounts after Loss
Partner A (includes $20,000 loan) ...	$101,200	(0.4 × $252,000) =	$(100,800)	$ 400
Partner B	135,200	(0.4 × $252,000) =	(100,800)	34,400
Partner C	38,600	(0.2 × $252,000) =	(50,400)	(11,800)
Totals	$275,000		$(252,000)	$23,000

Third, we assume that Partner C cannot invest additional capital and allocate C's $11,800 deficiency equally to A and B since they have equal (4:4) income shares, leading to the following:

	Capital Accounts before Loss	Loss Allocation		Capital Accounts after Loss
Partner A	$ 400	(0.5 × 11,800) =	$(5,900)	$ (5,500)
Partner B	34,400	(0.5 × 11,800) =	(5,900)	28,500
Partner C	(11,800)		—	0
Totals	$23,000		$(11,800)	$23,000

Fourth, we assume that A cannot invest additional capital, and allocate A's entire $5,500 deficiency to B, resulting in the following capital balances:

Partner A	$ 0
Partner B	23,000
Partner C	0
Total	$23,000

The $23,000 is therefore distributed entirely to Partner B. This is called a **safe payment** because it is based on the *worst possible circumstances;* namely, that no more cash will be generated by the sale of assets and that deficient partners are unable to invest additional capital. Following distribution of $30,000 to the creditors and $23,000 to Partner B, the accounts show the following:

Receivables	$15,000	Loan payable—A	$20,000
Land	25,000	Capital—A	81,200
Building, net	72,000	Capital—B ($135,200 − $23,000)	112,200
Equipment, net...................	140,000	Capital—C	38,600
Total assets	$252,000	Total liabilities and capital	$252,000

When more cash becomes available at the next stage in the liquidation, another safe payment is computed. Suppose that $6,000 of receivables is collected, the remaining receivables are uncollectible, and the equipment is sold for $90,000. After recording these transactions, including the $96,000 cash receipt, allocation of the $9,000 (= $15,000 − $6,000) loss from uncollectible receivables and the $50,000 (= $140,000 − $90,000) loss on sale of equipment to the partners in the 4:4:2 ratio, we have the following:

Cash..........................	$ 96,000	Loan payable—A	$ 20,000
Land	25,000	Capital—A	57,600
Building, net	72,000	Capital—B	88,600
		Capital—C	26,800
Total assets	$193,000	Total liabilities and capital	$193,000

As before, assume no recovery of the remaining assets having total book value of $97,000 (= $25,000 + $72,000) and allocate this potential loss to the partners as shown below:

	Capital Accounts before Loss	Loss Allocation		Capital Accounts after Loss
Partner A (includes $20,000 loan)	$ 77,600	(0.4 × $97,000) =	$(38,800)	$38,800
Partner B	88,600	(0.4 × $97,000) =	(38,800)	49,800
Partner C	26,800	(0.2 × $97,000) =	(19,400)	7,400
Totals	$193,000		$(97,000)	$96,000

Because this loss creates no capital deficiencies, the $96,000 is distributed: $38,800 to A, $49,800 to B, and $7,400 to C. After this cash distribution, an updated balance sheet is prepared, the next batch of assets is sold, and so forth, until the liquidation is complete. The safe payment approach to cash distribution in installments is a fairly easy procedure. Its principal disadvantages are that (1) new calculations must be made for each installment distribution and (2) no information on future installment distributions is provided. The cash distribution plan, discussed next, remedies these disadvantages.

Cash Distribution Plan   As an alternative to calculating safe payment at each cash installment, we can focus on the ability of the partners to absorb future losses at the beginning of the liquidation process. The resulting **cash distribution plan** provides a sequence of cash distributions satisfying safe payment criteria. Once prepared, we use the plan to determine how to distribute available cash.

The balances of the partners' capital accounts continue to be critical for determining cash distributions according to this plan. Throughout partnership accounting, we noted that partners' shares of capital and profits are not necessarily the same. Conceptually, the cash distribution plan integrates the partners' income shares and capital balances to develop standard measures of ability to absorb future losses.

This concept can be understood with a simple example. Suppose Black and Jones share profits and losses equally, but Black's capital account has a balance of $45,000, while Jones' capital account has a balance of $30,000. Despite the fact that they are equal partners for income-sharing purposes, Black has more capital, due to Black's having either invested more or withdrawn less than Jones. Fairness suggests that when the partnership is liquidated, Black should receive $15,000 before Jones receives anything so as to equalize their capital positions. Once Black's capital is reduced to $30,000, they should share any remaining cash in accordance with their equal income-sharing ratio. Thus the following cash distribution plan applies in this simple situation:

Jones' and Black's Cash Distribution Plan

1. All liabilities are paid.
2. Black receives the next $15,000.
3. Any further distributions are divided equally between Black and Jones.

When several partners with different income-sharing percentages liquidate their partnership in installments, derivation of the cash distribution plan requires the more formal approach explained in the following display. The logic is the same as in the simple example above: cash distributions should follow a sequence designed to bring the capital accounts of the partners into proper alignment with respect to each other. This means that the partner having the *largest capital balance relative to his or her income percentage* will be the first to receive cash. In the preceding example, Black, with more capital and a 50 percent income percentage, received the first distribution. After equalizing all the imbalances in relative capital strength, subsequent distributions are made to all partners in proportion to their income percentages.

The **cash distribution plan** is prepared before liquidation begins and incorporates the following steps:

1. **Standardize** the capital relationship among the partners by dividing each capital balance by that partner's income-sharing percentage. The results provide a **measure of each partner's ability to absorb losses** that may occur during liquidation. The larger a partner's standardized capital balance, the greater is that partner's ability to absorb losses before his or her capital balance is eliminated.

2. **Equalize** the standardized capital balances in steps. Begin with the largest balance, and determine the adjustment (subtraction) needed to equalize it with the next largest. Continue this process until all standardized capital amounts are equal. These equalization adjustments signify the **incremental amounts of loss** which can be absorbed by partners with larger standardized capital balances over what can be absorbed by partners with smaller standardized balances.

3. **Convert** the equalization adjustments back into the respective partners' capital accounts by multiplying each adjustment, in the order made, by that partner's income-sharing percentage. This gives the amounts and priorities of cash distributions to the partners.

4. **Organize** the results of Step 3 into a formal cash distribution plan. Remember to provide first for payment of all outside creditors.

Cash Distribution Plan Illustration   To illustrate preparation of a more complex cash distribution plan, refer to the ABC Partnership discussed in the previous section. Prior to the liquidation process, the right-hand side of the balance sheet appeared as follows:

ABC PARTNERSHIP Liabilities and Capital	
Liabilities.	$ 30,000
Loan payable—A	20,000
Capital—A	86,000
Capital—B	140,000
Capital—C	41,000
Total	$317,000

The partners share income in a 4:4:2 ratio. As before, A's capital of $86,000 and loan of $20,000 are combined prior to proceeding, so that Partner A has total capital of $106,000.

First, standardize the capital accounts to find each partner's *loss-absorption ability* by dividing each partner's actual capital by the income-sharing percentage:

	Actual Capital	Income Percentage	Standardized Capital
Partner A	$106,000	0.4	$265,000
Partner B	140,000	0.4	350,000
Partner C	41,000	0.2	205,000

This calculation tells us that when we standardize for the different income shares, Partner B has the greatest amount of relative capital, and Partner C has the least. Partner B can absorb the greatest amount of loss, and Partner C the least amount. It is reasonable to expect that B will receive money first, then A, then finally C.

Second, equalize the standardized capital balances, starting with the largest:

	Partner A	Partner B	Partner C
Standardized capital.	$265,000	$350,000	$205,000
a. Equalize B with A	—	(85,000)	—
	$265,000	$265,000	$205,000
b. Equalize A and B with C.	(60,000)	(60,000)	—
Totals	$205,000	$205,000	$205,000

This process is repeated until the standardized capital balances of all partners are equalized. *Each adjustment represents incremental loss-absorption ability.* Thus B can absorb a partnership loss on liquidation of $85,000 more than A, and $145,000 (= $85,000 + $60,000) more than C. When the equalization process is complete, all partners have the same loss-absorption ability remaining.

Third, convert these adjustments back into actual capital balances as follows:

	Partner A	Partner B	Partner C
a.	—	$85,000 × 0.4 = $34,000	—
b.	$60,000 × 0.4 = $24,000	$60,000 × 0.4 = $24,000	—

This calculation indicates that after paying the $30,000 of liabilities, Partner B receives $34,000, and then Partners A and B each receive $24,000. These distributions equalize the standardized capital balances of each partner, and convert their actual capital balances to their 4:4:2 income-sharing ratio. Any further distributions of cash should be made according to this income-sharing ratio.

Exhibit 14.4 shows a worksheet combining the second and third steps. The left side of the worksheet shows the equalization of standardized capital to determine the partners' incremental loss-absorption abilities. The right side shows the conversion back to the partners' actual capital account balances. The amounts on the left side are multiplied by the respective income percentages to get the figures on the right side. The adjustments equalizing the standardized capital represent the predetermined sequence of cash distributions that bring the partners' capital accounts into line with the income-sharing ratio.

EXHIBIT 14.4   Worksheet for Cash Distribution Plan

	Equalization of Standardized Capital				Actual Capital Accounts and Cash Distributions		
	Partner A	Partner B	Partner C		Partner A (40%)	Partner B (40%)	Partner C (20%)
Standardized capital.	$265,000	$350,000	$205,000	Actual capital	$106,000	$140,000	$41,000
a. Equalize B with A	—	(85,000)	—	Cash paid	—	(34,000)	—
	$265,000	$265,000	$205,000		$106,000	$106,000	$41,000
b. Equalize A and B with C.	(60,000)	(60,000)	—	Cash Paid	(24,000)	(24,000)	—
	$205,000	$205,000	$205,000		$ 82,000	$ 82,000	$41,000

Fourth, organize the results into a formal cash distribution plan, such as that shown below, that indicates how to distribute any amount of cash that becomes available. Remember that distributions are *cumulative:* each distribution starts where the previous one ended.

ABC Partnership's Cash Distribution Plan		
Distribution	**Amount**	**Payment Made to**
1.	First $30,000	Creditors
2.	Next $34,000	Partner B
3.	Next $48,000	Partners A and B in equal amounts up to $24,000 each
4.	Any further amount	Partners A, B and C in 4:4:2 ratio

Equivalence of Cash Distribution Plan and Safe Payments

To illustrate the equivalence of the cash distribution plan and safe payments, recall that we calculated the proper safe payment distribution of the first two installments in the liquidation of the ABC partnership—$53,000 ($30,000 to the creditors and $23,000 to B) and $96,000 ($38,800 to A, $49,800 to B and $7,400 to C). We now use the cash distribution plan to verify the safe payment amounts.

First, consider the $53,000. The cash distribution plan calls for paying the first $30,000 to creditors and the next $34,000 to Partner B. Available cash of $53,000 permits us to complete the first distribution—to pay the creditors $30,000—and to partially complete the second distribution—to pay Partner B $23,000 of the required $34,000, as follows:

Creditors.	$30,000
Partner B	23,000
Total	$53,000

Second, we have $96,000 to distribute. We must complete the second distribution called for by the plan—to pay Partner B an additional $11,000 (for a total of $34,000)—before moving to the third distribution. According to the cash distribution plan, we perform the following steps:

1. Pay $11,000 to Partner B to complete the second distribution, leaving $85,000 (= $96,000 − $11,000) available to pay out.
2. Divide the next $48,000 equally between A and B, completing the third distribution indicated by the plan, and leaving cash of $37,000 (= $85,000 − $48,000) to be paid.
3. Divide the $37,000 among A, B, and C in the 4:4:2 income-sharing ratio, as specified by the fourth and final distribution in the plan.

Proper payment of the entire $96,000 is summarized here:

		Payment Made To		
Distribution	**Amount**	**Partner A**	**Partner B**	**Partner C**
1	$11,000	$ 0	$11,000	$ 0
2	48,000	24,000	24,000	0
3	37,000	14,800	14,800	7,400
Totals	$96,000	$38,800	$49,800	$7,400

Observe that this result is identical to that achieved by the safe payment approach.

Deviations from the Plan and Distributions in Kind

Not all available cash need be paid to the partners immediately. Cash may be retained for anticipated liquidation expenses or other purposes. Both the safe payment approach and the cash distribution plan—which is actually a *schedule of safe payments*—specifically direct the distribution of *cash* in a partnership liquidation.

Occasionally, though, temporary deviations from the safe payments determined by either approach occur. For example, suppose a specific asset is distributed to a partner in lieu of cash, and the value of the asset exceeds the amount to which that partner is entitled. Subsequent payments must be adjusted in favor of other partners until the excess is absorbed. We illustrate how distribution of a noncash asset in liquidation can temporarily disrupt scheduled safe payments by using the following hypothetical cash distribution plan.

Distribution	**Amount**	**Payment Made to**
1	First $10,000	Creditors
2	Next $16,000	Partner D
3	Next $30,000	Partners D and E in 6:3 ratio
4	Any further amount	Partners D, E and F in 6:3:1 ratio

Suppose that when considering the third distribution, E receives a truck worth $14,200 in lieu of the $10,000 cash, effectively receiving an advance on the fourth distribution. Appropriate payments to

D and F in a 6:1 ratio must be made before making the fourth distribution in the 6:3:1 ratio. The excess payment of $4,200 to E (= $14,200 − $10,000 = 3 × $1,400) is remedied in the fourth distribution by paying $8,400 to D (= 6 × $1,400) and $1,400 to F (= 1 × $1,400) before E receives any further payment. In other words, of the next $14,000 considered in the fourth distribution, E's share of $4,200 (= 0.3 × $14,000) was *prepaid* as part of the truck value. D and F are paid the remaining $9,800 (= $14,000 − $4,200) in their 6:1 ratio. When more than $9,800 in cash is available in the fourth distribution, the excess is paid in the 6:3:1 ratio.

If we are working with individually calculated safe payments, distributing the truck to E could serve to prepay some of the next safe payment to which E is otherwise entitled. If so, calculation of that next safe payment is modified to incorporate the effect just illustrated on the cash distribution plan.

When dealing with partnership liquidations occurring over an extended period of time, the accountant must ensure an equitable distribution of partnership assets. Consideration must be given to actual and prospective losses on sales of assets and to the potential inability of partners to remedy capital deficiencies. These factors are considered, either directly or indirectly, in the two procedures discussed for installment liquidations—the safe payment approach and the cash distribution plan.

REVIEW 4   ●   Termination of the partnership

After 15 years of operation, the Abel, Baker and Cahn Agency is sold to new owners, as the existing partners either wish to retire or to pursue other business interests. The partnership has $65,000 of liabilities and capital accounts as follows: Baker (40% interest) $325,000; Cahn (40% interest), $180,000; Dexter (20% interest), $65,000. The agency's assets are sold for $800,000, which will be paid in four equal installments of $200,000.

Required
Determine the distribution of each $200,000 installment.

Solutions are located after the chapter assignments.

REVIEW OF KEY CONCEPTS   •

LO 1   **Distinguish between the characteristics of a partnership and a corporation. (p. 571)** Partnerships differ from corporations with respect to the rights and liabilities of their owners, and in certain aspects of accounting, particularly the measurement of net income. **Partnership law** specifies the general conditions under which partnerships operate. Many specific details are subject to the contractual terms established by the partners in the **partnership agreement**.

LO 2   **Record the formation of a partnership. (p. 576)** In the **formation of a partnership**, assets are recorded at **fair market value**. Initial capital balances may be based on amounts actually invested or on a pre-established capital ratio. In the latter case, either the **bonus** or **goodwill** approach is applied to reconcile any difference between the amount invested and the calculated share of capital.

LO 3   **Allocate partnership income to partners. (p. 578)** Because **net income of a partnership** represents **return to the partners**, it excludes deductions for salaries or interest to partners. Salaries, bonuses, interest on capital accounts, and percentage formulas all may be used to **allocate** net income to partners. **Full implementation** of such allocations is common.

LO 4   **Record the admission of a partner. (p. 582)** **Admission of a new partner** may occur by **purchase of an existing interest** or **direct investment in the partnership**. In the case of a purchase, transfer of capital accounts is the usual accounting method. In the case of investment, either the bonus or goodwill approach is used to account for any difference between the new partner's investment and the share of capital acquired. The **bonus** and **goodwill approaches** reflect different conceptual views of the nature of admission of a new partner. The **bonus method** recognizes **transfers of capital among partners**, similar to pooling-of-interests accounting formerly used in corporate business combinations. The **goodwill method** calls for **asset revaluations**, often in the form of intangibles, similar to acquisition accounting used in business combinations today.

LO 5   **Record the retirement of a partner. (p. 588)** The interest of a **retiring partner** may be purchased with the **personal assets** of one or more of the remaining partners or with **partnership assets**. In the latter case, the **bonus** and **goodwill** approaches are used to account for any difference between the payment to the retiring partner and the amount of the retiring partner's capital account. When the **partial goodwill** approach is used in retirement, asset revaluations are recognized only in connection with the **retiring partner's interest**. Use of the **total goodwill** approach infers asset revaluations pertaining to **all partners**, based on capitalizing the excess of the payment to the retiring partner over the retiree's capital balance.

Determine the appropriate cash distributions in partnership liquidations. (p. 592) If the partnership is to be liquidated, the **rights of creditors** are based on the applicable law. Loans payable to partners and loans receivable from partners are usually combined with those partners' capital balances under the **right of offset**. When a partner has a **capital deficiency**, that partner is obligated to invest additional assets in the partnership to remedy the deficiency; if this is impossible, the deficiency is allocated to the other partners in their income-sharing ratio. A **simple** or **lump-sum liquidation** occurs when all assets are sold before any cash is distributed to the partners. In an **installment liquidation**, cash is paid to the partners before the sale of assets is complete. Either the **safe payment approach** or the **cash distribution plan** provide for equitable division of each cash distribution among the partners. Both methods address the partners' relative abilities to absorb a total loss on all remaining assets and produce the same sequence of cash payments.

LO 6

MULTIPLE CHOICE QUESTIONS ••••••••••••••••••••••••••••••••••

1. In a partnership, *mutual agency* means that
　　　　　　　　　　　　　　　　　　　　　　　　　　　　　　LO 1

　　a. one partner is designated as agent, to act for all partners.
　　b. any partner may act on behalf of the partnership.
　　c. partners have unlimited liability for partnership debts.
　　d. partners are co-owners of partnership property.

2. In computing the net income of a partnership, expenses include operating expenses and
　　　　　　　　　　　　　　　　　　　　　　　　　　　　　　LO 1

　　a. partners' loan interest and partners' salaries.
　　b. partners' loan interest but not partners' salaries.
　　c. partners' salaries but not partners' loan interest.
　　d. no items related to partners.

Use the following information to answer questions 3 and 4 below.

　　Two individuals form a partnership. Amos invests $75,000 and Bemus invests $25,000, but each is to have an equal interest in partnership capital.

3. Under the bonus method, capital credited to Amos would be
　　　　　　　　　　　　　　　　　　　　　　　　　　　　　　LO 2

　　a. $75,000.
　　b. $50,000.
　　c. $37,500.
　　d. $25,000.

4. Under the goodwill method, capital credited to Bemus would be
　　　　　　　　　　　　　　　　　　　　　　　　　　　　　　LO 2

　　a. $25,000.
　　b. $37,500.
　　c. $50,000.
　　d. $75,000.

Use the following information to answer questions 5 and 6 below.

　　The Muldoon Partnership consists of three partners, Adam, Dawn, and Lorrie. The partnership agreement provides for annual salaries of $40,000 to Dawn and $60,000 to Lorrie. Residual profits are shared in a 3:3:4 ratio. Salaries are to be fully implemented, even if partnership net income is less than total salaries.

5. Partnership net income for the year is $140,000. Adam's share of net income is
　　　　　　　　　　　　　　　　　　　　　　　　　　　　　　LO 3

　　a. $14,000.
　　b. $12,000.
　　c. $42,000.
　　d. $ 4,000.

LO 3   **6.** Partnership net income for the year is $40,000. Adam's share of net income is

     a. $ 0.
     b. $(18,000).
     c. $ 42,000.
     d. $(12,000).

Use the following information to answer questions 7–12 below.

The balance sheet of the Troy Partnership at September 30, 2013 shows:

Various assets	$500,000	Various liabilities.	$100,000
		Capital, Thomas	160,000
		Capital, Renee	120,000
		Capital, Oscar.	80,000
		Capital, Yvonne	40,000
TOTAL	$500,000	TOTAL	$500,000

Consider each question independently.

LO 4   **7.** Zeke invests $150,000 and is admitted as an equal partner. The bonus method is used. Capital accounts of the partners after Zeke's admission are

     a.   Thomas $160,000, Renee $120,000, Oscar $80,000, Yvonne $40,000, Zeke $150,000.
     b.   Thomas $172,500, Renee $132,500, Oscar $92,500, Yvonne $52,500, Zeke $100,000.
     c.   Thomas $170,000, Renee $130,000, Oscar $90,000, Yvonne $50,000, Zeke $110,000.
     d.   Thomas $210,000, Renee $170,000, Oscar $130,000, Yvonne $90,000, Zeke $150,000.

LO 4   **8.** Zeke invests $150,000 and is admitted as an equal partner. The goodwill method is used. Capital accounts of the partners after Zeke's admission are

     a.   Thomas $160,000, Renee $120,000, Oscar $80,000, Yvonne $40,000, Zeke $150,000.
     b.   Thomas $172,500, Renee $132,500, Oscar $92,500, Yvonne $52,500, Zeke $100,000.
     c.   Thomas $170,000, Renee $130,000, Oscar $90,000, Yvonne $50,000, Zeke $110,000.
     d.   Thomas $210,000, Renee $170,000, Oscar $130,000, Yvonne $90,000, Zeke $150,000.

LO 5   **9.** Renee decides to retire as a partner. The remaining partners agree to pay Renee $300,000 from partnership funds, and to use the bonus method. The capital accounts of the remaining partners after Renee's retirement are

     a.   Thomas $160,000, Oscar $80,000, Yvonne $40,000.
     b.   Thomas $60,000, Oscar $(20,000), Yvonne $(60,000).
     c.   Thomas $100,000, Oscar $20,000, Yvonne $(20,000).
     d.   Thomas $90,000, Oscar $10,000, Yvonne $0.

LO 5   **10.** Renee decides to retire as a partner. The remaining partners agree to pay Renee $300,000 from partnership funds, and to use the partial goodwill method. The capital accounts of the remaining partners after Renee's retirement are

     a.   Thomas $160,000, Oscar $80,000, Yvonne $40,000.
     b.   Thomas $400,000, Oscar $320,000, Yvonne $280,000.
     c.   Thomas $260,000, Oscar $180,000, Yvonne $140,000.
     d.   Thomas $220,000, Oscar $140,000, Yvonne $100,000.

LO 6   **11.** The Troy Partnership decides to terminate operations and liquidate. To begin the process, assets with a book value of $292,000 are sold for $184,000. Under a safe payment approach, how much will be distributed to the partners?

     a.   Thomas $62,000, Renee $22,000, Oscar $0, Yvonne $0
     b.   Thomas $92,000, Renee $92,000, Oscar $0, Yvonne $0
     c.   Thomas $87,000, Renee $47,000, Oscar $25,000, Yvonne $25,000
     d.   Thomas $46,000, Renee $46,000, Oscar $46,000, Yvonne $46,000

12. Under a cash distribution plan, how would the first $150,000 be distributed?　　　LO 6

    a.　$100,000 to creditors, $50,000 equally among the four partners
    b.　$100,000 to creditors, $50,000 equally among Thomas, Renee, and Oscar
    c.　$100,000 to creditors, $50,000 equally to Thomas and Oscar
    d.　$100,000 to creditors, $45,000 to Thomas, $5,000 to Renee

**Assignments with the ✅ in the margin are available in an online homework system.
See the Preface of the book for details.**

EXERCISES

E14.1　Partnership Formation　On June 7, 2013, Cheng and Morales, two recent graduates of Upper State　LO 2
University, formed a computer consulting firm. Cheng contributed an extensive, up-to-date computer
installation, valued at $60,000. This equipment had been financed by a bank loan; the partnership as-
sumed the current balance of $28,000. Cheng also invested $4,000 cash. Morales had recently inherited
a small office building, valued at $130,000 and encumbered by a mortgage debt of $42,000. Morales
transferred both the building and the debt to the partnership. Cheng's extensive computer skills coupled
with Morales' sales and customer service skills suggest a profitable future for the firm. They agreed to
share profits in the ratio of 40 percent for Cheng and 60 percent for Morales, in part because of Morales'
larger investment.

Required

Compute the balance in each partner's capital account on June 7, 2013, and record the partnership formation entry if the:

    a.　Partners do not specify any capital relationship.
    b.　Partners agree that each is to have a 50 percent interest in partnership capital, and they specify the
       bonus approach to recording the formation.
    c.　Partners agree that each is to have a 50 percent interest in partnership capital, and they specify the
       goodwill approach to recording the formation.

E14.2　Partnership Formation　Max, Nat and Roberta formed a partnership to operate a dry-cleaning busi-　LO 2 ✅
ness. They agreed to share initial capital and subsequent income in a 3:2:1 ratio. Each partner's contributions to the new venture are listed next.

    Max: $20,000 cash, dry-cleaning equipment worth $150,000 and the ability to keep the equipment
    in good operating condition.

    Nat: $40,000 cash and extensive experience in the dry-cleaning business.

    Roberta: $15,000 cash and a 2-year $60,000 note, payable to the firm, with 12 percent interest on the
    unpaid balance.

Required
    a.　Record the formation using the goodwill approach.
    b.　Record the formation using the bonus approach.

E14.3　Partnership Income Allocation　Whitman and Greene are partners in a real estate venture. At Janu-　LO 3
ary 1, 2014, their respective capital balances were $134,000 and $160,000. Their partnership agreement
provides that Whitman is to receive a guaranteed salary of $65,000, and that remaining profits after
the salary are to be shared equally. Partnership operations for the year 2014 resulted in a net income of
$44,000. Whitman's salary is paid in cash during the year, but there are no other withdrawals or capital
changes. Assume full implementation.

Required
    a.　Compute the balance of each partner's capital account at December 31, 2014.
    b.　Compute the balance of each partner's capital account at December 31, 2014, assuming partnership
       net income was $88,000.

E14.4　Partnership Income Allocation—Various Options　The January 1, 2014, balance sheet of the　LO 3 ✅
partnership of Linda Kingston and Jeannette Allen is shown below.

Assets		Liabilities and Capital	
Cash......................	$ 20,000	Liabilities....................	$ 60,000
Other assets................	180,000	Capital—Kingston	56,000
		Capital—Allen................	84,000
Total assets	$200,000	Total liabilities and capital	$200,000

The partnership reported revenues of $80,000 and expenses of $55,000 for 2014. Neither partner withdrew funds from the partnership during the year. Kingston invested $8,000 in the firm on June 28, 2014.

Required

Compute the December 31, 2014, capital balance for each partner under each of the following assumptions:

a. The partnership agreement does not specify how income is to be divided.
b. The partnership agreement specifies that Kingston receives 65 percent of income and Allen 35 percent.
c. The partnership agreement specifies that income is divided equally after paying each partner 10 percent interest on her weighted average capital balance.
d. The partnership agreement specifies that Kingston and Allen receive salaries of $12,000 and $8,000, respectively, and that each partner receives 5 percent interest on her capital balance at the beginning of the year. Salary and interest allocations are to be fully implemented. Any remaining income is to be divided equally.

LO 3 **E14.5** **Multiple Income Allocation Provisions** Partners Johnson, Kane and Lehman agreed to the following provisions for sharing profit or loss from their partnership:

1. Johnson, Kane and Lehman receive salaries of $42,000, $35,000, and $50,000, respectively.
2. Interest on average capital investment is credited at the rate of 10 percent per annum.
3. Residual profit or loss is shared in the ratio 4:5:1.
4. All provisions are to be fully implemented.

The average capital investments for the year are:

Johnson	$186,000
Kane..	275,000
Lehman...	83,000

Required

a. Prepare a schedule to allocate partnership income of $217,000.
b. Repeat part *a* for income of $112,000.
c. Suppose Johnson, as managing partner, is entitled to a bonus of 15 percent of profit after the bonus but before other allocation provisions. Assume partnership income is $217,000. Without re-doing the entire schedule, calculate the effect of the bonus on the net allocation to Johnson and the other partners.

LO 4 **E14.6** **Admission of New Partner** Carson and Blake owned a successful insurance agency for many years. Currently their respective capital balances are $200,000 and $160,000; they share profits and losses in the ratio of 6:4. Manning, a famous pro athlete who recently retired, has expressed an interest in joining the agency. Carson and Blake believe that Manning's involvement would substantially boost sales and profits. They offer Manning a 20 percent interest in both capital and profits and losses without any requirement of an investment by Manning.

Required

a. Compute the balances in the capital accounts of Carson, Blake, and Manning after Manning's admission, assuming that the parties agree to record the admission by the bonus method.
b. Compute the balances in the capital accounts of Carson, Blake, and Manning after Manning's admission, assuming that the parties agree to record the admission by the goodwill method.

LO 4 **E14.7** **Admission of New Partner** Blackman and Coulter are highly successful criminal attorneys, practicing law in a partnership. Each earns approximately $600,000 annually, sharing profits equally. Since the firm has minimal capital needs, they withdraw most of their earnings. Their capital balances currently stand at $30,000 for Blackman and $40,000 for Coulter.

Xavier is a young staff attorney who has been with the firm for eight years. Xavier's research skills and case strategy plans have contributed significantly to the firm's success, but Xavier lacks the courtroom skills to be successful as a criminal trial attorney. Xavier currently receives an annual salary of $150,000.

Blackman and Coulter both anticipate retiring in ten years, at which point the firm will disband. To induce Xavier to remain with the firm over the next ten years, Blackman and Coulter propose to admit Xavier as an equal partner, though Xavier's role in the firm will not change. Blackman and Coulter will admit Xavier in exchange for a payment equal to Xavier's increased earnings (which is equal to Blackman and Coulter's decreased earnings), discounted at 20 percent.

Required

Assuming continuation of current earnings levels, how much must Xavier pay to be admitted to the partnership?

E14.8 Admission of New Partner   Following is the condensed balance sheet of Martinez, O'Neill and   LO 4 ✓
Clemens, partners who share profits or losses in the ratio of 2:3:5.

Cash.........................	$ 48,000	Liabilities......................	$200,000
Other assets..................	752,000	Capital—Martinez..............	108,000
		Capital—O'Neill	176,000
		Capital—Clemens	316,000
Total assets	$800,000	Total liabilities and capital	$800,000

Required

a. Assume that the partnership's assets and liabilities are fairly valued as shown. The partners wish to admit Jeter as a partner with a 30 percent interest in capital, profits, and losses. They require Jeter to invest an amount such that bonus or goodwill adjustments are not needed. How much should Jeter invest for the 30 percent share?

b. Assume instead that the existing partners, all of whom contemplate retirement relatively soon, decide to sell Jeter 30 percent of their respective partnership interests for a total payment of $210,000. This payment will be made proportionately to Martinez, O'Neill, and Clemens. The partners agree that implied goodwill is to be recorded prior to the transaction with Jeter. What are the capital balances of the four partners after the transaction with Jeter?

E14.9 Post-Retirement Capital Balances   On April 30, 2014, the partnership of ABC Associates had the   LO 5
following balance sheet:

Total assets, at cost...	$500,000
Loan payable to Atkins..	$195,000
Capital—Atkins (20% interest in profits)	60,000
Capital—Bodkins (30%)...	110,000
Capital—Calkins (50%)	135,000
Total liabilities and capital	$500,000

Atkins is retiring as of April 30, 2014. The partnership's assets have been appraised at $650,000, and the partnership records the appraised value. The partnership agrees to pay $150,000 for Atkins's capital interest. Atkins's loan will remain, and will continue to be paid, with interest, over the next several years. No goodwill is to be recorded in connection with Atkins's retirement.

Required

Calculate the capital balances of Bodkins and Calkins immediately after recording the retirement of Atkins.

E14.10 Retirement: Bonus and Goodwill Calculations   Ellery Stevens, senior partner in a rapidly grow-   LO 5
ing local CPA firm, has decided to retire. His share in the firm's profits and losses is 30 percent and his capital account, before considering drawings of $50,000, has a balance of $240,000. Total capital of the firm is $780,000, before considering total drawings of $180,000. Under the partnership agreement, Stevens will receive $250,000 upon retirement.

Required

a. Calculate the bonus to Stevens and the total capital of the firm after Stevens' retirement.
b. What balance sheet accounts will change after Stevens' retirement, and by what amounts, if the partial goodwill approach is used?
c. If the total goodwill method is used, calculate the amount of goodwill recognized and the total capital of the firm after Stevens' retirement.

LO 5   **E14.11 Retirement Journal Entries: Various Assumptions**   Baxter is planning to retire from the partnership of Baxter, Helman, and Caines. The partners' income-sharing ratio is 2:1:1. Helman and Caines will continue as a partnership, sharing profits and losses equally. The partners are considering various ways to pay Baxter $90,000, which is the fair market value of her interest in the business. Prior to retirement, Baxter's capital account balance is $70,000.

Required

Prepare the journal entry to record Baxter's retirement on the partnership books under each of the following assumptions:

a. Helman and Caines each pay Baxter $45,000 from personal funds.
b. Partnership cash is used to pay Baxter. The bonus method is followed.
c. Partnership cash is used to pay Baxter. The total goodwill approach is followed.
d. Partnership cash is used to pay Baxter. The partial goodwill approach is followed.
e. Helman and Caines each pay Baxter $10,000 from personal funds; the rest is paid with partnership cash.

LO 6   **E14.12 Lump-Sum Liquidation**   Three university students, Cho, Kenney, and Martinez, operated a successful business, renting furniture and appliances to students residing in dormitories and off-campus apartments. The three are now graduating and wish to sell the business before beginning their respective careers. They shared profits in a 7:5:4 ratio. The partnership's current balance sheet is as follows:

Cash	$ 7,000	Liabilities	$ 52,000
Receivables	15,000	Capital—Cho	40,000
Rental equipment, net	120,000	Capital—Kenney	5,600
		Capital—Martinez	44,400
Total assets	$142,000	Total liabilities and capital	$142,000

Another student group, organized as a corporation, wants to buy the business. Their offer of $95,000 for the equipment and $8,000 for the receivables is accepted. After receipt of the $103,000, the liabilities are paid and the partnership is liquidated.

Required

How much does each partner receive?

LO 6   **E14.13 Rights of Creditors**   The following are data for the AB Partnership and for A and B as individuals. Assume that A and B are equal partners.

AB Partnership	Case 1	Case 2
Assets	$48,000	$31,000
Liabilities	42,000	51,000
Capital—A	3,000	(8,000)
Capital—B	3,000	(12,000)
Partner A		
Assets	10,000	30,000
Liabilities	17,000	17,000
Partner B		
Assets	50,000	15,000
Liabilities	9,000	16,000

Required

For each case, indicate how the assets of the partnership and the assets of each partner are applied if creditor claims are satisfied as fully as possible.

E14.14 Safe Payment Calculation   Partners Rane, Snow, and Hale share profits and losses in the ratio of   LO 6
5:3:2, respectively. The partners vote to dissolve the partnership when its assets, liabilities, and capital are
as follows:

Cash......................	$ 10,000	Liabilities.....................	$ 90,000
Other assets.................	430,000	Capital—Rane	100,000
		Capital—Snow	170,000
		Capital—Hale.................	80,000
Total assets	$440,000	Total liabilities and capital	$440,000

The partnership will be liquidated over an extended period of time. As cash becomes available, it will
be distributed to the partners. The first sale of noncash assets having a book value of $190,000 realizes
$130,000.

Required

How much cash should be distributed to each partner after this sale?

E14.15 Cash Distribution Plan   At the time they decided to liquidate their partnership, Whitehead, Ellis   LO 6 ✓
and Riley had capital balances of $75,000, $60,000 and $100,000, respectively. Liabilities were $48,000
and the balance sheet showed a note receivable from Riley in the amount of $40,000. The partners share
income in a 5:3:2 ratio.

Required

Prepare a schedule showing how cash is to be distributed as it becomes available during the liquidation
process.

PROBLEMS ••

P14.1   Partnership Formation: Working Backward   Brian and two other friends from college decide to   LO 2
form a CPA firm specializing in forensic accounting. The three had worked for different Big Four firms
for several years and accumulated a wealth of experience as well as a variety of other assets the new firm
could use. After agreeing on a 2:3:1 capital and income ratio, the three listed what they intend to contribute to the new firm:

Brian: Cash ($12,000), office and computer equipment ($18,000), knowledge of potential client base.
Jennifer: Cash ($15,000), research materials ($11,000), specialized forensic skills
Eric: Note payable to the firm ($10,000), extensive computer audit experience

Pro-forma capital balances under three formation scenarios appear below.

	Scenario #1	Scenario #2	Scenario #3
Capital—Brian	$30,000	$22,000	$36,000
Capital—Jennifer	45,000	33,000	54,000
Capital—Eric	15,000	11,000	18,000

Required

a.   In each scenario, identify the flow of bonuses or the amount and beneficiaries of goodwill recorded.
b.   Discuss the relative advisability of the three scenarios, paying particular attention to their effects on
the new firm's future profitability and leverage (or credit-worthiness).

P14.2   Partnership Formation   Augustus Berrini, the sole proprietor of the Berrini Company, is planning to   LO 2
expand the company and establish a partnership with Fiedler and Wade. The partners plan to share profits
and losses as follows: Berrini, 50 percent; Fiedler, 25 percent; Wade 25 percent. They also agree that the
beginning capital balances of the partnership will reflect this same relationship.
    Berrini asked Fiedler to join the partnership because his many business contacts are expected to be
valuable during the expansion. Fiedler is also contributing $28,000. Wade is contributing $11,000 and a
block of marketable securities which the partnership expects to liquidate as needed during the expansion.
The securities, which cost Wade $42,000, are currently worth $57,500.

Berrini's investment in the partnership is the Berrini Company. The balance sheet for the Berrini Company appears below. He plans to pay off the notes with his personal assets. The other partners have agreed that the partnership will assume the accounts payable and the mortgage. The three partners agree that the inventory is worth $85,000; the equipment is worth half its original cost; the building and land are worth $65,000 and $25,000, respectively; and the allowance established for doubtful accounts is correct.

BERRINI COMPANY Balance Sheet Date of Partnership Formation			
Assets		**Liabilities and owner's equity**	
Cash.	$ 7,000	Accounts payable.	$ 53,000
Accounts receivable (net).	48,000	Notes payable	7,000
Inventory.	72,000	Mortgage payable	55,000
Equipment (net of $12,000		Total liabilities.	115,000
accumulated depreciation).	18,000	Owner's equity	
Building (net of $20,000		Capital, Berrini	85,000
accumulated depreciation).	40,000		
Land	15,000		
Total assets	$200,000	Total liabilities and owner's equity. . . .	$200,000

Required

Prepare the balance sheet of the partnership on the date of formation under each of the following independent assumptions:

a. The partners agree to follow the bonus approach to record the formation.
b. The partners agree to follow the goodwill approach to record the formation.

LO 3 **P14.3** **Partners' Disputes over Income Allocation** Nathan, Daniel and Kaitlyn generally get along well as business associates in their consulting firm. Recently, however, the income-sharing provisions of their partnership agreement have become contentious. These provisions require partnership net income to be shared as follows:

	Salary	Interest on Capital	% of Remainder
Nathan	$90,000	4%	20%
Daniel	75,000	4%	30%
Kaitlyn.	0	20%	50%

Note: Salary and interest provisions are to be implemented in that order only to the extent of the available income.

Kaitlyn was originally to have been a silent partner, an investor without active participation in the business. Daniel, on the other hand, was to have had a large voice in business decisions as well as a modest capital investment. As it turns out, Daniel has been shunted to the side whereas Kaitlyn appears to be running the business much of the time. Nathan spends a lot of time on practice development and generates few chargeable hours.

In the last three years, partnership income and partners' average capital balances were:

Partnership Net Income			Average Capital Balances		
2013	**2012**	**2011**	**Nathan**	**Daniel**	**Kaitlyn**
$140,000	$205,400	$250,000	$40,000	$70,000	$180,000

Required

a. Explain why the income-sharing provisions have become contentious.
b. Would a provision allowing Kaitlyn a 25 percent bonus of net income before any allocations satisfy her? What would Daniel's reaction be?
c. Suppose the partners adopt the provision in part *b* for 2014 except that the bonus is based on 25 percent of net income before allocations but after the bonus. Net income for 2014 amounts to $220,000

and average capital balances are unchanged. Compare the 2014 income allocations with and without the bonus. Comment on the income redistribution you observe.

P14.4 **Income Allocation; Schedule of Changes in Capital Accounts**   The December 31, 2013 bal-   LO 3
ance sheet for the Greystone Partnership appears below:

GREYSTONE PARTNERSHIP Balance Sheet December 31, 2013			
Assets		**Liabilities and Capital**	
Cash..........................	$ 20,000	Accounts payable................	$120,000
Accounts receivable.............	100,000	Long-term liabilities	200,000
Equipment	170,000	Capital—Burstein................	110,000
Buildings......................	250,000	Capital—Reeves.................	160,000
Land	60,000	Capital—Sills	10,000
Total assets	$600,000	Total liabilities and capital	$600,000

Additional information:
1.   The partners agreed that each will earn 6 percent interest on his or her beginning-of-year capital balance.
2.   Salaries are as follows: Burstein, $30,000; Reeves, $40,000; and Sills, $20,000.
3.   Sills is to receive a bonus of 10 percent of income before salaries, bonus, and interest to partners.
4.   Any income remaining after salaries, bonus, and interest to partners is to be allocated equally.
5.   During 2013, Burstein withdrew $6,600 from the firm. All other allocations to Burstein for salary, interest, and profit were retained in the business.
6.   Reeves withdrew all but $20,000 of 2013 allocations.
7.   In 2013 Sills withdrew $30,000 and all salary, bonus, interest, and profit allocations.
8.   Total capital investment at the beginning of the year was $240,000.
9.   Income for 2013 after deducting interest to partners but before deductions for salaries and bonus was $200,000.

Required
a.   Calculate the capital balances at January 1, 2013.
b.   Prepare a schedule of changes in capital accounts for the partners in the Greystone Partnership for 2013.

P14.5 **Financial Statement Effects of Partnership Expansion**   Graham and Hyde currently share profits   LO 4
and losses in a 3:1 ratio and are considering admitting Ingalls as a new partner with a 20 percent interest in capital and profits and losses. The different approaches to accounting for partnership expansion affect the financial statements of the new partnership. Condensed balance sheets for the Graham/Hyde partnership and the Graham/Hyde/Ingalls partnership under alternative admission approaches appear below.

	G/H	G/H/I #1	G/H/I #2	G/H/I #3	G/H/I #4
Cash and receivables.........	$ 37,000	$ 37,000	$ 77,000	$ 77,000	$ 49,000
Other assets...............	142,000	142,000	142,000	222,000	150,000
Total assets	$179,000	$179,000	$219,000	$299,000	$199,000
Accounts payable............	$ 48,000	$ 48,000	$ 48,000	$ 48,000	$ 48,000
Long-term debt	51,000	51,000	51,000	51,000	51,000
Capital—Graham	50,000	40,000	62,000	110,000	50,000
Capital—Hyde	30,000	24,000	34,000	50,000	30,000
Capital—Ingalls	—	16,000	24,000	40,000	20,000
Total liabilities and capital	$179,000	$179,000	$219,000	$299,000	$199,000

Required

a.   As a user of financial statements in credit-granting or investment decisions, which of the above balance sheets look strongest? Discuss any red flags that whet your appetite for additional information.

b.   Explain whether Ingalls will likely prefer a particular alternative. Which one?

c.   Reconstruct the journal entries recording the four alternatives.

LO 3, 4, 6   **P14.6   Investment Club: Admission and Income Allocation**   The Lucky Investment Club is a partnership of about 20 individuals who jointly invest in securities as a hobby. All are equal partners. There are occasional admissions of new partners who join the Club and occasional departures from the Club as individuals relocate or lose interest in Club activity. Thus the exact number of partners fluctuates somewhat over time. The Club maintains its books on a cost basis to facilitate its income tax reporting. Since it has no public reporting requirements, it chooses not to follow GAAP for marketable securities. However, upon admission, a new partner must invest an amount equal to a proportionate share of the fair market value of the Club's assets after the admission. Neither goodwill nor bonus is recorded upon admission of a new partner.

On January 1, 2014, the books of the Lucky Investment Club showed cash of $3,200 and a portfolio of securities with a cost of $78,300 and a fair market value of $122,800. The Club has no liabilities. The capital accounts of the 18 partners aggregate $81,500. No new partners have been admitted since February 2011.

On January 2, 2014, Grant and Lee are admitted to the Club, each investing cash equal to a 1/18 share of the Club's assets at fair market value, prior to their investment of new cash. During 2014, the Club earned interest and dividends of $4,200. Each of the 20 partners invested $500 in new funds. Two securities were sold; each had been bought in 2012:

Security	Cost	Fair Market Value January 1, 2014	Selling Price
A.	$ 3,000	$ 6,600	$ 8,600
B.	11,000	9,200	8,200
Totals	$14,000	$15,800	$16,800

$40,000 was invested in new securities during 2014. The fair market value of the portfolio at December 31, 2014 was $166,000.

Required

a.   Why must new partners joining the Club invest based on the fair market value of the portfolio rather than the recorded book value?

b.   How much must Grant and Lee each invest?

c.   Allocate the Club's 2014 income among Grant, Lee, and the other 18 partners as a group.

d.   In January 2015, a major stock market rally increases the portfolio value to $228,000. Club members vote to sell the entire portfolio and disband the Club. How much will Grant, Lee, and the other 18 partners as a group each receive?

LO 4   **P14.7   Admission – Various Cases**   Given below are account balances for the partnership of Simpson and Scott before the admission of a new partner, Lansing. Each case presents account balances of the partnership immediately after Lansing's admission. The cases are independent of each other.

Balance Sheet Accounts	Balances before Lansing's Admission	Balances after Lansing's Admission				
		Case 1	Case 2	Case 3	Case 4	Case 5
Cash.............	$10,000	$ 10,000	$10,000	$20,000	$ 10,000	$30,000
Other assets........	80,000	130,000	80,000	80,000	170,000	80,000
Goodwill..........	10,000	10,000	10,000	10,000	30,000	20,000
Liabilities..........	(30,000)	(30,000)	(30,000)	(30,000)	(80,000)	(30,000)
Capital—Simpson ...	(35,000)	(42,500)	(35,000)	(30,000)	(35,000)	(40,000)
Capital—Scott	(35,000)	(42,500)	—	(30,000)	(35,000)	(40,000)
Capital—Lansing	—	(35,000)	(35,000)	(20,000)	(60,000)	(20,000)

Required

For each independent case, answer the following questions. Show supporting calculations.

a. What method of accounting was used to record the admission (bonus, goodwill, neither)?
b. How much did Lansing invest in the partnership?
c. What percentage of ownership does Lansing have in the new partnership?

P14.8 Retirement of Two Partners   Thirty years ago, five mechanics formed a partnership and established   LO 5
an automobile repair shop. Two of the partners, Decker and Groth, are now retiring. The other three partners, Farmer, Wang, and Lux, are continuing the partnership. The original agreement called for an equal
division of income. The remaining partners plan to continue this arrangement. The following balance
sheet is prepared for the partnership as of the retirement date:

Cash.	$130,000	Accounts payable.	$180,000
Accounts receivable.	160,000	Loan payable	80,000
Inventory of parts	80,000	Capital—Decker.	100,000
Equipment, net.	180,000	Capital—Groth	80,000
Building, net	60,000	Capital—Farmer.	140,000
Land	50,000	Capital—Wang.	15,000
		Capital—Lux.	65,000
Total assets	$660,000	Total liabilities and capital	$660,000

All partners agreed that Decker should receive $125,000 for his interest in the business and Groth should
receive $100,000. Farmer proposed the bonus method for recording the retirements. Wang objects to this
method and suggests the partial goodwill approach.

Required

a. Prepare the journal entry to record the retirements under the bonus method.
b. Prepare the journal entry to record the retirements under the partial goodwill approach.
c. Why does Wang object to the bonus method of accounting?
d. Regardless of the accounting method employed, what immediate problem for the business can you
identify at the time of retirement? Propose a solution to this problem.

P14.9 Retirement – Various Cases   Given below are account balances for the partnership of Flint, Yancy,   LO 5
and Goldsmith before the retirement of Goldsmith. Each case presents account balances of the Flint and
Yancy partnership immediately after Goldsmith's retirement. The cases are independent of each other. In
Case 4, no bonus was recorded.

Balance Sheet Accounts	Balances before Goldsmith's Retirement	Balances after Goldsmith's Retirement				
		Case 1	Case 2	Case 3	Case 4	Case 5
Cash.	$ 50,000	$ 20,000	$ 0	$ 50,000	$ 50,000	$ 0
Other assets.	130,000	130,000	130,000	130,000	100,000	130,000
Goodwill	10,000	10,000	20,000	10,000	10,000	40,000
Liabilities.	(70,000)	(70,000)	(70,000)	(70,000)	(70,000)	(70,000)
Capital—Flint	(40,000)	(45,000)	(40,000)	(80,000)	(45,000)	(50,000)
Capital—Yancy.	(40,000)	(45,000)	(40,000)	(40,000)	(45,000)	(50,000)
Capital—Goldsmith	(40,000)	0	0	0	0	0

Required

For each independent case, answer the following questions.
a. What method of accounting was used to record the retirement (bonus, goodwill, neither)?
b. How much did Goldsmith receive upon retirement?

P14.10 Financial Statement Effects of Retirement/Admission   Moore, Mills, Sinclair & Co. (MMS)   LO 4, 5
is a rapidly-growing regional CPA firm. It actively recruits new staff accountants at major colleges and
universities and aggressively pursues exceptional partners and near-partners at other CPA firms. Concur-

rently, MMS's founders have been retiring. Moore left last year and Mills and Sinclair are contemplating retiring soon. Prior to retirement of Mills and Sinclair, who each have a 20 percent share in profits and losses, the firm's condensed balance sheet appears as follows:

MOORE, MILLS, SINCLAIR & CO.
Balance Sheet
December 31, 2013

Cash and cash equivalents	$ 178,000
Accounts receivable—clients	430,000
Notes receivable—Sinclair	100,000
Prepayments	60,000
Fixed assets, net	500,000
Goodwill, net	800,000
Total assets	$2,068,000
Trade payables	$47,000
Accrued liabilities	209,000
Notes payable—1st National Bank	600,000
Notes payable—Moore	200,000
Capital—Mills	270,000
Capital—Sinclair	195,000
Capital—Other Partners	547,000
Total liabilities and capital	$2,068,000

After some discussion, the firm agrees to pay Mills $350,000 upon retirement, intending to borrow the cash to do so from 1st National Bank. Shortly thereafter, Luh, a highly competent and entrepreneurial information systems specialist, is offered a 10 percent interest in capital and profits for a $50,000 cash investment.

Required

a. Discuss the ways in which the methods of accounting for the retirement could weaken the above balance sheet, and illustrate with calculations.
b. Suppose Mills' retirement is accounted for by the total goodwill method. After Mills' retirement is recorded by the total goodwill approach, prepare pro-forma balance sheets for MMS that reflect Luh's admission under the two alternative admission methods.
c. Briefly describe the principal differences between the two balance sheets in part *b*. Which seems to portray the healthier firm? Why?

LO 4, 6 **P14.11 Partnership Admission and Liquidation** Reitmyer, Simon, and Trybus are partners in a real estate partnership. The partnership's balance sheet shows:

Cash	$ 20,000	Mortgages payable	$300,000
Rental properties, net	700,000	Capital, Reitmyer (40%)	200,000
		Capital, Simon (40%)	150,000
		Capital, Trybus (20%)	70,000
Total assets	$720,000	Total liabilities and capital	$720,000

The partners are contemplating terminating their business, as they no longer wish to spend the time involved in managing the properties. Further, several properties are in need of renovation. They believe that the properties could be sold on a piecemeal basis for a total of $1,200,000. After paying off the mortgage debt, the remaining cash would be distributed to the partners.

Don and Mary Usher have approached the partnership with a proposal. Don is experienced at property maintenance and renovation, and Mary is experienced in property management. They are interested in getting into the real estate rental business. Both are currently employed, but they have little capital to invest. They offer $50,000 to be admitted as a 40 percent partner; the three existing partners would continue as partners, but would be relieved of all operating responsibilities. Each year for the next ten years, each old partner would receive a "salary" of $40,000 out of partnership earnings, though they would not be expected to render any services.

Because they would retain a collective 60 percent ownership, they could block any actions by Don and Mary that they deemed inadvisable. Their interests would be further protected by a security interest in the rental properties, though it would be subordinated to any present and future mortgage debt. At the end of the ten years, their remaining partnership interests would be transferred to the Ushers for $1,000 each. The Ushers could accelerate the process at any time by prepaying the future payments, at a 10 percent discount rate. The existing partners could terminate the agreement at any time and buy out the Ushers for a price of $50,000 times the number of years the agreement had been in effect. However, if the existing partners did not receive their specified salaries for two years, they could terminate the agreement without any payment due the Ushers.

Required

For each of the following five scenarios, determine the amount to be received, in present value terms, by each partner. Use a 10 percent discount rate.

a. Ushers' offer is not accepted. The properties are sold and the partnership is liquidated.
b. Ushers' offer is accepted and the agreement is completely fulfilled over the ten-year time span.
c. Ushers' offer is accepted. Despite their efforts, the Ushers are not able to turn the properties into money-makers, and have defaulted on the payments due the old partners for years 3 and 4. At the end of year 4, the old partners invoke their termination rights. The mortgage debt has grown to $400,000, as money was borrowed to finance renovations. It is estimated that the sales value of the various properties has fallen to $950,000.
d. Ushers' offer is accepted, and the Ushers have been quite successful in making the properties profitable. All payments to the old partners have been made as scheduled. However, tensions between the Ushers and the prior partners have escalated, due to different approaches to property management. By the end of year 5, the old partners are ready to invoke their termination rights, pay the Ushers the required buyout, and liquidate the partnership. The properties have an expected resale value of $2,000,000, and mortgage debt stands at $650,000. However, before the old partners act, the Ushers borrow money and exercise their prepayment rights.
e. Same as part d above, except that the Ushers do not exercise their prepayment rights.

P14.12 Partnership Liquidation—Safe Payments   Several years ago, Ann Dennis, Jill Edwards, Lee Lacy, and Sarah Ingram formed a partnership to operate the Deli Sisters Cafe. Rerouting of bus lines caused declines in patronage to the extent that the partners have agreed to dissolve the partnership and liquidate the assets. The November 2, 2014, balance sheet of the Deli Sisters Cafe and other data appear below. The partnership agreement did not specify how profits and losses were to be shared.

LO 6

DELI SISTERS CAFE Balance Sheet November 2, 2014			
Cash.	$ 30,000	Liabilities.	$ 45,000
Supplies	21,000	Loan—Ingram.	15,000
Equipment	80,000	Capital—Dennis	36,000
Fixtures.	27,000	Capital—Edwards.	23,000
		Capital—Lacy.	6,000
		Capital—Ingram	33,000
Total assets	$158,000	Total liabilities and capital	$158,000

Additional information:

1. During November, sold half of the fixtures for $9,000. Sold equipment with a book value of $20,000 for $12,000.
2. During December, paid all outside creditors. A neighboring restaurant bought Deli Sisters Cafe's supplies at 80 percent of cost. Sold the remaining fixtures for $6,000.
3. During January, sold equipment with a book value of $12,000 for $7,000.

Required

Following the safe payment approach, specify how cash is to be distributed at the end of November, December, and January.

LO 6 **P14.13 Partnership Liquidation – Safe Payments** Partners Dodge, Edsel, Ford and Harley share income in a ratio of 8:5:4:3, respectively. On January 1, 2014, they decide to terminate operations and begin a process of liquidation. The partnership's trial balance on that date shows the following:

	Debit	Credit
Cash.	$ 32,000	
Accounts receivable.	87,000	
Loan receivable—Edsel	25,000	
Inventory.	55,000	
Land	30,000	
Equipment	112,000	
Truck	37,000	
Bank loan payable		$ 75,000
Accounts payable.		48,000
Loan payable—Dodge		80,000
Capital—Dodge		71,000
Capital—Edsel		42,000
Capital—Ford.		53,000
Capital—Harley		9,000
Totals	$378,000	$378,000

To maximize proceeds, assets were sold over a three-month period. At the end of each month, available cash, less an amount retained to cover estimated future expenses, was distributed to the partners. The liquidation proceeded as follows:

January 2014:
1. Returned inventory costing $10,000 to the supplier, who granted a credit of $8,500 against the open accounts payable.
2. Collected $45,000 of the accounts receivable; collection of the remainder is uncertain.
3. Sold the remaining inventory to a competitor for $30,000.
4. Sold the equipment for $80,000.
5. Paid liquidation expenses of $5,500.
6. Paid the bank loan and the remaining accounts payable in full.
7. Retained $20,000 of cash for potential future obligations and liquidation expenses.

February 2014:
1. Collected $15,000 of the accounts receivable, and the remainder is determined to be uncollectible.
2. Transferred the truck to Dodge in exchange for a $30,000 reduction in the partnership's loan obligation to Dodge.
3. Paid liquidation expenses of $3,000.
4. Retained $10,000 of cash for potential future obligations and liquidation expenses.

March 2014:
1. Sold the land for $125,000.
2. Paid liquidation expenses of $8,000.
3. Distributed all remaining cash.

Required

Prepare a schedule to compute the safe installment payments to the partners at the end of January, February, and March 2014.

LO 3, 6 **P14.14 Close Books and Prepare Cash Distribution Plan** Arnold, Bell and Crane agree to liquidate their partnership as soon as possible. The partnership agreement calls for salaries of $30,000 and $40,000 for Arnold and Bell, respectively; any remaining profit or loss is divided in a 2:3:5 ratio. The preclosing trial balance for the partnership at July 31, 2014, the end of the firm's fiscal year, is:

Account	Debit	Credit
Cash	$ 84,500	
Other assets	260,000	
Liabilities		$110,000
Loan payable—Crane		30,000
Capital—Arnold		70,000
Capital—Bell		65,000
Capital—Crane		45,000
Sales		553,000
Operating expenses	438,000	
Drawings—Arnold	50,000	
Drawings—Bell	25,500	
Drawings—Crane	15,000	
Totals	$873,000	$873,000

Required

a. Prepare a schedule showing the balances in the capital accounts prior to liquidation.

b. Prepare a cash distribution plan for the liquidation.

c. Compute the amount that must be realized from the other assets to liquidate the liabilities and drive all capital accounts to zero.

P14.15 Analysis of Liquidation Scenario Partners Green and Blue have operated a coin laundry business LO 6 in a strip shopping center for several years. Their income-sharing ratio is 3:2. The business was generating decent operating cash flow but in the last 18 months, cash flow declined precipitously. On alternate days each partner empties the coins from the laundromat's machines and deposits them in the bank.

Green is experiencing personal financial problems relating to a messy divorce and investments that went "in the tank." She is urging Blue to sell out and liquidate their partnership. The following trial balance is prepared by the partners' accountant.

	Dr (Cr)
Cash	$2,300
Supplies and prepayments	900
Equipment	42,000
Accumulated depreciation	(17,000)
Accounts payable	(1,350)
Loan payable—Blue	(11,000)
Sales	(25,000)
Operating expenses	13,000
Depreciation expense	6,000
Capital—Green	(5,000)
Capital—Blue	(4,850)
Totals	$ 0

In addition, the partnership has a noncancellable lease (remaining term: 2 years) on the building where the laundromat is located, classified as an operating lease under *ASC Topic 840*. The monthly payments of $500 are based on an implicit annual interest rate of 9 percent and are consistently made on time. Although the lessor would like to rent the space to a pizza shop which would bring more traffic to the strip shopping center, he stands behind the lease agreement that requires a $10,000 payment to release the lessees.

Required

a. Identify the weakness in the partnership's internal control which could produce the pattern of declining cash flow.

b. If the partners decide to liquidate, explain whether they should pay the $10,000 or the present value of the remaining lease payments.

c. Using the cash distribution plan methodology, explain whether it is in Green's interest to liquidate at this time.

REVIEW SOLUTIONS ••

Review 1 Solution

Net assets invested amount to $222,000 ($130,000 cash, $200,000 building, $17,000 office equipment, less $125,000 mortgage payable).

a. Under the bonus method, $74,000 of capital (= $222,000/3) is credited to each partner. The entry to record the formation is:

Cash..	130,000	
Building	200,000	
Office equipment	17,000	
Mortgage payable		125,000
Capital, Abel		74,000
Capital, Baker		74,000
Capital, Cahn......................................		74,000
To record formation of partnership under the bonus method.		

b. Under the goodwill method, Abel's investment of $100,000 for a 1/3 interest would establish the value of the partnership at $300,000, resulting in goodwill of $78,000 (= $300,000 − $222,000). The entry to record the formation is:

Cash..	130,000	
Building	200,000	
Office equipment	17,000	
Goodwill	78,000	
Mortgage payable		125,000
Capital, Abel		100,000
Capital, Baker		100,000
Capital, Cahn......................................		100,000
To record formation of partnership under the goodwill method		

Review 2 Solution

a. Baker's bonus, 10 percent of net income over $100,000, is $7,700 (= 10 percent × $77,000). Abel receives interest of $11,100 (= 15 percent × $74,000) and Cahn receives interest of $5,920 (=8 percent × $74,000). After the salaries, bonus, and interest are allocated, $32,280 remains to be shared equally.

Partner	Salary	Bonus	Interest	Percentage	Total
Abel	—	—	$11,100	$10,760	$ 21,860
Baker	$ 80,000	$7,700	—	10,760	98,460
Cahn.............	40,000	—	5,920	10,760	56,680
Totals	$120,000	$7,700	$17,020	$32,280	$177,000

b. Capital balances at year-end:

Partner	Beginning Capital	Income Allocation	Distributions	Ending Capital
Abel	$ 74,000	$ 21,860	—	$ 95,860
Baker	74,000	98,460	$ 87,700	84,760
Cahn.............	74,000	56,680	40,000	90,680
Totals	$222,000	$177,000	$127,700	$271,300

Review 3 Solution

Abel receives $135,400 (= $100,000 original investment plus $35,400 (= 20 percent × $177,000)). Abel's capital balance is $95,860. Thus Abel receives $39,540 (= $135,400 − $95,860) in excess of capital balance.

a. Under the bonus approach, Baker and Cahn each transfer $19,770 (= $39,540/2) of capital to Abel. The entries are:

Capital, Baker.	19,770	
Capital, Cahn	19,770	
Capital, Abel		39,540
To record transfer of capital to Abel under the bonus method.		
Capital, Abel	135,400	
Cash		135,400
To record payment to Abel.		

b. Under the partial goodwill approach, the $39,540 excess payment to Abel is recorded as goodwill.

Goodwill	39,540	
Capital, Abel		39,540
To record partial goodwill based on payment to Abel.		
Capital, Abel.	135,400	
Cash		135,400
To record payment to Abel.		

c. Under the total goodwill approach, the $39,540 excess payment for Abel's 1/3 interest is multiplied by 3 to get total goodwill of $118,620.

Goodwill	118,620	
Capital, Abel		39,540
Capital, Baker		39,540
Capital, Cahn.		39,540
To record total goodwill based on payment to Abel.		
Capital, Abel.	135,400	
Cash		135,400
To record payment to Abel.		

Following Abel's withdrawal, recorded by the total goodwill approach, the partnership's capital is $244,520 (Baker $124,300 (= $84,760 + $39,540) and Cahn $120,220 (= $90,680 + $39,540)). Dexter is admitted as a 20 percent partner for an investment of $38,000. Total net assets of the partnership after Dexter's admission is $282,520 (= $244,520 + $38,000).

d. Under the bonus approach, Dexter's share of capital is $56,504 (= 20 percent × $282,520), which exceeds Dexter's investment by $18,504 (= $56,504 − $38,000). This amount, shared equally, is a bonus from Baker and Cahn to Dexter. The entry is:

Cash	38,000	
Capital, Baker.	9,252	
Capital, Cahn	9,252	
Capital, Dexter.		56,504
To record admission of Dexter under the bonus method.		

e. Under the goodwill approach, the value of the partnership based on the capital of Baker and Cahn is $305,650 (= $244,520/0.8). Thus Dexter's 20 percent share is $61,130 (= 20 percent × $305,650) and Dexter is presumed to have invested goodwill of $23,130 (= $61,130 − $38,000). The entry is:

Cash.	38,000	
Goodwill	23,130	
Capital, Dexter.		61,130
To record admission of Dexter under the goodwill method.		

Review 4 Solution

Partners' capital is $570,000 (= $325,000 + $180,000 + $65,000) and partnership assets are $635,000 (= $570,000 capital + $65,000 liabilities). The sale of partnership assets for $800,000 yields a gain on $165,000 (= $800,000 − $635,000). Preparation of a cash distribution plan, as shown below, indicates the following sequence of distributions:

    First $65,000 to creditors
    Next $145,000 to Baker
    Next $100,000 to Baker and Cahn in equal amounts
    All remaining funds to Baker, Cahn, and Dexter in 4:4:2 ratio

Cash Distribution Plan:

	Baker	Cahn	Dexter
Capital balances after gain.	$391,000	$246,000	$ 98,000
Standardized capital (divide by partner's percentage). . .	$977,500	$615,000	$490,000
Equalize Baker with Cahn	(362,500)		
Balance.	$615,000	$615,000	$490,000
Equalize Baker and Cahn with Dexter	(125,000)	(125,000)	
Balance.	$490,000	$490,000	$490,000

Convert back into profit sharing ratios:

1. Baker receives first $145,000 (= $362,500 × .40)
2. Baker and Cahn then receive $50,000 each (= $125,000 × .40)
3. All partners share remaining cash in 4:4:2 ratio

The allocation of each distribution is as follows:

	Assets	Liabilities	Baker (40%)	Cahn (40%)	Dexter (20%)
Balances.	$635,000	$65,000	$325,000	$180,000	$65,000
Gain on sale	165,000	—	66,000	66,000	33,000
Balances after gain.	800,000	65,000	391,000	246,000	98,000
First installment	(200,000)	(65,000)	(135,000)	—	—
Balances.	600,000	0	256,000	246,000	98,000
Partial second installment, to bring into 4:4:2 alignment	(110,000)	—	(60,000)	(50,000)	—
Balances.	490,000	0	196,000	196,000	98,000
Remainder of second installment.	(90,000)	—	(36,000)	(36,000)	(18,000)
Balances.	400,000	0	160,000	160,000	80,000
Third installment.	(200,000)	—	(80,000)	(80,000)	(40,000)
Balances.	200,000	0	80,000	80,000	40,000
Fourth installment.	(200,000)	—	(80,000)	(80,000)	(40,000)
Balances.	$ 0	$ 0	$ 0	$ 0	$ 0

15 Bankruptcy and Reorganization

LEARNING OBJECTIVES

BORDERS GROUP INC.

www.borders.com

Borders Group, Inc. was once the second-largest bookstore chain in the U.S., and soon will be a name from the past. The company had struggled financially for many years, in the face of strong competition from Barnes & Noble Inc. and online bookseller Amazon.com Inc. As more sales occurred online than in retail stores, Borders lacked a strong online presence and an e-book reader to compete with Amazon's *Kindle* and Barnes & Noble's *Nook*.

Founded in 1971, Borders had only 21 stores 20 years later. In 1992, it was purchased by Kmart, which rapidly expanded the chain to over 200 stores by 1997. There was talk of eventually expanding to 1,000 stores. But by the mid-2000's, Borders had severe financial problems resulting from the presence of online retailers and its own money-losing attempt to launch an e-commerce operation. The company sought to sell itself in 2008, but was unsuccessful.

Faced with growing obligations for unpaid purchases and rent, Borders declared bankruptcy in February 2011. It first filed for Chapter 11 protection to reorganize, listing liabilities of $1.29 billion and assets of $1.27 billion. The company planned to close about one-third of its 650-plus stores and hoped to sell or restructure the remaining stores. It immediately began "going-out-of-business" sales at about 200 stores targeted for closing. Because attempts to sell the remaining stores proved unsuccessful, Borders decided to liquidate under Chapter 7, closing its remaining 400-plus stores and putting its 11,000 employees out of work. Asset liquidation sales are underway, expected to bring in $250 million or more.

Had Borders been able to restructure, it would have faced several issues. How could it restructure its operations to achieve future profitability? What arrangements could it make with its creditors to ease its debt load? Creditors might have offered to restructure the interest rate or maturity of the debt, or even to settle for less than 100 percent of the full amount. What would have happened to stockholders? Would any of their equity interests have survived the reorganization? Having then decided to liquidate under Chapter 7 of the bankruptcy laws, how much can the assets yield upon sale, and how much will the creditors recover?

Sources: NYTimes.com DealBook, February 16, 2011 and Reuters.com July 18, 2011.

CHAPTER ORGANIZATION

Legal aspects of bankruptcy	Accounting for Chapter 7 bankruptcy (liquidation)	Accounting for Chapter 11 bankruptcy (reorganization)	Accounting for other forms of restructuring
• Chapters 7, 11 and 13 of Bankruptcy Code • Legal process of Chapter 7 liquidation • Legal process of Chapter 11 reorganization	• Categories of liabilities • Categories and valuation of assets • Statement of affairs • Transactions during liquidation • Statement of realization and liquidation	• Accounting for reorganization items • Reporting during reorganization • Determining reorganization value • Fresh start reporting	• Quasi-reorganization • Troubled debt restructuring

Many firms encounter serious financial difficulties that threaten their continued existence. Among the actions possible in the face of serious financial problems are liquidation, reorganization, and debt restructuring. *Liquidation* and *reorganization* usually proceed under the provisions of the bankruptcy laws, while debt restructuring typically involves a private agreement between a debtor and a creditor. This chapter examines the accounting and reporting implications of these actions.

Estates and trusts are entities created to manage assets on behalf of others. One common example is the estate of a deceased individual: an executor manages the estate's assets until they are distributed to the decedent's beneficiaries. Similarly, trusts can manage assets on behalf of someone unable to manage their own assets, such as a child or an infirm person. The estate concept also applies to the management of the assets of a "deceased" or financially ailing firm in bankruptcy until the assets can be properly distributed to creditors, bondholders, and stockholders. From an accounting perspective, the bankruptcy of a firm approximates the death of an individual. Both cases involve creation of an estate and appointment of a representative, known as a **fiduciary**, via a legal process to administer the estate on behalf of the beneficiaries.

In the case of a deceased individual, an **executor** is responsible for distributing assets to heirs in accord with the provisions of a will or intestacy law. In the case of a bankrupt firm, a **trustee** or **receiver** responsible primarily to the creditors of the firm must repay as much of their claims as possible, consistent with the security agreements contained in debt contracts and with the provisions of bankruptcy law. The trustee or receiver has secondary responsibility to the stockholders and seeks to preserve as much of their ownership equity as possible.

Adherence to laws affecting firms in bankruptcy proceedings influences the accounting for these entities. These laws safeguard the interests of creditors while the trustee or receiver manages the firm's assets. The accountant's mission of reporting on the management of the assets to the concerned parties involves accounting and special reporting that show how the trustee's responsibilities have been met. To carry out this reporting responsibility, the accountant must consider the legal framework that constrains the operation of bankrupt firms.

The **trustee/receiver** is responsible for payment of claims:

- First to creditors
- Second to stockholders

LEGAL ASPECTS OF BANKRUPTCY

LO1 Explain the basic legal aspects of bankruptcy.

A firm in financial difficulty can pursue several possible courses of action: initiate formal actions under federal bankruptcy law, or less formal actions outside the judicial system. The least formal action has the firm agree with one or more creditors to **restructure** debt—to modify the terms or to settle the debt at less than full payment. When several creditors agree to debt restructuring, the process often leads to a **composition** or **creditors' composition agreement**. In a somewhat more formal procedure, an **assignment for the benefit of creditors** has the firm voluntarily transfer its assets to a trustee, who liquidates the assets and offers partial payment to the creditors on a *pro rata* basis. Creditors accept the offer and discharge the remaining debt, or they reject the offer and initiate proceedings to force the firm into involuntary bankruptcy.

Federal law provides the legal process and remedies for **bankruptcy**, the condition that individuals and business firms face when unable to meet their debts. The bankruptcy process seeks to provide relief and protection to debtors, and to satisfy creditors, either by *liquidating and distributing the debtor's assets* to its creditors, or by *restructuring the organization to continue operations* in a way that offers better prospects for generating sufficient cash flows to satisfy obligations to creditors.

Federal bankruptcy law consists primarily of the *Bankruptcy Act of 1898*, its subsequent revisions, and case law. Major revisions included the *Chandler Act of 1938*, and the *Bankruptcy Reform Act of 1978* that remains the basis for much of current bankruptcy law. Most bankruptcy legislation between 1978 and 2005 dealt with administrative matters and the authority of bankruptcy judges. Major new legislation appeared in the *Bankruptcy Abuse Prevention and Consumer Protection Act of 2005*, that was generally viewed as making bankruptcy more difficult for individual and corporate debtors.

Three different situations are referred to as Chapter 7, 11, and 13 proceedings. It is common to refer to specific provisions by their chapter number.

Chapter 7, applicable to both individuals and firms, provides for **liquidation** of the debtor's assets to pay the creditors. A trustee takes control of the firm's assets, sells them and distributes the proceeds to creditors on a *pro rata* basis. A completed liquidation process results in most remaining debts being **discharged**—cancelled with the creditor having no further claim. Debts not discharged include certain taxes, alimony and child support, and certain student loans. This non-discharge applies mostly to individuals and these claims remain valid against the individual's future income. Chapter 7 proceedings are **voluntary** when initiated by the debtor, **involuntary** when initiated by one or more creditors.

Chapter 11 is most commonly used by business firms, although it also applies to individuals. Chapter 11 provides for **reorganization**, whereby the firm continues in business without liquidating its assets. The firm develops an equitable plan that modifies the rights and interests of its creditors and stockholders and often restructures its business operations. If a plan of reorganization allows the firm to remain in possession of its assets, the firm is called a **debtor-in-possession** and management usually continues to operate the business. To be implemented, the reorganization plan must be approved by creditors representing two-thirds of the dollar claims and a creditors' committee supervises administration of the plan. Creditors may agree to settle for partial payment, to lengthen the payment period, to modify terms, or to accept equity in place of debt. Creditors often prefer reorganization to liquidation because the prospects of collecting what the firm owes tends to improve when the company continues to operate instead of selling its assets.

Chapter 13 of the Bankruptcy Code applies the reorganization concept to an *individual debtor* with a regular income. Rather than liquidating the debtor's assets, a **repayment plan** is worked out with creditors. The 2005 bankruptcy legislation cited earlier made significant changes to individual bankruptcy that reduces the frequency with which a person can file for bankruptcy protection. This text does not examine Chapter 13 proceedings.

Bankruptcy filings are a common occurrence. According to U.S Bankruptcy Court statistics, in 2010 about 1,600,000 bankruptcy petitions were filed, an 8% increase from 1,475,000 filed in 2009. In 2005, before the change in the bankruptcy laws, over 2,000,000 petitions were filed. In 2010, approximately 56,000 petitions were filed by business entities and 1,536,000 by non-business entities, primarily individuals. Of the various types, about 1,140,000 filings fell under Chapter 7 of the Bankruptcy Code, 14,000 filings under Chapter 11, and 440,000 filings under Chapter 13.

Legal Process of Chapter 7 Liquidation

The legal process of a Chapter 7 bankruptcy begins with filing a petition in the federal bankruptcy court. This petition states that the debtor cannot meet obligations and requests that the provisions of the bankruptcy law be applied. When the debtor files the petition, it is a **voluntary petition**; when filed by creditors, it is an **involuntary petition**. The law requires that a specified number of creditors having a significant amount of claims against the firm must agree to file an involuntary petition.

When accepted by the bankruptcy judge, a properly filed petition subjects the debtor to an orderly process. Individual creditors cannot enforce liens or judgments, or repossess assets of the debtor. Rather, the claims of all creditors are processed and satisfied, to the extent possible, by applying the provisions of the law. The desire to be subject to this orderly process rather than face the lawsuits, repossessions, and liens of individual creditors explains why some debtors file voluntary petitions.

Chapter 7 mandates appointment of a **trustee** to take possession of the debtor's assets, convert them to cash over a period of time, and distribute cash to creditors according to their legal rights and priorities. Usually, the cash is insufficient to pay all debts fully. The trustee distributes all assets before **discharging** and releasing the debtor from all remaining debts. At that point the debtor company ceases to exist.

Legal Process of Chapter 11 Reorganization

The Chapter 11 reorganization process also begins when the debtor firm files a petition with the bankruptcy court. This filing begins the **reorganization proceeding** designed to preserve the company as a going concern while maximizing the recovery by creditors and stockholders.

Critical to the reorganization process is the **plan of reorganization**, a proposal to restructure the debt and equity interests of the company and fashion the entity that will emerge as the continuing operating firm. In a Chapter 11 filing the debtor usually remains in possession, although the court appoints a trustee when there is cause to do so. After the debtor proposes a reorganization plan, affected parties may respond and offer alternative plans. Ultimately, the bankruptcy court confirms the plan that it finds to be *feasible,* in the *best interests of the creditors*, and *fair and equitable* to any creditors unwilling to accept it. Once confirmed, the plan of reorganization binds all parties, including those that originally objected to it. Remaining corporate debts are not legally discharged as in a Chapter 7 liquidation.

FINANCIAL REPORTING FOR CHAPTER 7 LIQUIDATION

The financial reports for a Chapter 7 bankruptcy liquidation fall into two categories:

1. The **statement of affairs**, a balance sheet, shows the debtor firm's assets at their likely recoverable value, and the liabilities according to the legal status of the claims.

2. The **statement of realization and liquidation**, an operating statement, shows how the trustee has managed the bankrupt firm's assets on behalf of the creditors.

BUSINESS APPLICATION Stirling Energy Systems, Inc.

Many business bankruptcy filings are Chapter 11 filings, where the company hopes to restructure its obligations and continue in business. If reorganization cannot be accomplished, the company might opt for Chapter 7 liquidation. A few bankruptcy filings seek Chapter 7 liquidation from the start. Stirling Energy Systems Inc. of Scottsdale, Arizona, a financially-troubled manufacturer of solar-power equipment, filed for Chapter 7 bankruptcy on September 23, 2011, unable to find a buyer for its business. Various users of Stirling's technology saw their solar-power production plans scaled back due to lost contracts and abandoned projects, contributing to Stirling's demise. *Source: wsj.com, September 30, 2011.*

Statement of Affairs

LO2 Prepare a statement of affairs for a Chapter 7 bankruptcy.

The **statement of affairs** is a statement of financial condition for a company entering a Chapter 7 bankruptcy. Because such a company is no longer a going concern, **estimated realizable values** replace historical costs and going-concern fair values as the amounts reported for the debtor firm's assets. Thus the statement shows the amounts likely to be realized to satisfy creditors' claims.

Reporting the Debtor's Liabilities The statement of affairs presents the firm's liabilities according to the legal priorities for repayment and organizes liabilities into four categories:

1. **Fully secured liabilities.** Here the creditor has a lien on specific assets with estimated realizable values *equal to or greater than* the amount of the liability. For example, suppose a bank holds a $250,000 mortgage secured by a bankrupt firm's building that has an estimated realizable value of $430,000. Because the $430,000 proceeds expected from sale of the building exceed the mortgage amount, the mortgage is **fully secured**, and the bank is a **fully secured creditor**.

2. **Partially secured liabilities.** Here the creditor has a lien on specific assets with estimated realizable values *less* than the amount of the liability. For example, if a finance company holds a $20,000 note secured by equipment of a bankrupt firm with an estimated realizable value of only $13,000, the note is **partially secured**, and the finance company is a **partially secured creditor**.

3. **Unsecured liabilities with priority.** When the creditor has no lien on any specific assets of the bankrupt firm, but *by law* its claims rank ahead of other unsecured liabilities, the claims are considered **unsecured liabilities with priority**. Section 507 of the Bankruptcy Code lists the payment priority of such liabilities as follows:

   - Administrative expenses of the trustee.
   - Unpaid wages, up to $12,425 per employee, earned within 180 days prior to the bankruptcy petition.
   - Amounts due to employee benefit plans, up to $12,425 per employee, accrued within 180 days prior to the bankruptcy petition.
   - Deposits made with the bankrupt firm by consumers for the purchase, lease, or rental of property or services, up to $2,775 per claimant.
   - Taxes.

4. **Unsecured liabilities.** All other liabilities for which creditors have no liens on specific assets of the bankrupt firm are **unsecured.** This category includes the unsecured portion of the liability to partially secured creditors. In the partially secured liability discussed above, the $20,000 note payable to the finance company secured by equipment worth $13,000 means that the difference of $7,000 is added to the unsecured liabilities.

Reporting the Debtor's Assets The statement of affairs also presents the debtor firm's assets in order indicating the extent to which they secure specific creditor claims, and indicates amounts expected to be available for unsecured creditors. As mentioned, all assets are valued at their *estimated realizable value* rather than historical cost and are organized into three categories:

1. **Assets pledged to fully secured creditors.** Certain assets may be pledged as security for a particular liability, and the estimated realizable value of the assets *equals or exceeds* the amount of the liability. Liquidation of such assets can yield resources to cover unsecured liabilities. The building with an estimated realizable value of $430,000 that secures a $250,000 mortgage liability illustrates an asset pledged to a fully secured creditor. After paying the $250,000 mortgage, $180,000 remains for unsecured creditors.

2. **Assets pledged to partially secured creditors.** Other assets pledged as security for particular liabilities have estimated realizable values less than the amounts of the liabilities. Partial satisfaction of such secured liabilities consumes the entire asset value; nothing remains for the unsecured creditors. The equipment with an estimated realizable value of $13,000 that secures a $20,000 note payable illustrates an asset pledged to a partially secured creditor. The remaining $7,000 of the note is unsecured.

3. **Free assets.** Assets not pledged as security for any particular liability, and thus available to meet the claims of unsecured creditors, are labeled *free assets*. This category also includes the value of assets pledged to fully secured creditors in excess of the related liabilities. In the building/mortgage example, free assets include $180,000 of the building's value.

BUSINESS APPLICATION Peanut Corporation of America

Not all companies enter bankruptcy because of excessive liabilities. In 2009 the Peanut Corporation of America was implicated in several salmonella cases. It had shipped tainted peanuts to customers around the country. Hundreds of people became ill and at least nine died. Although the company was solvent at that point, the extensive adverse publicity caused major loss of customers, essentially wiping out the company's business. *Source: USA Today, May 13, 2009.*

Format of the Statement of Affairs   The statement of affairs presents assets and liabilities organized into the categories just discussed. Secured claims and corresponding assets are offset so that the statement of affairs shows both the *total amount of free assets* and the *total amount of unsecured liabilities*. We net these two amounts to show the **estimated deficiency to unsecured creditors**—the amount by which the unsecured liabilities exceed the assets available to pay them.

The **liability section** of the statement of affairs appears first and is structured as follows; all amounts are hypothetical:

(in thousands)	Creditors' Claims	Unsecured Liabilities
Fully secured creditors: (list)...........................	$275	
Partially secured creditors: (list).......................	155	
Less: Value of pledged assets	(80)	$ 75
Unsecured creditors with priority: (list).................	$ 24	
Unsecured creditors: (list)		315
Total unsecured liabilities.............................		$390

The total unsecured liabilities consists of the obligations to unsecured creditors plus the obligations to partially secured creditors in excess of the value of pledged assets. Observe also that because unsecured liabilities with priority must be paid before other unsecured liabilities, the former appear under creditors' claims but not in the total of unsecured liabilities. Instead, we offset unsecured liabilities with priority against free assets, as shown below.

Next, the **asset section** of the statement of affairs is structured as follows:

(in thousands)	Estimated Realizable Value	Free Assets
Assets pledged to fully secured creditors: (list)	$340	
Less: Amount of fully secured liabilities.....................	(275)	$ 65
Assets Pledged to Partially Secured Creditors: (List)............	$ 80	
Free assets: (list).....................................		137
Total free assets......................................		202
Less: Unsecured liabilities with priority		(24)
Net free assets.......................................		178
Estimated deficiency to unsecured creditors..................		212
Total unsecured liabilities..............................		$390

We see that **total free assets** consist of the value of unpledged assets plus the value of assets pledged to fully secured creditors in excess of the amount of the related liabilities. Total free assets are then reduced by the **unsecured liabilities with priority** to yield **net free assets**. The **estimated deficiency to unsecured creditors** explains the difference between the amount of **net free assets** and the total of **unsecured liabilities**, and makes the statement balance.

This simple format highlights the key aspects of bankruptcy reporting. In practice we might see more complex formats; for example, book values may appear on the statement of affairs along with the estimated realizable values. Because estimated realizable values are more relevant than historical costs for a company that is no longer a going concern, we present information directly related to the debtor's ability to repay the various classes of creditors. But the reported book values tie the statement of affairs to the conventional historical cost balance sheet and, when compared to the estimated realizable values, indicate the expected gains or losses upon liquidation. Such a statement of affairs appears in the format shown in Exhibit 15.1.

EXHIBIT 15.1   Format of the Statement of Affairs

X CORPORATION
Statement of Affairs (In thousands)
Date

Book Value		Estimated Realizable Value	Free Assets
$320	Assets pledged to fully secured creditors: (list)	$340	
	Less: Liabilities to fully secured creditors	(275)	$ 65
60	Assets pledged to partially secured creditors: (list)	$ 80	
400	Free assets: (list).		137
	Total free assets.		202
	Less: Unsecured liabilities with priority		(24)
	Net free assets		178
	Estimated deficiency to unsecured creditors.		212
$780	Total unsecured liabilities.		$390

Book Value		Creditors' Claims	Unsecured Liabilities
$275	Fully secured creditors: (list).	$275	
155	Partially secured creditors: (list)	$155	
	Less: Value of pledged assets	(80)	$ 75
24	Unsecured creditors with priority: (list).	$ 24	
315	Unsecured creditors: (list)		315
11	Stockholders' equity		—
$780	Total unsecured liabilities.		$390

Illustration of Statement of Affairs   Bristol Corporation enters Chapter 7 bankruptcy proceedings on October 31, 2014. Bristol's unclassified balance sheet on that date shows the following information:

BRISTOL CORPORATION
Balance Sheet
October 31, 2014

Assets		Liabilities and stockholders' equity	
Cash.	$ 4,000	Accounts payable.	$134,000
Marketable securities.	7,000	Loan payable	100,000
Accounts receivable.	27,000	Equipment note payable	30,000
Inventory.	63,000	Accrued wages.	41,000
Land	15,000	Taxes payable	12,000
Building	135,000	Mortgage payable	94,000
Equipment	163,000	Stockholders' equity	14,000
Goodwill	11,000		
Total assets	$425,000	Total liabilities and stockholders' equity ..	$425,000

A firm may enter bankruptcy even though it has positive stockholders' equity if the firm cannot meet its debt obligations. For example, when the Penn Central Railroad entered bankruptcy proceedings, its last annual report showed retained earnings of $495 million, and stockholders' equity of $1.8

billion. Nevertheless, the company's liquid assets were inadequate to meet its current obligations, and bankruptcy resulted.

Suppose Bristol's assets have the following realizable values:

Cash	$ 4,000
Marketable securities	9,000
Accounts receivable	20,000
Inventory	44,000
Land and building	190,000
Equipment	63,900
Goodwill	—
Total	$330,900

Bristol's assets cannot cover its $411,000 (= $425,000 − $14,000) in liabilities. The receivables and inventory are pledged as security for the $100,000 loan and the land and building secures the $94,000 mortgage. A machine with an estimated realizable value of $22,000 and a book value of $20,000 secures the $30,000 equipment note payable.

The statement of affairs for Bristol appears in Exhibit 15.2 and shows net free assets of $97,900, unsecured liabilities of $178,000, and an estimated deficiency to unsecured creditors of $80,100. This information can be converted into an **expected recovery percentage** for Bristol's unsecured creditors:

$$\text{Expected recovery percentage} = \text{Net free assets/Unsecured liabilities}$$
$$= \$97,900/\$178,000$$
$$= 55 \text{ percent}$$

Bristol's unsecured creditors can expect to receive 55 cents per dollar owed to them by the bankrupt firm. Fully secured creditors will receive the full amount owed them, as will the unsecured creditors with priority. The partially secured creditors receive less than 100 percent of what they are owed, but more than the percentage received by unsecured creditors. We can now calculate the total recovery expected by the two partially secured creditors in this example, as follows:

Loan payable of $100,000:	
Secured portion (full recovery) value of pledged assets	$64,000
Unsecured portion (partial recovery) $36,000 × 55%	19,800
Total recovery	$83,800

Equipment note payable of $30,000:	
Secured portion (full recovery) value of pledged asset	$22,000
Unsecured portion (partial recovery) $8,000 × 55%	4,400
Total recovery	$26,400

Thus the loan creditor recovers 83.8 percent (= $83,800/$100,000), and the equipment note creditor recovers 88 percent (= $26,400/$30,000).

REVIEW 1 • Chapter 7 Liquidation

Baines Corporation is undergoing liquidation under Chapter 7 of the bankruptcy code. Baines reports total liabilities of $820,000 and its assets have a liquidation value of $650,000. Of those assets, $300,000 are pledged as security on debt obligations of $220,000, and another $120,000 are pledged as security on $180,000 of liabilities. Unsecured liabilities with priority amount to $30,000.

Required Determine the expected recovery by unsecured creditors and the recovery percentage.

Solutions are located after the chapter assignments.

EXHIBIT 15.2   Statement of Affairs for Bristol Corporation

BRISTOL CORPORATION
Statement of Affairs
October 31, 2014

Book Value		Estimated Realizable Value	Free Assets
$150,000	Assets pledged to fully secured creditors:		
	Land and building.	$190,000	
	Less: Mortgage payable.	94,000	$96,000
	Assets pledged to partially secured creditors:		
27,000	Accounts receivable.	20,000	
63,000	Inventory.	44,000	
20,000	Equipment	22,000	
	Total assets pledged to partially secured creditors.	$ 86,000	
	Free assets:		
4,000	Cash.	$ 4,000	
7,000	Marketable securities.	9,000	
143,000	Equipment	41,900	
11,000	Goodwill.	0	54,900
	Total free assets.		150,900
	Less: Unsecured liabilities with priority		53,000
	Net free assets		97,900
	Estimated deficiency to unsecured creditors.		80,100
$425,000	Total unsecured liabilities.		$178,000

Book Value		Creditors' Claims	Unsecured Liabilities
	Fully secured creditors:		
$ 94,000	Mortgage payable	$ 94,000	
	Partially secured creditors:		
100,000	Loan payable	100,000	
	Less: Value of accounts receivable and inventory.	64,000	$ 36,000
30,000	Equipment note payable	30,000	
	Less: Value of machine	22,000	8,000
	Unsecured creditors with priority:		
41,000	Accrued wages.	41,000	
12,000	Taxes payable	12,000	
	Total unsecured creditors with priority.	$ 53,000	
	Unsecured creditors:		
134,000	Accounts payable.		134,000
14,000	Stockholders' equity		0
$425,000	Total unsecured liabilities.		$178,000

Statement of Realization and Liquidation

LO3
Prepare a statement of realization and liquidation.

The **statement of realization and liquidation** provides a complete record of the **receiver's transactions** during a period of time. Whereas the statement of affairs set forth the creditor claims and the expected realizable values of assets as the firm entered bankruptcy, the realization and liquidation statement reports on assets sold and liabilities paid during the liquidation process.

One task of the receiver is to **realize the assets**—to convert the noncash assets into cash to pay creditors. The process of realization takes several forms. Certain operating activities of the firm continue for a time and provide cash or other assets. Some assets are realized in normal business operations, such as collection of customer receivables. Other assets are realized through sale. Because the receiver acts in the best interest of the creditors, he or she selects the means of realization that provides the greatest return to the creditors. As a result, the realization process can extend over a considerable period of time, while gains and losses on asset sales occur, expenses are incurred, and revenues are earned.

Format of the Statement of Realization and Liquidation   Various formats are found in practice; Exhibit 15.3 shows one possibility. The statement *excludes* the following accounts, as the focus is only on the realization of assets and the liquidation of liabilities:

- The cash account
- Revenues and expenses
- The income accounts for gains and losses
- The equity account

EXHIBIT 15.3   Format of the Statement of Realization and Liquidation

X CORPORATION
(Name of Receiver or Trustee)
Statement of Realization and Liquidation
(Time Period Covered)

Assets to be realized:	Assets realized:
(List and amounts)	(List and amounts of proceeds)
Assets acquired:	Assets not realized:
(List and amounts)	(List and amounts)
Liabilities liquidated:	Liabilities to be liquidated:
(List and amounts of payments)	(List and amounts)
Liabilities not liquidated:	Liabilities incurred:
(List and amounts)	(List and amounts)
Gain on realization or liquidation:	Loss on realization or liquidation:
COMBINED TOTAL	COMBINED TOTAL

The assets realized and liabilities liquidated are reported at actual amounts received or paid, not at book value. The differences between book value and cash received or paid show up in the gain/loss sections of the statement.

A *balance sheet* and a *statement of estate deficit* should accompany the realization and liquidation statement. The **balance sheet of the trustee** has the following format:

Trustee
Balance Sheet

Cash	$ X	Liabilities not liquidated	$XX
Assets not realized	XX	Estate deficit	X
Total assets	$XX	Total liabilities and equity	$XX

A **statement of estate deficit** shows the periodic revenues, expenses, gains, and losses that produce a net change in the estate deficit. The initial balance of the estate deficit is *not equal* to the amount of the estimated deficiency to unsecured creditors reported on the statement of affairs. The statement of affairs reports assets at *estimated realizable values*, whereas *book values* continue to be used for the receiver's ongoing accounting of the firm's activities. Thus the initial balance of the estate deficit is simply the stockholders' equity of the firm, and subsequent transactions by the receiver increase or decrease this amount. Note the concept of *estate* used here; *the receiver acts as fiduciary to manage the assets of the bankrupt firm on behalf of its creditors*. The statement of estate deficit is analogous to a statement of income and retained earnings of a going concern. One format of this statement appears next:

Statement of Estate Deficit			
Revenues		$X	
Gains		X	$XX
Expenses		X	
Losses		X	XX
Net Change in estate deficit.			X
Estate deficit—beginning of period			X
Estate deficit—end of period			$XX

Reporting Perspective

When reporting changes in the estate deficit, a firm in receivership or bankruptcy must consider whether to recognize depreciation. In our view, when the firm continues its operating activities, recognition of depreciation is appropriate to measure the results of operations. If few or no operating activities are being conducted—often the case when assets are being sold and liabilities settled—no depreciation charges should be recorded.

Illustration of Statement of Realization and Liquidation   Joanne Willis is appointed receiver of the Weeks Corporation, a company in bankruptcy. Her responsibilities are to administer the bankrupt firm, to realize the assets, and to liquidate the liabilities. At the time of her appointment, the company's balance sheet appears as follows; none of the liabilities are secured.

WEEKS CORPORATION Balance Sheet March 31, 2013			
Cash.	$ 1,000	Accounts payable.	$27,000
Accounts receivable.	6,000	Accrued wages.	5,000
Inventories	11,000	Notes payable	40,000
Equipment, net.	35,000	Stockholders' equity	(19,000)
Total assets	$53,000	Total liabilities and equity.	$53,000

Willis takes control of the company's assets and has a statement of affairs prepared to show the estimated realizable values of the company's assets, and the estimated recovery by each class of creditors. She then establishes accounting records for herself as trustee. Her initial entry records the assets and liabilities that she is administering at their book values:

Cash.	1,000	
Accounts receivable.	6,000	
Inventories	11,000	
Equipment	35,000	
Estate deficit.	19,000	
Accounts payable		27,000
Accrued wages		5,000
Notes payable		40,000
To record assets and liabilities of Weeks Corporation, administered by Receiver Joanne Willis.		

Suppose that during the next three months, the following six transactions occur:

1. Collected $3,300 in settlement of $5,000 of accounts receivable; the remaining $1,000 is expected to be collectible.
2. Sold for $6,400 inventory items having a book value of $8,000.

3. Sold for $12,000 a machine with a book value of $7,000.
4. Paid the accrued wages.
5. Accrued administrative expenses of $4,000.
6. Made an initial payment of 20 cents per dollar of indebtedness to the unsecured creditors.

Receiver Willis records these transactions as follows:

1.

Cash...	3,300	
Loss on realization..	1,700	
Accounts receivable		5,000
To record collection of receivables.		

2.

Cash...	6,400	
Loss on realization..	1,600	
Inventory		8,000
To record sale of inventory.		

3.

Cash...	12,000	
Equipment...		7,000
Gain on realization..		5,000
To record sale of machine.		

4.

Accrued wages...	5,000	
Cash		5,000
To record payment of wages.		

5.

Administrative expenses	4,000	
Accrued expenses..		4,000
To accrue expenses of trustee.		

6.

Accounts payable..	5,400	
Notes payable	8,000	
Cash		13,400
To record partial payment of 20 percent of amount due to unsecured		
creditors; $13,400 = .2 × ($27,000 + $40,000).		

The statement of realization and liquidation, along with the receiver's balance sheet and the statement of estate deficit at June 30, 2013, appear in Exhibit 15.4.

FINANCIAL REPORTING FOR CHAPTER 11 REORGANIZATION

LO4
Account for a company undergoing Chapter 11 reorganization.

Because the bankruptcy process of Chapter 7 results in the *liquidation* of the firm, financial reporting focused on the realizable value of assets and the priority of settling liability claims. The bankruptcy process of Chapter 11, on the other hand, results in the *reorganization* of the firm and its continued operation in restructured form. Financial reporting emphasizes the various aspects of restructuring, including disposition and revaluation of assets, settlement and modification of liabilities, and changes in equity interests. Reporting requirements are found in *FASB ASC Topic 852*, Reorganizations.

Reporting During the Reorganization Process

Initiation of the Chapter 11 reorganization process does not have implications for *accounting valuation*. Unlike a Chapter 7 proceeding, which envisions liquidation, the going concern assumption continues to be valid in a Chapter 11 reorganization. Thus, changes in the existing historical cost valuation of assets and liabilities are not normally needed. If the needs of financial statement users change, however, *classification* and *disclosure* may be affected. The two major areas affected concern the *presentation of liability information* and the *distinction between operating transactions and transactions associated with the reorganization process.*

EXHIBIT 15.4   Receiver's Financial Statements

WEEKS CORPORATION
Joanne Willis, Receiver
Statement of Realization and Liquidation
For Three Months Ended June 30, 2013

Assets to be realized:			Assets realized:		
Accounts receivable	$ 6,000		Accounts receivable	$ 3,300	
Inventory	11,000		Inventory	6,400	
Equipment	35,000	$ 52,000	Equipment	12,000	$ 21,700
Assets acquired:			**Assets not realized:**		
None			Accounts receivable	1,000	
			Inventory	3,000	
			Equipment	28,000	32,000
Liabilities liquidated:			**Liabilities to be liquidated:**		
Accounts payable	5,400		Accounts payable	27,000	
Accrued wages	5,000		Accrued wages	5,000	
Notes payable	8,000	18,400	Notes payable	40,000	72,000
Liabilities not liquidated:			**Liabilities incurred:**		
Accounts payable	21,600		Accrued expenses		4,000
Notes payable	32,000				
Accrued expenses	4,000	57,600			
Gain on realization		5,000	Loss on realization		3,300
Combined total		$133,000	Combined total		$133,000

WEEKS CORPORATION
Joanne Willis, Receiver
Balance Sheet
June 30, 2013

Cash	$ 4,300	Accounts payable	$21,600
Accounts receivable	1,000	Notes payable	32,000
Inventory	3,000	Accrued expenses	4,000
Equipment	28,000	Estate deficit	(21,300)
Total assets	$36,300	Total liabilities and equity	$36,300

WEEKS CORPORATION
Joanne Willis, Receiver
Statement of Estate Deficit
June 30, 2013

Gain on realization		$ 5,000
Loss on realization	$ 3,300	
Administrative expenses	4,000	7,300
Net change in estate deficit		(2,300)
Estate deficit, March 31, 2013		(19,000)
Estate deficit, June 30, 2013		$(21,300)

Reporting Liabilities During a Reorganization   During reorganization, the balance sheet should separately classify the amount of liabilities *subject to compromise*. A liability is **subject to compromise** if it is a *prepetition* liability and is *not* fully secured. A **prepetition liability** arose *prior to filing* for Chapter 11 protection, or arose after filing but resulted from pre-bankruptcy events and is allowed by the court as a prepetition claim. An example of the latter is a liability incurred *after filing* for prematurely terminating a lease that existed prior to filing. A **fully secured liability** follows the previous Chapter 7 liquidation discussion: a liability secured by collateral with value exceeding the amount of the claim. When uncertainty exists over the collateral's sufficiency to fully secure the debt, we apply the conserva-

BUSINESS APPLICATION   The Crystal Cathedral

Bankruptcy is not limited to business enterprises; not-for-profits enter bankruptcy as well. The **Crystal Cathedral**, which takes its name from the 10,000-plus panes of glass on its façade, is a Protestant Christian church in Orange County, California, known for its "Hour of Power" broadcasts. It filed for bankruptcy on October 18, 2010, with over $50 million in debts. Its major asset is its campus and its distinctive building. Numerous bidders emerged for the property. Chapman University offered $50 million, would lease some of the property back to the church and provide a repurchase option. The Roman Catholic Diocese of Orange County submitted a $53.6 million bid, with plans to convert the building into a Catholic cathedral. Retailer Hobby Lobby and others also submitted bids. The church's leadership opposes any sale and is trying to raise the $50 million needed to satisfy creditors. However, the creditors' committee, which brought the bankruptcy proceeding, must approve any final settlement, and it leans toward sale. *Source: Reuters.com, August 10, 2011.*

tism principle and classify the liability as subject to compromise. If the uncertainty is later resolved and the liability becomes fully secured, we reclassify it as such.

The balance sheet of the firm in reorganization should report the total amount of liabilities subject to compromise under a separate caption, with disclosure of the major categories of these claims in the notes to the financial statements. Because payments on these liabilities cease upon initiating reorganization, pending development of a settlement plan, a current/noncurrent classification is not used. No payment of these liabilities is likely while the firm is in reorganization. On the other hand, the firm pays liabilities *not* subject to compromise on a timely basis, and reports them in the usual current and noncurrent categories.

Reporting liabilities subject to compromise separately from those not subject to compromise does not affect *valuation*. All liabilities are reported at the amounts expected to be *allowed* by the court, generally the existing book value, even though many of these liabilities are eventually *settled for lesser amounts*. Because the amounts of some claims need to be *estimated*, the recording of such *contingent claims* should be guided by *ASC Section 450-20-25*.

Recognition of Reorganization Items   The firm undergoing reorganization must next identify revenues, expenses, gains, and losses resulting from reorganization, and separate these items from the results of ongoing operations. The following elements are among those likely to appear as **reorganization items** on the income statement:

- Legal, accounting, and other costs directly resulting from the reorganization process.
- Gains and losses from asset dispositions, except that gains and losses from *disposals of a business segment* are reported according to the provisions of *ASC Subtopic 205-20*.
- Gains and losses resulting from adjusting existing book values of liabilities to the *amounts likely to be allowed*.
- Adjustments resulting from recording liabilities brought about by the reorganization process, such as cancellation of a purchase contract.
- Interest income. Because debt payments are typically halted during the reorganization process, pending the development and approval of the reorganization plan, a temporary accumulation and investment of cash is likely; the interest earned is deemed to be a reorganization item.

Settlements of prepetition liabilities do not normally occur *during* the reorganization process, and hence are not likely to appear in the category of reorganization items. Such settlements are governed by the reorganization plan, and are recorded as the firm *emerges from reorganization*, discussed later.

Although interest expense is included as an operating item rather than a reorganization item, the full contractual amount of interest is not likely to be recorded. Interest expense is recorded during reorganization only to the extent that it is *actually paid, or accrued when likely to be allowed as a claim*. Differences between contractual amounts of interest and recorded amounts should be disclosed in the notes to the financial statements.

The **statement of cash flows** also separately identifies reorganization items. A separate section for reorganization items, such as professional fees and interest revenue, appears in the operating activities section. We suggest reporting operating cash flows by the *direct method* to facilitate the separation of cash flows relating to the reorganization. The investing activities section reports proceeds from asset sales resulting from the reorganization process. Finally, the financing activities section distinguishes between payment of prepetition and postpetition liabilities.

Major differences in financial statements during reorganization:

- Liabilities subject to compromise are shown as a separate line on the balance sheet.
- Current/noncurrent classification of liabilities is not employed for liabilities subject to compromise.
- Liabilities are recorded at amounts expected to be allowed by the court
- Reorganization items are shown separately from the results of ongoing operations on the income statement.
- Reorganization items are also shown separately on the statement of cash flows.

Illustration of Financial Reporting During Reorganization Manson Corporation filed a petition for relief under Chapter 11 of the bankruptcy laws in April 2013. The company continued to operate while developing a plan of reorganization, and is considered a **debtor-in-possession**. The company considers all its prepetition liabilities to be subject to compromise, except for a mortgage secured by the company's headquarters building.

During the remaining months of 2013, Manson sold excess equipment and vehicles for $75,000, resulting in a $30,000 loss. Termination of a warehouse lease resulted in a $25,000 cancellation penalty. Other reorganization items included $42,000 paid for professional fees and $6,000 received in interest revenue. No prepetition liabilities were paid after the filing date, except for $13,000 in wages and customer warranty claims approved by the bankruptcy court. Manson's financial statements at December 31, 2013, appear as follows.

MANSON CORPORATION
(Debtor-in-Possession)
Balance Sheet
December 31, 2013

Current assets			Current liabilities (post-petition)	$ 360,000
Cash.........................	$ 150,000		Long-term liabilities (pre-petition,	
Accounts receivable..............	320,000		fully secured):	
Inventories	550,000		Mortgage payable.............	800,000
Prepayments	70,000		Liabilities subject to compromise...	2,500,000
	1,090,000		Stockholders' equity	
Property, plant and equipment, net ..	2,390,000		Preferred stock............... $400,000	
Intangible assets	120,000		Common stock............... 100,000	
			Retained earnings .... (560,000)	(60,000)
Total assets	$3,600,000		Total liabilities and equity.........	$3,600,000

The following liabilities are **subject to compromise**:

15% notes payable, partially secured by inventories and receivables	$1,000,000
Bank loan payable, unsecured...	300,000
Taxes payable (priority claims)..	150,000
Accounts payable and other liabilities	1,050,000
Total	$2,500,000

The income statement for the year is as follows:

MANSON CORPORATION
(Debtor-in-Possession)
Income Statement
For Year Ended December 31, 2013

Revenues		$3,100,000
Expenses		(2,980,000)
Income before reorganization items and taxes		120,000
Reorganization items:		
Professional fees	$(42,000)	
Loss on sale of equipment and vehicles	(30,000)	
Lease termination penalty.	(25,000)	
Interest revenue	6,000	(91,000)
Income before taxes		29,000
Income tax expense.		(10,000)
Net income.		$ 19,000

The following condensed statement of cash flows illustrates presentation of the reorganization items. Because the filing of the Chapter 11 petition temporarily halts payments on prepetition debt, the company's cash balance increased substantially.

MANSON CORPORATION
(Debtor-in-Possession)
Statement of Cash Flows
For Year Ended December 31, 2013

Cash flows from operating activities		$ 64,000
Operating cash flows from reorganization items:		
Interest received	$ 6,000	
Professional fees paid	(42,000)	(36,000)
		28,000
Cash flows from investing activities:		
Capital expenditures.	(10,000)	
Proceeds from sale of equipment and vehicles due to reorganization	75,000	65,000
Cash flows from financing activities:		
Net short-term borrowing (postpetition).	50,000	
Payments of prepetition debt authorized by court.	(13,000)	37,000
Net increase in cash.		$130,000

The reporting just illustrated applies while the company is in the reorganization process. As seen in the next section, different reporting considerations apply when the company *emerges from reorganization* as a restructured entity.

Reporting After Reorganization

The key element in the firm's **emergence from reorganization** as a new, restructured entity is the **confirmation of the plan of reorganization** by the Bankruptcy Court. Once confirmed, the plan binds all parties, even those creditors unwilling to agree to it. The confirmed plan typically provides for the *compromise* of prepetition liabilities and for reduction or elimination of prior equity interests. If certain conditions are met, the emerging firm is considered a *new entity for accounting purposes*.

Reorganization Value   In the new entity, assets must equal liabilities plus equity interests; any retained earnings deficit is eliminated. An important element affecting what the creditors and equity holders will receive under the reorganization plan is the value of the assets in the reorganized firm. **Reorganization value** is defined as the amount a willing buyer would pay for the *assets* of the firm immediately *after* the restructuring; essentially, reorganization value approximates the *fair value of the assets*.

The emerging firm classifies its assets into two groups for purposes of estimating the reorganization value. Some assets are needed to carry on the operations of the new entity; other assets (called **excess assets**) are scheduled for disposition. Fair value of the *excess assets* is measured by the *expected proceeds from disposition*. *Assets to be employed in the new entity*, taken as a whole, are considered to have a fair value equal to the *discounted cash flows* expected from the operation of the new entity. Thus:

> **Reorganization value** = Expected proceeds from sale of *excess assets*
> + Present value of future cash flows from the new entity's *operating assets*

The reorganization value establishes the total amount that the plan provides for liabilities and equity interests. Thus reorganization value can also be expressed in terms of the components of the right-hand side of the balance sheet.

> **Reorganization value** = Postpetition liabilities (in full)
> + Fully secured prepetition liabilities
> + Compromised amount of other prepetition liabilities
> + Valuation of new equity interests

New Basis of Accounting: Fresh Start Reporting   When certain conditions are met, the entity emerging from reorganization is deemed to be sufficiently distinct from the old entity to conclude that a **new basis of accounting** is appropriate for the entity's assets and liabilities. Financial reporting after adopting this new basis of accounting is referred to as **fresh start reporting**, initiated when these conditions are satisfied:

* Reorganization value of the entity's assets is *less than* the total amount of all postpetition liabilities plus all allowed prepetition claims, and
* The pre-confirmation holders of existing voting shares will receive *less than 50 percent* of the voting shares in the new entity.

The first condition requires that the asset value to be recorded—*reorganization value*—be less than total liabilities. Because fresh-start reporting eliminates any negative equity position, the reorganization also forces write-downs of debt to demonstrate that an economic revaluation in fact occurred. The second condition requires that there be a *change of control* of the entity, which also supports the conclusion that assets and liabilities should be revalued.

Fresh start reporting replaces previously existing book values with the entity's aggregate *reorganization value*. We then allocate the total reorganization value to specific assets by assigning fair market values to the various assets. When the assigned fair market values *exceed* the reorganization value, *noncurrent assets other than marketable securities are reduced*. When the assigned fair market values are less than the reorganization value, we recognize an intangible asset called **reorganization value in excess of amounts allocated to identifiable assets**, and account for it in accordance with *ASC Topic 350*. Reorganization value in excess of amounts allocated to identifiable assets parallels the concept of **goodwill**.

Fresh start reporting also typically involves reducing existing liability and equity amounts. The new entity reports each liability other than deferred taxes at its *fair value*. Deferred taxes are reported pursuant to *ASC Topic 740*. Benefits from net operating loss carryforwards should be used to reduce the intangible asset *reorganization value in excess of amounts allocated to identifiable assets*.

Entries to reflect fresh start reporting are made *on the books of the predecessor entity* to close out the reorganization process and to establish the new basis of accountability for the assets, liabilities, and equities of the new entity. These entries accomplish three objectives:

1. **Record the discharge of debt**: Eliminate the existing *liabilities subject to compromise* and record the *payments, new debt securities, and new equity securities* received by these creditors. Typically, the payments and new securities are *less than* the previously recorded amounts, leading to a **gain on debt discharge**.

2. **Record the new interests of the former equity holders**: Delete the old equity and establish the new equity interests, which are typically *much less than* the old interests. The difference produces a temporary increase in additional paid-in capital.

3. **Record the asset value adjustments and eliminate the existing deficit**: Increase or decrease assets to their fair market values determined in the allocation of reorganization value, and record the intangible *reorganization value in excess of amounts allocated to identifiable assets*. Canceling the deficit, net of the gain on discharge of debt recorded earlier, typically produces a charge against additional paid-in capital.

These entries reflect the provisions of the confirmed plan of reorganization that restructure the interests of the creditors and equity holders, and establish the new basis of accounting for the emerging entity. When it proves impossible to formulate an acceptable plan of reorganization, the company does not emerge from reorganization as a restructured firm and heads toward Chapter 7 liquidation.

BUSINESS APPLICATION   Harry and David Holdings, Inc.

Harry and David Holdings, Inc., a mail-order food company known for its fruit baskets and Moose Munch popcorn, emerged from Chapter 11 in September 2011. Under the reorganization plan, $200,000,000 in senior debt will be exchanged for equity in the restructured company. UBS AG and Ally Financial provided $100,000,000 in post-petition financing, and will continue to finance the restructured company. *Source:* Reuters, August 30, 2011.

Illustration of Fresh Start Reporting After Reorganization   Continuing with the earlier example of the Manson Corporation, suppose Manson adopts a plan of reorganization on January 1, 2014, that provides for the following:

1. The company's main building will be sold; future operations will be conducted in rented facilities. Proceeds from sale of the building (book value, $1,100,000) of $1,000,000 will fully pay the $800,000 mortgage.

2. After reflecting the above planned transaction, Manson estimates its reorganization value at $2,580,000, consisting of the following:

Cash in excess of normal operating requirements.	$ 250,000
Net realizable value of excess assets available for disposition	30,000
Present value of discounted operating cash flows of the emerging entity	2,300,000
Total reorganization value	$2,580,000

3. Its reorganized capital structure has these components:

Postpetition liabilities	$ 360,000
Note payable to IRS	100,000
Senior secured debt (12%, 10 years)	700,000
Subordinated debt (14%, 7 years)	950,000
Common stock	220,000
Total	$2,330,000

Observe that the total capital of $2,330,000 equals the reorganization value of $2,580,000 less the excess cash of $250,000, assumed paid to creditors immediately.

4. Settlement of the $2,500,000 of liabilities subject to compromise as follows:
    a. Exchange the 15 percent notes payable of $1,000,000 for (1) $150,000 immediate cash payment, (2) $500,000 of senior secured debt, (3) $250,000 of subordinated debt, and (4) 20 percent of the new common stock issue.
    b. Exchange the $300,000 bank loan for (1) $50,000 immediate cash payment, (2) $100,000 of senior secured debt, (3) $100,000 of subordinated debt, and (4) 10 percent of the new common stock issue.

  c. Settle the taxes payable of $150,000 by (1) $50,000 immediate cash payment and (2) two additional annual payments of $50,000, with interest at 15 percent.

  d. Exchange the $1,050,000 accounts payable and other liabilities for (1) $100,000 of senior secured debt, (2) $600,000 of subordinated debt, and (3) 50 percent of the new common stock issue.

5. Prior equity interests are adjusted as follows:

  a. The existing preferred stock is canceled; the preferred stockholders receive 15 percent of the new common stock issue.

  b. The existing common stock is canceled; the common stockholders receive 5 percent of the new common stock issue.

The emerging entity satisfies the *two conditions for fresh start reporting*:

- Reorganization value of $2,580,000 is less than the total amount of all postpetition liabilities ($360,000) plus all allowed prepetition claims ($2,500,000), and

- Pre-confirmation holders of the existing voting shares received less than 50 percent of the voting shares in the new entity (20 percent in this case).

Entries to Record the Restructuring Entries to reflect the above transactions follow. First, under provision 1 of the plan, record the sale of the building and repay the mortgage.

Cash.	1,000,000	
Loss on sale of building	100,000	
Property, plant and equipment, net.		1,100,000
To record sale of building		
Mortgage payable	800,000	
Cash		800,000
To record full settlement of the fully-secured liability.		

Next, pursuant to plan provision 4, record settlement of the prepetition liabilities subject to compromise.

Liabilities subject to compromise.	2,500,000	
Cash		250,000
Senior secured debt		700,000
Subordinated debt.		950,000
Note payable to IRS		100,000
Common stock (new).		176,000
Gain on discharge of debt.		324,000
To record settlement of prepetition liabilities according to terms of the plan of reorganization.		

The $176,000 credit to common stock represents the 80 percent share of the new equity of $220,000, specified in provision 3, granted to various creditors under terms of the reorganization plan. Because the total cash, new debt securities, and equity granted to the prepetition creditors fell short of the total claims by $324,000, this amount appears as a gain on discharge of debt.

  Restructuring the interests of the prior stockholders—plan provision 5—involves eliminating their existing interests, recording their new interests, and temporarily crediting additional paid-in capital with the difference.

Preferred stock.	400,000	
Common stock (old).	100,000	
Common stock (new).		44,000
Additional paid-In capital.		456,000
To record the elimination of existing equity interests and creation of new equity interests ($44,000 = .2 × new common stock equity of $220,000).		

The final step is the revaluation of assets of the emerging entity called for by provision 2 of the plan. After recording the building sale, total assets are $2,700,000:

Total assets at December 31, 2013 (from the balance sheet immediately prior to emerging from reorganization).	$3,600,000
Less: Book value of building sold	(1,100,000)
Plus: Cash from sale, net of mortgage repayment.	200,000
Total assets after building sale.	$2,700,000

Given the $2,580,000 reorganization value, assets must be written down by $120,000. Assume that estimates of the assets' fair values result in the following adjustments to pre-reorganization book values:

Accounts receivable are reduced from a book value of $320,000 to an estimated collectible value of $260,000.	$ (60,000)
Inventory is reduced from $550,000 to $450,000	(100,000)
Property, plant and equipment is increased from $1,290,000 to $1,380,000.	90,000
Intangibles are written off.	(120,000)
	(190,000)
Reorganization value in excess of amounts allocated to identifiable assets.	70,000
Net adjustment to book values	$(120,000)

The following **reorganization entry** reflects these adjustments, the elimination of the deficit net of gains and losses recorded above, and the reduction in the paid-in capital created by the restructuring of equity interests.

Property, plant and equipment.	90,000	
Reorganization value in excess of amounts allocable to identifiable assets	70,000	
Gain on discharge of debt	324,000	
Additional paid-in capital	456,000	
Accounts receivable		60,000
Inventories.		100,000
Intangible assets		120,000
Loss on sale of building.		100,000
Deficit on December 31, 2013 balance sheet		560,000
To adjust asset values to reorganization value and eliminate deficit.		

After posting these entries, Manson's balance sheet appears as follows:

MANSON CORPORATION
Balance Sheet
January 1, 2014

Assets		Liabilities and equity	
Cash.	$ 100,000	Postpetition	$ 360,000
Accounts receivable.	260,000	Current portion of long-term debt	255,700
Inventories	450,000	Current liabilities.	615,700
Prepayments	70,000		
Current assets	880,000	Long-term liabilities	
Property, plant and equipment, net	1,380,000	Senior secured debt.	700,000
Reorganization value in excess of amounts allocable to identifiable assets	70,000	Subordinated debt	950,000
		Note payable	100,000
			1,750,000
		Less current portion.	(255,700)
			1,494,300
		Stockholders' equity	
		Common stock.	220,000
		Retained earnings	0
Total assets	$2,330,000	Total liabilities and equity.	$2,330,000

BUSINESS APPLICATION   **Trump Entertainment Resorts**

....

Emerging from Chapter 11 does not guarantee future success. Some companies return again to Chapter 11. In 2009, Trump Entertainment Resorts entered Chapter 11 for the third time. About 10 other companies, including an airline, steel companies, and retailers, are believed to have used Chapter 11 three times each.   *Source: The Huffington Post, May 12, 2009.*

REVIEW 2 ● Chapter 11 Reorganization

Instead of filing under Chapter 7, Baines Corp. (see Review Problem 1) decides to reorganize under Chapter 11 of the bankruptcy code. Postpetition liabilities of $275,000 were incurred during the reorganization process. Adding the company's prepetition liabilities gives total liabilities of $1,095,000 (= $820,000 + $275,000). As Baines prepares to emerge from reorganization, it has $90,000 in cash, and the present value of future operating cash flows is $800,000. The prepetition liabilities will be discharged as follows:

* Fully-secured creditors ($220,000) will receive $40,000 in cash and $180,000 in 10 percent senior secured debt.
* Partially secured creditors ($180,000) will receive $20,000 in cash, $100,000 in 10 percent senior secured debt, $40,000 in subordinated debt, and 10 percent of the equity in the reorganized company.
* Unsecured creditors with priority ($30,000) will be paid in cash.
* Unsecured creditors ($390,000) will receive $250,000 in subordinated debt and 70 percent of the equity of the reorganized company.
* Prior stockholders will receive 20 percent of the equity of the reorganized company.

Required
Determine how much gain will be recorded on the settlement of debt.

Solutions are located after the chapter assignments.

OTHER FORMS OF RESTRUCTURING

LO5
Describe accounting for other forms of reorganization.

To this point, the chapter examined formal actions under the bankruptcy laws to deal with firms in financial difficulty: liquidation under Chapter 7 and reorganization under Chapter 11 of the Bankruptcy Code. We now briefly consider accounting for two other forms of restructuring.

Quasi-Reorganization

A *quasi-reorganization* normally does not involve a restructuring of debt. The usual situation is that the company has accumulated a deficit in retained earnings, and believes that its asset values are overstated and that future amortization of these overstated amounts will continue to produce losses. The **quasi-reorganization** uses fresh start accounting to accomplish the following:

* Write assets down to fair values further increasing the deficit.
* Restructure the common stock equity to create enough additional paid-in capital to absorb the deficit in retained earnings, reducing the per-share par value, reducing the number of shares, or both.
* Eliminate the deficit against the additional paid-in capital so that retained earnings has a zero balance.

Because a quasi-reorganization changes the interests of equity holders, formal stockholder approval is needed. Creditor approval is not needed, however, as debts are left unchanged. Further, there is no immediate effect on cash flows. The motivation for the quasi-reorganization is to enhance the prospects of profitable operations in the future and thereby create the ability to pay dividends, not possible with negative retained earnings. Past circumstances that produced the deficit imply that recorded asset values will not be recovered by future operations, and should be written down. To accomplish this, stockholders voluntarily restructure their own holdings.

The major impact on **post-quasi-reorganization financial reporting** is the establishment of a "new" retained earnings account, with an initial balance of zero, dated to show that the accumulation of retained earnings begins from the effective date of the restructuring. Dating the retained earnings account continues until enough time has passed so that the quasi-reorganization is no longer deemed significant in understanding the company's financial statements.

Troubled Debt Restructuring

As an alternative to the overall debt restructuring provided by bankruptcy law, a specific obligation may be restructured by negotiation between debtor and creditor. Such a restructuring is called a **troubled debt restructuring** when, in view of a debtor's financial difficulties, a creditor grants a concession to the debtor that it otherwise would not grant. The creditor seeks to make the best of a poor situation, hoping that the concession raises the probability or amount expected to be collected. The concession typically includes one or more of the following:

● Accepting noncash assets from the debtor, such as receivables or real estate, in full or partial settlement of the debt.

● Accepting an equity interest in the debtor in full or partial settlement of the debt.

● Modifying the terms of the obligation, by reducing the interest rate, extending the maturity date, reducing the principal amount, forgiving accrued interest, or some combination of the foregoing.

A troubled debt restructuring involves an **economic loss** to the creditor—the fair values of assets or equity interests accepted are *less than* the creditor's investment in the debt obligation being settled. However, modifying the terms of a debt obligation in response to changing market conditions, reduced risk, or competition from other lenders is *not* considered a troubled debt restructuring, even though the lender suffers an economic loss. For a troubled debt restructuring to occur, the modification must be one not granted under normal circumstances and be motivated by realization that collectibility is threatened in the absence of some concessions. Accounting principles for troubled debt restructurings are specified in *ASC Subtopics 470-60* and *310-40*. A 2011 Accounting Standards Update establishes two conditions that must exist for a transaction to be considered a troubled debt restructuring. The debtor must be experiencing financial difficulties, and the restructuring must constitute a concession by the creditor.

Accounting by Debtors   When assets are transferred in settlement of debt, the resulting gain to the debtor is likely to have two components. One component, the difference between the *fair value of the asset surrendered* and the asset's *carrying value*, is reported as a **gain or loss on asset disposition**. The second component, the difference between the *fair value of the asset surrendered* and the *carrying value of the debt settled*—face value plus accrued interest plus or minus unamortized premium, discount, or issue costs—is reported as a **gain on restructuring**. This latter gain is typically treated as an ordinary item.

When the debtor exchanges an equity interest for partial forgiveness of a debt, the debtor records the new equity at its fair value. The difference between the fair value of the equity granted and the carrying value of the debt settled also constitutes a *gain on restructuring*.

A modification of terms produces no adjustment to the carrying value of the debt unless the *total undiscounted future cash payments* specified by the new terms are *less than* the present carrying value. In this case, the debtor reduces the carrying value to the new total of the undiscounted future cash payments, and a gain on restructuring is recorded. When no reduction of carrying value is required, the change in terms is reflected *prospectively,* typically by modifying annual interest expense. The effective interest approach is used to calculate interest expense.

REVIEW OF KEY CONCEPTS ·····················

LO 1 **Explain the basic legal aspects of bankruptcy. (p. 624)** The **bankruptcy laws** provide two approaches for firms unable to meet their obligations. **Chapter 7** provides for **liquidation**—termination of operations and disposition of the firm's assets to pay creditors. **Chapter 11** provides for **reorganization**—continuation of operations while a plan is developed to restructure both creditor claims and equity interests so that the emerging entity has a prospect of profitable operations.

LO 2 **Prepare a statement of affairs for a Chapter 7 bankruptcy. (p. 626)** The trustee of **firms in liquidation** prepares a **statement of affairs** to show the financial condition of the company. Assets are valued at **estimated realizable value** and are classified according to any security interests held by creditors. Liabilities are classified according to their **legal preference**. The statement shows the **estimated deficiency to unsecured creditors**, the difference between the liabilities and the estimated realizable value of the assets.

LO 3 **Prepare a statement of realization and liquidation. (p. 630)** The **statement of realization and liquidation** details the activities of the **receiver or trustee** in administering the estate of the bankrupt firm during the liquidation process.

LO 4 **Account for a company undergoing Chapter 11 reorganization. (p. 633)** **Firms in reorganization** continue their accounting on a **going-concern basis**. Liabilities are classified to distinguish prepetition from postpetition claims, and to focus on those liabilities **subject to compromise**. During the reorganization phase, payments on prepetition liabilities are generally suspended while a **plan of reorganization** is developed. This plan restructures the interests of creditors and stockholders to enable the firm to continue to operate. When the company **emerges from reorganization** after approval of the plan, a **new accounting entity** results when **reorganization value** is less than total liabilities and prior stockholders have less than 50 percent of the voting shares in the new entity. **Fresh start reporting** follows from meeting these conditions and establishes a new basis of accountability for the firm's assets, liabilities, and equity interests.

LO 5 **Describe accounting for other forms of reorganization. (p. 642)** Restructurings may also occur in less formal ways, without resort to the bankruptcy laws. A **quasi-reorganization** revises asset values and restructures the equity interests to eliminate a deficit in retained earnings and enhance the prospects of future profitability. A **troubled debt restructuring** involves an agreement between a debtor and a creditor to settle a liability or modify its terms in light of the debtor's financial difficulties.

MULTIPLE CHOICE QUESTIONS ·····················

LO 1 **1.** Under the provisions of Chapter 7 of the bankruptcy laws

    a. all of a company's debts are forgiven.
    b. the company attempts to continue operations by restructuring its finances.
    c. the company ceases operations, disposes of assets, and settles its liabilities.
    d. the company is taken over by the creditors.

LO 1 **2.** Under the provisions of Chapter 11 of the bankruptcy laws

    a. all of a company's debts are forgiven.
    b. the company attempts to continue operations by restructuring its finances.
    c. the company ceases operations, disposes of assets, and settles its liabilities.
    d. the company is taken over by the creditors.

Use the following information to answer questions 3 and 4 below.

Inho Corporation has fully secured liabilities of $300,000 and unsecured liabilities of $1,500,000, of which $250,000 have legal priority. Inho's assets are expected to realize $1,000,000; of these, $420,000 is pledged to the fully-secured creditors.

LO 2 **3.** Inho's net free assets amount to

    a. $1,000,000.
    b. $ 700,000.
    c. $ 580,000.
    d. $ 450,000.

4. The estimated deficiency to Inho's unsecured creditors is   LO 2

 a. $800,000.
 b. $700,000.
 c. $500,000.
 d. $450,000.

Use the following information to answer questions 5 and 6 below.

 Borden Corporation is undergoing a Chapter 7 liquidation. Currently, it has cash of $130,000, inventory of $650,000, and equipment of $775,000. It owes an unsecured bank loan payable of $500,000 and unsecured accounts payable of $1,600,000. During the current month, the Receiver sells Borden's entire inventory to a liquidator for $290,000. The entire cash balance is then distributed to unsecured creditors.

5. Borden's statement of realization and liquidation shows   LO 3

 a. gain on liquidation of $1,680,000.
 b. assets not realized of $360,000 for inventory and $775,000 for equipment.
 c. assets to be realized of $1,555,000 (cash, inventory, and equipment).
 d. loss on realization of $360,000.

6. The receiver's payment to the bank is   LO 3

 a. $500,000.
 b. $420,000.
 c. $100,000.
 d. $290,000.

Use the following information to answer questions 7 and 8 below.

 Mannheim Corporation is ready to emerge from Chapter 11 bankruptcy under a reorganization plan accepted by all parties. Mannheim's balance sheet shows:

Various assets	$2,000,000	Prepetition liabilities, fully secured...............	$ 400,000
		Prepetition liabilities subject to compromise	1,360,000
		Postpetition liabilities	820,000
		Stockholders' equity	(580,000)
TOTAL	$2,000,000	TOTAL	$2,000,000

7. There are no excess assets. The present value of future cash flows from the reorganized company's operating assets is $2,370,000. Mannheim's reorganization value is LO 4

 a. $2,370,000.
 b. $2,000,000.
 c. $2,580,000.
 d. $1,760,000.

8. New equity interests in the reorganized company are $160,000. The compromised amount of Mannheim's prepetition liabilities is LO 4

 a. $1,360,000.
 b. $1,390,000.
 c. $2,210,000.
 d. $ 990,000.

9. Jones Inc. has common stock of $3,000,000, additional paid-in capital of $200,000, and a retained earnings deficit of $1,440,000. As part of a quasi-reorganization, Jones writes down its assets by $800,000. To eliminate its deficit, Jones must restructure its common equity, reducing it by LO 5

 a. $1,240,000.
 b. $1,440,000.
 c. $2,040,000.
 d. $2,240,000.

LO 5   **10.** Kiefer Company has negotiated with its major creditor to undertake a troubled debt restructuring. Under the agreement, Kiefer transfers a parcel of real estate in full settlement of a debt of $1,800,000. The real estate has a carrying value on Kiefer's books of $920,000 and a fair value of $1,460,00. As a result of this transaction, Kiefer reports

    a. $340,000 gain on debt restructuring.
    b. $880,000 gain on asset disposition.
    c. $880,000 gain on debt restructuring.
    d. $540,000 gain on debt restructuring.

Assignments with the ✅ in the margin are available in an online homework system.
See the Preface of the book for details.

EXERCISES •••

LO 2   **E15.1**   **Deficiency to Unsecured Creditors**   Consider the following information for Evans, Inc. when the company entered bankruptcy proceedings:

Account	Balance per Books Dr (Cr)
Cash.	$ 31,700
Accounts receivable.	646,800
Inventory.	320,000
Prepaid expenses.	10,600
Buildings, net	750,000
Equipment, net.	123,500
Goodwill	88,000
Wages payable.	(77,300)
Taxes payable	(30,900)
Accounts payable.	(967,300)
Notes payable	(205,400)
Common stock.	(1,200,000)
Retained earnings—deficit.	510,300
Total	$ 0

Inventory with a book value of $240,000 is security for notes payable of $145,000. The equipment secures other notes payable. Expected realizable values of the assets are:

Accounts receivable.	$410,000
Inventory.	220,000
Buildings.	400,000
Equipment	50,000

Required
Compute the estimated deficiency to unsecured creditors.

LO 2   **E15.2**   **Bankruptcy Calculations**   Faced with an inability to meet its current debt payments, The Selbert Company entered bankruptcy on April 30, 2014. The appointed trustee will liquidate the company and pay the creditors in accord with the provisions of the bankruptcy laws. Selbert's balance sheet on April 30, 2014, shows the following:

THE SELBERT COMPANY
Balance Sheet
April 30, 2014

Assets		**Liabilities and equity**	
Cash......................	$ 3,200	Accounts payable..............	$131,900
Accounts receivable............	71,000	Loan payable to bank...........	60,000
Notes receivable...............	50,000	Notes payable to suppliers.......	83,900
Inventories	108,600	Accrued wages.................	94,700
Prepaid expenses..............	17,200	Accrued taxes	70,000
Land and buildings, net	172,000	Mortgage payable	195,000
Equipment, net.................	113,500	Common stock.................	100,000
Goodwill, net	28,000	Retained earnings	(172,000)
Total assets	$563,500	Total liabilities and equity........	$563,500

Additional information:

1. The trustee estimates that 60 percent of the accounts receivable will be collected, and she has agreed to settle the notes receivable for $42,500. The notes receivable serve as collateral for the loan payable to the bank.
2. The inventories will likely be sold to a competitor, at 40 percent of book value.
3. Other than a $2,000 insurance refund, no recovery of prepaid items is expected.
4. Appraised at $300,000, the land and buildings are pledged as security on the mortgage.
5. The equipment is expected to be sold for $40,000.
6. The notes payable to the suppliers are unsecured.
7. Accrued wages do not exceed statutory limits per employee.

Required

Compute the following:

a. Estimated gains and losses on asset dispositions.
b. Amount of priority claims.
c. Estimated payments to secured creditors.
d. Expected recovery percentage.

E15.3 Statement of Affairs   Dellwood Corporation is experiencing difficulty in paying its bills and is considering filing for bankruptcy. Current data as of September 30, 2014, show the following: LO 2 ✓

Assets	**Book Value**	**Expected Realizable Value**
Cash......................................	$ 40,000	$ 40,000
Accounts receivable........................	400,000	300,000
Inventory—materials........................	360,000	270,000
Inventory—finished goods	500,000	550,000
Prepaid expenses...........................	10,000	—
Land......................................	100,000	420,000
Building	700,000	1,600,000
Trucks....................................	200,000	60,000
Equipment	450,000	250,000
Intangibles	160,000	—
Total	$2,920,000	

continued

continued from prior page

Liabilities		Secured by
Accounts payable..........................	$ 770,000	
Bank loan.................................	250,000	80% of receivables
Wages payable............................	120,000	
Taxes payable	80,000	
Truck loan...............................	50,000	Trucks with $120,000 book value, $35,000 estimated realizable value
Mortgage payable	430,000	Land and building
Loan payable	500,000	Finished goods
Stockholder loan	1,100,000	Not subordinated to other debt
Stockholders' equity	(380,000)	
Total	$2,920,000	

Wages payable do not exceed statutory limits per employee.

Required

Prepare a statement of affairs.

✓ LO 3   E15.4   Journal Entries for Bankruptcy Trustee   The balance sheet of the Binder Company immediately prior to entering bankruptcy proceedings and a balance sheet prepared during liquidation follows:

BINDER COMPANY
Balance Sheet
June 30, 2013

Cash...........................	$ 2,000	Accounts payable.................	$ 40,000
Accounts receivable..............	10,000	Accrued wages*...................	7,000
Inventories	30,000	Taxes payable	8,000
Equipment, net..................	53,000	Notes payable**...................	70,000
Land...........................	15,000	Stockholders' equity	(15,000)
Total assets	$110,000	Total liabilities and equity..........	$110,000

* Amounts due do not exceed statutory limits per employee.
** Of the notes payable, $15,000 are secured with inventory having a book value of $15,000. The remaining notes payable and the accounts payable are unsecured.

BINDER COMPANY, Alfred Wade, Trustee,
Balance Sheet
December 31, 2013

Cash...........................	$10,000	Liabilities not liquidated:	
Assets not realized:		Accounts payable...............	$32,000
Equipment, net	53,000	Notes payable..................	48,000
		Estate deficit....................	(17,000)
Total assets	$63,000	Total liabilities and equity...........	$63,000

The inventory was sold at two-thirds its book value. Half the accounts receivable were collected; the rest were written off.

Required

Reconstruct the journal entries made by Alfred Wade, Trustee for Binder Company, from June 30 to December 31, 2013.

LO 3   E15.5   Statement of Realization and Liquidation   At January 1, 2014, the records of Sharon Thomson, trustee in bankruptcy for Davis Corporation, showed the following:

	Dr (Cr)
Cash...	$17,700
Assets not realized:	
Land	40,000
Building..	217,000
Equipment..	68,000
Patents	21,600
Liabilities not liquidated:	
Accounts payable...	(400,000)
Loans payable	(120,000)
Estate deficit..	155,700

During January, Thomson sold equipment having a book value of $30,000 for $12,500, and sold the patents for $40,000. Thomson was paid $2,500 as a trustee's fee, and $62,400 was distributed proportionately to the creditors.

Required

Prepare a statement of realization and liquidation for January and a balance sheet and statement of estate deficit as of January 31, 2014.

E15.6 Reconstruct Realization and Liquidation Transactions   A trustee's statement of realization and   LO 3
liquidation is presented below:

Assets to be realized:			**Assets realized:**		
Accounts receivable.........	$ 15,000		Accounts receivable.........	$ 9,000	
Inventory..................	41,000		Inventory..................	18,000	
Equipment	88,000	$144,000	Equipment	23,000	$ 50,000
Assets acquired:			**Assets not realized:**		
None			Accounts receivable.........	6,000	
			Inventory..................	20,000	
			Equipment	72,000	98,000
Liabilities liquidated:			**Liabilities to be liquidated:**		
Notes payable		45,000	Accounts payable...........	90,000	
			Notes payable	160,000	250,000
Liabilities not liquidated:			**Liabilities incurred:**		
Accounts payable...........	90,000		None		
Notes payable	110,000	200,000			
Gain on realization		7,000	Loss on realization		3,000
Gain on liquidation		5,000			
Combined total.............		$401,000	Combined total.............		$401,000

Required

Reconstruct, in journal form, the trustee's transactions for the period.

E15.7 Liabilities During Reorganization   Francona Corporation is undergoing reorganization under the   LO 4
provisions of Chapter 11 of the bankruptcy code. Francona is currently continuing in operation as a
debtor-in-possession while a plan of reorganization is developed. The following occurred during the
reorganization period:

1.   Liabilities existing at the time of filing the petition for reorganization are $1,500,000, all unsecured.
     The full amount of these liabilities is expected to be allowed by the court, although the eventual
     settlement is projected to be about 70 percent of face value.
2.   Liabilities of $300,000 were incurred since filing the petition.
3.   Legal costs connected with the reorganization process amounted to $75,000.
4.   Sold three executive cars, generating $30,000 cash and an $8,000 gain.
5.   Cancelled a contract to purchase a new machine and forfeited the company's $30,000 deposit.

Required

Describe how each of the above would be presented on Francona's financial statements during reorganization. Give the specific statement and caption for each item.

LO 4   **E15.8   Calculation of Reorganization Value**   Weihong Corporation is about to emerge from a Chapter 11 reorganization. Assets of the emerging entity have a total book value of $1,520,000. Of these, assets with a book value of $195,000 are not needed to operate the emerging entity and will be sold for an expected price of $180,000. The remaining assets will be used in operations. Operations are expected to generate an annual net cash flow of $85,000. This amount is projected for the next ten years; a discount rate of 10 percent is deemed appropriate.

Required

Calculate Weihong Corporation's reorganization value.

LO 4   **E15.9   Fresh Start Reporting**   Rudolph Corporation is about to emerge from a Chapter 11 reorganization. The following data are available:

Reorganization value of assets	$2,000,000
Prepetition liabilities—allowed claims	1,600,000
Prepetition liabilities—expected settlement (value of cash, debt securities, and	
equity securities to be given in settlement)	1,150,000
Postpetition liabilities	600,000

Pre-confirmation equity structure:
    Preferred stock (nonvoting), 500,000 shares
    Common stock (voting), 500,000 shares

New equity structure:
    All existing stock canceled
    New voting common stock issued as follows:
        40 percent to prepetition creditors
        40 percent to previous preferred stockholders
        20 percent to previous common stockholders

Required

Is Rudolph Corporation entitled to adopt fresh start reporting for the emerging entity? Explain.

LO 5   **E15.10   Quasi-Reorganization**   Zoyhofski Corporation has incurred losses for several years, and currently has a $620,000 deficit in retained earnings. It has 40,000 shares of $10 par value common stock issued and outstanding, and has additional paid-in capital of $500,000. Due to a permanent decline in its economic prospects, Zoyhofski believes its assets are overvalued. As part of a quasi-reorganization, a $250,000 writedown is proposed to reflect the changed conditions. The present $10 par common stock is to be exchanged for a new issue bearing a $1 par value; each stockholder will receive one new share for every eight old shares.

Required

a.   Prepare journal entries to record the quasi-reorganization.
b.   Prepare the stockholders' equity section of Zoyhofski's balance sheet after the quasi-reorganization.

LO 5   **E15.11   Troubled Debt Restructuring**   Bakert Company's $1,000,000 note payable to a private investor just matured. Interest was not paid on the note for the past three years and accrued interest now totals $300,000. Bakert is in serious financial difficulty and is unable to pay off the note. In an attempt to help the company survive, the company and the investor agree to the following:

1.   Bakert transfers a parcel of vacant land to the investor in settlement of $400,000 of the total obligation. The land has a book value of $150,000, and $400,000 is a reasonable estimate of its fair value.
2.   Bakert issues $300,000 par value of 10 percent cumulative preferred stock in settlement of $300,000 of the obligation.
3.   The remaining $600,000 of the total obligation is replaced by a five-year note in the principal amount of $300,000, with interest at 15 percent.

Required

Prepare journal entries to record these arrangements for Bakert Company.

PROBLEMS ••

P15.1 **Statement of Affairs** The following items of information appear on the statement of affairs of Shaw   **LO 2**
Corporation:

1. Estimated deficiency to unsecured creditors, $72,000.
2. Unsecured liabilities with priority, $37,000.
3. Assets pledged to fully secured creditors ($200,000) exceed the related liabilities by $40,000.
4. Liabilities to partially secured creditors, $83,000.
5. Assets not pledged to any creditors, $185,000.
6. Total assets, book value $523,000, estimated realizable value $435,000.

Required

Determine the following amounts:

a. Assets pledged to partially secured creditors.
b. Total unsecured liabilities (excluding those with priority).
c. Total liabilities.
d. Total stockholders' equity.

P15.2 **Statement of Affairs** The Janes Corporation has filed a petition for protection under Chapter 7 of the   **LO 2**
bankruptcy laws. Its financial data as of March 10, 2014, the filing date, are as follows.

Assets	
Cash	$ 12,000
Accounts receivable, net	82,000
Inventory of raw materials	112,000
Inventory of finished goods	158,000
Prepaid advertising and insurance.	14,000
Marketable securities, fair market value at December 31, 2013	27,000
Land	50,000
Building, net	675,000
Machinery and equipment, net.	238,000
Goodwill	50,000
Total assets	$1,418,000
Liabilities and equity	
Accounts payable.	$ 370,000
Bank loan payable	113,000
Accrued federal taxes payable.	150,000
Accrued salaries and wages payable.	60,000
Notes payable	250,000
Mortgage payable	422,000
Common stock.	120,000
Retained earnings (deficit)	(67,000)
Total liabilities and equity.	$1,418,000

Additional data:

1. The cash balance includes $3,000 of NSF customer checks; collection of these is unlikely.
2. Accounts receivable include $41,000 in numerous small balances under $500. These customers would probably take advantage of Janes' bankruptcy filing and never pay, knowing that the amount owed is too small to justify collection procedures.
3. Accounts receivable also include $6,500 of credit balances owed to customers for overpayments, returns, and credit memos.
4. The inventory of raw materials could be sold for $70,000, or could be converted into finished goods at an additional cost of $52,000. These finished goods have a normal selling price of $220,000 (but see next item).
5. The inventory of finished goods has a normal selling price of $250,000, but when sold in bankruptcy to a liquidator, these goods are likely to yield only 55 percent of the normal selling price.
6. The prepaid advertising ($6,000) has no refund clause in its contract. The prepaid insurance ($8,000) has a cancellation value at the filing date of $1,700, but by the time bankruptcy proceedings are completed and the policy could safely be terminated, it is likely to have expired.

7. Since December 31, 2013, the marketable securities declined in value by $5,000.

8. The land and building have an estimated selling price of $800,000; the machinery and equipment have an estimated selling price of $90,000.

9. The goodwill balance results from an acquisition eight years ago, and has no liquidation value.

10. The notes payable are secured by the accounts receivable and by the current inventory of finished goods. The mortgage payable is secured by the land and building. All other liabilities are unsecured.

11. Accrued salaries and wages do not exceed statutory limits per employee.

12. Janes is defendant in a lawsuit, not reported on its balance sheet. A loss of $48,000 is probable, of which $25,000 will be covered by insurance.

13. Janes has noncancelable operating leases for several vehicles used in its business; $80,000 of lease payments remain. However, the leases can be terminated early by paying half the remaining balance.

14. Expected legal, accounting, and administrative costs of the bankruptcy are $100,000.

Required

a. Prepare a statement of affairs.

b. Compute the estimated settlement per dollar of unsecured liabilities.

c. Assume that $200,000 of the accounts payable is owed to a single major supplier and that, prior to the bankruptcy, the supplier had acquired a security interest in the inventory of raw materials and the machinery and equipment. What would be the effect on the estimated settlement per dollar of unsecured liabilities?

LO 2 **P15.3** **Statement of Affairs** Bridges Furniture Store is finding it increasingly difficult to meet its obligations despite satisfactory sales volume is satisfactory and profitability. Bridges cannot meet its working capital requirements for inventory and payments on current liabilities. Finally, after pledging all of its installment receivables, Bristol failed to meet the bills due on October 10, 2014. Management feels that if the company could obtain an extension of time in which to pay its obligations it could meet its liabilities in full. The corporation arranged for a meeting of creditors to determine whether the company should be granted an extension or be forced into bankruptcy.

The pre-closing trial balance for the current calendar year of the company on September 30, 2014, follows:

	Debit	Credit
Cash.	$ 6,360	
Installment receivables, pledged	645,000	
Allowance for doubtful installment receivables		$ 40,320
Accounts receivable.	62,490	
Allowance for doubtful accounts		3,150
Inventories, January 1, 2014	453,450	
Prepaid insurance	4,470	
Autos and trucks	67,140	
Accumulated depreciation, autos and trucks		44,880
Furniture and equipment	37,500	
Accumulated depreciation, furniture and equipment.		6,420
Buildings.	269,280	
Accumulated depreciation, buildings.		22,590
Land.	30,720	
Organization costs	2,640	
Trade accounts payable.		396,300
Furniture and equipment loan payable.		17,400
Installment loan on auto and trucks.		30,000
Bank loan, secured by installment receivables		483,750
Taxes payable (prior years)		42,660
Accrued salaries and wages		14,040
Accrued interest.		32,970
Notes payable, stockholder		300,000
Mortgage payable		147,000
Capital stock		300,000
Retained earnings	195,870	
Sales.		2,126,700
Purchases.	1,582,890	
Other expenses and income, net.	650,370	
Totals	$4,008,180	$4,008,180

Further investigation produced the following additional data:

1. Depreciation, allowances for doubtful accounts, prepaid and accrued items are all adjusted as of September 30, 2014.
2. All installment receivables are pledged with the bank on September 30, 2014, the bank had deducted its interest to date and loaned the company loan 75 percent of the face amount of the receivables. Bridges estimates that a forced liquidation will result in a loss of $120,000 of the receivables' face amount.
3. Accounts receivable are not pledged, and Bridges estimates collectibility of $49,500 on a liquidation basis.
4. Since January 1, 2014, the company made a gross profit of 33 1/3 percent but the inventory on hand will likely provide only $300,000 in a forced liquidation.
5. Cancellation of the insurance will provide $2,970.
6. All autos and trucks are pledged as security for an installment loan, and their total market value is $24,000.
7. The store was remodeled in 2013, and the furniture and equipment are financed by a loan; the furniture and equipment is pledged as security for the loan. Because of its specialized nature, Bridges estimates that a forced sale would realize no more than $15,000.
8. The land and buildings are subject to a 6 percent mortgage, on which interest is paid to July 30, 2014. It is estimated the property could be sold for $225,000.
9. The accrued salaries and wages do not exceed statutory limits per employee.
10. The notes payable to stockholders are not subordinated to general creditors. The notes carried a 6 percent rate of interest, but no interest has been paid since December 31, 2012.
11. Since prior income tax returns disclosed a large available net operating loss carryover, no current income taxes need be considered.
12. Bridges estimates the cost of liquidation proceedings to be $15,000.
13. There appeared to be no other realizable values on liquidation and no unrecorded liabilities.

Required

a. Prepare a statement of affairs for Bridges Furniture Store as of September 30, 2014.
b. Compute the percentages of recovery by the unsecured creditors and the partially-secured creditors if Bridges Furniture Store is forced into bankruptcy. *Hint:* Be sure to estimate ending inventory and cost of goods sold using information in item 4.

P15.4 **Statement of Realization and Liquidation**   Barnwell Corporation had a history of profitable operations until recently encountering serious difficulty paying its bills. Attempts to acquire bank financing have been unsuccessful, due to the advanced age and ill health of the firm's sole owner and manager, Amos Barnwell, as have attempts to sell the company. Faced with the prospect of the firm's bankruptcy, Barnwell's creditors met and proposed the following terms to Mr. Barnwell: **LO 3**

1. Operations will be continued until the present raw materials and work-in-process inventories are used or completed and sold.
2. The creditors will advance $9,000 to finance the necessary operating costs.
3. A trustee will be appointed by the creditors to manage the remaining operations and subsequent liquidation.

Amos Barnwell agreed to these terms and on August 1, 2013, Frank Carrington was appointed trustee. The company's balance sheet on that date showed the following:

BARNWELL CORPORATION			
Balance Sheet			
August 1, 2013			
Cash............................	$ 397	Accounts payable................	$ 37,933
Accounts receivable.............	6,093	Common stock, $10 par...........	30,000
Raw materials inventory...........	24,000	Additional paid-in capital..........	60,000
Work-in-process inventory.........	51,600	Retained earnings	12,783
Finished goods..................	8,550		
Equipment, net.................	50,076		
Total assets	$140,716	Total liabilities and equity..........	$140,716

During the first six months of Carrington's term as trustee, the following occurred:

1. The creditors advanced the company $9,000.
2. Purchased additional raw materials on account for $9,450.

3. Incurred expenses on account of $22,500. Paid expenses of $31,732, of which $24,937 was for labor. All expenses are charged to work in process.
4. Expended cash in the amount of $1,125 for new equipment.
5. Of the accounts receivable outstanding on August 1, $570 is deemed uncollectible. The balance was collected.
6. Recorded depreciation of $1,500 and charged it to work in process.
7. Collected sales on account of $108,450 during the 6-month period.
8. No equipment was sold.

On January 31, 2014, account balances are as follows: accounts receivable (new), $5,073; accounts payable (new), $133; raw materials, $3,000; and finished goods, $45,000.

Required

a. Prepare a schedule showing transactions affecting the cash account of Barnwell Corporation.
b. Prepare a statement of realization and liquidation for Barnwell Corporation for the six-month period ending January 31, 2014.

⊘ LO 3   P15.5   Statement of Realization and Liquidation   Comfort Mattress Corporation, a retailer, decided to liquidate in the face of an extreme cash shortage. By agreement with creditors, a receiver was appointed to manage the liquidation. Upon appointment, the receiver found the company's financial condition to be as follows:

COMFORT MATTRESS CORPORATION			
Balance Sheet			
March 17, 2013			
Cash.......................	$ 15,000	Accounts payable.................	$510,000
Accounts receivable.............	120,000	Loan payable (secured by inventory)..	200,000
Inventory of merchandise.........	500,000	Note payable (secured by fixtures)....	60,000
Store fixtures, net..............	150,000	Stockholders' equity	15,000
Total assets	$785,000	Total liabilities and equity...........	$785,000

From March 17 through June 30, the following occurred:

1. Collected accounts receivable of $85,000; the remaining accounts are deemed to be uncollectible.
2. Held a "going out of business sale." Sold inventory costing $310,000 for $388,000. Paid expenses of conducting the sale, amounting to $65,000.
3. Sold the remaining inventory to a liquidator for $75,000.
4. The receiver terminated the store's lease; the lease provides for a termination penalty of $30,000, which was accrued.
5. Sold the store fixtures at auction for a net of $37,000.
6. Accrued the receiver's fee of $52,000.
7. Paid the secured creditors to the extent of the value of their security.

Required

a. Prepare a statement of realization and liquidation as of June 30, 2013.
b. Compute the remaining cash and determine how it is disbursed, assuming no further expenses.

LO 4   P15.6   Accounting and Reporting During Reorganization   On April 1, 2015, the Axell Corporation entered formal reorganization proceedings under Chapter 11 of the bankruptcy laws. The company's **liabilities** at that date consisted of the following:

Accounts payable to trade creditors	$ 900,000
Loan payable to bank (unsecured)...	100,000
Note payable on equipment (uncertain as to whether the value of the equipment equals the amount of the note)...........................	150,000
Mortgage payable on building (fully secured)	1,000,000
Accrued interest on mortgage (payments are in arrears).............................	130,000
Total	$2,280,000

The company's assets were as follows:

Cash	$ 120,000
Accounts receivable, net	480,000
Equipment, net	350,000
Land and building, net	1,250,000
Investment (equity method)	200,000
Total	$2,400,000

During the next eight months, the company continued to operate while developing the reorganization plan. It made no payments on the above liabilities during this period. The following transactions occurred between April 1 and December 31:

1. Sales amounted to $1,400,000, with net cash collections of $1,200,000.
2. Operating expenses (including selling, general, and administrative expenses) were $1,120,000. Of this amount, $700,000 was paid in cash, $30,000 represented depreciation of equipment, and $80,000 represented depreciation of building.
3. Interest of $77,000 accrued on the company's liabilities: $7,000 on the loan, $10,000 on the note, and $60,000 on the mortgage. None of this amount was paid. Axell expects that half of each amount will be allowed as a claim.
4. Accrued income taxes of $100,000 for the period April 1 through December 31, and made estimated tax payments of $75,000.
5. Earned interest on cash balances of $65,000.
6. Accrued $100,000 in legal and accounting fees connected with the reorganization.
7. The accounts payable existing at April 1 include a $90,000 invoice from a subcontractor that is subject to dispute. It is expected that one-half of this amount is likely to be allowed as a claim.
8. Sold the investment in May for $350,000 cash. No further equity method income accruals or dividends were recordable after April 1. This sale did not constitute a disposal of a business segment.
9. Settled an employment contract with the company's executive vice president and agreed on $75,000 of deferred compensation. The $75,000 is likely to be allowed as a claim.

Required

Prepare Axell's December 31, 2015, balance sheet and its income statement and statement of cash flows for the period ended December 31, 2015.

P15.7 Classification of Liabilities in Reorganization The Spring Hill Corporation entered Chapter 11   **LO 3**
reorganization on March 19, 2014. At December 31, 2014, the accountant prepared the following list of liabilities, and seeks your assistance in determining the amount to classify as liabilities subject to compromise in the December 31, 2014, balance sheet:

1. The balance of accounts payable to suppliers is $742,000 on December 31, and was $588,000 on March 19. The company's attorney instructed that no payments are to be made on the March 19 balances. Incurred new accounts payable of $504,000 since March 19; some of these have been paid.
2. In April, the company terminated leases on several executives' automobiles, incurring a cancellation penalty of $26,000 that remains unpaid.
3. Accrued legal fees of $90,000. An $8,000 balance existed on March 19; the remainder was incurred since that date, in connection with the reorganization proceedings.
4. Notes payable for trucks amount to $57,000. An additional $7,000 in accrued interest accumulated, as no payments were made on the note since March 19. The market value of the trucks is estimated to be $50,000 to $70,000.
5. An unsecured line of credit loan from First National Bank has a balance of $150,000, plus $15,000 interest accrued since March 19.
6. Negotiated a new line of credit loan with Second National Bank after Spring Hill filed for reorganization. The current balance of this loan, including accrued interest, is $70,000.
7. The mortgage payable on the company's land and building stands at $350,000, plus $20,000 interest accrued since March 19. The land and building have an estimated market value of $500,000.
8. Canceled maintenance contracts, at an agreed cancellation charge of $10,000 that is not yet paid.

Required

Prepare a classification of liabilities for use in presenting the December 31, 2014, balance sheet.

LO 4   **P15.8**   **Reorganization Value**   Lopez Corporation is emerging from Chapter 11 reorganization proceedings. The company's balance sheet shows total assets of $9,000,000. Liabilities subject to compromise amount to $7,400,000, and fully secured liabilities are $1,800,000. Liabilities incurred since filing the reorganization petition amount to $900,000. The plan of reorganization identifies assets not needed in the new operation that have a $1,300,000 book value These assets will be sold in the near future for an expected $400,000. The remaining assets will be used in the new operations of the emerging company; the estimated present value of their future cash flows is $7,500,000. The plan also provides for the new equity interests in the emerging company to be valued at $900,000; 70 percent of this equity will be held by unsecured prepetition creditors, with the remainder held by the former stockholders of Lopez.

Required

a.   Determine the reorganization value.
b.   Determine the amount of gain on the restructuring of the company's debt.
c.   Prepare a summary balance sheet after implementing the reorganization plan.

LO 4   **P15.9**   **Emerging from Reorganization**   Salem-Winston Corporation is emerging from reorganization proceedings under Chapter 11 of the bankruptcy laws. The company's balance sheet shows total assets of $3,900,000, liabilities subject to compromise of $3,600,000, and postpetition liabilities of $700,000. For purposes of determining reorganization value, Salem-Winston has the following:

Excess cash (accumulated because no payments were made on prepetition debt during the reorganization period)...........................	$ 600,000
Net realizable value of excess assets available for disposition (book value is $100,000)....	60,000
Present value of future operating cash flows of the emerging entity....................	3,000,000
Total...	$3,660,000

The new capital structure of Salem-Winston will be as follows:

Postpetition liabilities......................................	$ 700,000
Senior secured debt (10%, 15-year maturity)	1,800,000
Subordinated debt (13%, 8-year maturity).........................	500,000
Common stock..	60,000
Total...	$3,060,000

The creditors represented in the amount of liabilities subject to compromise receive an immediate cash payment of $600,000 (the excess cash), all of the new debt securities, and 60 percent of the new common stock. The existing equity holders receive 40 percent of the new common stock.

Required

Prepare journal entries to record Salem-Winston's emergence from reorganization.

LO 5   **P15.10**   **Quasi-Reorganization**   The Hassani Corporation has the following balance sheet:

Current assets	$ 700,000	Current liabilities................	$ 600,000
Noncurrent assets	3,600,000	Long-term liabilities	2,950,000
		Common stock ($10 par)	1,700,000
		Retained earnings	(950,000)
Total assets	$4,300,000	Total liabilities and equity........	$4,300,000

Company profitability has been marginal, in part due to book values of noncurrent assets that do not adequately reflect the reduced earning power of the assets. To give its balance sheet a better basis for future profitability, the company decides to undertake a quasi-reorganization. Hassani writes down noncurrent assets to their fair value of $3,000,000 and replaces the current common stock with 100,000 shares of a new issue having a $1 par value.

Required

a.   Prepare journal entries to record the quasi-reorganization.
b.   Prepare a balance sheet following the quasi-reorganization.

P15.11 Troubled Debt Restructuring Herbert Company holds a variety of investment assets (land and securities) in addition to its operating assets. The company is experiencing cash flow problems because of marginally-profitable operations and a substantial operating debt burden. The investments produce very little cash flow, although the market values appreciated substantially. The current balance sheet follows: LO 5

Operating assets	$2,000,000	Accounts payable	$1,500,000
Land	700,000	Notes payable	300,000
Securities	1,200,000	Loan payable	500,000
		Officer loans	600,000
		Accrued liabilities	300,000
		Stockholders' equity	700,000
Total assets	$3,900,000	Total liabilities and equity	$3,900,000

Reluctantly, management decided to use some of its investment assets to reduce its operating debt burden, and negotiated the following agreements with creditors:

1. Settled the $300,000 note payable, currently secured by operating assets, by the transfer of securities with a fair market value of $290,000 (book value = $140,000). The creditor agreed to the $10,000 discount to get immediate settlement of the note, which does not mature for another two years.
2. Settled the 9 percent unsecured $500,000 bank loan, maturing in seven years, by the transfer of securities having a fair market value of $450,000 and a book value of $300,000. The bank agreed to the settlement because it can currently lend funds at 12 percent.
3. Settled the officer's loan of $600,000, plus $60,000 accrued interest, by the transfer of a parcel of land worth $600,000 (book value = $125,000).
4. Suppliers representing $1,200,000 of accounts payable agreed to accept a two-year, 8 percent note in the amount of $1,200,000.

Required

Prepare a balance sheet after the above transactions. Assume a 30 percent tax rate when accruing income taxes.

REVIEW SOLUTIONS ••

Review 1 Solution

Assets pledged to fully-secured creditors	$300,000
Less: Liabilities to fully secured creditors	220,000
Available as free assets	80,000
Unpledged assets (= $650,000 − $300,000 − $120,000)	230,000
Less: Unsecured liabilities with priority	(30,000)
Free assets	$280,000
Liabilities to partially-secured creditors	$180,000
Less: Assets pledged to partially-secured creditors	120,000
Unsecured portion	60,000
Unsecured liabilities (= $820,000 − $220,000 − $180,000 − $30,000)	390,000
Total unsecured liabilities	$450,000

Unsecured creditors expect to recover $280,000 of the $450,000 owed to them, or 62.22 percent.

••

Review 2 Solution

The company has $890,000 in assets ($90,000 cash plus $800,000 present value of future cash flows). With new liabilities of $845,000 (= $275,000 postpetition liabilities + $280,000 10 percent senior secured debt + $290,000 subordinated debt), the value of the new equity is $45,000.

The entry to record settlement of the prepetition debt follows:

Liabilities to fully-secured creditors	220,000	
Liabilities to partially-secured creditors	180,000	
Unsecured liabilities with priority	30,000	
Unsecured liabilities	390,000	
Cash		90,000
10% senior secured debt		280,000
Subordinated debt		290,000
Equity (= 80% × $45,000 assigned to creditors)		36,000
Gain on debt discharge		124,000

Thus, a gain of $124,000 is recognized on debt discharge.

16 The SEC and Financial Reporting

UNITED STATES SECURITIES AND EXCHANGE COMMISSION
www.sec.gov

Advanced accounting students are familiar with standard-setting organizations such as the Financial Accounting Standards Board (FASB) and the International Accounting Standards Board (IASB). They also know that the federal government plays a standard-setting role, primarily through the Securities and Exchange Commission (SEC). Because it has the statutory authority (1) to set accounting principles (this authority is delegated to the FASB) and (2) to regulate the securities markets, the SEC deserves detailed consideration in an advanced financial accounting course. Moreover, the SEC plays a major role in the move to International Financial Reporting Standards (IFRS) and copes with criticism emanating from the 2008 financial crisis in the financial markets.

Complying with SEC regulations in professional practice requires highly specialized expertise, and many professional accountants dedicate themselves to becoming experts in this field. It represents another important way for the professional to contribute to sound financial reporting and efficient securities markets.

One reason that investors rely on published financial reports relates to the SEC's **full disclosure** mission of providing the capital markets with all material financial information about public companies. Even though the SEC reviews only a fraction of the reports submitted to it, companies whose reports are not reviewed are subject to the same requirements for accurate and complete financial information as those whose reports are reviewed. This chapter describes reports filed with the SEC that are aimed to level the playing field in the securities markets.

CHAPTER ORGANIZATION

Introduction to the SEC	SEC organization and structure	Registration of new securities	Periodic reporting requirements	Corporate accountability and governance	SEC and accounting standards
• Establishing the SEC • Relevant securities legislation • Definition of "security"	• Divisions and offices • Accounting and auditing pronouncements	• 1933 Act requirements • Registration statement and forms • Underwriting scenarios	• EDGAR and IDEA disclosure systems • Annual (10-K), quarterly (10-Q) and special reports (8-K) • Regulation S-X • General accounting rules	• Treadway Commission • Audit committees • Sarbanes-Oxley Act and PCAOB • Antifraud provisions • Proxy statements	• SEC/FASB relationships • IFRS, mark-to-market and other issues

SEC IN THE NEWS

Legislation charges the SEC with monitoring securities markets and keeping investors informed of developments affecting publicly-traded companies, primarily through requirements emphasizing full disclosure. Here are some illustrations of the SEC in its investor-advocate role.

The **executive stock-option backdating scandal of 2006** and the **Bernard Madoff Ponzi scheme of 2008** put the spotlight on SEC activities. In the former, the SEC investigated companies accused of backdating option grants to "low-price" days, providing executives with built-in gains. In the latter, the SEC was criticized for ignoring analyst and whistle-blower Harry Markopolos' research findings that Madoff's investment returns were fraudulent.

Most financial reporting frauds involve **premature revenue recognition** that creates a false impression of financial health. A May 20, 2008 *Wall Street Journal* article reported an SEC investigation alleging that **America Online** (AOL) overstated revenue by $1 billion during 2000-2002. At the end of 2009, Reuters reported that auditors Ernst & Young paid an $8.5 million fine in connection with an earlier fraud at **Bally Total Fitness Holding Corp.**, pursuant to another SEC investigation. The Bally case featured premature revenue recognition and improper deferral of costs.

Concerns over **potential SEC employee ethical lapses** prompted the Commission in 2009 to retain Federal Tracking Technologies LLC to monitor employees' security trading activities. Unfortunately, *Bloomberg News* reported on October 14, 2011, that such data were inappropriately shared with entities not previously vetted by the SEC.

A growing rash of **cyber attacks** on companies' information systems caused the SEC in late 2011 to issue guidelines for public companies to follow in disclosing such attacks, potential losses therefrom, and remediation activities. U.S. banks in particular have been hard-pressed to deal with debit- and credit-card fraud.

In Release No. 34-62921, the SEC acknowledged that new whistle-blower rules contained in the **Dodd-Frank Wall Street Reform and Consumer Protection Act** (2010) repealed former Sec. 21A(e) of the Securities Exchange Act of 1934. Release No. 34-62921 rescinds rules issued to implement the prior SEC whistle-blower program. The Dodd-Frank Act's new and broader program goes beyond insider trading and compensates whistle-blowers for original information on any violation of the securities laws. It is codified as new Sec. 21F of the 1934 Act.

LO1 Discuss why the SEC was established and the principal legislation it enforces.

ESTABLISHMENT OF THE SEC AND KEY SECURITIES LEGISLATION

Long before 2008's near melt-down in the credit and financial markets, the 1929 stock market crash started a financial panic unparalleled in American history. Stock market averages lost about **50 percent** of their value during the autumn of 1929. The averages hit bottom in the summer of 1932, having lost about **80 percent** of their pre-crash levels. By contrast, the summer 2008 crisis saw market averages drop about **40 percent** from pre-crisis levels.

Concurrently in the 1929-1932 period, the value of extensive holdings of foreign bonds by U.S. citizens had collapsed. One estimate suggests that by 1932 the bonds of 16 European nations had lost about 43 percent of par; similar losses for bonds of Latin American nations amounted to 74 percent of par, including a drop of 93 percent in Peruvian bonds.

Establishment of the SEC

Following the 1929 crash, considerable discussion ensued as to the role the federal government might play in regulating the issuance and trading of securities. Several years of debate led to passage of the Securities Act of 1933 and the Securities Exchange Act of 1934. The latter act established the Securities and Exchange Commission. Securities legislation was conceived during the worst financial and social crisis in our history and became part of a much broader program of social reform that promised to give a New Deal to the average American at a time when the economy was prostrate. Twenty-five percent of the labor force was unemployed in 1933. Four thousand banks failed that year, and 252,400 nonfarm properties were foreclosed. The gross national product in 1933 declined to 53 percent of its 1929 level.

Enactment of the securities legislation, however, did not end the debate over the federal government's role in regulating the securities markets. That conversation still continues, as evidenced by the controversy over the 2008-2009 government intervention in the financial services industry, and the fact that some studies of security price behavior during periods before and after the SEC was formed fail to establish a strong empirical case for SEC regulation of financial disclosures.

Reporting Perspective

One consequence of the 2008-2009 financial crisis, driven by improper identification and pricing of risks in many mortgage-backed securities, was the collapse of some banks and the bailout of others. In 2010, Congress passed the controversial **Dodd-Frank Wall Street Reform and Consumer Protection Act**. In addition to its whistle-blowing provisions cited earlier, the Dodd-Frank Act seeks to provide the following safeguards against recurrence of the 2008-2009 debacle.

- **Consumer protections with authority and independence:** Creates a new independent watchdog to help American consumers get the clear, accurate information they need to shop for financial products, and protect them from abusive and deceptive practices.

- **Ends "too big to fail" bailouts:** Ends or at least reduces the likelihood of bailing out financial firms by creating a safe way to liquidate failed financial firms and imposing stronger capital and leverage requirements that make getting too big undesirable.

- **Advance warning system:** forms a new council to identify and address systemic risks posed by complex products and activities before they threaten the stability of the economy.

- **Transparency and accountability for exotic instruments and activities:** new disclosure requirements for derivatives, asset-backed securities, hedge funds, mortgage brokers and payday lenders.

- **Executive compensation and corporate governance:** enables shareholders to cast a non-binding vote on executive compensation and golden parachutes.

- **Protects investors:** new rules for transparency and accountability for credit rating agencies.

- **Enforces regulations on the books:** strengthens oversight and empowers regulators to aggressively pursue financial fraud, conflicts of interest and manipulation favoring special interests.

Only time will tell whether Dodd-Frank can deliver what it promises. To the extent it affects investors, it influences the SEC's **investor-protection mission**.

Securities Legislation and the SEC

The SEC's mission is to administer federal legislation that promotes efficient capital allocation by ensuring that securities markets function fairly and honestly. Embedded in the SEC's mission are (1) protection of investors by requiring full disclosure of material information by issuers of securities, and (2) prevention of fraudulent activities in securities trading and markets. The SEC is charged with administering these federal securities laws, discussed in detail below:

- Securities Act of 1933
- Securities Exchange Act of 1934
- Public Utility Holding Company Act of 1935
- Trust Indenture Act of 1939
- Investment Company Act of 1940
- Investment Advisers Act of 1940
- Sarbanes-Oxley Act of 2002

Other laws that significantly affect the SEC, also discussed below, include:

- Securities Investor Protection Act of 1970
- Foreign Corrupt Practices Act of 1977
- Insider Trading Sanctions Act of 1984
- Private Securities Litigation Reform Act of 1995
- Economic Recovery and Stabilization Act of 2008

The **Securities Act of 1933** deals primarily with the issuance of new securities. It regulates the public offering of securities and prohibits (subject to certain exemptions) the offering and sale of securities unless they are registered with the government as well as fraudulent or deceptive practices in the offering or sale of securities. The **Securities Exchange Act of 1934** established the **Securities and Exchange Commission,** granting it jurisdiction over the securities markets. The 1934 act governs trading in securities once they are issued and outstanding. This act authorizes the government, through the SEC, to establish accounting, reporting, and disclosure requirements for publicly-owned corporations, and prohibits deceptive and manipulative practices in the purchase or sale of securities.

Although the 1933 and 1934 acts are the primary focus of our discussion, several other laws related to the securities markets contribute to the work of the SEC. To prevent abuse of the holding company device in controlling and manipulating public utility operating companies, the **Public Utility Holding Company Act of 1935** was enacted. This act requires public utility holding companies to register with the SEC, provides for SEC-influenced reorganization of such holding companies when dictated by the public interest, and calls for equitable distribution of voting power among security holders in a public utility system. The **Trust Indenture Act of 1939** deals with the issuance of bonds. It requires a formal trust agreement, or *indenture,* specifying the rights of the bondholders, and provides for the appointment, by the issuing company, of an independent trustee to represent the bondholders.

The **Investment Company Act of 1940** regulates investment companies, such as *open-end mutual funds* and *closed-end investment companies*. When such companies register with the SEC, they fulfill certain disclosure requirements involving their investment policies and management fees, and solicit shareholder participation in company policy. **The Investment Advisers Act of 1940** requires those who provide paid advice to the public concerning securities to register with the SEC. Activities of such advisers are also regulated; for example, they may not receive a share of the gains in their clients' portfolios.

The **Securities Investor Protection Act of 1970** created the Securities Investor Protection Corp. (SIPC), which insures customer accounts held by brokers. The SIPC must file annual reports and financial statements with the SEC, and all of its activities are subject to SEC inspection. The **Foreign Corrupt Practices Act of 1977** (FCPA), enacted to stop U.S. companies from making illegal payments to foreign entities, requires companies to maintain accurate accounting records and to maintain a system of effective internal accounting controls. Provisions of the FCPA that are administered by the SEC apply to all companies that register with or report to the commission. Another key law, the **Insider Trading Sanctions Act of 1984,** drastically increased penalties assessed for violating insider trading rules. Under this legislation the SEC can seek fines of up to the greater of $1 million or three times the profits gained or losses avoided by those insiders who inappropriately use material nonpublic information.

The **Private Securities Litigation Reform Act of 1995** limits the liability of public accountants to their "fair share" in certain securities suits. It also creates new safe harbors—protection against lawsuits—that apply to certain forward-looking financial information reported by registrants to the SEC and illegal acts reported by auditors to the SEC.

Congress enacted the **Sarbanes-Oxley Act of 2002 (SOX)** in the wake of numerous financial reporting scandals and corporate governance failures in the early years of the 21st century. SOX requires new reports on internal controls, top management certifications of financial statements filed with the SEC, and created the *Public Company Accounting Oversight Board (PCAOB),* to monitor auditing firms and set auditing standards.

The "financial rescue plan" passed by Congress in October, 2008—the **Economic Recovery and Stabilization Act of 2008**—involved actions by the SEC. One provision reminds the SEC of its ability to suspend or modify accounting standards, in this case the FASB's mark-to-market fair value accounting rules provided in *FASB ASC Topic 820,* Fair Value Measurements and Disclosures. Some observers believe that the financial crisis was worsened by requiring banks to book large losses on securities normally traded in markets that simply froze up and became inactive. Later the FASB issued additional guidance relaxing some of the strict mark-to-market interpretations that had been controversial.

Separate but related was the *SEC's temporary ban on certain short sales.* In the phenomenon of **short-selling,** traders sell (short) stock they do not own. Short-sellers anticipate a fall in share prices that will enable them to purchase the borrowed shares at lower prices for return to the brokers. To counter the tendency of short-sellers to depress share prices, in October 2008 the SEC imposed a temporary ban on short-selling of several hundred individual stocks.

Definition of a Security

The Securities Act of 1933 established a broad definition of the meaning of a **security,** as follows:

> Any note, stock, treasury stock, bond, debenture, evidence of indebtedness, certificate of interest or participation in any profit-sharing agreement, collateral trust certificate, preorganization certificate or subscription, transferable share, investment contract, voting trust certificate, certificate of deposit for a security, fractional undivided interest in oil, gas, or other mineral rights, or, in general, any interest or instrument commonly known as a "security," or any certificate of interest or participation in, temporary or interim certificate for, receipt of, guarantee of, or warrant or right to subscribe to or to purchase, any of the foregoing. *(Sec. 2.1)*

The law provided several categories of securities that are exempt from the SEC's registration and reporting rules, although other provisions, such as the antifraud rules, generally apply to these securities. The following are among the **exempt securities:**

- Securities issued or guaranteed by federal, state, or local governments.
- Securities issued or guaranteed by a bank or savings and loan association. These securities, however, are subject to the provisions of the 1934 act.
- Commercial paper, that is, short-term notes (original maturity not exceeding nine months) issued for working capital purposes.
- Securities issued by not-for-profit organizations. These also are subject to the provisions of the 1934 act.

Subsequent legislation and litigation clarified the securities status of other financial instruments. In *SEC v. W. J. Howey Co.* (1946), the court concluded that the basic question to be addressed in deciding whether a financial instrument is a *security* is whether "the person invests his money in a common enterprise and is led to expect profits solely from the efforts of the promoter or a third party." Thus interests in real estate condominiums, interests in oil drilling programs, variable annuities (where the return depends on the performance of a portfolio of securities), and commodity option contracts have all been held to be securities. But bank certificates of deposit, savings and loan "shares," life insurance policies, and notes representing ordinary bank loans are not securities. Because the definition of a security is so broad, many financial transactions fall under the jurisdiction of the securities laws.

ORGANIZATION AND STRUCTURE OF THE SEC

The SEC administers and enforces the federal securities laws, and consists of five commissioners, collectively known as the *commission*. The president of the U.S. appoints one commissioner each year for a staggered five-year term. No more than three of the five commissioners can be from the President's political party. As an independent, nonpartisan agency, the SEC is not part of the legislative or executive branches of government. It is funded by a combination of user charges and congressional appropriations. The commission has a support staff of about 4,000 employees; the staff position best known to accountants is that of *Chief Accountant of the SEC*.

LO2 Examine the SEC's organization and structure.

The SEC is organized into several divisions. The division most frequently encountered by accountants is the **Division of Corporation Finance.** It processes documents that are filed with the SEC, such as registration statements and periodic reports, closely examines recurring **filings** on a rolling basis at least once every three years, and examines all first-time registration statements when filed. This division primarily administers the disclosure requirements of the securities laws and also participates in matters concerning proxy statements and tender offers.

The **Division of Enforcement** is charged with enforcing all securities laws except the Public Utility Holding Company Act. It investigates possible violations by market participants, such as corporate officers, brokers, financial analysts, and accountants. The division makes recommendations to the Justice Department concerning administrative proceedings, injunctions, and criminal prosecution.

The **Division of Trading and Markets** oversees the operations of the secondary securities markets, where already-outstanding securities are traded, and monitors trading activities and stock market operations. The **Division of Investment Management** has oversight and investigative responsibilities for the Investment Company Act of 1940, the Investment Advisers Act of 1940, and the Public Utility Holding Company Act of 1935. These duties include monitoring sales practices, advertising, and new products of mutual funds; processing investment company filings; and analyzing the legal and financial structure of public utility holding companies.

Several staff offices serve as technical advisors to the commission. They cooperate extensively with the SEC divisions in fulfilling the SEC's mission. Current staff offices include:

- Office of the General Counsel
- Division of Risk, Strategy and Financial Innovation
- Office of International Affairs
- Office of Administrative Law Judges
- Office of the Chief Accountant

The **Chief Accountant of the SEC**—the SEC's expert on accounting principles, auditing standards, and financial disclosures—supervises preparation of SEC accounting and auditing pronouncements, and reviews Division of Enforcement investigations of questionable accounting and auditing practices. Assisted by over 40 technical experts, the Chief Accountant serves as the link between the SEC and the accounting profession, has oversight powers over the FASB and the PCAOB, and expresses the SEC's views in speeches, papers, and appearances before standard-setting groups.

SEC Pronouncements on Accounting and Auditing

Recall that the goal of the SEC is to promote efficient allocation of capital by helping to maintain honest and fair securities markets. One important means for accomplishing this goal is by disclosures that communicate relevant information about securities to market participants. This in turn should lead to improved methods of security analysis and increased public confidence in the securities markets. Although the SEC delegates its authority to set accounting principles—recognition, measurement and accounting disclosure issues—to the FASB, it occasionally imposes additional requirements on its registrants and frequently comments on accounting and auditing matters. The SEC communicates its views on accounting and auditing-related matters in formal published pronouncements and through less formal methods, as follows.

- *Financial Reporting Releases (FRR* or *FR)* are formal pronouncements of the commission and are somewhat analogous to FASB *Statements*. By law, the SEC has the power to establish accounting and reporting standards for companies with securities under its jurisdiction. The *FRR*s therefore are viewed as the highest-ranking authoritative source of accounting principles for publicly-held companies. The SEC's **Codification of Financial Reporting Policies** organizes the *FRR*s and the predecessor *ASR*s (*Accounting Series Releases*) into a coherent reference document; it is included in the **SEC Accounting Guide**, updated and published periodically by Commerce Clearing House.

- *Staff Accounting Bulletins (SAB)* are similar but not identical to FASB *Technical Bulletins*. *SAB*s are issued by the SEC staff, including the Chief Accountant, without due process, and without a vote by the commission, and represent the staff's current position on various accounting issues in SEC filings.

- *Accounting and Auditing Enforcement Releases (AAER)* report disciplinary or other enforcement actions against accountants and others whose conduct affects public companies' financial reporting. Unlike the *SAB*s, all *AAER*s require an affirmative vote by the SEC commissioners.

- **Private rulings** to companies concerning particular transactions. Referred to as *no-action* and *interpretive letters,* these rulings indicate that the SEC will not object if a transaction is handled in the proposed manner.

- **Informal statements** by commissioners or top staff, such as the Chief Accountant. These statements, often in the form of speeches or written releases, convey informally the views of key individuals on certain matters. This format is frequently used to express views on matters being considered by the FASB or by the accounting profession.

- **Emerging Issues Task Force (EITF) Abstracts.** Issued by the FASB, these EITF discussions address certain narrow, technical accounting issues requiring quick resolution. However, as a key participant in EITF deliberations, the *Chief Accountant of the SEC has the authority to not permit an EITF consensus to apply to public companies* and may make statements at EITF meetings that have the force of *Staff Accounting Bulletins.*

REVIEW 1 • Mission and Organization of the SEC

Required

a. Explain why the SEC exists and its fundamental mission.
b. Describe three pieces of legislation that the SEC is responsible for, other than the 1933 and 1934 acts.
c. Describe in your own words the meaning of "security," and comment on whether that meaning is broad enough to encompass virtually all instruments likely to be traded in financial markets.
d. How does the SEC fulfill its statutory responsibility to set accounting and reporting standards?

Solutions are located after the chapter assignments.

REGISTRATION OF NEW SECURITIES

LO3 Describe principal SEC requirements for registering new securities.

The key feature of the **Securities Act of 1933** is the set of requirements for registration of new security issues, a direct response to the deceptive and manipulative environment frequently encountered by investors in the 1920s and early 1930s. Because the SEC acts as a conduit for information provided by issuers of securities to other market participants, the **full disclosure requirement** for new security issues of public companies provides adequate and accurate disclosure of material facts concerning the company and the securities it proposes to sell. Thus, investors may make a realistic appraisal of the merits of the securities and exercise informed judgment in determining whether or not to purchase them.

The 1933 act provides, with few exemptions, that no security may be offered or sold to the public unless it is registered with the SEC. Most corporate equity and publicly-held debt securities are registered. Achieving registration does not mean that the SEC passes judgment on the merits of the security; rather, it means only that certain disclosure requirements have been satisfied. Thus the SEC performs *compliance reviews,* not *merit reviews.* The 1933 act also sets forth the registration procedure and establishes liabilities for misstatements or omissions.

A prospective issuer becomes an SEC **registrant** and must file a **registration statement**—the set of documents needed to register securities—with the SEC. The registration statement consists of two parts: (1) a *prospectus* that must be furnished to each purchaser of the security, and (2) other information and exhibits that must be publicly available but need not be supplied to each investor. The **prospectus** describes the issuing company, its business operations and risks, its financial statements, historical financial information, the securities to be sold, and the expected uses of the proceeds. Typically, a **registration team** consisting of the issuer's chief financial officer and legal counsel, and the underwriter (investment banker) and underwriter's counsel, prepares the registration statement. The registrant's independent public accountant reviews and audits information in the registration statement.

Although a registration statement could become effective as early as 20 days after being filed, companies generally delay the effective date pending notification that the SEC will declare the registration statement "effective." The SEC's Division of Corporation Finance takes about 30 days to review the statement to see if it meets disclosure requirements. Reviews may be complete or partial, and the issuing company may receive a **letter of comment** stating any suggestions or criticisms. Responses to SEC comments and amendments to the registration statement frequently create additional 20-day waiting periods and delay the effective date. Even a cursory SEC review, however, does not waive the registrant's obligation to provide complete and accurate disclosures. Once the registration statement becomes effective, the issuer may sell the securities to the public.

Reporting Perspective

To help promote their securities before the registration process becomes effective, companies distribute *preliminary prospectuses*, with those words stamped in red on the cover, to a small group of potential investors. Because changes are often made to these red-stamped preliminary prospectuses after SEC review, they became known as **red herrings**. This term dates back at least to 19th century Britain where fugitives pulled strong smelling herrings that turned red after being smoked across the path to divert pursuing dogs to a false trail.

Form S-1, the basic form for the registration of new issues, consists of lists of required disclosures. Other commonly used forms are short **Form S-3** used by issuers meeting specified criteria and **Form S-4** for securities issued in exchanges, such as debt exchanges, and in business combinations. Companies may be able to file the simpler Form S-3 if they already filed an annual Form 10-K within the SEC's Integrated Disclosure System (discussed later in this chapter). The logic is that since information about such companies is already available to the market, less additional information is needed from them than from the company going public for the first time.

Financial data presented in a registration statement include a balance sheet dated within 90 days of filing, income statements and statements of cash flows for the past three years, and summaries of operations for the past five years. Such data must be accompanied by an auditor's report covering at least through the end of the last fiscal year. The period from the last audited statement to the date of the most recent interim period ending before the registration statement, known as the **stub period,** is generally covered by an accountant's review. Accountants also commonly write **comfort letters** to the underwriter providing negative assurance on non-financial statement information contained in the registration statement.

There are two major exemptions to the above detailed registration requirements. One is for "small" offerings: various rules limit the maximum dollar size and number of investors allowed under this provision. The second exemption is for **private placements,** securities issued to a single investor or small group of investors who have access to the kind of information otherwise disclosed during registration. Institutional investors such as insurance companies and pension funds frequently absorb private placements.

The flow of the securities in a typical issuance is

Issuer → Underwriter → Dealer → Public

The underwriter advises the company about the terms and structure of the issue, and markets the securities to the public under one of three types of arrangements.

- A **firm commitment** underwriting means that the underwriter buys the entire issue at a fixed price, and it is responsible for selling the issue to dealers, who will in turn sell it to the public. The underwriter bears the risk that the issue will not find market acceptance at the asking price.

- A **best efforts** underwriting means that the underwriter sells as many shares as possible, receiving a commission based on sales. The issuing company bears the risk of nonacceptance in the market.

- An **all-or-none** underwriting means that if the underwriter is unable to sell all, or a predetermined portion, of the issue, then the issue may be cancelled and the subscribed but unsold shares are rescinded. This arrangement relieves the issuing company of the risk that not enough capital will be raised to sustain the project or projects for which the securities are being sold.

After a new security issue is registered and sold, it normally is traded in a secondary market. Depending upon the size and nature of the issue, it may be traded *over-the-counter* by dealers or listed and traded on one of the organized securities exchanges. The issuing company has a continuing obligation to the SEC, and to the public, to provide full and complete disclosure of relevant information, and must satisfy the SEC's periodic reporting requirements.

PERIODIC REPORTING REQUIREMENTS

LO4 Explain the periodic reporting requirements for SEC registrants.

The **Securities Exchange Act of 1934** subjects issuers of currently traded securities to the same "full disclosure" philosophy that the 1933 act applies to newly offered securities. Thus issuers of currently traded securities also are SEC registrants that file periodic reports with the SEC so that important information about issuers' affairs becomes public. The periodic reporting requirements of the SEC cover all companies that have securities listed on a national securities exchange, along with all companies that have more than 500 stockholders and more than $10,000,000 in assets. About 15,000 listed companies were subject to the SEC's reporting and disclosure rules in 2008.

An **Integrated Disclosure System** reduces the burden of complying with SEC requirements, standardizes the disclosures required by the 1933 and 1934 acts, and brings financial statement data in annual reports to shareholders into conformity with reports required by the SEC. Sec. 102 of the SEC's *Codification of Financial Reporting Policies* discusses the Integrated Disclosure System.

"EDGAR" and "IDEA"

The SEC further expedites the filing process with the **Electronic Data Gathering, Analysis, and Retrieval System (EDGAR)** that reduces the amount of paperwork processed and stored by the SEC and reflects the following policy objectives:

- To provide investors, securities analysts, and the public with instant access to filers' disclosure documents.

- To allow companies to make required filings electronically by using their existing equipment.

- To allow the commission and its staff to process and analyze filings more efficiently.

Documents are filed by direct transmission using a modem or by physically delivering electronically readable media to the SEC. Hardcopy documents such as the annual report to shareholders are not always available in a word processing format compatible with EDGAR. When such documents are incorporated by reference into an SEC filing, they are filed separately in hardcopy form using Form SE.

In 2009 the SEC implemented the **Interactive Data Electronics Application (IDEA)** program, in conjunction with mandatory adoption of **XBRL**, the **eXtensible Business Reporting Language**. XBRL permits data submitted in electronically identified form to be easily retrievable and interactive. The new rules require domestic and foreign companies using U.S. GAAP to file their primary financial statements, notes, and financial statement schedules in XBRL. These rules supplement but do not replace or change disclosure using the traditional electronic filing formats in ASCII or HTML; EDGAR and IDEA run in parallel. IDEA is expected to provide significant new research and analysis capabilities based on publicly filed information.

The principal reports currently made by issuers to the SEC are the annual report (Form 10-K), quarterly reports (Form 10-Q), and special reports (Form 8-K) filed within a short period after specified events occur. Contents of these reports are largely governed by two sets of regulations: *Regulation S-X* addresses accounting and financial statement requirements for both annual and quarterly reports, and *Regulation S-K* covers all other disclosures.

The Annual Report: Form 10-K

The annual report to the SEC, or **Form 10-K,** is an extensive document presenting financial statements and a variety of disclosures and descriptive information. Exhibit 16.1 outlines the structure of the Form 10-K annual report. Note that financial statements comprise only one of the sixteen categories of information; financial disclosures and a variety of nonfinancial information account for the remainder.

In the interest of standardizing reporting and disclosure, the Integrated Disclosure System requires that a company's annual financial report to its stockholders conform to SEC financial statement requirements set forth in Regulation S-X. Moreover, the SEC specifies that other SEC-required disclosures be included in the annual report to stockholders. Such information can be *incorporated into the 10-K report by reference* to the annual report to shareholders.

EXHIBIT 16.1   Structure and Contents of Form 10-K

Item	Description
Part I	
1	Description of the business
1A	Risk factors
1B	Unresolved staff comments
2	Description of properties
3	Legal proceedings involving the company
4	Submission of matters to a vote of stockholders
Part II	
5	Market price of common stock, dividends, and related stockholder matters
6	Selected financial data
7	Management's discussion and analysis of financial condition and results of operations
7A	Quantitative and qualitative disclosures about market risk
8	Financial statements and supplementary financial information
9	Changes in and disagreements with accountants on accounting and financial disclosure
9A	Controls and procedures
Part III	
10	Directors and executive officers
11	Executive compensation and transactions with executives
12	Security ownership by certain beneficial owners and by management
13	Certain relationships and related-party transactions
14	Principal accountant fees and services
Part IV	
15	Exhibits
Signatures	
Certification	

Incorporation by reference means that the data already appear in another document but must legally be included in the required form. Typically the Form 10-K annual report filed with the SEC incorporates the audited financial statements by reference to the annual report to shareholders that includes these audited financial statements. When presenting a particular item in the 10-K, or in another report to the SEC, specific reference is made to the location of the information in the annual report. For example, note this disclosure in a 10-K filed by **Union Pacific Corporation**.

> **Item 8. Financial Statements and Supplementary Data**
> The consolidated financial statements and related notes of Union Pacific are presented on pages 31 through 40 of the Annual Report. Selected quarterly financial data are set forth under Selected Quarterly Data, appearing on page 41 of the Annual Report. Information about oil and gas producing activities is set forth under Supplementary Information, appearing on pages 41 though 44 of the Annual Report. All of this information is incorporated herein by reference.

Traditionally, a company filed its 10-K report with the SEC within 90 days of its fiscal year-end. But to get information about larger companies into investors' hands more quickly, SEC *Release 33–8128* as amended by *Release 33-8644* reduces the due date for *large accelerated filers* (companies with market caps > $700 million) to 60 days for fiscal years ending after December 15, 2006. *Accelerated filers* (companies with market caps > $75 million and < $700 million) are subject to a 75-day filing requirement.

The 90-day due date for filing continues to apply to all issuers other than large accelerated and accelerated filers. The registrant also files its 10-K with the exchange on which the stock is traded and makes copies available to company stockholders and others upon request. Registrants must disclose how investors can access reports on the company's Internet site. The public can also access filings on the SEC's website at www.sec.gov.

The 10-K is signed by the company, its principal executive officer, its principal financial officer, its principal accounting officer (usually the controller), and a majority of the board of directors, signifying the broad responsibility of officers and directors for proper reporting and disclosure. To further emphasize this responsibility, Section 302 of the Sarbanes-Oxley Act requires that CEOs and CFOs certify the accuracy and completeness of their companies' financial reports with personal sworn statements. SOX Section 404 requires similar certifications on the adequacy of internal controls in general and "internal control over financial reporting" in particular.

As stated, **Regulations S-X** and **S-K** set forth the accounting, reporting, and disclosure requirements for preparing the 10-K. Regulation S-X governs Item 8 in Exhibit 16.1—financial statements and supplementary financial information—whereas Regulation S-K governs the other items. The following brief discussion of the content of many of the 10-K items indicates the broad range of information required by the SEC, extending far beyond that commonly found in the annual financial report to stockholders.

Item 1A: Risk Factors   Item 1A requires disclosure of risk factors specific to the registrant's securities. These risk factors include but are not limited to: short operating history, lack of recent profitable periods, weak financial position, risky business-specific conditions and concerns over marketability of the registrant's securities

---

BUSINESS APPLICATION   Target Corporation's 2011 10-K, Item 1A

Target Corporation's 10-K for fiscal 2011 identifies the following risk factors, among others (Item 1A):

- Our success depends on our ability to positively differentiate ourselves from other retailers and on positive perceptions of Target.

- All of our stores are located within the United States, making us highly susceptible to deteriorations in U.S. macroeconomic conditions and consumer confidence.

- Interruptions with our vendors and within our supply chain could adversely affect our results.

- Product safety concerns could adversely affect our sales and results of operations.

- If we fail to protect the security of personal information about our guests, we could be subject to costly government enforcement actions or private litigation and our reputation could suffer.

- Given the geographic concentration of our stores, natural disasters could adversely affect our results of operations.

- If we are unable to access the capital markets or obtain bank credit, our growth plans, liquidity and results of operations could suffer.

Item 1B: Unresolved Staff Comments   Item 1B relates to accelerated and large accelerated filers, and well-known seasoned issuers who received SEC staff comments on their filings *more than* 180 days before the year-end. These registrants must disclose the substance of any unresolved staff comments believed to be material.

Item 2: Description of Properties   Item 2 contains descriptions of the location and general character of the company's principal plants; oil, gas, or other mineral deposits; and other physical properties. Users of the report need these physical descriptions to appreciate what lies behind the dollar amounts of plant assets reported in the corporate balance sheet. Property descriptions may be brief or very detailed.

Item 3: Legal Proceedings   Item 3 describes, in some detail, significant legal proceedings involving the company. Because this disclosure is usually more detailed than that presented in the annual report to stockholders, interested readers become better informed about the company's potential legal exposure and may be able to sense the adverse effects of significant liabilities lying beneath the surface.

Item 5: Stock Prices and Dividends   Data in Item 5 indicate the approximate number of stockholders of the company and the principal markets in which the stock is traded. Item 5 shows the high and low stock price for each quarter of the past two years, and the amount and frequency of dividends during the past two years. Companies are encouraged to make a statement that dividends will or will not be paid in the near future. This convenient item indicates in one place how widely held the stock is, a rough picture of the stock's recent price volatility, and the recent dividend payment record.

Item 6: Selected Financial Data   Item 6 presents summaries of financial data to highlight trends in the company's financial condition and operating results, and to provide a basis for evaluating the company's performance and financial position in the current year. These summaries include, for each of the past five years, at least the following:

- Net sales or operating revenues
- Income or loss from continuing operations
- Income or loss per share from continuing operations
- Total assets
- Long-term obligations and redeemable preferred stock
- Cash dividends declared per common share

Companies may disclose additional items that they believe are informative with respect to trends in their financial condition and operating results. Current value and/or constant dollar financial results, no longer mandatory, could be disclosed. The expanding use of fair values in contemporary financial statements, especially "mark-to-market" applied to financial instruments, provides some current value information.

Item 7: Management's Discussion and Analysis   The MD&A's principal objective is to allow the reader to examine the company through the eyes of management. It represents management's opportunity, indeed obligation, to provide analytical commentary on the current state of the company's business operations and likely significant future developments. The key areas to be discussed are *liquidity, capital resources,* and *operations.*

Liquidity refers to the company's ability to generate adequate amounts of cash to meet its needs. Registrants identify any known commitments or events that will significantly affect liquidity, or any major uncertainties that, if realized, will have a material effect on liquidity. When major liquidity problems exist, management should discuss actions it is taking or plans to remedy the problems.

Capital resources involve both sources of long-term funding and expenditures on long-term assets. Registrants discuss major commitments or plans for capital expenditures, such as plant expansions, pollution control equipment, or energy-saving investments. Discussion also includes trends or anticipated changes in the sources of long-term capital—debt, equity, and off-balance-sheet forms of financing.

With respect to **operations,** registrants disclose any unusual or infrequent events or transactions that materially affected income. Discussion also addresses trends or uncertainties that may significantly affect revenues—whether favorably or unfavorably—and events expected to change the relationship between costs and revenues. Registrants explain significant year-to-year changes in line items on the financial statements.

The SEC issued *FRR 36* in 1989, in response to finding major shortcomings in more than 350 companies' 10-K filings, 96% of which received comment letters. *FRR 36* addresses required disclosure of **prospective information:** management's expectations about future consequences of currently known trends, events, and uncertainties unless such consequences (1) are not reasonably likely to occur or (2) are not likely to have a material effect on the company's financial condition or operations. Although technically required, evaluating the significance and likelihood of future consequences of current events and trends becomes a judgment call by the company.

FRR 36 also calls for registrants to provide MD&A *on a line-of-business basis* when one or more business segments affect revenues, profits, or cash flow disproportionately. Companies that invest in *junk bonds* or other noninvestment-grade, high-yield financial instruments discuss the attendant unusual risks and returns in the MD&A.

Item 7A: Quantitative and Qualitative Disclosures about Market Risk The SEC added this item in 1997, responding to several high profile losses involving derivative financial instruments. It seeks to help financial statement users assess the reasons that companies use derivative financial instruments, and the likely exposure to market risk created by companies' positions in derivatives and other financial instruments. **Market risk** is the risk of loss from adverse movements in interest rates, exchange rates, commodity prices, and the like.

Registrants group their market risk sensitive instruments into those entered into (1) "for trading purposes" and (2) "for purposes other than trading" and have the flexibility to choose at least one of three alternative approaches to estimating and communicating market risk.

- **Tabular presentation** of estimated fair values and expected cash flows of derivatives and other financial instruments by expected maturity date.

- **Sensitivity analysis** indicates, for a selected time period, potential losses in future cash flows, earnings, or fair values from hypothetical changes of at least 10% in relevant interest and currency exchange rates, commodity prices, etc.

- **Value at risk (VAR)** indicates the potential loss, as in a sensitivity analysis, that has a selected likelihood of occurrence. For example, VAR could estimate the maximum loss expected to occur over the next ten days with probability ≤ 0.05.

BUSINESS APPLICATION **Microsoft Corporation's 2011 10-K, Item 7A**

Microsoft Corporation's 10-K for fiscal 2011 includes the following discussion of market risk (Item 7A):

> We are exposed to foreign currency, interest rate, equity, and commodity price risks. A portion of these risks is hedged, but fluctuations could impact our results of operations, financial position, and cash flows. We use a value-at-risk ("VaR") model to estimate and quantify our market risks. VaR is the expected loss, for a given confidence level, in fair value of our portfolio due to adverse market movements over a defined time horizon.
>
> VaR is calculated by computing the exposures of each holding's market value to a range of over 1,000 combinations of equity, interest rate, foreign exchange, and commodity risk factors. The exposures are then used to compute the parameters of a distribution of potential changes in the total market value of all holdings, taking into account the weighted historical volatilities of the different rates and prices and the weighted historical correlations among the different rates and prices, assuming normal market conditions. The VaR is then calculated as the total loss that will not be exceeded at the 97.5 percentile confidence level or, alternatively stated, the losses could exceed the VaR in 25 out of 1,000 cases. Total one-day VaR for the combined risk categories was $290 million at June 30, 2011 and $235 million at June 30, 2010.

Microsoft provides a one-day VaR for each of its risk categories, as follows:

Risk Categories *(in millions)*	June 30, 2011	June 30, 2010	Year ended June 30, 2011 Average	High	Low
Foreign currency	$ 86	$ 57	$ 67	$121	$ 40
Interest rate	58	58	56	65	50
Equity	212	183	211	230	184
Commodity	28	19	22	30	18

Why is the sum of the one-day VaR amounts for the four risk categories greater than the $290 million total one-day VaR at June 30, 2011? Portfolio diversification reduces the combined risk.

Item 9: Changes in and Disagreements with Accountants One area of concern is the extent to which firms replace their outside auditors because of disagreements over accounting or financial disclosure matters. A change of accountants is a special event that calls for filing a special report in accordance with the rules for Form 8-K (discussed later in this chapter). The report must indicate whether the registrant and the former auditors disagreed on an issue concerning auditing procedures, accounting principles, or financial statement disclosures. When such an 8-K was filed within the past 24 months, Item 9 of the annual 10-K must disclose, for the transactions or events under dispute, the difference between the company's reporting method and that proposed by the former auditors.

FRR 31 strengthens the 8-K reporting requirements after a change in independent auditors. Of particular concern is the phenomenon of **opinion shopping,** alleged to occur when a company seeks a new auditor willing to support a proposed accounting treatment that might be inconsistent with sound financial reporting.

Although opinion shopping can be viewed benignly—like medical patients, companies can request a second opinion—if not done professionally it impairs the auditing profession's credibility and the financial reporting process. Registrants replacing auditors must also disclose (1) former auditors' concerns that remain unresolved, (2) the substance of consultations with new auditors before their appointment and (3) whether the former auditors resigned or were discharged.

Item 9A: Controls and Procedures Here we find the report of the registrant's CEO and CFO about the effectiveness of the registrant's internal controls and procedures, and management's evaluation of the effectiveness of internal controls over financial reporting, required by SOX Section 404. Registrants discuss significant changes in and corrective actions to internal controls over financial reporting after the evaluation date that can materially affect internal control over financial reporting.

Item 10: Directors and Executive Officers Item 10 identifies the registrant's directors, executive officers, and certain other key employees, along with their business experience. It also requires disclosure of any family relationships among directors and executive officers and any involvement of directors or executive officers in certain legal proceedings.

Item 11: Executive Compensation and Transactions Item 11 describes various aspects of officer and director compensation. Registrants disclose the total compensation of all officers and directors as a group, the number of such individuals, and the names and amount of compensation (if over $60,000) of the five highest-paid officers and directors. Registrants present narrative descriptions of deferred compensation plans, pension and profit-sharing plans, stock option plans, and the like, and any proposed changes in officer and director compensation. Finally, registrants disclose management indebtedness to the company and other transactions with management exceeding $60,000.

Item 12: Security Ownership Item 12 discloses the security holdings of major stockholders and management of the company.

Item 13: Certain Relationships and Related Transactions Registrants describe transactions exceeding $60,000, including indebtedness, with related parties, such as executives and directors of the registrant, owners of more than 5% of the registrant's voting stock, and immediate family members of these individuals. In addition, certain business relationships and ownership interests involving directors or director nominees are to be disclosed.

Item 14: Principal Accountant Fees and Services This item relates to concerns over independence of a registrant's public accountant. It requires disclosure of aggregate fees billed by the principal accountant in each of the last two fiscal years for audit fees, audit-related fees, tax fees, and all other fees. The registrant must also describe its audit committee's procedures for approving such fees and the percentages of fees other than audit fees that the audit committee approved.

Certifications As stated earlier, to emphasize the responsibility of top management for the veracity of their companies' financial reports, first the SEC and then SOX Sections 302 and 404 require personal sworn statements by the registrant's CEO and CFO in three areas: (1) accuracy and completeness of financial statements, (2) effectiveness of internal controls and procedures related to financial reporting, and (3) deficiencies in and changes to internal controls, including corrective actions.

Regulation S-X

Regulation S-X governs the form and content of financial reporting to the SEC and related matters and is a collection of rules derived from original SEC pronouncements such as *FRR*s. Together with FASB *Statements* and *Interpretations,* Regulation S-X prescribes the body of accounting and reporting principles to be followed in SEC filings.

Regulation S-X is organized into the several articles outlined in Exhibit 16.2. Article 2 concerns the qualifications and actions of accountants. Disciplinary actions sanctioning the improper or unprofessional work of accountants who practice before the SEC are generally brought under *Rule 102(e)* of the Commission's Rules of Practice, often referred to as *Rule 2(e).* Articles 3 and 4 present the broad accounting and reporting rules applicable to most companies. Article 10 deals with interim reports and Article 12 prescribes disclosure of detailed information in schedules included in the 10-K report. Many of the other articles address accounting and reporting issues appropriate to particular industry types. Added in 2007, Article 8 replaces Regulation SB and related forms concerning smaller security offerings by smaller companies.

EXHIBIT 16.2   Contents of Regulation S-X

Article	Contents
1	Application of Regulation S-X
2	Qualifications and reports of accountants
3	General instructions as to financial statements
3A	Consolidated and combined financial statements
4	Rules of general application
5	Commercial and industrial companies
6	Registered investment companies
6A	Employee stock purchase, savings, and similar plans
7	Insurance companies other than life insurance
8	Financial statements of smaller reporting companies
9	Bank holding companies
10	Interim financial statements
11	*Pro forma* financial statements
12	Form and content of schedules

SEC accounting rules generally parallel generally accepted accounting principles (GAAP) issued by the FASB and its predecessors. Section 101 in the SEC's *Codification of Financial Reporting Policies* endorses the work of the FASB. The SEC automatically accepts pronouncements of the FASB and its predecessors unless the SEC issues its own pronouncement on the particular subject. Historically, most accounting standard-setting has been done directly by the private sector with SEC oversight, even though the SEC has the statutory authority to set accounting principles. The SEC accepts and encourages this procedure, except in a few cases where the SEC acted first to spur the private standard-setting body into action on some pressing matter.

Section 108 of SOX authorizes the SEC to recognize as generally accepted any accounting principles established by a standard-setting body that meets the Act's requirements. The FASB meets these requirements. In many respects, so does the International Accounting Standards Board (IASB), although its lack of an independent funding mechanism raised Congressional concerns. Presently the FASB is the SEC's "official" accounting standard-setter, but SOX leaves the door open for the SEC to recognize the work of other standard-setters that meet SOX's requirements, including independent funding.

General Accounting and Reporting Rules   Article 3 of Regulation S-X prescribes the financial statements to be prepared and the time periods covered. Registrants generally provide:

- Audited consolidated balance sheets as of the end of the two most recent fiscal years
- Audited consolidated statements of income and cash flows for the three most recent fiscal years
- Analysis of changes in the stockholders' equity accounts shown in the balance sheet for the three most recent fiscal years as a separate financial statement or a footnote schedule

Article 4 of Regulation S-X deals with selected accounting and reporting matters applicable to companies in general, independent of their industry. For example, in 2007 the SEC began permitting *foreign private issuers* to file financial statements using official IFRS without the previously required Form 20-F reconciliations of net income and stockholders' equity from IFRS to U. S. GAAP, effectively modifying Article 4. The SEC also accepts foreign security issuers' financial statements prepared according to a comprehensive set of accounting principles other than U.S. GAAP or IFRS, but requires the Form 20-F reconciliations of net income and stockholders' equity to U.S. GAAP. Examples of how Article 4 treats specific items appear in the following paragraphs.

Notes to the financial statements must provide summarized balance sheet and income statement information for certain significant unconsolidated subsidiaries and equity method investees. SEC rules for presenting *income tax expense* go beyond GAAP's tax allocation requirements and require separate disclosure of temporary differences whose effect exceeds 5% of the total tax expense. And the SEC requires a reconciliation of the amount reported as income tax expense and the amount computed by multiplying income before tax by the statutory federal tax rate. This often-difficult-to-understand reconciliation aids in determining the difference between the *statutory tax rate* and the registrant's *effective tax rate*.

Registrants disclose significant transactions with *related parties,* such as management, principal owners and affiliated companies. These rules encompass the provisions set forth in *ASC Topic 850,* Related Party Disclosures, and *Statement on Auditing Standards No. 6,* Related Party Transactions. When separate financial statements are prepared for the registrant or certain investees and subsidiaries, those statements must disclose amounts eliminated and not eliminated in the related consolidated statements. Similarly, the effect of intercompany profits/losses not eliminated in the separate statements shall be disclosed. Material related party items, such as receivables, payables, revenue, expense, gain or loss, or cash flows, must be identified on the face of the respective financial statement, not merely in the notes.

Schedules of Information   Article 12 of Regulation S-X requires schedules that provide considerable detail on several items. Their purpose is to enhance understanding of the financial statements through disclosure of details behind, and analysis of changes in, certain account balances. In general, schedules are required for the following items:

- Condensed financial information of the registrant (for certain bank holding companies).
- Valuation accounts; e.g., allowance for bad debts and valuation allowance for deferred tax assets.
- Real estate and accumulated depreciation.
- Mortgage loans on real estate.
- Supplemental insurance information.

The Quarterly Report: Form 10-Q

Firms required to file an annual report with the SEC must also file quarterly reports prescribed in Form 10-Q. Such quarterly reporting is intended to provide investors and others with an *update of the most recently filed 10-K report.* Quarterly reports are therefore not stand-alone documents and are not designed to forecast the next 10-K. Rather, they foster timely disclosure of important developments affecting the registrant such that the annual report should contain few major surprises. Registrants file the 10-Q report within 45 days after the end of each of the first three quarters of the company's fiscal year; no fourth quarter report is required. Quarterly report filing dates are 40 days after the end of the quarter for large accelerated and accelerated filers.

ASC Topic 270, Interim Reporting, *ASC Topic 250,* Accounting Changes and Error Corrections, and *ASC Subtopic 740-270,* Income Taxes—Interim Reporting, are the primary sources of accounting principles for interim reports. The SEC requires that quarterly data be presented in the annual reports of all registrants. Although these data need not be audited, the independent accountant checks for consistency between these data and those previously subjected to the auditor's review procedures. Quarterly reports are typically much shorter than the annual report. Form 10-Q contains:

- Balance sheets at the end of the quarter and the end of the prior fiscal year
- Quarterly and year-to-date income statements for the current quarter and the same quarter of the prior year
- Cumulative year-to-date statements of cash flow for the current and prior fiscal years

The statements may have fewer captions than the annual statements. For example, a balance sheet caption such as Receivables is needed only if the item exceeds 10 percent of total assets or if the item changed by more than 25 percent from the latest year-end balance. Otherwise, the caption may be combined with others so long as the general format of the statements is maintained; e.g., do not combine current items with noncurrent items.

Selected other disclosures also appear in the 10-Q, such as the **MD&A.** Others include legal proceedings, changes in the company's securities, defaults on senior securities, and matters reported on Form 8-K during the quarter. The extensive financial disclosures found in the annual report are not required on a quarterly basis.

Special Reports: Form 8-K

The SEC requires that registrants file a special report or *current report* known as **Form 8-K** within four days of the occurrence of events significant to investors, such as those in Exhibit 16.3.

EXHIBIT 16.3	**Events Reported on Form 8-K**
Item 1.01	Entry into a material definitive agreement.
Item 1.02	Termination of a material definitive agreement
Item 1.03	Bankruptcy or receivership
Item 2.01	Completion of acquisition or disposition of assets
Item 2.02	Results of operations and financial condition
Item 2.03	Creation of a direct financial obligation or an obligation under an off-balance sheet arrangement of a registrant
Item 2.04	Triggering events that accelerate or increase a direct financial obligation or an obligation under an off-balance sheet arrangement
Item 2.05	Costs associated with exit or disposal activities
Item 2.06	Material impairments
Item 3.01	Notice of delisting or failure to satisfy a continued listing rule or standard; transfer of listing
Item 3.02	Unregistered sales of equity securities
Item 3.03	Material modification to rights of security holders
Item 4.01	Changes in registrant's certifying accountant
Item 4.02	Non-reliance on previously issued financial statements or a related audit report or completed interim review
Item 5.01	Changes in control of registrant
Item 5.02	Departure of directors or certain officers; election of directors; appointment of certain officers; compensatory arrangements of certain officers
Item 5.03	Amendments to articles of incorporation or bylaws; change in fiscal year
Item 5.04	Temporary suspension of trading under registrant's employee benefit plans
Item 5.05	Amendments to the registrant's code of ethics, or waiver of a provision of the code of ethics
Item 5.06	Change in shell company status
Item 6.01	Asset-backed security informational and computational material
Item 6.02	Change of servicer or trustee
Item 6.03	Change in credit enhancement or other external support
Item 6.04	Failure to make a required distribution
Item 6.05	Securities act updating disclosure
Item 7.01	Regulation FD disclosure
Item 8.01	Other events

To illustrate an "other event" reported under Item 5.02, in a recent 8-K, **Cray Inc.** ("The Supercomputer Company") disclosed:

> **Item 5.02 Departure of Directors or Certain Officers; Election of Directors; Appointment of Certain Officers; Compensatory Arrangements of Certain Officers.**
>
> (b) On August 1, 2011, Steve Scott, Cray Inc.'s (the "Company's") Senior Vice President and Chief Technology Officer ("CTO"), informed the Company that he will leave the Company effective August 12, 2011. Mr. Scott will be taking a senior position at a technology partner of the Company. The Company greatly appreciates Mr. Scott's service as CTO and thanks him for his leadership contributions during his tenure.

Financial statements normally do not accompany Form 8-K. But when the 8-K reports a major acquisition, the 8-K filing includes the acquired company's financial statements. If not available by the filing deadline, the financial statements must follow within 75 days after the acquisition.

REVIEW 2 ● Registration and Periodic Reporting Requirements

Required

a. Summarize the process for registering new security issues with the SEC, including the forms used, the accountant's role, and the mechanics of typical underwriting.

b. Although Form 10-K is probably the best-known SEC filing, it contains much non-accounting information that is governed by Regulation S-K. Indicate which items in Regulation S-K relate to accounting and reporting.

c. Regulation S-X governs the financial statement information in the 10-K. Explain why Articles 3 and 4 are particularly important.

d. Explain the purpose of Form 8-K and comment briefly on the importance of Items 2.03, 2.04 and 4.01.

Solutions are located after the chapter assignments.

CORPORATE ACCOUNTABILITY AND GOVERNANCE

LO5 Describe the SEC's role in corporate accountability and governance, including the Sarbanes-Oxley Act (2002).

In addition to concerns over corporate *accounting,* capital market participants show considerable interest in the broader notion of corporate *accountability.* Complying with SEC requirements for periodic financial reporting helps the corporation fulfill its obligation to be accountable for its actions. How a corporation conducts its affairs and relates to its security holders, employees, and the public are major aspects of corporate accountability. The SEC plays an important role, both directly and indirectly, in setting guidelines for corporate accountability and governance.

One of its indirect influences appeared in the *Foreign Corrupt Practices Act (FCPA)* of 1978 that prohibits certain activities in the conduct of international transactions. This act also requires management to maintain accurate books and records that will reveal any illegal transactions, and to maintain an adequate system of internal control to reduce the occurrence of such transactions. Despite this apparently clear requirement, note that SOX revisits much of the same territory

The blockbuster Sarbanes-Oxley (SOX) legislation was enacted in 2002 in response to a series of corporate accounting scandals. One major provision of SOX established the **Public Company Accounting Oversight Board (PCAOB)** to regulate and monitor auditing firms, subject to SEC oversight. In an early decision, the PCAOB received authority to assume the AICPA's role in setting auditing standards for audits of public companies.

Another major SOX provision addresses auditor independence and conflict-of-interest concerns by severely limiting the types of non-audit services that CPA firms can provide to audit clients. Section 201 of SOX prohibits services such as bookkeeping, design and installation of financial information systems, internal audit outsourcing, and any other services that the PCAOB decides to prohibit. Finally, the growing importance of properly functioning committees of a company's board of directors leads us to summarize below some of the principal provisions of SOX relating to key board committees, especially the audit committee, and to director independence.

Audit Committees

The **board of directors** plays an important role in the governance of the corporation. Three key board committees are (1) the *audit committee,* (2) the *nominating committee* and (3) the *compensation committee.* Although SOX deals only with audit committees, as discussed below, the NYSE requires that all three committees be separate and composed of independent directors that cannot be current or prior employees of the firm or have other insider relationships. NASDAQ rules actually increase the influence of a company's independent directors.

The Dodd-Frank Act (2010) reaffirms these independence requirements. It also extends them to compensation committees' use of outside consultants.

The **audit committee** makes sure that management fulfills its responsibilities for accounting, reporting, controlling the operations, and safeguarding the assets of the corporation. It monitors the financial accounting and reporting system as well as the external and internal audit functions. Mandatory audit committee responsibilities include hiring the independent auditor and approving fees for audit and non-audit services. The auditor reports to the audit committee.

One significant implication of the independent director requirement for the three board committees mentioned above is that the company's Chief Executive Officer (CEO) can no longer serve on, and perhaps dominate, these committees. The independence and effectiveness of many corporate boards should increase as a result. Section 301 of SOX defines independence, makes the audit committee "directly responsible" for arrangements with and oversight of the company's external audit firm, and requires its active involvement in the company's financial reporting and internal control systems.

Although it is responsible to either the audit committee or management, the **internal audit department** needs direct access to the audit committee for special problems, and the audit committee can use the internal audit department for special investigations. The audit committee also interacts with top management on financial accounting, reporting, and control issues.

Antifraud Provisions and Insider Trading

A broad set of rules known as the **antifraud provisions**, found in both the 1933 and 1934 acts, promotes fair capital markets that allocate resources efficiently. These rules seek a "level playing field" for all capital market participants by prohibiting fraud, deceit, and manipulative practices in the issuance or trading of securities. For example,

- A corporation cannot issue false or misleading statements about the company or its stock. Underwriters of a stock issue cannot artificially stimulate demand or hold back stock in order to profit from a price rise.

- Prohibited corporate mismanagement includes issuing corporate stock for less than adequate compensation.

- Registrants cannot easily make mergers or acquisitions against minority shareholders' interests.

Insider trading is a special type of fraud that refers to the purchase or sale of a company's stock by individuals who have access to information not yet available either to those with whom they are dealing or to the market in general. An *insider* may be a company officer, director, major stockholder, or anyone else who utilizes confidential nonpublic information for the purpose of trading in securities. The exact definitions of *insider* and *inside information,* however, are still unsettled and are the subjects of many legal proceedings.

A major objective of the securities laws is to promote full disclosure of material information to all participants in the market. Trading by insiders having access to special knowledge compromises this objective. Although one cannot completely prevent use of inside knowledge, certain rules help to constrain it. One 1934 act rule requires officers, directors, and stockholders who directly or indirectly own more than 10% of a class of equity securities—*beneficial owners*—to report their holdings and transactions in these securities to the SEC. As a public record, this report discloses completed insider transactions. A second rule permits the company, or a stockholder acting on the company's behalf, to sue to recover "*shortswing profit*" earned by an insider from "in-and-out trading"—either purchase-sale or sale-purchase—within a six-month period.

• •

Reporting Perspective

The **National Commission on Fraudulent Financial Reporting**, also known as the **Treadway Commission**, was established in 1985 to address concerns shared by the SEC and others over the quality of financial reporting. The Commission focuses on **fraudulent financial reporting**, defined as "intentional

continued

or reckless conduct, whether act or omission, that results in materially misleading financial statements." Events that can produce fraudulent financial reporting include:

- deliberate distortion of company records, such as misstatement of inventory, which can manipulate reported income and financial position.

- fictitious transactions designed to increase reported income and financial position; for example, recording bogus sales and receivables.

- accounting principles applied improperly in the circumstances; for example, taking advantage of full absorption costing by raising production in order to bolster income by capitalizing excessive amounts of fixed manufacturing overhead.

- improperly timing the recognition of accounting events by, for example, recording next year's January sales at the end of December this year.

The Commission concluded that fraudulent financial reporting is a serious problem and found the potential for its occurrence to relate to the interplay of incentives provided by such factors as a company's operating environment, external business conditions (including the credit markets), internal controls, top management attitude, and ineffective external audits. The Commission's principal recommendations are that the SEC:

- obtain authority to assess monetary penalties in administrative proceedings, issue cease and desist orders, and suspend corporate officers and directors from future service in those capacities in public companies.

- increase criminal prosecution in cases of fraudulent financial reporting.

- mandate and monitor quality assurance programs for public accounting firms that audit public companies.

- secure the increase in resources needed to review a larger portion of SEC filings and implement the above recommendations.

After the major accounting frauds at **Enron, WorldCom**, and the **Baptist Foundation of Arizona**, the Sarbanes-Oxley Act adopted many of the Commission's original recommendations to the SEC.

Proxy Statements

Proxy statements are communications to shareholders of matters for shareholder action, such as election of directors, appointment of the independent auditor, a change in the corporate charter or bylaws, issuance of new securities, or approval of a business combination. The proxy statement discusses these matters and advises the shareholder of the voting procedure. When security issuances and business combinations are considered, accountants become involved to provide the proxy statement with the most recent annual report containing financial statements presented in accordance with Regulation S-X.

Because voting on policy matters frequently occurs at the stockholders' annual meeting that many stockholders cannot attend, management often solicits their voting right, or **proxy.** The proxy statement seeks to provide shareholders with the information they need to decide how to assign their proxies. SEC regulation of proxy statements follows from its emphasis on full disclosure and the belief that the capital markets work better when registrants' managers are accountable to the stockholders.

The proxy statement also provides a mechanism for action on *stockholder proposals not supported by management*. Notice of such a proposal must be given to the company at least 90 days prior to the mailing of the proxy statement. Stockholders' proposals must be personally presented at the annual meeting by a stockholder unless management previously agreed to put the proposal on the ballot. In addition, the proxy statement often contains detailed information on nonvoting matters, such as board committees, litigation, management compensation plans (including the amount of compensation paid to top management), and related-party transactions.

BUSINESS APPLICATION Shareholder Proposals

Increasing numbers of investors are presenting shareholder proposals related to social, environmental and governance issues. Recent data on these proposals relating to the 2011 proxy season revealed:

- The overall average support level cracked 20 percent, an historic first;
- Five proposals received majority support from investors; and
- Twenty-one resolutions garnered more than 40 percent support, another new record.

Of particular interest is that more than half of the votes (on 88 resolutions) were above 20 percent, compared with 11 percent on 18 proposals in 2002. Three of the proposals generating majority support were:

Company	Proposal	Proponent	Vote (%)
Layne Christensen	Publish sustainability report	Walden Asset Management	92.8%
KBR	Adopt sexual orientation/ gender ID nondiscrimination	NYC pension funds	61.7
Tesoro	Report on accident prevention efforts	AFL-CIO	54.3

These data suggest a growing activism on the part of shareholders advocating social and environmental changes within companies. Various aspects of executive compensation are no longer "the only thing" addressed in shareholder proposals.

THE SEC AND ACCOUNTING STANDARDS

LO6 Explain the SEC's role in accounting standards development and global standards convergence.

We previously mentioned that although the Securities Exchange Act of 1934 gave the SEC the statutory authority to set accounting standards for companies under its jurisdiction, the SEC historically left the bulk of this task to private-sector standard-setting bodies—the FASB and its predecessors. But as stated earlier, Section 108 of the Sarbanes-Oxley Act recognizes the SEC's authority and ability to designate another standard-setting body.

The SEC actively oversees the standard-setting process and continually reviews registrants' filings. It promotes a balance-sheet emphasis, favoring inclusion of "hard" assets and liabilities and readily challenges cost deferrals and potentially premature revenue recognition practices.

Although many accounting-related *ASR*s issued over the years deal with disclosure requirements for public companies rather than accounting measurement issues, the SEC began playing a more active role in standard-setting in the early 1970s. As inflation reared its ugly head in the 1970s, *inflation accounting* had not been adequately addressed by private standard-setting bodies, although the Accounting Principles Board (APB) issued nonbinding guidance on this subject in APB *Statement No. 3* (1969).

While the FASB gradually moved toward requiring supplemental disclosure of historical cost/constant dollar data, in 1976 the SEC struck first with *ASR 190,* requiring disclosure of current replacement cost data, not historical cost/constant dollar data. This action clearly signaled the SEC's opposition to the FASB's proposal, which later matured in 1979 with *SFAS 33,* calling for disclosure of historical cost/constant dollar *and* current cost data. The SEC then rescinded *ASR 190*. Disclosure of the effects of changing prices is now voluntary, per *ASC Topic 255.*

Another noteworthy conflict between the SEC and the private sector involved the controversy over oil and gas accounting when *SFAS 19* appeared. *SFAS 19* required immediate expensing of "dry-hole costs" incurred in drilling unsuccessful wells, a method called *successful efforts accounting.* Complaints by many companies that capitalized such costs under *full cost accounting* and Congressional pressure led the SEC to override the FASB and to seek a new method called *reserve-recognition accounting.* Later, *SFAS 25* amended *SFAS 19* to allow both full cost and successful efforts accounting. Provisions for oil and gas reporting are now found in *ASC Topic 932.*

More recently, the SEC moved faster than the FASB by issuing *SAB 100* (1999), which offered guidance on recognition, measurement and disclosure of restructuring charges and other costs of exit and disposal activities, three years before *SFAS 146* (2002), now in *ASC Topic 420,* dealt with those subjects. And a major codification of guidance on revenue recognition appeared in *SAB 101* (1999), well in advance of completion of the FASB revenue recognition project.

Reporting Perspective

The working relationship between the government's SEC and the private-sector's FASB is described by former FASB member Robert T. Sprouse as "mutually advantageous, eminently effective, and surprisingly sensible" in his "Commentary on the SEC-FASB Partnership" that appears in the December 1987 issue of *Accounting Horizons* (pp. 92-95). Sprouse stresses the spirit of cooperation among members of both bodies and identifies three ways that the SEC, primarily through its ongoing review of financial statements filed by registrants, contributes to the standard-setting process.

1. Observing lack of comparability among registrants' accounting treatments of apparently similar events, which can signify weaknesses or ambiguities in existing standards.
2. Detecting increasing use of questionable accounting methods which, although generally accepted, are not covered by existing pronouncements.
3. Noting the presence of new or unusual transactions which appear questionable and for which the accounting is evolving.

One example of #2 above involved *capitalization of interest during construction* that became controversial during an era of rising interest rates in the early 1970s because it allowed deferral of an otherwise immediately-expensed interest cost. Detecting use of this income-increasing treatment by growing numbers of registrants, in 1974 *ASR 163* placed a moratorium on this accounting practice until the FASB took a position on it. After the FASB issued *SFAS 34*, "Capitalization of Interest Cost," in 1979, the SEC withdrew *ASR 163*. Current standards for capitalization of interest are in *ASC Subtopic 835-20*.

As a more recent example of #3 above, and well after Sprouse's 1987 Commentary, the SEC pushed the FASB to get its project on consolidating special purpose entities on the "fast track" following the collapse of Enron in 2002. That guidance emerged quickly in 2003 and now appears in *ASC 810* as subsequently amended.

In 2008 the SEC began a Congressionally-mandated study of *SFAS 157*'s **mark-to-market accounting** (now in *ASC Topic 820*) as one response to the 2008 credit and financial crisis. Questions about mark-to-market accounting to be examined included:

- Effects on financial reporting of financial institutions
- Potential market responses to mark-to-market write-downs
- Usefulness to investors and regulators
- Improvements in current standards or alternative standards

Delivered to Congress in January 2009 *(http://sec.gov/news/studies/2008/marktomarket123008.pdf)*, the report's principal conclusion is that the financial crisis was not caused by fair value accounting measurements and that *SFAS 157* should be improved but not suspended.

Broader in scope is the August 1, 2008, Final Report of the [SEC] Advisory Committee on Improvements to Financial Reporting that contains 25 recommendations to make financial information more understandable and useful to investors, such as:

- Including an Executive Summary describing the company's main business activities and their principal performance metrics.
- More investor participation in the standard-setting process.
- Disaggregation of earnings into cash, value change and perhaps accrual components
- Increased disclosure of corrections of accounting errors with restatements limited to those that are material to current investors

A major ongoing SEC initiative relates to global convergence of accounting standards, focusing on **IFRS**, a comprehensive set of accounting standards with very little of the detailed guidance found in U.S. GAAP. In autumn 2008 the SEC had proposed a "roadmap" that would require all U.S. public companies to file under IFRS in 2014, following a phase-in beginning with certain 2010 filings. However, the initial fervor over rapid adoption of or convergence with IFRS has abated and a slower more measured approach now appears to be underway.

With the SEC's approval, the FASB entered into a memorandum of understanding with the IASB to work toward adopting common standards in a number of major areas including business combinations (now completed), financial instruments, leases and revenue recognition. While these projects move forward, the SEC is gathering data concerning the implications of moving U.S. public company accounting to international standards.

The initial goal was that the SEC would consider whether, when, and how to move toward IFRS sometime in 2011. In May 2011 the SEC staff issued a discussion paper exploring the approach of "endorsement" of IFRS, possibly on a standard-by-standard basis over a 5 to 7 year transition period. The SEC's objective was that at the end of that transition period, financial statements prepared based on U.S. GAAP would be substantially the same as those prepared using IFRS.

As this text goes to press, the timing and extent of overall adoption of IFRS or convergence between U.S. GAAP and IFRS remains uncertain.

Clearly, the SEC's statutory authority requires it to remain an active participant in the accounting standard-setting process. Even though the SEC is a key player in the financial reporting process, it consistently delegates that authority to private standard-setting bodies, currently the FASB. Like the FASB, though, the SEC faces its own challenges related to the bureaucratic nature of its operations and its dependence on Congress for sufficient financial resources to adequately carry out its multidimensional mission of investor protection.

REVIEW 3   •   Corporate Accountability and Governance, SEC Intervention in Standard-Setting

Required

a. Briefly explain the nature of fraudulent financial reporting and the ethical dilemma it poses.
b. Explain why strong audit committees are so important to good corporate governance.
c. Former FASB board member Robert Sprouse describes the SEC/FASB relationship very positively. In particular, how does Sprouse see the SEC's review of registrant's filings contributing to the standard-setting process?
d. Twenty-four years after Congress passed the Foreign Corrupt Practices Act (1978) requiring companies to maintain accurate books and records and an adequate system of internal control, Congress passed the Sarbanes-Oxley Act (2002), which contains similar provisions. Comment on whether this tells us anything about the state of corporate accountability in the U.S.

Solutions are located after the chapter assignments.

REVIEW OF KEY CONCEPTS

LO 1   **Discuss why the SEC was established and the principal legislation it enforces. (p. 662)** The 1929 stock market crash and ensuing economic depression led Congress to legislate governmental oversight for the financial markets and the companies with securities traded on those markets. Congress enacted the **Securities Act of 1933** to regulate the issuance of new securities. The subsequent **Securities Exchange Act of 1934** regulates the trading of already-issued securities and establishes the **Securities and Exchange Commission (SEC)**. The SEC is responsible for the administration and enforcement of the federal securities laws including the 1933 and 1934 acts.

LO 2   **Examine the SEC's organization and structure. (p. 665)** The **SEC is an independent non-partisan agency** funded by a combination of user charges and congressional appropriations. It is organized into four divisions with the **Division of Corporation Finance** being most relevant to accountants. Of its several supporting staff offices, the **Office of the Chief Accountant** has the most effect on the financial reporting process. The SEC has statutory authority to establish accounting and reporting principles for publicly held companies. Although it relies heavily on the private sector for standard-setting—currently the FASB—the SEC does issue its own pronouncements-*Financial Reporting Releases (FRR), Accounting and Auditing Enforcement Releases (AAER)* and *Staff Accounting Bulletins (SAB)*.

Describe principal SEC requirements for registering new securities. (p. 666) The **1933 Act** provides, with few **LO 3** exemptions, that **no security may be offered or sold to the public unless it is registered with the SEC.** A prospective issuer becomes an SEC **registrant** and must file a **registration statement**—the set of documents needed to register securities—that includes a **prospectus** and other information. The SEC does not pass judgment on the merits of the security and can be said to perform **compliance reviews, not merit reviews.** Typically, a **registration team**, consisting of the issuer's chief financial officer, legal counsel and independent public accountant, and the underwriter (investment banker) and underwriter's counsel, prepares the registration statement.

Explain the periodic reporting requirements for SEC registrants. (p. 668) Companies under SEC jurisdiction **LO 4** file annual reports (**Form 10-K**), quarterly reports (**Form 10-Q**), and special reports (**Form 8-K**) when certain events occur. The contents of these reports are largely governed by **Regulation S-X**, which covers accounting and financial statement requirements, and **Regulation S-K**, which covers all other disclosures.

Describe the SEC's role in corporate accountability and governance, including the Sarbanes-Oxley Act **LO 5** **(2002). (p. 677)** Besides its role in accounting and reporting, the SEC also plays an important role in **corporate governance**. It provides **proxy statement** requirements, encourages **audit committees**, and regulates **insider trading**. The landmark **Sarbanes-Oxley Act of 2002** made several reforms in the financial reporting process and strengthened the SEC's authority. These include the **Public Company Accounting Oversight Board** that reviews audit firms and sets auditing standards, top management sworn certifications of financial reports filed with the SEC, limits on non-audit services that external auditors can provide to audit clients, and reports on the effectiveness of registrants' internal controls over financial reporting.

Explain the SEC's role in accounting standards development and global standards convergence. (p. 680) The **LO 6** SEC has a history of involvement in accounting standard-setting. It continues to oversee the movement toward **adoption of or convergence with IFRS** although timetables have been fluid. Recently, it has been embroiled in the controversy over the propriety of **mark-to-market accounting** in the financial services industry and received a special report with recommendations to improve financial reporting's usefulness. Thus the SEC monitors the work of the FASB, contributes to it on a continuing basis, and occasionally overrules it.

MULTIPLE CHOICE QUESTIONS ·····································

1. The SEC was established in 1934 to help regulate the United States securities market. Which of the following statements is *true* concerning the SEC?   **LO 1**

   a. The SEC prohibits the sale of speculative securities.
   b. Registration with the SEC guarantees the accuracy of the registrant's prospectus.
   c. The SEC's initial influence and authority has diminished in recent years as stock exchanges have become more organized and better able to police themselves.
   d. The SEC regulates only securities offered for public sale.

2. Which of the following acts gives the SEC the ultimate power to suspend trading in a security, delist a security, and prevent brokers and dealers from working in the securities market?   **LO 1**

   a. Securities Investors Protection Act of 1934
   b. Securities Act of 1934
   c. Securities Exchange Act of 1934
   d. Investment Company Act of 1940

3. Assuming that all other criteria regarding the issuing organization and its "security" are met, which one of the following is not a "security" under the jurisdiction of the SEC?   **LO 1**

   a. A trust certificate
   b. A municipal bond
   c. An oil drilling venture participation unit
   d. A limited partnership share

4. Which of the SEC's organizational units—divisions and principal offices—reviews the registration statements, annual reports, and proxy statements filed with the commission?   **LO 2**

   a. Office of the Chief Accountant
   b. Division of Corporation Finance
   c. Division of Enforcement
   d. Division of the Comptroller

LO 2 **5.** *Financial Reporting Releases (FRRs)* and *Staff Accounting Bulletins (SABs)* are two pronouncements issues by the SEC. How do *FRRs* and *SABs* differ?

    a. *FRRs* are part of the 1934 Securities Exchange Act while *SABs* are not.

    b. *SABs* represent the official rules of the SEC while *FRRs* do not.

    c. *SABs* represent amendments to Regulation S-X, *FRRs* do not.

    d. *FRRs* represent requirements applicable to the form and content of financial statements filed with the SEC, *SABs* represent accounting interpretations followed by the SEC.

LO 3 **6.** Which of the following statements related to registration of new securities is *false*?

    a. Registration of new securities is governed by the Securities Act of 1933.

    b. Form S-1, the basic form for new security registration, is an elaborate checklist of rules to be followed and questions to be answered.

    c. A "private placement" may be exempt from detailed registration requirements.

    d. The independent public accountant reviews and audits information included in the registration statement.

LO 4 **7.** Which of the following statements related to the SEC's periodic reporting requirements is *false*?

    a. Form 10-K, the annual report, is governed only by *Regulation S-X*, not *Regulation S-K*.

    b. Financial statements in Form 10-Q, the quarterly report, follow typical interim reporting principles contained in *ASC Topic 270*.

    c. Required Form 10-Q financial statements include balance sheets, income statements and cash flow statements.

    d. Form 10-Q financial statements may include fewer line items than those in Form 10-K.

LO 4 **8.** A significant event affecting a company registered under the Securities and Exchange Act of 1934 should be reported on which of the following?

    a. Form 10-K

    b. Form S-1

    c. Form 8-K

    d. Form 11-K

LO 5 **9.** An audit committee of the board of directors consisting of outside directors should be objective in arbitrating disputes between a company's top management and the external auditor because audit committee members

    a. have no direct responsibility for the results of a company's operations.

    b. have only limited contacts with the external auditor.

    c. rely on senior management's opinions to resolve disputes with the external auditor.

    d. are required by the Securities Exchange Act of 1934 to oversee the progress of the annual external audit.

LO 6 **10.** The role of the SEC regarding financial accounting for public companies is that the SEC does which of the following?

    a. Promulgates generally accepted accounting principles

    b. Regularly adopts requirements that conflict with FASB pronouncements

    c. Makes regulations and rules pertaining to filings with the SEC but not to annual or quarterly reports to shareholders

    d. Makes regulations and rules pertaining more to disclosure outside the financial statements than to the setting of accounting principles

**Assignments with the ✔ in the margin are available in an online homework system.
See the Preface of the book for details.**

EXERCISES ••

LO 1, 2 **E16.1** **Multiple Choice—Securities Laws and SEC Functions** These questions involve the federal securities laws and the organization, structure, and authority of the SEC.

    Required

    a. Which of the following are *not* requirements imposed by the Securities Exchange Act of 1934 and its amendments?

    1. Proxy solicitation requirements.
    2. Prospectus requirements.
    3. Insider trading requirements.
    4. Tender offer requirements.
    5. Accounting, recordkeeping, and internal control requirements.

b. The Securities Exchange Act of 1934 specifies the types of companies that must periodically report to the SEC. Which of these types of companies is *not* required to report to the SEC under this act?
    1. Banks and carriers subject to the Interstate Commerce Act.
    2. Companies whose securities are listed on national securities exchanges.
    3. Companies whose securities are traded over the counter, if those companies have total assets in excess of $3 million and 500 or more stockholders.
    4. Companies whose securities are traded over the counter that voluntarily elect to comply with the reporting requirements even though they have total assets less than $3 million and less than 500 stockholders.
    5. Companies with over 300 stockholders of a class of securities that are registered under the Securities Act of 1933.

c. Which of the following is *not* a purpose of the Securities Exchange Act of 1934?
    1. To establish federal regulation over securities exchanges and markets.
    2. To prevent unfair practices on securities exchanges and markets.
    3. To discourage and prevent the use of credit in financing excessive speculation in securities.
    4. To approve the securities of corporations that are to be traded publicly.
    5. To control unfair use of information by corporate insiders.

d. Which of the following categories is *not* registered by the SEC?
    1. Securities brokers who deal in over-the-counter markets.
    2. Securities brokers who deal only in interstate markets.
    3. Public accounting firms.
    4. Securities exchanges.
    5. Securities of publicly traded companies.

E16.2 Multiple Choice—SEC Reporting Requirements These questions involve SEC reporting   LO 4
requirements.

Required

a. Nonfinancial statement disclosures are specified in which of the following?
    1. Regulation S-K
    2. *Financial Reporting Releases*
    3. *Staff Accounting Bulletins.*
    4. *Accounting and Auditing Enforcement Releases.*
    5. Regulation S-X

b. Which of these items is *not* required by the SEC in either the Securities Act of 1933 or the Securities Exchange Act of 1934?
    1. Identification of directors and executive officers with the principal occupation and employer of each.
    2. Line-of-business or product-line reports for the last five fiscal years.
    3. Identification of the principal markets in which the firm's securities are traded.
    4. Range of market prices and dividends for each quarter of the two most recent fiscal years.
    5. Comfort letter to the underwriter and legal counsel from the company's independent accountant.

c. SEC regulations provide for a procedure known as *incorporation by reference.* Which of the following best illustrates the concept of *incorporation by reference?*
    1. A partnership is incorporated by reference to the U.S. Tax Code.
    2. The incorporation of a proprietorship or partnership.
    3. Inclusion of information on officers' remuneration in Form 10-K by reference to the same information in the shareholders' proxy statement.
    4. Footnote reference to market data per share since incorporation.
    5. Footnote disclosure that financial statements are incorporated into the annual report by reference from Form 10-K.

d. The SEC requires Form 8-K to be filed with the commission within four days after the end of the month in which a significant event transpired. However, financial statements accompany Form 8-K only under certain conditions. Which events require financial statements to accompany Form 8-K?
    1. A material default on a senior security.

2. A write-down, write-off, or abandonment of assets, where such assets represent more than 15% of total assets.
3. An acquisition in which the acquired company represents more than 15% of total assets or revenues of the registering company.
4. An increase or decrease of more than 5% in any class of outstanding security.
5. A change in the registrant's certifying accountants.

✓ LO 4 **E16.3** **Multiple Choice—SEC Reporting Requirements** These questions involve SEC reporting requirements.

Required

a. Indicate the primary intent of the SEC's Integrated Disclosure System.
 1. To reduce the influence of SEC regulations in public financial reporting.
 2. To replace generally accepting accounting principles with Regulation S-X.
 3. To replace Regulation S-X with generally accepted accounting principles.
 4. To minimize the differences between published financial reports and financial reports filed on Form 10-K.
 5. To integrate the materiality criteria of Regulation S-X with generally accepted accounting principles.

b. The Management Discussion and Analysis section of Form 10-K was revised by the SEC's Integrated Disclosure System and no longer requires a description of which of the following?
 1. Factors affecting financial condition as well as the results of operations.
 2. Factors affecting international markets and currency exchange.
 3. Factors that are likely to increase or decrease liquidity materially.
 4. Material commitments for capital expenditures, including the purpose of and source of financing for such commitments.
 5. The impact of inflation and changing prices on net sales and revenues and on income from continuing operations.

c. At one point the SEC substantially increased the disclosure requirements on Form 10-Q quarterly reports. Which one of the following items need *not* be filed with Form 10-Q?
 1. Signature of either the chief financial officer or chief accounting officer.
 2. Management analysis of reasons for material changes in the amount of revenue and expense items from one quarter to the next.
 3. In case of a change in accounting principle, a letter showing the public accountant believes the new principle is preferable for measuring business operations.
 4. Income statements for the most recent quarter and for the equivalent quarter from the preceding year, and year-to-date data for both years.
 5. A statement by the public accountant that he or she has reviewed the financial data in Form 10-Q and that the statements reflect all necessary adjustments.

LO 4 **E16.4** **Multiple Choice—SEC Reporting Requirements** These questions involve SEC reporting requirements.

Required

a. Which of the following describes Regulation S-X?
 1. Specifies the information that can be incorporated by reference from the annual report into the registration statement filed with the SEC.
 2. Specifies the regulations and reporting requirements of proxy solicitations.
 3. Provides the basis for generally accepted accounting principles.
 4. Specifies the general form and content of financial statements filed with the SEC.
 5. Provides explanations and clarifications of changes in accounting or auditing procedures used in reports filed with the SEC.

b. The SEC integrated disclosure of financial information sets forth criteria for Management Discussion and Analysis of Financial Conditions and Results of Operations. Which of the following is one of these criteria?
 1. Disclosure of forward-looking information is encouraged but not required to be disclosed.
 2. A discussion of financial conditions for the most recent seven fiscal years is to be included.
 3. Disclosure of information on the effects of inflation is to be provided only when the registrant observes an inflation rate of 10 percent or more.
 4. An analysis of income from foreign operations is to be included even if such operations are not material to the results of the firm.

5. Identification of all equity security investments in defense contractors and oil and gas subsidiaries is to be included whether or not such investments are material to the overall financial statements and operations.

c. Within four days after any event of material importance to the stockholders occurs, a company must file a Form 8-K Information Report with the SEC to disclose the event. Which of these is an example of the type of event to be disclosed?
   1. Salary increases to the officers.
   2. A contract to employ the same certified public accounting firm used last year.
   3. A change in projected earnings per share from $12 to $12.11 per share.
   4. The purchase of bank certificates of deposit.
   5. Acquisition of a large subsidiary other than in the ordinary course of business.

d. Which of these items need not be included in a company's 8-K report filed with the SEC when significant events occur?
   1. Acquisition or disposition of a significant amount of assets.
   2. Instigation or termination of material legal proceedings other than routine litigation incidental to the business.
   3. Change in certifying public accountants.
   4. Election of new vice-president of finance to replace the retiring incumbent.
   5. Default in the payment of principal, interest, or sinking fund installment.

E16.5 Multiple Choice—Corporate Governance   These questions relate to corporate governance.   LO 5 ✓

Required

a. Formation and meaningful utilization of an audit committee of the board of directors is required of publicly traded companies that are subject to the rules of which of the following?
   1. Securities and Exchange Commission.
   2. Financial Accounting Standards Board.
   3. New York Stock Exchange.
   4. National Association of Securities Dealers.
   5. SEC Practice Section of the American Institute of Certified Public Accountants' Division of Firms.

b. The SEC's antifraud rules prohibit trading on the basis of inside information of a business corporation's stock by which of these?
   1. Officers.
   2. Officers and directors.
   3. All officers, directors, and stockholders.
   4. Officers, directors, and beneficial holders of 10% of the corporation's stock.
   5. Anyone who bases his or her trading activities on inside information.

c. Shareholders may ask or allow others to enter their vote at a shareholders meeting that they are unable to attend. The document furnished to shareholders to provide background information for their vote is a
   1. registration statement.
   2. proxy statement.
   3. 10-K report.
   4. prospectus.
   5. 8-K report.

E16.6 Multiple Choice—SEC and Accounting Standards   These questions examine the role of the   LO 6 ✓
SEC in establishing accounting and reporting standards.

Required

a. Two important topics concerning the SEC are the role it plays in developing accounting principles and the impact the SEC has on the accounting profession and business in general. Which statement concerning the SEC's authority relative to accounting practice is *false?*
   1. The SEC has the statutory authority to regulate and to prescribe the form and content of financial statements and other reports it receives.
   2. Regulation S-X of the SEC is the principal source relating to the form and content of financial statements to be included in registration statements and financial reports filed with the SEC.
   3. The SEC has little, if any, authority over disclosures in corporate annual reports mailed to shareholders with proxy solicitations. Here, the type of information disclosed and the format to be used are left to the discretion of management.
   4. If the SEC disagrees with some presentation in the registrant's financial statements but the principles used by the registrant have substantial authoritative support, the SEC may accept

footnotes to the statements in lieu of correcting the statements to the SEC view, provided the SEC has not previously expressed its opinion on the matter in published material.

5. The SEC reserves the right to rule against a registrant even if the registrant follows principles having substantial authoritative support, and to determine which accounting principles have substantive authoritative support.

b. While the SEC has generally allowed the private sector to establish accounting principles, it often exerts pressure to force the private sector into action. In some cases, the SEC establishes a moratorium on certain practices or requires that a particular principle be used. In oil and gas accounting, the SEC requires the use of
   1. full cost accounting.
   2. flow through accounting.
   3. successful efforts accounting.
   4. either full cost or successful efforts accounting.
   5. either full cost or flow through accounting.

⊘ LO 3   E16.7   Multiple Choice—Registration of Securities   These questions involve registration of new security issues with the SEC.

Required

a. In the registration and sale of new securities issues, the SEC
   1. allows a security's registration to go effective by endorsing its investment merit.
   2. provides a rating of the investment quality of the security.
   3. may not allow the registration to go effective if it judges the security's investment risk to be too great.
   4. allows all registrations to go effective if the issuing company's external accountant is satisfied that disclosures and representations are not misleading.
   5. makes no guarantees regarding the registration statement's material accuracy.

b. In cases of false or misleading disclosure in a registration statement that the SEC has allowed to become effective in conjunction with the public sale of securities, investors have the potential for legal recourse (for example, damage suits) against all of the following *except*
   1. the Securities and Exchange Commission.
   2. the issuing entity.
   3. the underwriter (managing broker) of the sale.
   4. the issuing entity's legal counsel.
   5. the issuing entity's external accountant.

c. Which of the following is *not* required for the registration statements filed under the Securities Act of 1933?
   1. Nature and history of the issuer's business
   2. Description of the securities being registered
   3. Estimate of the net proceeds and the expected uses of the proceeds
   4. Financial forecasts for the next two fiscal years
   5. Salaries and security holdings of officers and directors

d. The 1933 Securities Act provides for a 20-day waiting period between the filing and effective dates of the registration. During this waiting period the registrant is prohibited from engaging in which of these activities?
   1. Preparing any amendments to the registration statement.
   2. Announcing the prospective issue of the securities being registered.
   3. Accepting offers from potential investors to purchase securities being registered.
   4. Placing an advertisement indicating who will accept orders for the securities being registered.
   5. Issuing a prospectus in preliminary form.

LO 4   E16.8   Analysis of Form 10-Q   On August 5, 2011, **Ford Motor Company** filed its second quarter 10-Q for 2011. Its MD&A contains a table showing the effect of special items and noncontrolling interests on Ford's net income. Among the special items disclosed by Ford for the second quarter of 2011 are personnel-reduction programs ($110 million) and a Belgian pension settlement ($104 million).

FORD MOTOR COMPANY [F]

Required

Briefly explain the nature of these two items and indicate whether they increased or decreased Ford's net income.

E16.9 Possible Effect of SOX on the SEC's Designation of Standard-Setting Bodies   LO 5

Required

Write a two-page double-spaced essay speculating on how SOX could change the SEC's traditional delegation of its statutory authority to set accounting standards to private-sector standard-setting bodies in the U.S. Consider the implications of the new PCAOB and Section 108's recognition of the SEC's authority and ability to designate standard-setting bodies.

E16.10 Reporting Insider Trades   On February 18, 2011, Bradford L. Smith filed a Form 4 with the SEC in   LO 5
which he reported some insider transactions in **Microsoft** stock.

Required

MICROSOFT
[MSFT]

Access that Form 4 either by going to the Microsoft website or the SEC's website (sec.gov) and answer these questions.

a. Give the title of Form 4.
b. How many shares did Mr. Smith acquire and for what reason?
c. How many shares are owned by Mr. Smith?

E16.11 Use of Form 8-K   **Microsoft** filed a Form 8-K with the SEC on April 22, 2010, that described an event   LO 4
of potential significance to investors.

Required

MICROSOFT
[MSFT]

Access that Form 8-K either by going to the Microsoft website or the SEC's website (sec.gov) and answer these questions.

a. Briefly describe the event reported on that Form 8-K.
b. From the list of Microsoft's 2010 SEC filings, indicate how many SEC filings Microsoft made during 2010. Does this surprise you?

E16.12 Form 10-K Disclosure   Item 6 in **Molson Coors Brewing Company**'s 2010 Form 10-K, "Selected   LO 4
Financial Data," contains a table that includes net sales for the most recent five years and other information. Net sales for 2010 were down about 32% from 2008 net sales. Note (3) to that table offers an explanation for that decline in net sales.

**MOLSON COORS
BREWING
COMPANY**
[TAP]

Required

Explain in your own words the reason given for the decline in 2010 net sales compared with 2008.

E16.13 Effects of Sarbanes-Oxley Act on Financial Reporting Requirements   The Sarbanes-Oxley   LO 4
Act is expected to have a major positive effect on the proper functioning of the securities markets.

Required

Briefly describe three aspects of the Sarbanes-Oxley Act that are expected to improve the financial reporting process.

PROGRAMS ●●

PROBLEMS ●●

P16.1 Origins and Objectives of Securities Legislation   During the late 1920s, about 55% of all per-   LO 1
sonal savings in the United States were used to purchase securities. Public confidence in the business
community was extremely high as stock values doubled and tripled in short periods of time. People
believed the road to wealth was through the stock market, and everyone who was able participated. Thus,
the public was severely affected when the Dow Jones Industrial Average fell 89 percent between 1929
and 1933. The public outcry arising from this decline in stock prices motivated Congress to enact major
federal laws regulating the securities industry.

Required

a. Describe the investment practices of the 1920s that contributed to the erosion of the stock market.
b. Explain the basic objectives of each of the following:
1. Securities Act of 1933.
2. Securities Exchange Act of 1934.

    c. Subsequent legislation resulted from abuses in the securities industry. Explain the major provisions of each of the following:
1. Foreign Corrupt Practices Act of 1977.
2. Insider Trading Sanctions Act of 1984.

LO 4 **P16.2** **Annual Reports to Stockholders and Form 10-K** Marcon Inc. is a well-known manufacturing company with several wholly owned subsidiaries. The company's stock trades on the New York Stock Exchange, and the company files all appropriate reports with the SEC. Marcon's financial statements are audited by a public accounting firm. Marcon's Annual Report to Stockholders for the year ended December 31, 2012, contained the following phrase in boldface type: **The Company's 10-K is available upon written request.**

Required

    a. What is Form 10-K, and who requires that it be completed? Why is the phrase "The Company's 10-K is available upon written request" shown in the annual report?

    b. What information not normally included in the company's annual report could be ascertained from the 10-K?

    c. Indicate three items of financial information often included in annual reports that are not required for the 10-K.

    (CMA adapted)

LO 4 **P16.3** **Quarterly Reports to the SEC** In 1981 the SEC modified and expanded the financial information in Form 10-Q and better integrated it with quarterly reports to shareholders. The SEC set forth specific guidelines as to what information must be included on Form 10-Q.

Required

    a. Corporations are required by the SEC to file a Form 10-Q.
1. What is Form 10-Q, and how often is it filed with the SEC?
2. Explain why the SEC requires corporations to file Form 10-Q.

    b. Discuss the disclosure requirements now pertaining to Form 10-Q with specific regard to the following:
1. Condensed balance sheet.
2. Condensed income statement.
3. Condensed statements of cash flows.
4. Management's discussion and analysis of the interim period(s).
5. Footnote disclosures.

LO 4 **P16.4** **Special Reports to the SEC** To accomplish its regulatory objectives, the SEC requires that public companies register their securities and periodically prepare and file Forms 8-K, 10-K, and 10-Q.

Required

    a. With regard to Form 8-K, discuss
1. the purpose of the report.
2. the timing of the report.
3. the format of the report.
4. the role of financial statements in the filing of the report.

    b. Identify five circumstances under which the SEC requires the filing of Form 8-K.

    c. Discuss how the filing of Form 8-K fosters the purpose of the SEC.

    d. Explain whether the SEC passes judgment on securities based on information contained in periodic reports.

LO 5 **P16.5** **Audit Committees** Although audit committees are now very much a part of the corporate governance landscape, their evolution spans many decades. Today's audit committees reflect SEC recommendations, stock exchange listing requirements and the mandates of Section 301 of SOX.

Required

    a. Explain the role the audit committee generally assumes with respect to the annual audit conducted by the company's external auditors.

    b. Identify duties other than those associated with the annual audit that might be assigned to the audit committee by the board of directors.

    c. Discuss the relationship that should exist between the audit committee and a company's internal audit staff.

    d. Explain why board members appointed to serve on the audit committee should be outside (independent of management) board members.

P16.6 **Proxy Statements** The SEC was given the authority to regulate proxy solicitation by the Securities and Exchange Act of 1934. SEC regulations require that a proxy statement be mailed by a registrant's management to each shareholder shortly before the annual shareholders meeting. **LO 5**

Required

a. Explain the purpose of proxy statements.
b. Identify four types of events or actions for which proxy statements normally are solicited.
c. Identify the conditions that must be met in order to have a dissident shareholder proposal included in a proxy statement.

P16.7 **Registration of New Securities** In business for about twenty years, Trapper Inc.'s finance committee has been discussing alternative ways of financing a major proposed facilities expansion. Both short-term and long-term notes were ruled out because of high interest rates. Chief financial officer Bob Smith said, "It boils down to either bonds, preferred stock, or additional common stock." Maria Garza, a consultant helping in the financing decision, stated, "Regardless of your choice, you will have to file a Registration Statement with the SEC." Dave Brown, Trapper's chief accountant for the past five years, stated, "I've coordinated the filing of all the periodic reports required by the SEC—10-Ks, 10-Qs, and 8-Ks—and see no reason why I can't also prepare a Registration Statement." **LO 3**

Required

a. List the circumstances in which a firm files a Registration Statement with the SEC.
b. Explain the registration process's objectives given in the Securities Act of 1933.
c. Identify and explain the SEC publications Dave Brown would use for guidance in preparing the Registration Statement.

P16.8 **Role of the SEC in Standard Setting** Many organizations and individuals influenced the development of accounting theory and practice over a long period of time. Today the most important source of accounting rules is the private-sector independent FASB, based in Norwalk, CT. In Washington the SEC administers the federal securities laws that began to emerge from Congress after the collapse of stock prices and economic activity in the early 1930s. **LO 6**

Required

a. What official role does the SEC have in the development of financial accounting theory and practice?
b. Explain the relationship between the FASB and SEC with respect to the development and establishment of financial accounting theory and practices.

P16.9 **Competition among Accounting Standards-Setters?** Read Ronald Dye and Shyam Sunder, "Why Not Allow FASB and IASB Standards to Compete in the U.S.?" (*Accounting Horizons,* 15:3, September 2001, 257-271). **LO 6**

Required

Write a two-page double-spaced essay summarizing the issues raised in that article.

P16.10 **Corporate Governance Guidelines** Go to the website for **AIG (American International Group)**, the much-maligned insurance giant that got into a lot of trouble over credit default swaps, examine AIG's Corporate Governance Guidelines, and answer these questions. **LO 5**

AMERICAN INTERNATIONAL GROUP, INC
[AIG]

Required

a. How does the document distinguish between the roles of management and the board of directors in running AIG's business operations?
b. What percentage of the board is to be filled by "independent" directors, as defined in the New York Stock Exchange's listing standards?
c. What do the Guidelines say about former CEOs of AIG serving on the board? Do those guidelines have any particular individual(s) in mind?
d. List three particular requirements of AIG's audit committee discussed in Section IX. of the Guidelines.

P16.11 **Sarbanes-Oxley Act and PCAOB Inspections** Established by the Sarbanes-Oxley Act (2002), the Public Company Accounting Oversight Board (PCAOB) conducts inspections of registered auditing firms for evidence of quality control issues in their audits. On the PCAOB website, examine its December 5, 2008, report of inspections covering the years 2004 - 2007. **LO 5** ✅

Required

a. How were the audit areas discussed in the report selected?
b. Briefly describe the audit deficiencies noted in the report.

LO 3   **P16.12 eBay Inc. Registration Statement**   eBay Inc. filed a Registration Statement with the SEC on May 16, 2011.

eBAY INC.
[EBAY]

Required

a.   Describe in your own words the purpose of the shares covered by this Registration Statement.
b.   Calculate the apparent registration fee percent.
c.   Identify the public accounting firm involved and describe the permission they are providing.
d.   Briefly describe the difference between the stock options and the restricted stock awards mentioned in Items 4. and 5. of Exhibit 99.1 accompanying the registration statement.

REVIEW SOLUTIONS ●

Review 1 Solution

a.   The SEC's fundamental mission is investor protection, principally by requiring registrants to publicly disclose all material facts and circumstances and prevent or correct deceptive and fraudulent practices in securities trading. Because no such investor protections, at least at the federal level, existed before the 1929 stock market crash, Congress realized in the early 1930s such protections needed to be enacted.

b.   The text cites ten such pieces of legislation. Although any three could be chosen for discussion, we offer:

1.   The **Investment Company Act of 1940** requires investment companies, including mutual funds (but not hedge funds) to register with the SEC and disclose their investment policies and management fees, and to solicit shareholder participation in company policy.

2.   The **Private Securities Litigation Reform Act of 1995** limits the liability of public accountants to their "fair share" in certain securities suits and protects registrants from lawsuits related to certain forward-looking financial information and illegal acts reported by auditors to the SEC.

3.   The **Sarbanes-Oxley Act of 2002** requires reports on internal controls, top management certifications of financial statements filed with the SEC, and created the *Public Company Accounting Oversight Board (PCAOB)* to monitor auditing firms and set auditing standards.

c.   The statutory definition is very broad, referring to ANY note, stock, bond and the like and, in general, any interest or instrument commonly known as a "security," including ANY certificate to subscribe to or to purchase, any of the foregoing. Any financial instrument that promises a return or protection from loss, other than insurance policies, and involves a third party, is likely to be a "security."

d.   Although the SEC delegates its authority to set accounting principles to the FASB, it occasionally issues its own pronouncements, such as *FRR*s and *SAB*s, and influences the standard-setting process through its participation in that process.

Review 2 Solution

a.   A prospective issuer registers with the SEC registrant and files a registration statement that consists of two parts: (1) information generally included in a prospectus, which must be furnished to each purchaser of the security, and (2) other information and exhibits, which must be publicly available but need not be supplied to each investor.

The independent CPA is part of the registration team that also includes the issuer's chief financial officer, legal counsel, the underwriter (investment banker) and the underwriter's counsel. Form S-1 is the basic registration form although Forms S-3 and S-4 are used in certain circumstances. The underwriter advises the issuer and markets the securities to the investing public under one of three alternative arrangements.

b.   Certainly items 6 (selected financial data) and 7 (MD&A) relate to accounting and reporting. Also items 7A (disclosures about market risk of derivatives), 9 (changes and disagreements with accountants) and 9A (reports on internal controls and specifically internal controls over financial reporting), deal with various aspects of accounting and reporting.

c.   Article 3 prescribes the audited financial statements to be prepared and the time periods covered, generally consolidated balance sheets as of the end of the two most recent fiscal years, consolidated statements of income and cash flows for the three most recent fiscal years, and analysis of changes in the stockholders' equity accounts shown in the balance sheet for the three most recent fiscal years as a separate financial statement or a footnote schedule

   Article 4 deals with selected accounting and reporting matters applicable to companies in general, independent of their industry. It provides for the usual form, order, and terminology, and addresses issues related to filings by foreign private security issuers.

d.   In addition to annual (10-K) and quarterly (10-Q) reporting, registrants must file an 8-K within four days of any event deemed significant enough to be of interest to investors, including proposed business combinations and large transactions in securities. Items 2.03 and 2.04 call for timely reporting of creation or expansion of "direct" (on balance sheet) financial obligations or liabilities and "off-balance sheet" financial obligations that effectively create liabilities for registrants. Item 4.01 alerts investors to a change in the registrant's independent public accountant and the circumstances surrounding it, perhaps raising concerns about the credibility of financial reporting before or after the change.

Review 3 Solution

a.   The Treadway Commission's 1987 report defined fraudulent financial reporting as "intentional or reckless conduct, whether act or omission, that results in materially misleading financial statements." The chapter describes events that can produce fraudulent financial reporting.

   But at what point do discretionary transactions entered at year-end to produce a particular reporting result that seems to overemphasize the positive in the underlying economics, become fraudulent? Intent must usually be proven in fraud cases. The ethical dilemma arises when the boss asks for a "credit" when there should be a "debit" or specifies the timing and amount of transactions or event recognition that have significant financial statement effects, or whenever the accountant senses even a hint of impropriety.

b.   The audit committee makes sure that management fulfills its responsibilities for accounting, reporting, and controlling the operations and safeguarding the assets of the corporation. It monitors the financial accounting and reporting system as well as the external and internal audit functions, hires the independent auditor, and the auditor reports to it. The internal audit department needs direct access to the audit committee for special problems, and the audit committee can use the internal audit department for special investigations.

   A weak audit committee will overlook or deliberately ignore problems, fail to confront top management on financial accounting, reporting, and control issues, and not take advantage of an effective internal audit function. Strong audit committees composed of truly independent, financially savvy directors should contribute to good corporate governance primarily by fostering credible external financial reporting that creates trust with investors and creditors.

c.   Sprouse identifies three ways that the SEC, primarily through its ongoing review of financial statements filed by registrants, contributes to the standard-setting process.

   1.   Observing lack of comparability among registrants' accounting treatments of apparently similar events, which can signify weaknesses or ambiguities in existing standards.
   2.   Detecting increasing use of questionable accounting methods which, although generally accepted, are not covered by existing pronouncements.
   3.   Noting the presence of new or unusual transactions which appear questionable and for which the accounting is evolving.

d.   Sadly, the passage of time appears to have eroded the spirit if not the letter of the Foreign Corrupt Practices Act—it seemed less relevant to the financial reporting environment of the first few years of the 21st century. As seen, though, the act relates to more than foreign corrupt practices. Those responsible for corporate accountability, including the independent public accountants, may need periodic reminders of their obligations to the public. The fact that certain provisions of SOX were deemed necessary despite the apparent redundancy with FCPA is unfortunate.

Index